Sullivan's Guide to Putting It Together

Putting It Together Sections	Objective	Page(s)
5.6 Putting It Together: Which Method Do I Use?	1 Determine the appropriate probability rule to use 2 Determine the appropriate counting technique to use	286–287 287–289
9.3 Putting It Together: Which Method Do I Use?	1 Determine the appropriate confidence interval to construct	420–421
10.4 Putting It Together: Which Method Do I Use?	1 Determine the appropriate hypothesis test to perform (one sample)	460
11.4 Putting It Together: Which Method Do I Use?	1 Determine the appropriate hypothesis test to perform (two samples)	506

Putting It Together Exercises	Skills Utilized	Section(s) Covered	Page(s)
1.2.23 Passive Smoke	Variables, observational studies, designed experiments	1.1, 1.2	21–22
1.4.37 Comparing Sampling Methods	Simple random sampling and other sampling techniques	1.3, 1.4	38
1.4.38 Thinking about Randomness	Random sampling	1.3, 1.4	38
1.5.35 Speed Limit	Population, variables, level of measurement, sampling, bias	1.1–1.5	44
1.6.33 Mosquito Control	Population, variables, design of experiments	1.1, 1.6	53–54
2.1.30 Online Homework	Variables, designed experiments, bar graphs	1.1, 1.2, 1.6, 2.1	74–75
2.2.59 Time Viewing a Webpage	Graphing data	2.2	98
2.2.60 Which Graphical Summary	Graphing data	2.1, 2.2	98
2.2.61 Shark!	Graphing data	2.2	98–99
3.1.43 Shape, Mean, and Median	Discrete vs. continuous data, histograms, shape of a distribution, mean, median, mode, bias	1.1, 1.4, 2.2, 3.1	129
3.5.17 Paternal Smoking	Observational studies, designed experiments, lurking variables, mean, median, standard deviation, quartiles, boxplots	1.2, 1.6, 3.1, 3.2, 3.4, 3.5	169–170
4.2.28 Housing Prices	Scatter diagrams, correlation, linear regression	4.1, 4.2	206
4.2.29 Smoking and Birth Weight	Observational study vs. designed experiment, prospective studies, scatter diagrams, linear regression, correlation vs. causation, lurking variables	1.2, 4.1, 4.2	206–207
4.3.15 Building a Financial Model	Scatter diagrams, correlation, linear regression	4.1, 4.2, 4.3	212
4.3.16 Exam Scores	Scatter diagrams, correlation, linear regression	4.1, 4.2, 4.3	213
5.1.54 Drug Side Effects	Variables, graphical summaries of data, experiments, probability	1.1, 1.6, 2.1, 5.1	246
5.2.47 Red Light Cameras	Variables, relative frequency distributions, bar graphs, mean, standard deviation, probability, Simpson's Paradox	1.1, 2.1, 3.1, 3.2, 4.4, 5.1, 5.2	257–258
5.2.48 Exam Scores	Relative frequency distributions, mean, median, standard deviation, interquartile range, classical probability, Addition Rule for Disjoint Events	2.2, 3.1, 3.2, 5.1, 5.2	258
6.1.37 Sullivan Statistics Survey	Mean, standard deviation, probability, probability distributions	3.1, 3.2, 5.1, 6.1	309
7.2.52 Birth Weights	Relative frequency distribution, histograms, mean and standard deviation from grouped data, normal probabilities	2.1, 2.2, 3.3, 7.2	348
8.1.33 Playing Roulette	Probability distributions, mean and standard deviation of a random variable, sampling distributions	6.1, 8.1	379
9.1.45 Hand Washing	Observational studies, bias, confidence intervals	1.2, 1.5, 9.1	403–404
9.2.53 Smoking Cessation Study	Experimental design, confidence intervals	1.6, 9.1, 9.2	418
9.2.54 How Many Drinks?	Histograms, mean, standard deviation, mode, probability, unusual events, confidence intervals	2.2, 3.1, 3.3, 5.1, 9.2	418
10.2.40 Lupus	Observational studies, retrospective vs. prospective studies, bar graphs, confidence intervals, hypothesis testing	1.2, 2.1, 9.1, 10.2	447
10.2.41 Naughty or Nice?	Experimental design, determining null and alternative hypotheses, binomial probabilities, interpreting *P*-values	1.6, 6.2, 10.1, 10.2	447–448
10.3.38 Analyzing a Study	Statistical process, confidence intervals, hypothesis testing, case-control studies	1.1, 1.2, 9.1, 10.1, 10.2	458
10.4.17 Ideal Number of Children	Relative frequency histogram, mode, mean, standard deviation, Central Limit Theorem, hypothesis testing	2.2, 3.1, 3.2, 8.1,10.2	462
11.1.41 Salk Vaccine	Completely randomized design, hypothesis testing	1.6, 11.1	482
11.2.18 Glide Testing	Matched pairs design, hypothesis testing	1.6, 11.2	492

Putting It Together Exercises	Skills Utilized	Section(s) Covered	Page(s)
11.3.25 Online Homework	Completely randomized design, confounding, hypothesis testing	1.6, 11.3	504
12.1.29 The V-2 Rocket in London	Mean of discrete data, expected value, Poisson probability distribution, goodness-of-fit	6.1, 6.3, 12.1	526
12.1.30 Weldon's Dice	Addition Rule for Disjoint Events, classical probability, goodness-of-fit	5.1, 5.2, 12.1	526
12.2.21 Women, Aspirin, and Heart Attacks	Population, sample, variables, observational study vs. designed experiment, experimental design, compare two proportions, chi-square test of homogeneity	1.1, 1.2, 1.6, 11.1, 12.2	540–541
12.4.17 30 Television Prices	Scatter diagrams, correlation coefficient, linear relations, least-squares regression, residual analysis, confidence and prediction intervals, lurking variables	4.1, 4.2, 4.3, 12.3, 12.4	562

New to this edition is the Student Activity Workbook. The Activity Workbook includes many tactile activities for the classroom. In addition, the workbook includes activities based on statistical applets. Below is a list of the applet activities.

Applet	Section	Activity Name	Description
Mean versus median	3.1	Understanding Measures of Center	Observe the effect of outliers on mean and median. Use Applet to construct data sets for a given relationship between the mean and median.
Standard deviation	3.2	Exploring Standard Deviation	Create data set with given standard deviation to learn properties of this measure of dispersion.
Correlation by Eye	4.1	Limitations of the Linear Correlation Coefficient	Explore the properties of Pearson's linear correlation coefficient.
Regression by Eye	4.2	Minimizing the Sum of the Squared Residuals	Experiment with identifying the line of best fit using the sum of squared residuals.
Regression by Eye	4.2	Investigating Outliers and Influential Points	Explore the role outliers and influential points play in determining the least-squares regression line.
Simulating Flipping a Coin	5.1	Demonstrating the Law of Large Numbers	Simulate flipping a fair and a biased coin to help understand the Law of Large Numbers and the interpretation of probability.
Binomial Distribution	6.2	Exploring a Binomial Distribution from Multiple Perspectives	Explore a binomial distribution through multiple methods. Use a card simulation to construct a probability distribution for a binomial situation. Then use an applet and compare the two distributions obtained. Finally develop a mathematical model.
Sampling Distributions	8.1	Sampling from Normal and Non-normal Populations	Obtain samples from normal, uniform, and skewed distributions and analyze center, spread, and shape of distribution of sample means.
Sampling Distributions	8.2	Describing the Distribution of the Sample Proportion	Obtain samples from binary population and analyze center, spread, and shape of distribution of sample proportions.
Confidence Intervals for a Proportion	9.1	Exploring the Effects of Confidence Level, Sample Size, and Shape	Explore the roles of confidence level and sample size when estimating a proportion.
Confidence Intervals for a Mean	9.2	Exploring the Effects of Confidence Level and Sample Size	Explore the roles of confidence level and sample size when estimating a mean.
Hypothesis Tests for a Proportion	10.2	Understanding Type I Error Rates	Explore effect of sample size on probability of making a type I error in hypothesis tests for a proportion.
Hypothesis Tests for a Mean	10.3	Understanding Type I Error Rates	Explore effect of sample size on probability of making a type I error in hypothesis tests for a mean.
Randomization Test for Two Proportions	11.1	Making an Inference about Two Proportions	Simulate randomly assigning treatments between two samples to approximate the *P*-value of the hypothesis test.
Randomization Test for Correlation	12.3	Using a Randomization Test for Correlation	Simulate randomly assigning observations for bivariate data to approximate the *P*-value for testing whether a significant relation exists between the explanatory and response variables.

Annotated Instructor's Edition

FOURTH EDITION

Fundamentals of Statistics

Informed Decisions Using Data

Michael Sullivan, III

Joliet Junior College

PEARSON

Boston Columbus Indianapolis New York San Francisco Upper Saddle River
Amsterdam Cape Town Dubai London Madrid Milan Munich Paris Montréal Toronto
Delhi Mexico City São Paulo Sydney Hong Kong Seoul Singapore Taipei Tokyo

Editor in Chief, Mathematics and Statistics Deirdre Lynch
Acquisitions Editor Christopher Cummings
Senior Content Editor Joanne Dill
Editorial Assistant Sonia Ashraf
Development Editor Lenore Parens
Senior Managing Editor Karen Wernholm
Associate Managing Editor Tamela Ambush
Marketing Manager Erin Lane
Marketing Assistant Kathleen DeChavez
Digital Assets Manager Marianne Groth
Supplements Production Coordinator Katherine Roz
Media Producer Audra Walsh
Senior Content Developer Mary Durnwald
Content Project Supervisor, MyStatLab Bob Carroll
Senior Author Support/Technology Specialist Joe Vetere
Rights and Permissions Advisor Michael Joyce
Image Manager Rachel Youdelman
Procurement Specialist Debbie Rossi
Procurement Manager/Boston Evelyn Beaton
Associate Director of Design, USHE North and West Andrea Nix
Senior Designer Heather Scott
Text Design Rokusek Design
Production Coordination Cenveo Publisher Services/Nesbitt Graphics, Inc.
Composition Cenveo Publisher Services/Nesbitt Graphics, Inc.
Illustrations Cenveo Publisher Services/Nesbitt Graphics, Inc. and Laserwords

Cover Design Heather Scott
Cover Image Exactostock/SuperStock

Library of Congress Cataloging-in-Publication Data

Sullivan, Michael, 1967 July 2-
Fundamentals of statistics / Michael Sullivan, III. —4th ed.
p. cm. ISBN-10: 0-321-83903-X (Annotated Instructor's Edition)
Includes index. ISBN-13: 978-0-321-83903-9 (Annotated Instructor's Edition)
ISBN 978-0-321-83870-4
1. Statistics—Textbooks. I. Title.
QA276.12.S846 2014
519.5–dc23

2012003719

1 2 3 4 5 6 7 8 9 10—RRD—16 15 14 13 12

PEARSON www.pearsonhighered.com

ISBN 13: 978-0-321-83870-4
ISBN 10: 0-321-83870-X

To My Wife Yolanda
and
My Children
Michael, Kevin, and Marissa

Contents

Preface to the Instructor

Capturing a Powerful and Exciting Discipline in a Textbook

Statistics is a powerful subject, and it is one of my passions. Bringing my passion for the subject together with my desire to create a text that would work for me, my students, and my school led me to write the first edition of this textbook. It continues to motivate me as I revise the book to reflect on changes in students, in the statistics community, and in the world around us.

When I started writing, I used the manuscript of this text in class. My students provided valuable, insightful feedback, and I made adjustments based on their comments. In many respects, this text was written by students and for students. I also received constructive feedback from a wide range of statistics faculty, which has refined ideas in the book and in my teaching. I continue to receive valuable feedback from both faculty and students, and this text continues to evolve with the goal of providing clear, concise, and readable explanations, while challenging students to think statistically.

In writing this edition, I continue to make a special effort to abide by the *Guidelines for Assessment and Instruction in Statistics Education* (GAISE) for the college introductory course endorsed by the American Statistical Association (ASA). The GAISE Report gives six recommendations for the course:

1. Emphasize statistical literacy and develop statistical thinking
2. Use real data in teaching statistics
3. Stress conceptual understanding
4. Foster active learning
5. Use technology for developing conceptual understanding
6. Use assessments to improve and evaluate student learning

Changes to this edition and the hallmark features of the text reflect a strong adherence to these important GAISE guidelines.

Putting It Together

When students are learning statistics, often they struggle with seeing the big picture of how it all fits together. One of my goals is to help students learn not just the important concepts and methods of statistics but also how to put them together.

On the inside front cover, you'll see a pathway that provides a guide for students as they navigate through the process of learning statistics. The features and chapter organization in the fourth edition reinforce this important process.

New to This Edition

Pedagogical Changes

- **Over 35% New and Updated Exercises** The fourth edition makes a concerted effort to require students to write a few sentences that explain the results of their statistical analysis. To reflect this effort, the answers in the back of the text provide recommended explanations of the statistical results. In addition, exercises have been written to require students to understand pitfalls in faulty statistical analysis.
- **Over 40% New and Updated Examples** The examples continue to engage and provide clear, concise explanations for the students while following the **Problem,**

Approach, Solution presentation. *Problem* lays out the scenario of the example, *Approach* provides insight into the thought process behind the methodology used to solve the problem, and *Solution* goes through the solution utilizing the methodology suggested in the approach.

- **Vocabulary and Skill Building** New fill-in-the-blank and true/false questions that open the section level exercise sets assess the student's understanding of vocabulary introduced in the section. These problems are followed by Skill Building exercises that allow the student to practice skills developed in the section.
- **Explaining the Concepts** These are new, thought-provoking problems that require a student to explain statistical concepts. These appear at the end of the exercise set after the student has had a chance to develop his or her skills and conceptual understanding of the material.
- **New Example Structure** presents by-hand solutions side by side with technology solutions. This allows flexibility for an instructor to present only by-hand, only technology, or both solutions.
- **StatCrunch®** is included in the technology solutions (along with Excel, MINITAB, and the TI-graphing calculator). In addition, the Technology Step-by-Step following each section's exercises illustrate StatCrunch's syntax required to obtain the output.

Hallmark Features

- **Classroom Activities** The classroom activities and applet activities that appeared throughout the text in the third edition have been updated and included in a new **Student Activity Workbook**. In addition, the activity workbook includes exercises that introduce resampling methods that help develop conceptual understanding of hypothesis testing. The workbook is accompanied by an instructor resource guide with suggestions for incorporating the activities into class.
- **Sullivan Statistics Survey** Through the power of StatCrunch's survey tool, a survey was administered to approximately 200 individuals throughout the country. The results of this survey are available on the StatCrunch website (just search Sullivan Statistics Survey) and on the CD that accompanies the text. Most exercise sets have problems that require students to analyze results from this survey.
- **Making an Informed Decision** Many of the "Making an Informed Decision" projects that open each chapter have been updated with new and exciting scenarios that allow students to make an informed decision using the skills developed in the section.
- Because the use of **Real Data** piques student interest and helps show the relevance of statistics, great efforts have been made to extensively incorporate real data in the exercises and examples.
- **Putting It Together** sections open each chapter to help students put the current material in context with previously studied material.
- **Step-by-Step Annotated Examples** guide a student from problem to solution in three easy-to-follow steps.
- **"Now Work"** problems follow most examples so students can practice the concepts shown.
- Multiple types of **Exercises** are used at the end of sections and chapters to test varying skills with progressive levels of difficulty. These exercises include **Vocabulary and Skill Building, Applying the Concepts,** and **Explaining the Concepts**.
- **Chapter Review** sections include:
  - **Chapter Summary**.
  - A list of key chapter **Vocabulary**.
  - A list of **Formulas** used in the chapter.
  - **Chapter Objectives** listed with corresponding review exercises.
  - **Review Exercises** with all answers available in the back of the book.
- Each chapter concludes with **Case Studies** that help students apply their knowledge and promote active learning.

Integration of Technology

This book can be used with or without technology. Should you choose to integrate technology in the course, the following resources are available for your students:

- **Technology Step-by-Step** guides are included in applicable sections that show how to use MINITAB®, Excel®, the TI-83/84, and StatCrunch to complete statistics processes.
- Any problem that has 12 or more observations in the **Data Set** has a CD icon ( ) indicating that data set is included on the companion CD in various formats.
- Where applicable, exercises and examples incorporate output screens from various software including MINITAB, the TI-83/84, Excel, and StatCrunch.
- 22 **Applets** are included on the companion CD and connected with certain activities from the Student Activity Workbook, allowing students to manipulate data and interact with animations. See the front inside cover for a list of applets.
- Accompanying **Technology Manuals** are available that contain detailed tutorial instructions and worked out examples and exercises for the TI-83/84 and 89, Excel, SPSS, and MINITAB.

Companion CD Contents

- **Data Sets**
- 22 **Applets** (See description on the insert in front of the text.)
- **Formula Cards and Tables** in PDF format
- **Additional Topics Folder** including:
  - Review of Lines
  - Confidence Intervals for Population Standard Deviation
  - Hypothesis Tests for Population Standard Deviation
  - One-Way Analysis of Variance
  - Appendix A Tables
- **Sullivan Statistics Survey**
  - A copy of the questions asked on the Sullivan Statistics Survey
  - A data set containing the results of the Sullivan Statistics Survey
- **Case Studies** corresponding to every chapter in the text

Key Chapter Content Changes

Chapter 2 Organizing and Summarizing Data

The exercise sets went through a major overhaul with the goal of increasing the number of problems with data students find interesting and relevant.

Chapter 3 Numerically Summarizing Data

The presentation of measures of dispersion has been reorganized so that the emphasis is on the standard deviation rather than the variance.

Chapter 4 Describing the Relation between Two Variables

A new by-hand example has been added to determine correlation and least-squares regression that is not computationally intensive with the goal of increasing conceptual understanding. The interpretation of a predicted value as the mean value of the response variable for the given value of the explanatory variable is emphasized. The interpretation of slope and intercept of least-squares regression line has been rewritten. Section 4.4 is new to this edition where the relation between two qualitative variables is described.

Chapter 7 The Normal Probability Distribution

The introduction of the normal probability distribution in Section 7.1 has been rewritten to emphasize the normal curve as a model. The discussion of the standard normal distribution has been incorporated into the presentation on Applications of the Normal Distribution. Finding the area under a normal curve is presented in each example using a by-hand approach with the normal table and a technology approach in a side-by-side presentation, allowing flexibility of method.

Chapter 9 Estimating the Value of a Parameter

The chapter now opens with estimation of a population proportion. The discussion of estimation of the mean with sigma known has been removed. All the examples illustrating the construction of a confidence interval now present a by-hand and technology solution side-by-side, which allows for flexibility in the approach taken in the course. In Section 9.2, estimating the mean, a new Example 2 is presented in which Student's *t*-distribution is compared to the standard normal distribution through simulation.

Chapter 10 Hypothesis Testing Regarding a Parameter

The chapter now presents hypothesis testing for a population proportion before hypothesis testing for a mean. The discussion of hypothesis testing for a population mean with sigma known has been removed. Each hypothesis test is now presented in a side-by-side example format, which includes the classical by-hand approach, a by-hand *P*-value approach, and a technology approach. Again, this provides the utmost in flexibility. Added exercises emphasize the difference between "accepting" and "not rejecting" the null hypothesis (Problem 36 in Section 10.2 and Problem 35 in Section 10.3).

Chapter 11 Inference on Two Samples

The chapter now begins with a discussion of inference on two proportions (both independent and dependent samples) and then presents a discussion of inference on means. Again, all examples present the solutions in a side-by-side format that includes technology solutions.

Flexible to Work with Your Syllabus

To meet the varied needs of diverse syllabi, this book has been organized to be flexible. You will notice the "Preparing for This Section" material at the beginning of each section, which will tip you off to dependencies within the course. The two most common variations within an introductory statistics course are the treatment of regression analysis and the treatment of probability.

- **Coverage of Correlation and Regression** The text was written with the descriptive portion of bivariate data (Chapter 4) presented after the descriptive portion of univariate data (Chapter 3). Instructors who prefer to postpone the discussion of bivariate data can skip Chapter 4 and return to it before covering Sections 12.3 and 12.4.
- **Coverage of Probability** The text allows for light to extensive coverage of probability. Instructors wishing to minimize probability may cover Section 5.1 and skip the remaining sections. A mid-level treatment of probability can be accomplished by covering Sections 5.1 through 5.3. Instructors who will cover the chi-square test for independence will want to cover Sections 5.1 through 5.3. In addition, an instructor who will cover binomial probabilities will want to cover independence in Section 5.3 and combinations in Section 5.5.

Acknowledgments

Textbooks evolve into their final form through the efforts and contributions of many people. First and foremost, I would like to thank my family, whose dedication to this project was as much theirs as mine: my wife, Yolanda, whose words of encouragement and support were unabashed, and my children, Michael, Kevin, and Marissa, who would come and greet me every morning with smiles that only children can deliver. I owe each of them my sincerest gratitude. I would also like to thank the entire Mathematics Department at Joliet Junior College, my colleagues who provided support, ideas, and encouragement to help me complete this project. From Pearson Education, I thank Christopher Cummings, whose editorial expertise has been an invaluable asset; Deirdre Lynch, who has provided many suggestions that clearly demonstrate her expertise; Joanne Dill, who provided organizational skills that made this project go smoothly; Erin Lane, for her marketing savvy and dedication to getting the word out; Tamela Ambush, for her dedication in keeping everyone in the loop; Rose Kernan, for her ability to control the production process; and the Pearson Arts and Sciences Sales team, for their confidence and support of this book. Thanks also to the individuals who helped rigorously check the accuracy of this text: Kinnari Amin, Georgia Perimeter College; Jared Burch, College of the Sequoias; Toni Coombs Garcia, Arizona State University; Esmarie Kennedy, San Antonio College; Rose Jenkins, Midlands Technical College; and Rachid Makroz, San Antonio College. I also want to thank Brent Griffin, Craig Johnson, Kathleen McLaughlin, Alana Tuckey, and Dorothy Wakefield for help in creating supplements. A big thank-you goes to Brad Davis, who assisted in building the answer key for the back of the text and helped in proofreading. I would also like to acknowledge Kathleen Almy and Heather Foes for their help and expertise in developing the Student Activity Workbook. Many thanks to all the reviewers, whose insights and ideas form the backbone of this text. I apologize for any omissions.

CALIFORNIA Charles Biles, *Humboldt State University* • Carol Curtis, *Fresno City College* • Freida Ganter, *California State University–Fresno* • Craig Nance, *Santiago Canyon College* **COLORADO** Roxanne Byrne, *University of Colorado–Denver* **CONNECTICUT** Kathleen McLaughlin, *Manchester Community College* • Dorothy Wakefield, *University of Connecticut* • Cathleen M. Zucco-Teveloff, *Trinity College* **DISTRICT OF COLUMBIA** Jill McGowan, *Howard University* **FLORIDA** Randall Allbritton, *Daytona Beach Community College* • Franco Fedele, *University of West Florida* • Laura Heath, *Palm Beach Community College* • Perrian Herring, *Okaloosa Walton College* • Marilyn Hixson, *Brevard Community College* • Philip Pina, *Florida Atlantic University* • Mike Rosenthal, *Florida International University* • James Smart, *Tallahassee Community College* **GEORGIA** Virginia Parks, *Georgia Perimeter College* • Chandler Pike, *University of Georgia* • Jill Smith, *University of Georgia* **IDAHO** K. Shane Goodwin, *Brigham Young University* • Craig Johnson, *Brigham Young University* • Brent Timothy, *Brigham Young University* • Kirk Trigsted, *University of Idaho* **ILLINOIS** Grant Alexander, *Joliet Junior College* • Kathleen Almy, *Rock Valley College* • John Bialas, *Joliet Junior College* • Linda Blanco, *Joliet Junior College* • Kevin Bodden, *Lewis & Clark Community College* • Rebecca Bonk, *Joliet Junior College* • Joanne Brunner, *Joliet Junior College* • James Butterbach, *Joliet Junior College* • Elena Catoiu, *Joliet Junior College* • Faye Dang, *Joliet Junior College* • Laura Egner, *Joliet Junior College* • Jason Eltrevoog, *Joliet Junior College* • Erica Egizio, *Lewis University* • Heather Foes, *Rock Valley College* • Randy Gallaher, *Lewis & Clark Community College* • Iraj Kalantari, *Western Illinois University* • Donna Katula, *Joliet Junior College* • Diane Long, *College of DuPage* • Jean McArthur, *Joliet Junior College* • David McGuire, *Joliet Junior College* • Angela McNulty, *Joliet Junior College* • Linda Padilla, *Joliet Junior College* • David Ruffato, *Joliet Junior College* • Patrick Stevens, *Joliet Junior College* • Robert Tuskey, *Joliet Junior College* • Stephen Zuro, *Joliet Junior College* **INDIANA** Jason Parcon, *Indiana University–Purdue University Ft. Wayne* **KANSAS** Donna Gorton, *Butler Community College* • Ingrid Peterson, *University of Kansas* **MARYLAND** John Climent, *Cecil Community College* • Rita Kolb, *The Community College of Baltimore County* **MASSACHUSETTS** Daniel Weiner, *Boston University* • Pradipta Seal, *Boston University of Public Health* **MICHIGAN** Margaret M. Balachowski, *Michigan Technological University* • Diane Krasnewich, *Muskegon Community College* • Susan Lenker, *Central Michigan University* • Timothy D. Stebbins, *Kalamazoo Valley Community College* • Sharon Stokero, *Michigan Technological University* • Alana Tuckey, *Jackson Community College* **MINNESOTA** Mezbhur Rahman, *Minnesota State University* **MISSOURI** Farroll Tim Wright, *University of Missouri–Columbia* **NEBRASKA** Jane Keller, *Metropolitan Community College* **NEW YORK** Jacob Amidon, *Finger Lakes Community College* • Stella Aminova, *Hunter College* • Pinyuen Chen, *Syracuse University* • Rebecca Daggar, *Rochester Institute of Technology* • Bryan Ingham, *Finger Lakes Community College* • Anne M. Jowsey, *Niagara County Community College* • Maryann E. Justinger, *Erie Community College–South Campus* • Bernie Lanciaux, *Rochester Institute of Technology* • Kathleen Miranda, *SUNY at Old Westbury* • Robert Sackett, *Erie Community College–North Campus* **NORTH CAROLINA** Fusan Akman, *Coastal Carolina Community College* • Mohammad Kazemi, *University of North Carolina–Charlotte* • Janet Mays, *Elon University* • Marilyn McCollum, *North Carolina State University* • Claudia McKenzie, *Central Piedmont Community College* • Said E. Said, *East Carolina University* • Karen Spike, *University of North Carolina–Wilmington* • Jeanette Szwec, *Cape Fear Community College* **OHIO** Richard Einsporn, *The University of Akron* • Michael McCraith, *Cuyaghoga Community College* **OREGON** Daniel Kim, *Southern Oregon University* • Jong Sung Kin, *Portland State University* **SOUTH CAROLINA** Diana Asmus, *Greenville Technical College* • Dr. William P. Fox, *Francis Marion University* • Cheryl Hawkins, *Greenville Technical College* • Rose Jenkins, *Midlands Technical College* • Lindsay Packer, *College of Charleston* **TENNESSEE** Nancy Pevey, *Pellissippi State Technical Community College* • David Ray, *University of Tennessee–Martin* **TEXAS** Jada Hill, *Richland College* • David Lane, *Rice University* • Alma F. Lopez, *South Plains College* **UTAH** Joe Gallegos, *Salt Lake City Community College* **VIRGINIA** Kim Jones, *Virginia Commonwealth University* • Vasanth Solomon, *Old Dominion University* **WEST VIRGINIA** Mike Mays, *West Virginia University* **WISCONSIN** William Applebaugh, *University of Wisconsin–Eau Claire* • Carolyn Chapel, *Western Wisconsin Technical College* • Beverly Dretzke, *University of Wisconsin–Eau Claire* • Jolene Hartwick, *Western Wisconsin Technical College* • Thomas Pomykalski, *Madison Area Technical College*

Michael Sullivan, III
Joliet Junior College

Supplements

For the Instructor

Annotated Instructor's Edition

(ISBN 13: 978-0-321-83903-9; ISBN 10: 0-321-83903-X)

Margin notes include helpful teaching tips, suggest alternative presentations, and point out common student errors. Exercise answers are included in the exercise sets when space allows. The complete answer section is located in the back of the text.

Instructor's Resource Center

All instructor resources can be downloaded from *www.pearsonhighered.com/irc.* This is a password-protected site that requires instructors to set up an account or, alternatively, instructor resources can be ordered from your Pearson Higher Education sales representative.

Instructor's Solutions Manual (Download only) by Craig C. Johnson, *Brigham Young University*, *Idaho*.

Fully worked solutions to every textbook exercise, including the chapter review and chapter tests. Case Study Answers are also provided. Available from the Instructor's Resource Center and MyStatLab.

Mini Lectures (Download only) by Craig C. Johnson, *Brigham Young University, Idaho*.

Mini Lectures are provided to help with lecture preparation by providing learning objectives, classroom examples not found in the text, teaching notes, and the answers to these examples. Mini Lectures are available from the Instructor's Resource Center and MyStatLab.

Online Test Bank

A test bank derived from TestGen is available on the Instructor's Resource Center. There is also a link to the TestGen website within the Instructor Resource area of MyStatLab.

PowerPoint® Lecture Slides

Free to qualified adopters, this classroom lecture presentation software is geared specifically to the sequence and philosophy of *Statistics: Informed Decisions Using Data.* Key graphics from the book are included to help bring the statistical concepts alive in the classroom. Slides are available for download from the Instructor's Resource Center and MyStatLab.

New! **Instructor's Guide for Activities Manual** by Heather Foes and Kathleen Almy, *Rock Valley College* and Michael Sullivan, III, *Joliet Junior College*. Accompanies the activity workbook with suggestions for incorporating the activities into class. The Guide is available from the Instructor's Resource Center and MyStatLab.

For the Student

Video Resources on DVD

(ISBN 13: 978-0-321-75746-3; ISBN 10: 0-321-75746-7) A comprehensive set of Video Lectures, tied to the textbook, in which examples from each chapter are worked out by Michael Sullivan and master statistics teachers. The videos provide excellent support for students who require additional assistance, for distance learning and self-paced programs, or for students who missed class. There are two types of videos on the DVD. Video Lectures and Author in the Classroom videos are both on the DVD and in MyStatLab.

Author in the Classroom Videos by Michael Sullivan, III, *Joliet Junior College*

These are actual classroom lectures presented and filmed by the author using Camtasia. Students not only will see additional fully worked-out examples but also will hear and see the development of the material. The videos provide excellent support for students who require additional assistance, for distance learning and self-paced programs, or for students who miss class. Available on the DVD and in MyStatLab.

Student's Solutions Manual by Craig C. Johnson, *Brigham Young University, Idaho*

(ISBN 13: 978-0-321-83908-4; ISBN 10: 0-321-83908-0)

Fully worked solutions to odd-numbered exercises with all solutions to the chapter reviews and chapter tests.

Technology Manuals The following technology manuals contain detailed tutorial instructions and worked-out examples and exercises. Available on the Pearson site:
www.pearsonhighered.com/mathstatsresources

- **Excel Manual** by Alana Tuckey, *Jackson Community College*
- **Graphing Calculator Manual for the TI-83/84 Plus and TI-89** by Kathleen McLaughlin and Dorothy Wakefield

New! **Student Activity Workbook** by Heather Foes and Kathleen Almy, *Rock Valley College*, and Michael Sullivan, III, *Joliet Junior College*

(ISBN 13: 978-0-321-75912-2; ISBN 10: 0-321-75912-5) Includes classroom and applet activities that allow students to experience statistics firsthand in an active learning environment. Also introduces resampling methods that help develop conceptual understanding of hypothesis testing.

Technology Resources

MyStatLab™ Online Course (access code required)

MyStatLab is a course management systems that delivers **proven results** in helping individual students succeed.

- MyStatLab can be successfully implemented in any environment—lab-based, hybrid, fully online, traditional—and demonstrates the quantifiable difference that integrated usage has on student retention, subsequent success, and overall achievement.
- MyStatLab's comprehensive online gradebook automatically tracks students' results on tests, quizzes, homework, and in the study plan. Instructors can use the gradebook to provide positive feedback or intervene if students have trouble. Gradebook data can be easily exported to a variety of spreadsheet programs, such as Microsoft Excel.

MyStatLab provides **engaging experiences** that personalize, stimulate, and measure learning for each student. In addition to the resources below, each course includes a full interactive online version of the accompanying textbook.

- **Exercises with Multimedia Learning Aids:** The homework and practice exercises in MyStatLab align with the exercises in the textbook, and they regenerate algorithmically to give students unlimited opportunity for practice and mastery. Exercises offer immediate helpful feedback, guided solutions, sample problems, animations, videos, and eText clips for extra help at point-of-use. Many of the exercises in the MyStatLab course have been rewritten with the help of Michael Sullivan, an avid MyStatLab user.
- **StatTalk Videos:** *24 Conceptual Videos to Help You Actually Understand Statistics.* Fun-loving statistician Andrew Vickers takes to the streets of Brooklyn, NY to demonstrate important statistical concepts through interesting stories and real-life events. These fun and engaging videos will help students actually understand statistical concepts. Available with an instructor's user guide and assessment questions.
- **Getting Ready for Statistics:** A library of questions now appears within each MyStatLab course to offer the developmental math topics students need for the course. These can be assigned as a prerequisite to other assignments, if desired.
- **Conceptual Question Library:** In addition to algorithmically regenerated questions that are aligned with your textbook, there is a library of 1,000 Conceptual Questions available in the assessment manager that require students to apply their statistical understanding.
- **StatCrunch:** MyStatLab integrates the web-based statistical software, StatCrunch, within the online assessment platform so that students can easily analyze data sets from exercises and the text. In addition, MyStatLab includes access to **www.StatCrunch.com,** a web site where users can access more than 14,500 shared data sets, conduct online surveys, perform complex analyses using the powerful statistical software, and generate compelling reports.
- **Statistical Software Support:** Knowing that students often use external statistical software, we make it easy to copy our data sets, both from the ebook and the MyStatLab questions, into software such as StatCrunch, Minitab, Excel, and more. Students have access to a variety of support tools—Technology Instruction Videos, Technology Study Cards, and Manuals for select titles—to learn how to effectively use statistical software.
- **Expert Tutoring:** Although many students describe the whole of MyStatLab as 'like having your own personal tutor," students also have access to live tutoring from Pearson. Qualified statistics instructors provide tutoring sessions for students via MyStatLab.

And, MyStatLab comes from a **trusted partner** with educational expertise and an eye on the future.

Knowing that you are using a Pearson product means knowing that you are using quality content. That means that our eTexts are accurate, that our assessment tools work, and that our questions are error-free. And whether you are just getting started with MyStatLab, or have a question along the way, we're here to help you learn about our technologies and how to incorporate them into your course.

To learn more about how MyStatLab combines proven learning applications with powerful assessment, visit **www.mystatlab.com** or contact your Pearson representative.

MyStatLab™ Ready to Go Course (access code required)

These new Ready to Go courses provide students with all the same great MyStatLab features that you're used to, but make it easier for instructors to get started. Each course includes pre-assigned homework and quizzes to make creating your course even simpler. Ask your Pearson representative about the details for this particular course or to see a copy of this course.

Active Learning Questions

Prepared in PowerPoint®, these questions are intended for use with classroom response systems. Several multiple-choice questions are available for each chapter of the book, allowing instructors to quickly assess mastery of material in class. The Active Learning Questions are available to download from within MyStatLab and from Pearson Education's online catalog.

MathXL® for Statistics Online Course (access code required)
MathXL® for Statistics is an online homework, tutorial, and assessment system that accompanies Pearson's textbooks in statistics.

- **Interactive homework exercises**, correlated to your textbook at the objective level, are algorithmically generated for unlimited practice and mastery. Most exercises are free-response and provide guided solutions, sample problems, and learning aids for extra help. In addition, StatCrunch, a complete data analysis tool, is available with all online homework and practice exercises.
- **Personalized Homework** assignments are designed by the instructor to meet the needs of the class and then personalized for each student based on test or quiz results. As a result, each student receives a homework assignment where the problems cover only the objectives that he or she has not yet mastered.
- **Personalized Study Plan**, generated when students complete a test or quiz or homework, indicates which topics have been

mastered and links to tutorial exercises for topics students have not mastered. Instructors can customize the available topics in the study plan to match their course concepts.

- **Multimedia learning aids**, such as video lectures and animations, help students independently improve their understanding and performance. Applets are also available to display statistical concepts in a graphical manner for classroom demonstration or independent use. These are assignable as homework to further encourage their use.
- **Gradebook**, designed specifically for mathematics and statistics, automatically tracks students' results, lets you stay on top of student performance, and gives you control over how to calculate final grades.
- **MathXL Exercise Builder** allows you to create static and algorithmic exercises for your online assignments. You can use the library of sample exercises as an easy starting point or use the Exercise Builder to edit any of the course-related exercises.
- **Assessment Manager** lets you create online homework, quizzes, and tests that are automatically graded. Select just the right mix of questions from the MathXL exercise bank, instructor-created custom exercises, and/or TestGen test items.

MathXL for Statistics is available to qualified adopters. For more information, visit our website at www.mathxl.com or contact your Pearson representative.

ActivStats®

Developed by Paul Velleman and Data Description, Inc., ActivStats is an award-winning multimedia introduction to statistics and a comprehensive learning tool that works in conjunction with the book. It complements this text with interactive features such as videos of real-world stories, teaching applets, and animated expositions of major statistics topics. It also contains tutorials for learning a variety of statistics software, including Data Desk®, Excel®, JMP®, MINITAB®, and SPSS®. ActivStats for Windows and Macintosh ISBN 13: 978-0-321-50014-4; ISBN 10: 0-321-50014-8. Contact your Pearson Arts & Sciences sales representative for details or visit *www.aw-bc.com/activstats.*

The Student Edition of MINITAB

A condensed version of the Professional release of MINITAB statistical software. It offers the full range of statistical methods and graphical capabilities, along with worksheets that can include up to 10,000 data points. Individual copies of the software can be bundled with the text. ISBN 13: 978-0-321-11313-9. ISBN 10: 0-321-11313-6 (CD only).

JMP Student Edition

An easy-to-use, streamlined version of JMP desktop statistical discovery software from SAS Institute, Inc. is available for bundling with the text. ISBN-13: 978-0-321-89164-8; ISBN-10: 0-321-89164-3

Instructors can contact local sales representatives for details on purchasing and bundling supplements with the textbook or contact the company at exam@pearson.com for examination copies of many of these items.

TestGen®

TestGen (www.pearsonhighered.com/testgen) enables instructors to build, edit, print, and administer tests using a computerized bank of questions developed to cover all the objectives of the text. TestGen is algorithmically based, allowing instructors to create multiple but equivalent versions of the same question or test with the click of a button. Instructors can also modify test bank questions or add new questions. Tests can be printed or administered online. The software and test bank are available for download from Pearson Education's online catalog.

StatCrunch®

StatCrunch is powerful web-based statistical software that allows users to perform complex analyses, share data sets, and generate compelling reports of their data. The vibrant online community offers more than 14,500 data sets for students to analyze.

- **Collect.** Users can upload their own data to StatCrunch or search a large library of publicly shared data sets, spanning almost any topic of interest. Also, an online survey tool allows users to quickly collect data via web-based surveys.
- **Crunch.** A full range of numerical and graphical methods allow users to analyze and gain insights from any data set. Interactive graphics help users understand statistical concepts, and are available for export to enrich reports with visual representations of data.
- **Communicate.** Reporting options help users create a wide variety of visually-appealing representations of their data.

Full access to StatCrunch is available with a MyStatLab kit, and StatCrunch is available by itself to qualified adopters. StatCrunch Mobile now available to access from your mobile device. For more information, visit our website at **www.statcrunch.com,** or contact your Pearson representative.

Applications Index

PART

1 Getting the Information You Need

Statistics is a process—a series of steps that leads to a goal. This text is divided into four parts to help the reader see the process of statistics.

Part 1 focuses on the first step in the process, which is to determine the research objective or question to be answered. Then information is obtained to answer the questions stated in the research objective.

1 Data Collection

OUTLINE

Making an Informed Decision

It is your senior year of high school. You will have a lot of exciting experiences in the upcoming year, plus a major decision to make—which college should I attend? The choice you make may affect many aspects of your life—your career, where you live, your significant other, and so on, so you don't want to simply choose the college that everyone else picks. You need to design a questionnaire to help you make an informed decision about college. In addition, you want to know how well the college you are considering educates its students. See Making an Informed Decision on page 60.

PUTTING IT TOGETHER

Statistics plays a major role in many different areas of our lives. For example, it is used in sports to help a general manager decide which player might be the best fit for a team. It is used by politicians to help them understand how the public feels about various governmental policies. Statistics is used to help determine the effectiveness (efficacy) of experimental drugs.

Used appropriately, statistics can provide an understanding of the world around us. Used inappropriately, it can lend support to inaccurate beliefs. Understanding the methodologies of statistics will provide you with the ability to analyze and critique studies. With this ability, you will be an informed consumer of information, which will enable you to distinguish solid analysis from the bogus presentation of numerical "facts."

To help you understand the features of this text and for hints to help you study, read the Pathway to Success on the front inside cover of the text.

Note to Instructor

Due to the large number of terms in this chapter, you may want students to create a list of terms, definitions, and their own examples for each term. This will allow students to make a personal connection to the concepts and will lead to a greater understanding of the vocabulary. Remind students that many terms presented in this chapter will be presented again in later chapters, so they should not feel overwhelmed by the number of definitions.

1.1 INTRODUCTION TO THE PRACTICE OF STATISTICS

OBJECTIVES

1. Define statistics and statistical thinking
2. Explain the process of statistics
3. Distinguish between qualitative and quantitative variables
4. Distinguish between discrete and continuous variables
5. Determine the level of measurement of a variable

1 Define Statistics and Statistical Thinking

Note to Instructor

This first objective defines what statistics is, but also lists some key elements to solid statistical thinking.

1. Anecdotal claims can be refuted with statistical analysis.
2. Poorly collected data are not useful.
3. Watch out for lurking variables in a study.
4. Results in statistics are not certain.

The Guidelines for Assessment and Instruction in Statistics Education (GAISE) report suggests these as major components of statistical thinking.

What is statistics? Many people say that statistics is numbers. After all, we are bombarded by numbers that supposedly represent how we feel and who we are. For example, we hear on the radio that 50% of first marriages, 67% of second marriages, and 74% of third marriages end in divorce (Forest Institute of Professional Psychology, Springfield, MO).

Another interesting consideration about the "facts" we hear or read is that two different sources can report two different results. For example, a December 5–7, 2011, poll conducted by CBS News indicated that 82% of Americans disapproved of the job that Congress was doing. However, a December 15–18, 2011, Gallup poll indicated that 86% of Americans disapproved of the job that Congress was doing. Is it possible that Congress's disapproval rating could increase by 4% in less than 2 weeks or is something else going on? Statistics helps to provide the answer.

Certainly, statistics has a lot to do with numbers, but this definition is only partially correct. Statistics is also about where the numbers come from (that is, how they were obtained) and how closely the numbers reflect reality.

DEFINITION

Statistics is the science of collecting, organizing, summarizing, and analyzing information to draw conclusions or answer questions. In addition, statistics is about providing a measure of confidence in any conclusions.

Let's break this definition into four parts. The first part states that statistics involves the collection of information. The second refers to the organization and summarization of information. The third states that the information is analyzed to draw conclusions or answer specific questions. The fourth part states that results should be reported using some measure that represents how convinced we are that our conclusions reflect reality.

What is the information referred to in the definition? The information is **data**, which the *American Heritage Dictionary* defines as "a fact or proposition used to draw a conclusion or make a decision." Data can be numerical, as in height, or nonnumerical, as in gender. In either case, data describe characteristics of an individual. Data are important in statistics because data are used to draw a conclusion or make a decision.

In Other Words
Anecdotal means that the information being conveyed is based on casual observation, not scientific research.

Analysis of data can lead to powerful results. Data can be used to offset anecdotal claims, such as the suggestion that cellular telephones cause brain cancer. After carefully collecting, summarizing, and analyzing data regarding this phenomenon, it was determined that there is no link between cell phone usage and brain cancer. See Examples 1 and 2 in Section 1.2.

Because data are powerful, they can be dangerous when misused. The misuse of data usually occurs when data are incorrectly obtained or analyzed. For example, radio or television talk shows regularly ask poll questions for which respondents must call in or use the Internet to supply their vote. Most likely, the individuals who are going to call in are those who have a strong opinion about the topic. This group is not likely to be representative of people in general, so the results of the poll are not meaningful. Whenever we look at data, we should be mindful of where the data come from.

Even when data tell us that a relation exists, we need to investigate. For example, a study showed that breast-fed children have higher IQs than those who were not breast-fed. Does this study mean that a mother who breast-feeds her child will increase the child's IQ? Not necessarily. It may be that some factor other than breast-feeding contributes to the IQ of the children. In this case, it turns out that mothers who breast-feed generally have higher IQs than those who do not. Therefore, it may be genetics that leads to the higher IQ, not breast-feeding.* This illustrates an idea in statistics known as the *lurking variable*. In statistics, we must consider lurking variables, because two variables are often influenced by a third variable. A good statistical study will have a way of dealing with lurking variables.

A key aspect of data is that they vary. Consider the students in your classroom. Is everyone the same height? No. Does everyone have the same color hair? No. So, within groups there is variation. Now consider yourself. Do you eat the same amount of food each day? No. Do you sleep the same number of hours each day? No. So even considering an individual there is variation. Data vary. One goal of statistics is to describe and understand the sources of variation. Variability in data may help to explain the different results obtained by Gallup and CBS News described at the beginning of this section.

Because of this variability, the results that we obtain using data can vary. In a mathematics class, if Bob and Jane are asked to solve $3x + 5 = 11$, they will both obtain $x = 2$ as the solution when they use the correct procedures. In a statistics class, if Bob and Jane are asked to estimate the average commute time for workers in Dallas, Texas, they will likely get different answers, even though they both use the correct procedure. The different answers occur because they likely surveyed different individuals, and these individuals have different commute times. Bob and Jane would get the same result if they both asked *all* commuters or the same commuters about their commutes, but how likely is this?

So, in mathematics when a problem is solved correctly, the results can be reported with 100% certainty. In statistics, when a problem is solved, the results do not have 100% certainty. In statistics, we might say that we are 95% confident that the average commute time in Dallas, Texas, is between 20 and 23 minutes. Uncertain results may seem disturbing now but will be more reasonable as we proceed through the course.

Without certainty, how can statistics be useful? Statistics can provide an understanding of the world around us because recognizing where variability in data comes from can help us to control it. Understanding the techniques presented in this text will provide you with powerful tools that will give you the ability to analyze and critique media reports (which may help you decide how to vote), make investment decisions (such as what mutual fund to invest in), or conduct research on major purchases (such as what type of car you should buy). This will help to make you an informed citizen, consumer of information, and critical and statistical thinker.

2 Explain the Process of Statistics

Consider the following scenario.

> You are walking down the street and notice that a person walking in front of you drops $100. Nobody seems to notice the $100 except you. Since you could keep the money without anyone knowing, would you keep the money or return it to the owner?

Note: Obtaining a truthful response to a question such as this is challenging. In Section 1.5, we present some techniques for obtaining truthful responses to sensitive questions.

*In fact, a study found that a gene called FADS2 is responsible for higher IQ scores in breast-fed babies. *Source*: Duke University, "Breastfeeding Boosts IQ in Infants with 'Helpful' Genetic Variant," *Science Daily* 6 November 2007.

Suppose you wanted to use this scenario as a gauge of the morality of students at your school by determining the percent of students who would return the money. How might you do this? You could attempt to present the scenario to every student at the school, but this is likely to be difficult or impossible if the student body is large. A second possibility is to present the scenario to 50 students and use the results to make a statement about all the students at the school.

DEFINITIONS

The entire group to be studied is called the **population**. An **individual** is a person or object that is a member of the population being studied. A **sample** is a subset of the population that is being studied. See Figure 1.

Figure 1

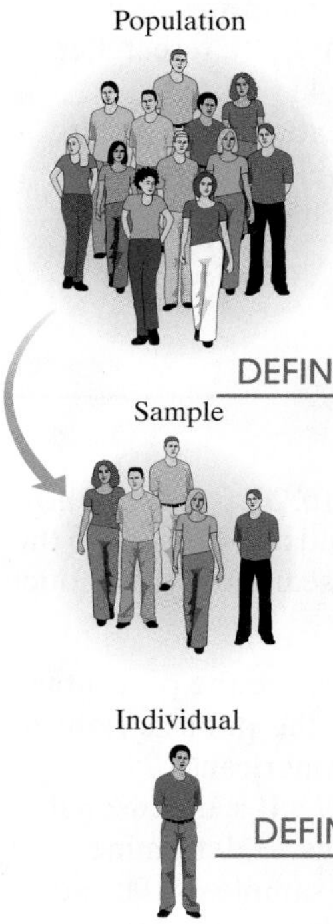

In the $100 study presented, the population is all the students at the school. Each student is an individual. The sample is the 50 students selected to participate in the study.

Suppose 39 of the 50 students stated that they would return the money to the owner. We could present this result by saying that the percent of students in the survey who would return the money to the owner is 78%. This is an example of a *descriptive statistic* because it describes the results of the sample without making any general conclusions about the population.

DEFINITIONS

A **statistic** is a numerical summary of a sample. **Descriptive statistics** consist of organizing and summarizing data. Descriptive statistics describe data through numerical summaries, tables, and graphs.

So 78% is a statistic because it is a numerical summary based on a sample. Descriptive statistics make it easier to get an overview of what the data are telling us.

If we extend the results of our sample to the population, we are performing *inferential statistics.*

DEFINITION

Inferential statistics uses methods that take a result from a sample, extend it to the population, and measure the reliability of the result.

The accuracy of a generalization always contains uncertainty because a sample cannot tell us everything about a population. Therefore, inferential statistics always includes a level of confidence in the results. So rather than saying that 78% of all students would return the money, we might say that we are 95% confident that between 74% and 82% of all students would return the money. Notice how this inferential statement includes a level of confidence (measure of reliability) in our results. It also includes a range of values to account for the variability in our results.

One goal of inferential statistics is to use statistics to estimate *parameters*.

DEFINITION

A **parameter** is a numerical summary of a population.

EXAMPLE 1 Parameter versus Statistic

Suppose the percentage of all students on your campus who own a car is 48.2%. This value represents a parameter because it is a numerical summary of a population. Suppose a sample of 100 students is obtained, and from this sample we find that 46% own a car. This value represents a statistic because it is a numerical summary of a sample.

Now Work Problem 7

The methods of statistics follow a process.

CAUTION

Many nonscientific studies are based on *convenience samples*, such as Internet surveys or phone-in polls. The results of any study performed using this type of sampling method are not reliable.

The Process of Statistics

1. *Identify the research objective.* A researcher must determine the question(s) he or she wants answered. The question(s) must be detailed so that it identifies the population that is to be studied.
2. *Collect the data needed to answer the question(s) posed in (1).* Conducting research on an entire population is often difficult and expensive, so we typically look at a sample. This step is vital to the statistical process, because if the data are not collected correctly, the conclusions drawn are meaningless. Do not overlook the importance of appropriate data collection. We discuss this step in detail in Sections 1.2 through 1.6.
3. *Describe the data.* Descriptive statistics allow the researcher to obtain an overview of the data and can help determine the type of statistical methods the researcher should use. We discuss this step in detail in Chapters 2 through 4.
4. *Perform inference.* Apply the appropriate techniques to extend the results obtained from the sample to the population and report a level of reliability of the results. We discuss techniques for measuring reliability in Chapters 5 through 8 and inferential techniques in Chapters 9 through 15.

Note to Instructor

Notice how the parts of the text are divided according to the process of statistics. As you enter a new part of the course, be sure to remind students where they are in the process of statistics.

EXAMPLE 2 The Process of Statistics: Gun Ownership

The AP-National Constitution Center conducted a poll August 11–16, 2010, to learn how adult Americans feel existing gun-control laws infringe on the second amendment to the U.S. Constitution. The following statistical process allowed the researchers to conduct their study.

1. *Identify the research objective.* The researchers wished to determine the percentage of adult Americans who believe gun-control laws infringe on the public's right to bear arms. Therefore, the population being studied was adult Americans.
2. *Collect the information needed to answer the question posed in (1).* It is unreasonable to expect to survey the more than 200 million adult Americans to determine how they feel about gun-control laws. So the researchers surveyed a sample of 1007 adult Americans. Of those surveyed, 514 stated they believe existing gun-control laws infringe on the public's right to bear arms.
3. *Describe the data.* Of the 1007 individuals in the survey, 51% (= 514/1007) believe existing gun-control laws infringe on the public's right to bear arms. This is a descriptive statistic because its value is determined from a sample.
4. *Perform inference.* The researchers at the AP-National Constitution Center wanted to extend the results of the survey to all adult Americans. Remember, when generalizing results from a sample to a population, the results are uncertain. To account for this uncertainty, researchers reported a 3% *margin of error.* This means that the researchers feel fairly certain (in fact, 95% certain) that the percentage of *all* adult Americans who believe existing gun-control laws infringe on the public's right to bear arms is somewhere between 48% (51% − 3%) and 54% (51% + 3%).

Now Work Problem 51

3 Distinguish between Qualitative and Quantitative Variables

Note to Instructor

Emphasize the point that variables vary. This is key to helping students to develop statistical thinking.

Once a research objective is stated, a list of the information we want to learn about the individuals must be created. **Variables** are the characteristics of the individuals within the population. For example, recently my son and I planted a tomato plant in our backyard.

We collected information about the tomatoes harvested from the plant. The individuals we studied were the tomatoes. The variable that interested us was the weight of a tomato. My son noted that the tomatoes had different weights even though they came from the same plant. He discovered that variables such as weight may vary.

If variables did not vary, they would be constants, and statistical inference would not be necessary. Think about it this way: If each tomato had the same weight, then knowing the weight of one tomato would allow us to determine the weights of all tomatoes. However, the weights of the tomatoes vary. One goal of research is to learn the causes of the variability so that we can learn to grow plants that yield the best tomatoes.

Variables can be classified into two groups: *qualitative* or *quantitative*.

DEFINITIONS

Qualitative, or categorical, variables allow for classification of individuals based on some attribute or characteristic.

Quantitative variables provide numerical measures of individuals. The values of a quantitative variable can be added or subtracted and provide meaningful results.

In Other Words
Typically, there is more than one correct approach to solving a problem. For example, if you turn the key in your car's ignition and it doesn't start, one approach would be to look under the hood to try to determine what is wrong. (Of course, this approach will work only if you know how to fix cars.) A second, equally valid approach would be to call an automobile mechanic to service the car.

Many examples in this text will include a suggested **approach**, or a way to look at and organize a problem so that it can be solved. The approach will be a suggested method of *attack* toward solving the problem. This does not mean that the approach given is the only way to solve the problem, because many problems have more than one approach leading to a correct solution.

EXAMPLE 3 Distinguishing between Qualitative and Quantitative Variables

Problem Determine whether the following variables are qualitative or quantitative.

(a) Gender
(b) Temperature
(c) Number of days during the past week that a college student studied
(d) Zip code

Approach Quantitative variables are numerical measures such that meaningful arithmetic operations can be performed on the values of the variable. Qualitative variables describe an attribute or characteristic of the individual that allows researchers to categorize the individual.

Solution

(a) Gender is a qualitative variable because it allows a researcher to categorize the individual as male or female. Notice that arithmetic operations cannot be performed on these attributes.
(b) Temperature is a quantitative variable because it is numeric, and operations such as addition and subtraction provide meaningful results. For example, 70°F is 10°F warmer than 60°F.
(c) Number of days during the past week that a college student studied is a quantitative variable because it is numeric, and operations such as addition and subtraction provide meaningful results.
(d) Zip code is a qualitative variable because it categorizes a location. Notice that, even though they are numeric, adding or subtracting zip codes does not provide meaningful results.

Now Work Problem 15

Example 3(d) shows us that a variable may be qualitative while having numeric values. Just because the value of a variable is numeric does not mean that the variable is quantitative.

4 Distinguish between Discrete and Continuous Variables

We can further classify quantitative variables into two types: *discrete* or *continuous*.

DEFINITIONS

A **discrete variable** is a quantitative variable that has either a finite number of possible values or a countable number of possible values. The term *countable* means that the values result from counting, such as 0, 1, 2, 3, and so on. A discrete variable cannot take on every possible value between any two possible values.

A **continuous variable** is a quantitative variable that has an infinite number of possible values that are not countable. A continuous variable may take on every possible value between any two values.

In Other Words
If you count to get the value of a quantitative variable, it is discrete. If you measure to get the value of a quantitative variable, it is continuous.

Figure 2 illustrates the relationship among qualitative, quantitative, discrete, and continuous variables.

Figure 2

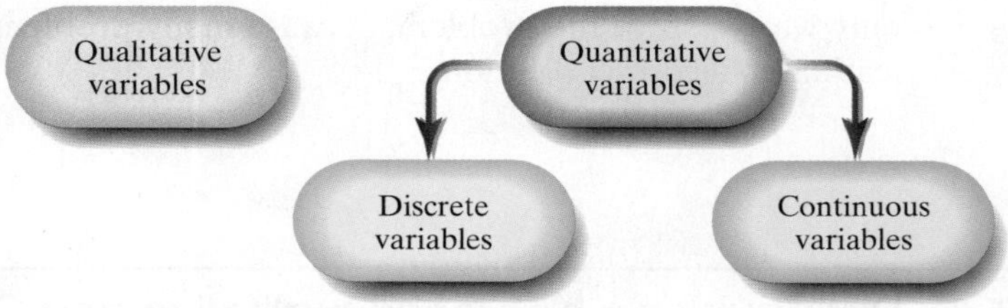

EXAMPLE 4 Distinguishing between Discrete and Continuous Variables

Problem Determine whether the quantitative variables are discrete or continuous.

(a) The number of heads obtained after flipping a coin five times.
(b) The number of cars that arrive at a McDonald's drive-thru between 12:00 P.M. and 1:00 P.M.
(c) The distance a 2012 Toyota Prius can travel in city driving conditions with a full tank of gas.

Approach A variable is discrete if its value results from counting. A variable is continuous if its value is measured.

Solution

(a) The number of heads obtained by flipping a coin five times is a discrete variable because we can count the number of heads obtained. The possible values of this discrete variable are 0, 1, 2, 3, 4, 5.
(b) The number of cars that arrive at a McDonald's drive-thru between 12:00 P.M. and 1:00 P.M. is a discrete variable because we find its value by counting the cars. The possible values of this discrete variable are 0, 1, 2, 3, 4, and so on. Notice that this number has no upper limit.
(c) The distance traveled is a continuous variable because we measure the distance (miles, feet, inches, and so on).

Now Work Problem 23

Continuous variables are often rounded. For example, if a certain make of car gets 24 miles per gallon (mpg) of gasoline, its miles per gallon must be greater than or equal to 23.5 and less than 24.5, or $23.5 \le \text{mpg} < 24.5$.

The type of variable (qualitative, discrete, or continuous) dictates the methods that can be used to analyze the data.

The list of observed values for a variable is **data**. Gender is a variable; the observations male and female are data. **Qualitative data** are observations corresponding to a qualitative variable. **Quantitative data** are observations corresponding to a quantitative variable. **Discrete data** are observations corresponding to a discrete variable. **Continuous data** are observations corresponding to a continuous variable.

Note to Instructor

Consider assigning the Student Data Survey Activity from the Student Activity Workbook.

EXAMPLE 5 Distinguishing between Variables and Data

Problem Table 1 presents a group of selected countries and information regarding these countries as of November, 2011. Identify the individuals, variables, and data in Table 1.

TABLE 1

Country	Government Type	Life Expectancy (years)	Population (in millions)
Australia	Federal parliamentary democracy	81.81	21.8
Canada	Constitutional monarchy	81.38	34.0
France	Republic	81.19	65.3
Morocco	Constitutional monarchy	75.90	32.0
Poland	Republic	76.05	38.4
Sri Lanka	Republic	75.73	21.3
United States	Federal republic	78.37	313.2

Source: CIA *World Factbook*

Approach An individual is an object or person for whom we wish to obtain data. The variables are the characteristics of the individuals, and the data are the specific values of the variables.

Solution The individuals in the study are the countries: Australia, Canada, and so on. The variables measured for each country are *government type*, *life expectancy*, and *population*. The variable *government type* is qualitative because it categorizes the individual. The variables *life expectancy* and *population* are quantitative.

The quantitative variable *life expectancy* is continuous because it is measured. The quantitative variable *population* is discrete because we count people. The observations are the data. For example, the data corresponding to the variable *life expectancy* are 81.81, 81.38, 81.19, 75.90, 76.05, 75.73, and 78.37. The following data correspond to the individual Poland: a republic government with residents whose life expectancy is 76.05 years and population is 38.4 million people. Republic is an instance of qualitative data that results from observing the value of the qualitative variable *government type.* The life expectancy of 76.05 years is an instance of quantitative data that results from observing the value of the quantitative variable *life expectancy*.

Now Work Problem 45

Note to Instructor
This objective is optional and can be skipped without loss of continuity.

5 Determine the Level of Measurement of a Variable

Rather than classify a variable as qualitative or quantitative, we can assign a level of measurement to the variable.

DEFINITIONS

A variable is at the **nominal level of measurement** if the values of the variable name, label, or categorize. In addition, the naming scheme does not allow for the values of the variable to be arranged in a ranked or specific order.

A variable is at the **ordinal level of measurement** if it has the properties of the nominal level of measurement, however the naming scheme allows for the values of the variable to be arranged in a ranked or specific order.

A variable is at the **interval level of measurement** if it has the properties of the ordinal level of measurement and the differences in the values of the variable have meaning. A value of zero does not mean the absence of the quantity. Arithmetic operations such as addition and subtraction can be performed on values of the variable.

A variable is at the **ratio level of measurement** if it has the properties of the interval level of measurement and the ratios of the values of the variable have meaning. A value of zero means the absence of the quantity. Arithmetic operations such as multiplication and division can be performed on the values of the variable.

In Other Words
The word *nominal* comes from the Latin word *nomen*, which means to name. When you see the word *ordinal*, think order.

Variables that are nominal or ordinal are qualitative variables. Variables that are interval or ratio are quantitative variables.

EXAMPLE 6 Determining the Level of Measurement of a Variable

Problem For each of the following variables, determine the level of measurement.
(a) Gender
(b) Temperature
(c) Number of days during the past week that a college student studied
(d) Letter grade earned in your statistics class

Approach For each variable, we ask the following: Does the variable simply categorize each individual? If so, the variable is nominal. Does the variable categorize *and* allow ranking of each value of the variable? If so, the variable is ordinal. Do differences in values of the variable have meaning, but a value of zero does not mean the absence of the quantity? If so, the variable is interval. Do ratios of values of the variable have meaning *and* there is a natural zero starting point? If so, the variable is ratio.

Solution
(a) Gender is a variable measured at the nominal level because it only allows for categorization of male or female. Plus, it is not possible to rank gender classifications.
(b) Temperature is a variable measured at the interval level because differences in the value of the variable make sense. For example, 70°F is 10°F warmer than 60°F. Notice that the ratio of temperatures does not represent a meaningful result. For example, 60°F is not twice as warm as 30°F. In addition, 0°F does not represent the absence of heat.

(c) Number of days during the past week that a college student studied is measured at the ratio level, because the ratio of two values makes sense and a value of zero has meaning. For example, a student who studies four days studies twice as many days as a student who studies two days.

(d) Letter grade is a variable measured at the ordinal level because the values of the variable can be ranked, but differences in values have no meaning. For example, an A is better than a B, but A − B has no meaning.

Now Work Problem 31

When classifying variables according to their level of measurement, it is extremely important that we recognize what the variable is intended to measure. For example, suppose we want to know whether cars with 4-cylinder engines get better gas mileage than cars with 6-cylinder engines. Here, engine size represents a category of data and so the variable is nominal. On the other hand, if we want to know the average number of cylinders in cars in the United States, the variable is classified as ratio (an 8-cylinder engine has twice as many cylinders as a 4-cylinder engine).

1.1 ASSESS YOUR UNDERSTANDING

VOCABULARY AND SKILL BUILDING

1. Define statistics.

2. Explain the difference between a population and a sample.

3. A(n) _individual_ is a person or object that is a member of the population being studied.

4. _Descriptive_ statistics consists of organizing and summarizing information collected, while _inferential_ statistics uses methods that generalize results obtained from a sample to the population and measure the reliability of the results.

5. A(n) _statistic_ is a numerical summary of a sample. A(n) _parameter_ is a numerical summary of a population.

6. _Variables_ are the characteristics of the individuals of the population being studied.

In Problems 7–14, determine whether the underlined value is a parameter or a statistic.

NW **7. State Government** Following the 2010 national midterm election, 12% of the governors of the 50 United States were female. *Source*: National Governors Association Parameter

8. Calculus Exam The average score for a class of 28 students taking a calculus midterm exam was 72%. Parameter

9. School Bullies In a national survey of 1300 high school students (grades 9 to 12), 32% of respondents reported that someone had bullied them at school. *Source*: Bureau of Justice Statistics

10. Drug Use In a national survey on substance abuse, 10.0% of respondents aged 12 to 17 reported using illicit drugs within the past month. *Source*: Substance Abuse and Mental Health Services Administration, *Results from the 2009 National Survey on Drug Use and Health: National Findings* Statistic

11. Batting Average Ty Cobb is one of major league baseball's greatest hitters of all time, with a career batting average of 0.366. *Source*: baseball-almanac.com Parameter

12. Moonwalkers Only 12 men have walked on the moon. The average age of these men at the time of their moonwalks was 39 years, 11 months, 15 days. *Source*: Wikipedia.org Parameter

13. Hygiene Habits A study of 6076 adults in public rest rooms (in Atlanta, Chicago, New York City, and San Francisco) found that 23% did not wash their hands before exiting. *Source*: American Society of Microbiology and the Soap and Detergent Association Statistic

14. Public Knowledge Interviews of 100 adults 18 years of age or older, conducted nationwide, found that 44% could state the minimum age required for the office of U.S. president. *Source*: *Newsweek Magazine* Statistic

In Problems 15–22, classify the variable as qualitative or quantitative.

NW **15.** Nation of origin Qualitative

16. Number of siblings Quantitative

17. Grams of carbohydrates in a doughnut Quantitative

18. Number on a football player's jersey Qualitative

19. Number of unpopped kernels in a bag of ACT microwave popcorn Quantitative

20. Assessed value of a house Quantitative

21. Phone number Qualitative

22. Student ID number Qualitative

In Problems 23–30, determine whether the quantitative variable is discrete or continuous. 24. Continuous

NW **23.** Goals scored in a season by a soccer player Discrete

24. Volume of water lost each day through a leaky faucet

25. Length (in minutes) of a country song Continuous

26. Number of Sequoia trees in a randomly selected acre of Yosemite National Park Discrete

27. Temperature on a randomly selected day in Memphis, Tennessee Continuous

28. Internet connection speed in kilobytes per second Continuous

29. Points scored in an NCAA basketball game Discrete

30. Air pressure in pounds per square inch in an automobile tire Continuous

In Problems 31–38, determine the level of measurement of each variable. 35. Ordinal

NW **31.** Nation of origin Nominal

32. Movie ratings of one star through five stars Ordinal

33. Volume of water used by a household in a day Ratio

34. Year of birth of college students Interval

35. Highest degree conferred (high school, bachelor's, and so on)

36. Eye color Nominal

37. Assessed value of a house Ratio

38. Time of day measured in military time Interval

In Problems 39–44, a research objective is presented. For each, identify the population and sample in the study.

39. The Gallup Organization contacts 1028 teenagers who are 13 to 17 years of age and live in the United States and asks whether or not they had been prescribed medications for any mental disorders, such as depression or anxiety.

40. A quality-control manager randomly selects 50 bottles of Coca-Cola that were filled on October 15 to assess the calibration of the filling machine.

41. A farmer wants to learn about the weight of his soybean crop. He randomly samples 100 plants and weighs the soybeans on each plant.

42. Every year the U.S. Census Bureau releases the *Current Population Report* based on a survey of 50,000 households. The goal of this report is to learn the demographic characteristics of all households within the United States, such as income.

43. Folate and Hypertension Researcher John P. Forman and co-workers want to determine whether or not higher folate intake is associated with a lower risk of hypertension (high blood pressure) in younger women (27 to 44 years of age). To make this determination, they look at 7373 cases of hypertension in younger women and find that younger women who consume at least 1000 micrograms per day (μg/d) of total folate (dietary plus supplemental) had a decreased risk of hypertension compared with those who consume less than 200 μg/d. *Source:* John P. Forman, MD; Eric B. Rimm, ScD; Meir J. Stampfer, MD; Gary C. Curhan, MD, ScD, "Folate Intake and the Risk of Incident Hypertension among US Women," *Journal of the American Medical Association* 293:320–329, 2005

44. A large community college notices that an increasing number of full-time students are working while attending the school. The administration randomly selects 128 students and asks this question: How many hours per week do you work?

In Problems 45–48, identify the individuals, variables, and data corresponding to the variables. Determine whether each variable is qualitative, continuous, or discrete.

NW **45. Smart Phones** The following represent information on smart phones recommended by CNET.

Model	Weight (ounces)	Service Provider	Depth (inches)
Motorola Droid X	5.47	Verizon	0.39
Motorola Droid 2	5.96	Verizon	0.53
Apple iPhone 4	4.8	ATT	0.37
Samsung Epic 4G	5.5	Sprint	0.6
Samsung Captivate	4.5	ATT	0.39

Source: cnet.com

46. BMW Cars The following information relates to the 2011 model year product line of BMW automobiles.

Model	Body Style	Weight (lb)	Number of Seats
3 Series	Coupe	3362	4
5 Series	Sedan	4056	5
6 Series	Convertible	4277	4
7 Series	Sedan	4564	5
X3	Sport utility	4012	5
Z4 Roadster	Coupe	3505	2

Source: www.motortrend.com

47. Driver's License Laws The following data represent driver's license laws for various states.

State	Minimum Age for Driver's License (unrestricted)	Mandatory Belt Use Seating Positions	Maximum Allowable Speed Limit (cars on rural interstate), mph, 2011
Alabama	17	Front	70
Colorado	17	Front	75
Indiana	18	All	70
North Carolina	16	All	70
Wisconsin	18	All	65

Source: Governors Highway Safety Association

48. MP3 Players The following represent information on MP3 players recommended by CNET.

49. (b) Adolescents 18 to 21; 20, 211; 18 year old Israeli Military recruits 49. (c) Average IQ of smokers: 94; average IQ of nonsmokers: 101
51. (a) To determine the proportion of adult Americans who believe the federal government wastes 51 cents or more of every dollar

Product	Rating	Memory (GB)	Audio Playback Time (hours)
Apple iPod Touch	Outstanding	32	40
Zune HD	Excellent	32	33
SanDisk Sansa Clip+	Excellent	4	15
Sony X-Series Walkman	Excellent	16	33
Apple iPod Nano	Very Good	8	24

Source: cnet.com

49. (a) To determine if adolescents who smoke have a lower IQ than nonsmokers
49. (d) Lower IQ individuals are more likely to choose to smoke

APPLYING THE CONCEPTS

49. Smoker's IQ A study was conducted in which 20,211 18-year-old Israeli male military recruits were given an exam to measure IQ. In addition, the recruits were asked to disclose their smoking status. An individual was considered a smoker if he smoked at least one cigarette per day. The goal of the study was to determine whether adolescents aged 18 to 21 who smoke have a lower IQ than nonsmokers. It was found that the average IQ of the smokers was 94, while the average IQ of the nonsmokers was 101. The researchers concluded that lower IQ individuals are more likely to choose to smoke, not that smoking makes people less intelligent. *Source*: Weiser, M., Zarka, S. Werbeloff, N., Kravitz, E. and Lubin, G. (2010). "Cognitive Test Scores in Male Adolescent Cigarette Smokers Compared to Non-smokers: A Population-Based Study." *Addiction*. 105:358–363. doi: 10.1111/j.1360-0443.2009.02740.x)

(a) What is the research objective?
(b) What is the population being studied? What is the sample?
(c) What are the descriptive statistics?
(d) What are the conclusions of the study?

50. A Cure for the Common Wart A study conducted by researchers was designed "to determine if application of duct tape is as effective as cryotherapy (liquid nitrogen applied to the wart for 10 seconds every 2 to 3 weeks) in the treatment of common warts." The researchers randomly divided 51 patients into two groups. The 26 patients in group 1 had their warts treated by applying duct tape to the wart for 6.5 days and then removing the tape for 12 hours, at which point the cycle was repeated for a maximum of 2 months. The 25 patients in group 2 had their warts treated by cryotherapy for a maximum of six treatments. Once the treatments were complete, it was determined that 85% of the patients in group 1 and 60% of the patients in group 2 had complete resolution of their warts. The researchers concluded that duct tape is significantly more effective in treating warts than cryotherapy. *Source*: Dean R. Focht III, Carole Spicer, Mary P. Fairchok. "The Efficacy of Duct Tape vs. Cryotherapy in the Treatment of Verruca Vulgaris (The Common Wart)," *Archives of Pediatrics and Adolescent Medicine*, 156(10), 2002

(a) What is the research objective?
(b) What is the population being studied? What is the sample?
(c) What are the descriptive statistics?
(d) What are the conclusions of the study?

NW **51. Government Waste** Gallup News Service conducted a survey of 1026 American adults aged 18 years or older, August 31–September, 2, 2009. The respondents were asked, "Of every tax dollar that goes to the federal government in Washington, D.C., how many cents of each dollar would you say are wasted?" Of the 1026 individuals surveyed, 35% indicated that 51 cents or more is wasted. Gallup reported that 35% of all adult Americans 18 years or older believe the federal government wastes at least 51 cents of each dollar spent, with a margin of error of 4% and a 95% level of confidence. 51. (b) American adults aged 18 years or older

(a) What is the research objective?
(b) What is the population?
(c) What is the sample? (c) 1026 American adults aged 18 years or older
(d) List the descriptive statistics.
(e) What can be inferred from this survey?

52. Retirement Planning The Principal Financial Group conducted a survey of 1172 employees in the United States between July 28, 2010, and August 8, 2010, and asked if they were currently participating in the employer-sponsored automatic payroll deduction for a 401(k) plan to save for retirement. Of the 1172 employees surveyed, 27% indicated they were participating. The Principal Group reported that 27% of all employees in the United States participate in automatic payroll deduction for a 401(k) plan to save for retirement with a 4% margin of error and 95% confidence.

(a) What is the research objective?
(b) What is the population? All employees in the United States
(c) What is the sample? 1172 employees in the United States
(d) List the descriptive statistics. 27% participate
(e) What can be inferred from this survey?

53. What Level of Measurement It is extremely important for a researcher to clearly define the variables in a study because this helps to determine the type of analysis that can be performed on the data. For example, if a researcher wanted to describe baseball players based on jersey number, what level of measurement would the variable *jersey number* be? Now suppose the researcher felt that certain players who were of lower caliber received higher numbers. Does the level of measurement of the variable change? If so, how?

54. Interpreting the Variable Suppose a fundraiser holds a raffle for which each person who enters the room receives a ticket. The tickets are numbered 1 to N, where N is the number of people at the fundraiser. The first person to arrive receives ticket number 1, the second person receives ticket number 2, and so on. Determine the level of measurement for each of the following interpretations of the variable *ticket number.*

(a) The winning ticket number. Nominal
(b) The winning ticket number was announced as 329. An attendee noted his ticket number was 294 and stated, "I guess I arrived too early." Ordinal
(c) The winning ticket number was announced as 329. An attendee looked around the room and commented, "It doesn't look like there are 329 people in attendance." Ratio

50. (a) To determine if duct tape is as effective as cryotherapy in the treatment of warts. (b) People with warts; 51 patients with warts
(c) 85% in group 1, 60% in group 2 had resolution of their warts (d) Duct tape is more effective in treating warts.
51. (d) Of the 1026 individuals surveyed, 35% indicated that 51 cents or more is wasted
52. (a) To determine the proportion of employees who participate in an employer-sponsored, automatic payroll deduction for a 401(k).

55. Analyze the Article Read the newspaper article and identify (a) the research question the study addresses, (b) the population, (c) the sample, (d) the descriptive statistics, and (e) the inferences of the study.

Study: Educational TV for Toddlers OK

CHICAGO (AP)—*Arthur* and *Barney* are OK for toddler TV-watching, but not *Rugrats* and certainly not *Power Rangers*, reports a new study of early TV-watching and future attention problems.

The research involved children younger than 3, so TV is mostly a no–no anyway, according to the experts. But if TV is allowed, it should be of the educational variety, the researchers said.

Every hour per day that kids under 3 watched violent child-oriented entertainment their risk doubled for attention problems five years later, the study found. Even nonviolent kids' shows like *Rugrats* and *The Flintstones* carried a still substantial risk for attention problems, though slightly lower.

On the other hand, educational shows, including *Arthur, Barney* and *Sesame Street* had no association with future attention problems.

Interestingly, the risks only occurred in children younger than age 3, perhaps because that is a particularly crucial period of brain development. Those results echo a different study last month that suggested TV-watching has less impact on older children's behavior than on toddlers.

The American Academy of Pediatrics recommends no television for children younger than 2 and limited TV for older children.

The current study by University of Washington researchers was prepared for release Monday in November's issue of the journal *Pediatrics.*

Previous research and news reports on TV's effects have tended to view television as a single entity, without regard to content. But "the reality is that it's not inherently good or bad. It really depends on what they watch," said Dr. Dimitri Christakis, who co-authored the study with researcher Frederick Zimmerman.

Their study was based on parent questionnaires. They acknowledge it's observational data that only suggests a link and isn't proof that TV habits cause attention problems. Still, they think the connection is plausible.

The researchers called a show violent if it involved fighting, hitting people, threats or other violence that was central to the plot or a main character. Shows listed included *Power Rangers, Lion King* and *Scooby Doo.*

These shows, and other kids' shows without violence, also tend to be very fast-paced, which may hamper children's ability to focus attention, Christakis said.

Shows with violence also send a flawed message, namely that "if someone gets bonked on the head with a rolling pin, it just makes a funny sound and someone gets dizzy for a minute and then everything is back to normal," Christakis said.

Dennis Wharton of the National Association of Broadcasters, a trade association for stations and networks including those with entertainment and educational children's TV shows, said he had not had a chance to thoroughly review the research and declined to comment on specifics.

Wharton said his group believes "there are many superb television programs for children, and would acknowledge that it is important for parents to supervise the media consumption habits of young children."

The study involved a nationally representative sample of 967 children whose parents answered government-funded child development questionnaires in 1997 and 2002. Questions involved television viewing habits in 1997. Parents were asked in 2002 about their children's behavior, including inattentiveness, difficulty concentrating and restlessness.

The researchers took into account other factors that might have influenced the results—including cultural differences and parents' education levels—and still found a strong link between the non-educational shows and future attention problems.

Peggy O'Brien, senior vice president for educational programming and services at the Corporation for Public Broadcasting, said violence in ads accompanying shows on commercial TV might contribute to the study results.

She said lots of research about brain development goes into the production of educational TV programming for children, and that the slower pace is intentional.

"We want it to be kind of an extension of play" rather than fantasy, she said. *Source:* "Study: Educational TV for Toddlers OK" by Chicago (AP), © 2008. Reprinted with permission by The Associated Press.

EXPLAINING THE CONCEPTS

56. Contrast the differences between qualitative and quantitative variables.

57. Discuss the differences between discrete and continuous variables.

58. In your own words, define the four levels of measurement of a variable. Give an example of each.

59. Explain what is meant when we say "data vary." How does this variability affect the results of statistical analysis?

60. Explain the process of statistics.

61. The age of a person is commonly considered to be a continuous random variable. Could it be considered a discrete random variable instead? Explain.

1.2 OBSERVATIONAL STUDIES VERSUS DESIGNED EXPERIMENTS

OBJECTIVES

1. Distinguish between an observational study and an experiment
2. Explain the various types of observational studies

Note to Instructor

If you like, you can wait to cover the material in Sections 1.2 through 1.6 until after Chapter 4. Provided you explain the concept of random sample, you can cover this material after Chapter 8.

1 Distinguish between an Observational Study and an Experiment

Once our research question is developed, we must develop methods for obtaining the data that can be used to answer the questions posed in our research objective. There are two methods for collecting data, *observational studies* and *designed experiments*. To see the difference between these two methods, read the following two studies.

EXAMPLE 1 Cellular Phones and Brain Tumors

Researcher Elisabeth Cardis and her colleagues wanted "to determine whether mobile phone use increases the risk of [brain] tumors." To do so, the researchers identified 5117 individuals from 13 countries who were 30–59 years of age who had brain tumors diagnosed between 2000 and 2004 and matched them with 5634 individuals who did not have brain tumors. The matching was based on age, gender, and region of residence. Both the individuals with tumors and the matched individuals were interviewed to learn about past mobile phone use, as well as sociodemographic background, medical history, and smoking status. The researchers found no significant difference in cell phone use between the two groups. The researchers concluded there is "no increased risk of brain tumors observed in association with use of mobile phones."
(*Source*: Elisabeth Cardis et al. "Brain Tumour Risk in Relation to Mobile Telephone Use," *International Journal of Epidemiology* 2010: 1–20)

EXAMPLE 2 Cellular Phones and Brain Tumors

Researchers Joseph L. Roti Roti and associates examined "whether chronic exposure to radio frequency (RF) radiation at two common cell phone signals—835.62 megahertz, a frequency used by analogue cell phones, and 847.74 megahertz, a frequency used by digital cell phones—caused brain tumors in rats." To do so, the researchers randomly divided 480 rats into three groups. The rats in group 1 were exposed to the analogue cell phone frequency; the rats in group 2 were exposed to the digital frequency; the rats in group 3 served as controls and received no radiation. The exposure was done for 4 hours a day, 5 days a week for 2 years. The rats in all three groups were treated the same, except for the RF exposure.

After 505 days of exposure, the researchers reported the following after analyzing the data. "We found no statistically significant increases in any tumor type, including brain, liver, lung or kidney, compared to the control group." (*Source*: M. La Regina, E. Moros, W. Pickard, W. Straube, J. L. Roti Roti, "The Effect of Chronic Exposure to 835.62 MHz FMCW or 847.74 MHz CDMA on the Incidence of Spontaneous Tumors in Rats," Bioelectromagnetic Society Conference, June 25, 2002)

In both studies, the goal was to determine if radio frequencies from cell phones increase the risk of contracting brain tumors. Whether or not brain cancer was contracted is the *response variable.* The level of cell phone usage is the *explanatory variable.* In research, we wish to determine how varying the amount of an **explanatory variable** affects the value of a **response variable**.

What are the differences between the studies in Examples 1 and 2? Obviously, in Example 1 the study was conducted on humans, while the study in Example 2 was conducted on rats. However, there is a bigger difference. In Example 1, no attempt was made to influence the individuals in the study. The researchers simply interviewed people to determine their historical use of cell phones. No attempt was made to influence the value of the explanatory variable, radio-frequency exposure (cell phone use). Because the researchers simply recorded the past behavior of the participants, the study in Example 1 is an *observational study.*

DEFINITION

An **observational study** measures the value of the response variable without attempting to influence the value of either the response or explanatory variables. That is, in an observational study, the researcher observes the behavior of the individuals without trying to influence the outcome of the study.

In the study in Example 2, the researchers obtained 480 rats and divided the rats into three groups. Each group was *intentionally* exposed to various levels of radiation. The researchers then compared the number of rats that had brain tumors. Clearly, there was an attempt to influence the individuals in this study because the value of the explanatory variable (exposure to radio frequency) was influenced. Because the researchers controlled the value of the explanatory variable, we call the study in Example 2 a *designed experiment.*

DEFINITION

If a researcher assigns the individuals in a study to a certain group, intentionally changes the value of an explanatory variable, and then records the value of the response variable for each group, the study is a **designed experiment**.

Now Work Problem 9

Which Is Better? A Designed Experiment or an Observational Study? To answer this question, let's consider another study.

EXAMPLE 3 Do Flu Shots Benefit Seniors?

Researchers wanted to determine the long-term benefits of the influenza vaccine on seniors aged 65 years and older. The researchers looked at records of over 36,000 seniors for 10 years. The seniors were divided into two groups. Group 1 were seniors who chose to get a flu vaccination shot, and group 2 were seniors who chose not to get a flu vaccination shot. After observing the seniors for 10 years, it was determined that seniors who get flu shots are 27% less likely to be hospitalized for pneumonia or influenza and 48% less likely to die from pneumonia or influenza. (*Source*: Kristin L. Nichol, MD, MPH, MBA, James D. Nordin, MD, MPH, David B. Nelson, PhD, John P. Mullooly, PhD, Eelko Hak, PhD. "Effectiveness of Influenza Vaccine in the Community-Dwelling Elderly," *New England Journal of Medicine* 357:1373–1381, 2007)

Wow! The results of this study sound great! All seniors should go out and get a flu shot. Right? Not necessarily. The authors were concerned about *confounding*. They were concerned that lower hospitalization and death rates may have been due to something other than the flu shot. Could it be that seniors who get flu shots are more health conscious or are able to get to the clinic more easily? Does race, income, or gender play a role in whether one might contract (and possibly die from) influenza?

DEFINITION

Confounding in a study occurs when the effects of two or more explanatory variables are not separated. Therefore, any relation that may exist between an explanatory variable and the response variable may be due to some other variable or variables not accounted for in the study.

Confounding is potentially a major problem with observational studies. Often, the cause of confounding is a *lurking variable.*

DEFINITION

A **lurking variable** is an explanatory variable that was not considered in a study, but that affects the value of the response variable in the study. In addition, lurking variables are typically related to explanatory variables considered in the study.

In the influenza study, possible lurking variables might be age, health status, or mobility of the senior. How can we manage the effect of lurking variables? One possibility is to look at the individuals in the study to determine if they differ in any significant way. For example, it turns out in the influenza study that the seniors who elected to get a flu shot were actually *less* healthy than those who did not. The researchers also accounted for race and income. The authors identified another potential lurking variable, *functional status*, meaning the ability of the seniors to conduct day-to-day activities on their own. The authors were able to adjust their results for this variable as well.

Even after accounting for all the potential lurking variables in the study, the authors were still careful to conclude that getting an influenza shot is *associated* with a lower risk of being hospitalized or dying from influenza. The authors used the term *associated*, instead of saying the influenza shots *caused* a lower risk of death, because the study was observational.

Observational studies do not allow a researcher to claim causation, only association.

Designed experiments, on the other hand, are used whenever control of certain variables is possible and desirable. This type of research allows the researcher to identify certain cause and effect relationships among the variables in the study.

So why ever conduct an observational study if we can't claim causation? Often, it is unethical to conduct an experiment. Consider the link between smoking and lung cancer. In a designed experiment to determine if smoking causes lung cancer in humans, a researcher would divide a group of volunteers into group 1 who would smoke a pack of cigarettes every day for the next 10 years, and group 2 who would not smoke. In addition, eating habits, sleeping habits, and exercise would be controlled so that the only difference between the two groups was smoking. After 10 years the experiment's researcher would compare the proportion of participants in the study who contract lung cancer in the smoking group to the nonsmoking group. If the two proportions differ significantly, it could be said that smoking causes cancer. This designed experiment is able to control many of the factors that might affect whether one contracts lung cancer that would not be controlled in an observational study, however, it is a very unethical study.

Other reasons exist for conducting observational studies over designed experiments. An article in support of observational studies states, "observational studies have several advantages over designed experiments, including lower cost, greater timeliness, and a broader range of patients." (*Source*: Kjell Benson, BA, and Arthur J. Hartz, MD, PhD. "A Comparison of Observational Studies and Randomized, Controlled Trials," *New England Journal of Medicine* 342:1878–1886, 2000).

We will continue to look at obtaining data through various types of observational studies until Section 1.6, when we will look at designed experiments.

2 Explain the Various Types of Observational Studies

There are three major categories of observational studies: (1) cross-sectional studies, (2) case-control studies, and (3) cohort studies.

Cross-sectional Studies These observational studies collect information about individuals at a specific point in time or over a very short period of time.

For example, a researcher might want to assess the risk associated with smoking by looking at a group of people, determining how many are smokers, and comparing the rate of lung cancer of the smokers to the nonsmokers.

An advantage of cross-sectional studies is that they are cheap and quick to do. However, they have limitations. For our lung cancer study, individuals might develop cancer after the data are collected, so our study will not give the full picture.

Case-control Studies These studies are **retrospective**, meaning that they require individuals to look back in time or require the researcher to look at existing records. In case-control studies, individuals who have a certain characteristic may be matched with those who do not.

For example, we might match individuals who smoke with those who do not. When we say "match" individuals, we mean that we would like the individuals in the study to be as similar (homogeneous) as possible in terms of demographics and other variables that may affect the response variable. Once homogeneous groups are established, we would ask the individuals in each group how much they smoked over the past 25 years. The rate of lung cancer between the two groups would then be compared.

A disadvantage to this type of study is that it requires individuals to recall information from the past. It also requires the individuals to be truthful in their responses. An advantage of case-control studies is that they can be done relatively quickly and inexpensively.

Cohort Studies A cohort study first identifies a group of individuals to participate in the study (the cohort). The cohort is then observed over a long period of time. During this period, characteristics about the individuals are recorded and some individuals will be exposed to certain factors (not intentionally) and others will not. At the end of the study the value of the response variable is recorded for the individuals.

Typically, cohort studies require many individuals to participate over long periods of time. Because the data are collected over time, cohort studies are **prospective**. Another problem with cohort studies is that individuals tend to drop out due to the long time frame. This could lead to misleading results. Cohort studies are the most powerful of the observational studies.

One of the largest cohort studies is the Framingham Heart Study. In this study, more than 10,000 individuals have been monitored since 1948. The study continues to this day, with the grandchildren of the original participants taking part in the study. This cohort study is responsible for many of the breakthroughs in understanding heart disease. Its cost is in excess of $10 million.

Some Concluding Remarks about Observational Studies versus Designed Experiments

Is a designed experiment superior to an observational study? Not necessarily. Plus, observational studies play a role in the research process. For example, because cross-sectional and case-control observational studies are relatively inexpensive, they allow researchers to explore possible associations prior to undertaking large cohort studies or designing experiments.

Also, it is not always possible to conduct an experiment. For example, we could not conduct an experiment to investigate the perceived link between high tension wires and leukemia (on humans). Do you see why?

Now Work Problem 19

Existing Sources of Data and Census Data

The saying "*There is no point in reinventing the wheel*" applies to spending energy obtaining data that already exist. If a researcher wishes to conduct a study and an appropriate data set exists, it would be silly to collect the data from scratch. For example, various federal agencies regularly collect data that are available to the public. Some of these agencies include the Centers for Disease Control and Prevention (www.cdc.gov), the Internal Revenue Service (www.irs.gov), and the Department of Justice (http://fjsrc.urban.org/index.cfm). A great Web site that lists virtually all the sources of federal data is www.fedstats.gov. Another great source of data is the General Social Survey (GSS) administered by the University of Chicago. This survey regularly asks "demographic and attitudinal questions" of individuals around the country. The Web site is www.gss.norc.org.

Another source of data is a *census*.

DEFINITION

A **census** is a list of all individuals in a population along with certain characteristics of each individual.

The United States conducts a census every 10 years to learn the demographic makeup of the United States. Everyone whose usual residence is within the borders of the United States must fill out a questionnaire packet. The cost of obtaining the census in 2010 was approximately $5.4 billion; about 635,000 temporary workers were hired to assist in collecting the data.

Why is the U.S. Census so important? The results of the census are used to determine the number of representatives in the House of Representatives in each state, congressional districts, distribution of funds for government programs (such as Medicaid), and planning for the construction of schools and roads. The first census of the United States was obtained in 1790 under the direction of Thomas Jefferson. It is a constitutional mandate that a census be conducted every 10 years.

Is the United States successful in obtaining a census? Not entirely. Some individuals go uncounted due to illiteracy, language issues, and homelessness. Given the political stakes that are based on the census, politicians often debate how to count these individuals. Statisticians have offered solutions to the counting problem. If you wish, go to www.census.gov and in the search box type *count homeless*. You will find many articles on the Census Bureau's attempt to count the homeless. The bottom line is that even census data can have flaws.

1.2 ASSESS YOUR UNDERSTANDING

VOCABULARY AND SKILL BUILDING

1. In your own words, define explanatory variable and response variable.

2. What is an observational study? What is a designed experiment? Which allows the researcher to claim causation between an explanatory variable and a response variable?

3. Explain what is meant by confounding. What is a lurking variable?

4. Given a choice, would you conduct a study using an observational study or a designed experiment? Why?

5. What is a cross-sectional study? What is a case-control study? Which is the superior observational study? Why?

17. (b) Whether the individual has heart disease or not; whether the individual is happy or not (c) Confounding due to lurking variables

6. The data used in the influenza study presented in Example 3 were obtained from a cohort study. What does this mean? Why is a cohort study superior to a case-control study?

7. Explain why it would be unlikely to use a designed experiment to answer the research question posed in Example 3.

8. What does it mean when an observational study is retrospective? What does it mean when an observational study is prospective?

In Problems 9–16, determine whether the study depicts an observational study or an experiment.

NW 9. Researchers wanted to know if there is a link between proximity to high-tension wires and the rate of leukemia in children. To conduct the study, researchers compared the rate of leukemia for children who lived within $^1/_2$ mile of high-tension wires to the rate of leukemia for children who did not live within $^1/_2$ mile of high-tension wires. Observational study

10. Rats with cancer are divided into two groups. One group receives 5 milligrams (mg) of a medication that is thought to fight cancer, and the other receives 10 mg. After 2 years, the spread of the cancer is measured. Experiment

11. Seventh-grade students are randomly divided into two groups. One group is taught math using traditional techniques; the other is taught math using a reform method. After 1 year, each group is given an achievement test to compare proficiency. Experiment

12. A poll is conducted in which 500 people are asked whom they plan to vote for in the upcoming election. Observational study

13. A survey is conducted asking 400 people, "Do you prefer Coke or Pepsi?" Observational study

14. While shopping, 200 people are asked to perform a taste test in which they drink from two randomly placed, unmarked cups. They are then asked which drink they prefer. Experiment

15. Sixty patients with carpal tunnel syndrome are randomly divided into two groups. One group is treated weekly with both acupuncture and an exercise regimen. The other is treated weekly with the exact same exercise regimen, but no acupuncture. After 1 year, both groups are questioned about their level of pain due to carpal tunnel syndrome. Experiment

16. Conservation agents netted 250 large-mouth bass in a lake and determined how many were carrying parasites. Observational study

APPLYING THE CONCEPTS

17. **Happiness and Your Heart** Researchers wanted to determine if there was an association between the level of happiness of an individual and their risk of heart disease. The researchers studied 1739 people over the course of 10 years. During this 10-year period, they interviewed the individuals and asked questions about their daily lives and the hassles they face. In addition, hypothetical scenarios were presented to determine how each individual would handle the situation. These interviews were videotaped and studied to assess the emotions of the individuals. The researchers also determined which individuals in the study experienced any type of heart disease over the 10-year period. After their analysis, the researchers concluded that the happy individuals were less likely to experience heart disease. *Source: European Heart Journal* 31 (9):1065–1070, February 2010.

(a) What type of observational study is this? Explain. Cohort

(b) What is the response variable? What is the explanatory variable?

(c) In the report, the researchers stated that "the research team also hasn't ruled out that a common factor like genetics could be causing both the emotions and the heart disease." Use the language introduced in this section to explain what this sentence means.

18. **Daily Coffee Consumption** Researchers wanted to determine if there was an association between daily coffee consumption and the occurrence of skin cancer. The researchers looked at 93,676 women enrolled in the Women's Health Initiative Observational Study and asked them to report their coffee-drinking habits. The researchers also determined which of the women had nonmelanoma skin cancer. After their analysis, the researchers concluded that consumption of six or more cups of caffeinated coffee per day was associated with a reduction in nonmelanoma skin cancer. *Source*: *European Journal of Cancer Prevention*, 16(5): 446–452, October 2007

(a) What type of observational study was this? Explain.

(b) What is the response variable in the study? What is the explanatory variable?

(c) In their report, the researchers stated that "After adjusting for various demographic and lifestyle variables, daily consumption of six or more cups was associated with a 30% reduced prevalence of nonmelanoma skin cancer." Why was it important to adjust for these variables?

NW 19. **Television in the Bedroom** Researchers Christelle Delmas and associates wanted to determine if having a television (TV) in the bedroom is associated with obesity. The researchers administered a questionnaire to 379 twelve-year-old French adolescents. After analyzing the results, the researchers determined that the body mass index of the adolescents who had a TV in their bedroom was significantly higher than that of the adolescents who did not have a TV in their bedroom. *Source*: Christelle Delmas, Carine Platat, Brigette Schweitzer, Aline Wagner, Mohamed Oujaa, and Chantal Simon. "Association Between Television in Bedroom and Adiposity Throughout Adolescence," *Obesity*, 15:2495–2503, 2007

(a) Why is this an observational study? What type of observational study is this? Cross-sectional

(b) What is the response variable in the study? What is the explanatory variable?

(c) Can you think of any lurking variables that may affect the results of the study?

(d) In the report, the researchers stated, "These results remain significant after adjustment for socioeconomic status." What does this mean?

(e) Can we conclude that a television in the bedroom causes a higher body mass index? Explain. No

20. **Get Married, Gain Weight** Researcher Penny Gordon-Larson and her associate wanted to determine whether young couples who marry or cohabitate are more likely to gain weight than those who stay single. The researchers followed 8000 men and women for 7 years as they matured from teens to young adults. When the study began, none of the participants were married or living with a romantic partner. By the end of the study, 14% of the participants were married and 16% were living with a romantic partner. The researchers found that married or cohabiting women gained, on average, 9 pounds more than single

18. (a) Cross-sectional (b) Whether the woman has nonmelanoma skin cancer or not; consumption of 6 or more cups of caffeinated coffee or not, daily. 19. (b) Body mass index; whether a TV is in the bedroom or not

women, and married or cohabiting men gained, on average, 6 pounds more than single men.

(a) Why is this an observational study? What type of observational study is this? Cohort study

(b) What is the response variable in the study? What is the explanatory variable?

(c) Identify some potential lurking variables in this study.

(d) Can we conclude that getting married or cohabiting causes one to gain weight? Explain. No

21. Analyze the Article Write a summary of the following opinion. The opinion was posted at abcnews.com. Include the type of study conducted, possible lurking variables, and conclusions. What is the message of the author of the article?

Power Lines and Cancer—To Move or Not to Move

New Research May Cause More Fear Than Warranted, One Physician Explains

OPINION by JOSEPH MOORE, M.D.

A recent study out of Switzerland indicates there might be an increased risk of certain blood cancers in people with prolonged exposure to electromagnetic fields, like those generated from high-voltage power lines.

If you live in a house near one of these high-voltage power lines, a study like this one might make you wonder whether you should move.

But based on what we know now, I don't think that's necessary. We can never say there is no risk, but we can say that the risk appears to be extremely small.

"Scare Science"

The results of studies like this add a bit more to our knowledge of potential harmful environmental exposures, but they should also be seen in conjunction with the results of hundreds of studies that have gone before. It cannot be seen as a definitive call to action in and of itself.

The current study followed more than 20,000 Swiss railway workers over a period of 30 years. True, that represents a lot of people over a long period of time.

However, the problem with many epidemiological studies, like this one, is that it is difficult to have an absolute control group of people to compare results with. The researchers compared the incidence of different cancers of workers with a high amount of electromagnetic field exposure to those workers with lower exposures.

These studies aren't like those that have identified definitive links between an exposure and a disease—like those involving smoking and lung cancer. In those studies, we can actually measure the damage done to lung tissue as a direct result of smoking. But usually it's very difficult for the conclusions of an epidemiological study to rise to the level of controlled studies in determining public policy.

Remember the recent scare about coffee and increased risk of pancreatic cancer? Or the always-simmering issue of cell phone use and brain tumors?

As far as I can tell, none of us have turned in our cell phones. In our own minds, we've decided that any links to cell phone use and brain cancer have not been proven definitively. While we can't say that there is absolutely no risk in using cell phones, individuals have determined on their own that the potential risks appear to be quite small and are outweighed by the benefits.

Findings Shouldn't Lead to Fear

As a society, we should continue to investigate these and other related exposures to try to prove one way or another whether they are disease-causing. If we don't continue to study, we won't find out. It's that simple.

When findings like these come out, and I'm sure there will be more in the future, I would advise people not to lose their heads. Remain calm. You should take the results as we scientists do—as intriguing pieces of data about a problem we will eventually learn more about, either positively or negatively, in the future. It should not necessarily alter what we do right now.

What we can do is take actions that we know will reduce our chances of developing cancer.

Stop smoking and avoid passive smoke. It is the leading cause of cancer that individuals have control over.

Whenever you go outside, put on sunscreen or cover up.

Eat a healthy diet and stay physically active.

Make sure you get tested or screened. Procedures like colonoscopies, mammograms, pap smears and prostate exams can catch the early signs of cancer, when the chances of successfully treating them are the best.

Taking the actions above will go much farther in reducing your risks for cancer than moving away from power lines or throwing away your cell phone.

Dr. Joseph Moore is a medical oncologist at Duke University Comprehensive Cancer Center. *Source:* Reprinted with the permission of the author.

22. Reread the article in Problem 55 from Section 1.1. What type of observational study does this appear to be? Name some lurking variables that the researchers accounted for.

23. Putting It Together: Passive Smoke? The following abstract appears in *The New England Journal of Medicine:*

BACKGROUND. The relation between passive smoking and lung cancer is of great public health importance. Some previous studies have suggested that exposure to environmental tobacco smoke in the household can cause lung cancer, but others have found no effect. Smoking by the spouse has been the most commonly used measure of this exposure.

METHODS. In order to determine whether lung cancer is associated with exposure to tobacco smoke within the household, we conducted a case-control study of 191 patients with lung cancer who had never smoked and an equal number of persons without lung cancer who had

20. (b) Weight gain; whether the individual is married/cohabitating or not (c) Having children; eating out more often

never smoked. Lifetime residential histories including information on exposure to environmental tobacco smoke were compiled and analyzed. Exposure was measured in terms of "smoker-years," determined by multiplying the number of years in each residence by the number of smokers in the household.

RESULTS. Household exposure to 25 or more smoker-years during childhood and adolescence doubled the risk of lung cancer. Approximately 15 percent of the control subjects who had never smoked reported this level of exposure. Household exposure of less than 25 smoker-years during childhood and adolescence did not increase the risk of lung cancer. Exposure to a spouse's smoking, which constituted less than one third of total household exposure on average, was not associated with an increase in risk.

CONCLUSIONS. The possibility of recall bias and other methodologic problems may influence the results of case-control studies of environmental tobacco smoke. Nonetheless, our findings regarding exposure during early life suggest that approximately 17 percent of lung cancers among nonsmokers can be attributed to high levels of exposure to cigarette smoke during childhood and adolescence.

(a) What is the research objective?

(b) What makes this study a case-control study? Why is this a retrospective study?

(c) What is the response variable in the study? Is it qualitative or quantitative?

(d) What is the explanatory variable in the study? Is it qualitative or quantitative?

(e) Can you identify any lurking variables that may have affected this study?

(f) What is the conclusion of the study? Can we conclude that exposure to smoke in the household causes lung cancer?

(g) Would it be possible to design an experiment to answer the research question in part (a)? Explain.

23. (c) Whether the individual has lung cancer; qualitative
23. (d) Number of smoker-years; quantitative
23. (e) Income; amount of exposure outside the home

1.3 SIMPLE RANDOM SAMPLING

OBJECTIVE 1 Obtain a simple random sample

Sampling

Besides the observational studies that we looked at in Section 1.2, observational studies can also be conducted by administering a survey. When administering a survey, the researcher must first identify the population that is to be targeted. For example, the Gallup Organization regularly surveys Americans about various pop-culture and political issues. Often, the population of interest is Americans aged 18 years or older. Of course, the Gallup Organization cannot survey *all* adult Americans (there are over 200 million), so instead the group typically surveys a *random sample* of about 1000 adult Americans.

DEFINITION

Random sampling is the process of using chance to select individuals from a population to be included in the sample.

Note to Instructor

Spend some time in class talking about the following: Suppose a grocery store manager wants to get a feel for how customers view the store. Why would a sample of the first 100 shoppers leaving a grocery store not be representative of the population? Why is this sampling method not random sampling?

For the results of a survey to be reliable, the characteristics of the individuals in the sample must be representative of the characteristics of the individuals in the population. The key to obtaining a sample representative of a population is to let *chance* or *randomness* play a role in dictating which individuals are in the sample, rather than convenience. **If convenience is used to obtain a sample, the results of the survey are meaningless.**

Suppose that Gallup wants to know the proportion of adult Americans who consider themselves to be baseball fans. If Gallup obtained a sample by standing outside of Fenway Park (home of the Boston Red Sox professional baseball team), the survey results are not likely to be reliable. Why? Clearly, the individuals in the sample do not accurately reflect the makeup of the entire population. As another example, suppose you wanted to learn the proportion of students on your campus who work. It might be convenient to survey the students in your statistics class, but do these students represent the overall student body? Does the proportion of freshmen, sophomores, juniors, and seniors in your class mirror the proportion of freshmen, sophomores, juniors, and seniors on campus? Does the proportion of males and females in your class resemble the proportion of males and females across campus? Probably not. For this reason, the convenient sample is not representative of the population, which means any results reported from your survey are misleading.

We will discuss four basic sampling techniques: *simple random sampling*, *stratified sampling*, *systematic sampling*, and *cluster sampling*. These sampling methods are designed so that any selection biases introduced (knowingly or unknowingly) by the surveyor during the selection process are eliminated. In other words, the surveyor does not have a choice as to which individuals are in the study. We will discuss simple random sampling now and the remaining three types of sampling in Section 1.4.

1 Obtain a Simple Random Sample

The most basic sample survey design is *simple random sampling.*

DEFINITION

A sample of size *n* from a population of size *N* is obtained through **simple random sampling** if every possible sample of size *n* has an equally likely chance of occurring. The sample is then called a **simple random sample**.

In Other Words
Simple random sampling is like selecting names from a hat.

The number of individuals in the sample is always less than the number of individuals in the population.

EXAMPLE 1 Illustrating Simple Random Sampling

Problem Sophia has four tickets to a concert. Six of her friends, Yolanda, Michael, Kevin, Marissa, Annie, and Katie, have all expressed an interest in going to the concert. Sophia decides to randomly select three of her six friends to attend the concert.

(a) List all possible samples of size $n = 3$ from the population of size $N = 6$. Once an individual is chosen, he or she cannot be chosen again.

(b) Comment on the likelihood of the sample containing Michael, Kevin, and Marissa.

Approach We list all possible combinations of three people chosen from the six. Remember, in simple random sampling, each sample of size 3 is equally likely to occur.

Solution

(a) The possible samples of size 3 are listed in Table 2

TABLE 2

Yolanda, Michael, Kevin	Yolanda, Michael, Marissa	Yolanda, Michael, Annie	Yolanda, Michael, Katie
Yolanda, Kevin, Marissa	Yolanda, Kevin, Annie	Yolanda, Kevin, Katie	Yolanda, Marissa, Annie
Yolanda, Marissa, Katie	Yolanda, Annie, Katie	Michael, Kevin, Marissa	Michael, Kevin, Annie
Michael, Kevin, Katie	Michael, Marissa, Annie	Michael, Marissa, Katie	Michael, Annie, Katie
Kevin, Marissa, Annie	Kevin, Marissa, Katie	Kevin, Annie, Katie	Marissa, Annie, Katie

From Table 2, we see that there are 20 possible samples of size 3 from the population of size 6. We use the term *sample* to mean the individuals in the sample.

(b) Only 1 of the 20 possible samples contains Michael, Kevin, and Marissa, so there is a 1 in 20 chance that the simple random sample will contain these three. In fact, all the samples of size 3 have a 1 in 20 chance of occurring.

Now Work Problem 7

Obtaining a Simple Random Sample

In Other Words
A frame lists all the individuals in a population. For example, a list of all registered voters in a particular precinct might be a frame.

The results of Example 1 leave one question unanswered: How do we select the individuals in a simple random sample? We could write the names of the individuals in the population on different sheets of paper and then select names from a hat. Often, however, the size of the population is so large that performing simple random sampling in this fashion is not practical. Typically, each individual in the population is assigned a unique number between 1 and N, where N is the size of the population. Then n distinct random numbers from this list are selected, where n represents the size of the sample. To number the individuals in the population, we need a **frame**—a list of all the individuals within the population.

EXAMPLE 2 Obtaining a Simple Random Sample Using a Table of Random Numbers

Note to Instructor
In practice, the approach used to obtain simple random samples presented in Example 2 is not done. If you like, you can skip the example without loss of continuity.

Problem The accounting firm of Senese and Associates has grown. To make sure their clients are still satisfied with the services they are receiving, the company decides to send a survey out to a simple random sample of 5 of its 30 clients.

Approach

Step 1 The clients must be listed (the frame) and numbered from 01 to 30.

Step 2 Five unique numbers will be randomly selected. The clients corresponding to the numbers are sent a survey. This process is called *sampling without replacement*. In a **sample without replacement**, an individual who is selected is removed from the population and cannot be chosen again. In a **sample with replacement**, a selected individual is placed back into the population and could be chosen a second time. We use sampling without replacement so that we don't select the same client twice.

Solution

Step 1 Table 3 shows the list of clients. We arrange them in alphabetical order, although this is not necessary, and number them from 01 to 30.

TABLE 3

01. ABC Electric	11. Fox Studios	21. R&Q Realty
02. Brassil Construction	12. Haynes Hauling	22. Ritter Engineering
03. Bridal Zone	13. House of Hair	23. Simplex Forms
04. Casey's Glass House	14. John's Bakery	24. Spruce Landscaping
05. Chicago Locksmith	15. Logistics Management, Inc.	25. Thors, Robert DDS
06. DeSoto Painting	16. Lucky Larry's Bistro	26. Travel Zone
07. Dino Jump	17. Moe's Exterminating	27. Ultimate Electric
08. Euro Car Care	18. Nick's Tavern	28. Venetian Gardens Restaurant
09. Farrell's Antiques	19. Orion Bowling	29. Walker Insurance
10. First Fifth Bank	20. Precise Plumbing	30. Worldwide Wireless

Step 2 A table of random numbers can be used to select the individuals to be in the sample. See Table 4.* We pick a starting place in the table by closing our eyes and placing a finger on it. This method accomplishes the goal of being random. Suppose we start in column 4, row 13. Because our data have two digits, we select two-digit numbers from the table using columns 4 and 5. We select numbers between 01 and 30, inclusive, and skip 00, numbers greater than 30, and numbers already selected.

Column 4

TABLE 4

Row Number	Column Number 01–05	06–10	11–15	16–20	21–25	26–30	31–35	36–40	41–45	46–50
01	89392	**23**212	74483	36590	25956	36544	68518	40805	09980	00467
02	61458	17639	96252	95649	73727	33912	72896	66218	52341	97141
03	11452	74197	81962	48433	90360	26480	73231	37740	26628	44690
04	27575	04429	31308	02241	01698	19191	18948	78871	36030	23980
05	36829	59109	88976	46845	28329	47460	88944	08264	00843	84592
06	81902	93458	42161	26099	09419	89073	82849	09160	61845	40906
07	59761	55212	33360	68751	86737	79743	85262	31887	37879	17525
08	46827	25906	64708	20307	78423	15910	86548	08763	47050	18513
09	24040	66449	32353	83668	13874	86741	81312	54185	78824	00718
10	98144	96372	50277	15571	82261	66628	31457	00377	63423	55141
11	14228	17930	30118	00438	49666	65189	62869	31304	17117	71489
12	55366	51057	90065	14791	62426	02957	85518	28822	30588	32798
Row 13 — 13	96**101**	30646	35526	90389	73634	79304	96635	06626	94683	16696
14	381**52**	55474	30153	26525	83647	31988	82182	98377	33802	80471
15	850**07**	18416	24661	95581	45868	15662	28906	36392	07617	50248
16	855**44**	15890	80011	18160	33468	84106	40603	01315	74664	20553
17	104**46**	20699	98370	17684	16932	80449	92654	02084	19985	59321
18	672**37**	45509	17638	65115	29757	80705	82686	48565	72612	61760
19	230**26**	89817	05403	82209	30573	47501	00135	33955	50250	72592
20	674**11**	58542	18678	46491	13219	84084	27783	34508	55158	78742

We skip 52 because it is larger than 30.

The first number in the list is 01, so the client corresponding to 01 will receive a survey. Reading down, the next number in the list is 52, which is greater than 30, so we skip it. Continuing down the list, the following numbers are selected from the list:

01, 07, 26, 11, 23

The clients corresponding to these numbers are

ABC Electric, Dino Jump, Travel Zone, Fox Studios, Simplex Forms

*Each digit is in its own column. The digits are displayed in groups of five for ease of reading. The digits in row 1 are 893922321274483, and so on. The first digit, 8, is in column 1; the second digit, 9, is in column 2; the ninth digit, 1, is in column 9.

We display each of the random numbers used to select the individuals in the sample in boldface type in Table 4 to help you to understand where they came from.

EXAMPLE 3 Obtaining a Simple Random Sample Using Technology

Note to Instructor

This text features the four most popular statistical software packages and calculators: MINITAB, Excel, TI83/TI84, and StatCrunch (as learned from our surveys). The technology used will vary from example to example, but the purpose of these examples is to illustrate how software can obtain the results we need to solve a problem. Once we have the results, work still must be done to determine its meaning. So, just because the software or calculator used in a technology example is not the one used by you, do not feel obligated to skip it.

Problem Find a simple random sample of five clients for the problem presented in Example 2.

Approach The approach is similar to that given in Example 2.

Step 1 We obtain the frame and assign the clients numbers from 01 to 30.

Step 2 We randomly select five numbers using a random number generator. To do this, we must first set the *seed*. The **seed** is an initial point for the generator to start creating random numbers—like selecting the initial point in the table of random numbers. The seed can be any nonzero number. Statistical software such as StatCrunch, MINITAB, or Excel can be used to generate random numbers, but we will use a TI-84 Plus graphing calculator. The steps for obtaining random numbers using StatCrunch, MINITAB, Excel, and the TI-83/84 graphing calculator can be found in the Technology Step-by-Step on page 29.

Solution

Step 1 Table 3 on page 24 shows the list of clients and numbers corresponding to the clients.

Step 2 Figure 3(a) shows the seed set at 34 on a TI-84 Plus graphing calculator. Now we can generate a list of random numbers, which are shown in Figure 3(b).

Using Technology

If you are using a different statistical package or type of calculator, the random numbers generated will likely be different. This does not mean you are wrong. There is no such thing as a wrong random sample as long as the correct procedures are followed.

Figure 3

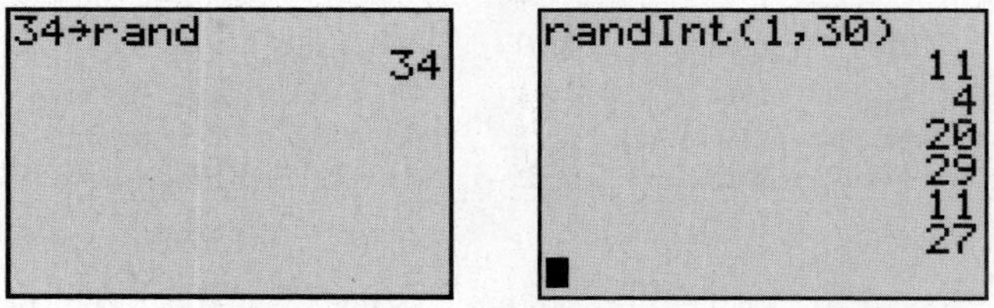

(a) (b)

The following numbers are generated by the calculator:

11, 4, 20, 29, 11, 27

We ignore the second 11 because we are sampling without replacement. The clients corresponding to these numbers are the clients to be surveyed: Fox Studios, Casey's Glass House, Precise Plumbing, Walker Insurance, and Ultimate Electric.

Now Work Problem 11

CAUTION

Random-number generators are not truly random, because they are programs, and programs do not act "randomly." The seed dictates the random numbers that are generated.

Notice an important difference in the solutions of Examples 2 and 3. Because both samples were obtained randomly, they resulted in different individuals in the sample! For this reason, each sample will likely result in different descriptive statistics. Any inference based on each sample *may* result in different conclusions regarding the population. This is the nature of statistics. Inferences based on samples will vary because the individuals in different samples vary.

1.3 ASSESS YOUR UNDERSTANDING

VOCABULARY AND SKILL BUILDING

1. What is a frame?

2. Define simple random sampling.

3. What does it mean when sampling is done without replacement?

4. What is random sampling? Why is it used and how does it compare with convenience sampling?

5. Literature As part of a college literature course, students must select three classic works of literature from the provided list and complete critical book reviews for each selected work. Obtain a simple random sample of size 3 from this list. Write a short description of the process you used to generate your sample.

Pride and Prejudice	*The Scarlet Letter*
As I Lay Dying	*The Jungle*
Death of a Salesman	*Huckleberry Finn*
The Sun Also Rises	*Crime and Punishment*
A Tale of Two Cities	

6. Team Captains A coach must select two players to serve as captains at the beginning of a soccer match. He has 10 players on his team and, to be fair, wants to randomly select 2 players to be the captains. Obtain a simple random sample of size 2 from the following list. Write a short description of the process you used to generate your sample.

Mady	Breanne
Evin	Tori
Emily	Claire
Caty	Jory
Payton	Jordyn

NW **7. Course Selection** A student entering a doctoral program in educational psychology is required to select two courses from the list of courses provided as part of his or her program.

EPR 616, Research in Child Development
EPR 630, Educational Research Planning and Interpretation
EPR 631, Nonparametric Statistics
EPR 632, Methods of Multivariate Analysis
EPR 645, Theory of Measurement
EPR 649, Fieldwork Methods in Educational Research
EPR 650, Interpretive Methods in Educational Research

(a) List all possible two-course selections.

(b) Comment on the likelihood that the pair of courses EPR 630 and EPR 645 will be selected.

8. Merit Badge Requirements To complete the Citizenship in the World merit badge, one must select TWO of the following organizations and describe their role in the world.

Source: Boy Scouts of America

1. The United Nations
2. The World Court
3. World Organization of the Scout Movement
4. The World Health Organization
5. Amnesty International
6. The International Committee of the Red Cross
7. CARE

(a) List all possible pairs of organizations.

(b) Comment on the likelihood that the pair "The United Nations" and "Amnesty International" will be selected.

APPLYING THE CONCEPTS

9. Sampling the Faculty A small community college employs 87 full-time faculty members. To gain the faculty's opinions about an upcoming building project, the college president wishes to obtain a simple random sample that will consist of 9 faculty members. He numbers the faculty from 1 to 87.

(a) Using Table I from Appendix A, the president closes his eyes and drops his ink pen on the table. It points to the digit in row 5, column 22. Using this position as the starting point and proceeding downward, determine the numbers for the 9 faculty members who will be included in the sample.

(b) If the president uses technology, determine the numbers for the 9 faculty members who will be included in the sample.

10. Sampling the Students The same community college from Problem 9 has 7656 students currently enrolled in classes. To gain the students' opinions about an upcoming building project, the college president wishes to obtain a simple random sample of 20 students. He numbers the students from 1 to 7656.

(a) Using Table I from Appendix A, the president closes his eyes and drops his ink pen on the table. It points to the digit in row 11, column 32. Using this position as the starting point and proceeding downward, determine the numbers for the 20 students who will be included in the sample.

(b) If the president uses technology, determine the numbers for the 20 students who will be included in the sample.

NW **11. Obtaining a Simple Random Sample** The table on the following page lists the 50 states.

(a) Obtain a simple random sample of size 10 using Table I in Appendix A, a graphing calculator, or computer software.

(b) Obtain a second simple random sample of size 10 using Table I in Appendix A, a graphing calculator, or computer software.

9. (a) 83, 67, 84, 38, 22, 24, 36, 58, 34
10. (a) 2869, 5518, 6635, 2182, 0603, 2654, 2686, 0135, 4080, 6621, 3774, 0826, 0916, 3188, 0876, 5418, 0037, 3130, 2882, 0662

1. Alabama	11. Hawaii	21. Massachusetts	31. New Mexico	41. South Dakota
2. Alaska	12. Idaho	22. Michigan	32. New York	42. Tennessee
3. Arizona	13. Illinois	23. Minnesota	33. North Carolina	43. Texas
4. Arkansas	14. Indiana	24. Mississippi	34. North Dakota	44. Utah
5. California	15. Iowa	25. Missouri	35. Ohio	45. Vermont
6. Colorado	16. Kansas	26. Montana	36. Oklahoma	46. Virginia
7. Connecticut	17. Kentucky	27. Nebraska	37. Oregon	47. Washington
8. Delaware	18. Louisiana	28. Nevada	38. Pennsylvania	48. West Virginia
9. Florida	19. Maine	29. New Hampshire	39. Rhode Island	49. Wisconsin
10. Georgia	20. Maryland	30. New Jersey	40. South Carolina	50. Wyoming

12. Obtaining a Simple Random Sample The following table lists the 44 presidents of the United States.

(a) Obtain a simple random sample of size 8 using Table I in Appendix A, a graphing calculator, or computer software.

(b) Obtain a second simple random sample of size 8 using Table I in Appendix A, a graphing calculator, or computer software.

1. Washington	10. Tyler	19. Hayes	28. Wilson	37. Nixon
2. J. Adams	11. Polk	20. Garfield	29. Harding	38. Ford
3. Jefferson	12. Taylor	21. Arthur	30. Coolidge	39. Carter
4. Madison	13. Fillmore	22. Cleveland	31. Hoover	40. Reagan
5. Monroe	14. Pierce	23. B. Harrison	32. F. D. Roosevelt	41. George H. Bush
6. J. Q. Adams	15. Buchanan	24. Cleveland	33. Truman	42. Clinton
7. Jackson	16. Lincoln	25. McKinley	34. Eisenhower	43. George W. Bush
8. Van Buren	17. A. Johnson	26. T. Roosevelt	35. Kennedy	44. Barack Obama
9. W. H. Harrison	18. Grant	27. Taft	36. L. B. Johnson	

13. Obtaining a Simple Random Sample Suppose you are the president of the student government. You wish to conduct a survey to determine the student body's opinion regarding student services. The administration provides you with a list of the names and phone numbers of the 19,935 registered students.

(a) Discuss the procedure you would follow to obtain a simple random sample of 25 students.

(b) Obtain this sample.

14. Obtaining a Simple Random Sample Suppose the mayor of Justice, Illinois, asks you to poll the residents of the village. The mayor provides you with a list of the names and phone numbers of the 5832 residents of the village.

(a) Discuss the procedure you would follow to obtain a simple random sample of 20 residents.

(b) Obtain this sample.

15. Future Government Club The Future Government Club wants to sponsor a panel discussion on the upcoming national election. The club wants four of its members to lead the panel discussion. Obtain a simple random sample of size 4 from the table. Write a short description of the process you used to generate your sample.

Blouin	Fallenbuchel	Niemeyer	Rice
Bolden	Grajewski	Nolan	Salihar
Bolt	Haydra	Ochs	Tate
Carter	Keating	Opacian	Thompson
Cooper	Khouri	Pawlak	Trudeau
Debold	Lukens	Pechtold	Washington
De Young	May	Ramirez	Wright
Engler	Motola	Redmond	Zenkel

16. Worker Morale The owner of a private food store is concerned about employee morale. She decides to survey the employees to see if she can learn about work environment and job satisfaction. Obtain a simple random sample of size 5 from the names in the given table. Write a short description of the process you used to generate your sample.

Archer	Foushi	Kemp	Oliver
Bolcerek	Gow	Lathus	Orsini
Bryant	Grove	Lindsey	Salazar
Carlisle	Hall	Massie	Ullrich
Cole	Hills	McGuffin	Vaneck
Dimas	Houston	Musa	Weber
Ellison	Kats	Nickas	Zavodny
Everhart			

Technology Step-By-Step

Obtaining a Simple Random Sample

TI-83/84 Plus

1. Enter any nonzero number (the seed) on the HOME screen.
2. Press the STO ▶ button.
3. Press the MATH button.
4. Highlight the PRB menu and select `1: rand`.
5. From the HOME screen press ENTER.
6. Press the MATH button. Highlight the PRB menu and select `5: randInt(`.
7. With `randInt(` on the HOME screen, enter 1, *N*, where *N* is the population size. For example, if $N = 500$, enter the following:

   `randInt(1,500)`

   Press ENTER to obtain the first individual in the sample. Continue pressing ENTER until the desired sample size is obtained.

MINITAB

1. Select the **Calc** menu and highlight **Set Base . . . .**
2. Enter any seed number you desire. Note that it is not necessary to set the seed, because MINITAB uses the time of day in seconds to set the seed.
3. Select the **Calc** menu, highlight **Random Data**, and select **Integer** . . . .
4. Fill in the following window with the appropriate values. To obtain a simple random sample for the situation in Example 2, we would enter the following:

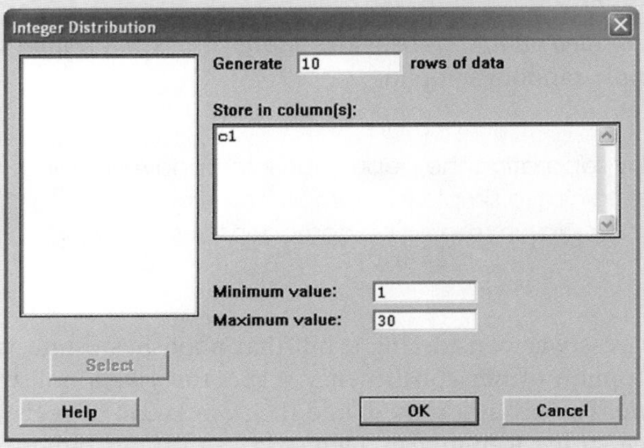

The reason we generate 10 rows of data (instead of 5) is in case any of the random numbers repeat. Select OK, and the random numbers will appear in column 1 (C1) in the spreadsheet.

Excel

1. Be sure the Data Analysis ToolPak is activated. This is done by selecting File, then selecting Options. Highlight Add-Ins. In the Manage: pull-down menu, choose Excel Add-ins and click Go . . . Check the Analysis ToolPak and click Okay.
2. Select **Data** and highlight **Data Analysis . . . .** Highlight **Random Number Generation** and select OK.
3. Fill in the window with the appropriate values. To obtain a simple random sample for the situation in Example 2, we would fill in the following:

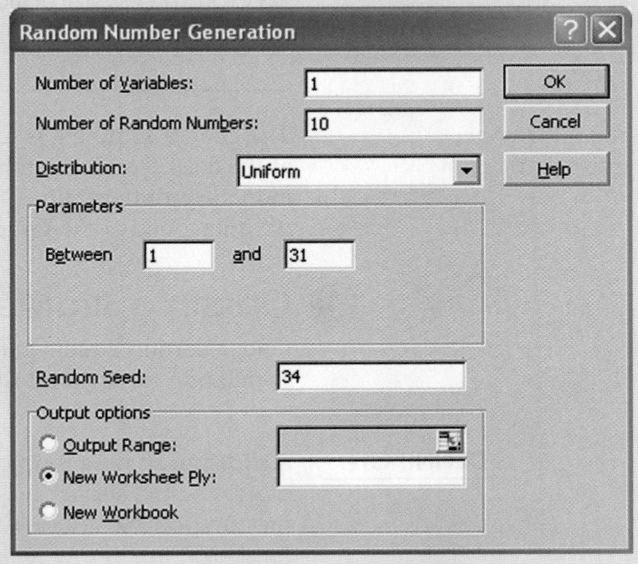

The reason we generate 10 rows of data (instead of 5) is in case any of the random numbers repeat. Notice also that the parameter is between 1 and 31, so any value greater than or equal to 1 and less than or equal to 31 is possible. In the unlikely event that 31 appears, simply ignore it. Select OK and the random numbers will appear in column 1 (A1) in the spreadsheet. Ignore any values to the right of the decimal place.

StatCrunch

1. Select **Data**, highlight **Simulate Data**, then highlight **Discrete Uniform**.
2. Fill in the window with the appropriate values. To obtain a simple random sample for the situation in Example 2, we would enter the values shown in the figure. The reason we generate 10 rows of data (instead of 5) is in case any of the random numbers repeat. Select Simulate, and the random numbers will appear in the spreadsheet. *Note:* You could also select the single dynamic seed radio button, if you like, to set the seed.

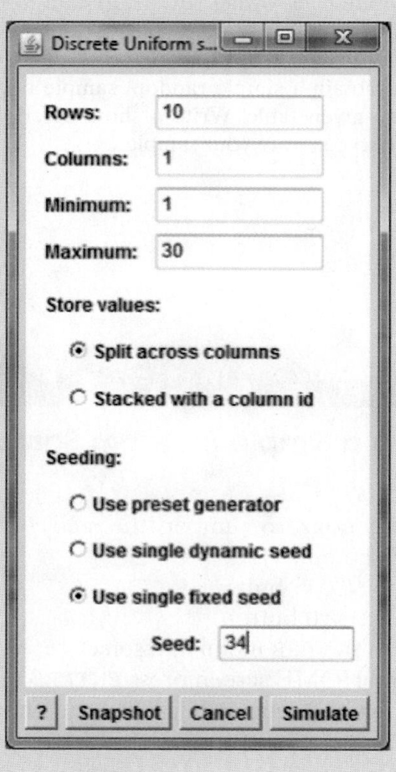

1.4 OTHER EFFECTIVE SAMPLING METHODS

OBJECTIVES

1 Obtain a stratified sample

2 Obtain a systematic sample

3 Obtain a cluster sample

Note to Instructor
The material in this section is optional and can be skipped without loss of continuity.

The goal of sampling is to obtain as much information as possible about the population at the least cost. Remember, we are using the word *cost* in a general sense. Cost includes monetary outlays, time, and other resources. With this goal in mind, we may find it advantageous to use sampling techniques other than simple random sampling.

1 Obtain a Stratified Sample

Under certain circumstances, *stratified sampling* provides more information about the population for less cost than simple random sampling.

DEFINITION

A **stratified sample** is obtained by separating the population into nonoverlapping groups called *strata* and then obtaining a simple random sample from each stratum. The individuals within each stratum should be homogeneous (or similar) in some way.

For example, suppose Congress was considering a bill that abolishes estate taxes. In an effort to determine the opinion of her constituency, a senator asks a pollster to conduct a survey within her state. The pollster may divide the population of registered voters within the state into three strata: Republican, Democrat, and Independent. This grouping makes sense because the members within each of the three parties may have the same opinion regarding estate taxes, but opinions among parties may differ. The main criterion in performing a stratified sample is that each group (stratum) must have a common attribute that results in the individuals being similar within the stratum.

In Other Words
Stratum is singular, while *strata* is plural. The word *strata* means divisions. So a stratified sample is a simple random sample of different divisions of the population.

An advantage of stratified sampling over simple random sampling is that it may allow fewer individuals to be surveyed while obtaining the same or more information. This result occurs because individuals within each subgroup have similar characteristics, so opinions within the group are not as likely to vary much from one individual to the next. In addition, a stratified sample guarantees that each stratum is represented in the sample.

EXAMPLE 1 Obtaining a Stratified Sample

Problem The president of DePaul University wants to conduct a survey to determine the community's opinion regarding campus safety. The president divides the DePaul community into three groups: resident students, nonresident (commuting) students, and staff (including faculty) so that he can obtain a stratified sample. Suppose there are 6204 resident students, 13,304 nonresident students, and 2401 staff, for a total of 21,909 individuals in the population. The president wants to obtain a sample of size 100, with the number of individuals selected from each stratum weighted by the population size. So resident students make up 6204/21,909 = 28%, nonresident students account for 61%, and staff constitute 11% of the sample. A sample of size 100 requires a stratified sample of 0.28(100) = 28 resident students, 0.61(100) = 61 nonresident students, and 0.11(100) = 11 staff.

Approach To obtain the stratified sample, conduct a simple random sample within each group. That is, obtain a simple random sample of 28 resident students (from the 6204 resident students), a simple random sample of 61 nonresident students, and a simple random sample of 11 staff. Be sure to use a different seed for each stratum.

Solution Using MINITAB, with the seed set to 4032 and the values shown in Figure 4, we obtain the following sample of staff:

240, 630, 847, 190, 2096, 705, 2320, 323, 701, 471, 744

Figure 4

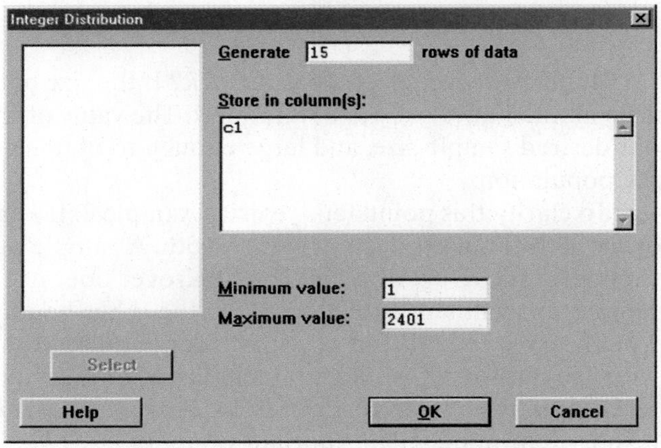

CAUTION
Do not use the same seed (or starting point in Table I) for all the groups in a stratified sample, because we want the simple random samples within each stratum to be independent of each other.

Repeat this procedure for the resident and nonresident students using a different seed.

Now Work Problem 25

An advantage of stratified sampling over simple random sampling is that the researcher can determine characteristics within each stratum. This allows an analysis to be performed on each stratum to see if any significant differences among them exist. For example, we could analyze the data obtained in Example 1 to see if there is a difference in the opinions of students versus staff.

2 Obtain a Systematic Sample

In both simple random sampling and stratified sampling, a frame—a list of the individuals in the population being studied—must exist. Therefore, these sampling techniques require some preliminary work before obtaining the sample. A sampling technique that does not require a frame is *systematic sampling*.

DEFINITION

A **systematic sample** is obtained by selecting every *k*th individual from the population. The first individual selected corresponds to a random number between 1 and *k*.

Because systematic sampling does not require a frame, it is a useful technique when you cannot obtain a list of the individuals in the population.

To obtain a systematic sample, select a number *k*, randomly select a number between 1 and *k* and survey that individual, then survey every *k*th individual there after. For example, we might decide to survey every $k = 8$th individual. We randomly select a number between 1 and 8, such as 5. This means we survey the 5th, $5 + 8 =$ 13th, $13 + 8 =$ 21st, $21 + 8 =$ 29th, and so on, individuals until we reach the desired sample size.

EXAMPLE 2 Obtaining a Systematic Sample without a Frame

Problem The manager of Kroger Food Stores wants to measure the satisfaction of the store's customers. Design a sampling technique that can be used to obtain a sample of 40 customers.

Approach A frame of Kroger customers would be difficult, if not impossible, to obtain. Therefore, it is reasonable to use systematic sampling by surveying every *k*th customer who leaves the store.

Solution The manager decides to obtain a systematic sample by surveying every 7th customer. He randomly determines a number between 1 and 7, say 5. He then surveys the 5th customer exiting the store and every 7th customer thereafter, until he has a sample of 40 customers. The survey will include customers 5, 12, 19, ..., 278.*

But how do we select the value of *k*? If the size of the population is unknown, there is no mathematical way to determine *k*. The value of *k* must be small enough to achieve our desired sample size, and large enough to obtain a sample that is representative of the population.

To clarify this point, let's revisit Example 2. If *k* is too large, say 30, we will survey every 30th shopper, starting with the 5th. A sample of size 40 would require that 1175 shoppers visit Kroger on that day. If Kroger does not have 1175 shoppers, the desired sample size will not be achieved. On the other hand, if *k* is too small, say 4, the store would survey the 5th, 9th, ..., 161st shopper. The 161st shopper might exit the store at 3 P.M., so our survey would not include any of the evening shoppers. This sample is not representative of *all* Kroger patrons! An estimate of the size of the population would help to determine an appropriate value for *k*.

To determine the value of *k* when the size of the population, *N*, is known is relatively straightforward. Suppose the population size is $N = 20{,}325$ and we desire a sample of size $n = 100$. To guarantee that individuals are selected evenly

*Because we are surveying 40 customers, the first individual surveyed is the 5th, the second is the $5 + 7 = 12$th, the third is the $5 + (2)7 = 19$th, and so on, until we reach the 40th, which is the $5 + (39)7 = 278$th shopper.

from both the beginning and the end of the population (such as early and late shoppers), we compute N/n and round down to the nearest integer. For example, $20{,}325/100 = 203.25$, so $k = 203$. Then we randomly select a number between 1 and 203 and select every 203rd individual thereafter. So, if we randomly selected 90 as our starting point, we would survey the 90th, 293rd, 496th, …, 20,187th individuals.

We summarize the procedure as follows:

Steps in Systematic Sampling

1. If possible, approximate the population size, N.
2. Determine the sample size desired, n.
3. Compute $\frac{N}{n}$ and round down to the nearest integer. This value is k.
4. Randomly select a number between 1 and k. Call this number p.
5. The sample will consist of the following individuals:

$$p, p + k, p + 2k, \ldots, p + (n - 1)k$$

Because systematic sampling does not require a frame, it typically provides more information for a given cost than does simple random sampling. In addition, systematic sampling is easier to employ, so there is less likelihood of interviewer error occurring, such as selecting the wrong individual to be surveyed.

Now Work Problem 27

3 Obtain a Cluster Sample

A fourth sampling method is called *cluster sampling*. Like the previous three sampling methods, this method has benefits under certain circumstances.

DEFINITION

A **cluster sample** is obtained by selecting all individuals within a randomly selected collection or group of individuals.

Suppose a school administrator wants to learn the characteristics of students enrolled in online classes. Rather than obtaining a simple random sample based on the frame of all students enrolled in online classes, the administrator could treat each online class as a cluster and then obtain a simple random sample of these clusters. The administrator would then survey *all* the students in the selected clusters. This reduces the number of classes that get surveyed.

In Other Words
Imagine a mall parking lot. Each subsection of the lot could be a cluster (Section F-4, for example).

EXAMPLE 3 Obtaining a Cluster Sample

Problem A sociologist wants to gather data regarding household income within the city of Boston. Obtain a sample using cluster sampling.

Approach The city of Boston can be set up so that each city block is a cluster. Once the city blocks have been identified, we obtain a simple random sample of the city blocks and survey all households on the blocks selected.

Note to Instructor
Consider doing the Comparing Sampling Methods activity in the Student Activity Workbook.

Solution Suppose there are 10,493 city blocks in Boston. First, the sociologist must number the blocks from 1 to 10,493. Suppose the sociologist has enough time and money to survey 20 clusters (city blocks). The sociologist should obtain a simple random sample of 20 numbers between 1 and 10,493 and survey all households from the clusters selected. Cluster sampling is a good choice in this example because it reduces the travel time

CAUTION

Stratified and cluster samples are different. In a stratified sample, we divide the population into two or more homogeneous groups. Then we obtain a simple random sample from each group. In a cluster sample, we divide the population into groups, obtain a simple random sample of some of the groups, and survey *all* individuals in the selected groups.

to households that is likely to occur with both simple random sampling and stratified sampling. In addition, there is no need to obtain a frame of all the households with cluster sampling. The only frame needed is one that provides information regarding city blocks.

The following are a few of the questions that arise in cluster sampling:

- How do I cluster the population?
- How many clusters do I sample?
- How many individuals should be in each cluster?

First, we must determine whether the individuals within the proposed cluster are homogeneous (similar individuals) or heterogeneous (dissimilar individuals). In Example 3, city blocks tend to have similar households. Survey responses from houses on the same city block are likely to be similar. This results in duplicate information. We conclude that if the clusters have homogeneous individuals it is better to have more clusters with fewer individuals in each cluster.

What if the cluster is heterogeneous? Under this circumstance, the heterogeneity of the cluster likely resembles the heterogeneity of the population. In other words, each cluster is a scaled-down representation of the overall population. For example, a quality-control manager might use shipping boxes that contain 100 light bulbs as a cluster, since the rate of defects within the cluster would resemble the rate of defects in the population, assuming the bulbs are randomly placed in the box. Thus, when each cluster is heterogeneous, fewer clusters with more individuals in each cluster are appropriate.

Now Work Problem 13

Convenience Sampling

In the four sampling techniques just presented, the individuals are selected randomly. Often, however, inappropriate sampling methods are used in which the individuals are not randomly selected.

Have you ever been stopped in the mall by someone holding a clipboard? These folks are responsible for gathering information, but their methods of data collection are inappropriate, and the results of their analysis are suspect because they obtained their data using a *convenience sample*.

DEFINITION

A **convenience sample** is a sample in which the individuals are easily obtained and not based on randomness.

CAUTION

Studies that use convenience sampling generally have results that are suspect. The results should be looked on with extreme skepticism.

The most popular of the many types of convenience samples are those in which the individuals in the sample are **self-selected** (the individuals themselves decide to participate in a survey). These are also called **voluntary response** samples. One example of self-selected sampling is phone-in polling; a radio personality will ask his or her listeners to phone the station to submit their opinions. Another example is the use of the Internet to conduct surveys. For example, a television news show will present a story regarding a certain topic and ask its viewers to "tell us what you think" by completing a questionnaire online or phoning in an opinion. Both of these samples are poor designs because the individuals who decide to be in the sample generally have strong opinions about the topic. A more typical individual in the population will not bother phoning or logging on to a computer to complete a survey. Any inference made regarding the population from this type of sample should be made with extreme caution.

Note to Instructor

Discuss some problems encountered in obtaining a sample from a nearby mall.

Convenience samples yield unreliable results because the individuals participating in the survey are not chosen using random sampling. Instead, the interviewer or participant selects who is in the survey. Would an interviewer select an ornery individual? Of course not! Therefore, the sample is likely not to be representative of the population.

Multistage Sampling

In practice, most large-scale surveys obtain samples using a combination of the techniques just presented.

As an example of multistage sampling, consider Nielsen Media Research. Nielsen randomly selects households and monitors the television programs these households are watching through a People Meter. The meter is an electronic box placed on each TV within the household. The People Meter measures what program is being watched and who is watching it. Nielsen selects the households with the use of a two-stage sampling process.

Stage 1 Using U.S. Census data, Nielsen divides the country into geographic areas (strata). The strata are typically city blocks in urban areas and geographic regions in rural areas. About 6000 strata are randomly selected.

Stage 2 Nielsen sends representatives to the selected strata and lists the households within the strata. The households are then randomly selected through a simple random sample.

Nielsen sells the information obtained to television stations and companies. These results are used to help determine prices for commercials.

As another example of multistage sampling, consider the sample used by the Census Bureau for the Current Population Survey. This survey requires five stages of sampling:

Stage 1 Stratified sample

Stage 2 Cluster sample

Stage 3 Stratified sample

Stage 4 Cluster sample

Stage 5 Systematic sample

This survey is very important because it is used to obtain demographic estimates of the United States in noncensus years. Details about the Census Bureau's sampling method can be found in *The Current Population Survey: Design and Methodology*, Technical Paper No. 40.

Sample Size Considerations

Throughout our discussion of sampling, we did not mention how to determine the sample size. Determining the sample size is key in the overall statistical process. Researchers need to know how many individuals they must survey to draw conclusions about the population within some predetermined margin of error. They must find a balance between the reliability of the results and the cost of obtaining these results. The bottom line is that time and money determine the level of confidence researchers will place on the conclusions drawn from the sample data. The more time and money researchers have available, the more accurate the results of the statistical inference.

In Sections 9.1 and 9.2, we will discuss techniques for determining the sample size required to estimate characteristics regarding the population within some margin of error. (For a detailed discussion of sample size considerations, consult a text on sampling techniques such as *Elements of Sampling Theory and Methods* by Z. Govindarajulu, Pearson, 1999.)

Summary

Figure 5 illustrates the four sampling techniques presented.

Figure 5

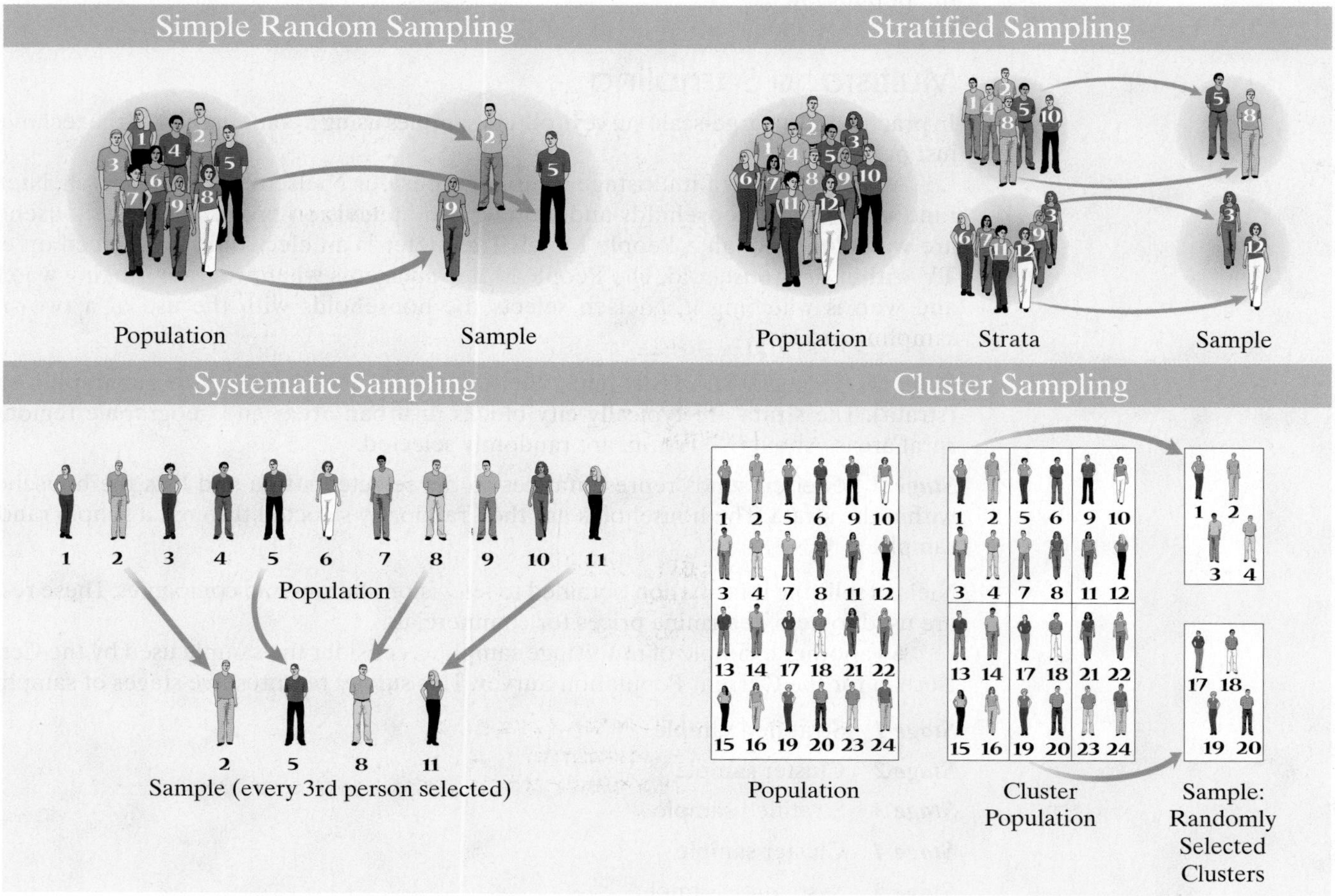

1.4 ASSESS YOUR UNDERSTANDING

VOCABULARY AND SKILL BUILDING

1. Describe a circumstance in which stratified sampling would be an appropriate sampling method. 2. Systematic

2. Which sampling method does not require a frame?

3. Why are convenience samples ill advised?

4. A(n) _____ sample is obtained by dividing the population into groups and selecting all individuals from within a random sample of the groups. cluster

5. A(n) _____ sample is obtained by dividing the population into homogeneous groups and randomly selecting individuals from each group. stratified

6. *True or False*: When taking a systematic random sample of size *n*, every group of size *n* from the population has the same chance of being selected. False

7. *True or False*: A simple random sample is always preferred because it obtains the same information as other sampling plans but requires a smaller sample size. False

8. *True or False*: When conducting a cluster sample, it is better to have fewer clusters with more individuals when the clusters are heterogeneous. True

9. *True or False*: Inferences based on voluntary response samples are generally not reliable. True

10. *True or False*: When obtaining a stratified sample, the number of individuals included within each stratum must be equal. False

In Problems 11–22, identify the type of sampling used.

11. To estimate the percentage of defects in a recent manufacturing batch, a quality-control manager at Intel selects every 8th chip that comes off the assembly line starting with the 3rd until she obtains a sample of 140 chips. Systematic

12. To determine the prevalence of human growth hormone (HGH) use among high school varsity baseball players, the State Athletic Commission randomly selects 50 high schools. All members of the selected high schools' varsity baseball teams are tested for HGH. Cluster

NW **13.** To determine customer opinion of its boarding policy, Southwest Airlines randomly selects 60 flights during a certain week and surveys all passengers on the flights. Cluster

14. A member of Congress wishes to determine her constituency's opinion regarding estate taxes. She divides her constituency into three income classes: low-income households, middle-income households, and upper-income households. She then takes a simple random sample of households from each income class. Stratified

15. In an effort to identify whether an advertising campaign has been effective, a marketing firm conducts a nationwide poll by randomly selecting individuals from a list of known users of the product. Simple random

16. A radio station asks its listeners to call in their opinion regarding the use of U.S. forces in peacekeeping missions. Convenience

17. A farmer divides his orchard into 50 subsections, randomly selects 4, and samples all the trees within the 4 subsections to approximate the yield of his orchard. Cluster

18. A college official divides the student population into five classes: freshman, sophomore, junior, senior, and graduate student. The official takes a simple random sample from each class and asks the members' opinions regarding student services. Stratified

19. A survey regarding download time on a certain Web site is administered on the Internet by a market research firm to anyone who would like to take it. Convenience

20. The presider of a guest-lecture series at a university stands outside the auditorium before a lecture begins and hands every fifth person who arrives, beginning with the third, a speaker evaluation survey to be completed and returned at the end of the program. Systematic

21. To determine his DSL Internet connection speed, Shawn divides up the day into four parts: morning, midday, evening, and late night. He then measures his Internet connection speed at 5 randomly selected times during each part of the day. Stratified

22. 24 Hour Fitness wants to administer a satisfaction survey to its current members. Using its membership roster, the club randomly selects 40 club members and asks them about their level of satisfaction with the club. Simple random

23. A salesperson obtained a systematic sample of size 20 from a list of 500 clients. To do so, he randomly selected a number from 1 of 25, obtaining the number 16. He included in the sample the 16th client on the list and every 25th client thereafter. List the numbers that correspond to the 20 clients selected.

24. A quality-control expert wishes to obtain a cluster sample by selecting 10 of 795 clusters. She numbers the clusters from 1 to 795. Using Table I from Appendix A, she closes her eyes and drops a pencil on the table. It points to the digit in row 8, column 38. Using this position as the starting point and proceeding downward, determine the numbers for the 10 clusters selected.

APPLYING THE CONCEPTS

NW **25. Stratified Sampling** The Future Government Club wants to sponsor a panel discussion on the upcoming national election. The club wants to have four of its members lead the panel discussion. To be fair, however, the panel should consist of two Democrats and two Republicans. From the list of current members of the club, obtain a stratified sample of two Democrats and two Republicans to serve on the panel.

Democrats		Republicans	
Bolden	Motola	Blouin	Ochs
Bolt	Nolan	Cooper	Pechtold
Carter	Opacian	De Young	Redmond
Debold	Pawlak	Engler	Rice
Fallenbuchel	Ramirez	Grajewski	Salihar
Haydra	Tate	Keating	Thompson
Khouri	Washington	May	Trudeau
Lukens	Wright	Niemeyer	Zenkel

26. Stratified Sampling The owner of a private food store is concerned about employee morale. She decides to survey the managers and hourly employees to see if she can learn about work environment and job satisfaction. From the list of workers at the store, obtain a stratified sample of two managers and four hourly employees to survey.

Managers		Hourly Employees		
Carlisle	Oliver	Archer	Foushi	Massie
Hills	Orsini	Bolcerek	Gow	Musa
Kats	Ullrich	Bryant	Grove	Nickas
Lindsey	McGuffin	Cole	Hall	Salazar
		Dimas	Houston	Vaneck
		Ellison	Kemp	Weber
		Everhart	Lathus	Zavodny

NW **27. Systematic Sample** The human resource department at a certain company wants to conduct a survey regarding worker morale. The department has an alphabetical list of all 4502 employees at the company and wants to conduct a systematic sample.

(a) Determine k if the sample size is 50. 90

(b) Determine the individuals who will be administered the survey. More than one answer is possible.

28. Systematic Sample To predict the outcome of a county election, a newspaper obtains a list of all 945,035 registered voters in the county and wants to conduct a systematic sample.

(a) Determine k if the sample size is 130. 7269

(b) Determine the individuals who will be administered the survey. More than one answer is possible.

29. Which Method? The mathematics department at a university wishes to administer a survey to a sample of students taking college algebra. The department is offering 32 sections of college algebra, similar in class size and makeup, with a total of 1280 students. They would like the sample size to be roughly 10% of the population of college algebra students this semester. How might the department obtain a simple random sample? A stratified

23. 16, 41, 66, 91, 116, 141, 166, 191, 216, 241, 266, 291, 316, 341, 366, 391, 416, 441, 466, 491
24. 763, 185, 377, 304, 626, 392, 315, 084, 565, 508

sample? A cluster sample? Which method do you think is best in this situation?

30. Good Sampling Method? To obtain students' opinions about proposed changes to course registration procedures, the administration of a small college asked for faculty volunteers who were willing to administer a survey in one of their classes. Twenty-three faculty members volunteered. Each faculty member gave the survey to all the students in one course of their choosing. Would this sampling method be considered a cluster sample? Why or why not?

31. Sample Design The city of Naperville is considering the construction of a new commuter rail station. The city wishes to survey the residents of the city to obtain their opinion regarding the use of tax dollars for this purpose. Design a sampling method to obtain the individuals in the sample. Be sure to support your choice.

32. Sample Design A school board at a local community college is considering raising the student services fees. The board wants to obtain the opinion of the student body before proceeding. Design a sampling method to obtain the individuals in the sample. Be sure to support your choice..

33. Sample Design Target wants to open a new store in the village of Lockport. Before construction, Target's marketers want to obtain some demographic information regarding the area under consideration. Design a sampling method to obtain the individuals in the sample. Be sure to support your choice.

34. Sample Design The county sheriff wishes to determine if a certain highway has a high proportion of speeders traveling on it. Design a sampling method to obtain the individuals in the sample. Be sure to support your choice.

35. Sample Design A pharmaceutical company wants to conduct a survey of 30 individuals who have high cholesterol. The company has obtained a list from doctors throughout the country of 6600 individuals who are known to have high cholesterol. Design a sampling method to obtain the individuals in the sample. Be sure to support your choice.

36. Sample Design A marketing executive for Coca-Cola, Inc., wants to identify television shows that people in the Boston area who typically drink Coke are watching. The executive has a list of all households in the Boston area. Design a sampling method to obtain the individuals in the sample. Be sure to support your choice.

37. Putting It Together: Comparing Sampling Methods Suppose a political strategist wants to get a sense of how American adults aged 18 years or older feel about health care and health insurance.

(a) In a political poll, what would be a good frame to use for obtaining a sample?

(b) Explain why simple random sampling may not guarantee that the sample has an accurate representation of registered Democrats, registered Republicans, and registered Independents.

(c) How can stratified sampling guarantee this representation?

38. Putting It Together: Thinking about Randomness What is random sampling? Why is it necessary for a sample to be obtained randomly rather than conveniently? Will randomness guarantee that a sample will provide accurate information about the population? Explain.

39. Research the origins of the Gallup Poll and the current sampling method the organization uses. Report your findings to the class.

40. Research the sampling methods used by a market research firm in your neighborhood. Report your findings to the class. The report should include the types of sampling methods used, number of stages, and sample size.

29. SRS: number from 1 to 1280; randomly select 128 students to survey. Stratified: randomly select 4 students from each section to survey. Cluster: randomly select 4 sections, survey all students in these 4 sections. Answers will vary. 30. No. The "clusters" were not randomly selected 37. (a) Registered voters who have voted in the past few elections

1.5 BIAS IN SAMPLING

OBJECTIVE **1** Explain the sources of bias in sampling

Note to Instructor

If you are pressed for time, this section can be given to the students as a reading assignment with light in-class coverage.

1 Explain the Sources of Bias in Sampling

So far we have looked at *how* to obtain samples, but not at some of the problems that inevitably arise in sampling. Remember, the goal of sampling is to obtain information about a population through a sample.

DEFINITION If the results of the sample are not representative of the population, then the sample has **bias**.

In Other Words

The word *bias* could mean to give preference to selecting some individuals over others; it could also mean that certain responses are more likely to occur in the sample than in the population.

There are three sources of bias in sampling:

1. Sampling bias
2. Nonresponse bias
3. Response bias

Sampling Bias

Sampling bias means that the technique used to obtain the sample's individuals tends to favor one part of the population over another. Any convenience sample has sampling bias because the individuals are not chosen through a random sample.

Sampling bias also results due to **undercoverage**, which occurs when the proportion of one segment of the population is lower in a sample than it is in the population. Undercoverage can result if the frame used to obtain the sample is incomplete or not representative of the population. Some frames, such as the list of all registered voters, may seem easy to obtain; but even this frame may be incomplete since people who recently registered to vote may not be on the published list of registered voters.

Sampling bias can lead to incorrect predictions. For example, the magazine *Literary Digest* predicted that Alfred M. Landon would defeat Franklin D. Roosevelt in the 1936 presidential election. The *Literary Digest* conducted a poll based on a list of its subscribers, telephone directories, and automobile owners. On the basis of the results, the *Literary Digest* predicted that Landon would win with 57% of the popular vote. However, Roosevelt won the election with about 62% of the popular vote. This election took place during the height of the Great Depression. In 1936, most subscribers to the magazine, households with telephones, and automobile owners were Republican, the party of Landon. Therefore, the choice of the frame used to conduct the survey led to an incorrect prediction due to sampling bias. Essentially, there was undercoverage of Democrats.

It is difficult to gain access to a *complete* list of individuals in a population. For example, public-opinion polls often use random telephone surveys, which implies that the frame is all households with telephones. This method of sampling excludes households without telephones, as well as homeless people. If these people differ in some way from people with telephones or homes, the results of the sample may not be valid. The federal government prohibits the random calling of cellular telephones. However, a study done by the Pew Research Center suggests that excluding cellphone-only homes from telephone surveys does not significantly affect the results.

Nonresponse Bias

Nonresponse bias exists when individuals selected to be in the sample who do not respond to the survey have different opinions from those who do. Nonresponse can occur because individuals selected for the sample do not wish to respond or the interviewer was unable to contact them.

All surveys will suffer from nonresponse. The federal government's Current Population Survey has a response rate of about 92%, but it varies depending on the age of the individual. For example, the response rate for 20- to 29-year-olds is 85%, and for individuals 70 and older, it is 99%. Response rates in random digit dialing (RDD) telephone surveys are typically around 70%, e-mail survey response rates hover around 40%, and mail surveys can have response rates as high as 60%.

Nonresponse bias can be controlled using callbacks. For example, if a mailed questionnaire was not returned, a callback might mean phoning the individual to conduct the survey. If an individual was not at home, a callback might mean returning to the home at other times in the day.

Another method to improve nonresponse is using rewards, such as cash payments for completing a questionnaire, or incentives such as a cover letter that states that the responses to the questionnaire will determine future policy. For example, I received $1 with a survey regarding my satisfaction with a recent purchase. The $1 "payment" was meant to make me feel guilty enough to fill out the questionnaire. As another example, a city may send out questionnaires to households and state in a cover letter that the responses to the questionnaire will be used to decide pending issues within the city.

Let's consider the *Literary Digest* poll again. The *Literary Digest* mailed out more than 10 million questionnaires and 2.3 million people responded. The rather low response rate (23%) contributed to the incorrect prediction. After all, Roosevelt was the incumbent president and only those who were unhappy with his administration were likely to respond. By the way, in the same election, the 35-year-old George Gallup predicted that Roosevelt would win the election in his survey involving 50,000 people.

Response Bias

Response bias exists when the answers on a survey do not reflect the true feelings of the respondent. Response bias can occur in a number of ways.

Interviewer Error A trained interviewer is essential to obtain accurate information from a survey. A skilled interviewer can elicit responses from individuals and make the interviewee feel comfortable enough to give truthful responses. For example, a good interviewer can obtain truthful answers to questions as sensitive as "Have you ever cheated on your taxes?" Do not be quick to trust surveys conducted by poorly trained interviewers. Do not trust survey results if the sponsor has a vested interest in the results of the survey. Would you trust a survey conducted by a car dealer that reports 90% of customers say they would buy another car from the dealer?

Misrepresented Answers Some survey questions result in responses that misrepresent facts or are flat-out lies. For example, a survey of recent college graduates may find that self-reported salaries are inflated. Also, people may overestimate their abilities. For example, ask people how many push-ups they can do in 1 minute, and then ask them to do the push-ups. How accurate were they?

CAUTION

The wording of questions can significantly affect the responses and, therefore, the validity of a study.

Wording of Questions The way a question is worded can lead to response bias in a survey, so questions must always be asked in balanced form. For example, the "yes/no" question

Do you oppose the reduction of estate taxes?

should be written

Do you favor or oppose the reduction of estate taxes?

The second question is balanced. Do you see the difference? Consider the following report based on studies from Schuman and Presser (*Questions and Answers in Attitude Surveys*, 1981, p. 277), who asked the following two questions:

(A) Do you think the United States should forbid public speeches against democracy?
(B) Do you think the United States should allow public speeches against democracy?

For those respondents presented with question A, 21.4% gave "yes" responses, while for those given question B, 47.8% gave "no" responses. The conclusion you may arrive at is that most people are not necessarily willing to forbid something, but more people are willing not to allow something. These results illustrate how wording a question can alter a survey's outcome.

Another consideration in wording a question is not to be vague. The question "How much do you study?" is too vague. Does the researcher mean how much do I study for all my classes or just for statistics? Does the researcher mean per day or per week? The question should be written "How many hours do you study statistics each week?"

Ordering of Questions or Words Many surveys will rearrange the order of the questions within a questionnaire so that responses are not affected by prior questions. Consider an example from Schuman and Presser in which the following two questions were asked:

Note to Instructor

Many of our students (and possibly even you) were not alive in 1980, so they may not be aware of the Cold War and American attitude toward Communism. Spend some time on this history lesson.

(A) Do you think the United States should let Communist newspaper reporters from other countries come in here and send back to their papers the news as they see it?
(B) Do you think a Communist country such as Russia should let American newspaper reporters come in and send back to America the news as they see it?

For surveys conducted in 1980 in which the questions appeared in the order (A, B), 54.7% of respondents answered "yes" to A and 63.7% answered "yes" to B. If the questions were ordered (B, A), then 74.6% answered "yes" to A and 81.9% answered "yes" to B. When Americans are first asked if U.S. reporters should be allowed to report Communist news, they are more likely to agree that Communists should be allowed to report American news. Questions should be rearranged as much as possible to help reduce effects of this type.

Pollsters will also rearrange words within a question. For example, the Gallup Organization routinely asks the following question of 1017 adults aged 18 years or older:

Do you [rotated: approve (or) disapprove] of the job Barack Obama is doing as president?

The words *approve* and *disapprove* are rotated to remove the effect that may occur by writing the word *approve* first in the question.

Type of Question One of the first considerations in designing a question is determining whether the question should be *open* or *closed*.

An **open question** allows the respondent to choose his or her response:

What is the most important problem facing America's youth today?

A **closed question** requires the respondent to choose from a list of predetermined responses:

What is the most important problem facing America's youth today?

(a) Drugs
(b) Violence
(c) Single-parent homes
(d) Promiscuity
(e) Peer pressure

In closed questions, the possible responses should be rearranged because respondents are likely to choose early choices in a list rather than later choices.

An open question should be phrased so that the responses are similar. (You don't want a wide variety of responses.) This allows for easy analysis of the responses. Closed questions limit the number of respondent choices and, therefore, the results are much easier to analyze. The limited choices, however, do not always include a respondent's desired choice. In that case, the respondent will have to choose a secondary answer or skip the question.

Survey designers recommend conducting pretest surveys with open questions and then using the most popular answers as the choices on closed-question surveys. Another issue to consider in the closed-question design is the number of possible responses. The option "no opinion" should be omitted, because this option does not allow for meaningful analysis. The goal is to limit the number of choices in a closed question without forcing respondents to choose an option they do not prefer, which would make the survey have response bias.

Data-entry Error Although not technically a result of response bias, data-entry error will lead to results that are not representative of the population. Once data are collected, the results typically must be entered into a computer, which could result in input errors. For example, 39 may be entered as 93. It is imperative that data be checked for accuracy. In this text, we present some suggestions for checking for data error.

Can a Census Have Bias?

The discussion so far has focused on bias in samples, but bias can also occur when conducting a census. A question on a census form could be misunderstood, thereby leading to response bias in the results. We also mentioned that it is often difficult to contact each individual in a population. For example, the U.S. Census Bureau is challenged to count each homeless person in the country, so the census data published by the U.S. government likely suffers from nonresponse bias.

Sampling Error versus Nonsampling Error

Nonresponse bias, response bias, and data-entry errors are types of *nonsampling error*. However, whenever a sample is used to learn information about a population, there will inevitably also be *sampling error.*

DEFINITIONS

Nonsampling errors result from undercoverage, nonresponse bias, response bias, or data-entry error. Such errors could also be present in a complete census of the population. **Sampling error** results from using a sample to estimate information about a population. This type of error occurs because a sample gives incomplete information about a population.

In Other Words
We can think of sampling error as error that results from using a subset of the population to describe characteristics of the population. Nonsampling error is error that results from obtaining and recording the information collected.

Note to Instructor
Consider administering the survey in the Student Activity Workbook. Then, the results can be analyzed throughout the semester. Better yet, build a survey in StatCrunch and administer it via email, Twitter, or Facebook.

By incomplete information, we mean that the individuals in the sample cannot reveal all the information about the population. Suppose we wanted to determine the average age of the students enrolled in an introductory statistics course. To do this, we obtain a simple random sample of four students and ask them to write their age on a sheet of paper and turn it in. The average age of these four students is 23.25 years. Assume that no students lied about their age or misunderstood the question, and the sampling was done appropriately. If the actual average age of all 30 students in the class (the population) is 22.91 years, then the sampling error is $23.25 - 22.91 = 0.34$ year. Now suppose the same survey is conducted, but this time one student lies about his age. Then the results of the survey will also have nonsampling error.

1.5 ASSESS YOUR UNDERSTANDING

VOCABULARY AND SKILL BUILDING

1. What is a closed question? What is an open question? Discuss the advantages and disadvantages of each type of question.

2. What does it mean when a part of the population is underrepresented?

3. What is bias? Name the three sources of bias and provide an example of each. How can a census have bias?

4. Distinguish between nonsampling error and sampling error.

In Problems 5–16, the survey has bias. (a) Determine the type of bias. (b) Suggest a remedy.

5. A retail store manager wants to conduct a study regarding the shopping habits of his customers. He selects the first 60 customers who enter his store on a Saturday morning. Sampling bias

6. The village of Oak Lawn wishes to conduct a study regarding the income level of households within the village. The village manager selects 10 homes in the southwest corner of the village and sends an interviewer to the homes to determine household income. Sampling bias

7. An antigun advocate wants to estimate the percentage of people who favor stricter gun laws. He conducts a nationwide survey of 1203 randomly selected adults 18 years old and older. The interviewer asks the respondents, "Do you favor harsher penalties for individuals who sell guns illegally?"
Response bias; poorly worded question

8. Suppose you are conducting a survey regarding the sleeping habits of students. From a list of registered students, you obtain a simple random sample of 150 students. One survey question is "How much sleep do you get?" Response bias; poorly worded question

9. A polling organization conducts a study to estimate the percentage of households that speaks a foreign language as the primary language. It mails a questionnaire to 1023 randomly selected households throughout the United States and asks the head of household if a foreign language is the primary language spoken in the home. Of the 1023 households selected, 12 responded. Nonresponse

10. Cold Stone Creamery is considering opening a new store in O'Fallon. Before opening the store, the company would like to know the percentage of households in O'Fallon that regularly visit an ice cream shop. The market researcher obtains a list of households in O'Fallon and randomly selects 150 of them. He mails a questionnaire to the 150 households that asks about ice cream eating habits and flavor preferences. Of the 150 questionnaires mailed, 4 are returned. Nonresponse

11. A newspaper article reported, "The *Cosmopolitan* magazine survey of more than 5000 Australian women aged 18–34 found about 42 percent considered themselves overweight or obese." *Source*: *Herald Sun*, September 9, 2007

12. A health teacher wishes to do research on the weight of college students. She obtains the weights for all the students in her 9 A.M. class by looking at their driver's licenses or state IDs. Sampling bias and possible response bias
11. Sampling bias and possible interviewer error

13. A magazine is conducting a study on the effects of infidelity in a marriage. The editors randomly select 400 women whose husbands were unfaithful and ask, "Do you believe a marriage can survive when the husband destroys the trust that must exist between husband and wife?" Response bias; poorly worded question

14. A textbook publisher wants to determine what percentage of college professors either require or recommend that their students purchase textbook packages with supplemental materials, such as study guides, digital media, and online tools. The publisher sends out surveys by e-mail to a random sample of 320 faculty members who have registered with its Web site and have agreed to receive solicitations. The publisher reports that 80% of college professors require or recommend that their students purchase some type of textbook package. Sampling bias; poor choice of a frame

15. Suppose you are conducting a survey regarding illicit drug use among teenagers in the Baltimore school district. You obtain a cluster sample of 12 schools within the district and sample all sophomore students in the randomly selected schools. The survey is administered by the teachers. Response bias

16. To determine the public's opinion of the police department, the police chief obtains a cluster sample of 15 census tracts within his jurisdiction and samples all households in the randomly selected tracts. Uniformed police officers go door to door to conduct the survey. Response bias

APPLYING THE CONCEPTS

17. Response Rates Surveys tend to suffer from low response rates. Based on past experience, a researcher determines that the typical response rate for an e-mail survey is 40%. She wishes to obtain a sample of 300 respondents, so she e-mails the survey to 1500 randomly selected e-mail addresses. Assuming the response rate for her survey is 40%, will the respondents form an unbiased sample? Explain.

18. Delivery Format The General Social Survey asked, "About how often did you have sex in the past 12 months?" About 47% of respondents indicated they had sex at least once a week. In a Web survey for a marriage and family wellness center, respondents were asked, "How often do you and your partner have sex (on average)?" About 31% of respondents indicated they had sex with their partner at least once a week. Explain how the delivery method for such a question could result in biased responses.

19. Order of the Questions Consider the following two questions:

(a) Suppose that a rape is committed in which the woman becomes pregnant. Do you think the criminal should or should not face additional charges if the woman becomes pregnant?

(b) Do you think abortions should be legal under any circumstances, legal under certain circumstances, or illegal in all circumstances?

Do you think the order in which the questions are asked will affect the survey results? If so, what can the pollster do to alleviate this response bias?

20. Order of the Questions Consider the following two questions:

(a) Do you believe that the government should or should not be allowed to prohibit individuals from expressing their religious beliefs at their place of employment?

(b) Do you believe that the government should or should not be allowed to prohibit teachers from expressing their religious beliefs in public school classrooms?

Do you think the order in which the questions are asked will affect the survey results? If so, what can the pollster do to alleviate this response bias? Discuss the choice of the word *prohibit* in the survey questions.

21. Improving Response Rates Suppose you are reading an article at psychcentral.com and the following text appears in a pop-up window:

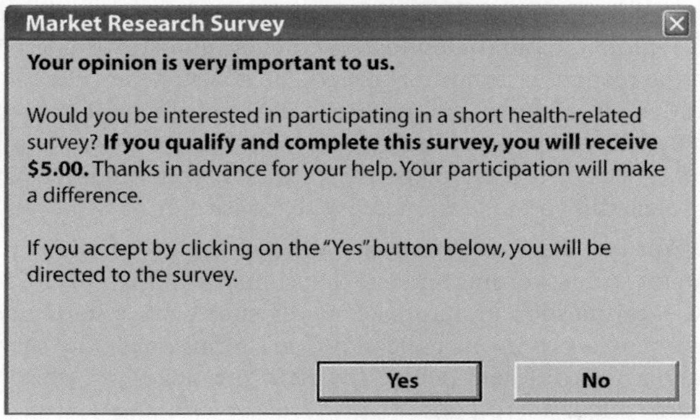

What tactic is the company using to increase the response rate for its survey?

22. Rotating Choices Consider this question from a recent Gallup poll:

Which of the following approaches to solving the nation's energy problems do you think the U.S. should follow right now—[ROTATED: emphasize production of more oil, gas and coal supplies (or) emphasize more conservation by consumers of existing energy supplies]?

Why is it important to rotate the two choices presented in the question?

23. Random Digit Dialing Many polls use random digit dialing (RDD) to obtain a sample, which means a computer randomly generates phone numbers of landlines. What is the frame for this type of sampling? Who would be excluded from the survey and how might this affect the results of the survey?

24. Caller ID How do you think caller ID has affected phone surveys?

25. Don't Call Me! The Telephone Consumer Protection Act (TCPA) allows consumers to put themselves on a do-not-call registry. If a number is on the registry, commercial telemarketers are not allowed to call you. Do you believe this has affected the ability of surveyors to obtain accurate polling results? If so, how?

26. Current Population Survey In the federal government's Current Population Survey, the response rate for 20- to 29-year-olds is 85%; for individuals at least 70 years of age it is 99%. Why do you think this is?

27. Exit Polling During every election, pollsters conduct exit polls to help determine which candidate people voted for. During the 2004 presidential election, pollsters incorrectly predicted John Kerry the winner over George Bush. When asked how this

17. No; undercoverage (sampling bias), nonresponse bias, and response bias

error could have happened, the pollsters cited interviewer error due to the fact that many of the interviewers were young, only young voters agreed to be interviewed, and young voters tended to favor Kerry. Plus, young interviewers tend to make more data-entry mistakes. In addition, the method of selecting individuals to be interviewed led to selecting a higher proportion of female voters, and Kerry was favored by females. In some precincts, interviewers were denied access to voters. Research the 2004 exit polling fiasco. Explain which nonsampling errors led to the incorrect conclusion regarding the 2004 election.

28. Write Your Own Survey Develop a survey that you could administer using online survey tools such as StatCrunch, surveymonkey.com, or polldaddy.com. Administer the survey. Did the responses accurately reflect the goals of each question? What types of nonsampling error did you encounter in the survey? If you invited individuals to take the survey via an e-mail, what type of response rate did you obtain? What approach did you take to increase response rate?

29. Wording Survey Questions Write a survey question that contains strong wording and one that contains tempered wording. Post each question in an online survey site such as StatCrunch, surveymonkey.com, or polldaddy.com. Administer the survey to at least 25 different people for each question. How does the wording affect the response?

30. Order in Survey Questions Write two questions that could have different responses, depending on the order in which the questions are presented. Or write a single question such that the order in which words are presented could affect the response. Administer the survey to at least 25 different people for each question. Did the results differ?

31. Research a survey method used by a company or government branch. Determine the sampling method used, the sample size, the method of collection, and the frame used.

32. Informed Opinions People often respond to survey questions without any knowledge of the subject matter. A common example of this is the discussion on banning dihydrogen monoxide. The Centers for Disease Control (CDC) reports that there were 1423 deaths due to asbestos in 2005, but over 3443 deaths were attributed to dihydrogen monoxide in 2007. Articles and Web sites such as www.dhmo.org tell how this substance is widely used despite the dangers associated with it. Many people have joined the cause to ban this substance without realizing that dihydrogen monoxide is simply water (H_2O). Their eagerness to protect the environment or their fear of seeming uninformed may be part of the problem. Put together a survey that asks individuals whether dihydrogen monoxide should or should not be banned. Give the survey to 20 randomly selected students around campus and report your results to the class. An example survey might look like the following:

Dihydrogen monoxide is colorless, odorless, and kills thousands of people every year. Most of these deaths are caused by accidental inhalation, but the dangers of dihydrogen monoxide do not stop there. Prolonged exposure to its solid form can severely damage skin tissue. Symptoms of ingestion can include excessive sweating and urination and possibly a bloated feeling, nausea, vomiting, and body electrolyte imbalance. Dihydrogen monoxide is a major component of acid rain and can cause corrosion after coming in contact with certain metals.

Do you believe that the government should or should not ban the use of dihydrogen monoxide?

33. Name two biases that led to the *Literary Digest* making an incorrect prediction in the presidential election of 1936.

34. Research on George Gallup Research the polling done by George Gallup in the 1936 presidential election. Write a report on your findings. Be sure to include information about the sampling technique and sample size. Now research the polling done by Gallup for the 1948 presidential election. Did Gallup accurately predict the outcome of the election? What lessons were learned by Gallup?

35. Putting It Together: Speed Limit In the state of California, speed limits are established through traffic engineering surveys. One aspect of the survey is for city officials to measure the speed of vehicles on a particular road.

Source: www.ci.eureka.ca.gov, www.nctimes.com

(a) What is the population of interest for this portion of the engineering survey?

(b) What is the variable of interest for this portion of the engineering survey? Speed

(c) Is the variable qualitative or quantitative? Quantitative

(d) What is the level of measurement for the variable? Ratio

(e) Is a census feasible in this situation? Explain why or why not. No

(f) Is a sample feasible in this situation? If so, explain what type of sampling plan could be used. If not, explain why not. Systematic

(g) In July 2007, the Temecula City Council refused a request to increase the speed limit on Pechanga Parkway from 40 to 45 mph despite survey results indicating that the prevailing speed on the parkway favored the increase. Opponents were concerned that it was visitors to a nearby casino who were driving at the increased speeds and that city residents actually favored the lower speed limit. Explain how bias might be playing a role in the city council's decision.

EXPLAINING THE CONCEPTS

36. Why is it rare for frames to be completely accurate?

37. What are some solutions to nonresponse?

38. Discuss the benefits of having trained interviewers.

39. What are the advantages of having a presurvey when constructing a questionnaire that has closed questions?

40. Discuss the pros and cons of telephone interviews that take place during dinner time in the early evening.

41. Why is a high response rate desired? How would a low response rate affect survey results?

42. Discuss why the order of questions or choices within a questionnaire are important in sample surveys.

43. Suppose a survey asks, "Do you own any CDs?" Explain how this could be interpreted in more than one way. Suggest a way in which the question could be improved.

44. Discuss a possible advantage of offering rewards or incentives to increase response rates. Are there any disadvantages?

1.6 THE DESIGN OF EXPERIMENTS

OBJECTIVES

1. Describe the characteristics of an experiment
2. Explain the steps in designing an experiment
3. Explain the completely randomized design
4. Explain the matched-pairs design

The major theme of this chapter has been data collection. Section 1.2 briefly discussed the idea of an experiment, but the main focus was on observational studies. Sections 1.3 through 1.5 focused on sampling and surveys. In this section, we further develop the idea of collecting data through an experiment.

1 Describe the Characteristics of an Experiment

Remember, in an observational study, if an association exists between an explanatory variable and response variable the researcher cannot claim causality. To demonstrate how changes in the explanatory variable *cause* changes in the response variable, the researcher needs to conduct an *experiment*.

DEFINITION

An **experiment** is a controlled study conducted to determine the effect varying one or more explanatory variables or **factors** has on a response variable. Any combination of the values of the factors is called a **treatment**.

Historical Note

Sir Ronald Fisher, often called the Father of Modern Statistics, was born in England on February 17, 1890. He received a BA in astronomy from Cambridge University in 1912. In 1914, he took a position teaching mathematics and physics at a high school. He did this to help serve his country during World War I. (He was rejected by the army because of his poor eyesight.) In 1919, Fisher took a job as a statistician at Rothamsted Experimental Station, where he was involved in agricultural research. In 1933, Fisher became Galton Professor of Eugenics at Cambridge University, where he studied Rh blood groups. In 1943 he was appointed to the Balfour Chair of Genetics at Cambridge. He was knighted by Queen Elizabeth in 1952. Fisher retired in 1957 and died in Adelaide, Australia, on July 29, 1962. One of his famous quotations is "To call in the statistician after the experiment is done may be no more than asking him to perform a postmortem examination: he may be able to say what the experiment died of."

In an experiment, the **experimental unit** is a person, object, or some other well-defined item upon which a treatment is applied. We often refer to the experimental unit as a **subject** when he or she is a person. The subject is analogous to the individual in a survey.

The goal in an experiment is to determine the effect various treatments have on the response variable. For example, we might want to determine whether a new treatment is superior to an existing treatment (or no treatment at all). To make this determination, experiments require a *control group*. A **control group** serves as a baseline treatment that can be used to compare to other treatments. For example, a researcher in education might want to determine if students who do their homework using an online homework system do better on an exam than those who do their homework from the text. The students doing the text homework might serve as the control group (since this is the currently accepted practice). The factor is the type of homework. There are two treatments: online homework and text homework. A second method for defining the control group is through the use of a *placebo*. A **placebo** is an innocuous medication, such as a sugar tablet, that looks, tastes, and smells like the experimental medication.

In an experiment, it is important that each group be treated the same way. It is also important that individuals do not adjust their behavior because of the treatment they are receiving. For this reason, many experiments use a technique called *blinding*. **Blinding** refers to nondisclosure of the treatment an experimental unit is receiving. There are two types of blinding: *single blinding* and *double blinding*.

DEFINITIONS

In **single-blind** experiments, the experimental unit (or subject) does not know which treatment he or she is receiving. In **double-blind** experiments, neither the experimental unit nor the researcher in contact with the experimental unit knows which treatment the experimental unit is receiving.

EXAMPLE 1 The Characteristics of an Experiment

Problem Lipitor is a cholesterol-lowering drug made by Pfizer. In the Collaborative Atorvastatin Diabetes Study (CARDS), the effect of Lipitor on cardiovascular disease was assessed in 2838 subjects, ages 40 to 75, with type 2 diabetes, without prior history of cardiovascular disease. In this placebo-controlled, double-blind experiment, subjects were randomly allocated to either Lipitor 10 mg daily (1428) or placebo (1410) and were followed for 4 years. The response variable was the occurrence of any major cardiovascular event.

Lipitor significantly reduced the rate of major cardiovascular events (83 events in the Lipitor group versus 127 events in the placebo group). There were 61 deaths in the Lipitor group versus 82 deaths in the placebo group.

(a) What does it mean for the experiment to be placebo-controlled?
(b) What does it mean for the experiment to be double-blind?
(c) What is the population for which this study applies? What is the sample?
(d) What are the treatments?
(e) What is the response variable? Is it qualitative or quantitative?

Approach We will apply the definitions just presented.

Solution

(a) The placebo is a medication that looks, smells, and tastes like Lipitor. The placebo control group serves as a baseline against which to compare the results from the group receiving Lipitor. The placebo is also used because people tend to behave differently when they are in a study. By having a placebo control group, the effect of this is neutralized.
(b) Since the experiment is double-blind, the subjects, as well as the individual monitoring the subjects, do not know whether the subjects are receiving Lipitor or the placebo. The experiment is double-blind so that the subjects receiving the medication do not behave differently from those receiving the placebo and so the individual monitoring the subjects does not treat those in the Lipitor group differently from those in the placebo group.
(c) The population is individuals from 40 to 75 years of age with type 2 diabetes without a prior history of cardiovascular disease. The sample is the 2838 subjects in the study.
(d) The treatments are 10 mg of Lipitor or a placebo daily.
(e) The response variable is whether the subject had any major cardiovascular event, such as a stroke, or not. It is a qualitative variable.

Now Work Problem 7

2 Explain the Steps in Designing an Experiment

To **design** an experiment means to describe the overall plan in conducting the experiment. Conducting an experiment requires a series of steps.

Step 1 *Identify the Problem to Be Solved.* The statement of the problem should be as explicit as possible and should provide the experimenter with direction. The statement must also identify the response variable and the population to be studied. Often, the statement is referred to as the *claim.*

Step 2 *Determine the Factors That Affect the Response Variable.* The factors are usually identified by an expert in the field of study. In identifying the factors, ask, "What things affect the value of the response variable?" After the factors are identified, determine which factors to fix at some predetermined level, which to manipulate, and which to leave uncontrolled.

Step 3 *Determine the Number of Experimental Units.* As a general rule, choose as many experimental units as time and money allow. Techniques (such as those in Sections 9.1 and 9.2) exist for determining sample size, provided certain information is available.

Step 4 *Determine the Level of Each Factor.* There are two ways to deal with the factors, control or randomize.

1. Control: There are two ways to control the factors.

(a) Set the level of a factor at one value throughout the experiment (if you are *not* interested in its effect on the response variable).

(b) Set the level of a factor at various levels (if you are interested in its effect on the response variable). The combinations of the levels of all varied factors constitute the treatments in the experiment.

2. Randomize: Randomly assign the experimental units to various treatment groups so that the effect of factors whose levels cannot be controlled is minimized. The idea is that randomization averages out the effects of uncontrolled factors (explanatory variables). It is difficult, if not impossible, to identify all factors in an experiment. This is why randomization is so important. It mutes the effect of variation attributable to factors not controlled.

Step 5 *Conduct the Experiment.*

(a) Randomly assign the experimental units to the treatments. **Replication** occurs when each treatment is applied to more than one experimental unit. Using more than one experimental unit for each treatment ensures the effect of a treatment is not due to some characteristic of a single experimental unit. It is a good idea to assign an equal number of experimental units to each treatment.

(b) Collect and process the data. Measure the value of the response variable for each replication. Then organize the results. The idea is that the value of the response variable for each treatment group is the *same* before the experiment because of randomization. Then any *difference* in the value of the response variable among the different treatment groups is a result of differences in the level of the treatment.

Step 6 *Test the Claim.* This is the subject of inferential statistics. **Inferential statistics** is a process in which generalizations about a population are made on the basis of results obtained from a sample. Provide a statement regarding the level of confidence in the generalization. Methods of inferential statistics are presented in Chapters 9 through 15.

3 Explain the Completely Randomized Design

The steps just given apply to any type of designed experiment. We now concentrate on the simplest type of experiment.

DEFINITION

A **completely randomized design** is one in which each experimental unit is randomly assigned to a treatment.

EXAMPLE 2 A Completely Randomized Design

Problem A farmer wishes to determine the optimal level of a new fertilizer on his soybean crop. Design an experiment that will assist him.

Approach We follow the steps for designing an experiment.

Note to Instructor
Consider doing the Designing an Experiment activity in the Student Activities Manual to illustrate the completely randomized design.

Solution

Step 1 The farmer wants to identify the optimal level of fertilizer for growing soybeans. We define *optimal* as the level that maximizes yield. So the response variable will be crop yield.

Step 2 Some factors that affect crop yield are fertilizer, precipitation, sunlight, method of tilling the soil, type of soil, plant, and temperature.

Step 3 In this experiment, we will plant 60 soybean plants (experimental units).

Step 4 We list the factors and their levels.

- **Fertilizer.** This factor will be controlled and set at three levels. We wish to measure the effect of varying the level of this variable on the response variable, yield. We will set the treatments (level of fertilizer) as follows:

  Treatment A: 20 soybean plants receive no fertilizer.

  Treatment B: 20 soybean plants receive 2 teaspoons of fertilizer per gallon of water every 2 weeks.

  Treatment C: 20 soybean plants receive 4 teaspoons of fertilizer per gallon of water every 2 weeks.

In Other Words
The various levels of the factor are the treatments in a completely randomized design.

See Figure 6.

Figure 6

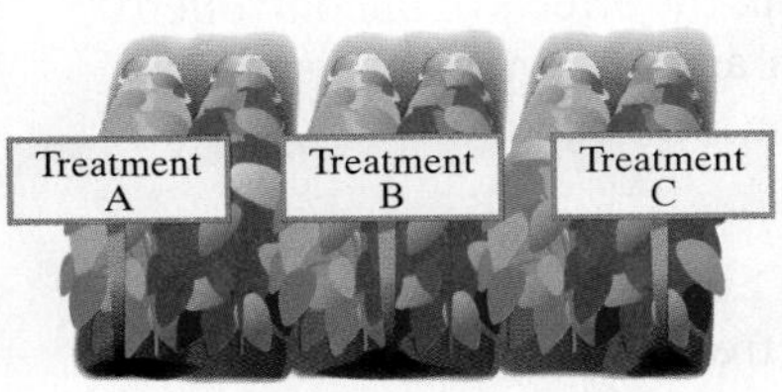

- **Precipitation.** We cannot control the amount of rainfall, but we can control the amount of watering we do, so that each plant receives the same amount of precipitation.
- **Sunlight.** This uncontrollable factor will be roughly the same for each plant.
- **Method of tilling.** We can control this factor and will use the round-up ready method of tilling for each plant.
- **Type of soil.** We can control certain aspects of the soil such as level of acidity. In addition, each plant will be planted within a 1-acre area, so it is reasonable to assume that the soil conditions for each plant are equivalent.
- **Plant.** There may be variation from plant to plant. To account for this, we randomly assign the plants to a treatment.
- **Temperature.** This factor is uncontrollable, but will be the same for each plant.

Step 5

(a) We need to assign each plant to a treatment group. First, we will number the plants from 1 to 60 and randomly generate 20 numbers. The plants corresponding to these numbers get treatment A. Next we number the remaining plants 1 to 40 and randomly generate 20 numbers. The plants corresponding to these numbers get treatment B. The remaining plants get treatment C. Now we till the soil, plant the soybean plants, and fertilize according to the schedule prescribed.

(b) At the end of the growing season, we determine the crop yield for each plant.

Step 6 We determine any differences in yield among the three treatment groups.

Figure 7 illustrates the experimental design.

Figure 7

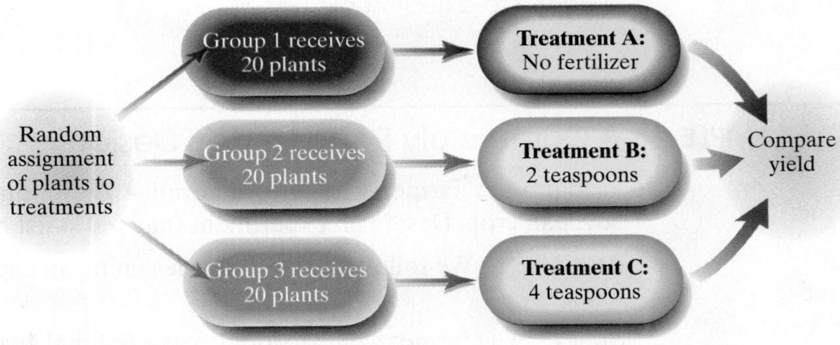

Note to Instructor
It is useful to diagram the experimental designs in this chapter to target the understanding of the visual learner.

Example 2 is a completely randomized design because the experimental units (the plants) were randomly assigned to the treatments. It is the most popular experimental design because of its simplicity, but it is not always the best. We discuss inferential procedures for the completely randomized design with two treatments and quantitative response variable in Section 11.3. We discuss inferential procedures for the completely randomized design for a qualitative response variable in Sections 11.1 and 12.2.

Now Work Problem 9

4 Explain the Matched-Pairs Design

Another type of experimental design is called a *matched-pairs design.*

DEFINITION

A **matched-pairs design** is an experimental design in which the experimental units are paired up. The pairs are selected so that they are related in some way (that is, the same person before and after a treatment, twins, husband and wife, same geographical location, and so on). There are only two levels of treatment in a matched-pairs design.

In matched-pairs design, one matched individual will receive one treatment and the other receives a different treatment. The matched pair is randomly assigned to the treatment using a coin flip or a random-number generator. We then look at the difference in the results of each matched pair. One common type of matched-pairs design is to measure a response variable on an experimental unit before and after a treatment is applied. In this case, the individual is matched against itself. These experiments are sometimes called before–after or pretest–posttest experiments.

EXAMPLE 3 A Matched-Pairs Design

Problem An educational psychologist wants to determine whether listening to music has an effect on a student's ability to learn. Design an experiment to help the psychologist answer the question.

Approach We will use a matched-pairs design by matching students according to IQ and gender (just in case gender plays a role in learning with music).

Solution We match students according to IQ and gender. For example, we match two females with IQs in the 110 to 115 range.

For each pair of students, we flip a coin to determine which student is assigned the treatment of a quiet room or a room with music playing in the background.

Each student will be given a statistics textbook and asked to study Section 1.1. After 2 hours, the students will enter a testing center and take a short quiz on the material in the section. We compute the difference in the scores of each matched pair. Any differences in scores will be attributed to the treatment. Figure 8 illustrates the design.

Figure 8

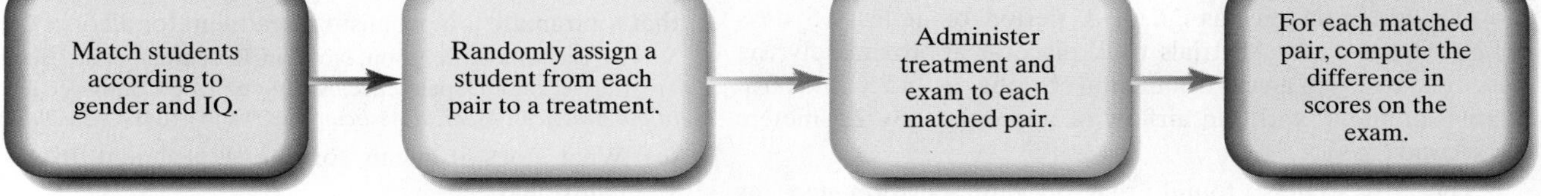

Now Work Problem 11

We discuss statistical inference for the matched-pairs design for a qualitative response variable in Section 11.1 and quantitative response variable in Section 11.2.

One note about the relation between a designed experiment and simple random sampling: It is often the case that the experimental units selected to participate in a study are not randomly selected. This is because we often need the experimental units to have some common trait, such as high blood pressure. For this reason, participants in experiments are recruited or volunteer to be in a study. However, once we have the experimental units, we use simple random sampling to assign them to treatment groups. With random assignment we assume that the participants are similar at the start of the experiment. Because the treatment is the only difference between the groups, we can say the treatment *caused* the difference observed in the response variable.

7. (c) Caffeinated sports drink, noncaffeinated sports drink, or flavored-water placebo 8. (d) All 18–65 year olds with alcohol dependence; 371 men and women aged 18 to 65 years of age with alcohol dependence (e) 300 mg of topiramate or a placebo daily (f) Percentage of heavy drinking days

1.6 ASSESS YOUR UNDERSTANDING

VOCABULARY

1. Define the following:

(a) Experimental unit
(b) Treatment
(c) Response variable
(d) Factor
(e) Placebo
(f) Confounding

2. What is replication in an experiment?

3. Explain the difference between a single-blind and a double-blind experiment.

4. A(n) ______ ______ design is one in which each experimental unit is randomly assigned to a treatment. A(n) ______ ______ design is one in which the experimental units are paired up. completely randomized; matched pairs

5. *True or False:* Observational studies are used to determine causality between explanatory and response variables. False

6. *True or False:* Generally, the goal of an experiment is to determine the effect that treatments will have on the response variable. True 7. (e) Caffeinated sports drink, noncaffeinated sports drink, or flavored-water placebo

APPLYING THE CONCEPTS

NW **7. Caffeinated Sports Drinks** Researchers conducted a double-blind, placebo-controlled, repeated-measures experiment to compare the effectiveness of a commercial caffeinated carbohydrate–electrolyte sports drink with a commercial noncaffeinated carbohydrate–electrolyte sports drink and a flavored-water placebo. Sixteen highly trained cyclists each completed three trials of prolonged cycling in a warm environment: one while receiving the placebo, one while receiving the noncaffeinated sports drink, and one while receiving the caffeinated sports drink. For a given trial, one beverage treatment was administered throughout a 2-hour variable-intensity cycling bout followed by a 15-minute performance ride. Total work in kilojoules (kJ) performed during the final 15 minutes was used to measure performance. The beverage order for the individual subjects was randomly assigned. A period of at least 5 days separated the trials. All trials took place at approximately the same time of day in an environmental chamber at 28.5°C and 60% relative humidity with fan airflow of approximately 2.5 meters per second (m/s).

The researchers found that cycling performance, as assessed by the total work completed during the performance ride, was 23% greater for the caffeinated sports drink than for the placebo and 15% greater for the caffeinated sports drink than for the noncaffeinated sports drink. Cycling performances for the noncaffeinated sports drink and the placebo were not significantly different. The researchers concluded that the caffeinated carbohydrate–electrolyte sports drink substantially enhanced physical performance during prolonged exercise compared with the noncaffeinated carbohydrate–electrolyte sports drink and the placebo. *Source*: Kirk J. Cureton, Gordon L. Warren et al. "Caffeinated Sports Drink: Ergogenic Effects and Possible Mechanisms," *International Journal of Sport Nutrition and Exercise Metabolism*, 17(1):35–55, 2007

(a) What does it mean for the experiment to be placebo-controlled?

(b) What does it mean for the experiment to be double-blind? Why do you think it is necessary for the experiment to be double-blind?

(c) How is randomization used in this experiment?

(d) What is the population for which this study applies? What is the sample? All athletes; 16 cyclists

(e) What are the treatments?

(f) What is the response variable? Total work

(g) This experiment used a *repeated-measures design*, a design type that has not been directly discussed in this textbook. Using this experiment as a guide, determine what it means for the design of the experiment to be repeated-measures. How does this design relate to the matched-pairs design?

8. Alcohol Dependence To determine if topiramate is a safe and effective treatment for alcohol dependence, researchers conducted a 14-week trial of 371 men and women aged 18 to 65 years diagnosed with alcohol dependence. In this double-blind, randomized, placebo-controlled experiment, subjects were randomly given either 300 milligrams (mg) of topiramate (183 subjects) or a placebo (188 subjects) daily, along with a weekly compliance enhancement intervention. The variable used to determine the effectiveness of the treatment was self-reported percentage of heavy drinking days. Results indicated that topiramate was more effective than placebo at reducing the percentage of heavy drinking days. The researchers concluded that topiramate is a promising treatment for alcohol dependence. *Source*: Bankole A. Johnson, Norman Rosenthal, et al. "Topiramate for Treating Alcohol Dependence: A Randomized Controlled Trial," *Journal of the American Medical Association*, 298(14):1641–1651, 2007

(a) What does it mean for the experiment to be placebo-controlled?

(b) What does it mean for the experiment to be double-blind? Why do you think it is necessary for the experiment to be double-blind?

(c) What does it mean for the experiment to be randomized?

9. (a) Score on achievement test (b) Method of teaching, grade level, intelligence, school district, teacher; Fixed: grade level, school district, teacher; Set to a predetermined level: method of teaching (f) Completely randomized design

14. (a) Completely randomized design (b) Adult outpatients diagnosed as having major depression and having a baseline Hamilton Rating Scale for Depression (HAM-D) score of at least 20 (c) Change in the HAM-D over the treatment period (d) Type of drug: St. John's wort extract or placebo

(d) What is the population for which this study applies? What is the sample?
(e) What are the treatments?
(f) What is the response variable?

NW **9. School Psychology** A school psychologist wants to test the effectiveness of a new method for teaching reading. She recruits 500 first-grade students in District 203 and randomly divides them into two groups. Group 1 is taught by means of the new method, while group 2 is taught by traditional methods. The same teacher is assigned to teach both groups. At the end of the year, an achievement test is administered and the results of the two groups are compared.

(a) What is the response variable in this experiment?
(b) Think of some of the factors in the study. How are they controlled?
(c) What are the treatments? How many treatments are there? New teaching method and traditional method; 2
(d) How are the factors that are not controlled dealt with? Random assignment
(e) Which group serves as the control group? Group 2
(f) What type of experimental design is this?
(g) Identify the subjects. 500 students
(h) Draw a diagram similar to Figure 7 or 8 to illustrate the design.

10. Pharmacy A pharmaceutical company has developed an experimental drug meant to relieve symptoms associated with the common cold. The company identifies 300 adult males 25 to 29 years old who have a common cold and randomly divides them into two groups. Group 1 is given the experimental drug, while group 2 is given a placebo. After 1 week of treatment, the proportions of each group that still have cold symptoms are compared. 10. (a) Proportion of subjects with cold

(a) What is the response variable in this experiment?
(b) Think of some of the factors in the study. How are they controlled?
(c) What are the treatments? How many treatments are there? Experimental drug and placebo; 2
(d) How are the factors that are not controlled dealt with? Random assignment
(e) What type of experimental design is this?
(f) Identify the subjects. 300 males
(g) Draw a diagram similar to Figure 7 or 8 to illustrate the design.

NW **11. Whiter Teeth** An ad for Crest Whitestrips Premium claims that the strips will whiten teeth in 7 days and the results will last for 12 months. A researcher who wishes to test this claim studies 20 sets of identical twins. Within each set of twins, one is randomly selected to use Crest Whitestrips Premium in addition to regular brushing and flossing, while the other just brushes and flosses. Whiteness of teeth is measured at the beginning of the study, after 7 days, and every month thereafter for 12 months. 11. (b) Whiteness level

(a) What type of experimental design is this? Matched pairs
(b) What is the response variable in this experiment?
(c) What are the treatments?
(d) What are other factors (controlled or uncontrolled) that could affect the response variable?
(e) What might be an advantage of using identical twins as subjects in this experiment?

12. Assessment To help assess student learning in her developmental math courses, a mathematics professor at a community college implemented pre- and posttests for her students. A knowledge-gained score was obtained by taking the difference of the two test scores.

(a) What type of experimental design is this? Matched pair
(b) What is the response variable in this experiment?
(c) What is the treatment? Math course

13. Insomnia Researchers Jack D. Edinger and associates wanted to test the effectiveness of a new cognitive behavioral therapy (CBT) compared with both an older behavioral treatment and a placebo therapy for treating insomnia. They identified 75 adults with chronic insomnia. Patients were randomly assigned to one of three treatment groups. Twenty-five patients were randomly assigned to receive CBT (sleep education, stimulus control, and time-in-bed restrictions), another 25 received muscle relaxation training (RT), and the final 25 received a placebo treatment. Treatment lasted 6 weeks, with follow-up conducted at 6 months. To measure the effectiveness of the treatment, researchers used wake time after sleep onset (WASO). Cognitive behavioral therapy produced larger improvements than did RT or placebo treatment. For example, the CBT-treated patients achieved an average 54% reduction in their WASO, whereas RT-treated and placebo-treated patients, respectively, achieved only 16% and 12% reductions in this measure. Results suggest that CBT treatment leads to significant sleep improvements within 6 weeks, and these improvements appear to endure through 6 months of follow-up. *Source*: Jack D. Edinger, PhD; William K. Wohlgemuth, PhD; Rodney A. Radtke, MD; Gail R. Marsh, PhD; Ruth E. Quillian, PhD. "Cognitive Behavioral Therapy for Treatment of Chronic Primary Insomnia," *Journal of the American Medical Association* 285:1856–1864, 2001

(a) What type of experimental design is this?
(b) What is the population being studied?
(c) What is the response variable in this study?
(d) What are the treatments?
(e) Identify the experimental units. 75 adults with insomnia
(f) Draw a diagram similar to Figure 7 or 8 to illustrate the design. 13. (a) Completely randomized design

14. Depression Researchers wanted to compare the effectiveness and safety of an extract of St. John's wort with placebo in outpatients with major depression. To do this, they recruited 200 adult outpatients diagnosed as having major depression and having a baseline Hamilton Rating Scale for Depression (HAM-D) score of at least 20. Participants were randomly assigned to receive either St. John's wort extract, 900 milligrams per day (mg/d) for 4 weeks, increased to 1200 mg/d in the absence of an adequate response thereafter, or a placebo for 8 weeks. The response variable was the change on the HAM-D over the treatment period. After analysis of the data, it was concluded that St. John's wort was not effective for treatment of major depression. *Source*: Richard C. Shelton, MD, et al. "Effectiveness of St. John's Wort in Major Depression," *Journal of the American Medical Association* 285:1978–1986, 2001

(a) What type of experimental design is this?
(b) What is the population that is being studied?
(c) What is the response variable in this study?

10. (b) Gender, age, geographic location, overall health, drug intervention; Fixed: gender, age, location; Set to a predetermined level: drug intervention (e) Completely randomized design 11. (c) Whitening method; Crest Whitestrips Premium with brushing and flossing versus brushing and flossing alone 12. (b) Difference in test scores 13. (b) Adults with insomnia (c) Wake time after sleep onset (WASO) (d) CBT, muscle relaxation training, placebo

17. (b) Distance yardstick falls (e) To eliminate bias due to starting on dominant or nondominant first for each trial
18. (a) Matched-pairs design (b) Distance ball hit (c) Shaft type: graphite shaft versus steel shaft

(d) What are the treatments?
(e) Identify the experimental units. 200 outpatients
(f) What is the control group in this study? Placebo group
(g) Draw a diagram similar to Figure 7 or 8 to illustrate the design.

15. The Memory Drug? Researchers wanted to evaluate whether ginkgo, an over-the-counter herb marketed as enhancing memory, improves memory in elderly adults as measured by objective tests. To do this, they recruited 98 men and 132 women older than 60 years and in good health. Participants were randomly assigned to receive ginkgo, 40 milligrams (mg) 3 times per day, or a matching placebo. The measure of memory improvement was determined by a standardized test of learning and memory. After 6 weeks of treatment, the data indicated that ginkgo did not increase performance on standard tests of learning, memory, attention, and concentration. These data suggest that, when taken following the manufacturer's instructions, ginkgo provides no measurable increase in memory or related cognitive function to adults with healthy cognitive function. *Source:* Paul R. Solomon et al. "Ginkgo for Memory Enhancement," *Journal of the American Medical Association* 288:835–840, 2002

(a) What type of experimental design is this?
(b) What is the population being studied?
(c) What is the response variable in this study?
(d) What is the factor that is set to predetermined levels? What are the treatments?
(e) Identify the experimental units.
(f) What is the control group in this study? Placebo group
(g) Draw a diagram similar to Figure 7 or 8 to illustrate the design.

16. Shrinking Stomach? Researchers wanted to determine whether the stomach shrinks as a result of dieting. To do this, they randomly divided 23 obese patients into two groups. The 14 individuals in the experimental group were placed on a diet that allowed them to consume 2508 kilojoules (kJ) per day for 4 weeks. The 9 subjects in the control group ate as they normally would. To assess the size of the stomach, a latex gastric balloon was inserted into each subject's stomach and filled with the maximum amount of water that could be tolerated by the patient. The volume of water was compared to the volume that could be tolerated at the beginning of the study. The experimental subjects experienced a 27% reduction in gastric capacity, while the subjects in the control group experienced no change in gastric capacity. It was concluded that a reduction in gastric capacity occurs after a restricted diet. *Source:* A. Geliebter et al. "Reduced Stomach Capacity in Obese Subjects after Dieting," *American Journal of Clinical Nutrition* 63(2):170–173, 1996 (a) Completely randomized design

(a) What type of experimental design is this?
(b) What is the population that the results of this experiment apply to? Obese individuals
(c) What is the response variable in this study? Is it qualitative or quantitative? Volume of stomach; quantitative
(d) What are the treatments? 2508 kJ diet vs. regular diet
(e) Identify the experimental units. The 23 obese patients
(f) Draw a diagram similar to Figure 7 or 8 to illustrate the design.

17. Dominant Hand Professor Andy Neill wanted to determine if the reaction time of people differs in their dominant hand versus their nondominant hand. To do this, he recruited 15 students. Each student was asked to hold a yardstick between the index finger and thumb. The student was asked to open the hand, release the yardstick, and then asked to catch the yardstick between the index finger and thumb. The distance that the yardstick fell served as a measure of reaction time. A coin flip was used to determine whether the student would use their dominant hand first or the nondominant hand. Results indicated that the reaction time in the dominant hand exceeded that of the nondominant hand.

(a) What type of experimental design is this?
(b) What is the response variable in this study?
(c) What is the treatment? Dominant versus nondominant hand
(d) Identify the experimental units. 15 students
(e) Why did Professor Neill use a coin flip to determine whether the student should begin with the dominant hand or the nondominant hand?
(f) Draw a diagram similar to Figure 7 or 8 to illustrate the design.

18. Golf Anyone? A local golf pro wanted to compare two styles of golf club. One golf club had a graphite shaft and the other had the latest style of steel shaft. It is a common belief that graphite shafts allow a player to hit the ball farther, but the manufacturer of the new steel shaft said the ball travels just as far with its new technology. To test this belief, the pro recruited 10 golfers from the driving range. Each player was asked to hit one ball with the graphite-shafted club and one ball with the new steel-shafted club. The distance that the ball traveled was determined using a range finder. A coin flip was used to determine whether the player hit with the graphite club or the steel club first. Results indicated that the distance the ball was hit with the graphite club was no different than the distance when using the steel club.

(a) What type of experimental design is this?
(b) What is the response variable in this study?
(c) What is the factor that is set to predetermined levels? What is the treatment?
(d) Identify the experimental units. 10 golfers
(e) Why did the golf pro use a coin flip to determine whether the golfer should hit with the graphite first or the steel first?
(f) Draw a diagram similar to Figure 7 or 8 to illustrate the design.

19. Drug Effectiveness A pharmaceutical company wants to test the effectiveness of an experimental drug meant to reduce high cholesterol. The researcher at the pharmaceutical company has decided to test the effectiveness of the drug through a completely randomized design. She obtains 20 volunteers with high cholesterol: Ann, John, Michael, Kevin, Marissa, Christina, Eddie, Shannon, Julia, Randy, Sue, Tom, Wanda, Roger, Laurie, Rick, Kim, Joe, Colleen, and Bill. Number the volunteers from 1 to 20. Use a random-number generator to randomly assign 10 of the volunteers to the experimental group. The remaining volunteers will go into the control group. List the individuals in each group.

15. (a) Completely randomized design (b) Adults older than 60 years in good health (c) Score on test of learning and memory
(d) Drug; 40 mg of ginkgo 3 times per day or a matching placebo (e) 98 men and 132 women older than 60 in good health
18. (e) To eliminate bias due to type of shaft used first

20. Effects of Alcohol A researcher has recruited 20 volunteers to participate in a study. The researcher wishes to measure the effect of alcohol on an individual's reaction time. The 20 volunteers are randomly divided into two groups. Group 1 serves as a control group in which participants drink four 1-ounce cups of a liquid that looks, smells, and tastes like alcohol in 15-minute increments. Group 2 will serve as an experimental group in which participants drink four 1-ounce cups of 80-proof alcohol in 15-minute increments. After drinking the last 1-ounce cup, the participants sit for 20 minutes. After the 20-minute resting period, the reaction time to a stimulus is measured.

(a) What type of experimental design is this?

(b) Use Table I in Appendix A or a random-number generator to divide the 20 volunteers into groups 1 and 2 by assigning the volunteers a number between 1 and 20. Then randomly select 10 numbers between 1 and 20. The individuals corresponding to these numbers will go into group 1.

21. Tomatoes An oncologist wants to perform a long-term study on the benefits of eating tomatoes. In particular, she wishes to determine whether there is a significant difference in the rate of prostate cancer among adult males after eating one serving of tomatoes per week for 5 years, after eating three servings of tomatoes per week for 5 years, and after eating five servings of tomatoes per week for 5 years. Help the oncologist design the experiment. Include a diagram to illustrate your design. Completely randomized design

22. Batteries An engineer wants to determine the effect of temperature on battery voltage. In particular, he is interested in determining if there is a significant difference in the voltage of the batteries when exposed to temperatures of 90°F, 70°F, and 50°F. Help the engineer design the experiment. Include a diagram to illustrate your design. Completely randomized design

23. The Better Paint Suppose you are interested in comparing Benjamin Moore's MoorLife Latex house paint with Sherwin Williams' LowTemp 35 Exterior Latex paint. Design an experiment that will answer this question: Which paint is better for painting the exterior of a house? Include a diagram to illustrate your design.

24. Tire Design An engineer has just developed a new tire design. However, before going into production, the tire company wants to determine if the new tire reduces braking distance on a car traveling 60 miles per hour compared with radial tires. Design an experiment to help the engineer determine if the new tire reduces braking distance.

25. Designing an Experiment Researchers wish to know if there is a link between hypertension (high blood pressure) and consumption of salt. Past studies have indicated that the consumption of fruits and vegetables offsets the negative impact of salt consumption. It is also known that there is quite a bit of person-to-person variability as far as the ability of the body to process and eliminate salt. However, no method exists for identifying individuals who have a higher ability to process salt. The U.S. Department of Agriculture recommends that daily intake of salt should not exceed 2400 milligrams (mg). The researchers want to keep the design simple, so they choose to conduct their study using a completely randomized design.

(a) What is the response variable in the study?

(b) Name three factors that have been identified.

(c) For each factor identified, determine whether the variable can be controlled or cannot be controlled. If a factor cannot be controlled, what should be done to reduce variability in the response variable?

(d) How many treatment levels would you recommend? Why?

26. Search a newspaper, magazine, or other periodical that describes an experiment. Identify the population, experimental unit, response variable, treatment, factors, and their levels.

27. Research the *placebo effect* and the *Hawthorne effect*. Write a paragraph that describes how each affects the outcome of an experiment.

28. Coke or Pepsi Suppose you want to perform an experiment whose goal is to determine whether people prefer Coke or Pepsi. Design an experiment that utilizes the completely randomized design. Design an experiment that utilizes the matched-pairs design. In both designs, be sure to identify the response variable, the role of blinding, and randomization. Which design do you prefer? Why?

29. Putting It Together: Mosquito Control In an attempt to identify ecologically friendly methods for controlling mosquito populations, researchers conducted field experiments in India where aquatic nymphs of the dragonfly *Brachytron pretense* were used against the larvae of mosquitoes. For the experiment, the researchers selected ten 300-liter (L) outdoor, open, concrete water tanks, which were natural breeding places for mosquitoes. Each tank was manually sieved to ensure that it was free of any nonmosquito larvae, nymphs, or fish. Only larvae of mosquitoes were allowed to remain in the tanks. The larval density in each tank was assessed using a 250-milliliter (ml) dipper. For each tank, 30 dips were taken and the mean larval density per dip was calculated. Ten freshly collected nymphs of *Brachytron pretense* were introduced into each of five randomly selected tanks. No nymphs were released into the remaining five tanks, which served as controls. After 15 days, larval densities in all the tanks were assessed again and all the introduced nymphs were removed. After another 15 days, the larval densities in all the tanks were assessed a third time.

In the nymph-treated tanks, the density of larval mosquitoes dropped significantly from 7.34 to 0.83 larvae per dip 15 days after the *Brachytron pretense* nymphs were introduced. Further, the larval density increased significantly to 6.83 larvae per dip 15 days after the nymphs were removed. Over the same time period, the control tanks did not show a significant difference in larval density, with density measurements of 7.12, 6.83, and 6.79 larvae per dip. The researchers concluded that *Brachytron pretense* can be used effectively as a strong, ecologically friendly control of mosquitoes and mosquito-borne diseases. *Source:* S. N. Chatterjee, A. Ghosh, and G. Chandra. "Eco-Friendly Control of Mosquito Larvae by *Brachytron pretense* Nymph," *Journal of Environmental Health* 69(8): 44–48, 2007

(a) Identify the research objective.

(b) What type of experimental design is this?

(c) What is the response variable? Is it quantitative or qualitative? If quantitative, is it discrete or continuous?

(d) What is the factor the researchers controlled and set to predetermined levels? What are the treatments?

20. (a) Completely randomized design 23. Matched-pair design (match by type of exterior finish) 24. Matched-pair design (match by car model) 25. (a) Blood pressure (b) Daily consumption of salt, daily consumption of fruits and vegetables, body's ability to process salt (c) Salt: controlled; Fruits and vegetables: controlled; Body: cannot be controlled. To deal with variability in body types, randomize experimental units to each treatment group. (d) Answers will vary, but three might be a good choice: one below RDA, one equal to RDA, one above RDA.

(e) Can you think of other factors that may affect larvae of mosquitoes? How are they controlled or dealt with?

(f) What is the population for which this study applies? What is the sample?

(g) List the descriptive statistics.

(h) How did the researchers control this experiment?

(i) Draw a diagram similar to Figure 7 or 8 to illustrate the design.

(j) State the conclusion made in the study.

EXPLAINING THE CONCEPTS

30. The Dictator Game In their book *SuperFreakonomics*, authors Steven Levitt and Stephen Dubner describe the research of behavioral economist John List. List recruited customers and dealers at a baseball-card show to participate in an experiment in which the customer would state how much he was willing to pay for a single baseball card. The prices ranged from \$4 (lowball) to \$50 (premium card). The dealer would then give the customer a card that was supposed to correspond to the offer price. In this setting, the dealer could certainly give the buyer a card worth less than the offer price, but this rarely happened. The card received by the buyer was close in value to the price offered. Next, List went to the trading floor at the show and again recruited customers. But this time the customers approached dealers at their booth. The dealers did not know they were being watched. The scenario went something like this: as the customer approached the dealer's booth, he would say, "Please give me the best Derek Jeter card you can for \$20." In this scenario, the dealers consistently ripped off the customers by giving them cards worth much less than the offer price. In fact, the dealers who were the worst offenders were the same dealers who refused to participate in List's study. Do you believe that individuals who volunteer for experiments are scientific do-gooders? That is, do you believe that in designed experiments subjects strive to meet the expectations of the researcher? In addition, do you believe that results of experiments may suffer because many experiments require individuals to volunteer, and individuals who are not do-gooders do not volunteer for studies? Now, explain why control groups are needed in designed experiments and the role they can play in neutralizing the impact of scientific do-gooders.

31. What is the role of randomization in a designed experiment? If you were conducting a completely randomized design with three treatments and 90 experimental units, describe how you would randomly assign the experimental units to the treatments.

29. (a) To determine if nymphs of Brachytron pretense will control mosquitoes (b) Completely randomized design (c) Mosquito larvae density; quantitative; discrete (d) Introduction of nymphs of Brachytron pretense into water tanks containing mosquito larvae; nymphs added or no nymphs added (e) Temperature, amount of rainfall, fish, other larvae, sunlight (f) All mosquito larvae in all breeding places; the mosquito larvae in the ten 300-liter outdoor, open concrete water tanks (g) During the study period, mosquito larvae density changed from 7.34 to 0.83 to 6.83 larvae per dip in the treatment tanks, while changing only from 7.12 to 6.83 to 6.79 larvae per dip in the control tanks. (j) Nymphs of Brachytron pretense can be used effectively as a strong, ecologically friendly control of mosquitoes and mosquito-borne diseases.

Consumer Reports® Emotional "Aspirin"

Americans have a long history of altering their moods with chemicals, ranging from alcohol and illicit drugs to prescription medications, such as diazepam (Valium) for anxiety and fluoxetine (Prozac) for depression. Today, there's a new trend: the over-the-counter availability of apparently effective mood modifiers in the form of herbs and other dietary supplements.

One problem is that many people who are treating themselves with these remedies may be sufficiently anxious or depressed to require professional care and monitoring. Self-treatment can be dangerous, particularly with depression, which causes some 20,000 reported suicides a year in the United States. Another major pitfall is that dietary supplements are largely unregulated by the government, so consumers have almost no protection against substandard preparations.

To help consumers and doctors, *Consumer Reports* tested the amounts of key ingredients in representative brands of several major mood-changing pills. To avoid potential bias, we tested samples from different lots of the pills using a randomized statistical design. The table contains a subset of the data from this study.

Each of these pills has a label claim of 200 mg of SAM-E. The column labeled Random Code contains a set of 3-digit random codes that were used so that the laboratory did not know which manufacturer was being tested. The column labeled Mg SAM-E contains the amount of SAM-E measured by the laboratory.

(a) Why is it important to label the pills with random codes?

(b) Why is it important to randomize the order in which the pills are tested instead of testing all of brand A first, followed by all of brand B, and so on?

Run Order	Brand	Random Code	Mg SAM-E
1	B	461	238.9
2	D	992	219.2
3	C	962	227.1
4	A	305	231.2
5	B	835	263.7
6	D	717	251.1
7	A	206	232.9
8	D	649	192.8
9	C	132	213.4
10	B	923	224.6
11	A	823	261.1
12	C	515	207.8

(c) Sort the data by brand. Does it appear that each brand is meeting its label claims?

(d) Design an experiment that follows the steps presented to answer the following research question: "Is there a difference in the amount of SAM-E contained in brands A, B, C, and D?"

Note to Readers: *In many cases, our test protocol and analytical methods are more complicated than described in this example. The data and discussion have been modified to make the material more appropriate for the audience.*

CHAPTER 1 REVIEW

Summary

We defined statistics as a science in which data are collected, organized, summarized, and analyzed to infer characteristics regarding a population. Statistics also provides a measure of confidence in the conclusions that are drawn. Descriptive statistics consists of organizing and summarizing information, while inferential statistics consists of drawing conclusions about a population based on results obtained from a sample. The population is a collection of individuals about which information is desired and the sample is a subset of the population.

Data are the observations of a variable. Data can be either qualitative or quantitative. Quantitative data are either discrete or continuous.

Data can be obtained from four sources: a census, an existing source, an observational study, or a designed experiment. A census will list all the individuals in the population, along with certain characteristics. Due to the cost of obtaining a census, most researchers opt for obtaining a sample. In observational studies, the response variable is measured without attempting to influence its value. In addition, the explanatory variable is not manipulated. Designed experiments are used when control of the individuals in the study is desired to isolate the effect of a certain treatment on a response variable.

We introduced five sampling methods: simple random sampling, stratified sampling, systematic sampling, cluster sampling, and convenience sampling. All the sampling methods, except for convenience sampling, allow for unbiased statistical inference to be made. Convenience sampling typically leads to an unrepresentative sample and biased results.

Vocabulary

Statistics (p. 3)
Data (pp. 3, 9)
Population (p. 5)
Individual (p. 5)
Sample (p. 5)
Statistic (p. 5)
Descriptive statistics (p. 5)
Inferential statistics (pp. 5, 47)
Parameter (p. 5)
Variable (p. 6)
Qualitative or categorical variable (p. 7)
Quantitative variable (p. 7)
Discrete variable (p. 8)
Continuous variable (p. 8)
Qualitative data (p. 9)
Quantitative data (p. 9)
Discrete data (p. 9)
Continuous data (p. 9)
Nominal level of measurement (p. 10)
Ordinal level of measurement (p. 10)
Interval level of measurement (p. 10)
Ratio level of measurement (p. 10)
Explanatory variable (p. 16)
Response variable (p. 16)
Observational study (p. 16)
Designed experiment (p. 16)
Confounding (p. 17)
Lurking variable (p. 17)
Retrospective (p. 18)
Prospective (p. 18)
Census (p. 19)
Random sampling (p. 22)
Simple random sampling (p. 23)
Simple random sample (p. 23)
Frame (p. 24)

Sampling without replacement (p. 24)
Sampling with replacement (p. 24)
Seed (p. 26)
Stratified sample (p. 30)
Systematic sample (p. 32)
Cluster sample (p. 33)
Convenience sample (p. 34)
Self-selected (p. 34)
Voluntary response (p. 34)
Bias (p. 38)
Sampling bias (p. 39)
Undercoverage (p. 39)
Nonresponse bias (p. 39)
Response bias (p. 40)
Open question (p. 41)
Closed question (p. 41)
Nonsampling error (p. 42)
Sampling error (p. 42)
Experiment (p. 45)
Factors (p. 45)
Treatment (p. 45)
Experimental unit (p. 45)
Subject (p. 45)
Control group (p. 45)
Placebo (p. 45)
Blinding (p. 45)
Single-blind (p. 46)
Double-blind (p. 46)
Design (p. 46)
Replication (p. 47)
Completely randomized design (p. 47)
Matched-pairs design (p. 49)

Objectives

Section	You should be able to . . .	Example(s)	Review Exercises
1.1	**1** Define statistics and statistical thinking (p. 3)	pp. 3–4	1
	2 Explain the process of statistics (p. 4)	2	7, 14, 15
	3 Distinguish between qualitative and quantitative variables (p. 6)	3	11–13
	4 Distinguish between discrete and continuous variables (p. 8)	4, 5	11–12
	5 Determine the level of measurement of a variable (p. 10)	6	16–19
1.2	**1** Distinguish between an observational study and an experiment (p. 15)	1–3	20–21, 31(b)
	2 Explain the various types of observational studies (p. 18)	pp. 18–19	6, 22
1.3	**1** Obtain a simple random sample (p. 23)	1–3	28, 30
1.4	**1** Obtain a stratified sample (p. 30)	1	25
	2 Obtain a systematic sample (p. 32)	2	26, 29
	3 Obtain a cluster sample (p. 33)	3	24
1.5	**1** Explain the sources of bias in sampling (p. 38)	pp. 38–42	8, 9, 27
1.6	**1** Describe the characteristics of an experiment (p. 45)	1	5
	2 Explain the steps in designing an experiment (p. 46)	pp. 46–47	10
	3 Explain the completely randomized design (p. 47)	2	31, 34, 35
	4 Explain the matched-pairs design (p. 49)	3	32, 35

Review Exercises

In Problems 1–5, provide a definition using your own words.

1. Statistics

2. Population

3. Sample

4. Observational study

5. Designed experiment

6. List and describe the three major types of observational studies.

7. What is meant by the *process of statistics*?

8. List and explain the three sources of bias in sampling. Provide some methods that might be used to minimize bias in sampling.

9. Distinguish between sampling and nonsampling error.

10. Explain the steps in designing an experiment.

In Problems 11–13, classify the variable as qualitative or quantitative. If the variable is quantitative, state whether it is discrete or continuous.

11. Number of new automobiles sold at a dealership on a given day Quantitative; discrete

12. Weight in carats of an uncut diamond

13. Brand name of a pair of running shoes Qualitative

12. Quantitative; continuous

In Problems 14 and 15, determine whether the underlined value is a parameter or a statistic.

14. In a survey of 1011 people age 50 or older, 73% agreed with the statement "I believe in life after death." Statistic

Source: Bill Newcott. "Life after Death," *AARP Magazine*, Sept./Oct. 2007

15. Completion Rate In the 2011 NCAA Football Championship Game, quarterback Cam Newton completed 59% of his passes for a total of 265 yards and 2 touchdowns. Parameter

In Problems 16–19, determine the level of measurement of each variable.

16. Birth year Interval

17. Marital status Nominal

18. Stock rating (strong buy, buy, hold, sell, strong sell) Ordinal

19. Number of siblings Ratio

In Problems 20 and 21, determine whether the study depicts an observational study or a designed experiment.

20. A parent group examines 25 randomly selected PG-13 movies and 25 randomly selected PG movies and records the number of sexual innuendos and curse words that occur in each. They then compare the number of sexual innuendos and curse words between the two movie ratings. Observational study

21. A sample of 504 patients in early stages of Alzheimer's disease is divided into two groups. One group receives an experimental drug; the other receives a placebo. The advance of the disease in the patients from the two groups is tracked at 1-month intervals over the next year. Experiment

22. Read the following description of an observational study and determine whether it is a cross-sectional, a case-control, or a cohort study. Explain your choice.

> The Cancer Prevention Study II (CPS-II) examines the relationship among environmental and lifestyle factors of cancer cases by tracking approximately 1.2 million men and women. Study participants completed an initial study questionnaire in 1982 providing information on a range of lifestyle factors, such as diet, alcohol and tobacco use, occupation, medical history, and family cancer history. These data have been examined extensively in relation to cancer mortality. The vital status of study participants is updated biennially. Cohort study 23. Convenience sample
>
> *Source*: American Cancer Society

In Problems 23–26, determine the type of sampling used.

23. On election day, a pollster for Fox News positions herself outside a polling place near her home. She then asks the first 50 voters leaving the facility to complete a survey.

24. An Internet service provider randomly selects 15 residential blocks from a large city. It then surveys every household in these 15 blocks to determine the number that would use a high-speed Internet service if it were made available.

25. Thirty-five sophomores, 22 juniors, and 35 seniors are randomly selected to participate in a study from 574 sophomores, 462 juniors, and 532 seniors at a certain high school.

26. Officers for the Department of Motor Vehicles pull aside every 40th tractor trailer passing through a weigh station, starting with the 12th, for an emissions test.

27. Each of the following surveys has bias. Determine the type of bias and suggest a remedy. (b) Response bias; interviewer error

(a) A politician sends a survey about tax issues to a random sample of subscribers to a literary magazine.

(b) An interviewer with little foreign language knowledge is sent to an area where her language is not commonly spoken.

(c) A data-entry clerk mistypes survey results into his computer. Data-entry error

28. **Obtaining a Simple Random Sample** The mayor of a small town wants to conduct personal interviews with small business owners to determine if there is anything the mayor could do to help improve business conditions. The following list gives the names of the companies in the town. Obtain a simple random sample of size 5 from the companies in the town.

Allied Tube and Conduit	Lighthouse Financial	Senese's Winery
Bechstien Construction Co.	Mill Creek Animal Clinic	Skyline Laboratory
Cizer Trucking Co.	Nancy's Flowers	Solus, Maria, DDS
D & M Welding	Norm's Jewelry	Trust Lock and Key
Grace Cleaning Service	Papoose Children's Center	Ultimate Carpet
Jiffy Lube	Plaza Inn Motel	Waterfront Tavern
Levin, Thomas, MD	Risky Business Security	WPA Pharmacy

29. **Obtaining a Systematic Sample** A quality-control engineer wants to be sure that bolts coming off an assembly line are within prescribed tolerances. He wants to conduct a systematic sample by selecting every 9th bolt to come off the assembly line. The machine produces 30,000 bolts per day, and the engineer wants a sample of 32 bolts. Which bolts will be sampled?

30. **Obtaining a Simple Random Sample** Based on the Military Standard 105E (ANS1/ASQC Z1.4, ISO 2859) Tables, a lot of 91 to 150 items with an acceptable quality level (AQL) of 1% and a normal inspection plan would require a sample of size 13 to be inspected for defects. If the sample contains no defects, the entire lot is accepted. Otherwise, the entire lot is rejected. A shipment of 100 night-vision goggles is received and must be inspected. Discuss the procedure you would follow to obtain a simple random sample of 13 goggles to inspect.

31. **Tooth-Whitening Gum** Smoking and drinking coffee have a tendency to stain teeth. In an effort to determine the ability of chewing gum to remove stains on teeth, researchers conducted an experiment in which 64 bovine incisors (teeth) were stained with natural pigments such as coffee for 10 days. Each tooth was randomly assigned to one of four treatments: gum A, gum B, gum C, or saliva. Each tooth group was placed into a device that simulated a human chewing gum. The temperature of the device was maintained at body temperature and the tooth was in the device for 20 minutes. The process was repeated six times (for a total of 120 minutes of chewing). The researcher conducting the experiment did not know which treatment was being applied to each experimental unit. Upon removing a tooth from the chewing apparatus, the color change was measured using a spectrophotometer. The percentage of stain removed by each treatment after 120 minutes is given in the table.

Gum A	Gum B	Gum C	Saliva
47.6%	45.2%	21.4%	2.1%

The researchers concluded that gums A and B removed significantly more stain than gum C or saliva. In addition, gum C removed significantly more stain than saliva.

Source: Michael Moore et al. "In Vitro Tooth Whitening Effect of Two Medicated Chewing Gums Compared to a Whitening Gum and Saliva," *BioMed Central Oral Health* 8:23, 2008

24. Cluster sample 25. Stratified sample 26. Systematic sample 27. (a) Sampling bias; undercoverage or nonrepresentative sample due to poor sampling frame

(a) Identify the research objective.

(b) Is this an observational study or designed experiment? Why? Designed experiment

(c) If observational, what type of observational study is this? If an experiment, what type of experimental design is this? Completely randomized design

(d) What is the response variable?

(e) What is the explanatory variable? Is it qualitative or quantitative? Type of stain remover (gum or saliva); qualitative

(f) Identify the experimental units.

(g) State a factor that could affect the value of the response variable that is fixed at a set level. Chewing simulator

(h) What is the conclusion of the study?

32. Reaction Time Researchers wanted to assess the effect of low alcohol consumption on reaction time in seniors. Their belief was that even low levels of alcohol consumption can impair the ability to walk, thereby increasing the likelihood of falling. They identified 13 healthy seniors who were not heavy consumers of alcohol. The experiment took place in late afternoon. Each subject was instructed to have a light lunch (such as a sandwich) and not to drink any caffeinated drinks in the 4 hours prior to arriving at the lab. The seniors were asked to walk on a treadmill on which an obstacle would appear randomly. The reaction time was measured by determining the time it took the senior to lift his or her foot upon the appearance of the obstacle. First, each senior walked the treadmill by consuming a drink consisting of water mixed with orange juice with the scent and taste of vodka. The senior was then asked to walk on the treadmill. The senior was then asked to drink two additional drinks (40% vodka mixed with orange juice). The goal was to have the senior reach a blood alcohol concentration around 0.05%. The senior then walked on the treadmill again. The average response time increased by 19 milliseconds after the alcohol treatment. The researchers concluded that response times are significantly delayed even for low levels of alcohol consumption.

Source: Judith Hegeman et al. "Even Low Alcohol Concentrations Affect Obstacle Avoidance Reactions in Healthy Senior Individuals," *BMC Research Notes* 3:243, 2010

(a) What type of experimental design is this?

(b) What is the response variable in this experiment? Is it quantitative or qualitative? Reaction time; quantitative

(c) What is the treatment? Alcohol

(d) What factors were controlled and set at a fixed level in this experiment? Food consumption, caffeine intake

(e) Can you think of any factors that may affect reaction to alcohol that were not controlled? Weight, gender

(f) Why do you think the researchers used a drink that had the scent and taste of vodka to serve as the treatment for a baseline measure?

(g) What was the conclusion of the study? To whom does this conclusion apply?

33. Multiple Choice A common tip for taking multiple-choice tests is to always pick (b) or (c) if you are unsure. The idea is that instructors tend to feel the answer is more hidden if it is surrounded by distractor answers. An astute statistics instructor is aware of this and decides to use a table of random digits to select which choice will be the correct answer. If each question has five choices, use Table I in Appendix A or a random-number generator to determine the correct answers for a 20-question multiple-choice exam.

34. Humor in Advertising A marketing research firm wants to know whether information presented in a commercial is better recalled when presented using humor or serious commentary by adults between 18 and 35 years of age. They will use an exam that asks questions of 50 subjects about information presented in the ad. The response variable will be percentage of information recalled. Create a completely randomized design to answer the question. Be sure to include a diagram to illustrate your design.

35. Describe what is meant by a matched-pairs design. Contrast this experimental design with a completely randomized design.

36. Internet Search Go to an online science magazine such as *Science Daily* (www.sciencedaily.com) or an open source online medical journal such as BioMed Central (www.biomedcentral.com) and identify an article that includes statistical research.

(a) Was the study you selected a designed experiment or an observational study?

(b) What was the research objective?

(c) What was the response variable in the study?

(d) Summarize the conclusions of the study.

37. Cell Phones Many newspaper articles discuss the dangers of teens texting while driving. Suppose you are a journalist and want to chime in on the discussion. However, you want your article to be more compelling, so you decide to conduct an experiment with one hundred 16- to 19-year-old volunteers. Design an experiment that will assess the dangers of texting while driving. Decide on the type of experiment (completely randomized, matched-pair, or other), a response variable, the explanatory variables, and any controls that will be imposed. Also, explain how you are going to obtain the data without potentially harming your subjects. Write an article that presents the experiment to your readers so that they know what to anticipate in your follow-up article. Remember, your article is for the general public, so be sure to clearly explain the various facets of your experiment.

31. (a) To determine the ability of chewing gum to remove stains from teeth (d) Percentage of stain removed (f) 64 stained bovine incisors (h) Gums A and B remove significantly more stain 32. (a) Matched-pairs (f) To act as a placebo to control psychosomatic effects of alcohol (g) Alcohol delays reaction time significantly in seniors for low levels of alcohol consumption; healthy seniors that are not regular drinkers

Problems in the chapter test are labeled by section.objective. For example, 1.3 means Section 1, Objective 3.

CHAPTER TEST

1.1 **1.** List the four components that comprise the definition of statistics.

1.2 **2.** What is meant by the *process of statistics*?

In Problems 3–5, determine if the variable is qualitative or quantitative. If the variable is quantitative, determine if it is discrete or continuous. State the level of measurement of the variable. 3. Quantitative, continuous, ratio

1.3, 1.4, 1.5 **3.** Time to complete the 500-meter race in speed skating.

1.3, 1.5 **4.** Video game rating system by the Entertainment Software Rating Board (EC, E, E10+, T, M, AO, RP) Ordinal, qualitative

1.3, 1.4, 1.5 **5.** The number of surface imperfections on a camera lens. Quantitative, discrete, ratio

In Problems 6 and 7, determine whether the study depicts an observational study or a designed experiment. Identify the response variable in each case.

2.1 **6.** A random sample of 30 digital cameras is selected and divided into two groups. One group uses a brand-name battery, while the other uses a generic plain-label battery. All variables besides battery type are controlled. Pictures are taken under identical conditions and the battery life of the two groups is compared. Experiment, battery life

2.1 **7.** A sports reporter asks 100 baseball fans if Barry Bonds's 756th homerun ball should be marked with an asterisk when sent to the Baseball Hall of Fame. Observational study, asterisk or not

2.2 **8.** Contrast the three major types of observational studies in terms of the time frame when the data are collected.

2.1 **9.** Compare and contrast observational studies and designed experiments. Which study allows a researcher to claim causality? Experiment

6.1 **10.** Explain why it is important to use a control group and blinding in an experiment.

6.2 **11.** List the steps required to conduct an experiment.

3.1 **12.** A cellular phone company is looking for ways to improve customer satisfaction. They want to select a simple random sample of four stores from their 15 franchises in which to conduct customer satisfaction surveys. Discuss the procedure you would use, and then use the procedure to select a simple random sample of size $n = 4$. The locations are as follows:

Afton	Ballwin	Chesterfield	Clayton	Deer Creek
Ellisville	Farmington	Fenton	Ladue	Lake St. Louis
O'Fallon	Pevely	Shrewsbury	Troy	Warrenton

4.1 **13.** A congresswoman wants to survey her constituency regarding public policy. She asks one of her staff members to obtain a sample of residents of the district. The frame she has available lists 9012 Democrats, 8302 Republicans, and 3012 Independents. Obtain a stratified random sample of 8 Democrats, 7 Republicans, and 3 Independents. Be sure to discuss the procedure used.

4.3 **14.** A farmer has a 500-acre orchard in Florida. Each acre is subdivided into blocks of 5. Altogether, there are 2500 blocks of trees on the farm. After a frost, he wants to get an idea of the extent of the damage. Obtain a sample of 10 blocks of trees using a cluster sample. Be sure to discuss the procedure used.

4.2 **15.** A casino manager wants to inspect a sample of 14 slot machines in his casino for quality-control purposes. There are 600 sequentially numbered slot machines operating in the casino. Obtain a systematic sample of 14 slot machines. Be sure to discuss how you obtained the sample.

6.3 **16.** Describe what is meant by an experiment that has a completely randomized design.

5.1 **17.** Each of the following surveys has bias. Identify the type of bias. 17. (a) Sampling bias (voluntary response)

(a) A television survey that gives 900 phone numbers for viewers to call with their vote. Each call costs \$2.00.

(b) An employer distributes a survey to her 450 employees asking them how many hours each week, on average, they surf the Internet during business hours. Three of the employees complete the survey. 17. (b) Nonresponse bias

(c) A question on a survey asks, "Do you favor or oppose a minor increase in property tax to ensure fair salaries for teachers and properly equipped school buildings?"

(d) A researcher conducting a poll about national politics sends a survey to a random sample of subscribers to *Time* magazine. Sampling bias (undercoverage)

6.4 **18.** The four members of Skylab had their lymphocyte count per cubic millimeter measured 1 day before lift-off and measured again on their return to Earth. 18. (a) Lymphocyte count

(a) What is the response variable in this experiment?

(b) What is the treatment? Space flight

(c) What type of experimental design is this? Matched pair

(d) Identify the experimental units. 4 members

(e) Draw a diagram similar to Figure 7 or 8 to illustrate the design.

6.3 **19.** Nucryst Pharmaceuticals, Inc., announced the results of its first human trial of NPI 32101, a topical form of its skin ointment. A total of 225 patients diagnosed with skin irritations were randomly divided into three groups as part of a double-blind, placebo-controlled study to test the effectiveness of the new topical cream. The first group received a 0.5% cream, the second group received a 1.0% cream, and the third group received a placebo. Groups were treated twice daily for a 6-week period. *Source*: www.nucryst.com

(a) What type of experimental design is this?

(b) What is the response variable in this experiment?

(c) What is the factor that is set to predetermined levels? What are the treatments? Topical cream; 0.5%, 1.0%, 0%

(d) What does it mean for this study to be double-blind?

(e) What is the control group for this study?

(f) Identify the experimental units.

(g) Draw a diagram similar to Figure 7 or 8 to illustrate the design.

2.2 **20.** Researchers Katherine Tucker and associates wanted to determine whether consumption of cola is associated with lower bone mineral density. They looked at 1125 men and 1413 women in the Framingham Osteoporosis Study, which is a cohort that began in 1971. The first examination in this study began between 1971 and 1975, with participants returning for an examination every 4 years. Based on results of questionnaires, the researchers were able to determine cola consumption on a weekly basis. Analysis of the results indicated that women

who consumed at least one cola per day (on average) had a bone mineral density that was significantly lower at the femoral neck than those who consumed less than one cola per day. The researchers did not find this relation in men.
Source: "Colas, but not other carbonated beverages, are associated with low bone mineral density in older women: The Framingham Osteoporosis Study," *American Journal of Clinical Nutrition* 84: 936–942, 2006

(a) Why is this a cohort study?

(b) What is the response variable in this study? What is the explanatory variable?

(c) Is the response variable qualitative or quantitative?

(d) The following appears in the article: "Variables that could potentially confound the relation between carbonated beverage consumption and bone mineral density were obtained from information collected (in the questionnaire)." What does this mean?

(e) Can you think of any lurking variables that should be accounted for?

(f) What are the conclusions of the study? Does increased cola consumption cause a lower bone mineral density?

17. (c) Response bias (poorly worded question) 19. (a) Completely randomized design (b) Condition (dermatitis) improvement (e) Subjects who get the 0% cream treatment (f) 225 patients with skin irritations 20. (b) Bone mineral density; amount of cola consumed per week (c) Quantitative (e) Smoking status; alcohol consumption; physical activity; calcium intake (f) Women who consumed at least one cola per day had a bone mineral density that was significantly lower at the femoral neck than those who consumed less than one cola per day. No, they are associated.

Making an Informed Decision

What College Should I Attend?

One of the most difficult tasks of surveying is phrasing questions so that they are not misunderstood. In addition, questions must be phrased so that the researcher obtains answers that allow for meaningful analysis. We wish to create a questionnaire that can be used to make an informed decision about what college to attend. In addition, we want to develop a plan for determining how well a particular college educates its students.

1. Using the school you are currently attending, determine a sampling plan to obtain a random sample of 20 students.

2. Develop a questionnaire that can be administered to the students. The questions in the survey should obtain demographic information about the student (age, gender) as well as questions that pertain to why they chose the school. Also, develop questions that answer the student's satisfaction with their school choice. Finally, develop questions that relate to things you consider important in a college environment. Administer the survey either by paper or use an online survey program such as Poll Monkey, Google, or StatCrunch.

3. Summarize your findings. Based on your findings, would you choose the school for yourself?

4. A second gauge in determining college choice is how well the school educates its students. Certainly, some schools have higher-caliber students as incoming freshmen than others, but you do not want academic ability upon entering the school to factor in your decision. Rather, you want to measure how much the college has increased its students' skill set. Design an experiment that would allow you to measure the response variable "increase in academic skill set" for a particular college. Provide detail for controls in obtaining this information.

The Chapter 1 Case Study is located on the CD that accompanies this text.

PART

2 Descriptive Statistics

Remember, statistics is a process. The first chapter (Part 1) dealt with the first two steps in the statistical process: (1) identify the research objective and (2) collect the information needed to answer the questions in the research objective. The next three chapters deal with organizing, summarizing, and presenting the data collected. This step in the process is called *descriptive statistics*.

2 Summarizing Data in Tables and Graphs

OUTLINE

Making an Informed Decision

Suppose you work for the school newspaper. Your editor approaches you with a special reporting assignment. Your task is to write an article that describes the "typical" student at your school, complete with supporting information. How are you going to do this assignment? See the Decisions project on page 115.

PUTTING IT TOGETHER

Chapter 1 discussed how to identify the research objective and collect data. We learned that data can be obtained from either observational studies or designed experiments. When data are obtained, they are referred to as **raw data**. Raw data must be organized into a meaningful form, so we can understand what the data are telling us.

The purpose of this chapter is to learn how to organize raw data in tables or graphs, which allow for a quick overview of the information collected. Describing data is the third step in the statistical process. The procedures used in this step depend on whether the data are qualitative, discrete, or continuous.

2.1 ORGANIZING QUALITATIVE DATA

Preparing for This Section Before getting started, review the following:

- Qualitative data (Section 1.1, p. 9)
- Level of measurement (Section 1.1 pp. 10–11)

OBJECTIVES

1. Organize qualitative data in tables
2. Construct bar graphs
3. Construct pie charts

Note to Instructor

If you like, you can print out and distribute the *Preparing for This Section* quiz located in the *Instructor's Resource Center.* The purpose of the quiz is to verify the students have the prerequisite knowledge for the section.

In this section we will concentrate on tabular and graphical summaries of qualitative data. In Section 2.2 we discuss methods for summarizing quantitative data.

1 Organize Qualitative Data in Tables

Recall that qualitative (or categorical) data provide measures that categorize or classify an individual. When raw qualitative data are collected, we often first determine the number of individuals within each category.

DEFINITION

A **frequency distribution** lists each category of data and the number of occurrences for each category of data.

EXAMPLE 1 Organizing Qualitative Data into a Frequency Distribution

Problem A physical therapist wants to determine types of rehabilitation required by her patients. To do so, she obtains a simple random sample of 30 of her patients and records the body part requiring rehabilitation. See Table 1. Construct a frequency distribution of location of injury.

TABLE 1

Back	Back	Hand
Wrist	Back	Groin
Elbow	Back	Back
Back	Shoulder	Shoulder
Hip	Knee	Hip
Neck	Knee	Knee
Shoulder	Shoulder	Back
Back	Back	Back
Knee	Knee	Back
Hand	Back	Wrist

Source: Krystal Catton, student at Joliet Junior College

Approach To construct a frequency distribution, we create a list of the body parts (categories) and tally each occurrence. Finally, we add up the number of tallies to determine the frequency.

Solution Table 2 shows that the back is the most common body part requiring rehabilitation, with a total of 12.

TABLE 2

Body Part	Tally	Frequency
Back	卌 卌 ||	12
Wrist	||	2
Elbow	|	1
Hip	||	2
Shoulder	||||	4
Knee	卌	5
Hand	||	2
Groin	|	1
Neck	|	1

CAUTION

The data in Table 2 are still qualitative. The frequency simply represents the count of each category.

In any frequency distribution, it is a good idea to add up the frequency column to make sure that it equals the number of observations. In Example 1, the frequency column adds up to 30, as it should.

Often, we want to know the *relative frequency* of the categories, rather than the frequency.

DEFINITION

The **relative frequency** is the proportion (or percent) of observations within a category and is found using the formula

$$\text{Relative frequency} = \frac{\text{frequency}}{\text{sum of all frequencies}} \quad (1)$$

A **relative frequency distribution** lists each category of data together with the relative frequency.

In Other Words
A frequency distribution shows the number of observations that belong in each category. A relative frequency distribution shows the proportion of observations that belong in each category.

EXAMPLE 2 Constructing a Relative Frequency Distribution of Qualitative Data

Problem Using the summarized data in Table 2, construct a relative frequency distribution.

Approach Add all the frequencies, and then use Formula (1) to compute the relative frequency of each category of data.

Solution The sum of all the values in the frequency column in Table 2 is 30.

We now compute the relative frequency of each category. For example, the relative frequency of the category *Back* is 12/30 = 0.4. The relative frequency distribution is shown in Table 3.

TABLE 3

Body Part	Frequency	Relative Frequency
Back	12	$\frac{12}{30} = 0.4$
Wrist	2	$\frac{2}{30} \approx 0.0667$
Elbow	1	0.0333
Hip	2	0.0667
Shoulder	4	0.1333
Knee	5	0.1667
Hand	2	0.0667
Groin	1	0.0333
Neck	1	0.0333
Total	**30**	**1**

Using Technology
Some statistical spreadsheets such as MINITAB have a Tally command. This command will construct a frequency and relative frequency distribution of raw qualitative data.

From the distribution, the most common body part for rehabilitation is the back.

Now Work Problems 21(a)–(b)

It is a good idea to add up the relative frequencies to be sure they sum to 1. In fraction form, the sum should be exactly 1. In decimal form, the sum may differ slightly from 1 due to rounding.

2 Construct Bar Graphs

Once raw data are organized in a table, we can create graphs. Graphs allow us to see the data and help us understand what the data are saying about the individuals in the study.

Just as "a picture is worth a thousand words," pictures of data result in a more powerful message than tables. Try the following exercise: Open a newspaper and look at a table and a graph. Study each. Now put the paper away and close your eyes. What do you see in your mind's eye? Can you recall information more easily from the table or the graph? In general, people are more likely to recall information obtained from a graph than they are from a table.

A common device for graphically representing qualitative data is a bar graph.

DEFINITION A **bar graph** is constructed by labeling each category of data on either the horizontal or vertical axis and the frequency or relative frequency of the category on the other axis. Rectangles of equal width are drawn for each category. The height of each rectangle represents the category's frequency or relative frequency.

EXAMPLE 3 Constructing a Frequency and a Relative Frequency Bar Graph

Problem Use the data summarized in Table 3 to construct a frequency bar graph and a relative frequency bar graph.

Approach We will use a horizontal axis to indicate the categories of the data (body parts) and a vertical axis to represent the frequency or relative frequency. We draw rectangles of equal width to the height that is the frequency or relative frequency for each category. The bars do not touch each other.

Solution Figure 1(a) shows the frequency bar graph, and Figure 1(b) shows the relative frequency bar graph.

Figure 1

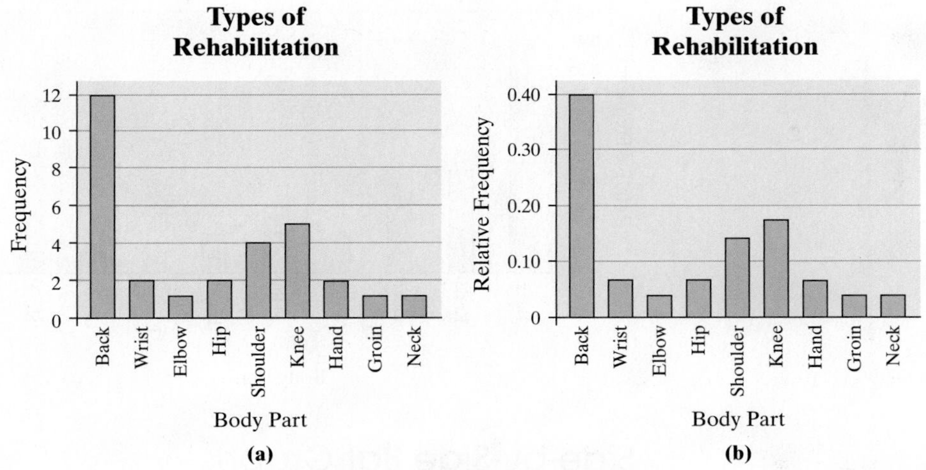

CAUTION

Graphs that start the scale at some value other than 0 or have bars with unequal widths, bars with different colors, or three-dimensional bars can misrepresent the data.

EXAMPLE 4 Constructing a Frequency or Relative Frequency Bar Graph Using Technology

Using Technology

The graphs obtained from a different statistical package may differ from those in Figure 2. Some packages use the word *count* in place of *frequency* or *percent* in place of *relative frequency.*

Problem Use a statistical spreadsheet to construct a frequency or relative frequency bar graph.

Approach We will use Excel to construct the frequency and relative frequency bar graph. The steps for constructing the graphs using MINITAB, Excel, and StatCrunch are given in the Technology Step-by-Step on page 76. **Note:** The TI-83 and TI-84 Plus graphing calculators cannot draw frequency or relative frequency bar graphs.

Solution Figure 2 on the following page shows the frequency and relative frequency bar graphs obtained from Excel.

Figure 2

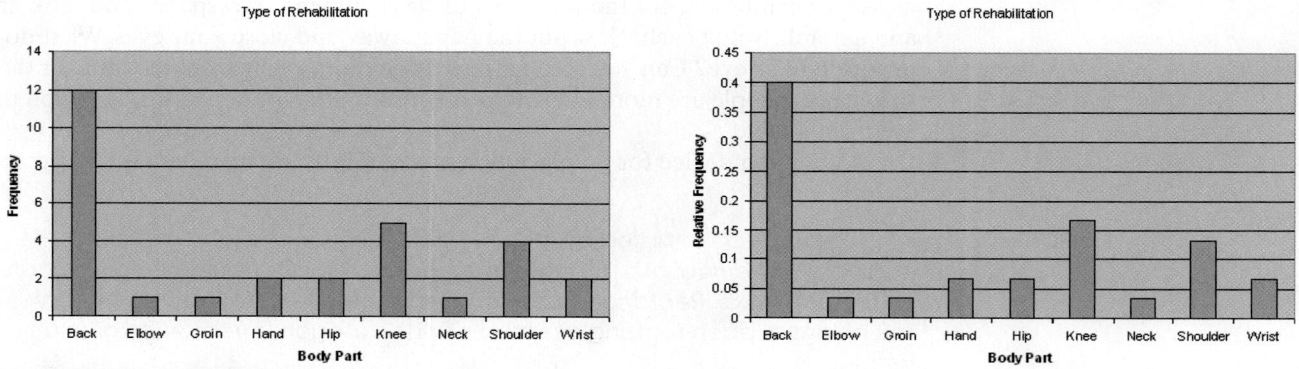

Now Work Problems 21(c)–(d)

In bar graphs, the order of the categories does not usually matter. However, bar graphs that have categories arranged in decreasing order of frequency help prioritize categories for decision-making purposes in areas such as quality control, human resources, and marketing.

DEFINITION A **Pareto chart** is a bar graph whose bars are drawn in decreasing order of frequency or relative frequency.

Figure 3 illustrates a relative frequency Pareto chart for the data in Table 3.

Figure 3

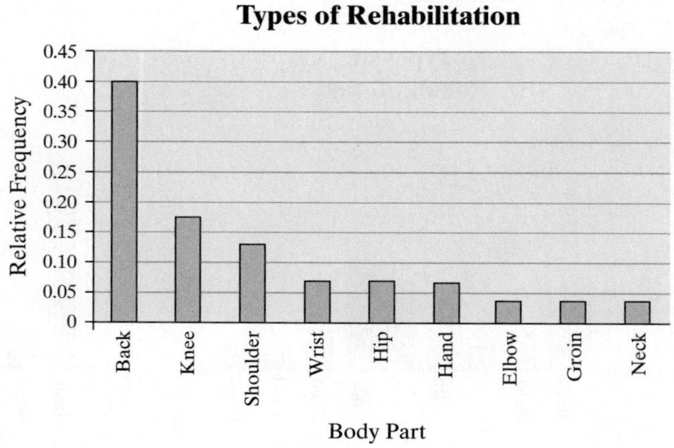

Side-by-Side Bar Graphs

Suppose we want to know whether more people are finishing college today than in 1990. We could draw a **side-by-side bar graph** to compare the data for the two different years. Data sets should be compared by using relative frequencies, because different sample or population sizes make comparisons using frequencies difficult or misleading.

EXAMPLE 5 Comparing Two Data Sets

Problem The data in Table 4 represent the educational attainment in 1990 and 2009 of adults 25 years and older who are residents of the United States. The data are in thousands. So 39,344 represents 39,344,000.

(a) Draw a side-by-side relative frequency bar graph of the data.

(b) Are a greater proportion of Americans attending college, but not earning a degree?

TABLE 4

Educational Attainment	1990	2009
Not a high school graduate	39,344	26,414
High school diploma	47,643	61,626
Some college, no degree	29,780	33,832
Associate's degree	9,792	17,838
Bachelor's degree	20,833	37,635
Graduate or professional degree	11,478	20,938
Totals	**158,870**	**198,283**

Source: U.S. Census Bureau

Approach First, we determine the relative frequencies of each category for each year. To construct side-by-side bar graphs, we draw two bars for each category of data, one for 1990, the other for 2009.

Solution Table 5 shows the relative frequency for each category.
(a) The side-by-side bar graph is shown in Figure 4.

TABLE 5

Educational Attainment	1990	2009
Not a high school graduate	0.2476	0.1332
High school diploma	0.2999	0.3108
Some college, no degree	0.1874	0.1706
Associate's degree	0.0616	0.0900
Bachelor's degree	0.1311	0.1898
Graduate or professional degree	0.0722	0.1056

Figure 4

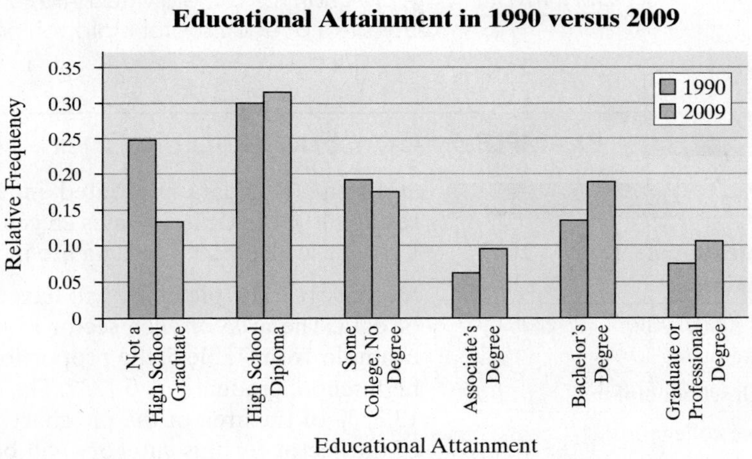

(b) The graph illustrates that the proportion of Americans 25 years and up who had some college, but no degree, was higher in 1990. This information is not clear from the frequency table because the population sizes are different. The increase in the number of Americans who did not complete a degree is due partly to the increase in the size of the population.

Now Work Problem 17

Horizontal Bars

So far we have only looked at bar graphs with vertical bars. However, the bars may also be horizontal. Horizontal bars are preferable when category names are lengthy. For example, Figure 5 on the next page uses horizontal bars to display the same data as in Figure 4.

Figure 5

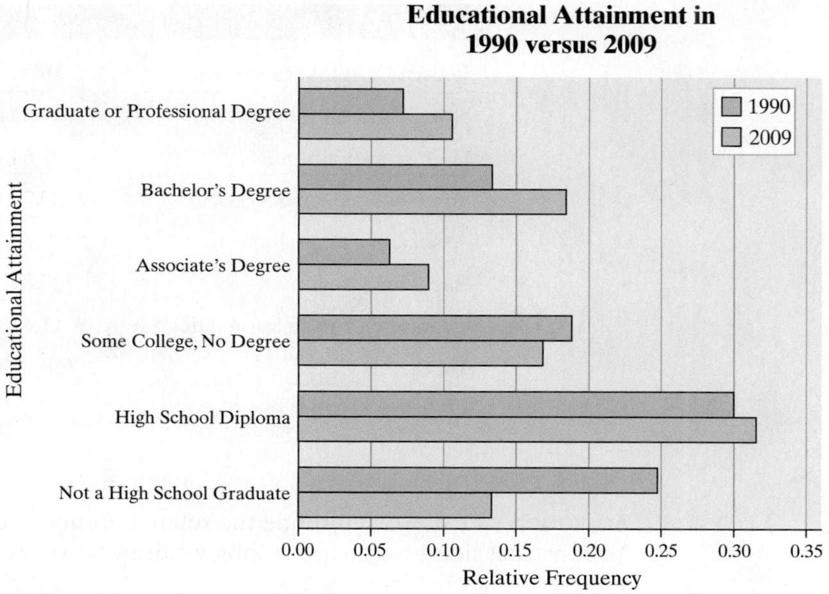

Note to Instructor

The by-hand approach to constructing pie charts is given so that students will have a conceptual understanding of the process. Encourage students to construct pie charts using technology.

Note to Instructor

Ask students to compare and contrast the similarities and differences of pie charts and bar graphs.

3 Construct Pie Charts

Pie charts are typically used to present the relative frequency of qualitative data. In most cases the data are nominal, but ordinal data can also be displayed in a pie chart.

DEFINITION A **pie chart** is a circle divided into sectors. Each sector represents a category of data. The area of each sector is proportional to the frequency of the category.

EXAMPLE 6 Constructing a Pie Chart

TABLE 6

Educational Attainment	2009
Not a high school graduate	26,414
High school diploma	61,626
Some college, no degree	33,832
Associate's degree	17,838
Bachelor's degree	37,635
Graduate or professional degree	20,938
Totals	**198,283**

Problem The data presented in Table 6 represent the educational attainment of residents of the United States 25 years or older in 2009, based on data obtained from the U.S. Census Bureau. The data are in thousands. Construct a pie chart of the data.

Approach The pie chart will have one part or sector corresponding to each category of data. The area of each sector is proportional to the frequency of each category. For example, from Table 5, the proportion of all U.S. residents 25 years or older who are not high school graduates is 0.1332. The category "not a high school graduate" will make up 13.32% of the area of the pie chart. Since a circle has 360 degrees, the degree measure of the sector for this category will be $(0.1332)360° \approx 48°$. Use a protractor to measure each angle.

Solution We use the same approach for the remaining categories to obtain Table 7.

TABLE 7

Educational Attainment	Frequency	Relative Frequency	Degree Measure of Each Sector
Not a high school graduate	26,414	0.1332	48
High school diploma	61,626	0.3108	112
Some college, no degree	33,832	0.1706	61
Associate's degree	17,838	0.0900	32
Bachelor's degree	37,635	0.1898	68
Graduate or professional degree	20,938	0.1056	38

Using Technology

Most statistical spreadsheets are capable of drawing pie charts. See the Technology Step-by-Step on page 76 for instructions on drawing pie charts using MINITAB, Excel, and StatCrunch. The TI-83 and TI-84 Plus graphing calculators do not draw pie charts.

To construct a pie chart by hand, we use a protractor to approximate the angles for each sector. See Figure 6.

Figure 6

Educational Attainment, 2009

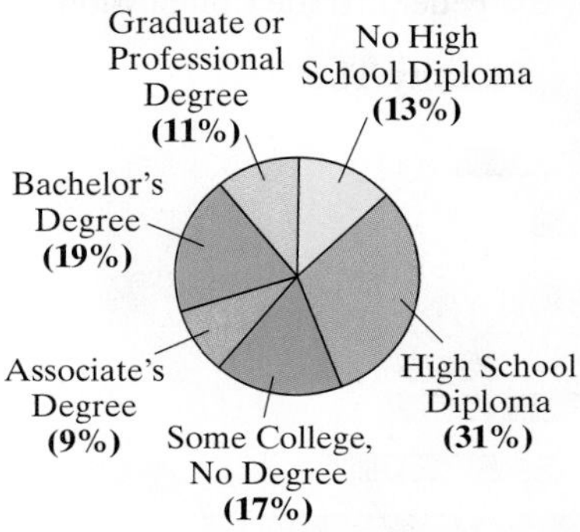

Now Work Problem 21(e)

To make a pie chart, we need all the categories of the variable under consideration. For example, using Example 1, we could create a bar graph that lists the proportion of patients requiring back, shoulder, or knee rehabilitation, but it would not make sense to construct a pie chart for this situation. Do you see why? Only 70% of the data would be represented.

When should a bar graph or a pie chart be used? Pie charts are useful for showing the division of all possible values of a qualitative variable into its parts. However, because angles are often hard to judge in pie charts, they are not as useful in comparing two specific values of the qualitative variable. Instead the emphasis is on comparing the part to the whole. Bar graphs are useful when we want to compare the different parts, not necessarily the parts to the whole. For example, to get the "big picture" regarding educational attainment in 2009, a pie chart is a good visual summary. However, to compare bachelor's degrees to high school diplomas, a bar graph is a good visual summary. Since bars are easier to draw and compare, some practitioners forgo pie charts in favor of Pareto charts when comparing parts to the whole.

2.1 ASSESS YOUR UNDERSTANDING

VOCABULARY AND SKILL BUILDING

1. Define raw data in your own words.

2. A frequency distribution lists the _number_ of occurrences of each category of data, while a relative frequency distribution lists the _proportion_ of occurrences of each category of data.

3. In a relative frequency distribution, what should the relative frequencies add up to? One

4. What is a bar graph? What is a Pareto chart?

5. Flu Season The pie chart shown, the type we see in *USA Today*, depicts the approaches people use to avoid getting the flu.

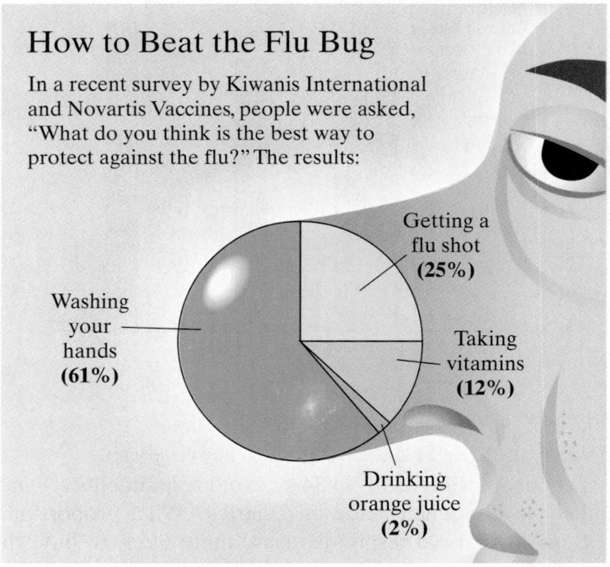

Source: Kiwanis International and Novartis Vaccines

(a) What is the most common approach? What percentage of the population chooses this method? Washing your hands; 61%

(b) What is the least used approach? What percentage of the population chooses this method? Drinking orange juice; 2%

(c) What percentage of the population thinks flu shots are the best way to beat the flu? 25%

6. Cosmetic Surgery This *USA Today*–type chart shows the most frequent cosmetic surgeries for women in 2009.

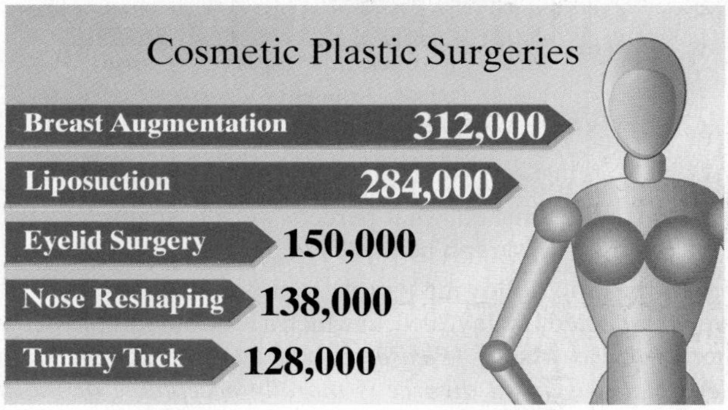

By Anne R. Carey and Suzy Parker, USA Today
Source: American Society of Plastic Surgeons (plasticsurgery.org)

(a) If women had 1.35 million cosmetic surgeries in 2009, what percent were for tummy tucks? 9.5% (c) 338,000

(b) What percent were for nose reshaping? 10.2%

(c) How many surgeries are not accounted for in the graph?

7. Internet Users The following Pareto chart represents Internet users in the top 10 countries as of June 2010.

Top 10 Internet Users

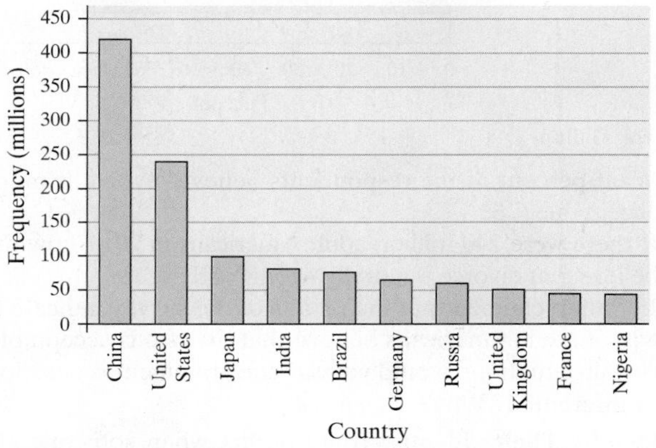

Source: www.internetworldstats.com

(a) Which country had the most Internet users in 2010? China

(b) Approximately how many Internet users did the United Kingdom have in 2010? 50 million

(c) Approximately how many more users were in China than in Germany in 2010? 350 million (d) Should use relative frequency

(d) How might this graph be misleading?

8. Poverty Every year the U.S. Census Bureau counts the number of people living in poverty. The bureau uses money income thresholds to define poverty, so noncash benefits such as Medicaid and food stamps do not count toward poverty thresholds. For example, in 2009 the poverty threshold for a family of four with two children was $21,756. The bar graph represents the number of people living in poverty in the United States in 2009, by ethnicity. (c) Should use relative frequencies

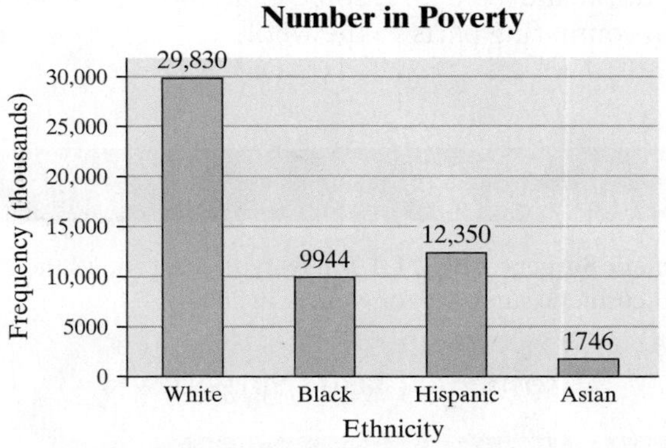

Source: U.S. Census Bureau

(a) How many whites were living in poverty in 2009? 29,830,000

(b) Of the impoverished, what percent were Hispanic? 22.9%

(c) How might this graph be misleading?

9. Divorce The following graph represents the results of a survey, conducted in May 2010, in which a random sample of adult Americans was asked, "*Please tell me whether you personally believe that in general divorce is morally acceptable or morally wrong.*"

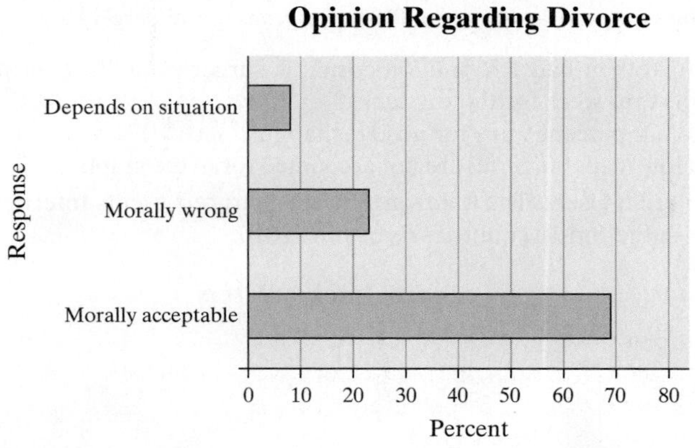

Source: Gallup

(a) What percent of the respondents believe divorce is morally acceptable? 69%

(b) If there were 240 million adult Americans in 2010, how many believe that divorce is morally wrong? 55.2 million

(c) If Gallup claimed that the results of the survey indicate that 8% of adult Americans believe that divorce is acceptable in certain situations, would you say this statement is descriptive or inferential? Why? Inferential

10. Identity Theft Identity fraud occurs when someone else's personal information is used to open credit card accounts, apply for a job, receive benefits, and so on. The following relative frequency bar graph represents the various types of identity theft based on a study conducted by the Federal Trade Commission.

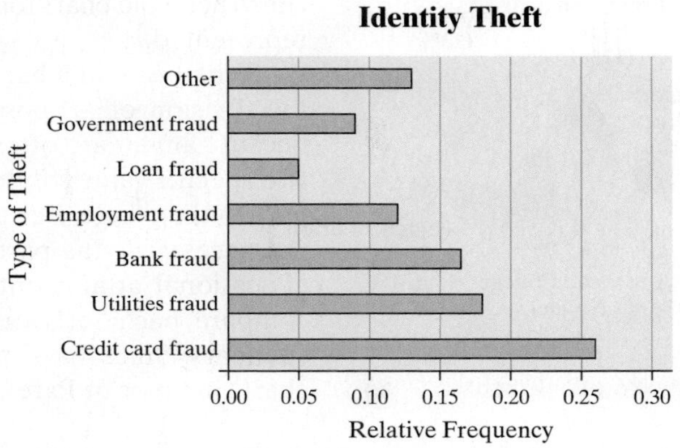

Source: Federal Trade Commission

(a) Approximately what percentage of identity theft was loan fraud (such as applying for a loan in someone else's name)? 5%

(b) If there were 10 million cases of identity fraud in 2008, how many were credit card fraud (someone uses someone else's credit card to make a purchase)? 2.6 million

11. Made in America In a poll conducted July 27–29, 2010, a random sample of 2163 adults (aged 18 and over) was asked, "When you see an ad emphasizing that a product is 'Made in America', are you more likely to buy it, less likely to buy it, or neither more nor less likely to buy it?" The results of the survey are presented in the side-by-side bar graph.

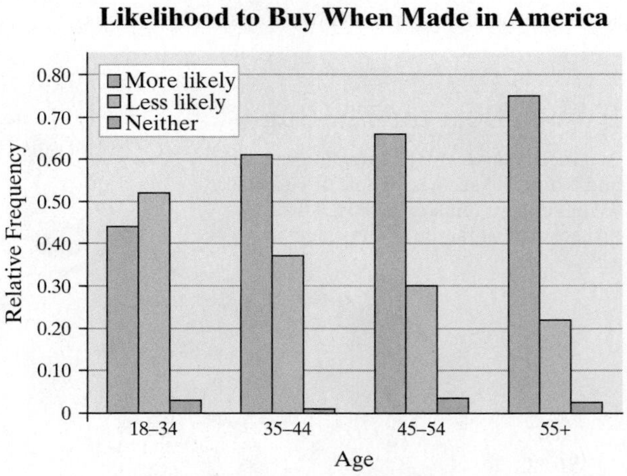

Source: Harris Interactive

(d) As age increases, so does likelihood to buy American.

(a) What proportion of 18- to 34-year-old respondents are more likely to buy when made in America? What proportion of 35- to 44-year-old respondents are more likely to buy when made America? 0.42; 0.61

(b) Which age group has the greatest proportion who are more likely to buy when made in America? 55+

(c) Which age group has a majority of respondents who are less likely to buy when made in America? 18 to 34

(d) What is the apparent association between age and likelihood to buy when made in America?

12. Desirability Attributes In a poll conducted July 27–29, 2010, a random sample of 2163 adults (aged 18 and over) was asked,

"Given a choice of the following, which one would you most want to be?" The results of the survey are presented in the side-by-side bar graph.

Desirability Attributes

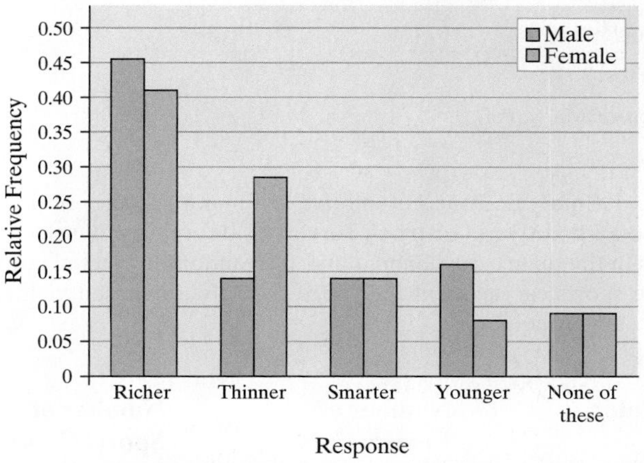

Source: Harris Interactive (a) 0.46; 0.41 (b) Thinner

(a) What proportion of males would like to be richer? What proportion of females would like to be richer?

(b) Which attribute do females desire more than males?

(c) Which attribute do males prefer over females two-to-one? Younger

(d) Which attribute do males and females desire in equal proportion? Smarter

APPLYING THE CONCEPTS

13. College Survey In a national survey conducted by the Centers for Disease Control to determine health-risk behaviors among college students, college students were asked, "How often do you wear a seat belt when riding in a car driven by someone else?" The frequencies were as follows:

Response	Frequency
Never	125
Rarely	324
Sometimes	552
Most of the time	1257
Always	2518

(b) 52.7%

(a) Construct a relative frequency distribution.

(b) What percentage of respondents answered "Always"?

(c) What percentage of respondents answered "Never" or "Rarely"? 9.4%

(d) Construct a frequency bar graph.

(e) Construct a relative frequency bar graph.

(f) Construct a pie chart.

(g) Suppose that a representative from the Centers for Disease Control says, "52.7% of all college students always wear a seat belt." Is this a descriptive or inferential statement? Inferential

14. College Survey In a national survey conducted by the Centers for Disease Control to determine health-risk behaviors among college students, college students were asked, "How often do you wear a seat belt when driving a car?" The frequencies were as follows:

Response	Frequency
I do not drive a car	249
Never	118
Rarely	249
Sometimes	345
Most of the time	716
Always	3093

(a) Construct a relative frequency distribution.

(b) What percentage of respondents answered "Always"?

(c) What percentage of respondents answered "Never" or "Rarely"? 7.7% (b) 64.8%

(d) Construct a frequency bar graph.

(e) Construct a relative frequency bar graph.

(f) Construct a pie chart.

(g) Compute the relative frequencies of "Never," "Rarely," "Sometimes," "Most of the time," and "Always," excluding those that do not drive. Compare with those in Problem 13. What might you conclude?

(h) Suppose that a representative from the Centers for Disease Control says, "2.5% of the college students in this survey responded that they never wear a seat belt." Is this a descriptive or inferential statement? Descriptive

15. Use the Internet? The Gallup organization conducted a survey in which 1025 randomly sampled adult Americans were asked, "How much time, if at all, do you personally spend using the Internet—more than 1 hour a day, up to 1 hour a day, a few times a week, a few times a month or less, or never?" The results of the survey were as follows:

Response	Frequency
More than 1 hour a day	377
Up to 1 hour a day	192
A few times a week	132
A few times a month or less	81
Never	243

(a) Construct a relative frequency distribution.

(b) What proportion of those surveyed never use the Internet? 0.2371 (about 24%)

(c) Construct a frequency bar graph.

(d) Construct a relative frequency bar graph.

(e) Construct a pie chart.

(f) A local news broadcast reported that 37% of adult Americans use the Internet more than 1 hour a day. What is wrong with this statement? No level of confidence

16. Dining Out In a poll taken in April 2010, a sample of 521 adults was asked, "How often do you dine out?" The results of the survey are given in the table on the following page.

(a) Construct a relative frequency distribution.

(b) What proportion of those surveyed dine out once or twice a week? 0.39

(c) Construct a frequency bar graph.

(d) Construct a relative frequency bar graph.

Response	Frequency
Several times a week	103
Once or twice a week	204
A few times a month	130
Very rarely	79
Never	5

Source: http://kingdomfirstmom.com

NW **17. Texting** A survey of U.S. adults and teens (ages 12–17) was administered by Pew Research April 29–May 30, 2010, to determine the number of texts sent in a single day.

Number of Texts	Adults	Teens
None	173	13
1–10	978	138
11–20	249	69
21–50	249	113
51–100	134	113
101+	153	181

Source: PewInternet

(a) Construct a relative frequency distribution for adults.
(b) Construct a relative frequency distribution for teens.
(c) Construct a side-by-side relative frequency bar graph.
(d) Compare the texting habits of adults and teens.

18. Educational Attainment On the basis of the 2009 Current Population Survey, there were 94.5 million males and 102 million females 25 years old or older in the United States. The educational attainment of the males and females was as follows:

Educational Attainment	Males (in millions)	Females (in millions)
Not a high school graduate	13.3	13.0
High school graduate	29.5	31.7
Some college, but no degree	15.8	18.0
Associate's degree	7.5	9.8
Bachelor's degree	18.0	19.6
Advanced degree	10.4	9.9

Source: U.S. Census Bureau

(a) Construct a relative frequency distribution for males.
(b) Construct a relative frequency distribution for females.
(c) Construct a side-by-side relative frequency bar graph.
(d) Compare each gender's educational attainment. Make a conjecture about the reasons for the differences.

19. Dream Job A survey of adult men and women asked, "Which one of the following jobs would you most like to have?" The results of the survey are shown in the table.

(a) Construct a relative frequency distribution for men and women.
(b) Construct a side-by-side relative frequency bar graph.
(c) What are the apparent differences in gender as it pertains to this question?

Response	Men	Women
Professional athlete	40	18
Actor/actress	26	37
President of the United States	13	13
Rock star	13	13
Not sure	7	19

Source: Marist Poll

20. Car Color DuPont Automotive is a major supplier of paint to the automotive industry. A survey of 100 randomly selected autos in the luxury car segment and 100 randomly selected autos in the sports car segment that were recently purchased yielded the following colors.

Color	Number of Luxury Cars	Number of Sports Cars
White	25	10
Black	22	15
Silver	16	18
Gray	12	15
Blue	7	13
Red	7	15
Gold	6	5
Green	3	2
Brown	2	7

Source: Based on results from www.infoplease.com

(a) Construct a relative frequency distribution for each car type.
(b) Draw a side-by-side relative frequency bar graph.
(c) Compare the colors for the two car types. Make a conjecture about the reasons for the differences.

NW **21. Olympic Gold Medals in Hockey** The table shows the gold medal winners in hockey in the Winter Olympics since 1920.

Year	Winner	Year	Winner
1920	Canada	1972	Soviet Union
1924	Canada	1976	Soviet Union
1928	Canada	1980	U.S.A.
1932	Canada	1984	Soviet Union
1936	Great Britain	1988	Soviet Union
1948	Canada	1992	Unified Team
1952	Canada	1994	Sweden
1956	Soviet Union	1998	Czech Republic
1960	U.S.A.	2002	Canada
1964	Soviet Union	2006	Sweden
1968	Soviet Union	2010	Canada

Source: Chicago Tribune

(a) Construct a frequency distribution.
(b) Construct a relative frequency distribution.
(c) Construct a frequency bar graph.
(d) Construct a relative frequency bar graph.
(e) Construct a pie chart.

22. Bachelor Party In a survey conducted by Opinion Research, participants were asked, "If you had an 'X-rated' bachelor party, would you tell your fiancé all, edit details, or say nothing?" The following data are based on their results.

(a) Construct a frequency distribution.
(b) Construct a relative frequency distribution.
(c) Construct a frequency bar graph.
(d) Construct a relative frequency bar graph.
(e) Construct a pie chart.

Tell all	Edit details	Tell all	Edit details	Tell all
Edit details	Say nothing	Edit details	Tell all	Tell all
Tell all	Tell all	Edit details	Tell all	Say nothing
Edit details	Tell all	Tell all	Say nothing	Tell all
Tell all	Edit details	Tell all	Tell all	Say nothing

Source: Based on results from Opinion Research

23. Favorite Day to Eat Out A survey was conducted by Wakefield Research in which participants were asked to disclose their favorite night to order takeout for dinner. The following data are based on their results.

Thursday	Saturday	Friday	Friday	Sunday
Wednesday	Saturday	Friday	Tuesday	Friday
Saturday	Monday	Friday	Friday	Sunday
Friday	Tuesday	Wednesday	Saturday	Friday
Wednesday	Monday	Wednesday	Wednesday	Friday
Friday	Wednesday	Thursday	Tuesday	Friday
Tuesday	Saturday	Friday	Tuesday	Friday
Saturday	Saturday	Saturday	Sunday	Friday

Source: Based on results from Wakefield Research

(a) Construct a frequency distribution.
(b) Construct a relative frequency distribution.
(c) If you own a restaurant, which day would you purchase an advertisement in the local newspaper? Are there any days you would avoid purchasing advertising space?
(d) Construct a frequency bar graph.
(e) Construct a relative frequency bar graph.
(f) Construct a pie chart.

24. Blood Type A phlebotomist draws the blood of a random sample of 50 patients and determines their blood types as shown:

O	O	A	A	O
B	O	B	A	O
AB	B	A	B	AB
O	O	A	A	O
AB	O	A	B	A
O	A	A	O	A
O	A	O	AB	A
O	B	A	A	O
O	O	O	A	O
O	A	O	A	O

(a) Construct a frequency distribution.
(b) Construct a relative frequency distribution.
(c) According to the data, which blood type is most common? O
(d) According to the data, which blood type is least common? AB
(e) Use the results of the sample to conjecture the percentage of the population that has type O blood. Is this an example of descriptive or inferential statistics? 44%; inferential
(f) Contact a local hospital and ask them the percentage of the population that is blood type O. Why might the results differ?
(g) Draw a frequency bar graph.
(h) Draw a relative frequency bar graph.
(i) Draw a pie chart.

25. Foreign Language According to the Modern Language Association, the number of college students studying foreign language is increasing. The following data represent the foreign language being studied based on a simple random sample of 30 students learning a foreign language.

Spanish	Chinese	Spanish	Spanish	Spanish
Chinese	German	Spanish	Spanish	French
Spanish	Spanish	Japanese	Latin	Spanish
German	German	Spanish	Italian	Spanish
Italian	Japanese	Chinese	Spanish	French
Spanish	Spanish	Russian	Latin	French

Source: Based on data obtained from the Modern Language Association

(a) Construct a frequency distribution.
(b) Construct a relative frequency distribution.
(c) Construct a frequency bar graph.
(d) Construct a relative frequency bar graph.
(e) Construct a pie chart.

26. President's State of Birth The following table lists the presidents of the United States (as of October 2010) and their state of birth.

Birthplace of U.S. President

President	State of Birth	President	State of Birth	President	State of Birth
Washington	Virginia	Lincoln	Kentucky	Hoover	Iowa
J. Adams	Massachusetts	A. Johnson	North Carolina	F. D. Roosevelt	New York
Jefferson	Virginia	Grant	Ohio	Truman	Missouri
Madison	Virginia	Hayes	Ohio	Eisenhower	Texas
Monroe	Virginia	Garfield	Ohio	Kennedy	Massachusetts
J. Q. Adams	Massachusetts	Arthur	Vermont	L. B. Johnson	Texas
Jackson	South Carolina	Cleveland	New Jersey	Nixon	California
Van Buren	New York	B. Harrison	Ohio	Ford	Nebraska
W. H. Harrison	Virginia	Cleveland	New Jersey	Carter	Georgia
Tyler	Virginia	McKinley	Ohio	Reagan	Illinois
Polk	North Carolina	T. Roosevelt	New York	George H. Bush	Massachusetts
Taylor	Virginia	Taft	Ohio	Clinton	Arkansas
Fillmore	New York	Wilson	Virginia	George W. Bush	Connecticut
Pierce	New Hampshire	Harding	Ohio	Barack Obama	Hawaii
Buchanan	Pennsylvania	Coolidge	Vermont		

(a) Construct a frequency bar graph for state of birth.
(b) Which state has yielded the most presidents? Virginia
(c) Explain why the answer obtained in part (b) may be misleading.

30. (a) To determine if online homework improves student learning.
30. (b) Experiment

27. Highest Elevation The following data represent the land area and highest elevation for each of the seven continents.

Continent	Land Area (square miles)	Highest Elevation (feet)
Africa	11,608,000	19,340
Antarctica	5,100,000	16,066
Asia	17,212,000	29,035
Australia	3,132,000	7,310
Europe	3,837,000	18,510
North America	9,449,000	20,320
South America	6,879,000	22,834

Source: www.infoplease.com

(a) Would it make sense to draw a pie chart for land area? Why? If so, draw a pie chart. Yes
(b) Would it make sense to draw a pie chart for the highest elevation? Why? If so, draw a pie chart. No

28. StatCrunch Survey Choose a qualitative variable from the Sullivan StatCrunch survey data set and summarize the variable.

29. StatCrunch Survey Choose a qualitative variable from the Sullivan StatCrunch survey data set and summarize the variable by gender. What are the differences, if any, in the value of the variable for males and females?

30. Putting It Together: Online Homework Keeping students engaged in the learning process greatly increases their chance of success in a course. Traditional lecture-based math instruction has been giving way to a more student-engaged approach where students interact with the teacher in class and receive immediate feedback to their responses. The teacher presence allows students, when incorrect in a response, to be guided through a solution and then immediately be given a similar problem to attempt.

A researcher conducted a study to investigate whether an online homework system using an attempt–feedback–reattempt approach improved student learning over traditional pencil-and-paper homework. The online homework system was designed to increase student engagement outside class, something commonly missing in traditional pencil-and-paper assignments, ultimately leading to increased learning.

The study was conducted using two first-semester calculus classes taught by the researcher in a single semester. One class was assigned traditional homework and the other was assigned online homework that used the attempt–feedback–reattempt approach. The summaries on the next page are based on data from the study.

(a) What is the research objective?
(b) Is this study an observational study or experiment?
(c) Give an example of how the researcher attempted to control variables in the study.
(d) Explain why assigning homework type to entirely separate classes can confound the conclusions of the study.
(e) For the data in the table, (i) identify the variables, (ii) indicate whether the variables are qualitative or quantitative, and (iii) for each quantitative variable, indicate whether the variable is discrete or continuous.

	Prior College Experience		No Prior College Experience	
	Traditional	**Online**	**Traditional**	**Online**
Number of students	10	9	23	18
Average age	22.8	19.4	18.13	18.11
Average exam score	84.52	68.9	79.38	80.61

Grades Earned on Exams (no prior college experience)

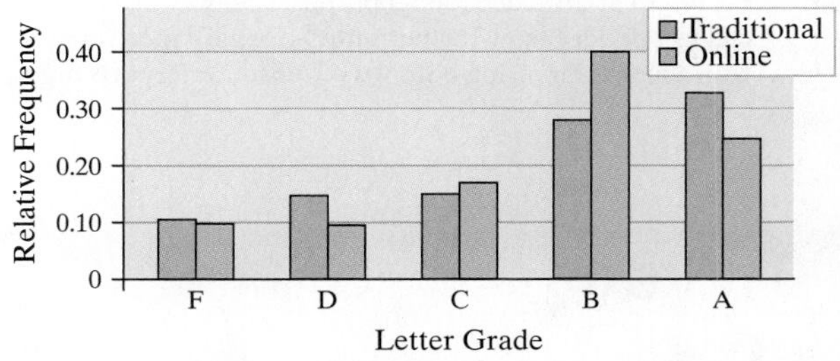

Source: Journal of Computers in Mathematics and Science Teaching 26(1):55–73, 2007

(f) What type of variable is letter grade? What level of measurement is letter grade? Do you think presenting the data in a table from A to F would be a better representation of the data than presenting it in a graph?

(g) What type of graph is displayed?

(h) Could the data in the graph be presented in a pie chart? If so, what is the "whole"? If not, why not?

(i) Considering the students with no prior college experience, how might the table and the graph generate conflicting conclusions?

EXPLAINING THE CONCEPTS

31. When should relative frequencies be used when comparing two data sets? Why?

32. Suppose you need to summarize ordinal data in a bar graph. How would you arrange the categories of data on the horizontal axis? Is it possible to make the order of the data apparent in a pie chart?

33. Describe the circumstances in which a bar graph is preferable to a pie chart. When is a pie chart preferred over a bar graph? Are there circumstances in which a pie chart cannot be drawn, but a bar graph could be drawn? What are these circumstances?

34. Consider the information in the chart shown next, which is in the *USA Today* style of graph. Could the information provided be organized into a pie chart? Why or why not? No

30. (g) Side-by-side relative frequency bar graph 30. (h) Yes; all students who received a grade in the course

Consumer Reports® Consumer Reports Rates Treadmills

A study that compared exercisers who worked out equally hard for the same time on several different types of machines found that they generally burned the most calories on treadmills. Our own research has shown that treadmills are less likely than other machines to sit unused. So it should come as no surprise that treadmills are the best-selling home exercise machine in the United States.

In a study by *Consumer Reports*, we tested 11 best-selling brands of treadmills ranging in price from \$500 to \$3000. The treadmills were rated on ease of use, ergonomics, exercise factors, construction, and durability. Ease of use is based on how straightforward the treadmill is to use. Ergonomics, including safety factors, belt size, and handrail placement, indicates how well the treadmill fits people of different sizes. Exercise includes evaluations of the minimum incline level, speed control, and heart-rate monitoring. Construction covers factors like the motor's continuous-duty horsepower rating and weld quality.

To help compare the treadmills, the individual attribute scores were combined into an overall score. The figure on the next page is a ratings chart for the 11 treadmills based on our test results. In addition to the performance ratings, other useful information, such as the models' price and belt size, is included.

(a) What type of graph is illustrated to display overall score in the figure?

(b) Which model has the highest construction score? Which models have the lowest ease of use score?

(c) For ease of use, how many treadmills rated excellent? very good? good? fair? poor?

(d) Draw a frequency bar graph for each rating category. In other words, draw a bar graph for ease of use, ergonomics, and so on.

(e) Does there appear to be a relationship between price and overall score? Explain your opinion.

Note to Readers: *In many cases, our test protocol and analytical methods are more complicated than described in these examples. The data and discussions have been modified to make the material more appropriate for the audience.*

Ratings Chart for Treadmills

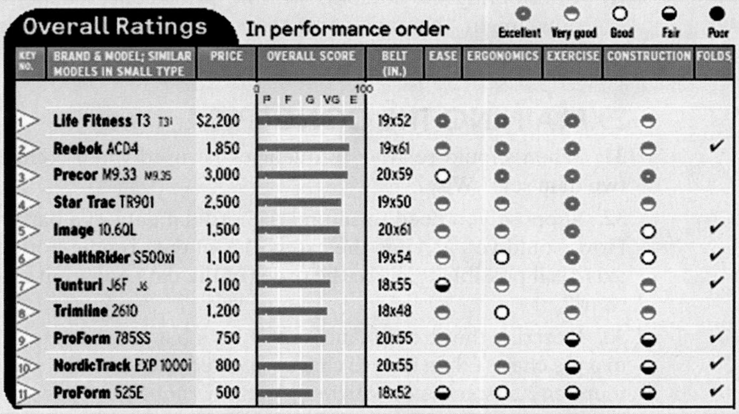

Technology Step-By-Step

Drawing Bar Graphs and Pie Charts

TI-83/84 Plus

The TI-83 or TI-84 Plus does not have the ability to draw bar graphs or pie charts.

MINITAB

Frequency or Relative Frequency Distributions from Raw Data

1. Enter the raw data in C1.
2. Select **Stat** and highlight **Tables** and select Tally Individual Variables …
3. Fill in the window with appropriate values. In the "Variables" box, enter C1. Check "counts" for a frequency distribution and/or "percents" for a relative frequency distribution. Click OK.

Bar Graphs from Summarized Data

1. Enter the categories in C1 and the frequency or relative frequency in C2.
2. Select **Graph** and highlight **Bar Chart**.
3. In the "Bars represent" pull-down menu, select "Values from a table" and highlight "Simple." Press OK.
4. Fill in the window with the appropriate values. In the "Graph variables" box, enter C2. In the "Categorical variable" box, enter C1. By pressing Labels, you can add a title to the graph. Click OK to obtain the bar graph.

Bar Graphs from Raw Data

1. Enter the raw data in C1.
2. Select **Graph** and highlight **Bar Chart.**
3. In the "Bars represent" pull-down menu, select "Counts of unique values" and highlight "Simple." Press OK.
4. Fill in the window with the appropriate values. In the "Categorical variable" box, enter C1. By pressing Labels, you can add a title to the graph. Click OK to obtain the bar graph.

Pie Chart from Raw or Summarized Data

1. If the data are in a summarized table, enter the categories in C1 and the frequency or relative frequency in C2. If the data are raw, enter the data in C1.
2. Select **Graph** and highlight **Pie Chart.**
3. Fill in the window with the appropriate values. If the data are summarized, click the "Chart values from a table" radio button; if the data are raw, click the "Chart counts of unique values" radio button. For summarized data, enter C1 in the "Categorical variable" box and C2 in the "Summary variable" box. If the data are raw, enter C1 in the "Categorical variable" box. By pressing Labels, you can add a title to the graph. Click OK to obtain the pie chart.

Excel

Bar Graphs from Summarized Data

1. Enter the categories in column A and the frequency or relative frequency in column B.
2. Use the mouse to highlight the data to be graphed.
3. Select the Insert menu. Click the "column"or "bar" chart type. Select the chart type in the upper-left corner.
4. Click the "Layout" tab to enter *x*-axis, *y*-axis, and chart titles.

Pie Charts from Summarized Data

1. Enter the categories in column A and the frequencies in column B.

2. Use the mouse to highlight the data to be graphed.
3. Select the Insert menu and click the "pie" chart type. Select the pie chart in the upper-left corner.
4. Click the "Layout" tab to add a title and labels.

StatCrunch

Frequency or Relative Frequency Distributions from Raw Data

1. Enter the raw data into the spreadsheet. Name the column variable.
2. Select **Stat**, highlight **Tables**, and select **Frequency**.
3. Click on the variable you wish to summarize and click Calculate.

Bar Graphs from Summarized Data

1. Enter the summarized data table into the spreadsheet. Name the variable and frequency (or relative frequency) column.
2. Select **Graphics**, highlight **Bar Plot**, then highlight **with summary**.
3. Select the "Categories in:" column and "Counts in:" column. Click Next>.
4. Choose the type of bar graph (frequency or relative frequency) and click Next>.
5. Enter labels for the x- and y-axes, and enter a title for the graph. Click Create Graph!

Bar Graphs from Raw Data

1. Enter the raw data into the spreadsheet. Name the column variable.
2. Select **Graphics**, highlight **Bar Plot**, then highlight **with data**.
3. Click on the variable you wish to summarize and click Next>.
4. Choose the type of bar graph (frequency or relative frequency) and click Next>.
5. Enter labels for the x- and y-axes, and enter a title for the graph. Click Create Graph!

Pie Chart from Summarized Data

1. Enter the summarized data table into the spreadsheet. Name the variable and frequency (or relative frequency) column.
2. Select **Graphics**, highlight **Pie Chart**, then highlight **with summary**.
3. Select the "Categories in:" column and "Counts in:" column. Click Next>.
4. Choose which displays you would like and click Next>.
5. Enter a title for the graph. Click Create Graph!

Pie Chart from Raw Data

1. Enter the raw data into the spreadsheet. Name the column variable.
2. Select **Graphics**, highlight **Pie Chart**, then highlight **with data**.
3. Click on the variable you wish to summarize and click Next>.
4. Choose which displays you would like and click Next>.
5. Enter a title for the graph. Click Create Graph!

2.2 ORGANIZING QUANTITATIVE DATA: THE POPULAR DISPLAYS

Preparing for This Section Before getting started, review the following:

- Quantitative variable (Section 1.1, pp. 6–8)
- Discrete variable (Section 1.1, pp. 8–9)
- Continuous variable (Section 1.1, pp. 8–9)

OBJECTIVES

1 Organize discrete data in tables
2 Construct histograms of discrete data
3 Organize continuous data in tables
4 Construct histograms of continuous data
5 Draw stem-and-leaf plots
6 Draw dot plots
7 Identify the shape of a distribution
8 Draw time-series graphs

Note to Instructor

If you like, you can print out and distribute the Preparing for This Section quiz located in the Instructor's Resource Center. The purpose is to verify the students have the prerequisite knowledge for this section.

In summarizing quantitative data, we first determine whether the data are discrete or continuous. If the data are discrete with relatively few different values of the variable,

Note to Instructor
Remind students of the differences between discrete and continuous data.

then the categories of data (called **classes**) will be the observations (as in qualitative data). If the data are discrete, but with many different values of the variable or if the data are continuous, then the categories of data (the *classes*) must be created using intervals of numbers. We will first present the techniques required to organize discrete quantitative data when there are relatively few different values and then proceed to organizing continuous quantitative data.

1 Organize Discrete Data in Tables

We use the values of a discrete variable to create the classes when the number of distinct data values is small.

EXAMPLE 1 Constructing Frequency and Relative Frequency Distributions from Discrete Data

Problem The manager of a Wendy's fast-food restaurant wants to know the typical number of customers who arrive during the lunch hour. The data in Table 8 represent the number of customers who arrive at Wendy's for 40 randomly selected 15-minute intervals of time during lunch. For example, during one 15-minute interval, seven customers arrived. Construct a frequency and relative frequency distribution.

TABLE 8

Number of Arrivals at Wendy's

7	6	6	6	4	6	2	6
5	6	6	11	4	5	7	6
2	7	1	2	4	8	2	6
6	5	5	3	7	5	4	6
2	2	9	7	5	9	8	5

Approach The number of people arriving could be 0, 1, 2, 3, ... Table 8 shows there are 11 categories of data from this study: 1, 2, 3, ..., 11. We tally the number of observations for each category, count each tally, and create the frequency and relative frequency distributions.

Solution The two distributions are shown in Table 9.

TABLE 9

Number of Customers	Tally	Frequency	Relative Frequency
1	𝍷	1	$\frac{1}{40} = 0.025$
2	𝍸 𝍷	6	0.15
3	𝍷	1	0.025
4	𝍷𝍷𝍷𝍷	4	0.1
5	𝍸 𝍷𝍷	7	0.175
6	𝍸 𝍸 𝍷	11	0.275
7	𝍸	5	0.125
8	𝍷𝍷	2	0.05
9	𝍷𝍷	2	0.05
10		0	0.0
11	𝍷	1	0.025

On the basis of the relative frequencies, 27.5% of the 15-minute intervals had 6 customers arrive at Wendy's during the lunch hour.

Now Work Problems 33(a)–(e)

2 Construct Histograms of Discrete Data

The *histogram*, a graph used to present quantitative data, is similar to the bar graph.

DEFINITION

A **histogram** is constructed by drawing rectangles for each class of data. The height of each rectangle is the frequency or relative frequency of the class. The width of each rectangle is the same and the rectangles touch each other.

EXAMPLE 2 Drawing a Histogram for Discrete Data

Problem Construct a frequency histogram and a relative frequency histogram using the data in Table 9.

Approach On the horizontal axis, we place the value of each category of data (number of customers). The vertical axis is the frequency or relative frequency of each category. We draw rectangles of equal width centered at the value of each category. For example, the first rectangle is centered at 1. For the frequency histogram, the height of the rectangle is the frequency of the category; for the relative frequency histogram, the height is the relative frequency of the category. Remember, the rectangles touch.

CAUTION

The rectangles in histograms touch, but the rectangles in bar graphs do not touch.

Solution Figures 7(a) and (b) show the frequency and relative frequency histograms, respectively.

Figure 7

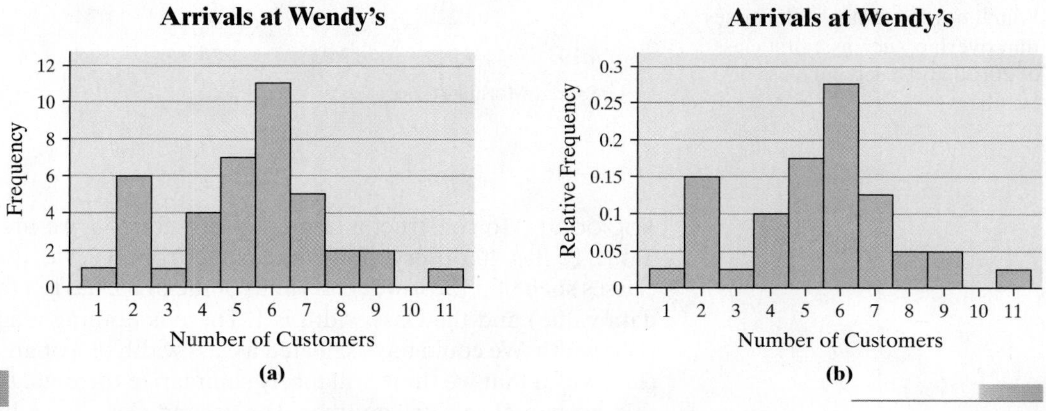

Now Work Problems 33(f)–(g)

3 Organize Continuous Data in Tables

Classes are categories into which data are grouped. When a data set consists of a large number of different discrete data values or when a data set consists of continuous data, we must create classes by using intervals of numbers.

Table 10 is a typical frequency distribution created from continuous data. The data represent the number of U.S. residents ages 25 to 74, who have earned a bachelor's degree or higher.

TABLE 10

Age	Number (in thousands)
25–34	12,967
35–44	13,904
45–54	13,005
55–64	10,357
65–74	4,584

Source: Current Population Survey, 2008

Notice that the data are categorized, or grouped, by intervals of numbers. Each interval represents a class. For example, the first class is 25- to 34-year-old U.S. residents who have a bachelor's degree or higher. We read this interval as follows: "The number of U.S. residents in 2008, ages 25 to 34, with a bachelor's degree or higher was 12,967,000." There are five classes in the table, each with a **lower class limit** (the smallest value within the class) and an **upper class limit** (the largest value within the class). The lower class limit for the first class in Table 10 is 25; the upper class limit is 34. The **class width** is the difference between consecutive lower class limits. In Table 10 the class width is $35 - 25 = 10$.

TABLE 11

Age	Number
20–29	266
30–39	952
40–49	1118
50–59	639
60 and older	232

Source: U.S. Justice Department

Notice that the classes in Table 10 do not overlap. This is necessary to avoid confusion as to which class a data value belongs. Notice also that the class widths are equal for all classes. One exception to the requirement of equal class widths occurs in open-ended tables. A table is **open ended** if the first class has no lower class limit or the last class has no upper class limit. The data in Table 11 represent the number of persons under sentence of death as of December 31, 2008, in the United States. The last class in the table, "60 and older," is open ended.

One final thought. In Table 10, the data are continuous. So the class 25–34 actually represents 25–34.999 . . . , or 25 up to every value less than 35.

EXAMPLE 3 Organizing Continuous Data into a Frequency and Relative Frequency Distribution

In Other Words
For qualitative and many discrete data, the classes are formed by using the data. For continuous data, the classes are formed by using intervals of numbers, such as 30–39.

Problem Suppose you are considering investing in a Roth IRA. You collect the data in Table 12 which represent the 5-year rate of return (in percent, adjusted for sales charges) for a simple random sample of 40 large-blended mutual funds. Construct a frequency and relative frequency distribution of the data.

TABLE 12

Five-Year Rate of Return of Mutual Funds (as of 10/7/10)

3.27	3.53	3.45	5.98	4.55	3.54	4.91	4.75
3.30	10.87	3.25	3.98	5.78	4.43	4.44	10.90
5.38	4.37	4.27	3.33	8.56	11.70	3.54	5.93
4.04	3.22	4.86	3.28	11.74	6.64	3.25	3.57
4.19	4.91	12.03	3.24	4.18	4.10	3.28	3.23

Source: Morningstar.com

CAUTION
Watch out for tables with classes that overlap, such as a first class of 20–30 and a second class of 30–40.

Approach To construct a frequency distribution, we first create classes of equal width. Table 12 has 40 observations that range from 3.22 to 12.03, so we decide to create the classes such that the lower class limit of the first class is 3 (a little smaller than the smallest data value) and the class width is 1. There is nothing magical about the choice of 1 as a class width. We could have selected a class width of 3 or any other class width. We choose a class width that we think will nicely summarize the data. If our choice doesn't accomplish this, we can always try another. The second class has a lower class limit $3 + 1 = 4$. The classes cannot overlap, so the upper class limit of the first class is 3.99. Continuing in this fashion, we obtain the following classes:

$$\begin{array}{c} 3-3.99 \\ 4-4.99 \\ \vdots \\ 12-12.99 \end{array}$$

This gives us 10 classes. We tally the number of observations in each class, count the tallies, and create the frequency distribution. By dividing each class's frequency by 40, the number of observations, we create the relative frequency distribution.

Solution We tally the data as shown in the second column of Table 13. The third column shows the frequency of each class. From the frequency distribution, we conclude that a 5-year rate of return between 3% and 3.99% occurs with the most frequency. The fourth column shows the relative frequency of each class. So, 40% of the large-blended mutual funds had a 5-year rate of return between 3% and 3.99%.

Using Technology
Many technologies have a "sort" feature that makes tallying data by hand much easier.

Note to Instructor
Consider assigning the "Exploring Histograms with StatCrunch" activity From the Student Activity Workbook.

TABLE 13

Class (5-year rate of return)	Tally	Frequency	Relative Frequency
3–3.99	卌 卌 卌 |	16	16/40 = 0.4
4–4.99	卌 卌 |||	13	13/40 = 0.325
5–5.99	||||	4	0.1
6–6.99	|	1	0.025
7–7.99		0	0
8–8.99	|	1	0.025
9–9.99		0	0
10–10.99	||	2	0.05
11–11.99	||	2	0.05
12–12.99	|	1	0.025

One mutual fund had a 5-year rate of return between 12% and 12.99%. We might consider this mutual fund worthy of our investment. This type of information would be more difficult to obtain from the raw data.

HISTORICAL NOTE

Florence Nightingale was born in Italy on May 12, 1820. She was named after the city of her birth. Nightingale was educated by her father, who attended Cambridge University. Between 1849 and 1851, she studied nursing throughout Europe. In 1854, she was asked to oversee the introduction of female nurses into the military hospitals in Turkey. While there, she greatly improved the mortality rate of wounded soldiers. She collected data and invented graphs (the polar area diagram), tables, and charts to show that improving sanitary conditions would lead to decreased mortality rates. In 1869, Nightingale founded the Nightingale School Home for Nurses. After a long and eventful life as a reformer of health care and contributor to graphics in statistics, Florence Nightingale died on August 13, 1910.

The choices of the lower class limit of the first class and the class width were rather arbitrary. Though formulas and procedures exist for creating frequency distributions from raw data, they do not necessarily provide better summaries. There is no one correct frequency distribution for a particular set of data. However, some frequency distributions can better illustrate patterns within the data than others. So constructing frequency distributions is somewhat of an art form. Use the distribution that seems to provide the best overall summary of the data.

Consider the frequency distributions in Tables 14 and 15 (on the following page), which also summarize the 5-year rate-of-return data discussed in Example 3. In both tables, the lower class limit of the first class is 3, but the class widths are 3 and 0.5, respectively. Do you think Table 13, 14, or 15 provides the best summary of the distribution? In forming your opinion, consider that too few classes will cause a bunching effect, and too many classes will spread the data out, thereby not revealing any pattern.

TABLE 14

Class (5-year rate of return)	Frequency
3–5.99	33
6–8.99	2
9–11.99	4
12–14.99	1

TABLE 15

Class (5-year rate of return)	Frequency
3–3.49	11
3.5–3.99	5
4–4.49	8
4.5–4.99	5
5–5.49	1
5.5–5.99	3
6–6.49	0
6.5–6.99	1
7–7.49	0
7.5–7.99	0
8–8.49	0
8.5–8.99	1
9–9.49	0
9.5–9.99	0
10–10.49	0
10.5–10.99	2
11–11.49	0
11.5–11.99	2
12–12.49	1

Now Work Problems 35(a)–(b)

The goal in constructing a frequency distribution is to reveal interesting features of the data, but we also typically want the number of classes to be between 5 and 20. When the data set is small, we usually want fewer classes. When the data set is large, we usually want more classes. Why do you think this is reasonable?

Although there is no "right" frequency distribution, there are bad ones. Use the following guidelines to help determine an appropriate lower class limit of the first class and class width.

Guidelines for Determining the Lower Class Limit of the First Class and Class Width

Choosing the Lower Class Limit of the First Class

Choose the smallest observation in the data set or a convenient number slightly lower than the smallest observation in the data set. For example, in Table 12, the smallest observation is 3.22. A convenient lower class limit of the first class is 3.

Determining the Class Width

- Decide on the number of classes. Generally, there should be between 5 and 20 classes. The smaller the data set, the fewer classes you should have. For example, we might choose 10 classes for the data in Table 12.
- Determine the class width by computing

$$\text{Class width} \approx \frac{\text{largest data value} - \text{smallest data value}}{\text{number of classes}}$$

In Other Words

Creating the classes for summarizing continuous data is an art form. There is no such thing as *the* correct frequency distribution. However, there can be less desirable frequency distributions. The larger the class width, the fewer classes a frequency distribution will have.

Note to Instructor

You could present Sturge's Formula for the number of classes, m.

$$m = 1 + 3.3 \log n$$

where n is the number of observations.

In Other Words
Rounding *up* is different from rounding *off*. For example, 6.2 rounded *up* would be 7, while 6.2 rounded *off* would be 6.

Round this value *up* to a convenient number. For example, using the data in Table 12, we obtain class width $\approx \frac{12.03 - 3.22}{10} = 0.881$. We round this up to 1 because this is an easy number to work with. Rounding up may result in fewer classes than were originally intended.

Now Work Problems 39(a)–(c)

Applying these guidelines, to the 5-year rate of return data, we would end up with the frequency distribution shown in Table 13.

4 Construct Histograms of Continuous Data

We are now ready to draw histograms of continuous data.

EXAMPLE 4 Drawing a Histogram of Continuous Data

Problem Construct a frequency and relative frequency histogram of the 5-year rate-of-return data discussed in Example 3.

Approach To draw the frequency histogram, we use the frequency distribution in Table 13. First, we label the lower class limits of each class on the horizontal axis. Then, for each class, we draw a rectangle whose width is the class width and whose height is the frequency. For the relative frequency histogram, the height of the rectangle is the relative frequency.

Note to Instructor
Have students think about the factors to consider in determining an appropriate class width. Are there any ways that a histogram can be used to distort the data?

Solution Figures 8(a) and (b) show the frequency and relative frequency histograms, respectively.

Figure 8

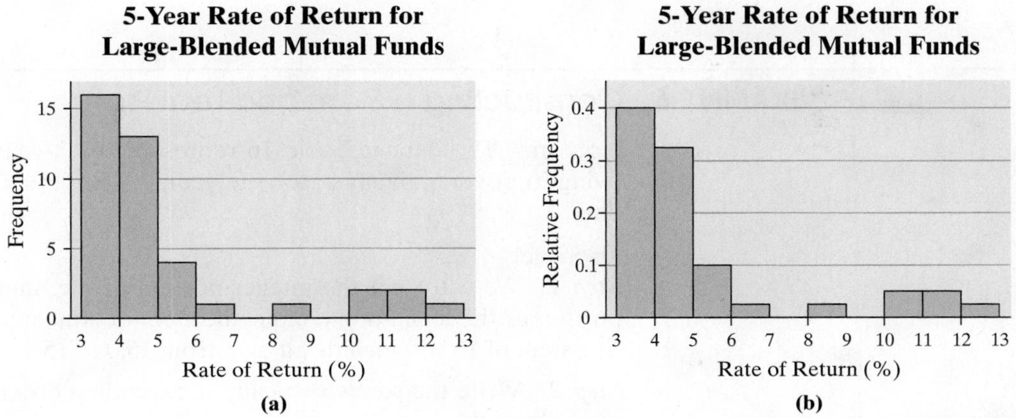

EXAMPLE 5 Drawing a Histogram for Continuous Data Using Technology

Problem Construct a frequency and relative frequency histogram of the 5-year rate-of-return data discussed in Example 3.

Approach We will use StatCrunch to construct the frequency and relative frequency histograms. The steps for constructing the graphs using the TI-83/84 Plus graphing calculators, MINITAB, Excel, and StatCrunch, are given in the Technology Step-by-Step on page 99.

Solution Figures 9(a) and (b) show the frequency and relative frequency histograms, respectively, obtained from StatCrunch.

Figure 9

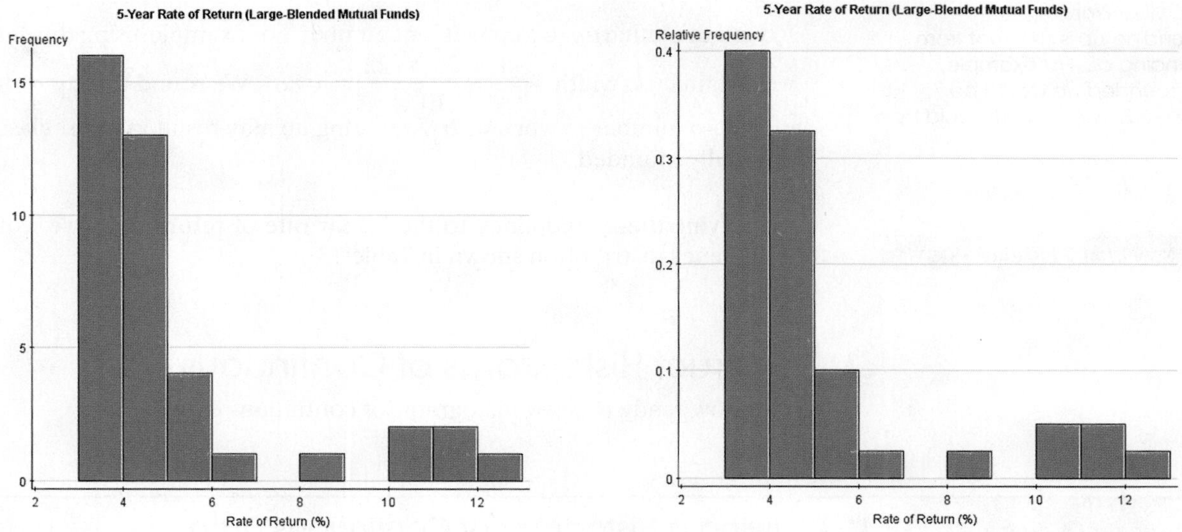

Now Work Problems 35(c)–(d)

Using technology to construct histograms is a convenient and efficient way to explore patterns in data using different class widths.

5 Draw Stem-and-Leaf Plots

A **stem-and-leaf plot** is another way to represent quantitative data graphically. In a stem-and-leaf plot (or *stem plot*), we use the digits to the left of the rightmost digit to form the **stem**. Each rightmost digit forms a **leaf**. For example, a data value of 147 would have 14 as the stem and 7 as the leaf.

EXAMPLE 6 Constructing a Stem-and-Leaf Plot

Note to Instructor

Spend some time discussing how the stems are chosen.

Problem The data in Table 16 represent the 2-year average percentage of persons living in poverty, by state, for the years 2008–2009. Draw a stem-and-leaf plot of the data.

Approach

Step 1 We will treat the integer portion of the number as the stem and the decimal portion as the leaf. For example, the stem of Alabama will be 15 and the leaf will be 4. The stem of 15 will include all data from 15.0 to 15.9.

Step 2 Write the stems vertically in ascending order, and then draw a vertical line to the right of the stems.

Step 3 Write the leaves corresponding to the stem.

Step 4 Within each stem, rearrange the leaves in ascending order. Title the plot and include a legend to indicate what the values represent.

Solution

Step 1 The stem from Alabama is 15 and the corresponding leaf is 4. The stem from Alaska is 9 and its leaf is 9, and so on.

Step 2 Since the lowest data value is 7.4 and the highest data value is 20.6, we let the stems range from 7 to 20. We write the stems vertically in Figure 10(a), along with a vertical line to the right of the stem.

Step 3 We write the leaves corresponding to each stem. See Figure 10(b).

Step 4 We rearrange the leaves in ascending order, give the plot a title, and add a legend. See Figure 10(c).

TABLE 16

Two-Year Average Percentage of Persons Living in Poverty (2008–2009)

State	Percent	State	Percent	State	Percent
Alabama	15.4	Kentucky	17.0	North Dakota	11.4
Alaska	9.9	Louisiana	16.2	Ohio	13.5
Arizona	19.6	Maine	11.7	Oklahoma	13.3
Arkansas	17.1	Maryland	9.1	Oregon	12.0
California	15.0	Massachusetts	11.1	Pennsylvania	11.0
Colorado	11.7	Michigan	13.5	Rhode Island	12.9
Connecticut	8.2	Minnesota	10.5	South Carolina	13.9
Delaware	10.9	Mississippi	20.6	South Dakota	13.6
D.C.	17.2	Missouri	14.4	Tennessee	15.8
Florida	13.9	Montana	13.2	Texas	16.6
Georgia	16.9	Nebraska	10.2	Utah	8.6
Hawaii	11.2	Nevada	11.9	Vermont	9.2
Idaho	13.0	New Hampshire	7.4	Virginia	10.5
Illinois	12.8	New Jersey	9.3	Washington	11.0
Indiana	15.2	New Mexico	19.3	West Virginia	15.2
Iowa	10.1	New York	15.0	Wisconsin	10.3
Kansas	13.2	North Carolina	15.4	Wyoming	9.7

Source: U.S. Census Bureau, *Current Population Survey*, 2009

Figure 10

```
 7 |
 8 |
 9 |
10 |
11 |
12 |
13 |
14 |
15 |
16 |
17 |
18 |
19 |
20 |
```

(a)

```
 7 | 4
 8 | 2 6
 9 | 9 1 3 2 7
10 | 9 1 5 2 5 3
11 | 7 2 7 1 9 4 0 0
12 | 8 0 9
13 | 9 0 2 5 2 5 3 9 6
14 | 4
15 | 4 0 2 0 4 8 2
16 | 9 2 6
17 | 1 2 0
18 |
19 | 6 3
20 | 6
```

(b)

Percentage of Persons Living in Poverty

```
 7 | 4
 8 | 2 6
 9 | 1 2 3 7 9
10 | 1 2 3 5 5 9
11 | 0 0 1 2 4 7 7 9
12 | 0 8 9
13 | 0 2 2 3 5 5 6 9 9
14 | 4
15 | 0 0 2 2 4 4 8
16 | 2 6 9
17 | 0 1 2
18 |
19 | 3 6
20 | 6
Legend: 7|4 represents 7.4%
```

(c)

The following summarizes the method for constructing a stem-and-leaf plot.

Construction of a Stem-and-Leaf Plot

Step 1 The stem of a data value will consist of the digits to the left of the right-most digit. The leaf of a data value will be the rightmost digit.

Step 2 Write the stems in a vertical column in increasing order. Draw a vertical line to the right of the stems.

Step 3 Write each leaf corresponding to the stems to the right of the vertical line.

Step 4 Within each stem, rearrange the leaves in ascending order, title the plot, and include a legend to indicate what the values represent.

EXAMPLE 7 Constructing a Stem-and-Leaf Plot Using Technology

Using Technology
In MINITAB, there is a column of numbers left of the stem. The (9) indicates that there are 9 observations in the class containing the middle value (called the *median*). The values above the (9) represent the number of observations less than or equal to the upper class limit of the class. For example, 14 states have percentages in poverty less than or equal to 10.9. The values in the left column below the (9) indicate the number of observations greater than or equal to the lower class limit of the class. For example, 16 states have percentages in poverty greater than or equal to 15.0.

Now Work Problem 41(a)

Problem Construct a stem-and-leaf plot of the poverty data discussed in Example 6.

Approach We will use MINITAB. The steps for constructing the graphs using MINITAB or StatCrunch are given in the Technology Step-by-Step on page 99. **Note:** The TI graphing calculators and Excel are not capable of drawing stem-and-leaf plots.

Solution Figure 11 shows the stem-and-leaf plot obtained from MINITAB.

Figure 11

```
Stem-and-leaf of Poverty  N  = 51
Leaf Unit = 0.10


  1   7   4
  3   8   26
  8   9   12379
 14  10   123559
 22  11   00124779
 25  12   089
 (9) 13   022355699
 17  14   4
 16  15   0022448
  9  16   269
  6  17   012
  3  18
  3  19   36
  1  20   6
```

In Other Words
The choice of the stem in the construction of a stem-and-leaf plot is also an art form. It acts just like the class width. For example, the stem of 7 in Figure 11 represents the class 7.0–7.9. The stem of 8 represents the class 8.0–8.9. Notice that the class width is 1.0. The number of leaves is the frequency of each category.

Notice that the stem-and-leaf plot looks much like a histogram turned on its side. The stem serves as the class. For example, the stem 10 contains all data from 10.0 to 10.9. The leaves represent the frequency (height of the rectangle). Therefore, it is important to space the leaves evenly.

One advantage of the stem-and-leaf plot over frequency distributions and histograms is that the raw data can be retrieved from the stem-and-leaf plot. So, in a stem-and-leaf plot, we could determine the maximum observation. We cannot learn this information from a histogram.

On the other hand, stem-and-leaf plots lose their usefulness when data sets are large or consist of a large range of values. In addition, the steps listed for creating stem-and-leaf plots sometimes must be modified to meet the needs of the data, as in the next example.

EXAMPLE 8 Constructing a Stem-and-Leaf Plot after Modifying the Data

Problem Construct a stem-and-leaf plot of the 5-year rate-of-return data listed in Table 12 on page 80.

Approach

Step 1 If we use the integer portion as the stem and the decimals as the leaves, the stems will be 3, 4, 5, . . . , 12; but the leaves will be two digits (such as 27, 30, and so on). This is not acceptable since each leaf must be a single digit. To solve this problem, we will round the data to the nearest tenth.

Step 2 Create a vertical column of the integer stems in increasing order.

Step 3 Write the leaves corresponding to each stem.

Step 4 Rearrange the leaves in ascending order, title the plot, and include a legend.

Solution

Step 1 We round the data to the nearest tenth as shown in Table 17.

Note to Instructor
Discuss the similarities and differences of histograms and stem-and-leaf diagrams. Remind students that they can determine the shape of the distribution just as they did with histograms, by turning the stem-and-leaf plot on its side.

TABLE 17

3.3	3.5	3.5	6.0	4.6	3.5	4.9	4.8
3.3	10.9	3.3	4.0	5.8	4.4	4.4	10.9
5.4	4.4	4.3	3.3	8.6	11.7	3.5	5.9
4.0	3.2	4.9	3.3	11.7	6.6	3.3	3.6
4.2	4.9	12.0	3.2	4.2	4.1	3.3	3.2

Step 2 Write the stems vertically in ascending order as shown in Figure 12(a).

Step 3 Write the leaves corresponding to each stem as shown in Figure 12(b).

Step 4 Rearrange the leaves in ascending order, title the plot, and include a legend as shown in Figure 12(c).

Figure 12 **Five-Year Rate of Return of Mutual Funds**

(a)

3
4
5
6
7
8
9
10
11
12

(b)

3	3 3 5 2 5 3 3 3 2 5 5 3 3 6 2
4	0 2 4 9 3 9 0 6 2 4 1 9 4 8
5	4 8 9
6	0 6
7	
8	6
9	
10	9 9
11	7 7
12	0

(c)

3	2 2 2 3 3 3 3 3 3 3 5 5 5 5 6
4	0 0 1 2 2 3 4 4 4 6 8 9 9 9
5	4 8 9
6	0 6
7	
8	6
9	
10	9 9
11	7 7
12	0

Legend: 12|0 represents 12.0%

In Other Words
Stem-and-leaf plots are best used when the data set is small and the range of values is not too wide.

Altering the data to construct the graph in Figure 12(c) means that we cannot retrieve the original data. A second limitation appearing in Example 8 is that we are effectively forced to use a "class width" of 1.0 even though a larger "width" may be more desirable. This illustrates that we must weigh the advantages against the disadvantages when choosing the type of graph to summarize data.

Split Stems

In Other Words
Using split stems is like adding more classes to a frequency distribution.

The data in Table 18 range from 11 to 48. Figure 13 shows a stem-and-leaf plot using the tens digit as the stem and the ones digit as the leaf. The data appear rather bunched. To resolve this problem, we can use **split stems.** For example, rather than using one stem for the class of data 10–19, we could use two stems, one for the 10–14 interval and the second for the 15–19 interval. We do this in Figure 14.

TABLE 18

27	17	11	24	36
13	29	22	18	17
23	30	12	46	17
32	48	11	18	23
18	32	26	24	38
24	15	13	31	22
18	21	27	20	16
15	37	19	19	29

Figure 13

1	1 1 2 3 3 5 5 6 7 7 7 8 8 8 8 9 9
2	0 1 2 2 3 3 4 4 4 6 7 7 9 9
3	0 1 2 2 6 7 8
4	6 8

Legend: 1|1 represents 11

Figure 14

1	1 1 2 3 3
1	5 5 6 7 7 7 8 8 8 8 9 9
2	0 1 2 2 3 3 4 4 4
2	6 7 7 9 9
3	0 1 2 2
3	6 7 8
4	
4	6 8

Legend: 1|1 represents 11

The stem-and-leaf plot shown in Figure 14 reveals the distribution of the data better. As with the determination of class intervals in the creation of frequency histograms, judgment plays a major role. There is no such thing as the correct stem-and-leaf plot. However, a quick comparison of Figures 13 and 14 shows that some plots are better than others.

Now Work Problem 47

6 Draw Dot Plots

One more graph! We draw a **dot plot** by placing each observation horizontally in increasing order and placing a dot above the observation each time it is observed. Though limited in usefulness, dot plots provide a quick picture of the data.

EXAMPLE 9 Drawing a Dot Plot

Problem Draw a dot plot for the number of arrivals at Wendy's data from Table 8 on page 78.

Approach The smallest observation in the data set is 1 and the largest is 11. We write the numbers 1 through 11 horizontally. For each observation, we place a dot above the value of the observation.

Solution Figure 15 shows the dot plot.

Figure 15

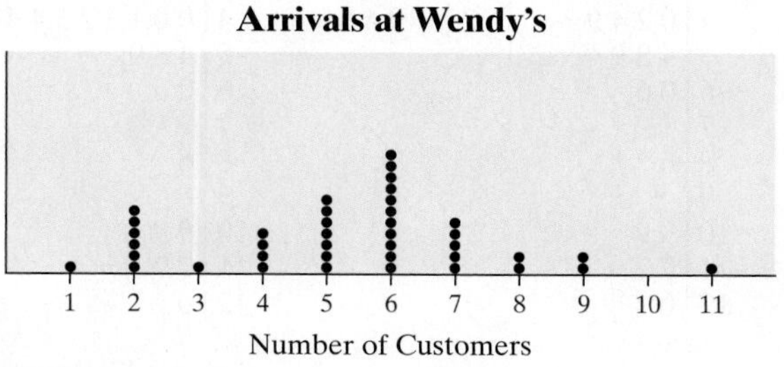

Now Work Problem 53

7 Identify the Shape of a Distribution

One way that a variable is described is through the shape of its distribution. Distribution shapes are typically classified as symmetric, skewed left, or skewed right. Figure 16 displays various histograms and the shape of the distribution.

Figures 16(a) and (b) show symmetric distributions. They are symmetric because, if we split the histogram down the middle, the right and left sides are mirror images. Figure 16(a) is a **uniform distribution** because the frequency of each value of the variable is evenly spread out across the values of the variable. Figure 16(b) displays a **bell-shaped distribution** because the highest frequency occurs in the middle and frequencies tail off to the left and right of the middle.The distribution in Figure 16(c) is **skewed right**. Notice that the tail to the right of the peak is longer than the tail to the left of the peak. Finally, Figure 16(d) illustrates a distribution that is **skewed left**, because the tail to the left of the peak is longer than the tail to the right of the peak.

Note to Instructor

Give examples of data sets that may be uniform, bell shaped, and skewed right. For example, rolling a single die, IQ scores, and income, respectively.

CAUTION

We do not describe qualitative data as skewed left, skewed right, or uniform.

CAUTION

It is important to recognize that data will not always exhibit behavior that perfectly matches any of the shapes given in Figure 16. To identify the shape of a distribution, some flexibility is required. In addition, people may disagree on the shape, since identifying shape is subjective.

Figure 16

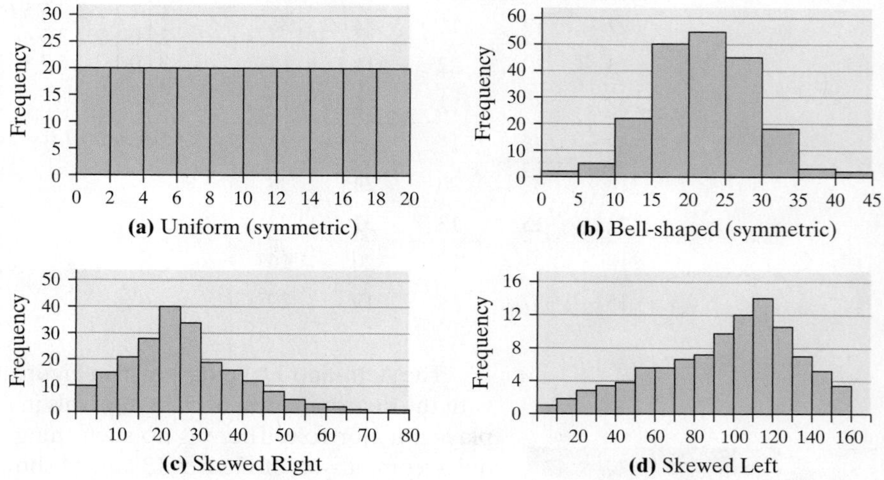

(a) Uniform (symmetric) **(b)** Bell-shaped (symmetric) **(c)** Skewed Right **(d)** Skewed Left

EXAMPLE 10 Identifying the Shape of a Distribution

Note to Instructor

Consider assigning the "Sorting Histograms by Shape" or "Predicting Distribution Shape" activities from the Student Activity Workbook.

Problem Figure 17 displays the histogram obtained in Example 4 for the 5-year rate of return for large-blended mutual funds. Describe the shape of the distribution.

Approach We compare the shape of the distribution displayed in Figure 17 with those in Figure 16.

Solution Since the histogram looks most like Figure 16(c), the distribution is skewed right.

Figure 17 **5-Year Rate of Return for Large-Blended Mutual Funds**

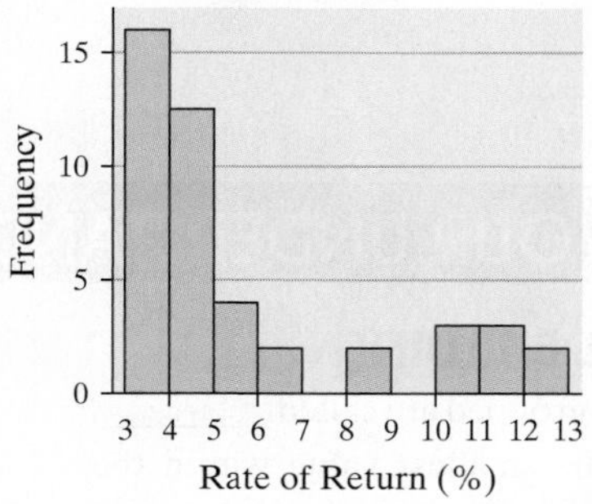

Now Work Problem 35(e)

8 Draw Time-Series Graphs

If the value of a variable is measured at different points in time, the data are referred to as **time-series data**. The closing price of Cisco Systems stock at the end of each month for the past 12 years is an example of time-series data.

DEFINITION

A **time-series plot** is obtained by plotting the time in which a variable is measured on the horizontal axis and the corresponding value of the variable on the vertical axis. Line segments are then drawn connecting the points.

Time-series plots are very useful in identifying trends in the data over time.

EXAMPLE 11 Drawing a Time-Series Plot

TABLE 19

Year	Housing Permits (000s)
2000	1592.3
2001	1636.7
2002	1747.7
2003	1889.2
2004	2070.1
2005	2155.3
2006	1838.9
2007	1398.4
2008	905.4
2009	583.0
2010	592.9

Source: U.S. Census Bureau

Problem A housing permit is authorization from a governing body to construct a privately owned housing unit. The data in Table 19 represent the number of housing permits issued from 2000 to 2010 in the United States. Construct a time-series plot of the data. In what year was the number of housing permits issued highest? What was the percentage change in housing permits from 2008 to 2009?

Approach

Step 1 Plot points for each month, with the date on the horizontal axis and the number of housing permits on the vertical axis.

Step 2 Connect the points with line segments.

Solution Figure 18 shows the time-series plot. The overall trend is dismal if you are in the home-building business. Housing permits peaked at 2155.3 thousand in 2005. The percentage change in housing permits issued from 2008 to 2009 is

$$\text{Percentage change in permits issued} = \frac{583.0 - 905.4}{905.4} \approx -0.356 = -35.6\%$$

$\% \text{ change} = \frac{P_2 - P_1}{P_1}$

Housing permits issued declined 35.6% from 2008 to 2009, but increased 1.7% from 2009 to 2010.

Figure 18

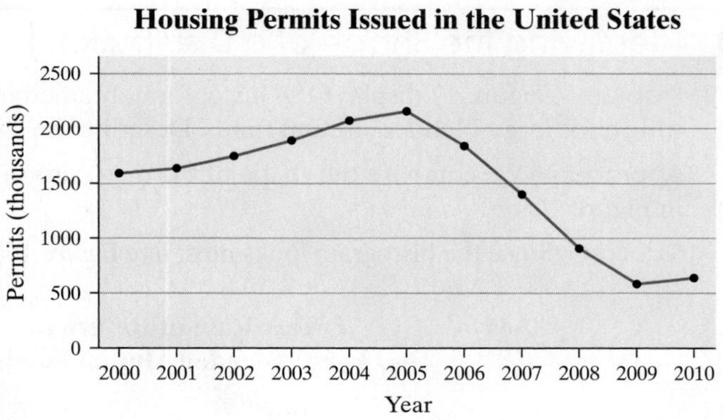

Using Technology
Statistical spreadsheets, such as StatCrunch, Excel, or MINITAB, and certain graphing calculators, such as the TI-83 or TI-84 Plus, can create time-series graphs.

Now Work Problem 55

2.2 ASSESS YOUR UNDERSTANDING

VOCABULARY AND SKILL BUILDING

1. The categories by which data are grouped are called __classes__.

2. The __lower__ class limit is the smallest value within the class and the __upper__ class limit is the largest value within the class.

3. The __class__ __width__ is the difference between consecutive lower class limits.

4. What does it mean if a distribution is said to be "skewed left"?

5. *True or False*: There is not one particular frequency distribution that is correct, but there are frequency distributions that are less desirable than others. True

6. *True or False*: Stem-and-leaf plots are particularly useful for large sets of data. False

7. *True or False*: The shape of the distribution shown is best classified as skewed left. False

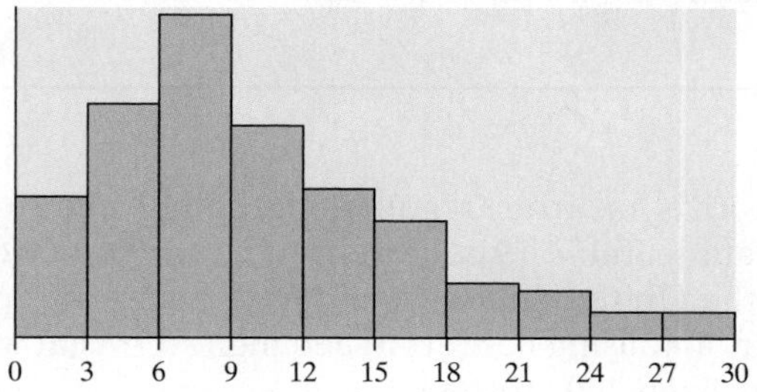

8. *True or False*: The shape of the distribution shown is best classified as uniform. False

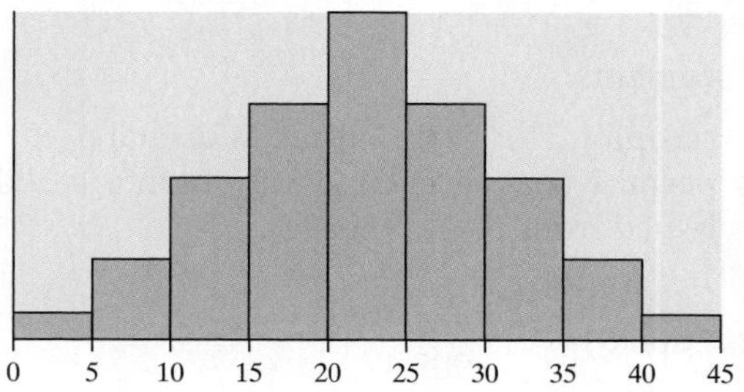

9. Rolling the Dice An experiment was conducted in which two fair dice were thrown 100 times. The sum of the pips showing on the dice was then recorded. The following frequency histogram gives the results.

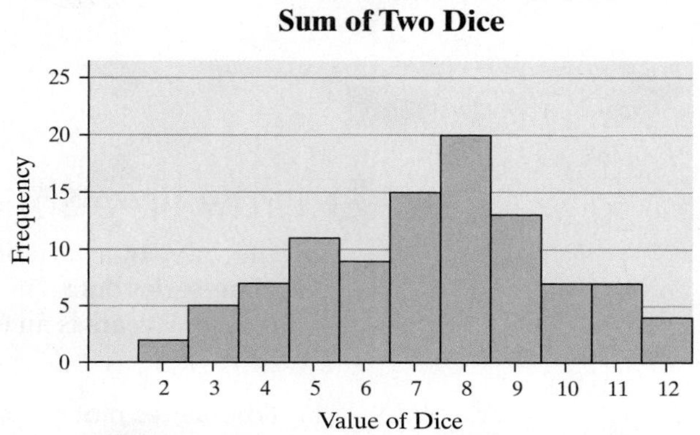

(a) What was the most frequent outcome of the experiment? 8

(b) What was the least frequent? 2

(c) How many times did we observe a 7? 15

(d) How many more 5's were observed than 4's? 4

(e) Determine the percentage of time a 7 was observed. 15%

(f) Describe the shape of the distribution. Bell shaped

10. Car Sales A car salesman records the number of cars he sold each week for the past year. The following frequency histogram shows the results.

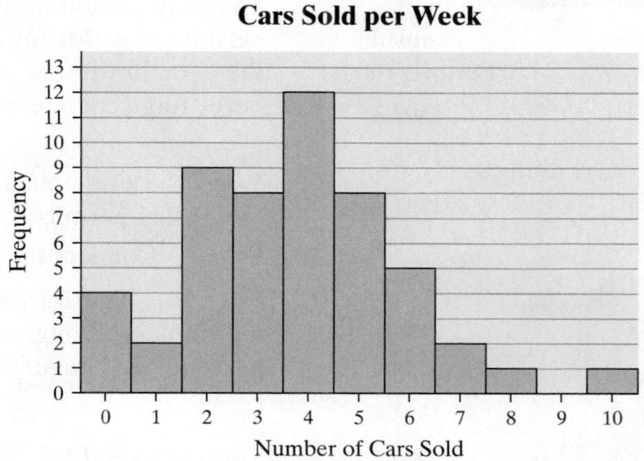

(a) What is the most frequent number of cars sold in a week? 4

(b) For how many weeks were two cars sold? 9

(c) Determine the percentage of time two cars were sold. 17.3%

(d) Describe the shape of the distribution. Skewed right

11. IQ Scores The following frequency histogram represents the IQ scores of a random sample of seventh-grade students. IQs are measured to the nearest whole number. The frequency of each class is labeled above each rectangle.

IQs of 7th Grade Students

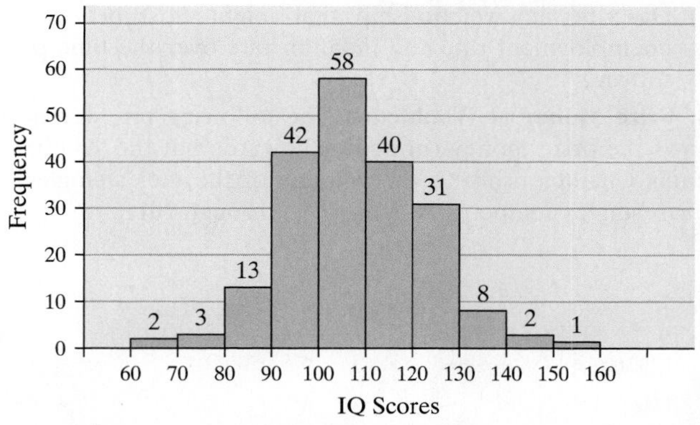

(a) How many students were sampled? 200
(b) Determine the class width. 10
(c) Identify the classes and their frequencies.
(d) Which class has the highest frequency? 100–109
(e) Which class has the lowest frequency? 150–159
(f) What percent of students had an IQ of at least 130? 5.5%
(g) Did any students have an IQ of 165? No

12. Alcohol-Related Traffic Fatalities The frequency histogram in the next column represents the number of alcohol-related traffic fatalities by state (including Washington, D.C.) in 2008 according to the National Highway Traffic Safety Administration.

(a) Determine the class width. 200
(b) Identify the classes.
(c) Which class has the highest frequency? 0–199
(d) Describe the shape of the distribution. Skewed right
(e) A reporter writes the following statement: "According to the data, Texas had 1463 alcohol-related deaths, while Vermont had only 15. So the roads in Vermont are much safer." Explain what is wrong with this statement and how a fair comparison can be made between alcohol-related traffic fatalities in Texas versus Vermont.

Alcohol-Related Traffic Fatalities

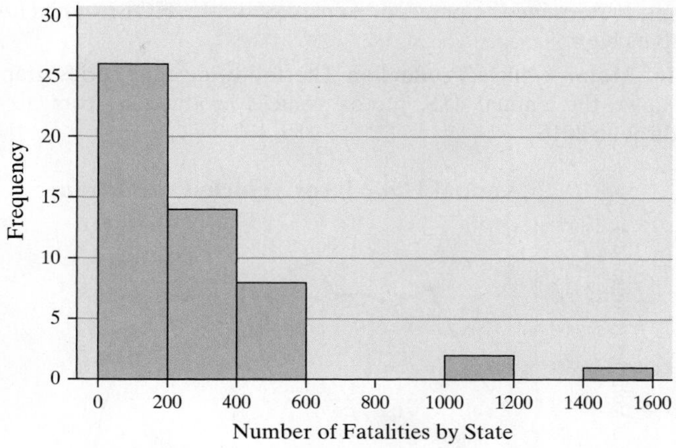

In Problems 13 and 14, for each variable presented, state whether you would expect a histogram of the data to be bell-shaped, uniform, skewed left, or skewed right. Justify your reasoning.

13. (a) Annual household incomes in the United States
(b) Scores on a standardized exam such as the SAT
(c) Number of people living in a household skewed right
(d) Ages of patients diagnosed with Alzheimer's disease

14. (a) Number of alcoholic drinks consumed per week
(b) Ages of students in a public school district Uniform
(c) Ages of hearing-aid patients Skewed left
(d) Heights of full-grown men Bell shaped

13. (a) skewed right (b) bell shaped (d) skewed left
14. (a) skewed right

15. Housing Affordability The National Association of Home Builders in conjunction with Wells Fargo compiles a housing affordability index called the Housing Opportunity Index (HOI). The index represents the proportion of homes considered to be affordable according to standard mortgage practices for individuals earning the national median income.

Housing Opportunity Index

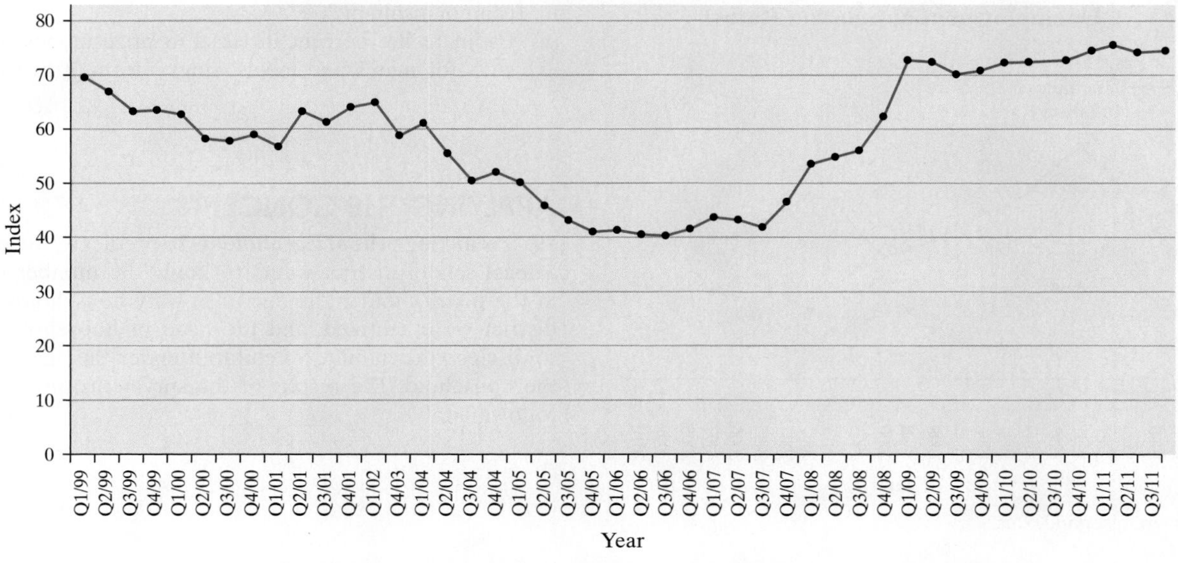

(a) Estimate the HOI in the first quarter of 1999 (Q1/99). 70%
(b) What was the lowest value of the HOI (meaning homes were least affordable)? In what year did this occur? 40%; 2006
(c) What was the highest value of the HOI? In what year did this occur? Approximately 75%; 2011
(d) Determine the percentage decrease in the HOI from the first quarter of 1999 to the third quarter of 2006. Decrease about 43%
(e) Determine the percentage increase in the HOI from its low to its high. Increase about 87.5%

16. Motor Vehicle Production The following time-series graph shows the annual U.S. motor vehicle production from 1990 through 2010.

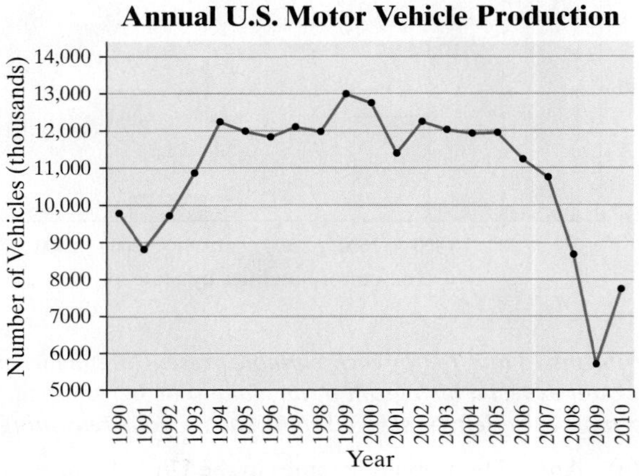

Source: Bureau of Transportation Statistics

(a) Estimate the number of motor vehicles produced in the United States in 1991. 8.8 million
(b) Estimate the number of motor vehicles produced in the United States in 1999. 13.0 million
(c) Use your results from (a) and (b) to estimate the percent increase in the number of motor vehicles produced from 1991 to 1999. 47.7%
(d) Estimate the percent decrease in the number of vehicles produced from 1999 to 2008. 56%

17. Unemployment and Inflation The following time-series plot shows the annual unemployment and inflation rates for the years 1988 through 2010.

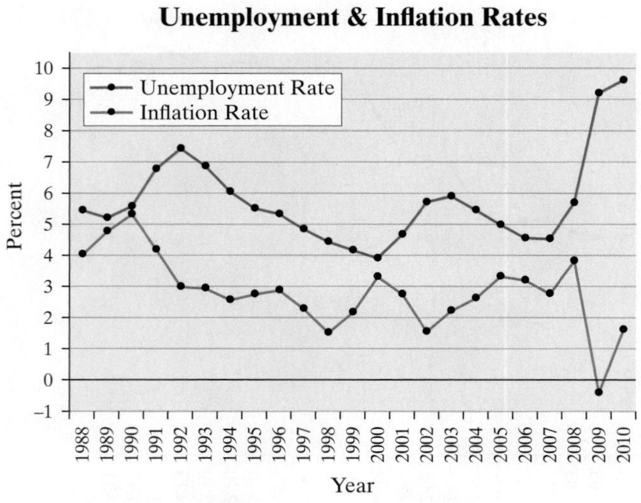

Source: www.miseryindex.us

(a) Estimate the unemployment and inflation rates for 1992.
(b) Estimate the unemployment and inflation rates for 2009.
(c) The misery index is defined as the sum of the unemployment rate and the inflation rate. Use your results from (a) and (b) to estimate the misery index for the years 1992 and 2009. (a) 7.5%; 3.0% (b) 9.2%; −0.4% (c) 10.5%; 8.8%
(d) Describe any relationship that might exist between the unemployment rate and inflation rate over the time period shown.

18. Prize Money at Wimbledon The following time-series plot shows the prize money (in pounds) awarded at the Wimbledon Tennis Championship to the winners of the men's singles and ladies' singles competitions from 1995 through 2011.

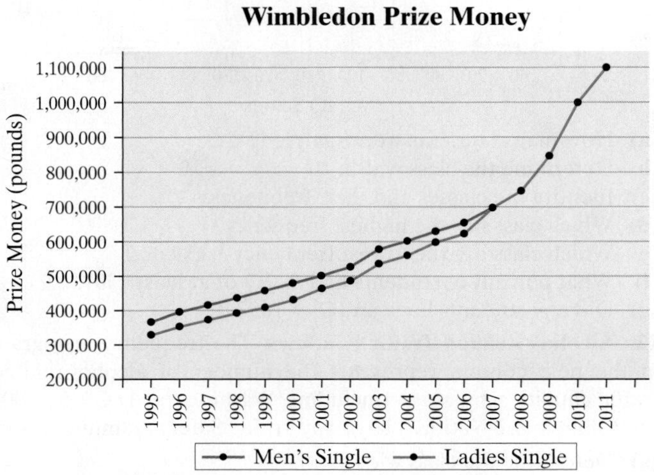

Source: www.wimbledon.org

(a) Estimate the prize money awarded to each for men's and ladies' singles in 1996. £400,000; £350,000
(b) Estimate the prize money awarded to each for men's and ladies' singles in 2006. £655,000; £625,000
(c) Describe any relationship that might exist between the prize money awarded for men's and ladies' singles over the time period shown.
(d) Use the graph to determine what happened for the first time in 2007. Estimate the prize money awarded for each championship in 2007.
(e) Estimate the percent increase in prize money awarded to each for men's and ladies' singles from 2010 to 2011. 10%

12. (d) Equal prize money was awarded; £700,000 each

APPLYING THE CONCEPTS

19. Predicting School Enrollment To predict future enrollment, a local school district wants to know the number of children in the district under the age of 5. Fifty households within the district were sampled, and the head of household was asked to disclose the number of children under the age of 5 living in the household. The results of the survey are presented in the following table.

Number of Children under 5	Number of Households
0	16
1	18
2	12
3	3
4	1

(a) Construct a relative frequency distribution of the data.
(b) What percentage of households has two children under the age of 5? 24%
(c) What percentage of households has one or two children under the age of 5? 60%

20. Free Throws A basketball player habitually makes 70% of her free throws. In an experiment, a researcher asks this basketball player to record the number of free throws she shoots until she misses. The experiment is repeated 50 times. The following table lists the distribution of the number of free throws attempted until a miss is recorded.

Number of Free Throws until a Miss	Frequency
1	16
2	11
3	9
4	7
5	2
6	3
7	0
8	1
9	0
10	1

(a) Construct a relative frequency distribution of the data.
(b) What percentage of the time did she first miss on her fourth free throw? 14%
(c) What percentage of the time did she first miss the tenth free throw? 2%
(d) What percentage of the time did she make at least five in a row? 10%

In Problems 21–24, determine the original set of data.

21.
1|0 1 4
2|1 4 4 7 9
3|3 5 5 5 7 7 8
4|0 0 1 2 6 6 8 9 9
5|3 3 5 8
6|1 2

Legend: 1|0 represents 10

22.
24|0 4 7
25|2 2 3 9 9
26|3 4 5 8 8 9
27|0 1 1 3 6 6
28|2 3 8

Legend: 24|0 represents 240

23.
1|2 4 6
2|1 4 7 7 9
3|3 3 3 5 7 7 8
4|0 1 1 3 6 6 8 8 9
5|3 4 5 8
6|2 4

Legend: 1|2 represents 1.2

24.
12|3 7 9 9
13|0 4 5 7 8 9 9
14|2 4 4 7 7 8 9
15|1 2 2 5 6
16|0 3

Legend: 12|3 represents 12.3

In Problems 25–28, find (a) the number of classes, (b) the class limits, and (c) the class width. 21. (a) 8 (c) $25

25. Tuition The following data represent the tuition for all 2-year public community colleges in California in 2009–2010.

Tuition (dollars)	Number of Community Colleges
775–799	22
800–824	68
825–849	15
850–874	5
875–899	0
900–924	0
925–949	0
950–974	1

Source: Chronicle of Higher Education

26. Earthquakes The following data represent the number of earthquakes worldwide in 2010 with magnitudes less than 9.0 (as of October 15, 2010). (a) 9 (c) 1.0

Magnitude	Number
0–0.9	22
1.0–1.9	22
2.0–2.9	3201
3.0–3.9	3332
4.0–4.9	7276
5.0–5.9	1430
6.0–6.9	130
7.0–7.9	18
8.0–8.9	1

Source: U.S. Geological Survey, Earthquake Hazards Program

27. Live Births The following data represent the number of live births in the United States in 2007 for women 15 to 49 years old. (a) 7 (c) 5

Age	Live Births
15–19	445,045
20–24	1,082,837
25–29	1,208,405
30–34	962,179
35–39	499,916
40–44	105,071
45–49	7,349

Source: National Center for Health Statistics

28. Community College Enrollments The following data represent the fall 2009 student headcount enrollments for all public community colleges in the state of Illinois. (a) 6 (c) 5000

Number of Students Enrolled	Number of Community Colleges
0–4,999	17
5,000–9,999	18
10,000–14,999	7
15,000–19,999	5
20,000–24,999	0
25,000–29,999	1

Source: Illinois Board of Higher Education

In Problems 29–32, construct (a) a relative frequency distribution, (b) a frequency histogram, and (c) a relative frequency histogram for the given data. Then answer the questions that follow.

29. Using the data in Problem 25, what percentage of California community colleges have tuition below \$800? What percentage of California community colleges have tuition of \$850 or more? 19.82%; 5.4%

30. Using the data in Problem 26, what percentage of earthquakes registered 4.0 to 4.9? What percentage of earthquakes registered 4.9 or less? 47.15%; 89.77%

31. Using the data in Problem 27, what percentage of live births was to women 40 to 44 years old? What percentage of live births was to women 24 years or younger? 2.44%; 35.44%

32. Using the data in Problem 28, what percentage of public community colleges in Illinois enrolled between 5000 and 9999 students? What percentage of public community colleges in Illinois enrolled 15,000 or more students? 37.5%; 12.5%

NW **33. Televisions in the Household** A researcher with A. C. Nielsen wanted to determine the number of televisions in households. He conducts a survey of 40 randomly selected households and obtains the following data.

1	1	4	2	3	3	5	1
1	2	2	4	1	1	0	3
1	2	2	1	3	1	1	3
2	3	2	2	1	2	3	2
1	2	2	2	2	1	3	1

Source: Based on data from the U.S. Department of Energy

(a) Are these data discrete or continuous? Explain. Discrete
(b) Construct a frequency distribution of the data.
(c) Construct a relative frequency distribution of the data.
(d) What percentage of households in the survey have 3 televisions? 20%
(e) What percentage of households in the survey have 4 or more televisions? 7.5%
(f) Construct a frequency histogram of the data.
(g) Construct a relative frequency histogram of the data.
(h) Describe the shape of the distribution. Skewed right

34. Waiting The following data represent the number of customers waiting for a table at 6:00 P.M. for 40 consecutive Saturdays at Bobak's Restaurant.

11	5	11	3	6	8	6	7
4	5	13	9	6	4	14	11
13	10	9	6	8	10	9	5
10	8	7	3	8	8	7	8
7	9	10	4	8	6	11	8

34. (a) Discrete

(a) Are these data discrete or continuous? Explain.
(b) Construct a frequency distribution of the data.
(c) Construct a relative frequency distribution of the data.
(d) What percentage of the Saturdays had 10 or more customers waiting for a table at 6:00 P.M.? 27.5%
(e) What percentage of the Saturdays had 5 or fewer customers waiting for a table at 6:00 P.M.? 20%
(f) Construct a frequency histogram of the data.
(g) Construct a relative frequency histogram of the data.
(h) Describe the shape of the distribution. Symmetric

NW **35. Average Income** The following data represent the per capita (average) disposable income (income after taxes) for the 50 states and the District of Columbia in 2009.

30,103	33,096	35,507	37,916	41,344	43,874
30,875	33,725	35,667	38,081	41,411	45,705
31,632	33,786	35,676	38,503	41,552	46,957
31,799	34,004	36,484	38,578	41,751	48,285
31,883	34,025	36,745	39,530	42,009	49,875
31,946	34,089	36,751	39,578	42,325	50,313
32,219	34,453	36,822	39,817	42,603	54,397
32,935	35,268	36,935	41,003	42,831	66,000
32,992	35,381	37,780			

Source: U.S. Bureau of Economic Analysis, March 2010

With the first class having a lower class limit of 30,000 and a class width of 6000:

(a) Construct a frequency distribution.
(b) Construct a relative frequency distribution.
(c) Construct a frequency histogram of the data.
(d) Construct a relative frequency histogram of the data.
(e) Describe the shape of the distribution. Skewed right
(f) Repeat parts (a)–(e) using a class width of 3000.
(g) Does one frequency distribution provide a better summary of the data than the other? Explain.

36. Uninsured Rates The following data represent the percentage of people without health insurance for the 50 states and the District of Columbia in 2009.

4.2	10.6	12.6	14.8	17.8	18.9	21.4
8.6	10.6	13.0	15.5	18.1	19.4	22.2
9.2	10.9	13.3	15.9	18.3	19.6	25.0
9.6	10.9	13.4	15.9	18.3	19.7	
9.6	11.3	13.9	16.1	18.4	20.6	
9.7	11.4	14.0	16.1	18.4	21.1	
10.2	11.6	14.3	16.1	18.6	21.2	
10.5	12.3	14.7	16.2	18.7	21.3	

Source: Gallup

With the first class having a lower class limit of 4 and a class width of 2:

(a) Construct a frequency distribution.
(b) Construct a relative frequency distribution.
(c) Construct a frequency histogram of the data.
(d) Construct a relative frequency histogram of the data.
(e) Describe the shape of the distribution. Symmetric
(f) Repeat parts (a)–(e) using a class width of 4.
(g) Does one frequency distribution provide a better summary of the data than the other? Explain.

37. Cigarette Tax Rates The table shows the tax, in dollars, on a pack of cigarettes in each of the 50 states and Washington, DC, as of September 2010. **Note:** The state with the lowest tax is Virginia and the state with the highest tax is New York.

3.025	1.18	0.87	1.70	0.57
0.80	2.00	1.70	0.60	0.44
1.53	1.56	2.52	0.64	0.84
1.66	1.41	1.03	0.79	1.36
0.17	1.15	0.36	0.68	0.62
0.60	0.98	2.00	1.25	0.995
1.60	4.35	2.00	0.55	0.30
0.45	0.57	0.37	0.425	1.339
1.78	2.24	2.51	3.46	3.00
2.70	1.60	2.00	2.50	2.00
3.00				

Source: Bureaus of Alcohol, Tobacco, Firearms, and Explosives

With a first class having a lower class limit of 0 and a class width of 0.50:

(a) Construct a frequency distribution.
(b) Construct a relative frequency distribution.
(c) Construct a frequency histogram of the data.
(d) Construct a relative frequency histogram of the data.
(e) Describe the shape of the distribution. Skewed right
(f) Repeat parts (a)–(e) using a class width of 1.
(g) Does one frequency distribution provide a better summary of the data than the other? Explain.

38. Dividend Yield A dividend is a payment from a publicly traded company to its shareholders. The dividend yield of a stock is determined by dividing the annual dividend of a stock by its price. The following data represent the dividend yields (in percent) of a random sample of 28 publicly traded stocks of companies with a value of at least $5 billion.

1.7	0	1.15	0.62	1.06	2.45	2.38
2.83	2.16	1.05	1.22	1.68	0.89	0
2.59	0	1.7	0.64	0.67	2.07	0.94
2.04	0	0	1.35	0	0	0.41

Source: Yahoo! Finance

With the first class having a lower class limit of 0 and a class width of 0.40:

(a) Construct a frequency distribution.
(b) Construct a relative frequency distribution.
(c) Construct a frequency histogram of the data.
(d) Construct a relative frequency histogram of the data.
(e) Describe the shape of the distribution. Skewed right
(f) Repeat parts (a)–(e) using a class width of 0.8.
(g) Which frequency distribution seems to provide a better summary of the data?

NW **39. Violent Crimes** Violent crimes include murder, forcible rape, robbery, and aggravated assault. The following data represent the violent-crime rate (crimes per 100,000 population) by state plus the District of Columbia in 2009.

449.8	1345.9	400.1	281.3	384.7	670.8	296.5
633.0	612.5	258.7	491.8	404.3	185.6	257.0
408.3	426.1	620.0	253.6	200.7	667.7	228.2
517.7	274.8	119.8	281.6	332.1	490.9	
472.0	228.4	589.9	702.2	501.1	212.7	
337.8	497.2	457.1	159.6	254.7	131.4	
298.7	333.2	497.0	311.5	380.5	226.8	
636.6	279.2	243.9	619.0	252.6	331.0	

Source: Federal Bureau of Investigation

(a) If thirteen classes are to be formed, choose an appropriate lower class limit for the first class and a class width.
(b) Construct a frequency distribution.
(c) Construct a relative frequency distribution.
(d) Construct a frequency histogram of the data.
(e) Construct a relative frequency histogram of the data.
(f) Describe the shape of the distribution. Skewed right

40. Volume of Altria Group Stock The volume of a stock is the number of shares traded on a given day. The following data, in millions, so that 6.42 represents 6,420,000 shares traded, represent the volume of Altria Group stock traded for a random sample of 35 trading days in 2010.

6.42	23.59	18.91	7.85	7.76
8.51	9.05	14.83	14.43	8.55
6.37	10.30	10.16	10.90	11.20
13.57	9.13	7.83	15.32	14.05
7.84	7.88	17.10	16.58	7.68
7.69	10.22	10.49	8.41	7.85
10.94	20.15	8.97	15.39	8.32

Source: TD Ameritrade

(a) If six classes are to be formed, choose an appropriate lower class limit for the first class and a class width.
(b) Construct a frequency distribution.
(c) Construct a relative frequency distribution.
(d) Construct a frequency histogram of the data.
(e) Construct a relative frequency histogram of the data.
(f) Describe the shape of the distribution. Skewed right

In Problems 41–44, (a) construct a stem-and-leaf plot and (b) describe the shape of the distribution.

NW 41. Age at Inauguration The following data represent the ages of the presidents of the United States (from George Washington through Barack Obama) on their first days in office.

Note: President Cleveland's age is listed twice, 47 and 55, because he is historically counted as two different presidents, numbers 22 and 24, since his terms were not consecutive.

42	47	50	52	54	55	57	61	64
43	48	51	52	54	56	57	61	65
46	49	51	54	55	56	57	61	68
46	49	51	54	55	56	58	62	69
47	50	51	54	55	57	60	64	

Source: factmonster.com

42. Divorce Rates The following data represent the divorce rate (per 1000 population) for most states in the United States in the year 2006. (b) Slightly skewed right

Note: The list includes the District of Columbia, but excludes California, Georgia, Hawaii, Indiana, Louisiana, and Oklahoma because of failure to report.

4.8	4.5	3.3	4.7	3.0	5.3	4.3	4.7
4.4	2.1	5.1	3.9	4.3	3.9	3.3	2.9
3.9	4.9	3.6	3.6	2.9	2.2	3.8	5.4
5.7	5.1	3.0	3.5	4.1	2.9	3.5	
4.4	2.5	2.3	6.7	2.6	3.0	4.1	
2.8	2.7	3.5	4.0	3.6	3.2	3.8	

Source: U.S. Census Bureau

43. Grams of Fat in a McDonald's Breakfast The following data represent the number of grams of fat in breakfast meals offered at McDonald's. (b) Bell shaped

12	22	27	3	25	30
32	37	27	31	11	16
21	32	22	46	51	55
59	16	36	30	9	24

Source: McDonald's Corporation, *McDonald's USA Nutrition Facts*, November 2007

44. Gasoline Mileages The following data represent the number of miles per gallon achieved on the highway for small cars for the model year 2011. (b) Bell shaped

35	34	35	34	36	35	38	37	40
35	34	34	36	29	36	43	36	34
36	34	36	35	33	33	29	28	25
35	36	37	36	35	30	36	34	36
34	32	32	31	31	33	33	33	33
31	30	25	23	22	34	31	30	28
34	34	31	33	32	31	31	33	33
27	26	25	23	35	34	32	33	32
30	36	35	33	31	42	42	34	31
33	29	29	30					

Source: fueleconomy.gov

45. Electric Rates The following data represent the average retail prices for electricity (cents/kWh) in 2010 for the 50 states plus the District of Columbia.

17.33	10.48	8.68	9.41	8.83	6.69	6.52
12.29	9.58	8.86	13.12	8.81	7.47	15.39
14.46	7.47	8.11	8.63	7.84	10.23	25.33
14.63	10.42	7.70	8.58	7.62	8.96	
14.56	9.35	8.14	8.78	8.07	7.58	
13.17	9.97	12.34	7.14	9.77	6.12	
15.65	7.81	13.89	9.17	10.52	14.41	
17.15	8.62	10.72	6.87	9.98	7.69	

Source: Energy Information Administration

(a) Round each observation to the nearest tenth of a cent and draw a stem-and-leaf plot.
(b) Describe the shape of the distribution. Skewed right
(c) Hawaii has the highest retail price for electricity. What is Hawaii's average retail price for electricity? Why might Hawaii's rate be so much higher than the others? 25.33 cents/kWh

46. Home Appreciation The following data represent the price appreciation in home values between the first quarter of 1991 and the second quarter of 2010 for homes in each of the 50 states plus the District of Columbia. **Note:** The best price appreciation was in the District of Columbia and the worst was in Nevada.

68.46	99.81	93.50	221.93	120.72	121.22	96.94
118.06	85.59	96.32	130.62	94.11	111.69	169.79
90.98	89.35	87.32	122.58	192.78	80.10	92.51
58.80	91.65	124.09	126.33	58.76	202.46	87.13
117.69	118.64	74.86	70.56	90.17	88.89	112.50
180.13	79.53	108.43	137.86	85.78	161.76	85.30
119.34	97.87	48.66	106.23	84.64	33.36	90.50
89.36	111.39					

Source: Federal Housing Finance Agency

(a) Round each observation to the nearest whole number and draw a stem-and-leaf plot.

(b) Describe the shape of the distribution.

(c) Do you think the stem-and-leaf plot does a good job of visually summarizing the data, or would you recommend a different graphical representation of the data? If you recommend a different graph, which would you recommend? Why?

NW **47. Violent Crimes** Use the violent crime rate data from Problem 39 to answer each of the following:

(a) Round the data to the nearest ten (for example, round 449.8 as 450).

(b) Draw a stem-and-leaf plot, treating the hundreds position as the stem and the tens position as the leaf (so that 4|3 represents 430).

(c) Redraw the stem-and-leaf plot using split stems.

(d) In your opinion, which of these plots better summarizes the data? Why?

In Problems 48 and 49, we compare data sets. A great way to compare two data sets is through back-to-back stem-and-leaf plots. The figure represents the number of grams of fat in 20 sandwiches served at McDonald's and 20 sandwiches served at Burger King.

Fat (g) in Fast Food Sandwiches

McDonald's		Burger King
9 8	0	7
9 8 7 6 6 4 2 0	1	2 2 3 6 6 7
9 8 8 6 6 4 3 3 1	2	1 2 9
	3	0 3 9 9
2	4	4 7
	5	4 7
	6	5 8

Legend: 8 |0|7 represents 8 g of fat for McDonald's and 7 g of fat for Burger King

Source: McDonald's Corporation, *McDonald's USA Nutrition Facts,* November 2007; Burger King Corporation, *Nutritional Information,* October 2007

48. Academy Award Winners The following data represent the ages on the ceremony date of the Academy Award winners for Best Actor and Best Actress in a leading role for the 33 years from 1977 to 2009.

Best Actor Ages

30	40	42	37	76	39	50
53	45	36	62	43	51	48
32	42	54	52	37	38	60
32	45	60	46	40	36	
47	29	43	37	38	45	

Best Actress Ages

32	41	33	31	74	33	32
49	38	61	21	41	26	33
80	42	29	33	36	45	45
49	39	34	26	25	33	
35	35	28	30	29	61	

(a) Construct a back-to-back stem-and-leaf plot.

(b) Compare the two populations. What can you conclude from the back-to-back stem-and-leaf plot?

49. Home Run Distances In 1998, Mark McGwire of the St. Louis Cardinals set the record for the most home runs hit in a season by hitting 70 home runs. Three years later in 2001, Barry Bonds of the San Francisco Giants broke McGwire's record by hitting 73 home runs. The following data represent the distances, in feet, of each player's home runs in his record-setting season.

(a) Construct a back-to-back stem-and-leaf plot.

(b) Compare the two populations. What can you conclude from the back-to-back stem-and-leaf plot?

Mark McGwire

360	370	370	430	420	340	460
410	440	410	380	360	350	527
380	550	478	420	390	420	425
370	480	390	430	388	423	410
360	410	450	350	450	430	461
430	470	440	400	390	510	430
450	452	420	380	470	398	409
385	369	460	390	510	500	450
470	430	458	380	430	341	385
410	420	380	400	440	377	370

Barry Bonds

420	417	440	410	390	417	420
410	380	430	370	420	400	360
410	420	391	416	440	410	415
436	430	410	400	390	420	410
420	410	410	450	320	430	380
375	375	347	380	429	320	360
375	370	440	400	405	430	350
396	410	380	430	415	380	375
400	435	420	420	488	361	394
410	411	365	360	440	435	454
442	404	385				

50. StatCrunch Survey Choose a discrete quantitative variable from the Sullivan StatCrunch survey data set and obtain an appropriate graphical summary of the variable.

51. StatCrunch Survey Choose a continuous quantitative variable from the Sullivan StatCrunch survey data set and obtain an appropriate graphical summary of the variable.

52. StatCrunch Survey Draw a dot plot of the variable "ideal number of children" from the Sullivan StatCrunch survey data set. Now draw a dot plot of the variable "ideal number of children" from the Sullivan StatCrunch survey data set by "gender." Do there appear to be any differences in the ideal number of children for males and females? Is there a better graph that could be drawn to make the comparison easier?

NW **53. Televisions in the Household** Draw a dot plot of the televisions per household data from Problem 33.

54. Waiting Draw a dot plot of the waiting data from Problem 34.

NW **55. Walt Disney Company** The following data represent the stock price for the Walt Disney Company at the end of each month in 2010. Construct a time-series plot and comment on any trends. What was the percent change in the stock price of Disney from January 2010 to December 2010? 30.7%

Date	Closing Price	Date	Closing Price
1/10	28.71	7/10	30.72
2/10	28.99	8/10	31.55
3/10	31.34	9/10	32.68
4/10	35.01	10/10	36.13
5/10	31.00	11/10	36.51
6/10	31.36	12/10	37.51

Source: TD Ameritrade

56. Google, Inc. The following data represent the closing stock price for Google, Inc. at the end of each year since it first went public in 2004 until the end of 2010. Construct a time-series plot and comment on any trends. What was the percent change in Google stock from 2009 to 2010? −4.2%

Date	Closing Price	Date	Closing Price
2004	192.79	2008	307.65
2005	414.86	2009	619.98
2006	460.48	2010	593.97
2007	691.48		

Source: TD Ameritrade

57. Federal Debt The following data represent the percentage of total federal debt as a percentage of gross domestic product (GDP). The GDP of a country is the total value of all goods and services produced within the country in a given year. Construct a time-series plot and comment on any trends.

Year	Debt as % of GDP	Year	Debt as % of GDP
1991	61.17	2001	56.46
1992	64.09	2002	58.52
1993	66.17	2003	60.88
1994	66.23	2004	62.18
1995	67.08	2005	62.77
1996	66.66	2006	63.49
1997	64.97	2007	63.99
1998	62.84	2008	69.15
1999	60.47	2009	83.29
2000	57.02	2010	94.27

Source: http://www.usgovernmentspending.com/federal_debt_chart.html

58. College Enrollment The data in the next column represent the percentage of 18- to 24-year-olds enrolled in college. Construct a time-series plot and comment on any trends.

Year	Percent Enrolled	Year	Percent Enrolled
1991	33.3	2000	35.5
1992	34.4	2001	36.3
1993	34.0	2002	36.7
1994	34.6	2003	37.8
1995	34.3	2004	38.0
1996	35.5	2005	38.9
1997	36.8	2006	37.3
1998	36.5	2007	38.8
1999	35.6	2008	39.6

Source: U.S. Center for Education Statistics

59. Putting It Together: Time Viewing a Web Page Nielsen/NetRatings is an Internet media and market research firm. One variable they measure is the amount of time an individual spends viewing a specific Web page. The following data represent the amount of time, in seconds, a random sample of 40 surfers spent viewing a Web page. Decide on an appropriate graphical summary and create the graphical summary. Write a few sentences that describe the data. Be sure to include in your description any interesting features the data may exhibit.

19	86	27	42	11	12	13	5
27	20	83	4	69	10	12	65
15	26	75	27	19	31	23	14
111	185	51	51	156	48	16	81
9	73	45	27	104	257	40	114

Source: Based on information provided by Nielsen/NetRatings

60. Putting It Together: Which Graphical Summary? Suppose you just obtained data from a survey in which you learned the following information about 50 individuals: age, income, marital status, number of vehicles in household. For each variable, explain the type of graphical summary you might be able to draw to provide a visual summary of the data.

61. Putting It Together: Shark! The following two graphics represent the number of reported shark attacks worldwide since 1900 and the worldwide fatality rate of shark attacks since 1900. Write a report about the trends in the graphs. In your report discuss the apparent contradiction between the increase in shark attacks, but the decrease in fatality rate.

Unprovoked Shark Attacks Worldwide

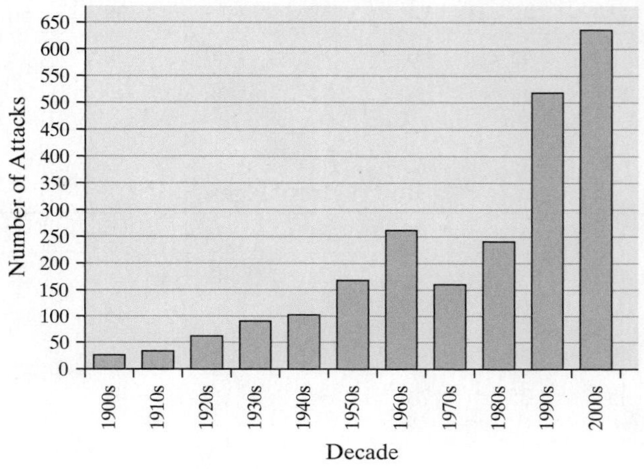

Worldwide Shark Attack Fatality Rate, 1900–2009

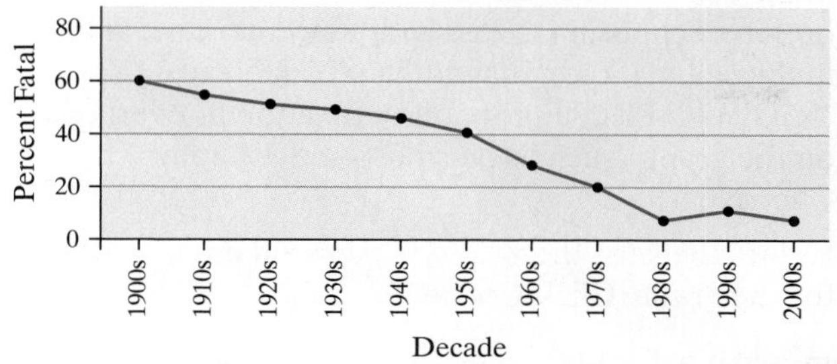

Source: Florida Museum of Natural History

EXPLAINING THE CONCEPTS

62. Why shouldn't classes overlap when summarizing continuous data in a frequency or relative frequency distribution?

63. Discuss the advantages and disadvantages of histograms versus stem-and-leaf plots.

64. Is there such a thing as the correct choice for a class width? Is there such a thing as a poor choice for a class width? Explain your reasoning.

65. Describe the situations in which it is preferable to use relative frequencies over frequencies when summarizing quantitative data.

66. StatCrunch Choose any data set that has at least 50 observations of a quantitative variable (you may choose a variable from the Sullivan Statistics survey if you like). In StatCrunch, open the "Histogram with Sliders" applet. Adjust the bin width and starting point of the histogram. Can the choice of bin width (class width) affect the shape of the histogram? Explain.

67. Sketch four histograms—one skewed right, one skewed left, one bell-shaped, and one uniform. Label each histogram according to its shape. What makes a histogram skewed left? Skewed right? Symmetric?

68. What type of variable is required when drawing a time-series plot? Why do we draw time-series plots?

68. Quantitative; to see trends

Technology Step-By-Step

Drawing Histograms, Stem-and-Leaf Plots, and Dot Plots

TI-83/84 Plus

Histograms

1. Enter the raw data in L1 by pressing STAT and selecting `1: Edit`.
2. Press 2nd Y = to access the StatPlot menu. Select `1: Plot1`.
3. Place the cursor on "ON" and press ENTER.
4. Place the cursor on the histogram icon (see the figure) and press ENTER. Press 2nd QUIT to exit Plot 1 menu.

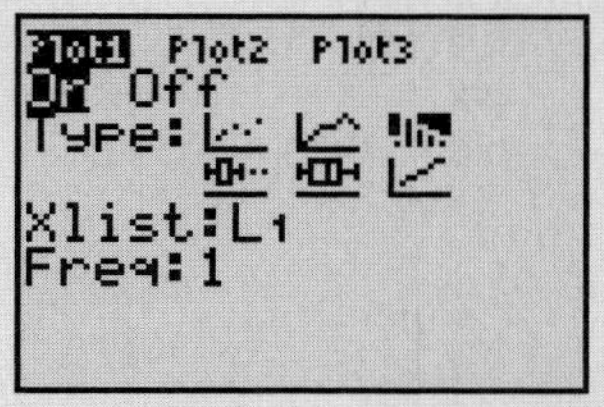

5. Press WINDOW. Set Xmin to the lower class limit of the first class. Set Xmax to the lower class limit of the class following the class containing the largest value. For example, if the first class is 0–9, set Xmin to 0. If the class width is 10 and the last class is 90–99, set Xmax to 100. Set Xscl to the class width. Set Ymin to 0. Set Ymax to a value larger than the frequency of the class with the highest frequency.
6. Press GRAPH.
   Helpful Hints: To determine each class frequency, press TRACE and use the arrow keys to scroll through each class. If you decrease the value of Ymin to a value such as −5, you can see the values displayed on the screen easier. The TI graphing calculators do not draw stem-and-leaf plots or dot plots.

MINITAB

Histograms

1. Enter the raw data in C1.
2. Select the **Graph** menu and highlight **Histogram**...
3. Highlight the "simple" icon and press OK.
4. Put the cursor in the "Graph variables" box. Highlight C1 and press Select. Click SCALE and select the Y-Scale Type tab. For a frequency histogram, click the frequency radio button. For a relative frequency histogram, click the percent radio button. Click OK twice.

Note: To adjust the class width and to change the labels on the horizontal axis to the lower class limit, double-click inside one of the bars in the histogram. Select the "binning" tab in the window that opens. Click the cutpoint button and the midpoint/cutpoint positions radio button. In the midpoint/cutpoint box, enter the lower class limits of each class. Click OK.

Stem-and-Leaf Plots

1. With the raw data entered in C1, select the **Graph** menu and highlight **Stem-and-Leaf**.
2. Select the data in C1 and press OK.

Dot Plots

1. Enter the raw data in C1.
2. Select the **Graph** menu and highlight **Dotplot.**
3. Highlight the "simple" icon and press OK.
4. Put the cursor in the "Graph variables" box. Highlight C1 and press Select. Click OK.

Excel

Histograms

1. Load the XLSTAT Add-in.
2. Enter the raw data in column A.
3. Select XLSTAT. Click Describing data, then select Histograms.
4. With the cursor in the Data cell, highlight the data in Column A.
5. Click either the Continuous or Discrete radio button.
6. Click the Options tab. Decide on either a certain number of intervals or enter your own lower class limits. To enter your own intervals, enter the lower class limits in Column B.
7. Click the Charts tab. Choose either Frequency or Relative Frequency. Click OK.

StatCrunch

Histograms

1. Enter the raw data into the spreadsheet. Name the column variable.
2. Select **Graphics** and highlight **Histogram**.
3. Click on the variable you wish to summarize and click Next>.
4. Choose the type of histogram (frequency or relative frequency) You have the option of choosing a lower class limit for the first class by entering a value in the cell marked "Start bins at:". You have the option of choosing a class width by entering a value in the cell marked "Binwidth:". Click Next>.
5. You could select a probability function to overlay on the graph (such as Normal—see Chapter 7). Click Next>.
6. Enter labels for the x- and y-axes, and enter a title for the graph. Click Create Graph!

Steam-and-Leaf Plots

1. Enter the raw data into the spreadsheet. Name the column variable.
2. Select **Graphics** and highlight **Stem and Leaf**.
3. Click on the variable you wish to summarize and click Next>.
4. Select None for Outlier trimming. Click Create Graph!

Dot Plots

1. Enter the raw data into the spreadsheet. Name the column variable.
2. Select **Graphics** and highlight **Dotplot**.
3. Click on the variable you wish to summarize and click Next>.
4. Enter labels for the x- and y-axes, and enter a title for the graph. Click Create Graph!

2.3 GRAPHICAL MISREPRESENTATIONS OF DATA

OBJECTIVE 1 Describe what can make a graph misleading or deceptive

1 Describe What Can Make a Graph Misleading or Deceptive

Statistics: The only science that enables different experts using the same figures to draw different conclusions.—EVAN ESAR

Note to Instructor

The material in this section can be omitted without loss of continuity. For those instructors who are pressed for time, it can be assigned for reading.

Often, statistics gets a bad rap for having the ability to manipulate data to support any position. One method of distorting the truth is through graphics. We mentioned in Section 2.1 how visual displays send more powerful messages than raw data or even tables of data. Since graphics are so powerful, care must be taken in constructing graphics and in interpreting their messages. Graphics may *mislead* or *deceive*. We will call graphs misleading if they unintentionally create an incorrect impression. We consider graphs deceptive if they purposely create an incorrect impression. In either case, a reader's incorrect impression can have serious consequences. Therefore, it is important to be able to recognize misleading and deceptive graphs.

Note to Instructor

Consider assigning the "Recognizing and Correcting Misleading Graphs" activity from the Student Activity Workbook.

The most common graphical misrepresentations of data involve the scale of the graph, an inconsistent scale, or a misplaced origin. Increments between tick marks should be constant, and scales for comparative graphs should be the same. Also, because readers usually assume that the baseline, or zero point, is at the bottom of the graph, a graph that begins at a higher or lower value can be misleading.

EXAMPLE 1 Misrepresentation of Data

Problem A home security company's summer ad campaign had the slogan "When you leave for vacation, burglars leave for work." According to the FBI, roughly 18% of home burglaries in 2009 occurred during the peak vacation months of July and August. The advertisement contains the graph shown in Figure 19. Explain what is wrong with the graphic.

Approach We need to find any characteristics that may mislead a reader, such as inconsistent scales or poorly defined categories.

Solution Let's consider how the categories of data are defined. The sum of the percentages (the relative frequencies) over all 12 months should be 1. Because $10(0.082) + 0.18 = 1$, it is clear that the bar for Other Months represents an average percent for *each* month, while the bar for July–August represents the average percent for the months July and August *combined*. The unsuspecting reader is mislead into thinking that July and August each have a burglary rate of 18%.

Figure 20 gives a better picture of the burglary distribution. The increase during the months of July and August is not as dramatic as the bar graph in Figure 19 implies. In fact, Figure 19 would be considered deceitful because the security company is intentionally trying to convince consumers that July and August are much higher burglary months.

Figure 19

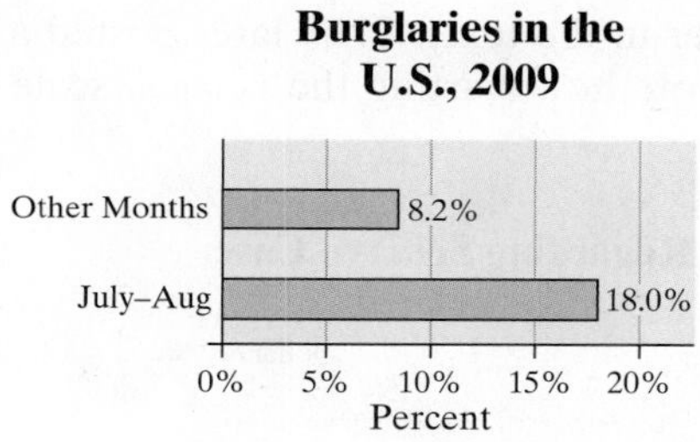

Figure 20

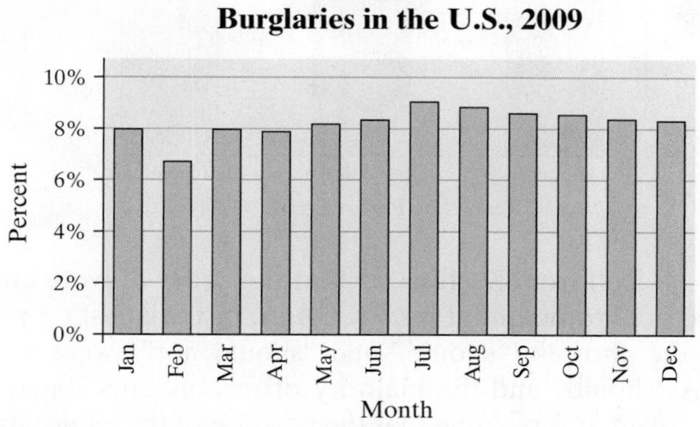

Source: FBI, Crime in the United States, 2009

Now Work Problem 5

EXAMPLE 2 Misrepresentation of Data by Manipulating the Vertical Scale

Problem In 2005, Terri Schiavo was the center of a right-to-die battle. At issue was whether her husband had the right to remove her feeding tube on which she had been dependent for 15 years. A CNN/USA Today/Gallup poll conducted March 18–20, 2005, asked respondents, "*As you may know, on Friday the feeding tube keeping Terri Schiavo alive was removed. Based on what you have heard or read about the case, do you think that the feeding tube should or should not have been removed?*" The results were presented in a graph similar to Figure 21. Explain what is wrong with the graphic.

Figure 21

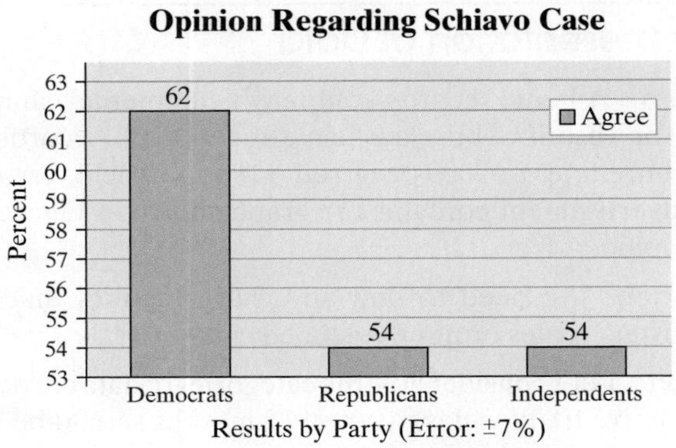

Approach We need to find any characteristics that may mislead a reader, such as manipulation of the vertical scale.

Solution The graphic suggests that Democrats supported the removal of the feeding tube much more than either Republicans or Independents. The vertical scale does not begin at 0, so it may appear that Democrats were 9 times more likely to support the decision (because the bar is 9 times as high as the others) when the difference is really only 8 percentage points. Note that the majority of each party sampled supported the decision. In addition, given a ±7 percentage point margin of error for each sample, the actual difference of 8 percentage points is not *statistically significant* (we will learn more about this later in the text). CNN later posted a corrected graphic similar to the one in Figure 22. Note how starting the vertical scale at 0 allows for a more accurate comparison.

Figure 22

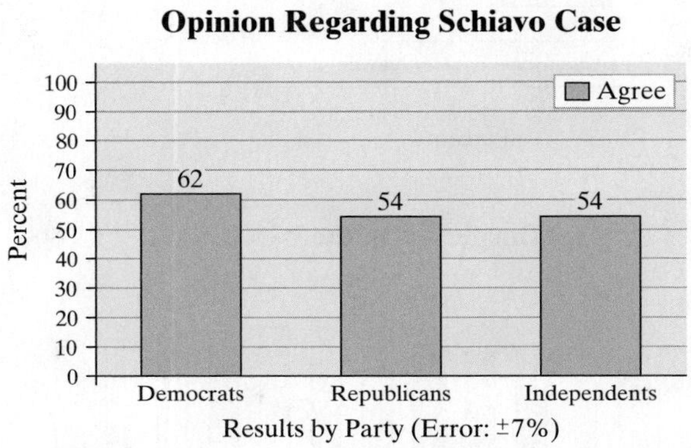

Recall from Section 1.5 that the order of words in a question can affect responses and lead to potential *response bias*. In the question presented in Example 2, the order of the choices ("should" and "should not") were not rotated. The first choice given was "should" and the majority of respondents stated that the feeding tube should be removed. It is possible that the position of the choice in the question could have affected the responses. A better way to present the question would be, "*As you may know, on Friday the feeding tube keeping Terri Schiavo alive was removed. Based on what you have heard or read about the case, do you [Rotated – agree (or) disagree] that the feeding tube should have been removed?*"

EXAMPLE 3 Misrepresentation of Data by Manipulating the Vertical Scale

Problem The time-series graph in Figure 23 depicts the average SAT math scores of college-bound seniors for the years 1991–2009. Why might this graph be considered misrepresentative?

Approach We need to find any characteristics that may mislead a reader, such as manipulation of the vertical scale.

Figure 23

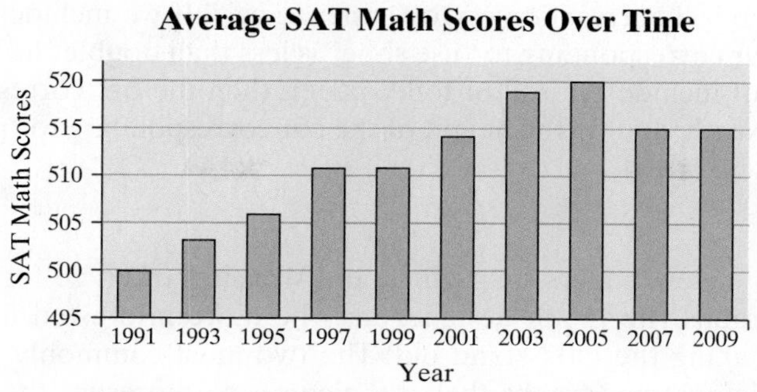

Source: College Board, College-Bound Seniors, 2009

Solution The graph may lead a reader to believe that SAT math scores have doubled or quadrupled since 1991 because the bar for 2009 is 4 times as tall as the bar for 1991. We notice in the figure that the vertical axis begins at 495 instead of the baseline of 200 (the minimum SAT math score). This type of scaling is common when the smallest observed data value is a rather large number. It is not necessarily done purposely to confuse or mislead the reader. Often, the main purpose in graphs (particularly time-series graphs) is to discover a trend, rather than the actual differences in the data. The trend is clearer in Figure 23 than in Figure 24, where the vertical axis begins at the baseline.

Remember that the goal of a good graph is to make the data stand out. When displaying time-series data, it is better to use a time-series plot to discover any trends. Also, instead of beginning the axis of a graph at 0 as in Figure 24, scales are frequently truncated so they begin at a value slightly less than the smallest value in the data set. There is nothing wrong with doing this, but care must be taken to make the reader aware of the scaling that is used. Figure 25 shows the proper construction of the graph of the SAT math scores, with the graph beginning at 495. The symbol ϟ indicates that the scale has been truncated and the graph has a gap. Notice that the lack of bars allows us to focus on the trend in the data, rather than the relative size (or area) of the bars.

Figure 24

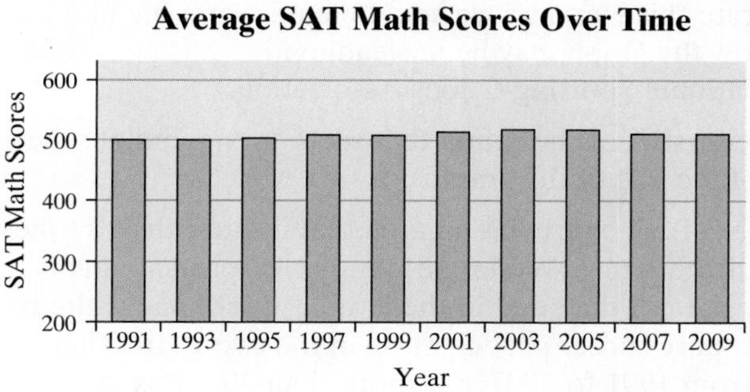

Figure 25

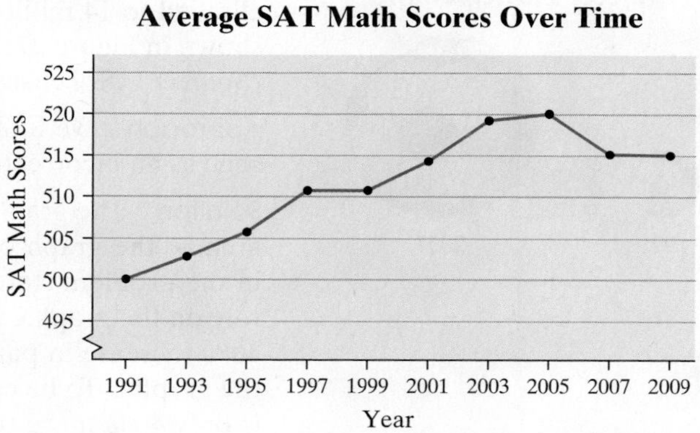

Now Work Problem 3

EXAMPLE 4 Misrepresentation of Data

Figure 26

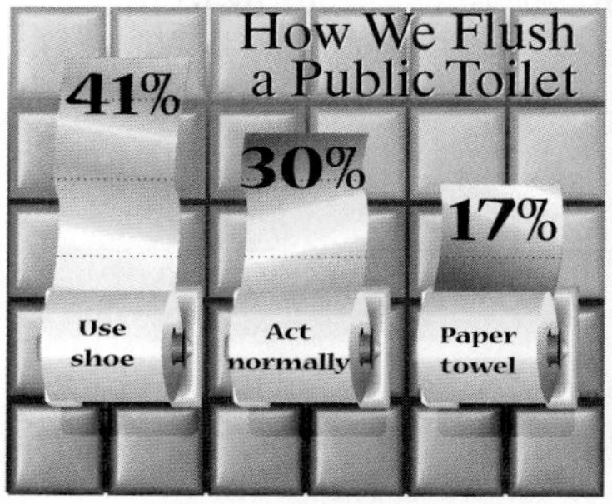

Problem The bar graph illustrated in Figure 26 is a *USA Today* type graph. A survey was conducted by Impulse Research for Quilted Northern Confidential in which individuals were asked how they would flush a toilet when the facilities are not sanitary. What's wrong with the graphic?

Approach We need to compare the vertical scales of each bar to see if they accurately depict the given percentages.

Solution First, it is unclear whether the bars include the roll of toilet paper or not. In either case, the roll corresponding to "use shoe" should be 2.4 (= 41/17) times taller than the roll corresponding to "paper towel." If we include the roll of toilet paper, then the bar corresponding to "use shoe" is less than double the height of "paper towel." If we do not include the roll of toilet paper, then the bar corresponding to "use shoe" is almost exactly double the height of the bar corresponding to "paper towel." The vertical scaling is incorrect.

Now Work Problem 11

Newspapers, magazines, and Websites often go for a "wow" factor when displaying graphs. The graph designer may be more interested in catching the reader's eye than making the data stand out. The two most commonly used tactics are 3-D graphs and pictograms (graphs that use pictures to represent the data). The use of 3-D effects is strongly discouraged, because such graphs are often difficult to read, add little value to the graph, and distract the reader from the data.

When comparing bars, our eyes are really comparing the *areas* of the bars. That is why we emphasized that the bars or classes should be of the same width. Uniform width ensures that the area of the bar is proportional to its height, so we can simply compare the heights of the bars. However, when we use two-dimensional pictures in place of bars, it is not possible to obtain a uniform width. To avoid distorting the picture when values increase or decrease, both the height and width of the picture must be adjusted. This often leads to misleading graphs.

EXAMPLE 5 Misleading Graphs

Problem Soccer continues to grow in popularity as a sport in the United States. High-profile players such as Mia Hamm and Landon Donovan have helped to generate renewed interest in the sport at various age levels. In 1991 there were approximately 10 million participants in the United States aged 7 years or older. By 2007 this number had climbed to 14 million. To illustrate this increase, we could create a graphic like the one shown in Figure 27. Describe how the graph may be misleading.
(*Source:* U.S. Census Bureau; National Sporting Goods Association.)

Figure 27

Approach We look for characteristics of the graph that seem to manipulate the facts, such as an incorrect depiction of the size of the graphics.

Solution The graph on the right of the figure has an area that is more than 4 times the area of the graph on the left of the figure. While the number of participants is given in the problem statement, they are not included in the graph, which makes the reader rely on the graphic alone to compare soccer participation in the two years. There was a 40% increase in participation from 1991 to 2007, not more than 300% as indicated by the graphic. To be correct, the graph on the right of the figure should have an area that is only 40% more than the area of the graph on the left of the figure. Adding the data values to the graphic would help reduce the chance of misinterpretation due to the oversized graph.

Now Work Problem 17

A variation on pictograms is to use a smaller picture repeatedly, with each picture representing a certain quantity. For example, we could present the data from Figure 27 by using a smaller soccer ball to represent 1 million participants. The resulting graphic is displayed in Figure 28. Note how the uniform size of the graphic allows us to make a more accurate comparison of the two quantities.

Figure 28

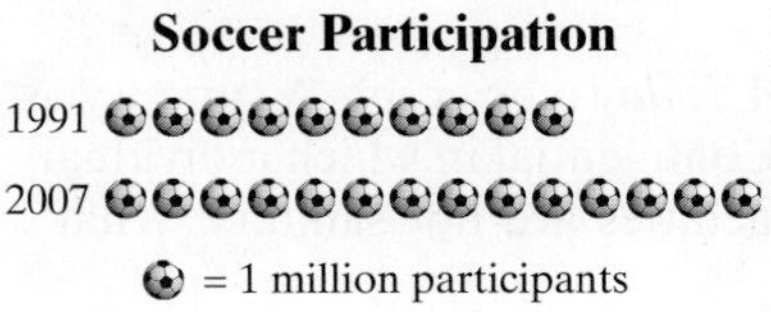

EXAMPLE 6 Misleading Graphs

Problem Figure 29 represents the number of active-duty military personnel in the United States as of May 2009. Describe how this graph is misleading. (*Source:* infoplease.com)

Figure 29

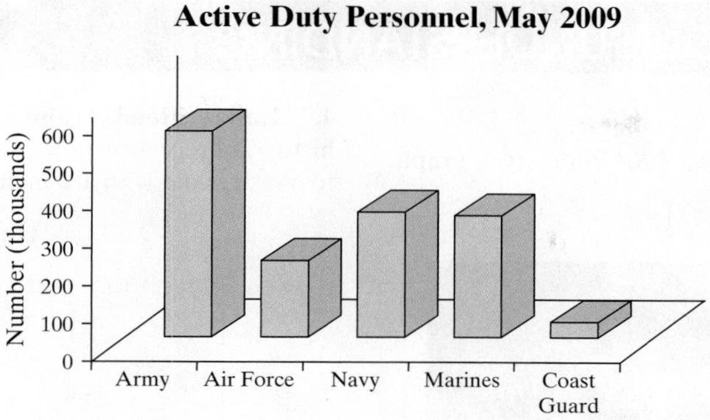

Approach Again, we look for characteristics of the graph that seem to distort the facts or distract the reader.

Solution The three-dimensional bar graph in the figure may draw the reader's attention, but the bars seem to stand out more than the data they represent. The perspective angle of the graph makes it difficult to estimate the data values being presented, resulting in estimates that are typically lower than the true values. This in turn makes comparing the data difficult. The only dimension that matters is bar height, so this is what should be emphasized. Figure 30 displays the same data in a two-dimensional bar graph. Which graphic is easier to read?

Figure 30

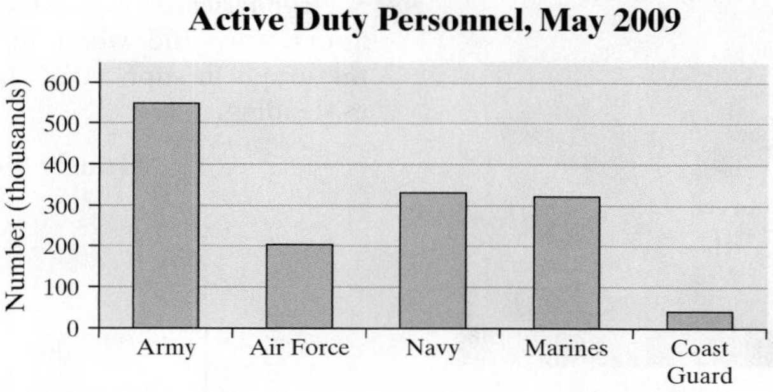

The material presented in this section is by no means all-inclusive. There are many ways to create graphs that mislead. Two popular texts written about ways that graphs mislead or deceive are *How to Lie with Statistics* (W. W. Norton & Company, Inc., 1982) by Darrell Huff and *The Visual Display of Quantitative Information* (Graphics Press, 2001) by Edward Tufte.

We conclude this section with some guidelines for constructing good graphics.

- Title and label the graphic axes clearly, providing explanations if needed. Include units of measurement and a data source when appropriate.
- Avoid distortion. Never lie about the data.
- Minimize the amount of white space in the graph. Use the available space to let the data stand out. If you truncate the scales, clearly indicate this to the reader.
- Avoid clutter, such as excessive gridlines and unnecessary backgrounds or pictures. Don't distract the reader.
- Avoid three dimensions. Three-dimensional charts may look nice, but they distract the reader and often lead to misinterpretation of the graphic.
- Do not use more than one design in the same graphic. Sometimes graphs use a different design in one portion of the graph to draw attention to that area. Don't try to force the reader to any specific part of the graph. Let the data speak for themselves.
- Avoid relative graphs that are devoid of data or scales.

2.3 ASSESS YOUR UNDERSTANDING

APPLYING THE CONCEPTS

1. **Inauguration Cost** The following is a *USA Today* type graph. Explain how it is misleading.

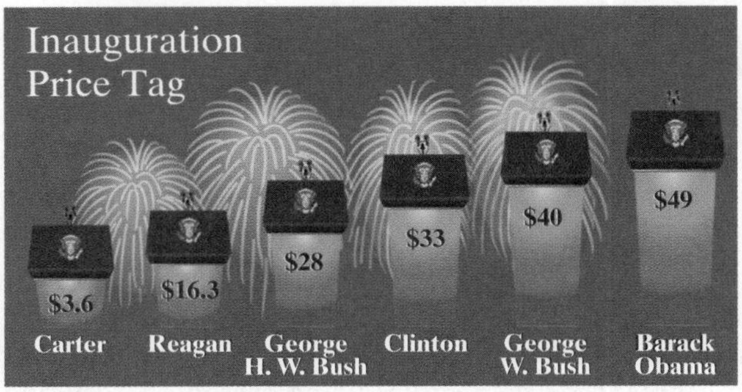

2. **Burning Calories** The following is a *USA Today* type graph.

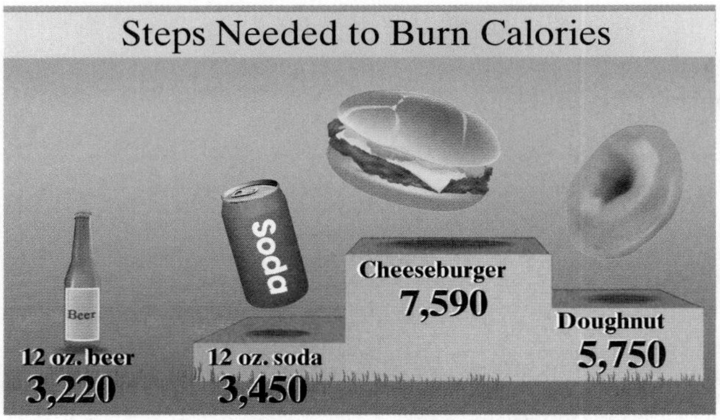

(a) Explain how it is misleading.
(b) What could be done to improve the graphic?

NW 3. **Median Earnings** The graph in the next column shows the median earnings for females from 2005 to 2009 in constant 2009 dollars.

(a) How is the bar graph misleading? What does the graph seem to convey?
(b) Redraw the graph so that it is not misleading. What does the new graph seem to convey?

Median Earnings for Females in Constant 2009 Dollars

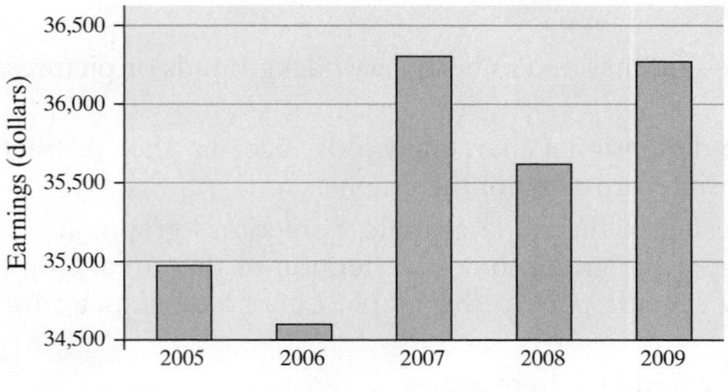

Source: U.S. Census Bureau

4. **Union Membership** The following relative frequency histogram represents the proportion of employed people aged 25 to 64 years old who are members of a union.

Union Membership

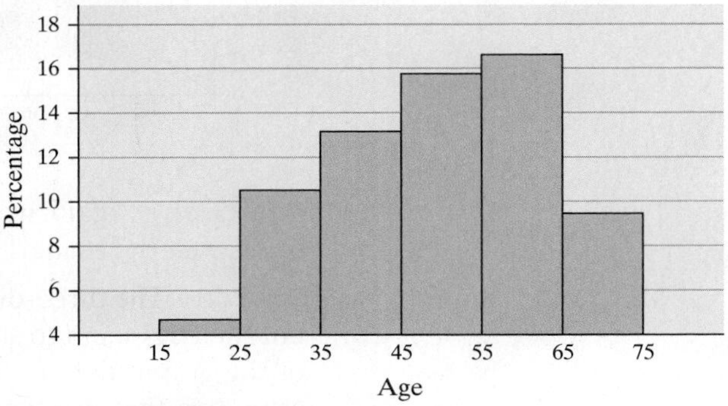

Source: U.S. Bureau of Labor Statistics

(a) Describe how this graph is misleading. What might a reader conclude from the graph?
(b) Redraw the histogram so that it is not misleading.

NW 5. **Robberies** A newspaper article claimed that the afternoon hours were the worst in terms of robberies and provided the graph in support of this claim. Explain how this graph is misleading.

Hourly Crime Distribution (Robbery)

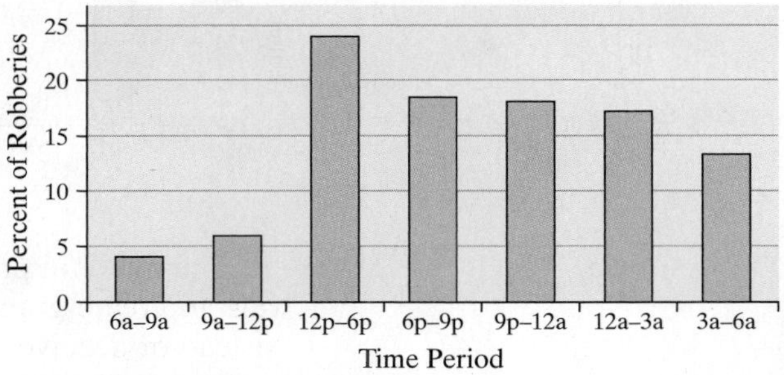

Source: U.S. Statistical Abstract

6. **Car Accidents** An article in a student newspaper claims that younger drivers are safer than older drivers and provides the following graph to support the claim. Explain how this graph is misleading.

Number of Motor Vehicle Accidents, 2007

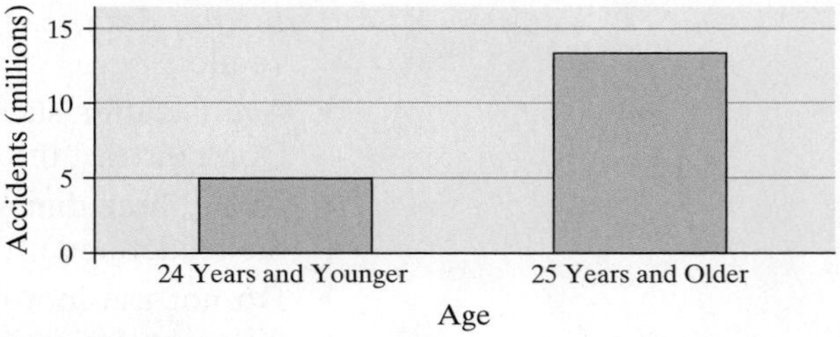

Source: U.S. Statistical Abstract

7. **Health Insurance** The following relative frequency histogram represents the proportion of people aged 25 to 64 years old not covered by any health insurance in 2009.

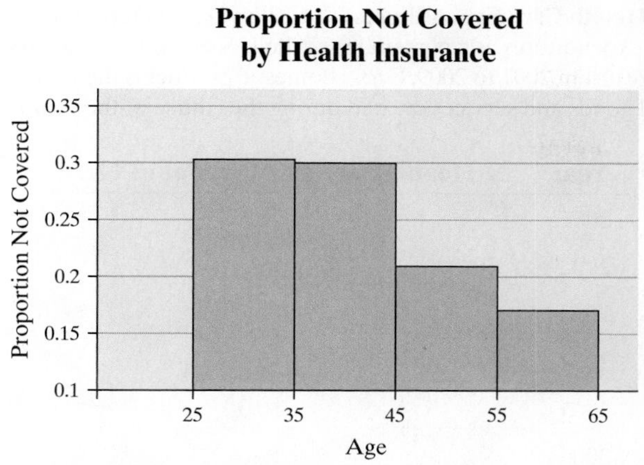

Source: U.S. Census Bureau

(a) Describe how this graph is misleading. What might a reader conclude from the graph?

(b) Redraw the histogram so that it is not misleading.

8. New Homes The time-series plot in the next column shows the number of new homes built in the Midwest from 2000 to 2009.

(a) Describe how this graph is misleading.

(b) What is the graph trying to convey?

(c) In January 2006, the National Association of Realtors reported, "*A lot of demand has been met over the last five years, and a modest rise in mortgage interest rates is causing some market cooling. Along with regulatory tightening on nontraditional mortgages, there will be fewer investors in the market this year.*" Does the graph support this view? Explain why or why not. Do you think the National Association of Realtors was correct in their assessment of the new home market?

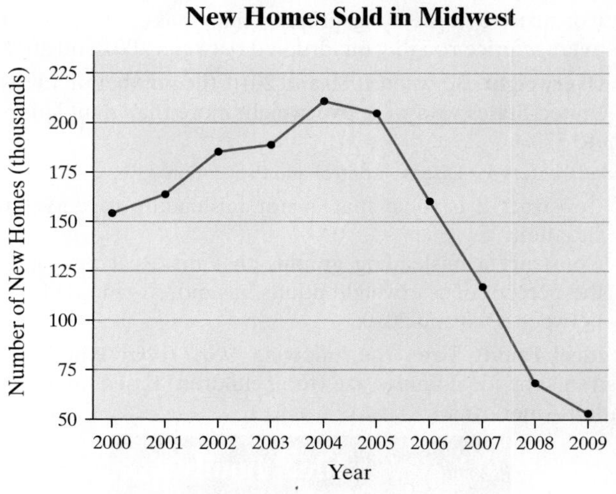

Source: U.S. Census Bureau

9. Tax Revenue The following histogram drawn in StatCrunch represents the total tax collected by the Internal Revenue Service for each state plus Washington, D.C. Explain why the graph is misleading.

Note: Vermont paid the least in tax ($3.3 million), while California paid the most ($264.9 million).

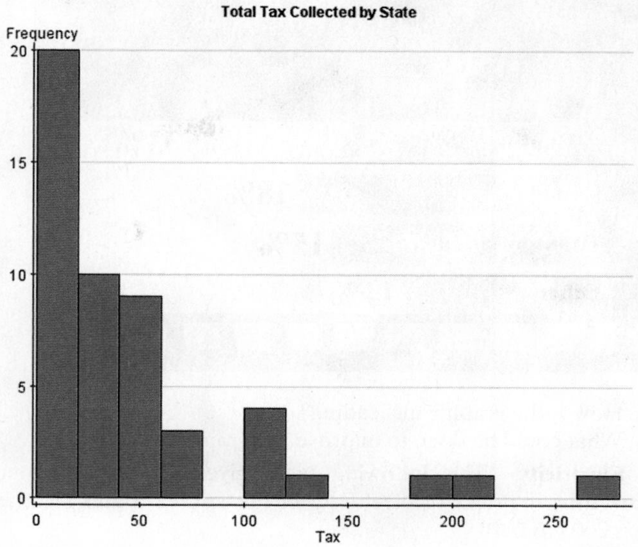

10. You Explain It! Oil Reserves The U.S. Strategic Oil Reserve is a government-owned stockpile of crude oil. It was established after the oil embargo in the mid-1970s and is meant to serve as a national defense fuel reserve, as well as to offset reductions in commercial oil supplies that would threaten the U.S. economy.

(a) How many times larger should the graphic for 2009 be than the 1977 graphic (to the nearest whole number)? 97 times

(b) The United States imported approximately 10 million barrels of oil per day in 2009. At that rate, assuming no change in U.S. oil production, how long would the U.S. strategic oil reserve last if no oil were imported? About 73 days

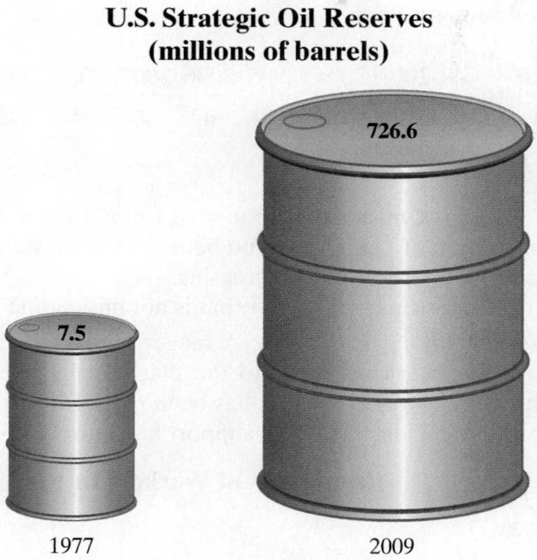

Source: U.S. Energy Information Administration

NW **11. Cost of Kids** The *USA Today* type graph on the following page is based on data from the Department of Agriculture. It represents the percentage of income a middle-income family will spend on their children.

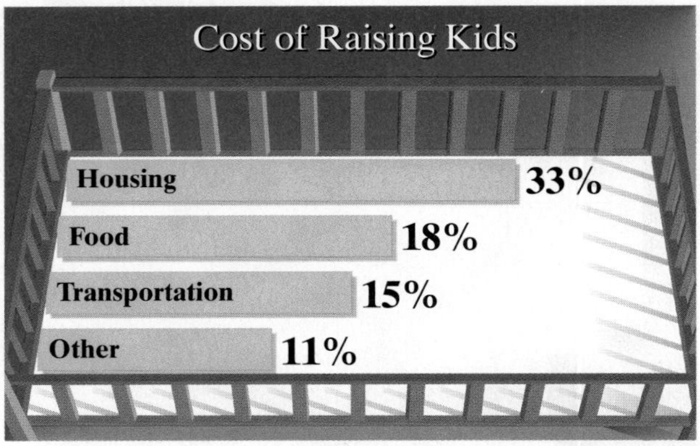

(a) How is the graphic misleading?
(b) What could be done to improve the graphic?

12. Electricity The following table gives the average per kilowatt-hour prices of electricity in the United States for the years 2003 to 2010.

Year	2003	2004	2005	2006	2007	2008	2009	2010
Price per kwh (cents)	7.44	7.61	8.14	8.90	9.13	9.74	9.89	9.81

Source: U.S. Energy Information Administration

(a) Construct a misleading graph indicating that the price per kilowatt-hour has more than tripled since 2003.
(b) Construct a graph that is not misleading.

13. Moral Values The Gallup Organization conducts an annual poll in which it asks a random sample of U.S. adults "How would you rate the overall state of moral values in this country today: excellent, good, only fair, or poor?" The following table represents the percentage of respondents who believe the state of moral values is poor.

Year	2003	2004	2005	2006	2007	2008	2009	2010
Percentage	35	40	39	42	44	44	45	45

Source: Gallup

(a) Construct a misleading time-series plot that indicates the proportion of U.S. adults who believe that the state of moral values is poor is rapidly increasing.
(b) Construct a time-series plot that is not misleading.

14. Worker Injury The safety manager at Klutz Enterprises provides the following graph to the plant manager and claims that the rate of worker injuries has been reduced by 67% over a 12-year period. Does the graph support his claim? Explain.

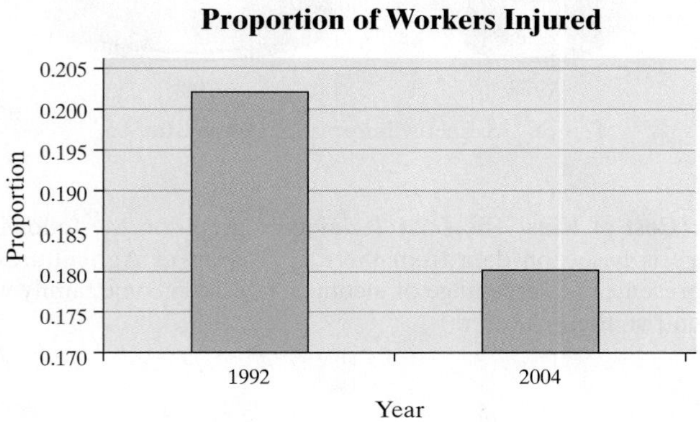

15. Health Care Expenditures The following data represent health care expenditures as a percentage of the U.S. gross domestic product (GDP) from 2001 to 2009. Gross domestic product is the total value of all goods and services created during the course of the year.

Year	Health Care as a Percent of GDP
2001	14.5
2002	15.3
2003	15.8
2004	15.9
2005	16.0
2006	16.0
2007	16.2
2008	16.2
2009	17.3

Source: Center for Medicare and Medicaid Services, Office of the Actuary

(a) Construct a time-series plot that a politician would create to support the position that health care expenditures, as a percentage of GDP, are increasing and must be slowed.
(b) Construct a time-series plot that the health care industry would create to refute the opinion of the politician. Is your graph convincing?
(c) Construct a time-series plot that is not misleading.

16. Gas Hike The average per gallon price for regular unleaded gasoline in the United States rose from $1.46 in 2001 to $3.83 in 2011. *Source:* U.S. Energy Information Administration

(a) Construct a graphic that is not misleading to depict this situation.
(b) Construct a misleading graphic that makes it appear the average price roughly quadrupled between 2001 and 2011.

NW **17. Overweight** Between 1980 and 2010, the number of adults in the United States who were overweight more than doubled from 15% to 37%.

Source: Centers for Disease Control and Prevention

(a) Construct a graphic that is not misleading to depict this situation.
(b) Construct a misleading graphic that makes it appear that the percent of overweight adults has more than quadrupled between 1980 and 2010.

18. Ideal Family Size The following *USA Today* type graphic illustrates the ideal family size (total children) based on a survey of adult Americans.

(a) What type of graphic is being displayed?
(b) Describe any problems with the graphic.
(c) Construct a graphic that is not misleading and makes the data stand out.

19. Inauguration Day The following graph appears on the Wikipedia Web site. The intention of the graph is to display the ages of United States presidents on Inauguration Day. Explain any problems you see with the graph.

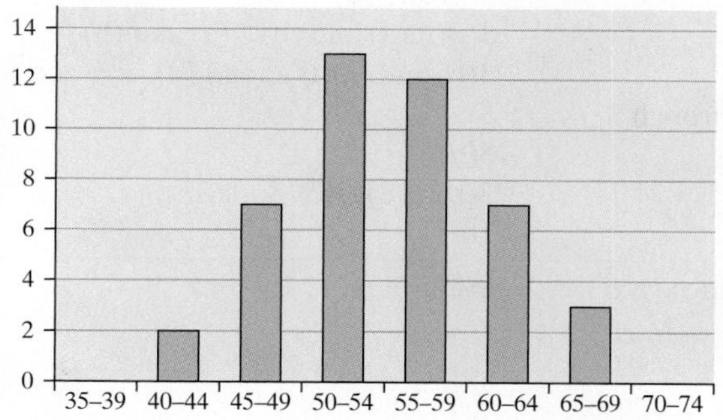

Source: http://en.wikipedia.org/wiki/List_of_Presidents_of_the_United_States_by_age

20. Putting It Together: College Costs The cover of the *Ithaca Times* from December 7, 2000, is shown.

(a) Identify the two variables being graphed and describe them in terms of type and measurement level.
(b) What type of data collection method was likely used to create this graph?
(c) What type of graph is displayed? Time-series
(d) What message does the graph convey to you? How might this graph be misleading?
(e) Describe at least three things that are wrong with the graph.

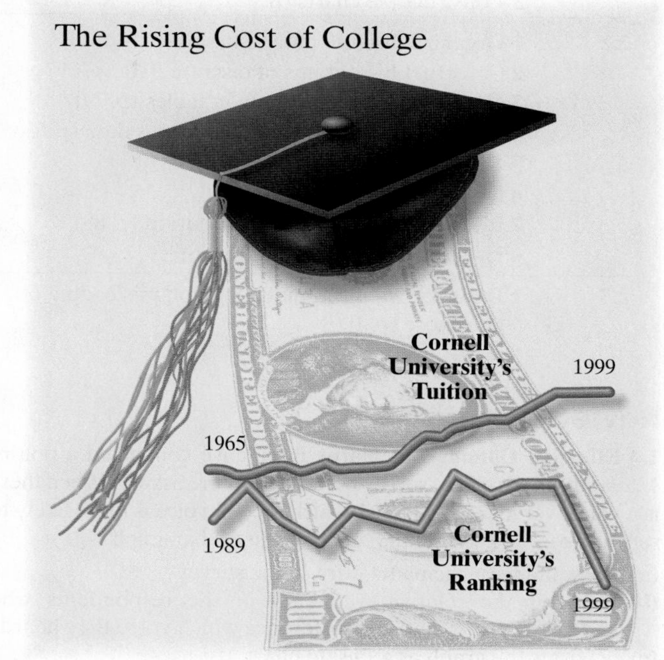

CHAPTER 2 REVIEW

Summary

Raw data are first organized into tables. Data are organized by creating classes into which they fall. Qualitative data and discrete data have values that provide clear-cut categories of data. However, with continuous data the categories, called classes, must be created. Typically, the first table created is a frequency distribution, which lists the frequency with which each class of data occurs. Other types of distributions include the relative frequency distribution and the cumulative frequency distribution.

Once data are organized into a table, graphs are created. For data that are qualitative, we can create bar charts and pie charts. For data that are quantitative, we can create histograms, stem-and-leaf plots, frequency polygons, and ogives.

In creating graphs, care must be taken not to draw a graph that misleads or deceives the reader. If a graph's vertical axis does not begin at zero, the symbol ϟ should be used to indicate the gap that exists in the graph.

Vocabulary

Raw data (p. 62)
Frequency distribution (p. 63)
Relative frequency (p. 64)
Relative frequency distribution (p. 64)
Bar graph (p. 65)
Pareto chart (p. 66)
Side-by-side bar graph (p. 66)
Pie chart (p. 68)
Class (p. 78)
Histogram (p. 79)
Lower and upper class limits (p. 79)
Class width (p. 79)
Open ended (p. 80)
Stem-and-leaf plot (p. 84)
Stem (p. 84)
Leaf (p. 84)
Split stems (p. 87)
Dot plot (p. 88)
Uniform distribution (p. 88)
Bell-shaped distribution (p. 88)
Skewed right (p. 88)
Skewed left (p. 88)
Time-series data (p. 89)
Time series plot (p. 89)

Objectives

Section	You should be able to . . .	Example(s)	Review Exercises
2.1	1 Organize qualitative data in tables (p. 63)	1, 2	2(a), 4(a) and (b)
	2 Construct bar graphs (p. 64)	3 through 5	2(c) and (d), 4(c)
	3 Construct pie charts (p. 68)	6	2(e), 4(d)
2.2	1 Organize discrete data in tables (p. 78)	1	5(a) and (b)
	2 Construct histograms of discrete data (p. 79)	2	5(c) and (d)
	3 Organize continuous data in tables (p. 79)	3	3(a), 6(a) and (b), 7(a) and (b)
	4 Construct histograms of continuous data (p. 83)	4, 5	3(b) and (c), 6(c) and (d), 7(c) and (d)
	5 Draw stem-and-leaf plots (p. 84)	6 through 8	8
	6 Draw dot plots (p. 88)	9	5(g)
	7 Identify the shape of a distribution (p. 88)	10	3(b), 6(e), 7(c), 8
	8 Draw time-series graphs (p. 89)	11	10
2.3	1 Describe what can make a graph misleading or deceptive (p. 100)	1 through 6	9(c), 10, 11, 12

Review Exercises

1. Effective Commercial Harris Interactive conducted a poll of U.S. adults in which the survey participants were asked, "When there is a voiceover in a commercial, which type of voice is more likely to sell me a car?" Results of the survey are in the bar graph. 1. (b) 0.653

(a) How many participants were in the survey? 2216

(b) What is the relative frequency of the respondents who indicated that it made no difference which voice they heard?

(c) Redraw the graph as a Pareto chart.

(d) Research automotive commercials. Do you believe that auto manufacturers use the results of this survey when developing their commercials?

Convincing Voice in Purchasing a Car

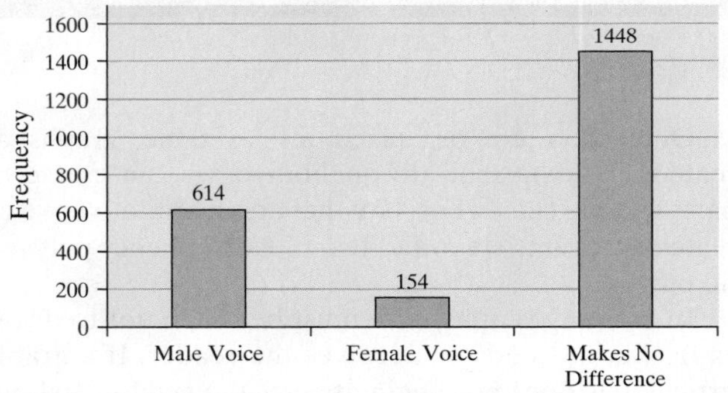

2. Weapons Used in Homicide The following frequency distribution represents the cause of death in homicides for the year 2009.

Type of Weapon	Frequency
Firearms	9146
Knives or cutting instruments	1825
Blunt objects (clubs, hammers, etc.)	611
Personal weapons (hands, fists, etc.)	801
Strangulation	121
Fire	99
Other weapon or not stated	895

Source: Crime in the United States, 2009, FBI, Uniform Crime Reports

(a) Construct a relative frequency distribution.

(b) What percentage of homicides was committed using a blunt object? 4.5%

(c) Construct a frequency bar graph.

(d) Construct a relative frequency bar graph.

(e) Construct a pie chart.

3. Live Births The following frequency distribution represents the number of live births (in thousands) in the United States in 2008 by age of mother.

Age of Mother (years)	Births (thousands)
10–14	6
15–19	435
20–24	1053
25–29	1197
30–34	958
35–39	489
40–44	106

Source: National Center for Health Statistics

(a) Construct a relative frequency distribution.

(b) Construct a frequency histogram. Describe the shape of the distribution.

(c) Construct a relative frequency histogram.

(d) What percentage of live births were to mothers aged 20 to 24? 24.81%

(e) What percentage of live births were to mothers of age 30 or older? 36.59%

4. Political Affiliation A sample of 100 randomly selected registered voters in the city of Naperville was asked their political affiliation: Democrat (D), Republican (R), or Independent (I). The results of the survey are shown on the next page.

(a) Construct a frequency distribution of the data.

(b) Construct a relative frequency distribution of the data.

(c) Construct a relative frequency bar graph of the data.

D	R	D	R	D	R	D	D	R	D
R	D	D	D	R	R	D	D	D	D
R	R	I	I	D	R	D	R	R	R
I	D	D	R	I	I	R	D	R	R
D	I	R	D	D	D	D	I	I	R
R	I	R	R	I	D	D	D	D	R
D	I	I	D	D	R	R	R	R	D
D	R	R	R	D	D	I	I	D	D
D	D	I	D	R	I	D	D	D	D
R	R	R	R	R	D	R	D	R	D

(d) Construct a pie chart of the data.
(e) What appears to be the most common political affiliation in Naperville? Democrat

5. Family Size A random sample of 60 couples married for 7 years were asked to give the number of children they have. The results of the survey are as follows:

0	0	3	1	2	3	2	4
3	4	3	3	0	3	4	2
1	2	1	3	0	3	2	2
4	2	3	2	2	4	2	2
2	1	3	4	1	3	2	3
0	3	3	3	2	1	2	3
2	0	3	1	2	3		
4	3	3	5	2	0		

(a) Construct a frequency distribution of the data.
(b) Construct a relative frequency distribution of the data.
(c) Construct a frequency histogram of the data. Describe the shape of the distribution. Symmetric
(d) Construct a relative frequency histogram of the data.
(e) What percentage of couples married 7 years has two children? 30%
(f) What percentage of couples married 7 years has at least two children? 76.7%
(g) Draw a dot plot of the data.

6. Home Ownership Rates The table shows the home ownership rate in each of the 50 states and Washington, DC, in 2009. **Note:** The state with the highest home ownership rate is West Virginia and the lowest is Washington, DC.

65.5	68.2	57.0	75.5	62.4
70.7	73.8	74.1	68.9	65.7
69.6	70.2	68.4	67.4	69.1
69.6	65.4	72.9	70.4	72.4
69.1	72.0	68.5	71.9	74.5
72.0	71.2	71.1	74.1	75.5
69.7	78.7	69.7	70.1	74.4
67.4	70.9	44.9	72.2	54.4
74.3	76.0	74.0	65.1	62.9
70.5	65.9	76.5	69.6	66.8
59.5				

Source: U.S. Census Bureau

With a first class of 40 and a class width of 5:

(a) Construct a frequency distribution.
(b) Construct a relative frequency distribution.
(c) Construct a frequency histogram of the data.
(d) Construct a relative frequency histogram of the data.
(e) Describe the shape of the distribution.
(f) Repeat parts (a)–(e) using a class width of 10.
(g) Does one frequency distribution provide a better summary of the data than the other? Explain.

7. Diameter of a Cookie The following data represent the diameter (in inches) of a random sample of 34 Keebler Chips Deluxe™ Chocolate Chip Cookies.

2.3414	2.3010	2.2850	2.3015	2.2850	2.3019	2.2400
2.3005	2.2630	2.2853	2.3360	2.3696	2.3300	2.3290
2.2303	2.2600	2.2409	2.2020	2.3223	2.2851	2.2382
2.2438	2.3255	2.2597	2.3020	2.2658	2.2752	2.2256
2.2611	2.3006	2.2011	2.2790	2.2425	2.3003	

Source: Trina S. McNamara, student at Joliet Junior College

(a) Construct a frequency distribution.
(b) Construct a relative frequency distribution.
(c) Construct a frequency histogram. Describe the shape of the distribution.
(d) Construct a relative frequency histogram.

8. Time Online The following data represent the average number of hours per week that a random sample of 40 college students spend online.

18.9	14.0	24.4	17.4	13.7	16.5	14.8	20.8
22.9	22.2	13.4	18.8	15.1	21.9	21.1	14.7
18.6	18.0	21.1	15.6	16.6	20.6	17.3	17.9
15.2	16.4	14.5	17.1	25.7	17.4	18.8	17.1
13.6	20.1	15.3	19.2	23.4	14.5	18.6	23.8

The data are based on the ECAR Study of Undergraduate Students and Information Technology, 2007. Construct a stem-and-leaf diagram of the data, and comment on the shape of the distribution. Skewed right

9. Grade Inflation The side-by-side bar graph on the next page shows the average grade point average for the years 1991–1992, 1996–1997, 2001–2002, and 2006–2007 for colleges and universities.

(a) Does the graph suggest that grade inflation is a problem in colleges?

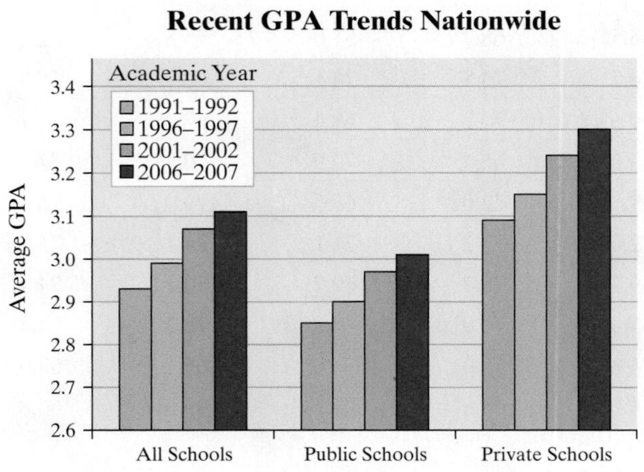

Source: gradeinflation.com

(b) Determine the percentage increase in GPAs for public schools from 1991 to 2006. Determine the percentage increase in GPAs for private schools from 1991 to 2006. Which type of institution appears to have the higher inflation? 5.6%; 6.8%; private schools

(c) Do you believe the graph is misleading? Explain.

10. Income Distribution The following data represent the percentage of total adjusted gross income (AGI) earned by various income classes. The top 1% represents the percentage of total AGI earned by those whose income is higher than 99% of all earners. The bottom 50% represents the percentage of total AGI earned by those whose income is in the bottom 50% of all income earners. For example, in 2001, 17.53% of all income earned in the United States was earned by those in the top 1% of all income earners, while 13.81% of all income earned in the United States was earned by those in the bottom 50% of income earners.

(a) Use the data to make a strong argument that adjusted gross incomes are diverging among Americans.

Year	Adjusted Gross Income Share of Top 1% of Earners	Adjusted Gross Income Share of Bottom 50% of Earners
2001	17.53	13.81
2002	16.12	14.23
2003	16.77	13.99
2004	19.00	13.42
2005	21.20	12.83
2006	22.06	12.51
2007	22.83	12.26
2008	20.00	12.75
2009	16.93	13.48

Source: The Tax Foundation

The following data represent the percentage of total tax paid by the top 1% of all income earners and the bottom 50% of all income earners.

(b) Use the data to make an argument that, while incomes are diverging between the top 1% and bottom 50%, the total taxes paid as a share of income are also diverging.

Year	Income Tax Share of Top 1% of Earners	Income Tax Share of Bottom 50% of Earners
2001	33.89	3.97
2002	33.71	3.50
2003	34.27	3.46
2004	36.89	3.30
2005	39.38	3.07
2006	39.89	2.99
2007	40.41	2.89
2008	38.02	2.70
2009	36.73	2.25

Source: The Tax Foundation

11. Misleading Graphs In 2009 the average earnings of a high school graduate were $32,272. At $62,394, the average earnings of a recipient of a bachelor's degree were about 93% higher. *Source:* U.S. Census Bureau

(a) Construct a misleading graph that a college recruiter might create to convince high school students that they should attend college.

(b) Construct a graph that does not mislead.

12. High Heels The following graphic is a *USA Today*-type graph displaying women's preference for shoes.

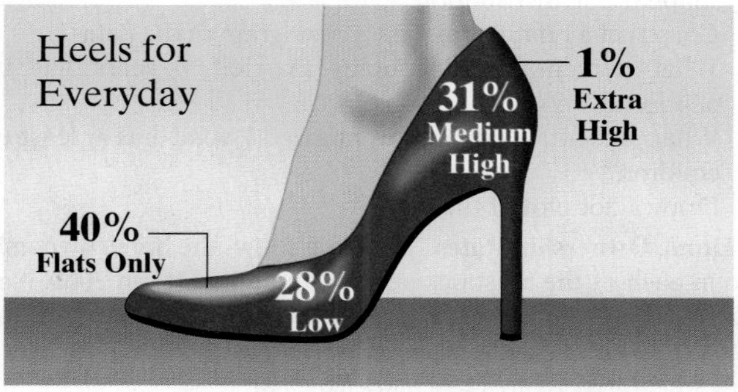

(a) Which type of shoe is preferred the most? The least?

(b) How is the graph misleading?

Problems in the chapter test are labeled by section.objective. For example, 2.3 means Section 2, Objective 3.

CHAPTER TEST

1.2 **1.** The following graph shows the country represented by the champion of the men's singles competition at the Wimbledon Tennis Championship from 1968 (when professional players were first allowed to participate in the tournament) through 2010.

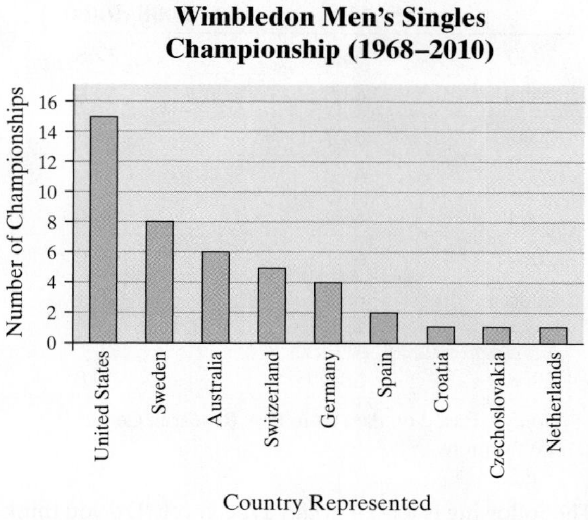

Source: www.wimbledon.org

(a) United States; 15

(a) Which country's representatives won the most championships from 1968 to 2010? How many did they win?

(b) How many more championships were won by representatives of Australia than Germany? 2

(c) What percentage of championships from 1968 to 2010 was won by representatives of Sweden? 18.6%

(d) Is it appropriate to describe the shape of the distribution as skewed right? Why or why not? No; qualitative data

2. A random sample of 1005 adult Americans was asked, "How would you prefer to pay for new road construction?" Results of the survey are below.

Response	Frequency
New tolls	412
Increase gas tax	181
No new roads	412

Source: HNTB Corporation

1.1 **(a)** Construct a relative frequency distribution.

(b) What percent of the respondents indicated they would like to see an increase in gas taxes? 18.01%

1.2 **(c)** Construct a frequency bar graph.

1.2 **(d)** Construct a relative frequency bar graph.

1.3 **(d)** Construct a pie chart.

3. The Metra Train Company was interested in knowing the educational background of its customers. The company contracted a marketing firm to conduct a survey with a random sample of 50 commuters at the train station. In the survey, commuters were asked to disclose their educational attainment. The results shown were obtained.

1.1 **(a)** Construct a frequency distribution of the data.

1.1 **(b)** Construct a relative frequency distribution of the data.

1.2 **(c)** Construct a relative frequency bar graph of the data.

1.3 **(d)** Construct a pie chart of the data.

(e) What is the most common educational level of a commuter? High school graduate

No high school diploma	Some college
High school graduate	No high school diploma
Some college	No high school diploma
No high school diploma	High school graduate
Associate's degree	High school graduate
Bachelor's degree	High school graduate
Bachelor's degree	High school graduate
High school graduate	Associate's degree
Associate's degree	High school graduate
Some college	No high school diploma
Some college	High school graduate
High school graduate	Advanced degree
High school graduate	High school graduate
Bachelor's degree	Bachelor's degree
High school graduate	Some college
Bachelor's degree	Advanced degree
Advanced degree	No high school diploma
Bachelor's degree	High school graduate
Bachelor's degree	No high school diploma
Associate's degree	Some college
Advanced degree	Some college
High school graduate	No high school diploma
Bachelor's degree	No high school diploma
Some college	Some college
High school graduate	High school graduate

4. The following data represent the number of cars that arrived at a McDonald's drive-through between 11:50 A.M. and 12:00 noon each Wednesday for the past 50 weeks:

1	7	3	8	2	3	8	2	6	3
6	5	6	4	3	4	3	8	1	2
5	3	6	3	3	4	3	2	1	2
4	4	9	3	5	2	3	5	5	5
2	5	6	1	7	1	5	3	8	4

2.1 **(a)** Construct a frequency distribution of the data.
2.1 **(b)** Construct a relative frequency distribution of the data.
2.2 **(c)** Construct a frequency histogram of the data. Describe the
2.7 shape of the distribution. Skewed right
2.2 **(d)** Construct a relative frequency histogram of the data.
(e) What percentage of weeks did exactly three cars arrive between 11:50 A.M. and 12:00 noon? 24%
(f) What percentage of weeks did three or more cars arrive between 11:50 A.M. and 12:00 noon? 76%
2.6 **(g)** Draw a dot plot of the data.

5. Serum HDL Dr. Paul Oswiecmiski randomly selects 40 of his 20- to 29-year-old patients and obtains the following data regarding their serum HDL cholesterol:

70	56	48	48	53	52	66	48
36	49	28	35	58	62	45	60
38	73	45	51	56	51	46	39
56	32	44	60	51	44	63	50
46	69	53	70	33	54	55	52

Source: Paul Oswiecmiski

2.3 **(a)** Construct a frequency distribution.
2.3 **(b)** Construct a relative frequency distribution.
2.4 **(c)** Construct a frequency histogram of the data.
2.4 **(d)** Construct a relative frequency histogram of the data.
2.7 **(e)** Describe the shape of the distribution. Bell shaped

6. Time Spent on Homework The following data represent
2.5 the time (in minutes) students spent working their Section 1.1 homework from Sullivan's College Algebra course (based on time logged into MyMathLab). Draw a stem-and-leaf diagram of the data and comment on the shape of the distribution.

46	47	110	56	71	109
63	91	111	93	125	78
85	108	73	118	70	89
99	45	73	125	96	109
110	61	40	52	103	126

7. Fertility Rates and Income The following data are based on
2.8 a study conducted by the Pew Research Center, which shows birth rates and per capita income (in thousands of 2008 dollars) from 2000 through 2008. Draw a time series plot for both birth rate and per capita income. Comment on any similarities in the trends.

Year	Birth Rate (births per 1000 women age 15–44)	Per capita Income (thousands of 2008 dollars)
2000	65.8	37.8
2001	64.9	37.6
2002	64.7	37.5
2003	66.0	37.9
2004	66.4	38.6
2005	67.1	39.0
2006	69.2	40.1
2007	70.0	40.6
2008	68.8	39.8

Source: Based on data from Pew Research Center Publications

3.1 **8.** The following is a *USA Today* type graph. Do you think the graph is misleading? Why? If you think it is misleading, what might be done to improve the graph?

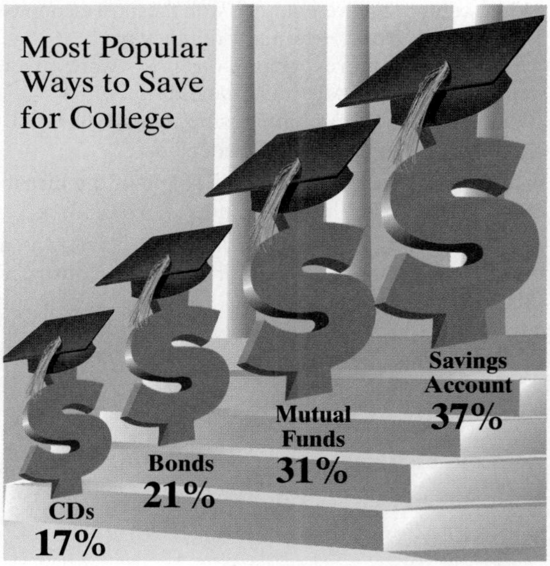

Making an Informed Decision

Tables or Graphs?

You work for the school newspaper. Your editor approaches you with a special reporting assignment. Your task is to write an article that describes the "typical" student at your school, complete with supporting information. To write this article, you have to survey at least 40 students and ask them to respond to a questionnaire. The editor would like to have at least two qualitative and two quantitative variables that describe the typical student. The results of the survey will be presented in your article, but you are unsure whether you should present tabular or graphical summaries, so you decide to perform the following experiment.

1. Develop a questionnaire that results in obtaining the values of two qualitative and two quantitative variables. Administer the questionnaire to at least 40 students on your campus.

2. Summarize the data in both tabular and graphical form.

3. Select 20 individuals. (They don't have to be students at your school.) Give the tabular summaries to 10 individuals and the graphical summaries to the other 10. Ask each individual to study the table or graph for 5 seconds. After 1 minute, give a questionnaire that asks various questions regarding the information contained in the table or graph. For example, if you summarize age data, ask the individual which age group has the highest frequency. Record the number of correct answers for each individual. Which summary results in a higher percentage of correct answers, the tables or the graphs? Write a report that discusses your findings.

4. Now use the data collected from the questionnaire to create some misleading graphs. Again, select 20 individuals. Give 10 individuals the misleading graphs and 10 individuals the correct graphs. Ask each individual to study each graph for 5 seconds. After 1 minute has elapsed, give a questionnaire that asks various questions regarding the information contained in the graphs. Record the number of correct answers for each individual. Did the misleading graphs mislead? Write a report that discusses your findings.

Note: Be sure to check with your school's administration regarding privacy laws and policies regarding studies involving human subjects. ◀

The Chapter 2 Case Study is located on the CD that accompanies this text.

3 Numerically Summarizing Data

OUTLINE

Making an Informed Decision

Informed Decisions Using Data

Suppose that you are in the market for a used car. To make an informed decision regarding your purchase, you decide to collect as much information as possible. What information is important in helping you make this decision? See the Decisions project on page 176.

PUTTING IT TOGETHER

When we look at a distribution of data, we should consider three characteristics of the distribution: shape, center, and spread. In the last chapter, we discussed methods for organizing raw data into tables and graphs. These graphs (such as the histogram) allow us to identify the shape of the distribution: symmetric (in particular, bell shaped or uniform), skewed right, or skewed left.

The center and spread are numerical summaries of the data. The center of a data set is commonly called the *average*. There are many ways to describe the *average* value of a distribution. In addition, there are many ways to measure the spread of a distribution. The most appropriate measure of center and spread depends on the distribution's shape.

Once these three characteristics of the distribution are known, we can analyze the data for interesting features, including unusual data values, called *outliers*.

3.1 MEASURES OF CENTRAL TENDENCY

Preparing for This Section Before getting started, review the following:

- Population versus sample (Section 1.1, p. 5)
- Parameter versus statistic (Section 1.1, p. 5)
- Quantitative data (Section 1.1, p. 9)
- Qualitative data (Section 1.1, p. 9)
- Simple random sampling (Section 1.3, pp. 23–26)

OBJECTIVES

1. Determine the arithmetic mean of a variable from raw data
2. Determine the median of a variable from raw data
3. Explain what it means for a statistic to be resistant
4. Determine the mode of a variable from raw data

Note to Instructor
If you like, you can print out and distribute the Preparing for this Section quiz located in the Instructor's Resource Center.

Note to Instructor
Discuss with students that we describe distributions using three characteristics: shape, center, and spread. Shape can be determined from pictures of data, like the histogram. Center is discussed in this section, and spread is discussed in Section 3.2.

A measure of central tendency numerically describes the average or typical data value. We hear the word *average* in the news all the time:

- The average miles per gallon of gasoline of the 2012 Chevrolet Corvette Z06 in highway driving is 24.
- According to the U.S. Census Bureau, the national average commute time to work in 2010 was 25.3 minutes.
- According to the U.S. Census Bureau, the average household income in 2010 was $49,455.
- The average American woman is 5′4″ tall and weighs 142 pounds.

In this chapter, we discuss the three most widely-used measures of central tendency: the *mean*, the *median*, and the *mode*. In the media (newspapers, blogs, and so on), *average* usually refers to the mean. But beware: some reporters use *average* to refer to the median or mode. As we shall see, these three measures of central tendency can give very different results!

CAUTION
Whenever you hear the word *average*, be aware that the word may not always be referring to the mean. One average could be used to support one position, while another average could be used to support a different position.

1 Determine the Arithmetic Mean of a Variable from Raw Data

In everyday language, the word *average* often represents the arithmetic mean. To compute the arithmetic mean of a set of data, the data must be quantitative.

DEFINITIONS

The **arithmetic mean** of a variable is computed by adding all the values of the variable in the data set and dividing by the number of observations. The **population arithmetic mean**, μ (pronounced "mew"), is computed using all the individuals in a population. The population mean is a parameter.

The **sample arithmetic mean**, $\bar{x}$ (pronounced "*x*-bar"), is computed using sample data. The sample mean is a statistic.

While other types of means exist (see Problems 41 and 42), the arithmetic mean is generally referred to as the **mean**. We will follow this practice for the remainder of the text.

We usually use Greek letters to represent parameters and Roman letters to represent statistics. The formulas for computing population and sample means follow:

In Other Words
To find the mean of a set of data, add up all the observations and divide by the number of observations.

If $x_1, x_2, \ldots, x_N$ are the N observations of a variable from a population, then the population mean, μ, is

$$\mu = \frac{x_1 + x_2 + \cdots + x_N}{N} = \frac{\sum x_i}{N} \tag{1}$$

If $x_1, x_2, \ldots, x_n$ are n observations of a variable from a sample, then the sample mean, $\bar{x}$, is

$$\bar{x} = \frac{x_1 + x_2 + \cdots + x_n}{n} = \frac{\sum x_i}{n} \qquad \textbf{(2)}$$

Note to Instructor

If you decided to postpone the discussion of Sections 1.2–1.6, let students know they should not dwell on how the sample is obtained.

Note that N represents the size of the population, and n represents the size of the sample. The symbol Σ (the Greek letter capital sigma) tells us to add the terms. The subscript i shows that the various values are distinct and does not serve as a mathematical operation. For example, x_1 is the first data value, x_2 is the second, and so on.

EXAMPLE 1 Computing a Population Mean and a Sample Mean

TABLE 1

Student	Score
1. Michelle	82
2. Ryanne	77
3. Bilal	90
4. Pam	71
5. Jennifer	62
6. Dave	68
7. Joel	74
8. Sam	84
9. Justine	94
10. Juan	88

Problem The data in Table 1 represent the first exam score of 10 students enrolled in Introductory Statistics. Treat the 10 students as a population.

(a) Compute the population mean.

(b) Find a simple random sample of size $n = 4$ students.

(c) Compute the sample mean of the sample found in part (b).

Approach

(a) To compute the population mean, we add all the data values (test scores) and divide by the number of individuals in the population.

(b) Recall from Section 1.3 that we can use Table I in Appendix A, a calculator with a random-number generator, or computer software to obtain simple random samples. We will use a TI-84 Plus graphing calculator.

(c) We find the sample mean by adding the data values corresponding to the individuals in the sample and then dividing by $n = 4$, the sample size.

Solution

(a) Compute the population mean by adding the scores of all 10 students:

$$\begin{aligned}\sum x_i &= x_1 + x_2 + x_3 + \cdots + x_{10} \\ &= 82 + 77 + 90 + 71 + 62 + 68 + 74 + 84 + 94 + 88 \\ &= 790\end{aligned}$$

Note to Instructor

Consider assigning the "Comparing Statistics to Parameters" activity from the Student Activity Workbook.

Divide this result by 10, the number of students in the class.

$$\mu = \frac{\sum x_i}{N} = \frac{790}{10} = 79$$

Although it was not necessary in this problem, we will agree to round the mean to one more decimal place than that in the raw data.

Figure 1

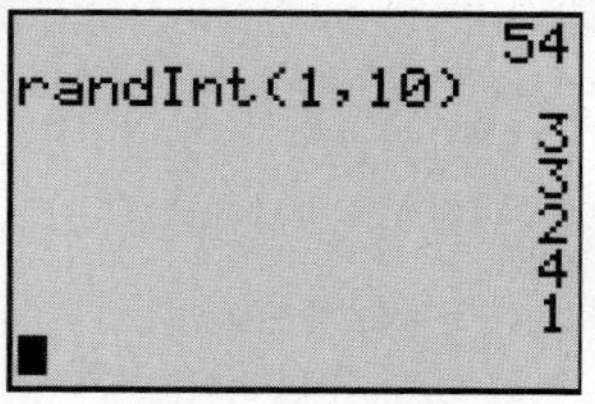

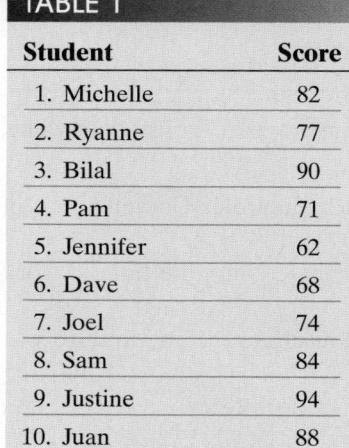

(b) To find a simple random sample of size $n = 4$ from a population of size $N = 10$, we will use the TI-84 Plus random-number generator with a seed of 54. (Recall that this gives the calculator its starting point to generate the list of random numbers.) Figure 1 shows the students in the sample: Bilal (90), Ryanne (77), Pam (71), and Michelle (82).

(c) We compute the sample mean by adding the scores of the four students:

$$\begin{aligned}\sum x_i &= x_1 + x_2 + x_3 + x_4 \\ &= 90 + 77 + 71 + 82 \\ &= 320\end{aligned}$$

Divide this result by 4, the number of individuals in the sample.

$$\bar{x} = \frac{\sum x_i}{n} = \frac{320}{4} = 80$$

Now Work Problem 21

It helps to think of the mean of a data set as the center of gravity. In other words, the mean is the value such that a histogram of the data is perfectly balanced, with equal weight on each side of the mean. Figure 2 shows a histogram of the data in Table 1 with the mean labeled. The histogram balances at $\mu = 79$.

Figure 2

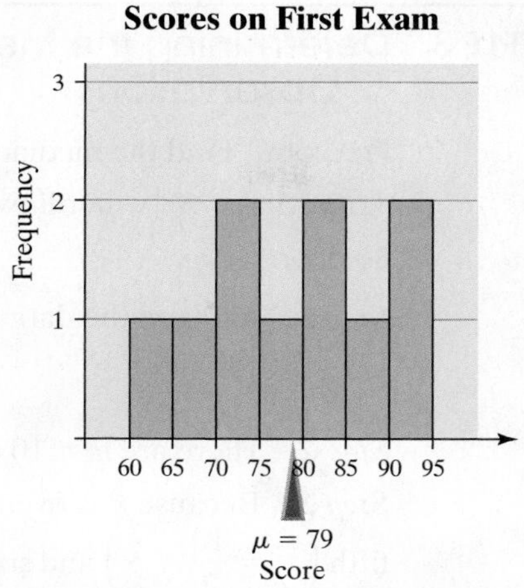

2 Determine the Median of a Variable from Raw Data

A second measure of central tendency is the median. To compute the median of a set of data, the data must be quantitative.

DEFINITION

The **median** of a variable is the value that lies in the middle of the data when arranged in ascending order. We use *M* to represent the median.

In Other Words
To help remember the idea behind the median, think of the median of a highway; it divides the highway in half. So the median divides the data in half, with at most half the data below the median and at most half above it.

Note to Instructor
Suppose that a data set has 10 observations. In class, have students explain in their own words how to find the median. What if the data set has 11 observations?

Steps in Finding the Median of a Data Set

Step 1 Arrange the data in ascending order.

Step 2 Determine the number of observations, *n*.

Step 3 Determine the observation in the middle of the data set.

- If the number of observations is odd, then the median is the data value exactly in the middle of the data set. That is, the median is the observation that lies in the $\frac{n+1}{2}$ position.
- If the number of observations is even, then the median is the mean of the two middle observations in the data set. That is, the median is the mean of the observations that lie in the $\frac{n}{2}$ position and the $\frac{n}{2}+1$ position.

EXAMPLE 2 Determining the Median of a Data Set with an Odd Number of Observations

TABLE 2

Song Name	Length
"Sister Golden Hair"	201
"Black Water"	257
"Free Bird"	284
"The Hustle"	208
"Southern Nights"	179
"Stayin' Alive"	222
"We Are Family"	217
"Heart of Glass"	206
"My Sharona"	240

Problem The data in Table 2 represent the length (in seconds) of a random sample of songs released in the 1970s. Find the median length of the songs.

Approach We will follow the steps listed above.

Solution

Step 1 Arrange the data in ascending order:

$$179, 201, 206, 208, 217, 222, 240, 257, 284$$

Step 2 There are $n = 9$ observations.

Step 3 Since *n* is odd, the median, *M*, is the observation exactly in the middle of the data set, 217 seconds (the $\frac{n+1}{2} = \frac{9+1}{2} = 5$th data value). We list the data in ascending order and show the median in blue.

$$179, 201, 206, 208, 217, 222, 240, 257, 284$$

Notice there are four observations on each side of the median.

EXAMPLE 3 Determining the Median of a Data Set with an Even Number of Observations

Problem Find the median score of the data in Table 1 on page 118.

Approach We will follow the steps listed on the previous page.

Solution

Step 1 Arrange the data in ascending order:

62, 68, 71, 74, 77, 82, 84, 88, 90, 94

Step 2 There are $n = 10$ observations.

Step 3 Because n is even, the median is the mean of the two middle observations, the fifth $\left(\frac{n}{2} = \frac{10}{2} = 5\right)$ and sixth $\left(\frac{n}{2} + 1 = \frac{10}{2} + 1 = 6\right)$ observations with the data written in ascending order. So the median is the mean of 77 and 82:

$$M = \frac{77 + 82}{2} = 79.5$$

Notice that there are five observations on each side of the median.

62, 68, 71, 74, 77, 82, 84, 88, 90, 94
↑
$M = 79.5$

We conclude that 50% (or half) of the students scored less than 79.5 and 50% (or half) of the students scored above 79.5.

Now compute the median of the data in Problem 15 by hand

EXAMPLE 4 Finding the Mean and Median Using Technology

Figure 3

Summary statistics:

Column	n	Mean	Median
Scores	10	79	79.5

Problem Use statistical software or a calculator to determine the population mean and median of the student test score data in Table 1 on page 118.

Approach We will use StatCrunch to obtain the mean and median. The steps for obtaining measures of central tendency using the TI-83/84 Plus graphing calculator, MINITAB, Excel, and StatCrunch are given in the Technology Step-by-Step on page 129.

Solution Figure 3 shows the output obtained from StatCrunch.The results agree with the "by hand" solution from Examples 1 and 3.

3 Explain What It Means for a Statistic to Be Resistant

So far, we have discussed two measures of central tendency, the mean and the median. Perhaps you are asking yourself which measure is better. It depends.

EXAMPLE 5 Comparing the Mean and the Median

Note to Instructor
Consider assigning the "Understanding Measures of Center" activity from the Student Activity Workbook.

Problem Yolanda wants to know how much time she typically spends on her cell phone. She goes to her phone's Web site and records the call length for a random sample of 12 calls, shown in Table 3. Find the mean and median length of a cell phone call. Which measure of central tendency better describes the length of a typical phone call?

Approach We will find the mean and median using MINITAB. To help judge which is the better measure of central tendency, we will also draw a dot plot of the data.

TABLE 3

1	7	4	1
2	4	3	48
3	5	3	6

Source: Yolanda Sullivan's cell phone records

Solution Figure 4 indicates that the mean call length is $\bar{x} = 7.3$ minutes and the median call length is 3.5 minutes. Figure 5 shows a dot plot of the data using MINITAB.

Figure 4

Descriptive Statistics: TalkTime

```
Variable  N N* Mean SE Mean StDev Minimum    Q1 Median    Q3 Maximum
TalkTime 12  0 7.25    3.74 12.96    1.00 2.25   3.50 5.75   48.00
```

Figure 5

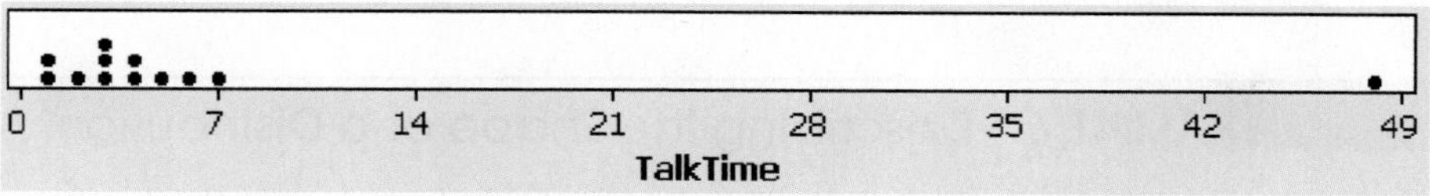

Which measure of central tendency do you think better describes the typical call length? Since only one phone call is longer than the mean, we conclude that the mean is not representative of the typical call length. So the median is the better measure of central tendency.

Note to Instructor

In-class concept check: Ask students to discuss how extreme observations affect the mean and median. Which measure of center is best when extreme values exist? Which is a better measure of central tendency for the following variables: income, price of housing, height, or IQ?

Look back at the data in Table 3. Suppose Yolanda's 48-minute call was actually a 5-minute call. Then the mean call length would be 3.7 minutes and the median call length would still be 3.5 minutes. So the one extreme observation (48 minutes) can cause the mean to increase substantially, but have no effect on the median. In other words, the mean is sensitive to extreme values while the median is not. In fact, if Yolanda's 48-minute call had actually been 148 minutes long, the median would still be 3.5 minutes, but the mean would increase to 15.6 minutes. The median is based on the value of the middle observation, so the value of the largest observation does not affect its computation. Because extreme values do not affect the value of the median, we say that the median is *resistant.*

DEFINITION

A numerical summary of data is said to be **resistant** if extreme values (very large or small) relative to the data do not affect its value substantially.

So the median is resistant, while the mean is not resistant.

When data are skewed, there are extreme values in the tail, which tend to pull the mean in the direction of the tail. For example, in skewed-right distributions, there are large observations in the right tail. These observations increase the value of the mean, but have little effect on the median. Similarly, if a distribution is skewed left, the mean tends to be smaller than the median. In symmetric distributions, the mean and the median are close in value. We summarize these ideas in Table 4 and Figure 6.

Note to Instructor

We use the term resistant to describe the effect extreme observations have on the value of a statistic. The term robust will be introduced in Chapter 9 to describe the ability of a procedure to overcome departures from underlying assumptions, such as normality.

TABLE 4

Relation Between the Mean, Median, and Distribution Shape

Distribution Shape	Mean versus Median
Skewed left	Mean substantially smaller than median
Symmetric	Mean roughly equal to median
Skewed right	Mean substantially larger than median

Figure 6
Mean or median versus skewness

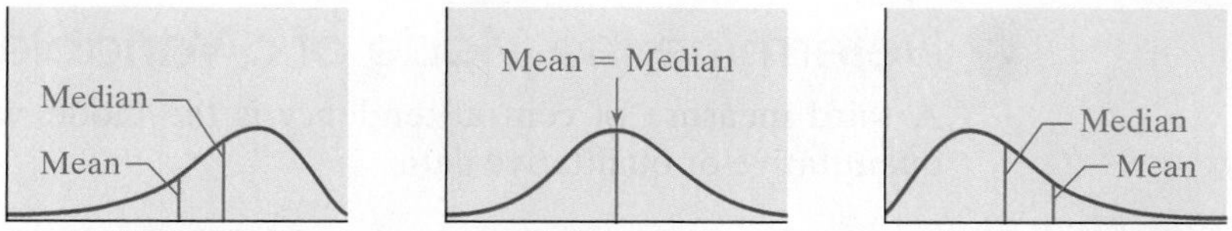

(a) Skewed Left
Mean < Median

(b) Symmetric
Mean = Median

(c) Skewed Right
Mean > Median

A word of caution is in order. The relation between the mean, median, and skewness are guidelines. The guidelines tend to hold up well for continuous data, but when the data are discrete, the rules can be easily violated. See Problem 43.*

You may be asking yourself, "Why would I ever compute the mean?" After all, the mean and median are close in value for symmetric data, and the median is the better measure of central tendency for skewed data. The reason we compute the mean is that much of the statistical inference that we perform is based on the mean. We will have more to say about this in Chapter 8. Plus, the mean uses all the data, while the median relies only on the position of the data.

EXAMPLE 6 Describing the Shape of a Distribution

TABLE 5

5.8	7.4	9.2	7.0	8.5	7.6
7.9	7.8	7.9	7.7	9.0	7.1
8.7	7.2	6.1	7.2	7.1	7.2
7.9	5.9	7.0	7.8	7.2	7.5
7.3	6.4	7.4	8.2	9.1	7.3
9.4	6.8	7.0	8.1	8.0	7.5
7.3	6.9	6.9	6.4	7.8	8.7
7.1	7.0	7.0	7.4	8.2	7.2
7.6	6.7				

Problem The data in Table 5 represent the birth weights (in pounds) of 50 randomly sampled babies.

(a) Find the mean and the median.

(b) Describe the shape of the distribution.

(c) Which measure of central tendency better describes the average birth weight?

Approach

(a) This can be done either by hand or technology. We will use a TI-84 Plus.

(b) We will draw a histogram to identify the shape of the distribution.

(c) If the data are roughly symmetric, the mean is the better measure of central tendency. If the data are skewed, the median is the better measure.

Solution

(a) Using a TI-84 Plus, we find $\bar{x} = 7.49$ and $M = 7.35$. See Figure 7.

Figure 7

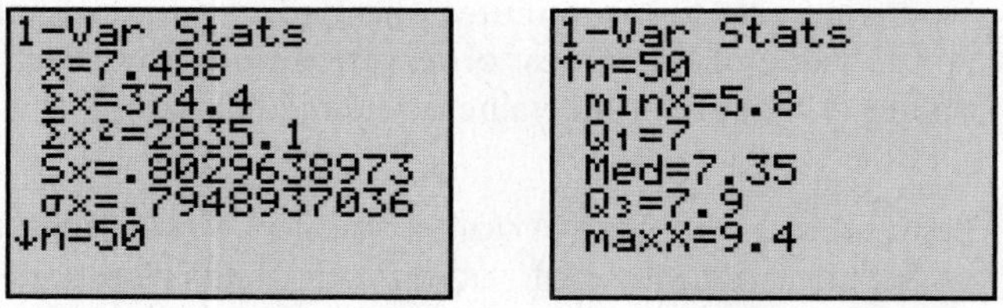

(a) (b)

(b) Figure 8 shows the frequency histogram with the mean and median labeled. The distribution is bell shaped. We have further evidence of the shape because the mean and median are close to each other.

Figure 8 Birth weights of 50 randomly selected babies

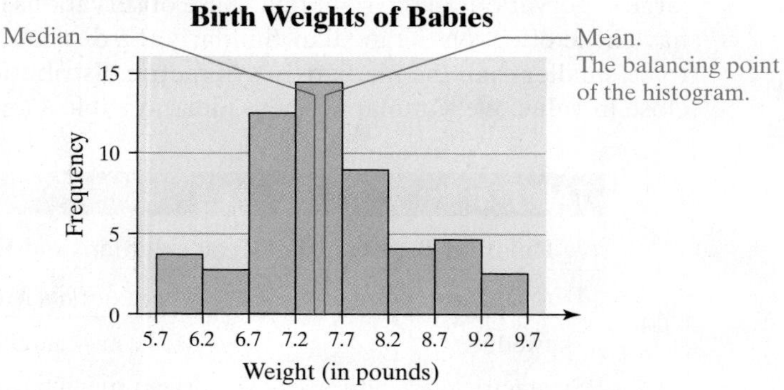

(c) Because the mean and median are close in value, we use the mean as the measure of central tendency.

Now Work Problem 25

4 Determine the Mode of a Variable from Raw Data

A third measure of central tendency is the mode, which can be computed for either quantitative or qualitative data.

*This idea is discussed in "Mean, Median, and Skew: Correcting a Textbook Rule" by Paul T. von Hippel. *Journal of Statistics Education,* Volume 13, Number 2 (2005).

DEFINITION

The **mode** of a variable is the most frequent observation of the variable that occurs in the data set.

To compute the mode, tally the number of observations that occur for each data value. The data value that occurs most often is the mode. A set of data can have no mode, one mode, or more than one mode. If no observation occurs more than once, we say the data have **no mode**.

EXAMPLE 7 Finding the Mode of Quantitative Data

Problem The following data represent the number of O-ring failures on the shuttle *Columbia* for its 17 flights prior to its fatal flight:

$$0, 0, 0, 0, 0, 0, 0, 0, 0, 0, 0, 1, 1, 1, 1, 2, 3$$

Find the mode number of O-ring failures.

Approach We tally the number of times we observe each data value. The data value with the highest frequency is the mode.

Solution The mode is 0 because it occurs most frequently (11 times).

EXAMPLE 8 Finding the Mode of Quantitative Data

Problem Find the mode of the exam score data listed in Table 1, which is repeated here:

$$82, 77, 90, 71, 62, 68, 74, 84, 94, 88$$

Approach Tally the number of times we observe each data value. The data value with the highest frequency is the mode.

Solution Since each data value occurs only once, there is no mode.

Now compute the mode of the data in Problem 15

Figure 9

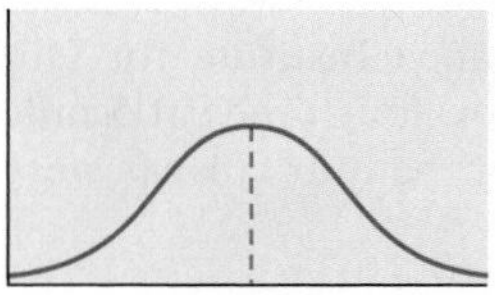

(a) One mode

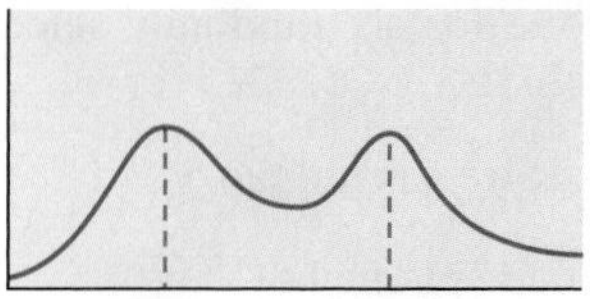

(b) Bimodal

A data set can have more than one mode. For example, if the data set in Table 1 had two scores of 77 and 88, the data set would have two modes: 77 and 88. In this case, we say the data are **bimodal**. If a data set has three or more data values that occur with the highest frequency, the data set is **multimodal**. The mode is usually not reported for multimodal data because it is not representative of a typical value. Figure 9(a) shows a distribution with one mode. Figure 9(b) shows a distribution that is bimodal.

We cannot determine the value of the mean or median of data that are nominal. The only measure of central tendency that can be determined for nominal data is the mode.

EXAMPLE 9 Determining the Mode of Qualitative Data

Problem The data in Table 6 represent the location of injuries that required rehabilitation by a physical therapist. Determine the mode location of injury.

In Other Words
Remember, nominal data are qualitative data that cannot be written in any meaningful order.

TABLE 6

Back	Back	Hand	Neck	Knee	Knee
Wrist	Back	Groin	Shoulder	Shoulder	Back
Elbow	Back	Back	Back	Back	Back
Back	Shoulder	Shoulder	Knee	Knee	Back
Hip	Knee	Hip	Hand	Back	Wrist

Source: Krystal Catton, student at Joliet Junior College

Now Work Problem 31

Approach Determine the location of injury that occurs with the highest frequency.

Solution The mode location of injury is the back, with 12 instances.

Summary

The chart below explains when to use each measure of central tendency.

Measure of Central Tendency	Computation	Interpretation	When to Use
Mean	Population mean: $\mu = \frac{\Sigma x_i}{N}$ Sample mean: $\bar{x} = \frac{\Sigma x_i}{n}$	Center of gravity	When data are quantitative and the frequency distribution is roughly symmetric
Median	Arrange data in ascending order and divide the data set in half	Divides the bottom 50% of the data from the top 50%	When the data are quantitative and the frequency distribution is skewed left or right
Mode	Tally data to determine most frequent observation	Most frequent observation	When the most frequent observation is the desired measure of central tendency or the data are qualitative

Note to Instructor *If you postponed discussion of Sections 1.2–1.6, do not assign Problems 21 or 22.*

3.1 ASSESS YOUR UNDERSTANDING

VOCABULARY AND SKILL BUILDING

1. What does it mean if a statistic is resistant?

2. In the 2011 Current Population Survey conducted by the U.S. Census Bureau, two average household incomes were reported: $49,445 and $67,530. One of these averages is the mean and the other is the median. Which is the mean? Support your answer. Mean = $67,530 3. Data skewed right

3. The U.S. Department of Housing and Urban Development (HUD) uses the median to report the average price of a home in the United States. Why do you think HUD uses the median?

4. A histogram of a set of data indicates that the distribution of the data is skewed right. Which measure of central tendency will likely be larger, the mean or the median? Why? Mean

5. If a data set contains 10,000 values arranged in increasing order, where is the median located?

6. *True or False*: A data set will always have exactly one mode. False

5. The median is between the 5000th and 5001st ordered values.

In Problems 7–10, find the population mean or sample mean as indicated.

7. Sample: 20, 13, 4, 8, 10 $\bar{x} = 11$

8. Sample: 83, 65, 91, 87, 84 $\bar{x} = 82$

9. Population: 3, 6, 10, 12, 14 $\mu = 9$

10. Population: 1, 19, 25, 15, 12, 16, 28, 13, 6 $\mu = 15$

11. For Super Bowl XLIV, CBS television sold 55 ad slots for a total revenue of roughly $165.5 million. What was the mean price per ad slot? $3.01 million

12. The median for the given set of six ordered data values is 26.5. What is the missing value? 7 12 21 ___32___ 41 50

13. Crash Test Results The Insurance Institute for Highway Safety crashed the 2010 Ford Fusion four times at 5 miles per hour. The costs of repair for each of the four crashes were

$2529, $1889, $2610, $1073

Compute the mean, median, and mode cost of repair.

14. Cell Phone Use The following data represent the monthly cell phone bill for my wife's phone for six randomly selected months. $41.41; $40.76; none 13. $2025.25; $2209; none

$35.34, $42.09, $39.43, $38.93, $43.39, $49.26

Compute the mean, median, and mode phone bill.

NW **15. Concrete Mix** A certain type of concrete mix is designed to withstand 3000 pounds per square inch (psi) of pressure. The strength of concrete is measured by pouring the mix into casting cylinders 6 inches in diameter and 12 inches tall. The concrete is allowed to set for 28 days. The concrete's strength is then measured. The following data represent the strength of nine randomly selected casts (in psi).

3960, 4090, 3200, 3100, 2940, 3830, 4090, 4040, 3780

Compute the mean, median, and mode strength of the concrete (in psi). 3670; 3830; 4090 16. 266; 266; 260

16. Flight Time The following data represent the flight time (in minutes) of a random sample of seven flights from Las Vegas, Nevada, to Newark, New Jersey, on Continental Airlines.

282, 270, 260, 266, 257, 260, 267

Compute the mean, median, and mode flight time.

17. For each of the three histograms shown, determine whether the mean is greater than, less than, or approximately equal to the median. Justify your answer. (a) $\bar{x} > M$ (b) $\bar{x} = M$ (c) $\bar{x} < M$

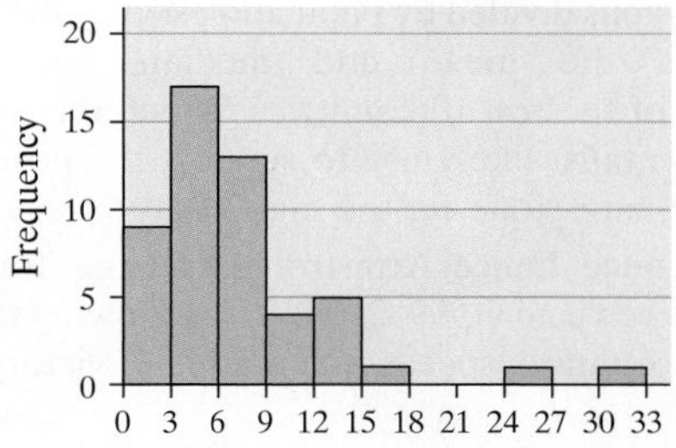

(a)

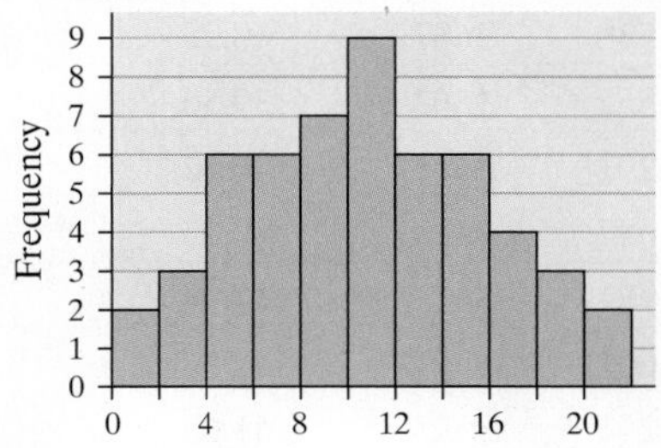

(b)

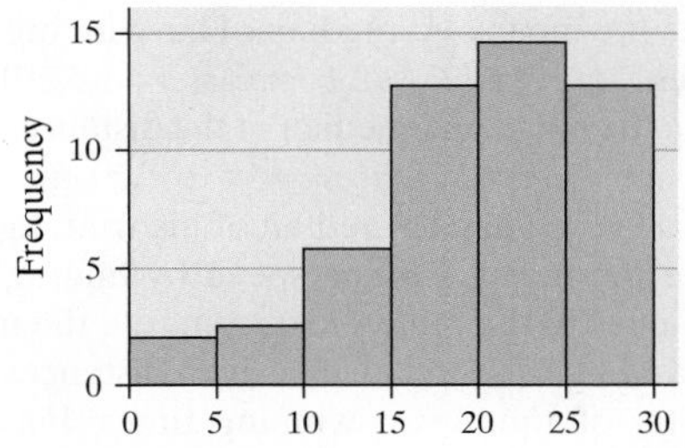

(c)

18. Match the histograms shown to the summary statistics:

	Mean	Median
I	42	42
II	31	36
III	31	26
IV	31	32

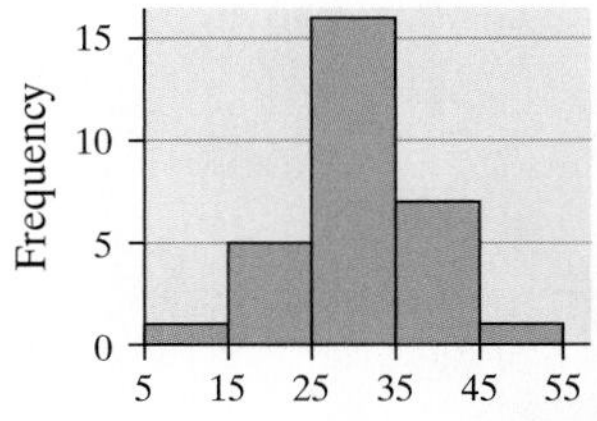

(a)

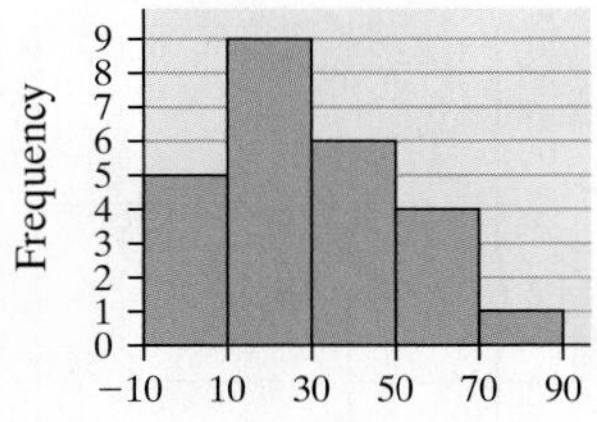

(b)

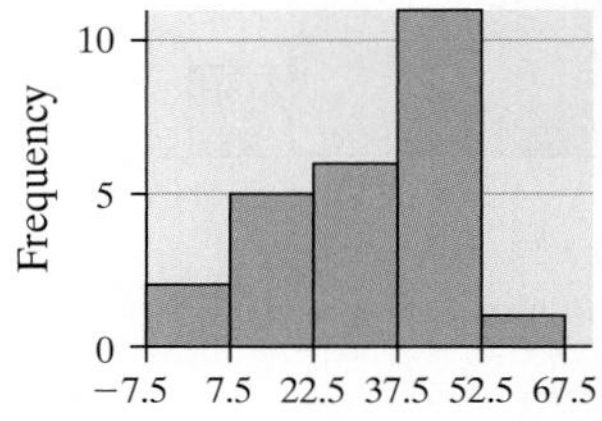

(c)

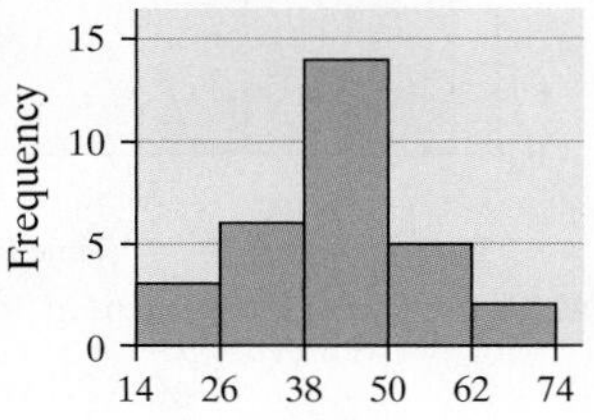

(d)

(a) IV (b) III (c) II (d) I

APPLYING THE CONCEPTS

19. pH in Water The acidity or alkalinity of a solution is measured using pH. A pH less than 7 is acidic; a pH greater than 7 is alkaline. The following data represent the pH in samples of bottled water and tap water.

Tap	7.64	7.45	7.47	7.50	7.68	7.69
	7.45	7.10	7.56	7.47	7.52	7.47
Bottled	5.15	5.09	5.26	5.20	5.02	5.23
	5.28	5.26	5.13	5.26	5.21	5.24

Source: Emily McCarney, student at Joliet Junior College

(a) Determine the mean, median, and mode pH for each type of water. Comment on the differences between the two water types. (b) $\bar{x} = 7.05$; $M = 7.485$; resistance

(b) Suppose the pH of 7.10 in tap water was incorrectly recorded as 1.70. How does this affect the mean? the median? What property of the median does this illustrate?

20. Reaction Time In an experiment conducted online at the University of Mississippi, study participants are asked to react to a stimulus. In one experiment, the participant must press a key upon seeing a blue screen. The time (in seconds) to press the key is measured. The same person is then asked to press a key upon seeing a red screen, again with the time to react measured. The table shows the results for six study participants.

Participant Number	Reaction Time to Blue	Reaction Time to Red
1	0.582	0.408
2	0.481	0.407
3	0.841	0.542
4	0.267	0.402
5	0.685	0.456
6	0.450	0.533

Source: PsychExperiments at the University of Mississippi (www.olemiss.edu/psychexps)

(a) Determine the mean, median, and mode reaction time for both blue and red.

(b) Does there appear to be a difference in the reaction time? What might account for any difference? How might this information be used?

(c) Suppose the reaction time of 0.841 for blue was incorrectly recorded as 8.41. How does this affect the mean? the median? What property of the median does this illustrate? $\bar{x} = 1.8125$; $M = 0.5315$; resistance

NW **21. Pulse Rates** The data on the following page represent the pulse rates (beats per minute) of nine students enrolled in a section of Sullivan's Introductory Statistics course. Treat the nine students as a population.

19. (a) Tap: $\bar{x} = 7.50$; $M = 7.485$; mode $= 7.47$
Bottled: $\bar{x} = 5.194$; $M = 5.22$; mode $= 5.26$
20. (a) Blue: 0.551 sec; 0.5315 sec; none; Red: 0.458 sec; 0.432 sec; none.

23. (a) 536,237 thousand metric tons (c) 2.693 thousand metric tons; 2.660 thousand metric tons; mean

Student	Pulse
Perpectual Bempah	76
Megan Brooks	60
Jeff Honeycutt	60
Clarice Jefferson	81
Crystal Kurtenbach	72
Janette Lantka	80
Kevin McCarthy	80
Tammy Ohm	68
Kathy Wojdyla	73

(a) Determine the population mean pulse. 72.2

(b) Find three simple random samples of size 3 and determine the sample mean pulse of each sample.

(c) Which samples result in a sample mean that overestimates the population mean? Which samples result in a sample mean that underestimates the population mean? Do any samples lead to a sample mean that equals the population mean?

22. Travel Time The following data represent the travel time (in minutes) to school for nine students enrolled in Sullivan's College Algebra course. Treat the nine students as a population.

Student	Travel Time	Student	Travel Time
Amanda	39	Scot	45
Amber	21	Erica	11
Tim	9	Tiffany	12
Mike	32	Glenn	39
Nicole	30		

(a) Determine the population mean for travel time. 26.4 min

(b) Find three simple random samples of size 4 and determine the sample mean for travel time of each sample.

(c) Which samples result in a sample mean that overestimates the population mean? Which samples result in a sample mean that underestimates the population mean? Do any samples lead to a sample mean that equals the population mean?

23. Carbon Dioxide Emissions The given data represent the fossil-fuel carbon dioxide (CO_2) emissions (in thousands of metric tons) of the top 10 emitters in 2007.

Country	Emissions	Per Capita Emissions
China	1,783,029	1.35
United States	1,591,756	5.20
India	439,695	0.39
Russia	419,241	2.95
Japan	342,117	2.71
Germany	214,872	2.61
Canada	151,988	4.61
United Kingdom	147,155	2.41
South Korea	137,257	2.82
Iran	135,257	1.88

Source: Carbon Dioxide Information Analysis Center

(a) Determine the mean CO_2 emissions of the top 10 countries.

(b) Explain why the total emissions of a country is likely not the best gauge of CO_2 emissions; instead, the emissions per capita (total emissions divided by population size) is the better gauge.

(c) Determine the mean and median per capita CO_2 emissions of the top 10 countries. Which measure would an environmentalist likely use to support the position that per capita CO_2 emissions are too high? Why?

24. Tour de Lance Lance Armstrong won the Tour de France seven consecutive years (1999–2005). The following table gives the winning times, distances, speeds, and margin of victory.

Year	Winning Time (h)	Distance (km)	Winning Speed (km/h)	Winning Margin (min)
1999	91.538	3687	40.28	7.617
2000	92.552	3662	39.56	6.033
2001	86.291	3453	40.02	6.733
2002	82.087	3278	39.93	7.283
2003	83.687	3427	40.94	1.017
2004	83.601	3391	40.56	6.317
2005	86.251	3593	41.65	4.667

Source: cyclingnews.com

(a) Determine the mean and median of his winning times for the seven races. Mean = 86.572 h; median = 86.251 h

(b) Determine the mean and median of the distances for the seven races. Mean = 3498.7 km; median = 3453 km

(c) Determine the mean and median of his winning margin.

(d) Determine the mean winning speed by finding the mean of the data values in the table. Next, compute the mean winning speed by finding the total of the seven distances and dividing by the total of the seven winning times. Finally, compute the mean winning speed by dividing the mean distance by the mean winning time. Do the three values agree or are there differences? (c) Mean = 5.667 min; median = 6.317 min

NW **25. Connection Time** A histogram of the connection time, in seconds, to an Internet service provider for 30 randomly selected connections is shown. The mean connection time is 39.007 seconds and the median connection time is 39.065 seconds. Identify the shape of the distribution. Which measure of central tendency better describes the "center" of the distribution? Symmetric; mean

Connection Time

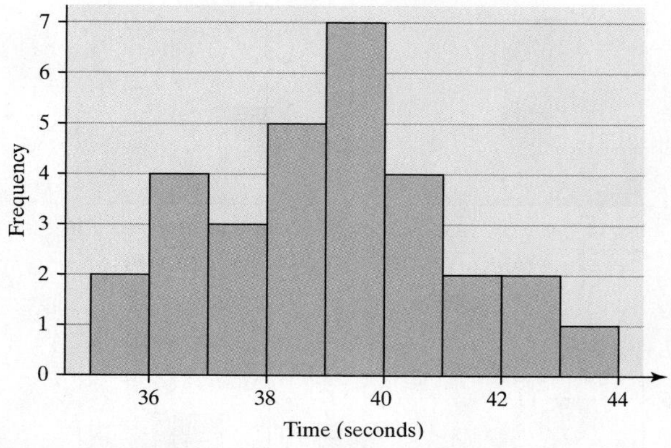

Source: Nicole Spreitzer, student at Joliet Junior College

24. (d) Method 1: mean = 40.420 km/h; method 2: mean = 40.414 km/h; method 3: mean = 40.414 km/h

26. Journal Costs A histogram of the annual subscription cost (in dollars) for 26 biology journals is shown. The mean subscription cost is \$1846 and the median subscription cost is \$1142. Identify the shape of the distribution. Which measure of central tendency better describes the "center" of the distribution? Skewed right; median

Cost of Biology Journals

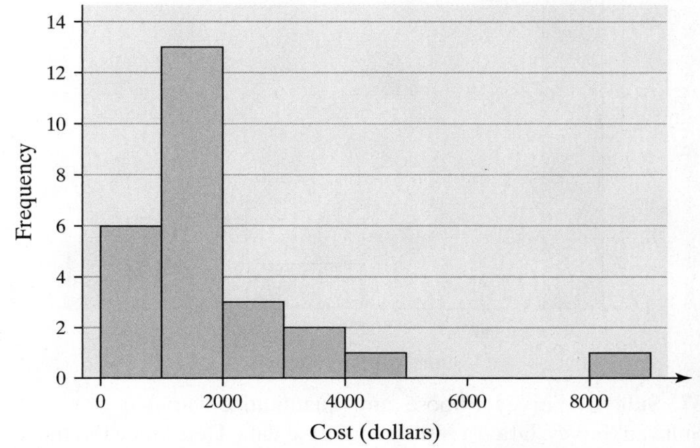

Source: Carol Wesolowski, student at Joliet Junior College

27. M&Ms The following data represent the weights (in grams) of a simple random sample of 50 M&M plain candies.

0.87	0.88	0.82	0.90	0.90	0.84	0.84
0.91	0.94	0.86	0.86	0.86	0.88	0.87
0.89	0.91	0.86	0.87	0.93	0.88	
0.83	0.95	0.87	0.93	0.91	0.85	
0.91	0.91	0.86	0.89	0.87	0.84	
0.88	0.88	0.89	0.79	0.82	0.83	
0.90	0.88	0.84	0.93	0.81	0.90	
0.88	0.92	0.85	0.84	0.84	0.86	

Source: Michael Sullivan

Determine the shape of the distribution of weights of M&Ms by drawing a frequency histogram. Find the mean and median. Which measure of central tendency better describes the weight of a plain M&M? Symmetric; $\bar{x} = 0.875$ g; $M = 0.875$ g; mean

28. Old Faithful We have all heard of the Old Faithful geyser in Yellowstone National Park. However, there is another, less famous, Old Faithful geyser in Calistoga, California. The following data represent the length of eruption (in seconds) for a random sample of eruptions of the California Old Faithful.

108	108	99	105	103	103	94
102	99	106	90	104	110	110
103	109	109	111	101	101	
110	102	105	110	106	104	
104	100	103	102	120	90	
113	116	95	105	103	101	
100	101	107	110	92	108	

Source: Ladonna Hansen, Park Curator

Determine the shape of the distribution of length of eruption by drawing a frequency histogram. Find the mean and median. Which measure of central tendency better describes the length of eruption? Symmetric; $\bar{x} = 104.1$ s; $M = 104$ s; mean

29. Hours Working A random sample of 25 college students was asked, "How many hours per week typically do you work outside the home?" Their responses were as follows:

0	0	15	20	30
40	30	20	35	35
28	15	20	25	25
30	5	0	30	24
28	30	35	15	15

Skewed left; $\bar{x} = 22$ hr; $M = 25$ hr; median

Determine the shape of the distribution of hours worked by drawing a frequency histogram. Find the mean and median. Which measure of central tendency better describes hours worked?

30. A Dealer's Profit The following data represent the profit (in dollars) of a new-car dealer for a random sample of 40 sales.

781	1038	453	1446	3082
501	451	1826	1348	3001
1342	1889	580	0	2909
2883	480	1664	1064	2978
149	1291	507	261	540
543	87	798	673	2862
1692	1783	2186	398	526
730	2324	2823	1676	4148

Source: Ashley Hudson, student at Joliet Junior College

Determine the shape of the distribution of new-car profit by drawing a frequency histogram. Find the mean and median. Which measure of central tendency better describes the profit? Skewed right; $\bar{x} = \$1392.83$; $M = \$1177.50$; median

NW **31. Political Views** A sample of 30 registered voters was surveyed in which the respondents were asked, "Do you consider your political views to be conservative, moderate, or liberal?" The results of the survey are shown in the table.

Liberal	Conservative	Moderate
Moderate	Liberal	Moderate
Liberal	Moderate	Conservative
Moderate	Conservative	Moderate
Moderate	Moderate	Liberal
Liberal	Moderate	Liberal
Conservative	Moderate	Moderate
Liberal	Conservative	Liberal
Liberal	Conservative	Liberal
Conservative	Moderate	Conservative

Source: Based on data from the General Social Survey

(a) Determine the mode political view. Moderate

(b) Do you think it would be a good idea to rotate the choices conservative, moderate, or liberal in the question? Why? Yes, to avoid response bias

32. Hospital Admissions The following data represent the diagnosis of a random sample of 20 patients admitted to a hospital. Determine the mode diagnosis. Gunshot wound

Cancer	Motor vehicle accident	Congestive heart failure
Gunshot wound	Fall	Gunshot wound
Gunshot wound	Motor vehicle accident	Gunshot wound
Assault	Motor vehicle accident	Gunshot wound
Motor vehicle accident	Motor vehicle accident	Gunshot wound
Motor vehicle accident	Gunshot wound	Motor vehicle accident
Fall	Gunshot wound	

Source: Tamela Ohm, student at Joliet Junior College

33. Resistance and Sample Size Each of the following three data sets represents the IQ scores of a random sample of adults. IQ scores are known to have a mean and median of 100. For each data set, determine the mean and median. For each data set recalculate the mean and median, assuming that the individual whose IQ is 106 is accidentally recorded as 160. For each sample size, state what happens to the mean and the median. Comment on the role the number of observations plays in resistance.

SAMPLE OF SIZE 5				
106	92	98	103	100

SAMPLE OF SIZE 12					
106	92	98	103	100	102
98	124	83	70	108	121

SAMPLE OF SIZE 30					
106	92	98	103	100	102
98	124	83	70	108	121
102	87	121	107	97	114
140	93	130	72	81	90
103	97	89	98	88	103

34. Mr. Zuro finds the mean height of all 14 students in his statistics class to be 68.0 inches. Just as Mr. Zuro finishes explaining how to get the mean, Danielle walks in late. Danielle is 65 inches tall. What is the mean height of the 15 students in the class? 67.8 inches

35. Missing Exam Grade A professor has recorded exam grades for 20 students in his class, but one of the grades is no longer readable. If the mean score on the exam was 82 and the mean of the 19 readable scores is 84, what is the value of the unreadable score? 44

36. Survival Rates Unfortunately, a friend of yours has been diagnosed with cancer. You obtain a histogram of the survival time (in months) of patients diagnosed with this form of cancer as shown in the figure. The median survival time for individuals with this form of cancer is 11 months, while the mean survival time is 69 months. What words of encouragement should you share with your friend from a statistical point of view?

Survival Time of Patients

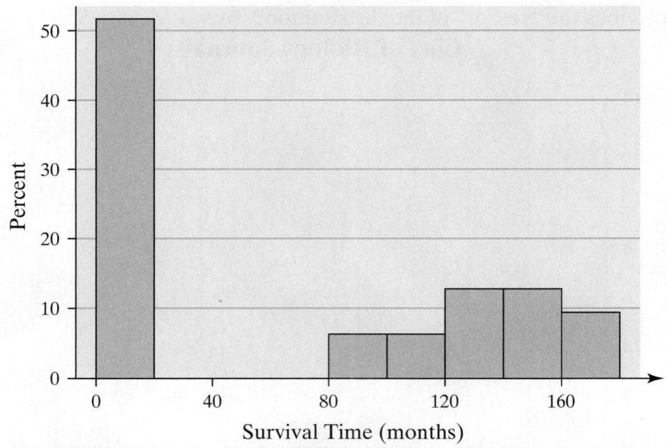

37. Sullivan Survey Choose any quantitative variable from the Sullivan Survey. Draw a histogram of the data. Determine the mean and the median. Based on the mean, median, and histogram, describe the shape of the distribution. Which measure of central tendency better describes the "center" of the distribution?

38. Sullivan Survey Choose any quantitative variable from the Sullivan Survey. Now choose a qualitative variable, such as gender or political philosophy. Determine the mean and the median by the qualitative variable chosen. For example, if you chose gender as the qualitative variable, determine the mean and median by gender. Does there appear to be any difference in the measure of central tendency for each level of the qualitative variable?

39. Linear Transformations Benjamin owns a small Internet business. Besides himself, he employs nine other people. The salaries earned by the employees are given next in thousands of dollars (Benjamin's salary is the largest, of course):

30, 30, 45, 50, 50, 50, 55, 55, 60, 75

(a) Determine the mean, median, and mode for salary.

(b) Business has been good! As a result, Benjamin has a total of \$25,000 in bonus pay to distribute to his employees. One option for distributing bonuses is to give each employee (including himself) \$2500. Add the bonuses under this plan to the original salaries to create a new data set. Recalculate the mean, median, and mode. How do they compare to the originals? mean = 52.5; median = 52.5; mode = 52.5

(c) As a second option, Benjamin can give each employee a bonus of 5% of his or her original salary. Add the bonuses under this second plan to the original salaries to create a new data set. Recalculate the mean, median, and mode. How do they compare to the originals? mean = 52.5; median = 52.5; mode = 52.5

(d) As a third option, Benjamin decides not to give his employees a bonus at all. Instead, he keeps the \$25,000 for himself. Use this plan to create a new data set. Recalculate the mean, median, and mode. How do they compare to the originals? mean = 52.5; median = 50; mode = 50

40. Linear Transformations Use the five test scores of 65, 70, 71, 75, and 95 to answer the following questions:

(a) Find the sample mean. 75.2

(b) Find the median. 71

(c) Which measure of central tendency best describes the typical test score? Median

(d) Suppose the professor decides to curve the exam by adding 4 points to each test score. Compute the sample mean based on the adjusted scores. 79.2

(e) Compare the unadjusted test score mean with the curved test score mean. What effect did adding 4 to each score have on the mean? The mean increased by 4.

41. Trimmed Mean Another measure of central tendency is the trimmed mean. It is computed by determining the mean of a data set after deleting the smallest and largest observed values. Compute the trimmed mean for the data in Problem 27. Is the trimmed mean resistant? Explain. 0.875 g

42. Midrange The midrange is also a measure of central tendency. It is computed by adding the smallest and largest observed values of a data set and dividing the result by 2; that is,

$$\text{Midrange} = \frac{\text{largest data value} + \text{smallest data value}}{2}$$

Compute the midrange for the data in Problem 27. Is the midrange resistant? Explain. 0.87g; no

43. Putting It Together: Shape, Mean and Median As part of a semester project in a statistics course, Carlos surveyed a sample of 50 high school students and asked, "How many days in the past week have you consumed an alcoholic beverage?" The results of the survey are shown next.

0	0	1	4	1	1	1	5	1	3
0	1	0	1	0	4	0	1	0	1
0	0	0	0	2	0	0	0	0	0
1	0	2	0	0	0	1	2	1	1
2	0	1	0	1	3	1	1	0	3

43. (b) Skewed right

(a) Is this data discrete or continuous? Discrete

(b) Draw a histogram of the data and describe its shape.

(c) Based on the shape of the histogram, do you expect the mean to be more than, equal to, or less than the median? $\bar{x} > M$

(d) Determine the mean and the median. What does this tell you? Mean: 0.94; Median: 1

(e) Determine the mode. 0

(f) Do you believe that Carlos's survey suffers from sampling bias? Why? Yes

EXPLAINING THE CONCEPTS

44. FICO Scores The Fair Isaacs Corporation has devised a model that is used to determine creditworthiness of individuals, called a FICO score. FICO scores range in value from 300 to 850, with a higher score indicating a more credit-worthy individual. The distribution of FICO scores is skewed left with a median score of 723. (b) 50%

(a) Do you think the mean FICO score is greater than, less than, or equal to 723? Justify your response. Less than

(b) What proportion of individuals have a FICO score above 723?

45. Why is the median resistant, but the mean is not?

46. A researcher with the Department of Energy wants to determine the mean natural gas bill of households throughout the United States. He knows the mean natural gas bill of households for each state, so he adds together these 50 values and divides by 50 to arrive at his estimate. Is this a valid approach? Why or why not? No

47. Net Worth According to the *Statistical Abstract of the United States*, the mean net worth of all households in the United States in 2007 was $556,300, while the median net worth was $120,300.

(a) Which measure do you believe better describes the typical U.S. household's net worth? Support your opinion. Median

(b) What shape would you expect the distribution of net worth to have? Why? Skewed right

(c) What do you think causes the disparity in the two measures of central tendency?

48. You are negotiating a contract for the Players Association of the NBA. Which measure of central tendency will you use to support your claim that the average player's salary needs to be increased? Why? As the chief negotiator for the owners, which measure would you use to refute the claim made by the Players Association? median; mean

49. In January 2012, the mean amount of money lost per visitor to a local riverboat casino was $135. Do you think the median was more than, less than, or equal to this amount? Why?

50. For each of the following situations, determine which measure of central tendency is most appropriate and justify your reasoning.

(a) Average price of a home sold in Pittsburgh, Pennsylvania, in 2011 Median

(b) Most popular major for students enrolled in a statistics course Mode

(c) Average test score when the scores are distributed symmetrically Mean

(d) Average test score when the scores are skewed right Median

(e) Average income of a player in the National Football League Median

(f) Most requested song at a radio station Mode

Technology Step-By-Step

Determining the Mean and Median

TI-83/84 Plus

1. Enter the raw data in L1 by pressing STAT and selecting `1:Edit`.
2. Press STAT, highlight the CALC menu, and select `1:1-Var Stats`.
3. With `1-Var Stats` appearing on the HOME screen, press 2nd then `1` to insert `L1` on the HOME screen. Press ENTER.

MINITAB

1. Enter the data in C1.
2. Select the **Stat** menu, highlight **Basic Statistics,** and then highlight **Display Descriptive Statistics.**
3. In the **Variables** window, enter C1. Click OK.

Excel

1. Enter the data in column A.
2. Select the **Data** menu and click **Data Analysis**.
3. In the Data Analysis window, highlight **Descriptive Statistics** and click OK.
4. With the cursor in the **Input Range** window, use the mouse to highlight the data in column A.
5. Select the **Summary statistics** option and click OK.

StatCrunch

1. Enter the raw data into the spreadsheet. Name the column variable.
2. Select **Stat**, highlight **Summary Stats**, and select **Columns**.
3. Click on the variable you wish to summarize and click Next>.
4. Deselect any statistics you do not wish to compute. Click Calculate.

3.2 MEASURES OF DISPERSION

OBJECTIVES

1. Determine the range of a variable from raw data
2. Determine the standard deviation of a variable from raw data
3. Determine the variance of a variable from raw data
4. Use the Empirical Rule to describe data that are bell shaped
5. Use Chebyshev's Inequality to describe any set of data

In Section 3.1, we discussed measures of central tendency. These measures describe the typical *value* of a variable. We would also like to know the amount of *dispersion* in the variable. **Dispersion** is the degree to which the data are spread out. Example 1 demonstrates why measures of central tendency are not sufficient in describing a distribution.

EXAMPLE 1 Comparing Two Sets of Data

Problem The data in Table 7 represent the IQ scores of a random sample of 100 students from two different universities. For each university, compute the mean IQ score and draw a histogram, using a lower class limit of 55 for the first class and a class width of 15. Comment on the results.

TABLE 7

University A										University B									
73	103	91	93	136	108	92	104	90	78	86	91	107	94	105	107	89	96	102	96
108	93	91	78	81	130	82	86	111	93	92	109	103	106	98	95	97	95	109	109
102	111	125	107	80	90	122	101	82	115	93	91	92	91	117	108	89	95	103	109
103	110	84	115	85	83	131	90	103	106	110	88	97	119	90	99	96	104	98	95
71	69	97	130	91	62	85	94	110	85	87	105	111	87	103	92	103	107	106	97
102	109	105	97	104	94	92	83	94	114	107	108	89	96	107	107	96	95	117	97
107	94	112	113	115	106	97	106	85	99	98	89	104	99	99	87	91	105	109	108
102	109	76	94	103	112	107	101	91	107	116	107	90	98	98	92	119	96	118	98
107	110	106	103	93	110	125	101	91	119	97	106	114	87	107	96	93	99	89	94
118	85	127	141	129	60	115	80	111	79	104	88	99	97	106	107	112	97	94	107

Approach We will use MINITAB to compute the mean and draw a histogram for each university.

Solution We enter the data into MINITAB and determine that the mean IQ score of both universities is 100.0. Figure 10 shows the histograms.

Figure 10

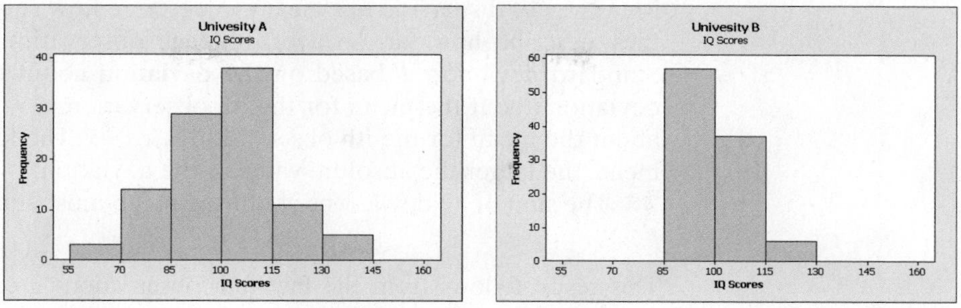

Both universities have the same mean IQ, but the histograms indicate the IQs from University A are more spread out, that is, more dispersed. While an IQ of 100.0 is typical for both universities, it appears to be a more reliable description of the typical student from University B than from University A. That is, a higher proportion of students from University B have IQ scores within, say, 15 points of the mean of 100.0 than students from University A.

Note to Instructor

You may want to share with students that the smallest data value is also referred to as the minimum and the largest data value is referred to as the maximum, as a preview of the five-number summary.

Our goal in this section is to discuss numerical measures of dispersion so that we can quantify the spread of data. We will discuss three numerical measures for describing the dispersion, or spread, of data: the *range*, *standard deviation*, and *variance*. In Section 3.4, we will discuss another measure of dispersion, the *interquartile range* (IQR).

1 Determine the Range of a Variable from Raw Data

The simplest measure of dispersion is the range. To compute the range, the data must be quantitative.

DEFINITION

The **range**, ***R***, of a variable is the difference between the largest and the smallest data value. That is,

$$\text{Range} = R = \text{largest data value} - \text{smallest data value}$$

EXAMPLE 2 Computing the Range of a Set of Data

Problem The data in Table 8 represent the scores on the first exam of 10 students enrolled in Introductory Statistics. Compute the range.

Approach The range is the difference between the largest and smallest data values.

Solution The highest test score is 94 and the lowest test score is 62. The range is

$$R = 94 - 62 = 32$$

All the students in the class scored between 62 and 94 on the exam. The difference between the best score and the worst score is 32 points.

Now compute the range of the data in Problem 13

TABLE 8

Student	Score
1. Michelle	82
2. Ryanne	77
3. Bilal	90
4. Pam	71
5. Jennifer	62
6. Dave	68
7. Joel	74
8. Sam	84
9. Justine	94
10. Juan	88

Notice that the range is affected by extreme values in the data set, so the range is not resistant. If Jennifer scored 28, the range becomes $R = 94 - 28 = 66$. Also, the range is computed using only two values in the data set (the largest and smallest). The *standard deviation*, on the other hand, uses all the data values in the computations.

2 Determine the Standard Deviation of a Variable from Raw Data

Measures of dispersion are meant to describe how spread out data are. In other words, they describe how far, on average, each observation is from the typical data value. Standard deviation is based on the **deviation about the mean**. For a population, the deviation about the mean for the ith observation is $x_i - \mu$. For a sample, the deviation about the mean for the ith observation is $x_i - \bar{x}$. The further an observation is from the mean, the larger the absolute value of the deviation.

The sum of all deviations about the mean must equal zero. That is,

$$\Sigma(x_i - \mu) = 0 \quad \text{and} \quad \Sigma(x_i - \bar{x}) = 0$$

This result follows from the fact that observations greater than the mean are offset by observations less than the mean. Because this sum is zero, we cannot use the average deviation about the mean as a measure of spread. There are two possible solutions to this "problem." We could either find the mean of the absolute values of the deviations about the mean, or we could find the mean of the squared deviations because squaring a nonzero number always results in a positive number. The first approach yields a measure of dispersion called the mean absolute deviation (MAD) (see Problem 42). The second approach leads to *variance*. The problem with variance is that squaring the deviations about the mean leads to squared units of measure, such as dollars squared. It is difficult to have a reasonable interpretation of dollars squared, so we "undo" the squaring process by taking the square root of the sum of squared deviations. We have the following definition for the *population standard deviation*.

Note
Recall, $|a| = a$ if $a \geq 0$, and $|a| = -a$ if $a < 0$ so $|3| = 3$ and $|-3| = 3$. ■

DEFINITION

The **population standard deviation** of a variable is the square root of the sum of squared deviations about the population mean divided by the number of observations in the population, N. That is, it is the square root of the mean of the squared deviations about the population mean.

The population standard deviation is symbolically represented by σ (lowercase Greek sigma).

$$\sigma = \sqrt{\frac{(x_1 - \mu)^2 + (x_2 - \mu)^2 + \cdots + (x_N - \mu)^2}{N}} = \sqrt{\frac{\Sigma(x_i - \mu)^2}{N}} \qquad \textbf{(1)}$$

where $x_1, x_2, \ldots, x_N$ are the N observations in the population and μ is the population mean.

A formula that is equivalent to Formula (1), called the **computational formula**, for determining the population standard deviation is

$$\sigma = \sqrt{\frac{\Sigma x_i^2 - \frac{(\Sigma x_i)^2}{N}}{N}} \qquad \textbf{(2)}$$

where Σx_i^2 means to square each observation and then sum these squared values, and $(\Sigma x_i)^2$ means to add up all the observations and then square the sum.

Example 3 illustrates how to use both formulas.

Note to Instructor
Consider assigning the "Exploring Standard Deviation" activity from the Student Activity Workbook.

EXAMPLE 3 Computing a Population Standard Deviation

Problem Compute the population standard deviation of the test scores in Table 8.

Approach Using Formula (1)

Step 1 Create a table with four columns. Enter the population data in Column 1. In Column 2, enter the population mean.

Step 2 Compute the deviation about the mean for each data value, $x_i - \mu$. Enter the result in Column 3.

Approach Using Formula (2)

Step 1 Create a table with two columns. Enter the population data in Column 1. Square each value in Column 1 and enter the result in Column 2.

Step 2 Sum the entries in Column 1. That is, find Σx_i. Sum the entries in Column 2. That is, find Σx_i^2.

Step 3 In Column 4, enter the squares of the values in Column 3.

Step 4 Sum the entries in Column 4, and divide this result by the size of the population, N.

Step 5 Determine the square root of the value found in Step 4.

Solution Using Formula (1)

Step 1 See Table 9. Column 1 lists the observations in the data set, and Column 2 contains the population mean.

TABLE 9

Score, x_i	Population Mean, μ	Deviation about the Mean, $x_i - \mu$	Squared Deviations about the Mean, $(x_i - \mu)^2$
82	79	$82 - 79 = 3$	$3^2 = 9$
77	79	$77 - 79 = -2$	$(-2)^2 = 4$
90	79	11	121
71	79	−8	64
62	79	−17	289
68	79	−11	121
74	79	−5	25
84	79	5	25
94	79	15	225
88	79	9	81
		$\Sigma(x_i - \mu) = 0$	$\Sigma(x_i - \mu)^2 = 964$

Step 2 Column 3 contains the deviations about the mean for each observation. For example, the deviation about the mean for Michelle is $82 - 79 = 3$. It is a good idea to add the entries in this column to make sure they sum to 0.

Step 3 Column 4 shows the squared deviations about the mean. Notice the farther an observation is from the mean, the larger the squared deviation.

Step 4 We sum the entries in Column 4 to obtain $\Sigma(x_i - \mu)^2$. We divide this sum by the number of students, 10:

$$\frac{\Sigma(x_i - \mu)^2}{N} = \frac{964}{10} = 96.4 \text{ points}^2$$

Step 5 The square root of the result in Step 4 is the population standard deviation.

$$\sigma = \sqrt{\frac{\Sigma(x_i - \mu)^2}{N}} = \sqrt{96.4 \text{ points}^2} \approx 9.8 \text{ points}$$

Step 3 Substitute the values found in Step 2 and the value for N into the computational formula and simplify.

Solution Using Formula (2)

Step 1 See Table 10. Column 1 lists the observations in the data set, and Column 2 contains the values in column 1 squared.

TABLE 10

Score, x_i	Score Squared, x_i^2
82	$82^2 = 6724$
77	$77^2 = 5929$
90	8100
71	5041
62	3844
68	4624
74	5476
84	7056
94	8836
88	7744
$\Sigma x_i = 790$	$\Sigma x_i^2 = 63{,}374$

Step 2 The last rows of Columns 1 and 2 show that $\Sigma x_i = 790$ and $\Sigma x_i^2 = 63{,}374$.

Step 3 We substitute 790 for Σx_i, 63,374 for Σx_i^2, and 10 for N into Formula (2):

$$\sigma = \sqrt{\frac{\Sigma x_i^2 - \frac{(\Sigma x_i)^2}{N}}{N}} = \sqrt{\frac{63{,}374 - \frac{(790)^2}{10}}{10}}$$

$$= \sqrt{\frac{964}{10}}$$

$$= \sqrt{96.4 \text{ points}^2}$$

$$\approx 9.8 \text{ points}$$

Formula (1) is sometimes referred to as the **conceptual formula** because it allows us to see how standard deviation measures spread. Look at Table 9 in Example 3. Notice that observations that are "far" from the mean, 79, result in larger squared deviations about the mean. For example, because the second observation, 77, is not "far" from 79, the squared deviation, 4, is not large, whereas the fifth observation, 62, is rather "far" from 79, so the squared deviation, 289, is much larger. So, if a data set has many observations that are "far" from the mean, the sum of the squared deviations will be large, and therefore the standard deviation will be large.

Now let's look at the definition of the *sample standard deviation.*

DEFINITION

The **sample standard deviation**, *s*, of a variable is the square root of the sum of squared deviations about the sample mean divided by $n - 1$, where *n* is the sample size.

$$s = \sqrt{\frac{(x_1 - \bar{x})^2 + (x_2 - \bar{x})^2 + \cdots + (x_n - \bar{x})^2}{n-1}} = \sqrt{\frac{\Sigma(x_i - \bar{x})^2}{n-1}} \quad \textbf{(3)}$$

where $x_1, x_2, \ldots, x_n$ are the *n* observations in the sample and $\bar{x}$ is the sample mean.

CAUTION
When using Formula (3), be sure to use $\bar{x}$ with as many decimal places as possible to avoid round-off error.

Formula (3) is often referred to as the conceptual formula for determining the sample standard deviation.

A computational formula that is equivalent to Formula (3) for computing the sample standard deviation is

$$s = \sqrt{\frac{\Sigma x_i^2 - \dfrac{\left(\Sigma x_i\right)^2}{n}}{n-1}} \quad \textbf{(4)}$$

CAUTION
When computing the sample standard deviation, be sure to divide by $n - 1$, not n.

Notice that the sample standard deviation is obtained by dividing by $n - 1$. Although showing why we divide by $n - 1$ is beyond the scope of the text, the following explanation has intuitive appeal. We already know that the sum of the deviations about the mean, $\Sigma(x_i - \bar{x})$, must equal zero. Therefore, if the sample mean is known and the first $n - 1$ observations are known, then the *n*th observation must be the value that causes the sum of the deviations to equal zero. For example, suppose $\bar{x} = 4$ based on a sample of size 3. In addition, if $x_1 = 2$ and $x_2 = 3$, then we can determine x_3.

$$\frac{x_1 + x_2 + x_3}{3} = \bar{x}$$

$$\frac{2 + 3 + x_3}{3} = 4 \qquad x_1 = 2, x_2 = 3, \bar{x} = 4$$

$$5 + x_3 = 12$$

$$x_3 = 7$$

Note to Instructor
A visual to help students understand degrees of freedom: Suppose there are six doughnuts in a box. The first five people to pick a doughnut have a choice (or freedom) about which doughnut to pick. The sixth person does not.

Note to Instructor
Consider assigning the "Understanding the Standard Deviation Formula: Why Divide by $n - 1$?" activity from the Student Activity Workbook.

We call $n - 1$ the **degrees of freedom** because the first $n - 1$ observations have freedom to be whatever value they wish, but the *n*th value has no freedom. It must be whatever value forces the sum of the deviations about the mean to equal zero.

Again, you should notice that typically Greek letters are used for parameters, while Roman letters are used for statistics. Do not use rounded values of the sample mean in Formula (3).

In Other Words
We have $n - 1$ degrees of freedom in the computation of *s* because an unknown parameter, μ, is estimated with $\bar{x}$. For each parameter estimated, we lose 1 degree of freedom.

EXAMPLE 4 Computing a Sample Standard Deviation

Problem Compute the sample standard deviation of the sample obtained in Example 1(b) on page 118 from Section 3.1.

Approach We follow the same approach that we used to compute the population standard deviation, but this time using the sample data. In looking back at Example 1(b) from Section 3.1, we see that Bilal (90), Ryanne (77), Pam (71), and Michelle (82) are in the sample.

Solution Using Formula (3)

Step 1 Create a table with four columns. Enter the sample data in Column 1. In Column 2, enter the sample mean. See Table 11.

TABLE 11

Score, x_i	Sample Mean, $\bar{x}$	Deviation about the Mean, $x_i - \bar{x}$	Squared Deviations about the Mean, $(x_i - \bar{x})^2$
90	80	$90 - 80 = 10$	$10^2 = 100$
77	80	-3	9
71	80	-9	81
82	80	2	4
		$\Sigma(x_i - \bar{x}) = 0$	$\Sigma(x_i - \bar{x})^2 = 194$

Step 2 Column 3 contains the deviations about the mean for each observation. For example, the deviation about the mean for Bilal is $90 - 80 = 10$. It is a good idea to add the entries in this column to make sure they sum to 0.

Step 3 Column 4 shows the squared deviations about the mean.

Step 4 We sum the entries in Column 4 to obtain $\Sigma(x_i - \bar{x})^2$. We divide the sum of the entries in Column 4 by one fewer than the number of students, $4 - 1$:

$$\frac{\Sigma(x_i - \bar{x})^2}{n - 1} = \frac{194}{4 - 1} = 64.7 \text{ points}^2$$

Step 5 The square root of the result in Step 4 is the sample standard deviation.

$$s = \sqrt{\frac{\Sigma(x_i - \bar{x})^2}{n - 1}}$$
$$= \sqrt{64.7 \text{ points}^2}$$
$$\approx 8.0 \text{ points}$$

Solution Using Formula (4)

Step 1 See Table 12. Column 1 lists the observations in the data set, and Column 2 contains the values in Column 1 squared.

TABLE 12

Score, x_i	Score squared, x_i^2
90	$90^2 = 8100$
77	$77^2 = 5929$
71	5041
82	6724
$\Sigma x_i = 320$	$\Sigma x_i^2 = 25{,}794$

Step 2 The last rows of Columns 1 and 2 show that $\Sigma x_i = 320$ and $\Sigma x_i^2 = 25{,}794$.

Step 3 We substitute 320 for Σx_i, 25,794 for Σx_i^2, and 4 for n into the computational Formula (4).

$$s = \sqrt{\frac{\Sigma x_i^2 - \frac{(\Sigma x_i)^2}{n}}{n - 1}} = \sqrt{\frac{25{,}794 - \frac{(320)^2}{4}}{4 - 1}}$$
$$= \sqrt{\frac{194}{3}}$$
$$= \sqrt{64.7 \text{ points}^2}$$
$$\approx 8.0 \text{ points}$$

EXAMPLE 5 Determining the Standard Deviation Using Technology

Problem Use statistical software or a calculator to determine the population standard deviation of the data listed in Table 8. Also determine the sample standard deviation of the sample data from Example 4.

Approach We will use a TI-84 Plus graphing calculator. The steps for determining the standard deviation using the TI-83 or TI-84 Plus graphing calculator, MINITAB, Excel, and StatCrunch are given in the Technology Step-by-Step on page 146.

Solution Figure 11(a) shows the population standard deviation, and Figure 11(b) shows the sample standard deviation. Notice that the TI graphing calculators provide both a population and sample standard deviation as output. This is because the calculator does not know whether the data entered are population data or sample data. It is up to the user of the calculator to choose the correct standard deviation. The results agree with those found in Examples 3 and 4.

Figure 11

Population standard deviation

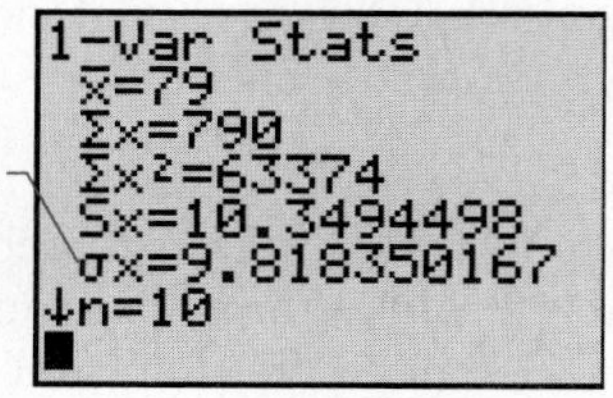

(a)

Sample standard deviation

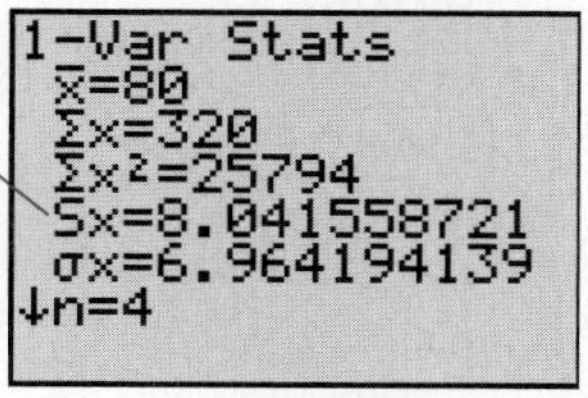

(b)

Now Work Problem 19

Is the standard deviation resistant? To help determine the answer, suppose Jennifer's exam score (Table 8 on page 131) is 26, not 62. The population standard deviation increases from 9.8 to 18.3. Clearly, the standard deviation is *not* resistant.

Interpretations of the Standard Deviation

Note to Instructor

To help students understand the concept of standard deviation, ask them whether they would prefer to invest in a stock with a standard deviation rate of return of 8% or one of 20%. Why? Or would they rather stand in a line with a standard deviation wait time of 3 minutes or 6 minutes? Why? In both examples, assume the means are equal.

The standard deviation is used along with the mean to numerically describe distributions that are bell shaped and symmetric. The mean measures the center of the distribution, while the standard deviation measures the spread of the distribution. So how does the value of the standard deviation relate to the spread of the distribution?

We can interpret the standard deviation as the typical deviation from the mean. So, in the data from Table 8, a typical deviation from the mean, $\mu = 79$ points, is 9.8 points.

If we are comparing two populations, then **the larger the standard deviation, the more dispersion the distribution has**, provided that the variable of interest from the two populations has the same unit of measure. The units of measure must be the same so that we are comparing apples with apples. For example, $100 is not the same as 100 Japanese yen, because $1 is equivalent to about 109 yen. This means a standard deviation of $100 is substantially higher than a standard deviation of 100 yen.

EXAMPLE 6 Comparing the Standard Deviation of Two Data Sets

Problem Refer to the data in Example 1. Use the standard deviation to determine whether University A or University B has more dispersion in its students' IQ scores.

Approach We will use MINITAB to determine the standard deviation of IQ for each university. The university with the higher standard deviation will be the university with more dispersion in IQ scores. The histograms shown in Figure 10 on page 131 imply that University A has more dispersion. Therefore, we expect University A to have a higher sample standard deviation.

Solution We enter the data into MINITAB and compute the descriptive statistics. See Figure 12.

Figure 12 **Descriptive statistics**

Variable	N	N*	Mean	SE Mean	StDev	Minimum
Univ A	100	0	100.00	1.61	16.08	60
Univ B	100	0	100.00	0.83	8.35	86

Variable	Q1	Median	Q3	Maximum
Univ A	90	102	110	141
Univ B	94	98	107	119

The sample standard deviation is larger for University A (16.1) than for University B (8.4). Therefore, University A has IQ scores that are more dispersed.

3 Determine the Variance of a Variable from Raw Data

A third measure of dispersion is called the *variance*.

DEFINITION

The **variance** of a variable is the square of the standard deviation. The **population variance** is σ^2 and the **sample variance** is s^2.

The units of measure in variance are squared values. So, if the variable is measured in dollars, the variance is measured in dollars squared. This makes interpreting the variance difficult. However, the variance is important for conducting certain types of statistical inference, which we discuss later in the text.

EXAMPLE 7 Determining the Variance of a Variable for a Population and a Sample

Problem Use the results of Examples 3 and 4 to determine the population and sample variance of test scores on the statistics exam.

Approach The population variance is found by squaring the population standard deviation. The sample variance is found by squaring the sample standard deviation.

Solution The population standard deviation in Example 3 was found to be $\sigma = 9.8$ points, so the population variance is $\sigma^2 = (9.8 \text{ points})^2 = 96.04 \text{ points}^2$. The sample standard deviation in Example 4 was found to be $s = 8.0$ points, so the sample variance is $s^2 = (8.0 \text{ points})^2 = 64.0 \text{ points}^2$.

If you look carefully at Formulas (1) and (3), you will notice that the value under the radical $(\sqrt{\ })$ represents the variance. So we could also find the population or sample variance while in the process of finding the population or sample standard deviation. Using this approach, we obtain a population variance of 96.4 points^2 and a sample variance of 64.7 points^2. Using a rounded value of the standard deviation to obtain the variance results in round-off error. To deal with this issue, it is recommended that you use as many decimal places as possible when using the standard deviation to obtain the variance.

A Final Thought on Variance and Standard Deviation

The sample variance is obtained using the formula $s^2 = \frac{\Sigma(x_i - \bar{x})^2}{n - 1}$. Suppose we divide by n instead of $n - 1$ in this formula to obtain the sample variance, as we might expect. Then the sample variance will consistently underestimate the population variance. Whenever a statistic consistently underestimates a parameter, it is said to be **biased.** To obtain an unbiased estimate of the population variance, we divide the sum of squared deviations about the sample mean by $n - 1$.

As an example of a biased estimator, suppose you work for a carnival in which you must guess a person's age. After 20 people come to your booth, you notice that you have a tendency to underestimate people's age. (You guess too low.) What would you do about this? You would probably adjust your guess higher to avoid underestimating. In other words, originally your guesses were biased. To remove the bias, you increase your guess. This is what dividing by $n - 1$ in the sample variance formula accomplishes.

Note to Instructor

To help students understand the concept of bias, draw a dart board on the board. Have all the darts congregate in the upper-left quadrant of the board.

Unfortunately, the sample standard deviation given in Formulas (3) and (4) is not an unbiased estimate of the population standard deviation. In fact, it is not possible to provide an unbiased estimator of the population standard deviation for all distributions. The explanation for this concept is beyond the scope of this class (it has to do with the shape of the graph of the square root function). Nonetheless, for the applications presented in this text, the bias (when dividing by $n - 1$) is minor and will not affect our results.

4 Use the Empirical Rule to Describe Data That Are Bell Shaped

If data have a distribution that is bell shaped, the *Empirical Rule* can be used to determine the percentage of data that will lie within k standard deviations of the mean.

The Empirical Rule

If a distribution is roughly bell shaped, then

- Approximately 68% of the data will lie within 1 standard deviation of the mean. That is, approximately 68% of the data lie between $\mu - 1\sigma$ and $\mu + 1\sigma$.

- Approximately 95% of the data will lie within 2 standard deviations of the mean. That is, approximately 95% of the data lie between $\mu - 2\sigma$ and $\mu + 2\sigma$.
- Approximately 99.7% of the data will lie within 3 standard deviations of the mean. That is, approximately 99.7% of the data lie between $\mu - 3\sigma$ and $\mu + 3\sigma$.

Note: We can also use the Empirical Rule based on sample data with $\bar{x}$ used in place of μ and s used in place of σ.

Figure 13 illustrates the Empirical Rule.

Figure 13

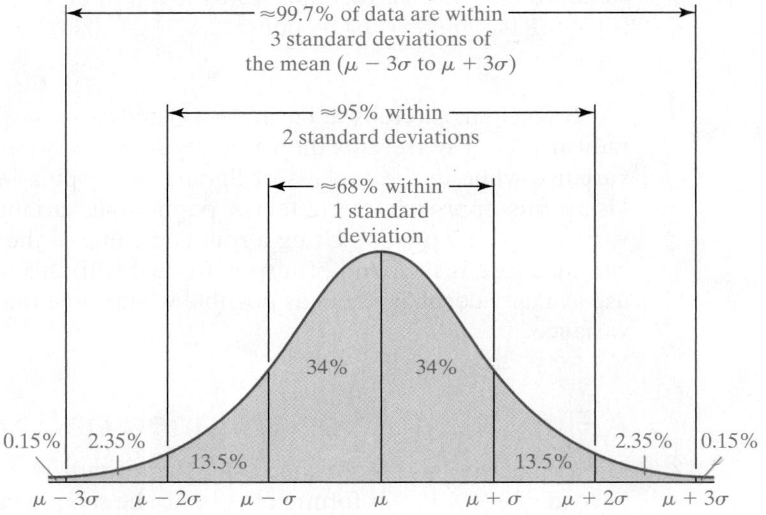

EXAMPLE 8 Using the Empirical Rule

Problem Use the data from University A in Table 7.

(a) Determine the percentage of students who have IQ scores within 3 standard deviations of the mean according to the Empirical Rule.

(b) Determine the percentage of students who have IQ scores between 67.8 and 132.2 according to the Empirical Rule.

(c) Determine the actual percentage of students who have IQ scores between 67.8 and 132.2.

(d) According to the Empirical Rule, what percentage of students have IQ scores above 132.2?

Approach To use the Empirical Rule, a histogram of the data must be roughly bell shaped. Figure 14 shows the histogram of the data from University A.

Solution The histogram is roughly bell shaped. From Examples 1 and 7, we know that the mean IQ score of the students enrolled in University A is 100 and the standard deviation is 16.1. To help organize our thoughts and make the analysis easier, we draw a bell-shaped curve like the one in Figure 13, with $\bar{x} = 100$ and $s = 16.1$. See Figure 15.

Figure 14

University A IQ Scores

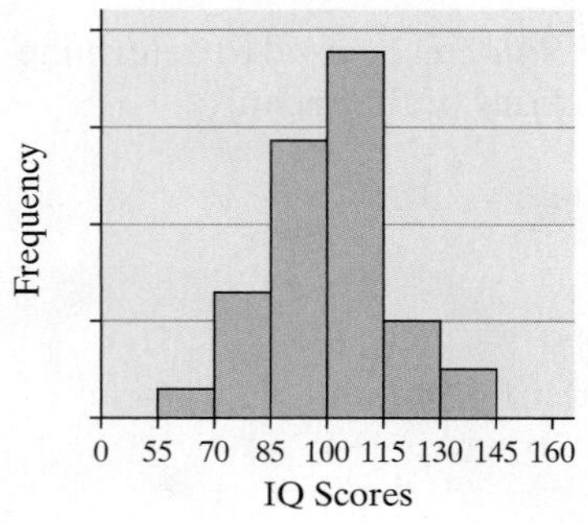

Figure 15

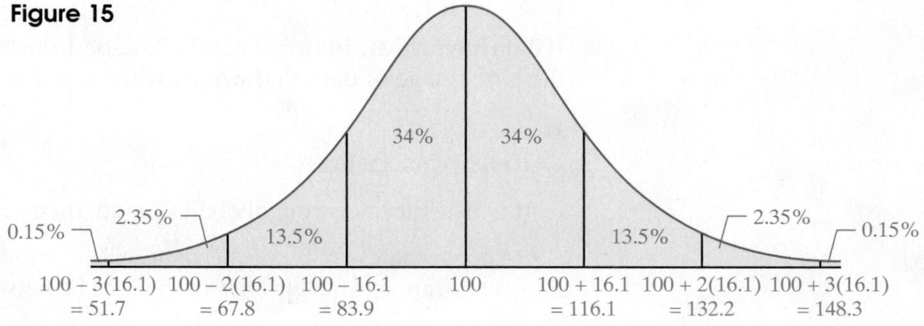

(a) According to the Empirical Rule, approximately 99.7% of the IQ scores are within 3 standard deviations of the mean [that is, greater than or equal to $100 - 3(16.1) = 51.7$ and less than or equal to $100 + 3(16.1) = 148.3$].

(b) Since 67.8 is exactly 2 standard deviations below the mean $[100 - 2(16.1) = 67.8]$ and 132.2 is exactly 2 standard deviations above the mean $[100 + 2(16.1) = 132.2]$, the Empirical Rule tells us that approximately 95% of the IQ scores lie between 67.8 and 132.2.

(c) Of the 100 IQ scores listed in Table 7, 96, or 96%, are between 67.8 and 132.2. This is very close to the Empirical Rule's approximation.

(d) Based on Figure 15, approximately $2.35\% + 0.15\% = 2.5\%$ of students at University A will have IQ scores above 132.2.

Now Work Problem 29

5 Use Chebyshev's Inequality to Describe Any Set of Data

Note to Instructor
Chebyshev's Inequality can be skipped without loss of continuity.

The Russian mathematician Pafnuty Chebyshev (1821–1894) developed an inequality that determines a minimum percentage of observations that lie within k standard deviations of the mean, where $k > 1$. What's amazing about this is that the result is obtained regardless of the basic shape of the distribution (skewed left, skewed right, or symmetric).

Chebyshev's Inequality

For any data set or distribution, at least $\left(1 - \frac{1}{k^2}\right)100\%$ of the observations lie within k standard deviations of the mean, where k is any number greater than 1. That is, at least $\left(1 - \frac{1}{k^2}\right)100\%$ of the data lie between $\mu - k\sigma$ and $\mu + k\sigma$ for $k > 1$.

Note: We can also use Chebyshev's Inequality based on sample data.

CAUTION
The Empirical Rule holds only if the distribution is bell shaped. Chebyshev's Inequality holds regardless of the shape of the distribution.

For example, at least $\left(1 - \frac{1}{2^2}\right)100\% = 75\%$ of all observations lie within $k = 2$ standard deviations of the mean and at least $\left(1 - \frac{1}{3^2}\right)100\% = 88.9\%$ of all observations lie within $k = 3$ standard deviations of the mean.

Notice the result does not state that exactly 75% of all observations lie within 2 standard deviations of the mean, but instead states that 75% or more of the observations will lie within 2 standard deviations of the mean.

EXAMPLE 9 Using Chebyshev's Inequality

Historical Note

Pafnuty Chebyshev was born on May 16, 1821, in Okatovo, Russia. In 1847, he began teaching mathematics at the University of St. Petersburg. Some of his more famous work was done on prime numbers. In particular, he discovered a way to determine the number of prime numbers less than or equal to a given number. Chebyshev also studied mechanics, including rotary motion. Chebyshev was elected a Fellow of the Royal Society in 1877. He died on November 26, 1894, in St. Petersburg.

Problem Use the data from University A in Table 7.

(a) Determine the minimum percentage of students who have IQ scores within 3 standard deviations of the mean according to Chebyshev's Inequality.

(b) Determine the minimum percentage of students who have IQ scores between 67.8 and 132.2, according to Chebyshev's Inequality.

(c) Determine the actual percentage of students who have IQ scores between 67.8 and 132.2.

Approach

(a) We use Chebyshev's Inequality with $k = 3$.

(b) We have to determine the number of standard deviations 67.8 and 132.2 are from the mean of 100.0. We then substitute this value for k in Chebyshev's Inequality.

(c) We refer to Table 7 and count the number of observations between 67.8 and 132.2. We divide this result by 100, the number of observations in the data set.

Solution

(a) Using Chebyshev's Inequality with $k = 3$, we find that at least $\left(1 - \frac{1}{3^2}\right)100\% = 88.9\%$ of all students have IQ scores within 3 standard deviations of the mean. Since the mean of the data set is 100.0 and the standard deviation is 16.1, at least 88.9%

of the students have IQ scores between $\bar{x} - ks = 100.0 - 3(16.1) = 51.7$ and $\bar{x} + ks = 100 + 3(16.1) = 148.3$.

(b) Since 67.8 is exactly 2 standard deviations below the mean $[100 - 2(16.1) = 67.8]$ and 132.2 is exactly 2 standard deviations above the mean $[100 + 2(16.1) = 132.2]$, Chebyshev's Inequality (with $k = 2$) says that at least $\left(1 - \frac{1}{2^2}\right)100\% = 75\%$ of all IQ scores lie between 67.8 and 132.2.

(c) Of the 100 IQ scores listed, 96 or 96% are between 67.8 and 132.2. Notice that Chebyshev's Inequality provides a conservative result.

Now Work Problem 35

Because the Empirical Rule requires that the distribution be bell shaped, while Chebyshev's Inequality applies to all distributions, the Empirical Rule gives more precise results.

3.2 ASSESS YOUR UNDERSTANDING

VOCABULARY AND SKILL BUILDING

1. The sum of the deviations about the mean always equals ___zero___.

2. The standard deviation is used in conjunction with the ___mean___ to numerically describe distributions that are bell shaped. The ___mean___ measures the center of the distribution, while the standard deviation measures the ___spread___ of the distribution.

3. *True or False:* When comparing two populations, the larger the standard deviation, the more dispersion the distribution has, provided that the variable of interest from the two populations has the same unit of measure. True

4. *True or False:* Chebyshev's Inequality applies to all distributions regardless of shape, but the Empirical Rule holds only for distributions that are bell shaped. True

In Problems 5–10, by hand, find the population variance and standard deviation or the sample variance and standard deviation as indicated.

5. Sample: 20, 13, 4, 8, 10 $s^2 = 36; s = 6$

6. Sample: 83, 65, 91, 87, 84 $s^2 = 100; s = 10$

7. Population: 3, 6, 10, 12, 14 $\sigma^2 = 16; \sigma = 4$

8. Population: 1, 19, 25, 15, 12, 16, 28, 13, 6 $\sigma^2 = 64; \sigma = 8$

9. Sample: 6, 52, 13, 49, 35, 25, 31, 29, 31, 29 $s^2 = 196; s = 14$

10. Population: 4, 10, 12, 12, 13, 21 $\sigma^2 = 25; \sigma = 5$

11. Crash Test Results The Insurance Institute for Highway Safety crashed the 2010 Ford Fusion four times at 5 miles per hour. The cost of repair for each of the four crashes are as follows:

$2529, $1889, $2610, $1073

Compute the range, sample variance, and sample standard deviation cost of repair. $1537; 507,013.6; $712.0

12. Cell Phone Use The following data represent the monthly cell phone bill for my wife's phone for six randomly selected months:

$35.34, $42.09, $39.43, $38.93, $43.39, $49.26

Compute the range, sample variance, and sample standard deviation phone bill. $13.92; 22.584; $4.752

NW 13. Concrete Mix A certain type of concrete mix is designed to withstand 3000 pounds per square inch (psi) of pressure. The strength of concrete is measured by pouring the mix into casting cylinders 6 inches in diameter and 12 inches tall. The concrete is allowed to set up for 28 days. The concrete's strength is then measured (in psi). The following data represent the strength of nine randomly selected casts:

3960, 4090, 3200, 3100, 2940, 3830, 4090, 4040, 3780

Compute the range and sample standard deviation for the strength of the concrete (in psi). 1150; 459.6

14. Flight Time The following data represent the flight time (in minutes) of a random sample of seven flights from Las Vegas, Nevada, to Newark, New Jersey, on Continental Airlines.

282, 270, 260, 266, 257, 260, 267

Compute the range and sample standard deviation of flight time. 25; 8.4 min

15. Which histogram depicts a higher standard deviation? Justify your answer. (b)

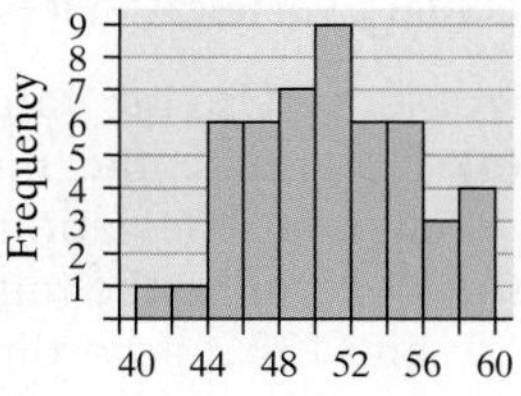

(a)

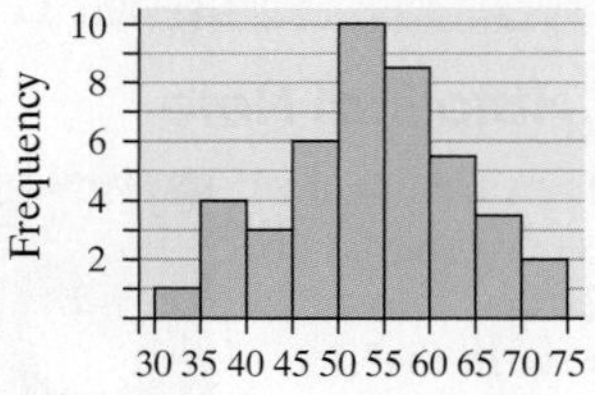

(b)

16. Match the histograms on the following page to the summary statistics given.

	Mean	Median	Standard Deviation
I	53	53	1.8
II	60	60	11
III	53	53	10
IV	53	53	22

(a) III (b) I (c) IV (d) II

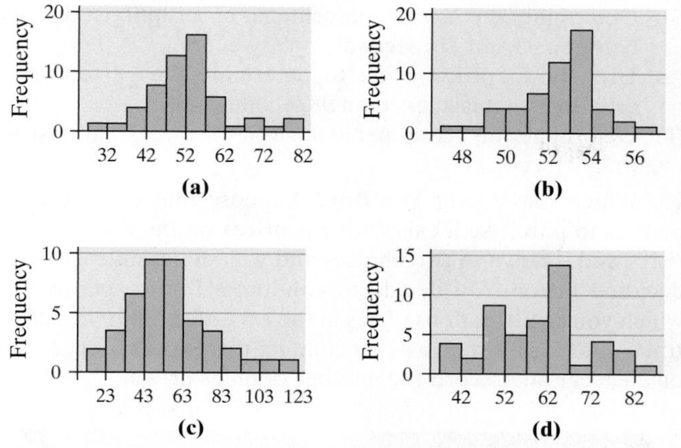

APPLYING THE CONCEPTS

17. pH in Water The acidity or alkalinity of a solution is measured using pH. A pH less than 7 is acidic, while a pH greater than 7 is alkaline. The following data represent the pH in samples of bottled water and tap water. (b) Tap water (0.154 vs. 0.081)

Tap	7.64	7.45	7.47	7.50	7.68	7.69
	7.45	7.10	7.56	7.47	7.52	7.47
Bottled	5.15	5.09	5.26	5.20	5.02	5.23
	5.28	5.26	5.13	5.26	5.21	5.24

Source: Emily McCarney, student at Joliet Junior College

(a) Which type of water has more dispersion in pH using the range as the measure of dispersion? Tap water (0.59 vs. 0.26)

(b) Which type of water has more dispersion in pH using the standard deviation as the measure of dispersion?

18. Reaction Time In an experiment conducted online at the University of Mississippi, study participants are asked to react to a stimulus. In one experiment, the participant must press a key upon seeing a blue screen. The time (in seconds) to press the key is measured. The same person is then asked to press a key upon seeing a red screen, again with the time to react measured. The results for six study participants are listed in the table.

Participant Number	Reaction Time to Blue	Reaction Time to Red
1	0.582	0.408
2	0.481	0.407
3	0.841	0.542
4	0.267	0.402
5	0.685	0.456
6	0.450	0.533

Source: PsychExperiments at the University of Mississippi (www.olemiss.edu/psychexps)

(a) Which color has more dispersion using the range as the measure of dispersion? Blue

(b) Which color has more dispersion using the standard deviation as the measure of dispersion? Blue

NW **19. Pulse Rates** The following data represent the pulse rates (beats per minute) of nine students enrolled in a section of Sullivan's course in Introductory Statistics. Treat the nine students as a population. 19. (a) 7.7 beats per minute

Student	Pulse
Perpectual Bempah	76
Megan Brooks	60
Jeff Honeycutt	60
Clarice Jefferson	81
Crystal Kurtenbach	72
Janette Lantka	80
Kevin McCarthy	80
Tammy Ohm	68
Kathy Wojdyla	73

(a) Determine the population standard deviation.

(b) Find three simple random samples of size 3, and determine the sample standard deviation of each sample.

(c) Which samples underestimate the population standard deviation? Which overestimate the population standard deviation?

20. Travel Time The following data represent the travel time (in minutes) to school for nine students enrolled in Sullivan's College Algebra course. Treat the nine students as a population.

Student	Travel Time	Student	Travel Time
Amanda	39	Scot	45
Amber	21	Erica	11
Tim	9	Tiffany	12
Mike	32	Glenn	39
Nicole	30		

(a) Determine the population standard deviation. 12.8 minutes

(b) Find three simple random samples of size 4, and determine the sample standard deviation of each sample.

(c) Which samples underestimate the population standard deviation? Which overestimate the population standard deviation?

21. A Fish Story Ethan and Drew went on a 10-day fishing trip. The number of smallmouth bass caught and released by the two boys each day was as follows:

Ethan	9	24	8	9	5	8	9	10	8	10
Drew	15	2	3	18	20	1	17	2	19	3

(a) Find the population mean and the range for the number of smallmouth bass caught per day by each fisherman. Do these values indicate any differences between the two fishermen's catches per day? Explain. $\mu = 10$; range $= 19$

(b) Find the population standard deviation for the number of smallmouth bass caught per day by each fisherman. Do these values present a different story about the two fishermen's catches per day? Which fisherman has the more consistent record? Explain. Ethan: $\sigma = 4.9$; Drew: $\sigma = 7.9$

(c) Discuss limitations of the range as a measure of dispersion.

22. Soybean Yield The data on the next page represent the number of pods on a sample of soybean plants for two different plot types. Which plot type do you think is superior? Why? Liberty

Plot Type	Pods								
Liberty	32	31	36	35	44	31	39	37	38
No Till	35	31	32	30	43	33	37	42	40

Source: Andrew Dieter and Brad Schmidgall, students at Joliet Junior College

23. The Empirical Rule The following data represent the weights (in grams) of a random sample of 50 M&M plain candies.

0.87	0.88	0.82	0.90	0.90	0.84	0.84
0.91	0.94	0.86	0.86	0.86	0.88	0.87
0.89	0.91	0.86	0.87	0.93	0.88	
0.83	0.95	0.87	0.93	0.91	0.85	
0.91	0.91	0.86	0.89	0.87	0.84	
0.88	0.88	0.89	0.79	0.82	0.83	
0.90	0.88	0.84	0.93	0.81	0.90	
0.88	0.92	0.85	0.84	0.84	0.86	

Source: Michael Sullivan

(a) Determine the sample standard deviation weight. Express your answer rounded to three decimal places. 0.036 gram
(b) On the basis of the histogram drawn in Section 3.1, Problem 27, comment on the appropriateness of using the Empirical Rule to make any general statements about the weights of M&Ms. Okay to use
(c) Use the Empirical Rule to determine the percentage of M&Ms with weights between 0.803 and 0.947 gram. *Hint:* $\bar{x} = 0.875$. 95%
(d) Determine the actual percentage of M&Ms that weigh between 0.803 and 0.947 gram, inclusive. 96%
(e) Use the Empirical Rule to determine the percentage of M&Ms with weights more than 0.911 gram. 16%
(f) Determine the actual percentage of M&Ms that weigh more than 0.911 gram. 12%

24. The Empirical Rule The following data represent the length of eruption for a random sample of eruptions at the Old Faithful geyser in Calistoga, California.

108	108	99	105	103	103	94
102	99	106	90	104	110	110
103	109	109	111	101	101	
110	102	105	110	106	104	
104	100	103	102	120	90	
113	116	95	105	103	101	
100	101	107	110	92	108	

Source: Ladonna Hansen, Park Curator

(a) Determine the sample standard deviation length of eruption. Express your answer rounded to the nearest whole number.
(b) On the basis of the histogram drawn in Section 3.1, Problem 28, comment on the appropriateness of using the Empirical Rule to make any general statements about the length of eruptions. Okay to use (a) 6 seconds
(c) Use the Empirical Rule to determine the percentage of eruptions that last between 92 and 116 seconds. *Hint:* $\bar{x} = 104$. 95%
(d) Determine the actual percentage of eruptions that last between 92 and 116 seconds, inclusive. 93%
(e) Use the Empirical Rule to determine the percentage of eruptions that last less than 98 seconds. 16%
(f) Determine the actual percentage of eruptions that last less than 98 seconds. 11%

25. Which Car Would You Buy? Suppose that you are in the market to purchase a car. With gas prices on the rise, you have narrowed it down to two choices and will let gas mileage be the deciding factor. You decide to conduct a little experiment in which you put 10 gallons of gas in the car and drive it on a closed track until it runs out gas. You conduct this experiment 15 times on each car and record the number of miles driven.

CAR 1				
228	223	178	220	220
233	233	271	219	223
217	214	189	236	248

CAR 2				
277	164	326	215	259
217	321	263	160	257
239	230	183	217	230

Describe each data set. That is, determine the shape, center, and spread. Which car would you buy and why?

26. Which Investment Is Better? You have received a year-end bonus of $5000. You decide to invest the money in the stock market and have narrowed your investment options down to two mutual funds. The following data represent the historical quarterly rates of return of each mutual fund for the past 20 quarters (5 years).

MUTUAL FUND A				
1.3	−0.3	0.6	6.8	5.0
5.2	4.8	2.4	3.0	1.8
7.3	8.6	3.4	3.8	−1.3
6.4	1.9	−0.5	−2.3	3.1

MUTUAL FUND B				
−5.4	6.7	11.9	4.3	4.3
3.5	10.5	2.9	3.8	5.9
−6.7	1.4	8.9	0.3	−2.4
−4.7	−1.1	3.4	7.7	12.9

Describe each data set. That is, determine the shape, center, and spread. Which mutual fund would you invest in and why?

27. Rates of Return of Stocks Stocks may be categorized by industry. The data on the following page represent the 5-year rates of return (in percent) for a sample of consumer goods stocks and energy stocks ending November 10, 2010.
(a) Determine the mean and the median rate of return for each industry. Which sector has the higher mean rate of return? Which sector has the higher median rate of return?
(b) Determine the standard deviation for each industry. In finance, the standard deviation rate of return is called **risk**. Typically, an investor "pays" for a higher return by accepting more risk. Is the investor paying for higher returns in this instance? Do you think the higher returns are worth the cost?

27. (a) CG: $\bar{x} = 9.805\%$, M = 10.11%; Energy: $\bar{x} = 11.679\%$, M = 10.76%; Energy; energy (b) CG: s = 8.993%; Energy: s = 9.340%; yes

CONSUMER GOODS STOCKS

9.83	10.11	11.06	9.32	7.5
8.66	13.7	15.04	17.24	16.83
6.22	8.86	11.79	9.64	−14.12
16.83	14.85	15.24	34.17	−8.32
0.52	1.46	11.26	6.79	10.66

ENERGY STOCKS

11.02	11.08	20.26	15.18	−0.13
4.13	1.61	1.58	16.14	−0.42
17.11	15.32	8.49	7.44	11.01
8.53	37.83	5.21	10.68	10.27
10.76	34.32	3.97	19.3	11.28

Source: morningstar.com

28. Temperatures It is well known that San Diego has milder weather than Chicago, but which city has more deviation from normal temperatures over the course of a month? Use the following data, which represent the deviation from normal high temperatures for each day in October 2010. In which city would you rather be a meteorologist? Why?

DEVIATION FROM NORMAL HIGH TEMPERATURE, CHICAGO (°F)

8	13	19	6	−9	7	−13
−7	11	11	0	0	1	
−9	15	−2	−5	2	−17	
−5	22	1	−4	8	−15	
2	17	−3	6	7	−2	

DEVIATION FROM NORMAL HIGH TEMPERATURE, SAN DIEGO (°F)

4	−6	−2	−3	−3	−3	−6
5	−1	−1	−5	−4	10	
1	−2	−1	−5	−5	8	
−4	3	−4	−4	−3	4	
−5	7	−5	−6	−4	−6	

Source: National Climatic Data Center

NW **29. The Empirical Rule** One measure of intelligence is the Stanford–Binet Intelligence Quotient (IQ). IQ scores have a bell-shaped distribution with a mean of 100 and a standard deviation of 15.

(a) What percentage of people has an IQ score between 70 and 130?

(b) What percentage of people has an IQ score less than 70 or greater than 130? (a) 95% (b) 5% (c) 2.5%

(c) What percentage of people has an IQ score greater than 130?

30. The Empirical Rule SAT Math scores have a bell-shaped distribution with a mean of 515 and a standard deviation of 114. *Source:* College Board, 2010

(a) What percentage of SAT scores is between 401 and 629? 68%

(b) What percentage of SAT scores is less than 401 or greater than 629? 32%

(c) What percentage of SAT scores is greater than 743? 2.5%

31. The Empirical Rule The weight, in grams, of the pair of kidneys in adult males between the ages of 40 and 49 has a bell-shaped distribution with a mean of 325 grams and a standard deviation of 30 grams. (a) 265 and 385 grams

(a) About 95% of kidney pairs will be between what weights?

(b) What percentage of kidney pairs weighs between 235 grams and 415 grams? 99.7%

(c) What percentage of kidney pairs weighs less than 235 grams or more than 415 grams? 0.3%

(d) What percentage of kidney pairs weighs between 295 grams and 385 grams? 81.5%

32. The Empirical Rule The distribution of the length of bolts has a bell shape with a mean of 4 inches and a standard deviation of 0.007 inch.

(a) About 68% of bolts manufactured will be between what lengths? 3.993 and 4.007 inches

(b) What percentage of bolts will be between 3.986 inches and 4.014 inches? 95%

(c) If the company discards any bolts less than 3.986 inches or greater than 4.014 inches, what percentage of bolts manufactured will be discarded? 5%

(d) What percentage of bolts manufactured will be between 4.007 inches and 4.021 inches? 15.85%

33. Which Professor? Suppose Professor Alpha and Professor Omega each teach Introductory Biology. You need to decide which professor to take the class from and have just completed your Introductory Statistics course. Records obtained from past students indicate that students in Professor Alpha's class have a mean score of 80% with a standard deviation of 5%, while past students in Professor Omega's class have a mean score of 80% with a standard deviation of 10%. Decide which instructor to take for Introductory Biology using a statistical argument.

34. Larry Summers Lawrence Summers (former secretary of the treasury and former president of Harvard) infamously claimed that women have a lower standard deviation IQ than men. He went on to suggest that this was a potential explanation as to why there are fewer women in top math and science positions. Suppose an IQ of 145 or higher is required to be a researcher at a top-notch research institution. Use the idea of standard deviation, the Empirical Rule, and the fact that the mean and standard deviation IQ of humans is 100 and 15, respectively, to explain Summers' argument.

NW **35. Chebyshev's Inequality** In December 2010, the average price of regular unleaded gasoline excluding taxes in the United States was \$3.06 per gallon, according to the Energy Information Administration. Assume that the standard deviation price per gallon is \$0.06 per gallon to answer the following.

(a) What minimum percentage of gasoline stations had prices within 3 standard deviations of the mean? 88.9%

(b) What minimum percentage of gasoline stations had prices within 2.5 standard deviations of the mean? What are the gasoline prices that are within 2.5 standard deviations of the mean? 84%; \$2.91 to \$3.21

(c) What is the minimum percentage of gasoline stations that had prices between \$2.94 and \$3.18? 75%

36. Chebyshev's Inequality According to the U.S. Census Bureau, the mean of the commute time to work for a resident of Boston, Massachusetts, is 27.3 minutes. Assume that the standard deviation of the commute time is 8.1 minutes to answer the following:

(a) What minimum percentage of commuters in Boston has a commute time within 2 standard deviations of the mean? 75%

(b) What minimum percentage of commuters in Boston has a commute time within 1.5 standard deviations of the mean?

28. Chicago: $R = 39$°F; $\sigma = 9.7$°F; San Diego: $R = 16$°F; $\sigma = 4.4$°F; Chicago has more dispersion.

What are the commute times within 1.5 standard deviations of the mean? 55.6%; 15.15 minutes to 39.45 minutes

(c) What is the minimum percentage of commuters who have commute times between 3 minutes and 51.6 minutes? 88.9%

37. Comparing Standard Deviations The standard deviation of batting averages of all teams in the American League is 0.008. The standard deviation of all players in the American League is 0.02154. Why is there less variability in team batting averages?

38. Linear Transformations Benjamin owns a small Internet business. Besides himself, he employs nine other people. The salaries earned by the employees are given next in thousands of dollars (Benjamin's salary is the largest, of course):

30, 30, 45, 50, 50, 50, 55, 55, 60, 75

(a) Determine the range, population variance, and population standard deviation for the data.

(b) Business has been good! As a result, Benjamin has a total of \$25,000 in bonus pay to distribute to his employees. One option for distributing bonuses is to give each employee (including himself) \$2500. Add the bonuses under this plan to the original salaries to create a new data set. Recalculate the range, population variance, and population standard deviation. How do they compare to the originals? $R = \$45, \sigma^2 = 160, \sigma = \$12.6$

(c) As a second option, Benjamin can give each employee a bonus of 5% of his or her original salary. Add the bonuses under this second plan to the original salaries to create a new data set. Recalculate the range, population variance, and population standard deviation. How do they compare to the originals? $R = \$47.25, \sigma^2 = 176.4, \sigma = \$13.3$

(d) As a third option, Benjamin decides not to give his employees a bonus at all. Instead, he keeps the \$25,000 for himself. Use this plan to create a new data set. Recalculate the range, population variance, and population standard deviation. How do they compare to the originals? $R = \$70, \sigma^2 = 341.3, \sigma = \$18.5$

39. Resistance and Sample Size Each of the following three data sets represents the IQ scores of a random sample of adults. IQ scores are known to have a mean and median of 100. For each data set, determine the sample standard deviation. Then recompute the sample standard deviation assuming that the individual whose IQ is 106 is accidentally recorded as 160. For each sample size, state what happens to the standard deviation. Comment on the role that the number of observations plays in resistance.

SAMPLE OF SIZE 5				
106	92	98	103	100

SAMPLE OF SIZE 12					
106	92	98	103	100	102
98	124	83	70	108	121

SAMPLE OF SIZE 30					
106	92	98	103	100	102
98	124	83	70	108	121
102	87	121	107	97	114
140	93	130	72	81	90
103	97	89	98	88	103

40. Identical Values Compute the sample standard deviation of the following test scores: 78, 78, 78, 78. What can be said about a data set in which all the values are identical? $s = 0$

41. Blocking and Variability Blocking refers to the idea that we can reduce the variability in a variable by segmenting the data by some other variable. The given data represent the recumbent length (in centimeters) of a sample of 10 males and 10 females who are 40 months of age.

MALES		FEMALES	
104.0	94.4	102.5	100.8
93.7	97.6	100.4	96.3
98.3	100.6	102.7	105.0
86.2	103.0	98.1	106.5
90.7	100.9	95.4	114.5

Source: National Center for Health Statistics

(a) Determine the standard deviation of recumbent length for all 20 observations. 6.11 cm

(b) Determine the standard deviation of recumbent length for the males. 5.67 cm

(c) Determine the standard deviation of recumbent length for the females. 5.59 cm

(d) What effect does blocking by gender have on the standard deviation of recumbent length for each gender?

42. Mean Absolute Deviation Another measure of variation is the mean absolute deviation. It is computed using the formula

$$\text{MAD} = \frac{\Sigma|x_i - \bar{x}|}{n}$$

Compute the mean absolute deviation of the data in Problem 11 and compare the results with the sample standard deviation. MAD = \$544.25; $s = \$712.05$

43. Coefficient of Skewness Karl Pearson developed a measure that describes the skewness of a distribution, called the **coefficient of skewness**. The formula is

$$\text{Skewness} = \frac{3(\text{mean} - \text{median})}{\text{standard deviation}}$$

The value of this measure generally lies between −3 and +3. The closer the value lies to −3, the more the distribution is skewed left. The closer the value lies to +3, the more the distribution is skewed right. A value close to 0 indicates a symmetric distribution. Find the coefficient of skewness of the following distributions and comment on the skewness.

(a) Mean = 50, median = 40, standard deviation = 10 3

(b) Mean = 100, median = 100, standard deviation = 15 0

(c) Mean = 400, median = 500, standard deviation = 120 −2.50

(d) Compute the coefficient of skewness for the data in Problem 23. 0

(e) Compute the coefficient of skewness for the data in Problem 24. 0.05

44. Diversification A popular theory in investment states that you should invest a certain amount of money in foreign investments to reduce your risk. The risk of a portfolio is defined as the standard deviation of the rate of return. Refer to the following graph, which depicts the relation between risk (standard deviation of rate of return) and reward (mean rate of return).

44. (d) Between −12.8% and 44.4%; between −27.1% and 58.7%; no

How Foreign Stocks Benefit a Domestic Portfolio

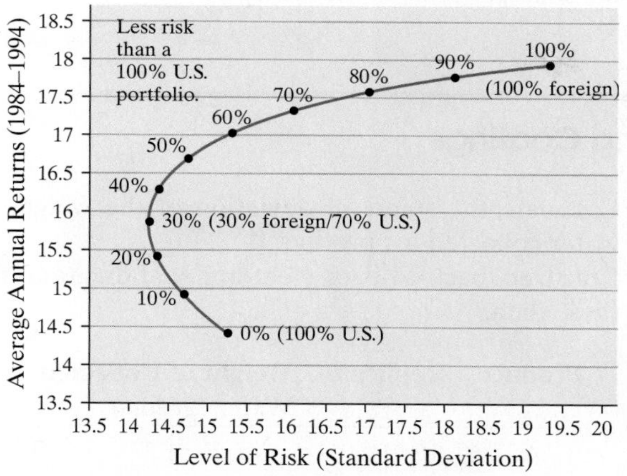

Source: T. Rowe Price

(a) Determine the average annual return and level of risk in a portfolio that is 10% foreign. 14.9%; 14.7%

(b) Determine the percentage that should be invested in foreign stocks to best minimize risk. 30%

(c) Why do you think risk initially decreases as the percent of foreign investments increases?

(d) A portfolio that is 30% foreign and 70% American has a mean rate of return of about 15.8%, with a standard deviation of 14.3%. According to Chebyshev's Inequality, at least 75% of returns will be between what values? According to Chebyshev's Inequality, at least 88.9% of returns will be between what two values? Should an investor be surprised if she has a negative rate of return? Why?

45. More Spread? The data set on the left represents the annual rate of return (in percent) of eight randomly sampled bond mutual funds, and the data set on the right represents the annual rate of return (in percent) of eight randomly sampled stock mutual funds.

2.0	2.4
3.2	2.7
1.6	1.8
1.9	3.4

8.4	6.9
7.4	8.1
9.1	7.6
7.2	9.4

(a) Bond: $\bar{x} = 2.375$, $s = 0.669$; Stock: $\bar{x} = 8.0125$; $s = 0.903$

(a) Determine the mean and standard deviation of each data set.

(b) Based only on the standard deviation, which data set has more spread? Stock (c) Bond: 0.625; stock: = 0.625

(c) What proportion of the observations is within one standard deviation of the mean for each data set?

(d) The **coefficient of variation**, CV, is defined as the ratio of the standard deviation to the mean of a data set, so

$$\text{CV} = \frac{\text{standard deviation}}{\text{mean}}$$

The coefficient of variation is unitless and allows for comparison in spread between two data sets by describing the amount of spread per unit mean. After all, larger numbers will likely have a larger standard deviation simply due to the size of the numbers. Compute the coefficient of variation for both data sets. Which data set do you believe has more "spread"? Bond: 0.28; stock: 0.11; bond

(e) Let's take this idea one step further. The following data represent the height of a random sample of 8 male college students. The data set on the left has their height measured in inches, and the data set on the right has their height measured in centimeters. Inches: mean = 70; $s = 2.5$; cm: mean = 177.8; $s = 6.368$; CV = 0.036 for both

74	72
66	71
69	71
68	69

187.96	182.88
167.64	180.34
175.26	180.34
172.72	175.26

For each data set, determine the mean and the standard deviation. Would you say that the height of the males is more dispersed based on the standard deviation of height measured in centimeters? Why? Now, determine the coefficient of variation for each data set. What did you find?

46. Sullivan Survey Choose any two quantitative variables from the Sullivan Survey for which a comparison is reasonable, such as number of hours of television versus number of hours of Internet. Draw a histogram for each variable. Which variable appears to have more dispersion? Determine the range and standard deviation of each variable. Based on the numerical measure, which variable has more dispersion?

47. Sullivan Survey Choose any quantitative variable from the Sullivan Survey. Now choose a qualitative variable, such as gender or political philosophy. Determine the range and standard deviation by the qualitative variable chosen. For example, if you chose gender as the qualitative variable, determine the range and standard deviation by gender. Does there appear to be any difference in the measure of dispersion for each level of the qualitative variable?

EXPLAINING THE CONCEPTS

48. Would it be appropriate to say that a distribution with a standard deviation of 10 centimeters is more dispersed than a distribution with a standard deviation of 5 inches? Support your position.

49. What is meant by the phrase *degrees of freedom* as it pertains to the computation of the sample standard deviation?

50. Are any of the measures of dispersion mentioned in this section resistant? Explain.

51. What does it mean when a statistic is biased?

52. What makes the range less desirable than the standard deviation as a measure of dispersion?

53. In one of Sullivan's statistics sections, the standard deviation of the heights of all students was 3.9 inches. The standard deviation of the heights of males was 3.4 inches and the standard deviation of females was 3.3 inches. Why is the standard deviation of the entire class more than the standard deviation of the males and females considered separately?

54. Explain how standard deviation measures spread. In your explanation include the computation of the same standard deviation for two data sets: Data set 1: 3, 4, 5; Data set 2: 0, 4, 8.

55. Which of the following would have a higher standard deviation? (a) IQ of students on your campus or (b) IQ of residents in your home town? Why?

56. Develop a sample of size $n = 8$ such that $\bar{x} = 15$ and $s = 0$.

57. Draw two histograms with different standard deviations and label them I and II. Which histogram has the larger standard deviation?

58. Fast Pass In 2000, the Walt Disney Company created the "fast pass." A fast-pass ticket is issued to a rider for the popular rides and the rider is told to return at a specific time during the day. At that time, the rider is allowed to by-pass the regular line, thereby reducing the wait time for that particular rider. When compared to wait times prior to creating the fast pass, overall wait times for rides at the park increased, on average. Yet patrons to the park indicated they were happier with the fast-pass system. Use the concepts of central tendency and dispersion to explain why.

Consumer Reports® Basement Waterproofing Coatings

A waterproofing coating can be an inexpensive and easy way to deal with leaking basements. But how effective are they? In a study, *Consumer Reports* tested nine waterproofers to rate their effectiveness in controlling water seepage though concrete foundations.

To compare the products' ability to control water seepage, we applied two coats of each product to slabs cut from concrete block. For statistical validity, this process was repeated at least six times. In each test run, four blocks (each coated with a different product) were simultaneously placed in a rectangular aluminum chamber. See the picture.

The chamber was sealed and filled with water and the blocks were subjected to progressively increasing hydrostatic pressures. Water that leaked out during each period was channeled to the bottom of the chamber opening, collected, and weighed.

The table contains a subset of the data collected for two of the products tested. Using these data:

(a) Calculate the mean, median, and mode weight of water collected for product A.

(b) Calculate the standard deviation of the weight of water collected for product A.

(c) Calculate the mean, median, and mode weight of water collected for product B.

Basement Waterproofer Test Chamber

(d) Calculate the standard deviation of the weight of water collected for product B.

(e) Construct back-to-back stem-and-leaf diagrams for these data.

Product	Replicate	Weight of Collected Water (grams)
A	1	91.2
A	2	91.2
A	3	90.9
A	4	91.3
A	5	90.8
A	6	90.8
B	1	87.1
B	2	87.2
B	3	86.8
B	4	87.0
B	5	87.2
B	6	87.0

Does there appear to be a difference in these two products' abilities to mitigate water seepage? Why?

Note to Readers: *In many cases, our test protocol and analytical methods are more complicated than described in these examples. The data and discussions have been modified to make the material more appropriate for the audience.*

Technology Step-By-Step

Determining the Range, Variance, and Standard Deviation

The same steps followed to obtain the measures of central tendency from raw data can be used to obtain the measures of dispersion.

Refer to the Technology Step-by-Step beginning on page 129.

3.3 MEASURES OF CENTRAL TENDENCY AND DISPERSION FROM GROUPED DATA

Preparing for This Section Before getting started, review the following:

- Organizing discrete data in tables (Section 2.2, pp. 78–79)
- Organizing continuous data in tables (Section 2.2, pp. 79–83)

OBJECTIVES

1. Approximate the mean of a variable from grouped data
2. Compute the weighted mean
3. Approximate the standard deviation of a variable from grouped data

Note to Instructor
This section can be skipped without loss of continuity. If covered, the formulas used in this section can be overwhelming. Therefore, it is recommended that "by hand" computations be de-emphasized. Use the TI calculator or Excel.

We have discussed how to compute descriptive statistics from raw data, but often the only available data have already been summarized in frequency distributions (**grouped data**). Although we cannot find exact values of the mean or standard deviation without raw data, we can approximate these measures using the techniques discussed in this section.

1 Approximate the Mean of a Variable from Grouped Data

Note to Instructor
If you like, you can print out and distribute the Preparing for this Section quiz located in the Instructor's Resource Center.

Since raw data cannot be retrieved from a frequency table, we assume that within each class the mean of the data values is equal to the *class midpoint*. The **class midpoint** is found by adding consecutive lower class limits and dividing the result by 2. We then multiply the class midpoint by the frequency. This product is expected to be close to the sum of the data that lie within the class. We repeat the process for each class and add the results. This sum approximates the sum of all the data.

DEFINITION

Approximate the Mean of a Variable from a Frequency Distribution

Population Mean

$$\mu = \frac{\sum x_i f_i}{\sum f_i} = \frac{x_1 f_1 + x_2 f_2 + \cdots + x_n f_n}{f_1 + f_2 + \cdots + f_n}$$

Sample Mean

$$\bar{x} = \frac{\sum x_i f_i}{\sum f_i} = \frac{x_1 f_1 + x_2 f_2 + \cdots + x_n f_n}{f_1 + f_2 + \cdots + f_n} \quad (1)$$

where x_i is the midpoint or value of the ith class
f_i is the frequency of the ith class
n is the number of classes

In Formula (1), $x_1 f_1$ approximates the sum of all the data values in the first class, $x_2 f_2$ approximates the sum of all the data values in the second class, and so on. Notice that the formulas for the population mean and sample mean are essentially identical, just as they were for computing the mean from raw data.

EXAMPLE 1 Approximating the Mean for Continuous Quantitative Data from a Frequency Distribution

Problem The frequency distribution in Table 13 on the next page represents the 5-year rate of return of a random sample of 40 large-blended mutual funds. Approximate the mean 5-year rate of return.

TABLE 13

Class (5-year rate of return)	Frequency
3–3.99	16
4–4.99	13
5–5.99	4
6–6.99	1
7–7.99	0
8–8.99	1
9–9.99	0
10–10.99	2
11–11.99	2
12–12.99	1

Note to Instructor

Some instructors may be used to using the formula $\frac{LL + UL}{2}$ to determine the class midpoint. While this method is acceptable, we choose the method presented here for two reasons: (1) The upper class limit of the first class in Table 13 is technically, $3.\overline{9}$, so the first class can be thought of as $3 - < 4$, in which case the class midpoint is 3.5. (2) The math is typically easier using consecutive lower class limits. The bottom line is that we are approximating the typical value of an observation in each class, and, regardless of which approach is used to obtain the class midpoint, there is likely some error.

Approach

Step 1 Determine the class midpoint of each class: add consecutive lower class limits and divide the result by 2.

Step 2 Compute the sum of the frequencies, Σf_i.

Step 3 Multiply the class midpoint by the frequency to obtain $x_i f_i$ for each class.

Step 4 Compute $\Sigma x_i f_i$.

Step 5 Substitute into Sample Mean Formula (1) to obtain the mean from grouped data.

Solution

Step 1 The first two lower class limits are 3 and 4. Therefore, the class midpoint of the first class is $\frac{3 + 4}{2} = 3.5$, so $x_1 = 3.5$. The remaining class midpoints are listed in column 2 of Table 14.

TABLE 14

Class (5-year rate of return)	Class Midpoint, x_i	Frequency, f_i	$x_i f_i$
3–3.99	$\frac{3+4}{2} = 3.5$	16	$(3.5)(16) = 56$
4–4.99	4.5	13	$(4.5)(13) = 58.5$
5–5.99	5.5	4	22
6–6.99	6.5	1	6.5
7–7.99	7.5	0	0
8–8.99	8.5	1	8.5
9–9.99	9.5	0	0
10–10.99	10.5	2	21
11–11.99	11.5	2	23
12–12.99	12.5	1	12.5
		$\sum f_i = 40$	$\sum x_i f_i = 208$

Step 2 We add the frequencies in column 3 to obtain $\Sigma f_i = 16 + 13 + \cdots + 1 = 40$.

Step 3 Compute the values of $x_i f_i$ by multiplying each class midpoint by the corresponding frequency and obtain the results shown in column 4 of Table 14.

Step 4 We add the values in column 4 of Table 14 to obtain $\Sigma x_i f_i = 208$.

Step 5 Substituting into Sample Mean Formula (1), we obtain

$$\bar{x} = \frac{\sum x_i f_i}{\sum f_i} = \frac{208}{40} = 5.2$$

The approximate mean 5-year rate of return is 5.2%.

CAUTION

We computed the mean from grouped data in Example 1 even though the raw data is available. The reason for doing this was to illustrate how close the two values can be. In practice, use raw data whenever possible.

The mean 5-year rate of return from the raw data listed in Example 3 on page 80 from Section 2.2 is 5.194%.

Now compute the approximate mean of the frequency distribution in Problem 1

2 Compute the Weighted Mean

Sometimes, certain data values have a higher importance or weight associated with them. In this case, we compute the *weighted mean*. For example, your grade-point average is a weighted mean, with the weights equal to the number of credit hours in each course. The value of the variable is equal to the grade converted to a point value.

DEFINITION

The **weighted mean**, $\bar{x}_w$, of a variable is found by multiplying each value of the variable by its corresponding weight, adding these products, and dividing this sum by the sum of the weights. It can be expressed using the formula

$$\bar{x}_w = \frac{\sum w_i x_i}{\sum w_i} = \frac{w_1 x_1 + w_2 x_2 + \cdots + w_n x_n}{w_1 + w_2 + \cdots + w_n} \quad \textbf{(2)}$$

where w_i is the weight of the ith observation

x_i is the value of the ith observation

Note to Instructor

Idea for a classroom discussion: Suppose a company owns three cars that get 20 miles per gallon, two cars that get 22 miles per gallon, and one car that gets 24 miles per gallon. Would the mean miles per gallon be 22? Discuss.

EXAMPLE 2 Computing the Weighted Mean

Problem Marissa just completed her first semester in college. She earned an A in her 4-hour statistics course, a B in her 3-hour sociology course, an A in her 3-hour psychology course, a C in her 5-hour computer programming course, and an A in her 1-hour drama course. Determine Marissa's grade-point average.

Approach We must assign point values to each grade. Let an A equal 4 points, a B equal 3 points, and a C equal 2 points. The number of credit hours for each course determines its weight. So a 5-hour course gets a weight of 5, a 4-hour course gets a weight of 4, and so on. We multiply the weight of each course by the points earned in the course, add these products, and divide this sum by the sum of the weights, number of credit hours.

Solution

$$\text{GPA} = \bar{x}_w = \frac{\sum w_i x_i}{\sum w_i} = \frac{4(4) + 3(3) + 3(4) + 5(2) + 1(4)}{4 + 3 + 3 + 5 + 1} = \frac{51}{16} = 3.19$$

Marissa's grade-point average for her first semester is 3.19.

Now Work Problem 9

3 Approximate the Standard Deviation of a Variable from Grouped Data

The procedure for approximating the standard deviation from grouped data is similar to that of finding the mean from grouped data. Again, because we do not have access to the original data, the standard deviation is approximate.

DEFINITION

Approximate the Standard Deviation of a Variable from a Frequency Distribution

Population Standard Deviation

$$\sigma = \sqrt{\frac{\sum (x_i - \mu)^2 f_i}{\sum f_i}}$$

Sample Standard Deviation

$$s = \sqrt{\frac{\sum (x_i - \bar{x})^2 f_i}{\left(\sum f_i\right) - 1}} \quad \textbf{(3)}$$

where x_i is the midpoint or value of the ith class

f_i is the frequency of the ith class

An algebraically equivalent formula for the population standard deviation is

$$\sqrt{\frac{\sum x_i^2 f_i - \frac{\left(\sum x_i f_i\right)^2}{\sum f_i}}{\sum f_i}}$$

EXAMPLE 3 Approximating the Standard Deviation from a Frequency Distribution

Problem The data in Table 13 on page 148 represent the 5-year rate of return of a random sample of 40 large-blended mutual funds. Approximate the standard deviation of the 5-year rate of return.

Approach We will use the sample standard deviation Formula (3).

Step 1 Create a table with the class in column 1, the class midpoint in column 2, the frequency in column 3, and the unrounded mean in column 4.

Step 2 Compute the deviation about the mean, $x_i - \bar{x}$, for each class, where x_i is the class midpoint of the ith class and $\bar{x}$ is the sample mean. Enter the results in column 5.

Step 3 Square the deviation about the mean and multiply this result by the frequency to obtain $(x_i - \bar{x})^2 f_i$. Enter the results in column 6.

Step 4 Add the entries in columns 3 and 6 to obtain Σf_i and $\Sigma (x_i - \bar{x})^2 f_i$.

Step 5 Substitute the values found in Step 4 into Formula (3) to obtain an approximate value for the sample standard deviation.

Solution

Step 1 We create Table 15. Column 1 contains the classes. Column 2 contains the class midpoint of each class. Column 3 contains the frequency of each class. Column 4 contains the unrounded sample mean obtained in Example 1.

TABLE 15

Class (5-year rate of return)	Class Midpoint, x_i	Frequency, f_i	$\bar{x}$	$x_i - \bar{x}$	$(x_i - \bar{x})^2 f_i$
3–3.99	$\frac{3+4}{2} = 3.5$	16	5.2	−1.7	46.24
4–4.99	4.5	13	5.2	−0.7	6.37
5–5.99	5.5	4	5.2	0.3	0.36
6–6.99	6.5	1	5.2	1.3	1.69
7–7.99	7.5	0	5.2	2.3	0
8–8.99	8.5	1	5.2	3.3	10.89
9–9.99	9.5	0	5.2	4.3	0
10–10.99	10.5	2	5.2	5.3	56.18
11–11.99	11.5	2	5.2	6.3	79.38
12–12.99	12.5	1	5.2	7.3	53.29
		$\sum f_i = 40$			$\sum (x_i - \bar{x})^2 f_i = 254.4$

Step 2 Column 5 contains the deviation about the mean, $x_i - \bar{x}$, for each class.

Step 3 Column 6 contains the values of the squared deviation about the mean multiplied by the frequency, $(x_i - \bar{x})^2 f_i$.

Step 4 Add the entries in columns 3 to 6 to obtain $\Sigma f_i = 40$ and $\Sigma (x_i - \bar{x})^2 f_i = 254.4$.

Step 5 Substitute these values into Formula (3) to obtain an approximate value for the sample standard deviation.

$$s = \sqrt{\frac{\sum (x_i - \bar{x})^2 f_i}{\left(\sum f_i\right) - 1}} = \sqrt{\frac{254.4}{40 - 1}} \approx 2.55$$

The approximate standard deviation of the 5-year rate of return is 2.55%. The standard deviation from the raw data listed in Example 3 from Section 2.2 is 2.64%.

EXAMPLE 4 Approximating the Mean and Standard Deviation of Grouped Data Using Technology

Problem Approximate the mean and standard deviation of the 5-year rate of return data in Table 13 using a TI-83/84 Plus graphing calculator.

Approach The steps for approximating the mean and standard deviation of grouped data using the TI-83/84 Plus graphing calculator are given in the Technology Step-by-Step on page 153.

Solution Figure 16 shows the result from the TI-84 Plus. From the output, we can see that the approximate mean is 5.2% and the approximate standard deviation is 2.55%. The results agree with our by-hand solutions.

Figure 16

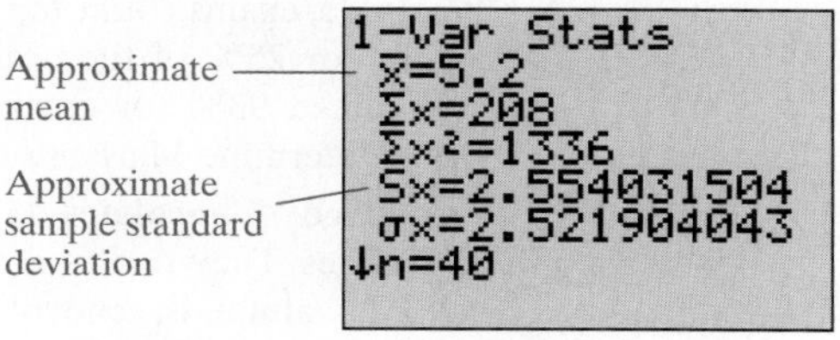

Now compute the approximate standard deviation from the frequency distribution in Problem 1

3.3 ASSESS YOUR UNDERSTANDING

APPLYING THE CONCEPTS

1. $\mu = 3289.5$ g; $\sigma = 657.2$ g

NW **1. Birth Weight** The following frequency distribution represents the birth weight of all babies born in the United States in 2004. Approximate the mean and standard deviation birth weight.

Weight (grams)	Number of Babies (thousands)
0–999	30
1000–1999	97
2000–2999	935
3000–3999	2698
4000–4999	344
5000–5999	5

Source: National Vital Statistics Report, Volume 55, No. 1

2. Square Footage of Housing The frequency distribution below represents the square footage of a random sample of 500 houses that are owner occupied year round. Approximate the mean and standard deviation square footage. $\bar{x} = 2419$ sq ft; $s = 907.0$ sq ft

Square Footage	Frequency
0–499	5
500–999	17
1000–1499	36
1500–1999	121
2000–2499	119
2500–2999	81
3000–3499	47
3500–3999	45
4000–4499	22
4500–4999	7

Source: Based on data from the U.S. Census Bureau

3. Household Winter Temperature Often, frequency distributions are reported using unequal class widths because the frequencies of some groups would otherwise be small or very large. Consider the following data, which represent the daytime household temperature the thermostat is set to when someone is home for a random sample of 750 households. Determine the class midpoint, if necessary, for each class and approximate the mean and standard deviation temperature. $\bar{x} = 70.6$°F; $s = 3.5$°F

Temperature (°F)	Frequency
61–64	31
65–67	67
68–69	198
70	195
71–72	120
73–76	89
77–80	50

Source: Based on data from the U.S. Department of Energy

4. Living in Poverty (See Problem 3.) The frequency distribution on the following page represents the age of people living in poverty in 2009 (in thousands). In this frequency distribution, the class widths are not the same for each class. Approximate the mean and standard deviation age of a person living in poverty. For the open-ended class 65 and older, use 70 as the class midpoint. $\mu = 29.9$ years; $\sigma = 20.3$ years

Age	Frequency
0–17	15,451
18–24	6071
25–34	6123
35–44	4756
45–54	4421
55–59	1792
60–64	1520
65 and older	3433

Source: U.S. Census Bureau

5. Multiple Births The following data represent the number of live multiple-delivery births (three or more babies) in 2007 for women 15 to 54 years old.

Age	Number of Multiple Births
15–19	100
20–24	467
25–29	1620
30–34	2262
35–39	1545
40–44	328
45–49	85
50–54	20

Source: National Vital Statistics Reports, Vol. 58, No. 24, August 2010

(a) Approximate the mean and standard deviation for age.
(b) Draw a frequency histogram of the data to verify that the distribution is bell shaped. (a) $\mu = 32.3$ years; $\sigma \approx 5.7$ years
(c) According to the Empirical Rule, 95% of mothers of multiple births will be between what two ages? 20.9 years and 43.7 years

6. SAT Scores The following data represent SAT Mathematics scores for 2010.

SAT Math Score	Number
200–299	36,305
300–399	193,968
400–499	459,010
500–599	467,855
600–699	286,518
700–800	104,334

Source: The College Board

6. (c) 285.6 and 754.8

(a) Approximate the mean and standard deviation of the score.
(b) Draw a frequency histogram of the data to verify that the distribution is bell shaped. (a) $\mu = 520.2$; $\sigma \approx 117.3$
(c) According to the Empirical Rule, 95% of these students will have SAT Mathematics scores between what two values?

7. Cigarette Tax Rates Use the frequency distribution whose class width is 0.5 obtained in Problem 37 in Section 2.2 to approximate the mean and standard deviation for cigarette tax rates. Compare these results to the actual mean and standard deviation.

$\bar{x} = \$1.505$; $\sigma = \$0.982$

8. $\bar{x} \approx 1.214\%$ $s \approx 0.865\%$

8. Dividend Yield Use the frequency distribution whose class width is 0.4 obtained in Problem 38 in Section 2.2 to approximate the mean and standard deviation of the dividend yield. Compare these results to the actual mean and standard deviation.

NW **9. Grade-Point Average** Marissa has just completed her second semester in college. She earned a B in her 5-hour calculus course, an A in her 3-hour social work course, an A in her 4-hour biology course, and a C in her 3-hour American literature course. Assuming that an A equals 4 points, a B equals 3 points, and a C equals 2 points, determine Marissa's grade-point average for the semester. 3.27

10. Computing Class Average In Marissa's calculus course, attendance counts for 5% of the grade, quizzes count for 10% of the grade, exams count for 60% of the grade, and the final exam counts for 25% of the grade. Marissa had a 100% average for attendance, 93% for quizzes, 86% for exams, and 85% on the final. Determine Marissa's course average. 87.15%

11. Mixed Chocolates Michael and Kevin want to buy chocolates. They can't agree on whether they want chocolate–covered almonds, chocolate-covered peanuts, or chocolate-covered raisins. They agree to create a mix. They bought 4 pounds of chocolate-covered almonds at \$3.50 per pound, 3 pounds of chocolate-covered peanuts for \$2.75 per pound, and 2 pounds of chocolate-covered raisins for \$2.25 per pound. Determine the cost per pound of the mix. \$2.97

12. Nut Mix Michael and Kevin return to the candy store, but this time they want to purchase nuts. They can't decide among peanuts, cashews, or almonds. They again agree to create a mix. They bought 2.5 pounds of peanuts for \$1.30 per pound, 4 pounds of cashews for \$4.50 per pound, and 2 pounds of almonds for \$3.75 per pound. Determine the price per pound of the mix. \$3.38

13. Population The following data represent the male and female population, by age, of the United States in 2008. **Note:** Use 95 for the class midpoint of ≥90.

Age	Male Resident Pop (in thousands)	Female Resident Pop (in thousands)
0–9	929	19,992
10–19	21,074	20,278
20–29	21,105	20,482
30–39	19,780	20,042
40–49	21,754	22,346
50–59	19,303	20,302
60–69	12,388	13,709
70–79	6940	8837
80–89	3106	9154
≥90	479	1263

Source: U.S. Census Bureau

(a) Approximate the population mean and standard deviation of age for males. $\mu \approx 36.2$ years; $\sigma \approx 22.0$ years
(b) Approximate the population mean and standard deviation of age for females. $\mu \approx 39.6$ years; $\sigma \approx 23.9$ years
(c) Which gender has the higher mean age? Female
(d) Which gender has more dispersion in age? Female

14. Age of Mother The following data represent the age of the mother at childbirth for 1980 and 2007.

Age	1980 Births (thousands)	2007 Births (thousands)
10–14	9.8	7.0
15–19	551.9	488.5
20–24	1226.4	1172.1
25–29	1108.2	1298.2
30–34	549.9	1035.3
35–39	140.7	544.0
40–44	23.2	116.6
45–49	1.1	7.3

Source: National Vital Statistics Reports, Vol. 55, No. 10

(a) Approximate the population mean and standard deviation of age for mothers in 1980. $\mu \approx 25.5$ years; $\sigma \approx 5.4$ years
(b) Approximate the population mean and standard deviation of age for mothers in 2007. $\mu \approx 27.9$ years; $\sigma \approx 6.4$ years
(c) Which year has the higher mean age? 2007
(d) Which year has more dispersion in age? 2007

Problems 15–18 use the following steps to approximate the median from grouped data.

Approximating the Median from Grouped Data

Step 1 Construct a cumulative frequency distribution.

Step 2 Identify the class in which the median lies. Remember, the median can be obtained by determining the observation that lies in the middle.

Step 3 Interpolate the median using the formula

$$\text{Median} = M = L + \frac{\frac{n}{2} - CF}{f}(i)$$

where L is the lower class limit of the class containing the median
n is the number of data values in the frequency distribution
CF is the cumulative frequency of the class immediately preceding the class containing the median
f is the frequency of the median class
i is the class width of the class containing the median

15. Approximate the median of the frequency distribution in Problem 1. 3367.9 g

16. Approximate the median of the frequency distribution in Problem 2. 2298.3 ft^2

17. Approximate the median of the frequency distribution in Problem 3. 70.4°F

18. Approximate the median of the frequency distribution in Problem 4. 25.4 years

Problems 19 and 20 use the following definition of the modal class. The **modal class** *of a variable can be obtained from data in a frequency distribution by determining the class that has the largest frequency.*

19. Determine the modal class of the frequency distribution in Problem 1. 3000–3999 g

20. Determine the modal class of the frequency distribution in Problem 2. 1500–1999 ft^2

Technology Step-By-Step

Determining the Mean and Standard Deviation from Grouped Data

TI-83/84 Plus

1. Enter the class midpoint in L1 and the frequency or relative frequency in L2 by pressing STAT and selecting `1:Edit`.
2. Press STAT, highlight the CALC menu, and select `1:1-Var Stats`
3. With `1-Var Stats` appearing on the HOME screen, press 2nd then 1 to insert L1 on the HOME screen. Then press the comma and press 2nd 2 to insert L2 on the HOME screen. So the HOME screen should have the following:

```
1-Var Stats L1, L2
```

Press ENTER to obtain the mean and standard deviation.

3.4 MEASURES OF POSITION AND OUTLIERS

OBJECTIVES

1. Determine and interpret *z*-scores
2. Interpret percentiles
3. Determine and interpret quartiles
4. Determine and interpret the interquartile range
5. Check a set of data for outliers

In Section 3.1, we determined measures of central tendency, which describe the *typical* data value. Section 3.2 discussed measures of dispersion, which describe the amount of *spread* in a set of data. In this section, we discuss measures of position, which describe the *relative position* of a certain data value within the entire set of data.

1 Determine and Interpret z-Scores

At the end of the 2010 season, the New York Yankees led the American League with 859 runs scored, while the Cincinnati Reds led the National League with 790 runs scored. It appears that the Yankees are the better run-producing team. However, this comparison is unfair because the two teams play in different leagues. The Yankees play in the American League, where the designated hitter bats for the pitcher, whereas the Reds play in the National League, where the pitcher must bat (pitchers are typically poor hitters). To compare the two teams' scoring of runs, we need to determine their relative standings in their respective leagues. We can do this using a *z-score*.

DEFINITION

The **z-score** represents the distance that a data value is from the mean in terms of the number of standard deviations. We find it by subtracting the mean from the data value and dividing this result by the standard deviation. There is both a population z-score and a sample z-score:

Population z-Score	**Sample z-Score**	
$z = \frac{x - \mu}{\sigma}$	$z = \frac{x - \bar{x}}{s}$	**(1)**

The z-score is unitless. It has mean 0 and standard deviation 1.

In Other Words
The z-score provides a way to compare apples to oranges by converting variables with different centers or spreads to variables with the same center (0) and spread (1).

If a data value is larger than the mean, the z-score is positive. If a data value is smaller than the mean, the z-score is negative. If the data value equals the mean, the z-score is zero. A z-score measures the number of standard deviations an observation is above or below the mean. For example, a z-score of 1.24 means the data value is 1.24 standard deviations above the mean. A z-score of −2.31 means the data value is 2.31 standard deviations below the mean.

Now we can determine whether the Yankees or Reds had a better year in run production.

EXAMPLE 1 Comparing z-Scores

Problem Determine whether the New York Yankees or the Cincinnati Reds had a relatively better run-producing season. The Yankees scored 859 runs and play in the American League, where the mean number of runs scored was $\mu = 721.2$ and the standard deviation was $\sigma = 93.5$ runs. The Reds scored 790 runs and play in the National League, where the mean number of runs scored was $\mu = 700.7$ and the standard deviation was $\sigma = 58.4$ runs.

Approach To determine which team had the relatively better run-producing season, we compute each team's z-score. The team with the higher z-score had the better season. Because we know the values of the population parameters, we will compute the population z-score.

Solution We compute each team's z-score, rounded to two decimal places.

$$\text{Yankees:} \quad z\text{-score} = \frac{x - \mu}{\sigma} = \frac{859 - 721.2}{93.5} = 1.47$$

$$\text{Reds:} \quad z\text{-score} = \frac{x - \mu}{\sigma} = \frac{790 - 700.7}{58.4} = 1.53$$

So the Yankees had run production 1.47 standard deviations above the mean, while the Reds had run production 1.53 standard deviations above the mean. Therefore, the Reds had a relatively better year at scoring runs than the Yankees.

Now Work Problem 5

Note to Instructor

It really does not make sense to talk about percentiles (other than quartiles) for small data sets. After all, how can one divide a data set with 40 observations into 100 parts? When data sets are large, it makes more sense to determine percentiles using a model, such as the normal model. For that reason, we will postpone determining percentiles until we can use the normal model to find their values.

In Example 1, the team with the higher z-score was said to have a relatively better season in producing runs. With negative z-scores, we need to be careful when deciding the better outcome. For example, suppose Bob and Mary run a marathon. If Bob finished the marathon in 213 minutes, where the mean finishing time among all men was 242 minutes with a standard deviation of 57 minutes, and Mary finished the marathon in 241 minutes, where the mean finishing time among all women was 273 minutes with a standard deviation of 52 minutes, who did better in the race? Since Bob's z-score is $z_{Bob} = \dfrac{213 - 242}{57} = -0.51$ and Mary's z-score is $z_{Mary} = \dfrac{241 - 273}{52} = -0.62$, Mary did better. Even though Bob's z-score is larger, Mary did better because she is more standard deviations below the mean.

2 Interpret Percentiles

Recall that the median divides the lower 50% of a set of data from the upper 50%. The median is a special case of a general concept called the *percentile*.

DEFINITION

The ***k*th percentile**, denoted P_k, of a set of data is a value such that k percent of the observations are less than or equal to the value.

So percentiles divide a set of data that is written in ascending order into 100 parts; thus 99 percentiles can be determined. For example, P_1 divides the bottom 1% of the observations from the top 99%, P_2 divides the bottom 2% of the observations from the top 98%, and so on. Figure 17 displays the 99 possible percentiles.

Figure 17

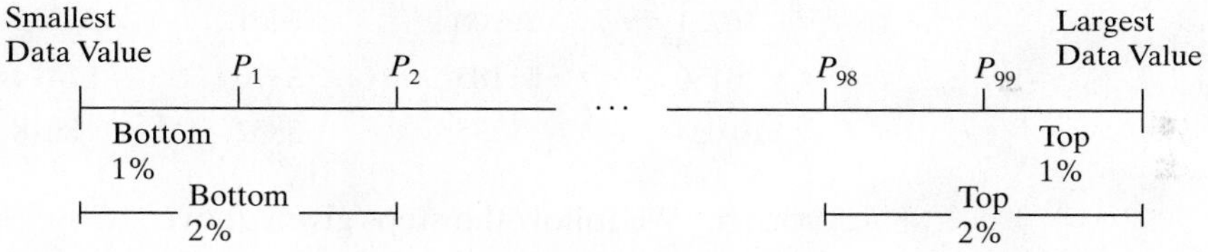

Percentiles are used to give the relative standing of an observation. Many standardized exams, such as the SAT college entrance exam, use percentiles to let students know how they scored on the exam in relation to all other students who took the exam.

EXAMPLE 2 Interpret a Percentile

Problem Jennifer just received the results of her SAT exam. Her SAT Mathematics score of 600 is at the 74th percentile. What does this mean?

Approach The kth percentile of an observation means that k percent of the observations are less than or equal to the observation.

Interpretation A percentile rank of 74% means that 74% of SAT Mathematics scores are less than or equal to 600 and 26% of the scores are greater. So 26% of the students who took the exam scored better than Jennifer.

Now Work Problem 15

3 Determine and Interpret Quartiles

The most common percentiles are quartiles. **Quartiles** divide data sets into fourths, or four equal parts. The first quartile, denoted Q_1, divides the bottom 25% of the data from the top 75%. Therefore, the first quartile is equivalent to the 25th percentile. The second quartile, Q_2, divides the bottom 50% of the data from the top 50%; it is equivalent to

In Other Words
The first quartile, Q_1, is equivalent to the 25th percentile, P_{25}. The 2nd quartile, Q_2, is equivalent to the 50th percentile, P_{50}, which is equivalent to the median, *M*. Finally, the third quartile, Q_3, is equivalent to the 75th percentile, P_{75}.

the 50th percentile or the median. Finally, the third quartile, Q_3, divides the bottom 75% of the data from the top 25%; it is equivalent to the 75th percentile. Figure 18 illustrates the concept of quartiles.

Figure 18

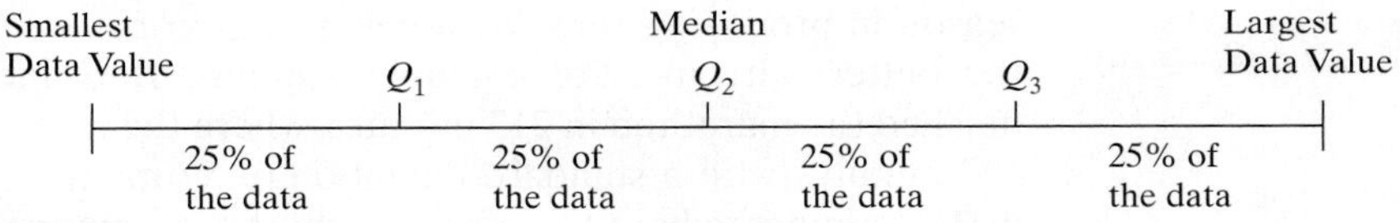

Using Technology
The technique presented here agrees with the method used by TI graphing calculators. It will agree with MINITAB output when the number of observations is odd. When the number of observations is even, MINITAB gives different results.

Finding Quartiles

Step 1 Arrange the data in ascending order.

Step 2 Determine the median, *M*, or second quartile, Q_2.

Step 3 Divide the data set into halves: the observations below (to the left of) *M* and the observations above *M*. The first quartile, Q_1, is the median of the bottom half and the third quartile, Q_3, is the median of the top half.

EXAMPLE 3 Finding and Interpreting Quartiles

In Other Words
To find Q_2, determine the median of the data set. To find Q_1, determine the median of the "lower half" of the data set. To find Q_3, determine the median of the "upper half" of the data set.

Problem The Highway Loss Data Institute routinely collects data on collision coverage claims. Collision coverage insures against physical damage to an insured individual's vehicle. The data in Table 16 represent a random sample of 18 collision coverage claims based on data obtained from the Highway Loss Data Institute for 2007 models. Find and interpret the first, second, and third quartiles for collision coverage claims.

Note to Instructor
Ask your students whether quartiles are resistant.

TABLE 16

$6751	$9908	$3461	$2336	$21,147	$2332
$189	$1185	$370	$1414	$4668	$1953
$10,034	$735	$802	$618	$180	$1657

Approach We follow the steps given above.

Solution

Step 1 The data written in ascending order are given as follows:

$180	$189	$370	$618	$735	$802	$1185	$1414	$1657
$1953	$2332	$2336	$3461	$4668	$6751	$9908	$10,034	$21,147

Step 2 There are $n = 18$ observations, so the median, or second quartile, Q_2, is the mean of the 9th and 10th observations. Therefore, $M = Q_2 = \frac{\$1657 + \$1953}{2} = \$1805$.

Step 3 The median of the bottom half of the data is the first quartile, Q_1. As shown next, the median of these data is the 5th observation, so $Q_1 = \$735$.

$180 $189 $370 $618 $735 $802 $1185 $1414 $1657
↑ Q_1 (at $735)

The median of the top half of the data is the third quartile, Q_3. As shown next, the median of these data is the 5th observation, so $Q_3 = \$4668$.

$1953 $2332 $2336 $3461 $4668 $6751 $9908 $10,034 $21,147
↑ Q_3 (at $4668)

Note
If the number of observations is odd, do not include the median when determining Q_1 and Q_3 by hand. ■

Interpretation We interpret the quartiles as percentiles. For example, 25% of the collision claims are less than or equal to the first quartile, \$735, and 75% of the collision claims are greater than \$735. Also, 50% of the collision claims are less than or equal to \$1805, the second quartile, and 50% of the collision claims are greater than \$1805. Finally, 75% of the collision claims are less than or equal to \$4668, the third quartile, and 25% of the collision claims are greater than \$4668.

EXAMPLE 4 Finding Quartiles Using Technology

Problem Find the quartiles of the collision coverage claims data in Table 16.

Approach We will use both StatCrunch and MINITAB to obtain the quartiles. The steps for obtaining quartiles using a TI-83/84 Plus graphing calculator, MINITAB, Excel, and StatCrunch are given in the Technology Step-by-Step on page 163.

Using Technology
Statistical packages may use different formulas for obtaining the quartiles, so results may differ slightly.

Solution The results obtained from StatCrunch [Figure 19(a)] agree with our "by hand" solution. In Figure 19(b), notice that the first quartile, 706, and the third quartile, 5189, reported by MINITAB disagree with our "by hand" and StatCrunch result. This difference is due to the fact that StatCrunch and MINITAB use different algorithms for obtaining quartiles.

Note to Instructor
Ask students to conjecture the method that MINITAB uses in finding the quartiles.

Figure 19

Summary statistics:

Column	n	Median	Min	Max	Q1	Q3
Claim	18	1805	180	21147	735	4668

(a)

Descriptive statistics: Claim

```
Variable  N N* Mean  SE Mean StDev Minimum  Q1 Median   Q3 Maximum
Claim    18  0 3874     1250  5302     180 706   1805 5189   21447
```

(b)

Now Work Problem 21(b)

4 Determine and Interpret the Interquartile Range

In Section 3.2 we introduced two measures of dispersion, the range and the standard deviation, which are not resistant to extreme values. Quartiles, on the other hand, are resistant to extreme values. For this reason, we would like to find a measure of dispersion that is based on quartiles.

DEFINITION

The **interquartile range, IQR,** is the range of the middle 50% of the observations in a data set. That is, the IQR is the difference between the third and first quartiles and is found using the formula

$$\text{IQR} = Q_3 - Q_1$$

The interpretation of the interquartile range is similar to that of the range and standard deviation. That is, the more spread a set of data has, the higher the interquartile range will be.

EXAMPLE 5 Determining and Interpreting the Interquartile Range

Problem Determine and interpret the interquartile range of the collision claim data from Example 3.

Approach We will use the quartiles found by hand in Example 3. The interquartile range, IQR, is found by computing the difference between the third and first quartiles. It represents the range of the middle 50% of the observations.

Solution The interquartile range is

$$\begin{aligned} \text{IQR} &= Q_3 - Q_1 \\ &= \$4668 - \$735 \\ &= \$3933 \end{aligned}$$

Interpretation The IQR, that is, the range of the middle 50% of the observations, in the collision claim data is \$3933.

Now Work Problem 21(c)

Let's compare the measures of central tendency and dispersion discussed thus far for the collision claim data. The mean collision claim is \$3874.4 and the median is \$1805. The median is more representative of the "center" because the data are skewed to the right (only 5 of the 18 observations are greater than the mean). The range is \$21,147 − \$180 = \$20,967. The standard deviation is \$5301.6 and the interquartile range is \$3933. The values of the range and standard deviation are affected by the extreme claim of \$21,147. In fact, if this claim had been \$120,000 (let's say the claim was for a totaled Mercedes S-class AMG), then the range and standard deviation would increase to \$119,820 and \$27,782.5, respectively. The interquartile range would not be affected. Therefore, when the distribution of data is highly skewed or contains extreme observations, it is best to use the interquartile range as the measure of dispersion because it is resistant.

SUMMARY: WHICH MEASURES TO REPORT

Shape of Distribution	Measure of Central Tendency	Measure of Dispersion
Symmetric	Mean	Standard deviation
Skewed left or skewed right	Median	Interquartile range

For the remainder of this text, the direction **describe the distribution** will mean to describe its shape (skewed left, skewed right, symmetric), its center (mean or median), and its spread (standard deviation or interquartile range).

5 Check a Set of Data for Outliers

When performing any type of data analysis, we should always check for extreme observations in the data set. Extreme observations are referred to as **outliers**. Outliers in a data set should be investigated. They can occur by chance, because of error in the measurement of a variable, during data entry, or from errors in sampling. For example, in the 2000 presidential election, a precinct in New Mexico accidentally recorded 610 absentee ballots for Al Gore as 110. Workers in the Gore camp discovered the data-entry error through an analysis of vote totals.

CAUTION

Outliers distort both the mean and the standard deviation, because neither is resistant. Because these measures often form the basis for most statistical inference, any conclusions drawn from a set of data that contains outliers can be flawed.

Outliers do not always occur because of error. Sometimes extreme observations are common within a population. For example, suppose we wanted to estimate the mean price of a European car. We might take a random sample of size 5 from the population of all European automobiles. If our sample included a Ferrari F430 Spider (approximately \$175,000), it probably would be an outlier, because this car costs much more than the typical European automobile. The value of this car would be considered *unusual* because it is not a typical value from the data set.

Note to Instructor

A second method for identifying outliers uses z-scores. If the z-score is less than −2 or greater than 2, the data value can be considered to be an outlier. However, this method should be used only if the distribution is symmetric, because it is based on the Empirical Rule.

We can use the following steps to check for outliers using quartiles.

Checking for Outliers by Using Quartiles

Step 1 Determine the first and third quartiles of the data.

Step 2 Compute the interquartile range.

Step 3 Determine the fences. **Fences** serve as cutoff points for determining outliers.

$$\text{Lower fence} = Q_1 - 1.5(\text{IQR})$$

$$\text{Upper fence} = Q_3 + 1.5(\text{IQR})$$

Step 4 If a data value is less than the lower fence or greater than the upper fence, it is considered an outlier.

EXAMPLE 6 Checking for Outliers

Problem Check the data that represent the collision coverage claims for outliers.

Approach We follow the preceding steps. Any data value that is less than the lower fence or greater than the upper fence will be considered an outlier.

Solution

Step 1 The quartiles found in Example 3 are $Q_1 = \$735$ and $Q_3 = \$4668$.

Step 2 The interquartile range, IQR, is

$$\begin{aligned}\text{IQR} &= Q_3 - Q_1\\ &= \$4668 - \$735\\ &= \$3933\end{aligned}$$

Step 3 The lower fence, LF, is

$$\begin{aligned}\text{LF} &= Q_1 - 1.5(\text{IQR})\\ &= \$735 - 1.5(\$3933)\\ &= -\$5164.5\end{aligned}$$

The upper fence, UF, is

$$\begin{aligned}\text{UF} &= Q_3 + 1.5(\text{IQR})\\ &= \$4668 + 1.5(\$3933)\\ &= \$10{,}567.5\end{aligned}$$

Now Work Problem 21(d)

Step 4 There are no observations below the lower fence. However, there is an observation above the upper fence. The claim of \$21,147 is an outlier.

3.4 ASSESS YOUR UNDERSTANDING

VOCABULARY

1. The _______ represents the number of standard deviations an observation is from the mean. *z-score*

2. The _______ _______ of a data set is a value such that k percent of the observations are less than or equal to the value. *kth percentile*

3. _______ divide data sets into fourths. *Quartiles*

4. The _______ _______ is the range of the middle 50% of the observations in a data set. *interquartile range*

APPLYING THE CONCEPTS

NW **5. Birth Weights** In 2010, babies born after a gestation period of 32 to 35 weeks had a mean weight of 2600 grams and a standard deviation of 660 grams. In the same year, babies born after a gestation period of 40 weeks had a mean weight of 3500 grams and a standard deviation of 470 grams. Suppose a 34-week gestation period baby weighs 2400 grams and a 40-week gestation period baby weighs 3300 grams. What is the z-score for the

34-week gestation period baby? What is the z-score for the 40-week gestation period baby? Which baby weighs less relative to the gestation period? -0.30; -0.43; 40-week gestation

6. Birth Weights In 2010, babies born after a gestation period of 32 to 35 weeks had a mean weight of 2600 grams and a standard deviation of 660 grams. In the same year, babies born after a gestation period of 40 weeks had a mean weight of 3500 grams and a standard deviation of 470 grams. Suppose a 34-week gestation period baby weighs 3000 grams and a 40-week gestation period baby weighs 3900 grams. What is the z-score for the 34-week gestation period baby? What is the z-score for the 40-week gestation period baby? Which baby weighs less relative to the gestation period? 0.61; 0.85; 34-week gestation

7. Men versus Women The average 20- to 29-year-old man is 69.6 inches tall, with a standard deviation of 3.0 inches, while the average 20- to 29-year-old woman is 64.1 inches tall, with a standard deviation of 3.8 inches. Who is relatively taller, a 75-inch man or a 70-inch woman? *Source:* CDC Vital and Health Statistics, Advance Data, Number 361, July 5, 2005 Man

8. Men versus Women The average 20- to 29-year-old man is 69.6 inches tall, with a standard deviation of 3.0 inches, while the average 20- to 29-year-old woman is 64.1 inches tall, with a standard deviation of 3.8 inches. Who is relatively taller, a 67-inch man or a 62-inch woman? *Source:* CDC Vital and Health Statistics, Advance Data, Number 361, July 5, 2005 Woman

9. ERA Champions In 2010, Josh Johnson of the Florida Marlins had the lowest earned-run average (ERA is the mean number of runs yielded per nine innings pitched) of any starting pitcher in the National League, with an ERA of 2.30. Also in 2010, Felix Hernandez of the Seattle Mariners had the lowest ERA of any starting pitcher in the American League with an ERA of 2.27. In the National League, the mean ERA in 2010 was 3.622 and the standard deviation was 0.743. In the American League, the mean ERA in 2010 was 3.929 and the standard deviation was 0.775. Which player had the better year relative to his peers, Johnson or Hernandez? Why? Hernandez

10. Batting Champions The highest batting average ever recorded in major league baseball was by Ted Williams in 1941 when he hit 0.406. That year, the mean and standard deviation for batting average were 0.2806 and 0.0328. In 2010, Josh Hamilton was the American League batting champion, with a batting average of 0.359. In 2010, the mean and standard deviation for batting average were 0.2711 and 0.0292. Who had the better year relative to his peers, Williams or Hamilton? Why? Williams

11. IndyCar Races The 2010 Indianapolis 500 was a very competitive race with 1 minute separating the time between the winning car and fourteenth car to finish the race. The mean finishing time of cars in the Indy 500 was 186.15 minutes with a standard deviation of 0.359 minute. The winning car, driven by Dario Franchitti, finished in 185.62 minutes. The 2010 Indy Grand Prix of Sonoma was also very competitive with 25 seconds separating the time between the winning car and the fifteenth car to finish the race. The mean finishing time of the cars finishing the Sonoma race was 112.8 minutes with a standard deviation of 0.131 minute. The winning car, driven by Will Power, finished in 112.57 minutes. Who had the more convincing victory? Will Power

12. Triathlon Roberto finishes a triathlon (750-meter swim, 5-kilometer run, and 20-kilometer bicycle) in 63.2 minutes. Among all men in the race, the mean finishing time was 69.4 minutes with a standard deviation of 8.9 minutes. Zandra finishes the same triathlon in 79.3 minutes. Among all women in the race, the mean finishing time was 84.7 minutes with a standard deviation of 7.4 minutes. Who did better in relation to their gender? Zandra

13. School Admissions A highly selective boarding school will only admit students who place at least 1.5 standard deviations above the mean on a standardized test that has a mean of 200 and a standard deviation of 26. What is the minimum score that an applicant must make on the test to be accepted? 239

14. Quality Control A manufacturer of bolts has a quality-control policy that requires it to destroy any bolts that are more than 2 standard deviations from the mean. The quality-control engineer knows that the bolts coming off the assembly line have a mean length of 8 cm with a standard deviation of 0.05 cm. For what lengths will a bolt be destroyed? <7.9 cm or >8.1 cm

NW **15. You Explain It! Percentiles** Explain the meaning of the following percentiles. *Source:* Advance Data from Vital and Health Statistics

(a) The 15th percentile of the head circumference of males 3 to 5 months of age is 41.0 cm.

(b) The 90th percentile of the waist circumference of females 2 years of age is 52.7 cm.

(c) Anthropometry involves the measurement of the human body. One goal of these measurements is to assess how body measurements may be changing over time. The following table represents the standing height of males aged 20 years or older for various age groups. Based on the percentile measurements of the different age groups, what might you conclude?

	Percentile				
Age	**10th**	**25th**	**50th**	**75th**	**90th**
20–29	166.8	171.5	176.7	181.4	186.8
30–39	166.9	171.3	176.0	181.9	186.2
40–49	167.9	172.1	176.9	182.1	186.0
50–59	166.0	170.8	176.0	181.2	185.4
60–69	165.3	170.1	175.1	179.5	183.7
70–79	163.2	167.5	172.9	178.1	181.7
80 or older	161.7	166.1	170.5	175.3	179.4

16. You Explain It! Percentiles Explain the meaning of the following percentiles. *Source:* National Center for Health Statistics.

(a) The 5th percentile of the weight of males 36 months of age is 12.0 kg.

(b) The 95th percentile of the length of newborn females is 53.8 cm.

17. You Explain It! Quartiles Violent crimes include rape, robbery, assault, and homicide. The following is a summary of the violent-crime rate (violent crimes per 100,000 population) for all 50 states in the United States plus Washington, D.C., in 2009.

$$Q_1 = 255.3 \quad Q_2 = 335.5 \quad Q_3 = 497.2$$

(a) Provide an interpretation of these results.

(b) Determine and interpret the interquartile range. 241.9

(c) The violent-crime rate in Washington, D.C., in 2009 was 1345.9. Would this be an outlier? Yes

(d) Do you believe that the distribution of violent-crime rates is skewed or symmetric? Why? Skewed right

18. You Explain It! Quartiles One variable that is measured by online homework systems is the amount of time a student spends on homework for each section of the text. The following is a summary of the number of minutes a student spends for each section of the text for the fall 2010 semester in a College Algebra class at Joliet Junior College.

$$Q_1 = 42 \quad Q_2 = 51.5 \quad Q_3 = 72.5$$

(a) Provide an interpretation of these results.
(b) Determine and interpret the interquartile range. 30.5
(c) Suppose a student spent 2 hours doing homework for a section. Is this an outlier? Yes
(d) Do you believe that the distribution of time spent doing homework is skewed or symmetric? Why? Skewed right

19. Ogives and Percentiles The following graph is an *ogive* of IQ scores. The vertical axis in an ogive is the cumulative relative frequency and can also be interpreted as a percentile.

Percentile Ranks of IQ Scores

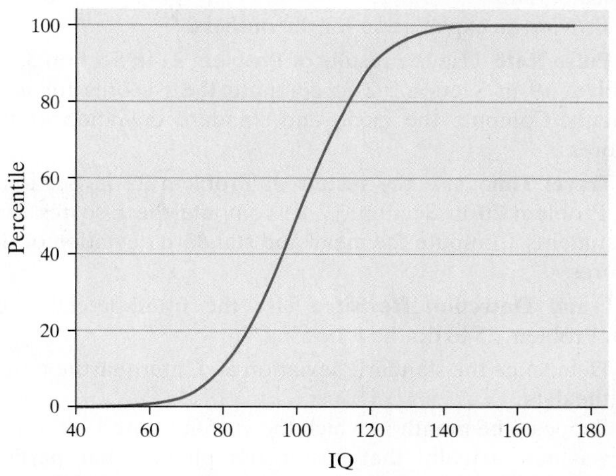

(a) Find and interpret the percentile rank of an individual whose IQ is 100. 50th
(b) Find and interpret the percentile rank of an individual whose IQ is 120. 90th
(c) What score corresponds to the 60th percentile for IQ? 105

20. Ogives and Percentiles The following graph is an *ogive* of the mathematics scores on the SAT for the class of 2010. The vertical axis in an ogive is the cumulative relative frequency and can also be interpreted as a percentile.

Class of 2010 SAT Mathematics Scores

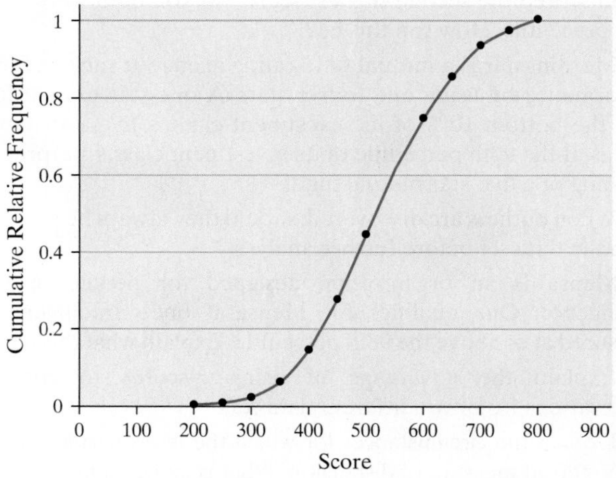

(a) Find and interpret the percentile rank of a student who scored 450 on the SAT mathematics exam. 28th
(b) Find and interpret the percentile rank of a student who scored 750 on the SAT mathematics exam. 96th
(c) If Jane scored at the 44th percentile, what was her score? 500

NW **21. SMART Car** The following data represent the miles per gallon of a random sample of SMART cars with a three-cylinder, 1.0-liter engine. (d) 30.625 mpg, 47.225 mpg; yes, 47.5 mpg

31.5	36.0	37.8	38.4	40.1	42.3
34.3	36.3	37.9	38.8	40.6	42.7
34.5	37.4	38.0	39.3	41.4	43.5
35.5	37.5	38.3	39.5	41.5	47.5

Source: www.fueleconomy.gov

(a) Compute the z-score corresponding to the individual who obtained 36.3 miles per gallon. Interpret this result. −0.73
(b) Determine the quartiles. 36.85 mpg; 38.35 mpg; 41.0 mpg
(c) Compute and interpret the interquartile range, IQR. 4.15 mpg
(d) Determine the lower and upper fences. Are there any outliers?

22. Hemoglobin in Cats The following data represent the hemoglobin (in g/dL) for 20 randomly selected cats.

5.7	8.9	9.6	10.6	11.7
7.7	9.4	9.9	10.7	12.9
7.8	9.5	10.0	11.0	13.0
8.7	9.6	10.3	11.2	13.4

Source: Joliet Junior College Veterinarian Technology Program

(a) Compute the z-score corresponding to the hemoglobin of Blackie, 7.8 g/dL. Interpret this result. −1.21
(b) Determine the quartiles. 9.15 g/dL; 9.95 g/dL; 11.1 g/dL
(c) Compute and interpret the interquartile range, IQR. 1.95
(d) Determine the lower and upper fences. Are there any outliers? 6.23 g/dL; 14.03 g/dL; Yes, 5.7 g/dL

23. Rate of Return of Google The following data represent the monthly rate of return of Google common stock from its inception in January 2007 through October 2010.

−0.10	−0.02	0.00	0.02	−0.10	0.03	0.04	−0.15	−0.08
0.02	0.01	−0.18	−0.10	−0.18	0.14	0.07	−0.01	0.09
0.03	0.10	−0.17	−0.10	0.05	0.05	0.08	0.08	−0.07
0.06	0.25	−0.07	−0.02	0.10	0.01	0.09	−0.07	0.17
0.05	−0.02	0.30	−0.14	0.00	0.05	0.06	−0.08	0.17

Source: Yahoo!Finance

(a) Determine and interpret the quartiles. −0.075, 0.02, 0.075
(b) Check the data set for outliers.

24. CO_2 Emissions The data on the following page represent the carbon dioxide emissions from the consumption of energy per capita (total carbon dioxide emissions, in tons, divided by total population) for the countries of Europe in 2008.

(a) Determine and interpret the quartiles. 6.12, 8.46, 10.06
(b) Is the observation corresponding to Albania, 1.31, an outlier? No

1.31	5.38	10.36	5.73	3.57	5.40	6.24
8.59	9.46	6.48	11.06	7.94	4.63	6.12
14.87	9.94	10.06	10.71	15.86	6.93	3.58
4.09	9.91	161.57	7.82	8.70	8.33	9.38
7.31	16.75	9.95	23.87	7.76	8.86	

Source: Carbon Dioxide Information Analysis Center

25. Fraud Detection As part of its "Customers First" program, a cellular phone company monitors monthly phone usage. The program identifies unusual use and alerts the customer that their phone may have been used by another person. The following data represent the monthly phone use in minutes of a customer enrolled in this program for the past 20 months.

346	345	489	358	471
442	466	505	466	372
442	461	515	549	437
480	490	429	470	516

The phone company decides to use the upper fence as the cutoff point for the number of minutes at which the customer should be contacted. What is the cutoff point? 574 minutes

26. Stolen Credit Card A credit card company has a fraud-detection service that determines if a card has any unusual activity. The company maintains a database of daily charges on a customer's credit card. Days when the card was inactive are excluded from the database. If a day's worth of charges appears unusual, the customer is contacted to make sure that the credit card has not been compromised. Use the following daily charges (rounded to the nearest dollar) to determine the amount the daily charges must exceed before the customer is contacted. \$219

143	166	113	188	133
90	89	98	95	112
111	79	46	20	112
70	174	68	101	212

27. Student Survey of Income A survey of 50 randomly selected full-time Joliet Junior College students was conducted during the Fall 2010 semester. In the survey, the students were asked to disclose their weekly income from employment. If the student did not work, \$0 was entered.

0	262	0	635	0
244	521	476	100	650
12,777	567	310	527	0
83	159	0	547	188
719	0	367	316	0
479	0	82	579	289
375	347	331	281	628
0	203	149	0	403
0	454	67	389	0
671	95	736	300	181

(a) Check the data set for outliers. \$12,777
(b) Draw a histogram of the data and label the outliers on the histogram.
(c) Provide an explanation for the outliers.

28. Student Survey of Entertainment Spending A survey of 40 randomly selected full-time Joliet Junior College students was conducted in the Fall 2010 semester. In the survey, the students were asked to disclose their weekly spending on entertainment. The results of the survey are as follows:

21	54	64	33	65	32	21	16
22	39	67	54	22	51	26	14
115	7	80	59	20	33	13	36
36	10	12	101	1000	26	38	8
28	28	75	50	27	35	9	48

(a) Check the data set for outliers. \$115 and \$1000
(b) Draw a histogram of the data and label the outliers on the histogram.
(c) Provide an explanation for the outliers.

29. Pulse Rate Use the results of Problem 21 in Section 3.1 and Problem 19 in Section 3.2 to compute the z-scores for all the students. Compute the mean and standard deviation of these z-scores.

30. Travel Time Use the results of Problem 22 in Section 3.1 and Problem 20 in Section 3.2 to compute the z-scores for all the students. Compute the mean and standard deviation of these z-scores.

31. Fraud Detection Revisited Use the fraud-detection data from Problem 25 to do the following.
(a) Determine the standard deviation and interquartile range of the data. 58.0 min; 56.5 min
(b) Suppose the month in which the customer used 346 minutes was not actually that customer's phone. That particular month, the customer did not use her phone at all, so 0 minutes were used. How does changing the observation from 346 to 0 affect the standard deviation and interquartile range? What property does this illustrate? $s = 115.0$ min; IQR = 56.5 min

32. Sullivan Survey Choose a quantitative variable from the Sullivan Survey and check it for outliers.

EXPLAINING THE CONCEPTS

33. Write a paragraph that explains the meaning of percentiles.

34. Suppose you received the highest score on an exam. Your friend scored the second-highest score, yet you both were in the 99th percentile. How can this be?

35. Morningstar is a mutual fund rating agency. It ranks a fund's performance by using one to five stars. A one-star mutual fund is in the bottom 10% of its investment class; a five-star mutual fund is at the 90th percentile of its investment class. Interpret the meaning of a five-star mutual fund.

36. When outliers are discovered, should they always be removed from the data set before further analysis?

37. Mensa is an organization designed for people of high intelligence. One qualifies for Mensa if one's intelligence is measured at or above the 98th percentile. Explain what this means.

38. Explain the advantage of using z-scores to compare observations from two different data sets.

39. Explain the circumstances for which the interquartile range is the preferred measure of dispersion. What is an advantage that the standard deviation has over the interquartile range?

40. Explain what each quartile represents.

Technology Step-By-Step

Determining Quartiles

TI-83/84 Plus
Follow the same steps given to compute the mean and median from raw data. (Section 3.1)

MINITAB
Follow the same steps given to compute the mean and median from raw data. (Section 3.1)

StatCrunch
Follow the same steps given to compute the mean and median from raw data. (Section 3.1)

Excel
1. Enter the raw data into column A.
2. With the data analysis Tool Pak enabled, select the Data tab and click on **Data Analysis**.
3. Select **Rank and Percentile** from the Data Analysis window. Press OK.
4. With the cursor in the **Input Range** cell, highlight the data. Press OK.

3.5 THE FIVE-NUMBER SUMMARY AND BOXPLOTS

OBJECTIVES
1. Compute the five-number summary
2. Draw and interpret boxplots

Historical Note

John Tukey was born on July 16, 1915, in New Bedford, Massachusetts. His parents graduated numbers 1 and 2 from Bates College and were voted "the couple most likely to give birth to a genius." Tukey earned his undergraduate and master's degrees in chemistry from Brown University. In 1939, he earned his doctorate in mathematics from Princeton University. He remained at Princeton and, in 1965, became the founding chair of the Department of Statistics. Among his many accomplishments, Tukey is credited with coining the terms *software* and *bit*. In the early 1970s, he discussed the negative effects of aerosol cans on the ozone layer. In December 1976, he published *Exploratory Data Analysis*, from which the following quote appears: "Exploratory data analysis can never be the whole story, but nothing else can serve as the foundation stone—as the first step" (p. 3). Tukey also recommended that the 1990 Census be adjusted by means of statistical formulas. John Tukey died in New Brunswick, New Jersey, on July 26, 2000.

Let's consider what we have learned so far. In Chapter 2, we discussed techniques for graphically representing data. These summaries included bar graphs, pie charts, histograms, stem-and-leaf plots, and time series graphs. In Sections 3.1 to 3.4, we presented techniques for measuring the center of a distribution, spread in a distribution, and relative position of observations in a distribution of data. Why do we want these summaries? What purpose do they serve?

Well, we want these summaries to see what the data can tell us. We *explore* the data to see if they contain interesting information that may be useful in our research. The summaries make this exploration much easier. In fact, because these summaries represent an exploration, a famous statistician named John Tukey called this material **exploratory data analysis**.

Tukey defined exploratory data analysis as "detective work—numerical detective work—or graphical detective work." He believed exploration of data is best carried out the way a detective searches for evidence when investigating a crime. Our goal is only to collect and present evidence. Drawing conclusions (or inference) is like the deliberations of the jury. What we have done so far falls under the category of exploratory data analysis. We have only collected information and presented summaries, not reached any conclusions.

We have already seen one of Tukey's graphical summaries, the stem-and-leaf plot. In this section, we look at two more summaries: the five-number summary and the boxplot.

1 Compute the Five-Number Summary

Remember that the median is a measure of central tendency that divides the lower 50% of the data from the upper 50%. It is resistant to extreme values and is the preferred measure of central tendency when data are skewed right or left.

The three measures of dispersion presented in Section 3.2 (range, variance, and standard deviation) are not resistant to extreme values. However, the interquartile range, $Q_3 - Q_1$, the difference between the 75th and 25th percentiles, is resistant. It is interpreted as the range of the middle 50% of the data. However, the median, Q_1, and Q_3 do not provide information about the extremes of the data, the smallest and largest values in the data set.

The **five-number summary** of a set of data consists of the smallest data value, Q_1, the median, Q_3, and the largest data value. We organize, the five-number summary as follows:

Five-Number Summary

MINIMUM Q_1 M Q_3 MAXIMUM

EXAMPLE 1 Obtaining the Five-Number Summary

Problem The data shown in Table 17 show the finishing times (in minutes) of the men in the 60- to 64-year-old age group in a 5-kilometer race. Determine the five-number summary of the data.

TABLE 17

19.95	23.25	23.32	25.55	25.83	26.28	42.47
28.58	28.72	30.18	30.35	30.95	32.13	49.17
33.23	33.53	36.68	37.05	37.43	41.42	54.63

Source: Laura Gillogly, student at Joliet Junior College

Approach The five-number summary requires that we list the minimum data value, Q_1, M (the median), Q_3, and the maximum data value. We need to arrange the data in ascending order and then use the procedures introduced in Section 3.4 to obtain Q_1, M, and Q_3.

Solution The data in ascending order are as follows:

19.95, 23.25, 23.32, 25.55, 25.83, 26.28, 28.58, 28.72, 30.18, 30.35, 30.95, 32.13, 33.23, 33.53, 36.68, 37.05, 37.43, 41.42, 42.47, 49.17, 54.63

The smallest number (the fastest time) in the data set is 19.95. The largest number in the data set is 54.63. The first quartile, Q_1, is 26.06. The median, M, is 30.95. The third quartile, Q_3, is 37.24. The five-number summary is

19.95 26.06 30.95 37.24 54.63

EXAMPLE 2 Obtaining the Five-Number Summary Using Technology

Problem Using statistical software or a graphing calculator, determine the five-number summary of the data presented in Table 17.

Approach We will use MINITAB to obtain the five-number summary.

Solution Figure 20 shows the output supplied by MINITAB. The five-number summary is highlighted.

Figure 20

Descriptive statistics: Times

Variable	N	N*	Mean	SE Mean	StDev	Minimum	Q1	Median	Q3	Maximum
Times	21	0	33.37	2.20	10.10	19.95	26.06	30.95	37.24	54.63

2 Draw and Interpret Boxplots

The five-number summary can be used to create another graph, called the **boxplot**.

Note to Instructor

Some call the boxplot described here the modified boxplot.

Drawing a Boxplot

Step 1 Determine the lower and upper fences:

$$\text{Lower fence} = Q_1 - 1.5(\text{IQR}) \qquad \text{where IQR} = Q_3 - Q_1$$
$$\text{Upper fence} = Q_3 + 1.5(\text{IQR})$$

Step 2 Draw a number line long enough to include the maximum and minimum values. Insert vertical lines at Q_1, M, and Q_3. Enclose these vertical lines in a box.

Step 3 Label the lower and upper fences.

Step 4 Draw a line from Q_1 to the smallest data value that is larger than the lower fence. Draw a line from Q_3 to the largest data value that is smaller than the upper fence. These lines are called **whiskers**.

Step 5 Any data values less than the lower fence or greater than the upper fence are outliers and are marked with an asterisk (*).

EXAMPLE 3 Constructing a Boxplot

Problem Use the results from Example 1 to construct a boxplot of the finishing times of the men in the 60- to 64-year-old age group.

Approach Follow the steps presented above.

Solution In Example 1, we found that $Q_1 = 26.06$, $M = 30.95$, and $Q_3 = 37.24$. Therefore, the interquartile range $= \text{IQR} = Q_3 - Q_1 = 37.24 - 26.06 = 11.18$. The difference between the 75th percentile and 25th percentile is a time of 11.18 minutes.

Step 1 We compute the lower and upper fences:

$$\text{Lower fence} = Q_1 - 1.5(\text{IQR}) = 26.06 - 1.5(11.18) = 9.29$$

$$\text{Upper fence} = Q_3 + 1.5(\text{IQR}) = 37.24 + 1.5(11.18) = 54.01$$

Step 2 Draw a horizontal number line with a scale that will accommodate our graph. Draw vertical lines at $Q_1 = 26.06$, $M = 30.95$, and $Q_3 = 37.24$. Enclose these lines in a box. See Figure 21(a).

Figure 21(a)

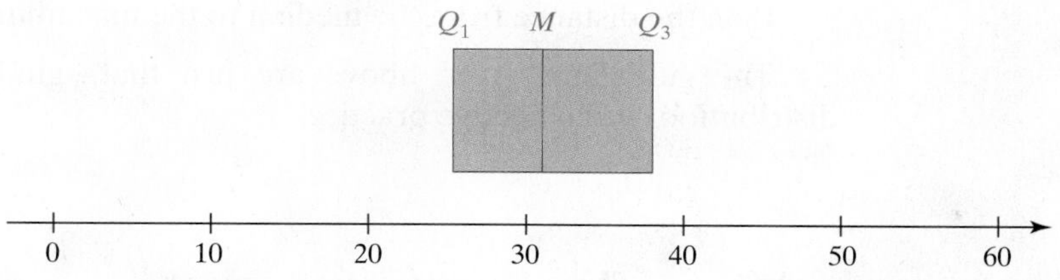

Step 3 Temporarily mark the location of the lower and upper fence with brackets ([and]). See Figure 21(b).

Figure 21(b)

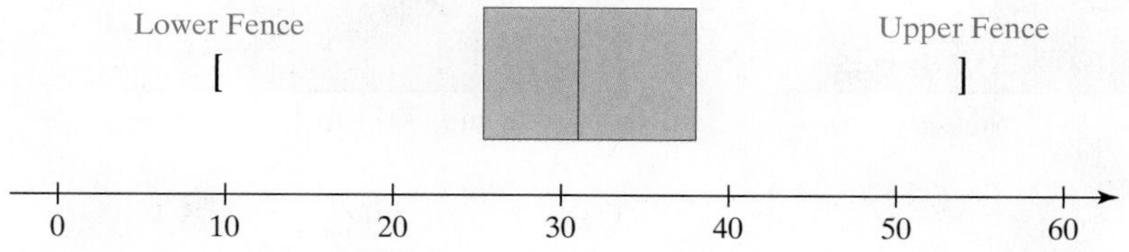

Step 4 Draw a horizontal line from Q_1 to 19.95, the smallest data value that is larger than 9.29 (the lower fence). Draw a horizontal line from Q_3 to 49.17, the largest data value that is smaller than 54.01 (the upper fence). See Figure 21(c).

Figure 21(c)

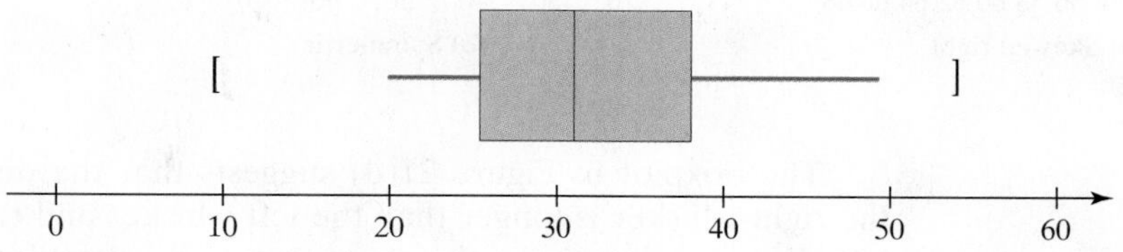

Step 5 Plot any outliers, which are values less than 9.29 (the lower fence) or greater than 54.01 (the upper fence) using an asterisk (*). So 54.63 is an outlier. Remove the temporary brackets from the graph. See Figure 21(d) on the next page.

Figure 21(d)

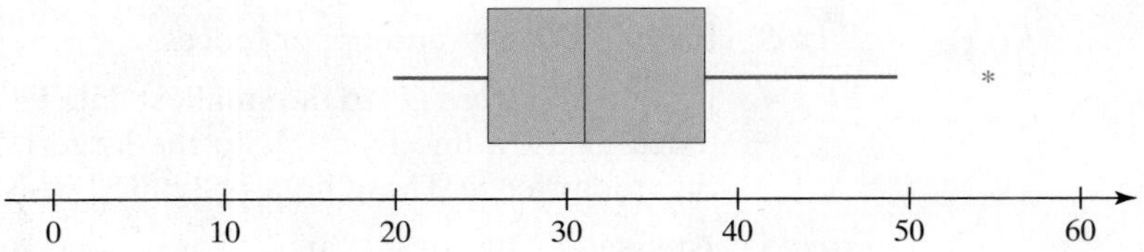

Using a Boxplot and Quartiles to Describe the Shape of a Distribution

Figure 22 shows three histograms and their corresponding boxplots with the five-number summary labeled. We should notice the following from the figure.

- In Figure 22(a), the histogram shows the distribution is skewed right. Notice that the median is left of center in the box, which means the distance from M to Q_1 is less than the distance from M to Q_3. In addition, the right whisker is longer than the left whisker. Finally, the distance from the median to the minimum value in the data set is less than the distance from the median to the maximum value in the data set.
- In Figure 22(b), the histogram shows the distribution is symmetric. Notice that the median is in the center of the box, so the distance from M to Q_1 is the same as the distance from M to Q_3. In addition, the left and right whiskers are roughly the same length. Finally, the distance from the median to the minimum value in the data set is the same as the distance from the median to the maximum value in the data set.
- In Figure 22(c), the histogram shows the distribution is skewed left. Notice that the median is right of center in the box, so the distance from M to Q_1 is more than the distance from M to Q_3. In addition, the left whisker is longer than the right whisker. Finally, the distance from the median to the minimum value in the data set is more than the distance from the median to the maximum value in the data set.

The guidelines given above are just that—guidelines. Judging the shape of a distribution is a subjective practice.

CAUTION

Identifying the shape of a distribution from a boxplot (or from a histogram, for that matter) is subjective. When identifying the shape of a distribution from a graph, be sure to support your opinion.

Note to Instructor

Consider assigning the "Matching Boxplots and Histograms" activity from the Student Activity Workbook.

Figure 22

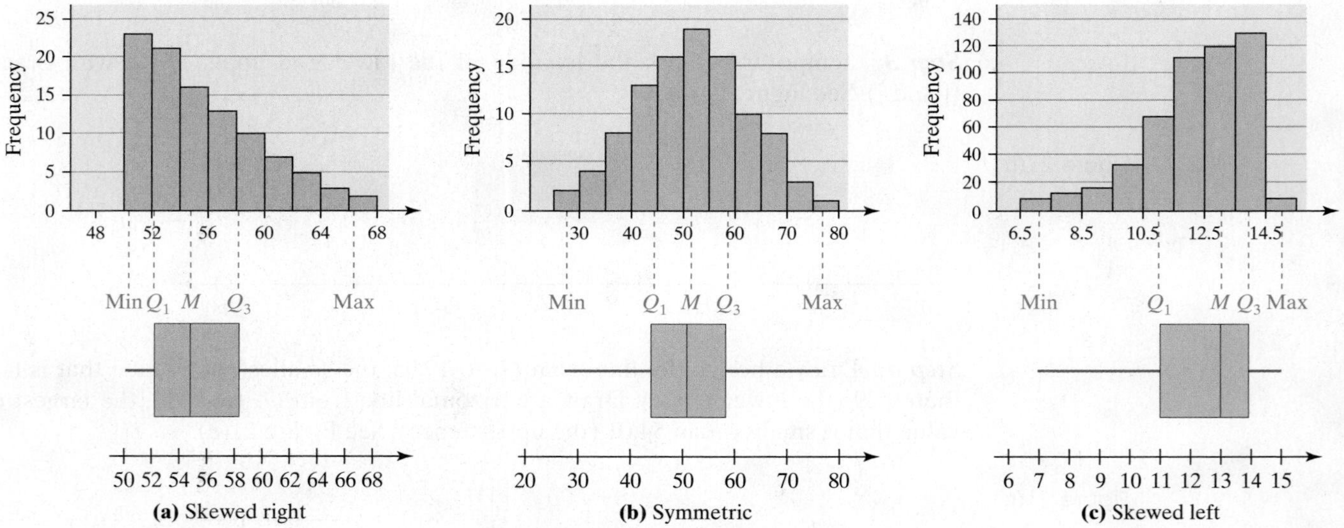

The boxplot in Figure 21(d) suggests that the distribution is skewed right, since the right whisker is longer than the left whisker and the median is left of center in the box. We can also assess the shape using the quartiles. The distance from M to Q_1 is 4.89 ($= 30.95 - 26.06$), while the distance from M to Q_3 is 6.29 ($= 37.24 - 30.95$). Also, the distance from M to the minimum value is 11 ($= 30.95 - 19.95$), while the distance from M to the maximum value is 23.68 ($= 54.63 - 30.95$).

Now Work Problem 11

EXAMPLE 4 Comparing Two Distributions by Using Boxplots

Problem In the Spacelab Life Sciences 2, led by Paul X. Callahan, 14 male rats were sent to space. The red blood cell mass (in milliliters) of the rats was determined when they returned. A control group of 14 male rats was held under the same conditions (except for space flight) as the space rats, and their red blood cell mass was also measured when the space rats returned. The data are in Table 18. Construct side-by-side boxplots for red blood cell mass for the flight group and control group. Does it appear that space flight affected the rats' red blood cell mass?

TABLE 18

Flight				Control			
7.43	7.21	8.59	8.64	8.65	6.99	8.40	9.66
9.79	6.85	6.87	7.89	7.62	7.44	8.55	8.70
9.30	8.03	7.00	8.80	7.33	8.58	9.88	9.94
6.39	7.54			7.14	9.14		

Source: NASA Life Sciences Data Archive

Approach Comparing two data sets is easy if we draw side-by-side boxplots on the same horizontal number line. Graphing calculators with advanced statistical features, as well as statistical spreadsheets such as MINITAB, Excel, and StatCrunch, can draw boxplots. We will use StatCrunch to draw the boxplots. The steps for drawing boxplots using a TI-83/84 Plus graphing calculator, MINITAB, Excel, and StatCrunch are given in the Technology Step-by-Step on page 170.

Solution Figure 23 shows the side-by-side boxplots drawn in StatCrunch. It appears that the space flight has reduced the red blood cell mass of the rats since the median for the flight group ($M \approx 7.7$) is less than the median for the control group ($M \approx 8.6$). The spread, as measured by the interquartile range, appears to be similar for both groups.

Figure 23

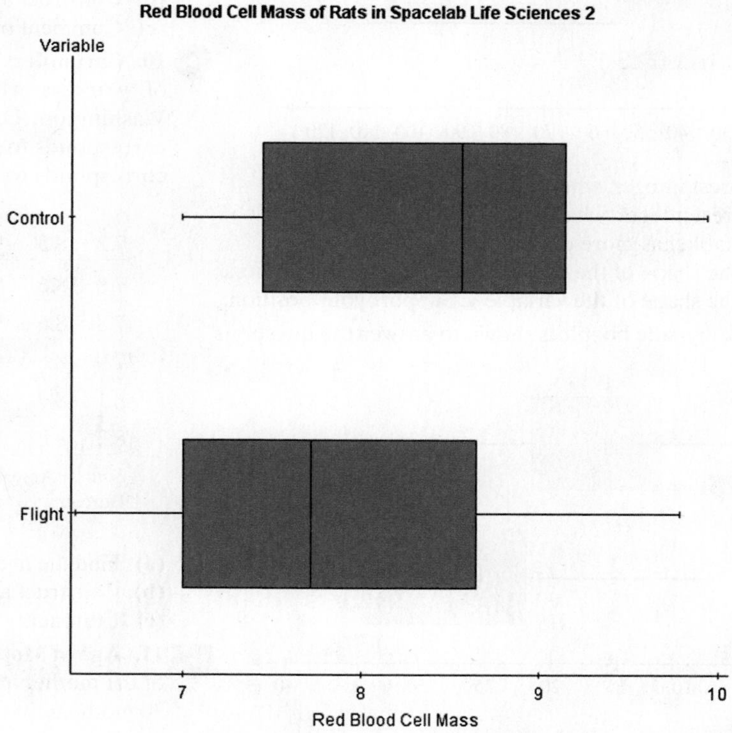

Now Work Problem 15

3.5 ASSESS YOUR UNDERSTANDING

VOCABULARY AND SKILL BUILDING

1. What does the five-number summary consist of?

2. In a boxplot, if the median is to the left of the center of the box and the right whisker is substantially longer than the left whisker, the distribution is skewed ________. right

In Problems 3 and 4, (a) identify the shape of the distribution and (b) determine the five-number summary. Assume that each number in the five-number summary is an integer.

3.

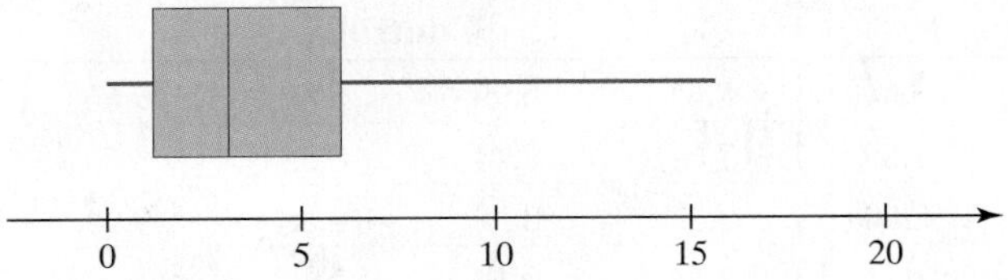

(a) skewed right (b) 0, 1, 3, 6, 16

4.

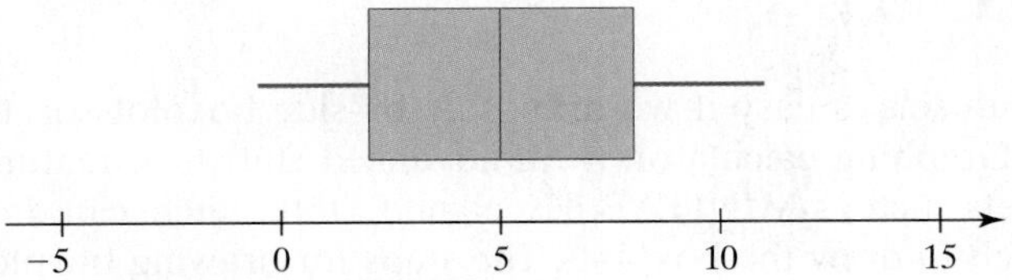

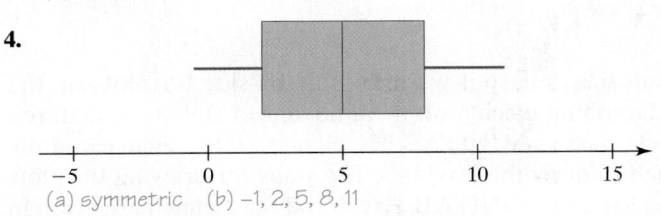

(a) symmetric (b) −1, 2, 5, 8, 11

5. Use the side-by-side boxplots shown to answer the questions that follow.

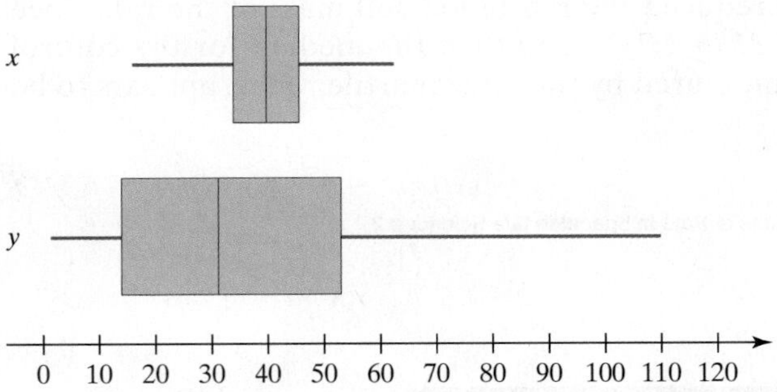

(a) To the nearest integer, what is the median of variable *x*? 40
(b) To the nearest integer, what is the third quartile of variable *y*?
(c) Which variable has more dispersion? Why? y
(d) Describe the shape of the variable *x*. Support your position.
(e) Describe the shape of the variable *y*. Support your position.

6. Use the side-by-side boxplots shown to answer the questions that follow.

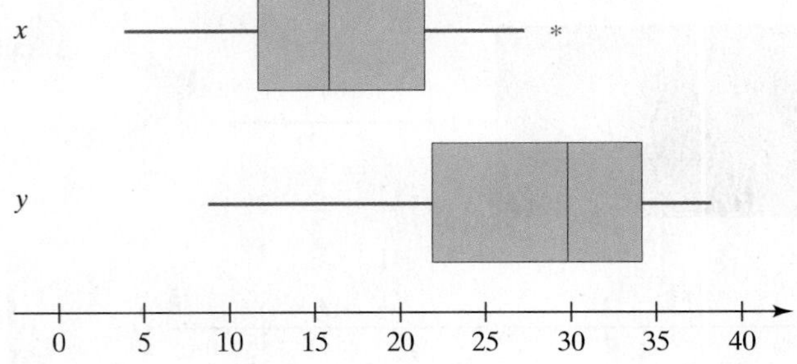

5. (b) 52 (d) Symmetric (e) Skewed right

(a) To the nearest integer, what is the median of variable *x*? 16
(b) To the nearest integer, what is the first quartile of variable *y*?
(c) Which variable has more dispersion? Why? y (b) 22
(d) Does the variable *x* have any outliers? If so, what is the value of the outlier(s)? Yes; 30 (e) Skewed left
(e) Describe the shape of the variable *y*. Support your position.

7. Exam Scores After giving a statistics exam, Professor Dang determined the following five-number summary for her class results: 60 68 77 89 98. Use this information to draw a boxplot of the exam scores.

8. Speed Reading Jessica enrolled in a course that promised to increase her reading speed. To help judge the effectiveness of the course, Jessica measured the number of words per minute she could read prior to enrolling in the course. She obtained the following five-number summary: 110 140 157 173 205. Use this information to draw a boxplot of the reading speed.

APPLYING THE CONCEPTS

9. Age at Inauguration The following data represent the age of U.S. presidents on their respective inauguration days (through Barack Obama).

42	47	50	52	54	55	57	61	64
43	48	51	52	54	56	57	61	65
46	49	51	54	55	56	57	61	68
46	49	51	54	55	56	58	62	69
47	50	51	54	55	57	60	64	

Source: factmonster.com

(a) Find the five-number summary. 42, 50.5, 54.5, 57.5, 69
(b) Construct a boxplot.
(c) Comment on the shape of the distribution. symmetric

10. Carpoolers The following data represent the percentage of workers who carpool to work for the 50 states plus Washington, D.C. **Note:** The minimum observation of 7.2% corresponds to Maine and the maximum observation of 16.4% corresponds to Hawaii.

7.2	8.5	9.0	9.4	10.0	10.3	11.2	11.5	13.8
7.8	8.6	9.1	9.6	10.0	10.3	11.2	11.5	14.4
7.8	8.6	9.2	9.7	10.0	10.3	11.2	11.7	16.4
7.9	8.6	9.2	9.7	10.1	10.7	11.3	12.4	
8.1	8.7	9.2	9.9	10.2	10.7	11.3	12.5	
8.3	8.8	9.4	9.9	10.3	10.9	11.3	13.6	

Source: American Community Survey by the U.S. Census Bureau

(a) Find the five-number summary. 7.2, 9.0, 10.0, 11.2, 16.4
(b) Construct a boxplot.
(c) Comment on the shape of the distribution. Skewed right

11. Age of Mother at Birth The following data represent the age of the mother at the time of her first birth for a random sample of 30 mothers.

21	35	33	25	22	26
21	24	16	32	25	20
30	20	20	29	21	19
18	24	33	22	23	25
17	23	25	29	25	19

Source: General Social Survey

(a) Construct a boxplot of the data.
(b) Use the boxplot and quartiles to describe the shape of the distribution. Slightly skewed right

12. Got a Headache? The following data represent the weight (in grams) of a random sample of 25 Tylenol tablets.

0.608	0.601	0.606	0.602	0.611
0.608	0.610	0.610	0.607	0.600
0.608	0.608	0.605	0.609	0.605
0.610	0.607	0.611	0.608	0.610
0.612	0.598	0.600	0.605	0.603

Source: Kelly Roe, student at Joliet Junior College

(a) Construct a boxplot.
(b) Use the boxplot and quartiles to describe the shape of the distribution. Skewed left

13. M&Ms In Problem 27 from Section 3.1, we drew a histogram of the weights of M&Ms and found that the distribution is symmetric. Draw a boxplot of these data. Use the boxplot and quartiles to confirm the distribution is symmetric. For convenience, the data are displayed again.

0.87	0.88	0.82	0.90	0.90	0.84	0.84
0.91	0.94	0.86	0.86	0.86	0.88	0.87
0.89	0.91	0.86	0.87	0.93	0.88	
0.83	0.95	0.87	0.93	0.91	0.85	
0.91	0.91	0.86	0.89	0.87	0.84	
0.88	0.88	0.89	0.79	0.82	0.83	
0.90	0.88	0.84	0.93	0.81	0.90	
0.88	0.92	0.85	0.84	0.84	0.86	

Source: Michael Sullivan

14. Old Faithful In Problem 28 from Section 3.1, we drew a histogram of the length of eruption of California's Old Faithful geyser and found that the distribution is symmetric. Draw a boxplot of these data. Use the boxplot and quartiles to confirm the distribution is symmetric. For convenience, the data are displayed again.

108	108	99	105	103	103	94
102	99	106	90	104	110	110
103	109	109	111	101	101	
110	102	105	110	106	104	
104	100	103	102	120	90	
113	116	95	105	103	101	
100	101	107	110	92	108	

Source: Ladonna Hansen, Park Curator

NW **15. Dissolving Rates of Vitamins** A student wanted to know whether Centrum vitamins dissolve faster than the corresponding generic brand. The student used vinegar as a proxy for stomach acid and measured the time (in minutes) it took for a vitamin to completely dissolve. The results are shown next.

Centrum					Generic Brand				
2.73	3.07	3.30	3.35	3.12	6.57	6.23	6.17	7.17	5.77
2.95	2.15	2.67	2.80	2.25	6.73	5.78	5.38	5.25	5.55
2.60	2.57	4.02	3.02	2.15	5.50	6.50	7.42	6.47	6.30
3.03	3.53	2.63	2.30	2.73	6.33	7.42	5.57	6.35	5.92
3.92	2.38	3.25	4.00	3.63	5.35	7.25	7.58	6.50	4.97
3.02	4.17	4.33	3.85	2.23	7.13	5.98	6.60	5.03	7.18

Source: Amanda A. Sindewald, student at Joliet Junior College

(a) Draw side-by-side boxplots for each vitamin type.
(b) Which vitamin type has more dispersion? Generic
(c) Which vitamin type appears to dissolve faster? Centrum

16. Chips per Cookie Do store-brand chocolate chip cookies have fewer chips per cookie than Keebler's Chips Deluxe Chocolate Chip Cookies? To find out, a student randomly selected 21 cookies of each brand and counted the number of chips in the cookies. The results are shown next.

Keebler			Store Brand		
32	23	28	21	23	24
28	28	29	24	25	27
25	20	25	26	26	21
22	21	24	18	16	24
21	24	21	21	30	17
26	28	24	23	28	31
33	20	31	27	33	29

Source: Trina McNamara, student at Joliet Junior College

(a) Draw side-by-side boxplots for each brand of cookie.
(b) Does there appear to be a difference in the number of chips per cookie? Not really
(c) Does one brand have a more consistent number of chips per cookie? Keebler

17. Putting It Together: Paternal Smoking It is well-documented that active maternal smoking during pregnancy is associated with lower-birth-weight babies. Researchers Fernando D. Martinez and associates wanted to determine if there is a relationship between paternal smoking habits and birth weight. The researchers administered a questionnaire to each parent of newborn infants. One question asked whether the individual smoked regularly. Because the survey was administered within 15 days of birth, it was assumed that any regular smokers were also regular smokers during pregnancy. Birth weights for the babies (in grams) of nonsmoking mothers were obtained and divided into two groups, nonsmoking fathers and smoking fathers. The given data on the next page are representative of the data collected by the researchers. The researchers concluded that the birth weight of babies whose father smoked was less than the birth weight of babies whose father did not smoke. *Source:* "The Effect of Paternal Smoking on the Birthweight of Newborns Whose Mothers Did Not Smoke," Fernando D. Martinez, Anne L. Wright, Lynn M. Taussig, *American Journal of Public Health* Vol. 84, No. 9

Nonsmokers			Smokers		
4194	3522	3454	3998	3455	3066
3062	3771	3783	3150	2986	2918
3544	3746	4019	4216	3502	3457
4054	3518	3884	3493	3255	3234
4248	3719	3668	2860	3282	2746
3128	3290	3423	3686	2851	3145
3471	4354	3544	3807	3548	4104
3994	2976	4067	3963	3892	2768
3732	3823	3302	3769	3509	3629
3436	3976	3263	4131	3129	4263

(a) Is this an observational study or a designed experiment? Why? Observational study

(b) What is the explanatory variable? What is the response variable? Whether the father smoked or not; birth weight

(c) Can you think of any lurking variables that may affect the results of the study?

(d) In the article, the researchers stated that "birthweights were adjusted for possible confounders . . . ." What does this mean?

(e) Determine summary statistics (mean, median, standard deviation, quartiles) for each group.

(f) Interpret the first quartile for both the nonsmoker and smoker group.

(g) Draw a side-by-side boxplot of the data. Does the side-by-side boxplot confirm the conclusions of the study?

EXPLAINING THE CONCEPTS

18. Which boxplot likely has the data with a larger standard deviation? Why? Boxplot II

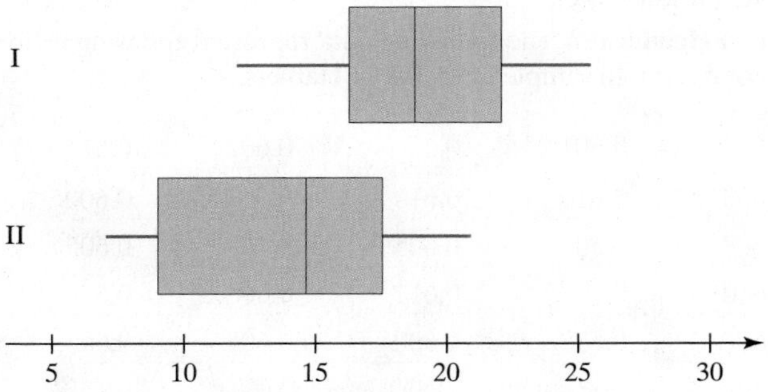

19. Explain how to determine the shape of a distribution using the boxplot and quartiles.

Technology Step-By-Step

Drawing Boxplots Using Technology

TI-83/84 Plus

1. Enter the raw data into `L1`.
2. Press `2nd Y=` and select `1:Plot 1`.
3. Turn the plots `ON`. Use the cursor to highlight the modified boxplot icon. Your screen should appear as follows:

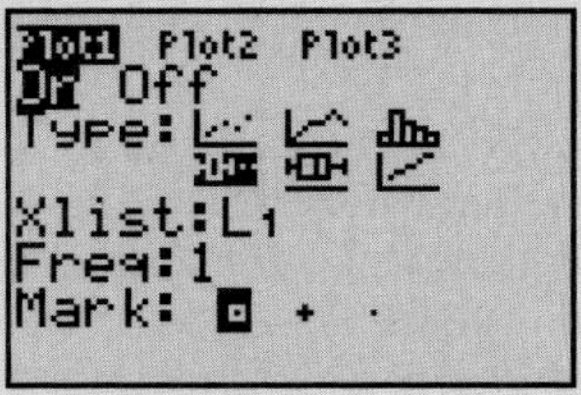

4. Press `ZOOM` and select `9:ZoomStat`.

MINITAB

1. Enter the raw data into column C1.
2. Select the **Graph** menu and highlight **Boxplot . . .**
3. For a single boxplot, select `One Y, simple`. For two or more boxplots, select `Multiple Y's, simple`.
4. Select the data to be graphed. If you want the boxplot to be horizontal rather than vertical, select the Scale button, then transpose value and category scales. Click OK.

Excel

1. Load the XLSTAT Add-in.
2. Enter the raw data into column A. If you are drawing side-by-side boxplots, enter each category of data in a separate column.
3. Select the **XLSTAT** menu and highlight **Describing data**. Then select **Descriptive statistics.**
4. In the Descriptive statistics dialogue box, place the cursor in the Quantitative data cell. Then highlight the data in column A. If you are drawing side-by-side boxplots, highlight all the data. Select the Charts tab.
5. Check Boxplots. Also check Outliers. If you want the graph drawn horizontal, select the Horizontal radio button. If you are drawing side-by-side boxplots, check the Group plots box. Click Okay.

StatCrunch

1. Enter the raw data into the spreadsheet. Name the column variable.
2. Select **Graphics** and highlight **Boxplot.**
3. Click on the variable whose boxplot you want to draw and click Next>.
4. Check whether you wish to identify outliers or draw the boxes horizontally. Click Next>.
5. Enter labels for the *x*-axis and enter a title for the graph. Click Create Graph!

CHAPTER 3 REVIEW

Summary

This chapter concentrated on describing distributions numerically. Measures of central tendency are used to indicate the typical value in a distribution. Three measures of central tendency were discussed. The mean measures the center of gravity of the distribution. The data must be quantitative to compute the mean. The median separates the bottom 50% of the data from the top 50%. The data must be at least ordinal to compute the median. The mode measures the most frequent observation. The data can be either quantitative or qualitative to compute the mode. The median is resistant to extreme values, while the mean is not.

Measures of dispersion describe the spread in the data. The range is the difference between the highest and lowest data values. The standard deviation is based on the average squared deviation about the mean. The variance is the square of the standard deviation. The range, standard deviation, and variance, are not resistant. The mean and standard deviation are used in many types of statistical inference.

The mean, median, and mode can be approximated from grouped data. The standard deviation can also be approximated from grouped data.

We can determine the relative position of an observation in a data set using z-scores and percentiles. A z-score denotes how many standard deviations an observation is from the mean. Percentiles determine the percent of observations that lie above and below an observation. The interquartile range is a resistant measure of dispersion. The upper and lower fences can be used to identify potential outliers. Any potential outlier must be investigated to determine whether it was the result of a data-entry error or some other error in the data-collection process, or is an unusual value in the data set.

The five-number summary provides an idea about the center and spread of a data set through the median and the interquartile range. The length of the tails in the distribution can be determined from the smallest and largest data values. The five-number summary is used to construct boxplots. Boxplots can be used to describe the shape of the distribution and to visualize outliers.

Vocabulary

Arithmetic mean (p. 117)
Population arithmetic mean (p. 117)
Sample arithmetic mean (p. 117)
Mean (p. 117)
Median (p. 119)
Resistant (p. 121)
Mode (p. 123)
No mode (p. 123)
Bimodal (p. 123)
Multimodal (p. 123)
Dispersion (p. 130)
Range (p. 131)
Deviation about the mean (p. 132)
Population standard deviation (p. 132)
Sample standard deviation (p. 134)
Degrees of freedom (p. 134)
Population variance (p. 136)
Sample variance (p. 136)
Biased (p. 137)
The Empirical Rule (p. 137)
Chebyshev's Inequality (p. 139)
Weighted mean (p. 149)
z-score (p. 154)
kth percentile (p. 155)
Quartiles (p. 155)
Interquartile range (p. 157)
Describe the distribution (p. 158)
Outlier (p. 158)
Fences (p. 159)
Exploratory data analysis (p. 163)
Five-number summary (p. 163)
Boxplot (p. 164)
Whiskers (p. 165)

Formulas

Population Mean

$$\mu = \frac{\sum x_i}{N}$$

Sample Mean

$$\bar{x} = \frac{\sum x_i}{n}$$

Population Standard Deviation

$$\sigma = \sqrt{\frac{\sum (x_i - \mu)^2}{N}} = \sqrt{\frac{\sum x_i^2 - \dfrac{\left(\sum x_i\right)^2}{N}}{N}}$$

Sample Standard Deviation

$$s = \sqrt{\frac{\sum (x_i - \bar{x})^2}{n-1}} = \sqrt{\frac{\sum x_i^2 - \dfrac{\left(\sum x_i\right)^2}{n}}{n-1}}$$

Population Variance

σ^2

Sample Variance

s^2

Range = Largest Data Value − Smallest Data Value

Weighted Mean

$$\bar{x}_w = \frac{\sum w_i x_i}{\sum w_i}$$

Population Mean from Grouped Data

$$\mu = \frac{\sum x_i f_i}{\sum f_i}$$

Sample Mean from Grouped Data

$$\bar{x} = \frac{\sum x_i f_i}{\sum f_i}$$

Population Standard Deviation from Grouped Data

$$\sigma = \sqrt{\frac{\Sigma(x_i - \mu)^2 f_i}{\Sigma f_i}}$$

Sample Standard Deviation from Grouped Data

$$s = \sqrt{\frac{\Sigma(x_i - \bar{x})^2 f_i}{(\Sigma f_i) - 1}}$$

Population *z*-Score

$$z = \frac{x - \mu}{\sigma}$$

Sample *z*-Score

$$z = \frac{x - \bar{x}}{s}$$

Interquartile Range

$$\text{IQR} = Q_3 - Q_1$$

Lower and Upper Fences

$$\text{Lower Fence} = Q_1 - 1.5(\text{IQR})$$

$$\text{Upper Fence} = Q_3 + 1.5(\text{IQR})$$

Objectives

Section	You should be able to . . .	Example	Review Exercises
3.1	1 Determine the arithmetic mean of a variable from raw data (p. 117)	1, 4, 6	1(a), 2(a), 3(a), 4(c), 10(a)
	2 Determine the median of a variable from raw data (p. 119)	2, 3, 4, 6	1(a), 2(a), 3(a), 4(c), 10(a)
	3 Explain what it means for a statistic to be resistant (p. 120)	5	2(c), 10(h), 10(i), 12
	4 Determine the mode of a variable from raw data (p. 122)	7, 8, 9	3(a), 4(d)
3.2	1 Determine the range of a variable from raw data (p. 131)	2	1(b), 2(b), 3(b)
	2 Determine the standard deviation of a variable from raw data (p. 132)	3–6	1(b), 2(b), 3(b), 10(d)
	3 Determine the variance of a variable from raw data (p. 136)	7	1(b)
	4 Use the Empirical Rule to describe data that are bell shaped (p. 137)	8	5(a)–(d)
	5 Use Chebyshev's Inequality to describe any set of data (p. 139)	9	5(e)–(f)
3.3	1 Approximate the mean of a variable from grouped data (p. 147)	1, 4	6(a)
	2 Compute the weighted mean (p. 148)	2	7
	3 Approximate the standard deviation of a variable from grouped data (p. 149)	3, 4	6(b)
3.4	1 Determine and interpret *z*-scores (p. 154)	1	8
	2 Interpret percentiles (p. 155)	2	11
	3 Determine and interpret quartiles (p. 155)	3, 4	10(b)
	4 Determine and interpret the interquartile range (p. 157)	5	2(b), 10(d)
	5 Check a set of data for outliers (p. 158)	6	10(e)
3.5	1 Compute the five-number summary (p. 163)	1, 2	10(c)
	2 Draw and interpret boxplots (p. 164)	3, 4	9, 10(f)–10(g)

Review Exercises

1. Muzzle Velocity The following data represent the muzzle velocity (in meters per second) of rounds fired from a 155-mm gun.

793.8	793.1	792.4	794.0	791.4
792.4	791.7	792.3	789.6	794.4

Source: Christenson, Ronald, and Blackwood, Larry, "Tests for Precision and Accuracy of Multiple Measuring Devices," *Technometrics*, 35(4): 411–421, 1993.

(a) Compute the sample mean and median muzzle velocity.

(b) Compute the range, sample variance, and sample standard deviation. *Range = 4.8 m/s, $s^2 = 2.03$, s = 1.42 m/s*

1. (a) $\bar{x} = 792.51$ m/s; M = 792.40 m/s

2. Price of Chevy Cobalts The following data represent the sales price in dollars for nine 2-year-old Chevrolet Cobalts in the Los Angeles area. *2. (a) $\bar{x} = \$10{,}178.9$; M = \$9980*

(b) Range = \$8550, s = \$3074.9, IQR = \$5954.5,

14050	13999	12999	10995	9980
8998	7889	7200	5500	

Source: cars.com

(a) Determine the sample mean and median price.

(b) Determine the range, sample standard deviation, and interquartile range.

(c) Redo (a) and (b) if the data value 14,050 was incorrectly entered as 41,050. How does this change affect the mean? the

2. (c) Median and IQR are resistant.

median? the range? the standard deviation? the interquartile range? Which of these values is resistant?

3. Chief Justices The following data represent the ages of chief justices of the U.S. Supreme Court when they were appointed.

Justice	Age
John Jay	44
John Rutledge	56
Oliver Ellsworth	51
John Marshall	46
Roger B. Taney	59
Salmon P. Chase	56
Morrison R. Waite	58
Melville W. Fuller	55
Edward D. White	65
William H. Taft	64
Charles E. Hughes	68
Harlan F. Stone	69
Frederick M. Vinson	56
Earl Warren	62
Warren E. Burger	62
William H. Rehnquist	62
John G. Roberts	50

Source: Information Please Almanac

3. (a) $\mu = 57.8$, $M = 58.0$, bimodal: 58 and 62
(b) Range $= 25$, $\sigma = 7.0$

(a) Determine the population mean, median, and mode ages.
(b) Determine the range and population standard deviation ages.
(c) Obtain two simple random samples of size 4, and determine the sample mean and sample standard deviation ages.

4. Number of Tickets Issued As part of a statistics project, a student surveys 30 randomly selected students and asks them how many speeding tickets they have been issued in the past month. The results of the survey are as follows:

1	1	0	1	0	0
0	0	0	1	0	1
0	1	2	0	1	1
0	0	0	0	1	1
0	0	0	0	1	0

(a) Draw a frequency histogram of the data and describe its shape. Skewed right (b) Mean > median
(b) Based on the shape of the histogram, do you expect the mean to be more than, equal to, or less than the median?
(c) Determine the mean and the median of the number of tickets issued. $\bar{x} = 0.4$; $M = 0$
(d) Determine the mode of the number of tickets issued. 0

5. Chebyshev's Inequality and the Empirical Rule Suppose that a certain brand of light bulb has a mean life of 600 hours and a standard deviation of 53 hours.

(a) A histogram of the data indicates the sample data follow a bell-shaped distribution. According to the Empirical Rule, 99.7% of light bulbs have lifetimes between ______ and ______ hours. 441, 759
(b) Assuming the data are bell shaped, determine the percentage of light bulbs that will have a life between 494 and 706 hours. 95%
(c) Assuming the data are bell shaped, what percentage of light bulbs will last between 547 and 706 hours. 81.5%
(d) If the company that manufactures the light bulb guarantees to replace any bulb that does not last at least 441 hours, what percentage of light bulbs can the firm expect to have to replace, according to the Empirical Rule? 0.15%
(e) Use Chebyshev's Inequality to determine the minimum percentage of light bulbs with a life within 2.5 standard deviations of the mean. 84%
(f) Use Chebyshev's Inequality to determine the minimum percentage of light bulbs with a life between 494 and 706 hours. 75%

6. Travel Time to Work The frequency distribution listed in the table represents the travel time to work (in minutes) for a random sample of 895 U.S. adults.

Travel Time (minutes)	Frequency
0–9	125
10–19	271
20–29	186
30–39	121
40–49	54
50–59	62
60–69	43
70–79	20
80–89	13

Source: Based on data from the 2009 American Community Survey

(a) Approximate the mean travel time to work for U.S. adults.
(b) Approximate the standard deviation travel time to work for U.S. adults. 19.1 minutes (a) 27.7 minutes

7. Weighted Mean Michael has just completed his first semester in college. He earned an A in his 5-hour calculus course, a B in his 4-hour chemistry course, an A in his 3-hour speech course, and a C in his 3-hour psychology course. Assuming an A equals 4 points, a B equals 3 points, and a C equals 2 points, determine Michael's grade-point average if grades are weighted by class hours. 3.33

8. Weights of Males versus Females According to the National Center for Health Statistics, the mean weight of a 20- to 29-year-old female is 156.5 pounds, with a standard deviation of 51.2 pounds. The mean weight of a 20- to 29-year-old male is 183.4 pounds, with a standard deviation of 40.0 pounds. Who is relatively heavier: a 20- to 29-year-old female who weighs 160 pounds or a 20- to 29-year-old male who weighs 185 pounds? Female

9. Halladay No-No On October 6, 2010, Roy Halladay of the Philadelphia Phillies threw the second post-season no-hitter in major league history. The side-by-side boxplot on the next page shows the pitch speed (in miles per hour) for all of Halladay's pitches during the game.

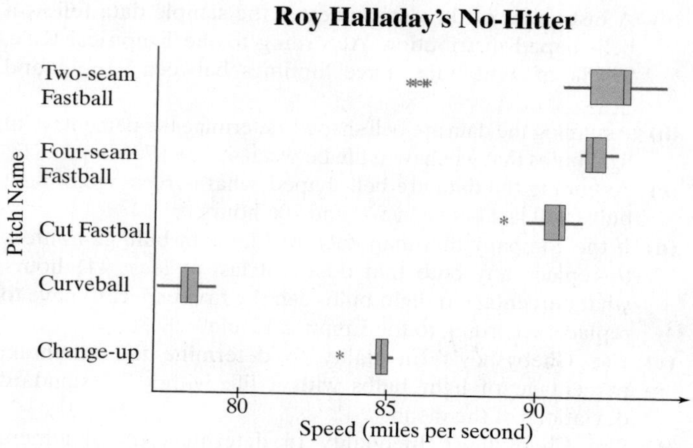

(b) Two-seam fastball

(a) Which pitch is typically thrown the fastest? Two-seam fastball

(b) Which pitch is most erratic as far as pitch speed goes?

(c) Which pitch is most consistent as far as pitch speed goes, the cut fastball or the four-seam fastball? Four-seam fastball

(d) Are there any outliers for Halladay's cut fastball? If so, approximate the pitch speed of the outlier. 88 mph

(e) Describe the shape of the distribution of Halladay's curveball. Symmetric

(f) Describe the shape of the distribution of Halladay's four-seam fastball. Skewed right

10. Presidential Inaugural Addresses Ever wonder how many words are in a typical inaugural address? The following data represent the lengths of all the inaugural addresses (measured in word count) for all presidents up to Barack Obama.

1425	1125	1128	5433	2242	2283
135	1172	1337	1802	2446	1507
2308	3838	2480	1526	2449	2170
1729	8445	2978	3318	1355	1571
2158	4776	1681	4059	1437	2073
1175	996	4388	3801	2130	2406
1209	3319	2015	1883	1668	
3217	2821	3967	1807	1087	
4467	3634	2217	1340	2463	
2906	698	985	559	2546	

Source: infoplease.com

(a) Determine the mean and median number of words in a presidential inaugural address.

(b) Determine and interpret the quartiles for the number of words in a presidential inaugural address.

(c) Determine the five-number summary for the number of words in a presidential inaugural address.

(d) Determine the standard deviation and interquartile range for the number of words in a presidential inaugural address.

(e) Are there any outliers in the data set? If so, what is (are) the value(s)? Yes, 5433 and 8445

(f) Draw a boxplot of the data.

(g) Describe the shape of the distribution. Support your position using the boxplot and quartiles. Skewed right

(h) Which measure of central tendency do you think better describes the typical number of words in an inaugural address? Why? Median

(i) Which measure of dispersion do you think better describes the spread of the typical number of words in an inaugural address? Why? IQR

11. You Explain It! Percentiles According to the National Center for Health Statistics, a 19-year-old female whose height is 67.1 inches has a height that is at the 85th percentile. Explain what this means.

12. Skinfold Thickness Procedure One method of estimating body fat is through skinfold thickness measurement. The measurement can use from three to nine different standard anatomical sites around the body. The right side is usually only measured (for consistency). The tester pinches the skin at the appropriate site to raise a double layer of skin and the underlying adipose tissue, but not the muscle. Calipers are then applied 1 centimeter below and at right angles to the pinch and a reading is taken 2 seconds later. The mean of two measurements should be taken. If the two measurements differ greatly, a third should be done and then the median value taken. Explain why a median is used as the measure of central tendency when three measures are taken, rather than the mean. Resistance

10. (a) $\mu = 2358.8$ words; $M = 2144$ words
(b) 1390, 2144, 2942 words
(c) 135, 1390, 2144, 2942, 8445
(d) $\sigma = 1393.2$ words; IQR = 1552 words

Problems in the chapter test are labeled by section.objective. For example, 2.3 means Section 2, Objective 3.

CHAPTER TEST

1. The following data represent the amount of time (in minutes) a random sample of eight students enrolled in Sullivan's Intermediate Algebra course spent on the homework from Section 4.5, Factoring Polynomials.

48	88	57	109
111	93	71	63

Source: MyMathLab

1.1 **(a)** Determine the mean amount of time spent doing Section 4.5 homework. 80 minutes

1.2 **(b)** Determine the median amount of time spent doing Section 4.5 homework. 79.5 minutes

1.3 **(c)** Suppose the observation 109 minutes is incorrectly recorded as 1009 minutes. Recompute the mean and the median. What do you notice? What property of the median does this illustrate? $\bar{x} = 192.5$ minutes, $M = 79.5$ minutes; resistance

1.4 **2.** The Federal Bureau of Investigation classifies various larcenies. The following data represent the type of larcenies based on a random sample of 15 larcenies. What is the mode type of larceny? From motor vehicles

Pocket picking and purse snatching	Bicycles	From motor vehicles
From motor vehicles	From motor vehicles	From buildings
From buildings	Shoplifting	Motor vehicle accessories
From motor vehicles	Shoplifting	From motor vehicles
From motor vehicles	Pocket picking and purse snatching	From motor vehicles

2.1 **3.** Determine the range of the homework data from Problem 1. 63 minutes

2.2 **4. (a)** Determine the standard deviation of the homework data from Problem 1. 23.8 minutes

3.4 **(b)** By hand, determine and interpret the interquartile range of the homework data from Problem 1. 41 minutes

1.3 **(c)** Which of these two measures of dispersion is resistant? Why? IQR

5. In a random sample of 250 toner cartridges, the mean number of pages a toner cartridge can print is 4302 and the standard deviation is 340.

2.4 **(a)** Suppose a histogram of the data indicates that the sample data follow a bell-shaped distribution. According to the Empirical Rule, 99.7% of toner cartridges will print between 3282 and 5322 pages.

2.4 **(b)** Assuming that the distribution of the data are bell shaped, determine the percentage of toner cartridges whose print total is between 3622 and 4982 pages. 95%

2.4 **(c)** If the company that manufactures the toner cartridges guarantees to replace any cartridge that does not print at least 3622 pages, what percent of cartridges can the firm expect to be responsible for replacing, according to the Empirical Rule? 2.5%

2.5 **(d)** Use Chebyshev's inequality to determine the minimum percentage of toner cartridges with a page count within 1.5 standard deviations of the mean. 55.6%

2.5 **(e)** Use Chebyshev's inequality to determine the minimum percentage of toner cartridges that print between 3282 and 5322 pages. 88.9%

6. The following data represent the length of time (in minutes) between eruptions of Old Faithful in Yellowstone National Park.

Time (minutes)	Frequency
40–49	8
50–59	44
60–69	23
70–79	6
80–89	107
90–99	11
100–109	1

3.1 **(a)** Approximate the mean length of time between eruptions.

3.3 **(b)** Approximate the standard deviation length of time between eruptions. 14.7 minutes (a) 74.9 minutes

3.2 **7.** Yolanda wishes to develop a new type of meatloaf to sell at her restaurant. She decides to combine 2 pounds of ground sirloin (cost \$2.70 per pound), 1 pound of ground turkey (cost \$1.30 per pound), and $\frac{1}{2}$ pound of ground pork (cost \$1.80 per pound). What is the cost per pound of the meatloaf? \$2.17

8. An engineer is studying bearing failures for two different materials in aircraft gas turbine engines. The following data are failure times (in millions of cycles) for samples of the two material types.

Material A		Material B	
3.17	5.88	5.78	9.65
4.31	6.91	6.71	13.44
4.52	8.01	6.84	14.71
4.66	8.97	7.23	16.39
5.69	11.92	8.20	24.37

1.1 **(a)** Determine the sample mean failure time for each material.

1.2 **(b)** By hand, compute the median failure time for each material.

2.2 **(c)** Determine the sample standard deviation of the failure times for each material. Which material has its failure times more dispersed?

5.1 **(d)** By hand, compute the five-number summary for each material.

5.2 **(e)** On the same graph, draw boxplots for the two materials. Annotate the graph with some general remarks comparing the failure times.

(f) Describe the shape of the distribution of each material using the boxplot and quartiles. Skewed right

9. The following data represent the weights (in grams) of 50 randomly selected quarters. Determine and interpret the quartiles. Does the data set contain any outliers?
4.3
4.5
5.58 g; 5.60 g; 5.67 g; yes, 5.84 g

5.49	5.58	5.60	5.62	5.68
5.52	5.58	5.60	5.63	5.70
5.53	5.58	5.60	5.63	5.71
5.53	5.58	5.60	5.63	5.71
5.53	5.58	5.60	5.65	5.72
5.56	5.58	5.60	5.66	5.73
5.57	5.59	5.60	5.66	5.73
5.57	5.59	5.61	5.66	5.73
5.57	5.59	5.62	5.67	5.74
5.57	5.59	5.62	5.67	5.84

8. (a) $\bar{x}_A = 6.404$ million cycles; $\bar{x}_B = 11.332$ million cycles
(b) $M_A = 5.785$ million cycles; $M_B = 8.925$ million cycles
(c) $s_A = 2.626$ million cycles; $s_B = 5.900$ million cycles; Material B
(d) A (in million cycles); 3.17, 4.52, 5.785, 8.01, 11.92
B (in million cycles); 5.78, 6.84, 8.925, 14.71, 24.37

4.1 **10.** Armando is filling out a college application. The application requires that Armando supply either his SAT math score or his ACT math score. Armando scored 610 on the SAT math and 27 on the ACT math. Which score should Armando report, given that the mean SAT math score is 515 with a standard deviation of 114, and the mean ACT math score is 21.0 with a standard deviation of 5.1? Why? ACT

4.2 **11.** According to the National Center for Health Statistics, a 10-year-old male whose height is 53.5 inches has a height that is at the 15th percentile. Explain what this means.

1.2 **12.** The distribution of income tends to be skewed to the right. Suppose you are running for a congressional seat and wish to portray that the average income in your district is low. Which measure of central tendency, the mean or the median, would you report? Why? Median

13. Answer the following based on the histograms shown to the right.

1.2 **(a)** Which measure of central tendency would you recommend reporting for the data whose histogram is shown in Figure I? Why? Mean

2.2 **(b)** Which one has more dispersion? Explain. I

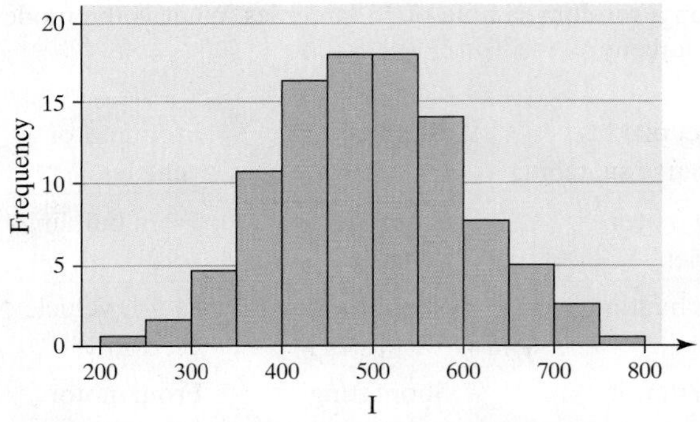

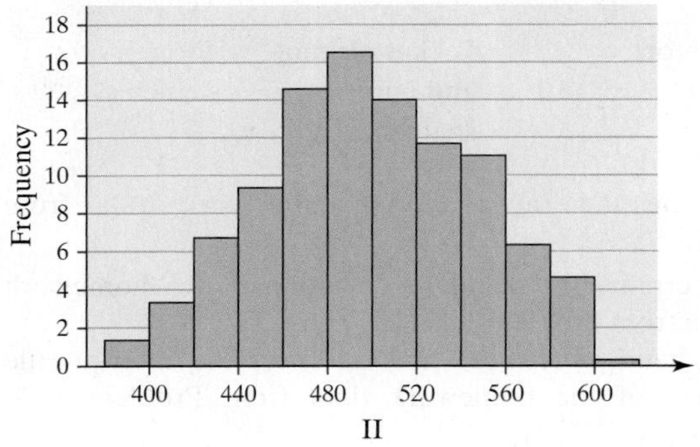

Making an Informed Decision

What Car Should I Buy?

Suppose you are in the market to purchase a used car. To make an informed decision regarding your purchase, you would like to collect as much information as possible. Among the information you might consider are the typical price of the car, the typical number of miles the car should have, its crash test results, insurance costs, and expected repair costs.

1. Make a list of at least three cars that you would consider purchasing. To be fair, the cars should be in the same class (such as compact, midsize, and so on). They should also be of the same age.

2. Collect information regarding the three cars in your list by finding at least eight cars of each type that are for sale. Obtain information such as the asking price and the number of miles the car has. Sources of data include your local newspaper, classified ads, and car websites (such as www.cars.com). Compute summary statistics for asking price, number of miles, and other variables of interest. Using the same scale, draw boxplots of each variable considered.

3. Go to the Insurance Institute for Highway Safety website (www.iihs.org). Select the Vehicle Ratings link. Choose the make and model for each car you are considering. Obtain information regarding crash testing for each car under consideration. Compare cars in the same class. How does each car compare? Is one car you are considering substantially safer than the others? What about repair costs? Compute summary statistics for crash tests and repair costs.

4. Obtain information about insurance costs. Contact various insurance companies to determine the cost of insuring the cars you are considering. Compute summary statistics for insurance costs and draw boxplots.

5. Write a report supporting your conclusion regarding which car you would purchase.

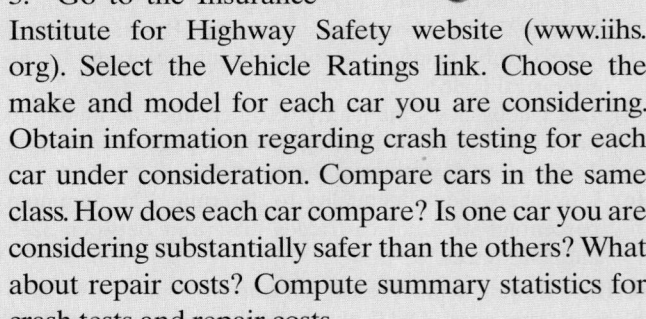

The Chapter 3 Case Study is located on the CD that accompanies this text.

4 Describing the Relation between Two Variables

OUTLINE

Making an Informed Decision

The world is a very interesting and dynamic place. How do quantitative variables relate to each other on a world scale? A Web site that allows us to see how the world is changing over time and, in particular, how relationships among variables in our world change over time is www.gapminder.org. See the Decisions Project on page 230.

PUTTING IT TOGETHER

In Chapters 2 and 3 we examined data in which a single variable was measured for each individual in the study (**univariate data**), such as the 5-year rate of return (the variable) for various mutual funds (the individuals). We found both graphical and numerical descriptive measures for the variable.

In this chapter, we discuss graphical and numerical methods for describing **bivariate data**, data in which two variables are measured on an individual. For example, we might want to know whether the amount of cola consumed per week is related to one's bone density. The individuals would be the people in the study, and the two variables would be the amount of cola and bone density. In this study, both variables are quantitative. We present methods for describing the relation between two quantitative variables in Sections 4.1–4.3.

Suppose we want to know whether level of education is related to one's employment status (employed or unemployed). Here, both variables are qualitative. We present methods for describing the relation between two qualitative variables in Section 4.4.

Situations may also occur in which one variable is quantitative and the other is qualitative. We have already presented a technique for describing this situation. Look back at Example 4 in Section 3.5 where we considered whether space flight affected red blood cell mass. There, space flight is qualitative (rat sent to space or not), and red blood cell mass is quantitative.

Note to Instructor

Remind students that Problems 15 to 17 in Section 3.5 discussed how we can graphically represent relations between a quantitative and qualitative variable. We now look at a graph of two quantitative variables. Section 4.4 will look at relations between two qualitative variables.

4.1 SCATTER DIAGRAMS AND CORRELATION

Preparing for This Section Before getting started, review the following:

- Mean (Section 3.1, pp. 117–119)
- z-scores (Section 3.4, pp. 154–155)
- Standard deviation (Section 3.2, pp. 132–136)
- Lurking variable and confounding (Section 1.2, p. 17)

OBJECTIVES

1. Draw and interpret scatter diagrams
2. Describe the properties of the linear correlation coefficient
3. Compute and interpret the linear correlation coefficient
4. Determine whether a linear relation exists between two variables
5. Explain the difference between correlation and causation

Note to Instructor
If you like, you can print out and distribute the Preparing for This Section quiz located in the Instructor's Resource Center. The purpose of the quiz is to verify that the students have the prerequisite knowledge for the section.

Before we can graphically represent bivariate data, we need to decide which variable we want to use to predict the value of the other variable. For example, it seems reasonable to think that as the speed at which a golf club is swung increases, the distance the golf ball travels also increases. Therefore, we might use club-head speed to predict distance. We call distance the *response* (or *dependent*) *variable* and club-head speed the *explanatory* (or *predictor* or *independent*) *variable*.

DEFINITION

The **response variable** is the variable whose value can be explained by the value of the **explanatory** or **predictor variable**.

In Other Words
We use the term *explanatory variable* because it helps to explain variability in the response variable.

1 Draw and Interpret Scatter Diagrams

The first step in identifying the type of relation that might exist between two variables is to draw a picture. We can represent bivariate data graphically through a *scatter diagram*.

DEFINITION

A **scatter diagram** is a graph that shows the relationship between two quantitative variables measured on the same individual. Each individual in the data set is represented by a point in the scatter diagram. The explanatory variable is plotted on the horizontal axis, and the response variable is plotted on the vertical axis.

EXAMPLE 1

Drawing a Scatter Diagram

TABLE 1

Club-head Speed (mph)	Distance (yards)
100	257
102	264
103	274
101	266
105	277
100	263
99	258
105	275

Source: Paul Stephenson, student at Joliet Junior College

Problem A golf pro wants to investigate the relation between the club-head speed of a golf club (measured in miles per hour) and the distance (in yards) that the ball will travel. He realizes other variables besides club-head speed determine the distance a ball will travel (such as club type, ball type, golfer, and weather conditions). To eliminate the variability due to these variables, the pro uses a single model of club and ball, one golfer, and a clear, 70-degree day with no wind. The pro records the club-head speed, measures the distance the ball travels, and collects the data in Table 1. Draw a scatter diagram of the data.

Approach Because the pro wants to use club-head speed to predict the distance the ball travels, club-head speed is the explanatory variable (horizontal axis) and distance is the response variable (vertical axis). We plot the ordered pairs (100, 257), (102, 264), and so on, in a rectangular coordinate system.

Solution The scatter diagram is shown in Figure 1. It appears from the graph that as club-head speed increases, the distance the ball travels increases as well.

Figure 1

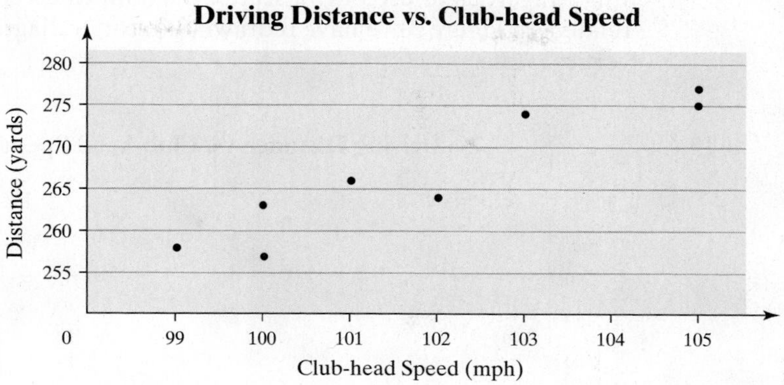

CAUTION

Do not connect points when drawing a scatter diagram.

Note to Instructor

You might want to discuss how a qualitative variable can be included in a scatter diagram. See Problems 33 and 34.

It is not always clear which variable should be considered the response variable and which the explanatory variable. For example, does high school GPA predict a student's SAT score or can the SAT score predict GPA? The researcher must determine which variable plays the role of explanatory variable based on the questions he or she wants answered. For example, if the researcher wants to predict SAT scores based on high school GPA, then high school GPA is the explanatory variable.

Now Work Problems 25(a) and 25(b)

Scatter diagrams show the type of relation that exists between two variables. Our goal in interpreting scatter diagrams is to distinguish scatter diagrams that imply a linear relation, a nonlinear relation, or no relation. Figure 2 displays various scatter diagrams and the type of relation implied.

Figure 2

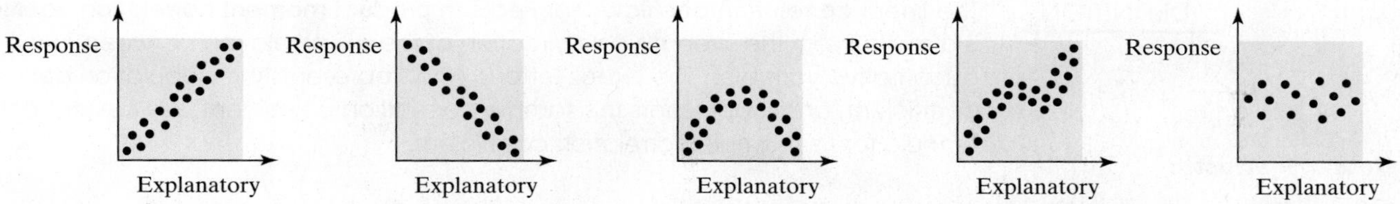

(a) Linear **(b)** Linear **(c)** Nonlinear **(d)** Nonlinear **(e)** No relation

Notice the difference between Figure 2(a) and Figure 2(b). The data follow a linear pattern that slants upward to the right in Figure 2(a) and downward to the right in Figure 2(b). Figures 2(c) and 2(d) show nonlinear relations. In Figure 2(e), there is no relation between the explanatory and response variables.

DEFINITIONS

Two variables that are linearly related are **positively associated** when above-average values of one variable are associated with above-average values of the other variable and below-average values of one variable are associated with below-average values of the other variable. That is, two variables are positively associated if, whenever the value of one variable increases, the value of the other variable also increases.

Two variables that are linearly related are **negatively associated** when above-average values of one variable are associated with below-average values of the other variable. That is, two variables are negatively associated if, whenever the value of one variable increases, the value of the other variable decreases.

In Other Words

If two variables are positively associated, then as one goes up the other also tends to go up. If two variables are negatively associated, then as one goes up the other tends to go down.

The scatter diagram in Figure 1 implies that club-head speed is positively associated with the distance a golf ball travels.

Now Work Problem 9

2 Describe the Properties of the Linear Correlation Coefficient

It is dangerous to use only a scatter diagram to determine if two variables are linearly related. In Figure 3, we have redrawn the scatter diagram from Figure 1 using a different vertical scale.

Figure 3

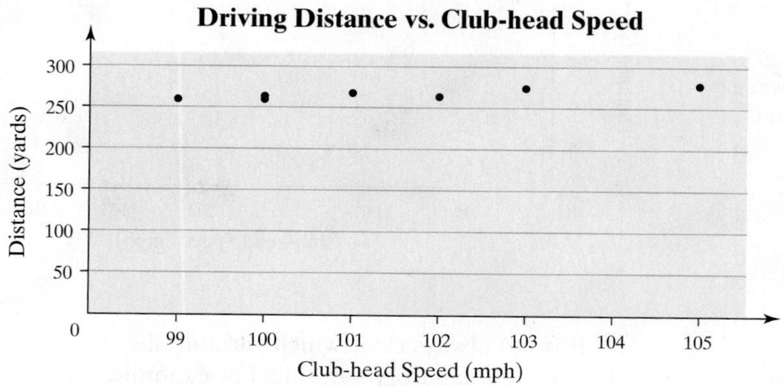

⚠ CAUTION

The horizontal and vertical scales of a scatter diagram should be set so that the scatter diagram does not mislead a reader.

It is more difficult to conclude that the variables are related in Figure 3 than in Figure 1. The moral of the story is this: Just as we can manipulate the scale of graphs of univariate data, we can also manipulate the scale of the graphs of bivariate data, possibly resulting in incorrect conclusions. Therefore, numerical summaries of bivariate data should be used in addition to graphs to determine any relation that exists between two variables.

DEFINITION

The **linear correlation coefficient** or **Pearson product moment correlation coefficient** is a measure of the strength and direction of the linear relation between two quantitative variables. The Greek letter ρ (rho) represents the population correlation coefficient, and r represents the sample correlation coefficient. We present only the formula for the sample correlation coefficient.

Sample Linear Correlation Coefficient*

$$r = \frac{\sum \left(\frac{x_i - \bar{x}}{s_x}\right)\left(\frac{y_i - \bar{y}}{s_y}\right)}{n - 1} \qquad (1)$$

where $\bar{x}$ is the sample mean of the explanatory variable

s_x is the sample standard deviation of the explanatory variable

$\bar{y}$ is the sample mean of the response variable

s_y is the sample standard deviation of the response variable

n is the number of individuals in the sample

Note to Instructor

Consider assigning the "Limitations of the Linear Correlation Coefficient" activity from the Student Activity Workbook.

*An equivalent computational formula for the linear correlation coefficient is

$$r = \frac{\sum x_i y_i - \frac{\sum x_i \sum y_i}{n}}{\sqrt{\left(\sum x_i^2 - \frac{(\sum x_i)^2}{n}\right)}\sqrt{\left(\sum y_i^2 - \frac{(\sum y_i)^2}{n}\right)}}$$

The Pearson linear correlation coefficient is named in honor of Karl Pearson (1857–1936).

Properties of the Linear Correlation Coefficient

1. The linear correlation coefficient is always between -1 and 1, inclusive. That is, $-1 \le r \le 1$.
2. If $r = +1$, then a perfect positive linear relation exists between the two variables. See Figure 4(a).
3. If $r = -1$, then a perfect negative linear relation exists between the two variables. See Figure 4(d).
4. The closer r is to $+1$, the stronger is the evidence of positive association between the two variables. See Figures 4(b) and 4(c).
5. The closer r is to -1, the stronger is the evidence of negative association between the two variables. See Figures 4(e) and 4(f).
6. If r is close to 0, then little or no evidence exists of a *linear* relation between the two variables. So **r close to 0 does not imply no relation, just no *linear* relation.** See Figures 4(g) and 4(h).
7. The linear correlation coefficient is a unitless measure of association. So the unit of measure for x and y plays no role in the interpretation of r.
8. The correlation coefficient is not resistant. Therefore, an observation that does not follow the overall pattern of the data could affect the value of the linear correlation coefficient.

Figure 4

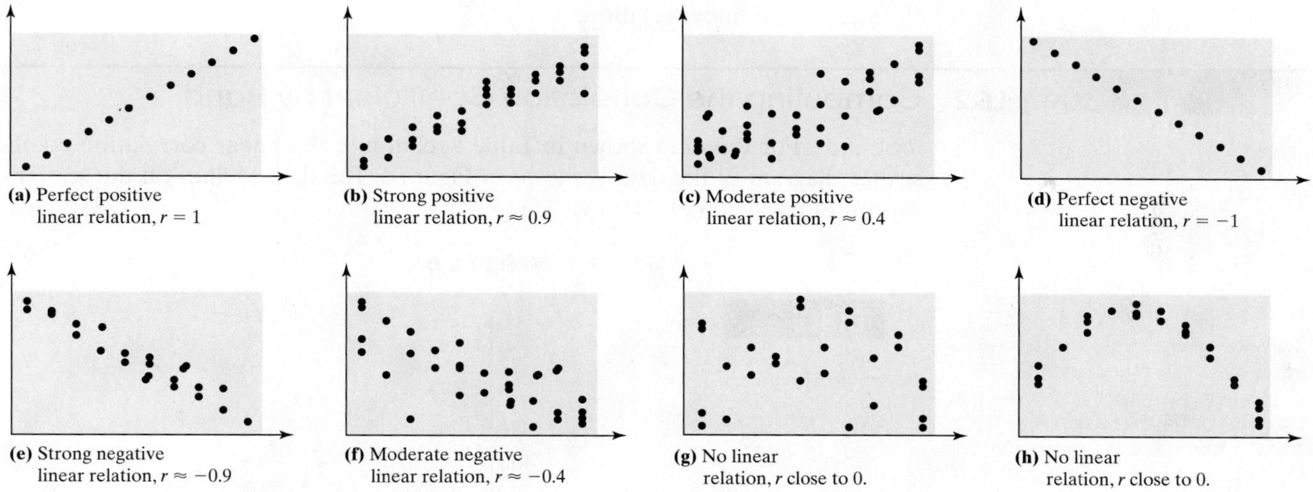

(a) Perfect positive linear relation, $r = 1$
(b) Strong positive linear relation, $r \approx 0.9$
(c) Moderate positive linear relation, $r \approx 0.4$
(d) Perfect negative linear relation, $r = -1$
(e) Strong negative linear relation, $r \approx -0.9$
(f) Moderate negative linear relation, $r \approx -0.4$
(g) No linear relation, r close to 0.
(h) No linear relation, r close to 0.

In Formula (1), notice that the numerator is the sum of the products of z-scores for the explanatory (x) and response (y) variables. A positive linear correlation coefficient means that the sum of the products of the z-scores for x and y must be positive. How does this occur? Figure 5 on the following page shows a scatter diagram with positive association between x and y. The vertical dashed line represents the value of $\bar{x}$, and the horizontal dashed line represents the value of $\bar{y}$. These two dashed lines divide our scatter diagram into four quadrants, labeled I, II, III, and IV.

Consider the data in quadrants I and III. If a certain x-value is above its mean, $\bar{x}$, then the corresponding y-value will be above its mean, $\bar{y}$. If a certain x-value is below its mean, $\bar{x}$, then the corresponding y-value will be below its mean, $\bar{y}$. Therefore, for data in quadrant I, we have $\frac{x_i - \bar{x}}{s_x}$ positive and $\frac{y_i - \bar{y}}{s_y}$ positive, so their product is positive. For data in quadrant III, we have $\frac{x_i - \bar{x}}{s_x}$ negative and $\frac{y_i - \bar{y}}{s_y}$ negative, so their product is positive. The sum of these products is positive, so the linear correlation coefficient is positive. A similar argument can be made for negative correlation.

CAUTION

A linear correlation coefficient close to 0 does not imply that there is no relation, just no linear relation. For example, although the scatter diagram drawn in Figure 4(h) indicates that the two variables are related, the linear correlation coefficient is close to 0.

Figure 5

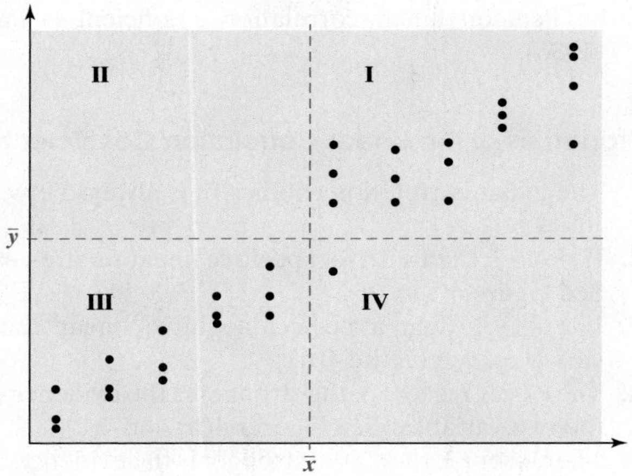

Now suppose that the data are equally dispersed in the four quadrants. Then the negative products (resulting from data in quadrants II and IV) will offset the positive products (resulting from data in quadrants I and III). The result is a linear correlation coefficient close to 0.

Now Work Problem 13

3 Compute and Interpret the Linear Correlation Coefficient

In the next example, we illustrate how to compute a linear correlation coefficient by hand. In practice, linear correlation coefficients are found using technology. However, we present the example so that you may gain an appreciation of how the formula measures the strength of linear relation.

EXAMPLE 2 Computing the Correlation Coefficient by Hand

Problem For the data shown in Table 2, compute the linear correlation coefficient. A scatter diagram of the data is shown in Figure 6. The dashed lines on the scatter diagram represent the mean of x and y.

Note to Instructor

This example is presented to help students understand how the correlation coefficient measures the strength of linear relation between two variables. It is recommended that students obtain correlation coefficients using technology.

TABLE 2

x	y
1	18
3	13
3	9
6	6
7	4

Figure 6

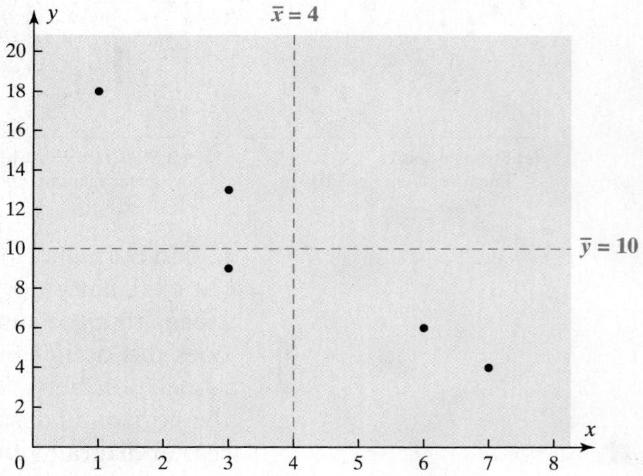

Approach

Step 1 Compute $\bar{x}, s_x, \bar{y}$, and s_y.

Step 2 Determine $\frac{x_i - \bar{x}}{s_x}$ and $\frac{y_i - \bar{y}}{s_y}$ for each observation.

Step 3 Compute $\left(\frac{x_i - \bar{x}}{s_x}\right)\left(\frac{y_i - \bar{y}}{s_y}\right)$ for each observation.

Step 4 Determine $\sum\left(\frac{x_i - \bar{x}}{s_x}\right)\left(\frac{y_i - \bar{y}}{s_y}\right)$ and substitute this value into Formula (1).

Historical Note

Karl Pearson was born March 27, 1857. Pearson's statistical proficiency was recognized early in his life. It is said that his mother told him not to suck his thumb, because otherwise it would wither away. Pearson analyzed the size of each thumb and said to himself, "They look alike to me. I can't see that the thumb I suck is any smaller than the other. I wonder if she could be lying to me."

Karl Pearson graduated from Cambridge University in 1879. From 1893 to 1911, he wrote 18 papers on genetics and heredity. Through this work, he developed ideas regarding correlation and the chi-square test. (See Chapter 12.) In addition, Pearson coined the term *standard deviation.*

Pearson and Ronald Fisher (see page 45) didn't get along. Their dispute was severe enough that Fisher turned down the post of chief statistician at the Galton Laboratory in 1919 because it would have meant working under Pearson.

Pearson died on April 27, 1936.

Solution

Step 1 We find $\bar{x} = 4$, $s_x = 2.44949$, $\bar{y} = 10$, and $s_y = 5.612486$.

Step 2 Columns 1 and 2 of Table 3 contain the data from Table 2. We determine $\dfrac{x_i - \bar{x}}{s_x}$ and $\dfrac{y_i - \bar{y}}{s_y}$ in Columns 3 and 4 of Table 3.

TABLE 3

x	y	$\dfrac{x_i - \bar{x}}{s_x}$	$\dfrac{y_i - \bar{y}}{s_y}$	$\left(\dfrac{x_i - \bar{x}}{s_x}\right)\left(\dfrac{y_i - \bar{y}}{s_y}\right)$
1	18	−1.2247	1.4254	−1.7457
3	13	−0.4083	0.5345	−0.2182
3	9	−0.4083	−0.1782	0.0727
6	6	0.8165	−0.7127	−0.5819
7	4	1.2247	−1.0690	−1.3093
				$\sum\left(\dfrac{x_i - \bar{x}}{s_x}\right)\left(\dfrac{y_i - \bar{y}}{s_y}\right) = -3.7824$

Step 3 Multiply the entries in Columns 3 and 4 to obtain the entries in Column 5 of Table 3.

Step 4 Add the entries in Column 5 and substitute this value into Formula (1) to obtain the correlation coefficient.

$$r = \frac{\sum\left(\dfrac{x_i - \bar{x}}{s_x}\right)\left(\dfrac{y_i - \bar{y}}{s_y}\right)}{n - 1} = \frac{-3.7824}{5 - 1} = -0.946$$

We will agree to round the correlation coefficient to three decimal places. The correlation coefficient suggests a strong negative association between the two variables.

Compare the signs of the entries in Columns 3 and 4 in Table 3. Notice that negative values in Column 3 correspond with positive values in Column 4 and that positive values in Column 3 correspond with negative values in Column 4 (except for the third observation). Look back at the scatter diagram in Figure 6 where the mean of x and y is drawn on the scatter diagram. Notice that below-average values of x are associated with above-average values of y, and above-average values of x are associated with below-average values of y. This is why the linear correlation coefficient is negative.

EXAMPLE 3 Determining the Linear Correlation Coefficient Using Technology

Problem Use a statistical spreadsheet or a graphing calculator with advanced statistical features to draw a scatter diagram of the data in Table 1. Then determine the linear correlation between club-head speed and distance.

Approach We will use Excel to draw the scatter diagram and obtain the linear correlation coefficient. The steps for drawing scatter diagrams and obtaining the linear correlation coefficient using the TI-83/84 Plus graphing calculators, MINITAB, Excel, and StatCrunch are given in the Technology Step-by-Step on pages 193–194.

Solution Figure 7(a) on the next page shows the scatter diagram, and Figure 7(b) shows the linear correlation coefficient of 0.939 obtained from Excel. Notice that Excel provides a **correlation matrix**, which means that for every pair of columns in the spreadsheet it will compute and display the correlation in the bottom triangle of the matrix.

Because the linear correlation coefficient is positive, we know above-average values of x, club-head speed, are associated with above-average values of y, driving distance, and below-average values of x are associated with below-average values of y.

Figure 7

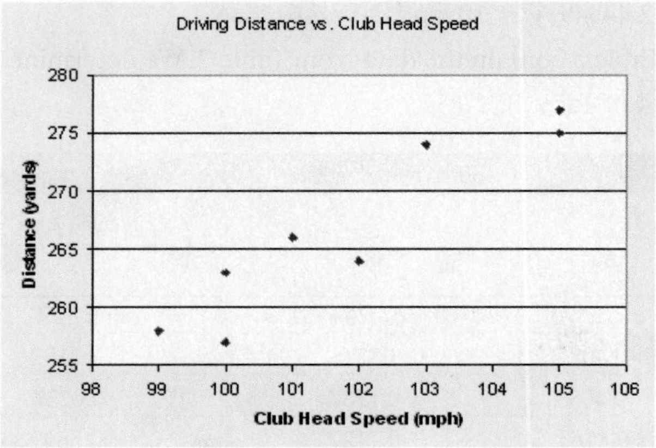

(a)

	Driving Distance	*Club Head Speed*
Driving Distance	1	
Club Head Speed	0.938695838	1

(b)

Now Work Problem 25(c)

We stated in Property 8 that the linear correlation coefficient is not resistant. For example, suppose the golfer in Examples 1 and 3 hits one more golf ball. As he swings, a car driving by blows its horn, which distracts the golfer. His swing speed is 105 mph, but the mis-hit golf ball travels only 255 yards. The linear correlation coefficient with this additional observation decreases to 0.535.

4 Determine Whether a Linear Relation Exists between Two Variables

A question you may be asking yourself is "How do I know the correlation between two variables is strong enough for me to conclude that a linear relation exists between them?" Although rigorous tests can answer this question, for now we will be content with a simple comparison test.

Note to Instructor

We are conducting this test using a 0.05 level of significance.

In Other Words

We use two vertical bars to denote absolute value, as in $|5|$ or $|-4|$. Recall, $|5| = 5$, $|-4| = 4$, and $|0| = 0$.

Testing for a Linear Relation

Step 1 Determine the absolute value of the correlation coefficient.

Step 2 Find the critical value in Table II from Appendix A for the given sample size.

Step 3 If the absolute value of the correlation coefficient is greater than the critical value, we say a linear relation exists between the two variables. Otherwise, no linear relation exists.

Another way to think about the procedure is to consider Figure 8. If the correlation coefficient is positive and greater than the critical value, the variables are positively associated. If the correlation coefficient is negative and less than the opposite of the critical value, the variables are negatively associated.

Figure 8

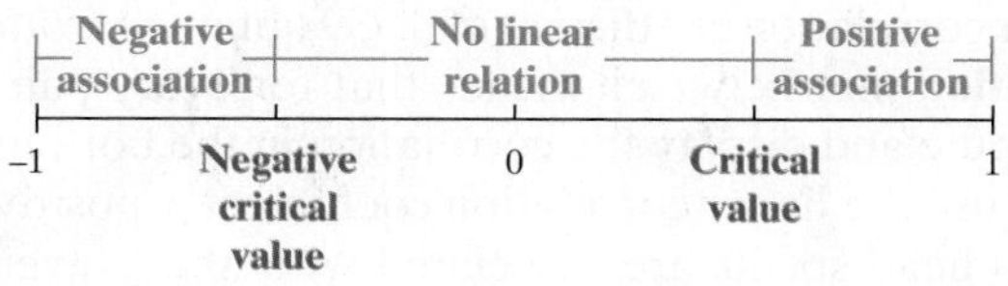

EXAMPLE 4 Does a Linear Relation Exist?

Problem Using the results from Example 3, determine whether a linear relation exists between club-head speed and distance.

Approach Follow Steps 1 through 3 given on the previous page.

Solution

Step 1 The linear correlation coefficient between club-head speed and distance is 0.939, so $|0.939| = 0.939$.

Step 2 Table II shows the critical value with $n = 8$ is 0.707.

Step 3 Since $|0.939| = 0.939 > 0.707$, we conclude a positive association (positive linear relation) exists between club-head speed and distance.

Now Work Problem 25(d)

5 Explain the Difference between Correlation and Causation

CAUTION
A linear correlation coefficient that implies a strong positive or negative association does not imply causation if it was computed using observational data.

In Chapter 1 we stated that there are two types of studies: observational studies and designed experiments. The data examined in Examples 1, 3 and 4 are the result of an experiment. Therefore, we can claim that a faster club-head speed causes the golf ball to travel a longer distance.

If data used in a study are observational, we cannot conclude the two correlated variables have a causal relationship. For example, the correlation between teenage birthrate and homicide rate since 1993 is 0.9987, but we cannot conclude that higher teenage birthrates cause a higher homicide rate because the data are observational. In fact, time-series data are often correlated because both variables happen to move in the same (or opposite) direction over time. Both teenage birthrates and homicide rates have been declining since 1993, so they have a high positive correlation.

Is there another way two variables can be correlated without there being a causal relation? Yes—through a *lurking variable.* A **lurking variable** is related to both the explanatory variable and response variable. For example, as air-conditioning bills increase, so does the crime rate. Does this mean that folks should turn off their air conditioners so that crime rates decrease? Certainly not! In this case, the lurking variable is air temperature. As air temperatures rise, both air-conditioning bills and crime rates rise.

EXAMPLE 5 Lurking Variables in a Bone Mineral Density Study

Problem Because colas tend to replace healthier beverages and colas contain caffeine and phosphoric acid, researchers Katherine L. Tucker and associates wanted to know whether cola consumption is associated with lower bone mineral density in women. Table 4 lists the typical number of cans of cola consumed in a week and the femoral neck bone mineral density for a sample of 15 women. The data were collected through a prospective cohort study.

Figure 9 on the next page shows the scatter diagram of the data. The correlation between number of colas per week and bone mineral density is -0.806. The critical value for correlation with $n = 15$ from Table II in Appendix A is 0.514. Because $|-0.806| > 0.514$, we conclude a negative linear relation exists between number of colas consumed and bone mineral density. Can the authors conclude that an increase in the number of colas consumed causes a decrease in bone mineral density? Identify some lurking variables in the study.

In Other Words
Confounding means that any relation that may exist between two variables may be due to some other variable not accounted for in the study.

Approach To claim causality, we must collect the data through a designed experiment. Remember, lurking variables are related to both the explanatory and response variables in a study.

TABLE 4

Number of Colas per Week	Bone Mineral Density (g/cm^2)
0	0.893
0	0.882
1	0.891
1	0.881
2	0.888
2	0.871
3	0.868
3	0.876
4	0.873
5	0.875
5	0.871
6	0.867
7	0.862
7	0.872
8	0.865

Source: Based on data obtained from Katherine L. Tucker et. al., "Colas, but not other carbonated beverages, are associated with low bone mineral density in older women: The Framingham Osteoporosis Study." *American Journal of Clinical Nutrition* 2006, 84:936–942.

Now Work Problem 41

Figure 9

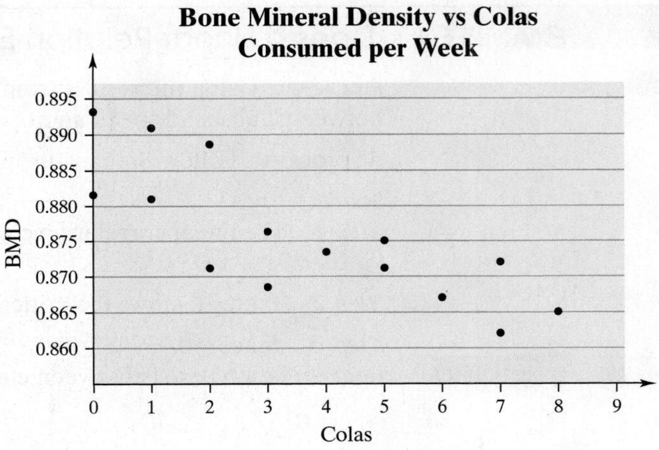

Solution In prospective cohort studies, data are collected on a group of subjects through questionnaires and surveys over time. Therefore, the data are observational. So the researchers cannot claim that increased cola consumption causes a decrease in bone mineral density.

In their article, the authors identified a number of lurking variables that could confound the results:

> Variables that could potentially confound the relation between cola consumption and bone mineral density ... included the following: age, body mass index, height, smoking, average daily intakes of alcohol, calcium, caffeine, total energy intake, physical activity, season of measurement, estrogen use, and menopause status.

The authors were careful to say that increased cola consumption is *associated* with lower bone mineral density because of potential lurking variables. They never stated that increased cola consumption *causes* lower bone mineral density.

4.1 ASSESS YOUR UNDERSTANDING

VOCABULARY AND SKILL BUILDING

1. What is the difference between univariate data and bivariate data?

2. The _______ variable is the variable whose value can be explained by the value of the explanatory variable. response

3. A _______ _______ is a graph that shows the relation between two quantitative variables. scatter diagram

4. What does it mean to say two variables are positively associated? Negatively associated?

5. If $r =$ _______, then a perfect negative linear relation exists between the two quantitative variables. -1

6. *True or False*: If the linear correlation coefficient is close to 0, then the two variables have no relation. False

7. A _______ variable is a variable that is related to both the explanatory and response variable. lurking

8. *True or False*: Correlation implies causation. False

In Problems 9–12, determine whether the scatter diagram indicates that a linear relation may exist between the two variables. If the relation is linear, determine whether it indicates a positive or negative association between the variables.

NW **9.** Nonlinear

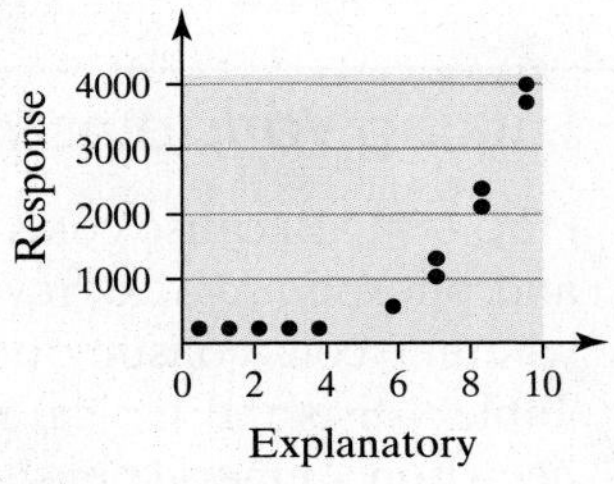

10. Linear, negative

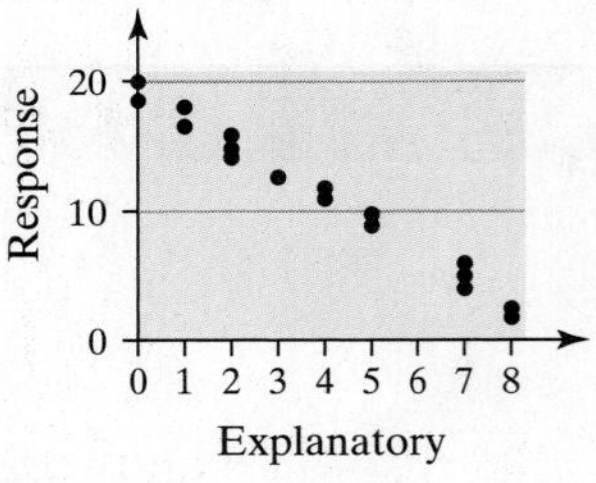

11. Linear, positive

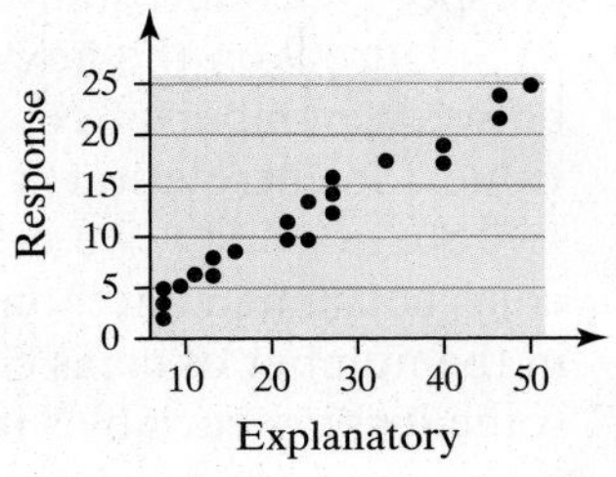

12. Nonlinear

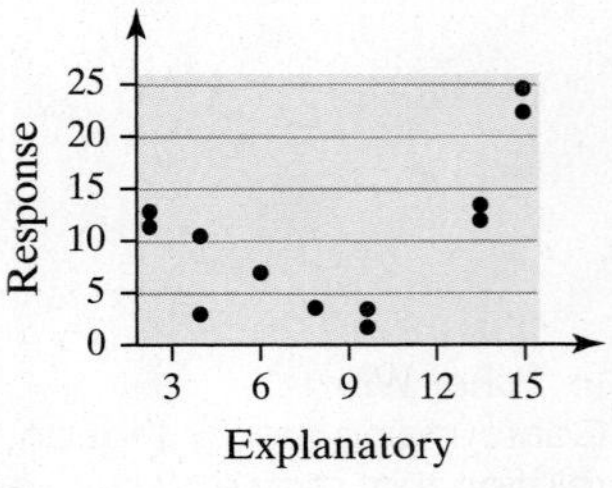

NW **13.** Match the linear correlation coefficient to the scatter diagrams. The scales on the x- and y-axes are the same for each diagram.

(a) $r = 0.787$ III **(b)** $r = 0.523$ IV
(c) $r = 0.053$ II **(d)** $r = 0.946$ I

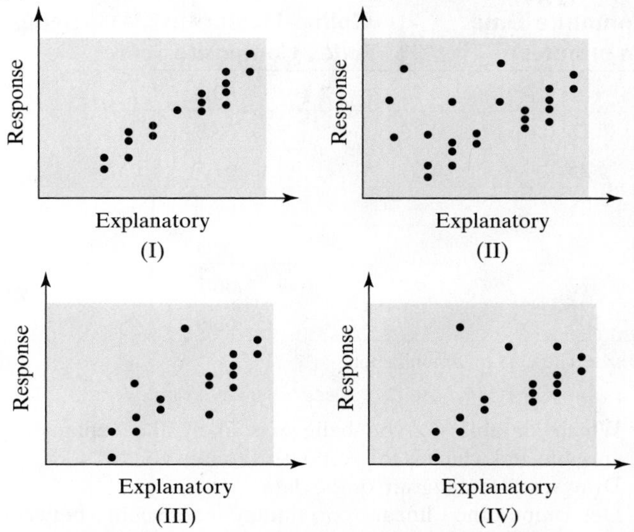

14. Match the linear correlation coefficient to the scatter diagram. The scales on the x- and y-axes are the same for each diagram.

(a) $r = -0.969$ IV **(b)** $r = -0.049$ III
(c) $r = -1$ I **(d)** $r = -0.992$ II

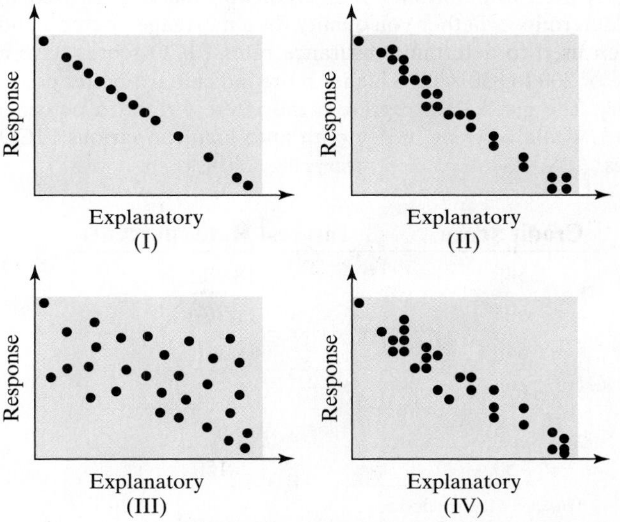

15. Does Education Pay? The scatter diagram drawn in MINITAB shows the relation between the percentage of the population of a state plus Washington, DC, that has at least a bachelor's degree and the median income (in dollars) of the state for 2009. *Source:* U.S. Census Bureau

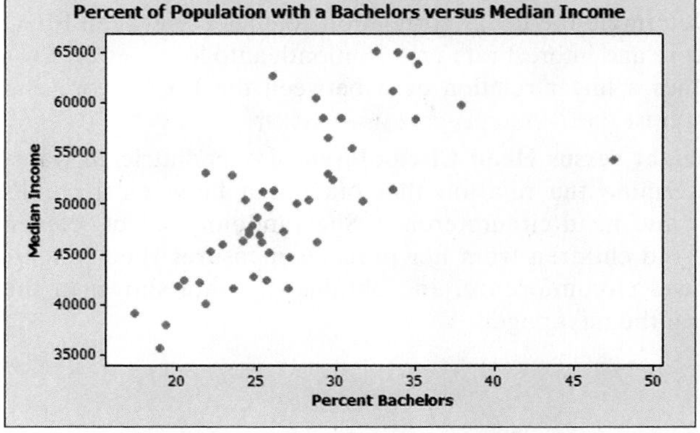

(a) Describe any relation that exists between level of education and median income. Linear; positive association

(b) One observation appears to stick out from the rest. Which one? This particular observation is for Washington, DC. Can you think of any reasons why Washington, DC, might have a high percentage of residents with a bachelor's degree, but a lower than expected median income?

(c) The correlation coefficient between the percentage of the population with a bachelor's degree and median income with Washington, DC, included in the data set is 0.718. The correlation coefficient without Washington, DC, included is 0.802. What property does this illustrate about the linear correlation coefficient? Not resistant

16. Relation between Income and Birthrate? The following scatter diagram drawn in StatCrunch shows the relation between median income (in dollars) in a state and birthrate (births per 1000 women 15 to 44 years old).

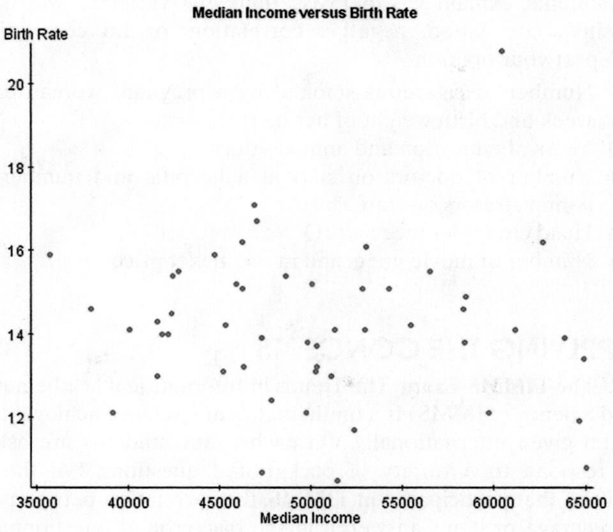

(a) Describe any relation that exists between median income and birthrate.

(b) One observation sticks out from the rest. Which one? This particular observation is for the state of Utah. Are there any explanations for this result?

(c) The correlation coefficient between median income and birthrate is -0.070. What does this imply about the relation between median income and birthrate? No linear relation

In Problems 17–20, (a) draw a scatter diagram of the data, (b) by hand, compute the correlation coefficient, and (c) determine whether there is a linear relation between x and y.

17.

x	2	4	6	6	7
y	4	8	10	13	20

(b) $r = 0.896$
(c) linear relation

18.

x	2	3	5	6	6
y	10	9	7	4	2

(b) $r = -0.933$
(c) linear relation

19.

x	2	6	6	7	9
y	8	7	6	9	5

(b) $r = -0.496$
(c) no linear relation

20.

x	0	5	7	8	9
y	3	8	6	9	4

(b) $r = 0.440$
(c) no linear relation

21. Name the Relation, Part I For each of the following statements, explain whether you think the variables will have positive correlation, negative correlation, or no correlation. Support your opinion. 21. (b) Negative

(a) Number of children in the household under the age of 3 and expenditures on diapers Positive
(b) Interest rates on car loans and number of cars sold
(c) Number of hours per week on the treadmill and cholesterol level Negative
(d) Price of a Big Mac and number of McDonald's French fries sold in a week Negative
(e) Shoe size and IQ No correlation

22. Name the Relation, Part II For each of the following statements, explain whether you think the variables will have positive correlation, negative correlation, or no correlation. Support your opinion.

(a) Number of cigarettes smoked by a pregnant woman each week and birth weight of her baby Negative
(b) Years of education and annual salary Positive
(c) Number of doctors on staff at a hospital and number of administrators on staff Positive
(d) Head circumference and IQ No correlation
(e) Number of movie goers and movie ticket price Negative

APPLYING THE CONCEPTS

23. The TIMMS Exam The Trends in International Mathematics and Science (TIMMS) is a mathematics and science achievement exam given internationally. On each exam, students are asked to respond to a variety of background questions. For the 41 nations that participated in TIMMS, the correlation between the percentage of items answered in the background questionnaire (used as a proxy for student task persistence) and mean score on the exam was 0.79. Does this suggest there is a linear relation between student task persistence and achievement score? Write a sentence that explains what this result might mean. Yes

24. The TIMMS Exam Part II (See Problem 23) For the 41 nations that participated in TIMMS, the correlation between the percentage of students who skipped class at least once in the past month and the mean score on the exam was −0.52. Does this suggest there is a linear relation between attendance and achievement score? Write a sentence that explains what this result might mean. Yes

NW **25. An Unhealthy Commute** The Gallup Organization regularly surveys adult Americans regarding their commute time to work. In addition, they administer a Well-Being Survey. According to the Gallup Organization, "The Gallup-Healthways Well-Being Index Composite Score is comprised of six sub-indices: Life Evaluation, Emotional Health, Physical Health, Healthy Behavior, Work Environment and Basic Access." A complete description of the index can be found at http://www.well-beingindex.com/. The data in the following table are based on the results of the survey, which represent commute time to work (in minutes) and well-being index score.

Commute Time (in minutes)	Gallup-Healthways Well-Being Index Composite Score
5	69.2
15	68.3
25	67.5
35	67.1
50	66.4
72	66.1
105	63.9

Source: The Gallup Organization

(a) Explanatory: commute time; Response: well-being score

(a) Which variable do you believe is likely the explanatory variable and which is the response variable?
(b) Draw a scatter diagram of the data.
(c) Determine the linear correlation coefficient between commute time and well-being index score. −0.981
(d) Does a linear relation exist between the commute time and well-being index score? Yes; negative association

26. Credit Scores Your Fair Isaacs Corporation (FICO) credit score is used to determine your creditworthiness. It is used to help determine whether you qualify for a mortgage or credit and is even used to determine insurance rates. FICO scores have a range of 300 to 850, with a higher score indicating a better credit history. The given data represent the interest rate (in percent) a bank would offer on a 36-month auto loan for various FICO scores. (a) Explanatory: credit score; Response: interest rate

Credit Score	Interest Rate (percent)
545	18.982
595	17.967
640	12.218
675	8.612
705	6.680
750	5.150

Source: www.myfico.com

(a) Which variable do you believe is likely the explanatory variable and which is the response variable?
(b) Draw a scatter diagram of the data.
(c) Determine the linear correlation coefficient between FICO score and interest rate on a 36-month auto loan. −0.976
(d) Does a linear relation exist between the FICO score and interest rate? Yes; negative association

27. Height versus Head Circumference A pediatrician wants to determine the relation that may exist between a child's height and head circumference. She randomly selects eleven 3-year-old children from her practice, measures their heights and head circumference, and obtains the data shown in the table on the next page.

Height (inches)	Head Circumference (inches)	Height (inches)	Head Circumference (inches)
27.75	17.5	26.5	17.3
24.5	17.1	27	17.5
25.5	17.1	26.75	17.3
26	17.3	26.75	17.5
25	16.9	27.5	17.5
27.75	17.6		

Source: Denise Slucki, student at Joliet Junior College

(a) Explanatory: height; Response: head circumference

(a) If the pediatrician wants to use height to predict head circumference, determine which variable is the explanatory variable and which is the response variable.
(b) Draw a scatter diagram.
(c) Compute the linear correlation coefficient between the height and head circumference of a child. 0.911
(d) Does a linear relation exist between height and head circumference? Yes; positive association

28. American Black Bears The American black bear (*Ursus americanus*) is one of eight bear species in the world. It is the smallest North American bear and the most common bear species on the planet. In 1969, Dr. Michael R. Pelton of the University of Tennessee initiated a long-term study of the population in the Great Smoky Mountains National Park. One aspect of the study was to develop a model that could be used to predict a bear's weight (since it is not practical to weigh bears in the field). One variable thought to be related to weight is the length of the bear. The following data represent the lengths and weights of 12 American black bears.

Total Length (cm)	Weight (kg)
139.0	110
138.0	60
139.0	90
120.5	60
149.0	85
141.0	100
141.0	95
150.0	85
166.0	155
151.5	140
129.5	105
150.0	110

Source: fieldtripearth.org

(a) Which variable is the explanatory variable based on the goals of the research? Length
(b) Draw a scatter diagram of the data.
(c) Determine the linear correlation coefficient between weight and height. 0.704
(d) Does a linear relation exist between the weight of the bear and its height? Yes; positive association

29. Weight of a Car versus Miles per Gallon An engineer wanted to determine how the weight of a car affects gas mileage. The following data represent the weights of various domestic cars and their gas mileages in the city for the 2011 model year.

Car	Weight (lb)	Miles per Gallon
Buick Lucerne	3735	17
Cadillac CTS	3860	16
Chevrolet Cobalt	2721	25
Chevrolet Impala	3555	19
Chrysler Sebring Sedan	3319	21
Dodge Caliber	2966	23
Dodge Charger	3727	17
Ford Focus	2605	24
Ford Mustang	3473	19
Lincoln MKZ	3796	17
Mercury Sable	3310	18

Source: www.roadandtrack.com

(a) Explanatory: weight; Response: mpg

(a) Determine which variable is the likely explanatory variable and which is the likely response variable.
(b) Draw a scatter diagram of the data.
(c) Compute the linear correlation coefficient between the weight of a car and its miles per gallon in the city. −0.960
(d) Does a linear relation exist between the weight of a car and its miles per gallon in the city? Yes; negative association

30. Bone Length Research performed at NASA and led by Emily R. Morey-Holton measured the lengths of the right humerus and right tibia in 11 rats that were sent to space on Spacelab Life Sciences 2. The following data were collected.

Right Humerus (mm)	Right Tibia (mm)	Right Humerus (mm)	Right Tibia (mm)
24.80	36.05	25.90	37.38
24.59	35.57	26.11	37.96
24.59	35.57	26.63	37.46
24.29	34.58	26.31	37.75
23.81	34.20	26.84	38.50
24.87	34.73		

Source: NASA Life Sciences Data Archive

(a) Draw a scatter diagram treating the length of the right humerus as the explanatory variable and the length of the right tibia as the response variable.
(b) Compute the linear correlation coefficient between the length of the right humerus and the length of the right tibia. 0.951
(c) Does a linear relation exist between the length of the right humerus and the length of the right tibia?
(d) Convert the data to inches (1 mm = 0.03937 inch), and recompute the linear correlation coefficient. What effect did the conversion from millimeters to inches have on the linear correlation coefficient? None (c) Yes; positive association

31. CEO Performance The data on the following page represent the total compensation for 10 randomly selected chief executive officers (CEO) and the company's stock performance in 2009.

Company	Compensation (millions of dollars)	Stock Return (%)
Kraft Foods	26.35	5.91
Sara Lee	12.48	30.39
Boeing	19.44	31.72
Middleby	13.37	79.76
Exelon	12.21	−8.40
Northern Trust	11.89	2.69
Abbott Laboratories	26.21	4.53
Archer Daniels Midland	14.95	10.80
McDonald's	17.57	4.01
Baxter International	14.36	11.76

Source: Chicago Tribune, May 23, 2010

(a) One would think that a higher stock return would lead to a higher compensation. Based on this, what would likely be the explanatory variable? Stock return

(b) Draw a scatter diagram of the data.

(c) Determine the linear correlation coefficient between compensation and stock return. −0.206

(d) Does a linear relation exist between compensation and stock return? Does stock performance appear to play a role in determining the compensation of a CEO? No; no

32. Age versus HDL Cholesterol A doctor wanted to determine whether a relation exists between a male's age and his HDL (so-called good) cholesterol. He randomly selected 17 of his patients and determined their HDL cholesterol levels. He obtained the following data.

Age	HDL Cholesterol	Age	HDL Cholesterol
38	57	38	44
42	54	66	62
46	34	30	53
32	56	51	36
55	35	27	45
52	40	52	38
61	42	49	55
61	38	39	28
26	47		

Source: Data based on information obtained from the National Center for Health Statistics

(a) Draw a scatter diagram of the data treating age as the explanatory variable. What type of relation, if any, appears to exist between age and HDL cholesterol?

(b) Compute the linear correlation coefficient between age and HDL cholesterol. −0.164 (c) No

(c) Does a linear relation exist between age and HDL cholesterol?

33. Does Size Matter? Researchers wondered whether the size of a person's brain was related to the individual's mental capacity. They selected a sample of right-handed introductory psychology students who had SAT scores higher than 1350. The subjects took the Wechsler Adult Intelligence Scale-Revised to obtain their IQ scores. MRI scans were performed at the same facility for the subjects. The scans consisted of 18 horizontal MR images. The computer counted all pixels with a nonzero gray scale in each of the 18 images, and the total count served as an index for brain size.

Gender	MRI Count	IQ	Gender	MRI Count	IQ
Female	816,932	133	Male	949,395	140
Female	951,545	137	Male	1,001,121	140
Female	991,305	138	Male	1,038,437	139
Female	833,868	132	Male	965,353	133
Female	856,472	140	Male	955,466	133
Female	852,244	132	Male	1,079,49	141
Female	790,619	135	Male	924,059	135
Female	866,662	130	Male	955,003	139
Female	857,782	133	Male	935,494	141
Female	948,066	133	Male	949,589	144

Source: L. Willerman, R. Schultz, J. N. Rutledge, and E. Bigler (1991). "In Vivo Brain Size and Intelligence," *Intelligence*, 15, 223–228.

(a) Draw a scatter diagram treating MRI count as the explanatory variable and IQ as the response variable. Comment on what you see. (b) 0.548; yes, (d) F: 0.359; M: 0.236; no

(b) Compute the linear correlation coefficient between MRI count and IQ. Are MRI count and IQ linearly related?

(c) A lurking variable in the analysis is gender. Draw a scatter diagram treating MRI count as the explanatory variable and IQ as the response variable, but use a different plotting symbol for each gender. For example, use a circle for males and a triangle for females. What do you notice? Linear relation goes away

(d) Compute the linear correlation coefficient between MRI count and IQ for females. Compute the linear correlation coefficient between MRI count and IQ for males. Are MRI count and IQ linearly related? What is the moral?

34. Male versus Female Drivers The following data represent the number of licensed drivers in various age groups and the number of fatal accidents within the age group by gender.

Age	Number of Male Licensed Drivers (000s)	Number of Fatal Crashes	Number of Female Licensed Drivers (000s)	Number of Fatal Crashes
<16	12	227	12	77
16–20	6,424	5,180	6,139	2,113
21–24	6,941	5,016	6,816	1,531
25–34	18,068	8,595	17,664	2,780
35–44	20,406	7,990	20,063	2,742
45–54	19,898	7,118	19,984	2,285
55–64	14,340	4,527	14,441	1,514
65–74	8,194	2,274	8,400	938
<74	4,803	2,022	5,375	980

Source: National Highway and Traffic Safety Institute

(a) On the same graph, draw a scatter diagram for both males and females. Be sure to use a different plotting symbol for each group. For example, use a square (□) for males and a plus sign (+) for females. Treat number of licensed drivers as the explanatory variable.

(b) Based on the scatter diagrams, do you think that insurance companies are justified in charging different insurance rates for males and females? Why? (c) 0.883

(c) Compute the linear correlation coefficient between number of licensed drivers and number of fatal crashes for males.

(d) Compute the linear correlation coefficient between number of licensed drivers and number of fatal crashes for females. 0.836

(e) Which gender has the stronger linear relation between number of licensed drivers and number of fatal crashes. Why? Males

35. Weight of a Car versus Miles per Gallon Suppose that we add the Ford Taurus to the data in Problem 29. A Ford Taurus weighs 3305 pounds and gets 19 miles per gallon.

(a) Redraw the scatter diagram with the Taurus included.

(b) Recompute the linear correlation coefficient with the Taurus included. −0.954

(c) Compare the results of parts (a) and (b) with the results of Problem 29. Why are the results here reasonable?

(d) Now suppose that we add the Ford Fusion Hybrid to the data in Problem 29 (remove the Taurus). A Fusion Hybrid weighs 3720 pounds and gets 41 miles per gallon. Redraw the scatter diagram with the Fusion included. What do you notice?

(e) Recompute the linear correlation coefficient with the Fusion included. How did this new value affect your result? −0.195

(f) Why does this observation not follow the pattern of the data?

36. American Black Bears The Web site that contained the American black bear data listed in Problem 28 actually had a bear whose height is 141.0 cm and weight is 100 kg incorrectly listed as 41.0 cm tall.

(a) Redraw the scatter diagram with the incorrect entry.

(b) Recompute the linear correlation coefficient using the data with the incorrect entry. 0.254

(c) Explain how the scatter diagram can be used to identify incorrectly entered data values. Explain how the incorrectly entered data value affects the correlation coefficient.

37. Draw Your Data! Consider the four data sets shown below.

Data Set 1		Data Set 2		Data Set 3		Data Set 4	
x	y	x	y	x	y	x	y
10	8.04	10	9.14	10	7.46	8	6.58
8	6.95	8	8.14	8	6.77	8	5.76
13	7.58	13	8.74	13	12.74	8	7.71
9	8.81	9	8.77	9	7.11	8	8.84
11	8.33	11	9.26	11	7.81	8	8.47
14	9.96	14	8.10	14	8.84	8	7.04
6	7.24	6	6.13	6	6.08	8	5.25
4	4.26	4	3.10	4	5.39	8	5.56
12	10.84	12	9.13	12	8.15	8	7.91
7	4.82	7	7.26	7	6.42	8	6.89
5	5.68	5	4.47	5	5.73	19	12.50

Source: Frank Anscombe. "Graphs in Statistical Analysis," *American Statistician* 27: 17–21, 1993.

(a) Compute the linear correlation coefficient for each data set. 1: 0.816; 2: 0.817; 3: 0.816; 4: 0.817

(b) Draw a scatter diagram for each data set. Conclude that linear correlation coefficients and scatter diagrams must be used together in any statistical analysis of bivariate data.

38. The Best Predictor of the Winning Percentage The ultimate goal in any sport (besides having fun) is to win. One measure of how well a team does is the winning percentage. In baseball, a lot of effort goes into figuring out the variable that best predicts a team's winning percentage. The following data represent the winning percentages of teams in the National League along with potential explanatory variables based on the 2010 season. Which variable do you think is the best predictor of winning percentage? Why? Team ERA

Team	Winning Percentage	Runs	Home Runs	Team Batting Average	On-Base Percentage	Batting Average Against	Team ERA
Philadelphia	0.599	772	166	0.260	0.332	0.254	3.67
Atlanta	0.562	738	139	0.258	0.339	0.246	3.56
San Francisco	0.568	697	162	0.257	0.321	0.236	3.36
Chicago Cubs	0.463	685	149	0.257	0.320	0.255	4.18
Florida	0.494	719	152	0.254	0.321	0.261	4.08
LA Dodgers	0.494	667	120	0.252	0.322	0.244	4.01
Washington	0.426	655	149	0.250	0.318	0.266	4.13
Arizona	0.401	713	180	0.250	0.325	0.271	4.81
NY Mets	0.488	656	128	0.249	0.314	0.260	3.70
Houston	0.469	611	108	0.247	0.303	0.261	4.09
San Diego	0.556	665	132	0.246	0.317	0.240	3.39
Pittsburgh	0.352	587	126	0.242	0.304	0.282	5.00

Source: espn.com

39. Diversification One basic theory of investing is diversification. The idea is that you want to have a basket of stocks that do not all "move in the same direction." In other words, if one investment goes down, you don't want a second investment in your portfolio that is also likely to go down. One hallmark of a good portfolio is a low correlation between investments. The following data represent the annual rates of return for various stocks. If you only wish to invest in two stocks, which two would you select if your goal is to have low correlation between the two investments? Which two would you select if your goal is to have one stock go up when the other goes down? Dell and Exxon Mobil; Dell and TECO Energy

	Rate of Return					
Year	**Cisco Systems**	**Walt Disney**	**General Electric**	**Exxon Mobil**	**TECO Energy**	**Dell**
1999	1.31	−0.015	0.574	0.151	−0.303	−0.319
2000	−0.286	−0.004	−0.055	0.127	0.849	−0.661
2001	−0.527	−0.277	−0.151	−0.066	−0.150	0.553
2002	−0.277	−0.203	−0.377	−0.089	−0.369	−0.031
2003	0.850	0.444	0.308	0.206	0.004	0.254
2004	−0.203	0.202	0.207	0.281	0.128	0.234
2005	0.029	−0.129	−0.014	0.118	0.170	−0.288
2006	0.434	0.443	0.093	0.391	0.051	−0.164
2007	0.044	−0.043	0.126	0.243	0.058	−0.033
2008	−0.396	−0.306	−0.593	−0.193	−0.355	−0.580
2009	0.459	0.417	−0.102	−0.171	0.249	0.393
2010	−0.185	0.155	0.053	0.023	0.044	−0.323

Source: Yahoo!Finance

40. Lyme Disease versus Drownings Lyme disease is an inflammatory disease that results in a skin rash and flulike symptoms. It is transmitted through the bite of an infected deer tick. The following data represent the number of reported cases of Lyme disease and the number of drowning deaths for a rural county in the United States.

Month	**J**	**F**	**M**	**A**	**M**	**J**	**J**	**A**	**S**	**O**	**N**	**D**
Cases of Lyme Disease	3	2	2	4	5	15	22	13	6	5	4	1
Drowning Deaths	0	1	2	1	2	9	16	5	3	3	1	0

(a) Draw a scatter diagram of the data using cases of Lyme disease as the explanatory variable.
(b) Compute the correlation coefficient for the data. 0.961
(c) Based on your results from parts (a) and (b), what type of relation exists between the number of reported cases of Lyme disease and drowning deaths? Do you believe that an increase in cases of Lyme disease causes an increase in drowning deaths? What is a likely lurking variable between cases of Lyme disease and drowning deaths?

NW **41. Television Stations and Life Expectancy** Based on data obtained from the *CIA World Factbook,* the linear correlation coefficient between the number of television stations in a country and the life expectancy of residents of the country is 0.599. What does this correlation imply? Do you believe that the more television stations a country has, the longer its population can expect to live? Why or why not? What is a likely lurking variable between number of televisions and life expectancy?

42. Obesity In a study published in the *Journal of the American Medical Association*, researchers found that the length of time a mother breast-feeds is negatively associated with the likelihood a child is obese. In an interview, the head investigator stated, "It's not clear whether breast milk has obesity-preventing properties or the women who are breast-feeding are less likely to have obese kids because they are less likely to be obese themselves." Using the researcher's statement, explain what might be wrong with concluding that breast-feeding prevents obesity. Identify some lurking variables in the study.

43. Crime Rate and Cell Phones The linear correlation between violent crime rate and percentage of the population that has a cell phone is −0.918 for years since 1995. Do you believe that increasing the percentage of the population that has a cell phone will decrease the violent crime rate? What might be a lurking variable between percentage of the population with a cell phone and violent crime rate?

44. Faulty Use of Correlation On the basis of the scatter diagram, explain what is wrong with the following statement: "Because the linear correlation coefficient between age and median income is 0.012, there is no relation between age and median income."

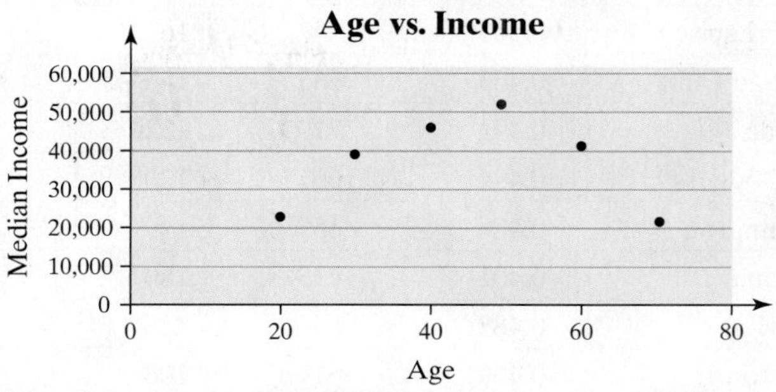

45. Influential Consider the following set of data:

x	2.2	3.7	3.9	4.1	2.6	4.1	2.9	4.7
y	3.9	4.0	1.4	2.8	1.5	3.3	3.6	4.9

(a) Draw a scatter diagram of the data and compute the linear correlation coefficient. 0.228

(b) Draw a scatter diagram of the data and compute the linear correlation coefficient with the additional data point (10.4, 9.3). Comment on the effect the additional data point has on the linear correlation coefficient. Explain why correlations should always be reported with scatter diagrams. 0.860

46. Transformations Consider the following data set:

x	5	6	7	7	8	8	8	8
y	4.2	5	5.2	5.9	6	6.2	6.1	6.9
x	9	9	10	10	11	11	12	12
y	7.2	8	8.3	7.4	8.4	7.8	8.5	9.5

(a) Draw a scatter diagram with the x-axis starting at 0 and ending at 30 and with the y-axis starting at 0 and ending at 20.

(b) Compute the linear correlation coefficient. 0.952

(c) Now multiply both x and y by 2.

(d) Draw a scatter diagram of the new data with the x-axis starting at 0 and ending at 30 and with the y-axis starting at 0 and ending at 20. Compare the scatter diagrams.

(e) Compute the linear correlation coefficient. 0.952

(f) Conclude that multiplying each value in the data set by a nonzero constant does not affect the correlation between the variables. Explain why this is the case.

47. RateMyProfessors.com Professors Theodore Coladarci and Irv Kornfield from the University of Maine found a correlation of 0.68 between responses to questions on the RateMyProfessors.com Web site and typical in-class evaluations. Use this correlation to make an argument in favor of the validity of RateMyProfessors.com as a legitimate evaluation tool. RateMyProfessors.com also has a chili pepper icon, which is meant to indicate a "hotness scale" for the professor. This hotness scale serves as a proxy for the sexiness of the professor. It was found that the correlation between quality and sexiness is 0.64. In addition, it was found that the correlation between easiness of the professor and quality is 0.85 for instructors with at least 70 posts. Use this information to make an argument against RateMyProfessors.com as a legitimate evaluation tool. *Source:* Theodore Coladarci and Irv Kornfield. "RateMyProfessors.com versus Formal In-class Student Evaluations of Teaching," *Practical Assessment, Research, & Evaluation,* 12:6, May, 2007.

EXPLAINING THE CONCEPTS

48. What does it mean to say that the linear correlation coefficient between two variables equals 1? What would the scatter diagram look like?

49. What does it mean if $r = 0$? No linear relation

50. Explain what is wrong with the following statement: "We have concluded that a high correlation exists between the gender of drivers and rates of automobile accidents." Suggest a better way to write the sentence.

51. Write a paragraph that explains the concept of correlation. Include a discussion of the role that $x_i - \bar{x}$ and $y_i - \bar{y}$ play in the computation.

52. Explain the difference between correlation and causation. When is it appropriate to state that the correlation implies causation?

53. Draw a scatter diagram that might represent the relation between the number of minutes spent exercising on an elliptical and calories burned. Draw a scatter diagram that might represent the relation between number of hours each week spent on Facebook and grade point average.

54. Suppose you work a part-time job and earn $15 per hour. Draw a scatter diagram that might represent the relation between your gross pay and hours worked. Is this a deterministic relation or a probabilistic relation? Deterministic

55. Suppose that two variables, X and Y, are negatively associated. Does this mean that above-average values of X will always be associated with below-average values of Y? Explain. No

Technology Step-By-Step

Drawing Scatter Diagrams and Determining the Correlation Coefficient

TI-83/84 Plus

Scatter Diagrams

1. Enter the explanatory variable in `L1` and the response variable in `L2`.
2. Press 2nd Y = to bring up the StatPlot menu. Select `1: Plot1`.
3. Turn Plot 1 on by highlighting the `On` button and pressing ENTER.
4. Highlight the scatter diagram icon (see the figure) and press ENTER. Be sure that Xlist is L1 and Ylist is L2.

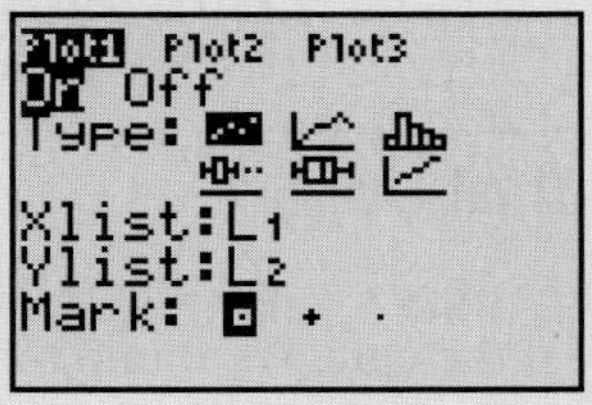

5. Press `ZOOM` and select `9:ZoomStat`.

Correlation Coefficient

1. Turn the diagnostics on by selecting the catalog (2nd 0). Scroll down and select `DiagnosticOn`. Hit ENTER twice to activate diagnostics.
2. With the explanatory variable in `L1` and the response variable in `L2`, press `STAT`, highlight `CALC` and select `4: LinReg (ax + b)`. With `LinReg` on the HOME screen, press ENTER.

MINITAB

Scatter Diagrams

1. Enter the explanatory variable in C1 and the response variable in C2. You may want to name the variables.

2. Select the **Graph** menu and highlight **Scatterplot . . . .**
3. Highlight the Simple icon and click OK.
4. With the cursor in the Y column, select the response variable. With the cursor in the X column, select the explanatory variable. Click OK.

Correlation Coefficient

1. With the explanatory variable in C1 and the response variable in C2, select the **Stat** menu and highlight **Basic Statistics**. Highlight **Correlation**.
2. Select the variables whose correlation you wish to determine and click OK.

Excel

Scatter Diagrams

1. Enter the explanatory variable in column A and the response variable in column B.
2. Highlight both sets of data.
3. Select Insert. Choose Scatter.

Correlation Coefficient

1. Select Formulas and highlight More Functions. Select Statistical.
2. Click CORREL.
3. With the cursor in Array 1, highlight the data containing the explanatory variable. With the cursor in Array 2, highlight the data containing the response variable. Click OK.

StatCrunch

Scatter Diagrams

1. Enter the explanatory variable in column var1 and the response variable in column var2. Name each column variable.
2. Select **Graphics** and highlight **Scatter Plot**.
3. Choose the explanatory variable for the X variable and the response variable for the Y variable. Click Next>.
4. Be sure to display data as points. Click Next>.
5. Enter the labels for the *x*- and *y*-axes, and enter a title for the graph. Click Create Graph!.

Correlation Coefficient

1. Enter the explanatory variable in column var1 and the response variable in column var2. Name each column variable.
2. Select **Stat**, highlight **Summary Stats**, and select **Correlation**.
3. Click on the variables whose correlation you wish to determine. Click Calculate.

4.2 LEAST-SQUARES REGRESSION

Preparing for This Section Before getting started, review the following:

- Lines (Appendix B on CD, pp. B1–B5)

OBJECTIVES

1. Find the least-squares regression line and use the line to make predictions
2. Interpret the slope and the *y*-intercept of the least-squares regression line
3. Compute the sum of squared residuals

Note to Instructor
If you like, you can print out and distribute the Preparing for This Section quiz located in the Instructor's Resource Center. The purpose of the quiz is to verify that the students have the prerequisite knowledge for the section.

Once the scatter diagram and linear correlation coefficient show that two variables have a linear relation, we then find a linear equation that describes this relation. One way to find a line that describes the relation is to select two points from the data that appear to provide a good fit and to find the equation of the line through these points.

EXAMPLE 1 Finding an Equation That Describes Linearly Related Data

Problem The data in Table 5 represent the club-head speed and the distance a golf ball travels for eight swings of the club. We found that these data are linearly related in Section 4.1.

Note to Instructor

Encourage students to review lines in Appendix B on the CD.

TABLE 5

Club-head Speed (mph) x	Distance (yd) y	(x, y)
100	257	(100, 257)
102	264	(102, 264)
103	274	(103, 274)
101	266	(101, 266)
105	277	(105, 277)
100	263	(100, 263)
99	258	(99, 258)
105	275	(105, 275)

Source: Paul Stephenson, student at Joliet Junior College

CAUTION

Example 1 *does not* present the least-squares method. It is used to set up the concepts of determining the line that best fits the data.

(a) Find a linear equation that relates club-head speed, x (the explanatory variable), and distance, y (the response variable), by selecting two points and finding the equation of the line containing the points.

(b) Graph the line on the scatter diagram.

(c) Use the equation to predict the distance a golf ball will travel if the club-head speed is 104 miles per hour.

Approach

(a) We perform the following steps:

In Other Words

A *good fit* means that the line drawn appears to describe the relation between the two variables well.

Step 1 Select two points so that a line drawn through the points appears to give a good fit. Call the points (x_1, y_1) and (x_2, y_2). See the scatter diagram in Figure 1 on page 179.

Step 2 Find the slope of the line containing the two points using $m = \frac{y_2 - y_1}{x_2 - x_1}$.

Step 3 Use the point–slope formula, $y - y_1 = m(x - x_1)$, to find the equation of the line through the points selected in Step 1. Express the equation in the form $y = mx + b$, where m is the slope and b is the y-intercept.

(b) Draw a line through the points selected in Step 1 of part (a).

(c) Let $x = 104$ in the equation found in part (a).

Solution

(a) ***Step 1*** We select $(x_1, y_1) = (99, 258)$ and $(x_2, y_2) = (105, 275)$, because a line drawn through these two points seems to give a good fit.

Step 2 $m = \frac{y_2 - y_1}{x_2 - x_1} = \frac{275 - 258}{105 - 99} = \frac{17}{6} = 2.8333$

Step 3 We use the point–slope formula to find the equation of the line.

CAUTION

The line found in Step 3 of Example 1 is not the least-squares regression line.

$$y - y_1 = m(x - x_1)$$

$$y - 258 = 2.8333(x - 99) \qquad m = 2.8333, x_1 = 99, y_1 = 258$$

$$y - 258 = 2.8333x - 280.4967$$

$$y = 2.8333x - 22.4967 \qquad (1)$$

CAUTION

Unless otherwise noted, we will round the slope and y-intercept to four decimal places. As always, do not round until the last computation.

The slope of the line is 2.8333, and the y-intercept is -22.4967.

(b) Figure 10 on the following page shows the scatter diagram along with the line drawn through the points (99, 258) and (105, 275).

(c) We let $x = 104$ in equation (1) to predict the distance.

$$y = 2.8333(104) - 22.4967$$
$$= 272.2 \text{ yards}$$

We predict that a golf ball will travel 272.2 yards when it is hit with a club-head speed of 104 miles per hour.

Figure 10

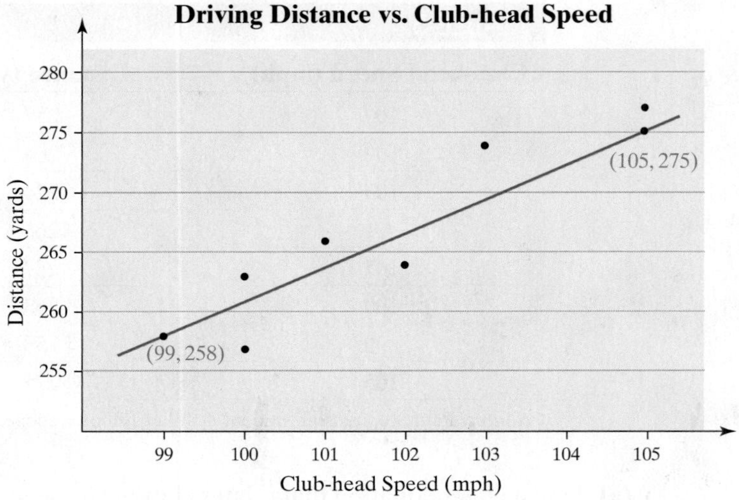

Now Work Problems 7(a)–(c)

1 Find the Least-Squares Regression Line and Use the Line to Make Predictions

The line that we found in Example 1 appears to describe the relation between club-head speed and distance quite well. However, is there a line that fits the data better? Is there a line that fits the data *best*?

Whenever we are attempting to determine the best of something, we need a criterion for determining best. For example, suppose that we are trying to identify the best domestic car. What do we mean by best? Best gas mileage? Best horsepower? Best reliability? In attempting to find the best line for describing the relation between two variables, we need a criterion for determining the best line as well. To understand this criterion, consider Figure 11. Each *y*-coordinate on the line corresponds to a predicted distance for a given club-head speed. For example, if club-head speed is 103 miles per hour, the predicted distance is $2.8333(103) - 22.4967 = 269.3$ yards. The observed distance for this club-head speed is 274 yards. The difference between the observed and predicted values of *y* is the error, or **residual**. For a club-head speed of 103 miles per hour, the residual is

In Other Words
The residual represents how close our prediction comes to the actual observation. The smaller the residual, the better the prediction.

$$\begin{aligned}\text{Residual} &= \text{observed } y - \text{predicted } y\\ &= 274 - 269.3\\ &= 4.7 \text{ yards}\end{aligned}$$

The residual for a club-head speed of 103 miles per hour is labeled in Figure 11.

Figure 11

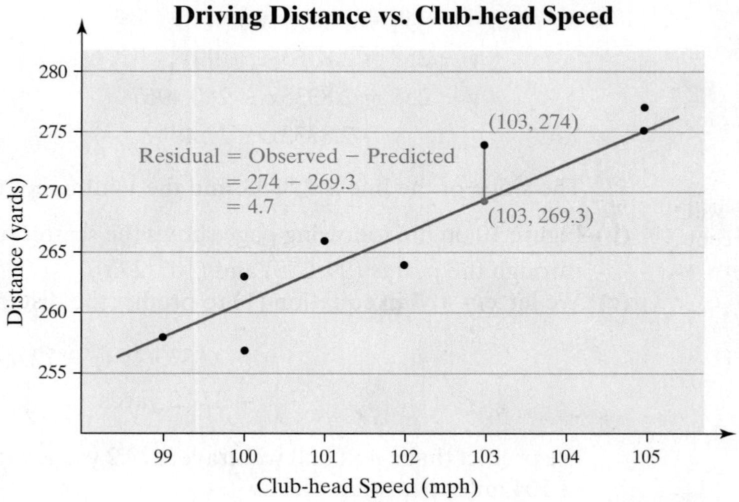

The criterion to determine the line that *best* describes the relation between two variables is based on the residuals. The most popular technique for making the residuals as small as possible is the *method of least squares*, developed by Adrien Marie Legendre.

DEFINITION

Least-Squares Regression Criterion

The **least-squares regression line** is the line that minimizes the sum of the squared errors (or residuals). This line minimizes the sum of the squared vertical distance between the observed values of y and those predicted by the line, $\hat{y}$ (read "y-hat"). We represent this as "minimize $\sum$ residuals^2".

Historical Note

Adrien Marie Legendre was born on September 18, 1752, into a wealthy family and was educated in mathematics and physics at the College Mazarin in Paris. From 1775 to 1780, he taught at École Militaire. In 1783, Legendre was appointed an adjoint in the Académie des Sciences. He became a member of the committee of the Académie des Sciences in 1791 and was charged with the task of standardizing weights and measures. The committee worked to compute the length of the meter. During the French Revolution, Legendre lost his small fortune. In 1794, Legendre published *Éléments de géométrie*, which was the leading elementary text in geometry for around 100 years. In 1806, Legendre published a book on orbits, in which he developed the theory of least squares. He died on January 10, 1833.

The advantage of the least-squares criterion is that it allows for statistical inference on the predicted value and slope (Chapter 14). Another advantage of the least-squares criterion is explained by Legendre in his text *Nouvelles méthodes pour la determination des orbites des comètes*, published in 1806.

> Of all the principles that can be proposed for this purpose, I think there is none more general, more exact, or easier to apply, than that which we have used in this work; it consists of making the sum of squares of the errors a *minimum*. By this method, a kind of equilibrium is established among the errors which, since it prevents the extremes from dominating, is appropriate for revealing the state of the system which most nearly approaches the truth.

The Least-Squares Regression Line

The equation of the least-squares regression line is given by

$$\hat{y} = b_1 x + b_0$$

where

$$b_1 = r \cdot \frac{s_y}{s_x} \text{ is the \textbf{slope} of the least-squares regression line}^* \qquad \textbf{(2)}$$

and

$$b_0 = \bar{y} - b_1\bar{x} \text{ is the \textbf{y-intercept} of the least-squares regression line} \qquad \textbf{(3)}$$

Note: $\bar{x}$ is the sample mean and s_x is the sample standard deviation of the explanatory variable x; $\bar{y}$ is the sample mean and s_y is the sample standard deviation of the response variable y.

*An equivalent formula is

$$b_1 = \frac{S_{xy}}{S_{xx}} = \frac{\sum x_i y_i - \frac{(\sum x_i)(\sum y_i)}{n}}{\sum x_i^2 - \frac{(\sum x_i)^2}{n}}$$

The notation $\hat{y}$ is used in the least-squares regression line to remind us that it is a predicted value of y for a given value of x. The least-squares regression line, $\hat{y} = b_1x + b_0$, always contains the point $(\bar{x}, \bar{y})$. This property can be useful when drawing the least-squares regression line by hand.

Since s_y and s_x must both be positive, the sign of the linear correlation coefficient, r, and the sign of the slope of the least-squares regression line, b_1, are the same. For example, if r is positive, then b_1 will also be positive.

The predicted value of y, $\hat{y}$, has an interesting interpretation. It is an estimate of the mean value of the response variable for any value of the explanatory variable. For example, suppose a least-squares regression equation is obtained that relates students' grade point average (GPA) to the number of hours studied each week. If the equation results in a predicted GPA of 3.14 when a student studies 20 hours each week, we would say the mean GPA of *all* students who study 20 hours each week is 3.14.

EXAMPLE 2 Finding the Least-Squares Regression Line by Hand

Note to Instructor
This example is presented to help students get comfortable with the least-squares method, especially the relation between the sign of the correlation coefficient and the slope of the least-squares regression line. It is recommended that students obtain the least-squares regression equation using technology.

Problem Find the least-squares regression line for the data in Table 2 from Section 4.1.

Approach In Example 2 of Section 4.1 (page 182), we found

$$r = -0.946, \bar{x} = 4, s_x = 2.44949, \bar{y} = 10, \text{ and } s_y = 5.612486$$

Substitute the values in Formulas (2) and (3) to find the slope and intercept of the least-squares regression line.

Solution Substitute $r = -0.946$, $s_x = 2.44949$, and $s_y = 5.612486$ into Formula (2):

$$b_1 = r \cdot \frac{s_y}{s_x} = -0.946 \cdot \frac{5.612486}{2.44949} = -2.1676$$

Substitute $\bar{x} = 4$, $\bar{y} = 10$, and $b_1 = -2.1676$ into Formula (3):

$$b_0 = \bar{y} - b_1\bar{x} = 10 - (-2.1676)(4) = 18.6704$$

The least-squares regression line is

$$\hat{y} = -2.1676x + 18.6704$$

In practice, the least-squares regression line is obtained using technology.

EXAMPLE 3 Finding the Least-Squares Regression Line Using Technology

Note to Instructor
Consider assigning the "Finding a Least-Squares Regression Line" activity from the Student Activity Workbook.

Problem Use the golf data in Table 5.

(a) Find the least-squares regression line.
(b) Draw the least-squares regression line on the scatter diagram of the data.
(c) Predict the distance a golf ball will travel when hit with a club-head speed of 103 miles per hour (mph).
(d) Determine the residual for the predicted value found in part (c). Is this distance above average or below average among all balls hit with a swing speed of 103 mph?

Approach Because technology plays a major role in obtaining the least-squares regression line, we will use a TI-84 Plus graphing calculator, MINITAB, Excel, and StatCrunch to obtain the least-squares regression line. The steps for obtaining regression lines are given in the Technology Step-by-Step on page 207.

Solution

(a) Figure 12 shows the output obtained from the various technologies. The least-squares regression line is $\hat{y} = 3.1661x - 55.7966$.

Figure 12

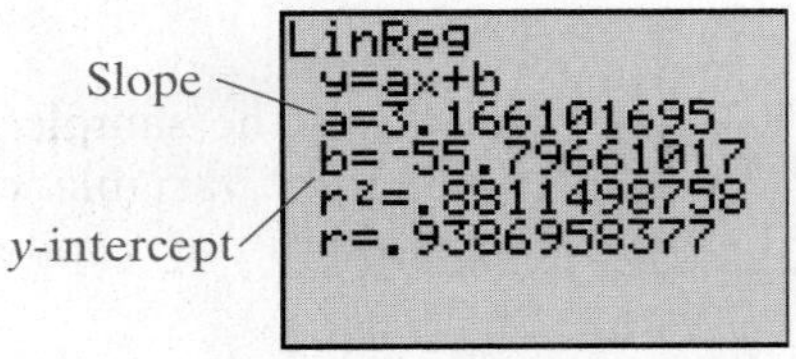

(a) TI-84 Plus output

⚠ CAUTION
Throughout the text, we will round the slope and y-intercept values to four decimal places. Predictions will be rounded to one more decimal place than the response variable.

```
The regression equation is
Distance (yards) = -55.8 + 3.17 Club Head Speed (mph)
Predictor              Coef    SE Coef        T        P
Constant             -55.80      48.37    -1.15    0.293
Club Head Speed (mph) 3.1661    0.4747     6.67    0.001

S = 2.88264     R - Sq = 88.1%    R - Sq(adj) = 86.1%
```

(b) MINITAB output

	Coefficients	*Standard Error*	*t Stat*	*P-value*
Intercept	−55.79661017	48.37134953	−1.153505344	0.29257431
Club Head Speed (mph)	3.166101695	0.47470539	6.669613957	0.00054983

(c) Excel output

Historical Note

Sir Francis Galton was born on February 16, 1822. Galton came from a wealthy and well-known family. Charles Darwin was his first cousin. Galton studied medicine at Cambridge. After receiving a large inheritance, he left the medical field and traveled the world. He explored Africa from 1850 to 1852. In the 1860s, his study of meteorology led him to discover anticyclones. Influenced by Darwin, Galton always had an interest in genetics and heredity. He studied heredity through experiments with sweet peas. He noticed that the weight of the "children" of the "parent" peas reverted or *regressed* to the mean weight of all peas—hence, the term *regression analysis*. Galton died January 17, 1911.

Figure 12(d)

Simple linear regression results:
Dependent Variable: Distance
Independent Variable: Club-head Speed
Distance = -55.79661 + 3.1661017 Club-head Speed
Sample size: 8
R (correlation coefficient) = 0.9387
R-sq = 0.8811499
Estimate of error standard deviation: 2.8826385

(d) StatCrunch output

(b) Figure 13 shows the least-squares regression line drawn on the scatter diagram using StatCrunch.

Figure 13

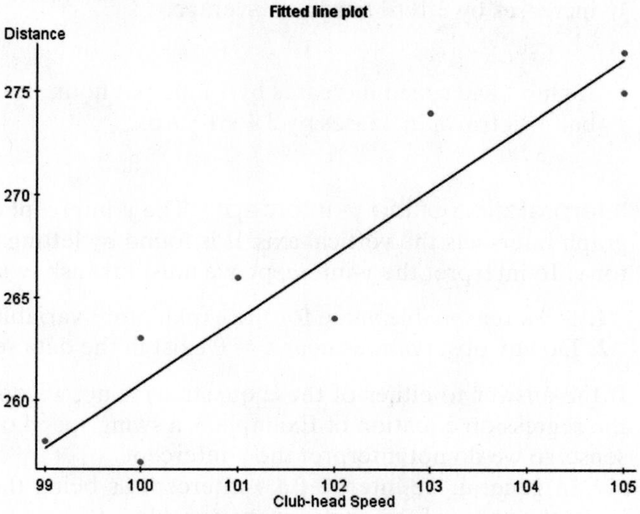

Note to Instructor
Consider assigning the "Examining the Relationship between Arm Length and Height" activity from the Student Activity Workbook.

(c) Let $x = 103$ in the least-squares regression equation $\hat{y} = 3.1661x - 55.7966$ to predict the distance the ball will travel when hit with a club-head speed of 103 mph.

$$\hat{y} = 3.1661(103) - 55.7966$$
$$= 270.3 \text{ yards}$$

We predict the distance the golf ball will travel is 270.3 yards.

(d) From the data in Table 1 from Section 4.1, we see the observed distance the ball traveled when the swing speed is 103 mph was 274 yards. So,

$$\text{Residual} = y - \hat{y} \quad \text{Residual = observed } y - \text{predicted } y$$
$$= 274 - 270.3$$
$$= 3.7 \text{ yards}$$

Since the residual is positive (the observed value of 274 yards is greater than the predicted value of 270.3 yards), the distance of 274 yards is above average for a swing speed of 103 mph.

Now Work Problems 17(a), (c), and (d)

2 Interpret the Slope and the *y*-Intercept of the Least-Squares Regression Line

Interpretation of Slope In algebra, we learned that the definition of slope is $\frac{\text{rise}}{\text{run}}$ or $\frac{\text{change in } y}{\text{change in } x}$. If a line has slope $\frac{2}{3}$, then if x increases by 3, y will increase by 2. Or if the slope of a line is $-4 = \frac{-4}{1}$, then if x increases by 1, y will decrease by 4.

Interpreting slope for least-squares regression lines has a minor twist, however. Statistical models such as a least-squares regression equation are *probabilistic*. This means that any predictions or interpretations made as a result of the model are based on uncertainty. Therefore, when we interpret the slope of a least-squares regression equation, we do not want to imply that there is 100% certainty behind the interpretation. For example, the slope of the least-squares regression line from Example 3 is 3.1661 yards per mph. In algebra, we would interpret the slope to mean "if x increases by 1 mph, then y will increase by 3.1661 yards." In statistics, this interpretation is close, but not quite accurate, because increasing the club-head speed by 1 mph does not guarantee the distance the ball will travel will increase by 3.1661 yards. Instead, over the course of data we observed, an increase in club-head speed of 1 mph increased distance 3.1661 yards, *on average*—sometimes the ball might travel a shorter additional distance, sometimes a longer additional distance, but on average this is the change in distance. So two interpretations of slope are acceptable:

> If club-head speed increases by 1 mile per hour, the distance the golf ball travels increases by 3.1661 yards, on average.
>
> or
>
> If club-head speed increases by 1 mile per hour, the expected distance the golf ball will travel increases by 3.1661 yards.

Interpretation of the y-Intercept The y-intercept of any line is the point where the graph intersects the vertical axis. It is found by letting $x = 0$ in an equation and solving for y. To interpret the y-intercept, we must first ask two questions:

1. Is 0 a reasonable value for the explanatory variable?
2. Do any observations near $x = 0$ exist in the data set?

If the answer to either of these questions is no, we do not interpret the y-intercept. In the regression equation of Example 3, a swing speed of 0 miles per hour does not make sense, so we do not interpret the y-intercept.

In general, we interpret a y-intercept as being the value of the response variable when the value of the explanatory variable is 0.

CAUTION
Be careful when using the least-squares regression line to make predictions for values of the explanatory variable that are much larger or much smaller than those observed.

The second condition for interpreting the y-intercept is especially important because we should not use the regression model to make predictions **outside the scope of the model**, meaning we should not use the regression model to make predictions for values of the explanatory variable that are much larger or much smaller than those observed. This is a dangerous practice because we cannot be certain of the behavior of data for which we have no observations.

For example, we should not use the line in Example 3 to predict distance when club-head speed is 140 mph. The highest observed club-head speed is 105 mph. The linear relation between distance and club-head speed might not continue. See Figure 14.

Figure 14

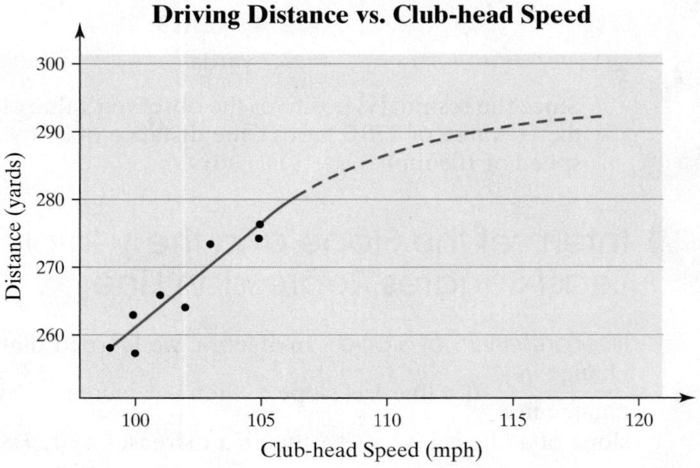

Now Work Problem 13

Note to Instructor

Consider assigning the "Minimizing the Sum of Squared Residuals" activity from the Student Activity Workbook.

Predictions When There Is No Linear Relation

When the correlation coefficient indicates no linear relation between the explanatory and response variables, and the scatter diagram indicates no relation at all between the variables, then we use the mean value of the response variable as the predicted value so that $\hat{y} = \bar{y}$.

3 Compute the Sum of Squared Residuals

Note to Instructor

The purpose of this material is to allow students to see that the least-squares regression line has the smallest sum of squared residuals. It can be skipped without loss of continuity.

Recall that the least-squares regression line is the line that minimizes the sum of the squared residuals. This means that the sum of the squared residuals, Σ residuals^2, is smaller for the least-squares line than for any other line that may describe the relation between the two variables. In particular, the sum of the squared residuals is smaller for the least-squares regression line in Example 3 than for the line obtained in Example 1. It is worthwhile to verify this result.

EXAMPLE 4 Comparing the Sum of Squared Residuals

Problem Compare the sum of squared residuals for the lines in Examples 1 and 3.

Approach We will use a table to compute Σ residuals^2 using the predicted values of y, $\hat{y}$, for the equations in Examples 1 and 3.

Solution Table 6 contains the value of the explanatory variable in Column 1. Column 2 contains the corresponding response variable. Column 3 contains the predicted values using the equation found in Example 1, $\hat{y} = 2.8333x - 22.4967$. In Column 4, we compute the residuals for each observation: residual = observed y − predicted $y = y - \hat{y}$. For example, the first residual is $y - \hat{y} = 257 - 260.8 = -3.8$. Column 5 contains the squares of the residuals. Column 6 contains the predicted values using the least-squares regression equation found in Example 3: $\hat{y} = 3.1661x - 55.7966$. Column 7 represents the residuals for each observation, and Column 8 represents the squared residuals.

TABLE 6

Club-head Speed (mph)	Distance (yd)	Example 1 ($\hat{y} = 2.8333x - 22.4967$)	Residual $y - \hat{y}$	Residual^2 $(y - \hat{y})^2$	Example 3 ($\hat{y} = 3.1661x - 55.7966$)	Residual $y - \hat{y}$	Residual $(y - \hat{y})^2$
100	257	260.8	−3.8	14.44	260.8	−3.8	14.44
102	264	266.5	−2.5	6.25	267.1	−3.1	9.61
103	274	269.3	4.7	22.09	270.3	3.7	13.69
101	266	263.7	2.3	5.29	264.0	2.0	4.00
105	277	275.0	2.0	4.00	276.6	0.4	0.16
100	263	260.8	2.2	4.84	260.8	2.2	4.84
99	258	258.0	0.0	0.00	257.6	0.4	0.16
105	275	275.0	0.0	0.00	276.6	−1.6	2.56
				Σ residual^2 = 56.91			Σ residual^2 = 49.46

The sum of the squared residuals for the line in Example 1 is 56.91; the sum of the squared residuals for the least-squares regression line is 49.46. Again, any line other than the least-squares regression line will have a sum of squared residuals that is greater than 49.46.

Now Work Problems 7(d)–(h)

We draw the graphs of the two lines obtained in Examples 1 and 3 on the same scatter diagram in Figure 15 to help the reader visualize the difference.

Figure 15

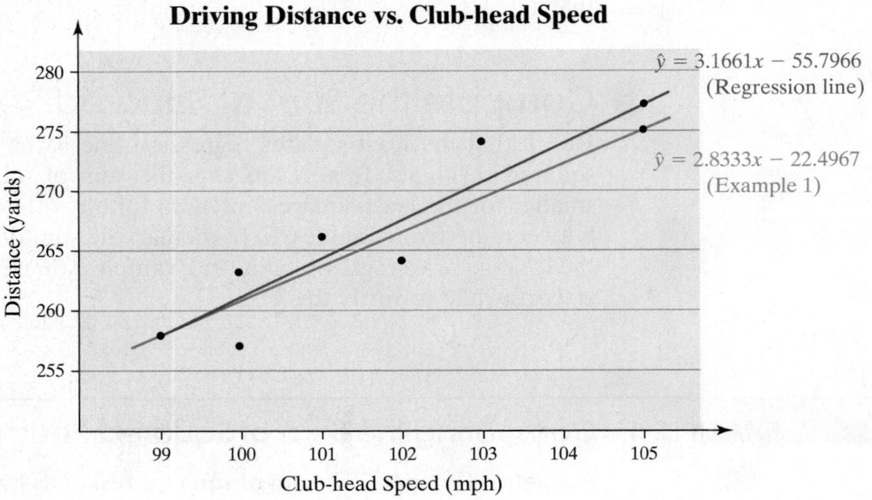

4.2 ASSESS YOUR UNDERSTANDING

VOCABULARY AND SKILL BUILDING

1. The difference between the observed and predicted value of y is the error, or ______. residual

2. If the linear correlation between two variables is negative, what can be said about the slope of the regression line? Negative

3. *True or False*: The least-squares regression line always travels through the point $(\bar{x}, \bar{y})$. True

4. If the linear correlation coefficient is 0, what is the equation of the least-squares regression line? $\hat{y} = \bar{y}$

5. For the data set

x	0	2	3	5	6	6
y	5.8	5.7	5.2	2.8	1.9	2.2

(a) Draw a scatter diagram. Comment on the type of relation that appears to exist between x and y.

(b) Given that $\bar{x} = 3.6667$, $s_x = 2.4221$, $\bar{y} = 3.9333$, $s_y = 1.8239$, and $r = -0.9477$, determine the least-squares regression line. $\hat{y} = -0.7136x + 6.5498$

(c) Graph the least-squares regression line on the scatter diagram drawn in part (a).

6. For the data set

x	2	4	8	8	9
y	1.4	1.8	2.1	2.3	2.6

(a) Draw a scatter diagram. Comment on the type of relation that appears to exist between x and y.

(b) Given that $\bar{x} = 6.2$, $s_x = 3.03315$, $\bar{y} = 2.04$, $s_y = 0.461519$, and $r = 0.957241$, determine the least-squares regression line. $\hat{y} = 0.1457x + 1.1370$

(c) Graph the least-squares regression line on the scatter diagram drawn in part (a).

In Problems 7–12:

(a) *By hand, draw a scatter diagram treating x as the explanatory variable and y as the response variable.*

(b) *Select two points from the scatter diagram and find the equation of the line containing the points selected.*

(c) *Graph the line found in part (b) on the scatter diagram.*

(d) *By hand, determine the least-squares regression line.*

(e) *Graph the least-squares regression line on the scatter diagram.*

(f) *Compute the sum of the squared residuals for the line found in part (b).*

(g) *Compute the sum of the squared residuals for the least-squares regression line found in part (d).*

(h) *Comment on the fit of the line found in part (b) versus the least-squares regression line found in part (d).*

NW 7.

x	3	4	5	7	8
y	4	6	7	12	14

8.

x	3	5	7	9	11
y	0	2	3	6	9

9.

x	−2	−1	0	1	2
y	−4	0	1	4	5

10.

x	−2	−1	0	1	2
y	7	6	3	2	0

11.

x	20	30	40	50	60
y	100	95	91	83	70

12.

x	5	10	15	20	25
y	2	4	7	11	18

NW **13. You Explain It! Video Games and GPAs** A student at Joliet Junior College conducted a survey of 20 randomly selected full-time students to determine the relation between the number of hours of video game playing each week, x, and grade-point average, y. She found that a linear relation exists between the two variables. The least-squares regression line that describes this relation is $\hat{y} = -0.0526x + 2.9342$.

(a) Predict the grade-point average of a student who plays video games 8 hours per week. 2.51

(b) Interpret the slope.

(c) If appropriate, interpret the y-intercept.

(d) A student who plays video games 7 hours per week has a grade-point average of 2.68. Is this student's grade-point average above or below average among all students who play video games 7 hours per week? Above

14. You Explain It! Study Time and Exam Scores After the first exam in a statistics course, Professor Katula surveyed 14 randomly selected students to determine the relation between the amount of time they spent studying for the exam and exam score. She found that a linear relation exists between the two variables. The least-squares regression line that describes this relation is $\hat{y} = 6.3333x + 53.0298$.

(a) Predict the exam score of a student who studied 2 hours. 65.7

(b) Interpret the slope.

(c) What is the mean score of students who did not study? 53.0

(d) A student who studied 5 hours for the exam scored 81 on the exam. Is this student's exam score above or below average among all students who studied 5 hours? Below

15. You Explain It! Winning Percentage and On-base Percentage In his best-selling book *Moneyball*, author Michael Lewis discusses how statistics can be used to judge both a baseball player's potential and a team's ability to win games. One aspect of this analysis is that a team's on-base percentage is the best predictor of winning percentage. The on-base percentage is the proportion of time a player reaches a base. For example, an on-base percentage of 0.3 would mean the player safely reaches bases 3 times out of 10, on average. For the 2010 baseball season, winning percentage, y, and on-base percentage, x, are linearly related by the least-squares regression equation $\hat{y} = 3.4722x - 0.6294$. *Source*: www.espn.com

(a) Interpret the slope.

(b) For 2010, the lowest on-base percentage was 0.298 and the highest on-base percentage was 0.350. Use this information to explain why it does not make sense to interpret the y-intercept.

(c) Would it be a good idea to use this model to predict the winning percentage of a team whose on-base percentage was 0.250? Why or why not? Bad idea

(d) The 2010 World Series Champion San Francisco Giants had an on-base percentage of 0.321 and a winning percentage of 0.568. What is the residual for San Francisco? How would you interpret this residual? 0.0828

16. You Explain It! CO_2 and Energy Production The least-squares regression equation $\hat{y} = 0.7676x - 52.6841$ relates the carbon dioxide emissions (in hundred thousands of tons), y, and energy produced (hundred thousands of megawatts), x, for all countries in the world in 2010. *Source*: CARMA (www.carma.org)

(a) Interpret the slope. (b) No; expect it to be 0.

(b) Is the y-intercept of the model reasonable? Why? What would you expect the y-intercept of the model to equal? Why?

(c) For 2010, the lowest energy-producing country was Rwanda, which produced 0.094 hundred thousand megawatts of energy. The highest energy-producing country was the United States, which produced 4190 hundred thousand megawatts of energy in 2010. Would it be reasonable to use this model to predict the CO_2 emissions of a country if it produced 6394 hundred thousand megawatts of energy in 2010? Why or why not? No

(d) In 2010, China produced 3260 hundred thousand megawatts of energy and emitted 3120 hundred thousand tons of carbon dioxide. What is the residual for China? How would you interpret this residual? 670 hundred thousand tons

APPLYING THE CONCEPTS

Problems 17–22 use the results from Problems 25–30 in Section 4.1.

NW **17. An Unhealthy Commute** (Refer to Problem 25, Section 4.1.) The following data represent commute times (in minutes) and score on a well-being survey.

Commute Time (minutes), x	Gallup-Healthways Well-Being Index Composite Score, y
5	69.2
15	68.3
25	67.5
35	67.1
50	66.4
72	66.1
105	63.9

Source: The Gallup Organization

(a) Find the least-squares regression line treating the commute time, x, as the explanatory variable and the index score, y, as the response variable. $\hat{y} = -0.0479x + 69.0296$

(b) Interpret the slope and y-intercept, if appropriate.

(c) Predict the well-being index of a person whose commute is 30 minutes. 67.6

(d) Suppose Barbara has a 20-minute commute and scores 67.3 on the survey. Is Barbara more "well-off" than the typical individual who has a 20-minute commute? Less well-off

18. Credit Scores (Refer to Problem 26, Section 4.1.) An economist wants to determine the relation between one's FICO score, x, and the interest rate of a 36-month auto loan, y. The given data represent the interest rate (in percent) a bank would offer on a 36-month auto loan for various FICO scores.

Credit Score, x	Interest Rate (percent), y
545	18.982
595	17.967
640	12.218
675	8.612
705	6.680
750	5.150

Source: www.myfico.com

(a) Find the least-squares regression line treating the FICO score, x, as the explanatory variable and the interest rate, y, as the response variable. $\hat{y} = -0.0764x + 61.3687$

(b) Interpret the slope and y-intercept, if appropriate. *Note:* Credit scores have a range of 300 to 850.

(c) Predict the interest rate a person would pay if her FICO scores were the median score of 723. 6.1315%

(d) Suppose Bob has a FICO score of 680 and he is offered an interest rate of 8.3%. Is this a good offer? Why? Good offer

19. Height versus Head Circumference (Refer to Problem 27, Section 4.1.) A pediatrician wants to determine the relation that exists between a child's height, x, and head circumference, y. She randomly selects 11 children from her practice, measures their heights and head circumferences, and obtains the following data.

Height (inches), x	Head Circumference (inches), y	Height (inches), x	Head Circumference (inches), y
27.75	17.5	26.5	17.3
24.5	17.1	27	17.5
25.5	17.1	26.75	17.3
26	17.3	26.75	17.5
25	16.9	27.5	17.5
27.75	17.6		

Source: Denise Slucki, student at Joliet Junior College

(a) Find the least-squares regression line treating height as the explanatory variable and head circumference as the response variable. $\hat{y} = 0.1827x + 12.4932$

(b) Interpret the slope and y-intercept, if appropriate.

(c) Use the regression equation to predict the head circumference of a child who is 25 inches tall. 17.06 inches

(d) Compute the residual based on the observed head circumference of the 25-inch-tall child in the table. Is the head circumference of this child above average or below average? −0.16 inch; below

(e) Draw the least-squares regression line on the scatter diagram of the data and label the residual from part (d).

(f) Notice that two children are 26.75 inches tall. One has a head circumference of 17.3 inches; the other has a head circumference of 17.5 inches. How can this be?

(g) Would it be reasonable to use the least-squares regression line to predict the head circumference of a child who was 32 inches tall? Why? No

20. American Black Bears (Refer to Problem 28, Section 4.1.) The American black bear (*Ursus americanus*) is one of eight bear species in the world. It is the smallest North American bear and the most common bear species on the planet. In 1969, Dr. Michael R. Pelton of the University of Tennessee initiated a long-term study of the population in Great Smoky Mountains National Park. One aspect of the study was to develop a model that could be used to predict a bear's weight (since it is not practical to weigh bears in the field). One variable thought to be related to weight is the length of the bear. The following data represent the lengths of 12 American black bears.

Total Length (cm), x	Weight (kg), y
139.0	110
138.0	60
139.0	90
120.5	60
149.0	85
141.0	100
141.0	95
150.0	85
166.0	155
151.5	140
129.5	105
150.0	110

Source: www.fieldtripearth.org

(a) Find the least-squares regression line, treating total length as the explanatory variable and weight as the response variable.

(b) Interpret the slope and y-intercept, if appropriate.

(c) Suppose a 149.0-cm bear is captured in the field. Use the least-squares regression line to predict the weight of the bear. 110.0 kg (a) $\hat{y} = 1.6942x - 142.4709$, (d) −25.0 kg; below

(d) What is the residual of the 149.0-cm bear? Is this bear's weight above or below average for a bear of this length?

21. Weight of a Car versus Miles per Gallon (Refer to Problem 29, Section 4.1.) An engineer wants to determine how the weight of a car, x, affects gas mileage, y. The following data represent the weights of various domestic cars and their miles per gallon in the city for the 2011 model year.

Car	Weight (pounds), x	Miles per Gallon, y
Buick Lucerne	3735	17
Cadillac CTS	3860	16
Chevrolet Cobalt	2721	25
Chevrolet Impala	3555	19
Chrysler Sebring Sedan	3319	21
Dodge Caliber	2966	23
Dodge Charger	3727	17
Ford Focus	2605	24
Ford Mustang	3473	19
Lincoln MKZ	3796	17
Mercury Sable	3310	18

Source: www.roadandtrack.com

(a) Find the least-squares regression line treating weight as the explanatory variable and miles per gallon as the response variable. $\hat{y} = -0.0069x + 42.9068$

(b) Interpret the slope and y-intercept, if appropriate.

(c) A Buick Regal weighs 3600 pounds and gets 18 miles per gallon. Is the miles per gallon of a Regal above average or below average for cars of this weight? Below

22. (a) $\hat{y} = 1.3902x + 1.1140$, (c) 0.548 mm; above, (e) 36.300 mm

(d) Would it be reasonable to use the least-squares regression line to predict the miles per gallon of a Toyota Prius, a hybrid gas and electric car? Why or why not? No

22. Bone Length (Refer to Problem 30, Section 4.1.) Research performed at NASA and led by Emily R. Morey-Holton measured the lengths of the right humerus and right tibia in 11 rats who were sent to space on Spacelab Life Sciences 2. The following data were collected.

Right Humerus (mm), *x*	Right Tibia (mm), *y*	Right Humerus (mm), *x*	Right Tibia (mm), *y*
24.80	36.05	25.90	37.38
24.59	35.57	26.11	37.96
24.59	35.57	26.63	37.46
24.29	34.58	26.31	37.75
23.81	34.20	26.84	38.50
24.87	34.73		

Source: NASA Life Sciences Data Archive

(a) Find the least-squares regression line treating the length of the right humerus, x, as the explanatory variable and the length of the right tibia, y, as the response variable.
(b) Interpret the slope and y-intercept, if appropriate.
(c) Determine the residual if the length of the right humerus is 26.11 mm and the actual length of the right tibia is 37.96 mm. Is the length of this tibia above or below average?
(d) Draw the least-squares regression line on the scatter diagram.
(e) Suppose one of the rats sent to space experienced a broken right tibia due to a severe landing. The length of the right humerus is determined to be 25.31 mm. Use the least-squares regression line to estimate the length of the right tibia.

23. Cola Consumption vs. Bone Density Example 5 in Section 4.1 on page 185 discussed the effect of cola consumption on bone mineral density in the femoral neck of women.
(a) Find the least-squares regression line treating cola consumption per week as the explanatory variable.
(b) Interpret the slope. (a) $\hat{y} = -0.0029x + 0.8861$
(c) Interpret the intercept.
(d) Predict the bone mineral density of the femoral neck of a woman who consumes four colas per week. 0.8745 g/cm^2
(e) The researchers found a woman who consumed four colas per week to have a bone mineral density of 0.873 g/cm^2. Is this woman's bone mineral density above or below average among all women who consume four colas per week? Below
(f) Would you recommend using the model found in part (a) to predict the bone mineral density of a woman who consumes two cans of cola per day? Why? No; outside the scope of the model

24. Attending Class The following data represent the number of days absent, x, and the final grade, y, for a sample of college students in a general education course at a large state university.

No. of absences, *x*	0	1	2	3	4	5	6	7	8	9
Final grade, *y*	89.2	86.4	83.5	81.1	78.2	73.9	64.3	71.8	65.5	66.2

Source: College Teaching, 53(1), 2005.

(a) Find the least-squares regression line treating number of absences as the explanatory variable and final grade as the response variable. $\hat{y} = -2.8273x + 88.7327$
(b) Interpret the slope and y-intercept, if appropriate.
(c) Predict the final grade for a student who misses five class periods and compute the residual. Is the final grade above or below average for this number of absences?
(d) Draw the least-squares regression line on the scatter diagram of the data. (c) 74.60; −0.70; below
(e) Would it be reasonable to use the least-squares regression line to predict the final grade for a student who has missed 15 class periods? Why or why not? No

25. CEO Performance (Refer to Problem 31 in Section 4.1.) The following data represent the total compensation for 10 randomly selected chief executive officers (CEO) and the company's stock performance in 2009. Based on the analysis from Problem 31 in Section 4.1, what would be the predicted stock return for a company whose CEO made \$15 million? What would be the predicted stock return for a company whose CEO made \$25 million? $\hat{y} = \bar{y} = 17.3\%$

Company	Compensation (millions of dollars)	Stock Return (%)
Kraft Foods	26.35	5.91
Sara Lee	12.48	30.39
Boeing	19.44	31.72
Middleby	13.37	79.76
Exelon	12.21	−8.40
Northern Trust	11.89	2.69
Abbott Laboratories	26.21	4.53
Archer Daniels Midland	14.95	10.80
McDonald's	17.57	4.01
Baxter International	14.36	11.76

Source: Chicago Tribune, May 23, 2010

26. Does Size Matter? (Refer to Problem 33, Section 4.1) Researchers wondered whether the size of a person's brain was related to the individual's mental capacity. They selected a sample of right-handed introductory psychology students who had SAT scores higher than 1350. The subjects were administered the Wechsler Adult Intelligence Scale-Revised to obtain their IQ scores. MRI scans, performed at the same facility, consisted of 18 horizontal MR images. The computer counted all pixels with non-zero gray scale in each of the 18 images, and the total count served as an index for brain size. The resulting data for the females in the study are presented in the table.

MRI Count, *x*	IQ, *y*
816,932	133
951,545	137
991,305	138
833,868	132
856,472	140
852,244	132
790,619	135
866,662	130
857,782	133
948,066	133

Source: L. Willerman, R. Schultz, J. N. Rutledge, and E. Bigler. "In Vivo Brain Size and Intelligence." *Intelligence*, 15: 223–228, 1991.

(a) Find the least-squares regression line for females treating MRI count as the explanatory variable and IQ as the response variable. $\hat{y} = 0.00002x + 119.1662$

(b) What do you notice about the value of the slope? Why does this result seem reasonable based on the scatter diagram and linear correlation coefficient obtained in Problem 33(d) of Section 4.1?

(c) Predict the IQ of a female whose MRI count is 1,000,000. Predict the IQ of a female whose MRI count is 830,000. 134.3; 134.3

27. Male vs. Female Drivers (Refer to Problem 34, Section 4.1.) The following data represent the number of licensed drivers in various age groups and the number of fatal accidents within the age group by gender.

Age	Number of Male Licensed Drivers (000s)	Number of Fatal Crashes	Number of Female Licensed Drivers (000s)	Number of Fatal Crashes
<16	12	227	12	77
16–20	6,424	5,180	6,139	2,113
21–24	6,941	5,016	6,816	1,531
25–34	18,068	8,595	17,664	2,780
35–44	20,406	7,990	20,063	2,742
45–54	19,898	7,118	19,984	2,285
55–64	14,340	4,527	14,441	1,514
65–74	8,194	2,274	8,400	938
>74	4,803	2,022	5,375	980

Source: National Highway and Traffic Safety Institute

(a) Find the least-squares regression line for males treating number of licensed drivers as the explanatory variable, x, and number of fatal crashes, y, as the response variable. Repeat this procedure for females.

(b) Interpret the slope of the least-squares regression line for each gender, if appropriate. How might an insurance company use this information?

(c) Was the number of fatal accidents for 16- to 20-year-old males above or below average? Was the number of fatal accidents for 21- to 24-year-old-males above or below average? Was the number of fatal accidents for males greater than 74 years old above or below average? How might an insurance company use this information? Does the same relationship hold for females?

28. Putting It Together: Housing Prices One of the biggest factors in determining the value of a home is the square footage. The following data represent the square footage and asking price (in thousands of dollars) for a random sample of homes for sale in Naples, Florida, in December 2010.

Square Footage, x	Asking Price ($000s), y
1148	154
1096	159.9
1142	169
1288	169.9
1322	170
1466	179.9
1344	180
1544	189
1494	189.9

Source: realtor.com

27. (a) Males: $\hat{y} = 0.3428x + 998.4488$; Females: $\hat{y} = 0.1045x + 514.1520$

(a) Which variable is the explanatory variable? Square footage

(b) Draw a scatter diagram of the data.

(c) Determine the linear correlation coefficient between square footage and asking price. 0.916

(d) Is there a linear relation between the square footage and asking price? Yes

(e) Find the least-squares regression line treating square footage as the explanatory variable. $\hat{y} = 0.0686x + 83.2366$

(f) Interpret the slope.

(g) Is it reasonable to interpret the y-intercept? Why? No

(h) One home that is 1092 square feet is listed at $189,900. Is this home's price above or below average for a home of this size? What might be some reasons for this price? Above

29. Putting It Together: Smoking and Birth Weight It is well known that women should not smoke while pregnant, but what is the effect of smoking on a baby's birth weight? Researchers Ira M. Bernstein and associates "sought to estimate how the pattern of maternal smoking throughout pregnancy influences newborn size." To conduct this study, 160 pregnant, smoking women were enrolled in a prospective study. During the third trimester of pregnancy, the woman self-reported the number of cigarettes smoked. Urine samples were collected to measure cotinine levels (to assess nicotine levels). Birth weights (in grams) of the babies were obtained upon delivery. *Source*: Ira M. Bernstein et. al. "Maternal Smoking and Its Association with Birthweight." *Obstetrics & Gynecology* 106 (Part 1) 5, 2005.

(a) The histogram, drawn in MINITAB, shows the birth weight of babies whose mothers did not smoke in the third trimester of pregnancy (but did smoke prior to the third trimester). Describe the shape of the distribution. What is the class width of the histogram? Bell-shaped; 200

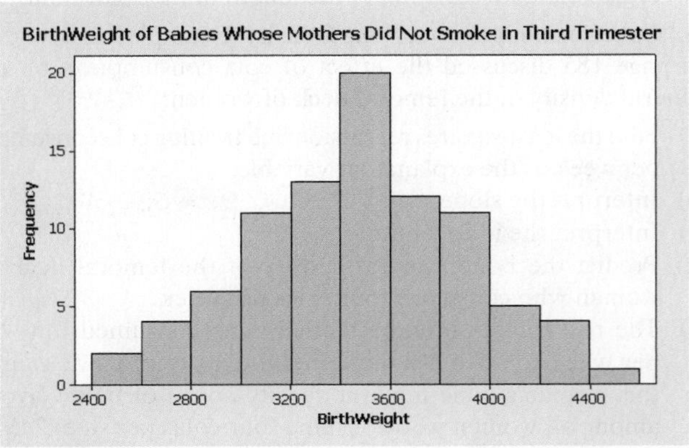

(b) Is this an observational study or a designed experiment?

(c) What does it mean for the study to be prospective?

(d) Why would the researchers conduct a urinalysis to measure cotinine levels? (b) Observational study

(e) What is the explanatory variable in the study? What is the response variable? Number of cigarettes; birth weight

(f) The scatter diagram of the data drawn using MINITAB is shown on the next page. What type of relation appears to exist between cigarette consumption in the third trimester and birth weight? Negative association

(g) Use the regression output from MINITAB to report the least-squares regression line between cigarette consumption and birth weight. $\hat{y} = -31.014x + 3456.04$

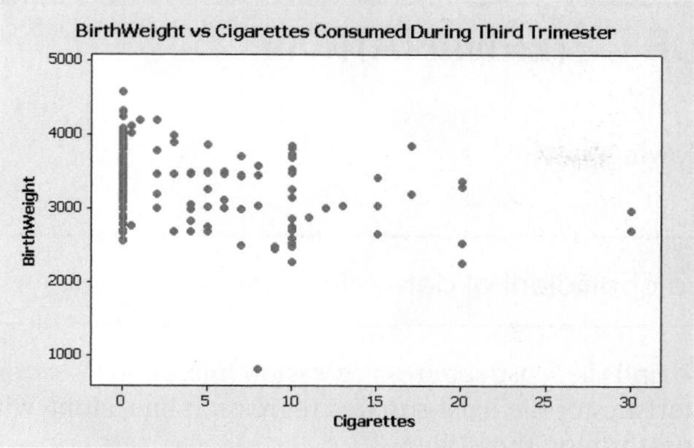

Regression Analysis: BirthWeight versus Cigarettes

```
The regression equation is
BirthWeight = 3456 − 31.0 Cigarettes

Predictor        Coef  SE Coef      T      P
Constant      3456.04    45.44  76.07  0.000
Cigarettes    −31.014    6.498  −4.77  0.000

S = 482.603    R − Sq = 12.6%    R − Sq(adj) = 12.0%
```

(h) Interpret the slope.

(i) Interpret the y-intercept.

(j) Would you recommend using this model to predict the birth weight of a baby whose mother smoked 10 cigarettes per day during the third trimester? Why? No

(k) Does this study demonstrate that smoking during the third trimester causes lower-birth-weight babies? No

(l) Cite some lurking variables that may confound the results of the study.

EXPLAINING THE CONCEPTS

30. What is a residual? What does it mean when a residual is positive?

31. Explain the phrase *outside the scope of the model*. Why is it dangerous to make predictions outside the scope of the model?

32. Explain the meaning of Legendre's quote given on page 197.

33. Explain what each point on the least-squares regression line represents.

34. Mark Twain, in his book *Life on the Mississippi* (1884), makes the following observation:

> *Therefore, the Mississippi between Cairo and New Orleans was twelve hundred and fifteen miles long one hundred and seventy-six years ago. It was eleven hundred and eighty after the cut-off of 1722. It was one thousand and forty after the American Bend cut-off. It has lost sixty-seven miles since. Consequently its length is only nine hundred and seventy-three miles at present.*
>
> *Now, if I wanted to be one of those ponderous scientific people, and "let on" to prove what had occurred in the remote past by what had occurred in a given time in the recent past, or what will occur in the far future by what has occurred in late years, what an opportunity is here! Geology never had such a chance, nor such exact data to argue from! Nor "development of species," either! Glacial epochs are great things, but they are vague—vague. Please observe:*
>
> *In the space of one hundred and seventy-six years the Lower Mississippi has shortened itself two hundred and forty-two miles. That is an average of a trifle over one mile and a third per year. Therefore, any calm person, who is not blind or idiotic, can see that in the Old Oolitic Silurian Period, just a million years ago next November, the Lower Mississippi River was upwards of one million three hundred thousand miles long, and stuck out over the Gulf of Mexico like a fishing-rod. And by the same token any person can see that seven hundred and forty-two years from now the Lower Mississippi will be only a mile and three-quarters long, and Cairo and New Orleans will have joined their streets together, and be plodding comfortably along under a single mayor and a mutual board of aldermen. There is something fascinating about Science. One gets such wholesale returns of conjecture out of such a trifling investment of fact.*

Discuss how Twain's observation relates to the material presented in this section.

Technology Step-By-Step

Determining the Least-Squares Regression Line

TI-83/84 Plus

Use the same steps that were followed to obtain the correlation coefficient. (See Section 4.1.)

MINITAB

1. With the explanatory variable in C1 and the response variable in C2, select the **Stat** menu and highlight **Regression**. Highlight **Regression . . . .**
2. Select the explanatory (predictor) variable and response variable and click OK.

Excel

1. Enter the explanatory variable in column A and the response variable in column B.
2. Select the **Data** menu and highlight **Data Analysis**.
3. Select the **Regression** option.
4. With the cursor in the Y-range cell, highlight the column that contains the response variable. With the cursor in the X-range cell, highlight the column that contains the explanatory variable. Select the Output Range. Press OK.

StatCrunch

1. Enter the explanatory variable in column var1 and the response variable in column var2. Name each column variable.
2. Select **Stat**, highlight **Regression**, and select **Simple Linear**.
3. Choose the explanatory variable for the X variable and the response variable for the Y variable. Click Calculate.

4.3 THE COEFFICIENT OF DETERMINATION

Preparing for This Section Before getting started, review the following:

- Outliers (Section 3.4, pp. 158–159)

OBJECTIVE **1** Compute and interpret the coefficient of determination

Note to Instructor
If you like, you can print out and distribute the Preparing for This Section quiz located in the Instructor's Resource Center. The purpose of the quiz is to verify that the students have the prerequisite knowledge for the section.

In Section 4.2, we showed how to find the least-squares regression line. In this section, we discuss additional characteristics of the least-squares regression line, along with graphical diagnostic tests to perform on these lines.

1 Compute and Interpret the Coefficient of Determination

Consider the club-head speed versus distance data introduced in Section 4.1. How could we predict the distance of a randomly selected shot? Our best guess might be the mean distance of all shots from the sample data given in Table 1, $\bar{y} = 266.75$ yards.

Now suppose we were told this particular shot resulted from a swing with a club-head speed of 103 mph. Knowing that a linear relation exists between club-head speed and distance, let's improve our estimate of the distance of the shot. In fact, we could use the least-squares regression line to adjust our guess to $\hat{y} = 3.1661(103) - 55.7966 = 270.3$ yards. In statistical terms, we say that some of the variation in distance is explained by the linear relation between club-head speed and distance.

The proportion of variation in the response variable that is explained by the least-squares regression line is called the *coefficient of determination*.

DEFINITION The **coefficient of determination, R^2,** measures the proportion of total variation in the response variable that is explained by the least-squares regression line.

In Other Words
The coefficient of determination is a measure of how well the least-squares regression line describes the relation between the explanatory and response variables. The closer R^2 is to 1, the better the line describes how changes in the explanatory variable affect the value of the response variable.

The coefficient of determination is a number between 0 and 1, inclusive. That is, $0 \le R^2 \le 1$. If $R^2 = 0$, the least-squares regression line has no explanatory value. If $R^2 = 1$, the least-squares regression line explains 100% of the variation in the response variable.

In Figure 16 a horizontal line is drawn at $\bar{y} = 266.75$, the predicted distance of a shot without any knowledge of club-head speed. If we know that the club-head speed is 103 miles per hour, we increase our guess to 270.3 yards. The difference between the predicted distance of 266.75 yards and the predicted distance of 270.3 yards is due to the fact that the club-head speed is 103 miles per hour. In other words, the difference between the prediction of $\hat{y} = 270.3$ and $\bar{y} = 266.75$ is explained by the linear relation between club-head speed and distance. The observed distance when club-head speed is 103 miles per hour is 274 yards (see Table 5 on page 195). The difference between our predicted value, $\hat{y} = 270.3$, and the actual value, $y = 274$, is due to factors (variables) other than the club-head speed (wind speed, position of the ball on the club face, and so on) and also to random error. The differences just discussed are called **deviations**.

In Other Words
The word *deviations* comes from deviate. To deviate means "to stray."

The deviation between the observed and mean values of the response variable is called the **total deviation**, so total deviation $= y - \bar{y}$. The deviation between the predicted and mean values of the response variable is called the **explained deviation**, so

Figure 16

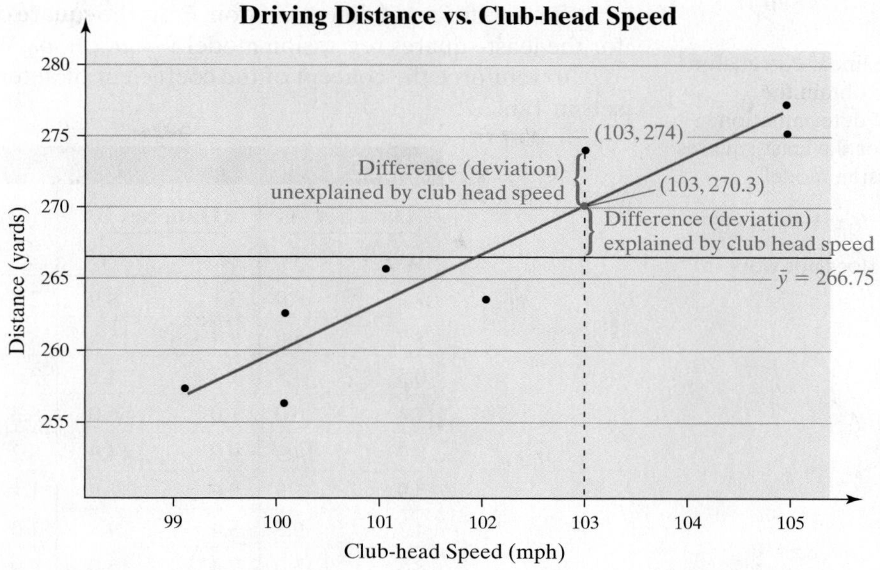

explained deviation $= \hat{y} - \bar{y}$. Finally, the deviation between the observed and predicted values of the response variable is called the **unexplained deviation**, so unexplained deviation $= y - \hat{y}$. See Figure 17.

Figure 17

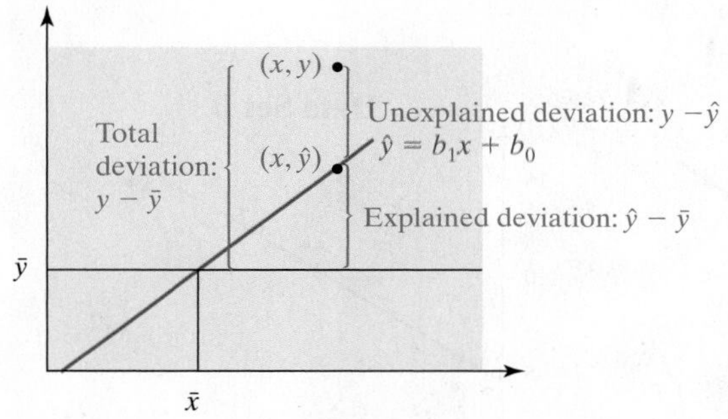

The figure illustrates that

$$\begin{aligned} \text{Total deviation} &= \text{unexplained deviation} + \text{explained deviation} \\ y - \bar{y} &= (y - \hat{y}) + (\hat{y} - \bar{y}) \end{aligned}$$

Although beyond the scope of this text, it can be shown that

$$\begin{aligned} \text{Total variation} &= \text{unexplained variation} + \text{explained variation} \\ \sum (y - \bar{y})^2 &= \sum (y - \hat{y})^2 + \sum (\hat{y} - \bar{y})^2 \end{aligned}$$

Dividing both sides by total variation, we obtain

$$1 = \frac{\text{unexplained variation}}{\text{total variation}} + \frac{\text{explained variation}}{\text{total variation}}$$

Subtracting $\dfrac{\text{unexplained variation}}{\text{total variation}}$ from both sides, we get

$$R^2 = \frac{\text{explained variation}}{\text{total variation}} = 1 - \frac{\text{unexplained variation}}{\text{total variation}}$$

Unexplained variation is found by summing the squares of the residuals, $\sum \text{residuals}^2 = \sum (y - \hat{y})^2$. So the smaller the sum of squared residuals, the smaller the unexplained variation and, therefore, the larger R^2 will be. Therefore, the closer the observed y's are to the regression line (the predicted y's), the larger R^2 will be.

CAUTION

Squaring the linear correlation coefficient to obtain the coefficient of determination works only for the least-squares linear regression model

$$\hat{y} = b_1x + b_0$$

The method does not work in general.

The coefficient of determination, R^2, is the square of the linear correlation coefficient for the least-squares regression model $\hat{y} = b_1x + b_0$. Written in symbols, $R^2 = r^2$.

To reinforce the concept of the coefficient of determination, consider the three data sets in Table 7.

TABLE 7

Data Set A		Data Set B		Data Set C	
x	y	x	y	x	y
3.6	8.9	3.1	8.9	2.8	8.9
8.3	15.0	9.4	15.0	8.1	15.0
0.5	4.8	1.2	4.8	3.0	4.8
1.4	6.0	1.0	6.0	8.3	6.0
8.2	14.9	9.0	14.9	8.2	14.9
5.9	11.9	5.0	11.9	1.4	11.9
4.3	9.8	3.4	9.8	1.0	9.8
8.3	15.0	7.4	15.0	7.9	15.0
0.3	4.7	0.1	4.7	5.9	4.7
6.8	13.0	7.5	13.0	5.0	13.0

Figures 18(a), (b), and (c) represent the scatter diagrams of data sets A, B, and C, respectively.

Figure 18

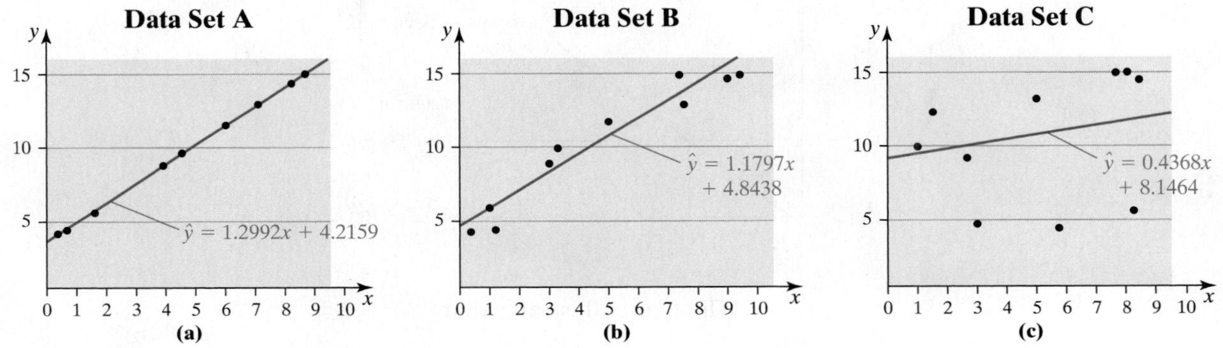

Notice that the y-values in each of the three data sets are the same. The variance of y is 17.49. In Figure 18(a), almost 100% of the variability in y can be explained by the least-squares regression line, because the data lie almost perfectly on a straight line. In Figure 18(b), a high percentage of the variability in y can be explained by the least-squares regression line because the data have a strong linear relation. Finally, in Figure 18(c), a low percentage of the variability in y is explained by the least-squares regression line. If x increases, we cannot easily predict the change in y. If we compute the coefficient of determination, R^2, for the three data sets in Table 7, we obtain the following results:

Data Set	Coefficient of Determination, R^2	Interpretation
A	99.99%	99.99% of the variability in y is explained by the least-squares regression line.
B	94.7%	94.7% of the variability in y is explained by the least-squares regression line.
C	9.4%	9.4% of the variability in y is explained by the least-squares regression line.

Notice that, as the explanatory ability of the line decreases, the coefficient of determination, R^2, also decreases.

EXAMPLE 1 Determining the Coefficient of Determination

Problem Determine and interpret the coefficient of determination, R^2, for the club-head speed versus distance data shown in Table 5 on page 195.

By Hand Approach

To compute R^2, we square the linear correlation coefficient, r, found in Example 3 from Section 4.1 on page 196.

By Hand Solution

$R^2 = r^2 = 0.939^2 = 0.882 = 88.2\%$

Technology Approach

We will use Excel to determine R^2. The steps for obtaining the coefficient of determination using the TI-83/84 Plus graphing calculator, MINITAB, Excel, and StatCrunch are given in the Technology Step-by Step on page 214.

Technology Solution

Figure 19 shows the results from Excel. The coefficient of determination is highlighted.

Figure 19 Summary Output

Regression Statistics	
Multiple R	0.938695838
R Square	0.881149876
Adjusted R Square	0.861341522
Standard Error	2.882638465
Observations	8

Interpretation 88.2% [Tech: 88.1%] of the variation in distance is explained by the least-squares regression line, and 11.8% of the variation in distance is explained by other factors.

Now Work Problems 5 and 7

4.3 ASSESS YOUR UNDERSTANDING

VOCABULARY AND SKILL BUILDING

1. The _____ _____ _____, R^2, measures the proportion of total variation in the response variable that is explained by the least-squares regression line. coefficient of determination

2. Total deviation = _____ deviation + _____ deviation

NW **3.** Match the coefficient of determination to the scatter diagram. The scales on the horizontal and vertical axis are the same for each scatter diagram.

(a) $R^2 = 0.58$ III **(b)** $R^2 = 0.90$ II

(c) $R^2 = 1$ IV **(d)** $R^2 = 0.12$ I

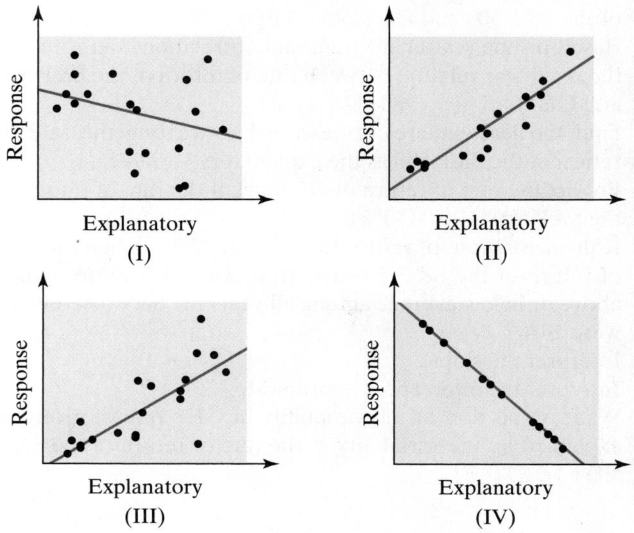

4. Use the linear correlation coefficient given to determine the coefficient of determination, R^2. Interpret each R^2.

(a) $r = -0.32$ $R^2 = 10.24\%$ **(b)** $r = 0.13$ $R^2 = 1.69\%$

(c) $r = 0.40$ $R^2 = 16\%$ **(d)** $r = 0.93$ $R^2 = 86.49\%$

2. explained; unexplained

APPLYING THE CONCEPTS

NW **5. The Other Old Faithful** Perhaps you are familiar with the famous Old Faithful geyser in Yellowstone National Park. Another Old Faithful geyser is located in Calistoga in California's Napa Valley. The following data represent the time (in minutes) between eruptions and the length of eruption for 11 randomly selected eruptions.

Time between Eruptions, x	Length of Eruption, y	Time between Eruptions, x	Length of Eruption, y
12.17	1.88	11.70	1.82
11.63	1.77	12.27	1.93
12.03	1.83	11.60	1.77
12.15	1.83	11.72	1.83
11.30	1.70		

Source: Ladonna Hansen, Park Curator

The coefficient of determination is 83.0%. Provide an interpretation of this value.

6. Concrete As concrete cures, it gains strength. The following data represent the 7-day and 28-day strength (in pounds per square inch) of a certain type of concrete.

7-Day Strength, x	28-Day Strength, y	7-Day Strength, x	28-Day Strength, y
2300	4070	2480	4120
3390	5220	3380	5020
2430	4640	2660	4890
2890	4620	2620	4190
3330	4850	3340	4630

The coefficient of determination is 57.5%. Provide an interpretation of this value.

Problems use the results from Problems 25–30 in Section 4.1 and Problems 17–22 in Section 4.2.

NW **7. An Unhealthy Commute** Use the results from Problem 25 in Section 4.1 and Problem 17 in Section 4.2 to:

(a) Determine the coefficient of determination, R^2. 96.1%

(b) Interpret the coefficient of determination and comment on the adequacy of the linear model.

8. Credit Scores Use the results from Problem 26 in Section 4.1 and Problem 18 in Section 4.2 to:

(a) Determine the coefficient of determination, R^2. 95.2%

(b) Interpret the coefficient of determination and comment on the adequacy of the linear model.

9. Height versus Head Circumference Use the results from Problem 27 in Section 4.1 and Problem 19 in Section 4.2 to:

(a) Compute the coefficient of determination, R^2. 83.0%

(b) Interpret the coefficient of determination and comment on the adequacy of the linear model.

10. American Black Bears Use the results from Problem 28 in Section 4.1 and Problem 20 in Section 4.2 to:

(a) Compute the coefficient of determination, R^2. 49.5%

(b) Interpret the coefficient of determination and comment on the adequacy of the linear model.

11. Weight of a Car versus Miles per Gallon Use the results from Problem 29 in Section 4.1 and Problem 21 in Section 4.2.

(a) What proportion of the variability in miles per gallon is explained by the relation between weight of the car and miles per gallon? 92.1%

(b) Interpret the coefficient of determination and comment on the adequacy of the linear model.

12. Bone Length Use the results from Problem 30 in Section 4.1 and Problem 22 in Section 4.2.

(a) What proportion of the variability in the length of the right tibia is explained by the relation between the length of the right humerus and the length of the right tibia? 90.5%

(b) Interpret the coefficient of determination and comment on the adequacy of the linear model.

13. Weight of a Car versus Miles per Gallon Suppose that we add the Dodge Viper to the data in Problem 21 in Section 4.2. A Dodge Viper weighs 3425 pounds and gets 11 miles per gallon.

Compute the coefficient of determination of the expanded data set. What effect does the addition of the Viper to the data set have on R^2? 58.0%; decreases

14. American Black Bears Suppose that we find a bear that is 205 cm tall and weighs 187 kg and add the bear to the data in Problem 20 from Section 4.2. (a) 71.7%; increases

Compute the coefficient of determination of the expanded data set. What effect does the additional bear have on R^2?

15. Putting It Together: Building a Financial Model In Section 3.2, we introduced one measure of risk used by financial analysts, the standard deviation of rate of return. In this problem we will learn about a second measure of risk of a stock, the beta of a stock. The following data represent the annual rate of return of General Electric (GE) stock and the annual rate of return of the Standard & Poor's 500 (S&P 500) Index for the past 15 years.

Year	Rate of Return of S&P 500	Rate of Return of GE
1996	0.203	0.402
1997	0.310	0.510
1998	0.267	0.410
1999	0.195	0.536
2000	−0.101	−0.060
2001	−0.130	−0.151
2002	−0.234	−0.377
2003	0.264	0.308
2004	0.090	0.207
2005	0.030	−0.014
2006	0.128	0.093
2007	−0.035	0.027
2008	−0.385	−0.593
2009	0.235	−0.102
2010	0.067	0.053

Source: finance.yahoo.com

(a) Draw a scatter diagram of the data treating the rate of return of the S&P 500 as the explanatory variable.

(b) Determine the correlation coefficient between rate of return of the S&P 500 and GE stock. 0.884

(c) Based on the scatter diagram and correlation coefficient, is there a linear relation between rate of return of the S&P 500 and GE? Yes, (d) $\hat{y} = 1.4020x - 0.0012$

(d) Find the least-squares regression line treating the rate of return of the S&P 500 as the explanatory variable.

(e) Predict the rate of return of GE stock if the rate of return of the S&P 500 is 0.10 (10%). 0.1390

(f) If the actual rate of return for GE was 13.2% when the rate of return of the S&P 500 was 10%, was GE's performance above or below average among all years the S&P 500 returns were 10%? Below

(g) Interpret the slope.

(h) Interpret the intercept, if appropriate.

(i) What proportion of the variability in GE's rate of return is explained by the variability in the rate of return of the S&P 500? 78.2%

16. Putting It Together: Exam Scores The following data represent scores earned by students in Sullivan's Elementary Algebra course for Chapter 2 (Linear Equations and Inequalities in One Variable) and Chapter 3 (Linear Equations and Inequalities in Two Variables). Completely summarize the relation between Chapter 2 and Chapter 3 exam scores, treating Chapter 2 exam scores as the explanatory variable. Write a report detailing the results of the analysis. What does the relationship say about the role Chapter 2 plays in a student's understanding of Chapter 3?

Chapter 2 Score	Chapter 3 Score
71.4	76.1
76.2	82.6
60.3	60.9
88.1	91.3
95.2	78.3
82.5	100
100	95.7
87.3	81.5
71.4	50.7
95.2	81.5
95.2	87.0
85.7	73.9
71.4	74.6
33.3	45.7
78.0	37.3
83.3	88.0
100	100
81.0	76.1
76.2	63.0

Source: Michael Sullivan

Consumer Reports® Fit to Drink

The taste, color, and clarity of the water coming out of home faucets have long concerned consumers. Recent reports of lead and parasite contamination have made unappetizing water a health, as well as an esthetic, concern. Water companies are struggling to contain cryptosporidium, a parasite that has caused outbreaks of illness that may be fatal to people with a weakened immune system. Even chlorination, which has rid drinking water of infectious organisms that once killed people by the thousands, is under suspicion as an indirect cause of miscarriages and cancer.

Concerns about water quality and taste have made home filtering increasingly popular. To find out how well they work, technicians at Consumer Reports tested 14 models to determine how well they filtered contaminants and whether they could improve the taste of our cabbage-soup testing mixture.

To test chloroform and lead removal, we added concentrated amounts of both to our water, along with calcium nitrate to increase water hardness. Every few days we analyzed the water to measure chloroform and lead content. The table contains the lead measurements for one of the models tested.

No. Gallons Processed	% Lead Removed
25	85
26	87
73	86
75	88
123	90
126	87
175	92
177	94

(a) Construct a scatter diagram of the data using % Lead Removed as the response variable.
(b) Does the relationship between No. Gallons Processed and % Lead Removed appear to be linear? If not, describe the relationship.
(c) Calculate the linear correlation coefficient between No. Gallons Processed and % Lead Removed. Based on the scatter diagram constructed in part (a) and your answer to part (b), is this measure useful? What is R^2? Interpret R^2.
(d) Fit a linear regression model to these data. Using this model, construct a residual plot. What does the residual plot suggest?
(e) Using statistical software or a graphing calculator with advanced statistical features, fit a quadratic model to these data. Construct a residual plot. What is R^2? Which model appears to fit the data better?
(f) Given the nature of the variables being measured, describe the type of curve you would expect to show the true relationship between these variables (linear, quadratic, exponential, S-shaped). Support your position.

***Note to Readers:** In many cases, our test protocol and analytical methods are more complicated than described in these examples. The data and discussions have been modified to make the material more appropriate for the audience.*

Technology Step-By-Step

Determining R^2 and Residual Plots

TI-83/84 Plus

The Coefficient of Determination, R^2

Use the same steps that were followed to obtain the correlation coefficient to obtain R^2. Diagnostics must be on.

Residual Plots

1. Enter the raw data in `L1` and `L2`. Obtain the least-squares regression line.
2. Access `STAT PLOT`. Select `Plot1`. Choose the scatter diagram icon and let XList be `L1`. Let YList be `RESID` by moving the cursor to YList, pressing 2nd `STAT`, and choosing the list entitled `RESID` under the NAMES menu.
3. Press `ZOOM` and select `9: ZoomStat`.

MINITAB

The Coefficient of Determination, R^2

This is provided in the standard regression output.

Residual Plots

Follow the same steps as those used to obtain the regression output (Section 4.2). Before selecting OK, click GRAPHS. In the cell that says "Residuals versus the variables," enter the name of the explanatory variable. Click OK.

Excel

The Coefficient of Determination, R^2

This is provided in the standard regression output.

Residual Plots

Follow the same steps as those used to obtain the regression output (Section 4.2). Before selecting OK, click **Residual Plots**. Click OK.

StatCrunch

The Coefficient of Determination, R^2

Follow the same steps used to obtain the least-squares regression line. The coefficient of determination is given as part of the output (R-sq).

Residual Plots

1. Enter the explanatory variable in column var1 and the response variable in column var2. Name each column variable.
2. Select **Stat**, highlight **Regression**, and select **Simple Linear**.
3. Choose the explanatory variable for the X variable and the response variable for the Y variable. Click Next>.
4. Click Next> until you reach the Graphics window. Select Residuals vs. X-values. Click Calculate. *Note:* In the output window, click Next-> to see the residual plot.s

4.4 CONTINGENCY TABLES AND ASSOCIATION

Preparing for This Section Before getting started, review the following:

- Side-by-side bar graphs (Section 2.1, pp. 66–68)

OBJECTIVES

1. Compute the marginal distribution of a variable
2. Use the conditional distribution to identify association among categorical data
3. Explain Simpson's Paradox

Note to Instructor

If you like, you can print out and distribute the Preparing for This Section quiz located in the Instructor's Resource Center. The purpose of the quiz is to verify that the students have the prerequisite knowledge for the section.

In Sections 4.1 to 4.3, we looked at techniques for summarizing relations between two quantitative variables. We now look at techniques for summarizing relations between two qualitative variables.

Consider the data (measured in thousands) in Table 8, which represent the employment status and level of education of all U.S. residents 25 years old or older in 2010. By definition, an individual is unemployed if he or she is actively seeking but is unable to find work. An individual is not in the labor force if he or she is not employed and not actively seeking employment.

TABLE 8

Employment Status	Level of Education: Did Not Finish High School	High School Graduate	Some College	Bachelor's Degree or Higher
Employed	9,993	34,130	34,067	43,992
Unemployed	1,806	3,838	3,161	2,149
Not in the labor force	19,969	30,246	18,373	16,290

Source: Bureau of Labor Statistics

Table 8 is referred to as a **contingency table**, or a **two-way table**, because it relates two categories of data. The **row variable** is employment status, because each row in the table describes the employment status of a group. The **column variable** is level of education. Each box inside the table is called a **cell**. For example, the cell corresponding to employed high school graduates is in the first row, second column. Each cell contains the frequency of the category: In 2010, 9993 thousand employed individuals had not finished high school.

The data in Table 8 describe two characteristics regarding the population of U.S. residents who are 25 years or older: their employment status and their level of education. We want to investigate whether the two variables are associated. For example, are individuals who have a higher level of education more likely to be employed? Just as we did in Sections 4.1 to 4.3, we will discuss both numerical and graphical methods for summarizing the data.

1 Compute the Marginal Distribution of a Variable

The first step in summarizing data in a contingency table is to determine the distribution of each variable separately. To do so, we create *marginal distributions.*

DEFINITION

A **marginal distribution** of a variable is a frequency or relative frequency distribution of either the row or column variable in the contingency table.

In Other Words
The distributions are called *marginal distributions* because they appear in the right and the bottom margin of the contingency table.

A marginal distribution removes the effect of either the row variable or the column variable in the contingency table.

To create a marginal distribution for a variable, we calculate the row and column totals for each category of the variable. The row totals represent the distribution of the row variable. The column totals represent the distribution of the column variable.

EXAMPLE 1 Determining Frequency Marginal Distributions

Problem Find the frequency marginal distributions for employment status and level of education from the data in Table 8.

Approach Find the row total for the category "employed" by adding the number of employed individuals who did not finish high school, who finished high school, and so on. Repeat this process for each category of employment status.

Find the column total for the category "did not finish high school" by adding the number of employed individuals, unemployed individuals, and individuals not in the labor force who did not finish high school. Repeat this process for each level of education.

Solution In Table 9 on the following page, the blue entries represent the marginal distribution of the row variable "employment status." For example, there were 9,993 + 34,130 + 34,067 + 43,992 = 122,182 thousand employed individuals in 2010. The red entries represent the marginal distribution of the column variable "level of education."

The marginal distribution for employment status removes the effect of level of education; the marginal distribution for level of education removes the effect of employment status. The marginal distribution of level of education shows there were about twice as many Americans with a bachelor's degree or higher as there were Americans who did not finish high school (62,431 thousand versus 31,768 thousand) in 2010. The marginal distribution of employment status shows that 122,182 thousand Americans were employed. The table also indicates that there were 218,014 thousand U.S. residents 25 years old or older.

TABLE 9

	Level of Education				
Employment Status	**Did Not Finish High School**	**High School Graduate**	**Some College**	**Bachelor's Degree or Higher**	Totals
Employed	9,993	34,130	34,067	43,992	122,182
Unemployed	1,806	3,838	3,161	2,149	10,954
Not in the labor force	19,969	30,246	18,373	16,290	84,878
Totals	31,768	68,214	55,601	62,431	**218,014**

Now Work Problem 9(a)

We can use the row and column totals obtained in Example 1 to calculate the relative frequency marginal distribution for level of education and employment status.

EXAMPLE 2 Determining Relative Frequency Marginal Distributions

Problem Determine the relative frequency marginal distribution for level of education and employment status from the data in Table 9.

Approach The relative frequency marginal distribution for the row variable, employment status, is found by dividing the row total for each employment status by the table total, 218,014. The relative frequency marginal distribution for the column variable, level of education, is found by dividing the column total for each level of education by the table total.

Solution Table 10 represents the relative frequency marginal distribution for each variable.

CAUTION

For relative frequency marginal distributions (such as in Table 10), row or column totals might not sum exactly to 1 due to rounding.

TABLE 10

	Level of Education				
Employment Status	**Did Not Finish High School**	**High School Graduate**	**Some College**	**Bachelor's Degree or Higher**	Relative Frequency Marginal Distribution
Employed	9,993	34,130	34,067	43,992	$\frac{122,182}{218,014} = 0.560$
Unemployed	1,806	3,838	3,161	2,149	$\frac{10,954}{218,014} = 0.050$
Not in the labor force	19,969	30,246	18,373	16,290	$\frac{84,878}{218,014} = 0.389$
Relative Frequency Marginal Distribution	$\frac{31,768}{218,014} = 0.146$	$\frac{68,214}{218,014} = 0.313$	$\frac{55,601}{218,014} = 0.255$	$\frac{62,431}{218,014} = 0.286$	**1**

Table 10 shows that 14.6% of U.S. residents 25 years old or older did not graduate from high school, and 56.0% of U.S. residents 25 years old or older were employed in 2010.

Now Work Problems 9(b) and (c)

2 Use the Conditional Distribution to Identify Association among Categorical Data

As we look at the information in Tables 9 and 10, we might ask whether a higher level of education is associated with a higher likelihood of being employed. If level of education does not play any role, we would expect the relative frequencies for employment status at each level of education to be close to the relative frequency marginal distribution for employment status given in blue in Table 10. So we would expect 56.0% of individuals who did not finish high school, 56.0% of individuals who finished high school, 56.0% of individuals with some college, and 56.0% of individuals with at least a bachelor's degree to be employed. If the relative frequencies for these various levels of education are different, we might associate this difference with the level of education.

CAUTION

To describe the association between two categorical variables, relative frequencies must be used because there are different numbers of observations for the categories.

The marginal distributions in Tables 9 and 10 allow us to see the distribution of either the row variable (employment status) or the column variable (level of education) but we do not get a sense of association from these tables.

When describing any association between two categories of data, we must use relative frequencies instead of frequencies, because frequencies are difficult to compare when there are different numbers of observations for the categories of a variable.

EXAMPLE 3 Comparing Two Categories of a Variable

Problem What proportion of the following groups of individuals is employed?

(a) Those who did not finish high school **(b)** High school graduates
(c) Those who finished some college **(d)** Those who have at least a bachelor's degree

Approach In part (a), we are asking, "Of the individuals who did not finish high school, what proportion is employed?" To determine this proportion, divide the number of employed individuals who did not finish high school by the number of people who did not finish high school. Repeat this process to answer parts (b)–(d).

Solution

(a) In 2010, 31,768 thousand individuals 25 years old or older did not finish high school. (See Table 9.) Of this number, 9993 thousand were employed. Therefore, $\frac{9993}{31,768} = 0.315$ represents the proportion of individuals who did not finish high school who are employed.

(b) In 2010, 68,214 thousand individuals 25 years old or older were high school graduates. Of this number, 34,130 thousand were employed. Therefore, $\frac{34,130}{68,214} = 0.500$ represents the proportion of individuals who graduated from high school who are employed.

(c) In 2010, 55,601 thousand individuals 25 years old or older had some college. Of this number, 34,067 thousand were employed. Therefore, $\frac{34,067}{55,601} = 0.613$ were employed.

(d) In 2010, 62,431 thousand individuals 25 years old or older had at least a bachelor's degree. Of this number, 43,992 thousand were employed. Therefore, $\frac{43,992}{62,431} = 0.705$ were employed.

We can see from these relative frequencies that as the level of education increases, the proportion of individuals employed increases.

In Other Words
Since we are finding the conditional distribution of employment status by level of education, the level of education is the *explanatory variable* and the employment status is the *response variable*.

The results in Example 3 are only partial. In general, we create a relative frequency distribution for each value of the explanatory variable. For our example, this means we would construct a relative frequency distribution for individuals who did not finish high school, a second relative frequency distribution for individuals who are high school graduates, and so on. These relative frequency distributions are called *conditional distributions*.

DEFINITION A **conditional distribution** lists the relative frequency of each category of the response variable, given a specific value of the explanatory variable in the contingency table.

An example should help to solidify our understanding of the definition.

EXAMPLE 4 Constructing a Conditional Distribution

Problem Find the conditional distribution of the response variable employment status by level of education, the explanatory variable, for the data in Table 8 on page 215. What is the association between level of education and employment status?

Approach First compute the relative frequency for each employment status, given that the individual did not finish high school. Next, compute the relative frequency for each employment status, given that the individual is a high school graduate. Continue computing the relative frequency for each employment status for the next two levels of education. This is the same approach taken in Example 3 for employed individuals.

Solution We first use the number of individuals who did not finish high school (31,768 thousand) as the denominator in computing the relative frequencies for each employment status.

We then use the number of individuals who graduated from high school as the denominator in computing relative frequencies for each employment status.

Next, compute the relative frequency for each employment status, given that the individual had some college and then given that the individual had at least a bachelor's degree. We obtain Table 11. Notice that the "Employed" row in Table 11 shows the results from Example 3.

TABLE 11

	Level of Education			
Employment Status	**Did Not Finish High School**	**High School Graduate**	**Some College**	**Bachelor's Degree or Higher**
Employed	$\frac{9,993}{31,768} = 0.315$	$\frac{34,130}{68,214} = 0.500$	$\frac{34,067}{55,601} = 0.613$	$\frac{43,992}{62,431} = 0.705$
Unemployed	$\frac{1,806}{31,768} = 0.057$	$\frac{3,838}{68,214} = 0.056$	$\frac{3,161}{55,601} = 0.057$	$\frac{2,149}{62,431} = 0.034$
Not in the labor force	$\frac{19,969}{31,768} = 0.629$	$\frac{30,246}{68,214} = 0.443$	$\frac{18,373}{55,601} = 0.330$	$\frac{16,290}{62,431} = 0.261$
Totals	1	1	1	1

Looking at the conditional distributions of employment status by level of education, associations become apparent. Read the information in Table 11 from left to right. As the amount of schooling (the explanatory variable) increases, the proportion employed within each category also increases. As the amount of schooling increases, the proportion not in the labor force decreases. The proportion unemployed with a bachelor's degree is much lower than those unemployed in the other three levels of education.

Information about individuals' levels of education provides insight into their employment status. For example, we might predict the number of employed individuals out of 100 to be about 56 because the employment rate for the entire United States is 56.0%. (See Table 10.) However, we would change our "guess" to 71 if we knew the 100 individuals had at least a bachelor's degree. Do you see why? The association between level of education and employment status allows us to adjust our predictions.

Now Work Problem 9(d)

In Example 4, we were able to see how a change in level of education affected employment status. Therefore, we are treating level of education as the explanatory variable and employment status as the response variable.

We could also construct a conditional distribution of level of education by employment status. In this situation, we would be treating employment status as the explanatory variable. The procedure is the same, except the distribution uses the rows instead of the columns. In this case, the explanatory variable is employment status and the response variable is level of education.

As is usually the case, a graph can provide a powerful depiction of the data.

EXAMPLE 5 Drawing a Bar Graph of a Conditional Distribution

Problem Using the results of Example 4, draw a bar graph that represents the conditional distribution of employment status by level of education.

Approach When drawing conditional bar graphs, label the values of the response variable on the horizontal axis, and use different colored bars for each value of the explanatory variable. So, draw four bars, side by side, for each level of education. Let the horizontal axis represent employment status and the vertical axis represent the relative frequency.

Solution See Figure 20. It is clear that as level of education increases, the proportion employed also increases. As the level of education increases, the proportion not in the labor force decreases.

Figure 20

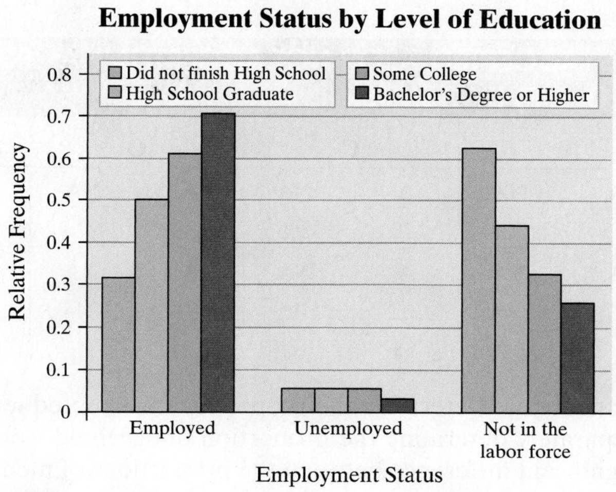

Now Work Problems 9(e) and (f)

The methods presented in this section for identifying the association between two categorical variables are different from the methods for measuring association between two quantitative variables. The measure of association in this section is based on whether there are differences in the relative frequencies of the response variable (employment status) for the different categories of the explanatory variable (level of education). If differences exist, we might attribute these differences to the explanatory variable.

In addition, because the data in Example 1 are observational, we do not make any statements regarding causation. Level of education is not said to be a cause of employment status, because a controlled experiment was not conducted.

3 Explain Simpson's Paradox

In Section 4.1, we discussed how a lurking variable can cause two quantitative variables to be correlated even though they are unrelated. This same phenomenon exists when exploring the relation between two qualitative variables.

EXAMPLE 6 Gender Bias at the University of California, Berkeley

Problem The data in Table 12 show the admission status and gender of students who applied to the University of California, Berkeley. From the data in Table 12, the proportion of accepted applications is $\frac{1748}{4425} = 0.395$. The proportion of accepted men is $\frac{1191}{2590} = 0.460$ and the proportion of accepted women is $\frac{557}{1835} = 0.304$. On the basis of these proportions, a gender bias suit was brought against the university. The university was shocked and claimed that program of study is a lurking variable that created the apparent association between admission status and gender. The university supplied Table 13 in its defense. Develop a conditional distribution by program of study to defend the university's admission policies.

Source: P. J. Bickel, E. A. Hammel, and J. W. O'Connell. "Sex Bias in Graduate Admissions: Data from Berkeley." *Science* 187(4175): 398–404, 1975.

TABLE 12

	Accepted (A)	Not Accepted (NA)	Total
Men	1191	1399	**2590**
Women	557	1278	**1835**
Total	**1748**	**2677**	**4425**

TABLE 13 ADMISSION STATUS (ACCEPTED, A, OR NOT ACCEPTED, NA), FOR SIX PROGRAMS OF STUDY (A, B, C, D, E, F) BY GENDER

	A		B		C		D		E		F	
Men	**A**	**NA**	**A**	**NA**	**A**	**NA**	**A**	**NA**	**A**	**NA**	**A**	**NA**
	511	314	353	207	120	205	138	279	53	138	16	256
Women	**A**	**NA**	**A**	**NA**	**A**	**NA**	**A**	**NA**	**A**	**NA**	**A**	**NA**
	89	19	17	8	202	391	131	244	94	299	24	317

Approach Determine the proportion of accepted men for each program of study and separately determine the proportion of accepted women for each program of study. A significant difference between the proportions of men and women accepted within each program of study may be evidence of discrimination; otherwise, the university should be exonerated.

Solution The proportion of men who applied to program A and were accepted is $\frac{511}{511 + 314} = 0.619$. The proportion of women who applied to program A and were accepted is $\frac{89}{89 + 19} = 0.824$. So, within program A, a higher proportion of women were accepted. Table 14 shows the conditional distribution for the remaining programs.

TABLE 14 CONDITIONAL DISTRIBUTION OF APPLICANTS ADMITTED FOR MEN AND WOMEN BY PROGRAM OF ADMISSION

	A	B	C	D	E	F
Men	$\frac{511}{825} = 0.619$	0.630	0.369	0.331	0.277	0.059
Women	0.824	0.680	0.341	0.349	0.239	0.070

Figure 21 shows the bar graph of the conditional distribution in Table 14. The blue bars represent the proportion of men admitted for each program; the green bars represent the proportion of women admitted for each program.

Figure 21

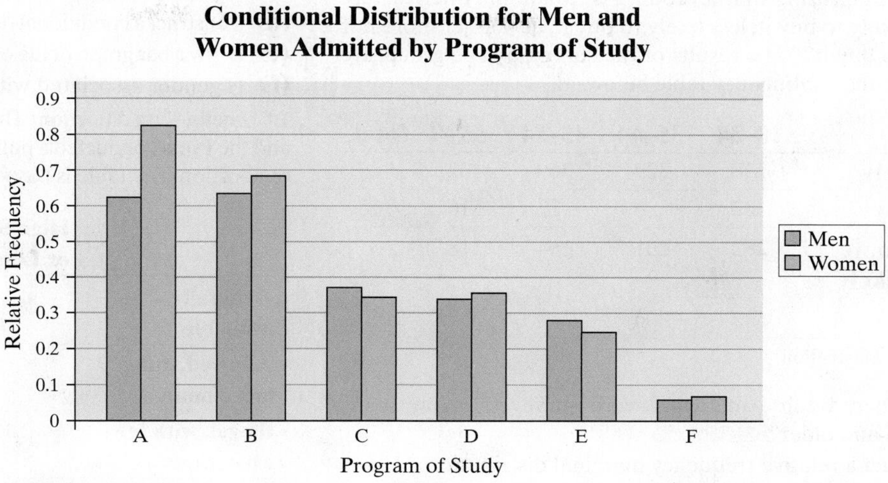

Four of the six programs actually had a higher proportion of women accepted! And the proportion of men accepted in programs C and E is not much higher than the proportion of women.

What caused the overall proportion of accepted men to be so much higher than the overall proportion of accepted women within the entire university, when, within each program, the proportions differ very little and may imply that women are accepted at a higher rate? The initial analysis did not account for the lurking variable, program of study. There were many more male applicants in programs A and B than female applicants, and these two programs happen to have higher acceptance rates. The higher acceptance rates in these programs led to the false conclusion that the University of California, Berkeley, was biased against gender in its admissions.

In Example 6, the association between gender and admission reverses when the lurking variable program of study is accounted for in the analysis. This illustrates a phenomenon known as **Simpson's Paradox**, which describes a situation in which an association between two variables inverts or goes away when a third variable is introduced to the analysis. The results of Example 6 serve as a warning that an apparent association between two variables may not exist once the effect of some third variable is accounted for in the study.

Now Work Problem 13

4.4 ASSESS YOUR UNDERSTANDING

VOCABULARY AND SKILL BUILDING

1. What is meant by a marginal distribution? What is meant by a conditional distribution?

2. Refer to Table 8. Is constructing a conditional distribution by level of education different from constructing a conditional distribution by employment status? If they are different, explain the difference.

3. Explain why we use the term *association* rather than *correlation* when describing the relation between two variables in this section.

4. Explain the idea behind Simpson's Paradox.

In Problems 5 and 6,

(a) Construct a frequency marginal distribution.

(b) Construct a relative frequency marginal distribution.

(c) Construct a conditional distribution by x.

(d) Draw a bar graph of the conditional distribution found in part (c).

5.

	x_1	x_2	x_3
y_1	20	25	30
y_2	30	25	50

6.

	x_1	x_2	x_3
y_1	35	25	20
y_2	65	75	80

APPLYING THE CONCEPTS

7. Made in America In a recent Harris Poll, a random sample of adult Americans (18 years and older) was asked, "When you see an ad emphasizing that a product is 'Made in America,' are you more likely to buy it, less likely to buy it, or neither more nor less likely to buy it?" The results of the survey, by age group, are presented in the contingency table below.

	18–34	35–44	45–54	55+	Total
More likely	238	329	360	402	1329
Less likely	22	6	22	16	66
Neither more nor less likely	282	201	164	118	765
Total	542	536	546	536	2160

Source: The Harris Poll

(a) How many adult Americans were surveyed? How many were 55 and older? 2160; 536

(b) Construct a relative frequency marginal distribution.

(c) What proportion of Americans are more likely to buy a product when the ad says "Made in America"? 0.615

(d) Construct a conditional distribution of likelihood to buy "Made in America" by age. That is, construct a conditional distribution treating age as the explanatory variable.

(e) Draw a bar graph of the conditional distribution found in part (d).

(f) Write a couple sentences explaining any relation between likelihood to buy and age.

8. Desirability Traits In a recent Harris Poll, a random sample of adult Americans (18 years and older) was asked, "Given a choice of the following, which one would you most want to be?" Results of the survey, by gender, are given in the contingency table.

	Richer	Thinner	Smarter	Younger	None of these	Total
Male	520	158	159	181	102	1120
Female	425	300	144	81	92	1042
Total	945	458	303	262	194	2162

Source: The Harris Poll

(a) How many adult Americans were surveyed? How many males were surveyed? 2162; 1120, (c) 0.437

(b) Construct a relative frequency marginal distribution.

(c) What proportion of adult Americans want to be richer?

(d) Construct a conditional distribution of desired trait by gender. That is, construct a conditional distribution treating gender as the explanatory variable.

(e) Draw a bar graph of the conditional distribution found in part (d).

(f) Write a couple sentences explaining any relation between desired trait and gender.

NW **9. Party Affiliation** Is there an association between party affiliation and gender? The following data represent the gender and party affiliation of registered voters based on a random sample of 802 adults.

	Female	Male
Republican	105	115
Democrat	150	103
Independent	150	179

Source: Star Tribune Minnesota Poll

(a) Construct a frequency marginal distribution.

(b) Construct a relative frequency marginal distribution.

(c) What proportion of registered voters considers themselves to be Independent? 0.410

(d) Construct a conditional distribution of party affiliation by gender.

(e) Draw a bar graph of the conditional distribution found in part (d).

(f) Is gender associated with party affiliation? If so, how? Yes

10. Feelings on Abortion The Pew Research Center for the People and the Press conducted a poll in which it asked about the availability of abortion. The table is based on the results of the survey.

	High School or Less	Some College	College Graduate
Generally available	90	72	113
Allowed, but more limited	51	60	77
Illegal, with few exceptions	125	94	69
Never permitted	51	14	17

Source: Pew Research Center for the People and the Press

(a) Construct a frequency marginal distribution.

(b) Construct a relative frequency marginal distribution.

(c) What proportion of college graduates feel that abortion should never be permitted? 0.062

(d) Construct a conditional distribution of people's feelings about the availability of abortion by level of education.

(e) Draw a bar graph of the conditional distribution found in part (d).

(f) Is level of education associated with opinion on the availability of abortion? If so, how? Yes

11. Health and Happiness The General Social Survey asks questions about one's happiness and health. One would think that health plays a role in one's happiness. Use the data in the table to determine whether healthier people tend to also be happier. Treat level of health as the explanatory variable.

	Poor	Fair	Good	Excellent	Total
Not too happy	696	1,386	1,629	732	4,443
Pretty happy	950	3,817	9,642	5,195	19,604
Very happy	350	1,382	4,520	5,095	11,347
Total	1,996	6,585	15,791	11,022	35,394

Source: General Social Survey

12. Happy in Your Marriage? The General Social Survey asks questions about one's happiness in marriage. Is there an association between gender and happiness in marriage? Use the data in the table to determine if gender is associated with happiness in marriage. Treat gender as the explanatory variable.

	Male	Female	Total
Very happy	7,609	7,942	15,551
Pretty happy	3,738	4,447	8,185
Not too happy	259	460	719
Total	11,606	12,849	24,455

Source: General Social Survey

NW **13. Smoking Is Healthy?** Could it be that smoking actually increases survival rates among women? The following data represent the 20-year survival status and smoking status of 1314 English women who participated in a cohort study from 1972 to 1992.

	Smoking Status		
	Smoker (S)	**Nonsmoker (NS)**	**Total**
Dead	139	230	369
Alive	443	502	945
Total	582	732	1314

Source: David R. Appleton et al. "Ignoring a Covariate: An Example of Simpson's Paradox." *American Statistician* 50(4), 1996

(a) What proportion of the smokers was dead after 20 years? What proportion of the nonsmokers was dead after 20 years? What does this imply about the health consequences of smoking? 0.239; 0.314

The data in the table above do not take into account a variable that is strongly related to survival status, age. The data shown next give the survival status of women and their age at the beginning of the study. For example, 14 women who were 35 to 44 at the beginning of the study were smokers and dead after 20 years.

	Age Group													
	18–24		25–34		35–44		45–54		55–64		65–74		75 or older	
	S	NS	S	NS	S	NS	S	NS	S	NS	S	NS	S	NS
Dead	2	1	3	5	14	7	27	12	51	40	29	101	13	64
Alive	53	61	121	152	95	114	103	66	64	81	7	28	0	0

(b) Determine the proportion of 18- to 24-year-old smokers who were dead after 20 years. Determine the proportion of 18- to 24-year-old nonsmokers who were dead after 20 years. 0.036; 0.016

(c) Repeat part (b) for the remaining age groups to create a conditional distribution of survival status by smoking status for each age group.

(d) Draw a bar graph of the conditional distribution from part (c).

(e) Write a short report detailing your findings.

14. Treating Kidney Stones Researchers conducted a study to determine which of two treatments, A or B, is more effective in the treatment of kidney stones. The results of their experiment are given in the table.

	Treatment A	Treatment B	Total
Effective	273	289	562
Not effective	77	61	138
Total	350	350	700

Source: C. R. Charig, D. R. Webb, S. R. Payne, and O. E. Wickham. "Comparison of Treatment Real Calculi by Operative Surgery, Percutaneous Nephrolithotomi, and Extracorporeal Shock Wave Lithoripsy." *British Medical Journal* 292(6524): 879–882.

(a) Which treatment appears to be more effective? Why? B

The data in the table above do not take into account the size of the kidney stone. The data shown next indicate the effectiveness of each treatment for both large and small kidney stones.

	Small Stones		Large Stones	
	A	**B**	**A**	**B**
Effective	81	234	273	55
Not effective	6	36	77	25

(b) Determine the proportion of small kidney stones that were effectively dealt with using treatment A. Determine the proportion of small kidney stones that were effectively dealt with using treatment B. 0.931; 0.867

(c) Repeat part (b) for the large stones to create a conditional distribution of effectiveness by treatment for each stone size. 0.78; 0.688

(d) Draw a bar graph of the conditional distribution from part (c).

(e) Write a short report detailing your findings.

Technology Step-By-Step

Contingency Tables and Association

MINITAB

1. Enter the values of the row variable in column C1 and the corresponding values of the column variable in C2. The frequency for the cell is entered in C3. For example, the data in Table 8 would be entered as follows:

↓	C1-T	C2-T	C3
1	Employed	No High School	9993
2	Unemployed	No High School	1806
3	Not in Labor Force	No High School	19969
4	Employed	HS	34130
5	Unemployed	HS	3838
6	Not in Labor Force	HS	30246
7	Employed	Some College	34067
8	Unemployed	Some College	3161
9	Not in Labor Force	Some College	18373
10	Employed	Bachelors	43992
11	Unemployed	Bachelors	2149
12	Not in Labor Force	Bachelors	16290

2. Select the Stat menu and highlight Tables. Then select Descriptive Statistics...
3. In the cell "For Rows:" enter C1. In the cell "For Columns:" enter C2. In the cell "Frequencies" enter C3. Click the Options button and make sure the radio button for Display marginal statistics for Rows and columns is checked. Click OK. Click the Categorical Variables button and then select the summaries you desire. Click OK twice.

StatCrunch

1. Enter the contingency table into the spreadsheet. The first column should be the row variable. For example, for the data in Table 8, the first column would be employment status. Each subsequent column would be the counts of each category of the column variable. For the data in Table 8, enter the counts for each level of education. Title each column (including the first column indicating the row variable).
2. Select **Stat**, highlight **Tables**, select **Contingency**, then highlight **with summary**.
3. Select the column variables. Then select the label of the row variable. For example, the data in Table 8 has four column variables (Did Not Finish High School, and so on) and the row label is employment status. Click Next>.
4. Decide what values you want displayed. Typically, we choose row percent and column percent for this section. Click Calculate.

CHAPTER 4 REVIEW

Summary

In this chapter we looked at describing the relation between two quantitative variables (Sections 4.1 to 4.3) and between two qualitative variables (Section 4.4).

The first step in describing the relation between two quantitative variables is to draw a scatter diagram. The explanatory variable is plotted on the horizontal axis and the corresponding response variable on the vertical axis. The scatter diagram can be used to discover whether the relation between the explanatory and the response variables is linear. In addition, for linear relations, we can judge whether the linear relation shows positive or negative association.

A numerical measure for the strength of linear relation between two quantitative variables is the linear correlation coefficient. It is a number between -1 and 1, inclusive. Values of the correlation coefficient near -1 are indicative of a negative linear relation between the two variables. Values of the correlation coefficient near $+1$ indicate a positive linear relation between the two variables. If the correlation coefficient is near 0, then little *linear* relation exists between the two variables.

Be careful! Just because the correlation coefficient between two quantitative variables indicates that the variables are linearly related, it does not mean that a change in one variable *causes* a change in a second variable. It could be that the correlation is the result of a lurking variable.

Once a linear relation between the two variables has been discovered, we describe the relation by finding the least-squares regression line. This line best describes the linear relation between the explanatory and response variables. We can use the least-squares regression line to predict a value of the response variable for a given value of the explanatory variable.

The coefficient of determination, R^2, measures the percent of variation in the response variable that is explained by the least-squares regression line. It is a measure between

0 and 1, inclusive. The closer R^2 is to 1, the more explanatory value the line has. Whenever a least-squares regression line is obtained, certain diagnostics must be performed. These include verifying that the linear model is appropriate, verifying the residuals have constant variance, and checking for outliers and influential observations.

Section 4.4 introduced methods that allow us to describe any association that might exist between two qualitative variables. This is done through contingency tables. Both marginal and conditional distributions allow us to describe the effect one variable might have on the other variable in the study. We also construct bar graphs to see the association between the two variables in the study. Again, just because two qualitative variables are associated does not mean that a change in one variable *causes* a change in a second variable. We also looked at Simpson's Paradox, which represents situations in which an association between two variables inverts or goes away when a third (lurking) variable is introduced into the analysis.

Vocabulary

Bivariate data (p. 177)
Response variable (p. 178)
Explanatory variable (p. 178)
Predictor variable (p. 178)
Scatter diagram (p. 178)
Positively associated (p. 179)
Negatively associated (p. 179)
Linear correlation coefficient (p. 180)
Correlation matrix (p. 183)
Lurking variable (p. 185)
Residual (p. 196)
Least-squares regression line (p. 197)
Slope (p. 197)
y-intercept (p. 197)
Outside the scope of the model (p. 200)
Coefficient of determination (p. 208)
Deviation (p. 208)
Total deviation (p. 208)
Explained deviation (p. 208)
Unexplained deviation (p. 209)
Contingency (or two-way) table (p. 215)
Row variable (p. 215)
Column variable (p. 215)
Cell (p. 215)
Marginal distribution (p. 215)
Conditional distribution (p. 218)
Simpson's Paradox (p. 221)

Formulas

Correlation Coefficient

$$r = \frac{\sum\left(\frac{x_i - \bar{x}}{s_x}\right)\left(\frac{y_i - \bar{y}}{s_y}\right)}{n - 1}$$

Equation of the Least-Squares Regression Line

$\hat{y} = b_1 x + b_0$

where

$\hat{y}$ is the predicted value of the response variable

$b_1 = r \cdot \frac{s_y}{s_x}$ is the slope of the least-squares regression line

$b_0 = \bar{y} - b_1\bar{x}$ is the y-intercept of the least-squares regression line

Coefficient of Determination, R^2

$$R^2 = \frac{\text{explained variation}}{\text{total variation}} = 1 - \frac{\text{unexplained variation}}{\text{total variation}}$$

$= r^2$ for the least-squares regression model $\hat{y} = b_1x + b_0$

Objectives

Section	You should be able to...	Example	Review Exercises
4.1	1 Draw and interpret scatter diagrams (p. 178)	1,3	2(b), 3(a), 6(a),
	2 Describe the properties of the linear correlation coefficient (p. 180)	page 181	13
	3 Compute and interpret the linear correlation coefficient (p. 182)	2,3	2(c), 3(b)
	4 Determine whether a linear relation exists between two variables (p. 184)	4	2(d), 3(c)
	5 Explain the difference between correlation and causation (p. 185)	5	9, 12
4.2	1 Find the least-squares regression line and use the line to make predictions (p. 196)	2,3	1(a), 1(b), 4(a), 4(d), 5(a), 5(c), 6(d), 14(c)
	2 Interpret the slope and y-intercept of the least-squares regression line (p. 199)	page 200	1(c), 1(d), 4(c), 5(b), 14(b)
	3 Compute the sum of squared residuals (p. 201)	4	6(f), 6(g)
4.3	1 Compute and interpret the coefficient of determination (p. 208)	1	1(e), 7, 8
4.4	1 Compute the marginal distribution of a variable (p. 215)	1, 2	10(b)
	2 Use the conditional distribution to identify association among categorical data (p. 217)	3–5	10(d), 10(e), 10(f)
	3 Explain Simpson's Paradox (p. 219)	6	11

Review Exercises

1. Basketball Spreads In sports betting, Las Vegas sports books establish winning margins for a team that is favored to win a game. An individual can place a wager on the game and will win if the team bet upon wins after accounting for the spread. For example, if Team A is favored by 5 points and wins the game by 7 points, then a bet on Team A is a winning bet. However, if Team A wins the game by only 3 points, then a bet on Team A is a losing bet. For NCAA Division I basketball games, a least-squares regression with explanatory variable home team Las Vegas spread, x, and response variable home team winning margin, y, is $\hat{y} = 1.007x - 0.012$. *Source:* Justin Wolfers. "Point Shaving: Corruption in NCAA Basketball"

(a) Predict the winning margin if the home team is favored by 3 points. 3.009 points

(b) Predict the winning margin (of the visiting team) if the visiting team is favored by 7 points (this is equivalent to the home team being favored by −7 points). 7.061 points

(c) Interpret the slope.

(d) Interpret the y-intercept.

(e) The coefficient of determination is 0.39. Interpret this value.

2. Fat and Calories in Cheeseburgers A nutritionist was interested in developing a model that describes the relation between the amount of fat (in grams) in cheeseburgers at fast-food restaurants and the number of calories. She obtains the following data from the Web sites of the companies.

Sandwich (Restaurant)	Fat Content (g)	Calories
Quarter-pound Single with Cheese (Wendy's)	20	430
Whataburger (Whataburger)	39	750
Cheeseburger (In-n-Out)	27	480
Big Mac (McDonald's)	29	540
Quarter-pounder with cheese (McDonald's)	26	510
Whopper with cheese (Burger King)	47	760
Jumbo Jack (Jack in the Box)	35	690
Double Steakburger with cheese (Steak 'n Shake)	38	632

Source: Each company's Web site

(a) The researcher wants to use fat content to predict calories. Which is the explanatory variable? Fat content

(b) Draw a scatter diagram of the data.

(c) Compute the linear correlation coefficient between fat content and calories. 0.944

(d) Does a linear relation exist between fat content and calories in fast-food restaurant sandwiches? Yes

3. Apartments The following data represent the square footage and rent for apartments in the borough of Queens and Nassau County, New York. (b) Queens: 0.909; Nassau: 0.867

Queens (New York City)		Nassau County (Long Island)	
Square Footage, x	Rent per Month, y	Square Footage, x	Rent per Month, y
500	650	1100	1875
588	1215	588	1075
1000	2000	1250	1775
688	1655	556	1050
825	1250	825	1300
460	1805	743	1475
1259	2700	660	1315
650	1200	975	1400
560	1250	1429	1900
1073	2350	800	1650
1452	3300	1906	4625
1305	3100	1077	1395

Source: apartments.com

(a) On the same graph, draw a scatter diagram for both Queens and Nassau County apartments treating square footage as the explanatory variable. Be sure to use a different plotting symbol for each group.

(b) Compute the linear correlation coefficient between square footage and rent for each location.

(c) Does a linear relation exist between the two variables for each location? Yes

(d) Does location appear to be a factor in rent?

4. Using the data and results from Problem 2, do the following:

(a) Find the least-squares regression line treating fat content as the explanatory variable. $\hat{y} = 13.7334x + 150.9469$

(b) Draw the least-squares regression line on the scatter diagram.

(c) Interpret the slope and y-intercept, if appropriate.

(d) Predict the number of calories in a sandwich that has 30 grams of fat. 562.9 calories

(e) A cheeseburger from Sonic has 700 calories and 42 grams of fat. Is the number of calories for this sandwich above or below average among all sandwiches with 42 grams? Below

5. Using the Queens data and results from Problem 3, do the following:

(a) Find the least-squares regression line, treating square footage as the explanatory variable. $\hat{y} = 2.2091x - 34.3148$

(b) Interpret the slope and y-intercept, if appropriate. (c) Below

(c) Is the rent on the 825-square-foot apartment in the data above or below average among 825-square-foot apartments?

6.

x	10	14	17	18	21
y	105	94	82	76	63

(a) Draw a scatter diagram treating x as the explanatory variable and y as the response variable.

(b) Select two points from the scatter diagram, and find the equation of the line containing the points selected.

(c) Graph the line found in part (b) on the scatter diagram.

(d) Determine the least-squares regression line.

(e) Graph the least-squares regression line on the scatter diagram.

(f) Compute the sum of the squared residuals for the line found in part (b). 24.406 (d) $\hat{y} = -3.8429x + 145.4857$

(g) Compute the sum of the squared residuals for the least-squares regression line found in part (d). 16.271

(h) Comment on the fit of the line found in part (b) versus the least-squares regression line found in part (d).

7. Use the results from Problem 2 to compute and interpret R^2. 89.1%

8. Use Queens data and the results from Problems 3 and 5 to compute and interpret R^2. 82.7%

9. Shark Attacks The correlation between the number of visitors to the state of Florida and the number of shark attacks since 1990 is 0.946. Should the number of visitors to Florida be reduced in an attempt to reduce shark attacks? Explain your reasoning.
Source: Florida Museum of Natural History

10. New versus Used Car Satisfaction Are you more likely to be satisfied with your automobile purchase when it is new or used? The following data represent the level of satisfaction of the buyer for both new and used cars.

	New	Used	Total
Not too satisfied	11	25	36
Pretty satisfied	78	79	157
Extremely satisfied	118	85	203
Total	207	189	396

Source: General Social Survey

(a) How many were extremely satisfied with their automobile purchase? 203

(b) Construct a relative frequency marginal distribution.

(c) What proportion of consumers was extremely satisfied with their automobile purchase? 0.513

(d) Construct a conditional distribution of satisfaction by purchase type (new or used).

(e) Draw a bar graph of the conditional distribution found in part (d).

(f) Do you think that the purchase type (new versus used) is associated with satisfaction? Yes

11. Unemployment Rates Recessions are an economic phenomenon that are often defined as two consecutive quarters of reduced national output. One measure to assess the severity of a recession is the rate of unemployment. The table shows the number of employed and unemployed residents of the United States at the peak of each recession (in thousands).

	Recession of 1982	Recession of 2009
Employed	98.9	130.1
Unemployed	11.3	14.5

Source: Bureau of Labor Statistics

(a) Determine the unemployment rate for each recession. Which recession appears worse as measured by unemployment rate? Note: Unemployment rate = unemployed/(employed + unemployed). 1982: 10.3%; 2009: 10.0%

The data in the table above do not account for level of education. The following data show the unemployment rate by level of education for each recession.

	Recession of 1982			Recession of 2009		
	Less than high school	**High school**	**Bachelor's degree or higher**	**Less than high school**	**High school**	**Bachelor's degree or higher**
Employed	20.3	58.2	20.4	10.0	76.7	43.4
Unemployed	3.9	6.6	0.8	2.0	10.3	2.2

Source: Bureau of Labor Statistics

(b) Determine the unemployment rate for each level of education for both recessions.

(c) Draw a bar graph of the conditional distribution from part (b).

(d) Write a report that suggests the recession of 2009 is worse than that of 1982.

12. (a) The correlation between number of married residents and number of unemployed residents in 2008 for the 50 states and Washington, DC, is 0.922. A scatter diagram of the data drawn in MINITAB is shown on the following page. What type of relation appears to exist between number of marriages and number unemployed?

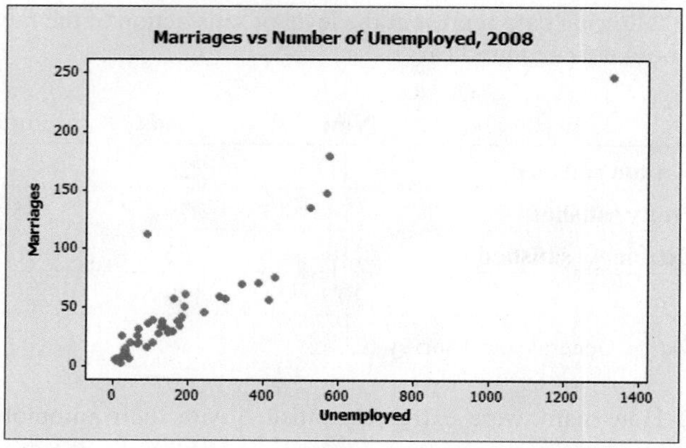

(b) A lurking variable is in the relation presented in part (a). Use the following correlation matrix to explain how population is a lurking variable.

Correlations: Unemployed, Population, Marriages

	Unemployed	Population
Population	0.979	
Marriages	0.922	0.947

Cell Contents: Pearson correlation

(c) The correlation between unemployment rate (number unemployed divided by population size) and marriage rate (number married divided by population size) in 2008 for the 50 states and Washington, DC, is 0.050. A scatter diagram between unemployment rate and marriage rate drawn in MINITAB is shown next. What type of relation appears to exist between unemployment rate and marriage rate?

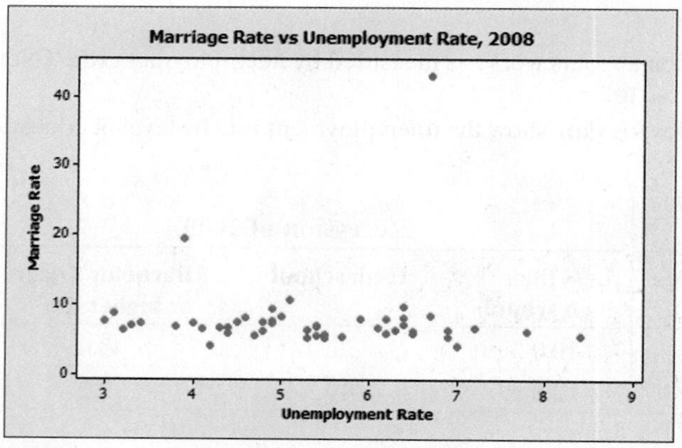

(d) Write a few sentences to explain the danger in using correlation to conclude that a relation exists between two variables without considering lurking variables.

13. List the eight properties of the linear correlation coefficient.

14. Analyzing a Newspaper Article In a newspaper article written in the *Chicago Tribune* on September 29, 2002, it was claimed that poorer school districts have shorter school days.

(a) The following scatter diagram was drawn using the data supplied in the article. In this scatter diagram, the response variable is length of the school day (in hours) and the explanatory variable is percent of the population that is low income. The correlation between length and income is -0.461. Do you think that the scatter diagram and correlation coefficient support the position of the article?

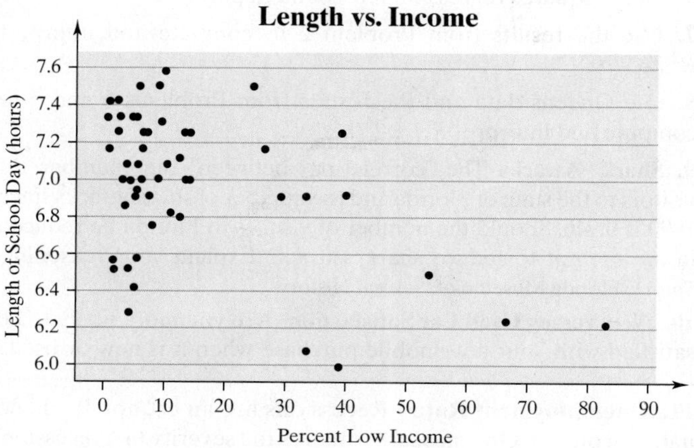

(b) The least-squares regression line between length, y, and income, x, is $\hat{y} = -0.0102x + 7.11$. Interpret the slope of this regression line. Does it make sense to interpret the y-intercept? If so, interpret the y-intercept.

(c) Predict the length of the school day for a district in which 20% of the population is low income by letting $x = 20$.

(d) This same article included average Prairie State Achievement Examination (PSAE) scores for each district. The article implied that shorter school days result in lower PSAE scores. The correlation between PSAE score and length of school day is 0.517. A scatter diagram treating PSAE as the response variable is shown next. Do you believe that a longer school day is positively associated with a higher PSAE score?

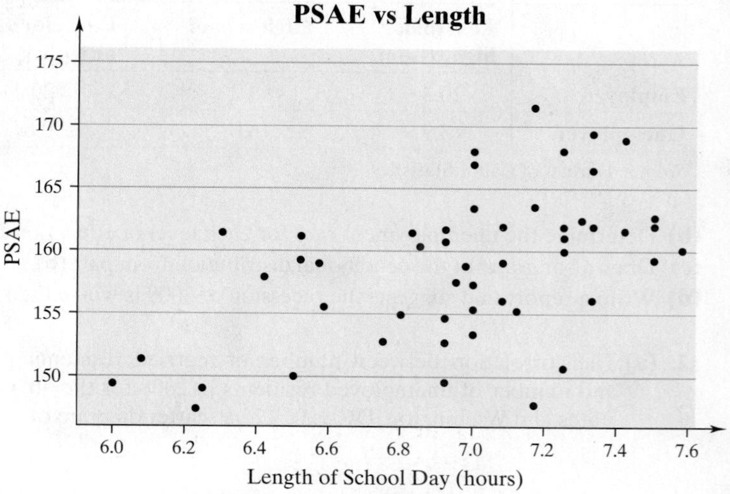

(e) The correlation between percentage of the population that is low income and PSAE score is −0.720. A scatter diagram treating PSAE score as the response variable is shown next. Do you believe that percentage of the population that is low income is negatively associated with PSAE score?

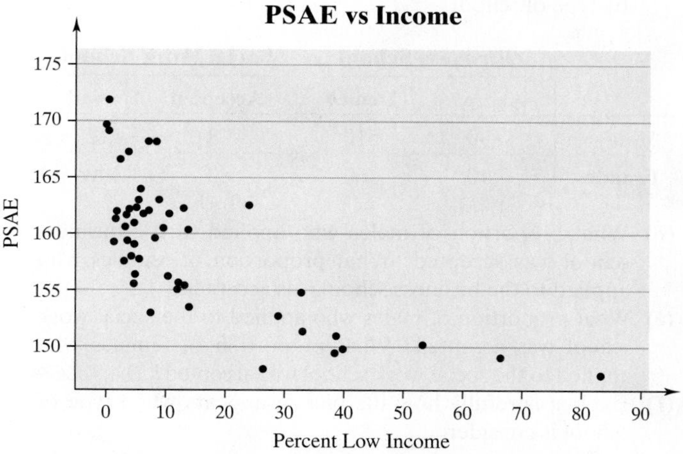

(f) Can you think of any lurking variables that are playing a role in this study?

Problems in the chapter test are labeled by section.objective. For example, 2.3 means Section 2, Objective 3.

CHAPTER TEST

1. Crickets make a chirping noise by sliding their wings rapidly over each other. Perhaps you have noticed that the number of chirps seems to increase with the temperature. The following data list the temperature (in degrees Fahrenheit) and the number of chirps per second for the striped ground cricket.

Temperature, x	Chirps per Second, y	Temperature, x	Chirps per Second, y
88.6	20.0	71.6	16.0
93.3	19.8	84.3	18.4
80.6	17.1	75.2	15.5
69.7	14.7	82.0	17.1
69.4	15.4	83.3	16.2
79.6	15.0	82.6	17.2
80.6	16.0	83.5	17.0
76.3	14.4		

Source: George W. Pierce. *The Songs of Insects*. Cambridge, MA: Harvard University Press, 1949, pp. 12–21.

(a) What is the likely explanatory variable in these data? Why?
1.1 **(b)** Draw a scatter diagram of the data. (a) Temperature
1.3 **(c)** Compute the linear correlation coefficient between temperature and chirps per second. 0.835
1.4 **(d)** Does a linear relation exist between temperature and chirps per second? Yes
2.1 **(e)** Find the least-squares regression line treating temperature as the explanatory variable and chirps per second as the response variable. $\hat{y} = 0.2119x - 0.3091$
2.2 **(f)** Interpret the slope and y-intercept, if appropriate.
(g) Predict the chirps per second if it is 83.3°F. 17.3
(h) A cricket chirps 15 times per second when the temperature is 82°F. Is this rate of chirping above or below average at this temperature? Below
(i) It is 55°F outside. Would you recommend using the linear model found in part (e) to predict the number of chirps per second of a cricket? Why or why not? No
3.1 **(j)** Compute and interpret R^2. 69.7%

1.5 **2.** A researcher collects data regarding the percent of all births to unmarried women and the number of violent crimes for the 50 states and Washington, DC. The scatter diagram along with the least-squares regression line obtained from MINITAB is shown. The correlation between percent of births to unmarried women and the number of violent crimes is 0.667. A politician looks over the data and claims that, for each 1% decrease in births to single mothers, violent crimes will decrease by 23. Therefore, percent of births to single mothers needs to be reduced in an effort to decrease violent crimes. Is there anything wrong with the reasoning of the politician? Explain.

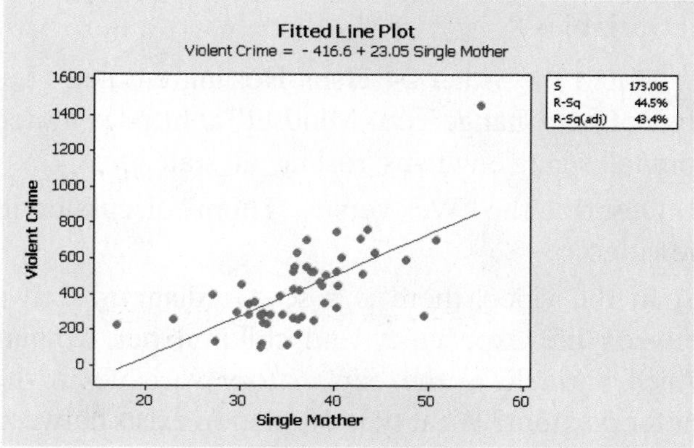

3. What is the relationship between education and belief in Heaven? The data on the following page represent the highest level of education and belief in Heaven for a random sample of adult Americans.

	Yes, Definitely	Yes, Probably	No, Probably Not	No, Definitely Not	Total
Less than high school	316	66	21	9	**412**
High school	956	296	122	65	**1439**
Bachelor's	267	131	62	64	**524**
Total	**1539**	**493**	**205**	**138**	**2375**

Source: General Social Survey

4.1 **(a)** Construct a relative frequency marginal distribution.
(b) What proportion of adult Americans in the survey definitely believe in Heaven? 0.648
4.2 **(c)** Construct a conditional distribution of belief in Heaven by level of education.
4.2 **(d)** Draw a bar graph of the conditional distribution found in part (c).
(e) Is there an association between level of education and belief in Heaven? Yes

4. Consider the following contingency table, which relates the number of applicants accepted to a college and gender.

	Accepted	Denied
Male	98	522
Female	90	200

4.2 **(a)** Construct a conditional distribution of acceptance status by gender.
(b) What proportion of males was accepted? What proportion of females was accepted? 0.158; 0.310
(c) What might you conclude about the admittance policies of the school?
A lurking variable is the type of school applied to. This particular college has two programs of study: business and social work. The following table shows applications by type of school.

	Business School		Social Work School	
	Accepted	Denied	Accepted	Denied
Male	90	510	8	12
Female	10	60	80	140

(d) What proportion of males who applied to the business school was accepted? What proportion of females who applied to the business school was accepted? 0.15; 0.143
(e) What proportion of males who applied to the social work school was accepted? What proportion of females who applied to the social work school was accepted? 0.4; 0.364
4.3 **(f)** Explain carefully how the bias disappears when type of school is considered.

1.2 **5.** What would you say about a set of quantitative bivariate data whose linear correlation coefficient is -1? What would a scatter diagram of the data look like?

6. If the slope of a least-squares regression line is negative, what could be said about the correlation between the explanatory and response variable? Negative

1.2 **7.** What does it mean if a linear correlation coefficient is close to zero? Draw two scatter diagrams for which the linear correlation coefficient is close to zero. No linear relation

Making an Informed Decision

Relationships among Variables on a World Scale

The purpose of this Decisions Project is to decide on two quantitative variables, see how the relationship between these variables has changed over time, and determine the most current relationship between the variables.

1. Watch the video by Hans Rosling entitled "Let My Dataset Change Your Mindset" at http://www.ted.com/talks/lang/eng/hans_rosling_at_state.html.

(a) Describe the "We" versus "Them" discussion in the video.

(b) In the video, there is a scatter diagram drawn between life expectancy and children per woman. Which variable is the explanatory variable in the scatter diagram? What type of relation exists between the two variables? How has the relationship changed over time when considering "We" versus "Them"?

2. Click the Data tab on the GapMinder Web site. Download the data for life expectancy and children per woman. Draw a scatter diagram of the data. Determine the linear correlation coefficient between the two variables. Be careful; some countries may not have both variables measured, so they will need to be excluded from the analysis.

3. Find the least-squares regression line between life expectancy and children per woman. Interpret the slope of the regression line.

4. Is the life expectancy of the United States above or below average given the number of children per woman?

5. Choose any two variables in the GapMinder library and write a report detailing the relationship between the variables over time. Does the data reflect your intuition about the relationship?

The Chapter 4 Case Study is located on the CD that accompanies this text.

PART

3 Probability and Probability Distributions

We now take a break from the statistical process. Why? In Chapter 1, we mentioned that inferential statistics uses methods that generalize results obtained from a sample to the population and measures their reliability. But how can we measure their reliability? It turns out that the methods we use to generalize results from a sample to a population are based on probability and probability models. Probability is a measure of the likelihood that something occurs. This part of the course will focus on methods for determining probabilities.

5 Probability

OUTLINE

Making an Informed Decision

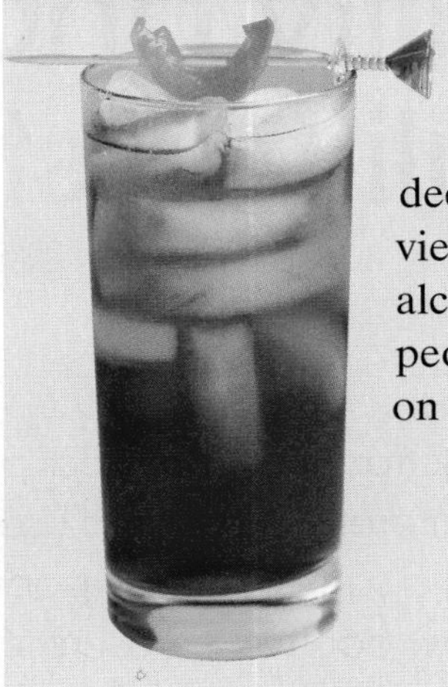

You are at a party and everyone is having a good time. Unfortunately, a few of the party-goers are having a little too much to drink. If they decide to drive home, what are the risks? Perhaps a view of some scary statistics about the effects of alcohol on one's driving skills will convince more people not to drink and drive. See the Decisions project on page 296.

PUTTING IT TOGETHER

In Chapter 1, we learned the methods of collecting data. In Chapters 2 through 4, we learned how to summarize raw data using tables, graphs, and numbers. As far as the statistical process goes, we have discussed the collecting, organizing, and summarizing parts of the process.

Before we begin to analyze data, we introduce probability, which forms the basis of inferential statistics. Why? Well, we can think of the probability of an outcome as the likelihood of observing that outcome. If something has a high likelihood of happening, it has a high probability (close to 1). If something has a small chance of happening, it has a low probability (close to 0). For example, it is unlikely that we would roll five straight sixes when rolling a single die, so this result has a low probability. In fact, the probability of rolling five straight sixes is 0.0001286. If we were playing a game in which a player threw five sixes in a row with a single die, we would consider the player to be lucky (or a cheater) because it is such an unusual occurrence. Statisticians use probability in the same way. If something occurs that has a low probability, we investigate to find out "what's up."

5.1 PROBABILITY RULES

Preparing for This Section Before getting started, review the following:

- Relative frequency (Section 2.1, p. 64)

OBJECTIVES

1. Apply the rules of probabilities
2. Compute and interpret probabilities using the empirical method
3. Compute and interpret probabilities using the classical method
4. Use simulation to obtain data based on probabilities
5. Recognize and interpret subjective probabilities

Note to Instructor
If you like, you can print out and distribute the Preparing for This Section quiz located in the Instructor's Resource Center. The purpose of the quiz is to verify that the students have the prerequisite knowledge for the section.

Flip a coin 100 times and compute the proportion of heads observed after each toss of the coin. Suppose the first flip is tails, so the proportion of heads is $\frac{0}{1}$; the second flip is heads, so the proportion of heads is $\frac{1}{2}$; the third flip is heads, so the proportion of heads is $\frac{2}{3}$, and so on. Plot the proportion of heads versus the number of flips and obtain the graph in Figure 1(a). We repeat this experiment with the results shown in Figure 1(b).

Figure 1

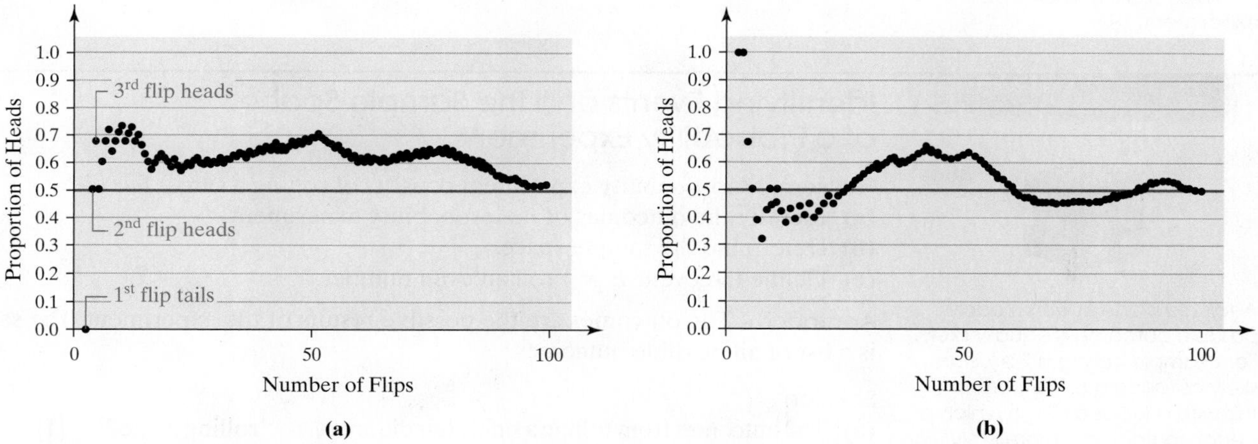

Note to Instructor
Consider assigning the "Demonstrating the Law of Large Numbers" activity from the Student Activity Workbook.

The graphs in Figures 1(a) and (b) show that in the short term (fewer flips) the observed proportion of heads is different and unpredictable for each experiment. As the number of flips increases, however, both graphs tend toward a proportion of 0.5. This is the basic premise of probability. **Probability** deals with experiments that yield random short-term results or **outcomes** yet reveal long-term predictability. **The long-term proportion in which a certain outcome is observed is the probability of that outcome.** So we say that the probability of observing a head is $\frac{1}{2}$ or 50% or 0.5 because, as we flip the coin more times, the proportion of heads tends toward $\frac{1}{2}$. This phenomenon, which is illustrated in Figure 1, is referred to as the *Law of Large Numbers.*

In Other Words
Probability describes how likely it is that some event will happen. If we look at the proportion of times an event has occurred over a long period of time (or over a large number of trials), we can be more certain of the likelihood of its occurrence.

The Law of Large Numbers

As the number of repetitions of a probability experiment increases, the proportion with which a certain outcome is observed gets closer to the probability of the outcome.

CAUTION
Probability is a measure of the likelihood of events that have yet to occur. Prior to flipping a coin, we say the probability of observing a head is $\frac{1}{2}$. However, once the coin is flipped, the probability is no longer $\frac{1}{2}$ since the outcome has been determined.

Note to Instructor
In-class activity: Have each student flip a coin three times. Use the results to find the probability of a head. Repeat this experiment a few times. Use the cumulative results to illustrate the Law of Large Numbers. You may also want to use the probability applet to demonstrate the Law of Large Numbers.

Jakob Bernoulli (a major contributor to the field of probability) believed that the Law of Large Numbers was common sense. This is evident in the following quote from his text *Ars Conjectandi*: "For even the most stupid of men, by some instinct of nature, by himself and without any instruction, is convinced that the more observations have been made, the less danger there is of wandering from one's goal."

In probability, an **experiment** is any process with uncertain results that can be repeated. The result of any single trial of the experiment is not known ahead of time. However, the results of the experiment over many trials produce regular patterns that enable us to predict with remarkable accuracy. For example, an insurance company cannot know whether a particular 16-year-old driver will have an accident over the course of a year. However, based on historical records, the company can be fairly certain that about three out of every ten 16-year-old male drivers will have a traffic accident during the course of a year. Therefore, of 816,000 male 16-year-old drivers (816,000 repetitions of the experiment), the insurance company is fairly confident that about 30%, or 244,800, will have an accident. This prediction helps to establish insurance rates for any particular 16-year-old male driver.

We now introduce some terminology that we will need to study probability.

DEFINITIONS

The **sample space,** *S*, of a probability experiment is the collection of all possible outcomes.

An **event** is any collection of outcomes from a probability experiment. An event consists of one outcome or more than one outcome. We will denote events with one outcome, sometimes called *simple events*, e_i. In general, events are denoted using capital letters such as *E*.

In Other Words
An outcome is the result of one trial of a probability experiment. The sample space is a list of all possible results of a probability experiment.

EXAMPLE 1

Identifying Events and the Sample Space of a Probability Experiment

A *fair die* is one in which each possible outcome is equally likely. For example, rolling a 2 is just as likely as rolling a 5. We contrast this with a *loaded* die, in which a certain outcome is more likely. For example, if rolling a 1 is more likely than rolling a 2, 3, 4, 5, or 6, the die is loaded.

Now Work Problem 19

Problem A probability experiment consists of rolling a single *fair* die.

(a) Identify the outcomes of the probability experiment.
(b) Determine the sample space.
(c) Define the event E = "roll an even number."

Approach The outcomes are the possible results of the experiment. The sample space is a list of all possible outcomes.

Solution

(a) The outcomes from rolling a single fair die are e_1 = "rolling a one" = {1}, e_2 = "rolling a two" = {2}, e_3 = "rolling a three" = {3}, e_4 = "rolling a four" = {4}, e_5 = "rolling a five" = {5}, and e_6 = "rolling a six" = {6}.
(b) The set of all possible outcomes forms the sample space, $S = \{1, 2, 3, 4, 5, 6\}$. There are 6 outcomes in the sample space.
(c) The event E = "roll an even number" = {2, 4, 6}.

1 Apply the Rules of Probabilities

In the following probability rules, the notation $P(E)$ means "the probability that event E occurs."

In Other Words
Rule 1 states that probabilities less than 0 or greater than 1 are not possible. Therefore, probabilities such as 1.32 or −0.3 are not possible. Rule 2 states when the probabilities of all outcomes are added, the sum must be 1.

Rules of Probabilities

1. The probability of any event E, $P(E)$, must be greater than or equal to 0 and less than or equal to 1. That is, $0 \le P(E) \le 1$.
2. The sum of the probabilities of all outcomes must equal 1. That is, if the sample space $S = \{e_1, e_2, \cdots, e_n\}$, then

$$P(e_1) + P(e_2) + \cdots + P(e_n) = 1$$

A **probability model** lists the possible outcomes of a probability experiment and each outcome's probability. A probability model must satisfy Rules 1 and 2 of the rules of probabilities.

EXAMPLE 2 A Probability Model

TABLE 1

Color	Probability
Brown	0.13
Yellow	0.14
Red	0.13
Blue	0.24
Orange	0.20
Green	0.16

Source: M&Ms

The color of a plain M&M milk chocolate candy can be brown, yellow, red, blue, orange, or green. Suppose a candy is randomly selected from a bag. Table 1 shows each color and the probability of drawing that color.

To verify that this is a probability model, we must show that Rules 1 and 2 on the previous page are satisfied.

Each probability is greater than or equal to 0 and less than or equal to 1, so Rule 1 is satisfied.

Because

$$0.13 + 0.14 + 0.13 + 0.24 + 0.20 + 0.16 = 1$$

Rule 2 is also satisfied. The table is an example of a probability model.

Now Work Problem 7

Note to Instructor

It is important to emphasize the interpretation of probability given here. We will use this interpretation again when we discuss confidence intervals.

If an event is **impossible**, the probability of the event is 0. If an event is a **certainty**, the probability of the event is 1.

The closer a probability is to 1, the more likely the event will occur. The closer a probability is to 0, the less likely the event will occur. For example, an event with probability 0.8 is more likely to occur than an event with probability 0.75. An event with probability 0.8 will occur about 80 times out of 100 repetitions of the experiment, whereas an event with probability 0.75 will occur about 75 times out of 100.

Be careful of this interpretation. An event with a probability of 0.75 does not have to occur 75 times out of 100. Rather, we *expect* the number of occurrences to be close to 75 in 100 trials. The more repetitions of the probability experiment, the closer the proportion with which the event occurs will be to 0.75 (the Law of Large Numbers).

One goal of this course is to learn how probabilities can be used to identify *unusual events*.

DEFINITION

An **unusual event** is an event that has a low probability of occurring.

In Other Words

An unusual event is an event that is not likely to occur.

Typically, an event with a probability less than 0.05 (or 5%) is considered unusual, but this *cutoff point* is not set in stone. The researcher and the context of the problem determine the probability that separates unusual events from *not so unusual events*.

For example, suppose that the probability of being wrongly convicted of a capital crime punishable by death is 3%. Even though 3% is below our 5% cutoff point, this probability is too high in light of the consequences (death for the wrongly convicted), so the event is not unusual (unlikely) enough. We would want this probability to be much closer to zero.

Note to Instructor

Ask students to cite some real-life examples of unusual events.

Now suppose that you are planning a picnic on a day having a 3% chance of rain. In this context, you would consider "rain" an unusual (unlikely) event and proceed with the picnic plans.

The point is this: Selecting a probability that separates unusual events from not so unusual events is subjective and depends on the situation. Statisticians typically use cutoff points of 0.01, 0.05, and 0.10.

CAUTION

A probability of 0.05 should not always be used to separate unusual events from not so unusual events.

Next, we introduce three methods for determining the probability of an event: the empirical method, the classical method, and the subjective method.

2 Compute and Interpret Probabilities Using the Empirical Method

Because probabilities deal with the long-term proportion a particular outcome is observed, we begin our discussion of determining probabilities using the idea of relative frequency. Probabilities computed in this manner rely on empirical evidence, that is, evidence based on the outcomes of a probability experiment.

Approximating Probabilities Using the Empirical Approach

The probability of an event E is approximately the number of times event E is observed divided by the number of repetitions of the experiment.

$$P(E) \approx \text{relative frequency of } E = \frac{\text{frequency of } E}{\text{number of trials of experiment}} \quad \textbf{(1)}$$

Note to Instructor
Consider assigning the "Finding the Probability of Getting Heads" activity from the Student Activity Workbook.

The probability obtained using the empirical approach is approximate because different *runs* of the probability experiment lead to different outcomes and, therefore, different estimates of $P(E)$. Consider flipping a coin 20 times and recording the number of heads. Use the results of the experiment to estimate the probability of obtaining a head. Now repeat the experiment. Because the results of the second run of the experiment do not necessarily yield the same results, we cannot say the probability *equals* the relative frequency; rather we say the probability is *approximately* the relative frequency. As we increase the number of trials of a probability experiment, our estimate becomes more accurate (again, the Law of Large Numbers).

EXAMPLE 3 Using Relative Frequencies to Approximate Probabilities

A pit boss wanted to approximate the probability of rolling a seven using a pair of dice that have been in use for a while. To do this, he rolls the dice 100 times and records 15 sevens. The probability of rolling a seven is approximately $\frac{15}{100} = 0.15$.

The probabilities computed from a survey of a random sample of individuals are approximate. We can think of a survey as a probability experiment, since the results of a survey are likely to be different each time the survey is conducted because different people are included.

EXAMPLE 4 Building a Probability Model from Survey Data

TABLE 2

Means of Travel	Frequency
Drive alone	153
Carpool	22
Public transportation	10
Walk	5
Other means	3
Work at home	7

Problem The data in Table 2 represent the results of a survey in which 200 people were asked their means of travel to work.

(a) Use the survey data to build a probability model for means of travel to work.

(b) Estimate the probability that a randomly selected individual carpools to work. Interpret this result.

(c) Would it be unusual to randomly select an individual who walks to work?

Approach To build a probability model, we estimate the probability of each outcome by determining its relative frequency.

Solution

(a) There are $153 + 22 + \cdots + 7 = 200$ individuals in the survey. The individuals can be thought of as trials of the probability experiment. The relative frequency

TABLE 3	
Means of Travel	**Probability**
Drive alone	0.765
Carpool	0.11
Public transportation	0.05
Walk	0.025
Other means	0.015
Work at home	0.035

for "drive alone" is $\frac{153}{200} = 0.765$. We compute the relative frequency of the other outcomes similarly and obtain the probability model in Table 3.

(b) From Table 3, we estimate the probability to be 0.11 that a randomly selected individual carpools to work. We interpret this result by saying, "If we were to survey 1000 individuals, we would expect about 110 to carpool to work."

(c) The probability that an individual walks to work is approximately 0.025. This means if we survey 1000 individuals, we would expect about 25 to walk to work. Therefore, it is unusual to randomly choose a person who walks to work.

Now Work Problem 35

3 Compute and Interpret Probabilities Using the Classical Method

The empirical method obtains an approximate probability of an event by conducting a probability experiment.

The classical method of computing probabilities does not require that a probability experiment actually be performed. Rather, it relies on counting techniques.

The classical method of computing probabilities requires *equally likely outcomes*. An experiment has **equally likely outcomes** when each outcome has the same probability of occurring. For example, in throwing a fair die once, each of the six outcomes in the sample space, {1, 2, 3, 4, 5, 6}, has an equal chance of occurring. Contrast this situation with a loaded die in which a five or six is twice as likely to occur as a one, two, three, or four.

Computing Probability Using the Classical Method

If an experiment has n equally likely outcomes and if the number of ways that an event E can occur is m, then the probability of E, $P(E)$, is

$$P(E) = \frac{\text{number of ways that } E \text{ can occur}}{\text{number of possible outcomes}} = \frac{m}{n} \qquad \textbf{(2)}$$

So, if S is the sample space of this experiment,

$$P(E) = \frac{N(E)}{N(S)} \qquad \textbf{(3)}$$

where $N(E)$ is the number of outcomes in E, and $N(S)$ is the number of outcomes in the sample space.

EXAMPLE 5 Computing Probabilities Using the Classical Method

Problem A pair of fair dice is rolled.

(a) Compute the probability of rolling a seven.

(b) Compute the probability of rolling "snake eyes"; that is, compute the probability of rolling a two.

(c) Comment on the likelihood of rolling a seven versus rolling a two.

Approach To compute probabilities using the classical method, count the number of outcomes in the sample space and count the number of ways the event can occur.

Solution

(a) There are 36 equally likely outcomes in the sample space, as shown in Figure 2 on the following page.

Figure 2

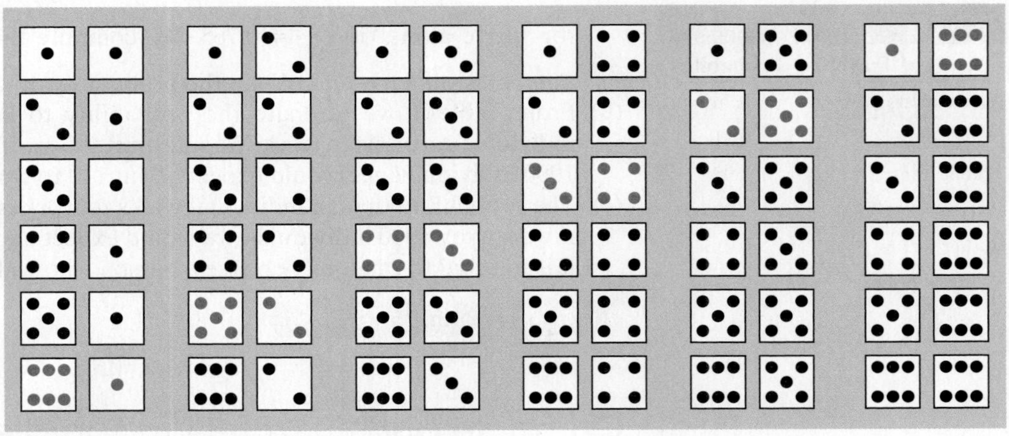

Historical Note

Girolamo Cardano (in English Jerome Cardan) was born in Pavia, Italy, on September 24, 1501. He was an illegitimate child whose father was Fazio Cardano, a lawyer in Milan. Fazio was a part-time mathematician and taught Girolamo. In 1526, Cardano earned his medical degree. Shortly thereafter, his father died. Unable to maintain a medical practice, Cardano spent his inheritance and turned to gambling to help support himself. Cardano developed an understanding of probability that helped him to win. Eventually, Cardano became a lecturer of mathematics at the Piatti Foundation. This position allowed him to practice medicine and develop a favorable reputation as a doctor. In 1545, he published his greatest work, *Ars Magna*. His booklet on probability, *Liber de Ludo Alaea*, was not printed until 1663, 87 years after his death. The booklet is a practical guide to gambling, including cards, dice, and cheating.

So, $N(S) = 36$. The event E = "roll a seven" = {(1, 6), (2, 5), (3, 4), (4, 3), (5, 2), (6, 1)}has six outcomes, so $N(E) = 6$. Using Formula (3),

$$P(E) = P(\text{roll a seven}) = \frac{N(E)}{N(S)} = \frac{6}{36} = \frac{1}{6}$$

(b) The event F = "roll a two" = {(1, 1)} has one outcome, so $N(F) = 1$.

$$P(F) = P(\text{roll a two}) = \frac{N(F)}{N(S)} = \frac{1}{36}$$ Use Formula (3).

(c) Since $P(\text{roll a seven}) = \frac{6}{36}$ and $P(\text{roll a two}) = \frac{1}{36}$, rolling a seven is six times as likely as rolling a two. In other words, in 36 rolls of the dice, we *expect* to observe about 6 sevens and only 1 two.

The empirical probability of rolling a seven, 0.15, obtained in Example 3, is not too different from the classical probability of rolling a seven, $\frac{1}{6} \approx 0.167$, obtained in Example 5(a). In fact, if the dice are fair, we expect the relative frequency of sevens to get closer to 0.167 as we increase the number of rolls of the dice. In other words, the empirical probability will get closer to the classical probability as the number of trials of the experiment increases. If the two probabilities do not get closer together, we may suspect that the dice are not fair.

In simple random sampling, each individual has the same chance of being selected. Therefore, we can use the classical method to compute the probability of obtaining a specific sample.

EXAMPLE 6 Computing Probabilities Using Equally Likely Outcomes

Problem Sophia has three tickets to a concert, but Yolanda, Michael, Kevin, and Marissa all want to go to the concert with her. To be fair, Sophia randomly selects the two people who can go with her.

(a) Determine the sample space of the experiment. In other words, list all possible simple random samples of size $n = 2$.
(b) Compute the probability of the event "Michael and Kevin attend the concert."
(c) Compute the probability of the event "Marissa attends the concert."
(d) Interpret the probability in part (c).

Approach First, determine the outcomes in the sample space by making a table. The probability of an event is the number of outcomes in the event divided by the number of outcomes in the sample space.

Solution

(a) The sample space is listed in Table 4.
(b) We have $N(S) = 6$, and there is one way the event "Michael and Kevin attend the concert" can occur. Therefore, the probability that Michael and Kevin attend the concert is $\frac{1}{6}$.

TABLE 4		
Yolanda, Michael	Yolanda, Kevin	Yolanda, Marissa
Michael, Kevin	Michael, Marissa	Kevin, Marissa

(c) We have $N(S) = 6$, and there are three ways the event "Marissa attends the concert" can occur. The probability that Marissa will attend is $\frac{3}{6} = 0.5 = 50\%$.

(d) If we conducted this experiment many times, about 50% of the experiments would result in Marissa attending the concert.

Now Work Problems 29 and 43

EXAMPLE 7 Comparing the Classical Method and Empirical Method

Problem Suppose that a survey asked 500 families with three children to disclose the gender of their children and found that 180 of the families had two boys and one girl.

(a) Estimate the probability of having two boys and one girl in a three-child family using the empirical method.

(b) Compute and interpret the probability of having two boys and one girl in a three-child family using the classical method, assuming boys and girls are equally likely.

Approach To answer part (a), determine the relative frequency of the event "two boys and one girl." To answer part (b), count the number of ways the event "two boys and one girl" can occur and divide this by the number of possible outcomes for this experiment.

Solution

(a) The empirical probability of the event E = "two boys and one girl" is

$$P(E) \approx \text{relative frequency of } E = \frac{180}{500} = 0.36 = 36\%$$

There is about a 36% probability that a family of three children will have two boys and one girl.

(b) To determine the sample space, we construct a **tree diagram** to list the equally likely outcomes of the experiment. We draw two branches corresponding to the two possible outcomes (boy or girl) for the first repetition of the experiment (the first child). For the second child, we draw four branches, and so on. See Figure 3 on the next page, where B stands for boy and G stands for girl.

We find the sample space S of this experiment by following each branch to identify all the possible outcomes of the experiment:

$$S = \{\text{BBB, BBG, BGB, BGG, GBB, GBG, GGB, GGG}\}$$

So, $N(S) = 8$.

For the event E = "two boys and a girl" = {BBG, BGB, GBB}, we have $N(E) = 3$. Since the outcomes are equally likely (for example, BBG is just as likely as BGB), we have

$$P(E) = \frac{N(E)}{N(S)} = \frac{3}{8} = 0.375 = 37.5\%$$

There is a 37.5% probability that a family of three children will have two boys and one girl. If we repeat this experiment 1000 times and the outcomes are equally likely (having a girl is just as likely as having a boy), we would expect about 375 of the trials to result in two boys and one girl.

Historical Note

Pierre de Fermat was born into a wealthy family. His father was a leather merchant and second consul of Beaumont-de-Lomagne. Fermat attended the University of Toulouse. By 1631, Fermat was a lawyer and government official. He rose quickly through the ranks because of deaths from the plague. In fact, in 1653, Fermat's death was incorrectly reported. In 1654, Fermat received a correspondence from Blaise Pascal in which Pascal asked Fermat to confirm his ideas on probability. Fermat and Pascal discussed the problem of how to divide the stakes in a game that is interrupted before completion, knowing how many points each player needs to win. Their short correspondence laid the foundation for the theory of probability. They are regarded as joint founders of the subject.

Mathematics was Fermat's passionate hobby and true love. He is most famous for his Last Theorem, which states that the equation $x^n + y^n = z^n$ has no nonzero integer solutions for $n > 2$. The theorem was scribbled in the margin of a book by Diophantus, a Greek mathematician. Fermat stated, "I have discovered a truly marvelous proof of this theorem, which, however, the margin is not large enough to contain." The status of Fermat's Last Theorem baffled mathematicians until Andrew Wiles proved it to be true in 1994.

Figure 3

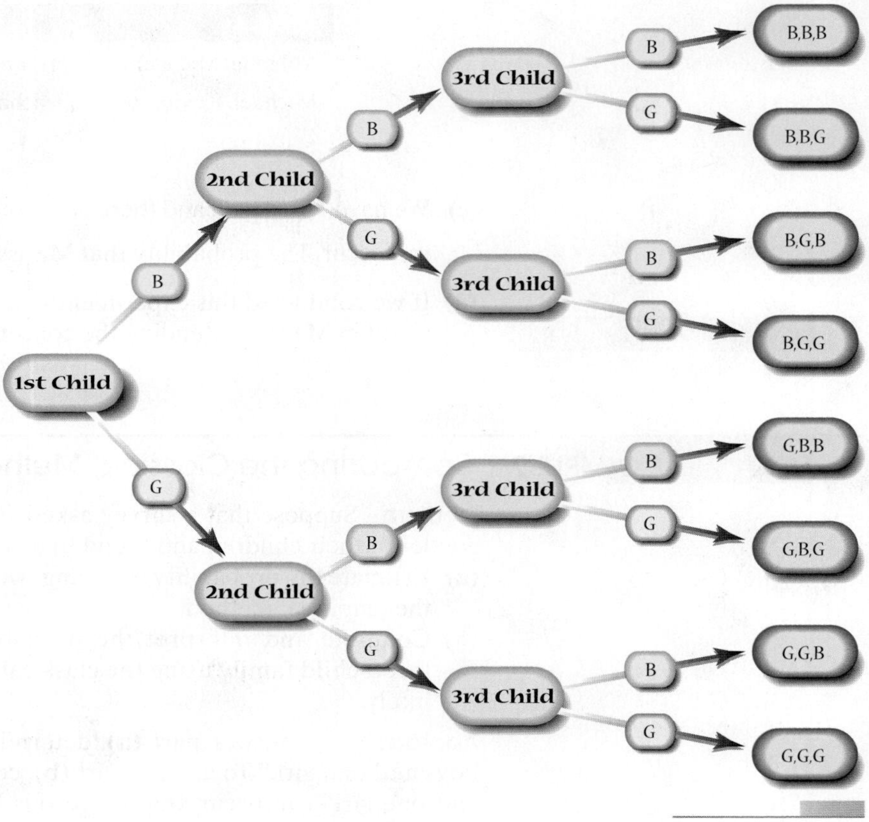

In comparing the results of Examples 7(a) and 7(b), we notice that the two probabilities are slightly different. We know empirical probabilities and classical probabilities often differ in value, but, as the number of repetitions of a probability experiment increases, the empirical probability should get closer to the classical probability. However, it is possible that the two probabilities differ because having a boy or having a girl are not equally likely events. (Maybe the probability of having a boy is 50.5% and the probability of having a girl is 49.5%.) If this is the case, the empirical probability will not get closer to the classical probability.

4 Use Simulation to Obtain Data Based on Probabilities

Suppose that we want to determine the probability of having a boy. We could approximate this probability by using the Vital Statistics data in the *Statistical Abstract of the United States*. In 2006, for example, 2,184,000 boys and 2,081,000 girls were born. Based on empirical evidence, the probability of a boy is approximately

$$\frac{2{,}184{,}000}{2{,}184{,}000 + 2{,}081{,}000} = 0.512 = 51.2\%.$$

The empirical evidence, which is based on a very large number of repetitions, differs from the value of 0.50 used for classical methods (which assumes boys and girls are equally likely). This suggests having a boy is not equally likely as having a girl.

Instead of obtaining data from existing sources, we could also simulate a probability experiment using a graphing calculator or statistical software to replicate the experiment as many times as we like. Simulation is particularly helpful for estimating the probability of more complicated events. In Example 7, we used a tree diagram and the classical approach to find the probability of an event (having two boys and one girl in a three-child family). In this next example, we use simulation to estimate the same probability.

EXAMPLE 8 Simulating Probabilities

Historical Note

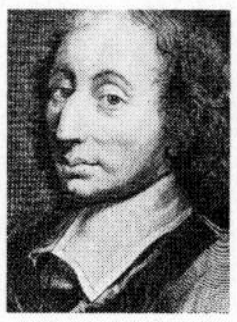

Blaise Pascal was born in 1623, in Clermont, France. Pascal's father felt that Blaise should not be taught mathematics before age 15. Pascal couldn't resist studying mathematics on his own, and at the age of 12 started to teach himself geometry. In December 1639, the Pascal family moved to Rouen, where Pascal's father had been appointed as a tax collector. Between 1642 and 1645, Pascal worked on developing a calculator to help his father collect taxes. In correspondence with Fermat, he helped develop the theory of probability. This correspondence consisted of five letters written in the summer of 1654. They considered the dice problem and the problem of points. The dice problem deals with determining the expected number of times a pair of dice must be thrown before a pair of sixes is observed. The problem of points asks how to divide the stakes if a game of dice is incomplete. They solved the problem of points for a two-player game, but did not solve it for three or more players.

Problem

(a) Simulate the experiment of sampling 100 three-child families to estimate the probability that a three-child family has two boys.

(b) Simulate the experiment of sampling 1000 three-child families to estimate the probability that a three-child family has two boys.

Approach To simulate probabilities, use the random-number generator available in statistical software and most graphing calculators. Assume that the outcomes "have a boy" and "have a girl" are equally likely.

Solution

(a) We use MINITAB to perform the simulation. Set the seed in MINITAB to any value you wish, say 1970. Use the Integer Distribution* to generate random data that simulate three-child families. If we agree to let 0 represent a girl and 1 represent a boy, we can approximate the probability of having 2 boys by summing each row (adding up the number of boys), counting the number of 2s (the number of times we observe two boys), and dividing by 100, the number of repetitions of the experiment. See Figure 4.

Figure 4

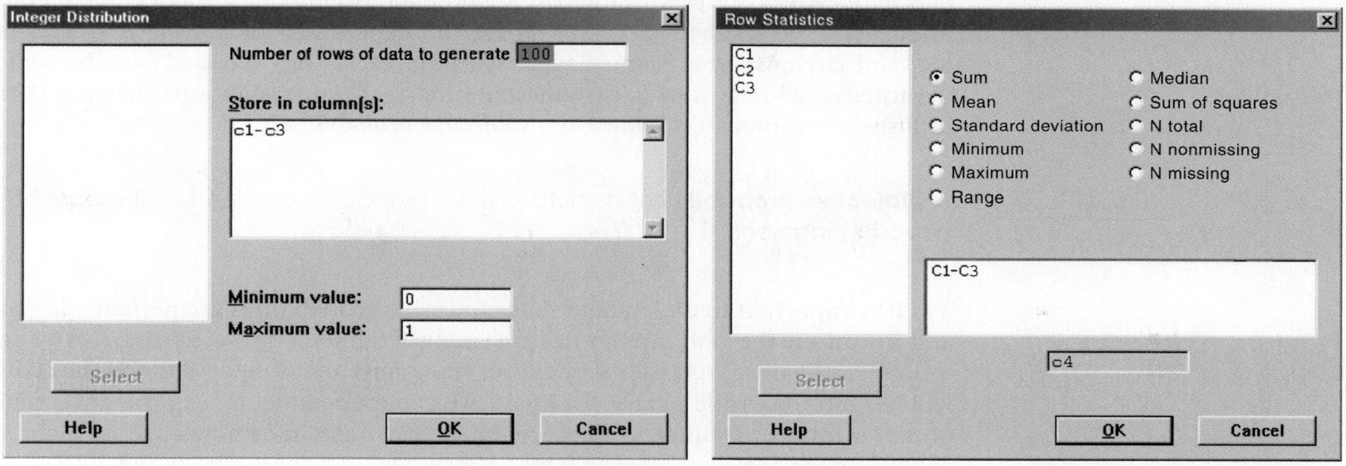

Using MINITAB's Tally command, we can determine the number of 2s that MINITAB randomly generated. See Figure 5.

Figure 5

Tally for Discrete Variables: C4

C4	Count	Percent
0	14	14.00
1	40	40.00
2	32	32.00
3	14	14.00
N = 100		

Based on this figure, we approximate that there is a 32% probability that a three-child family will have 2 boys.

*The Integer Distribution involves a mathematical formula that uses a seed number to generate a sequence of equally likely random integers. Consult the technology manuals for setting the seed and generating sequences of integers.

(b) Again, set the seed to 1970. Figure 6 shows the result of simulating 1000 three-child families.

Figure 6

Tally for Discrete Variables: C4

C4	Count	Percent
0	136	13.60
1	367	36.70
2	388	38.80
3	109	10.90
N =	1000	

We approximate that there is a 38.8% probability of a three-child family having 2 boys. Notice that more repetitions of the experiment (100 repetitions versus 1000 repetitions) results in a probability closer to 37.5% as found in Example 7(b).

Now Work Problem 47

5 Recognize and Interpret Subjective Probabilities

If a sports reporter is asked what he thinks the chances are for the Boston Red Sox to play in the World Series, the reporter would likely process information about the Red Sox (their pitching staff, lead-off hitter, and so on) and then make an educated guess of the likelihood. The reporter may respond that there is a 20% chance the Red Sox will play in the World Series. This forecast is a probability although it is not based on relative frequencies. We cannot, after all, repeat the experiment of playing a season under the same circumstances (same players, schedule, and so on) over and over. Nonetheless, the forecast of 20% does satisfy the criterion that a probability be between 0 and 1, inclusive. This forecast is known as a *subjective probability*.

DEFINITION

A **subjective probability** of an outcome is a probability obtained on the basis of personal judgment.

It is important to understand that subjective probabilities are perfectly legitimate and are often the only method of assigning likelihood to an outcome. As another example, a financial reporter may ask an economist about the likelihood the economy will fall into recession next year. Again, we cannot conduct an experiment n times to obtain a relative frequency. The economist must use her knowledge of the current conditions of the economy and make an educated guess about the likelihood of recession.

5.1 ASSESS YOUR UNDERSTANDING

VOCABULARY AND SKILL BUILDING

1. What is the probability of an event that is impossible? Suppose that a probability is approximated to be zero based on empirical results. Does this mean the event is impossible? 0; no

2. What does it mean for an event to be unusual? Why should the cutoff for identifying unusual events not always be 0.05?

3. *True or False:* In a probability model, the sum of the probabilities of all outcomes must equal 1. True

4. *True or False:* Probability is a measure of the likelihood of a random phenomenon or chance behavior. True

5. In probability, a(n)________ is any process that can be repeated in which the results are uncertain. experiment

6. A(n)_______ is any collection of outcomes from a probability experiment. event

NW **7.** Verify that the following is a probability model. What do we call the outcome "blue"? Impossible event

Color	Probability
Red	0.3
Green	0.15
Blue	0
Brown	0.15
Yellow	0.2
Orange	0.2

8. Verify that the following is a probability model. If the model represents the colors of M&Ms in a bag of milk chocolate M&Ms, explain what the model implies. All of the M&Ms are yellow.

Color	Probability
Red	0
Green	0
Blue	0
Brown	0
Yellow	1
Orange	0

9. Why is the following not a probability model? $P(\text{green}) < 0$

Color	Probability
Red	0.3
Green	−0.3
Blue	0.2
Brown	0.4
Yellow	0.2
Orange	0.2

10. Why is the following not a probability model? Sum of probabilities not 1

Color	Probability
Red	0.1
Green	0.1
Blue	0.1
Brown	0.4
Yellow	0.2
Orange	0.3

11. Which of the following numbers could be the probability of an event? 0, 0.01, 0.35, 1

$$0, 0.01, 0.35, -0.4, 1, 1.4$$

12. Which of the following numbers could be the probability of an event?

$$1.5, \frac{1}{2}, \frac{3}{4}, \frac{2}{3}, 0, -\frac{1}{4}$$

$\frac{1}{2}, \frac{3}{4}, \frac{2}{3}, 0$ (13) No

13. In five-card stud poker, a player is dealt five cards. The probability that the player is dealt two cards of the same value and three other cards of different value so that the player has a pair is 0.42. Explain what this probability means. If you play five-card stud 100 times, will you be dealt a pair exactly 42 times? Why or why not?

14. In seven-card stud poker, a player is dealt seven cards. The probability that the player is dealt two cards of the same value and five other cards of different value so that the player has a pair is 0.44. Explain what this probability means. If you play seven-card stud 100 times, will you be dealt a pair exactly 44 times? Why or why not? No

15. Suppose that you toss a coin 100 times and get 95 heads and 5 tails. Based on these results, what is the estimated probability that the next flip results in a head? 0.95

16. Suppose that you roll a die 100 times and get six 80 times. Based on these results, what is the estimated probability that the next roll results in six? 0.8

17. Bob is asked to construct a probability model for rolling a pair of fair dice. He lists the outcomes as 2, 3, 4, 5, 6, 7, 8, 9, 10, 11, 12. Because there are 11 outcomes, he reasoned, the probability of rolling a two must be $\frac{1}{11}$. What is wrong with Bob's reasoning? Not equally likely outcomes

18. Blood Types A person can have one of four blood types: A, B, AB, or O. If a person is randomly selected, is the probability they have blood type A equal to $\frac{1}{4}$? Why? No

NW **19.** If a person rolls a six-sided die and then flips a coin, describe the sample space of possible outcomes using 1, 2, 3, 4, 5, 6 for the die outcomes and H, T for the coin outcomes.

20. If a basketball player shoots three free throws, describe the sample space of possible outcomes using S for a made free throw and F for a missed free throw.

21. According to the U.S. Department of Education, 42.8% of 3-year-olds are enrolled in day care. What is the probability that a randomly selected 3-year-old is enrolled in day care? 0.428

22. According to the American Veterinary Medical Association, the proportion of households owning a dog is 0.372. What is the probability that a randomly selected household owns a dog? 0.372

For Problems 23–26, let the sample space be $S = \{1, 2, 3, 4, 5, 6, 7, 8, 9, 10\}$. *Suppose the outcomes are equally likely.*

23. Compute the probability of the event $E = \{1, 2, 3\}$. 0.3

24. Compute the probability of the event $F = \{3, 5, 9, 10\}$. 0.4

25. Compute the probability of the event E = "an even number less than 9." 0.4

26. Compute the probability of the event F = "an odd number." 0.5

APPLYING THE CONCEPTS

27. Play Sports? A survey of 500 randomly selected high school students determined that 288 played organized sports.

(a) What is the probability that a randomly selected high school student plays organized sports? 0.576

(b) Interpret this probability.

28. Volunteer? In a survey of 1100 female adults (18 years of age or older), it was determined that 341 volunteered at least once in the past year.

(a) What is the probability that a randomly selected adult female volunteered at least once in the past year? 0.31

(b) Interpret this probability.

NW **29. Planting Tulips** A bag of 100 tulip bulbs purchased from a nursery contains 40 red tulip bulbs, 35 yellow tulip bulbs, and 25 purple tulip bulbs.

(a) What is the probability that a randomly selected tulip bulb is red? 0.4

(b) What is the probability that a randomly selected tulip bulb is purple? 0.25

(c) Interpret these two probabilities.

30. Golf Balls The local golf store sells an "onion bag" that contains 80 "experienced" golf balls. Suppose the bag contains 35 Titleists, 25 Maxflis, and 20 Top-Flites.

(a) What is the probability that a randomly selected golf ball is a Titleist? 0.4375

(b) What is the probability that a randomly selected golf ball is a Top-Flite? 0.25

(c) Interpret these two probabilities.

31. Roulette In the game of roulette, a wheel consists of 38 slots numbered 0, 00, 1, 2, . . . , 36. (See the photo.) To play the game, a metal ball is spun around the wheel and is allowed to fall into one of the numbered slots.

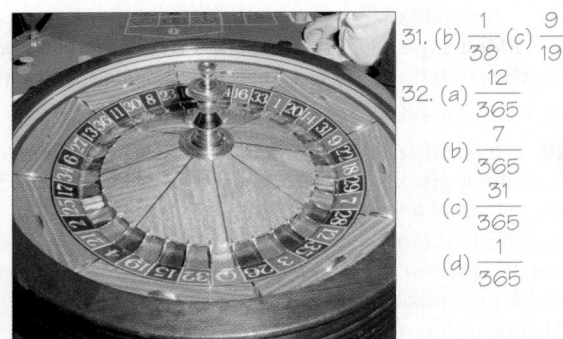

31. (b) $\frac{1}{38}$ (c) $\frac{9}{19}$
32. (a) $\frac{12}{365}$
(b) $\frac{7}{365}$
(c) $\frac{31}{365}$
(d) $\frac{1}{365}$

(a) Determine the sample space. {0, 00, 1, 2, . . . , 36}
(b) Determine the probability that the metal ball falls into the slot marked 8. Interpret this probability.
(c) Determine the probability that the metal ball lands in an odd slot. Interpret this probability.

32. Birthdays Exclude leap years from the following calculations and assume each birthday is equally likely:

(a) Determine the probability that a randomly selected person has a birthday on the 1st day of a month. Interpret this probability.
(b) Determine the probability that a randomly selected person has a birthday on the 31st day of a month. Interpret this probability.
(c) Determine the probability that a randomly selected person was born in December. Interpret this probability.
(d) Determine the probability that a randomly selected person has a birthday on November 8. Interpret this probability.
(e) If you just met somebody and she asked you to guess her birthday, are you likely to be correct? No
(f) Do you think it is appropriate to use the methods of classical probability to compute the probability that a person is born in December?

33. Genetics A gene is composed of two alleles. An allele can be either dominant or recessive. Suppose that a husband and wife, who are both carriers of the sickle-cell anemia allele but do not have the disease, decide to have a child. Because both parents are carriers of the disease, each has one dominant normal-cell allele (*S*) and one recessive sickle-cell allele (*s*). Therefore, the genotype of each parent is *Ss*. Each parent contributes one allele to his or her offspring, with each allele being equally likely.

(a) List the possible genotypes of their offspring. {SS, Ss, sS, ss}
(b) What is the probability that the offspring will have sickle-cell anemia? In other words, what is the probability that the offspring will have genotype *ss*? Interpret this probability.
(c) What is the probability that the offspring will not have sickle-cell anemia but will be a carrier? In other words, what is the probability that the offspring will have one dominant normal-cell allele and one recessive sickle-cell allele? Interpret this probability. 0.5 (b) 0.25

34. More Genetics In Problem 33, we learned that for some diseases, such as sickle-cell anemia, an individual will get the disease only if he or she receives both recessive alleles. This is not always the case. For example, Huntington's disease only requires one dominant gene for an individual to contract the disease. Suppose that a husband and wife, who both have a dominant Huntington's disease allele (*S*) and a normal recessive allele (*s*), decide to have a child.

(a) List the possible genotypes of their offspring. {SS, Ss, sS, ss}
(b) What is the probability that the offspring will not have Huntington's disease? In other words, what is the probability that the offspring will have genotype *ss*? Interpret this probability. 0.25
(c) What is the probability that the offspring will have Huntington's disease? 0.75

NW **35. College Survey** In a national survey conducted by the Centers for Disease Control to determine college students' health-risk behaviors, college students were asked, "How often do you wear a seatbelt when riding in a car driven by someone else?" The frequencies appear in the following table:

Response	Frequency
Never	125
Rarely	324
Sometimes	552
Most of the time	1257
Always	2518

(a) Construct a probability model for seatbelt use by a passenger.
(b) Would you consider it unusual to find a college student who never wears a seatbelt when riding in a car driven by someone else? Why? Yes

36. College Survey In a national survey conducted by the Centers for Disease Control to determine college students' health-risk behaviors, college students were asked, "How often do you wear a seatbelt when driving a car?" The frequencies appear in the following table:

Response	Frequency
Never	118
Rarely	249
Sometimes	345
Most of the time	716
Always	3093

(a) Construct a probability model for seatbelt use by a driver.
(b) Is it unusual for a college student to never wear a seatbelt when driving a car? Why? Yes

37. Larceny Theft A police officer randomly selected 642 police records of larceny thefts. The following data represent the number of offenses for various types of larceny thefts.

Type of Larceny Theft	Number of Offenses
Pocket picking	4
Purse snatching	6
Shoplifting	133
From motor vehicles	219
Motor vehicle accessories	90
Bicycles	42
From buildings	143
From coin-operated machines	5

Source: U.S. Federal Bureau of Investigation

(a) Construct a probability model for type of larceny theft.
(b) Are purse snatching larcenies unusual? Yes
(c) Are bicycle larcenies unusual? No

38. Multiple Births The following data represent the number of live multiple-delivery births (three or more babies) in 2007 for women 15 to 54 years old.

Age	Number of Multiple Births
15–19	100
20–24	467
25–29	1620
30–34	2262
35–39	1545
40–44	328
45–54	105

Source: National Vital Statistics Report, Vol. 58, No. 24, August, 2010

(a) Construct a probability model for number of multiple births.
(b) In the sample space of all multiple births, are multiple births for 15- to 19-year-old mothers unusual? Yes
(c) In the sample space of all multiple births, are multiple births for 40- to 44-year-old mothers unusual? Not too unusual

Problems 39–42 use the given table, which lists six possible assignments of probabilities for tossing a coin twice, to answer the following questions. 45. (a) $\frac{24}{73}$ (b) $\frac{2}{73}$

	Sample Space			
Assignments	**HH**	**HT**	**TH**	**TT**
A	$\frac{1}{4}$	$\frac{1}{4}$	$\frac{1}{4}$	$\frac{1}{4}$
B	0	0	0	1
C	$\frac{3}{16}$	$\frac{5}{16}$	$\frac{5}{16}$	$\frac{3}{16}$
D	$\frac{1}{2}$	$\frac{1}{2}$	$-\frac{1}{2}$	$\frac{1}{2}$
E	$\frac{1}{4}$	$\frac{1}{4}$	$\frac{1}{4}$	$\frac{1}{8}$
F	$\frac{1}{9}$	$\frac{2}{9}$	$\frac{2}{9}$	$\frac{4}{9}$

39. Which of the assignments of probabilities are consistent with the definition of a probability model? A, B, C, F

40. Which of the assignments of probabilities should be used if the coin is known to be fair? A

41. Which of the assignments of probabilities should be used if the coin is known to always come up tails? B

42. Which of the assignments of probabilities should be used if tails is twice as likely to occur as heads? F

NW **43. Going to Disney World** John, Roberto, Clarice, Dominique, and Marco work for a publishing company. The company wants to send two employees to a statistics conference in Orlando. To be fair, the company decides that the two individuals who get to attend will have their names randomly drawn from a hat.

(a) Determine the sample space of the experiment. That is, list all possible simple random samples of size $n = 2$.
(b) What is the probability that Clarice and Dominique attend the conference? 0.1
(c) What is the probability that Clarice attends the conference? 0.4
(d) What is the probability that John stays home? 0.6

44. Six Flags In 2011, Six Flags St. Louis had ten roller coasters: The Screamin' Eagle, The Boss, River King Mine Train, Batman the Ride, Mr. Freeze, Ninja, Tony Hawk's Big Spin, Evel Knievel, Xcalibur, and Sky Screamer. Of these, The Boss, The Screamin' Eagle, and Evel Knievel are wooden coasters. Ethan wants to ride two more roller coasters before leaving the park (not the same one twice) and decides to select them by drawing names from a hat.

(a) Determine the sample space of the experiment. That is, list all possible simple random samples of size $n = 2$.
(b) What is the probability that Ethan will ride Mr. Freeze and Evel Knievel? 0.022
(c) What is the probability that Ethan will ride the Screamin' Eagle? 0.2
(d) What is the probability that Ethan will ride two wooden roller coasters? 0.067
(e) What is the probability that Ethan will not ride any wooden roller coasters? 0.467

45. Barry Bonds On October 5, 2001, Barry Bonds broke Mark McGwire's home-run record for a single season by hitting his 71st and 72nd home runs. Bonds went on to hit one more home run before the season ended, for a total of 73. Of the 73 home runs, 24 went to right field, 26 went to right center field, 11 went to center field, 10 went to left center field, and 2 went to left field. *Source:* Baseball-almanac.com

(a) What is the probability that a randomly selected home run was hit to right field?
(b) What is the probability that a randomly selected home run was hit to left field?
(c) Was it unusual for Barry Bonds to hit a home run to left field? Explain. Yes

46. Rolling a Die

(a) Roll a single die 50 times, recording the result of each roll of the die. Use the results to approximate the probability of rolling a three.
(b) Roll a single die 100 times, recording the result of each roll of the die. Use the results to approximate the probability of rolling a three.
(c) Compare the results of (a) and (b) to the classical probability of rolling a three.

NW **47. Simulation** Use a graphing calculator or statistical software to simulate rolling a six-sided die 100 times, using an integer distribution with numbers one through six.

(a) Use the results of the simulation to compute the probability of rolling a one.
(b) Repeat the simulation. Compute the probability of rolling a one.
(c) Simulate rolling a six-sided die 500 times. Compute the probability of rolling a one.
(d) Which simulation resulted in the closest estimate to the probability that would be obtained using the classical method?

48. Classifying Probability Determine whether the probabilities on the following page are computed using classical methods, empirical methods, or subjective methods.

(a) The probability of having eight girls in an eight-child family is 0.390625%. Classical

(b) On the basis of a survey of 1000 families with eight children, the probability of a family having eight girls is 0.54%. Empirical

(c) According to a sports analyst, the probability that the Chicago Bears will win their next game is about 30%. Subjective

(d) On the basis of clinical trials, the probability of efficacy of a new drug is 75%. Empirical

49. Checking for Loaded Dice You suspect a pair of dice to be loaded and conduct a probability experiment by rolling each die 400 times. The outcome of the experiment is listed in the table below. Do you think the dice are loaded? Why? Yes

Value of Die	Frequency
1	105
2	47
3	44
4	49
5	51
6	104

50. Conduct a survey in your school by randomly asking 50 students whether they drive to school. Based on the results of the survey, approximate the probability that a randomly selected student drives to school.

51. In 2006, the median income of families in the United States was $58,500. What is the probability that a randomly selected family has an income greater than $58,500? 0.5

52. The middle 50% of enrolled freshmen at Washington University in St. Louis had SAT math scores in the range 700–780. What is the probability that a randomly selected freshman at Washington University has an SAT math score of 700 or higher? 0.75

53. Sullivan Survey Choose a qualitative variable from the Sullivan Survey. Build a probability model for the variable.

54. Putting It Together: Drug Side Effects In placebo-controlled clinical trials for the drug Viagra, 734 subjects received Viagra and 725 subjects received a placebo (subjects did not know which treatment they received). The table in the next column summarizes reports of various side effects that were reported. (a) Qualitative (b) Side-by-side relative frequency bar graph

Adverse Effect	Viagra (n = 734)	Placebo (n = 725)
Headache	117	29
Flushing	73	7
Dyspepsia	51	15
Nasal congestion	29	15
Urinary tract infection	22	15
Abnormal vision	22	0
Diarrhea	22	7
Dizziness	15	7
Rash	15	7

(a) Is the variable "adverse effect" qualitative or quantitative?

(b) Which type of graph would be appropriate to display the information in the table? Construct the graph.

(c) What is the estimated probability that a randomly selected subject from the Viagra group reported experiencing flushing? Would this be unusual? 0.099; no

(d) What is the estimated probability that a subject receiving a placebo would report experiencing flushing? Would this be unusual? 0.010; yes

(e) If a subject reports flushing after receiving a treatment, what might you conclude? They received the Viagra treatment.

(f) What type of experimental design is this? Completely randomized design

EXPLAINING THE CONCEPTS

55. Explain the Law of Large Numbers. How does this law apply to gambling casinos?

56. In computing classical probabilities, all outcomes must be equally likely. Explain what this means.

57. Describe what an unusual event is. Should the same cutoff always be used to identify unusual events? Why or why not?

58. You are planning a trip to a water park tomorrow. The weather forecaster says there is a 70% chance of rain tomorrow. Explain what this result means.

59. Describe the difference between classical and empirical probability.

60. Ask Marilyn In a September 19, 2010, article in *Parade Magazine* written to *Ask Marilyn*, Marilyn vos Savant was asked the following: Four identical sealed envelopes are on a table, one of which contains $100. You are to select one of the envelopes. Then the game host discards two of the remaining three envelopes and informs you that they do not contain the $100. In addition, the host offers you the opportunity to switch envelopes. What should you do? (a) Keep your envelope; (b) switch; (c) it does not matter.

Technology Step-By-Step

Simulation

TI-83/84 Plus

1. Set the seed by entering any number on the HOME screen. Press the STO ▶ button, press the MATH button, highlight the PRB menu, and highlight `1:rand` and hit ENTER. With the cursor on the HOME screen, hit ENTER.

2. Press the MATH button and highlight the PRB menu. Highlight `5:randInt (` and hit ENTER.

3. After the `randInt (` on the HOME screen, type `1, n, number of repetitions of experiment )`, where n is the number of equally likely outcomes. For example, to simulate rolling a single die 50 times, we type

```
randInt(1, 6, 50)
```

4. Press the STO ▶ button and then 2nd 1, and hit ENTER to store the data in L1.
5. Draw a histogram of the data using the outcomes as classes. TRACE to obtain outcomes.

MINITAB

1. Set the seed by selecting the **Calc** menu and highlighting **Set Base . . . .** Insert any seed you wish into the cell and click OK.
2. Select the **Calc** menu, highlight **Random Data**, and then highlight **Integer**. Fill in the cells as desired.
3. Select the **Stat** menu, highlight **Tables**, and then highlight **Tally . . . .** Enter C1 into the variables cell. Make sure that the Counts box is checked and click OK.

Excel

1. With cell A1 selected, select the Formulas menu.
2. Select Math & Trig in the Functions menu. Then highlight RANDBETWEEN.
3. To simulate rolling a die 100 times, enter 1 for the Bottom and 6 for the Top. Click OK.
4. Copy the contents of cell A1 into cells A2 through A100.
5. To count the number of "1s", enter

=CountIf(A1:A100, 1)

in any cell. Repeat this to obtain counts for 2 through 6.

StatCrunch

1. Select **Data**, highlight **Simulate Data**, then highlight **Discrete Uniform**.
2. Enter the number of random numbers you would like generated in the "Rows:" cell. For example, if we want to simulate rolling a die 100 times, enter 100. Enter 1 in the "Columns:" cell. Enter the smallest and largest integer in the "Minimum:" and "Maximum:" cell, respectively. For example, to simulate rolling a single die, enter 1 and 6, respectively.
3. Select either the dynamic seed or the fixed seed and enter a value of the seed. Click Simulate.
4. To get counts, select **Stat**, highlight **Summary Stats**, then select **Columns**.
5. Select the column the simulated data are located in. In the "Group by:" cell, also select the column the simulated data are located in. Click Next>.
6. In the "Statistics:" cell, only select *n*. Click Calculate.

5.2 THE ADDITION RULE AND COMPLEMENTS

Preparing for this Section Before getting started, review the following:

- Contingency Tables (Section 4.4, p. 215)

OBJECTIVES

1 Use the Addition Rule for Disjoint Events

2 Use the General Addition Rule

3 Compute the probability of an event using the Complement Rule

Note to Instructor

If you like, you can print out and distribute the Preparing for This Section quiz located in the Instructor's Resource Center. The purpose of the quiz is to verify that the students have the prerequisite knowledge for the section.

1 Use the Addition Rule for Disjoint Events

Before we present more rules for computing probabilities, we must discuss *disjoint events.*

DEFINITION

Two events are **disjoint** if they have no outcomes in common. Another name for disjoint events is **mutually exclusive** events.

In Other Words

Two events are disjoint if they cannot occur at the same time.

We can use **Venn diagrams** to represent events as circles enclosed in a rectangle. The rectangle represents the sample space, and each circle represents an event. For example, suppose we randomly select chips from a bag. Each chip is labeled 0, 1, 2, 3, 4, 5, 6, 7, 8, 9. Let E represent the event "choose a number less than or equal to 2," and let

F represent the event "choose a number greater than or equal to 8." Because E and F have no outcomes in common, they are disjoint. Figure 7 shows a Venn diagram of these disjoint events.

Figure 7

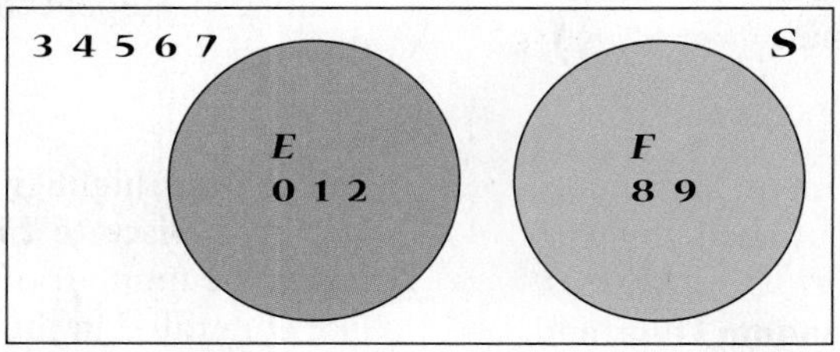

Notice that the outcomes in event E are inside circle E, and the outcomes in event F are inside circle F. All outcomes in the sample space that are not in E or F are outside the circles, but inside the rectangle. From this diagram, we know that $P(E) = \frac{N(E)}{N(S)} = \frac{3}{10} = 0.3$ and $P(F) = \frac{N(F)}{N(S)} = \frac{2}{10} = 0.2$. In addition, $P(E \text{ or } F) = \frac{N(E \text{ or } F)}{N(S)} = \frac{5}{10} = 0.5$ and $P(E \text{ or } F) = P(E) + P(F) = 0.3 + 0.2 = 0.5$. This result occurs because of the *Addition Rule for Disjoint Events.*

In Other Words
The Addition Rule for Disjoint Events states that, if you have two events that have no outcomes in common, the probability that one or the other occurs is the sum of their probabilities.

Addition Rule for Disjoint Events

If E and F are disjoint (or mutually exclusive) events, then

$$P(E \text{ or } F) = P(E) + P(F)$$

The Addition Rule for Disjoint Events can be extended to more than two disjoint events. In general, if $E, F, G, \ldots$ each have no outcomes in common (they are pairwise disjoint), then

$$P(E \text{ or } F \text{ or } G \text{ or} \ldots) = P(E) + P(F) + P(G) + \cdots$$

Let event G represent "the number is a 5 or 6." The Venn diagram in Figure 8 illustrates the Addition Rule for more than two disjoint events using the chip example. Notice that no pair of events has any outcomes in common. So, from the Venn diagram, we can see that $P(E) = \frac{N(E)}{N(S)} = \frac{3}{10} = 0.3$, $P(F) = \frac{N(F)}{N(S)} = \frac{2}{10} = 0.2$, and $P(G) = \frac{N(G)}{N(S)} = \frac{2}{10} = 0.2$. In addition, $P(E \text{ or } F \text{ or } G) = P(E) + P(F) + P(G) = 0.3 + 0.2 + 0.2 = 0.7$.

Figure 8

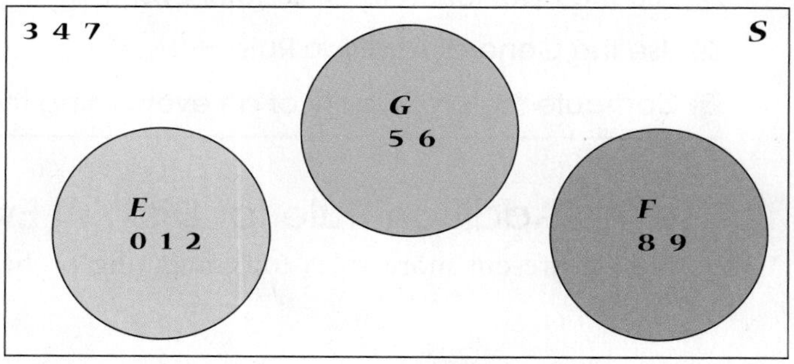

EXAMPLE 1 Benford's Law and the Addition Rule for Disjoint Events

Problem Our number system consists of the digits 0, 1, 2, 3, 4, 5, 6, 7, 8, and 9. Because we do not write numbers such as 12 as 012, the first significant digit in any number must be 1, 2, 3, 4, 5, 6, 7, 8, or 9. Although we may think that each digit appears with equal frequency so that each digit has a $\frac{1}{9}$ probability of being the first significant digit, this is not true. In 1881,

Simon Necomb discovered that digits do not occur with equal frequency. The physicist Frank Benford discovered the same result in 1938. After studying lots and lots of data, he assigned probabilities of occurrence for each of the first digits, as shown in Table 5.

TABLE 5

Digit	1	2	3	4	5	6	7	8	9
Probability	0.301	0.176	0.125	0.097	0.079	0.067	0.058	0.051	0.046

Source: The First Digit Phenomenon, T. P. Hill, *American Scientist*, July–August, 1998.

The probability model is now known as *Benford's Law* and plays a major role in identifying fraudulent data on tax returns and accounting books.

(a) Verify that Benford's Law is a probability model.

(b) Use Benford's Law to determine the probability that a randomly selected first digit is 1 or 2.

(c) Use Benford's Law to determine the probability that a randomly selected first digit is at least 6.

Approach For part (a), verify that each probability is between 0 and 1 and that the sum of all probabilities equals 1. For parts (b) and (c), use the Addition Rule for Disjoint Events.

Solution

(a) Each probability in Table 5 is between 0 and 1. In addition, the sum of all the probabilities, $0.301 + 0.176 + 0.125 + \cdots + 0.046$, is 1. Because Rules 1 and 2 are satisfied, Table 5 represents a probability model.

(b)

$$\begin{aligned} P(1 \text{ or } 2) &= P(1) + P(2) \\ &= 0.301 + 0.176 \\ &= 0.477 \end{aligned}$$

If we looked at 100 numbers, we would expect about 48 to begin with 1 or 2.

(c)

$$\begin{aligned} P(\text{at least } 6) &= P(6 \text{ or } 7 \text{ or } 8 \text{ or } 9) \\ &= P(6) + P(7) + P(8) + P(9) \\ &= 0.067 + 0.058 + 0.051 + 0.046 \\ &= 0.222 \end{aligned}$$

If we looked at 100 numbers, we would expect about 22 to begin with 6, 7, 8, or 9.

EXAMPLE 2 A Deck of Cards and the Addition Rule for Disjoint Events

Problem Suppose that a single card is selected from a standard 52-card deck, such as the one shown in Figure 9.

Figure 9

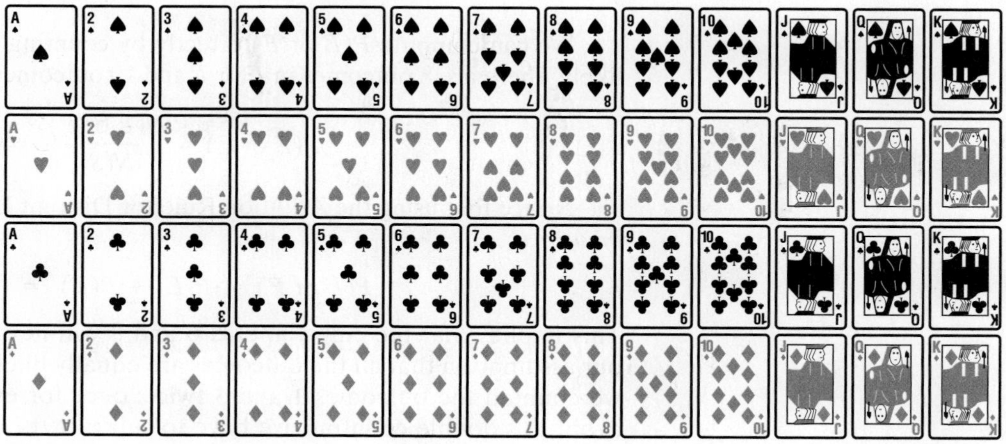

(a) Compute the probability of the event E = "drawing a king."
(b) Compute the probability of the event E = "drawing a king" or F = "drawing a queen" or G = "drawing a jack."

Approach Use the classical method for computing the probabilities because the outcomes are equally likely and easy to count. We use the Addition Rule for Disjoint Events to compute the probability in part (b) because the events are mutually exclusive. For example, you cannot simultaneously draw a king and a queen.

Solution The sample space consists of the 52 cards in the deck, so $N(S) = 52$.
(a) A standard deck of cards has four kings, so $N(E) = 4$. Therefore,

$$P(\text{king}) = P(E) = \frac{N(E)}{N(S)} = \frac{4}{52} = \frac{1}{13}$$

(b) A standard deck of cards has four kings, four queens, and four jacks. Because events E, F, and G are mutually exclusive, we use the Addition Rule for Disjoint Events extended to two or more disjoint events. So

$$\begin{aligned} P(\text{king or queen or jack}) &= P(E \text{ or } F \text{ or } G) \\ &= P(E) + P(F) + P(G) \\ &= \frac{4}{52} + \frac{4}{52} + \frac{4}{52} = \frac{12}{52} = \frac{3}{13} \end{aligned}$$

Now Work Problems 25(a)–(c)

2 Use the General Addition Rule

Note to Instructor
If you wish to design your course so that it minimizes probability coverage, the material in Objective 2 may be skipped without loss of continuity.

You may be asking yourself, "What if I need to compute the probability of two events that are not disjoint?"

Consider the chip example. Suppose we are randomly selecting chips from a bag. Each chip is labeled 0, 1, 2, 3, 4, 5, 6, 7, 8, or 9. Let E represent the event "choose an odd number," and let F represent the event "choose a number less than or equal to 4." Because $E = \{1, 3, 5, 7, 9\}$ and $F = \{0, 1, 2, 3, 4\}$ have the outcomes 1 and 3 in common, the events are not disjoint. Figure 10 shows a Venn diagram of these events.

Figure 10

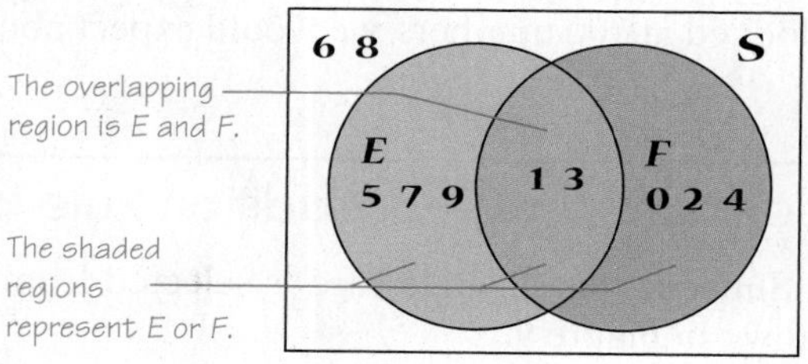

We can compute $P(E \text{ or } F)$ directly by counting because each outcome is equally likely. There are 8 outcomes in E or F and 10 outcomes in the sample space, so

$$P(E \text{ or } F) = \frac{N(E \text{ or } F)}{N(S)} = \frac{8}{10} = \frac{4}{5}$$

Notice that using the Addition Rule for Disjoint Events to find $P(E \text{ or } F)$ would be *incorrect*:

$$P(E \text{ or } F) \neq P(E) + P(F) = \frac{5}{10} + \frac{5}{10} = 1$$

This implies that the chips labeled 6 and 8 will never be selected, which contradicts our assumption that all the outcomes are equally likely. Our result is incorrect because we counted the outcomes 1 and 3 twice: once for event E and once for event F. To avoid this double counting, we have to subtract the probability corresponding to the overlapping region, E and F. That is, we have to subtract $P(E \text{ and } F) = \frac{2}{10}$ from the result and obtain

$$\begin{aligned} P(E \text{ or } F) &= P(E) + P(F) - P(E \text{ and } F) \\ &= \frac{5}{10} + \frac{5}{10} - \frac{2}{10} \\ &= \frac{8}{10} = \frac{4}{5} \end{aligned}$$

which agrees with the result we found by counting. The following rule generalizes these results.

The General Addition Rule

For any two events E and F,

$$P(E \text{ or } F) = P(E) + P(F) - P(E \text{ and } F)$$

EXAMPLE 3 Computing Probabilities for Events That Are Not Disjoint

Problem Suppose a single card is selected from a standard 52-card deck. Compute the probability of the event E = "drawing a king" or F = "drawing a diamond."

Approach The events are not disjoint because the outcome "king of diamonds" is in both events, so use the General Addition Rule.

Solution

$$\begin{aligned} P(E \text{ or } F) \quad &= \quad P(E) \quad + \quad P(F) \quad - \quad P(E \text{ and } F) \\ P(\text{king or diamond}) &= P(\text{king}) + P(\text{diamond}) - P(\text{king of diamonds}) \\ &= \frac{4}{52} + \frac{13}{52} - \frac{1}{52} \\ &= \frac{16}{52} = \frac{4}{13} \end{aligned}$$

Now Work Problem 31

Consider the data shown in Table 6, which represent the marital status of males and females 15 years old or older in the United States in 2010.

TABLE 6

	Males (in millions)	Females (in millions)
Never married	40.2	34.0
Married	62.2	62.0
Widowed	3.0	11.4
Divorced	10.0	13.8
Separated	2.4	3.2

Source: U.S. Census Bureau, *Current Population Reports*

Table 6 is called a **contingency table** or **two-way table**, because it relates two categories of data. The **row variable** is marital status, because each row in the table describes the marital status of an individual. The **column variable** is gender. Each box inside the table is called a **cell**. For example, the cell corresponding to married individuals who are male is in the second row, first column. Each cell contains the frequency of the category: There were 62.2 million married males in the United States in 2010. Put another way, in the United States in 2010, there were 62.2 million individuals who were male *and* married.

EXAMPLE 4 Using the Addition Rule with Contingency Tables

Problem Using the data in Table 6,

(a) Determine the probability that a randomly selected U.S. resident 15 years old or older is male.

(b) Determine the probability that a randomly selected U.S. resident 15 years old or older is widowed.

(c) Determine the probability that a randomly selected U.S. resident 15 years old or older is widowed or divorced.

(d) Determine the probability that a randomly selected U.S. resident 15 years old or older is male or widowed.

Approach Add the entries in each row and column to get the total number of people in each category. Then determine the probabilities using either the Addition Rule for Disjoint Events or the General Addition Rule.

Solution We first add the entries in each column. For example, the "male" column shows there are $40.2 + 62.2 + 3.0 + 10.0 + 2.4 = 117.8$ million males 15 years old or older in the United States. Add the entries in each row. For example, in the "never married" row we find there are $40.2 + 34.0 = 74.2$ million U.S. residents 15 years old or older who have never married. Adding the row totals or column totals, we find there are $117.8 + 124.4 = 74.2 + 124.2 + 14.4 + 23.8 + 5.6 = 242.2$ million U.S. residents 15 years old or older.

(a) There are 117.8 million males 15 years old or older and 242.2 million U.S. residents 15 years old or older. The probability that a randomly selected U.S. resident 15 years old or older is male is $\frac{117.8}{242.2} = 0.486$.

(b) There are 14.4 million U.S. residents 15 years old or older who are widowed. The probability that a randomly selected U.S. resident 15 years old or older is widowed is $\frac{14.4}{242.2} = 0.059$.

(c) The events widowed and divorced are disjoint. Do you see why? We use the Addition Rule for Disjoint Events.

$$
\begin{aligned}
P(\text{widowed or divorced}) &= P(\text{widowed}) + P(\text{divorced}) \\
&= \frac{14.4}{242.2} + \frac{23.8}{242.2} = \frac{38.2}{242.2} \\
&= 0.158
\end{aligned}
$$

(d) The events male and widowed are not mutually exclusive. In fact, there are 3.0 million males who are widowed in the United States. Therefore, we use the General Addition Rule to compute $P(\text{male or widowed})$:

$$
\begin{aligned}
P(\text{male or widowed}) &= P(\text{male}) + P(\text{widowed}) - P(\text{male and widowed}) \\
&= \frac{117.8}{242.2} + \frac{14.4}{242.2} - \frac{3.0}{242.2} \\
&= \frac{129.2}{242.2} = 0.533
\end{aligned}
$$

Now Work Problem 41

3 Compute the Probability of an Event Using the Complement Rule

Suppose that the probability of an event E is known and we would like to determine the probability that E does not occur. This can easily be accomplished using the idea of *complements*.

Note to Instructor

There are a number of ways to denote the complement of an event, such as $\overline{E}$, E', and $\sim E$. We choose E^c to avoid confusion with the notation for the sample mean.

DEFINITION

Complement of an Event

Let S denote the sample space of a probability experiment and let E denote an event. The **complement of E**, denoted E^c, is all outcomes in the sample space S that are not outcomes in the event E.

Because E and E^c are mutually exclusive,

$$P(E \text{ or } E^c) = P(E) + P(E^c) = P(S) = 1$$

Subtracting $P(E)$ from both sides, we obtain the following result.

In Other Words
For any event, either the event happens or it doesn't. Use the Complement Rule when you know the probability that some event will occur and you want to know the chance it will not occur.

Complement Rule

If E represents any event and E^c represents the complement of E, then

$$P(E^c) = 1 - P(E)$$

Figure 11 illustrates the Complement Rule using a Venn diagram.

Figure 11

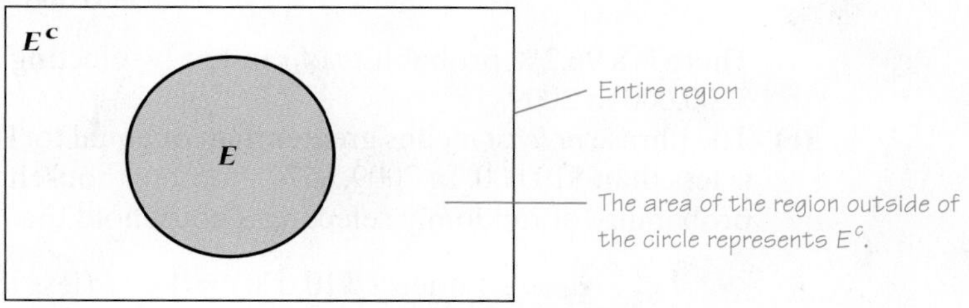

EXAMPLE 5 Computing Probabilities Using Complements

Problem According to the National Gambling Impact Study Commission, 52% of Americans have played state lotteries. What is the probability that a randomly selected American has not played a state lottery?

Approach Not playing a state lottery is the complement of playing a state lottery. We compute the probability using the Complement Rule.

Solution $P(\text{not played state lottery}) = 1 - P(\text{played state lottery}) = 1 - 0.52 = 0.48$

There is a 48% probability of randomly selecting an American who has not played a state lottery.

EXAMPLE 6 Computing Probabilities Using Complements

Problem The data in Table 7 represent the income distribution of households in the United States in 2009.

TABLE 7

Annual Income	Number (in thousands)	Annual Income	Number (in thousands)
Less than \$10,000	8,570	\$50,000 to \$74,999	21,280
\$10,000 to \$14,999	6,759	\$75,000 to \$99,999	13,549
\$15,000 to \$24,999	14,023	\$100,000 to \$149,999	14,034
\$25,000 to \$34,999	13,003	\$150,000 to \$199,999	5,209
\$35,000 to \$49,999	16,607	\$200,000 or more	4,506

Source: U.S. Census Bureau

Compute the probability that a randomly selected household earned the following incomes in 2009:

(a) \$200,000 or more
(b) Less than \$200,000
(c) At least \$10,000

Approach Determine the probabilities by finding the relative frequency of each event. We have to find the total number of households in the United States in 2009.

Solution

(a) There were a total of $8570 + 6759 + \cdots + 4506 = 117{,}540$ thousand households in the United States in 2009 and 4506 thousand of them earned \$200,000 or more, so

$$P(\text{earned \$200,000 or more}) = \frac{4506}{117{,}540} = 0.038.$$

(b) We could compute the probability of randomly selecting a household that earned less than \$200,000 in 2009 by adding the relative frequencies of each category less than \$200,000, but it is easier to use complements. The complement of earning less than \$200,000 is earning \$200,000 or more. Therefore,

$$P(\text{less than \$200,000}) = 1 - P(\text{\$200,000 or more}) = 1 - 0.038 = 0.962$$

There is a 96.2% probability of randomly selecting a household that earned less than \$200,000 in 2009.

(c) The phrase *at least* means greater than or equal to. The complement of at least \$10,000 is less than \$10,000. In 2009, 8570 thousand households earned less than \$10,000. The probability of randomly selecting a household that earned at least \$10,000 is

$$P(\text{at least \$10,000}) = 1 - P(\text{less than \$10,000}) = 1 - \frac{8570}{117{,}540} = 0.927$$

There is a 92.7% probability of randomly selecting a household that earned at least \$10,000 in 2009.

Now Work Problems 25(d) and 29

7. {5, 6, 7, 8, 9, 10, 11, 12}; $\frac{2}{3}$ 8. {2, 3, 4, 5, 6, 7}; $\frac{1}{2}$ 11. {1, 8, 9, 10, 11, 12}; $\frac{1}{2}$ 12. {1, 2, 3, 4, 10, 11, 12}; $\frac{7}{12}$ 21. $\frac{17}{20}$ 22. $\frac{11}{20}$ 23. $\frac{11}{20}$ 24. $\frac{17}{20}$

5.2 ASSESS YOUR UNDERSTANDING

VOCABULARY AND SKILL BUILDING

1. What does it mean when two events are disjoint?
2. If E and F are disjoint events, then $P(E \text{ or } F) =$ ________.
3. If E and F are not disjoint events, then $P(E \text{ or } F) =$ ________.
4. What does it mean when two events are complements?

2. $P(E) + P(F)$ 3. $P(E) + P(F) - P(E \text{ and } F)$

In Problems 5–12, a probability experiment is conducted in which the sample space of the experiment is $S = \{1, 2, 3, 4, 5, 6, 7, 8, 9, 10, 11, 12\}$. Let event $E = \{2, 3, 4, 5, 6, 7\}$, event $F = \{5, 6, 7, 8, 9\}$, event $G = \{9, 10, 11, 12\}$, and event $H = \{2, 3, 4\}$. Assume that each outcome is equally likely. 5. {5, 6, 7}; no 6. {9}; no

5. List the outcomes in E and F. Are E and F mutually exclusive?
6. List the outcomes in F and G. Are F and G mutually exclusive?
7. List the outcomes in F or G. Now find $P(F \text{ or } G)$ by counting the number of outcomes in F or G. Determine $P(F \text{ or } G)$ using the General Addition Rule.
8. List the outcomes in E or H. Now find $P(E \text{ or } H)$ by counting the number of outcomes in E or H. Determine $P(E \text{ or } H)$ using the General Addition Rule.
9. List the outcomes in E and G. Are E and G mutually exclusive? { }; yes
10. List the outcomes in F and H. Are F and H mutually exclusive? { }; yes
11. List the outcomes in E^c. Find $P(E^c)$.
12. List the outcomes in F^c. Find $P(F^c)$.

In Problems 13–18, find the probability of the indicated event if $P(E) = 0.25$ and $P(F) = 0.45$.

13. Find $P(E \text{ or } F)$ if $P(E \text{ and } F) = 0.15$. 0.55
14. Find $P(E \text{ and } F)$ if $P(E \text{ or } F) = 0.6$. 0.1
15. Find $P(E \text{ or } F)$ if E and F are mutually exclusive. 0.7
16. Find $P(E \text{ and } F)$ if E and F are mutually exclusive. 0
17. Find $P(E^c)$. 0.75
18. Find $P(F^c)$. 0.55
19. If $P(E) = 0.60$, $P(E \text{ or } F) = 0.85$, and $P(E \text{ and } F) = 0.05$, find $P(F)$. 0.30
20. If $P(F) = 0.30$, $P(E \text{ or } F) = 0.65$, and $P(E \text{ and } F) = 0.15$, find $P(E)$. 0.50

In Problems 21–24, a golf ball is selected at random from a golf bag. If the golf bag contains 9 Titleists, 8 Maxflis, and 3 Top-Flites, find the probability of each event.

21. The golf ball is a Titleist or Maxfli.
22. The golf ball is a Maxfli or Top-Flite.
23. The golf ball is not a Titleist.
24. The golf ball is not a Top-Flite.

APPLYING THE CONCEPTS

NW 25. **Weapon of Choice** The following probability model shows the distribution of murders by type of weapon for murder cases in 2009.

Weapon	Probability
Handgun	0.473
Rifle	0.026
Shotgun	0.031
Unknown firearm	0.141
Knives	0.134
Hands, fists, etc.	0.059
Other	0.136

Source: U.S. Federal Bureau of Investigation

(a) Verify that this is a probability model.

(b) What is the probability that a randomly selected murder resulted from a rifle or shotgun? Interpret this probability.

(c) What is the probability that a randomly selected murder resulted from a handgun, rifle, or shotgun? Interpret this probability. 0.53 (b) 0.057

(d) What is the probability that a randomly selected murder resulted from a weapon other than a gun? Interpret this probability.

(e) Are murders with a shotgun unusual? Yes (d) 0.329

26. Doctorates Conferred The following probability model shows the distribution of doctoral degrees from U.S. universities in 2009 by area of study.

Area of Study	Probability
Engineering	0.154
Physical sciences	0.087
Life sciences	0.203
Mathematics	0.031
Computer sciences	0.033
Social sciences	0.168
Humanities	0.094
Education	0.132
Professional and other fields	0.056
Health	0.042

Source: U.S. National Science Foundation

(a) Verify that this is a probability model.

(b) What is the probability that a randomly selected doctoral candidate who earned a degree in 2009 studied physical science or life science? Interpret this probability. 0.290

(c) What is the probability that a randomly selected doctoral candidate who earned a degree in 2009 studied physical science, life science, mathematics, or computer science? Interpret this probability. 0.354

(d) What is the probability that a randomly selected doctoral candidate who earned a degree in 2009 did not study mathematics? Interpret this probability. 0.969

(e) Are doctoral degrees in mathematics unusual? Does this result surprise you? Yes

27. If events E and F are disjoint and the events F and G are disjoint, must the events E and G necessarily be disjoint? Give an example to illustrate your opinion. No

28. Draw a Venn diagram like that in Figure 10 that expands the general addition rule to three events. Use the diagram to write the General Addition Rule for three events.

NW **29. Multiple Births** The following data represent the number of live multiple-delivery births (three or more babies) in 2007 for women 15 to 54 years old:

Age	Number of Multiple Births
15–19	100
20–24	467
25–29	1620
30–34	2262
35–39	1545
40–44	328
45–54	105
Total	**6427**

Source: National Vital Statistics Report, Vol. 58, No. 24, August, 2010

(a) Determine the probability that a randomly selected multiple birth in 2007 for women 15 to 54 years old involved a mother 30 to 39 years old. Interpret this probability. 0.592

(b) Determine the probability that a randomly selected multiple birth in 2007 for women 15 to 54 years old involved a mother who was not 30 to 39 years old. Interpret this probability. 0.408

(c) Determine the probability that a randomly selected multiple birth in 2007 for women 15 to 54 years old involved a mother who was less than 45 years old. Interpret this probability. 0.984

(d) Determine the probability that a randomly selected multiple birth in 2007 for women 15 to 54 years old involved a mother who was at least 20 years old. Interpret this probability. 0.984

30. Housing The following probability model shows the distribution for the number of rooms in U.S. housing units.

Rooms	Probability
One	0.005
Two	0.011
Three	0.088
Four	0.183
Five	0.230
Six	0.204
Seven	0.123
Eight or more	0.156

Source: U.S. Census Bureau

(a) Verify that this is a probability model.

(b) What is the probability that a randomly selected housing unit has four or more rooms? Interpret this probability. 0.896

(c) What is the probability that a randomly selected housing unit has fewer than eight rooms? Interpret this probability. 0.844

(d) What is the probability that a randomly selected housing unit has from four to six (inclusive) rooms? Interpret this probability. 0.617

(e) What is the probability that a randomly selected housing unit has at least two rooms? Interpret this probability. 0.995

NW **31. A Deck of Cards** A standard deck of cards contains 52 cards, as shown in Figure 9. One card is randomly selected from the deck.

(a) Compute the probability of randomly selecting a heart or club from a deck of cards. 1/2

(b) Compute the probability of randomly selecting a heart or club or diamond from a deck of cards. 3/4

(c) Compute the probability of randomly selecting an ace or heart from a deck of cards. 4/13

32. A Deck of Cards A standard deck of cards contains 52 cards, as shown in Figure 9. One card is randomly selected from the deck.

(a) Compute the probability of randomly selecting a two or three from a deck of cards. 2/13

(b) Compute the probability of randomly selecting a two or three or four from a deck of cards. 3/13

(c) Compute the probability of randomly selecting a two or club from a deck of cards. 4/13

33. Birthdays Exclude leap years from the following calculations:

(a) Compute the probability that a randomly selected person does not have a birthday on November 8. 364/365

(b) Compute the probability that a randomly selected person does not have a birthday on the 1st day of a month. 353/365

(c) Compute the probability that a randomly selected person does not have a birthday on the 31st day of a month. 358/365

(d) Compute the probability that a randomly selected person was not born in December. 334/365

34. Roulette In the game of roulette, a wheel consists of 38 slots numbered 0, 00, 1, 2, . . . , 36. The odd-numbered slots are red, and the even-numbered slots are black. The numbers 0 and 00 are green. To play the game, a metal ball is spun around the wheel and is allowed to fall into one of the numbered slots.

(a) What is the probability that the metal ball lands on green or red? 10/19

(b) What is the probability that the metal ball does not land on green? 18/19

35. Health Problems According to the Centers for Disease Control, the probability that a randomly selected citizen of the United States has hearing problems is 0.151. The probability that a randomly selected citizen of the United States has vision problems is 0.093. Can we compute the probability of randomly selecting a citizen of the United States who has hearing problems or vision problems by adding these probabilities? Why or why not? No

36. Visits to the Doctor A National Ambulatory Medical Care Survey administered by the Centers for Disease Control found that the probability a randomly selected patient visited the doctor for a blood pressure check is 0.593. The probability a randomly selected patient visited the doctor for urinalysis is 0.064. Can we compute the probability of randomly selecting a patient who visited the doctor for a blood pressure check or urinalysis by adding these probabilities? Why or why not? No

37. Foster Care A social worker for a child advocacy center has a caseload of 24 children under the age of 18. Her caseload by age is as follows:

Age (yr)	Under 1	1–5	6–10	11–14	15–17
Cases	1	6	5	7	5

What is the probability that one of her clients, selected at random, is:

(a) Between 6 and10 years old? Is this unusual? 0.208; no

(b) More than 5 years old? 0.708

(c) Less than 1 year old? Is this unusual? 0.042; yes

38. Language Spoken at Home According to the U.S. Census Bureau, the probability that a randomly selected household speaks only English at home is 0.81. The probability that a randomly selected household speaks only Spanish at home is 0.12.

(a) What is the probability that a randomly selected household speaks only English or only Spanish at home? 0.93

(b) What is the probability that a randomly selected household speaks a language other than only English or only Spanish at home? 0.07

(c) What is the probability that a randomly selected household speaks a language other than only English at home? 0.19

(d) Can the probability that a randomly selected household speaks only Polish at home equal 0.08? Why or why not? No

39. Getting to Work According to the U.S. Census Bureau, the probability that a randomly selected worker primarily drives a car to work is 0.867. The probability that a randomly selected worker primarily takes public transportation to work is 0.048.

(a) What is the probability that a randomly selected worker primarily drives a car or takes public transportation to work? 0.915

(b) What is the probability that a randomly selected worker neither drives a car nor takes public transportation to work? 0.085

(c) What is the probability that a randomly selected worker does not drive a car to work? 0.133

(d) Can the probability that a randomly selected worker walks to work equal 0.15? Why or why not? No

40. Working Couples A guidance counselor at a middle school collected the following information regarding the employment status of married couples within his school's boundaries.

	Number of Children under 18 Years Old			
Worked	**0**	**1**	**2 or More**	**Total**
Husband only	172	79	174	**425**
Wife only	94	17	15	**126**
Both spouses	522	257	370	**1149**
Total	**788**	**353**	**559**	**1700**

(a) What is the probability that, for a married couple selected at random, both spouses work? 0.676

(b) What is the probability that, for a married couple selected at random, the couple has one child under the age of 18? 0.208

(c) What is the probability that, for a married couple selected at random, the couple has two or more children under the age of 18 and both spouses work? 0.218

(d) What is the probability that, for a married couple selected at random, the couple has no children or only the husband works? 0.612

(e) Would it be unusual to select a married couple at random for which only the wife works? No

NW **41. Cigar Smoking** The data in the following table show the results of a national study of 137,243 U.S. men that investigated the association between cigar smoking and death from cancer. **Note:** Current cigar smoker means cigar smoker at time of death.

	Died from Cancer	Did Not Die from Cancer
Never smoked cigars	782	120,747
Former cigar smoker	91	7,757
Current cigar smoker	141	7,725

Source: Shapiro, Jacobs, and Thun. "Cigar Smoking in Men and Risk of Death from Tobacco-Related Cancers," *Journal of the National Cancer Institute*, February 16, 2000.

(a) If an individual is randomly selected from this study, what is the probability that he died from cancer? 0.007

(b) If an individual is randomly selected from this study, what is the probability that he was a current cigar smoker? 0.057

(c) If an individual is randomly selected from this study, what is the probability that he died from cancer and was a current cigar smoker? 0.001

(d) If an individual is randomly selected from this study, what is the probability that he died from cancer or was a current cigar smoker? 0.064

42. Civilian Labor Force The following table represents the employment status and gender of the civilian labor force ages 16 to 19 (in thousands).

	Male	Female
Employed	2328	2509
Unemployed	898	654
Not seeking employment	5416	5237

Source: U.S. Bureau of Labor Statistics, December 2007

(a) What is the probability that a randomly selected 16- to 19-year-old individual from the civilian labor force is employed? 0.284

(b) What is the probability that a randomly selected 16- to 19-year-old individual from the civilian labor force is male? 0.507

(c) What is the probability that a randomly selected 16- to 19-year-old individual from the civilian labor force is employed and male? 0.137

(d) What is the probability that a randomly selected 16- to 19-year-old individual from the civilian labor force is employed or male? 0.654

43. Sullivan Survey: Speeding Tickets The following data represent the number of speeding tickets issued to individuals in the past year and the gender of the individuals. Determine the following probabilities based on the results of the survey.

	0	1	2	3	Total
Female	97	14	3	1	**115**
Male	71	7	1	3	**82**
Total	**168**	**21**	**4**	**4**	**197**

Source: Sullivan Statistics Survey

(a) Determine the probability a randomly selected driver is female. 0.584

(b) Determine the probability a randomly selected driver has been issued 1 ticket in the past year. 0.107

(c) Determine the probability a randomly selected driver is female and has been issued 1 ticket in the past year. 0.071

(d) Determine the probability a randomly selected driver is female or has been issued 1 ticket in the past year. 0.619

44. The Placebo Effect A company is testing a new medicine for migraine headaches. In the study, 150 women were given the new medicine and an additional 100 women were given a placebo. Each participant was directed to take the medicine when the first symptoms of a migraine occurred and then to record whether the headache went away within 45 minutes or lingered. The results are recorded in the following table:

	Headache Went Away	Headache Lingered
Given medicine	132	18
Given placebo	56	44

(a) If a study participant is selected at random, what is the probability she was given the placebo? 0.40

(b) If a study participant is selected at random, what is the probability her headache went away within 45 minutes? 0.752

(c) If a study participant is selected at random, what is the probability she was given the placebo and her headache went away within 45 minutes? 0.224

(d) If a study participant is selected at random, what is the probability she was given the placebo or her headache went away within 45 minutes? 0.928

45. Social Media Harris Interactive conducted a survey in which they asked adult Americans (18 years or older) whether they used social media (Facebook, Twitter, and so on) regularly. The following table is based on the results of the survey.

	18–34	35–44	45–54	55+	Total
Use social media	117	89	83	49	**338**
Do not use social media	33	36	57	66	**192**
Total	**150**	**125**	**140**	**115**	**530**

Source: Harris Interactive

(a) If an adult American is randomly selected, what is the probability he or she uses social media? 0.638

(b) If an adult American is randomly selected, what is the probability he or she is 45 to 54 years of age? 0.264

(c) If an adult American is randomly selected, what is the probability he or she is a 35- to 44-year-old social media user? 0.168

(d) If an adult American is randomly selected, what is the probability he or she is 35- to 44-years-old or uses social media? 0.706

46. Driver Fatalities The following data represent the number of drivers involved in fatal crashes in the United States in 2009 by day of the week and gender.

	Male	Female	Total
Sunday	8,222	4,325	**12,547**
Monday	6,046	3,108	**9,154**
Tuesday	5,716	3,076	**8,792**
Wednesday	5,782	3,011	**8,793**
Thursday	6,315	3,302	**9,617**
Friday	7,932	4,113	**12,045**
Saturday	9,558	4,824	**14,382**
Total	**49,571**	**25,759**	**75,330**

Source: Fatality Analysis Reporting System, National Highway Traffic Safety Administration

(a) Determine the probability that a randomly selected fatal crash involved a male. 0.658

(b) Determine the probability that a randomly selected fatal crash occurred on Sunday. 0.167

(c) Determine the probability that a randomly selected fatal crash occurred on Sunday and involved a male. 0.109

(d) Determine the probability that a randomly selected fatal crash occurred on Sunday or involved a male. 0.715

(e) Would it be unusual for a fatality to occur on Wednesday and involve a female driver? Yes

47. Putting It Together: Red Light Cameras In a study of the feasibility of a red-light camera program in the city of

Crash Type	Current System	With Red-Light Cameras
Reported injury	289	221
Reported property damage only	392	333
Unreported injury	78	60
Unreported property damage only	362	308
Total	**1121**	**922**

Source: Krig, Moran, Regan. "An Analysis of a Red-Light Camera Program in the City of Milwaukee," Spring 2006, prepared for the city of Milwaukee Budget and Management Division

Milwaukee, the data above summarize the projected number of crashes at 13 selected intersections over a 5-year period.

(a) Identify the variables presented in the table.

(b) State whether each variable is qualitative or quantitative. If quantitative, state whether it is discrete or continuous.

(c) Construct a relative frequency distribution for each system.

(d) Construct a side-by-side relative frequency bar graph for the data.

(e) Determine the mean number of crashes per intersection in the study, if possible. If not possible, explain why.

(f) Determine the standard deviation number of crashes, if possible. If not possible, explain why.

(g) Based on the data shown, does it appear that the red-light camera program will be beneficial in reducing crashes at the intersections? Explain. *(e) Current: 86.2; Camera: 70.9*

(h) For the current system, what is the probability that a crash selected at random will have reported injuries? *0.258*

(i) For the camera system, what is the probability that a crash selected at random will have only property damage? *0.695*

The study classified crashes further by indicating whether they were red-light running crashes or rear-end crashes. The results are as follows:

	Rear End		Red-Light Running	
Crash Type	**Current**	**Cameras**	**Current**	**Cameras**
Reported injury	67	77	222	144
Reported property damage only	157	180	235	153
Unreported injury	18	21	60	39
Unreported property damage only	145	167	217	141
Total	**387**	**445**	**734**	**477**

(j) Using Simpson's Paradox, explain how the additional classification affects your response to part (g).

(k) What recommendation would you make to the city council regarding the implementation of the red-light camera program? Would you need any additional information before making your recommendation? Explain.

48. Putting It Together: Exam Scores The following data represent the homework scores for the material on Polynomial and Rational Functions in Sullivan's College Algebra course.

37	67	76	82	89
48	70	77	83	90
54	72	77	84	90
59	73	77	84	91
61	75	77	84	92
65	75	78	85	95
65	76	80	87	95
67	76	81	88	98

Source: Michael Sullivan, MyMathLab

(a) Construct a relative frequency distribution with a lower class limit of the first class equal to 30 and a class width of 10.

(b) Draw a relative frequency histogram of the data.

(c) Determine the mean and median score. *77; 77*

(d) Describe the shape of the distribution based on the results from parts (b) and (c). *Slightly skewed left*

(e) Determine the standard deviation and interquartile range.

(f) What is the probability a randomly selected student fails the homework (scores less than 70)? *0.225* *(e) 13.06; 15*

(g) What is the probability a randomly selected student earns an A or B on the homework (scores 80 or higher)? *0.45*

(h) What is the probability a randomly selected student scores less than 30 on the homework? *0*

5.3 INDEPENDENCE AND THE MULTIPLICATION RULE

OBJECTIVES

1. Identify independent events
2. Use the Multiplication Rule for Independent Events
3. Compute at-least probabilities

1 Identify Independent Events

We use the Addition Rule for Disjoint Events to compute the probability of observing an outcome in event E *or* event F. We now describe a probability rule for computing the probability that E *and* F both occur.

Before we can present this rule, we must discuss the idea of *independent events*.

DEFINITIONS

Two events E and F are **independent** if the occurrence of event E in a probability experiment does not affect the probability of event F. Two events are **dependent** if the occurrence of event E in a probability experiment affects the probability of event F.

Think about flipping a fair coin twice. Does the fact that you obtained a head on the first toss have any effect on the likelihood of obtaining a head on the second toss? Not unless you are a master coin flipper who can manipulate the outcome of a coin flip! For this reason, the outcome from the first flip is independent of the outcome from the second flip. Let's look at other examples.

EXAMPLE 1 Independent or Not?

(a) Suppose you flip a coin and roll a die. The events "obtain a head" and "roll a 5" are independent because the results of the coin flip do not affect the results of the die toss.

(b) Are the events "earned a bachelor's degree" and "earn more than \$100,000 per year" independent? No, because knowing that an individual has a bachelor's degree affects the likelihood that the individual is earning more than \$100,000 per year.

(c) Two 24-year-old male drivers who live in the United States are randomly selected. The events "male 1 gets in a car accident during the year" and "male 2 gets in a car accident during the year" are independent because the males were randomly selected. This means what happens with one of the drivers has nothing to do with what happens to the other driver.

In Other Words
In determining whether two events are independent, ask yourself whether the probability of one event is affected by the other event. For example, what is the probability that a 29-year-old male has high cholesterol? What is the probability that a 29-year-old male has high cholesterol, given that he eats fast food four times a week? Does the fact that the individual eats fast food four times a week change the likelihood that he has high cholesterol? If yes, the events are not independent.

In Example 1(c), we are able to conclude that the events "male 1 gets in an accident" and "male 2 gets in an accident" are independent because the individuals are randomly selected. By randomly selecting the individuals, it is reasonable to conclude that the individuals are not related in any way (related in the sense that they do not live in the same town, attend the same school, and so on). If the two individuals did have a common link between them (such as they both lived on the same city block), then knowing that one male had a car accident may affect the likelihood that the other male had a car accident. After all, they could hit each other!

Now Work Problem 7

Disjoint Events versus Independent Events It is important to know that disjoint events and independent events are different concepts. Recall that two events are disjoint if they have no outcomes in common, that is, if knowing that one of the events occurs, we know the other event did not occur. Independence means that one event occurring does not affect the probability of the other event occurring. Therefore, knowing two events are disjoint means that the events are not independent.

⚠ CAUTION
Two events that are disjoint are not independent.

Consider the experiment of rolling a single die. Let E represent the event "roll an even number," and let F represent the event "roll an odd number." We can see that E and F are mutually exclusive (disjoint) because they have no outcomes in common. In addition, $P(E) = \frac{1}{2}$ and $P(F) = \frac{1}{2}$. However, if we are told that the roll of the die is going to be an even number, then what is the probability of event F? Because the outcome will be even, the probability of event F is now 0 (and the probability of event E is now 1).

2 Use the Multiplication Rule for Independent Events

Suppose that you flip a fair coin twice. What is the probability that you obtain a head on both flips, that is, a head on the first flip *and* you obtain a head on the second flip? If H

represents the outcome "heads" and T represents the outcome "tails," the sample space of this experiment is

$$S = \{HH, HT, TH, TT\}$$

There is one outcome with both heads. Because each outcome is equally likely, we have

$$P(\text{heads on Flip 1 and heads on Flip 2}) = \frac{N(\text{heads on Flip 1 and heads on Flip 2})}{N(S)} = \frac{1}{4}$$

We may have intuitively figured this out by recognizing $P(\text{head}) = \frac{1}{2}$ for each flip. So it seems reasonable that

$$\begin{aligned} P(\text{heads on Flip 1 and heads on Flip 2}) &= P(\text{heads on Flip 1}) \cdot P(\text{heads on Flip 2}) \\ &= \frac{1}{2} \cdot \frac{1}{2} \\ &= \frac{1}{4} \end{aligned}$$

Because both approaches result in the same answer, $\frac{1}{4}$, we conjecture that $P(E \text{ and } F) = P(E) \cdot P(F)$. Our conjecture is correct.

Multiplication Rule for Independent Events

If E and F are independent events, then

$$P(E \text{ and } F) = P(E) \cdot P(F)$$

EXAMPLE 2 Computing Probabilities of Independent Events

Problem In the game of roulette, the wheel has slots numbered 0, 00, and 1 through 36. A metal ball rolls around a wheel until it falls into one of the numbered slots. What is the probability that the ball will land in the slot numbered 17 two times in a row?

Approach The sample space of the experiment has 38 outcomes. We use the classical method of computing probabilities because the outcomes are equally likely. In addition, we use the Multiplication Rule for Independent Events. The events "17 on Spin 1" and "17 on Spin 2" are independent because the ball does not remember it landed on 17 on the first spin, so this cannot affect the probability of landing on 17 on the second spin.

Solution There are 38 possible outcomes, so the probability of landing on 17 is $\frac{1}{38}$. Because the events "17 on Spin 1" and "17 on Spin 2" are independent, we have

$$\begin{aligned} P(\text{17 on Spin 1 and 17 on Spin 2}) &= P(\text{17 on Spin 1}) \cdot P(\text{17 on Spin 2}) \\ &= \frac{1}{38} \cdot \frac{1}{38} = \frac{1}{1444} \approx 0.0006925 \end{aligned}$$

We expect the ball to land on 17 twice in a row about 7 times in 10,000 trials.

We can extend the Multiplication Rule for three or more independent events.

Multiplication Rule for *n* Independent Events

If events $E_1, E_2, E_3, \ldots, E_n$ are independent, then

$$P(E_1 \text{ and } E_2 \text{ and } E_3, \text{ and} \ldots \text{ and } E_n) = P(E_1) \cdot P(E_2) \cdot \cdots \cdot P(E_n)$$

EXAMPLE 3 Life Expectancy

Problem The probability that a randomly selected 24-year-old male will survive the year is 0.9986 according to the *National Vital Statistics Report*, Vol. 56, No. 9. What is the probability that 3 randomly selected 24-year-old males will survive the year? What is the probability that 20 randomly selected 24-year-old males will survive the year?

In Other Words
In Example 3, if two of the males lived in the same house, a house fire could kill both males and we lose independence. (Knowledge that one male died in a house fire certainly affects the probability that the other died.) By randomly selecting the males, we minimize the chances that they are related in any way.

Approach It is safe to assume that the outcomes of the probability experiment are independent, because there is no indication that the survival of one male affects the survival of the others.

Solution

$$\begin{aligned} P(\text{all three males survive}) &= P(\text{1st survives and 2nd survives and 3rd survives}) \\ &= P(\text{1st survives}) \cdot P(\text{2nd survives}) \cdot P(\text{3rd survives}) \\ &= (0.9986)(0.9986)(0.9986) \\ &= 0.9958 \end{aligned}$$

There is a 99.58% probability that all three males survive the year.

$$\begin{aligned} P(\text{all 20 males survive}) &= P(\text{1st survives and 2nd survives and} \ldots \text{and 20th survives}) \\ &= P(\text{1st survives}) \cdot P(\text{2nd survives}) \cdot \cdots \cdot P(\text{20th survives}) \\ &= \overbrace{(0.9986) \cdot (0.9986) \cdot \cdots \cdot (0.9986)}^{\text{Multiply 0.9986 by itself 20 times.}} \\ &= (0.9986)^{20} \\ &= 0.9724 \end{aligned}$$

Now Work Problem 17(a) and (b)

There is a 97.24% probability that all 20 males survive the year.

3 Compute At-Least Probabilities

Probabilities involving the phrase "at least" typically use the Complement Rule. The phrase *at least* means "greater than or equal to." For example, a person must be at least 17 years old to see an R-rated movie.

EXAMPLE 4 Computing At-Least Probabilities

Note to Instructor
Remind students that at-least means greater than or equal to. At-least probabilities are usually determined using the Complement Rule. For Example 4, ask students to distinguish between $1 - 0.9986^{1000}$ and $(1 - 0.9986)^{1000}$.

Problem Compute the probability that at least 1 male out of 1000 aged 24 years will die during the course of the year if the probability that a randomly selected 24-year-old male survives the year is 0.9986.

Approach The phrase *at least* means "greater than or equal to," so we wish to know the probability that 1 or 2 or 3 or . . . or 1000 males will die during the year. These events are mutually exclusive, so

$$P(1 \text{ or } 2 \text{ or } 3 \text{ or} \ldots \text{or } 1000 \text{ die}) = P(1 \text{ dies}) + P(2 \text{ die}) + P(3 \text{ die}) + \cdots + P(1000 \text{ die})$$

Computing these probabilities is very time consuming. However, we notice that the complement of "at least one dying" is "none die." We use the Complement Rule to compute the probability.

Solution

$$\begin{aligned} P(\text{at least one dies}) &= 1 - P(\text{none die}) \\ &= 1 - P(\text{1st survives and 2nd survives and} \ldots \text{and 1000th survives}) \\ &= 1 - P(\text{1st survives}) \cdot P(\text{2nd survives}) \cdot \cdots \cdot P(\text{1000th survives}) \quad \text{Independent events} \\ &= 1 - (0.9986)^{1000} \\ &= 1 - 0.2464 \\ &= 0.7536 \\ &= 75.36\% \end{aligned}$$

There is a 75.36% probability that at least one 24-year-old male out of 1000 will die during the course of the year.

Now Work Problem 17(c)

Summary: Rules of Probability

1. The probability of any event must be between 0 and 1, inclusive. If we let E denote any event, then $0 \leq P(E) \leq 1$.
2. The sum of the probabilities of all outcomes in the sample space must equal 1. That is, if the sample space $S = \{e_1, e_2, \ldots, e_n\}$, then $P(e_1) + P(e_2) + \cdots + P(e_n) = 1$.
3. If E and F are disjoint events, then $P(E \text{ or } F) = P(E) + P(F)$. If E and F are not disjoint events, then $P(E \text{ or } F) = P(E) + P(F) - P(E \text{ and } F)$.
4. If E represents any event and E^c represents the complement of E, then $P(E^c) = 1 - P(E)$.
5. If E and F are independent events, then $P(E \text{ and } F) = P(E) \cdot P(F)$.

Notice that *or* probabilities use the Addition Rule, whereas *and* probabilities use the Multiplication Rule. Accordingly, *or* probabilities imply addition, while *and* probabilities imply multiplication.

5.3 ASSESS YOUR UNDERSTANDING

VOCABULARY AND SKILL BUILDING

1. Two events E and F are _____ if the occurrence of event E in a probability experiment does not affect the probability of event F.

2. The word *and* in probability implies that we use the _____ Rule. Multiplication 1. independent

3. The word *or* in probability implies that we use the _____ Rule. Addition

4. *True or False:* When two events are disjoint, they are also independent. False 5. $P(E) \cdot P(F)$

5. If two events E and F are independent, $P(E \text{ and } F) =$ _____.

6. Suppose events E and F are disjoint. What is $P(E \text{ and } F)$? 0

NW **7.** Determine whether the events E and F are independent or dependent. Justify your answer.

(a) E: Speeding on the interstate.
F: Being pulled over by a police officer. Dependent

(b) E: You gain weight.
F: You eat fast food for dinner every night. Dependent

(c) E: You get a high score on a statistics exam.
F: The Boston Red Sox win a baseball game. Independent

8. Determine whether the events E and F are independent or dependent. Justify your answer.

(a) E: The battery in your cell phone is dead.
F: The batteries in your calculator are dead. Independent

(b) E: Your favorite color is blue.
F: Your friend's favorite hobby is fishing. Independent

(c) E: You are late for school.
F: Your car runs out of gas. Dependent

9. Suppose that events E and F are independent, $P(E) = 0.3$ and $P(F) = 0.6$. What is the $P(E \text{ and } F)$? 0.18

10. Suppose that events E and F are independent, $P(E) = 0.7$ and $P(F) = 0.9$. What is the $P(E \text{ and } F)$? 0.63

APPLYING THE CONCEPTS

11. Flipping a Coin What is the probability of obtaining five heads in a row when flipping a fair coin? Interpret this probability.

12. Rolling a Die What is the probability of obtaining 4 ones in a row when rolling a fair, six-sided die? Interpret this probability. 0.0008 11. 0.03125

13. Southpaws About 13% of the population is left-handed. If two people are randomly selected, what is the probability that both are left-handed? What is the probability that at least one is right-handed? 0.0169; 0.9831

14. Double Jackpot Shawn lives near the border of Illinois and Missouri. One weekend he decides to play \$1 in both state lotteries in hopes of hitting two jackpots. The probability of winning the Missouri Lotto is about 0.00000028357 and the probability of winning the Illinois Lotto is about 0.000000098239.

(a) Explain why the two lotteries are independent.

(b) Find the probability that Shawn will win both jackpots.

15. False Positives The ELISA is a test to determine whether the HIV antibody is present. The test is 99.5% effective, which means that the test will come back negative if the HIV antibody is not present 99.5% of the time. The probability of a test coming back positive when the antibody is not present (a false positive) is 0.005. Suppose that the ELISA is given to five randomly selected people who do not have the HIV antibody.

(a) What is the probability that the ELISA comes back negative for all five people? 0.9752 14.(b) 0.0000000000000279

(b) What is the probability that the ELISA comes back positive for at least one of the five people? 0.0248

16. Christmas Lights Christmas lights are often designed with a series circuit. This means that when one light burns out the entire string of lights goes black. Suppose that the lights are designed so that the probability a bulb will last 2 years is 0.995. The success or failure of a bulb is independent of the success or failure of other bulbs.

(a) What is the probability that in a string of 100 lights all 100 will last 2 years? 0.6058

(b) What is the probability that at least one bulb will burn out in 2 years? 0.3942

NW **17. Life Expectancy** The probability that a randomly selected 40-year-old male will live to be 41 years old is 0.99757, according to the *National Vital Statistics Report*, Vol. 56, No. 9.

(a) What is the probability that two randomly selected 40-year-old males will live to be 41 years old? 0.99515

(b) What is the probability that five randomly selected 40-year-old males will live to be 41 years old? 0.98791

(c) What is the probability that at least one of five randomly selected 40-year-old males will not live to be 41 years old? Would it be unusual if at least one of five randomly selected 40-year-old males did not live to be 41 years old? 0.01209; yes

18. Life Expectancy The probability that a randomly selected 40-year-old female will live to be 41 years old is 0.99855 according to the *National Vital Statistics Report*, Vol. 56, No. 9.

(a) What is the probability that two randomly selected 40-year-old females will live to be 41 years old? 0.99710

(b) What is the probability that five randomly selected 40-year-old females will live to be 41 years old? 0.99277

(c) What is the probability that at least one of five randomly selected 40-year-old females will not live to be 41 years old? Would it be unusual if at least one of five randomly selected 40-year-old females did not live to be 41 years old? 0.00723; yes

19. Mental Illness According to the Department of Health and Human Services, 30% of 18- to 25-year-olds have some form of mental illness.

(a) What is the probability two randomly selected 18- to 25-year-olds have some form of mental illness? 0.09

(b) What is the probability six randomly selected 18- to 25-year-olds have some form of mental illness? 0.000729

(c) What is the probability at least one of six randomly selected 18- to 25-year-olds has some form of mental illness? 0.882

(d) Would it be unusual that among four randomly selected 18- to 25-year-olds, none has some form of mental illness? No

20. Quality Control Suppose that a company selects two people who work independently inspecting two-by-four timbers. Their job is to identify low-quality timbers. Suppose that the probability that an inspector does not identify a low-quality timber is 0.20.

(a) What is the probability that both inspectors do not identify a low-quality timber? 0.04

(b) How many inspectors should be hired to keep the probability of not identifying a low-quality timber below 1%? 3

(c) Interpret the probability from part (a).

21. Reliability For a parallel structure of identical components, the system can succeed if at least one of the components succeeds. Assume that components fail independently of each other and that each component has a 0.15 probability of failure.

(a) Would it be unusual to observe one component fail? Two components? No; yes

(b) What is the probability that a parallel structure with 2 identical components will succeed? 0.9775

(c) How many components would be needed in the structure so that the probability the system will succeed is greater than 0.9999? 5

22. E.P.T. Pregnancy Tests The packaging of an E.P.T. Pregnancy Test states that the test is "99% accurate at detecting typical pregnancy hormone levels." Assume that the probability that a test will correctly identify a pregnancy is 0.99 and that 12 randomly selected pregnant women with typical hormone levels are each given the test. (a) 0.8864

(a) What is the probability that all 12 tests will be positive?

(b) What is the probability that at least one test will not be positive? 0.1136

23. Cold Streaks Players in sports are said to have "hot streaks" and "cold streaks." For example, a batter in baseball might be considered to be in a slump, or cold streak, if he has made 10 outs in 10 consecutive at-bats. Suppose that a hitter successfully reaches base 30% of the time he comes to the plate.

(a) Find and interpret the probability that the hitter makes 10 outs in 10 consecutive at-bats, assuming that at-bats are independent events. *Hint:* The hitter makes an out 70% of the time. 0.02825

(b) Are cold streaks unusual? Yes

(c) Find the probability the hitter makes five consecutive outs and then reaches base safely. 0.0504

24. Hot Streaks In a recent basketball game, a player who makes 65% of his free throws made eight consecutive free throws. Assuming that free-throw shots are independent, determine whether this feat was unusual. Unusual

25. Bowling Suppose that Ralph gets a strike when bowling 30% of the time.

(a) What is the probability that Ralph gets two strikes in a row? 0.09

(b) What is the probability that Ralph gets a turkey (three strikes in a row)? 0.027

(c) When events are independent, their complements are independent as well. Use this result to determine the probability that Ralph gets a turkey, but fails to get a clover (four strikes in a row). 0.0189

26. NASCAR Fans Among Americans who consider themselves auto racing fans, 59% identify NASCAR stock cars as their favorite type of racing. Suppose that four auto racing fans are randomly selected. *Source:* ESPN/TNS Sports, reported in *USA Today*

(a) What is the probability that all four will identify NASCAR stock cars as their favorite type of racing? 0.1212

(b) What is the probability that at least one will not identify NASCAR stock cars as his or her favorite type of racing? 0.8788

(c) What is the probability that none will identify NASCAR stock cars as his or her favorite type of racing? 0.0283

(d) What is the probability that at least one will identify NASCAR stock cars as his or her favorite type of racing? 0.9717

27. Driving under the Influence Among 21- to 25-year-olds, 29% say they have driven while under the influence of alcohol. Suppose that three 21- to 25-year-olds are selected at random. *Source:* U.S. Department of Health and Human Services, reported in *USA Today*

(a) What is the probability that all three have driven while under the influence of alcohol? 0.0244

(b) What is the probability that at least one has not driven while under the influence of alcohol? 0.9756

(c) What is the probability that none of the three has driven while under the influence of alcohol? 0.3579

(d) What is the probability that at least one has driven while under the influence of alcohol? 0.6421

28. Defense System Suppose that a satellite defense system is established in which four satellites acting independently have a 0.9 probability of detecting an incoming ballistic missile. What is the probability that at least one of the four satellites detects an incoming ballistic missile? Would you feel safe with such a system? 0.9999

29. Audits and Pet Ownership According to Internal Revenue Service records, 6.42% of all household tax returns are audited. According to the Humane Society, 39% of all households own a dog. Assuming dog ownership and audits are independent events, what is the probability a randomly selected household is audited and owns a dog? 0.025

30. Weight Gain and Gender According to the National Vital Statistics Report, 20.1% of all pregnancies result in weight gain in excess of 40 pounds (for singleton births). In addition, 49.5% of all pregnancies result in the birth of a baby girl. Assuming gender and weight gain are independent, what is the probability a randomly selected pregnancy results in a girl and weight gain in excess of 40 pounds? 0.099

31. Stocks Suppose your financial advisor recommends three stocks to you. He claims the likelihood that the first stock will increase in value at least 10% within the next year is 0.7, the likelihood the second stock will increase in value at least 10% within the next year is 0.55, and the likelihood the third stock will increase at least 10% within the next year is 0.20. Would it be unusual for all three stocks to increase at least 10%, assuming the stocks behave independently of each other? No; 0.077 probability

32. Betting on Sports According to a Gallup Poll, about 17% of adult Americans bet on professional sports. Census data indicate that 48.4% of the adult population in the United States is male.

(a) Assuming that betting is independent of gender, compute the probability that an American adult selected at random is a male and bets on professional sports. 0.0823

(b) Using the result in part (a), compute the probability that an American adult selected at random is male or bets on professional sports. 0.5717

(c) The Gallup poll data indicated that 10.6% of adults in the United States are males and bet on professional sports. What does this indicate about the assumption in part (a)? Not independent

(d) How will the information in part (c) affect the probability you computed in part (b)? 0.548

33. Fingerprints Fingerprints are now widely accepted as a form of identification. In fact, many computers today use fingerprint identification to link the owner to the computer. In 1892, Sir Francis Galton explored the use of fingerprints to uniquely identify an individual. A fingerprint consists of ridgelines. Based on empirical evidence, Galton estimated the probability that a square consisting of six ridgelines that covered a fingerprint could be filled in accurately by an experienced fingerprint analyst as $\frac{1}{2}$.

(a) Assuming that a full fingerprint consists of 24 of these squares, what is the probability that all 24 squares could be filled in correctly, assuming that success or failure in filling in one square is independent of success or failure in filling in any other square within the region? (This value represents the probability that two individuals would share the same ridgeline features within the 24-square region.)

(b) Galton further estimated that the likelihood of determining the fingerprint type (e.g., arch, left loop, whorl, etc.) as $\left(\frac{1}{2}\right)^4$ and the likelihood of the occurrence of the correct number of ridges entering and exiting each of the 24 regions as $\left(\frac{1}{2}\right)^8$. Assuming that all three probabilities are independent, compute Galton's estimate of the probability that a particular fingerprint configuration would occur in nature (that is, the probability that a fingerprint match occurs by chance).

33. (a) $\left(\frac{1}{2}\right)^{24} \approx 5.96 \times 10^{-8}$ (b) $\left(\frac{1}{2}\right)^{36} \approx 1.46 \times 10^{-11}$

5.4 CONDITIONAL PROBABILITY AND THE GENERAL MULTIPLICATION RULE

OBJECTIVES
1 Compute conditional probabilities
2 Compute probabilities using the General Multiplication Rule

1 Compute Conditional Probabilities

In the last section, we learned that when two events are independent the occurrence of one event has no effect on the probability of the second event. However, we cannot generally assume that two events will be independent. Will the probability of being in a car accident change depending on driving conditions? We would expect so. For example,

Note to Instructor

For Instructors who want to offer a course that minimizes the coverage of probability, this section can be skipped without loss of continuity.

we would expect the probability of an accident to be higher for nighttime driving on icy roads than for daytime driving on dry roads.

According to data from the Centers for Disease Control, 33.3% of adult men in the United States are obese. So the probability is 0.333 that a randomly selected U.S. adult male is obese. However, 28% of adult men aged 20 to 39 are obese compared to 40% of adult men aged 40 to 59. The probability is 0.28 that an adult male is obese, *given* that he is aged 20 to 39. The probability is 0.40 that an adult male is obese, *given* that he is aged 40 to 59. The probability that an adult male is obese changes depending on his age group. This is called *conditional probability*.

DEFINITION

Conditional Probability

The notation $P(F|E)$ is read "the probability of event F given event E." It is the probability that the event F occurs, given that the event E has occurred.

EXAMPLE 1 An Introduction to Conditional Probability

Problem Suppose a single die is rolled. What is the probability that the die comes up 3? Now suppose that the die is rolled a second time, but we are told the outcome will be an odd number. What is the probability that the die comes up 3?

Approach We assume that the die is fair and compute the probabilities using equally likely outcomes.

Solution In the first instance, there are six possibilities in the sample space, $S = \{1, 2, 3, 4, 5, 6\}$, so $P(3) = \frac{1}{6}$. In the second instance, there are three possibilities in the sample space, because the only possible outcomes are odd, so $S = \{1, 3, 5\}$. We express this probability symbolically as $P(3|\text{outcome is odd}) = \frac{1}{3}$, which is read "the probability of rolling a 3, given that the outcome is odd, is one-third."

From Example 1, we notice that conditional probabilities reduce the size of the sample space under consideration. Let's look at another example. The data in Table 8 represent the marital status of males and females 15 years old or older in the United States in 2010.

TABLE 8

	Males (in millions)	Females (in millions)	Totals (in millions)
Never married	40.2	34.0	**74.2**
Married	62.2	62.0	**124.2**
Widowed	3.0	11.4	**14.4**
Divorced	10.0	13.8	**23.8**
Separated	2.4	3.2	**5.6**
Totals (in millions)	**117.8**	**124.4**	**242.2**

Source: U.S. Census Bureau, Current Population Reports

To find the probability that a randomly selected individual 15 years old or older is widowed, divide the number of widowed individuals by the total number of individuals who are 15 years old or older.

$$P(\text{widowed}) = \frac{14.4}{242.2}$$
$$= 0.059$$

Suppose that we know the individual is female. Does this change the probability that she is widowed? The sample space now consists only of females, so the probability that the individual is widowed, given that the individual is female, is

$$P(\text{widowed} \mid \text{female}) = \frac{N(\text{widowed females})}{N(\text{females})}$$

$$= \frac{11.4}{124.4} = 0.092$$

So, knowing that the individual is female increases the likelihood that the individual is widowed. This leads to the following rule.

Conditional Probability Rule

If E and F are any two events, then

$$P(F \mid E) = \frac{P(E \text{ and } F)}{P(E)} = \frac{N(E \text{ and } F)}{N(E)} \quad \textbf{(1)}$$

The probability of event F occurring, given the occurrence of event E, is found by dividing the probability of E and F by the probability of E, or by dividing the number of outcomes in E and F by the number of outcomes in E.

EXAMPLE 2 Conditional Probabilities on Marital Status and Gender

Problem The data in Table 8 on the previous page represent the marital status and gender of the residents of the United States aged 15 years old or older in 2010.

(a) Compute the probability that a randomly selected individual has never married given the individual is male.

(b) Compute the probability that a randomly selected individual is male given the individual has never married.

Approach

(a) Since the randomly selected person is male, concentrate on the male column. There are 117.8 million males and 40.2 million males who never married, so $N(\text{male}) = 117.8$ million and $N(\text{male and never married}) = 40.2$ million. Compute the probability using the Conditional Probability Rule.

(b) Since the randomly selected person has never married, concentrate on the never married row. There are 74.2 million people who have never married and 40.2 million males who have never married, so $N(\text{never married}) = 74.2$ million and $N(\text{male and never married}) = 40.2$ million. Compute the probability using the Conditional Probability Rule.

Solution

(a) Substituting into Formula (1), we obtain

$$P(\text{never married} \mid \text{male}) = \frac{N(\text{male and never married})}{N(\text{male})} = \frac{40.2}{117.8} = 0.341$$

There is a 34.1% probability that the randomly selected individual has never married, given that he is male.

(b) Substituting into Formula (1), we obtain

$$P(\text{male} \mid \text{never married}) = \frac{N(\text{male and never married})}{N(\text{never married})} = \frac{40.2}{74.2} = 0.542$$

There is a 54.2% probability that the randomly selected individual is male, given that he or she has never married.

What is the difference between the results of Example 2(a) and (b)? In Example 2(a), we found that 34.1% of males have never married, whereas in Example 2(b) we found that 54.2% of individuals who have never married are male. Do you see the difference?

Now Work Problem 17

EXAMPLE 3 Birth Weights of Preterm Babies

Problem In 2007, 12.7% of all births were preterm. (The gestation period of the pregnancy was less than 37 weeks.) Also in 2007, 0.22% of all births resulted in a preterm baby who weighed 8 pounds, 13 ounces or more. What is the probability that a randomly selected baby weighs 8 pounds, 13 ounces or more, given that the baby was preterm? Is this unusual?

Approach We want to know the probability that the baby weighs 8 pounds, 13 ounces or more, given that the baby was preterm. Since 0.22% of all babies weighed 8 pounds, 13 ounces or more and were preterm, $P(\text{weighs 8 lb, 13 oz or more and preterm}) = 0.22\%$. Since 12.7% of all births were preterm, $P(\text{preterm}) = 12.7\%$. Use the Conditional Probability Rule to compute the probability.

Solution $P(\text{weighs 8 lb, 13 oz or more} \mid \text{preterm})$

$$= \frac{P(\text{weighs 8 lb, 13 oz or more and preterm})}{P(\text{preterm})}$$

$$= \frac{0.22\%}{12.7\%} = \frac{0.0022}{0.127} \approx 0.0173 = 1.73\%$$

There is a 1.73% probability that a randomly selected baby will weigh 8 pounds, 13 ounces or more, given that the baby is preterm, which is unusual.

Now Work Problem 13

2 Compute Probabilities Using the General Multiplication Rule

If we solve the Conditional Probability Rule for $P(E \text{ and } F)$, we obtain the General Multiplication Rule.

General Multiplication Rule

The probability that two events E and F both occur is

$$P(E \text{ and } F) = P(E) \cdot P(F \mid E)$$

In words, the probability of E and F is the probability of event E occurring times the probability of event F occurring, given the occurrence of event E.

EXAMPLE 4 Using the General Multiplication Rule

Problem The probability that a driver who is speeding gets pulled over is 0.8. The probability that a driver gets a ticket, given that he or she is pulled over, is 0.9. What is the probability that a randomly selected driver who is speeding gets pulled over and gets a ticket?

Approach Let E represent the event "driver who is speeding gets pulled over," and let F represent the event "driver gets a ticket." We use the General Multiplication Rule to compute $P(E \text{ and } F)$.

Solution P(driver who is speeding gets pulled over and gets a ticket) $= P(E \text{ and } F) = P(E) \cdot P(F \mid E) = 0.8(0.9) = 0.72$. There is a 72% probability that a driver who is speeding gets pulled over and gets a ticket.

Now Work Problem 31

EXAMPLE 5 Acceptance Sampling

Problem Suppose that of 100 circuits sent to a manufacturing plant, 5 are defective. The plant manager receiving the circuits randomly selects 2 and tests them. If both circuits work, she will accept the shipment. Otherwise, the shipment is rejected. What is the probability that the plant manager discovers at least 1 defective circuit and rejects the shipment?

Approach To determine the probability that at least one of the tested circuits is defective, consider four possibilities. Neither of the circuits is defective, the first is defective while the second is not, the first is not defective while the second is defective, or both circuits are defective. Note that the outcomes are not equally likely.

One approach is to use a tree diagram to list all possible outcomes and the General Multiplication Rule to compute the probability for each outcome. Then determine the probability of at least 1 defective by adding the probability that only the first is defective, only the second is defective, or both are defective, using the Addition Rule (because they are disjoint).

A second approach is to compute the probability that both circuits are not defective and use the Complement Rule to determine the probability of at least 1 defective.

We will illustrate both approaches.

Solution Of the 100 circuits, 5 are defective, so 95 are not defective. To use our first approach, we construct a tree diagram to determine the possible outcomes for the experiment. We draw two branches corresponding to the two possible outcomes (defective or not defective) for the first repetition of the experiment (the first circuit). For the second circuit, two branches originate from the first defective circuit and two branches originate from the first nondefective circuit. See Figure 12, where D stands for defective and G stands for good (not defective). Since the outcomes are not equally likely, we include the probabilities in our diagram to show how the probability of each outcome is obtained. The probability for each outcome is obtained by multiplying the individual probabilities along the corresponding path in the diagram.

Figure 12

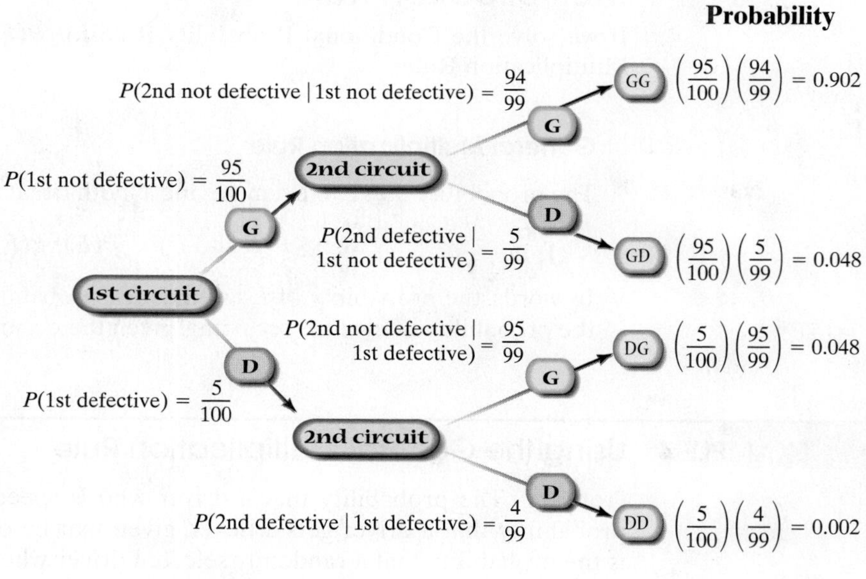

From our tree diagram, and using the Addition Rule, we can write

$$\begin{aligned} P(\text{at least 1 defective}) &= P(\text{GD}) + P(\text{DG}) + P(\text{DD}) \\ &= 0.048 + 0.048 + 0.002 \\ &= 0.098 \end{aligned}$$

There is a 9.8% probability that the shipment will not be accepted.

For our second approach, we compute the probability that both circuits are not defective and use the Complement Rule to determine the probability of at least 1 defective.

$$\begin{aligned} P(\text{at least 1 defective}) &= 1 - P(\text{none defective}) \\ &= 1 - P(\text{1st not defective}) \cdot P(\text{2nd not defective} \mid \text{1st not defective}) \\ &= 1 - \left(\frac{95}{100}\right) \cdot \left(\frac{94}{99}\right) \\ &= 1 - 0.902 \\ &= 0.098 \end{aligned}$$

There is a 9.8% probability that the shipment will not be accepted. This result is the same as that obtained using our tree diagram.

Now Work Problem 21

Whenever a small random sample is taken from a large population, it is reasonable to compute probabilities of events assuming independence. Consider the following example.

EXAMPLE 6 Sickle-Cell Anemia

Problem A survey of 10,000 African Americans found that 27 had sickle-cell anemia.

(a) Suppose we randomly select 1 of the 10,000 African Americans surveyed. What is the probability that he or she has sickle-cell anemia?

(b) If two individuals from this group are randomly selected, what is the probability that both have sickle-cell anemia?

(c) Compute the probability of randomly selecting two individuals from this group who have sickle-cell anemia, assuming independence.

Approach We let the event E = "sickle-cell anemia," so $P(E)$ = number of African Americans who have sickle-cell anemia divided by the number in the survey. To answer part (b), we let E_1 = "first person has sickle-cell anemia" and E_2 = "second person has sickle-cell anemia," and then we compute $P(E_1 \text{ and } E_2) = P(E_1) \cdot P(E_2 \mid E_1)$. To answer part (c), we use the Multiplication Rule for Independent Events.

Solution

(a) If one individual is selected, $P(E) = \dfrac{27}{10{,}000} = 0.0027$.

(b) Using the Multiplication Rule, we have

$$P(E_1 \text{ and } E_2) = P(E_1) \cdot P(E_2 \mid E_1) = \frac{27}{10{,}000} \cdot \frac{26}{9999} \approx 0.00000702$$

Notice that $P(E_2 \mid E_1) = \dfrac{26}{9999}$ because we are sampling without replacement, so after event E_1 occurs there is one less person with sickle-cell anemia and one less person in the sample space.

(c) The assumption of independence means that the outcome of the first trial of the experiment does not affect the probability of the second trial. (It is like sampling with replacement.) Therefore, we assume that

$$P(E_1) = P(E_2) = \frac{27}{10{,}000}$$

Then

$$P(E_1 \text{ and } E_2) = P(E_1) \cdot P(E_2) = \frac{27}{10{,}000} \cdot \frac{27}{10{,}000} \approx 0.00000729$$

The probabilities in Examples 6(b) and 6(c) are extremely close in value. Based on these results, we infer the principle on the following page.

Historical Note

Andrei Nikolaevich Kolmogorov was born on April 25, 1903, in Tambov, Russia. His parents were not married, and he was raised by his aunt. He graduated from Moscow State University in 1925. That year he published eight papers, including his first on probability. By the time he received his doctorate, in 1929, he already had 18 publications. He became a professor at Moscow State University in 1931. Kolmogorov is quoted as saying, "The theory of probability as a mathematical discipline can and should be developed from axioms in exactly the same way as Geometry and Algebra." Kolmogorov helped to educate gifted children. It did not bother him if the students did not become mathematicians; he simply wanted them to be happy. Andrei Kolmogorov died on October 20, 1987.

If small random samples are taken from large populations without replacement, it is reasonable to assume independence of the events. As a rule of thumb, if the sample size is less than 5% of the population size, we treat the events as independent.

For example, in Example 6, we can compute the probability of randomly selecting two African Americans who have sickle-cell anemia assuming independence because the sample size, 2, is only $\frac{2}{10{,}000}$, or 0.02% of the population size, 10,000.

Now Work Problem 39

We can now express independence using conditional probabilities.

DEFINITION Two events E and F are independent if $P(E \mid F) = P(E)$ or, equivalently, if $P(F \mid E) = P(F)$.

If either condition in our definition is true, the other is as well. In addition, for independent events,

$$P(E \text{ and } F) = P(E) \cdot P(F)$$

So the Multiplication Rule for Independent Events is a special case of the General Multiplication Rule.

Look back at Table 8 on page 265. Because $P(\text{widowed}) = 0.059$ does not equal $P(\text{widowed} \mid \text{female}) = 0.092$, the events "widowed" and "female" are not independent. In fact, knowing an individual is female increases the likelihood that the individual is also widowed.

Now Work Problem 41

5.4 ASSESS YOUR UNDERSTANDING

VOCABULARY AND SKILL BUILDING

1. The notation $P(F \mid E)$ means the probability of event __F__ given event __E__.

2. If $P(E) = 0.6$ and $P(E \mid F) = 0.34$, are events E and F independent? No

3. Suppose that E and F are two events and that $P(E \text{ and } F) = 0.6$ and $P(E) = 0.8$. What is $P(F \mid E)$? 0.75

4. Suppose that E and F are two events and that $P(E \text{ and } F) = 0.21$ and $P(E) = 0.4$. What is $P(F \mid E)$? 0.525

5. Suppose that E and F are two events and that $N(E \text{ and } F) = 420$ and $N(E) = 740$. What is $P(F \mid E)$? 0.568

6. Suppose that E and F are two events and that $N(E \text{ and } F) = 380$ and $N(E) = 925$. What is $P(F \mid E)$? 0.411

7. Suppose that E and F are two events and that $P(E) = 0.8$ and $P(F \mid E) = 0.4$. What is $P(E \text{ and } F)$? 0.32

8. Suppose that E and F are two events and that $P(E) = 0.4$ and $P(F \mid E) = 0.6$. What is $P(E \text{ and } F)$? 0.24

9. According to the U.S. Census Bureau, the probability that a randomly selected head of household in the United States earns more than $100,000 per year is 0.202. The probability that a randomly selected head of household in the United States earns more than $100,000 per year, given that the head of household has earned a bachelor's degree, is 0.412. Are the events "earn more than $100,000 per year" and "earned a bachelor's degree" independent? No

10. The probability that a randomly selected individual in the United States 25 years and older has at least a bachelor's degree is 0.279. The probability that an individual in the United States 25 years and older has at least a bachelor's degree, given that the individual lives in Washington D.C., is, 0.485. Are the events "bachelor's degree" and "lives in Washington, D.C.," independent? *Source: American Community Survey, 2009* No

APPLYING THE CONCEPTS

11. Drawing a Card Suppose that a single card is selected from a standard 52-card deck. What is the probability that the card drawn is a club? Now suppose that a single card is drawn from a standard 52-card deck, but we are told that the card is black. What is the probability that the card drawn is a club? 0.25; 0.5

12. Drawing a Card Suppose that a single card is selected from a standard 52-card deck. What is the probability that the card drawn is a king? Now suppose that a single card is drawn from a standard 52-card deck, but we are told that the card is a heart. What is the probability that the card drawn is a king? Did the knowledge that the card is a heart change the probability that the card was a king? What term is used to describe this result?

NW **13. Rainy Days** For the month of June in the city of Chicago, 37% of the days are cloudy. Also in the month of June in the city of Chicago, 21% of the days are cloudy and rainy. What is the probability that a randomly selected day in June will be rainy if it is cloudy? 0.568 12. 1/13; 1/13; no; independence

14. Cause of Death According to the U.S. National Center for Health Statistics, 0.15% of deaths in the United States are 25- to 34-year-olds whose cause of death is cancer. In addition, 1.71% of all those who die are 25 to 34 years old. What is the probability that a randomly selected death is the result of cancer if the individual is known to have been 25 to 34 years old? 0.088

15. High School Dropouts According to the U.S. Census Bureau, 8.0% of 16- to 24-year-olds are high school dropouts. In addition, 2.1% of 16- to 24-year-olds are high school dropouts and unemployed. What is the probability that a randomly selected 16- to 24-year-old is unemployed, given he or she is a dropout? 0.263

16. Income by Region According to the U.S. Census Bureau, 17.9% of U.S. households are in the Northeast. In addition, 5.4% of U.S. households earn $100,000 per year or more and are located in the Northeast. Determine the probability that a randomly selected U.S. household earns more than $100,000 per year, given that the household is located in the Northeast. 0.302

NW **17. Made in America** In a recent Harris Poll, a random sample of adult Americans (18 years and older) was asked, "When you see an ad emphasizing that a product is 'Made in America,' are you more likely to buy it, less likely to buy it, or neither more nor less likely to buy it?" The results of the survey, by age group, are presented in the following contingency table.

	18–34	35–44	45–54	55+	Total
More likely	238	329	360	402	**1329**
Less likely	22	6	22	16	**66**
Neither more nor less likely	282	201	164	118	**765**
Total	**542**	**536**	**546**	**536**	**2160**

Source: The Harris Poll

(a) What is the probability that a randomly selected individual is 35 to 44 years of age, given the individual is more likely to buy a product emphasized as "Made in America"? 0.248

(b) What is the probability that a randomly selected individual is more likely to buy a product emphasized as "Made in America," given the individual is 35 to 44 years of age? 0.614

(c) Are 18- to 34-year-olds more likely to buy a product emphasized as "Made in America" than individuals in general? No, less likely: 0.439 vs. 0.615

18. Sullivan Survey: Speeding Tickets The following data represent the number of speeding tickets issued to individuals in the past year and the gender of the individuals. Determine the following probabilities based on the results of the survey.

	0	1	2	3	Total
Female	97	14	3	1	**115**
Male	71	7	1	3	**82**
Total	**168**	**21**	**4**	**4**	**197**

Source: Sullivan Statistics Survey

(c) Not really, $P(\text{0 tickets} \mid F) = 0.843$; $P(\text{0 tickets} \mid M) = 0.866$

(a) What is the probability that a randomly selected individual was issued no tickets last year, given the individual is female? 0.843

(b) What is the probability that a randomly selected individual is female, given the individual has not been issued a ticket in the past year? 0.577

(c) Using the results of this survey, does it appear to be the case that females are more likely to get 0 speeding tickets than males?

19. Traffic Fatalities The following data represent the number of traffic fatalities in the United States in 2009 by seat location and gender.

	Male	Female	Total
Driver	32,873	11,856	**44,729**
Passenger	6,453	6,363	**12,816**
Total	**39,326**	**18,219**	**57,545**

Source: National Highway Traffic Safety Administration, Fatality Analysis Reporting System

(a) Among female fatalities, what is the probability that a randomly selected fatality is the driver? 0.651

(b) Among passenger fatalities, what is the probability that a randomly selected fatality is female? 0.496

(c) Suppose you are a police officer called to the scene of a traffic accident with a fatality. The dispatcher states that the victim was driving, but the gender is not known. Is the victim more likely to be male or female? Why? Male

20. Driver Fatalities The following data represent the number of drivers involved in fatal crashes in the United States in 2009 by day of the week and gender.

22. $\frac{2}{7}$ 23.(a) $\frac{1}{221}$ (b) $\frac{1}{169}$

	Male	Female	Total
Sunday	8,222	4,325	**12,547**
Monday	6,046	3,108	**9,154**
Tuesday	5,716	3,076	**8,792**
Wednesday	5,782	3,011	**8,793**
Thursday	6,315	3,302	**9,617**
Friday	7,932	4,113	**12,045**
Saturday	9,558	4,824	**14,382**
Total	**49,571**	**25,759**	**75,330**

Source: National Highway Traffic Safety Administration, Fatality Analysis Reporting System

(a) Among Sunday fatal crashes, what is the probability that a randomly selected fatality is female? 0.345

(b) Among female fatalities, what is the probability that a randomly selected fatality occurs on Sunday? 0.168

(c) Are there any days in which a fatality is more likely to be male? That is, is $P(\text{male} \mid \text{Sunday})$ much different from $P(\text{male} \mid \text{Monday})$ and so on? No

NW **21. Acceptance Sampling** Suppose that you just received a shipment of six televisions. Two of the televisions are defective. If two televisions are randomly selected, compute the probability that both televisions work. What is the probability that at least one does not work? 0.4; 0.6

22. Committee A committee consists of four women and three men. The committee will randomly select two people to attend a conference in Hawaii. Find the probability that both are women.

23. Suppose that two cards are randomly selected from a standard 52-card deck.

(a) What is the probability that the first card is a king and the second card is a king if the sampling is done without replacement?

(b) What is the probability that the first card is a king and the second card is a king if the sampling is done with replacement?

24. Suppose that two cards are randomly selected from a standard 52-card deck.

(a) What is the probability that the first card is a club and the second card is a club if the sampling is done without replacement?

(b) What is the probability that the first card is a club and the second card is a club if the sampling is done with replacement?

25. Board Work This past semester, I had a small business calculus section. The students in the class were Mike, Neta, Jinita, Kristin, and Dave. Suppose that I randomly select two people to go to the board to work problems. What is the probability that Dave is the first person chosen to go to the board and Neta is the second?

26. Party My wife has organized a monthly neighborhood party. Five people are involved in the group: Yolanda (my wife), Lorrie, Laura, Kim, and Anne Marie. They decide to randomly select the first and second home that will host the party. What is the probability that my wife hosts the first party and Lorrie hosts the second?

Note: Once a home has hosted, it cannot host again until all other homes have hosted.

27. Playing a CD on the Random Setting Suppose that a compact disc (CD) you just purchased has 13 tracks. After listening to the CD, you decide that you like 5 of the songs. With the random feature on your CD player, each of the 13 songs is played once in random order. Find the probability that among the first two songs played

(a) You like both of them. Would this be unusual?

(b) You like neither of them.

(c) You like exactly one of them.

(d) Redo (a)–(c) if a song can be replayed before all 13 songs are played (if, for example, track 2 can play twice in a row).

28. Packaging Error Due to a manufacturing error, three cans of regular soda were accidentally filled with diet soda and placed into a 12-pack. Suppose that two cans are randomly selected from the 12-pack.

(a) Determine the probability that both contain diet soda.

(b) Determine the probability that both contain regular soda. Would this be unusual?

(c) Determine the probability that exactly one is diet and one is regular?

29. Planting Tulips A bag of 30 tulip bulbs purchased from a nursery contains 12 red tulip bulbs, 10 yellow tulip bulbs, and 8 purple tulip bulbs. Use a tree diagram like the one in Example 5 to answer the following:

(a) What is the probability that two randomly selected tulip bulbs are both red? 0.152

(b) What is the probability that the first bulb selected is red and the second yellow? 0.138

(c) What is the probability that the first bulb selected is yellow and the second is red? 0.138

(d) What is the probability that one bulb is red and the other yellow? 0.276

30. Golf Balls The local golf store sells an "onion bag" that contains 35 "experienced" golf balls. Suppose that the bag contains 20 Titleists, 8 Maxflis, and 7 Top-Flites. Use a tree diagram like the one in Example 5 to answer the following:

(a) What is the probability that two randomly selected golf balls are both Titleists? 0.319

(b) What is the probability that the first ball selected is a Titleist and the second is a Maxfli? 0.134

(c) What is the probability that the first ball selected is a Maxfli and the second is a Titleist? 0.134

(d) What is the probability that one golf ball is a Titleist and the other is a Maxfli? 0.269

NW **31. Smokers** According to the National Center for Health Statistics, there is a 20.3% probability that a randomly selected resident of the United States aged 18 years or older is a smoker. In addition, there is a 44.5% probability that a randomly selected resident of the United States aged 18 years or older is female, given that he or she smokes. What is the probability that a randomly selected resident of the United States aged 18 years or older is female and smokes? Would it be unusual to randomly select a resident of the United States aged 18 years or older who is female and smokes? 0.090; no

32. Multiple Jobs According to the U.S. Bureau of Labor Statistics, there is a 4.9% probability that a randomly selected employed individual has more than one job (a multiple-job holder). Also, there is a 46.6% probability that a randomly selected employed individual is male, given that he has more than one job. What is the probability that a randomly selected employed individual is a multiple-job holder and male? Would it be unusual to randomly select an employed individual who is a multiple-job holder and male? 0.023; yes

33. The Birthday Problem Determine the probability that at least 2 people in a room of 10 people share the same birthday, ignoring leap years and assuming each birthday is equally likely, by answering the following questions:

(a) Compute the probability that 10 people have 10 different birthdays. 0.883

Hint: The first person's birthday can occur 365 ways, the second person's birthday can occur 364 ways, because he or she cannot have the same birthday as the first person, the third person's birthday can occur 363 ways, because he or she cannot have the same birthday as the first or second person, and so on.

(b) The complement of "10 people have different birthdays" is "at least 2 share a birthday." Use this information to compute the probability that at least 2 people out of 10 share the same birthday. 0.117

34. The Birthday Problem Using the procedure given in Problem 33, compute the probability that at least 2 people in a room of 23 people share the same birthday. 0.507

35. Teen Communication The following data represent the number of different communication activities (e.g., cell phone, text messaging, e-mail, Internet, and so on) used by a random sample of teenagers over the past 24 hours.

Activities	0	1–2	3–4	5+	Total
Male	21	81	60	38	**200**
Female	21	52	56	71	**200**
Total	**42**	**133**	**116**	**109**	**400**

(a) Are the events "male" and "0 activities" independent? Justify your answer. Yes

(b) Are the events "female" and "5+ activities" independent? Justify your answer. No

(c) Are the events "1–2 activities" and "3–4 activities" mutually exclusive? Justify your answer. Yes

(d) Are the events "male" and "1–2 activities" mutually exclusive? Justify your answer. No

24. (a) $\frac{1}{17}$ (b) $\frac{1}{16}$ 25. $\frac{1}{20}$ 26. $\frac{1}{20}$ 27. (a) $\frac{5}{39}$; no (b) $\frac{14}{39}$ (c) $\frac{20}{39}$ (d) $\frac{25}{169}$; $\frac{64}{169}$; $\frac{80}{169}$ 28. (a) $\frac{1}{22}$ (b) $\frac{6}{11}$; no (c) $\frac{9}{22}$

36. Party Affiliation The following data represent political party by age from a random sample of registered Iowa Voters.

	17–29	30–44	45–64	65+	Total
Republican	224	340	1075	561	**2200**
Democrat	184	384	773	459	**1800**
Total	**408**	**724**	**1848**	**1020**	**4000**

(a) Are the events "Republican" and "30–44" independent? Justify your answer. No

(b) Are the events "Democrat" and "65+" independent? Justify your answer. Yes

(c) Are the events "17–29" and "45–64" mutually exclusive? Justify your answer. Yes

(d) Are the events "Republican" and "45–64" mutually exclusive? Justify your answer. No

37. A Flush A flush in the card game of poker occurs if a player gets five cards that are all the same suit (clubs, diamonds, hearts, or spades). Answer the following questions to obtain the probability of being dealt a flush in five cards.

(a) We initially concentrate on one suit, say clubs. There are 13 clubs in a deck. Compute P(five clubs) $= P$(first card is clubs and second card is clubs and third card is clubs and fourth card is clubs and fifth card is clubs). 0.000495

(b) A flush can occur if we get five clubs or five diamonds or five hearts or five spades. Compute P(five clubs or five diamonds or five hearts or five spades). Note that the events are mutually exclusive. 0.002

38. A Royal Flush A royal flush in the game of poker occurs if the player gets the cards Ten, Jack, Queen, King, and Ace all in the same suit. Use the procedure given in Problem 37 to compute the probability of being dealt a royal flush. 0.00000154

NW **39. Independence in Small Samples from Large Populations** Suppose that a computer chip company has just shipped 10,000 computer chips to a computer company. Unfortunately, 50 of the chips are defective. (b) 0.000025

(a) Compute the probability that two randomly selected chips are defective using conditional probability. 0.0000245

(b) There are 50 defective chips out of 10,000 shipped. The probability that the first chip randomly selected is defective is $\frac{50}{10{,}000} = 0.005 = 0.5\%$. Compute the probability that two randomly selected chips are defective under the assumption of independent events. Compare your results to part (a). Conclude that, when small samples are taken from large populations without replacement, the assumption of independence does not significantly affect the probability.

40. Independence in Small Samples from Large Populations Suppose that a poll is being conducted in the village of Lemont. The pollster identifies her target population as all residents of Lemont 18 years old or older. This population has 6494 people.

(a) Compute the probability that the first resident selected to participate in the poll is Roger Cummings and the second is Rick Whittingham. 0.0000000237 (b) 0.0000000237

(b) The probability that any particular resident of Lemont is the first person picked is $\frac{1}{6494}$. Compute the probability that Roger is selected first and Rick is selected second, assuming independence. Compare your results to part (a). Conclude that, when small samples are taken from large populations without replacement, the assumption of independence does not significantly affect the probability.

NW **41. Independent?** Refer to the contingency table in Problem 17 that relates age and likelihood to buy American. Determine P(45–54 years old) and P(45–54 years old | more likely). Are the events "45–54 years old" and "more likely" independent? 0.253; 0.271; no

42. Independent? Refer to the contingency table in Problem 18 that relates number of speeding tickets and gender. Determine P(female) and P(female | 1 ticket). Are the events "1 ticket" and "female"independent? 0.584; 0.667; no

43. Independent? Refer to the contingency table in Problem 19 that relates person type in a traffic fatality to gender. Determine P(female) and P(female | driver). Are the events "female" and "driver" independent? 0.317; 0.265; no

44. Independent? Refer to the contingency table in Problem 20 that relates gender to day of the week. Determine P(male) and P(male | Wednesday). Are the events "male" and "Wednesday" independent? 0.658; 0.658; yes

45. Let's Make a Deal In 1991, columnist Marilyn Vos Savant posted her reply to a reader's question. The question posed was in reference to one of the games played on the gameshow *Let's Make a Deal* hosted by Monty Hall.

Suppose you're on a game show, and you're given the choice of three doors: Behind one door is a car; behind the others, goats. You pick a door, say No. 1, and the host, who knows what's behind the doors, opens another door, say No. 3, which has a goat. He then says to you, "Do you want to pick door No. 2?" Is it to your advantage to take the switch?

Her reply generated a tremendous amount of backlash, with many highly educated individuals angrily responding that she was clearly mistaken in her reasoning.

(a) Using subjective probability, estimate the probability of winning if you switch.

(b) Load the *Let's Make a Deal* applet. Simulate the probability that you will win if you switch by going through the simulation at least 100 times. How does your simulated result compare to your answer to part (a)?

(c) Research the Monty Hall Problem as well as the reply by Marilyn Vos Savant. How does the probability she gives compare to the two estimates you obtained?

(d) Write a report detailing why Marilyn was correct. One approach is to use a random variable on a wheel similar to the one shown. On the wheel, the innermost ring indicates the door where the car is located, the middle ring indicates the door you selected, and the outer ring indicates the door(s) that Monty could show you. In the outer ring, green indicates you lose if you switch while purple indicates you win if you switch.

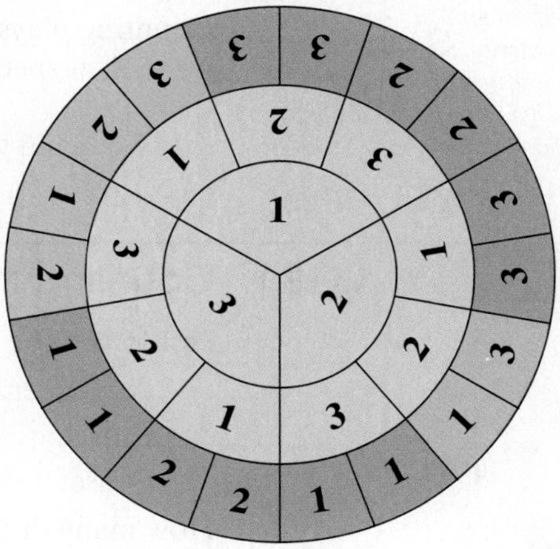

Consumer Reports® His 'N' Hers Razor?

With so many men's and women's versions of different products, you might wonder how different they really are. To help answer this question, technicians at Consumers Union compared a triple-edge razor for women with a leading double-edge razor for women and a leading triple-edge razor for men. The technicians asked 30 women panelists to shave with the razors over a 4-week period, following a random statistical design.

After each shave, the panelists were asked to answer a series of questions related to the performance of the razor. One question involved rating the razor. The following table contains a summary of the results for this question.

Survey Results for Razor Study

	Rating		
Razor	**Poor**	**Fair**	**Excellent**
A	1	8	21
B	0	11	19
C	6	11	13

Using the information in the table, answer the following questions:

(a) Calculate the probability that a randomly selected razor scored Excellent.

(b) Calculate the probability that a randomly selected razor scored Poor.

(c) Calculate the probability of randomly selecting Razor B, given the score was Fair.

(d) Calculate the probability of receiving an Excellent rating, given that Razor C was selected.

(e) Are razor type and rating independent?

(f) Which razor would you choose based on the information given? Support your decision.

***Note to Readers:** In many cases, our test protocol and analytical methods are more complicated than described in these examples. The data and discussions have been modified to make the material more appropriate for the audience.*

5.5 COUNTING TECHNIQUES

OBJECTIVES

1. Solve counting problems using the Multiplication Rule
2. Solve counting problems using permutations
3. Solve counting problems using combinations
4. Solve counting problems involving permutations with nondistinct items
5. Compute probabilities involving permutations and combinations

1 Solve Counting Problems Using the Multiplication Rule

Note to Instructor
Most of the material in this section is optional. However, the material on combinations should be covered if you intend to present binomial probabilities (Section 6.2).

Counting plays a major role in many diverse areas, including probability. In this section, we look at special types of counting problems and develop general techniques for solving them.

We begin with an example that demonstrates a general counting principle.

EXAMPLE 1 Counting the Number of Possible Meals

Problem The fixed-price dinner at Mabenka Restaurant provides the following choices:

Appetizer: soup or salad
Entrée: baked chicken, broiled beef patty, baby beef liver, or roast beef au jus
Dessert: ice cream or cheesecake

How many different meals can be ordered?

Approach Ordering such a meal requires three separate decisions:

Choose an Appetizer	Choose an Entrée	Choose a Dessert
2 choices	4 choices	2 choices

Figure 13 is a tree diagram that lists the possible meals that can be ordered.

Figure 13

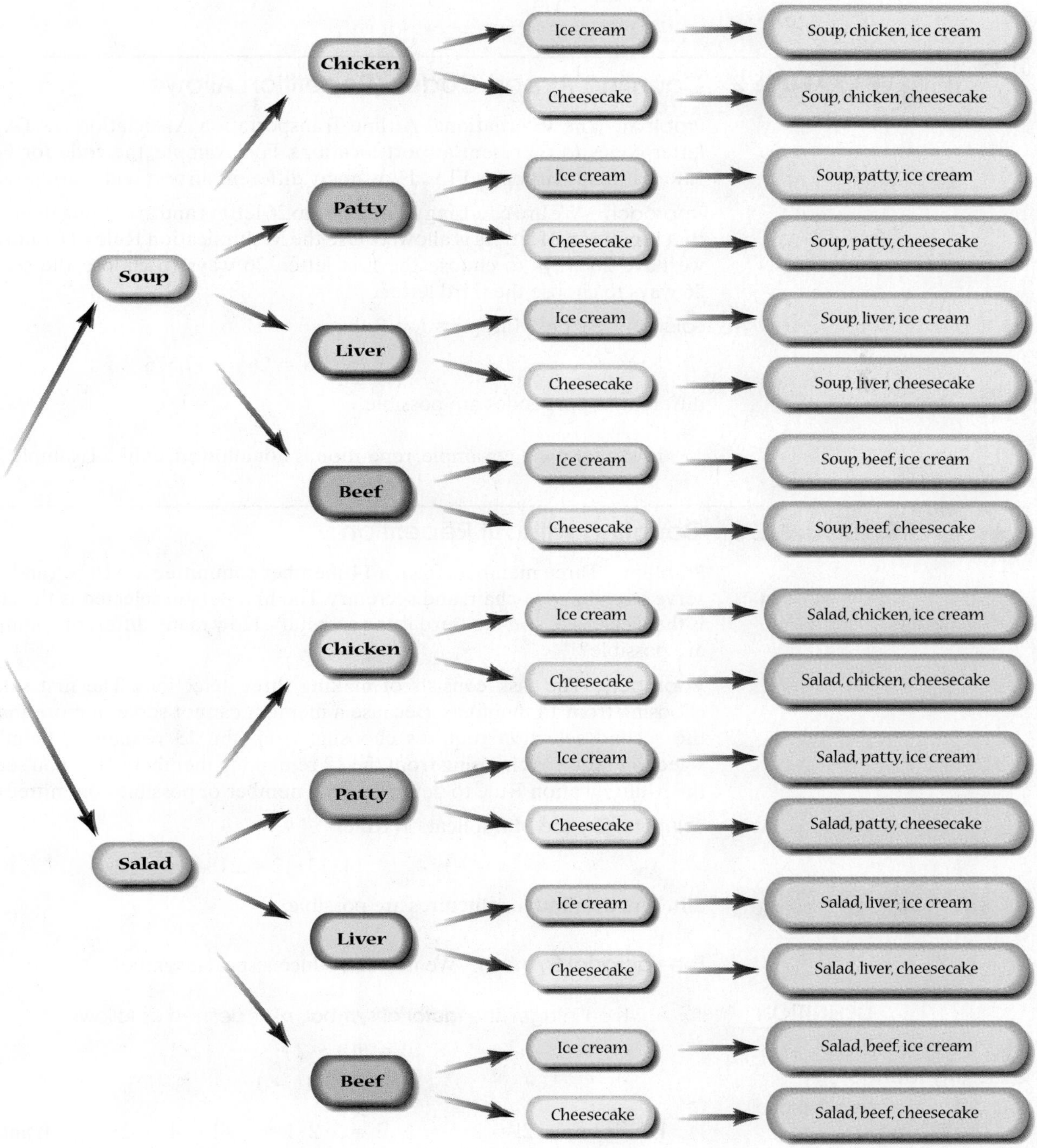

Solution Look at the tree diagram in Figure 13. For each choice of appetizer, we have 4 choices of entrée, and for each of these $2 \cdot 4 = 8$ choices, there are 2 choices for dessert. A total of $2 \cdot 4 \cdot 2 = 16$ different meals can be ordered.

Example 1 illustrates a general counting principle.

Multiplication Rule of Counting

If a task consists of a sequence of choices in which there are p selections for the first choice, q selections for the second choice, r selections for the third choice, and so on, then the task of making these selections can be done in

$$p \cdot q \cdot r \cdot \cdots$$

different ways.

EXAMPLE 2 Counting Airport Codes (Repetition Allowed)

Problem The International Airline Transportation Association (IATA) assigns three-letter codes to represent airport locations. For example, the code for Fort Lauderdale International Airport is FLL. How many different airport codes are possible?

Approach We are choosing 3 letters from 26 letters and arranging them in order. Notice that repetition of letters is allowed. Use the Multiplication Rule of Counting, recognizing we have 26 ways to choose the first letter, 26 ways to choose the second letter, and 26 ways to choose the third letter.

Solution By the Multiplication Rule,

$$26 \cdot 26 \cdot 26 = 26^3 = 17{,}576$$

different airport codes are possible.

In the following example, repetition is not allowed, unlike Example 2.

EXAMPLE 3 Counting without Repetition

Problem Three members from a 14-member committee are to be randomly selected to serve as chair, vice-chair, and secretary. The first person selected is the chair, the second is the vice-chair, and the third is the secretary. How many different committee structures are possible?

Approach The task consists of making three selections. The first selection requires choosing from 14 members. Because a member cannot serve in more than one capacity, the second selection requires choosing from the 13 remaining members. The third selection requires choosing from the 12 remaining members. (Do you see why?) We use the Multiplication Rule to determine the number of possible committees structures.

Solution By the Multiplication Rule,

$$14 \cdot 13 \cdot 12 = 2184$$

different committee structures are possible.

Now Work Problem 31

The Factorial Symbol We now introduce a special symbol.

DEFINITION

If $n \geq 0$ is an integer, the **factorial symbol, $n!$**, is defined as follows:

$$n! = n(n-1) \cdot \cdots \cdot 3 \cdot 2 \cdot 1$$

$$0! = 1 \qquad 1! = 1$$

Using Technology

Your calculator has a factorial key. Use it to see how fast factorials increase in value. Find the value of 69!. What happens when you try to find 70!? In fact, 70! is larger than 10^{100} (a *googol*), the largest number most calculators can display.

For example, $2! = 2 \cdot 1 = 2$, $3! = 3 \cdot 2 \cdot 1 = 6$, $4! = 4 \cdot 3 \cdot 2 \cdot 1 = 24$, and so on. Table 9 lists the values of $n!$ for $0 \leq n \leq 6$.

TABLE 9

n	0	1	2	3	4	5	6
$n!$	1	1	2	6	24	120	720

EXAMPLE 4 The Traveling Salesperson

Problem You have just been hired as a book representative for Pearson Education. On your first day, you must travel to seven schools to introduce yourself. How many different routes are possible?

Approach Call the seven schools A, B, C, D, E, F, and G. School A can be visited first, second, third, fourth, fifth, sixth, or seventh. So, there are seven choices for school A. There are six choices for school B, five choices for school C, and so on. Use the Multiplication Rule and the factorial to find the solution.

Now Work Problems 5 and 33

Solution $7 \cdot 6 \cdot 5 \cdot 4 \cdot 3 \cdot 2 \cdot 1 = 7! = 5040$ different routes are possible.

2 Solve Counting Problems Using Permutations

Examples 3 and 4 illustrate a type of counting problem referred to as a *permutation*.

DEFINITION

A **permutation** is an ordered arrangement in which r objects are chosen from n distinct (different) objects so that $r \le n$ and repetition is not allowed. The symbol ${}_nP_r$, represents the number of permutations of r objects selected from n objects.

So we could represent the solution in Example 3 as

$${}_nP_r = {}_{14}P_3 = 14 \cdot 13 \cdot 12 = 2184$$

and the solution to Example 4 as

$${}_7P_7 = 7 \cdot 6 \cdot 5 \cdot 4 \cdot 3 \cdot 2 \cdot 1 = 5040$$

To arrive at a formula for ${}_nP_r$, we note that there are n choices for the first selection, $n - 1$ choices for the second selection, $n - 2$ choices for the third selection, . . . , and $n - (r - 1)$ choices for the rth selection. By the Multiplication Rule, we have

$$\begin{aligned} & \quad\;\; \text{1st} \quad\; \text{2nd} \qquad \text{3rd} \qquad\qquad\quad r\text{th} \\ {}_nP_r &= n \cdot (n-1) \cdot (n-2) \cdot \cdots \cdot [n-(r-1)] \\ &= n \cdot (n-1) \cdot (n-2) \cdot \cdots \cdot (n-r+1) \end{aligned}$$

This formula for ${}_nP_r$ can be written in **factorial notation**:

$$\begin{aligned} {}_nP_r &= n \cdot (n-1) \cdot (n-2) \cdot \cdots \cdot (n-r+1) \\ &= n \cdot (n-1) \cdot (n-2) \cdot \cdots \cdot (n-r+1) \cdot \frac{(n-r) \cdot \cdots \cdot 3 \cdot 2 \cdot 1}{(n-r) \cdot \cdots \cdot 3 \cdot 2 \cdot 1} \\ &= \frac{n!}{(n-r)!} \end{aligned}$$

Number of Permutations of n Distinct Objects Taken r at a Time

The number of arrangements of r objects chosen from n objects, in which

1. the n objects are distinct,
2. repetition of objects is not allowed, and
3. order is important,

is given by the formula

$${}_nP_r = \frac{n!}{(n-r)!} \qquad \textbf{(1)}$$

In Other Words
"Order is important" means that *ABC* is different from *BCA*.

EXAMPLE 5 Computing Permutations

Problem Evaluate:
(a) ${}_7P_5$ **(b)** ${}_5P_5$

By Hand Approach

Use Formula (1): ${}_nP_r = \dfrac{n!}{(n-r)!}$

By Hand Solution

(a)
$$
\begin{aligned}
{}_7P_5 &= \frac{7!}{(7-5)!} = \frac{7!}{2!} = \frac{7\cdot 6\cdot 5\cdot 4\cdot 3\cdot \cancel{2!}}{\cancel{2!}}\\
&= \underbrace{7\cdot 6\cdot 5\cdot 4\cdot 3}_{\text{5 factors}}\\
&= 2520
\end{aligned}
$$

(b)
$$
\begin{aligned}
{}_5P_5 &= \frac{5!}{(5-5)!} = \frac{5!}{0!} = 5!\\
&= 5\cdot 4\cdot 3\cdot 2\cdot 1\\
&= 120
\end{aligned}
$$

Technology Approach

We will use a TI-84 Plus graphing calculator in part (a) and Excel in part (b) to evaluate each permutation. The steps for determining permutations using the TI-83/84 Plus graphing calculator and Excel can be found in the Technology Step-by-Step on page 285.

Technology Solution

(a) Figure 14(a) shows the results on a TI-84 Plus calculator, so ${}_7P_5 = 2520$.
(b) Figure 14(b) shows the results from Excel. Enter "=permut(5,5)" in any cell, so ${}_5P_5 = 120$.

Figure 14

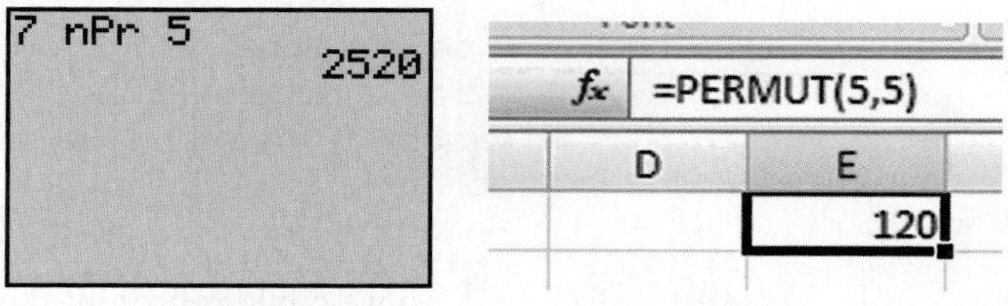

(a) (b)

Now Work Problem 11

EXAMPLE 6 Betting on the Trifecta

Problem In how many ways can horses in a 10-horse race finish first, second, and third?

Approach The 10 horses are distinct. Once a horse crosses the finish line, that horse will not cross the finish line again, and, in a race, finishing order is important. We have a permutation of 10 objects taken 3 at a time.

Solution The top three horses can finish a 10-horse race in

$$
\begin{aligned}
{}_{10}P_3 &= \frac{10!}{(10-3)!} = \frac{10!}{7!} = \frac{10\cdot 9\cdot 8\cdot 7!}{7!}\\
&= \underbrace{10\cdot 9\cdot 8}_{\text{3 factors}}\\
&= 720 \text{ ways}
\end{aligned}
$$

Now Work Problem 45

3 Solve Counting Problems Using Combinations

In a permutation, order is important. For example, the arrangements ABC and BAC are considered different arrangements of the letters A, B, and C. If order is unimportant, we do not distinguish ABC from BAC. In poker, the order in which the cards are received does not matter. The *combination* of the cards is what matters.

DEFINITION

A **combination** is a collection, without regard to order, in which r objects are chosen from n distinct objects with $r \le n$ and without repetition. The symbol ${}_nC_r$ represents the number of combinations of n distinct objects taken r at a time.

EXAMPLE 7 Listing Combinations

Problem Roger, Ken, Tom, and Jay are going to play golf. They will randomly select teams of two players each. List all possible team combinations. That is, list all the combinations of the four people Roger, Ken, Tom, and Jay taken two at a time. What is ${}_4C_2$?

Approach We list the possible teams. We note that order is unimportant, so {Roger, Ken} is the same as {Ken, Roger}.

Solution The list of all such teams (combinations) is

Roger, Ken   Roger, Tom   Roger, Jay   Ken, Tom   Ken, Jay   Tom, Jay

So,

$${}_4C_2 = 6$$

There are six ways of forming teams of two from a group of four players.

We can find a formula for ${}_nC_r$ by noting that the only difference between a permutation and a combination is that we disregard order in combinations. To determine ${}_nC_r$, we eliminate from the formula for ${}_nP_r$ the number of permutations that were rearrangements of a given set of r objects. In Example 7, for example, selecting {Roger, Ken} was the same as selecting {Ken, Roger}, so there were $2! = 2$ rearrangements of the two objects. This can be determined from the formula for ${}_nP_r$ by calculating ${}_rP_r = r!$. So, if we divide ${}_nP_r$ by $r!$, we will have the desired formula for ${}_nC_r$:

$${}_nC_r = \frac{{}_nP_r}{r!} = \frac{n!}{r!(n-r)!}$$

Number of Combinations of *n* Distinct Objects Taken *r* at a Time

The number of different arrangements of r objects chosen from n objects, in which

1. the n objects are distinct,
2. repetition of objects is not allowed, and
3. order is not important

is given by the formula

$${}_nC_r = \frac{n!}{r!(n-r)!} \qquad \textbf{(2)}$$

Using Formula (2) to solve the problem presented in Example 7, we obtain

$${}_4C_2 = \frac{4!}{2!(4-2)!} = \frac{4!}{2!2!} = \frac{4\cdot 3\cdot 2!}{2\cdot 1\cdot 2!} = \frac{12}{2} = 6$$

EXAMPLE 8 Computing Combinations

Problem Evaluate:

(a) ${}_4C_1$ **(b)** ${}_6C_4$ **(c)** ${}_6C_2$

By Hand Approach

Use Formula (2): ${}_nC_r = \dfrac{n!}{r!(n-r)!}$

Technology Approach

We will use a TI-84 Plus graphing calculator in part (a) and Excel in parts (b) and (c) to evaluate each combination. The steps for determining combinations using the TI-83/84 Plus graphing calculator and Excel can be found in the Technology Step-by-Step on page 285.

By Hand Solution

(a) $_4C_1 = \dfrac{4!}{1!(4-1)!} = \dfrac{4!}{1! \cdot 3!} = \dfrac{4 \cdot 3!}{1 \cdot 3!} = 4$

(b) $_6C_4 = \dfrac{6!}{4!(6-4)!} = \dfrac{6!}{4! \cdot 2!} = \dfrac{6 \cdot 5 \cdot 4!}{4! \cdot 2 \cdot 1} = \dfrac{30}{2} = 15$

(c) $_6C_2 = \dfrac{6!}{2!(6-2)!} = \dfrac{6!}{2! \cdot 4!} = \dfrac{6 \cdot 5 \cdot 4!}{2 \cdot 1 \cdot 4!} = \dfrac{30}{2} = 15$

Technology Solution

(a) Figure 15(a) shows the results on a TI-84 Plus calculator. So, $_4C_1 = 4$.

(b) Figure 15(b) shows the results from Excel. Enter "=combin(6,4)" in any cell. So $_6C_4 = 15$.

(c) If we enter "=combin(6,2)" into any cell in Excel, we obtain a result of 15.

Figure 15

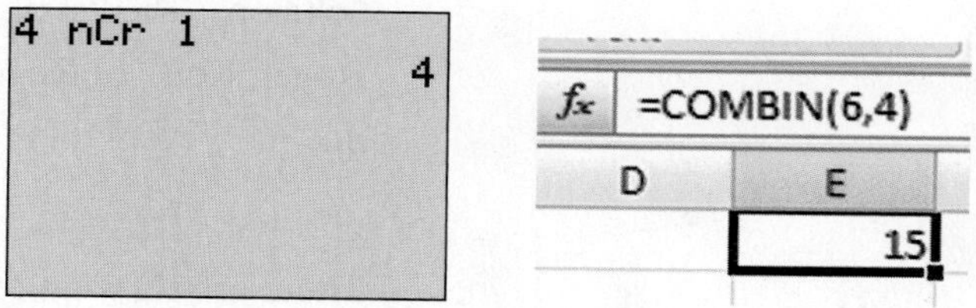

(a) (b)

Now Work Problem 19

Notice in Examples 8(b) and (c) that $_6C_4 = {}_6C_2$. This result can be generalized as

$$_nC_r = {}_nC_{n-r}$$

EXAMPLE 9 Simple Random Samples

Problem How many different simple random samples of size 4 can be obtained from a population whose size is 20?

Approach The 20 individuals in the population are distinct. In addition, the order in which individuals are selected is unimportant. Thus, the number of simple random samples of size 4 from a population of size 20 is a combination of 20 objects taken 4 at a time.

Solution Use Formula (2) with $n = 20$ and $r = 4$:

$$_{20}C_4 = \frac{20!}{4!(20-4)!} = \frac{20!}{4!16!} = \frac{20 \cdot 19 \cdot 18 \cdot 17 \cdot 16!}{4 \cdot 3 \cdot 2 \cdot 1 \cdot 16!} = \frac{116{,}280}{24} = 4845$$

There are 4845 different simple random samples of size 4 from a population whose size is 20.

Now Work Problem 51

4 Solve Counting Problems Involving Permutations with Nondistinct Items

Sometimes we wish to arrange objects in order, but some of the objects are not distinguishable.

EXAMPLE 10 DNA Sequence

Problem A DNA sequence consists of a series of letters representing a DNA strand that spells out the genetic code. There are four possible letters (A, C, G, and T), each representing a specific nucleotide base in the DNA strand (adenine, cytosine, guanine, and thymine, respectively). How many distinguishable sequences can be formed using two As, two Cs, three Gs, and one T?

Approach Each sequence formed will have eight letters. To construct each sequence, we need to fill in eight positions with the eight letters:

$$\overline{1}\ \ \overline{2}\ \ \overline{3}\ \ \overline{4}\ \ \overline{5}\ \ \overline{6}\ \ \overline{7}\ \ \overline{8}$$

The process of forming a sequence consists of four tasks:

Task 1: Choose the positions for the two As.

Task 2: Choose the positions for the two Cs.

Task 3: Choose the positions for the three Gs.

Task 4: Choose the position for the one T.

Task 1 can be done in ${}_8C_2$ ways because we are choosing the 2 positions for A, but order does not matter (because we cannot distinguish the two As). This leaves 6 positions to be filled, so task 2 can be done in ${}_6C_2$ ways. This leaves 4 positions to be filled, so task 3 can be done in ${}_4C_3$ ways. The last position can be filled in ${}_1C_1$ way.

Solution By the Multiplication Rule, the number of possible sequences that can be formed is

$$\begin{aligned} {}_8C_2 \cdot {}_6C_2 \cdot {}_4C_3 \cdot {}_1C_1 &= \frac{8!}{2! \cdot \cancel{6!}} \cdot \frac{\cancel{6!}}{2! \cdot \cancel{4!}} \cdot \frac{\cancel{4!}}{3! \cdot \cancel{1!}} \cdot \frac{\cancel{1!}}{1! \cdot 0!} \\ &= \frac{8!}{2! \cdot 2! \cdot 3! \cdot 1! \cdot 0!} \\ &= 1680 \end{aligned}$$

There are 1680 possible distinguishable sequences that can be formed.

Example 10 suggests a general result. Had the letters in the sequence each been different, ${}_8P_8 = 8!$ possible sequences would have been formed. This is the numerator of the answer. The presence of two As, two Cs, and three Gs reduces the number of different sequences, as the entries in the denominator illustrate. We are led to the following result:

Permutations with Nondistinct Items

The number of permutations of n objects of which n_1 are of one kind, n_2 are of a second kind, . . . , and n_k are of a kth kind is given by

$$\frac{n!}{n_1! \cdot n_2! \cdot \cdots \cdot n_k!} \qquad \textbf{(3)}$$

where $n = n_1 + n_2 + \cdots + n_k$.

EXAMPLE 11 Arranging Flags

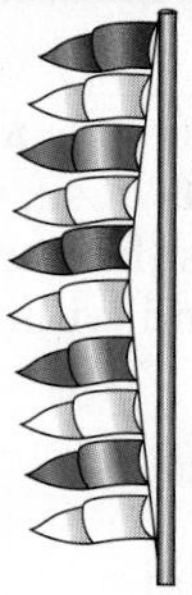

Problem How many different vertical arrangements are there of 10 flags if 5 are white, 3 are blue, and 2 are red?

Approach We seek the number of permutations of 10 objects, of which 5 are of one kind (white), 3 are of a second kind (blue), and 2 are of a third kind (red).

Solution Using Formula (3), we find that there are

$$\frac{10!}{5! \cdot 3! \cdot 2!} = \frac{10 \cdot 9 \cdot 8 \cdot 7 \cdot 6 \cdot 5!}{5! \cdot 3! \cdot 2!}$$

$$= 2520 \text{ different vertical arrangements}$$

Now Work Problem 55

Summary

Table 10 summarizes combinations and the various permutations we have studied.

TABLE 10

	Description	Formula
Combination	The selection of r objects from a set of n different objects when the order in which the objects are selected does not matter (so AB is the same as BA) and an object cannot be selected more than once (repetition is not allowed)	${}_nC_r = \dfrac{n!}{r!(n-r)!}$
Permutation of Distinct Items with Replacement	The selection of r objects from a set of n different objects when the order in which the objects are selected matters (so AB is different from BA) and an object may be selected more than once (repetition is allowed)	n^r
Permutation of Distinct Items without Replacement	The selection of r objects from a set of n different objects when the order in which the objects are selected matters (so AB is different from BA) and an object cannot be selected more than once (repetition is not allowed)	${}_nP_r = \dfrac{n!}{(n-r)!}$
Permutation of Nondistinct Items without Replacement	The number of ways n objects can be arranged (order matters) in which there are n_1 of one kind, n_2 of a second kind, …, and n_k of a kth kind, where $n = n_1 + n_2 + \cdots + n_k$	$\dfrac{n!}{n_1!n_2!\cdots n_k!}$

Note to Instructor

Consider assigning the "Calculating the Probability of Winning the Lottery" activity from the Student Activity Workbook.

5 Compute Probabilities Involving Permutations and Combinations

The counting techniques presented in this section can be used along with the classical method to compute certain probabilities. Recall that this method stated the probability of an event E is the number of ways event E can occur divided by the number of different possible outcomes of the experiment provided each outcome is equally likely.

EXAMPLE 12 Winning the Lottery

Problem In the Illinois Lottery, an urn contains balls numbered 1 to 52. From this urn, six balls are randomly chosen without replacement. For a \$1 bet, a player chooses two sets of six numbers. To win, all six numbers must match those chosen from the urn. The order in which the balls are picked does not matter. What is the probability of winning the lottery?

Approach The probability of winning is given by the number of ways a ticket could win divided by the size of the sample space. Each ticket has two sets of six numbers and therefore two chances of winning. The size of the sample space S is the number of ways 6 objects can be selected from 52 objects without replacement and without regard to order, so $N(S) = {}_{52}C_6$.

Solution The size of the sample space is

$$N(S) = {}_{52}C_6 = \frac{52!}{6! \cdot (52-6)!} = \frac{52 \cdot 51 \cdot 50 \cdot 49 \cdot 48 \cdot 47 \cdot 46!}{6! \cdot 46!} = 20{,}358{,}520$$

Each ticket has two chances of winning. If E is the event "winning ticket," then $N(E) = 2$ and

$$P(E) = \frac{2}{20{,}358{,}520} = 0.000000098$$

There is about a 1 in 10,000,000 chance of winning the Illinois Lottery!

EXAMPLE 13 Acceptance Sampling

Problem A shipment of 120 fasteners that contains 4 defective fasteners was sent to a manufacturing plant. The plant's quality-control manager randomly selects and inspects 5 fasteners. What is the probability that exactly 1 of the inspected fasteners is defective?

Approach Find the probability that exactly 1 fastener is defective by calculating the number of ways of selecting exactly 1 defective fastener in 5 fasteners and dividing this result by the number of ways of selecting 5 fasteners from 120 fasteners. To choose exactly 1 defective in the 5 requires choosing 1 defective from the 4 defectives and 4 nondefectives from the 116 nondefectives. The order in which the fasteners are selected does not matter, so we use combinations.

Solution The number of ways of choosing 1 defective fastener from 4 defective fasteners is ${}_4C_1$. The number of ways of choosing 4 nondefective fasteners from 116 nondefectives is ${}_{116}C_4$. Using the Multiplication Rule, we find that the number of ways of choosing 1 defective and 4 nondefective fasteners is

$$({}_4C_1) \cdot ({}_{116}C_4) = 4 \cdot 7{,}160{,}245 = 28{,}640{,}980$$

The number of ways of selecting 5 fasteners from 120 fasteners is ${}_{120}C_5 = 190{,}578{,}024$. The probability of selecting exactly 1 defective fastener is

$$P(\text{1 defective fastener}) = \frac{({}_4C_1)({}_{116}C_4)}{{}_{120}C_5} = \frac{28{,}640{,}980}{190{,}578{,}024} = 0.1503$$

Now Work Problem 61

There is a 15.03% probability of randomly selecting exactly 1 defective fastener.

5.5 ASSESS YOUR UNDERSTANDING

VOCABULARY AND SKILL BUILDING

1. A permutation is an ordered arrangement of r objects chosen from n distinct objects without repetition.

2. A combination is an arrangement of r objects chosen from n distinct objects without repetition and without regard to order.

3. *True or False:* In a combination problem, order is not important. True

4. The factorial symbol, $n!$, is defined as $n! =$ $n(n-1)\cdot \cdots \cdot 3 \cdot 2 \cdot 1$ and $0! =$ 1 .

In Problems 5–10, find the value of each factorial.

NW **5.** 5! 120 **6.** 7! 5040

7. 10! 3,628,800 **8.** 12! 479,001,600

9. 0! 1 **10.** 1! 1

In Problems 11–18, find the value of each permutation.

NW **11.** ${}_6P_2$ 30 **12.** ${}_7P_2$ 42

13. ${}_4P_4$ 24 **14.** ${}_7P_7$ 5040

15. ${}_5P_0$ 1 **16.** ${}_4P_0$ 1

17. ${}_8P_3$ 336 **18.** ${}_9P_4$ 3024

In Problems 19–26, find the value of each combination.

NW **19.** ${}_8C_3$ 56 **20.** ${}_9C_2$ 36

21. ${}_{10}C_2$ 45 **22.** ${}_{12}C_3$ 220

23. ${}_{52}C_1$ 52 **24.** ${}_{40}C_{40}$ 1

25. ${}_{48}C_3$ 17,296 **26.** ${}_{30}C_4$ 27,405

27. List all the permutations of five objects a, b, c, d, and e taken two at a time without repetition. What is ${}_5P_2$? 20

28. List all the permutations of four objects a, b, c, and d taken two at a time without repetition. What is ${}_4P_2$? 12

29. List all the combinations of five objects a, b, c, d, and e taken two at a time. What is ${}_5C_2$? 10

30. List all the combinations of four objects a, b, c, and d taken two at a time. What is ${}_4C_2$? 6

APPLYING THE CONCEPTS

NW **31. Clothing Options** A man has six shirts and four ties. Assuming that they all match, how many different shirt-and-tie combinations can he wear? 24

32. Clothing Options A woman has five blouses and three skirts. Assuming that they all match, how many different outfits can she wear? 15

NW **33. Arranging Songs on a CD** Suppose Dan is going to burn a compact disc (CD) that will contain 12 songs. In how many ways can Dan arrange the 12 songs on the CD? 12!

34. Arranging Students In how many ways can 15 students be lined up? 15!

35. Traveling Salesperson A salesperson must travel to eight cities to promote a new marketing campaign. How many different trips are possible if any route between cities is possible? 8!

36. Randomly Playing Songs A certain compact disc player randomly plays each of 10 songs on a CD. Once a song is played, it is not repeated until all the songs on the CD have been played. In how many different ways can the CD player play the 10 songs? 10!

37. Stocks on the NYSE Companies whose stocks are listed on the New York Stock Exchange (NYSE) have their company name represented by either one, two, or three letters (repetition of letters is allowed). What is the maximum number of companies that can be listed on the New York Stock Exchange? 18,278

38. Stocks on the NASDAQ Companies whose stocks are listed on the NASDAQ stock exchange have their company name represented by either four or five letters (repetition of letters is allowed). What is the maximum number of companies that can be listed on the NASDAQ? 12,338,352

39. Garage Door Code Outside a home there is a keypad that will open the garage if the correct four-digit code is entered.

(a) How many codes are possible? 10,000 (b) 0.0001

(b) What is the probability of entering the correct code on the first try, assuming that the owner doesn't remember the code?

40. Social Security Numbers A Social Security number is used to identify each resident of the United States uniquely. The number is of the form xxx–xx–xxxx, where each x is a digit from 0 to 9.

(a) How many Social Security numbers can be formed? 10^9

(b) What is the probability of correctly guessing the Social Security number of the president of the United States? $1/10^9$

41. User Names Suppose that a local area network requires eight letters for user names. Lower- and uppercase letters are considered the same. How many user names are possible for the local area network? 26^8 42. $10 \cdot 26^7 \approx 8.03 \times 10^{10}$

42. User Names How many user names are possible in Problem 41 if the last character must be a digit?

43. Combination Locks A combination lock has 50 numbers on it. To open it, you turn counterclockwise to a number, then rotate clockwise to a second number, and then counterclockwise to the third number. Repetitions are allowed.

(a) How many different lock combinations are there? 50^3

(b) What is the probability of guessing a lock combination on the first try? $1/50^3$

44. Forming License Plate Numbers How many different license plate numbers can be made by using one letter followed by five digits selected from the digits 0 through 9? 2,600,000

NW **45. INDY 500** Suppose 40 cars start at the Indianapolis 500. In how many ways can the top 3 cars finish the race? 59,280

46. Betting on the Perfecta In how many ways can the top 2 horses finish in a 10-horse race? 90

47. Forming a Committee Four members from a 20-person committee are to be selected randomly to serve as chairperson, vice-chairperson, secretary, and treasurer. The first person selected is the chairperson; the second, the vice-chairperson; the third, the secretary; and the fourth, the treasurer. How many different leadership structures are possible? 116,280

48. Forming a Committee Four members from a 50-person committee are to be selected randomly to serve as chairperson, vice-chairperson, secretary, and treasurer. The first person selected is the chairperson; the second, the vice-chairperson; the third, the secretary; and the fourth, the treasurer. How many different leadership structures are possible? ${}_{50}P_4$

49. Lottery A lottery exists where balls numbered 1 to 25 are placed in an urn. To win, you must match the four balls chosen in the correct order. How many possible outcomes are there for this game? 303,600 50. 293,930 51. 2,118,760

50. Forming a Committee In the U.S. Senate, there are 21 members on the Committee on Banking, Housing, and Urban Affairs. Nine of these 21 members are selected to be on the Subcommittee on Economic Policy. How many different committee structures are possible for this subcommittee?

NW **51. Simple Random Sample** How many different simple random samples of size 5 can be obtained from a population whose size is 50?

52. Simple Random Sample How many different simple random samples of size 7 can be obtained from a population whose size is 100? ${}_{100}C_7$ 53. 15

53. Children A family has six children. If this family has exactly two boys, how many different birth and gender orders are possible?

54. Children A family has eight children. If this family has exactly three boys, how many different birth and gender orders are possible? 56

NW **55. DNA Sequences** (See Example 10.) How many distinguishable DNA sequences can be formed using three As, two Cs, two Gs, and three Ts? 25,200

56. DNA Sequences (See Example 10.) How many distinguishable DNA sequences can be formed using one A, four Cs, three Gs, and four Ts? 138,600 57. 6930

57. Landscape Design A golf-course architect has four linden trees, five white birch trees, and two bald cypress trees to plant in a row along a fairway. In how many ways can the landscaper plant the trees in a row, assuming that the trees are evenly spaced?

58. Starting Lineup A baseball team consists of three outfielders, four infielders, a pitcher, and a catcher. Assuming that the outfielders and infielders are indistinguishable, how many batting orders are possible? 2520

59. Little Lotto In the Illinois Lottery game Little Lotto, an urn contains balls numbered 1 to 39. From this urn, 5 balls are chosen randomly, without replacement. For a \$1 bet, a player chooses one set of five numbers. To win, all five numbers must match those chosen from the urn. The order in which the balls are selected does not matter. What is the probability of winning Little Lotto with one ticket? 1/575,757

60. Mega Millions In Mega Millions, an urn contains balls numbered 1 to 56, and a second urn contains balls numbered 1 to 46. From the first urn, 5 balls are chosen randomly, without replacement and without regard to order. From the second urn, 1 ball is chosen randomly. For a \$1 bet, a player chooses one set of five numbers to match the balls selected from the first urn and one number to match the ball selected from the second urn. To win, all six numbers must match; that is, the player must match the first 5 balls selected from the first urn *and* the single ball selected from the second urn. What is the probability of winning the Mega Millions with a single ticket? $1/({}_{56}C_5 \cdot 46)$

NW **61. Selecting a Jury** The grade appeal process at a university requires that a jury be structured by selecting five individuals randomly from a pool of eight students and ten faculty.

(a) What is the probability of selecting a jury of all students? 56/8568 = 1/153

(b) What is the probability of selecting a jury of all faculty? 252/8568 = 1/34

(c) What is the probability of selecting a jury of two students and three faculty? 3360/8568 = 20/51

62. Selecting a Committee Suppose that there are 55 Democrats and 45 Republicans in the U.S. Senate. A committee of seven senators is to be formed by selecting members of the Senate randomly.

(a) What is the probability that the committee is composed of all Democrats? 0.0127

(b) What is the probability that the committee is composed of all Republicans? 0.0028

(c) What is the probability that the committee is composed of three Democrats and four Republicans? 0.2442

63. Acceptance Sampling Suppose that a shipment of 120 electronic components contains 4 defective components. To determine whether the shipment should be accepted, a quality-control engineer randomly selects 4 of the components and tests them. If 1 or more of the components is defective, the shipment is rejected. What is the probability that the shipment is rejected?

64. In the Dark A box containing twelve 40-watt light bulbs and eighteen 60-watt light bulbs is stored in your basement. Unfortunately, the box is stored in the dark and you need two 60-watt bulbs. What is the probability of randomly selecting two 60-watt bulbs from the box? 0.3517 63. 0.1283

65. Randomly Playing Songs Suppose a compact disc (CD) you just purchased has 13 tracks. After listening to the CD, you decide that you like 5 of the songs. The random feature on your CD player will play each of the 13 songs once in a random order. Find the probability that among the first 4 songs played

(a) you like 2 of them; 0.3916

(b) you like 3 of them; 0.1119

(c) you like all 4 of them. 0.0070

66. Packaging Error Through a manufacturing error, three cans marked "regular soda" were accidentally filled with diet soda and placed into a 12-pack. Suppose that three cans are randomly selected from the 12-pack.

(a) Determine the probability that exactly two contain diet soda. 0.1227

(b) Determine the probability that exactly one contains diet soda. 0.4909 (c) 0.0045

(c) Determine the probability that all three contain diet soda.

67. Three of a Kind You are dealt 5 cards from a standard 52-card deck. Determine the probability of being dealt three of a kind (such as three aces or three kings) by answering the following questions:

(a) How many ways can 5 cards be selected from a 52-card deck? 2,598,960 (b) 52

(b) Each deck contains 4 twos, 4 threes, and so on. How many ways can three of the same card be selected from the deck?

(c) The remaining 2 cards must be different from the 3 chosen and different from each other. For example, if we drew three kings, the 4th card cannot be a king. After selecting the three of a kind, there are 12 different ranks of card remaining in the deck that can be chosen. If we have three kings, then we can choose twos, threes, and so on. Of the 12 ranks remaining, we choose 2 of them and then select one of the 4 cards in each of the two chosen ranks. How many ways can we select the remaining 2 cards? $66 \cdot 4 \cdot 4 = 1056$

(d) Use the General Multiplication Rule to compute the probability of obtaining three of a kind. That is, what is the probability of selecting three of a kind and two cards that are not like? 0.0211

68. Two of a Kind Follow the outline presented in Problem 67 to determine the probability of being dealt exactly one pair. 0.4226

69. Acceptance Sampling Suppose that you have just received a shipment of 20 modems. Although you don't know this, 3 of the modems are defective. To determine whether you will accept the shipment, you randomly select 4 modems and test them. If all 4 modems work, you accept the shipment. Otherwise, the shipment is rejected. What is the probability of accepting the shipment? 0.4912

70. Acceptance Sampling Suppose that you have just received a shipment of 100 televisions. Although you don't know this, 6 are defective. To determine whether you will accept the shipment, you randomly select 5 televisions and test them. If all 5 televisions work, you accept the shipment; otherwise, the shipment is rejected. What is the probability of accepting the shipment? 0.7291

71. Password Policy According to the Sefton Council Password Policy (August 2007), the United Kingdom government recommends the use of "*Environ passwords with the following format: consonant, vowel, consonant, consonant, vowel, consonant, number, number (for example, pinray45).*"

(a) Assuming passwords are not case sensitive, how many such passwords are possible (assume that there are 5 vowels and 21 consonants)? 486,202,500

(b) How many passwords are possible if they are case sensitive? $420^4 \approx 3.11 \times 10^{10}$

Technology Step-By-Step

Factorials, Permutations, and Combinations

TI-83/84 Plus

Factorials

1. To compute 7!, type 7 on the HOME screen.
2. Press MATH, then highlight PRB, and then select 4 : ! With 7! on the HOME screen, press ENTER again.

Permutations and Combinations

1. To compute $_7P_3$, type 7 on the HOME screen.
2. Press MATH, then highlight PRB, and then select 2 : $_nP_r$.
3. Type 3 on the HOME screen, and press ENTER.

Note: To compute $_7C_3$, select 3 : $_nC_r$ instead of 2 : $_nP_r$.

Excel

Factorials In any cell, enter "=fact(*n*)" where *n* is the factorial desired.

Permutations In any cell, enter "=permut(*n*, *r*)" where *n* is the number of distinct objects and *r* is the number of objects to be selected.

Combinations In any cell, enter "=combin(*n*, *r*)" where *n* is the number of distinct objects and *r* is the number of objects to be selected.

5.6 PUTTING IT TOGETHER: WHICH METHOD DO I USE?

OBJECTIVES
1. Determine the appropriate probability rule to use
2. Determine the appropriate counting technique to use

1 Determine the Appropriate Probability Rule to Use

Working with probabilities can be challenging because of the number of different probability rules. This chapter provides the basic building blocks of probability theory, but knowing when to use a particular rule takes practice. To aid you in this learning process, consider the flowchart in Figure 16. While not all situations can be handled directly with the formulas provided, they can be combined and expanded to many more situations.

Figure 16

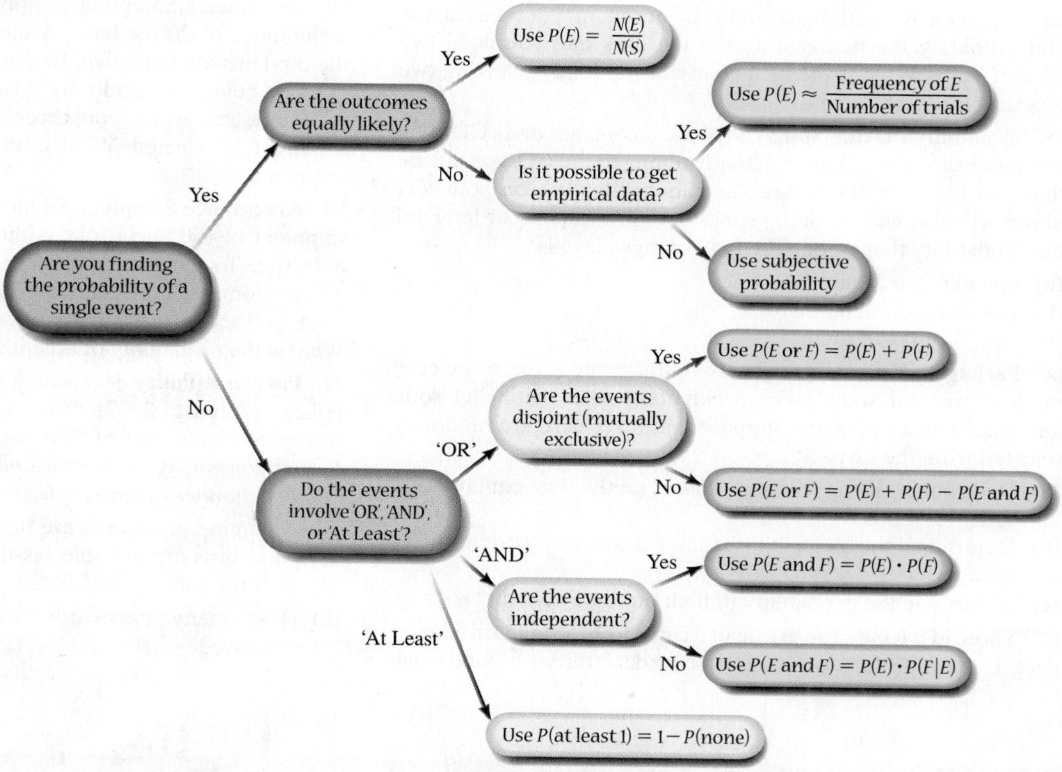

Note to Instructor
Consider assigning the "Exploring the Duplicate Birthday Problem" activity from the Student Activity Workbook.

The first step is to determine whether we are finding the probability of a single event. If we are dealing with a single event, we must decide whether to use the classical method (equally likely outcomes), the empirical method (relative frequencies), or subjective assignment. For experiments involving more than one event, we first decide which type of statement we have. For events involving 'AND', we must know if the events are independent. For events involving 'OR', we need to know if the events are disjoint (mutually exclusive).

EXAMPLE 1 Probability: Which Rule Do I Use?

Problem In the game show *Deal or No Deal?*, a contestant is presented with 26 suitcases that contain amounts ranging from \$0.01 to \$1,000,000. The contestant must pick an initial case that is set aside as the game progresses. The amounts are randomly distributed among the suitcases prior to the game as shown in Table 11. What is the probability that the contestant picks a case worth at least \$100,000?

TABLE 11

Prize	Number of Suitcases
\$0.01–\$100	8
\$200–\$1000	6
\$5,000–\$50,000	5
\$100,000–\$1,000,000	7

Approach Follow the flowchart in Figure 16.

Solution There is a single event, so we must decide among the empirical, classical, or subjective approaches to determine the probability. The probability experiment is selecting a suitcase. Each prize amount is randomly assigned to one of the 26 suitcases, so the outcomes are equally likely. Table 11 shows that 7 cases contain at least \$100,000. Letting E = "worth at least \$100,000," we compute $P(E)$ using the classical approach.

$$P(E) = \frac{N(E)}{N(S)} = \frac{7}{26} = 0.269$$

The chance the contestant selects a suitcase worth at least \$100,000 is 26.9%. In 100 different games, we would expect about 27 games to result in a contestant choosing a suitcase worth at least \$100,000.

EXAMPLE 2 Probability: Which Rule Do I Use?

Problem According to a Harris poll, 14% of adult Americans have one or more tattoos, 50% have pierced ears, and 65% of those with one or more tattoos also have pierced ears. What is the probability that a randomly selected adult American has one or more tattoos and pierced ears?

Approach Follow the flowchart in Figure 16.

Solution We are finding the probability of an event involving 'AND'. Letting T = "one or more tattoos" and E = "ears pierced," we must find $P(T \text{ and } E)$. We need to determine if the two events, T and E, are independent. The problem statement tells us that $P(E) = 0.50$ and $P(E \mid T) = 0.65$. Because $P(E) \neq P(E \mid T)$,the two events are not independent. We find $P(T \text{ and } E)$ using the General Multiplication Rule.

$$\begin{aligned} P(T \text{ and } E) &= P(T) \cdot P(E \mid T) \\ &= (0.14)(0.65) \\ &= 0.091 \end{aligned}$$

So the likelihood of selecting an adult American at random who has one or more tattoos and pierced ears is 9.1%.

2 Determine the Appropriate Counting Technique to Use

To determine the appropriate counting technique to use, we need the ability to distinguish between a sequence of choices and an arrangement of items. We also need to determine whether order matters in the arrangements. See Figure 17 on the following page. Keep in mind that one problem may require several counting rules.

Figure 17

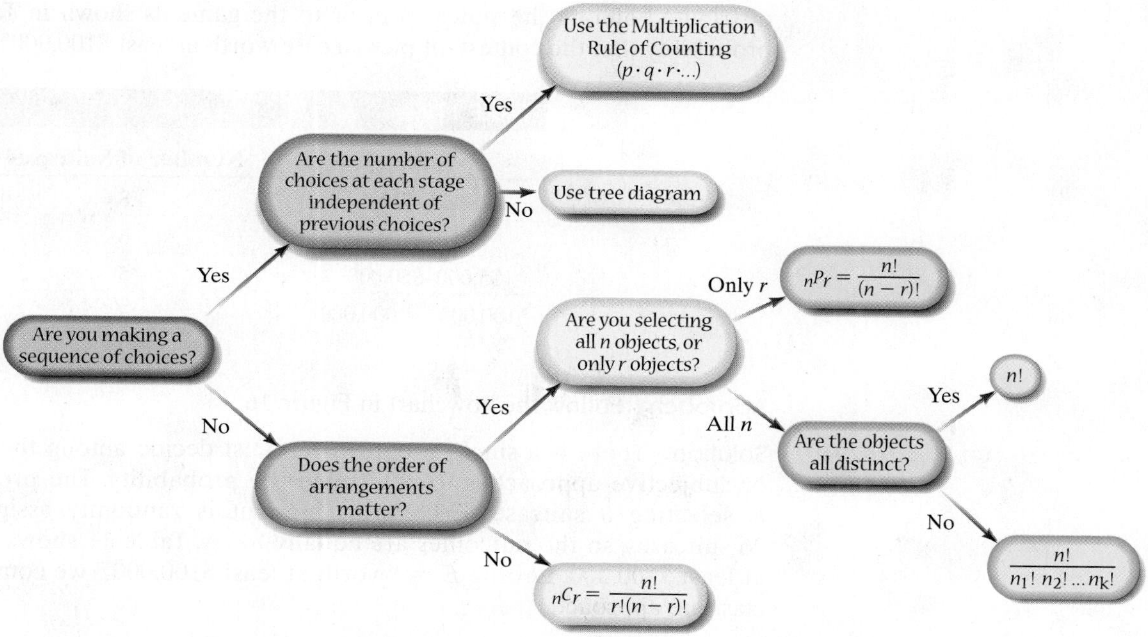

We first must decide whether we have a sequence of choices or an arrangement of items. For a sequence of choices, we use the Multiplication Rule of Counting if the number of choices at each stage is independent of previous choices. This may involve the rules for arrangements, since each choice in the sequence could involve arranging items. If the number of choices at each stage is not independent of previous choices, we use a tree diagram. When determining the number of arrangements of items, we want to know whether the order of selection matters. If order matters, we also want to know whether we are arranging all the items available or a subset of the items.

EXAMPLE 3 Counting: Which Technique Do I Use?

Problem The Hazelwood city council consists of 5 men and 4 women. How many different subcommittees can be formed that consist of 3 men and 2 women?

Approach Follow the flowchart in Figure 17.

Solution We need to find the number of subcommittees having 3 men and 2 women. So we consider a sequence of events: select the men, then select the women. Since the number of choices at each stage is independent of previous choices (the men chosen will not impact which women are chosen), we use the Multiplication Rule of Counting to obtain

$$N(\text{subcommittees}) = N(\text{ways to pick 3 men}) \cdot N(\text{ways to pick 2 women})$$

To select the men, we must consider the number of arrangements of 5 men taken 3 at a time. Since the order of selection does not matter, we use the combination formula.

$$N(\text{ways to pick 3 men}) = {}_5C_3 = \frac{5!}{3! \cdot 2!} = 10$$

To select the women, we must consider the number of arrangements of 4 women taken 2 at a time. Since the order of selection does not matter, we use the combination formula again.

$$N(\text{ways to pick 2 women}) = {}_4C_2 = \frac{4!}{2! \cdot 2!} = 6$$

Combining our results, we obtain $N(\text{subcommittees}) = 10 \cdot 6 = 60$. There are 60 possible subcommittees that contain 3 men and 2 women.

EXAMPLE 4 Counting: Which Technique Do I Use?

Problem On February 20, 2011, the Daytona International Speedway hosted the 53rd running of the Daytona 500, touted by many to be the most anticipated event in racing history. With 43 drivers in the race, in how many different ways could the top four finishers (1st, 2nd, 3rd, and 4th place) occur?

Approach Follow the flowchart in Figure 17.

Solution We need to find the number of ways to select the top four finishers. We can view this as a sequence of choices, where the first choice is the first-place driver, the second choice is the second-place driver, and so on. There are 43 ways to pick the first driver, 42 ways to pick the second, 41 ways to pick the third, and 40 ways to pick the fourth. The number of choices at each stage is independent of previous choices, so we can use the Multiplication Rule of Counting. The number of ways the top four finishers can occur is

$$N(\text{top four}) = 43 \cdot 42 \cdot 41 \cdot 40 = 2{,}961{,}840$$

We could also approach this problem as an arrangement of units. Since each race position is distinguishable, order matters. We are arranging the 43 drivers taken 4 at a time. Using our permutation formula, we get

$$N(\text{top four}) = {}_{43}P_4 = \frac{43!}{(43-4)!} = \frac{43!}{39!} = 43 \cdot 42 \cdot 41 \cdot 40 = 2{,}961{,}840$$

Again there are 2,961,840 different ways that the top four finishers could occur.

5.6 ASSESS YOUR UNDERSTANDING

VOCABULARY AND SKILL BUILDING

1. What is the difference between a permutation and a combination?

2. What method of assigning probabilities to a simple event uses relative frequencies? Empirical 3. 'AND'; 'OR'

3. Which type of compound event is generally associated with multiplication? Which is generally associated with addition?

4. Suppose that you roll a pair of dice 1000 times and get seven 350 times. Based on these results, what is the probability that the next roll results in seven? 0.35

For Problems 5 and 6, let the sample space be $S = \{1, 2, 3, 4, 5, 6, 7, 8, 9, 10\}$. Suppose that the outcomes are equally likely.

5. Compute the probability of the event $E = \{1, 3, 5, 10\}$. 0.4

6. Compute the probability of the event F = "a number divisible by three." 0.3

7. List all permutations of five objects a, b, c, d, and e taken three at a time without replacement.

In Problems 8 and 9, find the probability of the indicated event if $P(E) = 0.7$ and $P(F) = 0.2$.

8. Find $P(E \text{ or } F)$ if E and F are mutually exclusive. 0.9

9. Find $P(E \text{ or } F)$ if $P(E \text{ and } F) = 0.15$. 0.75

In Problems 10–12, evaluate each expression.

10. $\dfrac{6!2!}{4!}$ 60 **11.** ${}_7P_3$ 210 **12.** ${}_9C_4$ 126

13. Suppose that events E and F are independent, $P(E) = 0.8$, and $P(F) = 0.5$. What is $P(E \text{ and } F)$? 0.4

14. Suppose that E and F are two events and $P(E \text{ and } F) = 0.4$ and $P(E) = 0.9$. Find $P(F \mid E)$.

15. Suppose that E and F are two events and $P(E) = 0.9$ and $P(F \mid E) = 0.3$. Find $P(E \text{ and } F)$. 0.27

16. List all combinations of five objects a, b, c, d, and e taken three at a time without replacement.

14. $\frac{4}{9} = 0.444$

APPLYING THE CONCEPTS

17. Soccer? In a survey of 500 randomly selected Americans, it was determined that 22 play soccer. What is the probability that a randomly selected American plays soccer? 0.044

18. Apartment Vacancy A real estate agent conducted a survey of 200 landlords and asked how long their apartments remained vacant before a tenant was found. The results of the survey are shown in the table. The data are based on information obtained from the U.S. Census Bureau.

Duration of Vacancy	Frequency
Less than 1 month	42
1 to 2 months	38
2 to 4 months	45
4 to 6 months	30
6 to 12 months	24
1 to 2 years	13
2 years or more	8

(a) Construct a probability model for duration of vacancy.

(b) Is it unusual for an apartment to remain vacant for 2 years or more? Yes

(c) Determine the probability that a randomly selected apartment is vacant for 1 to 4 months. 0.415

(d) Determine the probability that a randomly selected apartment is vacant for less than 2 years. 0.96

19. Seating Arrangements In how many ways can three men and three women be seated around a circular table (that seats six) assuming that women and men must alternate seats? 36

20. Starting Lineups Payton's futsal team consists of 10 girls, but only 5 can be on the field at any given time (four fielders and a goalie).

(a) How many starting lineups are possible if all players are selected without regard to position played? 252

(b) How many starting lineups are possible if either Payton or Jordyn must play goalie? 252

21. Titanic Survivors The following data represent the survival data for the ill-fated *Titanic* voyage by gender. The males are adult males and the females are adult females.

	Male	Female	Child	Total
Survived	338	316	57	**711**
Died	1352	109	52	**1513**
Total	**1690**	**425**	**109**	**2224**

Suppose a passenger is selected at random.

(a) What is the probability that the passenger survived? 0.320

(b) What is the probability that the passenger was female? 0.191

(c) What is the probability that the passenger was female or a child? 0.240

(d) What is the probability that the passenger was female and survived? 0.142

(e) What is the probability that the passenger was female or survived? 0.369

(f) If a female passenger is selected at random, what is the probability that she survived? 0.744

(g) If a child passenger is selected at random, what is the probability that the child survived? 0.523

(h) If a male passenger is selected at random, what is the probability that he survived? 0.2

(i) Do you think the adage "women and children first" was adhered to on the *Titanic*? Yes

(j) Suppose two females are randomly selected. What is the probability both survived? 0.552

22. Marijuana Use According to the *Statistical Abstract of the United States*, about 17% of all 18- to 25-year-olds are current marijuana users.

(a) What is the probability that four randomly selected 18- to 25-year-olds are all marijuana users? 0.00084

(b) What is the probability that among four randomly selected 18- to 25-year-olds at least one is a marijuana user? 0.525

23. SAT Reports Shawn is planning for college and takes the SAT test. While registering for the test, he is allowed to select three schools to which his scores will be sent at no cost. If there are 12 colleges he is considering, how many different ways could he fill out the score report form? 220

24. National Honor Society The distribution of National Honor Society members among the students at a local high school is shown in the table. A student's name is drawn at random.

Class	Total	National Honor Society
Senior	92	37
Junior	112	30
Sophomore	125	20
Freshman	120	0

(a) What is the probability that the student is a junior? 0.249

(b) What is the probability that the student is a senior, given that the student is in the National Honor Society? 0.425

25. Instant Winner In 2002, Valerie Wilson won $1 million in a scratch-off game (Cool Million) from the New York lottery. Four years later, she won $1 million in another scratch-off game ($3,000,000 Jubilee), becoming the first person in New York state lottery history to win $1 million or more in a scratch-off game twice. In the first game, she beat odds of 1 in 5.2 million to win. In the second, she beat odds of 1 in 705,600.

(a) What is the probability that an individual would win $1 million in both games if they bought one scratch-off ticket from each game? $\approx$ 0.00000000000027

(b) What is the probability that an individual would win $1 million twice in the $3,000,000 Jubilee scratch-off game? $\approx$ 0.000000000002

26. Text Twist In the game Text Twist, 6 letters are given and the player must form words of varying lengths using the letters provided. Suppose that the letters in a particular game are ENHSIC.

(a) How many different arrangements are possible using all 6 letters? 720

(b) How many different arrangements are possible using only 4 letters? 360

(c) The solution to this game has three 6-letter words. To advance to the next round, the player needs at least one of the 6-letter words. If the player simply guesses, what is the probability that he or she will get one of the 6-letter words on their first guess of six letters?

27. Digital Music Players According to a survey by Pew Internet, 79% of teens own an iPod or other MP3 player. If the probability that both a teen and his or her parent own an iPod or other MP3 player is 0.430, what is the probability that a parent owns such a device given that his or her teenager owns one? 0.544

28. Weather Forecast The weather forecast says there is a 10% chance of rain on Thursday. Jim wakes up on Thursday and sees overcast skies. Since it has rained for the past three days, he believes that the chance of rain is more likely 60% or higher. What method of probability assignment did Jim use? Subjective

29. Essay Test An essay test in European History has 12 questions. Students are required to answer 8 of the 12 questions. How many different sets of questions could be answered? 495

30. Exercise Routines Todd is putting together an exercise routine and feels that the sequence of exercises can affect his overall performance. He has 12 exercises to select from, but only has enough time to do 9. How many different exercise routines could he put together? 79,833,600

31. New Cars If the 2011 Hyundai Genesis has 2 engine types, 2 vehicle styles, 3 option packages, 8 exterior color choices, and 2 interior color choices, how many different Genesis's are possible? 192

32. Lingo In the gameshow *Lingo*, the team that correctly guesses a mystery word gets a chance to pull two Lingo balls from a bin. Balls in the bin are labeled with numbers corresponding to the numbers remaining on their Lingo board. There are also three prize balls and three red "stopper" balls in the bin. If a stopper ball is drawn first, the team loses their second draw. To form a Lingo, the team needs five numbers in a vertical, horizontal, or diagonal row. Consider the sample Lingo board on the next page for a team that has just guessed a mystery word.

26. (c) $\frac{1}{240} = 0.0042$

L	I	N	G	O
10			48	66
		34		74
		22	58	68
4	16		40	70
	26	52		64

(a) What is the probability that the first ball selected is on the Lingo board? 0.714

(b) What is the probability that the team draws a stopper ball on its first draw? 0.143

(c) What is the probability that the team makes a Lingo on their first draw? 0

(d) What is the probability that the team makes a Lingo on their second draw? 0.0143

CHAPTER 5 REVIEW

Summary

In this chapter, we introduced the concept of probability. Probability is a measure of the likelihood of a random phenomenon or chance behavior. Because we are measuring a random phenomenon, there is short-term uncertainty. However, this short-term uncertainty gives rise to long-term predictability.

Probabilities are numbers between zero and one, inclusive. The closer a probability is to one, the more likely the event is to occur. If an event has probability zero, it is said to be impossible. Events with probability one are said to be certain.

We introduced three methods for computing probabilities: (1) the empirical method, (2) the classical method, and (3) subjective probabilities. Empirical probabilities rely on the relative frequency with which an event happens. Classical probabilities require the outcomes in the experiment to be equally likely. We count the number of ways an event can happen and divide this by the number of possible outcomes of the experiment. Empirical probabilities require that an experiment be performed, whereas classical probability does not. Subjective probabilities are probabilities based on the opinion of the individual providing the probability. They are educated guesses about the likelihood of an event occurring, but still represent a legitimate way of assigning probabilities.

We are also interested in probabilities of multiple outcomes. For example, we might be interested in the probability that either event E or event F happens. The Addition Rule is used to compute the probability of E *or* F; the Multiplication Rule is used to compute the probability that both E *and* F occur. Two events are mutually exclusive (or disjoint) if they do not have any outcomes in common. That is, mutually exclusive events cannot happen at the same time. Two events E and F are independent if knowing that one of the events occurs does not affect the probability of the other. The complement of an event E, denoted E^c, is all the outcomes in the sample space that are not in E.

Finally, we introduced counting methods. The Multiplication Rule of Counting is used to count the number of ways a sequence of events can occur. Permutations are used to count the number of ways r items can be arranged from a set of n distinct items. Combinations are used to count the number of ways r items can be selected from a set of n distinct items without replacement and without regard to order. These counting techniques can be used to calculate probabilities using the classical method.

Vocabulary

Probability (p. 233)
Outcome (p. 233)
Law of Large Numbers (p. 233)
Experiment (p. 234)
Sample space (p. 234)
Event (p. 234)
Probability model (p. 235)
Impossible event (p. 235)
Certainty (p. 235)
Unusual event (p. 235)
Equally likely outcomes (p. 237)
Tree diagram (p. 239)
Subjective probability (p. 242)
Disjoint (p. 247)
Mutually exclusive (p. 247)
Venn diagram (p. 247)
Contingency table (p. 251)
Two-way table (p. 251)
Row variable (p. 251)
Column variable (p. 251)
Cell (p. 251)
Complement (p. 252)
Independent (p. 259)
Dependent (p. 259)
Conditional probability (p. 265)
Factorial symbol (p. 276)
Permutation (p. 277)
Factorial notation (p. 277)
Combination (p. 278)

Formulas

Empirical Probability

$$P(E) \approx \frac{\text{frequency of } E}{\text{number of trials of experiment}}$$

Classical Probability

$$P(E) = \frac{\text{number of ways that } E \text{ can occur}}{\text{number of possible outcomes}} = \frac{N(E)}{N(S)}$$

Addition Rule for Disjoint Events

$P(E \text{ or } F) = P(E) + P(F)$

General Addition Rule

$P(E \text{ or } F) = P(E) + P(F) - P(E \text{ and } F)$

Probabilities of Complements

$P(E^c) = 1 - P(E)$

Multiplication Rule for Independent Events

$P(E \text{ and } F) = P(E) \cdot P(F)$

Multiplication Rule for *n* Independent Events

$P(E_1 \text{ and } E_2 \text{ and } E_3 \cdots \text{ and } E_n) = P(E_1) \cdot P(E_2) \cdot \cdots \cdot P(E_n)$

Conditional Probability Rule

$$P(F \mid E) = \frac{P(E \text{ and } F)}{P(E)} = \frac{N(E \text{ and } F)}{N(E)}$$

General Multiplication Rule

$P(E \text{ and } F) = P(E) \cdot P(F \mid E)$

Factorial Notation

$n! = n \cdot (n-1) \cdot (n-2) \cdot \cdots \cdot 3 \cdot 2 \cdot 1$

Combination

$${}_nC_r = \frac{n!}{r!(n-r)!}$$

Permutation

$${}_nP_r = \frac{n!}{(n-r)!}$$

Permutations with Nondistinct Items

$$\frac{n!}{n_1! \cdot n_2! \cdot \cdots \cdot n_k!}$$

Objectives

Section	You should be able to . . .	Examples	Review Exercises
5.1	1 Apply the rules of probabilities (p. 234)	2	1, 13(d), 15
	2 Compute and interpret probabilities using the empirical method (p. 236)	3, 4, 7(a)	14(a), 15, 16(a) and (b), 17(a), 30
	3 Compute and interpret probabilities using the classical method (p. 237)	5, 6, 7(b)	2–4, 13(a) and (d), 32(a) and (b)
	4 Use simulation to obtain data based on probabilities (p. 240)	8	27
	5 Recognize and interpret subjective probabilities (p. 242)		28
5.2	1 Use the Addition Rule for Disjoint Events (p. 247)	1 and 2	3, 4, 7, 13(b) and (c)
	2 Use the General Addition Rule (p. 250)	3 and 4	6, 16(d)
	3 Compute the probability of an event using the Complement Rule (p. 252)	5 and 6	5, 14(b), 17(b)
5.3	1 Identify independent events (p. 259)	1	9, 16(g), 32(f)
	2 Use the Multiplication Rule for Independent Events (p. 259)	2 and 3	8, 14(c) and (d), 17(c) and (e), 18, 19
	3 Compute at-least probabilities (p. 261)	4	14(e), 17(d) and (f)
5.4	1 Compute conditional probabilities (p. 264)	1 through 3	11, 16(f), 32(c) and (d)
	2 Compute probabilities using the General Multiplication Rule (p. 267)	4 through 6	10, 20, 29
5.5	1 Solve counting problems using the Multiplication Rule (p. 274)	1 through 4	21
	2 Solve counting problems using permutations (p. 277)	5 and 6	12(e) and (f), 22
	3 Solve counting problems using combinations (p. 278)	7 through 9	12(c) and (d), 24
	4 Solve counting problems involving permutations with nondistinct items (p. 280)	10 and 11	23
	5 Compute probabilities involving permutations and combinations (p. 282)	12 and 13	25, 26
5.6	1 Determine the appropriate probability rule to use (p. 286)	1, 2	13–20, 25, 26, 29(c) and (d), 30
	2 Determine the appropriate counting technique to use (p. 287)	3, 4	21–25

Review Exercises

1. (a) Which among the following numbers could be the probability of an event?

$$0, -0.01, 0.75, 0.41, 1.34$$ 0, 0.75, 0.41

(b) Which among the following numbers could be the probability of an event?

$$\frac{2}{5}, \frac{1}{3}, -\frac{4}{7}, \frac{4}{3}, \frac{6}{7}$$ $\frac{2}{5}, \frac{1}{3}, \frac{6}{7}$

For Problems 2–5, let the sample space be $S = \{\text{red, green, blue, orange, yellow}\}$. *Suppose that the outcomes are equally likely.*

2. Compute the probability of the event $E = \{\text{yellow}\}$. $\frac{1}{5}$

3. Compute the probability of the event $\frac{2}{5}$

$F = \{\text{green or orange}\}$.

4. Compute the probability of the event $\frac{3}{5}$

$E = \{\text{red or blue or yellow}\}$.

5. Suppose that $E = \{\text{yellow}\}$. Compute the probability of E^c. $\frac{4}{5}$

6. Suppose that $P(E) = 0.76$, $P(F) = 0.45$, and $P(E \text{ and } F) = 0.32$. What is $P(E \text{ or } F)$? 0.89

7. Suppose that $P(E) = 0.36$, $P(F) = 0.12$, and E and F are mutually exclusive. What is $P(E \text{ or } F)$? 0.48

8. Suppose that events E and F are independent. In addition, $P(E) = 0.45$ and $P(F) = 0.2$. What is $P(E \text{ and } F)$? 0.09

9. Suppose that $P(E) = 0.8$, $P(F) = 0.5$, and $P(E \text{ and } F) = 0.24$. Are events E and F independent? Why? No

10. Suppose that $P(E) = 0.59$ and $P(F|E) = 0.45$. What is $P(E \text{ and } F)$? 0.2655

11. Suppose that $P(E \text{ and } F) = 0.35$ and $P(F) = 0.7$. What is $P(E|F)$? 0.5

12. Determine the value of each of the following:

(a) $7!$ 5040 **(b)** $0!$ 1
(c) ${}_9C_4$ 126 **(d)** ${}_{10}C_3$ 120
(e) ${}_9P_2$ 72 **(f)** ${}_{12}P_4$ 11,880

13. (a) $\frac{1}{19}$ (b) $\frac{10}{19}$ (c) $\frac{1}{2}$

13. Roulette In the game of roulette, a wheel consists of 38 slots, numbered 0, 00, 1, 2, . . . , 36. (See the photo in Problem 31 from Section 5.1.) To play the game, a metal ball is spun around the wheel and allowed to fall into one of the numbered slots. The slots numbered 0 and 00 are green, the odd numbers are red, and the even numbers are black.

(a) Determine the probability that the metal ball falls into a green slot. Interpret this probability.

(b) Determine the probability that the metal ball falls into a green or a red slot. Interpret this probability.

(c) Determine the probability that the metal ball falls into 00 or a red slot. Interpret this probability.

(d) Determine the probability that the metal ball falls into the number 31 and a black slot simultaneously. What term is used to describe this event? 0; impossible

14. Traffic Fatalities In 2009, there were 33,722 traffic fatalities in the United States. Of these, 9817 were alcohol related.

(a) What is the probability that a randomly selected traffic fatality in 2009 was alcohol related? 0.291

(b) What is the probability that a randomly selected traffic fatality in 2009 was not alcohol related? 0.709

(c) What is the probability that two randomly selected traffic fatalities in 2009 were both alcohol related? 0.085

(d) What is the probability that neither of two randomly selected traffic fatalities in 2009 were alcohol related? 0.503

(e) What is the probability that of two randomly selected traffic fatalities in 2009 at least one was alcohol related? 0.497

15. Long Life? In a poll conducted by Genworth Financial, a random sample of adults was asked, "What age would you like to live to?" The results of the survey are given in the table.

Age	Number
18–79	126
80–89	262
90–99	263
100 or older	388

(a) Construct a probability model of the data.

(b) Is it unusual for an individual to want to live between 18 and 79 years? No

16. Gestation Period versus Weight The following data represent the birth weights (in grams) of babies born in 2007, along with the period of gestation.

	Period of Gestation			
Birth Weight (grams)	**Preterm**	**Term**	**Postterm**	**Total**
Less than 1000	30,985	251	31	31,267
1000–1999	88,962	11,504	1,082	101,548
2000–2999	263,667	713,797	39,212	1,016,676
3000–3999	152,073	2,498,255	175,221	2,825,549
4000–4999	9,107	290,478	26,197	325,782
Over 5000	203	3,919	396	4,518
Total	**544,997**	**3,518,204**	**242,139**	**4,305,340**

Source: National Vital Statistics Report, Vol. 56, No. 6, December 5, 2007

(a) What is the probability that a randomly selected baby born in 2007 was postterm? 0.056

(b) What is the probability that a randomly selected baby born in 2007 weighed 3000 to 3999 grams? 0.656

(c) What is the probability that a randomly selected baby born in 2007 weighed 3000 to 3999 grams and was postterm? 0.041

(d) What is the probability that a randomly selected baby born in 2007 weighed 3000 to 3999 grams or was postterm? 0.672

(e) What is the probability that a randomly selected baby born in 2007 weighed less than 1000 grams and was postterm? Is this event impossible? 0.000007; no

(f) What is the probability that a randomly selected baby born in 2007 weighed 3000 to 3999 grams, given the baby was postterm? 0.724

(g) Are the events "postterm baby" and "weighs 3000 to 3999 grams" independent? Why? No

17. Who Do You Trust? According to the National Constitution Center, 18% of Americans trust organized religion.

(a) If an American is randomly selected, what is the probability he or she trusts organized religion? 0.18

(b) If an American is randomly selected, what is the probability he or she does not trust organized religion? 0.82

(c) In a random sample of three Americans, all three indicated that they trust organized religion. Is this result surprising? Yes; P(all three trust) = 0.006

(d) If three Americans are randomly selected, what is the probability that at least one does not trust organized religion? 0.994 (e) No; P(all five do not trust) = 0.371

(e) Would it be surprising if a random sample of five Americans resulted in none indicating they trust organized religion?

(f) If five Americans are randomly selected, what is the probability that at least one trusts organized religion? 0.629

18. Pick 3 For the Illinois Lottery's PICK 3 game, a player must match a sequence of three repeatable numbers, ranging from 0 to 9, in exact order (for example, 3–7–2). With a single ticket, what is the probability of matching the three winning numbers? 0.001

19. Pick 4 The Illinois Lottery's PICK 4 game is similar to PICK 3, except a player must match a sequence of four repeatable numbers, ranging from 0 to 9, in exact order (for example, 5–8–5–1). With a single ticket, what is the probability of matching the four winning numbers? 0.0001

20. Drawing Cards Suppose that you draw 3 cards without replacement from a standard 52-card deck. What is the probability that all 3 cards are aces? 0.00018

21. Forming License Plates A license plate is designed so that the first two characters are letters and the last four characters are digits (0 through 9). How many different license plates can be formed assuming that letters and numbers can be used more than once? 6,760,000

22. Choosing a Seat If four students enter a classroom that has 10 vacant seats, in how many ways can they be seated? 5040

23. Arranging Flags How many different vertical arrangements are there of 10 flags if 4 are white, 3 are blue, 2 are green, and 1 is red?

24. Simple Random Sampling How many different simple random samples of size 8 can be obtained from a population whose size is 55? ${}_{55}C_8$ 23. 12,600

25. Arizona's Pick 5 In one of Arizona's lotteries, balls are numbered 1 to 35. Five balls are selected randomly, without replacement. The order in which the balls are selected does not matter. To win, your numbers must match the five selected. Determine your probability of winning Arizona's Pick 5 with one ticket. 1/324,632

26. Packaging Error Because of a mistake in packaging, a case of 12 bottles of red wine contained 5 Merlot and 7 Cabernet, each without labels. All the bottles look alike and have an equal probability of being chosen. Three bottles are randomly selected.

(a) What is the probability that all three are Merlot? 0.0455

(b) What is the probability that exactly two are Merlot? 0.3182

(c) What is the probability that none is a Merlot? 0.1591

27. Simulation Use a graphing calculator or statistical software to simulate the playing of the game of roulette, using an integer distribution with numbers 1 through 38. Repeat the simulation 100 times. Let the number 37 represent 0 and the number 38 represent 00. Use the results of the simulation to answer the following questions.

(a) What is the probability that the ball lands in the slot marked 7?

(b) What is the probability that the ball lands either in the slot marked 0 or in the one marked 00?

28. Explain what is meant by a subjective probability. List some examples of subjective probabilities.

29. Playing Five-Card Stud In the game of five-card stud, one card is dealt face down to each player and the remaining four cards are dealt face up. After two cards are dealt (one down and one up), the players bet. Players continue to bet after each additional card is dealt. Suppose three cards have been dealt to each of five players at the table. You currently have three clubs in your hand, so you will attempt to get a flush (all cards in the same suit). Of the cards dealt, there are two clubs showing in other player's hands.

(a) How many clubs are in a standard 52-card deck? 13

(b) How many cards remain in the deck or are not known by you? Of this amount, how many are clubs? 41; 8

(c) What is the probability that you get dealt a club on the next card? 8/41 (d) 0.034

(d) What is the probability that you get dealt two clubs in a row?

(e) Should you stay in the game? No

30. Mark McGwire During the 1998 major league baseball season, Mark McGwire of the St. Louis Cardinals hit 70 home runs. Of the 70 home runs, 34 went to left field, 20 went to left center field, 13 went to center field, 3 went to right center field, and 0 went to right field. *Source*: Miklasz, B., et al. *Celebrating 70: Mark McGwire's Historic Season*, Sporting News Publishing Co., 1998, p. 179.

(a) What is the probability that a randomly selected home run was hit to left field? Interpret this probability. 0.486

(b) What is the probability that a randomly selected home run was hit to right field? 0

(c) Was it impossible for Mark McGwire to hit a homer to right field? No

31. Lottery Luck In 1996, a New York couple won $2.5 million in the state lottery. Eleven years later, the couple won $5 million in the state lottery using the same set of numbers. The odds of winning the New York lottery twice are roughly 1 in 16 trillion, described by a lottery spokesperson as "galactically astronomical." Although it is highly unlikely that an individual will win the lottery twice, it is not "galactically astronomical" that *someone* will win a lottery twice. Explain why this is the case.

32. Coffee Sales The following data represent the number of cases of coffee or filters sold by four sales reps in a recent sales competition.

Salesperson	Gourmet	Single Cup	Filters	Total
Connor	142	325	30	**497**
Paige	42	125	40	**207**
Bryce	9	100	10	**119**
Mallory	71	75	40	**186**
Total	**264**	**625**	**120**	**1009**

(a) What is the probability that a randomly selected case was sold by Bryce? Is this unusual? 0.118; no

(b) What is the probability that a randomly selected case was Gourmet? 0.262

(c) What is the probability that a randomly selected Single-Cup case was sold by Mallory? 0.120

(d) What is the probability that a randomly selected Gourmet case was sold by Bryce? Is this unusual? 0.034; yes

(e) What can be concluded from the results of parts (a) and (d)?

(f) Are the events "Mallory" and "Filters" independent? Explain. No

(g) Are the events "Paige" and "Gourmet" mutually exclusive? Explain. No

Problems in the chapter test are labeled by section.objective. For example, 2.3 means Section 2, Objective 3.

CHAPTER TEST

1.1 **1.** Which among the following numbers could be the probability of an event? 0.23, 0, $\frac{3}{2}$, $\frac{3}{4}$, -1.32 0.23, 0, $\frac{3}{4}$

For Problems 2–4, let the sample space be S = {Chris, Adam, Elaine, Brian, Jason}. *Suppose that the outcomes are equally likely.*

1.3 **2.** Compute the probability of the event E = {Jason}. 1/5

1.3 **3.** Compute the probability of the event E = {Chris or Elaine}.

2.3 **4.** Suppose that E = {Adam}. Compute the probability of E^c.

5. Suppose that $P(E) = 0.37$ and $P(F) = 0.22$.

2.1 **(a)** Find $P(E \text{ or } F)$ if E and F are mutually exclusive. 0.59

3.2 **(b)** Find $P(E \text{ and } F)$ if E and F are independent. 0.0814

6. Suppose that $P(E) = 0.15$, $P(F) = 0.45$, and $P(F \mid E) = 0.70$.

4.2 **(a)** What is $P(E \text{ and } F)$? 0.105

2.2 **(b)** What is $P(E \text{ or } F)$? 0.495

4.1 **(c)** What is $P(E \mid F)$? 0.233

(d) Are E and F independent? No

7. Determine the value of each of the following:

(a) 8! 40,320

5.3 **(b)** $_{12}C_6$ 924

5.2 **(c)** $_{14}P_8$ 121,080,960

8. Craps is a dice game in which two fair dice are cast. If the roller shoots a 7 or 11 on the first roll, he or she wins. If the roller shoots a 2, 3, or 12 on the first roll, he or she loses.

1.3 **(a)** Compute the probability that the shooter wins on the first roll. Interpret this probability.

2.3 **(b)** Compute the probability that the shooter loses on the first roll. Interpret this probability.

1.2; 2.3 **9.** The National Fire Protection Association reports that 32% of fires in 2006 were in structures. What is the probability that a randomly selected fire from 2006 was in a structure? What is the probability that a randomly selected fire from 2006 occurred somewhere other than in a structure? 0.32; 0.68

10. The following probability model shows the distribution of the most-popular-selling Girl Scout Cookies®.

Cookie Type	Probability
Thin Mints	0.25
Samoas®/Caramel deLites™	0.19
Peanut Butter Patties®/Tagalongs™	0.13
Peanut Butter Sandwich/Do-si-dos™	0.11
Shortbread/Trefoils	0.09
Other varieties	0.23

Source: www.girlscouts.org

1.1 **(a)** Verify that this is a probability model.

2.1 **(b)** If a girl scout is selling cookies to people who randomly enter a shopping mall, what is the probability that the next box sold will be Peanut Butter Patties®/Tagalongs™ or Peanut Butter Sandwich/Do-si-dos™? 0.24

2.1 **(c)** If a girl scout is selling cookies to people who randomly enter a shopping mall, what is the probability that the next box sold will be Thin Mints, Samoas®/Caramel deLites™, or Shortbread/Trefoils? 0.53

2.3 **(d)** What is the probability that the next box sold will not be Thin Mints? 0.75

11. The following represent the results of a survey in which individuals were asked to disclose what they perceive to be the ideal number of children.

	0	1	2	3	4	5	6	Total
Female	5	2	87	61	28	3	2	**188**
Male	3	2	68	28	8	0	0	**109**
Total	**8**	**4**	**155**	**89**	**36**	**3**	**2**	**297**

Source: Sullivan Statistics Survey

1.2 **(a)** What is the probability an individual believes the ideal number of children is 2? 0.522

1.2 **(b)** What is the probability an individual is female and believes the ideal number of children is 2? 0.293

4.2 **(c)** What is the probability a randomly selected individual who took this survey is female or believes the ideal number of children is 2? 0.862

4.1 **(d)** Among the females, what is the probability the individual believes the ideal number of children is 2? 0.463

4.1 **(e)** If an individual who believes the ideal number of children is 4 is randomly selected, what is the probability the individual is male? 0.222

12. During the 2010 season, the Minnesota Twins won 58% of their games. Assuming that the outcomes of the baseball games are independent and that the percentage of wins this season will be the same as in 2010, answer the following questions:

3.2 **(a)** What is the probability that the Twins will win two games in a row? 0.336

3.2 **(b)** What is the probability that the Twins will win seven games in a row? 0.022

3.3 **(c)** What is the probability that the Twins will lose at least one of their next seven games? 0.978

4.2 **13.** You just received a shipment of 10 DVD players. One DVD player is defective. You will accept the shipment if two randomly selected DVD players work. What is the probability that you will accept the shipment? 0.8

5.1 **14.** In the game of Jumble, the letters of a word are scrambled. The player must form the correct word. In a recent game in a local newspaper, the Jumble "word" was LINCEY. How many different arrangements are there of the letters in this "word"? 6!

5.3 **15.** The U.S. Senate Appropriations Committee has 29 members and a subcommittee is to be formed by randomly selecting 5 of its members. How many different committees could be formed? $_{29}C_5$

5.5 **16.** In Pennsylvania's Cash 5 lottery, balls are numbered 1 to 43. Five balls are selected randomly, without replacement. The order in which the balls are selected does not matter. To win, your numbers must match the five selected. Determine your probability of winning Pennsylvania's Cash 5 with one ticket. 1/962,598

3. $\frac{2}{5}$ 4. $\frac{4}{5}$ 8. (a) $\frac{2}{9}$ (b) $\frac{1}{9}$

5.1 **17.** A local area network requires eight characters for a password. The first character must be a letter, but the remaining seven characters can be either a letter or a digit (0 through 9). Lower- and uppercase letters are considered the same. How many passwords are possible for the local area network? $26 \cdot 36^7$

18. In 1 second, a 3-GHz computer processor can generate about 3 million passwords. How long would it take such a processor to generate all the passwords for the scheme in Problem 17? 679,156 seconds

1.5 **19.** A survey distributed at the 28th Lunar and Planetary Science Conference in March 1997 asked respondents to estimate the chance that there was life on Mars. The median response was a 57% chance of life on Mars. Which method of finding probabilities was used to obtain this result? Explain why. Subjective

5.4 **20.** How many distinguishable DNA sequences can be formed using two As, four Cs, four Gs, and five Ts? 9,459,450

1.4 **21.** A student is taking a 40-question multiple-choice test. Each question has five possible answers. Since the student did not study for the test, he guesses on all the questions. Letting 0 or 1 indicate a correct answer, use the following line from a table of random digits to simulate the probability that the student will guess a question correctly. 0.225

73634 79304 78871 25956 59109 30573 18513 61760

Making an Informed Decision

The Effects of Drinking and Driving

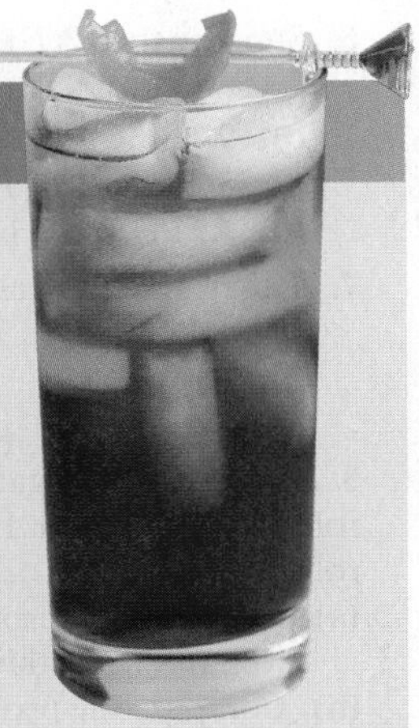

Everyone knows that alcohol impairs reaction time. For example, one study indicates that reaction time at a blood alcohol concentration of 0.08% doubles from 1.5 to 3 seconds. Your job is to compile some probabilities based on existing data to help convince people that it is a really bad idea to get behind the wheel of a car after consuming alcohol. It is also a bad idea to get into a car with an individual who has had a few drinks.

Go to the Fatality Analysis Reporting System Encyclopedia, which is online at the National Highway Traffic Safety Administration Web site. This encyclopedia contains records of all fatal car crashes for any given year. Click Query FARS data. You might consider reading the documentation provided to get a sense as to the type of data that can be obtained. Select a year you wish to analyze and click Submit.

You should see a table with variables that can be considered as it relates to fatal vehicle crashes. For example, if you want to determine the probability that a crash resulted from driver alcohol involvement, you could check the Driver Alcohol Involvement box. Then click Submit. In the drop-down menu, you can fine-tune the data obtained. Click Univariate Tabulation. The next screen allows for further refinement. Click Submit, and you will have the data for the current year. Compile a few probabilities for univariate analysis.

Next, consider relations among two variables. For example, is there a relation between gender and driver alcohol involvement? Check both variables and click Submit. Again, you can fine-tune the data obtained. Once this is complete, select Cross Tabulation. Now choose the appropriate column and row variables to create a contingency table and click Submit. Develop a few conditional probabilities to see the relation between your two variables. Are they independent? If not, what does the dependency tell us?

Write a report, complete with the probabilities showing variable dependencies, that can be used to convince people of the dangers of mixing alcohol consumption with driving.

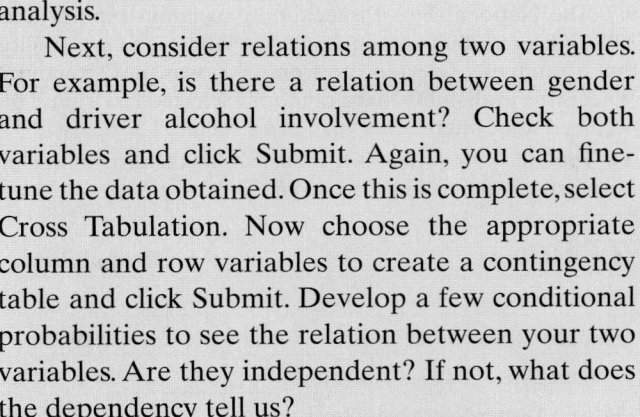

The Chapter 5 Case Study is located on the CD that accompanies this text.

6 Discrete Probability Distributions

OUTLINE

Making an Informed Decision

A woman who was shopping in Los Angeles had her purse stolen by a young, blonde female who was wearing a ponytail. Because there were no eyewitnesses and no real evidence, the prosecution used probability to make its case against the defendant. Your job is to play the role of both the prosecution and defense attorney to make probabilistic arguments both for and against the defendant. See the Decisions project on page 327.

PUTTING IT TOGETHER

In Chapter 5, we discussed the idea of probability. The probability of an event is the long-term proportion with which the event is observed. That is, if we conduct an experiment 1000 times and observe an outcome 300 times, we estimate that the probability of the outcome is 0.3. The more times we conduct the experiment, the more accurate this empirical probability will be. This is the Law of Large Numbers. We learned that we can use counting techniques to obtain theoretical probabilities if the outcomes in the experiment are equally likely. This is called *classical probability*.

We also learned that a probability model lists the possible outcomes of a probability experiment and each outcome's probability. A probability model must satisfy the rules of probability. In particular, all probabilities must be between 0 and 1, inclusive, and the sum of the probabilities must equal 1.

In this chapter, we introduce probability models for *random variables*. A random variable is a numerical measure of the outcome to a probability experiment. So, rather than listing specific outcomes of a probability experiment, such as heads or tails, we might list the number of heads obtained in, say, three flips of a coin. In Section 6.1, we discuss random variables and describe the distribution of discrete random variables (shape, center, and spread). We then discuss a specific discrete probability distribution: *the binomial probability distribution.*

6.1 DISCRETE RANDOM VARIABLES

Preparing for This Section Before getting started, review the following:

- Discrete versus continuous variables (Section 1.1, pp. 8–9)
- Relative frequency histograms for discrete data (Section 2.2, p. 79)
- Mean (Section 3.1, pp. 117–119)
- Standard deviation (Section 3.2, pp. 132–136)
- Mean from grouped data (Section 3.3, pp. 147–148)
- Standard deviation from grouped data (Section 3.3, pp. 149–151)

OBJECTIVES

1 Distinguish between discrete and continuous random variables

2 Identify discrete probability distributions

3 Construct probability histograms

4 Compute and interpret the mean of a discrete random variable

5 Interpret the mean of a discrete random variable as an expected value

6 Compute the standard deviation of a discrete random variable

1 Distinguish between Discrete and Continuous Random Variables

Note to Instructor

If you like, you can print out and distribute the Preparing for This Section quiz located in the Instructor's Resource Center. The purpose of the quiz is to verify that the students have the prerequisite knowledge for this section.

In Chapter 5, we presented the concept of a probability experiment and its outcomes. Suppose we flip a coin two times. The outcomes of the experiment are {HH, HT, TH, TT}. Rather than being interested in a particular outcome, we might be interested in the number of heads. If the outcome of a probability experiment is a numerical result, we say the outcome is a *random variable*.

DEFINITION

A **random variable** is a numerical measure of the outcome of a probability experiment, so its value is determined by chance. Random variables are typically denoted using capital letters such as *X*.

Note to Instructor

To help students understand the difference between a discrete and continuous random variable, tell them that a discrete random variable has values given by points on a number line, while continuous random variables have possible values given by an interval on a number line.

So, in our coin-flipping example, if the random variable X represents the number of heads in two flips of a coin, the possible values of X are $x = 0, 1,$ or 2. Notice that we follow the practice of using a capital letter, such as X, to identify the random variable and a lowercase letter, x, to list the possible values of the random variable, that is, the sample space of the experiment.

As another example, consider an experiment that measures the time between arrivals of cars at a drive-through. The random variable T describes the time between arrivals, so the sample space of the experiment is $t > 0$.

There are two types of random variables, *discrete* and *continuous*.

DEFINITIONS

A **discrete random variable** has either a finite or countable number of values. The values of a discrete random variable can be plotted on a number line with space between each point. See Figure 1(a).

A **continuous random variable** has infinitely many values. The values of a continuous random variable can be plotted on a line in an uninterrupted fashion. See Figure 1(b).

In Other Words
Discrete random variables typically result from counting (0, 1, 2, 3, and so on). Continuous random variables are variables that result from measurement.

Figure 1

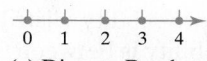

(a) Discrete Random Variable **(b)** Continuous Random Variable

EXAMPLE 1 Distinguishing between Discrete and Continuous Random Variables

(a) The number of As earned in a section of statistics with 15 students enrolled is a discrete random variable because its value results from counting. If the random variable X represents the number of As, then the possible values of X are $x = 0, 1, 2, \ldots, 15$.

(b) The number of cars that travel through a McDonald's drive-through in the next hour is a discrete random variable because its value results from counting. If the random variable X represents the number of cars, the possible values of X are $x = 0, 1, 2, \ldots$.

(c) The speed of the next car that passes a state trooper is a continuous random variable because speed is measured. If the random variable S represents the speed, the possible values of S are all positive real numbers; that is, $s > 0$.

CAUTION

Even though a radar gun may report the speed of a car as 37 miles per hour, it is actually any number greater than or equal to 36.5 mph and less than 37.5 mph. That is, $36.5 \le s < 37.5$.

Now Work Problem 5

In this chapter, we will concentrate on probabilities of discrete random variables. Chapter 7 discusses obtaining probabilities for certain continuous random variables.

2 Identify Discrete Probability Distributions

Because the value of a random variable is determined by chance, we may assign probabilities to the possible values of the random variable.

DEFINITION

The **probability distribution** of a discrete random variable X provides the possible values of the random variable and their corresponding probabilities. A probability distribution can be in the form of a table, graph, or mathematical formula.

EXAMPLE 2 A Discrete Probability Distribution

TABLE 1

x	$P(x)$
0	0.01
1	0.10
2	0.38
3	0.51

Suppose we ask a basketball player to shoot three free throws. Let the random variable X represent the number of shots made, so $x = 0, 1, 2$, or 3. Table 1 shows a probability distribution for the random variable X.

The probability distribution in Table 1 shows that the probability the player makes all three free-throw attempts is 0.51.

We will denote probabilities using the notation $P(x)$, where x is a specific value of the random variable. We read $P(x)$ as "the probability that the random variable X equals x." For example, $P(3) = 0.51$ is read "the probability that the random variable X equals 3 is 0.51."

Recall from Section 5.1 that probabilities must obey certain rules. We repeat the rules for a discrete probability distribution using the notation just introduced.

In Other Words
The first rule states that the sum of the probabilities must equal 1. The second rule states that each probability must be between 0 and 1, inclusive.

Rules for a Discrete Probability Distribution

Let $P(x)$ denote the probability that the random variable X equals x; then

1. $\sum P(x) = 1$
2. $0 \le P(x) \le 1$

Table 1 from Example 2 is a probability distribution because the sum of the probabilities equals 1 and each probability is between 0 and 1, inclusive.

EXAMPLE 3 Identifying Discrete Probability Distributions

Problem Which of the following is a discrete probability distribution?

(a)

x	$P(x)$
1	0.20
2	0.35
3	0.12
4	0.40
5	−0.07

(b)

x	$P(x)$
1	0.20
2	0.25
3	0.10
4	0.14
5	0.49

(c)

x	$P(x)$
1	0.20
2	0.25
3	0.10
4	0.14
5	0.31

Approach In a discrete probability distribution, the sum of the probabilities must equal 1, and all probabilities must be between 0 and 1, inclusive.

Solution

(a) This is not a discrete probability distribution because $P(5) = -0.07$, which is less than 0.

(b) This is not a discrete probability distribution because

$$\sum P(x) = 0.20 + 0.25 + 0.10 + 0.14 + 0.49 = 1.18 \neq 1$$

(c) This is a discrete probability distribution because the sum of the probabilities equals 1, and each probability is between 0 and 1, inclusive.

Now Work Problem 9

Table 1 is an example of a discrete probability distribution in table form. We discuss discrete probability distributions using graphs next and using mathematical formulas in Section 6.2.

3 Construct Probability Histograms

A discrete probability distribution is typically presented graphically with a *probability histogram*.

DEFINITION

In a **probability histogram,** the horizontal axis corresponds to the value of the random variable and the vertical axis represents the probability of each value of the random variable.

EXAMPLE 4 Constructing a Probability Histogram

Problem Construct a probability histogram of the discrete probability distribution given in Table 1 from Example 2.

Approach Construct probability histograms like relative frequency histograms, but let the vertical axis represent the probability of the random variable, rather than its relative frequency. Center each rectangle at the value of the discrete random variable.

Solution Figure 2 shows the probability histogram of the distribution in Table 1.

Figure 2

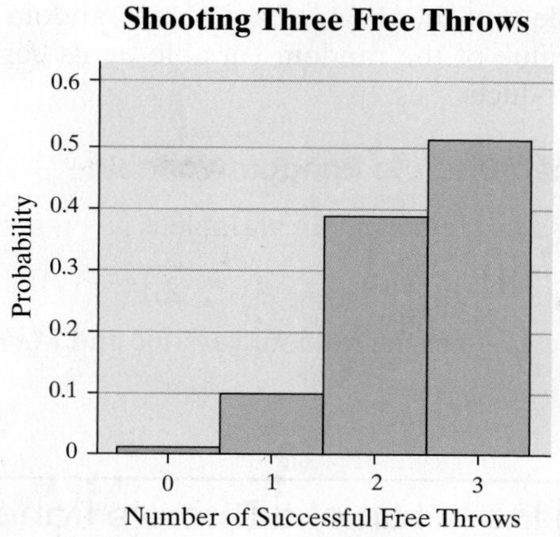

Now Work Problems 17(a) and (b)

Note to Instructor

Emphasize the relation between area and probability in probability histograms as a prelude to probabilities for continuous random variables.

Notice that the area of each rectangle in the probability histogram equals the probability that the random variable assumes the particular value. For example, the area of the rectangle corresponding to the value $x = 2$ is $1 \cdot (0.38) = 0.38$, where 1 represents the width and 0.38 represents the height of the rectangle.

Probability histograms help us determine the shape of the distribution. Recall that we describe distributions as skewed left, skewed right, or symmetric. The probability histogram in Figure 2 is skewed left.

4 Compute and Interpret the Mean of a Discrete Random Variable

Remember, when we describe the distribution of a variable, we describe its center, spread, and shape. We will use the mean to describe the center and use the standard deviation to describe the spread.

Let's see where the formula for computing the mean of a discrete random variable comes from. One semester I asked a small statistics class of 10 students to disclose the number of people living in their households. I obtained the following data:

$$2, 4, 6, 6, 4, 4, 2, 3, 5, 5$$

What is the mean number of people in the 10 households? We could find the mean by adding the observations and dividing by 10, but we will take a different approach. Letting the random variable X represent the number of people in the household, we obtain the probability distribution in Table 2.

TABLE 2

x	$P(x)$
2	$\frac{2}{10} = 0.2$
3	$\frac{1}{10} = 0.1$
4	$\frac{3}{10} = 0.3$
5	$\frac{2}{10} = 0.2$
6	$\frac{2}{10} = 0.2$

Now we compute the mean as follows:

$$\mu = \frac{\Sigma x_i}{N} = \frac{2 + 4 + 6 + 6 + 4 + 4 + 2 + 3 + 5 + 5}{10}$$

$$= \frac{\overbrace{2 + 2}^{2} + \overbrace{3}^{1} + \overbrace{4 + 4 + 4}^{3} + \overbrace{5 + 5}^{2} + \overbrace{6 + 6}^{2}}{10}$$

$$= \frac{2 \cdot 2 + 3 \cdot 1 + 4 \cdot 3 + 5 \cdot 2 + 6 \cdot 2}{10}$$

$$= 2 \cdot \frac{2}{10} + 3 \cdot \frac{1}{10} + 4 \cdot \frac{3}{10} + 5 \cdot \frac{2}{10} + 6 \cdot \frac{2}{10}$$

$$= 2 \cdot P(2) + 3 \cdot P(3) + 4 \cdot P(4) + 5 \cdot P(5) + 6 \cdot P(6)$$

$$= 2(0.2) + 3(0.1) + 4(0.3) + 5(0.2) + 6(0.2)$$

$$= 4.1$$

Note to Instructor

Point out to students that 4.1 is not a possible value of the random variable; it just represents the mean number of people in all households of the population.

We conclude that the mean of a discrete random variable is found by multiplying each possible value of the random variable by its corresponding probability and then adding these products.

The Mean of a Discrete Random Variable

The mean of a discrete random variable is given by the formula

$$\mu_X = \sum [x \cdot P(x)] \qquad (1)$$

where x is the value of the random variable and $P(x)$ is the probability of observing the value x.

In Other Words
To find the mean of a discrete random variable, multiply the value of each random variable by its probability. Then add these products.

EXAMPLE 5 Computing the Mean of a Discrete Random Variable

Problem Compute the mean of the discrete random variable given in Table 1 from Example 2.

Approach Find the mean of a discrete random variable by multiplying each value of the random variable by its probability and adding these products.

Solution Refer to Table 3. The first two columns represent the discrete probability distribution. The third column represents $x \cdot P(x)$.

TABLE 3

x	$P(x)$	$x \cdot P(x)$
0	0.01	$0 \cdot 0.01 = 0$
1	0.10	$1 \cdot 0.1 = 0.1$
2	0.38	$2 \cdot 0.38 = 0.76$
3	0.51	$3 \cdot 0.51 = 1.53$

We substitute into Formula (1) to find the mean number of free throws made.

$$\mu_X = \sum [x \cdot P(x)] = 0(0.01) + 1(0.10) + 2(0.38) + 3(0.51) = 2.39 \approx 2.4$$

We will follow the practice of rounding the mean and standard deviation to one more decimal place than the values of the random variable.

How to Interpret the Mean of a Discrete Random Variable

The mean of a discrete random variable can be thought of as the mean outcome of the probability experiment if we repeated the experiment many times. If we repeated the experiment in Example 5 of shooting three free throws many times, we would expect the mean number of free throws made to be around 2.4.

Interpretation of the Mean of a Discrete Random Variable

Suppose an experiment is repeated n independent times and the value of the random variable X is recorded. As the number of repetitions of the experiment increases, the mean value of the n trials will approach μ_X, the mean of the random variable X. In other words, let x_1 be the value of the random variable X after the first experiment, x_2 be the value of the random variable X after the second experiment, and so on. Then

$$\bar{x} = \frac{x_1 + x_2 + \cdots + x_n}{n}$$

The difference between $\bar{x}$ and μ_X gets closer to 0 as n increases.

In Other Words
Recall from Chapter 5 that independent means the results of one trial of the experiment do not affect the results of other trials of the experiment.

EXAMPLE 6 Interpretation of the Mean of a Discrete Random Variable

Problem The basketball player from Example 2 is asked to shoot three free throws 100 times. Compute the mean number of free throws made.

Approach The player shoots three free throws and the number made is recorded. We repeat this experiment 99 more times and then compute the mean number of free throws made.

Solution Table 4 shows the results.

TABLE 4

First experiment →	3	2	3	3	3	3	1	2	3	2	
Second experiment →	2	3	3	1	2	2	2	2	2	3	
Third experiment →	3	3	2	2	3	2	3	2	2	2	
	3	3	2	3	2	3	3	2	3	1	
	3	2	2	2	2	0	2	3	1	2	
	3	3	2	3	2	3	2	1	3	2	
	2	3	3	3	1	3	3	1	3	3	
	3	2	2	1	3	2	2	2	3	2	
	3	2	2	2	3	3	2	2	3	3	
	2	3	2	1	2	3	3	2	3	3	← Hundredth experiment

In the first experiment, the player made all three free throws. In the second experiment, the player made two out of three free throws. In the hundredth experiment, the player made three free throws. The mean number of free throws made was

$$\bar{x} = \frac{3 + 2 + 3 + \cdots + 3}{100} = 2.35$$

This is close to the theoretical mean of 2.4 (from Example 5). As the number of repetitions of the experiment increases, we expect $\bar{x}$ to get even closer to 2.4.

Figures 3(a) and (b) further illustrate the mean of a discrete random variable. Figure 3(a) shows the mean number of free throws made versus the number of repetitions of the experiment for the data in Table 4. Figure 3(b) shows the same information when the experiment of shooting three free throws is conducted a second time for 100 repetitions. In both plots the player starts "hot," since the mean number of free throws made is above the theoretical level of 2.4. However, both graphs approach the theoretical mean of 2.4 as the number of repetitions of the experiment increases.

Figure 3

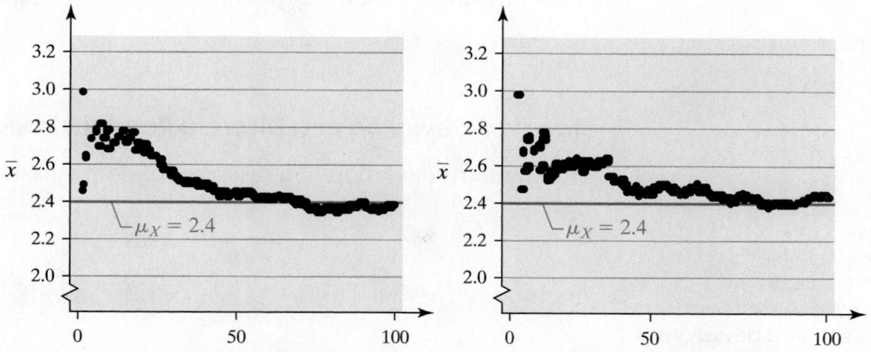

(a) Number of Repetitions **(b) Number of Repetitions**

Note to Instructor

Consider assigning the "Finding the Expected Value of Game" activity from the Student Activity Workbook.

Now Work Problem 17(c)

5 Interpret the Mean of a Discrete Random Variable as an Expected Value

In Other Words
The expected value of a discrete random variable is the mean of the discrete random variable.

Because the mean of a random variable represents what we would expect to happen in the long run, it is also called the **expected value**, $E(X)$. The interpretation of expected value is the same as the interpretation of the mean of a discrete random variable.

EXAMPLE 7 Finding the Expected Value

HISTORICAL NOTE

Christiaan Huygens was born on April 14, 1629, into an influential Dutch family. He studied Law and Mathematics at the University of Leiden from 1645 to 1647. From 1647 to 1649, he continued to study Law and Mathematics at the College of Orange at Breda. Among his many accomplishments, Huygens discovered the first moon of Saturn in 1655 and the shape of the rings of Saturn in 1656. While in Paris sharing his discoveries, he learned about probability through Fermat and Pascal. In 1657, Huygens published the first book on probability theory, in which he introduced the idea of expected value.

Problem A term life insurance policy will pay a beneficiary a certain sum of money upon the death of the policyholder. These policies have premiums that must be paid annually. Suppose an 18-year-old male buys a \$250,000 1-year term life insurance policy for \$350. According to the *National Vital Statistics Report*, Vol. 58, No. 21, the probability that the male will survive the year is 0.998937. Compute the expected value of this policy to the insurance company.

Approach The experiment has two possible outcomes: survival or death. Let the random variable X represent the *payout* (money lost or gained), depending on survival or death of the insured. Assign probabilities to each payout and substitute these values into Formula (1).

Solution

Step 1 We have $P(\text{survives}) = 0.998937$, so $P(\text{dies}) = 0.001063$. If the client survives the year, the insurance company makes \$350, so, $x = \$350$. If the client dies during the year, the insurance company must pay \$250,000 to the client's beneficiary, but still keeps the \$350 premium, so $x = \$350 - \$250{,}000 = -\$249{,}650$. The value is negative because it is money paid by the insurance company. The probability distribution is listed in Table 5.

TABLE 5

x	$P(x)$
\$350 (survives)	0.998937
−\$249,650 (dies)	0.001063

Step 2 Substituting into Formula (1), we obtain the expected value (from the point of view of the insurance company) of the policy.

$$E(X) = \mu_X = \sum xP(x) = \$350(0.998937) + (-\$249{,}650)(0.001063) = \$84.25$$

Interpretation The company expects to make \$84.25 for each 18-year-old male client it insures. The \$84.25 profit of the insurance company is a long-term result. It does not make \$84.25 on each 18-year-old male it insures, but rather the average profit per 18-year-old male insured is \$84.25. Because this is a long-term result, the insurance "idea" will not work with only a few insured.

Now Work Problem 27

6 Compute the Standard Deviation of a Discrete Random Variable

Note to Instructor

Insurance companies attempt to set premiums so that the expected value of the policy is zero.

We now introduce a method for computing the standard deviation of a discrete random variable.

Standard Deviation of a Discrete Random Variable

The standard deviation of a discrete random variable X is given by

$$\sigma_X = \sqrt{\Sigma[(x - \mu_X)^2 \cdot P(x)]} \qquad \textbf{(2a)}$$

$$= \sqrt{\Sigma[x^2 \cdot P(x)] - \mu_X^2} \qquad \textbf{(2b)}$$

where x is the value of the random variable, μ_X is the mean of the random variable, and $P(x)$ is the probability of observing a value of the random variable.

In Other Words

The standard deviation of a discrete random variable is the square root of a weighted average of the squared deviations for which the weights are the probabilities.

EXAMPLE 8 Computing the Standard Deviation of a Discrete Random Variable

Problem Find the standard deviation of the discrete random variable given in Table 1 from Example 2.

Approach We will use Formula (2a) with the unrounded mean $\mu_X = 2.39$.

Solution Refer to Table 6. Columns 1 and 2 represent the discrete probability distribution. Column 3 represents $(x - \mu_X)^2 \cdot P(x)$. Find the sum of the entries in Column 3.

TABLE 6

x	$P(x)$	$(x - \mu_X)^2 \cdot P(x)$
0	0.01	$(0 - 2.39)^2 \cdot 0.01 = 0.057121$
1	0.10	$(1 - 2.39)^2 \cdot 0.10 = 0.19321$
2	0.38	$(2 - 2.39)^2 \cdot 0.38 = 0.057798$
3	0.51	$(3 - 2.39)^2 \cdot 0.51 = 0.189771$
		$\sum (x - \mu_X)^2 \cdot P(x) = 0.4979$

The standard deviation of the discrete random variable X is

$$\sigma_X = \sqrt{\sum[(x - \mu_X)^2 \cdot P(x)]} = \sqrt{0.4979} \approx 0.7$$

Now Work Problem 17(d)

Approach We will use Formula (2b) with the unrounded mean $\mu_X = 2.39$.

Solution Refer to Table 7. Columns 1 and 2 represent the discrete probability distribution. Column 3 represents $x^2 \cdot P(x)$. Find the sum of the entries in Column 3.

TABLE 7

x	$P(x)$	$x^2 \cdot P(x)$
0	0.01	$0^2 \cdot 0.01 = 0$
1	0.10	$1^2 \cdot 0.10 = 0.10$
2	0.38	$2^2 \cdot 0.38 = 1.52$
3	0.51	$3^2 \cdot 0.51 = 4.59$
		$\sum x^2 \cdot P(x) = 6.21$

The standard deviation of the discrete random variable X is

$$\sigma_X = \sqrt{\sum[x^2 \cdot P(x)] - \mu_X^2} = \sqrt{6.21 - 2.39^2} = \sqrt{0.4979} \approx 0.7$$

The variance of the discrete random variable is the value under the square root in the computation of the standard deviation. The variance of the discrete random variable in Example 8 is

$$\sigma_X^2 = 0.4979 \approx 0.5$$

EXAMPLE 9 Obtaining the Mean and Standard Deviation of a Discrete Random Variable Using Technology

Problem Use statistical software or a graphing calculator to find the mean and the standard deviation of the random variable whose distribution is given in Table 1.

Approach We will use a TI-84 Plus graphing calculator to obtain the mean and standard deviation. The steps for determining the mean and standard deviation using a TI-83/84 Plus graphing calculator are given in the Technology Step-by-Step on page 309.

Figure 4

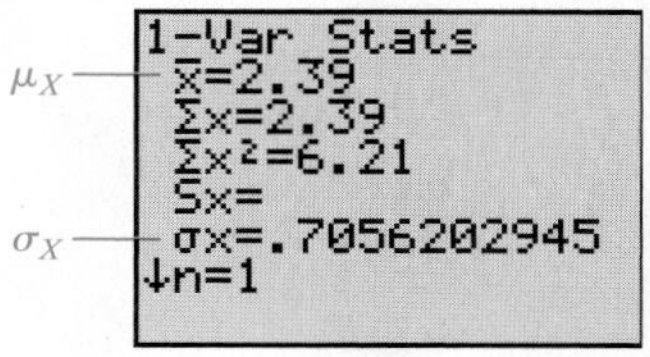

Solution Figure 4 shows the results from a TI-84 Plus graphing calculator.

Note: The TI-84 does not find s_X when the sum of L_2 is 1.

6.1 ASSESS YOUR UNDERSTANDING

VOCABULARY AND SKILL BUILDING

1. What is a random variable?

2. What is the difference between a discrete random variable and a continuous random variable? Provide your own examples of each.

3. What are the two requirements for a discrete probability distribution?

4. In your own words, provide an interpretation of the mean (or expected value) of a discrete random variable.

In Problems 5–8, determine whether the random variable is discrete or continuous. In each case, state the possible values of the random variable.

NW **5. (a)** The number of light bulbs that burn out in the next week in a room with 20 bulbs. Discrete; $x = 0, 1, \ldots, 20$

5. (c) Discrete, $x = 0, 1, 2, \ldots$
7. (a) Continuous, $r \geq 0$, (b) Discrete, $x = 0, 1, 2, \ldots$

(b) The time it takes to fly from New York City to Los Angeles. Continuous; $t > 0$ (d) Continuous, $s \geq 0$
(c) The number of hits to a Web site in a day.
(d) The amount of snow in Toronto during the winter.

6. (a) The time it takes for a light bulb to burn out.
(b) The weight of a T-bone steak. Continuous, $w > 0$
(c) The number of free-throw attempts before the first shot is made. Discrete, $x = 1, 2, \ldots$. (a) Continuous, $t > 0$
(d) In a random sample of 20 people, the number with type A blood. Discrete, $x = 0, 1, \ldots, 20$

7. (a) The amount of rain in Seattle during April.
(b) The number of fish caught during a fishing tournament.
(c) The number of customers arriving at a bank between noon and 1:00 P.M. Discrete, $x = 0, 1, 2, \ldots$ (d) Continuous, $t > 0$
(d) The time required to download a file from the Internet.

8. (a) The number of defects in a roll of carpet.
(b) The distance a baseball travels in the air after being hit.
(c) The number of points scored during a basketball game.
(d) The square footage of a house. Continuous, $a > 0$

In Problems 9–14, determine whether the distribution is a discrete probability distribution. If not, state why.

NW **9.** Yes

x	$P(x)$
0	0.2
1	0.2
2	0.2
3	0.2
4	0.2

10. Yes

x	$P(x)$
0	0.1
1	0.5
2	0.05
3	0.25
4	0.1

11. No; $P(50) < 0$

x	$P(x)$
10	0.1
20	0.23
30	0.22
40	0.6
50	−0.15

12. Yes

x	$P(x)$
1	0
2	0
3	0
4	0
5	1

13. No; $\sum P(x) \neq 1$

x	$P(x)$
100	0.1
200	0.25
300	0.2
400	0.3
500	0.1

14. No; $\sum P(x) \neq 1$

x	$P(x)$
100	0.25
200	0.25
300	0.25
400	0.25
500	0.25

In Problems 15 and 16, determine the required value of the missing probability to make the distribution a discrete probability distribution.

15. $P(4) = 0.3$

x	$P(x)$
3	0.4
4	?
5	0.1
6	0.2

16. $P(2) = 0.15$

x	$P(x)$
0	0.30
1	0.15
2	?
3	0.20
4	0.15
5	0.05

8. (a) Discrete, $x = 0, 1, 2, \ldots$ (b) Continuous, $d > 0$
(c) Discrete, $x = 0, 1, 2, \ldots$

APPLYING THE CONCEPTS

NW **17. Televisions** In the Sullivan Statistics Survey, individuals were asked to disclose the number of televisions in their household. In the following probability distribution, the random variable X represents the number of televisions in households.

Number of Televisions, x	$P(x)$
0	0
1	0.161
2	0.261
3	0.176
4	0.186
5	0.116
6	0.055
7	0.025
8	0.010
9	0.010

Source: Sullivan Statistics Survey

(a) Verify this is a discrete probability distribution.
(b) Draw a probability histogram. (c) $\mu_X = 3.2$ (d) $\sigma_X = 1.7$
(c) Determine and interpret the mean of the random variable X.
(d) Determine the standard deviation of the random variable X.
(e) What is the probability that a randomly selected household has three televisions? 0.176
(f) What is the probability that a randomly selected household has three or four televisions? 0.362
(g) What is the probability that a randomly selected household has no televisions? Would you consider this to be an impossible event? 0; no

18. Parental Involvement In the following probability distribution, the random variable X represents the number of activities a parent of a 6th- to 8th-grade student is involved in.

x	$P(x)$
0	0.073
1	0.117
2	0.258
3	0.322
4	0.230

Source: U.S. National Center for Education Statistics

(a) Verify that this is a discrete probability distribution.
(b) Draw a probability histogram. (c) $\mu_X = 2.5$ (d) $\sigma_X = 1.2$
(c) Compute and interpret the mean of the random variable X.
(d) Compute the standard deviation of the random variable X.
(e) What is the probability that a randomly selected student has a parent involved in three activities? 0.322
(f) What is the probability that a randomly selected student has a parent involved in three or four activities? 0.552

19. Ichiro's Hit Parade In the 2004 baseball season, Ichiro Suzuki of the Seattle Mariners set the record for the most hits in a season with a total of 262 hits. In the following probability distribution, the random variable X represents the number of hits Ichiro obtained in a game.

x	$P(x)$
0	0.1677
1	0.3354
2	0.2857
3	0.1491
4	0.0373
5	0.0248

Source: Chicago Tribune

(a) Verify that this is a discrete probability distribution.
(b) Draw a probability histogram. (c) $\mu_X = 1.6$, (d) $\sigma_X = 1.2$
(c) Compute and interpret the mean of the random variable X.
(d) Compute the standard deviation of the random variable X.
(e) What is the probability that in a randomly selected game Ichiro got 2 hits? 0.2857
(f) What is the probability that in a randomly selected game Ichiro got more than 1 hit? 0.4969

20. Waiting in Line A Wendy's manager performed a study to determine a probability distribution for the number of people, X, waiting in line during lunch. The results were as follows:

x	$P(x)$	x	$P(x)$
0	0.011	7	0.098
1	0.035	8	0.063
2	0.089	9	0.035
3	0.150	10	0.019
4	0.186	11	0.004
5	0.172	12	0.006
6	0.132		

(a) Verify that this is a discrete probability distribution.
(b) Draw a probability histogram. (c) $\mu_X = 4.9$ (d) $\sigma_X = 2.2$
(c) Compute and interpret the mean of the random variable X.
(d) Compute the standard deviation of the random variable X.
(e) What is the probability that eight people are waiting in line for lunch? 0.063
(f) What is the probability that 10 or more people are waiting in line for lunch? Would this be unusual? 0.029; yes

In Problems 21–24, (a) construct a discrete probability distribution for the random variable X [Hint: $P(x_i) = \frac{f_i}{N}$*], (b) draw the probability histogram, (c) compute and interpret the mean of the random variable X, and (d) compute the standard deviation of the random variable X.* 21. (c) $\mu_X = 5.8$ (d) $\sigma_X = 1.1$

21. The World Series The following data represent the number of games played in each World Series from 1923 to 2010.

x (games played)	Frequency
4	17
5	18
6	19
7	33

Source: Major League Baseball

22. Ideal Number of Children What is the ideal number of children to have in a family? The following data represent the ideal number of children for a random sample of 900 adult Americans. (c) $\mu_X = 2.4$ (d) $\sigma_X = 0.8$

x (number of children)	Frequency
0	10
1	30
2	520
3	250
4	70
5	17
6	3

Source:: Based on data from a Gallup poll

23. Paper Toss Paper Toss is a popular application for smart phones. The goal of the game is to toss crumbled paper into a trash can while accounting for wind from a fan. The following data represent the ratings (on a scale from 1 to 5) with 1 representing a poor rating. (c) $\mu_X = 3.7$ (d) $\sigma_X = 1.4$

Stars	Frequency
1	2752
2	2331
3	4215
4	3902
5	10,518

Source: iTunes

24. Tickets The following data, obtained from the Sullivan Statistics Survey, represent the number of speeding tickets individuals received in the past 12 months.
(c) $\mu_X = 0.2$ (d) $\sigma_X = 0.6$

Tickets	Frequency
0	169
1	21
2	4
3	4

Source: Sullivan Statistics Survey

25. Number of Births The probability histogram on the following page represents the number of live births by a mother 50 to 54 years old who had a live birth in 2007. *Source: National Vital Statistics Report*, 58(24): August 9, 2010.

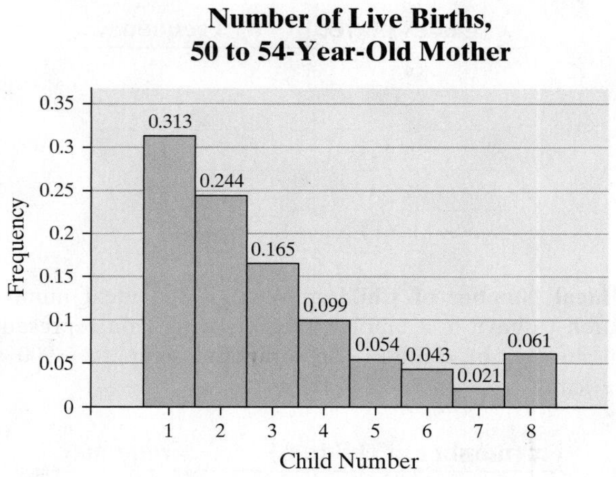

(a) What is the probability that a randomly selected 50- to 54-year-old mother who had a live birth in 2007 has had her fourth live birth? 0.099

(b) What is the probability that a randomly selected 50- to 54-year-old mother who had a live birth in 2007 has had her fourth or fifth live birth? 0.153

(c) What is the probability that a randomly selected 50- to 54-year-old mother who had a live birth in 2007 has had her sixth or more live birth? 0.125

(d) If a 50- to 54-year-old mother who had a live birth in 2007 is randomly selected, how many live births would you expect the mother to have had? 2.9

26. Rental Units The probability histogram represents the number of rooms in rented housing units in 2009. *Source*: 2009 American Housing Survey.

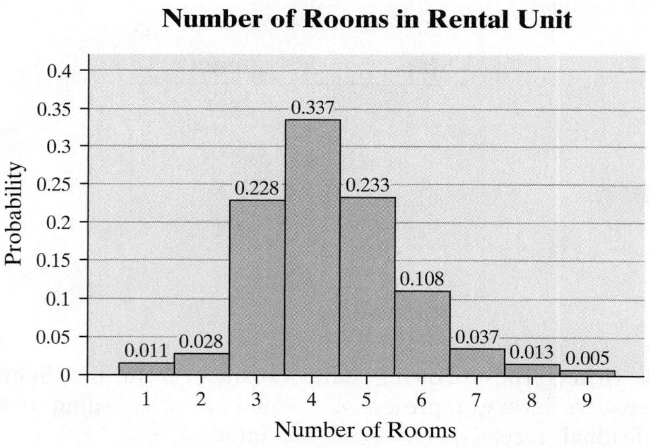

(a) What is the probability that a randomly selected rental unit has five rooms? 0.233

(b) What is the probability that a randomly selected rental unit has five or six rooms? 0.341

(c) What is the probability that a randomly selected rental unit has seven or more rooms? 0.055

(d) If a rental unit is randomly selected, how many rooms would you expect the unit to have? 4.3

NW **27. Life Insurance** A life insurance company sells a $250,000 1-year term life insurance policy to a 20-year-old female for $200. According to the *National Vital Statistics Report*, 58(21), the probability that the female survives the year is 0.999544. Compute and interpret the expected value of this policy to the insurance company. $86.00

28. Life Insurance A life insurance company sells a $250,000 1-year term life insurance policy to a 20-year-old male for $350. According to the *National Vital Statistics Report*, 58(21), the probability that the male survives the year is 0.998734. Compute and interpret the expected value of this policy to the insurance company. $33.50

29. Investment An investment counselor calls with a hot stock tip. He believes that if the economy remains strong, the investment will result in a profit of $50,000. If the economy grows at a moderate pace, the investment will result in a profit of $10,000. However, if the economy goes into recession, the investment will result in a loss of $50,000. You contact an economist who believes there is a 20% probability the economy will remain strong, a 70% probability the economy will grow at a moderate pace, and a 10% probability the economy will slip into recession. What is the expected profit from this investment? $12,000 30. $15,000

30. Real Estate Investment Shawn and Maddie purchase a foreclosed property for $50,000 and spend an additional $27,000 fixing up the property. They feel that they can resell the property for $120,000 with probability 0.15, $100,000 with probability 0.45, $80,000 with probability 0.25, and $60,000 with probability 0.15. Compute and interpret the expected profit for reselling the property.

31. Roulette In the game of roulette, a player can place a $5 bet on the number 17 and have a $\frac{1}{38}$ probability of winning. If the metal ball lands on 17, the player wins $175. Otherwise, the casino takes the player's $5. What is the expected value of the game to the player? If you played the game 1000 times, how much would you expect to lose? −$0.26; about $260 32. −$ 0.42

32. Connecticut Lottery In the Cash Five Lottery in Connecticut, a player pays $1 for a single ticket with five numbers. Five balls numbered 1 through 35 are randomly chosen from a bin without replacement. If all five numbers on a player's ticket match the five chosen, the player wins $100,000. The probability of this occurring is $\frac{1}{324{,}632}$. If four numbers match, the player wins $300. This occurs with probability $\frac{1}{2164}$. If three numbers match, the player wins $10. This occurs with probability $\frac{1}{75}$. Compute and interpret the expected value of the game from the player's point of view.

33. Powerball Powerball is a multistate lottery. The following probability distribution represents the cash prizes of Powerball with their corresponding probabilities.

x (cash prize, $)	*P*(*x*)
Grand prize	0.00000000684
200,000	0.00000028
10,000	0.000001711
100	0.000153996
7	0.004778961
4	0.007881463
3	0.01450116
0	0.9726824222

Source: www.powerball.com

(a) If the grand prize is $15,000,000, find and interpret the expected cash prize. If a ticket costs $1, what is your expected profit from one ticket? $0.30; −$0.70

(b) To the nearest million, how much should the grand prize be so that you can expect a profit? Assume nobody else wins so that you do not have to share the grand prize. $118,000,000

(c) Does the size of the grand prize affect your chance of winning? Explain. No

34. SAT Test Penalty Some standardized tests, such as the SAT test, incorporate a penalty for wrong answers. For example, a multiple-choice question with five possible answers will have 1 point awarded for a correct answer and $\frac{1}{4}$ point deducted for an incorrect answer. Questions left blank are worth 0 points.

(a) Find the expected number of points received for a multiple-choice question with five possible answers when a student just guesses. 0

(b) Explain why there is a deduction for wrong answers.

35. Simulation Use the probability distribution from Problem 19 and a DISCRETE command for some statistical software to simulate 100 repetitions of the experiment (100 games). The number of hits is recorded. Approximate the mean and standard deviation of the random variable X based on the simulation. Repeat the simulation by performing 500 repetitions of the experiment. Approximate the mean and standard deviation of the random variable. Compare your results to the theoretical mean and standard deviation. What property is being illustrated?

36. Simulation Use the probability distribution from Problem 20 and a DISCRETE command for some statistical software to simulate 100 repetitions of the experiment. Approximate the mean and standard deviation of the random variable X based on the simulation. Repeat the simulation by performing 500 repetitions of the experiment. Approximate the mean and standard deviation of the random variable. Compare your results to the theoretical mean and standard deviation. What property is being illustrated?

37. Putting It Together: Sullivan Statistics Survey One question from the Sullivan Statistics Survey was "How many credit cards do you currently have?" This question was asked of only those individuals who have a credit card. Answer the following questions based on the results of the survey.

(a) Determine the mean number of credit cards based on the raw data. 3.3

(b) Determine the standard deviation number of credit cards based on the raw data. 2.3 (e) $\mu_X = 3.3$; $\sigma_X = 2.3$

(c) Determine a probability distribution for the random variable, X, the number of credit cards issued to an individual.

(d) Draw a probability histogram for the random variable X. Describe the shape of the distribution.

(e) Determine the mean and standard deviation number of credit cards from the probability distribution found in part (c).

(f) Determine the probability of randomly selecting an individual whose number of credit cards is more than two standard deviations from the mean. Is this result unusual? 0.05; a little

(g) Determine the probability of randomly selecting two individuals who are issued exactly two credit cards. [*Hint:* Are the events independent?] Interpret this result. 0.0744

Technology Step-By-Step

Finding the Mean and Standard Deviation of a Discrete Random Variable Using Technology

TI-83/84 Plus

1. Enter the values of the random variable in L1 and their corresponding probabilities in L2.
2. Press STAT, highlight CALC, and select `1: 1-Var Stats.`
3. With 1-Var Stats on the HOME screen, type L1 followed by a comma, followed by L2 as follows:

```
1-Var Stats L1, L2
```

Hit ENTER.

6.2 THE BINOMIAL PROBABILITY DISTRIBUTION

Preparing for This Section Before getting started, review the following:

- Empirical Rule (Section 3.2, pp. 137–139)
- Addition Rule for Disjoint Events (Section 5.2, pp. 247–250)
- Complement Rule (Section 5.2, pp. 252–254)
- Independence (Section 5.3, p. 259)
- Multiplication Rule for Independent Events (Section 5.3, pp. 259–261)
- Combinations (Section 5.5, pp. 278–280)

OBJECTIVES

1. Determine whether a probability experiment is a binomial experiment
2. Compute probabilities of binomial experiments
3. Compute the mean and standard deviation of a binomial random variable
4. Construct binomial probability histograms

1 Determine Whether a Probability Experiment Is a Binomial Experiment

Note to Instructor
If you like, you can print out and distribute the Preparing for This Section quiz located in the Instructor's Resource Center. The purpose of the quiz is to verify that the students have the prerequisite knowledge for this section.

In Section 6.1, we stated that probability distributions could be presented using tables, graphs, or mathematical formulas. In this section, we introduce a specific type of discrete probability distribution that can be presented using a formula, the *binomial probability distribution.*

The binomial probability distribution is a discrete probability distribution that describes probabilities for experiments in which there are two mutually exclusive (disjoint) outcomes. These two outcomes are generally referred to as *success* (such as making a free throw) and *failure* (such as missing a free throw).

In Other Words
The prefix *bi* means "two." This should help remind you that binomial experiments deal with situations in which there are only two outcomes: success or failure.

Experiments in which only two outcomes are possible are referred to as *binomial experiments*, provided that certain criteria are met.

Criteria for a Binomial Probability Experiment

An experiment is said to be a **binomial experiment** if

1. The experiment is performed a fixed number of times. Each repetition of the experiment is called a **trial**.
2. The trials are independent. This means that the outcome of one trial will not affect the outcome of the other trials.
3. For each trial, there are two mutually exclusive (disjoint) outcomes: success or failure.
4. The probability of success is the same for each trial of the experiment.

Let the random variable X be the number of successes in n trials of a binomial experiment. Then X is called a **binomial random variable**. Before introducing the method for computing binomial probabilities, it is worthwhile to introduce some notation.

Notation Used in the Binomial Probability Distribution

- There are n independent trials of the experiment.
- Let p denote the probability of success for each trial so that $1 - p$ is the probability of failure for each trial.
- Let X denote the number of successes in n independent trials of the experiment. So $0 \leq x \leq n$.

EXAMPLE 1 Identifying Binomial Experiments

Problem Determine which of the following probability experiments qualify as a binomial experiment. For those that are binomial experiments, identify the number of trials, probability of success, probability of failure, and possible values of the random variable X.

(a) An experiment in which a basketball player who historically makes 80% of his free throws is asked to shoot three free throws, and the number of free throws made is recorded.

(b) The number of people with blood type O-negative based on a simple random sample of size 10 is recorded. According to the American Red Cross, 7% of people in the United States have blood type O-negative.

(c) A probability experiment in which three cards are drawn from a deck without replacement and the number of aces is recorded.

Historical Note

Jacob Bernoulli was born on December 27, 1654, in Basel, Switzerland. He studied philosophy and theology at the urging of his parents. (He resented this.) In 1671, he graduated from the University of Basel with a master's degree in philosophy. In 1676, he received a licentiate in theology.

(continued)

Approach Determine whether the four conditions for a binomial experiment are satisfied.

1. The experiment is performed a fixed number of times.
2. The trials are independent.

After earning his philosophy degree, Bernoulli traveled to Geneva to tutor. From there, he went to France to study with the great mathematicians of the time. One of Bernoulli's greatest works is *Ars Conjectandi*, published 8 years after his death. In this publication, Bernoulli proved the binomial probability formula. To this day, each trial in a binomial probability experiment is called a *Bernoulli trial.*

3. There are only two possible outcomes of the experiment.
4. The probability of success for each trial is constant.

Solution

(a) This is a binomial experiment because
1. There are $n = 3$ trials.
2. The trials are independent.
3. There are two possible outcomes: make or miss.
4. The probability of success (make) is 0.8 and the probability of failure (miss) is 0.2. The probabilities are the same for each trial.
The random variable X is the number of free throws made with $x = 0, 1, 2,$ or 3.

(b) This is a binomial experiment because
1. There are 10 trials (the 10 randomly selected people).
2. The trials are independent.*
3. There are two possible outcomes: finding a person with blood type O-negative or not.
4. The probability of success is 0.07 and the probability of failure is 0.93.
The random variable X is the number of people with blood type O-negative with $x = 0, 1, 2, 3, \ldots, 10$.

(c) This is not a binomial experiment because the trials are not independent. The probability of an ace on the first trial is $\frac{4}{52}$. Because we are sampling without replacement, if an ace is selected on the first trial, the probability of an ace on the second trial is $\frac{3}{51}$. If an ace is not selected on the first trial, the probability of an ace on the second trial is $\frac{4}{51}$.

Now Work Problem 9

⚠ CAUTION

The probability of success, p, is always associated with the random variable X, the number of successes. So if X represents the number of 18-year-olds involved in an accident, then p represents the probability of an 18-year-old being involved in an accident.

Note that the word *success* does not necessarily imply something positive. Success means that an outcome has occurred that corresponds with p, the probability of success. For example, a probability experiment might be to randomly select ten 18-year-old male drivers. If X denotes the number who have been involved in an accident within the last year, a success would mean obtaining an 18-year-old male who was involved in an accident. This outcome is not positive, but it is a success as far as the experiment goes.

2 Compute Probabilities of Binomial Experiments

We are now prepared to compute probabilities for a binomial random variable X. We present three methods for obtaining binomial probabilities: (1) the binomial probability distribution formula, (2) a table of binomial probabilities, and (3) technology. We develop the binomial probability formula in Example 2.

EXAMPLE 2 Constructing a Binomial Probability Distribution

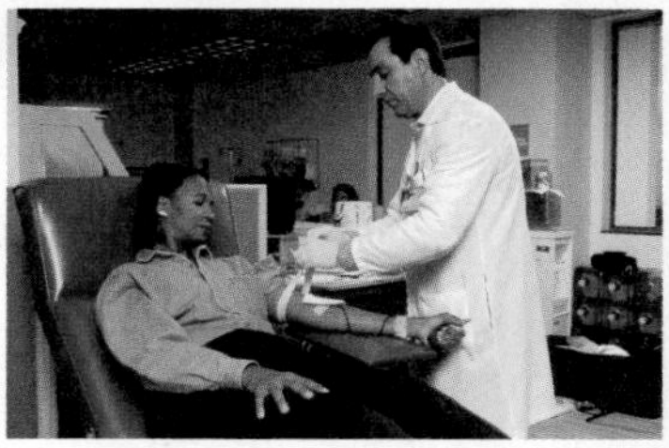

Problem According to the American Red Cross, 7% of people in the United States have blood type O-negative. A simple random sample of size 4 is obtained, and the number of people X with blood type O-negative is recorded. Construct a probability distribution for the random variable X.

Approach This is a binomial experiment with $n = 4$ trials. We define a success as selecting an individual with blood type O-negative. The probability of success, p, is 0.07, and X is the random variable representing the number of successes with $x = 0, 1, 2, 3,$ or 4.

Step 1 Construct a tree diagram listing the various outcomes of the experiment by listing each outcome as S (success) or F (failure).

*In sampling from large populations without replacement, the trials are assumed to be independent, provided that the sample size is small in relation to the size of the population. As a rule of thumb, if the sample size is less than 5% of the population size, the trials are assumed to be independent, although they are technically dependent. See Example 6 in Section 5.4.

Step 2 Compute the probabilities for each value of the random variable X.

Step 3 Construct the probability distribution.

Solution

Step 1 The tree diagram in Figure 5 lists the 16 possible outcomes of the experiment.

Figure 5

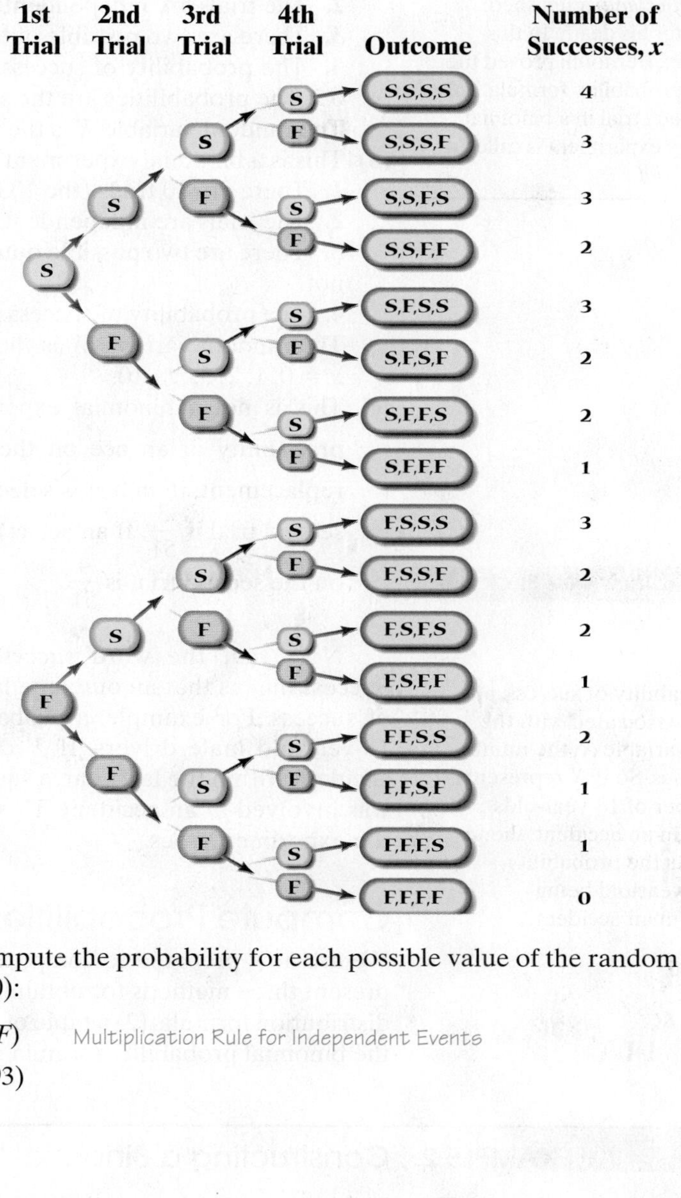

Step 2 We now compute the probability for each possible value of the random variable X. We start with $P(0)$:

$$P(0) = P(FFFF) = P(F) \cdot P(F) \cdot P(F) \cdot P(F) \quad \text{Multiplication Rule for Independent Events}$$
$$= (0.93)(0.93)(0.93)(0.93)$$
$$= (0.93)^4$$
$$= 0.74805$$

$$P(1) = P(SFFF \text{ or } FSFF \text{ or } FFSF \text{ or } FFFS)$$
$$= P(SFFF) + P(FSFF) + P(FFSF) + P(FFFS) \quad \text{Addition Rule for Disjoint Events}$$
$$= (0.07)^1(0.93)^3 + (0.07)^1(0.93)^3 + (0.07)^1(0.93)^3 + (0.07)^1(0.93)^3 \quad \text{Multiplication Rule for Independent Events}$$
$$= 4(0.07)^1(0.93)^3$$
$$= 0.22522$$

$$P(2) = P(SSFF \text{ or } SFSF \text{ or } SFFS \text{ or } FSSF \text{ or } FSFS \text{ or } FFSS)$$
$$= P(SSFF) + P(SFSF) + P(SFFS) + P(FSSF) + P(FSFS) + P(FFSS)$$
$$= (0.07)^2(0.93)^2 + (0.07)^2(0.93)^2 + (0.07)^2(0.93)^2 + (0.07)^2(0.93)^2 + (0.07)^2(0.93)^2 + (0.07)^2(0.93)^2$$
$$= 6(0.07)^2(0.93)^2$$
$$= 0.02543$$

TABLE 8

x	$P(x)$
0	0.74805
1	0.22522
2	0.02543
3	0.00128
4	0.00002

We compute $P(3)$ and $P(4)$ similarly and obtain $P(3) = 0.00128$ and $P(4) = 0.00002$. You are encouraged to verify these probabilities.

Step 3 We present these results in the probability distribution in Table 8.

Notice some interesting results in Example 2. Consider the probability of obtaining $x = 1$ success:

$$P(1) = 4(0.07)^1\,(0.93)^3$$

4 is the number of ways we obtain 1 success in 4 trials of the experiment. Here, it is ${}_4C_1$.

0.07 is the probability of success and the exponent 1 is the number of successes.

0.93 is the probability of failure and the exponent 3 is the number of failures.

The coefficient 4 is the number of ways of obtaining one success in four trials. In general, the coefficient is ${}_nC_x$, the number of ways of obtaining x successes in n trials. The second factor in the formula, $(0.07)^1$, is the probability of success, p, raised to the number of successes, x. The third factor in the formula, $(0.93)^3$, is the probability of failure, $1 - p$, raised to the number of failures, $n - x$. The following *binomial probability distribution function (pdf)* formula holds for all binomial experiments.

CAUTION

Before using the binomial probability distribution function, be sure the requirements for a binomial experiment are satisfied.

Binomial Probability Distribution Function

The probability of obtaining x successes in n independent trials of a binomial experiment is given by

$$P(x) = {}_nC_x\, p^x (1 - p)^{n-x} \qquad x = 0, 1, 2, \ldots, n \qquad (1)$$

where p is the probability of success.

When reading probability problems, pay special attention to key phrases that translate into mathematical symbols. Table 9 lists various phrases and their corresponding mathematical equivalent.

Note to Instructor

Consider assigning the "Exploring a Binomial Distribution from Multiple Perspectives" activity from the Student Activity Workbook.

TABLE 9

Phrase	Math Symbol
"at least" or "no less than" or "greater than or equal to"	$\geq$
"more than" or "greater than"	$>$
"fewer than" or "less than"	$<$
"no more than" or "at most" or "less than or equal to"	$\leq$
"exactly" or "equals" or "is"	$=$

EXAMPLE 3 Using the Binomial Probability Distribution Function

Problem According to CTIA, 25% of all U.S. households are wireless-only households (no landline). In a random sample of 20 households, what is the probability that

(a) Exactly 5 are wireless-only?

(b) Fewer than 3 are wireless-only?

(c) At least 3 are wireless-only?

(d) The number of households that are wireless-only is between 5 and 7, inclusive?

Approach This is a binomial experiment with $n = 20$ independent trials. We define a success as selecting a household that is wireless-only. The probability of success, p, is 0.25. The possible values of the random variable X are $x = 0, 1, 2, \ldots, 20$. We use Formula (1) to compute the probabilities.

Solution

(a) $P(5) = {}_{20}C_5(0.25)^5(1 - 0.25)^{20-5}$ $\quad n = 20, x = 5, p = 0.25$

$$= \frac{20!}{5!(20-5)!}(0.25)^5(0.75)^{15} \quad {}_nC_x = \frac{n!}{x!(n-x)!}$$

$$= 15{,}504(0.25)^5(0.75)^{15} = 0.2023$$

Note to Instructor

It is important to reinforce the relative frequency approach to interpreting probabilities. This will help students when we get to confidence intervals and P-values.

Interpretation The probability of getting exactly 5 households out of 20 that are wireless-only is 0.2023. In 100 trials of this experiment (that is, if we surveyed 20 households 100 different times), we would expect about 20 trials to result in 5 households that are wireless-only.

(b) The phrase *fewer than* means "less than." The values of the random variable X less than 3 are $x = 0, 1,$ or 2.

$$\begin{aligned} P(X < 3) &= P(0 \text{ or } 1 \text{ or } 2) \\ &= P(0) + P(1) + P(2) \quad \text{Addition Rule for Disjoint Events} \\ &= {}_{20}C_0(0.25)^0(1-0.25)^{20-0} + {}_{20}C_1(0.25)^1(1-0.25)^{20-1} + {}_{20}C_2(0.25)^2(1-0.25)^{20-2} \\ &= 0.0032 + 0.0211 + 0.0669 \\ &= 0.0912 \end{aligned}$$

Interpretation There is a 0.0912 probability that, in a random sample of 20 households, fewer than 3 will be a wireless-only household. In 100 trials of this experiment, we would expect about 9 trials to result in fewer than 3 wireless-only households.

(c) The values of the random variable X that are at least 3 are $x = 3, 4, 5, \ldots, 20$. Rather than compute $P(X \geq 3)$ directly by computing $P(3) + P(4) + \cdots + P(20)$, we can use the Complement Rule.

$$P(X \geq 3) = 1 - P(X < 3) = 1 - 0.0912 = 0.9088$$

Interpretation There is a 0.9088 probability that, in a random sample of 20 households, at least 3 will be a wireless-only household. In 100 trials of this experiment, we would expect about 91 trials to result in at least 3 being wireless-only households.

(d) The word *inclusive* means "including," so we want to determine the probability that 5, 6, or 7 households are wireless-only.

$$\begin{aligned} P(5 \leq X \leq 7) &= P(5 \text{ or } 6 \text{ or } 7) \\ &= P(5) + P(6) + P(7) \quad \text{Addition Rule for Disjoint Events} \\ &= {}_{20}C_5(0.25)^5(1-0.25)^{20-5} + {}_{20}C_6(0.25)^6(1-0.25)^{20-6} + {}_{20}C_7(0.25)^7(1-0.25)^{20-7} \\ &= 0.2023 + 0.1686 + 0.1124 \\ &= 0.4833 \end{aligned}$$

Interpretation The probability that the number of wireless-only households is between 5 and 7, inclusive, is 0.4833. In 100 trials of this experiment, we would expect about 48 trials to result in 5 to 7 households that are wireless-only.

Note to Instructor

Obtaining binomial probabilities from tables can be skipped without loss of continuity.

Obtaining Binomial Probabilities from Tables

Another method for obtaining probabilities is the binomial probability table. Table III in Appendix A gives probabilities for a binomial random variable X taking on a specific value, such as $P(10)$, for select values of n and p. Table IV in Appendix A gives cumulative probabilities of a binomial random variable X. This means that Table IV gives "less than or equal to" binomial probabilities, such as $P(X \leq 6)$. We illustrate how to use Tables III and IV in Example 4.

EXAMPLE 4 Computing Binomial Probabilities Using the Binomial Table

Problem According to the Gallup Organization, 65% of adult Americans are in favor of the death penalty for individuals convicted of murder. In a random sample of 15 adult Americans, what is the probability that

(a) Exactly 10 favor the death penalty?
(b) No more than 6 favor the death penalty?

Approach We use Tables III and IV in Appendix A to obtain the probabilities.

Solution

(a) We have $n = 15$, $p = 0.65$, and $x = 10$. In Table III, Appendix A, we go to the section that contains $n = 15$ and the column that contains $p = 0.65$. The value at which the $x = 10$ row intersects the $p = 0.65$ column is the probability we seek. See Figure 6. So $P(10) = 0.2123$.

Interpretation In 100 trials of this experiment (randomly selecting 15 adult Americans), we expect about 21 trials to result in exactly 10 adult Americans who favor the death penalty for individuals convicted of murder.

Figure 6

		p														
n	*x*	0.01	0.05	0.10	0.15	0.20	0.25	0.30	0.35	0.40	0.45	0.50	0.55	0.60	0.65	0.70
15	0	0.8601	0.4633	0.2059	0.0874	0.0352	0.0134	0.0047	0.0016	0.0005	0.0001	0.0000+	0.0000+	0.0000+	0.0000+	0.0000+
	1	0.1303	0.3658	0.3432	0.2312	0.1319	0.0668	0.0305	0.0126	0.0047	0.0016	0.0005	0.0001	0.0000+	0.0000+	0.0000+
	2	0.0092	0.1348	0.2669	0.2856	0.2309	0.1559	0.0916	0.0476	0.0219	0.0090	0.0032	0.0010	0.0003	0.0001	0.0000+
	3	0.0004	0.0307	0.1285	0.2184	0.2501	0.2252	0.1700	0.1110	0.0634	0.0318	0.0139	0.0052	0.0016	0.0004	0.0001
	4	0.0000+	0.0049	0.0428	0.1156	0.1876	0.2252	0.2186	0.1792	0.1268	0.0780	0.0417	0.0191	0.0074	0.0024	0.0006
	5	0.0000+	0.0006	0.0105	0.0449	0.1032	0.1651	0.2061	0.2123	0.1859	0.1404	0.0916	0.0515	0.0245	0.0096	0.0030
	6	0.0000+	0.0000+	0.0019	0.0132	0.0430	0.0917	0.1472	0.1906	0.2066	0.1914	0.1527	0.1048	0.0612	0.0298	0.0116
	7	0.0000+	0.0000+	0.0003	0.0030	0.0138	0.0393	0.0811	0.1319	0.1771	0.2013	0.1964	0.1647	0.1181	0.0710	0.0348
	8	0.0000+	0.0000+	0.0000+	0.0005	0.0035	0.0131	0.0348	0.0710	0.1181	0.1647	0.1964	0.2013	0.1771	0.1319	0.0811
	9	0.0000+	0.0000+	0.0000+	0.0001	0.0007	0.0034	0.0116	0.0298	0.0612	0.1048	0.1527	0.1914	0.2066	0.1906	0.1472
	10	0.0000+	0.0000+	0.0000+	0.0000+	0.0001	0.0007	0.0030	0.0096	0.0245	0.0515	0.0916	0.1404	0.1859	0.2123	0.2061
	11	0.0000+	0.0000+	0.0000+	0.0000+	0.0000+	0.0001	0.0006	0.0024	0.0074	0.0191	0.0417	0.0780	0.1268	0.1792	0.2186

(b) The phrase *no more than* means "less than or equal to." To compute $P(X \leq 6)$, we use the cumulative binomial table, Table IV in Appendix A, which lists binomial probabilities less than or equal to a specified value. We have $n = 15$, $p = 0.65$, so we go to the section that contains $n = 15$ and the column that contains $p = 0.65$. The value at which the $x = 6$ row intersects the $p = 0.65$ column represents $P(X \leq 6)$. See Figure 7. So $P(X \leq 6) = 0.0422$.

Interpretation In 100 trials of this experiment, we expect about 4 trials to result in no more than 6 adult Americans who favor the death penalty for individuals convicted of murder.

Note to Instructor

Be sure to inform students that discrepancies in answers can occur due to rounding in the binomial distribution table. For example, had we used Table III in Appendix A to solve part (b) of Example 4, we would obtain 0.0001 + 0.0004 + 0.0024 + 0.0096 + 0.0298 = 0.0423. Because of the rounding within Table III, this result differs from the answer 0.0422 found by using the cumulative table, Table IV. Point out to students that it is generally better to use the cumulative binomial table when the binomial probabilities must be summed.

Figure 7

		p														
n	*x*	0.01	0.05	0.10	0.15	0.20	0.25	0.30	0.35	0.40	0.45	0.50	0.55	0.60	0.65	0.70
15	0	0.8601	0.4633	0.2059	0.0874	0.0352	0.0134	0.0047	0.0016	0.0005	0.0001	0.0000+	0.0000+	0.0000+	0.0000+	0.0000+
	1	0.9904	0.8290	0.5490	0.3186	0.1671	0.0802	0.0353	0.0142	0.0052	0.0017	0.0005	0.0001	0.0000+	0.0000+	0.0000+
	2	0.9996	0.9638	0.8159	0.6042	0.3980	0.2361	0.1268	0.0617	0.0271	0.0107	0.0037	0.0011	0.0003	0.0001	0.0000+
	3	1.0000–	0.9945	0.9444	0.8227	0.6482	0.4613	0.2969	0.1727	0.0905	0.0424	0.0176	0.0063	0.0019	0.0005	0.0001
	4	1.0000–	0.9994	0.9873	0.9383	0.8358	0.6865	0.5155	0.3519	0.2173	0.1204	0.0592	0.0255	0.0093	0.0028	0.0007
	5	1.0000–	0.9999	0.9978	0.9832	0.9389	0.8518	0.7216	0.5643	0.4032	0.2608	0.1509	0.0769	0.0338	0.0124	0.0037
	6	1.0000–	1.0000–	0.9997	0.9964	0.9819	0.9434	0.8689	0.7548	0.6098	0.4522	0.3036	0.1818	0.0950	0.0422	0.0152
	7	1.0000–	1.0000–	1.0000–	0.9994	0.9958	0.9827	0.9500	0.8868	0.7869	0.6535	0.5000	0.3465	0.2131	0.1132	0.0500

Obtaining Binomial Probabilities Using Technology

Statistical software and graphing calculators also have the ability to compute binomial probabilities.

EXAMPLE 5 Obtaining Binomial Probabilities Using Technology

Note to Instructor
Consider assigning the "Randomness" activity from the Student Activity Workbook.

Problem According to the Gallup Organization, 65% of adult Americans are in favor of the death penalty for individuals convicted of murder. In a random sample of 15 adult Americans, what is the probability that

(a) Exactly 10 favor the death penalty?
(b) No more than 6 favor the death penalty?

Approach Statistical software or graphing calculators with advanced statistical features have the ability to determine binomial probabilities. The steps for determining binomial probabilities using the TI-83/84 Plus graphing calculators, MINITAB, Excel, and StatCrunch can be found in the Technology Step-by-Step on page 322.

Solution We will use StatCrunch to determine the probability for (a) and a TI-84 Plus to determine the probability for part (b).

(a) Using StatCrunch's binomial calculator, we obtain the results in Figure 8(a). So $P(10) = 0.2123$.

Interpretation In 100 trials of this experiment (randomly selecting 15 adult Americans), we expect about 21 trials to result in exactly 10 adult Americans who favor the death penalty for individuals convicted of murder.

(b) The phrase *no more than* means "less than or equal to." To compute $P(X \leq 6)$, we use the **cumulative distribution function (cdf)**, which computes probabilities less than or equal to a specified value. Using a TI-84 Plus graphing calculator to find $P(X \leq 6)$ with $n = 15$ and $p = 0.65$, we find $P(X \leq 6) = 0.0422$. See Figure 8(b).

Interpretation In 100 trials of this experiment, we expect about 4 trials to result in no more than 6 adult Americans who favor the death penalty for individuals convicted of murder.

Figure 8

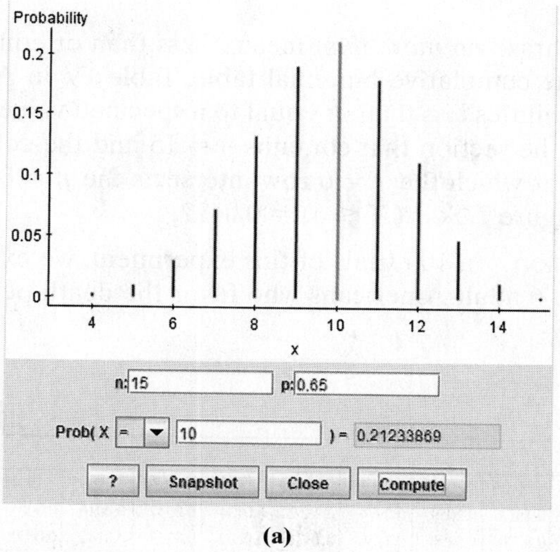

(a)

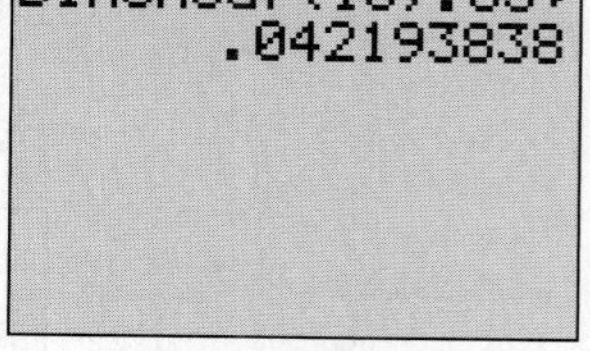

(b)

Now Work Problem 35

3 Compute the Mean and Standard Deviation of a Binomial Random Variable

We discussed finding the mean (or expected value) and standard deviation of a discrete random variable in Section 6.1. These formulas can be used to find the mean and standard deviation of a binomial random variable, but a simpler method exists.

In Other Words
The mean of a binomial random variable equals the product of the number of trials of the experiment and the probability of success. It can be interpreted as the expected number of successes in n trials of the experiment.

Mean (or Expected Value) and Standard Deviation of a Binomial Random Variable

A binomial experiment with n independent trials and probability of success p has a mean and standard deviation given by the formulas

$$\mu_X = np \quad \text{and} \quad \sigma_X = \sqrt{np(1-p)} \qquad \textbf{(2)}$$

EXAMPLE 6 Finding the Mean and Standard Deviation of a Binomial Random Variable

Note to Instructor
You may want to construct a binomial probability distribution with $n = 3$ and $p = 0.4$. Then use the formulas from Section 6.1 to compute μ_X and σ_X. Now use Formula (2) to compute μ_X and σ_X.

Problem According to CTIA, 25% of all U.S. households are wireless-only households. In a simple random sample of 300 households, determine the mean and standard deviation number of wireless-only households.

Approach This is a binomial experiment with $n = 300$ and $p = 0.25$. Use Formula (2) to find the mean and standard deviation, respectively.

Solution

$$\mu_X = np = 300(0.25) = 75$$

and

$$\sigma_X = \sqrt{np(1-p)} = \sqrt{300(0.25)(1-0.25))} = \sqrt{56.25} = 7.5$$

Interpretation We expect that, in a random sample of 300 households, 75 will be wireless-only.

Now Work Problems 29(a)–(c)

4 Construct Binomial Probability Histograms

Constructing binomial probability histograms is no different from constructing other probability histograms.

EXAMPLE 7 Constructing Binomial Probability Histograms

Problem

(a) Construct a binomial probability histogram with $n = 10$ and $p = 0.2$. Comment on the shape of the distribution.
(b) Construct a binomial probability histogram with $n = 10$ and $p = 0.5$. Comment on the shape of the distribution.
(c) Construct a binomial probability histogram with $n = 10$ and $p = 0.8$. Comment on the shape of the distribution.

Approach To construct a binomial probability histogram, we will first obtain the probability distribution and then construct its histogram.

Solution

(a) Table 10 shows the probability distribution with $n = 10$ and $p = 0.2$. Although $P(9)$ is 0.000004096, it is written as 0.0000 to four significant digits. The same idea applies to $P(10)$. Figure 9 shows the corresponding probability histogram with the mean $\mu_X = 10(0.2) = 2$ labeled. The distribution is skewed right.

TABLE 10

x	$P(x)$
0	0.1074
1	0.2684
2	0.3020
3	0.2013
4	0.0881
5	0.0264
6	0.0055
7	0.0008
8	0.0001
9	0.0000
10	0.0000

Figure 9

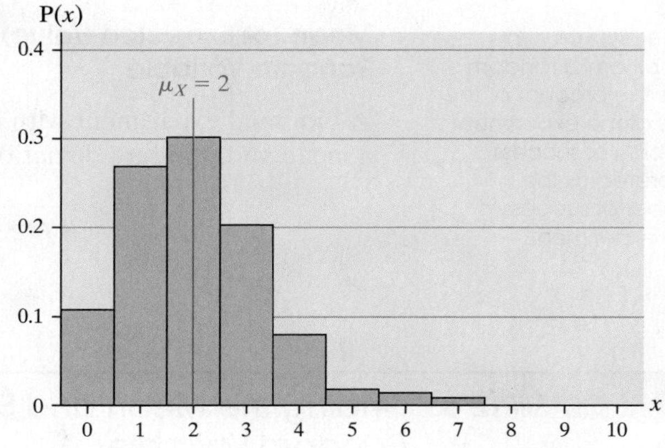

(b) Table 11 shows the probability distribution with $n = 10$ and $p = 0.5$. Figure 10 shows the corresponding probability histogram with the mean $\mu_X = 10(0.5) = 5$ labeled. The distribution is symmetric and approximately bell shaped.

TABLE 11

x	$P(x)$
0	0.0010
1	0.0098
2	0.0439
3	0.1172
4	0.2051
5	0.2461
6	0.2051
7	0.1172
8	0.0439
9	0.0098
10	0.0010

Figure 10

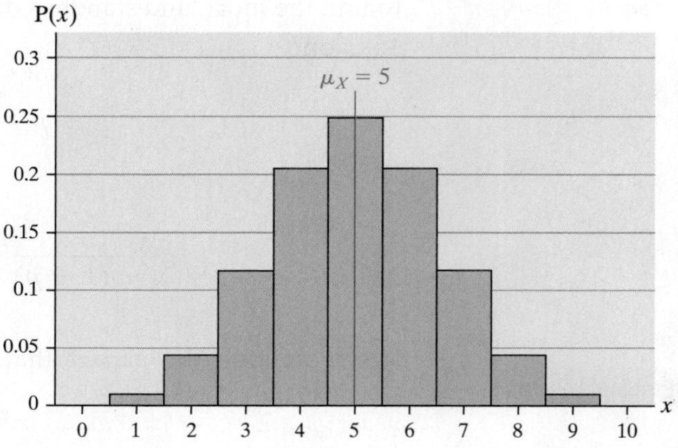

(c) Table 12 shows the probability distribution with $n = 10$ and $p = 0.8$. Figure 11 shows the corresponding probability histogram with the mean $\mu_X = 10(0.8) = 8$ labeled. The distribution is skewed left.

TABLE 12

x	$P(x)$
0	0.0000
1	0.0000
2	0.0001
3	0.0008
4	0.0055
5	0.0264
6	0.0881
7	0.2013
8	0.3020
9	0.2684
10	0.1074

Figure 11

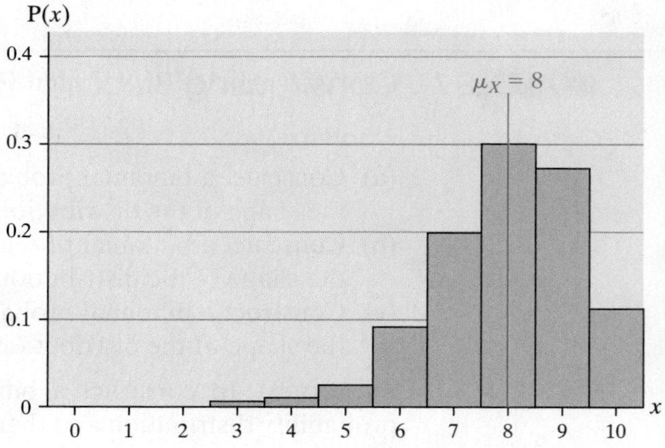

Now Work Problem 29(d)

Based on the results of Example 7, we conclude that the binomial probability distribution is skewed right if $p < 0.5$, symmetric and approximately bell shaped if $p = 0.5$, and skewed left if $p > 0.5$. Notice that Figure 9 ($p = 0.2$) and Figure 11 ($p = 0.8$) are mirror images of each other.

We have seen the role that p plays in the shape of a binomial distribution, but what role does n play in its shape? Let's compare the binomial probability histograms when $n = 10$ and $p = 0.2$ [see Figure 12(a)], when $n = 30$ and $p = 0.2$ [Figure 12(b)], and when $n = 70$ and $p = 0.2$ [Figure 12(c)].

Figure 12

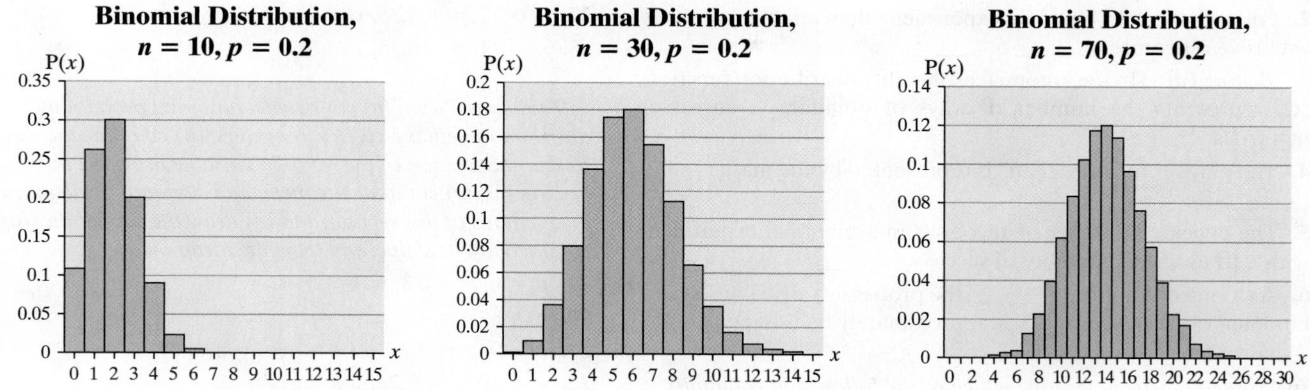

(a) (b) (c)

Figure 12(a) is skewed right, Figure 12(b) is slightly skewed right, and Figure 12(c) appears bell shaped. Our conclusion follows:

> For a fixed p, as the number of trials n in a binomial experiment increases, the probability distribution of the random variable X becomes bell shaped. As a rule of thumb, if $np(1 - p) \geq 10$,* the probability distribution will be approximately bell shaped.

In Other Words
Provided that $np(1 - p) \geq 10$, the interval $\mu - 2\sigma$ to $\mu + 2\sigma$ represents the "usual" observations. Observations outside this interval may be considered unusual.

This result allows us to use the Empirical Rule to identify unusual observations in a binomial experiment. Recall the Empirical Rule states that in a bell-shaped distribution about 95% of all observations lie within two standard deviations of the mean. That is, about 95% of the observations lie between $\mu - 2\sigma$ and $\mu + 2\sigma$. Any observation that lies outside this interval may be considered unusual because the observation occurs less than 5% of the time.

EXAMPLE 8 Using the Mean, Standard Deviation, and Empirical Rule to Check for Unusual Results in a Binomial Experiment

Problem According to CTIA, 25% of all U.S. households are wireless-only. In a simple random sample of 300 households, 92 were wireless-only. Is this result unusual?

Approach Because $np(1 - p) = 300(0.25)(1 - 0.25) = 56.25 \geq 10$, the binomial probability distribution is approximately bell shaped. Therefore, we can use the Empirical Rule: If the observation is less than $\mu - 2\sigma$ or greater than $\mu + 2\sigma$, it is unusual.

Solution

From Example 6, we have $\mu = 75$ and $\sigma = 7.5$.

$$\mu - 2\sigma = 75 - 2(7.5) = 75 - 15 = 60$$

and

$$\mu + 2\sigma = 75 + 2(7.5) = 75 + 15 = 90$$

Interpretation Since any value less than 60 or greater than 90 is unusual, 92 is an unusual result. We should try to identify the reason for its value. Perhaps the percentage of households that are wireless-only has increased.

Now Work Problem 43

*P. P. Ramsey and P. H. Ramsey, "Evaluating the Normal Approximation to the Binomial Test," *Journal of Educational Statistics* 13 (1998): 173–182.

6.2 ASSESS YOUR UNDERSTANDING

VOCABULARY AND SKILL BUILDING

1. A binomial experiment is performed a fixed number of times. Each repetition of the experiment is called a _______. trial

2. For each trial of a binomial experiment, there are two mutually exclusive outcomes: _______ or _______. success; failure

3. *True or False*: In the binomial probability distribution function, ${}_nC_x$ represents the number of ways of obtaining x successes in n trials. True

4. The phrase "no more than" is represented by the math symbol _______. $\leq$

5. The expected number of successes in a binomial experiment with n trials and probability of success p is_______. np

6. As a rule of thumb, if _______, the probability distribution of a binomial random variable X is approximately bell shaped.
6. $np(1 - p) \geq 10$

In Problems 7–16, determine which of the following probability experiments represents a binomial experiment. If the probability experiment is not a binomial experiment, state why.

7. A random sample of 15 college seniors is obtained, and the individuals selected are asked to state their ages. Not binomial

8. A random sample of 30 cars in a used car lot is obtained, and their mileages recorded. Not binomial

NW **9.** An experimental drug is administered to 100 randomly selected individuals, with the number of individuals responding favorably recorded. Binomial

10. A poll of 1200 registered voters is conducted in which the respondents are asked whether they believe Congress should reform Social Security. Binomial 11. Not binomial

11. Three cards are selected from a standard 52-card deck without replacement. The number of aces selected is recorded.

12. Three cards are selected from a standard 52-card deck with replacement. The number of kings selected is recorded. Binomial

13. A basketball player who makes 80% of her free throws is asked to shoot free throws until she misses. The number of free-throw attempts is recorded. Not binomial

14. A baseball player who reaches base safely 30% of the time is allowed to bat until he reaches base safely for the third time. The number of at-bats required is recorded. Not binomial

15. One hundred randomly selected U.S. parents with at least one child under the age of 18 are surveyed and asked if they have ever spanked their child. The number of parents who have spanked their child is recorded. Binomial

16. In a town with 400 citizens, 100 randomly selected citizens are asked to identify their religion. The number who identify with a Christian religion is recorded. Not binomial

In Problems 17–28, a binomial probability experiment is conducted with the given parameters. Compute the probability of x successes in the n independent trials of the experiment.

17. $n = 10, p = 0.4, x = 3$ 0.2150

18. $n = 15, p = 0.85, x = 12$ 0.2184

19. $n = 40, p = 0.99, x = 38$ 0.0532

20. $n = 50, p = 0.02, x = 3$ 0.0607

21. $n = 8, p = 0.35, x = 3$ 0.2786

22. $n = 20, p = 0.6, x = 17$ 0.0123

23. $n = 9, p = 0.2, x \leq 3$ 0.9144

24. $n = 10, p = 0.65, x < 5$ 0.0949

25. $n = 7, p = 0.5, x > 3$ 0.5

26. $n = 20, p = 0.7, x \geq 12$ 0.8867

27. $n = 12, p = 0.35, x \leq 4$ 0.5833

28. $n = 11, p = 0.75, x \geq 8$ 0.7133

In Problems 29–34, (a) construct a binomial probability distribution with the given parameters; (b) compute the mean and standard deviation of the random variable using the methods of Section 6.1; (c) compute the mean and standard deviation, using the methods of this section; and (d) draw the probability histogram, comment on its shape, and label the mean on the histogram.

NW **29.** $n = 6, p = 0.3$ $\mu_X = 1.8, \sigma_X = 1.1$

30. $n = 8, p = 0.5$ $\mu_X = 4, \sigma_X = 1.4$

31. $n = 9, p = 0.75$ $\mu_X = 6.75, \sigma_X = 1.3$

32. $n = 10, p = 0.2$ $\mu_X = 2, \sigma_X = 1.3$

33. $n = 10, p = 0.5$ $\mu_X = 5, \sigma_X = 1.6$

34. $n = 9, p = 0.8$ $\mu_X = 7.2, \sigma_X = 1.2$

APPLYING THE CONCEPTS

NW **35. On-Time Flights** According to flightstats.com, American Airlines flights from Dallas to Chicago are on time 80% of the time. Suppose 15 flights are randomly selected, and the number of on-time flights is recorded.

(a) Explain why this is a binomial experiment.

(b) Find and interpret the probability that exactly 10 flights are on time. 0.1032

(c) Find and interpret the probability that fewer than 10 flights are on time. 0.0611

(d) Find and interpret the probability that at least 10 flights are on time. 0.9389

(e) Find and interpret the probability that between 8 and 10 flights, inclusive, are on time. 0.16

36. Smokers According to the American Lung Association, 90% of adult smokers started smoking before turning 21 years old. Ten smokers 21 years old or older are randomly selected, and the number of smokers who started smoking before 21 is recorded.

(a) Explain why this is a binomial experiment.

(b) Find and interpret the probability that exactly 8 of them started smoking before 21 years of age. 0.1937

(c) Find and interpret the probability that fewer than 8 of them started smoking before 21 years of age. 0.0702

(d) Find and interpret the probability that at least 8 of them started smoking before 21 years of age. 0.9298 (e) 0.6385

(e) Find and interpret the probability that between 7 and 9 of them, inclusive, started smoking before 21 years of age.

37. Morality In a recent poll, the Gallup Organization found that 45% of adult Americans believe that the overall state of moral values in the United States is poor. Suppose a survey of a random sample of 25 adult Americans is conducted in which they are asked to disclose their feelings on the overall state of moral values in the United States.

(a) Find and interpret the probability that exactly 15 of those surveyed feel the state of morals is poor. 0.0520

(b) Find and interpret the probability that no more than 10 of those surveyed feel the state of morals is poor. 0.3843

(c) Find and interpret the probability that more than 16 of those surveyed feel the state of morals is poor. 0.0174

(d) Find and interpret the probability that 13 or 14 believe the state of morals is poor. 0.2103

(e) Would it be unusual to find 20 or more adult Americans who believe the overall state of moral values is poor in the United States? Why? Yes; $P(X \geq 20) = 0.0004$

38. Allergy Sufferers Clarinex-D is a medication whose purpose is to reduce the symptoms associated with a variety of allergies. In clinical trials of Clarinex-D, 5% of the patients in the study experienced insomnia as a side effect. A random sample of 20 Clarinex-D users is obtained, and the number of patients who experienced insomnia is recorded.

(a) Find the probability that exactly 3 experienced insomnia as a side effect. 0.0596

(b) Find the probability that 3 or fewer experienced insomnia as a side effect. 0.9841

(c) Find the probability that between 1 and 4 patients inclusive, experienced insomnia as a side effect. 0.6389

(d) Would it be unusual to find 4 or more patients who experienced insomnia as a side effect? Why? Yes

39. Sneeze According to a study done by Nick Wilson of Otago University Wellington, the probability a randomly selected individual will not cover his or her mouth when sneezing is 0.267. Suppose you sit on a bench in a mall and observe people's habits as they sneeze. (c) Yes; probability is 0.0272

(a) What is the probability that among 10 randomly observed individuals exactly 4 do not cover their mouth when sneezing? 0.1655

(b) What is the probability that among 10 randomly observed individuals fewer than 3 do not cover their mouth? 0.4752

(c) Would you be surprised if, after observing 10 individuals, fewer than half covered their mouth when sneezing? Why?

40. Sneeze Revisited According to a study done by Nick Wilson of Otago University Wellington, the probability a randomly selected individual will cover his or her mouth with a tissue, handkerchief, or elbow (the method recommended by public health officials) is 0.047. Suppose you sit on a bench in a mall and observe people's habits as they sneeze.

(a) What is the probability that among 15 randomly observed individuals exactly 2 cover their mouth with a tissue, handkerchief, or elbow? 0.1240

(b) What is the probability that among 15 randomly observed individuals fewer than 3 cover their mouth with a tissue, handkerchief, or elbow? 0.9691

(c) Would you be surprised if, after observing 15 randomly observed individuals, more than 4 covered the mouth with a tissue, handkerchief, or elbow? Yes; $P(X > 4) = 0.0005$

41. Jury Selection Twelve jurors are randomly selected from a population of 3 million residents. Of these 3 million residents, it is known that 45% are Hispanic. Of the 12 jurors selected, 2 are Hispanic. 48. Yes; $84 < \mu_X - 2\sigma_X = 121 - 2(10.4)$

(a) What proportion of the jury described is Hispanic? 0.1667

(b) If 12 jurors are randomly selected from a population that is 45% Hispanic, what is the probability that 2 or fewer jurors will be Hispanic? 0.0421

(c) If you were the lawyer of a Hispanic defendant, what might you argue?

42. Sullivan Survey: Car Color According to paint manufacturer DuPont, 6% of all cars worldwide are red. In the Sullivan Statistics Survey, of 175 respondents, 17, or 9.7%, indicated the color of their car is red. Determine if the results of the Sullivan Survey contradict those of DuPont by computing $P(X \geq 17)$, where X is a binomial random variable with $n = 175$ and $p = 0.06$. Explain what the probability represents. 0.0348

NW **43. On-Time Flights** According to flightstats.com, American Airlines flights from Dallas to Chicago are on time 80% of the time. Suppose 100 flights are randomly selected.

(a) Compute the mean and standard deviation of the random variable X, the number of on-time flights in 100 trials of the probability experiment. $\mu_X = 80, \sigma_X = 4$

(b) Interpret the mean.

(c) Would it be unusual to observe 75 on-time flights in a random sample of 100 flights from Dallas to Chicago? Why? No

44. Smokers According to the American Lung Association, 90% of adult smokers started smoking before turning 21 years old.

(a) Compute the mean and standard deviation of the random variable X, the number of smokers who started before turning 21 years old in 200 trials of the probability experiment.

(b) Interpret the mean. (a) $\mu_X = 180, \sigma_X = 4.2$

(c) Would it be unusual to observe 185 smokers who started smoking before turning 21 years old in a random sample of 200 adult smokers? Why? No

45. Morality In a recent poll, the Gallup Organization found that 45% of adult Americans believe that the overall state of moral values in the United States is poor.

(a) Compute the mean and standard deviation of the random variable X, the number of adults who believe that the overall state of moral values in the United States is poor based on a random sample of 500 adult Americans. $\mu_X = 225; \sigma_X = 11.1$

(b) Interpret the mean.

(c) Would it be unusual to identify 240 adult Americans who believe that the overall state of moral values in the United States is poor based on a random sample of 500 adult Americans? Why? No

46. Allergy Sufferers Clarinex-D is a medication whose purpose is to reduce the symptoms associated with a variety of allergies. In clinical trials of Clarinex-D, 5% of the patients in the study experienced insomnia as a side effect.

(a) If 240 users of Clarinex-D are randomly selected, how many would we expect to experience insomnia as a side effect? 12

(b) Would it be unusual to observe 20 patients experiencing insomnia as a side effect in 240 trials of the probability experiment? Why? Yes

47. Spanking In March 1995, The Harris Poll reported that 80% of parents spank their children. Suppose a recent poll of 1030 adult Americans with children finds that 781 indicated that they spank their children. If we assume parents' attitude toward spanking has not changed since 1995, how many of 1030 parents surveyed would we expect to spank? Do the results of the survey suggest that parents' attitude toward spanking may have changed since 1995? Why? 824; yes, $781 < \mu_X - 2\sigma_X = 824 - 2(12.8)$

48. Government Solutions? In May, 2000, the Gallup Organization reported that 11% of adult Americans had a great deal of trust and confidence in the federal government handling domestic issues. Suppose a survey of a random sample of 1100 adult Americans finds that 84 have a great deal of trust and confidence in the federal government handling domestic issues. Would these results be considered unusual? Why?

49. Internet Searches In August 2007, Google™ accounted for 53.6% of all U.S. Internet searches. Assuming this percentage is still accurate today, would it be unusual to observe 600 searches using Google™ in a random sample of 1000 U.S. Internet searches? Why?
Source: Nielsen NetRatings Yes

50. Asthma Control Singulair is a medication whose purpose is to control asthma attacks. In clinical trials of Singulair, 18.4% of the patients in the study experienced headaches as a side effect. Would it be unusual to observe 86 patients who experience headaches in a random sample of 400 patients who use this medication? Why? No

51. Racial Profiling in New York City The following excerpt is from the *Racial Profiling Data Collection Resource Center* (www.racialprofilinganalysis.neu.edu/).

In 2006, the New York City Police Department stopped a half-million pedestrians for suspected criminal involvement. Raw statistics for these encounters suggest large racial disparities—89 percent of the stops involved nonwhites. Do these statistics point to racial bias in police officers' decisions to stop particular pedestrians? Do they indicate that officers are particularly intrusive when stopping nonwhites?

Write a report that answers the questions posed using the fact that 44% of New York City residents were classified as white in 2006. In your report, cite some shortcomings in using the proportion of white residents in the city to formulate likelihoods.

52. Simulation According to the U.S. National Center for Health Statistics, there is a 98% probability that a 20-year-old male will survive to age 30.

(a) Using statistical software, simulate taking 100 random samples of size 30 from this population.

(b) Using the results of the simulation, compute the probability that exactly 29 of the 30 males survive to age 30.

(c) Compute the probability that exactly 29 of the 30 males survive to age 30, using the binomial probability distribution. Compare the results with part (b). 0.3340

(d) Using the results of the simulation, compute the probability that at most 27 of the 30 males survive to age 30.

(e) Compute the probability that at most 27 of the 30 males survive to age 30 using the binomial probability distribution. Compare the results with part (d). 0.0217

(f) Compute the mean number of male survivors in the 100 simulations of the probability experiment. Is it close to the expected value?

(g) Compute the standard deviation of the number of male survivors in the 100 simulations of the probability experiment. Compare the result to the theoretical standard deviation of the probability distribution.

(h) Did the simulation yield any unusual results?

53. Athletics Participation According to the High School Athletics Participation Survey, approximately 55% of students enrolled in high schools participate in athletic programs. You are performing a study of high school students and would like at least 11 students in the study to be participating in athletics.
Source: National Federation of State High School Associations

(a) How many high school students do you expect to have to randomly select? 20

(b) How many high school students do you have to select to have a 99% probability that the sample contains at least 12 who participate in athletics? 33

54. Educational Attainment According to the *2008 American Community Survey*, 27% of residents of the United States 25 years old or older had earned at least a bachelor's degree. You are performing a study and would like at least 10 people in the study to have earned at least a bachelor's degree.

(a) How many residents of the United States 25 years old or older do you expect to randomly select? 38

(b) How many residents of the United States 25 years old or older do you have to randomly select to have a probability 0.99 that the sample contains at least 10 who have earned at least a bachelor's degree? 65

EXPLAINING THE CONCEPTS

55. State the criteria for a binomial probability experiment.

56. Explain what "success" means in a binomial probability experiment.

57. Explain how the value of n, the number of trials in a binomial experiment, affects the shape of the binomial probability histogram.

58. Explain how the value of p, the probability of success, affects the shape of the binomial probability histogram.

59. When can the Empirical Rule be used to identify unusual results in a binomial experiment? Why can the Empirical Rule be used to identify results in a binomial experiment?

Technology Step-By-Step

Computing Binomial Probabilities via Technology

TI-83/84 Plus

Computing $P(x)$

1. Press 2nd VARS to access the probability distribution menu.
2. Highlight `binompdf(` and hit ENTER.
3. With `binompdf(` on the HOME screen, type the number of trials n, the probability of success, p, and the number of successes, x. For example, with $n = 15, p = 0.3$, and $x = 8$, type

```
binompdf(15, 0.3, 8)
```

Then hit ENTER.

Computing $P(X \leq x)$

1. Press 2nd VARS to access the probability distribution menu.
2. Highlight `binomcdf(` and hit ENTER.
3. With `binomcdf(` on the HOME screen, type the number of trials n, the probability of success, p, and the number of successes, x. For example, with $n = 15, p = 0.3$, and $x \leq 8$, type

```
binomcdf(15, 0.3, 8)
```

Then hit ENTER.

MINITAB

Computing $P(x)$

1. Enter the possible values of the random variable X in C1. For example, with $n = 15, p = 0.3$, enter $0, 1, 2, \ldots, 15$ into C1.

2. Select the **CALC** menu, highlight **Probability Distributions**, then highlight **Binomial . . .** .
3. Fill in the window as shown. Click OK.

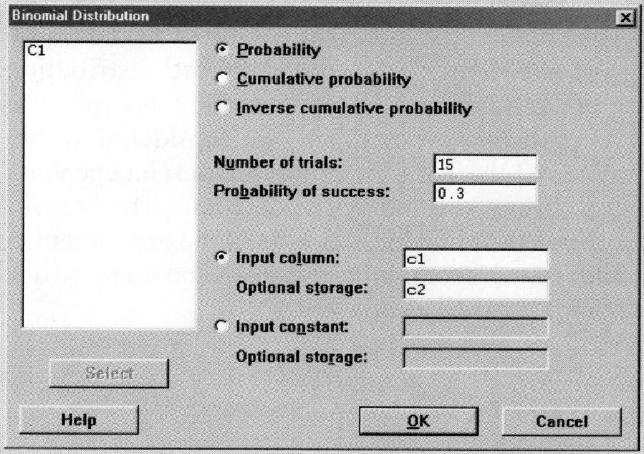

Computing $P(X \leq x)$

Follow the same steps as those for computing $P(x)$. In the window that comes up after selecting Binomial Distribution, select **Cumulative probability** instead of **Probability**.

Excel

Computing $P(x)$

1. Click Formulas tab. Select More Functions. Highlight Statistical in the Function category menu. Highlight BINOMDIST in the Function name menu.
2. Fill in the window with the appropriate values. Click OK.

Computing $P(X \leq x)$

Follow the same steps as those presented for computing $P(x)$. In the BINOMDIST window, type TRUE in the cumulative cell.

StatCrunch

1. Select **Stat**, highlight **Calculators**, select **Binomial**.
2. Enter the number of trials, n, and probability of success, p. In the pull-down menu, decide if you wish to compute $P(X \leq x)$, $P(X < x)$, and so on. Finally, enter the value of x. Click Compute.

Consumer Reports® Quality Assurance in Customer Relations

The Customer Relations Department at Consumers Union (CU) receives thousands of letters and e-mails from customers each month. Some people write asking how well a product performed during CU's testing, some people write sharing their own experiences with their household products, and the remaining people write for an array of other reasons.

To respond to each letter and e-mail that is received, Customer Relations recently upgraded its customer contact database. Although much of the process has been automated, it still requires employees to manually draft the responses. Given the current size of the department, each Customer Relations representative is required to draft approximately 300 responses each month.

As part of a quality assurance program, the Customer Relations manager would like to develop a plan that allows him to evaluate the performance of his employees. From past experience, he knows the probability that a new employee will write an initial draft of a response that contains errors is approximately 10%. The manager would like to know how many of the 300 responses he should sample to have a cost-effective quality assurance program.

(a) Let X be a discrete random variable that represents the number of the $n = 300$ draft responses that contain errors. Describe the probability distribution for X. Be sure to include the name of the probability distribution, possible values for the random variable X, and values of the parameters.

(b) To be effective, the manager would like to have a 95% probability of finding at least one draft document that contains an error. If the probability that a draft document will have errors is known to be 10%, determine the appropriate sample size to satisfy the manager's requirements.
Hint: We are required to find the number of draft documents that must be sampled so that the probability of finding at least one document containing an error is 95%. In other words, we have to determine n by solving: $P(X \geq 1) = 0.95$.

(c) Suppose that the error rate is really 20%. What sample size will the manager have to review to have a 95% probability of finding one or more documents containing an error?

Note to Readers: *In many cases, our test protocol and analytical methods are more complicated than described in these examples. The data and discussions have been modified to make the material more appropriate for the audience.*

CHAPTER 6 REVIEW

Summary

In this chapter, we discussed discrete probability distributions. A random variable represents the numerical measurement of the outcome from a probability experiment. Discrete random variables have either a finite or a countable number of outcomes. The term *countable* means that the values result from counting. Probability distributions must satisfy the following two criteria: (1) All probabilities must be between 0 and 1, inclusive, and (2) the sum of all probabilities must equal 1. Discrete probability distributions can be presented by a table, graph, or mathematical formula.

The mean and standard deviation of a random variable describe the center and spread of the distribution. The mean of a random variable is also called its expected value.

A probability experiment is considered a binomial experiment if there is a fixed number of n independent trials of the experiment with only two outcomes. The probability of success, p, is the same for each trial of the experiment. Special formulas exist for computing the mean and standard deviation of a binomial random variable.

Vocabulary

Random variable (p. 298)
Discrete random variable (p. 298)
Continuous random variable (p. 298)
Probability distribution (p. 299)
Probability histogram (p. 300)
Expected value (p. 303)
Binomial experiment (p. 310)
Trial (p. 310)
Binomial random variable (p. 310)
Binomial probability distribution (p. 313)
Cumulative distribution function (p. 316)

Formulas

Mean (or Expected Value) of a Discrete Random Variable

$$\mu_X = E(X) = \sum xP(x)$$

Standard Deviation of a Discrete Random Variable

$$\sigma_X = \sqrt{\sum (x - \mu_X)^2 \cdot P(x)} = \sqrt{\sum [x^2 \cdot P(x)] - \mu_X^2}$$

Binomial Probability Distribution Function

$$P(x) = {}_nC_x\, p^x(1 - p)^{n-x} \quad x = 0, 1, 2, \ldots, n$$

Mean of a Binomial Random Variable

$$\mu_X = np$$

Standard Deviation of a Binomial Random Variable

$$\sigma_X = \sqrt{np(1 - p)}$$

Objectives

Section	You should be able to . . .	Examples	Review Exercises
6.1	1 Distinguish between discrete and continuous random variables (p. 298)	1	1
	2 Identify discrete probability distributions (p. 299)	2 and 3	2, 3(a)
	3 Construct probability histograms (p. 300)	4	3(b)
	4 Compute and interpret the mean of a discrete random variable (p. 301)	5, 6, and 9	3(c)
	5 Interpret the mean of a discrete random variable as an expected value (p. 303)	7	4
	6 Compute the standard deviation of a discrete random variable (p. 304)	8 and 9	3(d)
6.2	1 Determine whether a probability experiment is a binomial experiment (p. 310)	1	5
	2 Compute probabilities of binomial experiments (p. 311)	2–5	6(a)–(e), 7(a)–(d), 8(a), 11
	3 Compute the mean and standard deviation of a binomial random variable (p. 316)	6	6(f), 7(e), 8(b)
	4 Construct binomial probability histograms (p. 317)	7	8(c)

2. (a) No; $\sum P(x) = 0.73 \neq 1$

Review Exercises

1. Determine whether the random variable is discrete or continuous. In each case, state the possible values of the random variable.

(a) The number of students in a randomly selected elementary school classroom Discrete; $s = 0, 1, 2, \ldots$

(b) The amount of snow that falls in Minneapolis during the winter season Continuous; $s \geq 0$

(c) The flight time accumulated by a randomly selected Air Force fighter pilot Continuous; $h \geq 0$

(d) The number of points scored by the Miami Heat in a randomly selected basketball game Discrete; $x = 0, 1, 2, \ldots$

2. Determine whether the distribution is a discrete probability distribution. If not, state why.

(a)

x	$P(x)$
0	0.34
1	0.21
2	0.13
3	0.04
4	0.01

(b) Yes

x	$P(x)$
0	0.40
1	0.31
2	0.23
3	0.04
4	0.02

3. Stanley Cup The Stanley Cup is a best-of-seven series to determine the champion of the National Hockey League. The following data represent the number of games played, X, in the Stanley Cup before a champion was determined from 1939 to 2011. *Note:* There was no champion in 2005. The season was cancelled due to a labor dispute.

x	Frequency
4	20
5	17
6	19
7	16

Source: Information Please Almanac

(a) Construct a probability model for the random variable X, the number of games in the Stanley Cup.

(b) Draw a probability histogram. (c) $\mu_X = 5.4$ (d) $\sigma_X = 1.1$

(c) Compute and interpret the mean of the random variable X.

(d) Compute the standard deviation of the random variable X.

4. Expected Value of Three-Card Poker A popular casino table game is three-card poker. One aspect of the game is the "pair plus" bet in which a player is paid a dollar amount for any hand of a pair or better, regardless of the hand the dealer has. The table shows the profit and probability of various hands of a player playing the $5 pair plus bet.

Outcome	Profit ($)	Probability
Straight flush	200	12/5525
Three of a kind	150	1/425
Straight	30	36/1105
Flush	20	274/5525
Pair	5	72/425
Other	−5	822/1105

Source: http://wizardofodds.com/threecardpoker

(a) What is the expected profit when playing the $5 pair plus bet in three card poker. −$0.12

(b) If you play the game for 4 hours with an average of 35 hands per hour, how much would you expect to lose? $16.80

5. Determine whether the probability experiment represents a binomial experiment. If not, explain why.

(a) According to the *Chronicle of Higher Education*, there is a 54% probability that a randomly selected incoming freshman will graduate from college within 6 years. Suppose that 10 incoming freshmen are randomly selected. After 6 years, each student is asked whether he or she graduated. Binomial

(b) An experiment is conducted in which a single die is cast until a 3 comes up. The number of throws required is recorded. Not binomial

6. Emergency Room Visits The probability that a randomly selected patient who visits the emergency room (ER) will die within 1 year of the visit is 0.05. *Source:* SuperFreakonomics (a) 0.3151

(a) What is the probability that exactly 1 of 10 randomly selected visitors to the ER will die within 1 year? Interpret this result.

(b) What is the probability that fewer than 2 of 25 randomly selected visitors to the ER will die within 1 year? Interpret this result. 0.6424 (c) 0.3576 (e) No; $P(X > 3) = 0.0608$

(c) What is the probability that at least 2 of 25 randomly selected visitors to the ER will die within 1 year? Interpret this result.

(d) What is the probability that at least 8 of 10 randomly selected visitors to the ER will *not* die within 1 year? 0.9885

(e) Would it be unusual if more than 3 of 30 randomly selected visitors to the ER died within 1 year? Why?

(f) In a random sample of 1000 visitors to the ER, how many visitors are expected to die within the next year? What is the standard deviation number of deaths? $\mu_X = 50$; $\sigma_X = 6.9$

(g) At a particular emergency room, a researcher obtains a random sample of 800 visitors and finds that after 1 year 51 of them have died. Do you think this particular emergency room should be investigated to see if something unusual is occurring? No

7. Driving Age According to a Gallup poll, 60% of U.S. women 18 years old or older stated that the minimum driving age should be 18. In a random sample of 15 U.S. women 18 years old or older, find the probability that: (a) 0.1859 (b) 0.0093 (c) 0.9907

(a) Exactly 10 believe that the minimum driving age should be 18.

(b) Fewer than 5 believe that the minimum driving age should be 18.

(c) At least 5 believe that the minimum driving age should be 18.

(d) Between 7 and 12, inclusive, believe that the minimum driving age should be 18. 0.8779 (e) $\mu_X = 120$; $\sigma_X = 6.9$

(e) In a random sample of 200 U.S. women 18 years old or older, what is the expected number who believe that the minimum driving age should be 18? What is the standard deviation?

(f) If a random sample of 200 U.S. women 18 years old or older resulted in 110 who believe that the minimum driving age should be 18, would this be unusual? Why? No

8. Consider a binomial probability distribution with parameters $n = 8$ and $p = 0.75$.

(a) Construct a binomial probability distribution with these parameters. (b) $\mu_X = 6$; $\sigma_X = 1.2$

(b) Compute the mean and standard deviation of the distribution.

(c) Draw the probability histogram, comment on its shape, and label the mean on the histogram.

9. State the condition required to use the Empirical Rule to check for unusual observations in a binomial experiment.

10. In sampling without replacement, the assumption of independence required for a binomial experiment is violated. Under what circumstances can we sample without replacement and still use the binomial probability formula to approximate probabilities?

11. Self-Injury According to the article "Self-injurious Behaviors in a College Population," 17% of undergraduate or graduate students have had at least one incidence of self-injurious behavior.

The researchers conducted a survey of 40 college students who reported a history of emotional abuse and found that 12 of them have had at least one incidence of self-injurious behavior. What do the results of this survey tell you about college students who report a history of emotional abuse? *Source:* Janis Whitlock, John Eckenrode, and Daniel Silverman. "Self-injurious Behaviors in a College Population," *Pediatrics* 117: 1939–1948

Problems in the chapter test are labeled by section.objective. For example, 2.3 means Section 2, Objective 3.

CHAPTER TEST

1.1 **1.** Determine whether the random variable is discrete or continuous. In each case, state the possible values of the random variable.

(a) The number of days with measurable rainfall in Honolulu, Hawaii, during a year Discrete; $r = 0, 1, 2, \ldots, 365$

(b) The miles per gallon of gasoline obtained by a randomly selected Toyota Prius Continuous; $m > 0$

(c) The number of golf balls hit into the ocean on the famous 18th hole at Pebble Beach on a randomly selected Sunday Discrete; $x = 0, 1, 2, \ldots$

(d) The weight (in grams) of a randomly selected robin's egg Continuous; $w > 0$

1.2 **2.** Determine whether the distribution is a discrete probability distribution. If not, state why.

(a)

x	$P(x)$
0	0.324
1	0.121
2	0.247
3	0.206
4	0.102

Yes

(b)

x	$P(x)$
0	0.34
1	0.28
2	0.26
3	0.23
4	–0.11

No; $P(4)$ is negative

3. At the Wimbledon Tennis Championship, to win a match in men's singles a player must win the best of five sets. The following data represent the number of sets played, X, in the men's singles final match for the years 1968 to 2011.

x	Frequency
3	19
4	12
5	13

Source: www.wimbledon.org

3. (c) $\mu_X = 3.9$ 3. (d) $\sigma_X = 0.8$

(a) Construct a probability model for the random variable, X, the number of sets played in the Wimbledon men's singles final match.

1.3 **(b)** Draw a probability histogram.

1.4 **(c)** Compute and interpret the mean of the random variable X.

1.6 **(d)** Compute the standard deviation of the random variable X.

1.5 **4.** A life insurance company sells a \$100,000 one-year term life insurance policy to a 35-year-old male for \$200. According to the *National Vital Statistics Report*, 56(9), the probability the male survives the year is 0.998725. Compute and interpret the expected value of this policy to the life insurance company. \$72.50

2.1 **5.** State the criteria that must be met for an experiment to be a binomial experiment.

2.1 **6.** Determine whether the probability experiment represents a binomial experiment. If not, explain why.

(a) An urn contains 20 colored golf balls: 8 white, 6 red, 4 blue, and 2 yellow. A child is allowed to draw balls until he gets a yellow one. The number of draws required is recorded.

(b) According to the *Uniform Crime Report, 2006,* 16% of property crimes committed in the United States were cleared by arrest or exceptional means. Twenty-five property crimes from 2006 are randomly selected and the number that was cleared is recorded. Binomial (a) Not binomial

2.2 **7.** According to a study conducted by CESI Debt Solutions, 80% of married people hide purchases from their mates. In a random sample of 20 married people, find and interpret:

(a) The probability exactly 15 hide purchases from their mates.

(b) The probability at least 19 hide purchases from their mates.

(c) The probability fewer than 19 hide purchases from their mates. 0.9308 (a) 0.1746 (b) 0.0692

(d) The probability between 15 and 17, inclusive, hide purchases from their mates. 0.5981

2.3 **8.** Suppose the adult American population is equally split in their belief that the amount of tax (federal, state, property, sales, and so on) they pay is too high.

(a) How many people would we expect to say they pay too much tax if we surveyed 1200 randomly selected adult Americans?

(b) Explain why we can use the Empirical Rule with the idea of unusual events (events that occur with relative frequency less than 0.05) to identify any unusual results in a survey of 1200 adult Americans. $np(1 - p) \geq 10$ (a) 600

(c) If a survey of 1200 adult Americans results in 640 stating they feel the amount of tax they pay is too high, would these results contradict the belief that adult Americans are equally split in their belief that the amount of tax they pay is too high? Why? Yes

9. Consider a binomial probability distribution with parameters $n = 5$ and $p = 0.2$.

2.2 **(a)** Construct a binomial probability distribution with these parameters.

2.3 **(b)** Compute the mean and standard deviation of the distribution. $\mu_X = 1$; $\sigma_X = 0.9$

2.4 **(c)** Draw the probability histogram, comment on its shape, and label the mean on the histogram.

Making an Informed Decision

Should We Convict?

A woman who was shopping in Los Angeles had her purse stolen by a young, blonde female who was wearing a ponytail. The blonde female got into a yellow car that was driven by a black male who had a mustache and a beard. The police located a blonde female named Janet Collins who wore her hair in a ponytail and had a friend who was a black male who had a mustache and beard and also drove a yellow car. The police arrested the two subjects.

Because there were no eyewitnesses and no real evidence, the prosecution used probability to make its case against the defendants. The probabilities listed below were presented by the prosecution for the known characteristics of the thieves.

Characteristic	Probability
Yellow car	$\frac{1}{10}$
Man with a mustache	$\frac{1}{4}$
Woman with a ponytail	$\frac{1}{10}$
Woman with blonde hair	$\frac{1}{3}$
Black man with beard	$\frac{1}{10}$
Interracial couple in car	$\frac{1}{1000}$

(a) Assuming that the characteristics listed are independent of each other, what is the probability that a randomly selected couple has all these characteristics? That is, what is P ("yellow car" and "man with a mustache" and ... and "interracial couple in a car")?

(b) Would you convict the defendants based on this probability? Why?

(c) Now let n represent the number of couples in the Los Angeles area who could have committed the crime. Let p represent the probability that a randomly selected couple has all six characteristics listed. Let the random variable X represent the number of couples who have all the characteristics listed in the table. Assuming that the random variable X follows the binomial probability function, we have

$$P(x) = {}_nC_x \cdot p^x(1-p)^{n-x} \qquad x = 0, 1, 2, \ldots, n$$

Assuming that there are $n = 1{,}000{,}000$ couples in the Los Angeles area, what is the probability that more than one of them has the characteristics listed in the table? Does this result cause you to change your mind regarding the defendants' guilt?

(d) Now let's look at this case from a different point of view. We will compute the probability that more than one couple has the characteristics described, given that at least one couple has the characteristics.

$$P(X > 1 \mid X \geq 1) = \frac{P(X > 1 \text{ and } X \geq 1)}{P(X \geq 1)}$$

$$= \frac{P(X > 1)}{P(X \geq 1)} \quad \text{Conditional Probability Rule}$$

Compute this probability, assuming that $n = 1{,}000{,}000$. Compute this probability again, but this time assume that $n = 2{,}000{,}000$. Do you think that the couple should be convicted "beyond all reasonable doubt"? Why?

The Chapter 6 Case Study is located on the CD that accompanies this text.

7 The Normal Probability Distribution

OUTLINE

Making an Informed Decision

You are interested in modeling the behavior of stocks. In particular, you want to build a model that describes the rate of return on a basket of stocks, such as large capitalization companies. To build this model, you must identify historical rates of returns on a basket of stocks, and use this history to build your model. Then your model can be used to identify high-performing companies that might be worthy of your investment. See the Decisions project on page 364.

PUTTING IT TOGETHER

In Chapters 6, we introduced discrete probability distributions and, in particular, the binomial probability distribution and Poisson probability distribution. We computed probabilities for these discrete distributions using their probability distribution function.

However, we could also determine the probability of any discrete random variable from its probability histogram. For example, the figure shows the probability histogram for the binomial random variable X with $n = 5$ and $p = 0.35$.

From the probability histogram, we can see $P(1) \approx 0.31$. Notice that the width of each rectangle in the probability histogram is 1. Since the area of a rectangle equals height times width, we can think of $P(1)$ as the area of the rectangle corresponding to $x = 1$. Thinking of probability in this fashion makes the transition from computing discrete probabilities to continuous probabilities much easier.

Binomial Probability Histogram; $n = 5, p = 0.35$

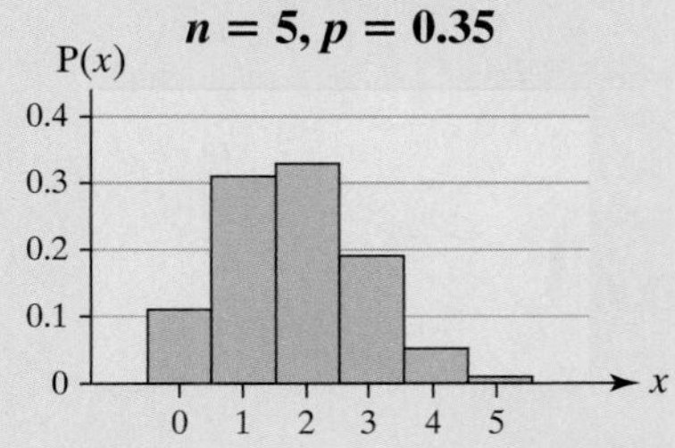

In this chapter, we discuss two continuous distributions, the *uniform distribution* and the *normal distribution*. The greater part of the discussion will focus on the normal distribution, which has many uses and applications.

7.1 PROPERTIES OF THE NORMAL DISTRIBUTION

Preparing for This Section Before getting started, review the following:

- Continuous variable (Section 1.1, p. 8)
- Rules for a discrete probability distribution (Section 6.1, p. 299)
- The Empirical Rule (Section 3.2, pp. 137–139)

OBJECTIVES

1. Use the uniform probability distribution
2. Graph a normal curve
3. State the properties of the normal curve
4. Explain the role of area in the normal density function

1 Use the Uniform Probability Distribution

We discuss a uniform distribution next in order to see the relation between area and probability.

EXAMPLE 1 The Uniform Distribution

Note to Instructor

If you like, you can print out and distribute the Preparing for This Section quiz located in the Instructor's Resource Center. The purpose of the quiz is to verify that the students have the prerequisite knowledge for the section.

Note to Instructor

To help students understand the relation between area and probability, we begin with a discussion of the uniform distribution. The graph of the uniform distribution is a rectangle. Tell students that we will be using the concept of area in this section and that the area of a rectangle is length times width.

Imagine that a friend of yours is always late. Let the random variable X represent the time from when you are supposed to meet your friend until he shows up. Suppose your friend could be on time ($x = 0$) or up to 30 minutes late ($x = 30$), with all intervals of equal time between $x = 0$ and $x = 30$ being equally likely. For example, your friend is just as likely to be from 3 to 4 minutes late as he is to be 25 to 26 minutes late. The random variable X can be any value in the interval from 0 to 30, that is, $0 \leq x \leq 30$. Because any two intervals of equal length between 0 and 30, inclusive, are equally likely, the random variable X is said to follow a **uniform probability distribution**.

When we compute probabilities for discrete random variables, we usually substitute the value of the random variable into a formula.

Things are not as easy for continuous random variables. Since an infinite number of outcomes are possible for continuous random variables, the probability of observing one *particular* value is zero. For example, the probability that your friend is exactly 12.9438823 minutes late is zero. This result is based on the fact that classical probability is found by dividing the number of ways an event can occur by the total number of possibilities: there is one way to observe 12.9438823, and there are an infinite number of possible values between 0 and 30. To resolve this problem, we compute probabilities of continuous random variables over an *interval* of values. For example, we might compute the probability that your friend is between 10 and 15 minutes late. To find probabilities for continuous random variables, we use *probability density functions*.

DEFINITION

A **probability density function (pdf)** is an equation used to compute probabilities of continuous random variables. It must satisfy the following two properties:

1. The total area under the graph of the equation over all possible values of the random variable must equal 1.

2. The height of the graph of the equation must be greater than or equal to 0 for all possible values of the random variable.

Property 1 is similar to the rule for discrete probability distributions that stated the sum of the probabilities must add up to 1. Property 2 is similar to the rule that stated all probabilities must be greater than or equal to 0.

Figure 1 illustrates these properties for Example 1. Since any value of the random variable between 0 and 30 is equally likely, the graph of the probability density function is a rectangle. Because the random variable is any number between 0 and 30 inclusive, the width of the rectangle is 30. Since the area under the graph of the probability density function must equal 1, and the area of a rectangle equals height times width, the height of the rectangle must be $\frac{1}{30}$.

Figure 1

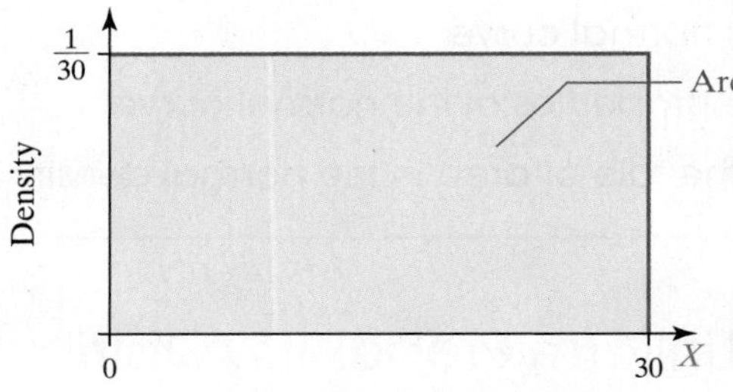

In Other Words
To find probabilities for continuous random variables, we do not use probability distribution functions (as we did for discrete random variables). Instead, we use probability density functions. The word *density* is used because it refers to the number of individuals per unit of area.

A pressing question remains: How do we use density functions to find probabilities of continuous random variables?

> The area under the graph of a density function over an interval represents the probability of observing a value of the random variable in that interval.

The following example illustrates this statement.

EXAMPLE 2 Area as a Probability

Problem Refer to the situation in Example 1.

(a) What is the probability your friend will be between 10 and 20 minutes late?

(b) It is 10 A.M. There is a 20% probability your friend will arrive within the next ______ minutes.

Approach Use the graph of the density function in Figure 1 to find the solutions.

Solution

(a) We want to find the shaded area in Figure 2(a). The width of the shaded rectangle is 10 and its height is $\frac{1}{30}$. The area between 10 and 20 is $10\left(\frac{1}{30}\right) = \frac{1}{3}$. The probability your friend is between 10 and 20 minutes late is $\frac{1}{3}$.

(b) We are given the area of the shaded region in Figure 2(b). Here we need to determine the width of the rectangle so that its area is 0.2. We solve $x_0 \cdot \frac{1}{30} = 0.2$ and find $x_0 = 30(0.2) = 6$. There is a 20% probability your friend will arrive within the next 6 minutes, or by 10:06 A.M.

Figure 2

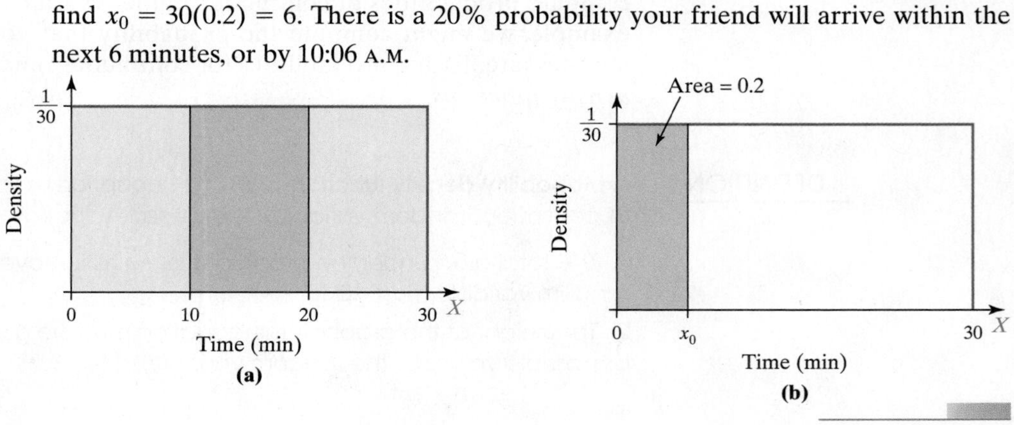

Now Work Problem 13

We introduced the uniform density function so we could associate probability with area. We are now better prepared to discuss the most frequently used continuous distribution, the *normal distribution*.

2 Graph a Normal Curve

When we described a uniform random variable using a probability distribution, we used a rectangle to find probabilities of observing an interval of numbers (such as 10 to 20 minutes late). Representing distributions of continuous random variables using smooth curves is commonplace; however, continuous random variables, such as IQ scores, birth weights of babies, or weights of M&Ms, do not have uniform distributions, but instead have distributions that are symmetric and bell shaped. For example, consider the histograms in Figure 3, drawn using StatCrunch, which represent the IQ scores of 10,000 randomly selected adults. Notice that as the class width of the histogram decreases the histogram is closely approximated by the smooth red curve. For this reason, we can use the curve to *model* the probability distribution of this continuous random variable.

Figure 3

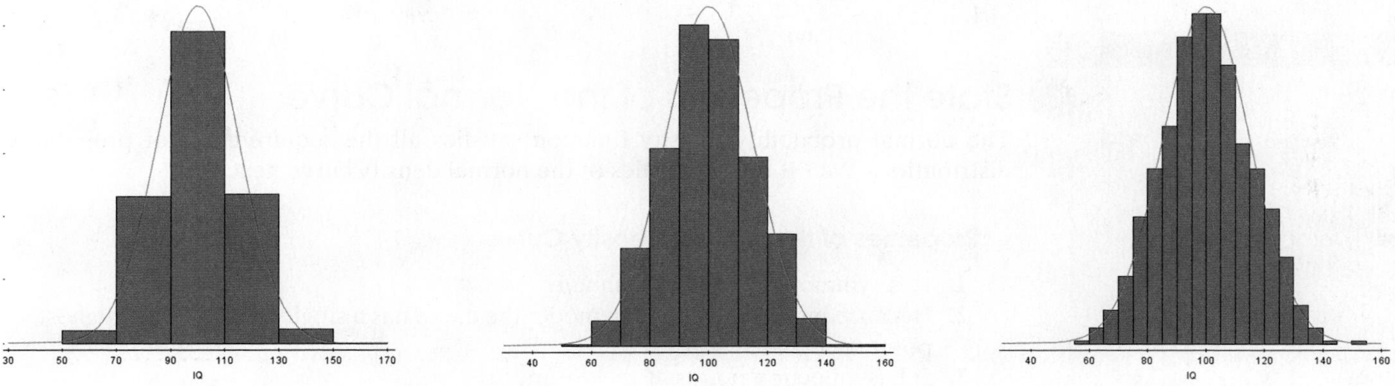

(a) **(b)** **(c)**

In mathematics, a **model** is an equation, table, or graph used to describe reality. The red curve shown in Figure 3 is a model called the **normal curve**, which is used to describe continuous random variables that are said to be *normally distributed.*

DEFINITION A continuous random variable is **normally distributed**, or has a **normal probability distribution**, if its relative frequency histogram has the shape of a normal curve.

Figure 4

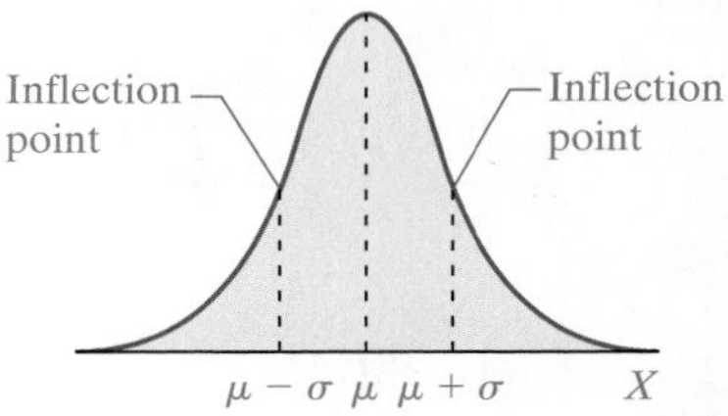

Figure 4* shows a normal curve, demonstrating the roles that the mean μ and standard deviation σ play in drawing the curve. The mode represents the "high point" of the graph of any distribution. The median represents the point where 50% of the area under the distribution is to the left and 50% is to the right. The mean represents the balancing point of the graph of the distribution (see Figure 2 on page 119 in Section 3.1). For symmetric distributions with a single peak, such as the normal distribution, the mean = median = mode. Because of this, the mean, μ, is the high point of the graph of the distribution.

The points at $x = \mu - \sigma$ and $x = \mu + \sigma$ are the **inflection points** on the normal curve, the points on the curve where the curvature of the graph changes. To the left of $x = \mu - \sigma$ and to the right of $x = \mu + \sigma$, the curve is drawn upward (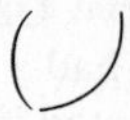 or 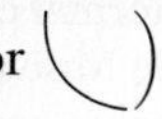).

Between $x = \mu - \sigma$ and $x = \mu + \sigma$, the curve is drawn downward (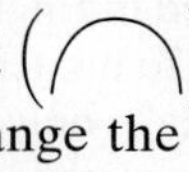).

Figure 5 on the next page shows how changes in μ and σ change the position or shape of a normal curve. In Figure 5(a), one density curve has $\mu = 0, \sigma = 1$, and the other has $\mu = 3, \sigma = 1$. We can see that increasing the mean from 0 to 3 caused the graph to shift three units to the right but maintained its shape. In Figure 5(b), one density

Note to Instructor

Consider using the normal curve applet to illustrate the role of μ and σ in the normal curve.

*The vertical scale on the graph, which indicates **density**, is purposely omitted. The vertical scale, while important, will not play a role in any of the computations using this curve.

Historical Note

Karl Pearson (of correlation fame) coined the phrase *normal curve*. He did not do this to imply that a distribution that is not normal is *abnormal*. Rather, Pearson wanted to avoid giving the name of the distribution a proper name, such as Gaussian (as in Carl Friedrich Gauss, who is incorrectly credited with the discovery of the normal curve.)

curve has $\mu = 0, \sigma = 1$, and the other has $\mu = 0, \sigma = 2$. We can see that increasing the standard deviation from 1 to 2 caused the graph to become flatter and more spread out but maintained its location of center.

Figure 5

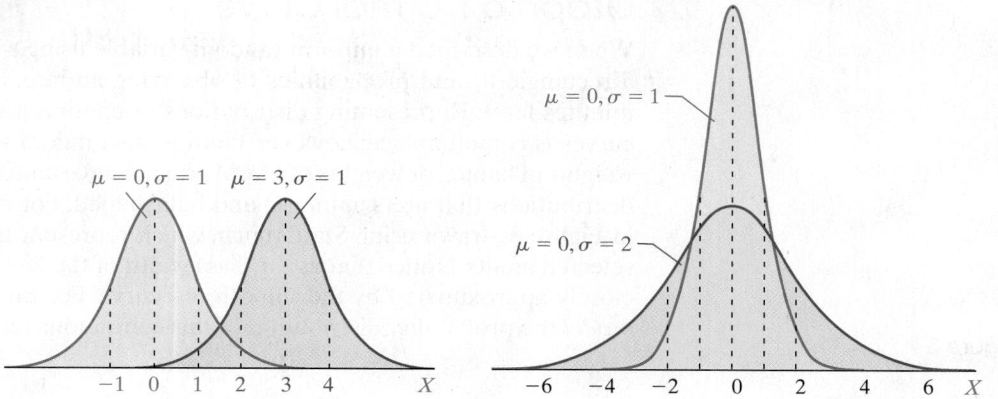

(a) (b)

Now Work Problem 25

3 State the Properties of the Normal Curve

The normal probability density function satisfies all the requirements of probability distributions. We list the properties of the normal density curve next.

Properties of the Normal Density Curve

1. It is symmetric about its mean, μ.
2. Because mean = median = mode, the curve has a single peak and the highest point occurs at $x = \mu$.
3. It has inflection points at $\mu - \sigma$ and $\mu + \sigma$.
4. The area under the curve is 1.
5. The area under the curve to the right of μ equals the area under the curve to the left of μ, which equals $\frac{1}{2}$.
6. As x increases without bound (gets larger and larger), the graph approaches, but never reaches, the horizontal axis. As x decreases without bound (gets more and more negative), the graph approaches, but never reaches, the horizontal axis.
7. The Empirical Rule: Approximately 68% of the area under the normal curve is between $x = \mu - \sigma$ and $x = \mu + \sigma$; approximately 95% of the area is between $x = \mu - 2\sigma$ and $x = \mu + 2\sigma$; approximately 99.7% of the area is between $x = \mu - 3\sigma$ and $x = \mu + 3\sigma$. See Figure 6.

Historical Note

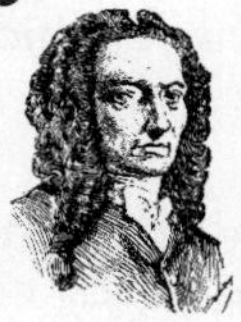

Abraham de Moivre was born in France on May 26, 1667. He is known as a great contributor to the areas of probability and trigonometry. In 1685, he moved to England. De Moivre was elected a fellow of the Royal Society in 1697. He was part of the commission to settle the dispute between Newton and Leibniz regarding who was the discoverer of calculus. He published *The Doctrine of Chance* in 1718. In 1733, he developed the equation that describes the normal curve. Unfortunately, de Moivre had a difficult time being accepted in English society (perhaps due to his accent) and was able to make only a meager living tutoring mathematics. An interesting piece of information regarding de Moivre: he correctly predicted the day of his death, November 27, 1754.

Figure 6 **Normal Distribution**

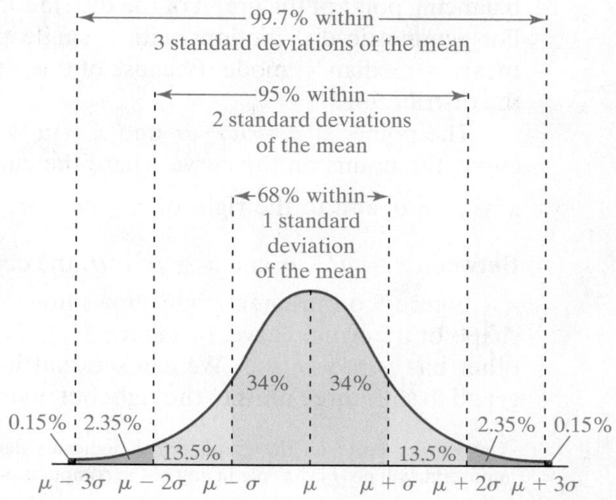

4 Explain the Role of Area in the Normal Density Function

Let's look at an example of a normally distributed random variable.

EXAMPLE 3 A Normal Random Variable

TABLE 1

Height (Inches)	Relative Frequency
29.0–29.9	0.005
30.0–30.9	0.005
31.0–31.9	0.005
32.0–32.9	0.025
33.0–33.9	0.02
34.0–34.9	0.055
35.0–35.9	0.075
36.0–36.9	0.09
37.0–37.9	0.115
38.0–38.9	0.15
39.0–39.9	0.12
40.0–40.9	0.11
41.0–41.9	0.07
42.0–42.9	0.06
43.0–43.9	0.035
44.0–44.9	0.025
45.0–45.9	0.025
46.0–46.9	0.005
47.0–47.9	0.005

Problem The relative frequency distribution given in Table 1 represents the heights of a pediatrician's 200 three-year-old female patients. The raw data indicate that the mean height of the patients is $\mu = 38.72$ inches with standard deviation $\sigma = 3.17$ inches.

(a) Draw a relative frequency histogram of the data. Comment on the shape of the distribution.

(b) Draw a normal curve with $\mu = 38.72$ inches and $\sigma = 3.17$ inches on the relative frequency histogram. Compare the area of the rectangle for heights between 40 and 40.9 inches to the area under the normal curve for heights between 40 and 40.9 inches.

Approach

(a) Draw the relative frequency histogram. If the histogram is shaped like Figure 4, the height is approximately normal. We say "approximately normal," rather than "normal," because the normal curve is an idealized description of the data, and data rarely follow the curve exactly.

(b) Draw the normal curve on the histogram with the high point at μ and the inflection points at $\mu - \sigma$ and $\mu + \sigma$. Shade the rectangle corresponding to heights between 40 and 40.9 inches.

Solution

(a) Figure 7 shows the relative frequency histogram, which is symmetric and bell shaped.

Figure 7

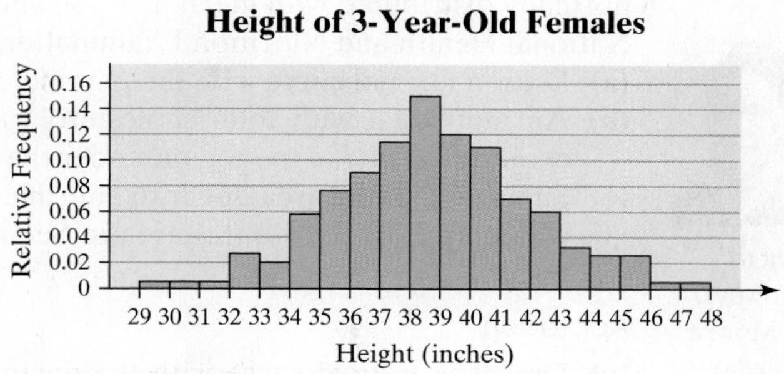

(b) In Figure 8, the normal curve with $\mu = 38.72$ and $\sigma = 3.17$ is superimposed on the relative frequency histogram. The normal curve describes the data fairly well. We conclude that the heights of 3-year-old females are approximately normal with $\mu = 38.72$ and $\sigma = 3.17$.

Figure 8 also shows the rectangle whose area represents the proportion of 3-year-old females between 40 and 40.9 inches. Notice that the area of this shaded region is very close to the area under the normal curve for the same region, so we can use the area under the normal curve to approximate the proportion of 3-year-old females with heights between 40 and 40.9 inches!

Figure 8

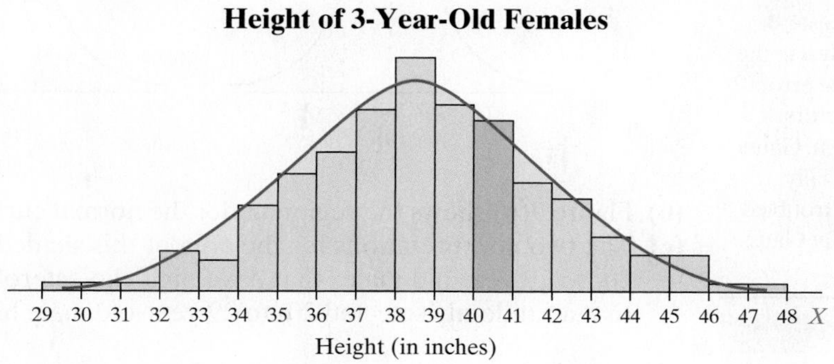

Note to Instructor
Consider assigning the "Constructing Probability Distributions Involving Dice" activity from the Student Activity Workbook.

The equation (or model) used to determine the probability of a continuous random variable is called a **probability density function** (or **pdf**). The **normal probability density function** is given by

$$y = \frac{1}{\sigma\sqrt{2\pi}} e^{\frac{-(x-\mu)^2}{2\sigma^2}} = \frac{1}{\sigma\sqrt{2\pi}} e^{-\frac{1}{2}\left(\frac{x-\mu}{\sigma}\right)^2}$$

where μ is the mean and σ is the standard deviation of the normal random variable. Do not feel threatened by this equation, because we will not be using it in this text. Instead, we will use the normal distribution in graphical form by drawing the normal curve.

We now summarize the role area plays in the normal curve.

Area under a Normal Curve

Suppose that a random variable X is normally distributed with mean μ and standard deviation σ. The area under the normal curve for any interval of values of the random variable X represents either

- the proportion of the population with the characteristic described by the interval of values or
- the probability that a randomly selected individual from the population will have the characteristic described by the interval of values.

EXAMPLE 4 Interpreting the Area under a Normal Curve

Historical Note

The normal probability distribution is often referred to as the Gaussian distribution in honor of Carl Gauss, the individual thought to have discovered the idea. However, it was actually Abraham de Moivre who first wrote down the equation of the normal distribution. Gauss was born in Brunswick, Germany, on April 30, 1777. Mathematical prowess was evident early in Gauss's life. At age 8 he was able to instantly add the first 100 integers. In 1799, Gauss earned his doctorate. The subject of his dissertation was the Fundamental Theorem of Algebra. In 1809, Gauss published a book on the mathematics of planetary orbits. In this book, he further developed the theory of least-squares regression by analyzing the errors. The analysis of these errors led to the discovery that errors follow a normal distribution. Gauss was considered to be "glacially cold" as a person and had troubled relationships with his family. Gauss died on February 23, 1855.

Problem The serum total cholesterol for males 20 to 29 years old is approximately normally distributed with mean $\mu = 180$ and $\sigma = 36.2$, based on data obtained from the National Health and Nutrition Examination Survey.

(a) Draw a normal curve with the parameters labeled.
(b) An individual with total cholesterol greater than 200 is considered to have high cholesterol. Shade the region under the normal curve to the right of $x = 200$.
(c) Suppose that the area under the normal curve to the right of $x = 200$ is 0.2903. (You will learn how to find this area in Section 7.2.) Provide two interpretations of this result.

Approach

(a) Draw the normal curve with the mean $\mu = 180$ labeled at the high point and the inflection points at $\mu - \sigma = 180 - 36.2 = 143.8$ and $\mu + \sigma = 180 + 36.2 = 216.2$.
(b) Shade the region under the normal curve to the right of $x = 200$.
(c) The two interpretations of the area under a normal curve are (1) a proportion and (2) a probability.

Solution

(a) Figure 9(a) shows the graph of the normal curve.

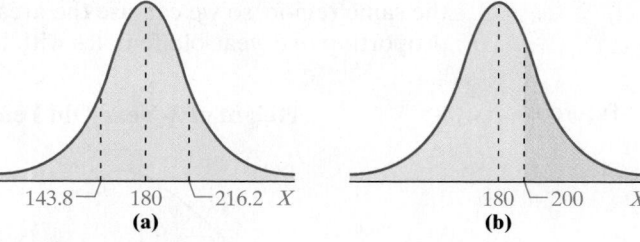

Figure 9

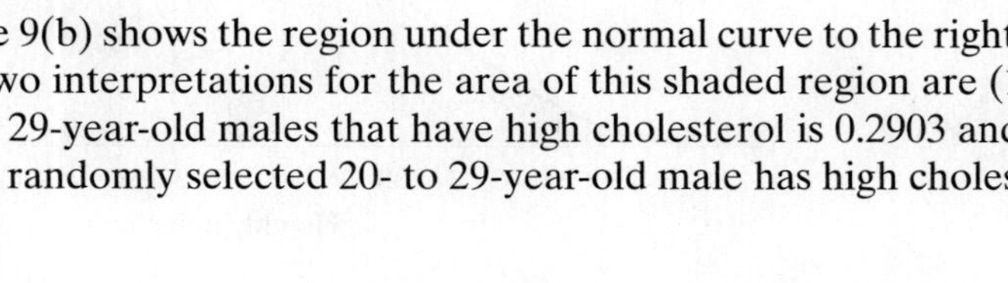

(b) Figure 9(b) shows the region under the normal curve to the right of $x = 200$ shaded.
(c) The two interpretations for the area of this shaded region are (1) the proportion of 20- to 29-year-old males that have high cholesterol is 0.2903 and (2) the probability that a randomly selected 20- to 29-year-old male has high cholesterol is 0.2903.

Now Work Problems 31 and 35

7.1 ASSESS YOUR UNDERSTANDING

VOCABULARY AND SKILL BUILDING

1. A probability density function is an equation used to compute probabilities of continuous random variables.

2. A model is an equation, table, or graph used to describe reality.

3. *True or False*: The normal curve is symmetric about its mean, μ. True

4. The area under the normal curve to the right of μ equals 1/2.

5. The points at $x = \mu - \sigma$ and $x = \mu + \sigma$ are the inflection points on the normal curve.

6. The area under a normal curve can be interpreted as a probability or proportion.

For Problems 7–12, determine whether the graph can represent a normal curve. If it cannot, explain why.

7. No

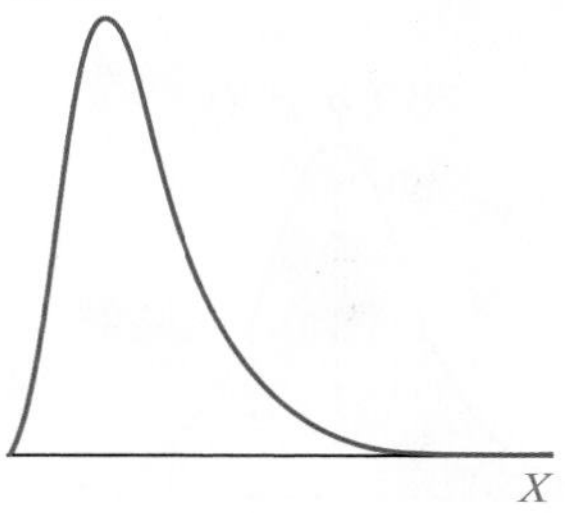

8. Yes

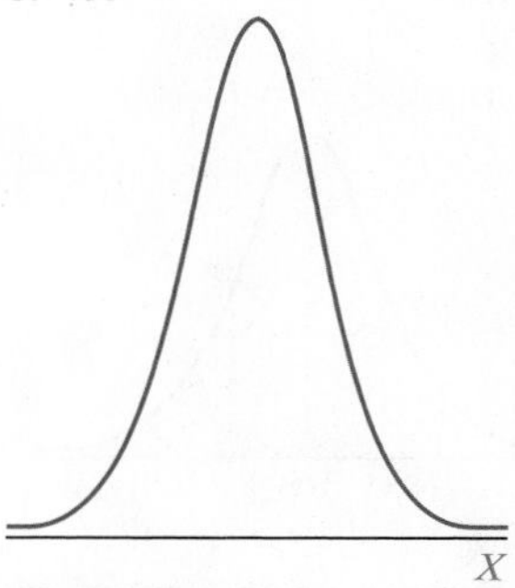

9. No

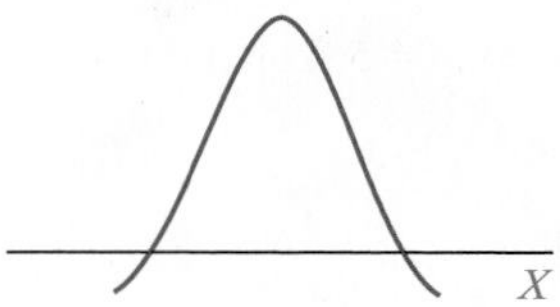

10. No

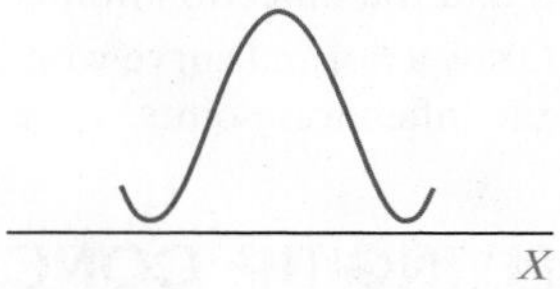

11. Yes

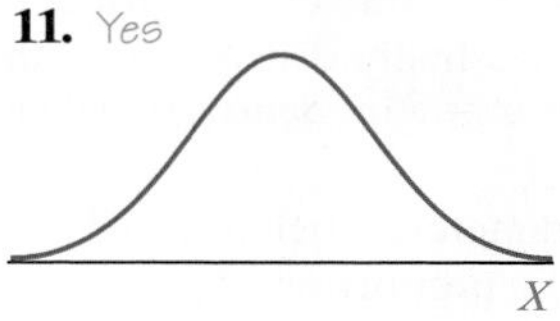

12. No

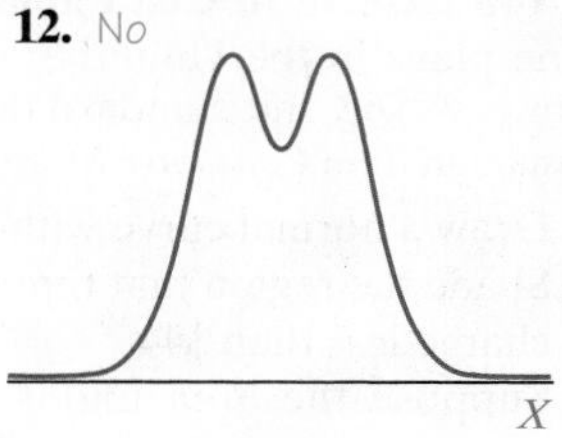

Problems 13–16 use the information presented in Examples 1 and 2.

NW **13.** **(a)** Find the probability that your friend is between 5 and 10 minutes late. 1/6

(b) It is 10 A.M. There is a 40% probability your friend will arrive within the next 12 minutes.

14. **(a)** Find the probability that your friend is between 15 and 25 minutes late. 1/3

(b) It is 10 A.M. There is a 90% probability your friend will arrive within the next 27 minutes.

15. Find the probability that your friend is at least 20 minutes late.

16. Find the probability that your friend is no more than 5 minutes late. 1/6 15. 1/3

17. Uniform Distribution The random-number generator on calculators randomly generates a number between 0 and 1. The random variable X, the number generated, follows a uniform probability distribution.

(a) Draw the graph of the uniform density function.

(b) What is the probability of generating a number between 0 and 0.2? 0.2

(c) What is the probability of generating a number between 0.25 and 0.6? 0.35

(d) What is the probability of generating a number greater than 0.95? 0.05

(e) Use your calculator or statistical software to randomly generate 200 numbers between 0 and 1. What proportion of the numbers are between 0 and 0.2? Compare the result with part (b).

18. Uniform Distribution The reaction time X (in minutes) of a certain chemical process follows a uniform probability distribution with $5 \leq X \leq 10$.

(a) Draw the graph of the density curve.

(b) What is the probability that the reaction time is between 6 and 8 minutes? 2/5

(c) What is the probability that the reaction time is between 5 and 8 minutes? 3/5

(d) What is the probability that the reaction time is less than 6 minutes? 1/5

In Problems 19–22, determine whether or not the histogram indicates that a normal distribution could be used as a model for the variable. 19. Normal

19. Birth Weights The relative frequency histogram represents the birth weights (in grams) of babies whose term was 36 weeks.

Birth Weights of Babies Whose Term Was 36 Weeks

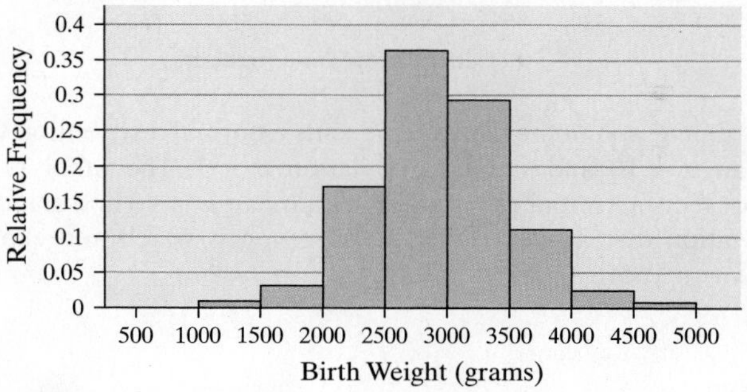

20. Waiting in Line The relative frequency histogram represents the waiting times (in minutes) to ride the Demon Roller Coaster for 2000 randomly selected people on a Saturday afternoon in the summer. Not normal

Waiting Time for the Demon Roller Coaster

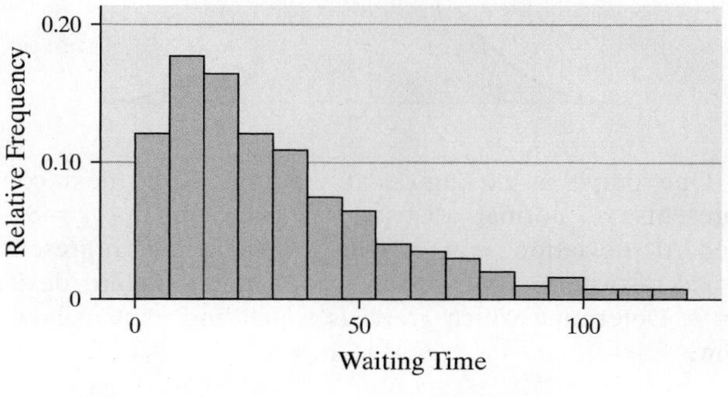

21. Length of Phone Calls The relative frequency histogram represents the length of phone calls on my wife's cell phone during the month of September. Not normal

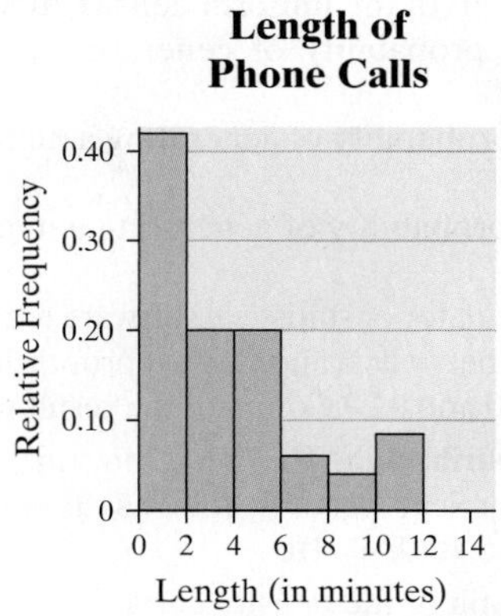

22. Incubation Times The relative frequency histogram represents the incubation times of a random sample of Rhode Island Red hens' eggs. Normal

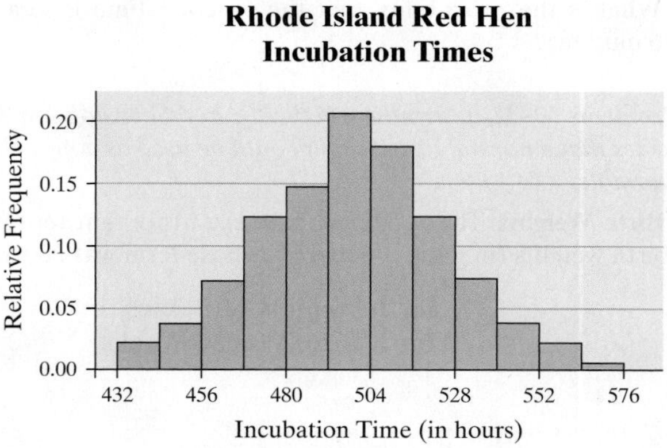

23. One graph in the figure represents a normal distribution with mean $\mu = 10$ and standard deviation $\sigma = 3$. The other graph represents a normal distribution with mean $\mu = 10$ and standard deviation $\sigma = 2$. Determine which graph is which and explain how you know. A: $\mu = 10$, $\sigma = 2$; B: $\mu = 10$, $\sigma = 3$

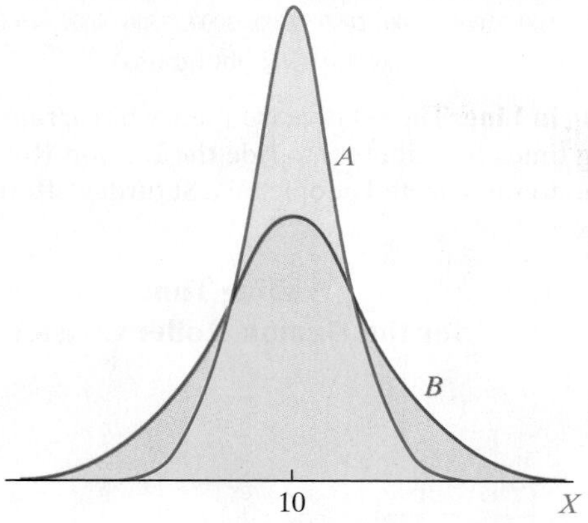

24. One graph in the figure at the top of the next column represents a normal distribution with mean $\mu = 8$ and standard deviation $\sigma = 2$. The other graph represents a normal distribution with mean $\mu = 14$ and standard deviation $\sigma = 2$. Determine which graph is which and explain how you know. A: $\mu = 8$, $\sigma = 2$; B: $\mu = 14$, $\sigma = 2$

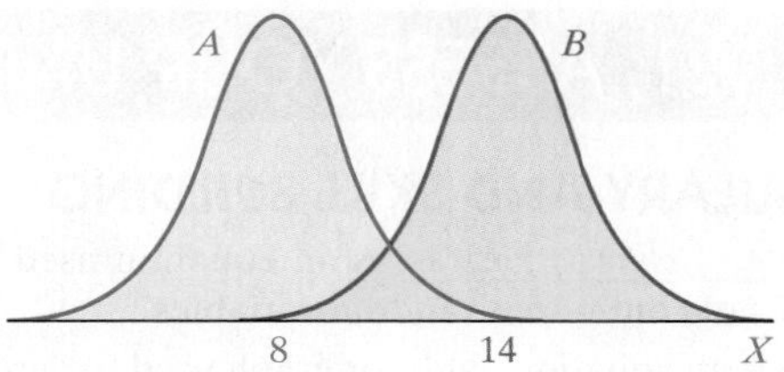

In Problems 25–28, the graph of a normal curve is given. Use the graph to identify the values of μ and σ.

NW **25.** $\mu = 2$, $\sigma = 3$

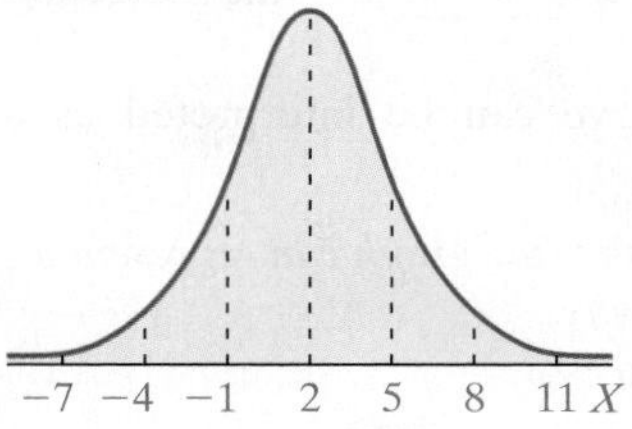

26. $\mu = 5$, $\sigma = 2$

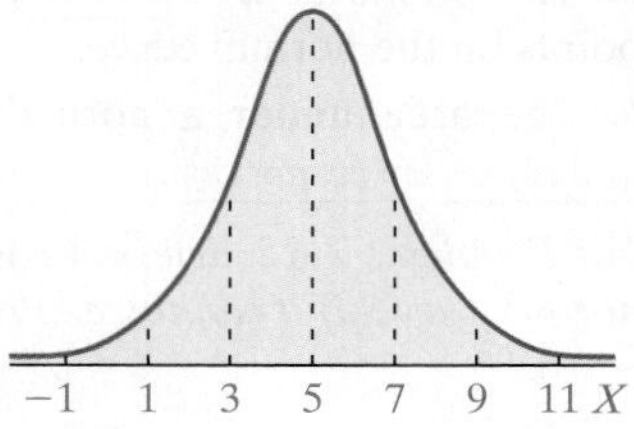

27. $\mu = 100$, $\sigma = 15$

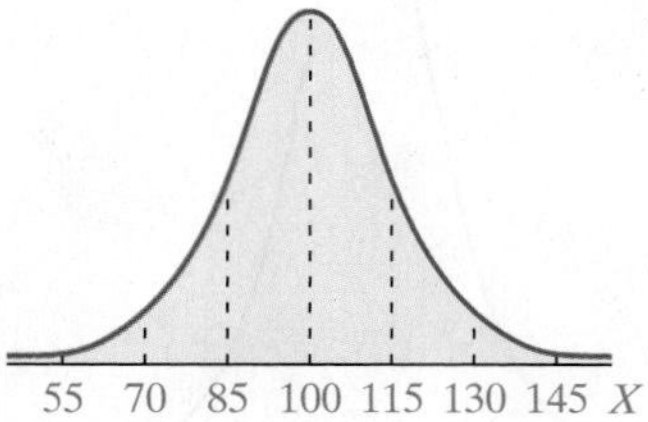

28. $\mu = 530$, $\sigma = 100$

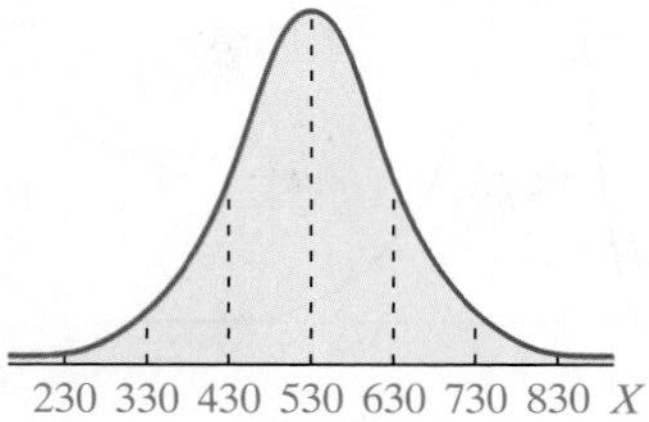

29. Draw a normal curve with $\mu = 30$ and $\sigma = 10$. Label the mean and the inflection points.

30. Draw a normal curve with $\mu = 50$ and $\sigma = 5$. Label the mean and the inflection points.

APPLYING THE CONCEPTS

NW **31. You Explain It! Cell Phone Rates** Monthly charges for cell phone plans in the United States are normally distributed with mean $\mu = \$62$ and standard deviation $\sigma = \$18$. *Source*: Based on information from *Consumer Reports*

(a) Draw a normal curve with the parameters labeled.
(b) Shade the region that represents the proportion of plans that charge less than \$44.
(c) Suppose the area under the normal curve to the left of $x = \$44$ is 0.1587. Provide two interpretations of this result.

32. You Explain It! Refrigerators The lives of refrigerators are normally distributed with mean $\mu = 14$ years and standard deviation $\sigma = 2.5$ years. *Source*: Based on information from *Consumer Reports*

(a) Draw a normal curve with the parameters labeled.
(b) Shade the region that represents the proportion of refrigerators that last for more than 17 years.
(c) Suppose the area under the normal curve to the right of $x = 17$ is 0.1151. Provide two interpretations of this result.

33. You Explain It! Birth Weights The birth weights of full-term babies are normally distributed with mean $\mu = 3400$ grams and $\sigma = 505$ grams. *Source:* Based on data obtained from the *National Vital Statistics Report*, Vol. 48, No. 3

(a) Draw a normal curve with the parameters labeled.
(b) Shade the region that represents the proportion of full-term babies who weigh more than 4410 grams.
(c) Suppose the area under the normal curve to the right of $x = 4410$ is 0.0228. Provide two interpretations of this result.

34. You Explain It! Height of 10-Year-Old Males The heights of 10-year-old males are normally distributed with mean $\mu = 55.9$ inches and $\sigma = 5.7$ inches.

(a) Draw a normal curve with the parameters labeled.
(b) Shade the region that represents the proportion of 10-year-old males who are less than 46.5 inches tall.
(c) Suppose the area under the normal curve to the left of $x = 46.5$ is 0.0496. Provide two interpretations of this result.

NW 35. You Explain It! Gestation Period The lengths of human pregnancies are normally distributed with $\mu = 266$ days and $\sigma = 16$ days.

(a) The figure represents the normal curve with $\mu = 266$ days and $\sigma = 16$ days. The area to the right of $x = 280$ is 0.1908. Provide two interpretations of this area.

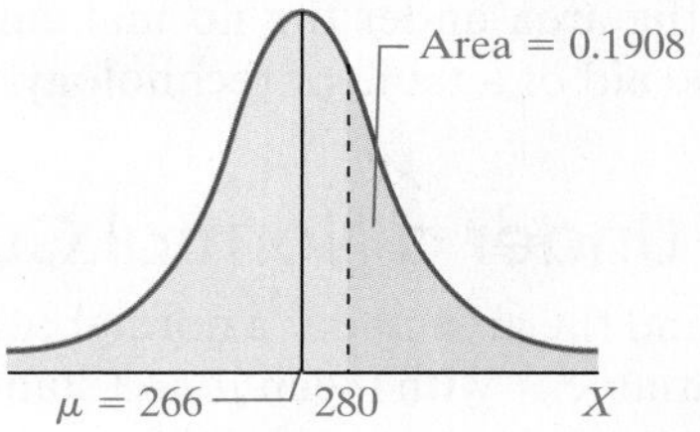

(b) The figure represents the normal curve with $\mu = 266$ days and $\sigma = 16$ days. The area between $x = 230$ and $x = 260$ is 0.3416. Provide two interpretations of this area.

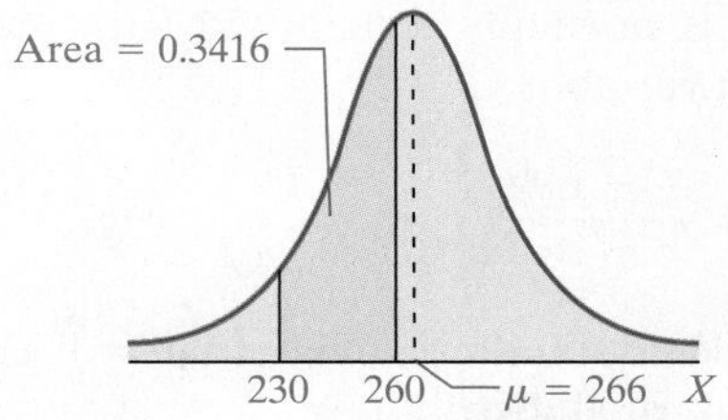

36. You Explain It! Miles per Gallon Elena conducts an experiment in which she fills up the gas tank on her Toyota Camry 40 times and records the miles per gallon for each fill-up. A histogram of the miles per gallon indicates that a normal distribution with a mean of 24.6 miles per gallon and a standard deviation of 3.2 miles per gallon could be used to model the gas mileage for her car.

(a) The figure represents the normal curve with $\mu = 24.6$ miles per gallon and $\sigma = 3.2$ miles per gallon. The area under the curve to the right of $x = 26$ is 0.3309. Provide two interpretations of this area.

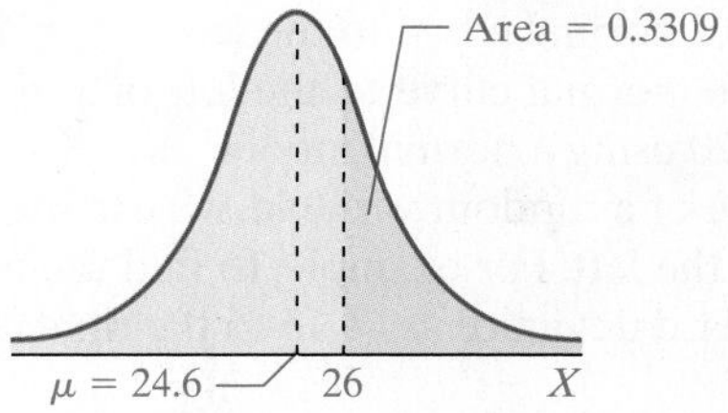

(b) The figure at the top of the next column represents the normal curve with $\mu = 24.6$ miles per gallon and $\sigma = 3.2$ miles per gallon. The area under the curve between $x = 18$ and $x = 21$ is 0.1107. Provide two interpretations of this area.

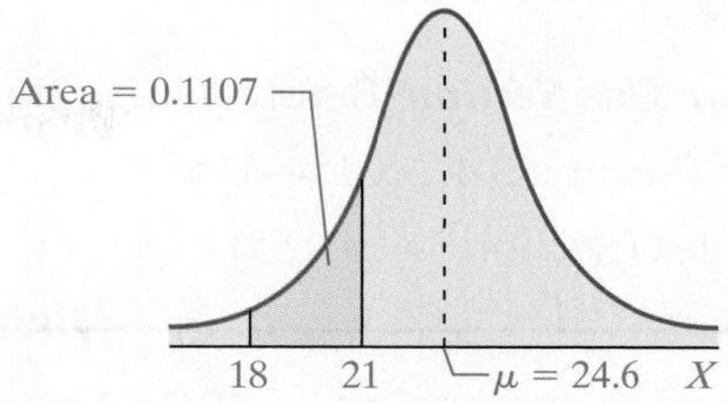

37. Hitting a Pitching Wedge In the game of golf, distance control is just as important as how far a player hits the ball. Michael went to the driving range with his range finder and hit 75 golf balls with his pitching wedge and measured the distance each ball traveled (in yards). He obtained the following data:

100	97	101	101	103	100	99	100	100
104	100	101	98	100	99	99	97	101
104	99	101	101	101	100	96	99	99
98	94	98	107	98	100	98	103	100
98	94	104	104	98	101	99	97	103
102	101	101	100	95	104	99	102	95
99	102	103	97	101	102	96	102	99
96	108	103	100	95	101	103	105	100
94	99	95						

(a) Use MINITAB or other statistical software to construct a relative frequency histogram. Comment on the shape of the distribution. Draw a normal density function on the relative frequency histogram.
(b) Do you think the normal density function accurately describes the distance Michael hits with a pitching wedge? Why?

38. Heights of 5-Year-Old Females The following frequency distribution represents the heights (in inches) of 80 randomly selected 5-year-old females.

44.5	42.4	42.2	46.2	45.7	44.8	43.3	39.5
45.4	43.0	43.4	44.7	38.6	41.6	50.2	46.9
39.6	44.7	36.5	42.7	40.6	47.5	48.4	37.5
45.5	43.3	41.2	40.5	44.4	42.6	42.0	40.3
42.0	42.2	38.5	43.6	40.6	45.0	40.7	36.3
44.5	37.6	42.2	40.3	48.5	41.6	41.7	38.9
39.5	43.6	41.3	38.8	41.9	40.3	42.1	41.9
42.3	44.6	40.5	37.4	44.5	40.7	38.2	42.6
44.0	35.9	43.7	48.1	38.7	46.0	43.4	44.6
37.7	34.6	42.4	42.7	47.0	42.8	39.9	42.3

(a) Use MINITAB or some other statistical software to construct a relative frequency histogram. Comment on the shape of the distribution. Draw a normal density curve on the relative frequency histogram.
(b) Do you think the normal density function accurately describes the heights of 5-year-old females? Why?

7.2 APPLICATIONS OF THE NORMAL DISTRIBUTION

Preparing for This Section Before getting started, review the following:

- z-scores (Section 3.4, pp. 154–155)
- Percentiles (Section 3.4, p. 155)
- Complement Rule (Section 5.2, pp. 253)

OBJECTIVES

1 Find and interpret the area under a normal curve

2 Find the value of a normal random variable

In Section 7.1, we introduced the normal distribution. We learned that if X is a normally distributed random variable, the area under the normal curve represents the proportion of a population with a certain characteristic, or the probability that a randomly selected individual from the population has the characteristic.

The question then is, "How do I find the area under the normal curve?" We have two options—by-hand calculations with the aid of a table or technology.

1 Find and Interpret the Area Under a Normal Curve

Note to Instructor
Consider assigning the "Modeling with the Normal Distribution" activity from the Student Activity Workbook.

The by-hand method uses z-scores to help find the area under a normal curve. Recall, the z-score allows us to transform a random variable X with mean μ and standard deviation σ into a random variable Z with mean 0 and standard deviation 1.

Standardizing a Normal Random Variable

Suppose that the random variable X is normally distributed with mean μ and standard deviation σ. Then the random variable

$$Z = \frac{X - \mu}{\sigma}$$

is normally distributed with mean $\mu = 0$ and standard deviation $\sigma = 1$. The random variable Z is said to have the **standard normal distribution**.

Figure 10

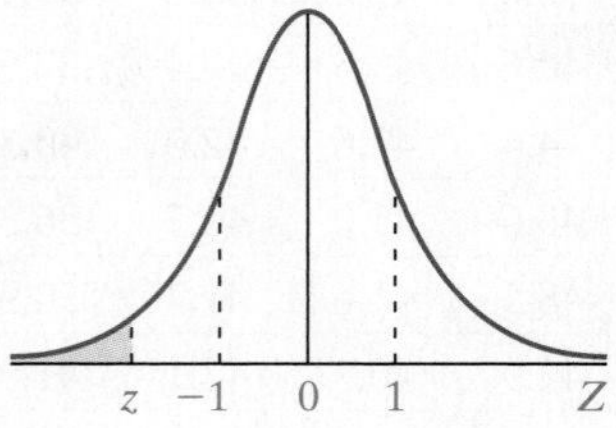

This result is powerful! If a normal random variable X has mean different from 0 or a standard deviation different from 1, we can transform X into a **standard normal random variable Z** whose mean is 0 and standard deviation is 1. Then we can use Table V (found in Appendix A) to find the area to the left of a specified z-score, z, as shown in Figure 10, which is also the area to the left of the value of x in the distribution of X. The graph in Figure 10 is called the **standard normal curve**.

For example, IQ scores can be modeled by a normal distribution with $\mu = 100$ and $\sigma = 15$. An individual whose IQ is 120, is $z = \frac{x - \mu}{\sigma} = \frac{120 - 100}{15} = 1.33$ standard deviations above the mean (recall, we round z-scores to two decimal places). We look in Table V and find the area under the standard normal curve to the left of $z = 1.33$ is 0.9082. See Figure 11. Therefore, the area under the normal curve to the left of $x = 120$ is 0.9082. Figure 12 illustrates the area to the left of 120 using a normal model.

To find the area to the right of the value of a random variable, we use the Complement Rule and determine one minus the area to the left. For example, to find the area under the normal curve with mean $\mu = 100$ and standard deviation $\sigma = 15$ to the right of $x = 120$, we compute

$$\text{Area} = 1 - 0.9082$$
$$= 0.0918$$

as shown in Figure 12.

Figure 11

Standard Normal Distribution

z	.00	.01	.02	.03	.04	.05	.06
0.0	0.5000	0.5040	0.5080	0.5120	0.5160	0.5199	0.5239
0.1	0.5398	0.5438	0.5478	0.5517	0.5557	0.5596	0.5636
0.2	0.5793	0.5832	0.5871	0.5910	0.5948	0.5987	0.6026
0.3	0.6179	0.6217	0.6255	0.6293	0.6331	0.6368	0.6406
0.4	0.6554	0.6591	0.6628	0.6664	0.6700	0.6736	0.6772
0.5	0.6915	0.6950	0.6985	0.7019	0.7054	0.7088	0.7123
0.6	0.7257	0.7291	0.7324	0.7357	0.7389	0.7422	0.7454
0.7	0.7580	0.7611	0.7642	0.7673	0.7704	0.7734	0.7764
0.8	0.7881	0.7910	0.7939	0.7967	0.7995	0.8023	0.8051
0.9	0.8159	0.8186	0.8212	0.8238	0.8264	0.8289	0.8315
1.0	0.8413	0.8438	0.8461	0.8485	0.8508	0.8531	0.8554
1.1	0.8643	0.8665	0.8686	0.8708	0.8729	0.8749	0.8770
1.2	0.8849	0.8869	0.8888	0.8907	0.8925	0.8944	0.8962
1.3	0.9032	0.9049	0.9066	0.9082	0.9099	0.9115	0.9131
1.4	0.9192	0.9207	0.9222	0.9236	0.9251	0.9265	0.927[illegible]
1.5	0.9332	[illegible]	0.9357	[illegible]	0.9382	0.9394	0.940[illegible]

Figure 12

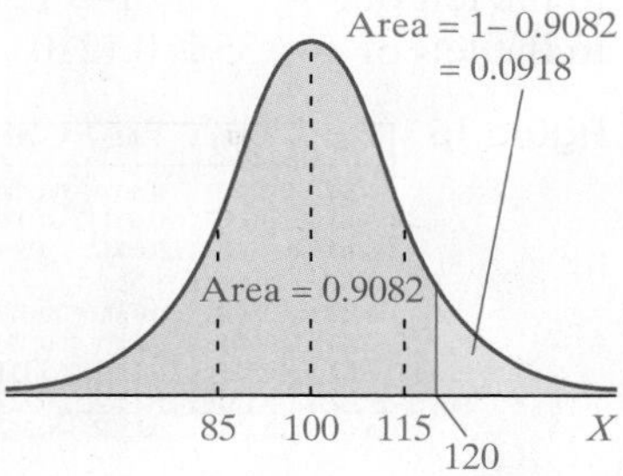

EXAMPLE 1 Finding Area under a Normal Curve

Problem A pediatrician obtains the heights of her 200 three-year-old female patients. The heights are approximately normally distributed, with mean 38.72 inches and standard deviation 3.17 inches. Use the normal model to determine the proportion of the 3-year-old females that have a height less than 35 inches.

By-Hand Approach

Step 1 Draw a normal curve and shade the desired area.

Step 2 Convert the value of x to a z-score using

$$z = \frac{x - \mu}{\sigma}$$

Step 3 Use Table V to find the area to the left of the z-score found in Step 2.

By-Hand Solution

Step 1 Figure 13 shows the normal curve with the area to the left of 35 shaded.

Figure 13

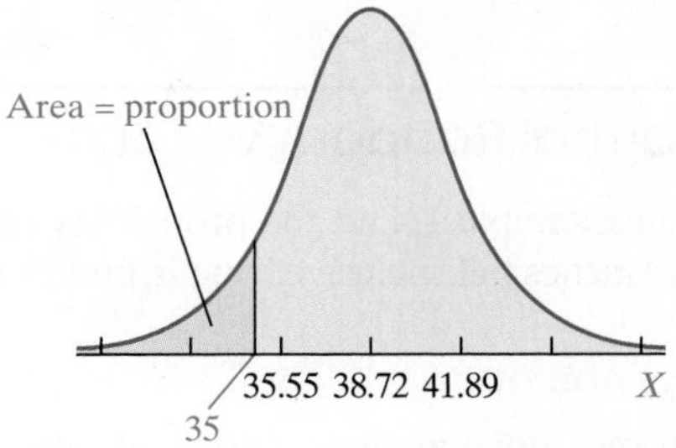

Step 2 Convert $x = 35$ to a z-score.

$$z = \frac{x - \mu}{\sigma} = \frac{35 - 38.72}{3.17} = -1.17$$

Technology Approach

Step 1 Draw a normal curve and shade the desired area.

Step 2 Use a statistical spreadsheet or calculator with advanced statistical features to find the area. The steps for determining the area under any normal curve using the TI-83/84 Plus graphing calculator, MINITAB, Excel, and StatCrunch are found in the Technology Step-by-Step on page 349.

Technology Solution

Step 1 Figure 14 shows the normal curve with the area left of 35 shaded.

Figure 14

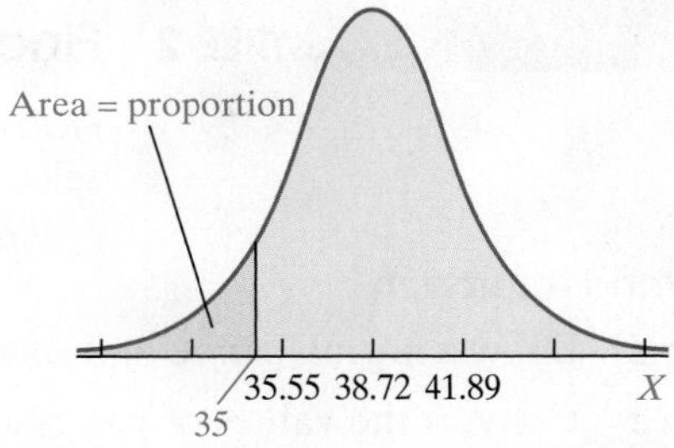

Step 2 Figure 16 shows the results from MINITAB. The area under the normal curve to the left of 35 is 0.1203.

Step 3 Look up $z = -1.17$ in Table V and find the entry. The area to the left of $z = -1.17$ is 0.1210. See Figure 15. Therefore, the area to the left of $x = 35$ is 0.1210.

Figure 15

z	.00	.01	.02	.03	.04	.05	.06	.07	.08
−3.4	0.0003	0.0003	0.0003	0.0003	0.0003	0.0003	0.0003	0.0003	0.0003
−3.3	0.0005	0.0005	0.0005	0.0004	0.0004	0.0004	0.0004	0.0004	0.0004
−3.2	0.0007	0.0007	0.0006	0.0006	0.0006	0.0006	0.0006	0.0005	0.0005
−1.4	0.0808	0.0793	0.0778	0.0764	0.0749	0.0735	0.0721	0.0708	0.0694
−1.3	0.0968	0.0951	0.0934	0.0918	0.0901	0.0885	0.0869	0.0853	0.0838
−1.2	0.1151	0.1131	0.1112	0.1093	0.1075	0.1056	0.1038	0.1020	0.1003
−1.1	0.1357	0.1335	0.1314	0.1292	0.1271	0.1251	0.1230	0.1210	0.1190
−1.0	0.1587	0.1562	0.1539	0.1515	0.1492	0.1469	0.1446	0.1423	0.1401

The normal model indicates that the proportion of the pediatrician's 3-year-old females who are less than 35 inches tall is 0.1210.

Figure 16

Cumulative Distribution Function

```
Normal with mean = 38.72 and standard deviation = 3.17

 x  P( X <= x )
35     0.120297
```

The normal model indicates that the proportion of the pediatrician's 3-year-old females who are less than 35 inches tall is 0.1203.

CAUTION

Notice the by-hand solution and technology solution in Example 1 differ. The difference exists because we rounded the z-score in Step 2 of the by-hand solution, which leads to rounding error.

TABLE 2

Height (inches)	Relative Frequency
29.0–29.9	0.005
30.0–30.9	0.005
31.0–31.9	0.005
32.0–32.9	0.025
33.0–33.9	0.02
34.0–34.9	0.055
35.0–35.9	0.075
36.0–36.9	0.09
37.0–37.9	0.115
38.0–38.9	0.15
39.0–39.9	0.12
40.0–40.9	0.11
⋮	⋮
47.0–47.9	0.005

According to the results of Example 1, the proportion of 3-year-old females who are shorter than 35 inches is approximately 0.12. If the normal curve is a good model for determining proportions (or probabilities), then about 12% of the 200 three-year-olds in Table 1 (from Section 7.1) should be shorter than 35 inches. For convenience, part of Table 1 is repeated in Table 2.

The relative frequency distribution in Table 2, shows that $0.005 + 0.005 + 0.005 + 0.025 + 0.02 + 0.055 = 0.115 = 11.5\%$ of the 3-year-old females are less than 35 inches tall. The results based on the normal curve are close to the actual results. The normal curve accurately models the heights.

If we wanted to know the proportion of 3-year-old females whose height is greater than 35 inches, we use the Complement Rule and find the proportion is $1 - 0.1210 = 0.879$ (using the "by-hand" computation).

Because the area under the normal curve represents a proportion, we can also use the area to find percentile ranks of scores. Recall that the kth percentile divides the lower $k\%$ of a data set from the upper $(100 - k)\%$. In Example 1, 12% of the females have a height less than 35 inches, and 88% of the females have a height greater than 35 inches, so a child whose height is 35 inches is at the 12th percentile.

EXAMPLE 2 Finding the Probability of a Normal Random Variable

Problem For the pediatrician presented in Example 1, find the probability that a randomly selected 3-year-old girl is between 35 and 40 inches tall, inclusive. That is, find $P(35 \le X \le 40)$.

By-Hand Approach

Step 1 Draw a normal curve and shade the desired area.

Step 2 Convert the values of x to z-scores using

$$z = \frac{x - \mu}{\sigma}$$

Step 3 Use Table V to find the area to the left of each z-score found in Step 2. Use this result to find the area between the z-scores.

Technology Approach

Step 1 Draw a normal curve and shade the desired area.

Step 2 Use a statistical spreadsheet or calculator with advanced statistical features to find the area. The steps for determining the area under any normal curve using the TI-83/84 Plus graphing calculator, MINITAB, Excel, and StatCrunch are found in the Technology Step-by-Step on page 349.

By-Hand Solution

Step 1 Figure 17 shows the normal curve with the area between 35 and 40 shaded.

Technology Solution

Step 1 Figure 18 shows the normal curve with the area between 35 and 40 shaded.

Figure 17

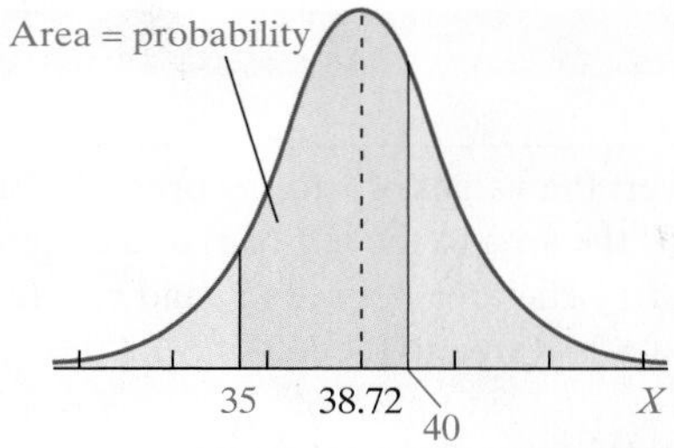

Step 2 Convert $x_1 = 35$ and $x_2 = 40$ to z-scores.

$$z_1 = \frac{x_1 - \mu}{\sigma} = \frac{35 - 38.72}{3.17} = -1.17$$

$$z_2 = \frac{x_2 - \mu}{\sigma} = \frac{40 - 38.72}{3.17} = 0.40$$

Step 3 Table V shows that the area to the left of $z_2 = 0.4$ (or $x_2 = 40$) is 0.6554 and the area to the left of $z_1 = -1.17$ (or $x_1 = 35$) is 0.1210, so the area between $z_1 = -1.17$ and $z_2 = 0.40$ is $0.6554 - 0.1210 = 0.5344$. The probability a randomly selected 3-year-old female is between 35 and 40 inches tall is 0.5344. That is, $P(35 \le X \le 40) = P(-1.17 \le Z \le 0.40) = 0.5344$.

Figure 18

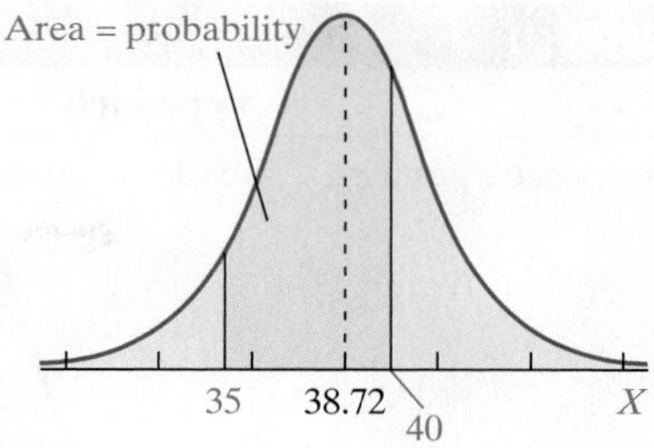

Step 2 Figure 19 shows the results from a TI-84 Plus graphing calculator.

Figure 19

The area between $x = 35$ and $x = 40$ is 0.5365. The probability a randomly selected 3-year-old female is between 35 and 40 inches tall is 0.5365. That is, $P(35 \le X \le 40) = 0.5365$.

Interpretation If we randomly selected one 3-year-old female 100 different times, we would expect to select a child whose height is between 35 and 40 inches tall about 53 or 54 times.

Now Work Problem 39

In Other Words
The normal probability density function is used to model random variables that appear to be normal (such as girls' heights). A good model is one that yields results that are close to reality.

According to the relative frequency distribution in Table 2, the proportion of the 200 three-year-old females with heights between 35 and 40 inches is $0.075 + 0.09 + 0.115 + 0.15 + 0.12 = 0.55 = 55\%$. This is very close to the probability found in Example 2.

We summarize the methods for obtaining the area under a normal curve in Table 3.

TABLE 3

Problem	Approach	Solution
Find the area to the left of x.	Shade the area to the left of x. 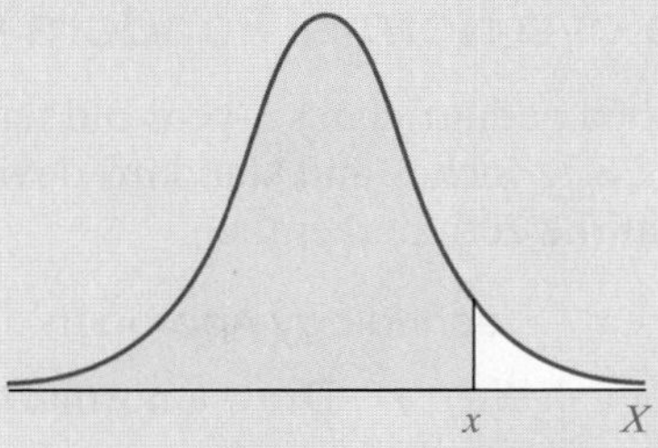	• Convert the value of x to a z-score. Use Table V to find the row and column that correspond to z. The area to the left of x is the value where the row and column intersect. or • Use technology to find the area.
Find the area to the right of x.	Shade the area to the right of x. 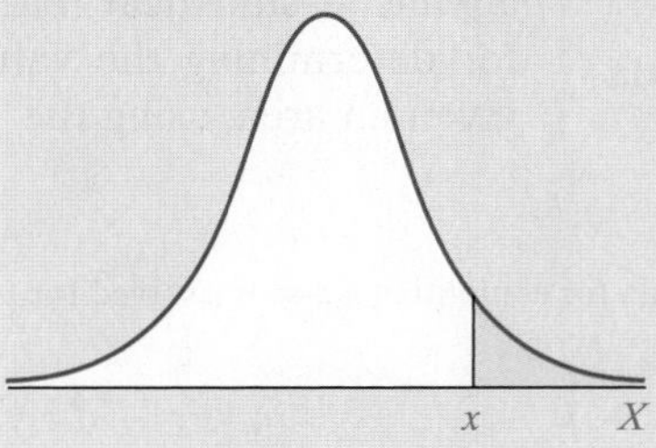	• Convert the value of x to a z-score. Use Table V to find the area to the left of z (which is also the area to the left of x). The area to the right of z (also x) is 1 minus the area to the left of z. or • Use technology to find the area.

continued

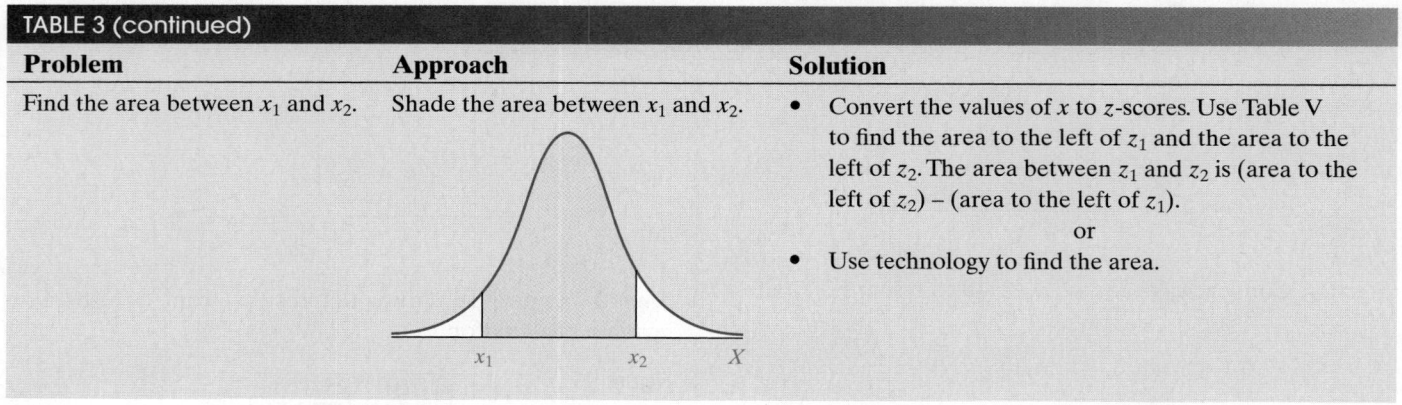

TABLE 3 (continued)

Problem	Approach	Solution
Find the area between x_1 and x_2.	Shade the area between x_1 and x_2. 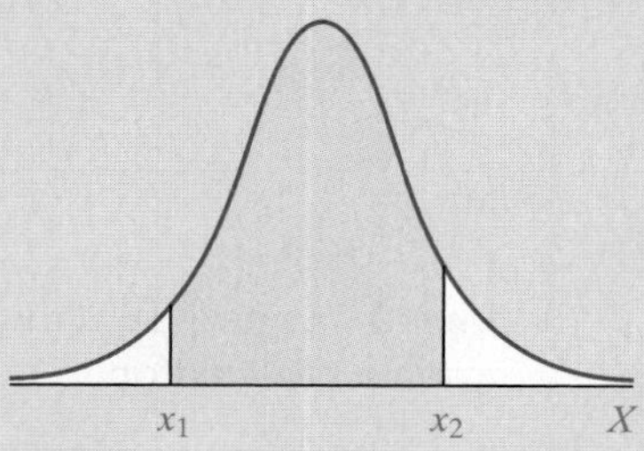	• Convert the values of x to z-scores. Use Table V to find the area to the left of z_1 and the area to the left of z_2. The area between z_1 and z_2 is (area to the left of z_2) − (area to the left of z_1). or • Use technology to find the area.

Some Cautionary Thoughts

Figure 20

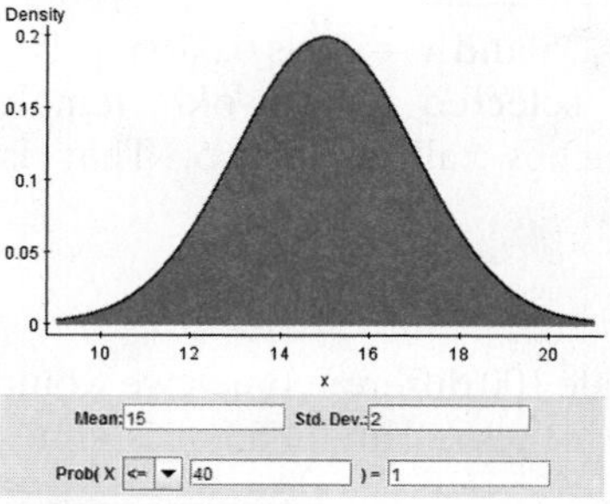

The normal curve extends indefinitely in both directions. For this reason, there is no range of values of a normal random variable for which the area under the curve is 1. For example, if asked to find the area under a normal curve to the left of $x = 40$ with $\mu = 15$ and $\sigma = 2$, StatCrunch (as well as other software and calculators) will state the area is 1, because it can only compute a limited number of decimal places. See Figure 20. However, the area under the curve to the left of $x = 40$ is not 1; it is some value slightly less than 1. So we will follow the practice of reporting such areas as >0.9999. Similarly, if software reports an area of 0, we will report the area as <0.0001.

When finding area under the normal curve by hand using Table V, we will report any area to the left of $z = -3.49$ (the smallest value of z in the table) or to the right of $z = 3.49$ (the largest value of z in the table) as <0.0001. Any area under the normal curve to the left of $z = 3.49$ or to the right of $z = -3.49$ is stated as >0.9999.

2 Find the Value of a Normal Random Variable

Often, we do not want to find the proportion, probability, or percentile given a value of a normal random variable. Rather, we want to find the value of a normal random variable that corresponds to a certain proportion, probability, or percentile. For example, we might want to know the height of a 3-year-old girl who is at the 20th percentile. Or we might want to know the scores on a standardized exam that separate the middle 90% of scores from the bottom and top 5%.

Note to Instructor

Consider assigning the "Grading on a Curve" activity from the Student Activity Workbook.

EXAMPLE 3 Finding the Value of a Normal Random Variable

Problem The heights of a pediatrician's 3-year-old females are approximately normally distributed, with mean 38.72 inches and standard deviation 3.17 inches. Find the height of a 3-year-old female at the 20th percentile.

By-Hand Approach

Step 1 Draw a normal curve and shade the desired area.

Step 2 Use Table V to find the z-score that corresponds to the shaded area.

Step 3 Obtain the normal value from the formula $x = \mu + z\sigma$.*

Technology Approach

Step 1 Draw a normal curve and shade the desired area.

Step 2 Use a statistical spreadsheet or calculator with advanced statistical features to find the score. The steps for determining the value of a normal random variable, given an area, using the TI-83/84 Plus graphing calculator,

*The formula provided in Step 3 of the by-hand approach is the formula for computing a z-score, solved for x.

$z = \dfrac{x - \mu}{\sigma}$ Formula for standardizing a value, x, for a random variable x

$z\sigma = x - \mu$ Multiply both sides by σ.

$x = \mu + z\sigma$ Add μ to both sides.

By-Hand Solution

Step 1 Figure 21 shows the normal curve with the unknown value of x at the 20th percentile, which separates the bottom 20% of the distribution from the top 80%.

Figure 21

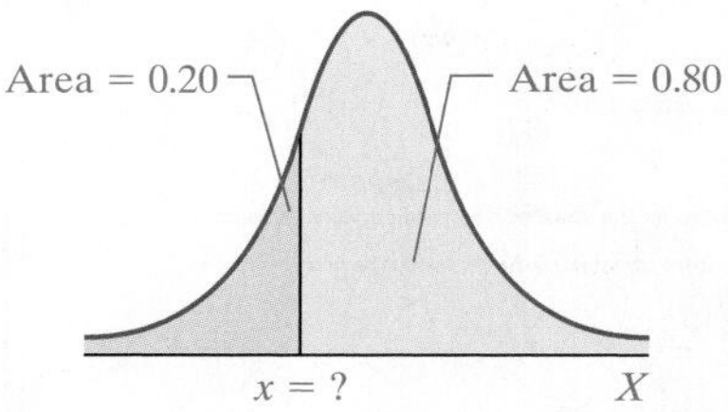

Step 2 We want to find the z-score such that the area to the left of the z-score is 0.20. We refer to Table V and look in the body of the table for the area closest to 0.20. The area closest to 0.20 is 0.2005, which corresponds to a z-score of -0.84. See Figure 22.

Figure 22

Standard Normal Distributio

z	.00	.01	.02	.03	.04	.05
−3.4	0.0003	0.0003	0.0003	0.0003	0.0003	0.0003
−3.3	0.0005	0.0005	0.0005	0.0004	0.0004	0.0004
−0.9	0.1841	0.1814	0.1788	0.1762	0.1736	0.1711
−0.8	0.2119	0.2090	0.2061	0.2033	0.2005	0.1977
−0.7	0.2420	0.2389	0.2358	0.2327	0.2296	0.2266

Step 3 The height of a 3-year-old female at the 20th percentile is

$$\begin{aligned} x &= \mu + z\sigma \\ &= 38.72 + (-0.84)(3.17) \\ &= 36.1 \text{ inches} \end{aligned}$$

Now Work Problem 47(a)

MINITAB, Excel, and StatCrunch are found in the Technology Step-by-Step on page 349.

Technology Solution

Step 1 Figure 23 shows the normal curve with the unknown value of X at the 20th percentile, which separates the bottom 20% of the distribution from the top 80%.

Figure 23

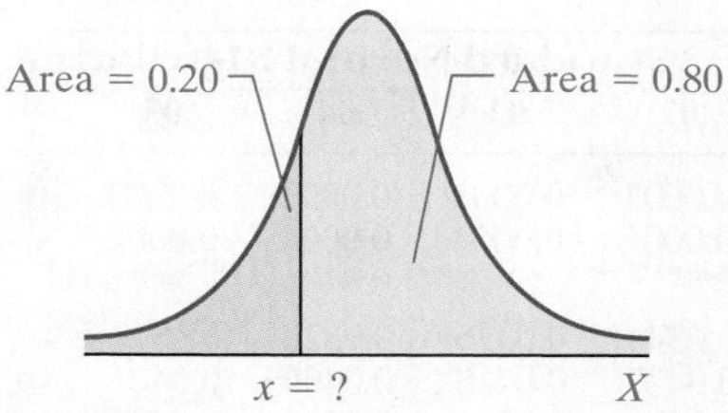

Step 2 Figure 24 shows the results obtained from StatCrunch. The height of a 3-year-old female at the 20th percentile is 36.1 inches.

Figure 24

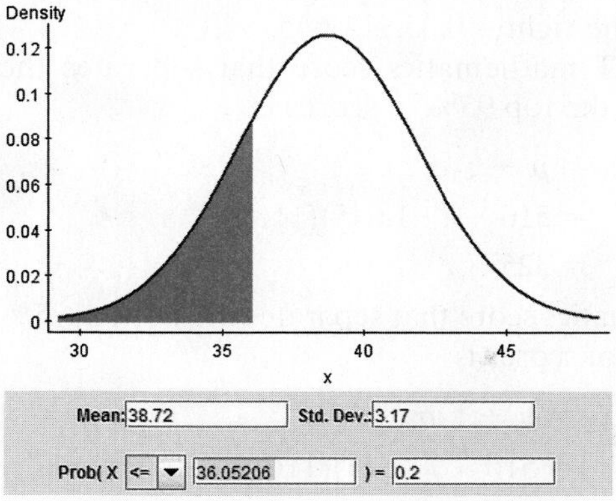

EXAMPLE 4 Finding the Value of a Normal Random Variable

Problem The scores earned on the mathematics portion of the SAT, a college entrance exam, are approximately normally distributed with mean 516 and standard deviation 116. What scores separate the middle 90% of test takers from the bottom and top 5%? In other words, find the 5th and 95th percentiles. *Source*: The College Board

By-Hand Solution

Step 1 Figure 25 shows the normal curve with the unknown values of x separating the bottom and top 5% of the distribution from the middle 90%.

Figure 25

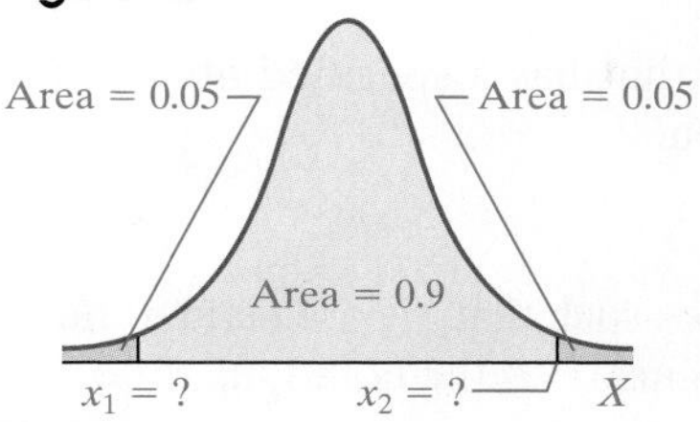

Technology Solution

Step 1 Figure 27 shows the normal curve with the unknown values of x separating the bottom and top 5% of the distribution from the middle 90%.

Figure 27

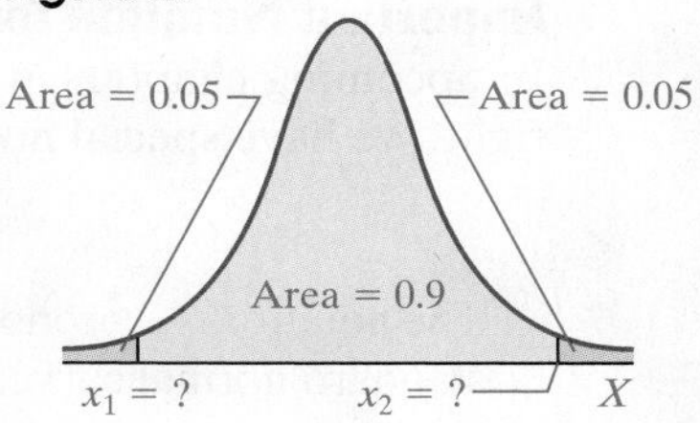

Step 2 First, we find the z-score that corresponds to an area of 0.05 to the left. In Table V, we look in the body of the table and find that 0.0495 and 0.0505 are equally close to 0.05. See Figure 26. We agree to take the mean of the two z-scores corresponding to the areas. The z-score corresponding to an area of 0.0495 is -1.65, and the z-score corresponding to an area of 0.0505 is -1.64. The approximate z-score corresponding to an area of 0.05 to the left is -1.645.

Figure 26

Standard Normal Distributio

z	.00	.01	.02	.03	.04	.05
−3.4	0.0003	0.0003	0.0003	0.0003	0.0003	0.0003
−3.3	0.0005	0.0005	0.0005	0.0004	0.0004	0.0004
−1.8	0.0359	0.0351	0.0344	0.0336	0.0329	0.0322
−1.7	0.0446	0.0436	0.0427	0.0418	0.0409	0.0401
−1.6	0.0548	0.0537	0.0526	0.0516	0.0505	0.0495
−1.5	0.0668	0.0655	0.0643	0.0630	0.0618	0.0606
−1.4	0.0808	0.0793	0.0778	0.0764	0.0749	0.0735

Now we find the z-score corresponding to an area of 0.05 to the right, which means the area to the left is 0.95. From Table V, we find an area of 0.9495 and 0.9505, which correspond to 1.64 and 1.65. The approximate z-score, such that the area to the right is 0.05, is 1.645.

Step 3 The SAT mathematics score that separates the bottom 5% from the top 95% of scores is

$$\begin{aligned} x_1 &= \mu + z_1\sigma \\ &= 516 + (-1.645)(116) \\ &= 325 \end{aligned}$$

The SAT mathematics score that separates the bottom 95% from the top 5% of scores is

$$\begin{aligned} x_2 &= \mu + z_2\sigma \\ &= 516 + (1.645)(116) \\ &= 707 \end{aligned}$$

Step 2 Figure 28 shows the results obtained from Excel with the values of x_1 and x_2 highlighted.

Figure 28

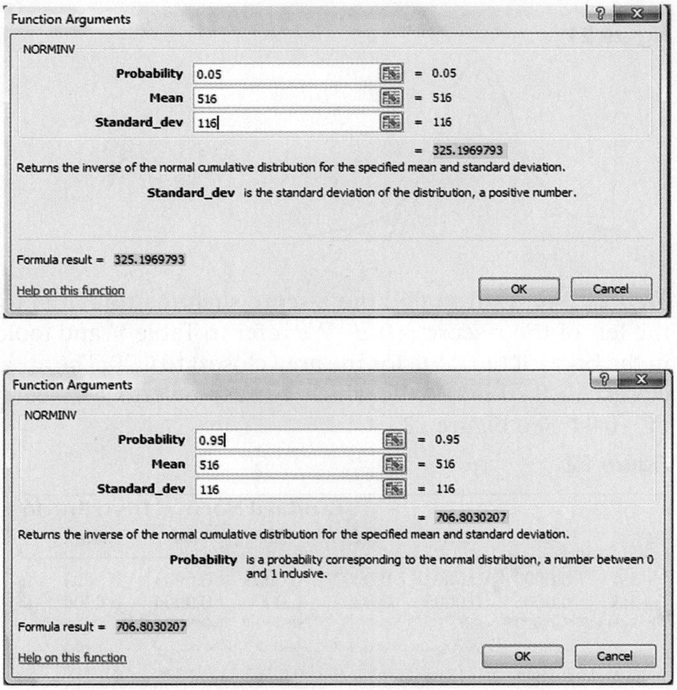

Interpretation SAT mathematics scores that separate the middle 90% of the scores from the bottom and top 5% are 325 and 707. Put another way, a student who scores 325 on the SAT math exam is at the 5th percentile. A student who scores 707 on the SAT math exam is at the 95th percentile. We might use these results to identify those scores that are unusual.

Now Work Problem 47

We could also obtain the by-hand solution to Example 4 using symmetry. Because the normal curve is symmetric about its mean, the z-score that corresponds to an area of 0.05 to the left will be the additive inverse (i.e., the opposite) of the z-score that corresponds to an area of 0.05 to the right. Since the area to the left of $z = -1.645$ is 0.05, the area to the right of $z = 1.645$ is 0.05.

Important Notation for the Future

In upcoming chapters, we will need to find the z-score that has a specified area to the right. We have special notation to represent this situation.

> The notation z_α (pronounced "z sub alpha") is the z-score such that the area under the standard normal curve to the right of z_α is α. Figure 29 illustrates the notation.

Figure 29

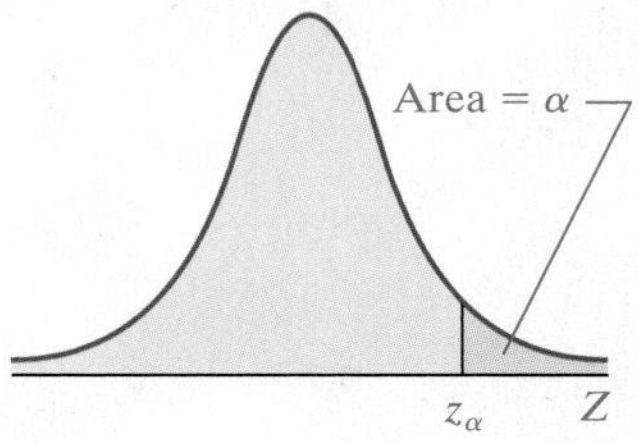

EXAMPLE 5 Finding the Value of z_α

Problem Find the value of $z_{0.10}$.

Approach We wish to find the z-value such that the area under the standard normal curve to the right of the z-value is 0.10.

By-Hand Solution The area to the right of the unknown z-value is 0.10, so the area to the left of the z-value is $1 - 0.10 = 0.90$. We look in Table V for the area closest to 0.90. The closest area is 0.8997, which corresponds to a z-value of 1.28. Therefore, $z_{0.10} = 1.28$.

Technology Solution The area to the right of the unknown z-value is 0.10, so the area to the left is $1 - 0.10 = 0.90$. A TI-84 Plus is used to find that the z-value such that the area to the left is 0.90 is 1.28. See Figure 30. Therefore, $z_{0.10} = 1.28$.

Figure 30

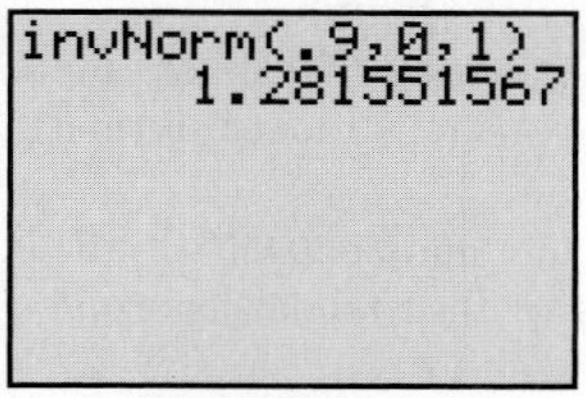

Figure 31 shows the z-value on the normal curve.

Figure 31

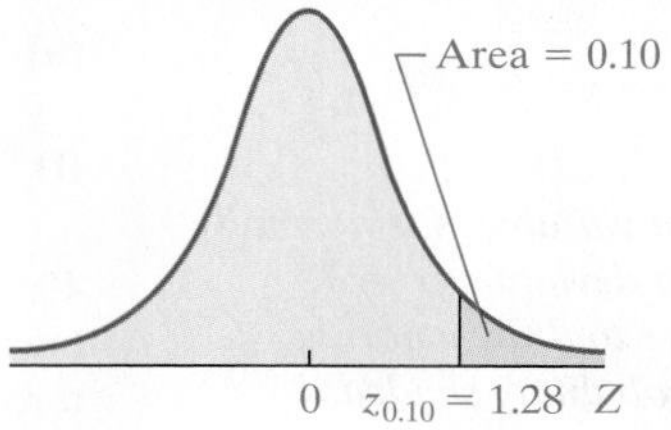

Now Work Problem 19

Note to Instructor
Be sure to emphasize this concept with students.

For any continuous random variable, the probability of observing a specific value of the random variable is 0. For example, for a normal random variable, $P(a) = 0$ for any value of a, because there is no area under the normal curve associated with a single value. Therefore, the following probabilities are equivalent:

$$P(a < X < b) = P(a \le X < b) = P(a < X \le b) = P(a \le X \le b)$$

7.2 ASSESS YOUR UNDERSTANDING

VOCABULARY AND SKILL BUILDING

1. A random variable Z that is normally distributed with mean $\mu = 0$ and standard deviation $\sigma = 1$ is said to have the standard normal distribution.

2. The notation z_α is the z-score that the area under the standard normal curve to the right of z_α is α.

3. If X is a normal random variable with mean 40 and standard deviation 10 and $P(X > 45) = 0.3085$, then $P(X < 35) =$ 0.3085.

4. If X is normal random variable with mean 40 and standard deviation 10 and $P(X < 38) = 0.4207$, then $P(X \le 38) =$ 0.4207.

In Problems 5–12, find the indicated areas. For each problem, be sure to draw a standard normal curve and shade the area that is to be found.

5. Determine the area under the standard normal curve that lies to the left of

(a) $z = -2.45$ 0.0071 **(b)** $z = -0.43$ 0.3336
(c) $z = 1.35$ 0.9115 **(d)** $z = 3.49$ 0.9998

6. Determine the area under the standard normal curve that lies to the left of

(a) $z = -3.49$ 0.0002 **(b)** $z = -1.99$ 0.0233
(c) $z = 0.92$ 0.8212 **(d)** $z = 2.90$ 0.9981

7. Determine the area under the standard normal curve that lies to the right of

(a) $z = -3.01$ 0.9987 **(b)** $z = -1.59$ 0.9441
(c) $z = 1.78$ 0.0375 **(d)** $z = 3.11$ 0.0009

8. Determine the area under the standard normal curve that lies to the right of

(a) $z = -3.49$ 0.9998 **(b)** $z = -0.55$ 0.7088
(c) $z = 2.23$ 0.0129 **(d)** $z = 3.45$ 0.0003

9. Determine the area under the standard normal curve that lies between

(a) $z = -2.04$ and $z = 2.04$ 0.9586
(b) $z = -0.55$ and $z = 0$ 0.2088
(c) $z = -1.04$ and $z = 2.76$ 0.8479

10. Determine the area under the standard normal curve that lies between

(a) $z = -2.55$ and $z = 2.55$ 0.9892
(b) $z = -1.67$ and $z = 0$ 0.4525
(c) $z = -3.03$ and $z = 1.98$ 0.9749

11. Determine the total area under the standard normal curve

(a) to the left of $z = -2$ or to the right of $z = 2$ 0.0456
(b) to the left of $z = -1.56$ or to the right of $z = 2.56$ 0.0646
(c) to the left of $z = -0.24$ or to the right of $z = 1.20$ 0.5203

12. Determine the total area under the standard normal curve

(a) to the left of $z = -2.94$ or to the right of $z = 2.94$ 0.0032
(b) to the left of $z = -1.68$ or to the right of $z = 3.05$ 0.0476
(c) to the left of $z = -0.88$ or to the right of $z = 1.23$ 0.2987

In Problems 13–18, find the indicated z-score. Be sure to draw a standard normal curve that depicts the solution.

13. Find the z-score such that the area under the standard normal curve to its left is 0.1. −1.28

14. Find the z-score such that the area under the standard normal curve to its left is 0.2. −0.84

15. Find the z-score such that the area under the standard normal curve to its right is 0.25. 0.67

16. Find the z-score such that the area under the standard normal curve to its right is 0.35. 0.39

17. Find z-scores that separate the middle 99% of the distribution from the area in the tails of the standard normal distribution. −2.575, 2.575

18. Find the z-scores that separate the middle 94% of the distribution from the area in the tails of the standard normal distribution. −1.88; 1.88

In Problems 19–22, find the value of z_α.

NW **19.** $z_{0.01}$ 2.33 **20.** $z_{0.02}$ 2.05

21. $z_{0.025}$ 1.96 **22.** $z_{0.15}$ 1.04

In Problems 23–32, assume that the random variable X is normally distributed, with mean $\mu = 50$ and standard deviation $\sigma = 7$. Compute the following probabilities. Be sure to draw a normal curve with the area corresponding to the probability shaded.

23. $P(X > 35)$ 0.9838 **24.** $P(X > 65)$ 0.0162

25. $P(X \leq 45)$ 0.2389 **26.** $P(X \leq 58)$ 0.8729

27. $P(40 < X < 65)$ 0.9074 **28.** $P(56 < X < 68)$ 0.1898

29. $P(55 \leq X \leq 70)$ 0.2368 **30.** $P(40 \leq X \leq 49)$ 0.3679

31. $P(38 < X \leq 55)$ 0.7175 **32.** $P(56 \leq X < 66)$ 0.1839

In Problems 33–36, assume that the random variable X is normally distributed, with mean $\mu = 50$ and standard deviation $\sigma = 7$. Find each indicated percentile for X.

33. The 9th percentile 40.62

34. The 90th percentile 58.96

35. The 81st percentile 56.16

36. The 38th percentile 47.83

APPLYING THE CONCEPTS

37. Egg Incubation Times The mean incubation time of fertilized chicken eggs kept at 100.5°F in a still-air incubator is 21 days. Suppose that the incubation times are approximately normally distributed with a standard deviation of 1 day. *Source:* University of Illinois Extension

(a) What is the probability that a randomly selected fertilized chicken egg hatches in less than 20 days? 0.1587

(b) What is the probability that a randomly selected fertilized chicken egg takes over 22 days to hatch? 0.1587

(c) What is the probability that a randomly selected fertilized chicken egg hatches between 19 and 21 days? 0.4772

(d) Would it be unusual for an egg to hatch in less than 18 days? Why? Yes

38. Reading Rates The reading speed of sixth-grade students is approximately normal, with a mean speed of 125 words per minute and a standard deviation of 24 words per minute.

(a) What is the probability that a randomly selected sixth-grade student reads less than 100 words per minute? 0.1492

(b) What is the probability that a randomly selected sixth-grade student reads more than 140 words per minute 0.2643

(c) What is the probability that a randomly selected sixth-grade student reads between 110 and 130 words per minute? 0.3189

(d) Would it be unusual for a sixth-grader to read more than 200 words per minute? Why? Yes

NW **39. Chips Ahoy! Cookies** The number of chocolate chips in an 18-ounce bag of Chips Ahoy! chocolate chip cookies is approximately normally distributed with a mean of 1262 chips and standard deviation 118 chips according to a study by cadets of the U.S. Air Force Academy. *Source:* Brad Warner and Jim Rutledge, *Chance* 12(1): 10–14, 1999

(a) What is the probability that a randomly selected 18-ounce bag of Chips Ahoy! contains between 1000 and 1400 chocolate chips, inclusive? 0.8658

(b) What is the probability that a randomly selected 18-ounce bag of Chips Ahoy! contains fewer than 1000 chocolate chips? 0.0132

(c) What proportion of 18-ounce bags of Chips Ahoy! contains more than 1200 chocolate chips? 0.7019

(d) What proportion of 18-ounce bags of Chips Ahoy! contains fewer than 1125 chocolate chips? 0.1230

(e) What is the percentile rank of an 18-ounce bag of Chips Ahoy! that contains 1475 chocolate chips? 96th percentile

(f) What is the percentile rank of an 18-ounce bag of Chips Ahoy! that contains 1050 chocolate chips? 4th percentile

40. Wendy's Drive-Through Fast-food restaurants spend quite a bit of time studying the amount of time cars spend in their drive-throughs. Certainly, the faster the cars get through the drive-through, the more the opportunity for making money. *QSR Magazine* studied drive-through times for fast-food restaurants and found Wendy's had the best time, with a mean time spent in the drive-through of 138.5 seconds. Assuming drive-through times are normally distributed with a standard deviation of 29 seconds, answer the following.

(a) What is the probability that a randomly selected car will get through Wendy's drive-through in less than 100 seconds? 0.0918

(b) What is the probability that a randomly selected car will spend more than 160 seconds in Wendy's drive-through? 0.2296

(c) What proportion of cars spend between 2 and 3 minutes in Wendy's drive-through? 0.6625

(d) Would it be unusual for a car to spend more than 3 minutes in Wendy's drive-through? Why? No

41. Gestation Period The lengths of human pregnancies are approximately normally distributed, with mean $\mu = 266$ days and standard deviation $\sigma = 16$ days.

(a) What proportion of pregnancies lasts more than 270 days? 0.4013 (b) 0.1587

(b) What proportion of pregnancies lasts less than 250 days?

(c) What proportion of pregnancies lasts between 240 and 280 days? 0.7590

(d) What is the probability that a randomly selected pregnancy lasts more than 280 days? 0.1894

(e) What is the probability that a randomly selected pregnancy lasts no more than 245 days? 0.0951

(f) A "very preterm" baby is one whose gestation period is less than 224 days. Are very preterm babies unusual? Yes; 0.0043

42. Light Bulbs General Electric manufactures a decorative Crystal Clear 60-watt light bulb that it advertises will last 1500 hours. Suppose that the lifetimes of the light bulbs are approximately normally distributed, with a mean of 1550 hours and a standard deviation of 57 hours.

(a) What proportion of the light bulbs will last less than the advertised time? 0.1894

(b) What proportion of the light bulbs will last more than 1650 hours? 0.0401

(c) What is the probability that a randomly selected GE Crystal Clear 60-watt light bulb will last between 1625 and 1725 hours? 0.0923

(d) What is the probability that a randomly selected GE Crystal Clear 60-watt light bulb will last longer than 1400 hours? 0.9957

43. Manufacturing Steel rods are manufactured with a mean length of 25 centimeters (cm). Because of variability in the manufacturing process, the lengths of the rods are approximately normally distributed, with a standard deviation of 0.07 cm.

(a) What proportion of rods has a length less than 24.9 cm? 0.0764

(b) Any rods that are shorter than 24.85 cm or longer than 25.15 cm are discarded. What proportion of rods will be discarded? 0.0324

(c) Using the results of part (b), if 5000 rods are manufactured in a day, how many should the plant manager expect to discard? 162

(d) If an order comes in for 10,000 steel rods, how many rods should the plant manager manufacture if the order states that all rods must be between 24.9 cm and 25.1 cm? 11,804

44. Manufacturing Ball bearings are manufactured with a mean diameter of 5 millimeters (mm). Because of variability in the manufacturing process, the diameters of the ball bearings are approximately normally distributed, with a standard deviation of 0.02 mm.

(a) What proportion of ball bearings has a diameter more than 5.03 mm? 0.0668

(b) Any ball bearings that have a diameter less than 4.95 mm or greater than 5.05 mm are discarded. What proportion of ball bearings will be discarded? 0.0124

(c) Using the results of part (b), if 30,000 ball bearings are manufactured in a day, how many should the plant manager expect to discard? 372

(d) If an order comes in for 50,000 ball bearings, how many bearings should the plant manager manufacture if the order states that all ball bearings must be between 4.97 mm and 5.03 mm? 57,711

45. NCAA Basketball Point Spreads In sports betting, Las Vegas sports books establish winning margins for a team that is favored to win a game. An individual can place a wager on the game and will win if the team bet upon wins after accounting for the spread. For example, if Team A is favored by 5 points, and wins the game by 7 points, then a bet on Team A is a winning bet. However, if Team A wins the game by only 3 points, then a bet on Team A is a losing bet. In games where a team is favored by 12 or fewer points, the margin of victory for the favored team relative to the spread is approximately normally distributed with a mean of 0 points and a standard deviation of 10.9 points. *Source:* Justin Wolfers, "Point Shaving: Corruption in NCAA Basketball"

(a) In games where a team is favored by 12 or fewer points, what is the probability that the favored team wins by 5 or more points relative to the spread? 0.3228

(b) In games where a team is favored by 12 or fewer points, what is the probability that the favored team loses by 2 or more points relative to the spread? 0.4286

(c) Explain the meaning of "the margin of victory relative to the spread has a mean of 0 points." Does this imply that the spreads are accurate for games in which a team is favored by 12 or fewer points? Yes

46. NCAA Basketball Point Spreads Revisited See Problem 45. In games where a team is favored by more than 12 points, the margin of victory for the favored team relative to the spread is normally distributed with a mean of −1.0 point and a standard deviation of 10.9 points. *Source:* Justin Wolfers, "Point Shaving: Corruption in NCAA Basketball"

(a) In games where a team is favored by more than 12 points, what is the probability that the favored team wins by 5 or more points relative to the spread? 0.2912

(b) In games where a team is favored by more than 12 points, what is the probability that the favored team loses by 2 or more points relative to the spread? 0.4641

(c) In games where a team is favored by more than 12 points, what is the probability that the favored team "beats the spread"? Does this imply that the possible point shaving spreads are accurate for games in which a team is favored by more than 12 points? 0.4641; No, possible point shaving

NW **47. Egg Incubation Times** The mean incubation time of fertilized chicken eggs kept at 100.5°F in a still-air incubator is 21 days. Suppose that the incubation times are approximately normally distributed with a standard deviation of 1 day. *Source:* University of Illinois Extension

(a) Determine the 17th percentile for incubation times of fertilized chicken eggs. 20 days

(b) Determine the incubation times that make up the middle 95% of fertilized chicken eggs. 19–23 days

48. Reading Rates The reading speed of sixth-grade students is approximately normal, with a mean speed of 125 words per minute and a standard deviation of 24 words per minute.

(a) What is the reading speed of a sixth-grader whose reading speed is at the 90th percentile? 156 words per minute

(b) A school psychologist wants to determine reading rates for unusual students (both slow and fast). Determine the reading rates of the middle 95% of all sixth-grade students. What are the cutoff points for unusual readers? 78 and 172 words per minute

49. Chips Ahoy! Cookies The number of chocolate chips in an 18-ounce bag of Chips Ahoy! chocolate chip cookies is approximately normally distributed, with a mean of 1262 chips and a standard deviation of 118 chips, according to a study by cadets of the U.S. Air Force Academy. *Source:* Brad Warner and Jim Rutledge, *Chance* 12(1): 10–14, 1999 (b) 958 to 1566 chips

(a) Determine the 30th percentile for the number of chocolate chips in an 18-ounce bag of Chips Ahoy! cookies. 1201 chips

(b) Determine the number of chocolate chips in a bag of Chips Ahoy! that make up the middle 99% of bags.

50. Wendy's Drive-Through Fast-food restaurants spend quite a bit of time studying the amount of time cars spend in their drive-through. Certainly, the faster the cars get through the drive-through, the more the opportunity for making money. *QSR Magazine* studied drive-through times for fast-food restaurants, and found Wendy's had the best time, with a mean time a car spent in the drive-through equal to 138.5 seconds. Assume that drive-through times are normally distributed, with a standard deviation of 29 seconds. Suppose that Wendy's wants to institute a policy at its restaurants that it will not charge any patron that must wait more than a certain amount of time for an order. Management does not want to give away free meals to more than 1% of the patrons. What time would you recommend Wendy's advertise as the maximum wait time before a free meal is awarded? 206 seconds

51. Speedy Lube The time required for Speedy Lube to complete an oil change service on an automobile approximately follows a normal distribution, with a mean of 17 minutes and a standard deviation of 2.5 minutes.

(a) Speedy Lube guarantees customers that the service will take no longer than 20 minutes. If it does take longer, the customer will receive the service for half-price. What percent of customers receive the service for half price? 11.51%

(b) If Speedy Lube does not want to give the discount to more than 3% of its customers, how long should it make the guaranteed time limit? 22 minutes

52. Putting It Together: Birth Weights The following data represent the distribution of birth weights (in grams) for babies in which the pregnancy went full term (37 to 41 weeks).

Birth Weight (g)	Number of Live Births
0–499	22
500–999	201
1000–1499	1,645
1500–1999	9,365
2000–2499	92,191
2500–2999	569,319
3000–3499	1,387,335
3500–3999	988,011
4000–4499	255,700
4500–4999	36,766
5000–5499	3,994

Source: National Vital Statistics Report 56(6): Dec 5, 2007.

(a) Construct a relative frequency distribution for birth weight.
(b) Draw a relative frequency histogram for birth weight. Describe the shape of the distribution.
(c) Determine the mean and standard deviation birth weight. $\mu = 3375$ g; $\sigma = 493$ g
(d) Use the normal model to determine the proportion of babies in each class.
(e) Compare the proportions predicted by the normal model to the relative frequencies found in part (a). Do you believe that the normal model is effective in describing the birth weights of babies? Yes

EXPLAINING THE CONCEPTS

53. Give three interpretations for the area under a normal curve. Probability, proportion, percentile

54. Explain why $P(X < 30)$ should be reported as <0.0001 if X is a normal random variable with mean 100 and standard deviation 15.

55. Explain why $P(X \geq 220)$ should be reported as >0.9999 if X is a normal random variable with mean 100 and standard deviation 15.

56. The ACT and SAT are two college entrance exams. The composite score on the ACT is approximately normally distributed with mean 21.1 and standard deviation 5.1. The composite score on the SAT is approximately normally distributed with mean 1026 with standard deviation 210. Suppose you scored 26 on the ACT and 1240 on the SAT. Which exam did you score better on? Justify your reasoning using the normal model. SAT

Consumer Reports® Sunscreens

More than 1 million skin cancers are expected to be diagnosed in the United States this year, accounting for almost half of all cancers diagnosed. The prevalence of skin cancer is attributable in part to a history of unprotected or underprotected sun exposure. Sunscreens have been shown to prevent certain types of lesions associated with skin cancer. They also protect skin against exposure to light that contributes to premature aging. As a result, sunscreen is now in moisturizers, lip balms, shampoos, hair-styling products, insect repellents, and makeup.

Consumer Reports tested 23 sunscreens and two moisturizers, all with a claimed sun-protection factor (SPF) of 15 or higher. SPF is defined as the degree to which a sunscreen protects the skin from UVB, the ultraviolet rays responsible for sunburn. (Some studies have shown that UVB, along with UVA, can increase the risk of skin cancers.) A person with untreated skin who can stay in the sun for 5 minutes before becoming sunburned should be able to stay in the sun for $15 \times 5 = 75$ minutes using a sunscreen rated at SPF 15.

To test whether products met their SPF claims for UVB, we used a solar simulator (basically a sun lamp) to expose people to measured amounts of sunlight. First we determined the exposure time (in minutes) that caused each person's untreated skin to turn pink within 24 hours. Then we applied sunscreen to new areas of skin and made the same determination. To avoid potential sources of bias, samples of the sunscreens were applied to randomly assigned sites on the subjects' skin.

To determine the SPF rating of a sunscreen for a particular individual, the exposure time with sunscreen was divided by the exposure time without sunscreen. The following table contains the mean and standard deviation of the SPF measurements for two particular sunscreens.

Product	Mean	Std Dev
A	15.5	1.5
B	14.7	1.2

(a) In designing this experiment, why is it important to obtain the exposure time without sunscreen first and then determine the exposure time with sunscreen for each person?
(b) Why is the random assignment of people and application sites to each treatment (the sunscreen) important?
(c) Assuming that the SPF ratings are approximately normal, calculate the proportion of SPF measurements that you expect to be less than 15, the advertised level of protection for each of the products.

(d) Calculate the proportion of SPF measurements that you expect to be greater than 17.5 for product A. Repeat this for product B.

(e) Calculate the proportion of SPF measurements that you expect to fall between 14.5 and 15.5 for product A. Repeat this for product B.

(f) Which product appears to be superior, A or B? Support your conclusion.

Note to Readers: *In many cases, our test protocol and analytical methods are more complicated than described in these examples. The data and discussions have been modified to make the material more appropriate for the audience.*

Technology Step-By-Step

The Normal Distribution

TI-83/84 Plus

Finding Areas under the Normal Curve

1. From the HOME screen, press 2nd VARS to access the DISTRibution menu.
2. Select `2:normalcdf(`.
3. With `normalcdf(` on the HOME screen, type *lowerbound, upperbound*, μ, σ). For example, to find the area to the left of $x = 35$ under the normal curve with $\mu = 40$ and $\sigma = 10$, type

```
normalcdf(-1E99, 35, 40, 10)
```

and hit ENTER.

Note: When there is no lowerbound, enter −1E99. When there is no upperbound, enter 1E99. The E shown is scientific notation; it is selected by pressing 2nd then ,.

Finding Normal Values Corresponding to an Area

1. From the HOME screen, press 2nd VARS to access the DISTRibution menu.
2. Select `3:invNorm(`.
3. With `invNorm(`on the HOME screen, type "*area left*", μ, σ). For example, to find the normal value such that the area under the normal curve to the left of the value is 0.68, with $\mu = 40$ and $\sigma = 10$, type

```
invNorm(0.68, 40, 10)
```

and hit ENTER.

MINITAB

Finding Areas under the Normal Curve

1. Select the **Calc menu**, highlight **Probability Distributions**, and highlight **Normal ...**.
2. Select **Cumulative Probability**. Enter the mean, μ, and the standard deviation, σ. Select **Input Constant**, and enter the observation. Click OK.

Finding Normal Values Corresponding to an Area

1. Select the **Calc** menu, highlight **Probability** Distributions, and highlight **Normal ...**.
2. Select **Inverse Cumulative Probability**. Enter the mean, μ, and the standard deviation, σ. Select **Input Constant**, and enter the area to the left of the unknown normal value. Click OK.

Excel

Finding Areas under the Normal Curve

1. Select the Formulas tab. Click "More Functions", then select "Statistical." In the drop-down menu, select "NORMDIST".
2. Enter the specified observation, μ, and σ, and set **Cumulative** to True. Click OK.

Finding Normal Values Corresponding to an Area

1. Select the Formulas tab. Click "More Functions", then select "Statistical." In the drop-down menu, select "NORMINV". Click OK.
2. Enter the area left of the unknown normal value, μ, and σ. Click OK.

StatCrunch

Finding Areas under the Standard Normal Curve

1. Select **Stats,** highlight **Calculator,** select **Normal.**
2. Enter the mean and the standard deviation. In the pull-down menu, decide if you wish to compute $P(X \le x)$ or $P(X \ge x)$. Finally, enter the value of x. Click Compute.

Finding Scores Corresponding to an Area

1. Select **Stats,** highlight **Calculator,** select **Normal.**
2. Enter the mean and the standard deviation. In the pull-down menu, decide if you are given the area to the left of the unknown score or the area to the right. If given the area to the left, in the pull-down menu choose the ≤ option; if given the area to the right, choose the ≥ option. Finally, enter the area in the right-most cell. Click Compute.

7.3 ASSESSING NORMALITY

Preparing for This Section Before getting started, review the following:

- Shape of a distribution (Section 2.2, pp. 88–89)

OBJECTIVE **1** Use normal probability plots to assess normality

Note to Instructor
If you like, you can print out and distribute the Preparing for This Section quiz located in the Instructor's Resource Center. The purpose of the quiz is to verify that the students have the prerequisite knowledge for the section.

Up to this point, we have said that a random variable X is normally distributed, or at least approximately normal, provided the histogram of the data is symmetric and bell shaped. This works well for large data sets, but the shape of a histogram drawn from a small sample of observations does not always accurately represent the shape of the population. For this reason, we need additional methods for assessing the normality of a random variable X when we are looking at a small set of sample data.

1 Use Normal Probability Plots to Assess Normality

A **normal probability plot** is a graph that plots observed data versus *normal scores*. A **normal score** is the expected z-score of the data value, assuming that the distribution of the random variable is normal. The expected z-score of an observed value depends on the number of observations in the data set.

In Other Words
Normal probability plots are used to assess normality in small data sets.

Drawing a normal probability plot requires the following steps:

Note to Instructor
The goal of this section is for students to be able to understand what a normal probability plot is. In addition, we want students to be able to read the output provided by a computer or calculator. Do not emphasize the by-hand solution. Rather, emphasize how to interpret normal probability plots.

Drawing a Normal Probability Plot

Step 1 Arrange the data in ascending order.

Step 2 Compute $f_i = \dfrac{i - 0.375}{n + 0.25}$,* where i is the index (the position of the data value in the ordered list) and n is the number of observations. The expected proportion of observations less than or equal to the ith data value is f_i.

Step 3 Find the z-score corresponding to f_i from Table V.

Step 4 Plot the observed values on the horizontal axis and the corresponding expected z-scores on the vertical axis.

Figure 32

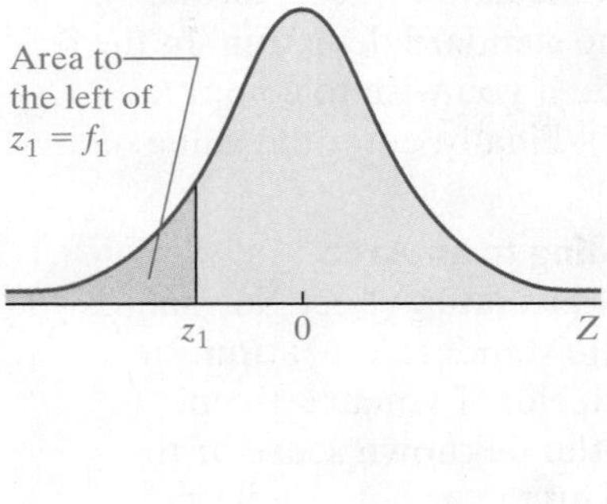

The idea behind finding the expected z-score is that, if the data come from a normally distributed population, we could predict the area to the left of each data value. The value of f_i represents the expected area to the left of the ith observation when the data come from a population that is normally distributed. For example, f_1 is the expected area to the left of the smallest data value, f_2 is the expected area to the left of the second-smallest data value, and so on. See Figure 32.

Once we determine each f_i, we find the z-scores corresponding to f_1, f_2, and so on. The smallest observation in the data set will be the smallest expected z-score, and the largest observation in the data set will be the largest expected z-score. Also, because of the symmetry of the normal curve, the expected z-scores are always paired as positive and negative values.

Values of normal random variables and their z-scores are linearly related ($x = \mu + z\sigma$), so a plot of observations of normal variables against their expected z-scores will be linear. We conclude the following:

If sample data are taken from a population that is normally distributed, a normal probability plot of the observed values versus the expected z-scores will be approximately linear.

*The derivation of this formula is beyond the scope of this text.

Normal probability plots are typically drawn using graphing calculators or statistical software. However, it is worthwhile to go through an example that demonstrates the procedure to better understand the results supplied by technology.

EXAMPLE 1 Constructing a Normal Probability Plot

TABLE 4

31.35	32.52
32.06	31.26
31.91	32.37

Source: Greyhound Park, Dubuque, IA

Note to Instructor
See note on page 352.

Sample Size, n	Critical Value
5	0.880
6	0.888
7	0.898
8	0.906
9	0.912
10	0.918
11	0.923
12	0.928
13	0.932
14	0.935
15	0.939
16	0.941
17	0.944
18	0.946
19	0.949
20	0.951
21	0.952
22	0.954
23	0.956
24	0.957
25	0.959
30	0.960

Source: S. W. Looney and T. R. Gulledge, Jr. "Use of the Correlation Coefficient with Normal Probability Plots," *American Statistician* 39(Feb. 1985): 75–79.

Problem The data in Table 4 represent the finishing time (in seconds) for six randomly selected races of a greyhound named Barbies Bomber in the $\frac{5}{16}$-mile race at Greyhound Park in Dubuque, Iowa. Is there evidence to support the belief that the variable "finishing time" is normally distributed?

Approach We follow Steps 1 through 4.

Solution

Step 1 Column 1 in Table 5 represents the index *i*. Column 2 represents the observed values in the data set, written in ascending order.

TABLE 5

Index, i	Observed Value	f_i	Expected z-score
1	31.26	$\frac{1-0.375}{6+0.25} = 0.10$	−1.28
2	31.35	$\frac{2-0.375}{6+0.25} = 0.26$	−0.64
3	31.91	0.42	−0.20
4	32.06	0.58	0.20
5	32.37	0.74	0.64
6	32.52	0.90	1.28

Step 2 Column 3 in Table 5 represents $f_i = \frac{i - 0.375}{n + 0.25}$ for each observation. This value is the expected area under the normal curve to the left of the *i*th observation, assuming normality. For example, $i = 1$ corresponds to the finishing time of 31.26, and

$$f_1 = \frac{1 - 0.375}{6 + 0.25} = 0.10$$

So the area under the normal curve to the left of 31.26 is 0.10 if the sample data come from a population that is normally distributed.

Step 3 We use Table V to find the z-scores that correspond to each f_i, then list them in Column 4 of Table 5. Look in Table V for the area closest to $f_1 = 0.1$. The expected z-score is −1.28. Notice that for each negative expected z-score there is a corresponding positive expected z-score, as a result of the symmetry of the normal curve.

Step 4 We plot the actual observations on the horizontal axis and the expected z-scores on the vertical axis. See Figure 33.

Figure 33

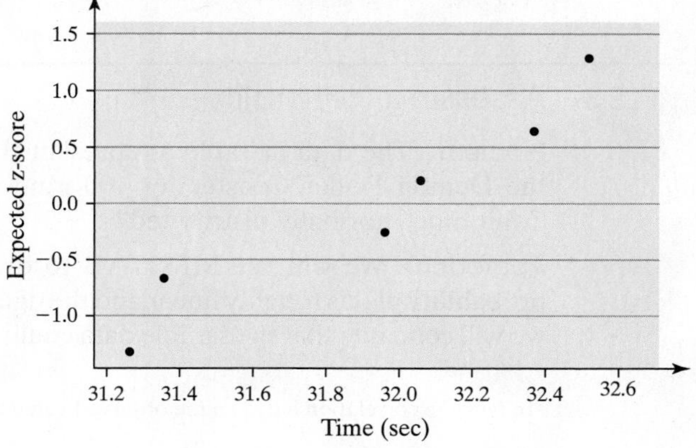

Although the normal probability plot in Figure 33 does show some curvature, it is roughly linear.* We conclude that the finishing times of Barbies Bomber in the $\frac{5}{16}$-mile race are approximately normally distributed.

Typically, normal probability plots are drawn using either a graphing calculator with advanced statistical features or statistical software. Certain software, such as MINITAB, will provide bounds that the data must lie within to support the belief that the sample data come from a population that is normally distributed.

EXAMPLE 2 Assessing Normality Using Technology

Problem Using MINITAB or some other statistical software, draw a normal probability plot of the data in Table 4 and determine whether the sample data come from a population that is normally distributed.

Approach We will use MINITAB, which provides curved *bounds* that can be used to assess normality. If the normal probability plot is roughly linear and all the data lie within the bounds, we have reason to believe the data come from a population that is approximately normal. The steps for constructing normal probability plots using TI-83/84 Plus graphing calculators, MINITAB, Excel, and StatCrunch can be found on page 355.

Solution Figure 34 shows the normal probability plot. Notice that MINITAB gives the area to the left of the expected z-score, rather than the z-score. For example, the area to the left of the expected z-score of -1.28 is 0.10. MINITAB writes 0.10 as 10 percent.

Figure 34

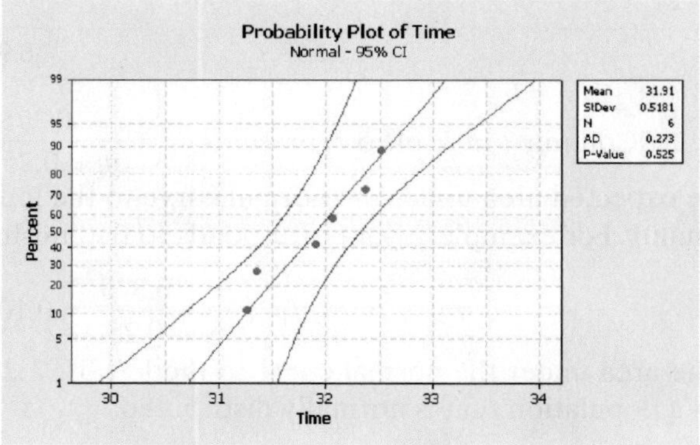

Note to Instructor

As an alternative to using MINITAB to assess the linearity of the normal probability plot, we can use the linear correlation coefficient, using the following:

Step 1: Compute the linear correlation between the data and the expected z-scores.

Step 2: Compare the linear correlation coefficient to the critical values supplied on page 351 ($\alpha = 0.05$). If the linear correlation coefficient is greater than or equal to the critical value, there is evidence to support the belief that the data come from a normally distributed population.

The normal probability plot is roughly linear, and all the data lie within the bounds provided by MINITAB. We conclude that the sample data could come from a population that is normally distributed.

Throughout the text, we will provide normal probability plots drawn with MINITAB so that assessing normality is straightforward.

EXAMPLE 3 Assessing Normality

Problem The data in Table 6 represent the time spent waiting in line (in minutes) for the Demon Roller Coaster for 100 randomly selected riders. Is the random variable "wait time" normally distributed?

Approach We will use MINITAB to draw a normal probability plot. If the normal probability plot is roughly linear and the data lie within the bounds provided by MINITAB, we will conclude that the sample data could come from a normally distributed population.

*In fact, the correlation between the observed value and expected z-score is 0.970.

TABLE 6

7	3	5	107	8	37	16	41	7	25	22	19	1	40	1	29	93
33	76	14	8	9	45	15	81	94	10	115	18	0	18	11	60	34
30	6	21	0	86	6	11	1	1	3	9	79	41	2	9	6	19
4	3	2	7	18	0	93	68	6	94	16	13	24	6	12	121	30
35	39	9	15	53	9	47	5	55	64	51	80	26	24	12	0	
94	18	4	61	38	38	21	61	9	80	18	21	8	14	47	56	

Solution Figure 35(a) shows a normal probability plot of the data drawn using MINITAB. Since the normal probability plot is not linear, the random variable "wait time" is not normally distributed. Figure 35(b) which shows a histogram of the data in Table 6, indicates that the data are skewed right.

Figure 35

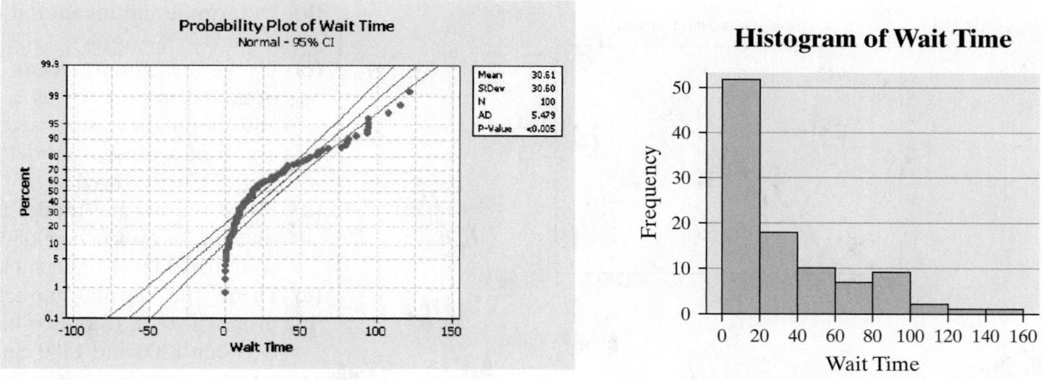

(a) (b)

Now Work Problems 3 and 7

7.3 ASSESS YOUR UNDERSTANDING

VOCABULARY AND SKILL BUILDING

1. A normal probability plot is a graph that plots observed data versus normal scores.

2. *True or False:* A normal score is the expected z-score of a data value, assuming the distribution of the random variable is normal. True

In Problems 3–8, determine whether the normal probability plot indicates that the sample data could have come from a population that is normally distributed.

NW 3. Not normal

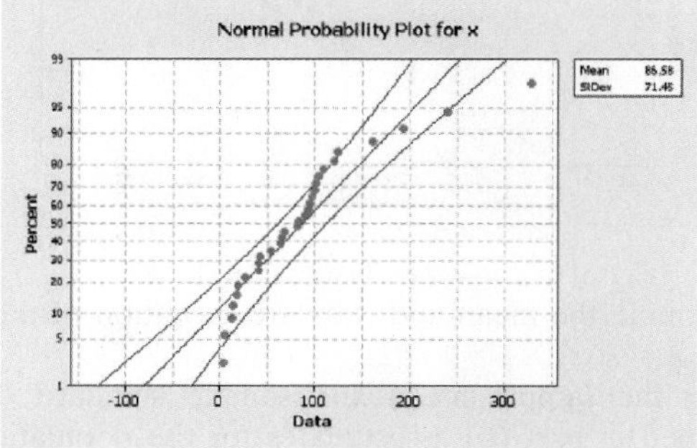

4. Normal

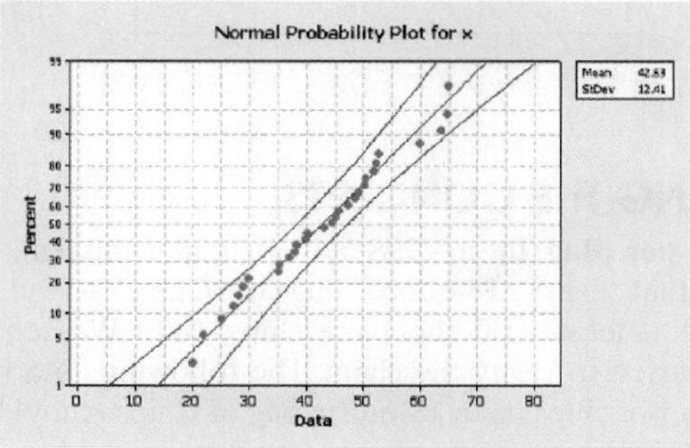

5. Not normal

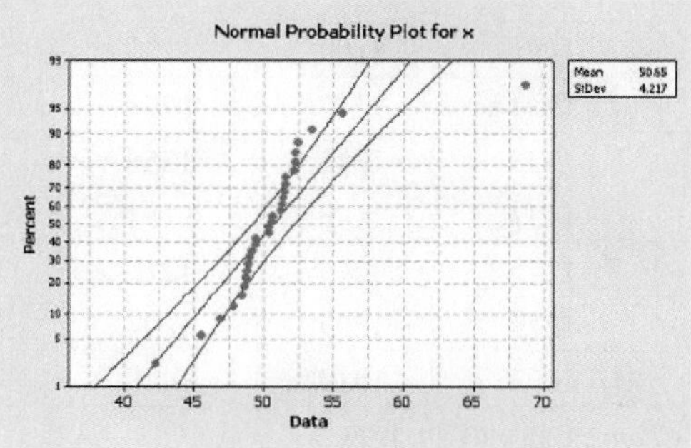

6. Not normal

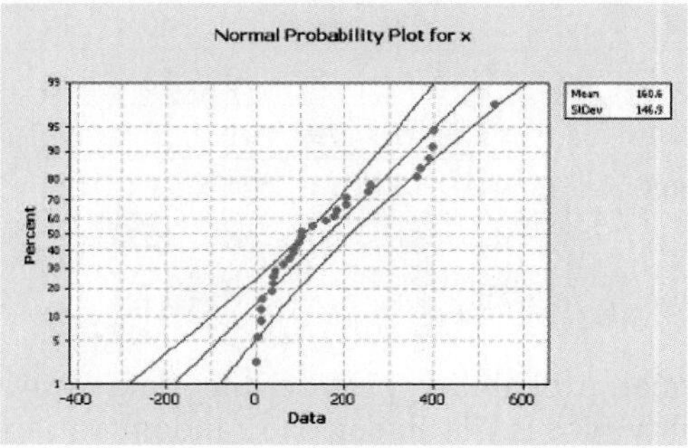

NW 7. Normal

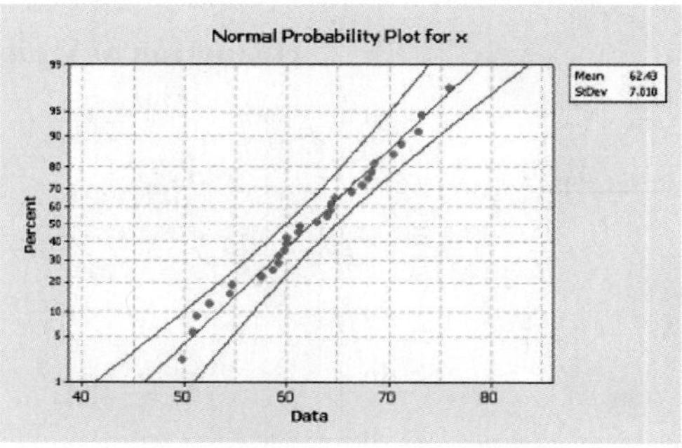

8. Normal

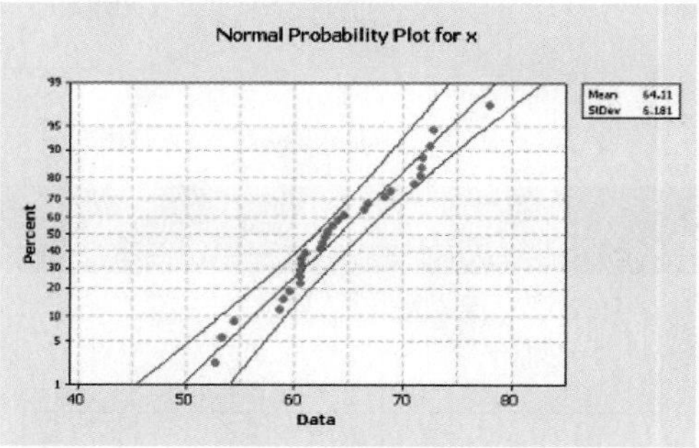

APPLYING THE CONCEPTS

9. Chips per Bag In a 1998 advertising campaign, Nabisco claimed that every 18-ounce bag of Chips Ahoy! cookies contained at least 1000 chocolate chips. Brad Warner and Jim Rutledge tried to verify the claim. The following data represent the number of chips in an 18-ounce bag of Chips Ahoy! based on their study.

1087	1098	1103	1121	1132
1185	1191	1199	1200	1213
1239	1244	1247	1258	1269
1307	1325	1345	1356	1363
1135	1137	1143	1154	1166
1214	1215	1219	1219	1228
1270	1279	1293	1294	1295
1377	1402	1419	1440	1514

Source: Chance 12(1): 10–14, 1999

(a) Use the following normal probability plot to determine if the data could have come from a normal distribution. Normal

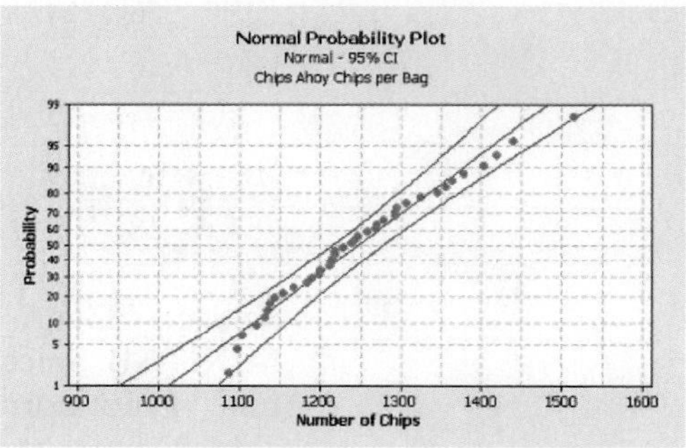

(b) Determine the mean and standard deviation of the sample data. $\bar{x} = 1247.4$, $s = 101.0$

(c) Using the sample mean and sample standard deviation obtained in part (b) as estimates for the population mean and population standard deviation, respectively, draw a graph of a normal model for the distribution of chips in a bag of Chips Ahoy!.

(d) Using the normal model from part (c), find the probability that an 18-ounce bag of Chips Ahoy! selected at random contains at least 1000 chips. 0.9929

(e) Using the normal model from part (c), determine the proportion of 18-ounce bags of Chips Ahoy! that contains between 1200 and 1400 chips, inclusive. 0.6153

10. Hours of TV A random sample of college students aged 18 to 24 years was obtained, and the number of hours of television watched in a typical week was recorded.

36.1	30.5	2.9	17.5	21.0
23.5	25.6	16.0	28.9	29.6
7.8	20.4	33.8	36.8	0.0
9.9	25.8	19.5	19.1	18.5
22.9	9.7	39.2	19.0	8.6

(a) Use the following normal probability plot to determine if the data could have come from a normal distribution. Normal

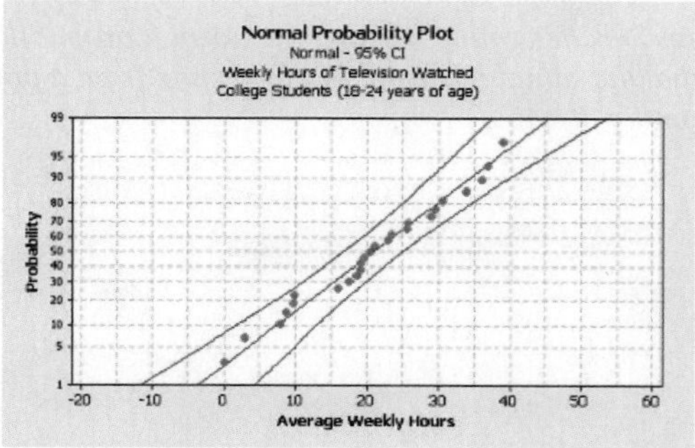

(b) Determine the mean and standard deviation of the sample data. $\bar{x} = 20.90$, $s = 10.52$

(c) Using the sample mean and sample standard deviation obtained in part (b) as estimates for the population mean and population standard deviation, respectively, draw a graph of a normal model for the distribution of weekly hours of television watched.

(d) Using the normal model from part (c), find the probability that a college student aged 18 to 24 years, selected at random, watches between 20 and 35 hours of television each week. 0.4458

(e) Using the normal model from part (c), determine the proportion of college students aged 18 to 24 years who watch more than 40 hours of television per week. 0.0344

In Problems 11–14, use a normal probability plot to assess whether the sample data could have come from a population that is normally distributed.

11. O-Ring Thickness A random sample of O-rings was obtained, and the wall thickness (in inches) of each was recorded. Normal

0.276	0.274	0.275	0.274	0.277
0.273	0.276	0.276	0.279	0.274
0.273	0.277	0.275	0.277	0.277
0.276	0.277	0.278	0.275	0.276

12. Customer Service A random sample of weekly work logs at an automobile repair station was obtained, and the average number of customers per day was recorded. Normal

26	24	22	25	23
24	25	23	25	22
21	26	24	23	24
25	24	25	24	25
26	21	22	24	24

13. School Loans A random sample of 20 undergraduate students receiving student loans was obtained, and the amount of their loans for the 2011–2012 school year was recorded. Not normal

2,500	1,000	2,000	14,000	1,800
3,800	10,100	2,200	900	1,600
500	2,200	6,200	9,100	2,800
2,500	1,400	13,200	750	12,000

14. Memphis Snowfall A random sample of 25 years between 1890 and 2011 was obtained, and the amount of snowfall, in inches, for Memphis was recorded. Not normal

24.0	7.9	1.5	0.0	0.3
0.4	8.1	4.3	0.0	0.5
3.6	2.9	0.4	2.6	0.1
16.6	1.4	23.8	25.1	1.6
12.2	14.8	0.4	3.7	4.2

Source: National Oceanic and Atmospheric Administration

Technology Step-By-Step

Normal Probability Plots

TI-83/84 Plus

1. Enter the raw data into L1.
2. Press 2nd Y = access STAT PLOTS.
3. Select `1:Plot1`.
4. Turn `Plot1` on by highlighting On and pressing ENTER. Press the down-arrow key. Highlight the *normal probability plot* icon. It is the icon in the lower-right corner under Type:. Press ENTER to select this plot type. The Data List should be set at L1. The Data Axis should be the *x*-axis.
5. Press ZOOM, and select `9:ZoomStat`.

MINITAB

1. Enter the raw data into C1.
2. Select the **Graph** menu. Highlight **Probability Plot . . . .** Select "Single." Click OK.
3. In the Graph variables cell, enter the column that contains the raw data. Make sure Distribution is set to Normal. Click OK.

Excel

1. Install XLSTAT.
2. Enter the raw data into column A.
3. Select the **XLSTAT** menu. Highlight **Visualizing Data** and select **Univariate Plots**.
4. In the general tab, check Quantitative data. With the cursor in the Quantitative data box, highlight the raw data. Uncheck the box "Sample Labels." Click the charts tab and check Normal P-P plots or Normal Q-Q plots. Click OK.

StatCrunch

1. Enter the raw data into var1.
2. Select Graphics. Highlight QQ Plot.
3. Select var1. Click Create Graph!

7.4 THE NORMAL APPROXIMATION TO THE BINOMIAL PROBABILITY DISTRIBUTION

Preparing for This Section Before getting started, review the following:

- Binomial probability distribution (Section 6.2, pp. 309–319)

OBJECTIVE **1** Approximate binomial probabilities using the normal distribution

1 Approximate Binomial Probabilities Using the Normal Distribution

Note to Instructor

If you like, you can print out and distribute the Preparing for This Section quiz located in the Instructor's Resource Center. The purpose of the quiz is to verify that the students have the prerequisite knowledge for the section.

Note to Instructor

The material in this section is optional and can be omitted without loss of continuity.

Note to Instructor

The concepts in this section can be illustrated using the Normal Approximation to the Binomial applet.

In Section 6.2, we discussed the binomial probability distribution. Now, we will review the criteria for a probability experiment to be a binomial experiment.

Criteria for a Binomial Probability Experiment

A probability experiment is a binomial experiment if all the following are true:

1. The experiment is performed n independent times. Each repetition of the experiment is called a **trial**. Independence means that the outcome of one trial will not affect the outcome of the other trials.
2. For each trial, there are two mutually exclusive outcomes—success or failure.
3. The probability of success, p, is the same for each trial of the experiment.

The binomial probability formula can be used to compute probabilities of events in a binomial experiment. A large number of trials of a binomial experiment, however, makes this formula difficult to use. For example, given 500 trials of a binomial experiment, to compute the probability of 400 or more successes requires that we compute the following probabilities:

$$P(X \geq 400) = P(400) + P(401) + \cdots + P(500)$$

This would be time consuming to compute by hand! Fortunately, we have an alternative means for approximating binomial probabilities, provided that certain conditions are met.

Historical Note

The normal approximation to the binomial was discovered by Abraham de Moivre in 1733. With the advance of computing technology, its importance has been diminished.

Recall, the following fact from page 319:

For a fixed p, as the number of trials n in a binomial experiment increases, the probability distribution of the random variable X becomes more nearly symmetric and bell shaped. As a rule of thumb, if $np(1 - p) \geq 10$, the probability distribution will be approximately symmetric and bell shaped.

This result suggests that binomial probabilities can be approximated by the area under a normal curve, provided that $np(1 - p) \geq 10$.

Note to Instructor

Consider assigning the "Playing Plinko" activity from the Student Activity Workbook.

The Normal Approximation to the Binomial Probability Distribution

If $np(1 - p) \geq 10$, the binomial random variable X is approximately normally distributed, with mean $\mu_X = np$ and standard deviation $\sigma_X = \sqrt{np(1 - p)}$.

Figure 36 shows a probability histogram for the binomial random variable X, with $n = 40$ and $p = 0.5$, and a normal curve, with $\mu_X = np = 40(0.5) = 20$ and standard deviation $\sigma_X = \sqrt{np(1-p)} = \sqrt{40(0.5)(0.5)} = \sqrt{10}$. Notice that $np(1-p) = 40(0.5)(1-0.5) = 10$.

Figure 36

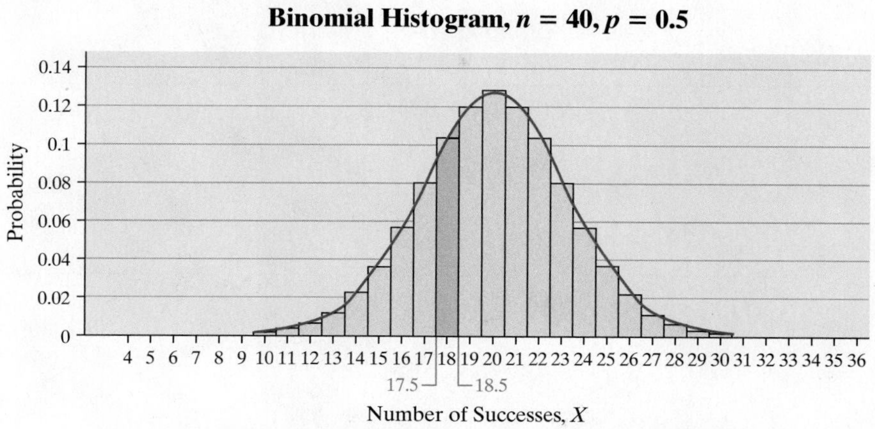

CAUTION

Don't forget about the correction for continuity. It is needed because we are using a continuous density function to approximate the probability of a discrete random variable.

We know from Section 6.2 that the area of the rectangle corresponding to $x = 18$ represents $P(18)$. The width of each rectangle is 1, so the rectangle extends from $x = 17.5$ to $x = 18.5$. The area under the normal curve from $x = 17.5$ to $x = 18.5$ is approximately equal to the area of the rectangle corresponding to $x = 18$. Therefore, the area under the normal curve between $x = 17.5$ and $x = 18.5$ is approximately equal to $P(18)$, where X is a binomial random variable with $n = 40$ and $p = 0.5$. We add and subtract 0.5 from $x = 18$ as a **correction for continuity**, because we are using a continuous density function to approximate a discrete probability.

Suppose we want to approximate $P(X \leq 18)$ as in Figure 37.

Figure 37

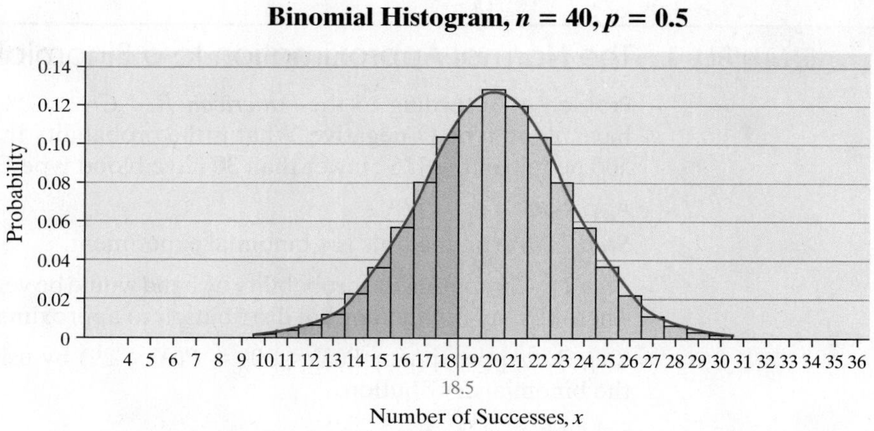

To approximate $P(X \leq 18)$, we compute the area under the normal curve for $X \leq 18.5$. Do you see why?

If we want to approximate $P(X \geq 18)$, we compute $P(X \geq 17.5)$. Do you see why? Table 7 on the next page summarizes how to use the correction for continuity.

TABLE 7

Exact Probability Using Binomial	Approximate Probability Using Normal	Graphical Depiction
$P(a)$	$P(a - 0.5 \leq X \leq a + 0.5)$	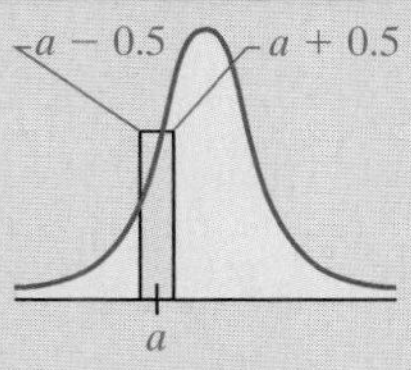
$P(X \leq a)$	$P(X \leq a + 0.5)$	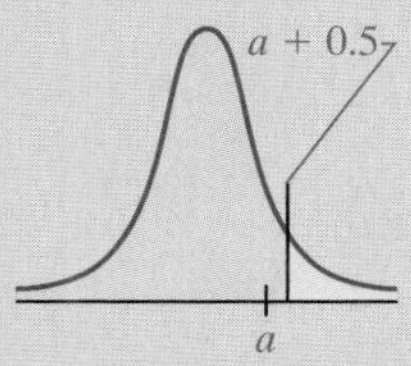
$P(X \geq a)$	$P(X \geq a - 0.5)$	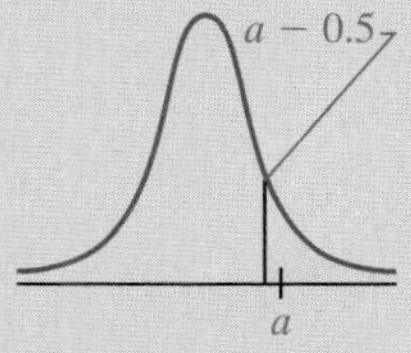
$P(a \leq X \leq b)$	$P(a - 0.5 \leq X \leq b + 0.5)$	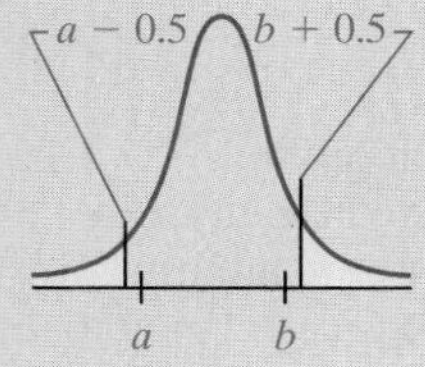

A question remains, however. What do we do if the probability is of the form $P(X > a)$, $P(X < a)$, or $P(a < X < b)$? The solution is to rewrite the inequality in a form with $\leq$ or $\geq$. For example, $P(X > 4) = P(X \geq 5)$ and $P(X < 4) = P(X \leq 3)$ for binomial random variables, because the values of the random variables must be whole numbers.

EXAMPLE 1 The Normal Approximation to a Binomial Random Variable

Problem According to the *American Red Cross*, 7% of people in the United States have blood type O-negative. What is the probability that, in a simple random sample of 500 people in the U.S., fewer than 30 have blood type O-negative?

Approach

Step 1 Verify that this is a binomial experiment.

Step 2 Computing the probability by hand would be very tedious. Verify $np(1 - p) \geq 10$. Then we may use the normal distribution to approximate the binomial probability.

Step 3 Approximate $P(X < 30) = P(X \leq 29)$ by using the normal approximation to the binomial distribution.

Solution

Step 1 Each of the 500 independent trials has a probability of success equal to 0.07. This is a binomial experiment.

Step 2 We verify $np(1 - p) \geq 10$.

$$np(1 - p) = 500(0.07)(0.93) = 32.55 \geq 10$$

We can use the normal distribution to approximate the binomial distribution.

Step 3 The probability that fewer than 30 people in the sample have blood type O-negative is $P(X < 30) = P(X \leq 29)$. This is approximately equal to the area under the normal curve to the left of $x = 29.5$, with $\mu_X = np = 500(0.07) = 35$ and $\sigma_X = \sqrt{np(1 - p)} = \sqrt{500(0.07)(1 - 0.07)} = \sqrt{32.55} \approx 5.71$. See Figure 38. We convert $x = 29.5$ to a z-score.

Figure 38

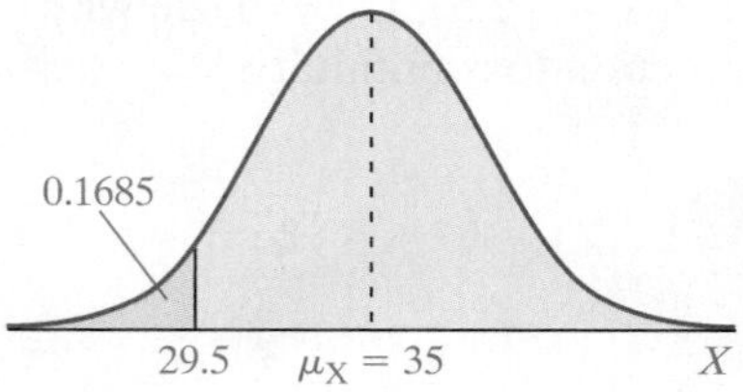

Figure 39

$$z = \frac{29.5 - 35}{\sqrt{32.55}} = -0.96$$

From Table V, we find that the area to the left of $z = -0.96$ is 0.1685. Therefore, the approximate probability that fewer than 30 people will have blood type O-negative is $0.1685 = 16.85\%$.

Using the *binomcdf(* command on a TI-84 Plus graphing calculator, we find that the exact probability is 0.1678. See Figure 39. The approximate result is close indeed!

Now Work Problem 21

EXAMPLE 2 A Normal Approximation to the Binomial

Problem According to the Gallup Organization, 65% of adult Americans are in favor of the death penalty for individuals convicted of murder. Erica selects a random sample of 1000 adult Americans in Will County, Illinois, and finds that 630 of them are in favor of the death penalty for individuals convicted of murder.

(a) Assuming that 65% of adult Americans in Will County are in favor of the death penalty, what is the probability of obtaining a random sample of no more than 630 adult Americans in favor of the death penalty from a sample of size 1000?

(b) Does the result from part (a) contradict the Gallup Organization's findings? Explain.

Approach This is a binomial experiment with $n = 1000$ and $p = 0.65$. Erica needs to determine the probability of obtaining a random sample of no more than 630 adult Americans who favor the death penalty, assuming 65% of adult Americans favor the death penalty. Computing this probability using the binomial probability formula would be difficult, so Erica will use the normal approximation to the binomial, since $np(1-p) = 1000(0.65)(1 - 0.65) = 227.5 \geq 10$. Approximate $P(X \leq 630)$ by computing the area under the normal curve to the left of $x = 630.5$ with $\mu_X = np = 650$ and $\sigma_X = \sqrt{np(1-p)} = \sqrt{1000(0.65)(1-0.65)} \approx 15.083$.

Solution

(a) Figure 40 shows the area we wish to compute. We convert $x = 630.5$ to a z-score.

$$z = \frac{630.5 - 650}{15.083} = -1.29$$

Figure 40

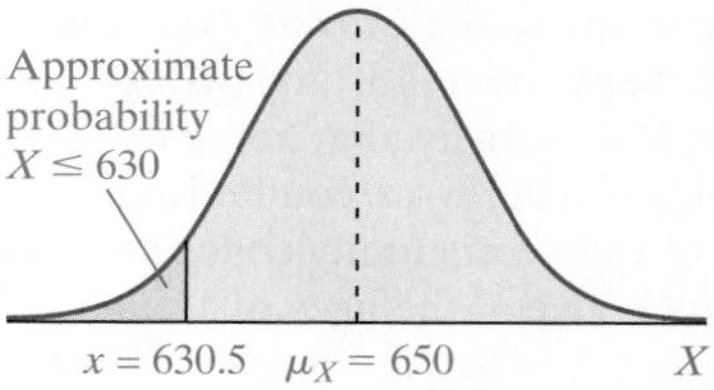

The area under the standard normal curve to the left of $z = -1.29$ is 0.0985. There is a 9.85% probability of obtaining 630 or fewer adult Americans who favor the death penalty from a sample of 1000 adult Americans, assuming the proportion of adult Americans who favor the death penalty is 0.65.

(b) The result of part (a) means that, if we had obtained 100 different simple random samples of size 1000, we would expect about 10 to result in 630 or fewer adult Americans favoring the death penalty if the true proportion is 0.65. Because the results obtained are not unusual under the assumption that $p = 0.65$, Erica finds that the results of her survey do not contradict those of Gallup.

Now Work Problem 27

7.4 ASSESS YOUR UNDERSTANDING

VOCABULARY AND SKILL BUILDING

1. In a binomial experiment with n trials and probability of success p, if $np(1-p) \geq 10$, the binomial random variable X is approximately normal with $\mu_X =$ np and $\sigma_X =$ $\sqrt{np(1-p)}$.

2. When adding or subtracting 0.5 from x, we are making a correction for continuity.

3. Suppose X is a binomial random variable. To approximate $P(X < 5)$, compute $P(X \leq 4.5)$.

4. Suppose X is a binomial random variable. To approximate $P(3 \leq X \leq 10)$, compute $P(2.5 \leq X \leq 10.5)$.

In Problems 5–14, a discrete random variable is given. Assume the probability of the random variable will be approximated using the normal distribution. Describe the area under the normal curve that will be computed. For example, if we wish to compute the *probability of finding at least five defective items in a shipment, we would approximate the probability by computing the area under the normal curve to the right of $x = 4.5$.*

5. The probability that at least 40 households have a gas stove Right of $x = 39.5$

6. The probability of no more than 20 people who want to see *Roe v. Wade* overturned Left of $x = 20.5$

7. The probability that exactly eight defective parts are in the shipment Between $x = 7.5$ and $x = 8.5$

8. The probability that exactly 12 students pass the course

9. The probability that the number of people with blood type O-negative is between 18 and 24, inclusive

10. The probability that the number of tornadoes that occur in the month of May is between 30 and 40, inclusive

11. The probability that more than 20 people want to see the marriage tax penalty abolished Right of $x = 20.5$

12. The probability that fewer than 40 households have a pet Left of $x = 39.5$

13. The probability that more than 500 adult Americans support a bill proposing to extend daylight savings time Right of $x = 500.5$

14. The probability that fewer than 35 people support the privatization of Social Security Left of $x = 34.5$

In Problems 15–20, compute P(x) using the binomial probability formula. Then determine whether the normal distribution can be used as an approximation for the binomial distribution. If so, approximate P(x) and compare the result to the exact probability.

15. $n = 60, p = 0.4, x = 20$ 0.0616; 0.0618

16. $n = 80, p = 0.15, x = 18$ 0.0221; 0.0220

17. $n = 40, p = 0.25, x = 30$ <0.0001; cannot be used

18. $n = 100, p = 0.05, x = 50$ <0.0001; cannot be used

19. $n = 75, p = 0.75, x = 60$ 0.0677; 0.0630

20. $n = 85, p = 0.8, x = 70$ 0.0970; 0.0926

APPLYING THE CONCEPTS

NW **21. On-Time Flights** According to American Airlines, Flight 215 from Orlando to Los Angeles is on time 90% of the time. Randomly select 150 flights and use the normal approximation to the binomial to

(a) approximate the probability that exactly 130 flights are on time. 0.0444

(b) approximate the probability that at least 130 flights are on time. 0.9332

(c) approximate the probability that fewer than 125 flights are on time. 0.0021

(d) approximate the probability that between 125 and 135 flights, inclusive, are on time. 0.5536

22. Smokers According to *Information Please Almanac*, 80% of adult smokers started smoking before they were 18 years old. Suppose 100 smokers 18 years old or older are randomly selected. Use the normal approximation to the binomial to

(a) approximate the probability that exactly 80 of them started smoking before they were 18 years old. 0.1034

(b) approximate the probability that at least 80 of them started smoking before they were 18 years old. 0.5517

(c) approximate the probability that fewer than 70 of them started smoking before they were 18 years old. 0.0043

(d) approximate the probability that between 70 and 90 of them, inclusive, started smoking before they were 18 years old. 0.9914

23. Morality In a recent poll, the Gallup Organization found that 45% of adult Americans believe that the overall state of moral values in the United States is poor. Suppose a survey of a random sample of 500 adult Americans is conducted in which they are asked to disclose their feelings on the overall state of moral values in the United States. Use the normal approximation to the binomial to approximate the probability that

(a) exactly 250 of those surveyed feel the state of morals is poor. 0.0029

(b) no more than 220 of those surveyed feel the state of morals is poor. 0.3446

(c) more than 250 of those surveyed feel the state of morals is poor. 0.0110

(d) between 220 and 250, inclusive, believe the state of morals is poor. 0.6769

(e) at least 260 adult Americans believe the overall state of moral values is poor. Would you find this result unusual? Why? Yes, $P(X \geq 260) \approx 0.0010$

24. Sneeze According to a study done by Nick Wilson of Otago University Wellington, the probability a randomly selected individual will not cover his or her mouth when sneezing is 0.267. Suppose you sit on a bench in a mall and observe 300 randomly selected individuals' habits as they sneeze.

(a) Use the normal approximation to the binomial to approximate the probability that of the 300 randomly observed individuals exactly 100 do not cover the mouth when sneezing. 0.0018

(b) Use the normal approximation to the binomial to approximate the probability that of the 300 randomly observed individuals fewer than 75 do not cover the mouth. 0.2327

(c) Would you be surprised if, after observing 300 individuals, more than 100 did not cover the mouth when sneezing? Why? Yes; probability is 0.0039

25. Males Living at Home According to the *Current Population Survey* (Internet release date: September 15, 2004), 55% of males between the ages of 18 and 24 years lived at home in 2003. (Unmarried college students living in a dorm are counted as living at home.) A survey is administered at a community college to 200 randomly selected male students between the ages of 18 and 24 years, and 130 of them respond that they live at home.

(a) Approximate the probability that such a survey will result in at least 130 of the respondents living at home under the assumption that the true percentage is 55%. 0.0028

(b) Does the result from part (a) contradict the results of the *Current Population Survey*? Explain. Yes

26. Females Living at Home According to the *Current Population Survey* (Internet release date: September 15, 2004), 46% of females between the ages of 18 and 24 years lived at home in 2003. (Unmarried college students living in a dorm are counted as living at home.) A survey is administered at a community college to 200 randomly selected female students between the ages of 18 and 24 years, and 110 of them respond that they live at home.

(a) Approximate the probability that such a survey will result in at least 110 of the respondents living at home under the assumption that the true percentage is 46%. 0.0066

(b) Does the result from part (a) contradict the results of the *Current Population Survey*? Explain. Yes

8. Between $x = 11.5$ and $x = 12.5$ 9. Between $x = 17.5$ and $x = 24.5$ 10. Between $x = 29.5$ and $x = 40.5$

NW **27. Boys Are Preferred** In a Gallup poll, 37% of survey respondents said that, if they only had one child, they would prefer the child to be a boy. You conduct a survey of 150 randomly selected students on your campus and find that 75 of them would prefer a boy.

(a) Approximate the probability that, in a random sample of 150 students, at least 75 would prefer a boy, assuming the true percentage is 37%. 0.0007

(b) Does this result contradict the Gallup poll? Explain. Yes

28. Liars According to a *USA Today* "Snapshot," 3% of Americans surveyed lie frequently. You conduct a survey of 500 college students and find that 20 of them lie frequently.

(a) Compute the probability that, in a random sample of 500 college students, at least 20 lie frequently, assuming the true percentage is 3%. 0.1190

(b) Does this result contradict the *USA Today* "Snapshot"? Explain. No

CHAPTER 7 REVIEW

Summary

In this chapter, we introduced continuous random variables and the normal probability density function. A continuous random variable is said to be approximately normally distributed if a histogram of its values is symmetric and bell-shaped. In addition, we can draw normal probability plots that are based on expected z-scores. If these normal probability plots are approximately linear, we say the distribution of the random variable is approximately normal. The area under the normal density function can be used to find proportions, probabilities, or percentiles for normal random variables. Also, we can find the value of a normal random variable that corresponds to a specific proportion, probability, or percentile.

If X is a binomial random variable with $np(1-p) \geq 10$, we can use the area under the normal curve to approximate the probability of a particular binomial random variable. The parameters of the normal curve are $\mu_X = np$ and $\sigma_X = \sqrt{np(1-p)}$, where n is the number of trials of the binomial experiment and p is the probability of success on a single trial.

Vocabulary

Uniform probability distribution (p. 329)
Probability density function (p. 329)
Model (p. 331)
Normal curve (p. 331)
Normally distributed (p. 331)
Normal probability distribution (p. 331)
Inflection points (p. 331)
Normal density curve (p. 332)
Normal probability density function (p. 334)
Standard normal distribution (p. 338)
Standard normal curve (p. 338)
Normal probability plot (p. 350)
Normal score (p. 350)
Trial (p. 356)
Normal approximation to the binomial distribution (p. 356)
Correction for continuity (p. 357)

Formulas

Standardizing a Normal Random Variable

$$z = \frac{x - \mu}{\sigma}$$

Finding the Score

$$x = \mu + z\sigma$$

Objectives

Section	You should be able to . . .	Examples	Review Exercises
7.1	1 Use the uniform probability distribution (p. 329)	1 and 2	18
	2 Graph a normal curve (p. 331)	pages 331–332	7–9
	3 State the properties of the normal curve (p. 332)	page 332	19
	4 Explain the role of area in the normal density function (p. 333)	3 and 4	1
7.2	1 Find and interpret the area under a normal curve (p. 338)	1 and 2	7–9, 10(a)–(c), 11(a)–(d), 12
	2 Find the value of a normal random variable (p. 342)	3 and 4	10(d), 11(e)–(f)
7.3	1 Use normal probability plots to assess normality (p. 350)	1–3	14–16, 20
7.4	1 Approximate binomial probabilities using the normal distribution (p. 356)	1 and 2	13, 17

Review Exercises

1. Use the figure to answer the questions that follow.

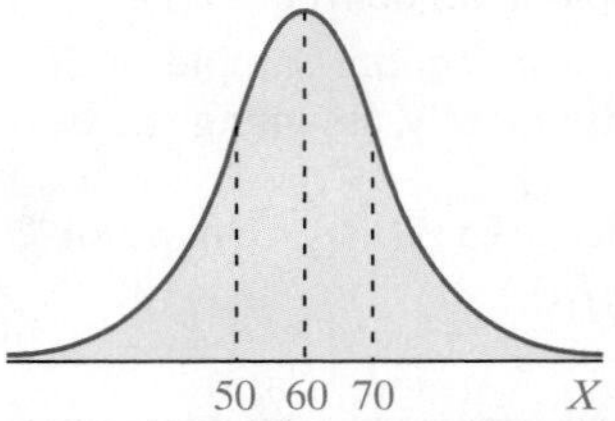

(a) What is μ? 60

(b) What is σ? 10

(c) Suppose that the area under the normal curve to the right of $x = 75$ is 0.0668. Provide two interpretations for this area.

(d) Suppose that the area under the normal curve between $x = 50$ and $x = 75$ is 0.7745. Provide two interpretations for this area.

In Problems 2 and 3, draw a standard normal curve and shade the area indicated. Then find the area of the shaded region.

2. The area to the left of $z = -1.04$. 0.1492

3. The area between $z = -0.34$ and $z = 1.03$. 0.4816

4. Find the z-score such that the area to the right of the z-score is 0.483. 0.04

5. Find the z-scores that separate the middle 92% of the data from the area in the tails of the standard normal distribution. −1.75, 1.75

6. Find the value of $z_{0.20}$. 0.84

In Problems 7–9, draw the normal curve with the parameters indicated. Then find the probability of the random variable X. Shade the area that represents the probability.

7. $\mu = 50, \sigma = 6, P(X > 55)$ 0.2033

8. $\mu = 30, \sigma = 5, P(X \le 23)$ 0.0808

9. $\mu = 70, \sigma = 10, P(65 < X < 85)$ 0.6247

10. Tire Wear Suppose that Dunlop Tire manufactures a tire with a lifetime that approximately follows a normal distribution with mean 70,000 miles and standard deviation 4400 miles.

(a) What proportion of the tires will last at least 75,000 miles? 0.1271

(b) Suppose that Dunlop warrants the tires for 60,000 miles. What proportion of the tires will last 60,000 miles or less? 0.0116

(c) What is the probability that a randomly selected Dunlop tire lasts between 65,000 and 80,000 miles? 0.8613

(d) Suppose that Dunlop wants to warrant no more than 2% of its tires. What mileage should the company advertise as its warranty mileage? 60,980 miles

11. Wechsler Intelligence Scale The Wechsler Intelligence Scale for Children is approximately normally distributed, with mean 100 and standard deviation 15.

(a) What is the probability that a randomly selected test taker will score above 125? 0.0475

(b) What is the probability that a randomly selected test taker will score below 90? 0.2514

(c) What proportion of test takers will score between 110 and 140?

(d) If a child is randomly selected, what is the probability that she scores above 150? 0.0004 (c) 0.2476

(e) What intelligence score will place a child in the 98th percentile? 131

(f) If normal intelligence is defined as scoring in the middle 95% of all test takers, figure out the scores that differentiate normal intelligence from abnormal intelligence. 71–129

12. Major League Baseballs According to major league baseball rules, the ball must weigh between 5 and 5.25 ounces. A factory produces baseballs whose weights are approximately normally distributed, with mean 5.11 ounces and standard deviation 0.062 ounce. *Source:* www.baseball-almanac.com

(a) What proportion of the baseballs produced by this factory are too heavy for use by major league baseball? 0.0119

(b) What proportion of the baseballs produced by this factory are too light for use by major league baseball? 0.0384

(c) What proportion of the baseballs produced by this factory can be used by major league baseball? 0.9497

(d) If 8000 baseballs are ordered, how many baseballs should be manufactured, knowing that some will need to be discarded? 8424

13. America Reads According to a Gallup poll, 46% of Americans 18 years old or older stated that they had read at least six books (fiction and nonfiction) within the past year. You conduct a random sample of 250 Americans 18 years old or older.

(a) Verify that the conditions for using the normal distribution to approximate the binomial distribution are met.

(b) Approximate the probability that exactly 125 read at least six books within the past year. Interpret this result. 0.0213

(c) Approximate the probability that fewer than 120 read at least six books within the past year. Interpret this result. 0.7157

(d) Approximate the probability that at least 140 read at least six books within the past year. Interpret this result. 0.0009

(e) Approximate the probability that between 100 and 120, inclusive, read at least six books within the past year. Interpret this result. 0.7336

In Problems 14 and 15, a normal probability plot of a simple random sample of data from a population whose distribution is unknown was obtained. Given the normal probability plot, is there reason to believe the population is normally distributed?

14. Normal

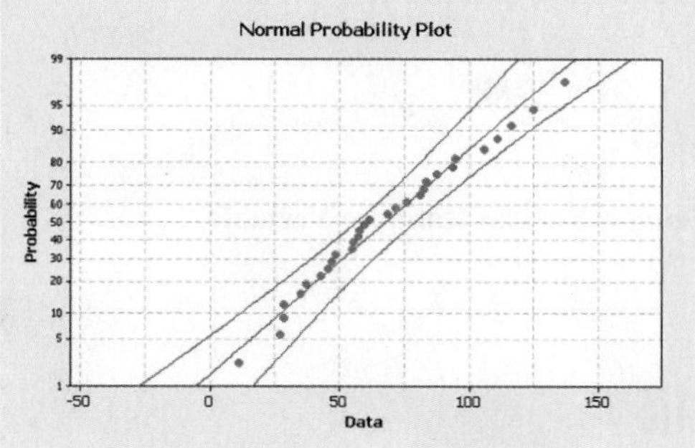

15. Not normal

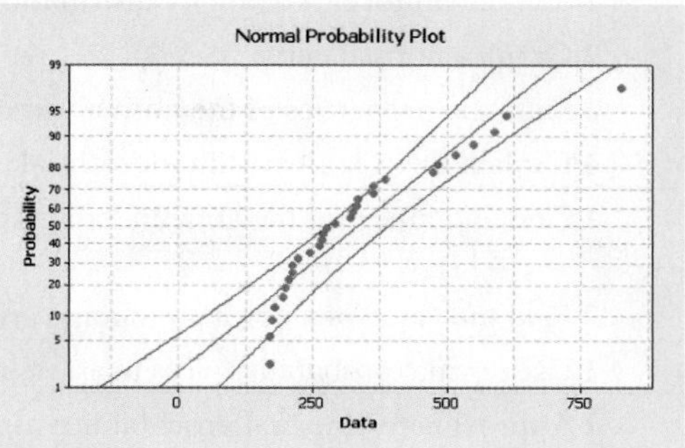

16. Density of Earth In 1798, Henry Cavendish obtained 27 measurements of the density of Earth, using a torsion balance. The following data represent his estimates, given as a multiple of the density of water. Is it reasonable to conclude that the sample data come from a population that is normally distributed? No

5.50	5.57	5.42	5.61	5.53
5.47	4.88	5.62	5.63	4.07
5.29	5.34	5.26	5.44	5.55
5.34	5.30	5.36	5.79	5.29
5.10	5.86	5.58	5.27	5.85
5.65	5.39			

Source: S. M. Stigler. "Do Robust Estimators Work with Real Data?" *Annals of Statistics* 5(1977), 1055–1078.

17. Creative Thinking According to a *USA Today* "Snapshot," 20% of adults surveyed do their most creative thinking while driving. You conduct a survey of 250 adults and find that 30 do their most creative thinking while driving.

(a) Compute the probability that, in a random sample of 250 adults, 30 or fewer do their most creative thinking while driving. 0.0010

(b) Does this result contradict the *USA Today* "Snapshot"? Explain. Yes

18. A continuous random variable X is uniformly distributed with $0 \le X \le 20$.

(a) Draw a graph of the uniform density function.

(b) What is $P(0 \le X \le 5)$? 0.25

(c) What is $P(10 \le X \le 18)$? 0.4

19. List the properties of the normal density curve.

20. Explain how to use a normal probability plot to assess normality.

Problems in the chapter test are labeled by section.objective. For example, 2.3 means Section 2, Objective 3.

CHAPTER TEST

1. Use the figure to answer the questions that follow:

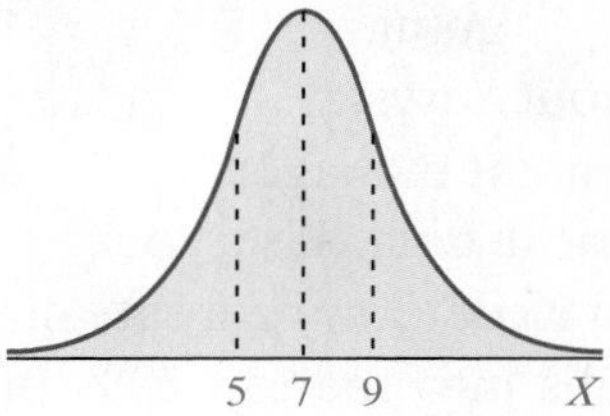

1.3 **(a)** What is μ? 7 1.3 **(b)** What is σ? 2

1.4 **(c)** Suppose that the area under the normal curve to the left of $x = 10$ is 0.9332. Provide two interpretations for this area.

1.4 **(d)** Suppose that the area under the normal curve between $x = 5$ and $x = 8$ is 0.5328. Provide two interpretations for this area.

1.2 **2.** Draw a standard normal curve and shade the area to the right of $z = 2.04$. Then find the area of the shaded region. 0.0207

2.2 **3.** Find the z-scores that separate the middle 88% of the data from the area in the tails of the standard normal distribution. −1.555, 1.555

2.2 **4.** Find the value of $z_{0.04}$. 1.75

1.2 **5. (a)** Draw a normal curve with $\mu = 20$ and $\sigma = 3$.

2.1 **(b)** Shade the region that represents $P(22 \le X \le 27)$ and find the probability. 0.2415

2.1 **6.** Suppose that the talk time on the Apple iPhone is approximately normally distributed with mean 7 hours and standard deviation 0.8 hour.

(a) What proportion of the time will a fully charged iPhone last at least 6 hours? 0.8944

(b) What is the probability a fully charged iPhone will last less than 5 hours? 0.0062

(c) What talk time would represent the cutoff for the top 5% of all talk times? 8.3 hours

(d) Would it be unusual for the phone to last more than 9 hours? Why? Yes

7. The waist circumference of males 20 to 29 years old is approximately normally distributed, with mean 92.5 cm and standard deviation 13.7 cm.

Source: M. A. McDowell, C. D. Fryar, R. Hirsch, and C. L. Ogden. *Anthropometric Reference Data for Children and Adults: U. S. Population, 1999–2002*. Advance data from vital and health statistics: No. 361. Hyattsville, MD: National Center for Health Statistics, 2005.

2.1 **(a)** Use the normal model to determine the proportion of 20- to 29-year-old males whose waist circumference is less than 100 cm. 0.7088

2.1 **(b)** What is the probability that a randomly selected 20- to 29-year-old male has a waist circumference between 80 and 100 cm? 0.5274

2.2 **(c)** Determine the waist circumferences that represent the middle 90% of all waist circumferences. 70 to 115 cm

2.2 **(d)** Determine the waist circumference that is at the 10th percentile. 75 cm

2.2 **8.** Suppose the scores earned on Professor McArthur's third statistics exam are normally distributed with mean 64 and standard deviation 8. Professor McArthur wants to curve the exam scores as follows: The top 6% get an A, the next 14% get a B, the middle 60% get a C, the bottom 6% fail, and the rest earn a D. Any student who can determine these cut-offs earns 5 bonus points. Determine the cut-offs for Professor McArthur.

4.1 **9.** In a poll conducted by the Gallup organization, 16% of adult, employed Americans were dissatisfied with the amount of their vacation time. You conduct a survey of 500 adult, employed Americans.

(a) Approximate the probability that exactly 100 are dissatisfied with their amount of vacation time. 0.0025

(b) Approximate the probability that less than 60 are dissatisfied with the amount of their vacation time. 0.0062

8. A: ≥ 76.4; B: 70.7–76.3; C: 57.3–70.6; D: 51.6–57.2; F: < 51.6

3.1 **10.** Jane obtained a random sample of 15 college students and asked how many hours they studied last week. Is it reasonable to believe that hours studied is normally distributed based on the following normal probability plot? No: not normal

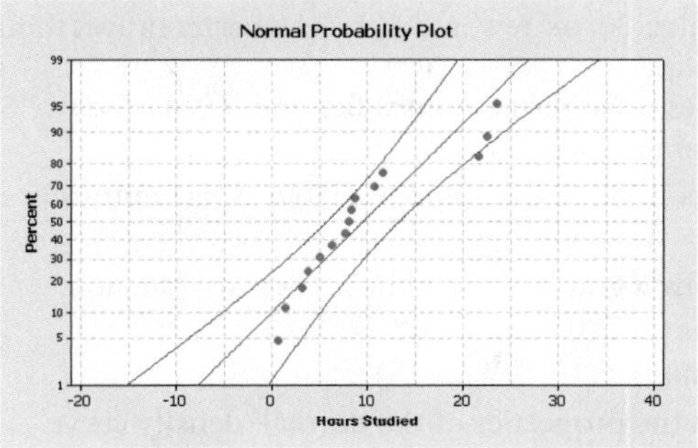

1.1 **11.** A continuous random variable X is uniformly distributed with $10 \le X \le 50$.

(a) Draw a graph of the uniform density function.

(b) What is $P(20 \le X \le 30)$? 0.25

(c) What is $P(X < 15)$? 0.125

Making an Informed Decision

Stock Picking

You are interested in modeling the behavior of stocks. In particular, you want to build a model that describes the rate of return on a basket of stocks, such as large capitalization companies.

(a) Go to a Web site that provides historical rates of return on a certain basket of stocks, such as www.morningstar.com. Decide on a certain sector of the economy you would like to model, such as consumer goods or energy. Choose the largest 100 companies in this sector and determine the time frame for which you want to build your model. For example, you might decide to build a model for the 1-year rate of return on the stock.

(b) Enter your data into statistical software and construct a relative frequency histogram. Does the data appear bell shaped? Do you think the normal model would be a good model to describe the rate of return for the sector you have chosen? Why or why not?

(c) Regardless of your answer to part (b), build a normal model by determining the mean and standard deviation for the rate of return. Draw the normal model on the relative frequency histogram from part (b).

(d) One purpose of financial models is to identify quality investments going forward. Without a crystal ball, all investment managers have is historical data. Use your historical data to determine a rate of return that falls into the top 20% of all companies within the sector. Use this rate of return as a criterion for choosing a company to invest in.

(e) Conduct further research on the stock you wish to invest in. For example, have the company's earnings been growing for the past 5 years? What is the company's market share? Does the company pay a dividend? If so, for how long has the company paid a dividend? Has the dividend been growing consistently?

(f) Write a report that lays out your recommendation regarding the particular stock you have researched. Perhaps include a few other models that might help to decide whether the company is a solid investment.

The Chapter 7 Case Study is located on the CD that accompanies this text.

PART

4 Inference: From Samples to Population

In Chapter 1, we presented the following process of statistics:

Step 1: Identify the research objective.
Step 2: Collect the data needed to answer the question(s) posed in Step 1.
Step 3: Describe the data.
Step 4: Perform inference.

The methods for conducting Steps 1 and 2 were discussed in Chapter 1. The methods for conducting Step 3 were discussed in Chapters 2 through 4. We took a break from the statistical process in Chapters 5 through 7 so that we could develop skills that allow us to tackle Step 4.

If the information (data) collected is from the entire population, we can use the summaries obtained in Step 3 to draw conclusions about the population being studied and the statistical process is over.

However, it is often difficult or impossible to gain access to populations, so the information obtained in Step 2 is often sample data. The sample data are used to make inferences about the population. For example, we might compute a sample mean from the data collected in Step 2 and use this information to draw conclusions regarding the population mean. The last part of this text discusses how sample data are used to draw conclusions about populations.

8 Sampling Distributions

OUTLINE

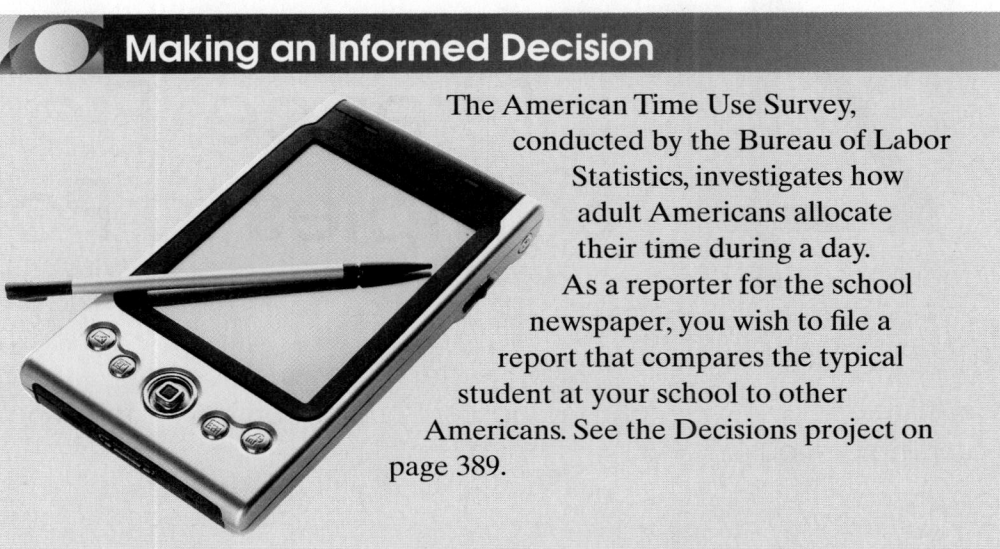

Making an Informed Decision

The American Time Use Survey, conducted by the Bureau of Labor Statistics, investigates how adult Americans allocate their time during a day.

As a reporter for the school newspaper, you wish to file a report that compares the typical student at your school to other Americans. See the Decisions project on page 389.

PUTTING IT TOGETHER

In Chapters 6 and 7, we learned about random variables and their probability distributions. A random variable is a numerical measure of the outcome to a probability experiment. A probability distribution provides a way to assign probabilities to the possible values of the random variable. For discrete random variables, we discussed the binomial probability distribution and the Poisson probability distribution. We assigned probabilities using a formula. For continuous random variables, we discussed the normal probability distribution. To compute probabilities for a normal random variable, we found the area under a normal density curve.

In this chapter, we continue our discussion of probability distributions where statistics, such as $\bar{x}$, will be the random variable. Statistics are random variables because the value of a statistic varies from sample to sample. For this reason, statistics have probability distributions associated with them. For example, there is a probability distribution for the sample mean, sample proportion, and so on. We use probability distributions to make probability statements regarding the statistic. So this chapter discusses the shape, center, and spread of statistics such as $\bar{x}$.

8.1 DISTRIBUTION OF THE SAMPLE MEAN

Preparing for This Section Before getting started, review the following:

- Simple random sampling (Section 1.3, pp. 22–26)
- The mean (Section 3.1, pp. 117–119)
- The standard deviation (Section 3.2, pp. 132–136)
- Applications of the normal distribution (Section 7.2, pp. 338–345)

OBJECTIVES

1 Describe the distribution of the sample mean: normal population

2 Describe the distribution of the sample mean: nonnormal population

Note to Instructor

If you like, you can print out and distribute the Preparing for This Section quiz located in the Instructor's Resource Center. The purpose of the quiz is to verify that the students have the prerequisite knowledge for the section.

Suppose the government wanted to determine the mean income of all U.S. households. One approach the government could take is to literally survey each U.S. household to determine the population mean, μ. This would be a very expensive and time-consuming survey!

A second approach the government could (and does) take is to survey a random sample of U.S. households and use the results to estimate the mean household income. This is done through the American Community Survey, which is administered to approximately 250,000 randomly selected households each month. Among the many questions on the survey, respondents are asked to report the income of each individual in the household. From this information, the federal government obtains a sample mean household income for U.S. households. For example, in 2009 the mean annual household income in the United States was estimated to be $\bar{x} = \$67{,}976$. The government might infer from this survey that the mean annual household income of *all* U.S. households in 2009 was $\mu = \$67{,}976$.

The households in the American Community Survey were determined by chance (random sampling). A second random sample of households would likely lead to a different sample mean, such as $\bar{x} = \$67{,}731$, and a third random sample of households would likely lead to a third sample mean, such as $\bar{x} = \$67{,}978$. Because the households selected will vary from sample to sample, the sample mean of household income will also vary from sample to sample. For this reason, the sample mean $\bar{x}$ is a random variable, so it has a probability distribution. Our goal in this section is to describe the distribution of the sample mean. Remember, when we describe a distribution, we do so in terms of its shape, center, and spread.

DEFINITIONS

The **sampling distribution** of a statistic is a probability distribution for all possible values of the statistic computed from a sample of size *n*.

The **sampling distribution of the sample mean** $\bar{x}$ is the probability distribution of all possible values of the random variable $\bar{x}$ computed from a sample of size *n* from a population with mean μ and standard deviation σ.

Note to Instructor

Consider assigning the "Creating a Sampling Distribution for the Mean" activity from the Student Activity Workbook.

In Other Words

If the number of individuals in a population is a positive integer, we say the population is finite. Otherwise, the population is infinite.

The idea behind obtaining the sampling distribution of the mean is as follows:

Step 1: Obtain a simple random sample of size *n*.

Step 2: Compute the sample mean.

Step 3: Assuming that we are sampling from a finite population, repeat Steps 1 and 2 until all distinct simple random samples of size *n* have been obtained.

Note: Once a particular sample is obtained, it cannot be obtained a second time.

1 Describe the Distribution of the Sample Mean: Normal Population

Note to Instructor

Consider assigning the "Simulating IQ Scores" activity from the Student Activity Workbook.

The probability distribution of the sample mean is determined from statistical theory. We will use simulation to help justify the result that statistical theory provides. We consider two possibilities. In the first case (Examples 1, 2, and 3), we sample from a population that is normally distributed. In the second case (Examples 4 and 5), we sample from a population that is not normally distributed.

EXAMPLE 1 Sampling Distribution of the Sample Mean: Normal Population

Note to Instructor

You could illustrate the sampling distribution of the sample mean using the sampling distributions applet. See the Student Activity Workbook.

Using Technology

We are using MINITAB's Random Data command under the Calc menu to generate these data. Select Normal . . . from the Random Data menu.

Problem An intelligence quotient, or IQ, is a measurement of intelligence derived from a standardized test, such as the Stanford Binet IQ test. Scores on this test are normally distributed with a mean score of 100 and a standard deviation of 15. What is the sampling distribution of the sample mean for a sample of size $n = 9$?

Approach The problem asks us to determine the shape, center, and spread of the distribution of the sample mean. Remember, the sampling distribution of the sample mean would be the distribution of *all* possible sample means of size $n = 9$. To get a sense of this distribution, use MINITAB to simulate obtaining 1000 samples of size $n = 9$ by randomly generating 1000 rows of IQs over 9 columns. Each row represents a random sample of size 9. For each of the 1000 samples (the 1000 rows), we determine the mean IQ score. Draw a histogram to gauge the shape of the distribution of the sample mean, determine the mean of the 1000 sample means to approximate the mean of the sampling distribution, and determine the standard deviation of the 1000 sample means to approximate the standard deviation of the sampling distribution.

Solution Figure 1 shows partial output from MINITAB. Row 1 contains the first sample, where the IQ scores of the nine individuals are 90, 74, 95, 88, 91, 91, 102, 91, and 96. The mean of these nine IQ scores is 90.9. Row 2 represents a second sample with nine different IQ scores; row 3 represents a third sample, and so on. Column C10 (xbar) lists the sample means for each of the different samples.

Figure 1

Worksheet 1 ***

↓	C1	C2	C3	C4	C5	C6	C7	C8	C9	C10 xbar	
Sample 1 — 1	90	74	95	88	91	91	102	91	96	90.9	$\bar{x} = 90.9$
Sample 2 — 2	114	86	96	82	80	68	93	136	111	96.2	$\bar{x} = 96.2$
3	89	89	86	98	96	96	89	99	107	94.3	
4	87	94	89	116	92	124	115	83	111	101.3	
5	107	103	86	86	109	104	94	82	110	97.8	
6	113	84	101	89	92	71	89	86	108	92.7	
7	75	116	107	118	112	86	104	97	106	102.4	
8	118	117	81	96	86	94	109	96	104	100.1	
9	91	91	79	80	109	89	97	81	99	90.6	
10	112	98	115	73	95	104	76	95	87	95.0	
11	103	92	100	75	95	108	105	125	62	96.1	
12	75	124	101	113	91	85	121	115	85	101.2	
13	104	103	81	134	111	108	101	88	115	105.1	
14	121	85	118	88	96	84	103	77	102	97.1	
15	119	84	119	80	99	98	88	88	89	95.9	
16	71	86	94	101	95	84	124	105	83	93.7	

Figure 2(a) shows the distribution of the population, and Figure 2(b) shows the distribution of the sample means from column C10 (using MINITAB). The shape of the distribution of the population is normal. The histogram in Figure 2(b) shows that the shape of the distribution of the sample means is also normal. In addition, we notice that the center of the distribution of the sample means is the same as the center of the distribution of the population, but the spread of the distribution of the sample means is smaller than the spread of the distribution of the population. In fact, the mean of the 1000 sample means is 99.92, which is close to the population mean, 100; the standard deviation of the sample means is 4.88, which is less than the population standard deviation, 15.

Figure 2

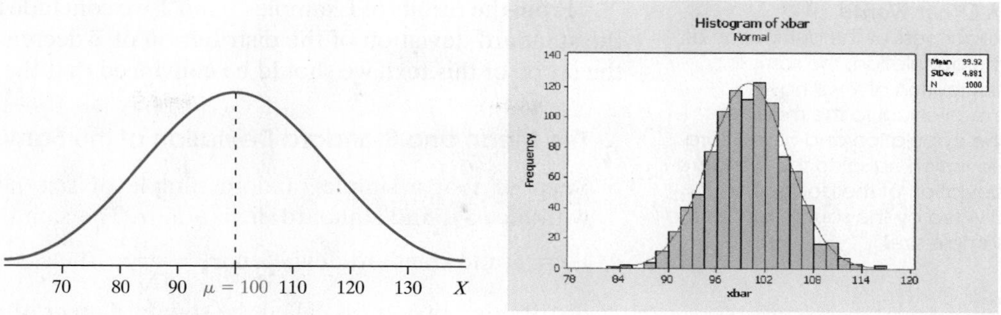

(a) (b)

We draw the following conclusions:

- **Shape:** The shape of the distribution of the sample mean is normal.
- **Center:** The mean of the distribution of the sample mean equals the mean of the population, 100.
- **Spread:** The standard deviation of the sample mean is less than the standard deviation of the population.

Why is the standard deviation of the sample mean less than the standard deviation of the population? Consider that, if we randomly select any one individual, there is about a 68% chance that the individual's IQ score is between 85 and 115 (that is, within 1 standard deviation of the mean). If we had a sample of 9 individuals; we would not expect as much spread in the sample as there is for a single individual, since individuals with lower IQs will offset individuals in the sample with higher IQs, resulting in a sample mean closer to the expected value of 100. Look back at Figure 1. In the first sample (row 1), the low-IQ individual (IQ = 74) is offset by the higher-IQ individual (IQ = 102), which is why the sample mean is closer to 100. In the second sample (row 2), the low-IQ individual (IQ = 68) is offset by the higher-IQ individual (IQ = 136), so the sample mean of the second sample is closer to 100. Therefore, the spread in the distribution of sample means should be less than the spread in the population from which the sample is drawn.

Based on this, what role do you think n, the sample size, plays in the standard deviation of the distribution of the sample mean?

EXAMPLE 2 The Impact of Sample Size on Sampling Variability

Problem Repeat the problem in Example 1 with a sample of size $n = 25$.

Approach Use the approach presented in Example 1, but let $n = 25$ instead of $n = 9$.

Solution Figure 3 shows the histogram of the sample means. Notice that the sample means appear to be normally distributed with the center at 100. The histogram in Figure 3 shows less dispersion than the histogram in Figure 2(b). This implies that the distribution of $\bar{x}$ with $n = 25$ has less variability than the distribution of $\bar{x}$ with $n = 9$. In fact, the mean of the 1000 sample means is 99.99, and the standard deviation is 3.00.

Figure 3

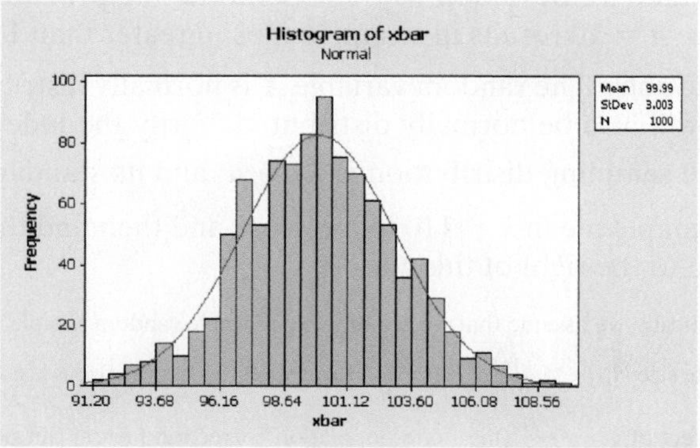

Note to Instructor

Consider assigning the "Analyzing the Variability in Sample Means" activity from the Student Activity Workbook.

In Other Words
Regardless of the distribution of the population, the sampling distribution of $\bar{x}$ will have a mean equal to the mean of the population and a standard deviation equal to the standard deviation of the population divided by the square root of the sample size!

CAUTION

It is important that two assumptions are satisfied with regard to sampling from a population.
1. The sample must be a random sample.
2. The sampled values must be independent. When sampling without replacement (which is the case when obtaining simple random samples), we shall verify this assumption, by checking that the size is less than 5% of the population size ($n < 0.05N$).

Now Work Problem 9

From the results of Examples 1 and 2, we conclude that, as the sample size n increases, the standard deviation of the distribution of $\bar{x}$ decreases. Although the proof is beyond the scope of this text, we should be convinced that the following result is reasonable.

The Mean and Standard Deviation of the Sampling Distribution of $\bar{x}$

Suppose that a simple random sample of size n is drawn from a population* with mean μ and standard deviation σ. The sampling distribution of $\bar{x}$ has mean $\mu_{\bar{x}} = \mu$ and standard deviation $\sigma_{\bar{x}} = \frac{\sigma}{\sqrt{n}}$. The standard deviation of the sampling distribution of $\bar{x}$, $\sigma_{\bar{x}}$, is called the **standard error of the mean.**

For the population presented in Example 1, if we draw a simple random sample of size $n = 9$, the sampling distribution $\bar{x}$ will have mean $\mu_{\bar{x}} = 100$ and standard deviation

$$\sigma_{\bar{x}} = \frac{\sigma}{\sqrt{n}} = \frac{15}{\sqrt{9}} = 5$$

This standard error of the mean is close to the approximate standard error of 4.88 found in our simulation in Example 1.

In Example 2, where the simple random sample was of size $n = 25$, the sampling distribution of $\bar{x}$ will have mean $\mu_{\bar{x}} = 100$ and standard deviation

$$\sigma_{\bar{x}} = \frac{\sigma}{\sqrt{n}} = \frac{15}{\sqrt{25}} = 3$$

This standard error of the mean equals the approximate standard error found in our simulation in Example 2.

Now that we can find the mean and standard deviation for any sampling distribution of $\bar{x}$, we can concentrate on the shape of the distribution. Refer back to Figures 2(b) and 3 from Examples 1 and 2: both histograms appear to be normal. Recall that the population from which the sample was drawn was normal. This leads us to believe that, if the population is normal, then the distribution of the sample mean is also normal.

Figure 4

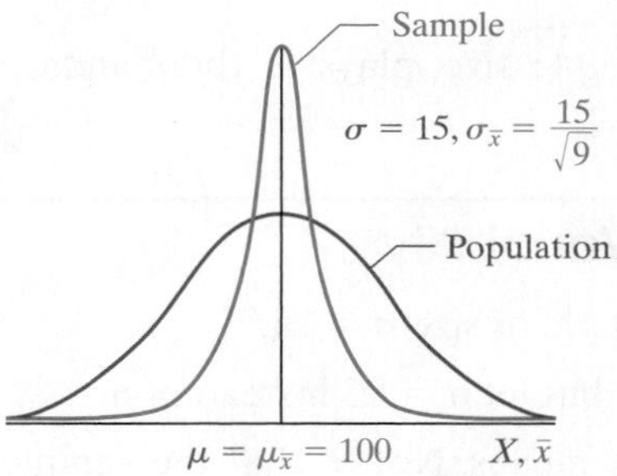

The Shape of the Sampling Distribution of $\bar{x}$ If X Is Normal

If a random variable X is normally distributed, the distribution of the sample mean, $\bar{x}$, is normally distributed.

For example, the IQ scores of individuals are modeled by a normal random variable with mean $\mu = 100$ and standard deviation $\sigma = 15$. The distribution of the sample mean, $\bar{x}$, the mean IQ of a simple random sample of $n = 9$ individuals, is normal, with mean $\mu_{\bar{x}} = 100$ and standard deviation $\sigma_{\bar{x}} = \frac{15}{\sqrt{9}}$. See Figure 4.

EXAMPLE 3 Describing the Distribution of the Sample Mean

Problem The IQ, X, of humans is approximately normally distributed with mean $\mu = 100$ and standard deviation $\sigma = 15$. Compute the probability that a simple random sample of size $n = 10$ results in a sample mean greater than 110. That is, compute $P(\bar{x} > 110)$.

Approach The random variable X is normally distributed, so the sampling distribution of $\bar{x}$ will also be normally distributed. Verify the independence requirement. The mean of the sampling distribution is $\mu_{\bar{x}} = \mu$, and its standard deviation is $\sigma_{\bar{x}} = \frac{\sigma}{\sqrt{n}}$. Convert the sample mean $\bar{x} = 110$ to a z-score and then find the area under the standard normal curve to the right of this z-score.

*Technically, we assume that we are drawing a simple random sample from an infinite population. For populations of finite size N, $\sigma_{\bar{x}} = \sqrt{\frac{N-n}{N-1}} \cdot \frac{\sigma}{\sqrt{n}}$. However, if the sample size is less than 5% of the population size ($n < 0.05N$), the effect of $\sqrt{\frac{N-n}{N-1}}$ (the finite population correction factor) can be ignored without significantly affecting the results.

Figure 5

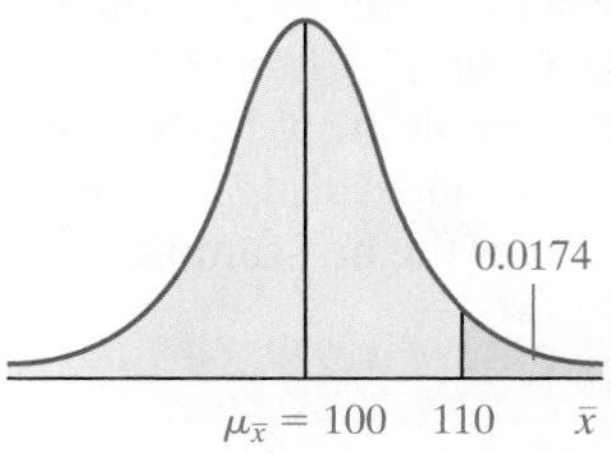

Solution The sample mean is normally distributed, with mean $\mu_{\bar{x}} = 100$ and standard deviation $\sigma_{\bar{x}} = \frac{\sigma}{\sqrt{n}} = \frac{15}{\sqrt{10}} = 4.743$. The sample size is definitely less than 5% of the population size.

Figure 5 displays the normal curve with the area we wish to compute shaded. To find the area by hand, we convert $\bar{x} = 110$ to a z-score and obtain

$$z = \frac{\bar{x} - \mu_{\bar{x}}}{\sigma_{\bar{x}}} = \frac{\bar{x} - \mu_{\bar{x}}}{\frac{\sigma}{\sqrt{n}}} = \frac{110 - 100}{\frac{15}{\sqrt{10}}} = 2.11$$

The area to the right of $z = 2.11$ is $1 - 0.9826 = 0.0174$.

Using technology, we find the area to the right of $\bar{x} = 110$ is 0.0175.

Note to Instructor
Emphasize the interpretation of the probabilities as a prelude to *P*-values.

Interpretation The probability of obtaining a sample mean IQ greater than 110 from a population whose mean is 100 is approximately 0.02. That is, $P(\bar{x} > 110) = 0.0174$ (or 0.0175 using technology). If we take 100 simple random samples of $n = 10$ individuals from this population and if the population mean is 100, about 2 of the samples will result in a mean IQ that is greater than 110.

Now Work Problem 19

2 Describe the Distribution of the Sample Mean: Nonnormal Population

Now we explore the distribution of the sample mean assuming the population from which the sample is drawn is not normal. Again we use simulation.

EXAMPLE 4 Sampling from a Population That Is Not Normal

Problem The data in Table 1 represent the probability distribution of the number of people living in households in the United States. Figure 6 shows a histogram of the data. From the data in Table 1, we determine the mean and standard deviation number of people living in households in the United States to be $\mu = 2.9$ and $\sigma = 1.48$.

Clearly, the distribution is not normal. Approximate the sampling distribution of the sample mean $\bar{x}$ by obtaining, through simulation, 1000 samples of size (a) $n = 4$, (b) $n = 10$, and (c) $n = 30$ from the population.

TABLE 1

Number in Household	Proportion
1	0.147
2	0.361
3	0.187
4	0.168
5	0.083
6	0.034
7	0.012
8	0.004
9	0.002
10	0.002

Source: General Social Survey

Figure 6

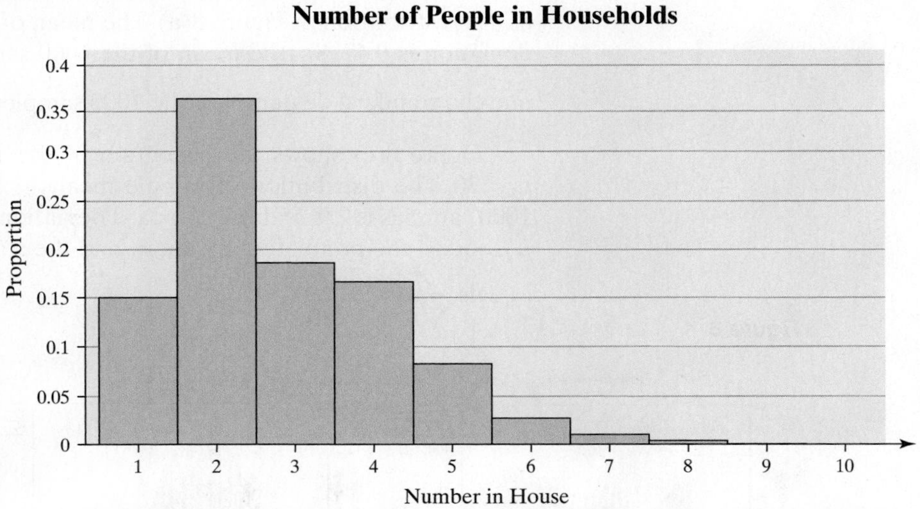

Approach Use MINITAB to obtain 1000 random samples of size $n = 4$ from the population. This simulates going to 4 households 1000 times and determining the number of people living in the household. Next, compute the mean of each of the 1000 random samples. Finally, draw a histogram, determine the mean, and determine the standard deviation of the 1000 sample means. Repeat this for samples of size $n = 10$ and $n = 30$.

Solution Figure 7 shows partial output from MINITAB for random samples of size $n = 4$. Columns 1 and 2 represent the probability distribution. Each row in Columns 3 through 6 lists the number of individuals in the household for each sample. Column 7 (xbar) lists the sample mean for each sample (each row). For example, in the first sample (row 1), there are 4 individuals in the first house surveyed, and 2 individuals in the second, third, and fourth houses surveyed. The mean number of individuals in the household for the first sample is 2.5.

Figure 7

Worksheet 2 ***

↓	C1	C2	C3	C4	C5	C6	C7
	Number	Proportion					xbar
1	1	0.147	4	2	2	2	2.50
2	2	0.361	1	3	4	2	2.50
3	3	0.187	4	4	2	4	3.50
4	4	0.168	5	4	2	6	4.25
5	5	0.083	7	2	4	4	4.25
6	6	0.034	2	2	6	2	3.00
7	7	0.012	4	8	3	1	4.00
8	8	0.004	3	2	2	2	2.25
9	9	0.002	2	2	4	2	2.50
10	10	0.002	2	2	4	1	2.25
11			2	1	7	2	3.00
12			3	7	2	1	3.25
13			5	3	2	3	3.25
14			1	5	2	2	2.50
15			1	1	4	7	3.25

Figure 8(a) shows the histogram of the 1000 sample means for a sample of size $n = 4$. The distribution of sample means is skewed right (just like the parent population, but not as strongly). The mean of the 1000 samples is 2.9, and the standard deviation is 0.73. So, the mean of the 1000 samples, $\mu_{\bar{x}}$, equals the population mean μ, and the standard deviation of the 1000 samples, $\sigma_{\bar{x}}$, is close to $\dfrac{\sigma}{\sqrt{n}} = \dfrac{1.48}{\sqrt{4}} = 0.74$.

Figure 8(b) shows the histogram of the 1000 sample means for a sample of size $n = 10$. The distribution of these sample means is also skewed right, but not as skewed as the distribution in Figure 8(a). The mean of the 1000 samples is 2.9, and the standard deviation is 0.47. So, the mean of the 1000 samples, $\mu_{\bar{x}}$ equals the population mean, μ, and the standard deviation of the 1000 samples, $\sigma_{\bar{x}}$, equals $\dfrac{\sigma}{\sqrt{n}} = \dfrac{1.48}{\sqrt{10}} = 0.47$.

Figure 8(c) shows the histogram of the 1000 sample means for a sample of size $n = 30$. The distribution of sample means is approximately normal! The mean of the 1000 samples is 2.9, and the standard deviation is 0.27. So, the mean of the 1000 samples, $\mu_{\bar{x}}$, equals the population mean, μ, and the standard deviation of the 1000 samples, $\sigma_{\bar{x}}$, equals $\dfrac{\sigma}{\sqrt{n}} = \dfrac{1.48}{\sqrt{30}} = 0.27$.

Figure 8

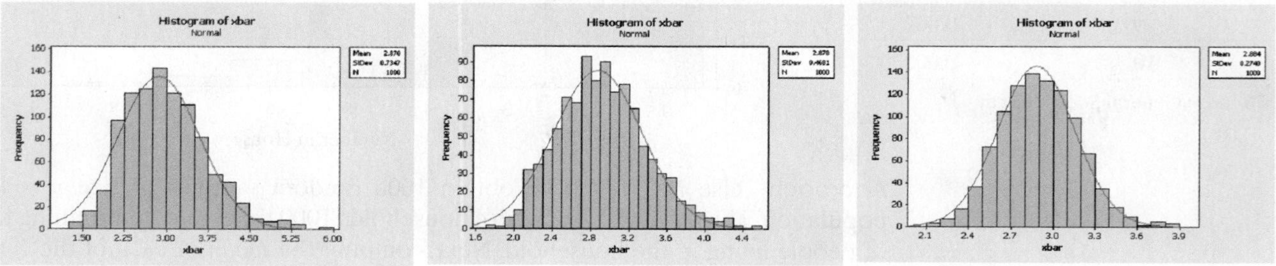

(a) (b) (c)

Note to Instructor

Technically, the parent population must have a finite variance.

There are two key concepts to understand in Example 4.

1. The mean of the sampling distribution of the sample mean is equal to the mean of the underlying population, and the standard deviation of the sampling distribution of the sample mean is $\frac{\sigma}{\sqrt{n}}$, regardless of the size of the sample.
2. The shape of the distribution of the sample mean becomes approximately normal as the sample size n increases, regardless of the shape of the underlying population.

We formally state point 2 as the *Central Limit Theorem.*

In Other Words

For any population, regardless of its shape, as the sample size increases, the shape of the distribution of the sample mean becomes more "normal."

The Central Limit Theorem

Regardless of the shape of the underlying population, the sampling distribution of $\bar{x}$ becomes approximately normal as the sample size, n, increases.

CAUTION

The Central Limit Theorem only has to do with the shape of the distribution of $\bar{x}$, not the center or spread. Regardless of the size of the sample, $\mu_{\bar{x}} = \mu$ and $\sigma_{\bar{x}} = \frac{\sigma}{\sqrt{n}}$.

How large does the sample size need to be before we can say that the sampling distribution of $\bar{x}$ is approximately normal? The answer depends on the shape of the distribution of the underlying population. Distributions that are highly skewed will require a larger sample size for the distribution of $\bar{x}$ to become approximately normal.

For example, the right-skewed distribution in Example 4 required a sample size of about 30 before the distribution of the sample mean became approximately normal. However, Figure 9(a) shows a uniform distribution for $0 \le X \le 10$. Figure 9(b) shows the distribution of the sample mean obtained via simulation using StatCrunch for $n = 4$. Even for samples as small as $n = 4$, the distribution of the sample mean is approximately normal.

Figure 9

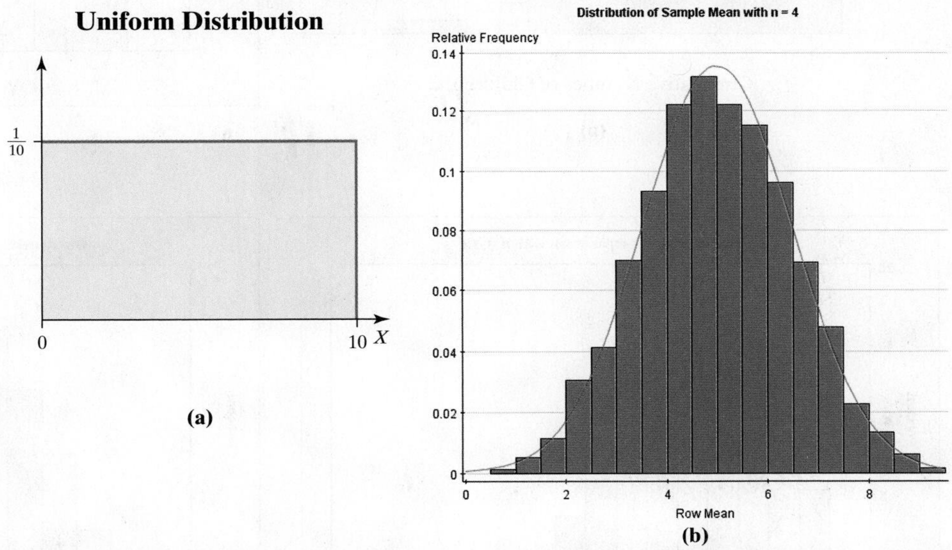

Historical Note

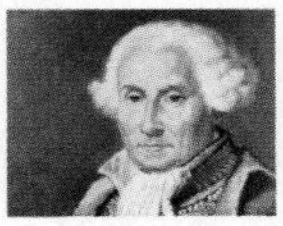

Pierre Simon Laplace was born on March 23, 1749, in Normandy, France. At age 16, Laplace attended Caen University, where he studied theology. While there, his mathematical talents were discovered, which led him to Paris, where he obtained a job as professor of mathematics at the École Militaire. In 1773, Laplace was elected to the Académie des Sciences. Laplace was not humble. It is reported that, in 1780, he stated that he was the best mathematician in Paris. In 1799, Laplace published the first two volumes of *Méchanique céleste*, in which he discussed methods for calculating the motion of the planets. On April 9, 1810, Laplace presented the Central Limit Theorem to the Academy.

Table 2 shows the distribution of the cumulative number of children for 50- to 54-year-old mothers who had a live birth in 2008.

TABLE 2

x (number of children)	P(x)
1	0.329
2	0.252
3	0.161
4	0.103
5	0.058
6	0.034
7	0.016
8	0.047

Source: National Vital Statistics Report

Figure 10(a) shows the probability histogram for this distribution. Figure 10(b) shows the distribution of the sample mean for a random sample of $n = 3$ mothers from MINITAB. Figure 10(c) shows the distribution of the sample mean for a random sample of $n = 12$ mothers, and Figure 10(d) shows the distribution of the sample mean for a random sample of $n = 20$ mothers, also from MINITAB. In this instance, the distribution of the sample mean is close to normal for $n = 20$.

Figure 10

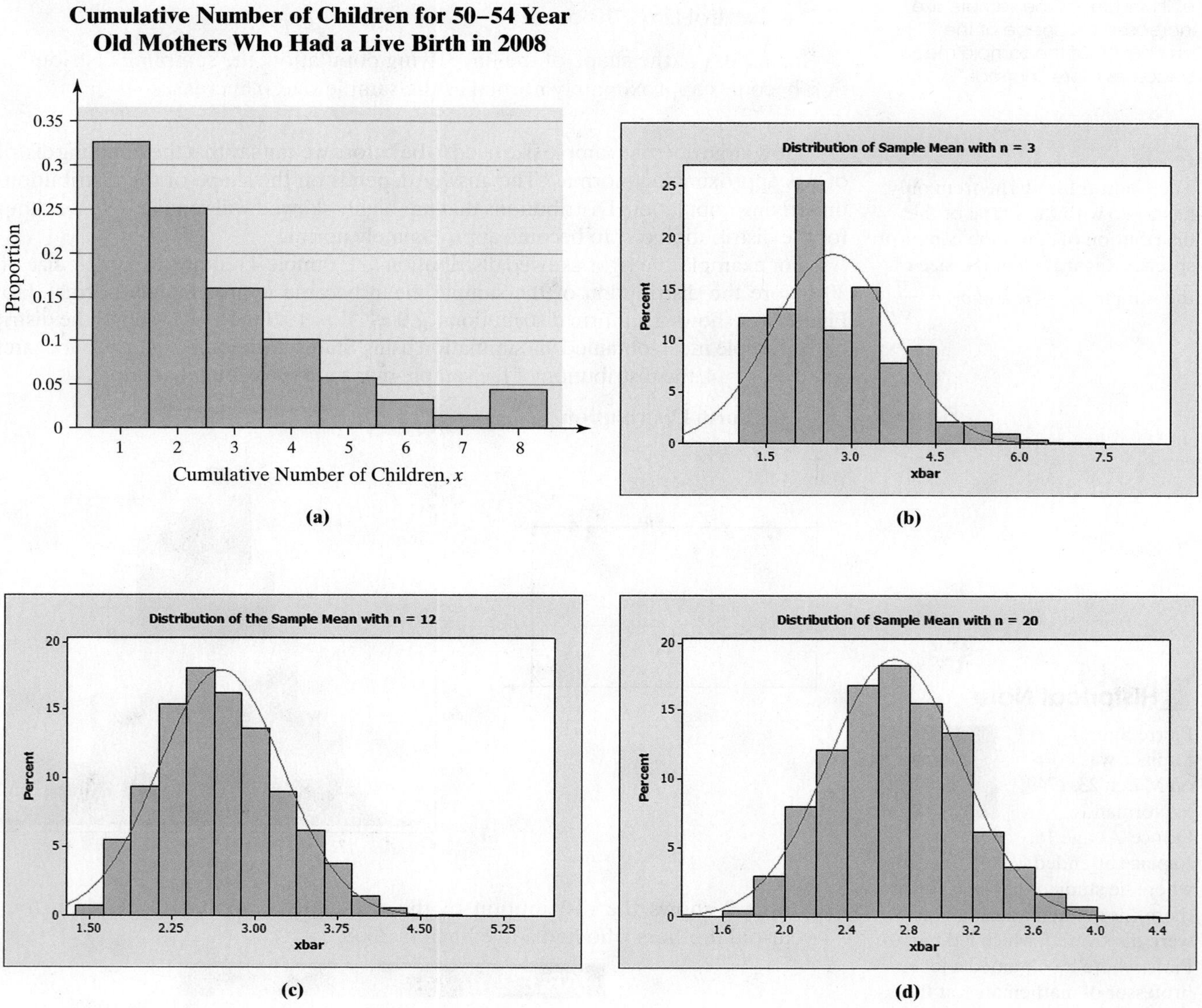

Note to Instructor

While admittedly conservative, requiring $n \geq 30$ for nonnormal distributions provides a clear-cut decision rule for students to use.

The results of Example 4 and Figures 9 and 10 confirm that the shape of the distribution of the population dictates the size of the sample required for the distribution of the sample mean to be normal. The more skewed the distribution of the population is, the larger the sample size needed to invoke the Central Limit Theorem. We will err on the side of caution and say that, if the distribution of the population is unknown or not normal, then the distribution of the sample mean is approximately normal provided that the sample size is greater than or equal to 30.

EXAMPLE 5 Weight Gain During Pregnancy

Problem The mean weight gain during pregnancy is 30 pounds, with a standard deviation of 12.9 pounds. Weight gain during pregnancy is skewed right. An obstetrician obtains a random sample of 35 low-income patients and determines their mean weight gain during pregnancy was 36.2 pounds. Does this result suggest anything unusual?

Approach We want to know whether the sample mean obtained is unusual. Therefore, determine the likelihood of obtaining a sample mean of 36.2 pounds or higher (if a 36.2 pound weight gain is unusual, certainly any weight gain above 36.2 pounds is also unusual). Assume that the patients come from the population whose mean weight gain is 30 pounds. Verify the independence assumption. Use the normal model to obtain the probability since the sample size is large enough to use the Central Limit Theorem. Determine the area under the normal curve to the right of 36.2 pounds with $\mu_{\bar{x}} = \mu = 30$ and $\sigma_{\bar{x}} = \frac{\sigma}{\sqrt{n}} = \frac{12.9}{\sqrt{35}}$.

Figure 11

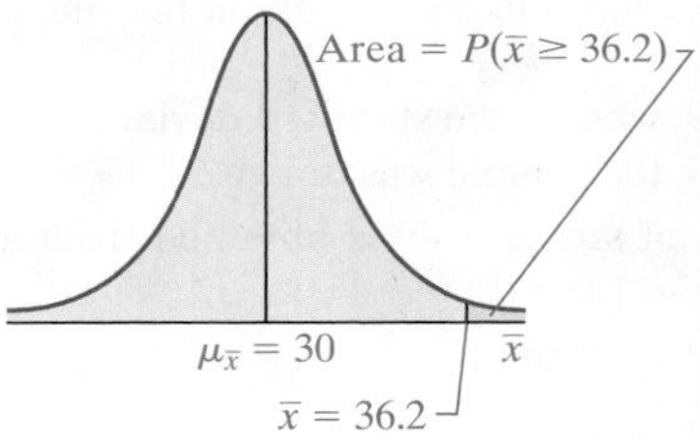

Solution It seems reasonable there are at least 1000 low-income pregnant women in the population. So the sample size is less than 5% of the population size. The probability is represented by the area under the normal curve to the right of 36.2. See Figure 11.

To find $P(\bar{x} \geq 36.2)$ by hand, we convert the sample mean $\bar{x} = 36.2$ to a z-score.

$$z = \frac{\bar{x} - \mu_{\bar{x}}}{\sigma_{\bar{x}}} = \frac{36.2 - 30}{\frac{12.9}{\sqrt{35}}} = 2.84$$

The area under the standard normal curve to the left of $z = 2.84$ is 0.9977. So the area to the right is 0.0023. Therefore, $P(\bar{x} \geq 36.2) = 0.0023$.

If we use technology to find the area to the right of $\bar{x} = 36.2$, we obtain 0.0022.

Interpretation If the population from which this sample is drawn has a mean weight gain of 30 pounds, the probability that a random sample of 35 women has a sample mean weight gain of 36.2 pounds (or more) is approximately 0.002. This means that about 2 samples in 1000 will result in a sample mean of 36.2 pounds or higher if the population mean is 30 pounds. We can conclude one of two things based on this result:

1. The mean weight gain for low-income patients is 30 pounds, and we happened to select women who, on average, gained more weight.

2. The mean weight gain for low-income patients is more than 30 pounds.

We are inclined to accept the second explanation over the first since our sample was obtained randomly. Therefore, the obstetrician should be concerned. Perhaps she should look at the diets and/or lifestyles of low-income patients while they are pregnant.

Now Work Problem 25

SUMMARY: SHAPE, CENTER, AND SPREAD OF THE DISTRIBUTION OF $\bar{x}$

	Distribution of the Sample Mean		
Shape, Center, and Spread of the Population	**Shape**	**Center**	**Spread**
Population is normal with mean μ and standard deviation σ	Regardless of the sample size n, the shape of the distribution of the sample mean is normal	$\mu_{\bar{x}} = \mu$	$\sigma_{\bar{x}} = \frac{\sigma}{\sqrt{n}}$
Population is not normal with mean μ and standard deviation σ	As the sample size n increases, the distribution of the sample mean becomes approximately normal	$\mu_{\bar{x}} = \mu$	$\sigma_{\bar{x}} = \frac{\sigma}{\sqrt{n}}$

12. $\mu_{\bar{x}} = 27, \sigma_{\bar{x}} = \frac{6}{\sqrt{15}} \approx 1.549$ 17. (a) Normal; normal with $\mu_{\bar{x}} = 64$ and $\sigma_{\bar{x}} = \frac{17}{\sqrt{12}}$

8.1 ASSESS YOUR UNDERSTANDING

VOCABULARY AND SKILL BUILDING

1. The _______ of the sample mean, $\bar{x}$, is the probability distribution of all possible values of the random variable $\bar{x}$ computed from a sample of size n from a population with mean μ and standard deviation σ. sampling distribution

2. Suppose a simple random sample of size n is drawn from a large population with mean μ and standard deviation σ. The sampling distribution of $\bar{x}$ has mean $\mu_{\bar{x}}$ = ___μ___ and standard deviation $\sigma_{\bar{x}}$ = _______. $\sigma/\sqrt{n}$

3. The standard deviation of the sampling distribution of $\bar{x}$, $\sigma_{\bar{x}}$, is called the _______ _______ of the_______. standard error, mean

4. *True or False*: The distribution of the sample mean, $\bar{x}$, will be normally distributed if the sample is obtained from a population that is normally distributed, regardless of the sample size. True 15. (a) Approximately normal with $\mu_{\bar{x}} = 80$ and $\sigma_{\bar{x}} = 2$

5. *True or False*: The distribution of the sample mean, $\bar{x}$, will be normally distributed if the sample is obtained from a population that is not normally distributed, regardless of the sample size. False 16. (a) Approximately normal with $\mu_{\bar{x}} = 64$ and $\sigma_{\bar{x}} = 3$

6. *True or False*: To cut the standard error of the mean in half, the sample size must be doubled. False

7. A simple random sample of size $n = 10$ is obtained from a population that is normally distributed with $\mu = 30$ and $\sigma = 8$. What is the sampling distribution of $\bar{x}$?

8. A simple random sample of size $n = 40$ is obtained from a population with $\mu = 50$ and $\sigma = 4$. Does the population need to be normally distributed for the sampling distribution of $\bar{x}$ to be approximately normally distributed? Why? What is the sampling distribution of $\bar{x}$?

In Problems 9–12, determine $\mu_{\bar{x}}$ and $\sigma_{\bar{x}}$ from the given parameters of the population and the sample size.

NW **9.** $\mu = 80, \sigma = 14, n = 49$ $\mu_{\bar{x}} = 80, \sigma_{\bar{x}} = 2$

10. $\mu = 64, \sigma = 18, n = 36$ $\mu_{\bar{x}} = 64, \sigma_{\bar{x}} = 3$

11. $\mu = 52, \sigma = 10, n = 21$

12. $\mu = 27, \sigma = 6, n = 15$

13. Answer the following questions for the sampling distribution of the sample mean shown.

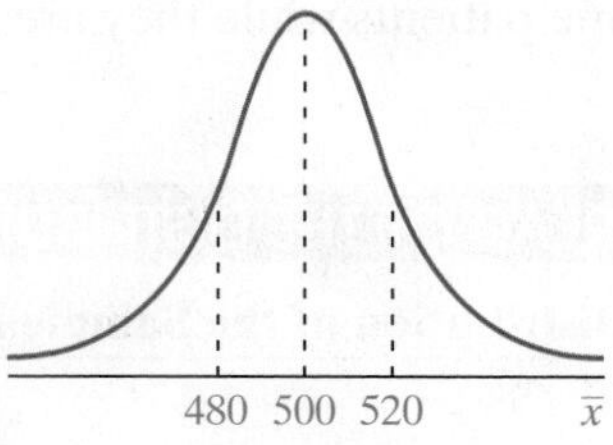

(a) What is the value of $\mu_{\bar{x}}$? 500

(b) What is the value of $\sigma_{\bar{x}}$? 20

(c) If the sample size is $n = 16$, what is likely true about the shape of the population? Normal

(d) If the sample size is $n = 16$, what is the standard deviation of the population from which the sample was drawn? 80

14. Answer the following questions for the sampling distribution of the sample mean shown.

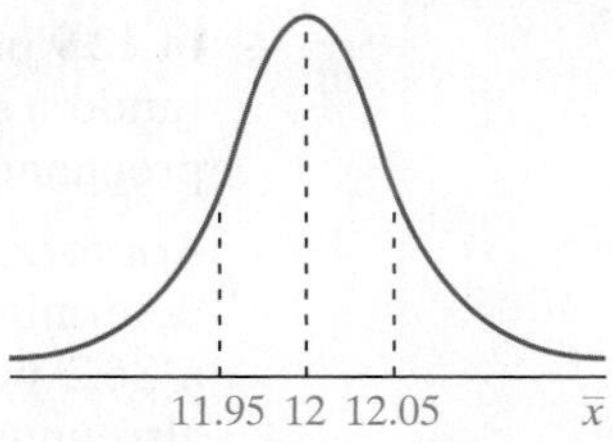

(a) What is the value of $\mu_{\bar{x}}$? 12

(b) What is the value of $\sigma_{\bar{x}}$? 0.05

(c) If the sample size is $n = 9$, what is likely true about the shape of the population? Normal

(d) If the sample size is $n = 9$, what is the standard deviation of the population from which the sample was drawn? 0.15

15. A simple random sample of size $n = 49$ is obtained from a population with $\mu = 80$ and $\sigma = 14$.

(a) Describe the sampling distribution of $\bar{x}$.

(b) What is $P(\bar{x} > 83)$? 0.0668

(c) What is $P(\bar{x} \le 75.8)$? 0.0179

(d) What is $P(78.3 < \bar{x} < 85.1)$? 0.7969

16. A simple random sample of size $n = 36$ is obtained from a population with $\mu = 64$ and $\sigma = 18$.

(a) Describe the sampling distribution of $\bar{x}$.

(b) What is $P(\bar{x} < 62.6)$? 0.3192

(c) What is $P(\bar{x} \ge 68.7)$? 0.0582

(d) What is $P(59.8 < \bar{x} < 65.9)$? 0.6549

17. A simple random sample of size $n = 12$ is obtained from a population with $\mu = 64$ and $\sigma = 17$.

(a) What must be true regarding the distribution of the population in order to use the normal model to compute probabilities involving the sample mean? Assuming that this condition is true, describe the sampling distribution of $\bar{x}$.

(b) Assuming that the requirements described in part (a) are satisfied, determine $P(\bar{x} < 67.3)$. 0.7486

(c) Assuming that the requirements described in part (a) are satisfied, determine $P(\bar{x} \ge 65.2)$. 0.4052

18. A simple random sample of size $n = 20$ is obtained from a population with $\mu = 64$ and $\sigma = 17$.

(a) What must be true regarding the distribution of the population in order to use the normal model to compute probabilities involving the sample mean? Assuming that this condition is true, describe the sampling distribution of $\bar{x}$.

(b) Assuming that the requirements described in part (a) are satisfied, determine $P(\bar{x} < 67.3)$. 0.8078

(c) Assuming that the requirements described in part (a) are satisfied, determine $P(\bar{x} \ge 65.2)$. 0.3745

(d) Compare the results obtained in parts (b) and (c) with the results obtained in parts (b) and (c) in Problem 17. What effect does increasing the sample size have on the probabilities? Why do you think this is the case?

18. (a) Normal; normal with $\mu_{\bar{x}} = 64$ and $\sigma_{\bar{x}} = \frac{17}{\sqrt{20}}$

APPLYING THE CONCEPTS

NW **19. Gestation Period** The length of human pregnancies is approximately normally distributed with mean $\mu = 266$ days and standard deviation $\sigma = 16$ days.

(a) What is the probability a randomly selected pregnancy lasts less than 260 days? 0.3520

7. Normal, $\mu_{\bar{x}} = 30, \sigma_{\bar{x}} = \frac{8}{\sqrt{10}}$ 8. No, $n \ge 30$, approx. normal, $\mu_{\bar{x}} = 50, \sigma_{\bar{x}} = \frac{4}{\sqrt{40}}$ 11. $\mu_{\bar{x}} = 52, \sigma_{\bar{x}} = \frac{10}{\sqrt{21}} \approx 2.182$

(b) Suppose a random sample of 20 pregnancies is obtained. Describe the sampling distribution of the sample mean length of human pregnancies.

(c) What is the probability that a random sample of 20 pregnancies has a mean gestation period of 260 days or less? 0.0465

(d) What is the probability that a random sample of 50 pregnancies has a mean gestation period of 260 days or less? 0.0040

(e) What might you conclude if a random sample of 50 pregnancies resulted in a mean gestation period of 260 days or less?

(f) What is the probability a random sample of size 15 will have a mean gestation period within 10 days of the mean? 0.9844

20. Upper Leg Length The upper leg length of 20- to 29-year-old males is normally distributed with a mean length of 43.7 cm and a standard deviation of 4.2 cm. *Source*: "Anthropometric Reference Data for Children and Adults: U.S. Population, 1999–2002; Volume 361, July 7, 2005.

(a) What is the probability that a randomly selected 20- to 29-year-old male has an upper leg length that is less than 40 cm?

(b) A random sample of 9 males who are 20 to 29 years old is obtained. What is the probability that the mean upper leg length is less than 40 cm? 0.0041 (a) 0.1894

(c) What is the probability that a random sample of 12 males who are 20 to 29 years old results in a mean upper leg length that is less than 40 cm? 0.0011

(d) What effect does increasing the sample size have on the probability? Provide an explanation for this result. Decreases

(e) A random sample of 15 males who are 20 to 29 years old results in a mean upper leg length of 46 cm. Do you find this result unusual? Why? Yes; $P(\bar{x} \geq 46) = 0.0170$

21. Reading Rates The reading speed of second grade students is approximately normal, with a mean of 90 words per minute (wpm) and a standard deviation of 10 wpm.

(a) What is the probability a randomly selected student will read more than 95 words per minute? 0.3085

(b) What is the probability that a random sample of 12 second grade students results in a mean reading rate of more than 95 words per minute? 0.0418

(c) What is the probability that a random sample of 24 second grade students results in a mean reading rate of more than 95 words per minute? 0.0071

(d) What effect does increasing the sample size have on the probability? Provide an explanation for this result. Decreases

(e) A teacher instituted a new reading program at school. After 10 weeks in the program, it was found that the mean reading speed of a random sample of 20 second grade students was 92.8 wpm. What might you conclude based on this result? $P(\bar{x} \geq 92.8) = 0.1056$; program not effective

(f) There is a 5% chance that the mean reading speed of a random sample of 20 second grade students will exceed what value? 93.9 wpm

22. Old Faithful The most famous geyser in the world, Old Faithful in Yellowstone National Park, has a mean time between eruptions of 85 minutes. If the interval of time between eruptions is normally distributed with standard deviation 21.25 minutes, answer the following questions: *Source:* www.unmuseum.org

(a) What is the probability that a randomly selected time interval between eruptions is longer than 95 minutes? 0.3192

(b) What is the probability that a random sample of 20 time intervals between eruptions has a mean longer than 95 minutes?

(c) What is the probability that a random sample of 30 time intervals between eruptions has a mean longer than 95 minutes?

(d) What effect does increasing the sample size have on the probability? Provide an explanation for this result. Decreases

(e) What might you conclude if a random sample of 30 time intervals between eruptions has a mean longer than 95 minutes?

(f) On a certain day, suppose there are 22 time intervals for Old Faithful. Treating these 22 eruptions as a random sample, the likelihood the mean length of time between eruptions exceeds __88.8__ minutes is 0.20. 22. (b) 0.0179 (c) 0.0049

23. Rates of Return in Stocks The S&P 500 is a collection of 500 stocks of publicly traded companies. Using data obtained from Yahoo! Finance, the monthly rates of return of the S&P 500 since 1950 are normally distributed. The mean rate of return is 0.007233 (0.7233%), and the standard deviation for rate of return is 0.04135 (4.135%).

(a) What is the probability that a randomly selected month has a positive rate of return? That is, what is $P(x > 0)$? 0.5675

(b) Treating the next 12 months as a simple random sample, what is the probability that the mean monthly rate of return will be positive? That is, with $n = 12$, what is $P(\bar{x} > 0)$? 0.7291

(c) Treating the next 24 months as a simple random sample, what is the probability that the mean monthly rate of return will be positive? 0.8051

(d) Treating the next 36 months as a simple random sample, what is the probability that the mean monthly rate of return will be positive? 0.8531

(e) Use the results of parts (b)–(d) to describe the likelihood of earning a positive rate of return on stocks as the investment time horizon increases.

24. Gas Mileage Based on tests of the Chevrolet Cobalt, engineers have found that the miles per gallon in highway driving are normally distributed, with a mean of 32 miles per gallon and a standard deviation of 3.5 miles per gallon.

(a) What is the probability that a randomly selected Cobalt gets more than 34 miles per gallon? 0.2843

(b) Ten Cobalts are randomly selected and the miles per gallon for each car are recorded. What is the probability that the mean miles per gallon exceeds 34 miles per gallon? 0.0351

(c) Twenty Cobalts are randomly selected and the miles per gallon for each car are recorded. What is the probability that the mean miles per gallon exceeds 34 miles per gallon? Would this result be unusual? 0.0052; yes

NW **25. Oil Change** The shape of the distribution of the time required to get an oil change at a 10-minute oil-change facility is unknown. However, records indicate that the mean time for an oil change is 11.4 minutes, and the standard deviation for oil-change time is 3.2 minutes. (a) At least 30

(a) To compute probabilities regarding the sample mean using the normal model, what size sample would be required?

(b) What is the probability that a random sample of $n = 40$ oil changes results in a sample mean time of less than 10 minutes? 0.0028 (c) 10.8 minutes

(c) Suppose the manager agrees to pay each employee a $50 bonus if they meet a certain goal. On a typical Saturday, the oil-change facility will perform 40 oil changes between 10 A.M. and 12 P.M. Treating this as a random sample, what mean oil-change time would there be a 10% chance of being at or below? This will be the goal established by the manager.

26. Time Spent in the Drive-Through The quality-control manager of a Long John Silver's restaurant wishes to analyze the length of time that a car spends at the drive-through window waiting for an order. According to records obtained from the restaurant, it is determined that the mean time spent at the window is 59.3 seconds with a standard deviation of 13.1 seconds. The distribution of time at the window is skewed right

27. (b) $\mu_{\bar{x}} = 3$, $\sigma_{\bar{x}} = \dfrac{\sqrt{3}}{\sqrt{50}}$ (c) 0.0071; yes 28. (a) Large sample size (b) $\mu_{\bar{x}} = 20$, $\sigma_{\bar{x}} = \dfrac{\sqrt{20}}{\sqrt{40}} = \dfrac{1}{\sqrt{2}}$

(data based on information provided by Danica Williams, student at Joliet Junior College).

(a) To obtain probabilities regarding a sample mean using the normal model, what size sample is required? At least 30

(b) The quality-control manager wishes to use a new delivery system designed to get cars through the drive-through system faster. A random sample of 40 cars results in a sample mean time spent at the window of 56.8 seconds. What is the probability of obtaining a sample mean of 56.8 seconds or less, assuming that the population mean is 59.3 seconds? Do you think that the new system is effective? 0.1131; no

(c) Treat the next 50 cars that arrive as a simple random sample. There is a 15% chance the mean time will be at or below __57.4__ seconds.

27. Insect Fragments The Food and Drug Administration sets Food Defect Action Levels (FDALs) for some of the various foreign substances that inevitably end up in the food we eat and liquids we drink. For example, the FDAL for insect filth in peanut butter is 3 insect fragments (larvae, eggs, body parts, and so on) per 10 grams. A random sample of 50 ten-gram portions of peanut butter is obtained and results in a sample mean of $\bar{x} = 3.6$ insect fragments per ten-gram portion. (a) Large sample size

(a) Why is the sampling distribution of $\bar{x}$ approximately normal?

(b) What is the mean and standard deviation of the sampling distribution of $\bar{x}$ assuming that $\mu = 3$ and $\sigma = \sqrt{3}$?

(c) What is the probability that a simple random sample of 50 ten-gram portions results in a mean of at least 3.6 insect fragments? Is this result unusual? What might we conclude?

28. Burger King's Drive-Through Suppose that cars arrive at Burger King's drive-through at the rate of 20 cars every hour between 12:00 noon and 1:00 P.M. A random sample of 40 one-hour time periods between 12:00 noon and 1:00 P.M. is selected and has 22.1 as the mean number of cars arriving.

(a) Why is the sampling distribution of $\bar{x}$ approximately normal?

(b) What is the mean and standard deviation of the sampling distribution of $\bar{x}$ assuming that $\mu = 20$ and $\sigma = \sqrt{20}$?

(c) What is the probability that a simple random sample of 40 one-hour time periods results in a mean of at least 22.1 cars? Is this result unusual? What might we conclude? 0.0015; yes

29. Watching Television The amount of time Americans spend watching television is closely monitored by firms such as A. C. Nielsen because this helps to determine advertising pricing for commercials.

(a) Do you think the variable "weekly time spent watching television" would be normally distributed? If not, what shape would you expect the variable to have? No; skewed right

(b) According to the American Time Use Survey, adult Americans spend 2.35 hours per day watching television on a weekday. Assume that the standard deviation for "time spent watching television on a weekday" is 1.93 hours. If a random sample of 40 adult Americans is obtained, describe the sampling distribution of $\bar{x}$, the mean amount of time spent watching television on a weekday.

(c) Determine the probability that a random sample of 40 adult Americans results in a mean time watching television on a weekday of between 2 and 3 hours. 0.8583

(d) One consequence of the popularity of the Internet is that it is thought to reduce television watching. Suppose that a random sample of 35 individuals who consider themselves to be avid Internet users results in a mean time of 1.89 hours watching television on a weekday. Determine the likelihood of obtaining a sample mean of 1.89 hours or less from a population whose mean is presumed to be 2.35 hours. Based on the result obtained, do you think avid Internet users watch less television? 0.0793; no

30. ATM Withdrawals According to Crown ATM Network, the mean ATM withdrawal is $67. Assume that the standard deviation for withdrawals is $35.

(a) Do you think the variable "ATM withdrawal" is normally distributed? If not, what shape would you expect the variable to have? No; skewed right

(b) If a random sample of 50 ATM withdrawals is obtained, describe the sampling distribution of $\bar{x}$, the mean withdrawal amount.

(c) Determine the probability of obtaining a sample mean withdrawal amount between $70 and $75. 0.2183

31. Sampling Distributions The following data represent the ages of the winners of the Academy Award for Best Actor for the years 2004–2009. (d) $\mu_{\bar{x}} \approx 46.3$ years

2004: Jamie Foxx	37
2005: Philip Seymour Hoffman	38
2006: Forest Whitaker	45
2007: Daniel Day-Lewis	50
2008: Sean Penn	48
2009: Jeff Bridges	60

Source: Wikipedia

(a) Compute the population mean, μ. $\mu \approx 46.3$ years

(b) List all possible samples with size $n = 2$. There should be ${}_6C_2 = 15$ samples.

(c) Construct a sampling distribution for the mean by listing the sample means and their corresponding probabilities.

(d) Compute the mean of the sampling distribution.

(e) Compute the probability that the sample mean is within 3 years of the population mean age. 0.467

(f) Repeat parts (b)–(e) using samples of size $n = 3$. Comment on the effect of increasing the sample size.

32. Sampling Distributions The following data represent the running lengths (in minutes) of the winners of the Academy Award for Best Picture for the years 2004–2009.

2004: *Million Dollar Baby*	132
2005: *Crash*	112
2006: *The Departed*	151
2007: *No Country for Old Men*	122
2008: *Slumdog Millionaire*	120
2009: *The Hurt Locker*	131

Source: The Internet Movie Database

(a) Compute the population mean, μ. $\mu = 128$ minutes

(b) List all possible samples with size $n = 2$. There should be ${}_6C_2 = 15$ samples. (d) $\mu_{\bar{x}} = 128$ minutes

(c) Construct a sampling distribution for the mean by listing the sample means and their corresponding probabilities.

(d) Compute the mean of the sampling distribution.

(e) Compute the probability that the sample mean is within 5 minutes of the population mean running time. 0.4

29. (b) Approx. normal; $\mu_{\bar{x}} = 2.35$, $\sigma_{\bar{x}} = \dfrac{1.93}{\sqrt{40}}$ 30. (b) Approx. normal; $\mu_{\bar{x}} = 67$; $\sigma_{\bar{x}} = \dfrac{35}{\sqrt{50}}$

(f) Repeat parts (b)–(e) using samples of size $n = 3$. Comment on the effect of increasing the sample size.

33. Putting It Together: Playing Roulette In the game of roulette, a wheel consists of 38 slots numbered 0, 00, 1, 2, . . . , 36. (See the photo.) To play the game, a metal ball is spun around the wheel and is allowed to fall into one of the numbered slots. If the number of the slot the ball falls into matches the number you selected, you win \$35; otherwise you lose \$1.

(a) Construct a probability distribution for the random variable X, the winnings of each spin. (b) $\mu_{\bar{x}} = -0.05$, $\sigma_{\bar{x}} = 5.76$

(b) Determine the mean and standard deviation of the random variable X. Round your results to the nearest penny.

(c) Suppose that you play the game 100 times so that $n = 100$. Describe the sampling distribution of $\bar{x}$, the mean amount won per game.

(d) What is the probability of being ahead after playing the game 100 times? That is, what is the probability that the sample mean is greater than 0 for $n = 100$? 0.4641

(e) What is the probability of being ahead after playing the game 200 times? 0.4522

(f) What is the probability of being ahead after playing the game 1000 times? 0.3936

(g) Compare the results of parts (d) and (e). What lesson does this teach you?

EXPLAINING THE CONCEPTS

34. Explain what a sampling distribution is.

35. State the Central Limit Theorem.

36. Technically, we assume that we are obtaining simple random samples from infinite populations when obtaining sampling distributions. If the size of the population is finite, we technically need a finite population correction factor. However, if the sample size is small relative to the size of the population, this factor can be ignored. Explain what an "infinite population" is. What is the finite population correction factor? How small must the sample size be relative to the size of the population so that we can ignore the factor? Finally, explain why the factor can be ignored for such samples.

37. Without doing any computation, decide which has a higher probability, assuming each sample is from a population that is normally distributed with $\mu = 100$ and $\sigma = 15$. Explain your reasoning. (b)

(a) $P(90 \le \bar{x} \le 110)$ for a random sample of size $n = 10$.

(b) $P(90 \le \bar{x} \le 110)$ for a random sample of size $n = 20$.

38. For the three probability distributions shown, rank each distribution from lowest to highest in terms of the sample size required for the distribution of the sample mean to be approximately normally distributed. Justify your choice. (b), (a), (c)

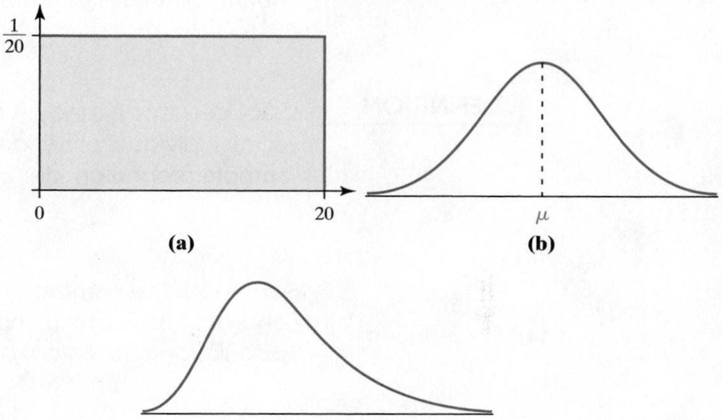

(a) (b) (c)

39. Suppose Jack and Diane are each attempting to use simulation to describe the sampling distribution from a population that is skewed left with mean 50 and standard deviation 10. Jack obtains 1000 random samples of size $n = 3$ from the population, finds the mean of the 1000 samples, draws a histogram of the means, finds the mean of the means, and determines the standard deviation of the means. Diane does the same simulation, but obtains 1000 random samples of size $n = 30$ from the population.

(a) Describe the shape you expect for Jack's distribution of sample means. Describe the shape you expect for Diane's distribution of sample means.

(b) What do you expect the mean of Jack's distribution to be? What do you expect the mean of Diane's distribution to be?

(c) What do you expect the standard deviation of Jack's distribution to be? What do you expect the standard deviation of Diane's distribution to be?

33. (c) $\mu_{\bar{x}} = -0.05$; $\sigma_{\bar{x}} = \dfrac{5.76}{\sqrt{100}} = 0.576$

8.2 DISTRIBUTION OF THE SAMPLE PROPORTION

Preparing for This Section Before getting started, review the following:

- Applications of the Normal Distribution (Section 7.2, pp. 338–345)

OBJECTIVES

1. Describe the sampling distribution of a sample proportion
2. Compute probabilities of a sample proportion

Note to Instructor

If you like, you can print out and distribute the Preparing for This Section quiz located in the Instructor's Resource Center. The purpose of the quiz is to verify that the students have the prerequisite knowledge for the section.

Note to Instructor

Although some texts use π to denote the population proportion to follow the convention of using Greek letters for population parameters, we use p to avoid confusion with the irrational number π.

1 Describe the Sampling Distribution of a Sample Proportion

Suppose we want to determine the proportion of households in a 100-house homeowners association that favor an increase in the annual assessments to pay for neighborhood improvements. We could survey all households to learn which are in favor of higher assessments. If 65 of the 100 households favor the higher assessment, the population proportion, p, of households in favor of a higher assessment is

$$p = \frac{65}{100} = 0.65$$

Of course, gaining access to all the individuals in a population is rare, so we usually obtain estimates of population parameters such as p.

DEFINITION

Suppose that a random sample of size n is obtained from a population in which each individual either does or does not have a certain characteristic. The **sample proportion**, denoted $\hat{p}$ (read "p-hat"), is given by

$$\hat{p} = \frac{x}{n}$$

where x is the number of individuals in the sample with the specified characteristic.* The sample proportion, $\hat{p}$, is a statistic that estimates the population proportion, p.

EXAMPLE 1 Computing a Sample Proportion

Problem Opinion Dynamics Corporation conducted a survey of 1000 adult Americans age 18 or older and asked, "Are you currently on some form of a low-carbohydrate diet?" Of those surveyed, 150 said they were on a low-carb diet. Find the sample proportion of individuals surveyed who were on a low-carb diet.

Approach Use the formula $\hat{p} = \frac{x}{n}$, where x is the number of individuals "on a low-carb diet" and n is the sample size.

Solution Substituting $x = 150$ and $n = 1000$ into $\hat{p} = \frac{x}{n}$, we find that $\hat{p} = \frac{150}{1000} = 0.15$, so Opinion Dynamics estimates that 0.15 or 15% of adult Americans age 18 or older are on some form of low-carbohydrate diet.

A second survey of 1000 American adults would likely have a different estimate of the proportion of Americans on a low-carbohydrate diet because different individuals would be in the sample. Because the value of $\hat{p}$ varies from sample to sample, it is a random variable and has a probability distribution.

To get a sense of the shape, center, and spread of the sampling distribution of $\hat{p}$, we could repeat the exercise of obtaining simple random samples of 1000 adult Americans over and over. This would lead to a list of sample proportions. A histogram of the sample proportions will give us a feel for the shape of the distribution of the sample proportion. The mean of the sample proportions will give us an idea of the center of the distribution, and the standard deviation of the sample proportions will give us an idea of the spread of the distribution.

Rather than literally surveying 1000 adult Americans over and over again, we will use simulation to get an idea of the shape, center, and spread of the sampling distribution of the proportion.

*For those who studied Section 6.2 on binomial probabilities, x can be thought of as the number of successes in n trials of a binomial experiment.

EXAMPLE 2 Using Simulation to Describe the Distribution of the Sample Proportion

Note to Instructor

Consider assigning the "Creating a Sampling Distribution for a Proportion" activity from the Student Activity Workbook.

Note to Instructor

Consider assigning the "Describing the Distribution of the Sample Proportion" activity from the Student Activity Workbook.

Problem Based on a study conducted by the Gallup organization, 76% of Americans believe that the state of moral values in the United States is getting worse. Describe the sampling distribution of the sample proportion for samples of size (a) $n = 10$, (b) $n = 25$, (c) $n = 60$.

Approach Describing a distribution means finding its shape, center, and spread. The actual sampling distribution of the sample proportion would be the distribution of *all* possible sample proportions of size $n = 10$. It is virtually impossible to find all possible samples of size $n = 10$ from the population of Americans. To get a sense as to the shape, center, and spread of the sampling distribution of the sample proportion, we will use StatCrunch's Bernoulli Random Data command with event probability 0.76 to simulate obtaining 2000 samples of size $n = 10$ by randomly generating 2000 rows of responses over 10 columns. Each row consists of a 0 or 1, with 0 representing a failure (individual does not believe the state of moral values is getting worse) and 1 representing a success (individual believes the state of moral values is getting worse). For each of the 2000 samples (the 2000 rows), determine the mean number of successes (the sample proportion). We draw a histogram of the 2000 sample proportions to gauge the shape of the distribution of the sample proportions. We determine the mean of the 2000 sample proportions to approximate the mean of the sampling distribution. We determine the standard deviation of the 2000 sample proportions to approximate the standard deviation of the sampling distribution. We repeat this process for samples of size $n = 20$ and $n = 60$.

Solution Figure 12 shows a partial output from StatCrunch. Row 1 contains the first sample, where the results of the survey are 1 (success), 1 (success), 1(success), …, 0 (failure), 1 (success). The mean number of successes, that is, the sample proportion, from the first sample of $n = 10$ adult Americans is 0.7.

Figure 12

Row	Bernoulli1	Bernoulli2	Bernoulli3	Bernoulli4	Bernoulli5	Bernoulli6	Bernoulli7	Bernoulli8	Bernoulli9	Bernoulli10	p-hat
1 (Sample 1)	1	1	1	1	0	1	0	1	0	1	0.7 ($\hat{p} = 0.7$)
2 (Sample 2)	1	1	1	1	0	1	0	1	0	1	0.7 ($\hat{p} = 0.7$)
3	1	0	1	1	0	1	1	1	1	1	0.8
4	1	1	0	1	1	1	1	1	0	1	0.8
5	1	1	1	1	1	1	1	1	1	1	1
6	0	1	1	0	0	0	1	1	1	1	0.6
7	1	0	1	1	1	1	1	0	1	1	0.8
8	1	1	1	1	1	1	0	0	1	1	0.8
9	1	1	1	0	1	1	1	0	0	0	0.6

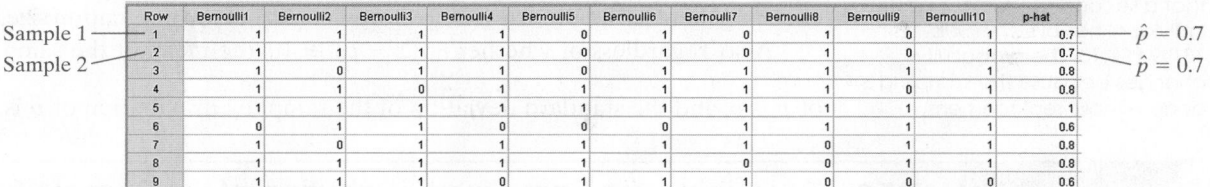

Figure 13(a) shows the histogram of the 2000 sample proportions from column p-hat. Notice that the shape of the distribution is skewed left. The mean of the 2000 sample proportions is 0.76 and the standard deviation is 0.136. Notice that the mean of the sample proportions equals the population proportion.

Figure 13(b) shows the histogram for 2000 sample proportions from samples of size $n = 20$. Notice that the histogram is slightly skewed left (although not as skewed as the

Figure 13

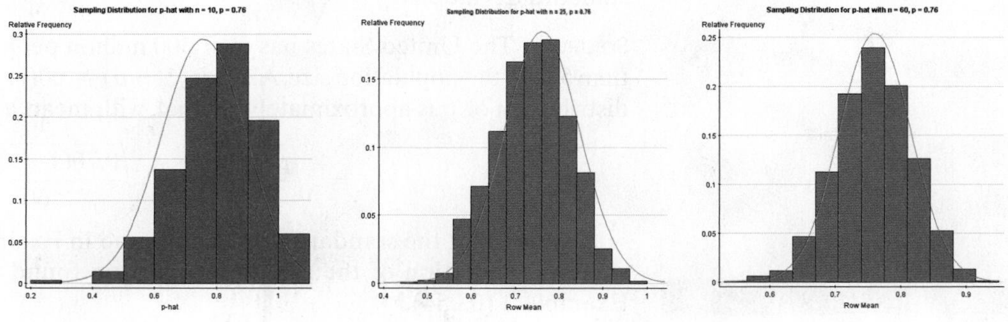

(a) (b) (c)

histogram with $n = 10$). The mean of the 2000 sample proportions for a sample of size $n = 20$ is 0.76 and the standard deviation is 0.096.

Figure 13(c) shows the histogram for 2000 sample proportions from samples of size $n = 60$. Notice that the histogram is approximately normal. The mean of the 2000 sample proportions is 0.76 and the standard deviation is 0.054.

We notice the following points regarding the sampling distribution of the sample proportion:

- **Shape:** As the size of the sample increases, the shape of the sampling distribution of the sample proportion becomes approximately normal.
- **Center:** The mean of the sampling distribution of the sampling proportion equals the population proportion, p.
- **Spread:** The standard deviation of the sampling distribution of the sample proportion decreases as the sample size increases.

Although the proof is beyond the scope of this text, we should be convinced that the following results are reasonable.

In Other Words
The sample size cannot be more than 5% of the population size because the success or failure of identifying an individual in the population that has the specified characteristic should not be affected by earlier observations. For example, in a population of size 100 where 14 of the individuals have brown hair, the probability that a randomly selected individual has brown hair is 14/100 = 0.14. The probability that a second randomly selected individual has brown hair is 13/99 = 0.13. The probability changes because the sampling is done without replacement.

Sampling Distribution of $\hat{p}$

For a simple random sample of size n with a population proportion p,

- The shape of the sampling distribution of $\hat{p}$ is approximately normal provided $np(1 - p) \geq 10$.
- The mean of the sampling distribution of $\hat{p}$ is $\mu_{\hat{p}} = p$.
- The standard deviation of the sampling distribution of $\hat{p}$ is $\sigma_{\hat{p}} = \sqrt{\dfrac{p(1-p)}{n}}$.

One requirement of this model is that the sampled values must be independent of each other—that is, one outcome cannot affect the success or failure of any other outcome. When sampling from finite populations, we verify the independence assumption by checking that the sample size n is no more than 5% of the population size, N ($n \leq 0.05N$).

Also, regardless of whether $np(1 - p) \geq 10$, the mean of the sampling distribution of $\hat{p}$ is p, and the standard deviation of the sampling distribution of $\hat{p}$ is $\sqrt{\dfrac{p(1-p)}{n}}$.

EXAMPLE 3 Describing the Sampling Distribution of the Sample Proportion

Problem Based on a study conducted by the Gallup organization, 76% of Americans believe that the state of moral values in the United States is getting worse. Suppose we obtain a simple random sample of $n = 60$ Americans and determine which believe that the state of the moral values in the United States is getting worse. Describe the sampling distribution of the sample proportion for Americans with this belief.

Approach If the sample size is less than 5% of the population size and $np(1 - p)$ is at least 10, the sampling distribution of $\hat{p}$ is approximately normal, with mean $\mu_{\hat{p}} = p$ and standard deviation $\sigma_{\hat{p}} = \sqrt{\dfrac{p(1-p)}{n}}$.

Solution The United States has over 300 million people, so the sample of $n = 60$ is less than 5% of the population size. Also, $np(1 - p) = 60(0.76)(1 - 0.76) = 10.944 \geq 10$. The distribution of $\hat{p}$ is approximately normal, with mean $\mu_{\hat{p}} = 0.76$ and standard deviation

$$\sigma_{\hat{p}} = \sqrt{\frac{p(1-p)}{n}} = \sqrt{\frac{0.76(1-0.76)}{60}} = 0.055$$

Notice that the standard deviation found in Example 3 (0.055) is very close to the standard deviation of the sample proportion found using simulation with $n = 60$ in Example 2 (0.054).

Now Work Problem 7

2 Compute Probabilities of a Sample Proportion

Now that we can describe the sampling distribution of the sample proportion, we can compute probabilities involving sample proportions.

EXAMPLE 4 Compute Probabilities of a Sample Proportion

Problem According to the National Center for Health Statistics, 15% of all Americans have hearing trouble.

(a) In a random sample of 120 Americans, what is the probability at most 12% have hearing trouble?

(b) Suppose that a random sample of 120 Americans who regularly listen to music using headphones results in 26 having hearing trouble. What might you conclude?

Approach First, determine whether the sampling distribution is approximately normal by verifying that the sample size is less than 5% of the population size and that $np(1-p) \geq 10$. Then use the normal distribution to determine the probabilities.

Solution There are over 300 million people in the United States, so the sample size of $n = 120$ is definitely less than 5% of the population size. We are told that $p = 0.15$. Because $np(1-p) = 120(0.15)(1-0.15) = 15.3 \geq 10$, the shape of the distribution of the sample proportion is approximately normal. The mean of the sample proportion $\hat{p}$ is $\mu_{\hat{p}} = 0.15$, and the standard deviation is $\sigma_{\hat{p}} = \sqrt{\dfrac{0.15(1-0.15)}{120}}$.

Figure 14

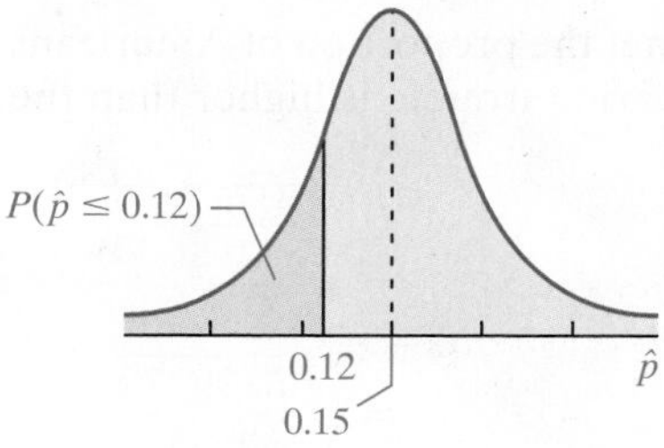

(a) We want to know the probability that a random sample of 120 Americans will result in a sample proportion of at most 0.12 (or 12%). That is, we want to know $P(\hat{p} \leq 0.12)$. Figure 14 shows the normal curve with the area to the left of 0.12 shaded.

To find this area by hand, we convert $\hat{p} = 0.12$ to a z-score by subtracting the mean and dividing by the standard deviation. Don't forget that we round z to two decimal places.

$$z = \frac{\hat{p} - \mu_{\hat{p}}}{\sigma_{\hat{p}}} = \frac{0.12 - 0.15}{\sqrt{\dfrac{0.15(1-0.15)}{120}}} = -0.92$$

The area under the standard normal curve left of $z = -0.92$ is 0.1788. Remember, the area to the left of $\hat{p} = 0.12$ is the same as the area to the left of $z = -0.92$, so $P(\hat{p} \leq 0.12) = 0.1788$.

If we use technology to find the area to the left of $\hat{p} = 0.12$, we obtain 0.1787, so $P(\hat{p} \leq 0.12) = 0.1787$.

Interpretation The probability that a random sample of $n = 120$ Americans results in at most 12% having hearing trouble is approximately 0.18. This means that about 18 out of 100 random samples of size 120 will result in at most 12% having hearing trouble if the population proportion of Americans with hearing trouble is 0.15.

(b) A random sample of 120 Americans who regularly listen to music using headphones results in 26 having hearing trouble. The sample proportion is $\hat{p} = \dfrac{26}{120} = 0.217$. We want to know if obtaining a sample proportion of 0.217 from a population whose proportion is assumed to be 0.15 is unusual. We compute $P(\hat{p} \geq 0.217)$, because if a sample proportion of 0.217 is unusual, then any sample proportion more than 0.217 is also unusual. Figure 15 on the next page shows the normal curve with the area to the right of 0.217 shaded.

Figure 15

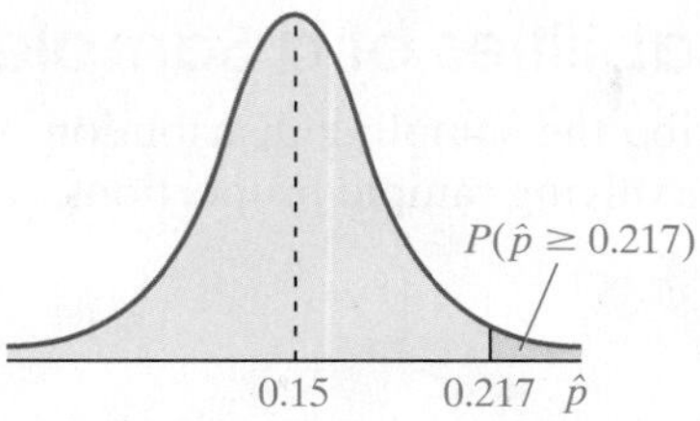

To find this area by hand, we convert $\hat{p} = 0.217$ to a z-score.

$$z = \frac{\hat{p} - \mu_{\hat{p}}}{\sigma_{\hat{p}}} = \frac{0.217 - 0.15}{\sqrt{\dfrac{0.15(1 - 0.15)}{120}}} = 2.06$$

The area under the standard normal curve to the right of 2.06 is 0.0197. The area to the right of $\hat{p} = 0.217$ is the same as the area to the right of $z = 2.06$, so $P(\hat{p} \geq 0.217) = 0.0197$.

If we use technology to find the area to the right of $\hat{p} = 0.217$, we obtain 0.0199, so $P(\hat{p} \geq 0.217) = 0.0199$.

Interpretation About 2 samples in 100 will result in a sample proportion of 0.217 or more from a population whose proportion is 0.15. We obtained a result that should only happen about 2 times in 100, so the results obtained are indeed unusual. We could make one of two conclusions:

- The population proportion of Americans with hearing trouble who regularly listen to music using headphones is 0.15, and we just happen to randomly select a higher proportion that have hearing trouble.
- The population proportion of Americans with hearing trouble who regularly listen to music using headphones is more than 0.15.

We are more likely to select the second conclusion, that the proportion of Americans who regularly listen using headphones who have hearing trouble is higher than the general population.

Now Work Problem 17

15. (a) Approximately normal; $\mu_{\hat{p}} = 0.47$; $\sigma_{\hat{p}} = \sqrt{\dfrac{0.47(0.53)}{200}}$
16. (a) Approximately normal; $\mu_{\hat{p}} = 0.82$; $\sigma_{\hat{p}} = \sqrt{\dfrac{0.82(0.18)}{100}}$
17. (a) Approximately normal; $\mu_{\hat{p}} = 0.39$; $\sigma_{\hat{p}} = \sqrt{\dfrac{0.39(0.61)}{500}}$
18. (a) Approximately normal; $\mu_{\hat{p}} = 0.29$; $\sigma_{\hat{p}} = \sqrt{\dfrac{0.29(0.71)}{500}}$

8.2 ASSESS YOUR UNDERSTANDING

VOCABULARY AND SKILL BUILDING

1. In a town of 500 households, 220 have a dog. The population proportion of dog owners in this town (expressed as a decimal) is $p =$ <u>0.44</u>.

2. The ______ ______, denoted $\hat{p}$, is given by the formula $\hat{p} =$ ______, where x is the number of individuals with a specified characteristic in a sample of n individuals.

3. *True or False:* The population proportion and sample proportion always have the same value. False

4. *True or False:* The mean of the sampling distribution of $\hat{p}$ is p. True 5. $n \leq 0.05N$, $np(1 - p) \geq 10$

5. Describe the circumstances under which the shape of the sampling distribution of $\hat{p}$ is approximately normal.

6. What happens to the standard deviation of $\hat{p}$ as the sample size increases? If the sample size is increased by a factor of 4, what happens to the standard deviation of $\hat{p}$? Decreases; halved

In Problems 7–10, describe the sampling distribution of $\hat{p}$. Assume that the size of the population is 25,000 for each problem. 7. Approximately normal; $\mu_{\hat{p}} = 0.4$, $\sigma_{\hat{p}} \approx 0.022$

NW 7. $n = 500, p = 0.4$ **8.** $n = 300, p = 0.7$

9. $n = 1000, p = 0.103$ **10.** $n = 1010, p = 0.84$

11. A simple random sample of size $n = 75$ is obtained from a population whose size is $N = 10{,}000$ and whose population proportion with a specified characteristic is $p = 0.8$.

(a) Describe the sampling distribution of $\hat{p}$. (c) 0.0047

(b) What is the probability of obtaining $x = 63$ or more individuals with the characteristic? That is, what is $P(\hat{p} \geq 0.84)$? 0.1922

(c) What is the probability of obtaining $x = 51$ or fewer individuals with the characteristic? That is, what is $P(\hat{p} \leq 0.68)$?

12. A simple random sample of size $n = 200$ is obtained from a population whose size is $N = 25{,}000$ and whose population proportion with a specified characteristic is $p = 0.65$.

2. sample proportion; $\dfrac{x}{n}$ 8. Approximately normal; $\mu_{\hat{p}} = 0.7$, $\sigma_{\hat{p}} \approx 0.026$ 9. Approximately normal; $\mu_{\hat{p}} = 0.103$, $\sigma_{\hat{p}} \approx 0.010$ 10. Approximately normal; $\mu_{\hat{p}} = 0.84$, $\sigma_{\hat{p}} \approx 0.012$ 11. (a) Approximately normal; $\mu_{\hat{p}} = 0.8$, $\sigma_{\hat{p}} \approx 0.046$

12. (a) Approximately normal; $\mu_{\hat{p}} = 0.65$, $\sigma_{\hat{p}} \approx 0.034$

(a) Describe the sampling distribution of $\hat{p}$.
(b) What is the probability of obtaining $x = 136$ or more individuals with the characteristic? That is, what is $P(\hat{p} \geq 0.68)$? 0.1867
(c) What is the probability of obtaining $x = 118$ or fewer individuals with the characteristic? That is, what is $P(\hat{p} \leq 0.59)$? 0.0375

13. A simple random sample of size $n = 1000$ is obtained from a population whose size is $N = 1{,}000{,}000$ and whose population proportion with a specified characteristic is $p = 0.35$.
(a) Describe the sampling distribution of $\hat{p}$.
(b) What is the probability of obtaining $x = 390$ or more individuals with the characteristic? 0.0040
(c) What is the probability of obtaining $x = 320$ or fewer individuals with the characteristic? 0.0233

14. A simple random sample of size $n = 1460$ is obtained from a population whose size is $N = 1{,}500{,}000$ and whose population proportion with a specified characteristic is $p = 0.42$.
(a) Describe the sampling distribution of $\hat{p}$.
(b) What is the probability of obtaining $x = 657$ or more individuals with the characteristic? 0.0102
(c) What is the probability of obtaining $x = 584$ or fewer individuals with the characteristic? 0.0606

APPLYING THE CONCEPTS

15. Foreign Language According to a study done by Wakefield Research, the proportion of Americans who can order a meal in a foreign language is 0.47.
(a) Suppose a random sample of 200 Americans is asked to disclose whether they can order a meal in a foreign language. Describe the sampling distribution of $\hat{p}$, the proportion of Americans who can order a meal in a foreign language. Be sure to verify the model requirements.
(b) In the sample obtained in part (a), what is the probability the proportion of Americans who can order a meal in a foreign language is greater than 0.5? 0.1977
(c) Would it be unusual that, in a survey of 200 Americans, 80 or fewer Americans can order a meal in a foreign language? Why? Yes; $P(\hat{p} \leq 0.4) = 0.0239$

16. Are You Satisfied? According to a study done by the Gallup organization, the proportion of Americans who are satisfied with the way things are going in their lives is 0.82.
(a) Suppose a random sample of 100 Americans is asked, "Are you satisfied with the way things are going in your life?" Describe the sampling distribution of $\hat{p}$, the proportion of Americans who are satisfied with the way things are going in their life. Be sure to verify the model requirements.
(b) In the sample obtained in part (a), what is the probability the proportion who are satisfied with the way things are going in their life exceeds 0.85? 0.2177
(c) Would it be unusual for a survey of 100 Americans to reveal that 75 or fewer are satisfied with the way things are going in their life? Why? Yes; $P(\hat{p} \leq 0.75) = 0.0344$

NW **17. Marriage Obsolete?** According to a study done by the Pew Research Center, 39% of adult Americans believe that marriage is now obsolete.
(a) Suppose a random sample of 500 adult Americans is asked whether marriage is obsolete. Describe the sampling distribution of $\hat{p}$, the proportion of adult Americans who believe marriage is obsolete.
(b) What is the probability that in a random sample of 500 adult Americans less than 38% believe that marriage is obsolete? 0.3228
(c) What is the probability that in a random sample of 500 adult Americans between 40% and 45% believe that marriage is obsolete? 0.3198
(d) Would it be unusual for a random sample of 500 adult Americans to result in 210 or more who believe marriage is obsolete? No; $P(\hat{p} \geq 0.42) = 0.0838$

18. Credit Cards According to creditcard.com, 29% of adults do not own a credit card.
(a) Suppose a random sample of 500 adults is asked, "Do you own a credit card?" Describe the sampling distribution of $\hat{p}$, the proportion of adults who own a credit card.
(b) What is the probability that in a random sample of 500 adults more than 30% do not own a credit card? 0.3121
(c) What is the probability that in a random sample of 500 adults between 25% and 30% do not own a credit card? 0.6635
(d) Would it be unusual for a random sample of 500 adults to result in 125 or fewer who do not own a credit card? Why? Yes; $P(\hat{p} \leq 0.25) = 0.0244$

19. Afraid to Fly According to a study conducted by the Gallup organization, the proportion of Americans who are afraid to fly is 0.10. A random sample of 1100 Americans results in 121 indicating that they are afraid to fly. Explain why this is not necessarily evidence that the proportion of Americans who are afraid to fly has increased since the time of the Gallup study.

20. Having Children? The Pew Research Center recently reported that 18% of women 40 to 44 years of age have never given birth. Suppose a random sample of 250 adult women 40 to 44 years of age results in 52 indicating they have never given birth. Explain why this is not necessarily evidence that the proportion of women 40 to 44 years of age who have not given birth has increased since the time of the Pew study. $P(\hat{p} \geq 0.208) = 0.1251$

21. Election Prediction Exit polling is a popular technique used to determine the outcome of an election prior to results being tallied. Suppose a referendum to increase funding for education is on the ballot in a large town (voting population over 100,000). An exit poll of 310 voters finds that 164 voted for the referendum. How likely are the results of your sample if the population proportion of voters in the town in favor of the referendum is 0.49? Based on your result, comment on the dangers of using exit polling to call elections. Include a discussion of the potential nonsampling error that could disrupt your findings. $P(\hat{p} \geq 0.529) = 0.0853$

22. Acceptance Sampling A shipment of 50,000 transistors arrives at a manufacturing plant. The quality control engineer at the plant obtains a random sample of 500 resistors and will reject the entire shipment if 10 or more of the resistors are defective. Suppose that 4% of the resistors in the whole shipment are defective. What is the probability the engineer accepts the shipment? Do you believe the acceptance policy of the engineer is sound? ≈0.01; yes

23. Social Security Reform A researcher studying public opinion of proposed Social Security changes obtains a simple random sample of 50 adult Americans and asks them whether or not they support the proposed changes. To say that the distribution of $\hat{p}$, the sample proportion of adults who respond yes, is approximately normal, how many more adult Americans does the researcher need to sample if
(a) 10% of all adult Americans support the changes? 62 more
(b) 20% of all adult Americans support the changes? 13 more

24. ADHD A researcher studying ADHD among teenagers obtains a simple random sample of 100 teenagers aged 13 to 17 and asks them whether or not they have ever been prescribed

13. (a) Approximately normal; $\mu_{\hat{p}} = 0.35$, $\sigma_{\hat{p}} \approx 0.015$ 14. (a) Approximately normal; $\mu_{\hat{p}} = 0.42$, $\sigma_{\hat{p}} \approx 0.013$ 19. $P(\hat{p} \geq 0.11) = 0.1335$

medication for ADHD. To say that the distribution of $\hat{p}$, the sample proportion of teenagers who respond no, is approximately normal, how many more teenagers aged 13 to 17 does the researcher need to sample if

(a) 90% of all teenagers aged 13 to 17 have never been prescribed medication for ADHD? 12 more

(b) 95% of all teenagers aged 13 to 17 have never been prescribed medication for ADHD? 111 more

25. Assessments Consider the homeowners association presented at the beginning of this section. A random sample of 20 households resulted in 15 indicating that they would favor an increase in assessments. Explain why the normal model could not be used to determine if a sample proportion of $\frac{15}{20} = 0.75$ or higher from a population whose proportion is 0.65 is unusual.

26. Finite Population Correction Factor In this section, we assumed that the sample size was less than 5% of the size of the population. When sampling without replacement from a finite population in which $n > 0.05N$, the standard deviation of the distribution of $\hat{p}$ is given by

$$\sigma_{\hat{p}} = \sqrt{\frac{p(1-p)}{n-1} \cdot \left(\frac{N-n}{N}\right)}$$

where N is the size of the population. A survey is conducted at a college having an enrollment of 6502 students. The student council wants to estimate the percentage of students in favor of establishing a student union. In a random sample of 500 students, it was determined that 410 were in favor of establishing a student union.

(a) Obtain the sample proportion, $\hat{p}$, of students surveyed who favor establishing a student union. 0.82

(b) Calculate the standard deviation of the sampling distribution of $\hat{p}$ using $\hat{p}$ as an estimate of p. 0.017

25. Events are not independent.

Consumer Reports® Tanning Salons

Medical groups have long warned about the dangers of indoor tanning. The American Medical Association and the American Academy of Dermatology unsuccessfully petitioned the Food and Drug Administration in 1994 to ban cosmetic-tanning equipment. Three years later, the Federal Trade Commission warned the public to beware of advertised claims that "unlike the sun, indoor tanning will not cause skin cancer or skin aging" or that you can "tan indoors with absolutely no harmful side effects."

In February 1999, still under pressure from the medical community, the FDA announced that current recommendations "may allow higher exposures" to UV radiation "than are necessary." The agency proposed reducing recommended exposures and requiring simpler wording on consumer warnings. But it has not yet implemented either of these changes. An FDA spokeswoman told us that "the agency decided to postpone amendment of its standard pending the results of ongoing research and discussions with other organizations."

To make matters worse, only about half the states have any rules for tanning parlors. In some of these states, the regulation is minimal and may not require licensing, inspections, training, record keeping, or parental consent for minors. Despite this, millions of Americans, including a growing number of teenage girls, will visit tanning salons this year.

In a recent survey of 296 indoor-tanning facilities around the country, to our knowledge the first nationwide survey of its kind, we found evidence of widespread failures to inform customers about the possible risks, including premature wrinkling and skin cancer, and to follow recommended safety procedures, such as wearing eye goggles. Many facilities made questionable claims about indoor tanning: that it's safer than sunlight, for example, and is well controlled.

(a) In designing this survey, why is it important to sample a large number of facilities? And why is it important to sample these facilities in multiple cities?

(b) Given the fact that there are over 150,000 tanning facilities in the United States, is the condition for independence of survey results satisfied? Why?

(c) Sixty-seven of the 296 tanning facilities surveyed stated that "tanning in a salon is the same as tanning in the sun with respect to causing skin cancer." Assuming that the true proportion of facilities that believe this is 25%, describe the sampling distribution of $\hat{p}$, the sample proportion of tanning facilities that state "tanning in a salon is the same as tanning in the sun with respect to causing skin cancer." Calculate the probability that less than 22.6% of randomly selected tanning salon facilities would state that tanning in a salon is the same as tanning in the sun with respect to causing skin cancer.

(d) Forty-two of the 296 tanning facilities surveyed stated "tanning in a salon does not cause wrinkled skin." Assuming that the true proportion of facilities that believe this is 18%, describe the sampling distribution of $\hat{p}$, the sample proportion of tanning facilities that state "tanning in a salon does not cause wrinkled skin." Calculate the probability that at least 14.2% will state that tanning in a salon does not cause wrinkled skin. Would it be unusual for 50 or fewer facilities to state that tanning in a salon does not cause wrinkled skin?

Note to Readers: *In many cases, our test protocol and analytical methods are more complicated than described in this example. The data and discussion have been modified to make the material more appropriate for the audience.*

CHAPTER 8 REVIEW

Summary

This chapter forms the bridge between probability and statistical inference. In Section 8.1, we discussed the distribution of the sample mean. We learned that the mean of the distribution of the sample mean equals the mean of the population ($\mu_{\bar{x}} = \mu$) and that the standard deviation of the distribution of the sample mean is the standard deviation of the population divided by the square root of the sample size $\left(\sigma_{\bar{x}} = \dfrac{\sigma}{\sqrt{n}}\right)$. If the sample is obtained from a population that is known to be normally distributed, the shape of the distribution of the sample mean is also normal. If the sample is obtained from a population that is not normal, the shape of the distribution of the sample mean becomes approximately normal as the sample size increases. This result is known as the Central Limit Theorem.

In Section 8.2, we discussed the distribution of the sample proportion. We learned that the mean of the distribution of the sample proportion is the population proportion ($\mu_{\hat{p}} = p$) and that the standard deviation of the distribution of the sample proportion is $\sigma_{\hat{p}} = \sqrt{\dfrac{p(1-p)}{n}}$. If $n \le 0.05N$ and $np(1-p) \ge 10$, then the shape of the distribution of $\hat{p}$ is approximately normal.

Vocabulary

Sampling distribution (p. 367)
Sampling distribution of the sample mean (p. 367)
Standard error of the mean (p. 370)
Central Limit Theorem (p. 373)
Sample proportion (p. 380)
Sampling distribution of $\hat{p}$ (p. 382)

Formulas

Mean and Standard Deviation of the Sampling Distribution of $\bar{x}$

$$\mu_{\bar{x}} = \mu \quad \text{and} \quad \sigma_{\bar{x}} = \frac{\sigma}{\sqrt{n}}$$

Sample Proportion

$$\hat{p} = \frac{x}{n}$$

Mean and Standard Deviation of the Sampling Distribution of $\hat{p}$

$$\mu_{\hat{p}} = p \quad \text{and} \quad \sigma_{\hat{p}} = \sqrt{\frac{p(1-p)}{n}}$$

Standardizing a Normal Random Variable

$$z = \frac{\bar{x} - \mu}{\dfrac{\sigma}{\sqrt{n}}} \quad \text{or} \quad z = \frac{\hat{p} - p}{\sqrt{\dfrac{p(1-p)}{n}}}$$

Objectives

Section	You should be able to . . .	Examples	Review Exercises
8.1	1 Describe the distribution of the sample mean: normal population (p. 368)	1–3	2, 4, 5
	2 Describe the distribution of the sample mean: nonnormal population (p. 371)	4 and 5	2, 6, 7
8.2	1 Describe the sampling distribution of a sample proportion (p. 380)	2 and 3	3, 4, 8(a), 10(a)
	2 Compute probabilities of a sample proportion (p. 383)	4	8(b), (c), 9, 10(b), (c)

Review Exercises

1. In your own words, explain what a sampling distribution is.

2. Under what conditions is the sampling distribution of $\bar{x}$ normal? Population normal; large sample size

3. Under what conditions is the sampling distribution of $\hat{p}$ approximately normal? when $np(1-p) \ge 10$

4. What are the mean and standard deviation of the sampling distribution of $\bar{x}$? What are the mean and standard deviation of the sampling distribution of $\hat{p}$?

5. Energy Need during Pregnancy The total energy need during pregnancy is normally distributed, with mean $\mu = 2600$ kcal/day and standard deviation $\sigma = 50$ kcal/day. *Source:* American Dietetic Association

(a) What is the probability that a randomly selected pregnant woman has an energy need of more than 2625 kcal/day? Is this result unusual? 0.3085; no

(b) Describe the sampling distribution of $\bar{x}$, the sample mean daily energy requirement for a random sample of 20 pregnant women.

(c) What is the probability that a random sample of 20 pregnant women has a mean energy need of more than 2625 kcal/day? Is this result unusual? 0.0125; yes

6. Copper Tubing A machine at K&A Tube & Manufacturing Company produces a certain copper tubing component in a refrigeration unit. The tubing components produced by the manufacturer have a mean diameter of 0.75 inch with a standard

4. $\mu_{\bar{x}} = \mu, \sigma_{\bar{x}} = \dfrac{\sigma}{\sqrt{n}}; \mu_{\hat{p}} = p, \sigma_{\hat{p}} = \sqrt{\dfrac{p(1-p)}{n}}$ 5. (b) Normal; $\mu_{\bar{x}} = 2600, \sigma_{\bar{x}} = \dfrac{50}{\sqrt{20}}$

deviation of 0.004 inch. The quality-control inspector takes a random sample of 30 components once each week and calculates the mean diameter of these components. If the mean is either less than 0.748 inch or greater than 0.752 inch, the inspector concludes that the machine needs an adjustment.

(a) Describe the sampling distribution of $\bar{x}$, the sample mean diameter, for a random sample of 30 such components.

(b) What is the probability that, based on a random sample of 30 such components, the inspector will conclude that the machine needs an adjustment when, in fact, the machine is correctly calibrated? 0.0062

7. Number of Televisions Based on data obtained from A. C. Nielsen, the mean number of televisions in a household in the United States is 2.24. Assume that the population standard deviation number of television sets in the United States is 1.38.

(a) Do you believe the shape of the distribution of number of television sets follows a normal distribution? Why or why not?

(b) A random sample of 40 households results in a total of 102 television sets. What is the mean number of televisions in these 40 households? 2.55 (a) No; skewed right (c) 0.0778; no

(c) What is the probability of obtaining the sample mean obtained in part (b) if the population mean is 2.24? Does the statistic from part (b) contradict the results reported by A. C. Nielsen?

8. Entrepreneurship A Gallup survey indicated that 72% of 18- to 29-year-olds, if given a choice, would prefer to start their own business rather than work for someone else. A random sample of 600 18- to 29-year-olds is obtained today.

(a) Describe the sampling distribution of $\hat{p}$, the sample proportion of 18- to 29-year-olds who would prefer to start their own business. Approximately normal; $\mu_{\hat{p}} = 0.72$, $\sigma_{\hat{p}} \approx 0.018$

(b) In a random sample of 600 18- to 29-year-olds, what is the probability that no more than 70% would prefer to start their own business? 0.1379

(c) Would it be unusual if a random sample of 600 18- to 29-year-olds resulted in 450 or more who would prefer to start their own business? a little unusual

9. Advanced Degrees According to the U.S. Census Bureau, 10% of adults 25 years and older in the United States had advanced degrees in 2009. A researcher with the U.S. Department of Education surveys 500 randomly selected adults 25 years of age or older and finds that 60 of them have an advanced degree. Explain why this is not necessarily evidence that the proportion of adults 25 years of age or older with advanced degrees has increased.

10. Variability in Baseball During the course of a typical season, suppose a batter has 500 at-bats. This means the player has the opportunity to get a hit 500 times during the course of a season. Further, suppose a batter is a career 0.280 hitter (he averages 280 hits every 1000 at-bats or he has 280 successes in 1000 trials of the experiment), so the population proportion of hits is 0.280.

(a) Assuming each at-bat is an independent event, describe the sampling distribution of $\hat{p}$, the proportion of hits in 500 at-bats over the course of a season.

(b) Would it be unusual for a player who is a career 0.280 hitter to have a season in which he hits 0.310?

(c) Would it be unusual for the player who hit 0.310 one season to hit below 0.255 the following season?

(d) Explain why a career 0.280 hitter could easily have a batting average between 0.260 and 0.300.

(e) Use the result of part (d) to explain that a player who hit 0.260 in a season may not be a worse player than one who hit 0.300.

6. (a) Approximately normal; $\mu_{\bar{x}} = 0.75$; $\sigma_{\bar{x}} = \dfrac{0.004}{\sqrt{30}}$

10. (a) Approximately normal; $\mu_{\hat{p}} = 0.280$; $\sigma_{\hat{p}} \approx \sqrt{\dfrac{0.28(0.72)}{500}}$

10. (b) No; $P(\hat{p} \geq 0.310) = 0.0681$ (c) No; $P(\hat{p} < 0.255) = 0.1056$

Problems in the chapter test are labeled by section.objective. For example, 2.3 means Section 2, Objective 3.

CHAPTER TEST

2. $\mu_{\bar{x}} = 50$, $\sigma_{\bar{x}} = \dfrac{24}{\sqrt{36}} = 4$ 3. (b) Normal; $\mu_{\bar{x}} = 90$, $\sigma_{\bar{x}} = \dfrac{35}{\sqrt{10}}$ 4. (a) Approximately normal; $\mu_{\bar{x}} = 2.0$, $\sigma_{\bar{x}} = \dfrac{0.05}{\sqrt{45}}$

1.2 **1.** State the Central Limit Theorem.

1.1 **2.** If a random sample of 36 is obtained from a population with mean 50 and standard deviation 24, what is the mean and standard deviation of the sampling distribution of the sample mean?

1.1 **3.** The charge life of a certain lithium ion battery for camcorders is normally distributed, with mean 90 minutes and standard deviation 35 minutes.

(a) What is the probability that a randomly selected battery of this type lasts more than 100 minutes on a single charge? Is this result unusual? 0.3859; no

(b) Describe the sampling distribution of $\bar{x}$, the sample mean charge life for a random sample of 10 such batteries.

(c) What is the probability that a random sample of 10 such batteries has a mean charge life of more than 100 minutes? Is this result unusual? 0.1841; no

(d) What is the probability that a random sample of 25 such batteries has a mean charge life of more than 100 minutes?

(e) Explain what causes the probabilities in parts (c) and (d) to be different. (d) 0.0764

1.2 **4.** A machine used for filling plastic bottles with a soft drink has a known standard deviation of $\sigma = 0.05$ liter. The target mean fill volume is $\mu = 2.0$ liters.

(a) Describe the sampling distribution of $\bar{x}$, the sample mean fill volume, for a random sample of 45 such bottles.

(b) A quality-control manager obtains a random sample of 45 bottles. He will shut down the machine if the sample mean of these 45 bottles is less than 1.98 liters or greater than 2.02 liters. What is the probability that the quality-control manager will shut down the machine even though the machine is correctly calibrated? 0.0074

5. According to the National Center for Health Statistics (2004), 22.4% of adults are smokers. A random sample of 300 adults is obtained.

2.1 **(a)** Describe the sampling distribution of $\hat{p}$, the sample proportion of adults who smoke. Normal; $\mu_{\hat{p}} = 0.224$, $\sigma_{\hat{p}} \approx 0.024$

2.2 **(b)** In a random sample of 300 adults, what is the probability that at least 50 are smokers? 0.9913

2.2 **(c)** Would it be unusual if a random sample of 300 adults results in 18% or less being smokers? Yes

6. Peanut and tree nut allergies are considered to be the most serious food allergies. According to the National Institute of Allergy and Infectious Diseases, roughly 1% of Americans are allergic to peanuts or tree nuts. A random sample of 1500 Americans is obtained.

2.1 **(a)** Explain why a large sample is needed for the distribution of the sample proportion to be approximately normal.

2.2 **(b)** Would it be unusual if a random sample of 1500 Americans results in fewer than 10 with peanut or tree nut allergies? No

2.2 **7.** According to Wikipedia.com, net worth is defined as total assets (value of house, cars, money, etc.) minus total liabilities (mortgage balance, credit card debt, etc.). According to a recent study by TNS Financial Services, 7% of American households had a net worth in excess of $1 million (excluding their primary residence). A random sample of 1000 American households results in 82 having a net worth in excess of $1 million. Explain why the results of this survey do not necessarily imply that the proportion of households with a net worth in excess of $1 million has increased.

Making an Informed Decision

How Much Time Do You Spend in a Day . . . ?

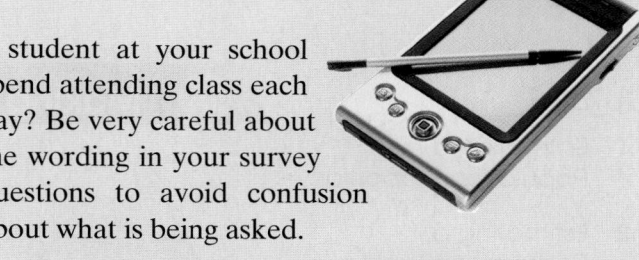

The American Time Use Survey is a survey of adult Americans conducted by the Bureau of Labor Statistics. The purpose of the survey is to learn how Americans allocate their time in a day. As a reporter for the school newspaper, you wish to file a report that compares the typical student at your school to other Americans.

1. Go to the American Time Use Survey web page. Research variables of interest to you (or that you believe would be of interest to your readers). Determine the mean amount of time Americans who are enrolled in school spend doing the activities you find interesting.

2. Use StatCrunch or an online polling site (such as surveymonkey.com) to conduct a survey of a random sample of students at your school. Write questions to learn how students at your school use their time. For example, how much time does a student at your school spend attending class each day? Be very careful about the wording in your survey questions to avoid confusion about what is being asked.

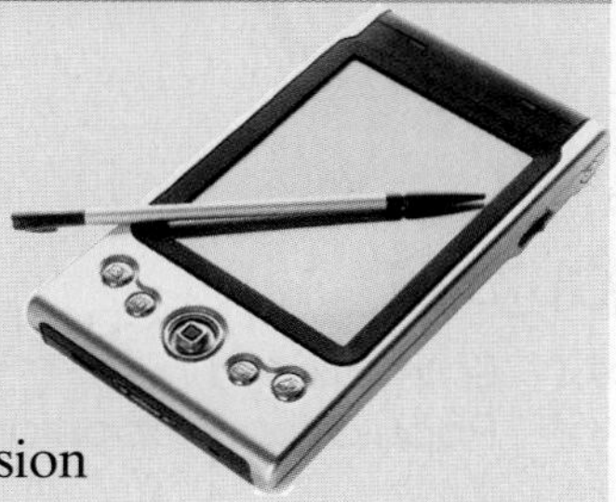

3. For each question, describe the sampling distribution of the sample mean. Use the national norms as the population mean for each variable. Use the sample standard deviation from your survey sample as the population standard deviation.

4. Compute probabilities regarding values of the statistics obtained from the study. Are any of the results unusual?

5. Write an article for your newspaper reporting your findings. Be sure any interpretations are written so they are statistically accurate, but understandable for the statistically untrained reader.

The Chapter 8 Case Study is located on the CD that accompanies this text.

9 Estimating the Value of a Parameter

OUTLINE

Making an Informed Decision

A home purchase is one of the biggest investment decisions we make in our lifetime. Buying a home involves consideration of location, price, features, and neighborhoods. This decision could also affect your family's social life. See the Decision Project on page 427.

PUTTING IT TOGETHER

Chapters 1 through 7 laid the groundwork for the remainder of the course. These chapters dealt with data collection (Chapter 1), descriptive statistics (Chapters 2 through 4), and probability (Chapters 5 through 7). Chapter 8 formed a bridge between probability and statistical inference by giving us a model we can use to make probability statements about the sample mean and sample proportion.

We know from Section 8.1 that the sample mean is a random variable and has a distribution associated with it. This distribution is called the sampling distribution of the sample mean. The mean of this distribution is equal to the mean of the population, μ, and the standard deviation is $\frac{\sigma}{\sqrt{n}}$. The shape of the distribution of the sample mean is normal if the population is normal; it is approximately normal if the sample size is large. We learned in Section 8.2 that $\hat{p}$ is also a random variable whose mean is p and whose standard deviation is $\sqrt{\frac{p(1-p)}{n}}$. If $np(1-p) \geq 10$, the distribution of the random variable $\hat{p}$ is approximately normal.

We now discuss inferential statistics—the process of generalizing information obtained from a sample to a population. We will study two areas of inferential statistics: (1) estimation—sample data are used to estimate the value of unknown parameters such as μ or p, and (2) hypothesis testing—statements regarding a characteristic of one or more populations are tested using sample data. In this chapter, we discuss estimation of an unknown parameter, and in the next chapter we discuss hypothesis testing.

9.1 ESTIMATING A POPULATION PROPORTION

Preparing for This Section Before getting started, review the following:

- Parameter versus statistic (Section 1.1, p. 5)
- Simple random sampling (Section 1.3, pp. 22–26)
- Sampling error (Section 1.5, p. 42)
- z_α notation (Section 7.2, pp. 344–345)
- Finding the value of a normal random variable(Section 7.2, pp. 342–344)
- Distribution of the sample proportion (Section 8.2, pp. 379–384)

OBJECTIVES

1. Obtain a point estimate for the population proportion
2. Construct and interpret a confidence interval for the population proportion
3. Determine the sample size necessary for estimating a population proportion within a specified margin of error

Note to Instructor
If you like, you can print out and distribute the Preparing for This Section quiz located in the Instructor's Resource Center. The purpose of the quiz is to verify that the students have the prerequisite knowledge for the section.

1 Obtain a Point Estimate for the Population Proportion

Suppose we want to estimate the proportion of adult Americans who believe the amount they pay in federal income taxes is too high. It is unreasonable to expect that we could survey every adult American. Instead, we use a sample of adult Americans to arrive at an estimate of the proportion. We call this estimate a *point estimate.*

DEFINITION A **point estimate** is the value of a statistic that estimates the value of a parameter.

For example, the point estimate for the population proportion is $\hat{p} = \frac{x}{n}$, where x is the number of individuals in the sample with the specified characteristic and n is the sample size.

EXAMPLE 1 Obtaining a Point Estimate of a Population Proportion

Problem The Gallup Organization conducted a poll in April 2010 in which a simple random sample of 1020 Americans age 18 or older were asked, "Do you consider the amount of federal income tax you have to pay is too high?" Of the 1020 adult Americans surveyed, 490 said yes. Obtain a point estimate for the proportion of Americans age 18 or older who believe the amount of federal income tax they pay is too high.

Approach The point estimate of the population proportion is $\hat{p} = \frac{x}{n}$, where $x = 490$ and $n = 1020$.

Solution Substituting into the formula, we get $\hat{p} = \frac{x}{n} = \frac{490}{1020} = 0.480 = 48.0\%$. We estimate that 48% of Americans age 18 or older believe the amount of federal income tax they have to pay is too high.

Now Work Problem 25(a)

Note: We agree to round proportions to three decimal places.

2 Construct and Interpret a Confidence Interval for the Population Proportion

Note to Instructor
Try this as a mini-in-class activity. Ask students to make a guess for the proportion of students in the class who are left-handed, for which they are 100% confident. Only possible answer: (0%, 100%).

Based on the point estimate of Example 1, can we conclude that less than a majority of the United States adult population believes the amount of federal income tax they have to pay is too high? Or is it possible that a majority (more than 50%) of adult Americans believe their federal income tax is too high, and we just happened to sample folks who do not believe they pay too much in taxes? After all, statistics such as $\hat{p}$ vary from sample to sample. So a different random sample of adult Americans might result in a different point estimate of the population proportion, such as $\hat{p} = 0.503$. If the method used to select the adult Americans was done appropriately, both point estimates would be good guesses of the population proportion. Due to variability in the sample proportion, we need to report a range (or *interval*) of values, including a measure of the likelihood that the interval includes the unknown population proportion.

To understand the idea of this interval, consider the following situation. Suppose you were asked to guess the proportion of students on your campus who use Facebook. If a survey of 80 students results in 60 who use Facebook, then $\hat{p} = 0.75$. From this you might guess the proportion of *all* students on your campus who use Facebook is 0.75. Because you did not survey every student on campus, your estimate may be incorrect. To account for this error, you might adjust your guess by stating the proportion of students on your campus who use Facebook is 0.75, give or take 0.05 (the *margin of error*). Mathematically, we write this as 0.75 ± 0.05. If asked how confident you are that the proportion is between 0.70 and 0.80, you might respond, "I am 80% confident that the proportion of students on my campus who use Facebook is between 0.70 and 0.80." If you want an interval for which your confidence increases to, say, 90%, what do you think will happen to the interval? More confidence that the interval will capture the unknown population proportion requires that your interval will need to increase to, say, 0.65 to 0.85.

In Other Words
The symbol $\pm$ is read "plus or minus." It means "to add and subtract the quantity following the $\pm$ symbol."

In statistics, we construct an interval for a population parameter based upon a guess along with a level of confidence. The guess is the point estimate of the population parameter, and the level of confidence plays a role in the width of the interval. See Figure 1.

Figure 1

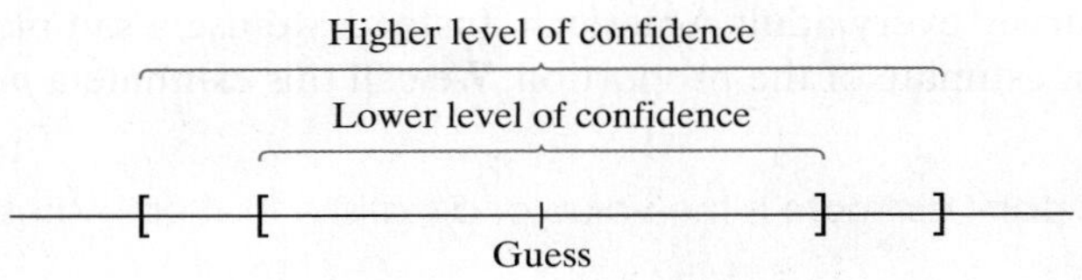

DEFINITIONS

- A **confidence interval** for an unknown parameter consists of an interval of numbers based on a point estimate.
- The **level of confidence** represents the expected proportion of intervals that will contain the parameter if a large number of different samples is obtained. The level of confidence is denoted $(1 - \alpha) \cdot 100\%$.

In Other Words
A confidence interval is a range of numbers, such as 22–30. The level of confidence is the proportion of intervals that will contain the unknown parameter if repeated samples are obtained.

For example, a 95% level of confidence ($\alpha = 0.05$) implies that if 100 different confidence intervals are constructed, each based on a different sample from the same population, then we will expect 95 of the intervals to include the parameter and 5 to not include the parameter.

Confidence interval estimates for the population proportion are of the form

$$\text{Point estimate} \pm \text{margin of error}$$

For example, in the poll in which Gallup was estimating the proportion of adult Americans who believe they are paying too much in federal income taxes, the point estimate is $\hat{p} = 0.480$. From the report, Gallup indicated the margin of error was 0.04. Gallup also reported the level of confidence to be 95%. So Gallup is 95% confident the proportion of adult Americans who believe they pay too much in federal income tax is between 0.44 $(= 0.48 - 0.04)$ and 0.52 $(= 0.48 + 0.04)$. Here are some unanswered questions at this point in the discussion:

- Why does the level of confidence represent the expected proportion of intervals that contain the parameter if a large number of different samples is obtained?
- How is the margin of error determined?

To help answer these questions, let's review what we know about the model that describes the sampling distribution of $\hat{p}$, the sample proportion.

- The shape of the distribution of all possible sample proportions is approximately normal provided $np(1 - p) \geq 10$ and the sample size is no more than 5% of the population size.
- The mean of the distribution of the sample proportion equals the population proportion. That is, $\mu_{\hat{p}} = p$.
- The standard deviation of the distribution of the sample proportion (the standard error) is $\sigma_{\hat{p}} = \sqrt{\frac{p(1-p)}{n}}$.

Because the distribution of the sample proportion is approximately normal, we know 95% of all sample proportions will lie within 1.96 standard deviations of the population proportion, p, and 2.5% of the sample proportions will lie in each tail. See Figure 2. The 1.96 comes from the fact that $z_{0.025}$ is the z-value such that 2.5% of the area under the standard normal curve is to its right. Recall, $z_{0.025} = 1.96$ and $-z_{0.025} = -1.96$.

Figure 2

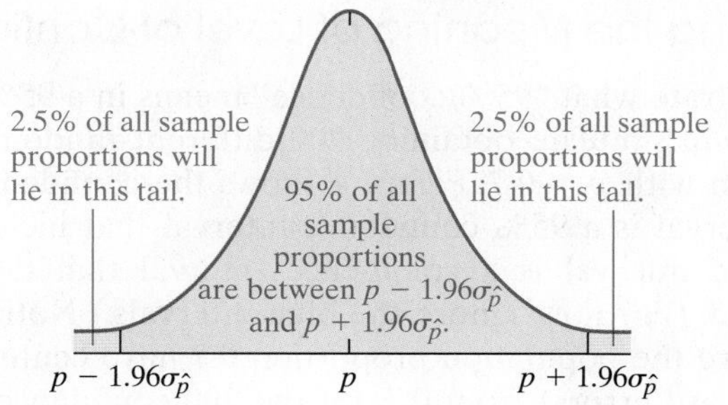

From Figure 2, we see that 95% of all sample proportions are in the inequality

$$p - 1.96\sigma_{\hat{p}} < \hat{p} < p + 1.96\sigma_{\hat{p}}$$

parameter − 1.96 standard error < point estimate < parameter + 1.96 standard error

With a little algebraic manipulation, we can rewrite this inequality with p in the middle and obtain

$$\hat{p} - 1.96\sigma_{\hat{p}} < p < \hat{p} + 1.96\sigma_{\hat{p}} \qquad \textbf{(1)}$$

point estimate − 1.96 standard error < parameter < point estimate + 1.96 standard error

This inequality states that 95% of *all* sample proportions will result in confidence interval estimates that contain the population proportion, while 5% of *all* sample proportions will result in confidence interval estimates that do not contain the population proportion. It is common to write the 95% confidence interval as

$$\hat{p} \pm 1.96\sigma_{\hat{p}}$$

point estimate ± 1.96 standard error

point estimate ± margin of error

So the **margin of error** for a 95% confidence interval for the population proportion is $1.96\sigma_{\hat{p}}$. This determines the width of the interval.

To visually illustrate the idea of a confidence interval, draw the sampling distribution of $\hat{p}$. Now create a "slider" that shows $\hat{p} - 1.96\sigma_{\hat{p}}$ and $\hat{p} + 1.96\sigma_{\hat{p}}$. As $\hat{p}$ leaves the blue-shaded region, the corresponding confidence interval does not capture the population proportion, p. See Figure 3.

Figure 3 tells us that, for a 95% confidence interval, 95% of all sample proportions will result in a confidence interval that includes the population proportion, while 5% of all sample proportions (those in the tails) will result in a confidence interval that does not include the population proportion.

Note to Instructor

Consider assigning the "Exploring the Effects of Confidence Level, Sample Size, and Shape" activity from the Student Activity Workbook.

Figure 3

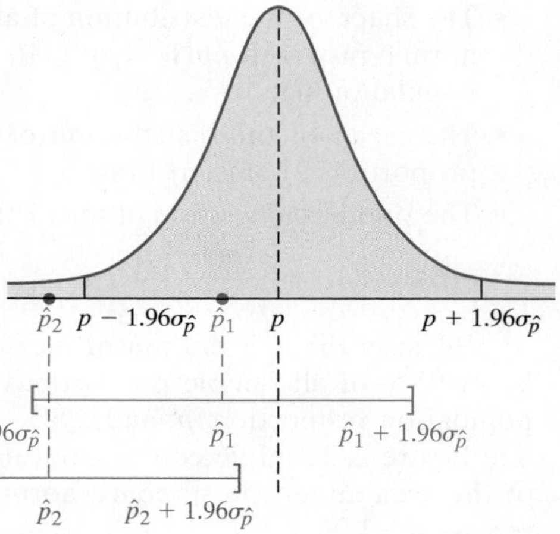

EXAMPLE 2 Illustrating the Meaning of Level of Confidence Using Simulation

Note to Instructor

Use the confidence interval applet to illustrate the concepts in Example 2.

Let's illustrate what "95% confidence" means in a 95% confidence interval in another way. We will simulate obtaining 200 different random samples of size $n = 50$ from a population with $p = 0.7$. Figure 4 shows the confidence intervals in groups of 100. A green interval is a 95% confidence interval that includes the population proportion, 0.7. A red interval is a confidence interval that does not include the population proportion. (For now, ignore the blue intervals.) Notice that the red intervals that do not capture the population proportion 0.7 have centers that are far away (more than 1.96 standard errors) from 0.7. Of the 200 confidence intervals obtained, 10 (the red intervals) do not include the population proportion. For example, the first interval to miss has a sample proportion that is too small to result in an interval that captures 0.7. So 190/200 = 0.95 (or 95%) of the samples have intervals that capture the population proportion.

A 95% level of confidence means that 95% of all possible samples result in confidence intervals that include the parameter (and 5% of all possible samples result in confidence intervals that do not include the parameter).

Figure 4

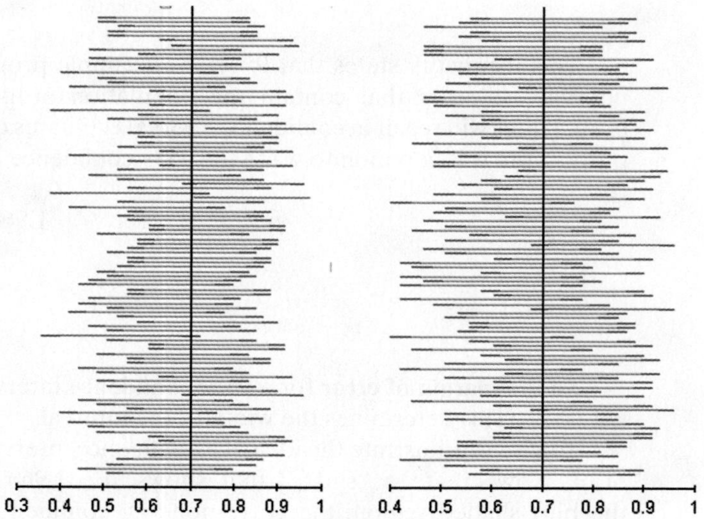

CAUTION

A 95% confidence interval does *not* mean that there is a 95% probability that the interval contains the parameter (such as p or μ). Remember, probability describes the likelihood of undetermined events. Therefore, it does not make sense to talk about the probability that the interval contains the parameter since the parameter is a fixed value. Think of it this way: I flip a coin and obtain a head. If I ask you to determine the probability that the flip resulted in a head, it would not be 0.5, because the outcome has already been determined. Instead, the probability is 0 or 1. Confidence intervals work the same way. Because p or μ is already determined, we do not say that there is a 95% probability that the interval contains p or μ.

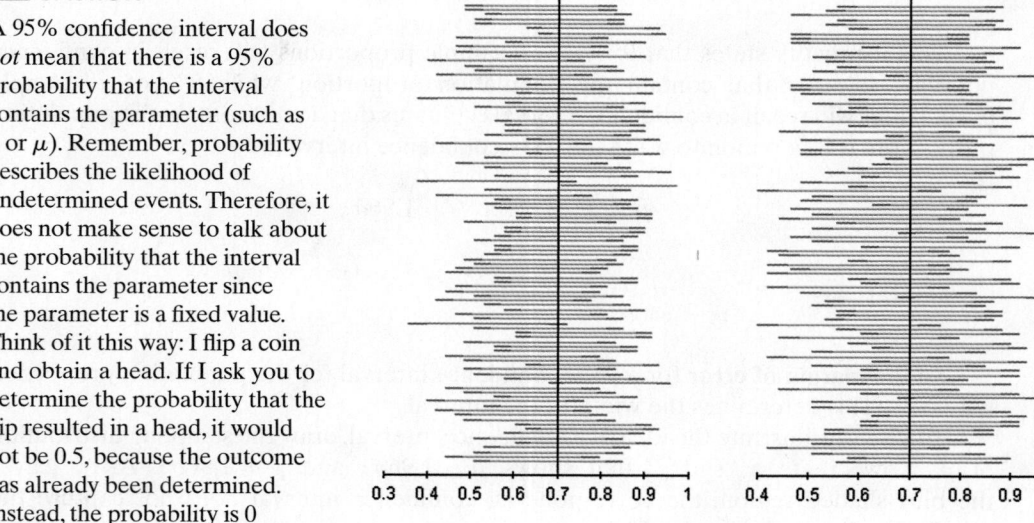

We can express the results of Example 2 in a different way. For a 95% confidence interval, any sample proportion that lies within 1.96 standard errors of the population proportion will result in a confidence interval that includes p, and any sample proportion that is more than 1.96 standard errors from the population proportion will result in a confidence interval that does not contain p. So, **whether a confidence interval contains the population parameter depends solely on the value of the sample statistic.**

In practice, we construct only one confidence interval. We do not know whether the sample results in a confidence interval that includes the parameter or not, but we do know that if we construct a 95% confidence interval it will include the unknown parameter 95% of the time.

We need a method for constructing any $(1 - \alpha) \cdot 100\%$ confidence interval. [When $\alpha = 0.05$, we are constructing a $(1 - 0.05) \cdot 100\% = 95\%$ confidence interval.]

We generalize Formula (1) on page 393 by first noting that $(1 - \alpha) \cdot 100\%$ of all sample proportions are in the interval

$$p - z_{\frac{\alpha}{2}} \cdot \sqrt{\frac{p(1-p)}{n}} < \hat{p} < p + z_{\frac{\alpha}{2}} \cdot \sqrt{\frac{p(1-p)}{n}}$$

as shown in Figure 5.

Figure 5

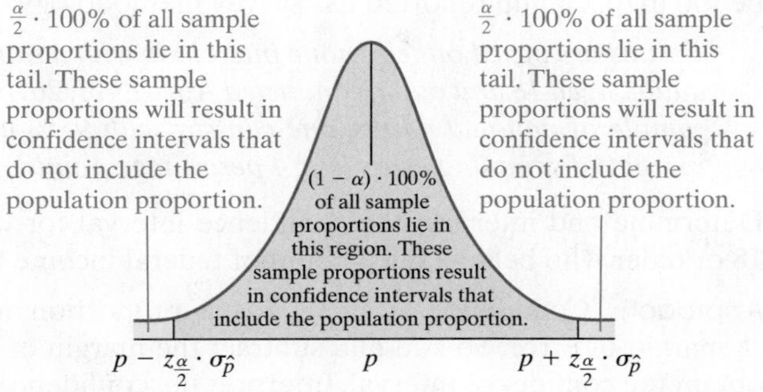
$\frac{\alpha}{2} \cdot 100\%$ of all sample proportions lie in this tail. These sample proportions will result in confidence intervals that do not include the population proportion.
$\frac{\alpha}{2} \cdot 100\%$ of all sample proportions lie in this tail. These sample proportions will result in confidence intervals that do not include the population proportion.
$(1 - \alpha) \cdot 100\%$ of all sample proportions lie in this region. These sample proportions result in confidence intervals that include the population proportion.
$p - z_{\frac{\alpha}{2}} \cdot \sigma_{\hat{p}}$
p
$p + z_{\frac{\alpha}{2}} \cdot \sigma_{\hat{p}}$

We rewrite this inequality with p in the middle and obtain

$$\hat{p} - z_{\frac{\alpha}{2}} \cdot \sqrt{\frac{p(1-p)}{n}} < p < \hat{p} + z_{\frac{\alpha}{2}} \cdot \sqrt{\frac{p(1-p)}{n}}$$

So $(1 - \alpha) \cdot 100\%$ of all sample proportions will result in confidence intervals that contain the population proportion. The sample proportions that are in the tails of the distribution in Figure 5 will not result in confidence intervals that contain the population proportion.

The value $z_{\frac{\alpha}{2}}$ is called the **critical value** of the distribution. It represents the number of standard deviations the sample statistic can be from the parameter and still result in an interval that includes the parameter. Table 1 shows some of the common critical values used in the construction of confidence intervals. Notice that higher levels of confidence correspond to higher critical values. After all, if your level of confidence that the interval includes the unknown parameter increases, the width of your interval (using the margin of error) should increase.

TABLE 1

Level of Confidence, $(1 - \alpha) \cdot 100\%$	Area in Each tail, $\frac{\alpha}{2}$	Critical Value, $z_{\frac{\alpha}{2}}$
90%	0.05	1.645
95%	0.025	1.96
99%	0.005	2.575

In Other Words
The interpretation of a confidence interval is this: We are (*insert level of confidence*) confident that the population proportion is between (*lower bound*) and (*upper bound*). This is an abbreviated way of saying that the method is correct $(1 - \alpha) \cdot 100\%$ of the time.

Interpretation of a Confidence Interval

A $(1 - \alpha) \cdot 100\%$ confidence interval indicates that $(1 - \alpha) \cdot 100\%$ of all simple random samples of size n from the population whose parameter is unknown will result in an interval that contains the parameter.

For example, a 90% confidence interval for a parameter suggests that 90% of all possible samples will result in an interval that includes the unknown parameter and 10% of the samples result in an interval that does not capture the parameter.

Look back at Figure 4 on page 394 from Example 2. The intervals, *including* the blue parts, represent 99% confidence intervals. Any interval entirely in red is an interval whose 99% confidence interval does not include the population proportion, 0.7. We can see that only 2 of the 200 intervals constructed do not include 0.7, so 198/200 or 99% of the 200 intervals do include the population proportion. Therefore, a 99% confidence interval for a parameter means that 99% of all possible samples result in an interval that includes the parameter and 1% of the samples result in an interval that does not capture the parameter.

EXAMPLE 3 Interpreting a Confidence Interval

Problem When the Gallup Organization conducted the poll introduced in Example 1, 48% of those surveyed considered the amount of federal income tax they have to pay to be too high. Gallup reported its "survey methodology" as follows:

> *Results are based on telephone interviews with a random sample of 1020 national adults, aged 18 and older, conducted April 8–11, 2010. For results based on the total sample of national adults, one can say with 95% confidence that the maximum margin of sampling error is* ± 4 *percentage points.*

Determine and interpret the confidence interval for the proportion of Americans age 18 or older who believe the amount of federal income tax they have to pay is too high.

Approach Confidence intervals for a proportion are of the form point estimate $\pm$ margin of error. So add and subtract the margin of error from the point estimate to obtain the confidence interval. Interpret the confidence interval, "We are 95% confident the proportion of Americans age 18 or older who believe the amount of federal income tax they have to pay is too high is between *lower bound* and *upper bound*."

Solution The point estimate is 0.48 and the margin of error is 0.04. The confidence interval is 0.48 ± 0.04. Therefore, the lower bound of the confidence interval is $0.48 - 0.04 = 0.44$ and the upper bound of the confidence interval is $0.48 + 0.04 = 0.52$. We are 95% confident the proportion of Americans age 18 or older who believe the amount of federal income tax they have to pay is too high is between 0.44 and 0.52.

Now Work Problem 21

An extremely important point is that the level of confidence refers to the confidence in the *method*, not in the specific interval. A 90% confidence interval means the method "works" (that is, the interval includes the unknown parameter) for 90% of all samples. We do not know whether the sample statistic we obtained is one of the 90% with an interval that includes the parameter, or one of the 10% whose interval does not include the parameter. **A 90% level of confidence *does not* tell us there is a 90% probability the parameter lies between the lower and upper bound.**

We are now prepared to present a method for constructing a $(1 - \alpha) \cdot 100\%$ confidence interval about the population proportion, p.

We repeat (from Section 8.2) the sampling distribution of the sample proportion, $\hat{p}$.

Sampling Distribution of $\hat{p}$

For a simple random sample of size n, the sampling distribution of $\hat{p}$ is approximately normal, with mean $\mu_{\hat{p}} = p$ and standard deviation $\sigma_{\hat{p}} = \sqrt{\dfrac{p(1-p)}{n}}$, provided that $np(1 - p) \geq 10$.

Note: We also require that each trial be independent. When sampling from finite populations, this means that the sample size can be no more than 5% of the population size ($n \leq 0.05N$).

We use the sampling distribution of $\hat{p}$ to construct a confidence interval for the population proportion, p.

Constructing a $(1 - \alpha) \cdot 100\%$ Confidence Interval for a Population Proportion

Suppose that a simple random sample of size n is taken from a population or the data are the result of a randomized experiment. A $(1 - \alpha) \cdot 100\%$ confidence interval for p is given by the following quantities:

$$\text{Lower bound: } \hat{p} - z_{\frac{\alpha}{2}} \cdot \sqrt{\frac{\hat{p}(1-\hat{p})}{n}}$$
$$\text{Upper bound: } \hat{p} + z_{\frac{\alpha}{2}} \cdot \sqrt{\frac{\hat{p}(1-\hat{p})}{n}} \qquad (2)$$

Note: It must be the case that $n\hat{p}(1 - \hat{p}) \geq 10$ and $n \leq 0.05N$ to construct this interval.

Note to Instructor

Consider assigning the "Constructing a Confidence Interval with M & Ms" activity from the Student Activity Workbook.

Notice that we use $\hat{p}$ in place of p in the standard deviation. This is because p is unknown, and $\hat{p}$ is the best point estimate of p.

EXAMPLE 4 Constructing a Confidence Interval for a Population Proportion

Problem In the 2009 Parent–Teen Cell Phone Survey conducted by Princeton Survey Research Associates International, 800 randomly sampled 16- to 17-year-olds living in the United States were asked whether they have ever used their cell phone to text while driving. Of the 800 teenagers surveyed, 272 indicated that they text while driving. Obtain a 95% confidence interval for the proportion of 16- to 17-year-olds who text while driving.

By Hand Approach

Step 1 Compute the value of $\hat{p}$.

Step 2 Verify that $n\hat{p}(1 - \hat{p}) \geq 10$ (the normality condition) and $n \leq 0.05N$ (the sample size is no more than 5% of the population size − the independence condition).

Step 3 Determine the critical value $z_{\frac{\alpha}{2}}$.

Step 4 Use Formula (2) to determine the lower and upper bounds of the confidence interval.

Step 5 Interpret the result.

By-Hand Solution

Step 1 There are $x = 272$ successes (teens who text while driving) out of $n = 800$ individuals in the survey, so

$$\hat{p} = \frac{x}{n} = \frac{272}{800} = 0.34$$

Step 2 $n\hat{p}(1 - \hat{p}) = 800(0.34)(1 - 0.34) = 179.52 \geq 10$. There are certainly more than 1,000,000 teenagers 16 to 17 years of age in the United States, so our sample size is definitely less than 5% of the population size. The independence requirement is satisfied.

Step 3 Because we want a 95% confidence interval, we have $\alpha = 1 - 0.95 = 0.05$, so $z_{\frac{\alpha}{2}} = z_{\frac{0.05}{2}} = z_{0.025} = 1.96$.

Technology Approach

Step 1 By hand, compute the value of $\hat{p}$.

Step 2 Verify that $n\hat{p}(1 - \hat{p})>10$ (the normality condition) and $n \leq 0.05N$ (the sample size is no more than 5% of the population size–the independence condition).

Step 3 Use a statistical spreadsheet or graphing calculator with advanced statistical features to obtain the confidence interval. We will use StatCrunch. The steps for constructing confidence intervals using StatCrunch, MINITAB, Excel, and the TI-83/84 Plus graphing calculators are given in the Technology Step-by-Step on page 404.

Step 4 Interpret the result.

Technology Solution

Step 1 There are $x = 272$ successes (teens who text while driving) out of $n = 800$ individuals in the survey, so

$$\hat{p} = \frac{x}{n} = \frac{272}{800} = 0.34$$

Step 2 $n\hat{p}(1 - \hat{p}) = 800(0.34)(1 - 0.34) = 179.52 \geq 10$. There are certainly more than 1,000,000 teenagers 16 to 17 years of age in the United States, so our sample size is definitely less than 5% of the population size. The independence requirement is satisfied.

Step 4 Substituting into Formula (2) with $n = 800$, we obtain the lower and upper bounds of the confidence interval:

Lower bound:

$$\begin{aligned}\hat{p} - z_{\frac{\alpha}{2}}\cdot\sqrt{\frac{\hat{p}(1-\hat{p})}{n}} &= 0.34 - 1.96\cdot\sqrt{\frac{0.34(1-0.34)}{800}}\\ &= 0.34 - 0.033\\ &= 0.307\end{aligned}$$

Upper bound:

$$\begin{aligned}\hat{p} + z_{\frac{\alpha}{2}}\cdot\sqrt{\frac{\hat{p}(1-\hat{p})}{n}} &= 0.34 + 1.96\cdot\sqrt{\frac{0.34(1-0.34)}{800}}\\ &= 0.34 + 0.033\\ &= 0.373\end{aligned}$$

Step 5 We are 95% confident that the proportion of 16- to 17-year-olds who text while driving is between 0.307 and 0.373.

Step 3 Figure 6 shows the results obtained from StatCrunch.

Figure 6

95% confidence interval results:
p : proportion of successes for population
Method: Standard-Wald

Proportion	Count	Total	Sample Prop.	Std. Err.	L. Limit	U. Limit
p	272	800	0.34	0.016748134	0.30717427	0.37282574

The lower bound (L. Limit) is 0.307 and the upper bound (U. Limit) is 0.373.

Step 4 We are 95% confident that the proportion of 16- to 17-year-olds who text while driving is between 0.307 and 0.373.

Using Technology
Confidence intervals constructed by hand may differ from those using technology because of rounding.

It is important to remember the correct interpretation of a confidence interval. The statement "95% confident" means that, if 1000 samples of size 800 were taken, we would expect 950 of the intervals to contain the parameter p, while 50 will not. Unfortunately, we cannot know whether the interval we constructed in Example 4 is one of the 950 intervals that contains p or one of the 50 that does not contain p.

Note: In this text we report the interval as *Lower bound:* 0.307; *Upper bound:* 0.373. Some texts will use interval notation as in (0.307, 0.373).

Now Work Problem 25 (b), (c) and (d)

The Effect of Level of Confidence on the Margin of Error

We stated on page 392 that logic suggests that a higher level of confidence leads to a wider interval. The width of the interval is determined by the margin of error.

DEFINITION

The **margin of error, *E*,** in a $(1-\alpha)\cdot 100\%$ confidence interval for a population proportion is given by

$$E = z_{\frac{\alpha}{2}}\cdot\sqrt{\frac{\hat{p}(1-\hat{p})}{n}} \quad \textbf{(3)}$$

EXAMPLE 5 Role of the Level of Confidence in the Margin of Error

Problem For the problem of estimating the proportion of 16- to 17-year-old teenagers who text while driving, determine the effect on the margin of error by increasing the level of confidence from 95% to 99%.

By-Hand Approach

With a 99% level of confidence, we have $\alpha = 1 - 0.99 = 0.01$. So, to compute the margin of error, E, we determine the value of $z_{\frac{\alpha}{2}} = z_{\frac{0.01}{2}} = z_{0.005}$. We then substitute this value into Formula (3) with $\hat{p} = 0.34$ and $n = 800$.

Technology Approach

Construct a 99% confidence interval using a statistical spreadsheet or graphing calculator with advanced statistical features. Then use the fact that a confidence interval about the population proportion is of the form $\hat{p} \pm E$. The midpoint of the upper and lower bound gives the point estimate. The difference between the point estimate and the lower bound is the margin of error.

By-Hand Solution

After consulting Table V (Appendix A), we determine that $z_{0.005} = 2.575$. Substituting into Formula (3), we obtain

$$E = z_{\frac{\alpha}{2}} \cdot \sqrt{\frac{\hat{p}(1-\hat{p})}{n}} = 2.575 \cdot \sqrt{\frac{0.34(1-0.34)}{800}}$$

$$= 0.043$$

Technology Solution

Figure 7 shows the 99% confidence interval using a TI-84 Plus graphing calculator.

Figure 7

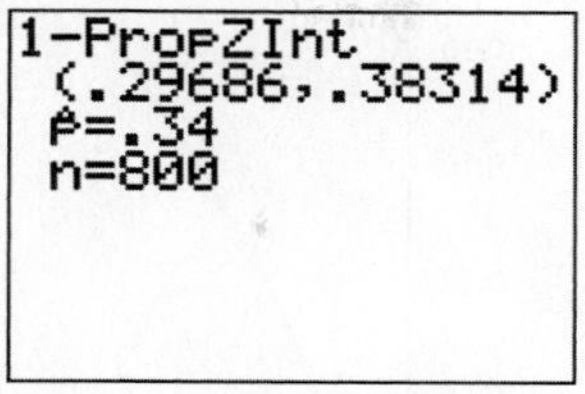

The lower bound is 0.297 and the upper bound is 0.383. The midpoint is $\hat{p} = \frac{0.297 + 0.383}{2} = 0.34$. The margin of error is $E = 0.34 - 0.297 = 0.043$.

In Other Words

As the level of confidence increases, the margin of error also increases.

The margin of error for the 95% confidence interval found in Example 4 is 0.033, so increasing the level of confidence increases the margin of error, therefore resulting in a wider confidence interval.

The Effect of Sample Size on the Margin of Error

We already know that larger sample sizes produce more precise estimates (the Law of Large Numbers). Given that the margin of error is $z_{\frac{\alpha}{2}} \cdot \sqrt{\frac{\hat{p}(1-\hat{p})}{n}}$, we can see that increasing the sample size n decreases the standard error, so the margin of error decreases. This means that larger sample sizes will result in narrower confidence intervals.

To illustrate this idea, suppose the survey conducted in Example 4 resulted in $\hat{p} = 0.34$ for the proportion of 16- to 17-year-old teenagers who text while driving, but the sample size is only 200. The margin of error would be

$$E = z_{\frac{\alpha}{2}} \cdot \sqrt{\frac{\hat{p}(1-\hat{p})}{n}} = 1.96 \cdot \sqrt{\frac{0.34(1-0.34)}{200}} = 0.066$$

In Other Words

As the sample size increases, the margin of error decreases.

So a sample size that is one-fourth the original size causes the margin of error to double. Put another way, if the sample size is quadrupled, the margin of error will be cut in half.

3 Determine the Sample Size Necessary for Estimating a Population Proportion within a Specified Margin of Error

Suppose you want to estimate a proportion with a 3% (0.03) margin of error and 95% confidence. How many individuals should be in your sample? From Formula (3), the margin of error is $E = z_{\frac{\alpha}{2}} \cdot \sqrt{\frac{\hat{p}(1-\hat{p})}{n}}$. If we solve this formula for n, we obtain $n = \hat{p}(1-\hat{p}) \cdot \left(\frac{z_{\frac{\alpha}{2}}}{E}\right)^2$.

Note to Instructor

You might have students experiment with various values of $\hat{p}$ to see which one maximizes $\hat{p}(1-\hat{p})$.

The problem with this formula is that it depends on $\hat{p}$, and $\hat{p} = \frac{x}{n}$ depends on the sample size, n, which is what we are trying to determine in the first place! How do we resolve this issue? There are two possibilities: (1) We could determine a preliminary value for $\hat{p}$ based on a pilot study or an earlier study, or (2) we could let $\hat{p} = 0.5$. When $\hat{p} = 0.5$, the maximum value of $\hat{p}(1-\hat{p}) = 0.25$ is obtained, as illustrated in Figure 8. Using the maximum value gives the largest possible value of n for a given level of confidence and a given margin of error.

Figure 8

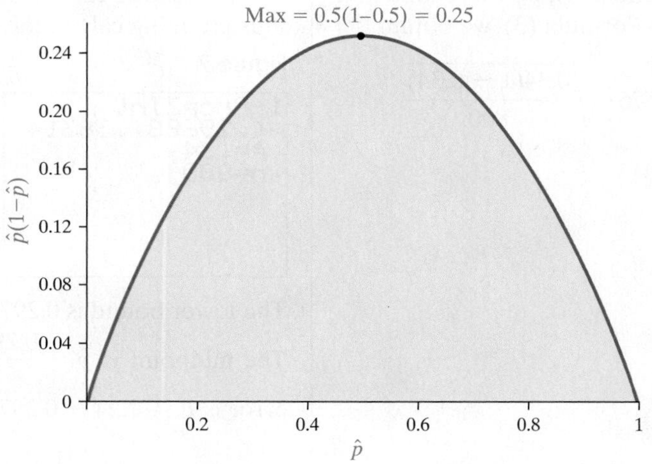

The disadvantage of the second option is that it could lead to a larger sample size than is necessary. Because of the time and expense of sampling, it is desirable to avoid too large a sample.

Sample Size Needed for Estimating the Population Proportion p

The sample size required to obtain a $(1 - \alpha) \cdot 100\%$ confidence interval for p with a margin of error E is given by

$$n = \hat{p}(1 - \hat{p})\left(\frac{z_{\frac{\alpha}{2}}}{E}\right)^2 \quad \textbf{(4)}$$

(rounded up to the next integer), where $\hat{p}$ is a prior estimate of p. If a prior estimate of p is unavailable, the sample size required is

$$n = 0.25\left(\frac{z_{\frac{\alpha}{2}}}{E}\right)^2 \quad \textbf{(5)}$$

rounded up to the next integer. The margin of error should always be expressed as a decimal when using Formulas (4) and (5).

CAUTION

Rounding *up* is different from rounding *off*. We round 12.3 up to 13; we round 12.3 off to 12.

EXAMPLE 6 Determining Sample Size

Problem An economist wants to know if the proportion of the U.S. population who commutes to work via car-pooling is on the rise. What size sample should be obtained if the economist wants an estimate within 2 percentage points of the true proportion with 90% confidence if

(a) the economist uses the 2006 estimate of 10.7% obtained from the American Community Survey?

(b) the economist does not use any prior estimates?

Approach In both cases, $E = 0.02$ $(2\% = 0.02)$ and $z_{\frac{\alpha}{2}} = z_{\frac{0.1}{2}} = z_{0.05} = 1.645$. To answer part (a), let $\hat{p} = 0.107$ in Formula (4). To answer part (b), use Formula (5).

Solution

(a) Substituting $E = 0.02$, $z_{0.05} = 1.645$, and $\hat{p} = 0.107$ into Formula (4), we obtain

$$n = \hat{p}(1 - \hat{p})\left(\frac{z_{\frac{\alpha}{2}}}{E}\right)^2 = 0.107(1 - 0.107)\left(\frac{1.645}{0.02}\right)^2 = 646.4$$

We round this value up to 647, so the economist must survey 647 randomly selected residents of the United States.

CAUTION

We always round up when determining sample size.

(b) Substituting $E = 0.02$ and $z_{0.05} = 1.645$ into Formula (5), we obtain

$$n = 0.25\left(\frac{z_{\frac{\alpha}{2}}}{E}\right)^2 = 0.25\left(\frac{1.645}{0.02}\right)^2 = 1691.3$$

We round this value up to 1692, so the economist must survey 1692 randomly selected residents of the United States.

We can see the effect of not having a prior estimate of p: In this case, the required sample size more than doubled!

Now Work Problem 33

9.1 ASSESS YOUR UNDERSTANDING

VOCABULARY AND SKILL BUILDING

1. A point estimate is the value of a statistic that estimates the value of a parameter.

2. The level of confidence represents the expected proportion of intervals that will contain the parameter if a large number of different samples is obtained. It is denoted $(1-\alpha)100\%$.

3. *True or False*: A 95% confidence interval for a population proportion with lower bound 0.45 and upper bound 0.51 means there is a 95% probability the population proportion is between 0.45 and 0.51. False

4. The value $z_{\frac{\alpha}{2}}$ represents the critical value of the distribution.

5. As the level of confidence of a confidence interval increases, the margin of error increases (increases/decreases).

6. As the sample size used to obtain a confidence interval increases, the margin of error decreases (increases/decreases).

In Problems 7–10, determine the critical value $z_{\alpha/2}$ that corresponds to the given level of confidence.

7. 90% 1.645 **8.** 99% 2.575

9. 98% 2.33 **10.** 92% 1.75

In Problems 11–14, determine the point estimate of the population proportion, the margin of error for each confidence interval, and the number of individuals in the sample with the specified characteristic, x, for the sample size provided.

11. Lower bound: 0.201, upper bound: 0.249, $n = 1200$

12. Lower bound: 0.051, upper bound: 0.074, $n = 1120$

13. Lower bound: 0.462, upper bound: 0.509, $n = 1680$

14. Lower bound: 0.853, upper bound: 0.871, $n = 10{,}732$
$\hat{p} = 0.862$, $E = 0.009$, $x = 9251$

In Problems 15–20, construct a confidence interval of the population proportion at the given level of confidence.

15. $x = 30$, $n = 150$, 90% confidence (0.146, 0.254)

16. $x = 80$, $n = 200$, 98% confidence (0.319, 0.481)

17. $x = 120$, $n = 500$, 99% confidence (0.191, 0.289)

18. $x = 400$, $n = 1200$, 95% confidence (0.306, 0.360)

19. $x = 860$, $n = 1100$, 94% confidence (0.759, 0.805)

20. $x = 540$, $n = 900$, 96% confidence (0.567, 0.633)

APPLYING THE CONCEPTS

NW **21. You Explain It! New Deal Policies** In response to the Great Depression, Franklin D. Roosevelt enacted many New Deal policies. One such policy was the enactment of the National Recovery Administration (NRA), which forced business to agree to wages and prices within their particular industry. The thought was that this would encourage higher wages among the working class, thereby spurring consumption. In a Gallup survey conducted in 1933 of 2025 adult Americans, 55% thought that wages paid to workers in industry were too low. The margin of error was 3 percentage points with 95% confidence. Which of the following represents a reasonable interpretation of the survey results? For those that are not reasonable, explain the flaw. (c) is correct

(a) We are 95% confident 55% of adult Americans during the Great Depression felt wages paid to workers in industry were too low.

(b) We are 92% to 98% confident 55% of adult Americans during the Great Depression felt wages paid to workers in industry were too low.

(c) We are 95% confident the proportion of adult Americans during the Great Depression who believed wages paid to workers in industry were too low was between 0.52 and 0.58.

(d) In 95% of samples of adult Americans during the Great Depression, the proportion who believed wages paid to workers in industry were too low is between 0.52 and 0.58.

22. You Explain It! Superstition A *USA Today*/Gallup poll asked 1006 adult Americans how much it would bother them to stay in a room on the 13th floor of a hotel. Interestingly, 13% said it would bother them. The margin of error was 3 percentage points with 95% confidence. Which of the following represents a reasonable interpretation of the survey results? For those not reasonable, explain the flaw. (a) is correct

(a) We are 95% confident that the proportion of adult Americans who would be bothered to stay in a room on the 13th floor is between 0.10 and 0.16.

(b) We are between 92% and 98% confident that 13% of adult Americans would be bothered to stay in a room on the 13th floor.

(c) In 95% of samples of adult Americans, the proportion who would be bothered to stay in a room on the 13th floor is between 0.10 and 0.16.

(d) We are 95% confident that 13% of adult Americans would be bothered to stay in a room on the 13th floor.

23. You Explain It! Valentine's Day A Rasmussen Reports national survey of 1000 adult Americans found that 18% dreaded Valentine's Day. The margin of error for the survey was 4.5 percentage points with 95% confidence. Explain what this means.

24. You Explain It! A Stressful Commute? A Gallup poll of 547 adult Americans employed full or part time asked, "Generally speaking, would you say your commute to work is—very stressful, somewhat stressful, not that stressful, or not stressful at all?" Gallup reported that 24% of American workers said that their commute was "very" or "somewhat" stressful. The margin of error was 4 percentage points with 95% confidence. Explain what this means.

11. $\hat{p} = 0.225$, $E = 0.024$, $x = 270$ 12. $\hat{p} = 0.0625$, $E = 0.0115$, $x = 70$ 13. $\hat{p} = 0.4855$, $E = 0.0235$, $x = 816$

NW **25. Smartphone Purchases** In a survey of 3611 adult Americans 18 years and older conducted in July 2010 by SmartRevenue, it was found that 542 have used their smartphone to make a purchase.

(a) Obtain a point estimate for the population proportion of adult Americans 18 years and older who have used their smartphone to make a purchase. 0.150

(b) Verify that the requirements for constructing a confidence interval about p are satisfied.

(c) Construct a 90% confidence interval for the population proportion of adult Americans who have used their smartphone to make a purchase. (0.140, 0.160)

(d) Interpret the interval.

26. Saving for Retirement? A Retirement Confidence Survey of 1153 workers and retirees in the United States 25 years of age and older conducted by Employee Benefit Research Institute in January 2010 found that 496 had less than $10,000 in savings.

(a) Obtain a point estimate for the population proportion of workers and retirees in the United States 25 years of age and older who have less than $10,000 in savings. 0.430

(b) Verify that the requirements for constructing a confidence interval about p are satisfied. (c) (0.401, 0.459)

(c) Construct a 95% confidence interval for the population proportion of workers and retirees in the United States 25 years of age and older who have less than $10,000 in savings.

(d) Interpret the interval.

27. Luxury or Necessity? A random sample of 1003 adult Americans was asked, "Do you pretty much think televisions are a necessity or a luxury you could do without?" Of the 1003 adults surveyed, 521 indicated that televisions are a luxury they could do without.

(a) Obtain a point estimate for the population proportion of adult Americans who believe that televisions are a luxury they could do without. 0.519

(b) Verify that the requirements for constructing a confidence interval about p are satisfied.

(c) Construct and interpret a 95% confidence interval for the population proportion of adult Americans who believe that televisions are a luxury they could do without. (0.488, 0.550)

(d) Is it possible that a supermajority (more than 60%) of adult Americans believe that television is a luxury they could do without? Is it likely? Yes; no

(e) Use the results of part (c) to construct a 95% confidence interval for the population proportion of adult Americans who believe that televisions are a necessity. (0.450, 0.512)

28. Family Values In a *USA Today*/Gallup poll, 768 of 1024 randomly selected adult Americans aged 18 or older stated that a candidate's positions on the issue of family value are extremely or very important in determining their vote for president.

(a) Obtain a point estimate for the proportion of adult Americans aged 18 or older for which the issue of family values is extremely or very important in determining their vote for president. $\hat{p} = 0.75$

(b) Verify that the requirements for constructing a confidence interval for p are satisfied.

(c) Construct a 99% confidence interval for the proportion of adult Americans aged 18 or older for which the issue of family values is extremely or very important in determining their vote for president. (0.715, 0.785)

(d) Is it possible that the proportion of adult Americans aged 18 or older for which the issue of family values is extremely or very important in determining their vote for president is below 70%? Is this likely? Yes; no 28. (e) (0.215, 0.285)

(e) Use the results of part (c) to construct a 99% confidence interval for the proportion of adult Americans aged 18 or older for which the issue of family values is not extremely or very important in determining their vote for president.

29. Tattoo Attitude A Harris Interactive poll conducted during January 2008 found that 944 of 1748 adult Americans 18 years or older who do not have a tattoo believe that individuals with tattoos are more rebellious.

(a) Obtain a point estimate for the proportion of adult Americans without tattoos who believe individuals with tattoos are more rebellious. 0.540

(b) Verify that the requirements for constructing a confidence interval for p are satisfied.

(c) Construct a 90% confidence interval for the proportion of adult Americans without tattoos who believe individuals with tattoos are more rebellious. (0.520, 0.560)

(d) Construct a 99% confidence interval for the proportion of adult Americans without tattoos who believe individuals with tattoos are more rebellious. (0.509, 0.571)

(e) What is the effect of increasing the level of confidence on the width of the interval? Width increases

30. Healthcare A Gallup poll conducted in November 2010 found that 493 of 1050 adult Americans believe it is the responsibility of the federal government to make sure all Americans have healthcare coverage.

(a) Obtain a point estimate for the proportion of adult Americans who believe it is the responsibility of the federal government to make sure all Americans have healthcare coverage. 0.470

(b) Verify that the requirements for constructing a confidence interval for p are satisfied.

(c) Construct a 95% confidence interval for the proportion of adult Americans who believe it is the responsibility of the federal government to make sure all Americans have healthcare coverage. (0.440, 0.500)

(d) Construct a 99% confidence interval for the proportion of adult Americans who believe it is the responsibility of the federal government to make sure all Americans have healthcare coverage. (0.430, 0.510)

(e) What is the effect of increasing the level of confidence on the width of the interval? Width increases

31. Sullivan Statistics Survey: Deficit Reduction One question on the Sullivan Statistics Survey is "Would you be willing to pay higher taxes if the tax revenue went directly toward deficit reduction?" Treat the survey respondents as a simple random sample of adult Americans. Construct and interpret a 90% confidence interval for the proportion of adult Americans who would be willing to pay higher taxes if the revenue went directly toward deficit reduction. (0.205, 0.307)

32. Sullivan Statistics Survey: Language One question on the Sullivan Statistics Survey is "Is a language other than English the primary language spoken in your home?" Treat the survey respondents as a simple random sample of adult Americans. Construct and interpret a 95% confidence interval for the proportion of adult Americans who speak a language other than English at home. (0.084, 0.177)

NW **33. High-Speed Internet Access** A researcher wishes to estimate the proportion of households that have broadband Internet access. What size sample should be obtained if she wishes the estimate to be within 0.03 with 99% confidence if

(a) she uses a 2009 estimate of 0.635 obtained from the National Telecommunications and Information Administration? 1708

(b) she does not use any prior estimates? 1842

34. Home Ownership An urban economist wishes to estimate the proportion of Americans who own their homes. What size sample should be obtained if he wishes the estimate to be within 0.02 with 90% confidence if

(a) he uses a 2010 estimate of 0.669 obtained from the U.S Census Bureau? 1499

(b) he does not use any prior estimates? 1692

35. A Penny for Your Thoughts A researcher for the U.S. Department of the Treasury wishes to estimate the percentage of Americans who support abolishing the penny. What size sample should be obtained if he wishes the estimate to be within 2 percentage points with 98% confidence if

(a) he uses a 2006 estimate of 15% obtained from a Coinstar National Currency Poll? 1731

(b) he does not use any prior estimate? 3394

36. Credit-Card Debt A school administrator is concerned about the amount of credit-card debt that college students have. She wishes to conduct a poll to estimate the percentage of full-time college students who have credit-card debt of $2000 or more. What size sample should be obtained if she wishes the estimate to be within 2.5 percentage points with 94% confidence if

(a) a pilot study indicates that the percentage is 34%? 1269

(b) no prior estimates are used? 1414

37. Football Fans A television sports commentator wants to estimate the proportion of Americans who "follow professional football." What sample size should be obtained if he wants to be within 3 percentage points with 95% confidence if

(a) he uses a 2010 estimate of 53% obtained from a Harris poll. 1064

(b) he does not use any prior estimates? 1068

(c) Why are the results from parts (a) and (b) so close?

38. Affirmative Action A sociologist wishes to conduct a poll to estimate the percentage of Americans who favor affirmative action programs for women and minorities for admission to colleges and universities. What sample size should be obtained if she wishes the estimate to be within 4 percentage points with 90% confidence if

(a) she uses a 2003 estimate of 55% obtained from a Gallup Youth Survey? 419

(b) she does not use any prior estimates? 423

(c) Why are the results from parts (a) and (b) so close?

39. Death Penalty In a Gallup poll conducted in October 2010, 64% of the people polled answered yes to the following question: "Are you in favor of the death penalty for a person convicted of murder?" The margin of error in the poll was 3%, and the estimate was made with 95% confidence. At least how many people were surveyed? 984

40. Gun Control In a Gallup Poll conducted October 2010, 44% of the people polled answered "more strict" to the following question: "Do you feel that the laws covering the sale of firearms should be made more strict, less strict, or kept as they are now?" Suppose the margin of error in the poll was 3.5% and the estimate was made with 95% confidence. At least how many people were surveyed? 773

41. 2004 Presidential Election The Gallup organization conducted a poll of 2014 likely voters just prior to the 2004 presidential election. The results of the survey indicated that George W. Bush would receive 49% of the popular vote and John Kerry would receive 47% of the popular vote. The margin of error was reported to be 3%. The Gallup organization reported that the race was too close to call. Use the concept of a confidence interval to explain what this means.

42. Simulation – When Model Requirements Fail A Bernoulli random variable is a variable that is either 0 (a failure) or 1 (a success). The probability of success is denoted p.

(a) Use StatCrunch, MINITAB, or some other statistical spreadsheet to generate 1000 Bernoulli samples of size $n = 20$ with $p = 0.15$.

(b) Estimate the population proportion for each of the 1000 Bernoulli samples.

(c) Draw a histogram of the 1000 proportions from part (b). What is the shape of the histogram?

(d) Construct a 95% confidence interval for each of the 1000 Bernoulli samples using the normal model.

(e) What proportion of the intervals do you expect to include the population proportion, p? What proportion of the intervals actually captures the population proportion? Explain any differences.

To deal with issues such as the distribution of $\hat{p}$ not following a normal distribution (Problem 42), A. Agresti and B. Coull (Approximate Is Better Than "Exact" for Interval Estimation of Binomial Proportion. *American Statistician,* 52:119–26, 1998) *proposed a modified approach to constructing confidence intervals for a proportion. A $(1 - \alpha) \cdot 100\%$ confidence interval for p is given by*

$$\text{Lower bound: } \tilde{p} - z_{\frac{\alpha}{2}} \cdot \sqrt{\frac{\tilde{p}(1-\tilde{p})}{n+4}}$$

$$\text{Upper bound: } \tilde{p} + z_{\frac{\alpha}{2}} \cdot \sqrt{\frac{\tilde{p}(1-\tilde{p})}{n+4}}$$

where $\tilde{p} = \dfrac{x+2}{n+4}$ *(x is the number of successes in n trials).*

Use this result to answer Problems 43 and 44.

43. Cauliflower? Jane wants to estimate the proportion of students on her campus who eat cauliflower. After surveying 20 students, she finds 2 who eat cauliflower. Obtain and interpret a 95% confidence interval for the proportion of students who eat cauliflower on Jane's campus using Agresti and Coull's method. (0.018, 0.316)

44. Walk to Work Alan wants to estimate the proportion of adults who walk to work. In a survey of 10 adults, he finds 0 who walk to work. Explain why a 95% confidence interval using the normal model yields silly results. Then compute and interpret a 95% confidence interval for the proportion of adults who walk to work using Agresti and Coull's method. (0, 0.326)

45. Putting It Together: Hand Washing The American Society for Microbiology (ASM) and the Soap and Detergent Association (SDA) jointly commissioned two separate studies during 2007, both of which were conducted by Harris Interactive. In one of the studies, 1001 adults were interviewed by telephone and asked about their hand-washing habits. In the other study, the hand-washing behavior of 6076 adults was inconspicuously observed within public rest rooms in four U.S. cities.

(a) In the telephone interviews, 921 of the adults said they always wash their hands in public rest rooms. Use this result to obtain a point estimate for the proportion of adults who say they always wash their hands in public rest rooms. $\hat{p} = 0.920$

(b) Verify that the requirements for constructing a confidence interval for p from part (a) are satisfied.

(c) Using the results from the telephone interviews, construct a 95% confidence interval for the proportion of adults who say they always wash their hands in public rest rooms. (0.903, 0.937)

(d) Is it possible that the proportion of adults who say they always wash their hands in public rest rooms is less than 0.85? Is this likely? Yes; no

(e) In the observational study, 4679 of the 6076 adults were observed washing their hands. Use this result to obtain a point estimate for the proportion of adults who wash their hands in public rest rooms. $\hat{p} = 0.770$

(f) Verify that the requirements for constructing a confidence interval for p from part (e) are satisfied.

(g) Using the results from the observational study, construct a 95% confidence interval for the proportion of adults who wash their hands in public rest rooms. (0.759, 0.781)

(h) Is it possible that the proportion of adults who wash their hands in public rest rooms is greater than 0.85? Is this likely? Yes; no

(i) Based on your findings in parts (a) through (h), what might you conclude about the proportion of adults who say they always wash their hands versus the proportion of adults who actually wash their hands in public rest rooms? Why do you think this is? The proportion who say they wash their hands is larger than the proportion who actually do.

EXPLAINING THE CONCEPTS

46. Explain what "95% confidence" means in a 95% confidence interval.

47. Explain why quadrupling the sample size causes the margin of error to be cut in half.

48. Why do polling companies often survey 1060 individuals when they wish to estimate a population proportion with a margin of error of 3% with 95% confidence?

49. Katrina wants to estimate the proportion of adult Americans who read at least 10 books last year. To do so, she obtains a simple random sample of 100 adult Americans and constructs a 95% confidence interval. Matthew also wants to estimate the proportion of adult Americans who read at least 10 books last year. He obtains a simple random sample of 400 adult Americans and constructs a 99% confidence interval. Assuming both Katrina and Matthew obtained the same point estimate, whose estimate will have the smaller margin of error? Justify your answer. Matthew

50. Two researchers, Jaime and Mariya, are each constructing confidence intervals for the proportion of a population who is left-handed. They find the point estimate is 0.13. Each independently constructed a confidence interval based on the point estimate, but Jaime's interval has a lower bound of 0.097 and an upper bound of 0.163, while Mariya's interval has a lower bound of 0.117 and an upper bound of 0.173. Which interval is wrong? Why?

51. The 112th Congress of the United States of America has 535 members, of which 87 are women. An alien lands near the U.S. Capitol and treats members of Congress as a random sample of the human race. He reports to his superiors that a 95% confidence interval for the proportion of the human race that is female has a lower bound of 0.131 and an upper bound of 0.194. What is wrong with the alien's approach to estimating the proportion of the human race that is female? 48. Use margin of error formula with $\hat{p} = 0.5$.

Technology Step-By-Step

Confidence Intervals about *p*

TI-83/84 Plus

1. Press STAT, highlight TESTS, and select `A: 1-propZInt ...`
2. Enter the values of x and n.
3. Enter the confidence level following `C-Level:`
4. Highlight `Calculate:` press ENTER.

MINITAB

1. If you have raw data, enter the data in column C1.
2. Select the **Stat** menu, highlight **Basic Statistics,** then highlight **1 Proportion . . . .**
3. Enter C1 in the cell marked "Samples in Columns" if you have raw data. If you have summary statistics, click "Summarized data" and enter the number of trials, n, and the number of events (successes) x.
4. Click the **Options** ... button. Enter a confidence level. Click "Use test and interval based on a normal distribution" (provided that the assumptions stated are satisfied). Click OK twice.

Excel

1. Load the XLSTAT Add-in.
2. Select the XLSTAT menu. Highlight **Parametric tests**, then select **z-test for one proportion**.
3. In the Frequency cell, enter the number of successes. In the Sample size cell, enter the sample size. Be sure the Frequency radio button is checked for Data format and the z test box is checked. Click the Options tab.
4. Be sure the Sample radio button is checked under Variance and the Wald radio button is selected under Confidence Interval. For a 90% confidence interval, enter 10 for Significance Level; for a 95% confidence interval, enter 5 for Significance Level, and so on. Click OK.

StatCrunch

1. If you have raw data, enter them into the spreadsheet. Name the column variable.
2. Select **Stat**, highlight **Proportions**, select **One sample**, and then choose either **with data** or **with summary**.
3. If you chose **with data**, select the column that has the observations, choose which outcome represents a success, then click Next>. If you chose **with summary**, enter the number of successes and the number of trials. Click Next>.
4. Choose the confidence interval radio button. Enter the level of confidence. Leave the Method as the Standard-Wald. Click Calculate.

9.2 ESTIMATING A POPULATION MEAN

Preparing for This Section Before getting started, review the following:

- Parameter versus statistic (Section 1.1, p. 5)
- z-scores (Section 3.4, pp. 154–155)
- Standard normal distribution (Section 7.2, p. 338)
- Simple random sampling (Section 1.3, pp. 22–26)
- Degrees of freedom (Section 3.2, p. 134)
- Normal probability plots (Section 7.3, pp. 350–353)
- Distribution of the sample mean (Section 8.1, pp. 367–375)

OBJECTIVES

1. Obtain a point estimate for the population mean
2. State properties of Student's t-distribution
3. Determine t-values
4. Construct and interpret a confidence interval for a population mean
5. Find the sample size needed to estimate the population mean within a given margin of error

1 Obtain a Point Estimate for the Population Mean

Remember, the goal of statistical inference is to use information obtained from a sample and generalize the results to the population being studied. Just as with estimating the population proportion, the first step is to obtain a point estimate of the parameter. The point estimate of the population mean, μ, is the sample mean, $\bar{x}$.

EXAMPLE 1 Computing a Point Estimate of the Population Mean

TABLE 2

28.5	26.0	21.7
23.8	23.5	26.1
25.2	23.4	24.0
26.3	18.8	
28.4	18.0	

Source: www.fueleconomy.gov

Problem The Web site fueleconomy.gov allows drivers to report the miles per gallon of their vehicle. The data in Table 2 show the reported miles per gallon of 2007 Ford Taurus automobiles for 13 different owners. Obtain a point estimate of the population mean miles per gallon of a 2007 Ford Taurus.

Approach We will treat the 13 entries as a simple random sample of all 2007 Ford Taurus automobiles. To find the point estimate of the population mean, we compute the sample mean miles per gallon of the 13 cars.

Solution The sample mean is

$$\bar{x} = \frac{28.5 + 23.8 + \dots + 24.0}{13} = \frac{313.7}{13} = 24.13 \text{ miles per hour}$$

The point estimate of μ is 24.13 miles per hour. Remember, we round statistics to one more decimal point than the raw data.

2 State Properties of Student's t-distribution

In Example 1, a different random sample of 13 cars would likely result in a different point estimate of μ. For this reason, we would like to construct a confidence interval for the population mean, just as we did for the population proportion.

A confidence interval for the population mean is of the form point estimate $\pm$ margin of error (just like the confidence interval for a population proportion). To determine the margin of error, we need to know the sampling distribution of the sample mean. Recall, the distribution of $\bar{x}$ is approximately normal if the population from which the sample is drawn is normal or the sample size is sufficiently large. In addition, the distribution of $\bar{x}$ has the same mean as the parent population, $\mu_{\bar{x}} = \mu$, and a standard deviation equal to the parent population's standard deviation divided by the square root of the sample size, $\sigma_{\bar{x}} = \dfrac{\sigma}{\sqrt{n}}$. Following the same logic used in constructing a confidence interval about a population proportion, our confidence interval would be

$$\text{point estimate} \pm \text{margin of error}$$

$$\bar{x} \quad \pm \quad z_{\frac{\alpha}{2}} \cdot \frac{\sigma}{\sqrt{n}}$$

This presents a problem because we need to know the population standard deviation to construct this interval. It does not seem likely that we would know the population standard deviation, but not know the population mean. So, what can we do? A logical option is to use the sample standard deviation, s, as an estimate of σ. Then the standard deviation of the distribution of $\bar{x}$ would be estimated by $\dfrac{s}{\sqrt{n}}$ and our confidence interval would be

$$\bar{x} \pm z_{\frac{\alpha}{2}} \cdot \frac{s}{\sqrt{n}} \qquad \textbf{(1)}$$

Unfortunately, there is a problem with this approach. The sample standard deviation, s, is a statistic and therefore will vary from sample to sample. Using the normal model to determine the critical value, $z_{\frac{\alpha}{2}}$, in the margin of error does not take into account the additional variability introduced by using s in place of σ. This is not much of a problem for large samples because the variability in the sample standard deviation decreases as the sample size increases (Law of Large Numbers), but for small samples, we have a real problem. Put another way, the z-score of $\bar{x}$, $\dfrac{\bar{x} - \mu}{\dfrac{\sigma}{\sqrt{n}}}$, is normally distributed with mean 0 and standard deviation 1 (provided $\bar{x}$ is normally distributed). However, $\dfrac{\bar{x} - \mu}{\dfrac{s}{\sqrt{n}}}$ is *not* normally distributed with mean 0 and standard deviation 1. So a new model must be used to determine the margin of error that accounts for this additional variability. This leads to the story of William Gosset.

In the early 1900s, William Gosset worked for the Guinness brewery. Gosset was in charge of conducting experiments at the brewery to identify the best barley variety. When working with beer, Gosset was limited to small data sets. At the time, the model used for constructing confidence intervals about a mean was the normal mode, regardless of whether the population standard deviation was known. Gosset did not know the population standard deviation, so he simply substituted the sample standard deviation for the population standard deviation as suggested by Formula (1). While doing this, he was finding that his confidence intervals did not include the population mean at the rate expected. This led Gosset to develop a model that accounts for the additional variability introduced by using s in place of σ when determining the margin of error. Guinness would not allow Gosset to publish his results under his real name (Guinness was very secretive about its brewing practices), but did allow the results to be published under a pseudonym. Gosset chose Student. So we have Student's t-distribution.

Note to Instructor

Consider the following to help students understand degrees of freedom: You have five pens of different colors and five students want to borrow a pen. The first four students have some freedom as to which pen to select; however, the last person has no freedom, but must choose the last available pen.

Student's *t*-Distribution

Suppose that a simple random sample of size n is taken from a population. If the population from which the sample is drawn follows a normal distribution, the distribution of

$$t = \frac{\bar{x} - \mu}{\dfrac{s}{\sqrt{n}}}$$

follows Student's t-distribution with $n - 1$ degrees of freedom,* where $\bar{x}$ is the sample mean and s is the sample standard deviation.

*The reader may wish to review the discussion of degrees of freedom in Section 3.2 on p. 134.

The interpretation of t is the same as that of the z-score. The t-statistic represents the number of *sample* standard errors $\bar{x}$ is from the population mean, μ. It turns out that the shape of the t-distribution depends on the sample size, n.

To help see how the t-distribution differs from the standard normal (or z-) distribution and the role that the sample size n plays, we will go through the following simulation.

EXAMPLE 2 Comparing the Standard Normal Distribution to the *t*-Distribution Using Simulation

(a) Use statistical software such as MINITAB or StatCrunch to obtain 1500 simple random samples of size $n = 5$ from a normal population with $\mu = 50$ and $\sigma = 10$.

(b) Calculate the sample mean and sample standard deviation for each sample.

(c) Compute $z = \dfrac{\bar{x} - \mu_{\bar{x}}}{\dfrac{\sigma}{\sqrt{n}}}$ and $t = \dfrac{\bar{x} - \mu_{\bar{x}}}{\dfrac{s}{\sqrt{n}}}$ for each sample.

(d) Draw histograms for both z and t.

(e) Repeat parts (a)–(d) for 1500 simple random samples of size $n = 10$.

Solution We use MINITAB to obtain the 1500 simple random samples and compute the 1500 sample means and sample standard deviations. We then compute $z = \dfrac{\bar{x} - \mu_{\bar{x}}}{\dfrac{\sigma}{\sqrt{n}}} = \dfrac{\bar{x} - 50}{\dfrac{10}{\sqrt{5}}}$ and $t = \dfrac{\bar{x} - \mu_{\bar{x}}}{\dfrac{s}{\sqrt{n}}} = \dfrac{\bar{x} - 50}{\dfrac{s}{\sqrt{5}}}$ for each of the 1500 samples. Figure 9(a) shows the histogram for z, and Figure 9(b) shows the histogram for t.

Figure 9

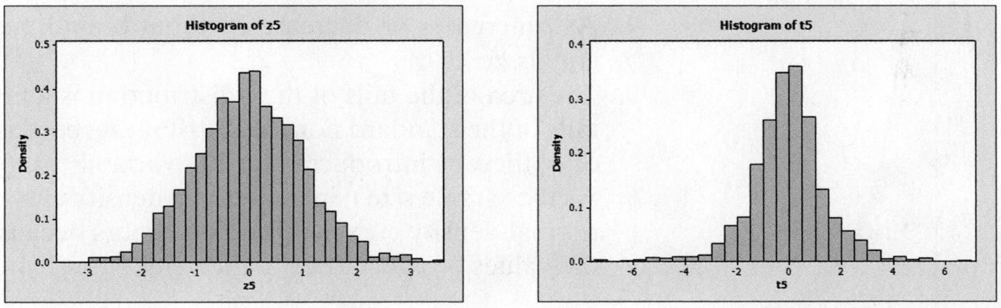

(a) (b)

We notice that the histogram in Figure 9(a) is symmetric and bell shaped, with the histogram centered at 0, and virtually all the rectangles lie between –3 and 3. In other words, z with $n = 5$ follows a standard normal distribution. The histogram of t with $n = 5$ is also symmetric, bell shaped, and centered at 0, but the histogram of t has longer tails (that is, t is more dispersed), so it is unlikely that t follows a standard normal distribution. This additional spread is due to the fact that we divided by $\dfrac{s}{\sqrt{n}}$ to find t instead of by $\dfrac{\sigma}{\sqrt{n}}$.

We repeat these steps for samples of size $n = 10$. Figure 10(a) shows the histogram for z, and Figure 10(b) shows the histogram for t. What do you notice?

Figure 10

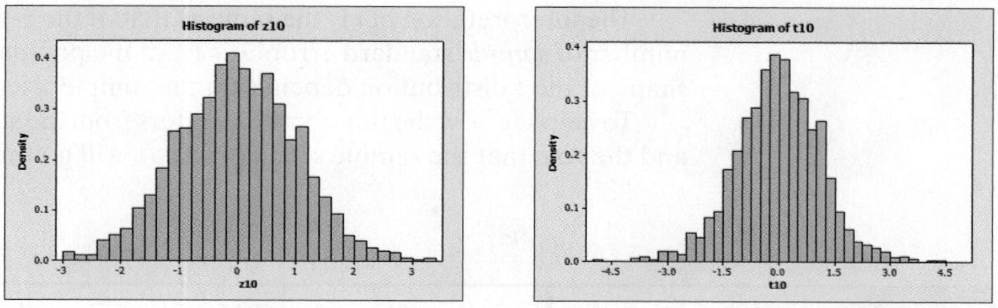

(a) (b)

The histogram in Figure 10(a) is symmetric, bell shaped, centered at 0, and virtually all the rectangles lie between −3 and 3. In other words, z with $n = 10$ follows a standard normal distribution. The histogram of t with $n = 10$ is also symmetric, bell shaped, and centered at 0, but the histogram has longer tails (that is, t is more dispersed) than the histogram of z with $n = 10$. So t with $n = 10$ also does not appear to follow the standard normal distribution.

One very important distinction must be made. We notice the distribution of t with $n = 10$ (Figure 10(b)) is less dispersed than the distribution of t with $n = 5$ (Figure 9(b)).

We conclude that there are different t distributions for different sample sizes. In addition, the spread in the distribution of t decreases as the sample size n increases. In fact, it can be shown that as the sample size n increases, the distribution of t behaves more and more like the standard normal distribution.

Note to Instructor

Ask students to cite some differences between the standard normal and the t-distribution. What are some similarities?

Properties of the *t*-Distribution

1. The t-distribution is different for different degrees of freedom.
2. The t-distribution is centered at 0 and is symmetric about 0.
3. The area under the curve is 1. The area under the curve to the right of 0 equals the area under the curve to the left of 0, which equals $\frac{1}{2}$.
4. As t increases or decreases without bound, the graph approaches, but never equals, zero.
5. The area in the tails of the t-distribution is a little greater than the area in the tails of the standard normal distribution, because we are using s as an estimate of σ, thereby introducing further variability into the t-statistic.
6. As the sample size n increases, the density curve of t gets closer to the standard normal density curve. This result occurs because, as the sample size increases, the values of s get closer to the value of σ, by the Law of Large Numbers.

Figure 11

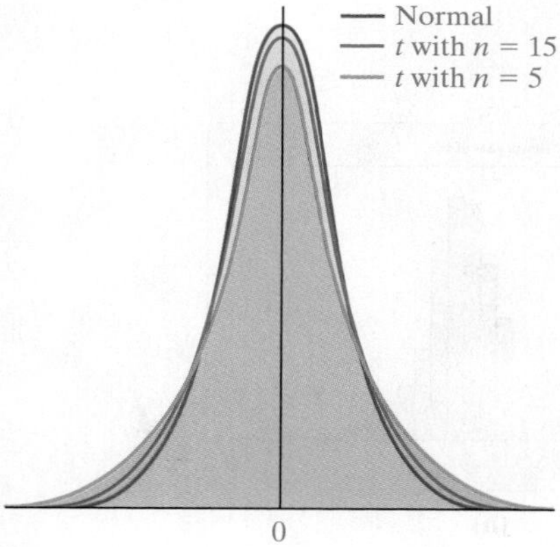

In Figure 11, we show the t-distribution for the sample sizes $n = 5$ and $n = 15$, along with the standard normal density curve.

Figure 12

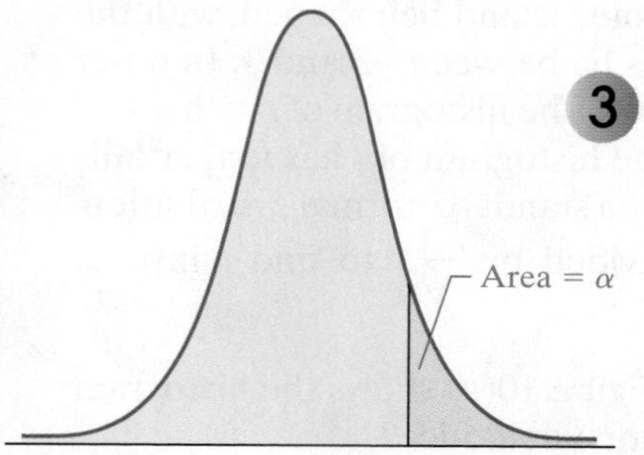

3 Determine *t*-Values

Recall that the notation z_α is used to represent the z-score whose area under the normal curve to the right of z_α is α. Similarly, we let t_α represent the t-value whose area under the t-distribution to the right of t_α is α. See Figure 12.

The shape of the t-distribution depends on the sample size, n. Therefore, the value of t_α depends not only on α, but also on the degrees of freedom, $n - 1$. In Table VI in Appendix A, the far left column gives the degrees of freedom. The top row represents the area under the t-distribution to the right of some t-value.

EXAMPLE 3 Finding *t*-Values

Problem Find the t-value such that the area under the t-distribution to the right of the t-value is 0.10, assuming 15 degrees of freedom (df). That is, find $t_{0.10}$ with 15 degrees of freedom.

Approach

Step 1 Draw a t-distribution with the unknown t-value labeled. Shade the area under the curve to the right of the t-value, as in Figure 12.

Step 2 Find the row in Table VI corresponding to 15 degrees of freedom and the column corresponding to an area in the right tail of 0.10. Identify where the row and column intersect. This is the unknown t-value.

Solution

Step 1 Figure 13 shows the graph of the t-distribution with 15 degrees of freedom. The unknown value of t is labeled, and the area under the curve to the right of t is shaded.

Figure 13

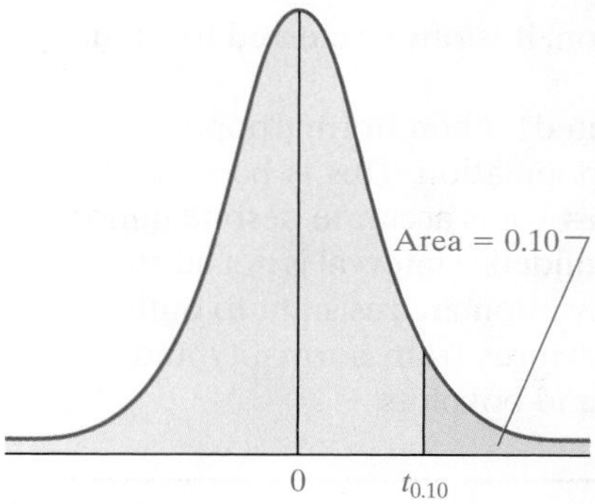

Step 2 A portion of Table VI is shown in Figure 14. We have enclosed the row that represents 15 degrees of freedom and the column that represents the area 0.10 in the right tail. The value where the row and column intersect is the t-value we are seeking. The value of $t_{0.10}$ with 15 degrees of freedom is 1.341; that is, the area under the t-distribution to the right of $t = 1.341$ with 15 degrees of freedom is 0.10.

Figure 14

	Area in Right Tail											
df	0.25	0.20	0.15	0.10	0.05	0.025	0.02	0.01	0.005	0.0025	0.001	0.0005
1	1.000	1.376	1.963	3.078	6.314	12.706	15.894	31.821	63.657	127.321	318.309	636.619
2	0.816	1.061	1.386	1.886	2.920	4.303	4.849	6.965	9.925	14.089	22.327	31.599
3	0.765	0.978	1.250	1.638	2.353	3.182	3.482	4.541	5.841	7.453	10.215	12.924
13	0.694	0.870	1.079	1.350	1.771	2.160	2.282	2.650	3.012	3.372	3.852	4.221
14	0.692	0.868	1.076	1.345	1.761	2.145	2.264	2.624	2.977	3.326	3.787	4.140
15	0.691	0.866	1.074	1.341	1.753	2.131	2.249	2.602	2.947	3.286	3.733	4.073
16	0.690	0.865	1.071	1.337	1.746	2.120	2.235	2.583	2.921	3.252	3.686	4.015

Notice that the critical value of z with an area of to the right of 0.10 is smaller—approximately 1.28. This is because the t-distribution has more spread than the z-distribution.

Now Work Problem 7

Using Technology

The TI-84 Plus graphing calculator has an invT feature, which finds the value of t given an area to the left of the unknown t-value and the degrees of freedom.

If the degrees of freedom we desire are not listed in Table VI, choose the closest number in the "df" column. For example, if we have 43 degrees of freedom, we use 40 degrees of freedom from Table VI. In addition, the last row of Table VI lists the z-values from the standard normal distribution. Use these values when the degrees of freedom are more than 1000 since the t-distribution starts to behave like the standard normal distribution as n increases.

4 Construct and Interpret a Confidence Interval for a Population Mean

We are now ready to construct a confidence interval for a population mean.

Note to Instructor

Emphasize to students that we construct Z-intervals when σ is known and t-intervals when σ is unknown.

Constructing a $(1 - \alpha)100\%$ Confidence Interval for μ

Provided

- sample data come from a simple random sample or randomized experiment
- sample size is small relative to the population size ($n \leq 0.05N$)

- the data come from a population that is normally distributed, or the sample size is large

A $(1-\alpha)100\%$ confidence interval for μ is given by

$$\text{Lower bound: } \bar{x} - t_{\frac{\alpha}{2}} \cdot \frac{s}{\sqrt{n}} \qquad \text{Upper bound: } \bar{x} + t_{\frac{\alpha}{2}} \cdot \frac{s}{\sqrt{n}} \qquad (2)$$

where $t_{\frac{\alpha}{2}}$ is the critical value with $n - 1$ degrees of freedom.

Because this confidence interval uses the t-distribution, it is often referred to as the ***t*-interval**.

Notice that a confidence interval about μ can be computed for non-normal populations even though Student's t-distribution requires a normal population. This is because the procedure for constructing the confidence interval is **robust**—it is accurate despite minor departures from normality. If a data set has outliers, the confidence interval is not accurate because neither the sample mean nor sample standard deviation are resistant to outliers. Sample data should always be inspected for serious departures from normality and for outliers. This is easily done with normal probability plots and boxplots.

Note to Instructor

Consider assigning the "Exploring the Effects of Confidence Level and Sample Size" activity from the Student Activity Workbook.

EXAMPLE 4 Constructing a Confidence Interval about a Population Mean

Problem The Web site fueleconomy.gov allows drivers to report the miles per gallon of their vehicle. The data in Table 3 show the reported miles per gallon of 2007 Ford Taurus automobiles for 13 different owners. Treat the sample as a simple random sample of all 2007 Ford Taurus automobiles. Construct a 95% confidence interval for the mean miles per gallon of a 2007 Ford Taurus. Interpret the interval.

TABLE 3

28.5	26.0	21.7	26.3	18.8
23.8	23.5	26.1	28.4	18.0
25.2	23.4	24.0		

Source: www.fueleconomy.gov

Approach

Step 1 Verify the data are obtained randomly and the sample size is small relative to the population size. Because the sample size is small, draw a normal probability plot to verify the data come from a population that is normally distributed and a boxplot to verify that there are no outliers.

By-Hand Approach

Step 2 Compute the value of $\bar{x}$ and s.

Step 3 Determine the critical value $t_{\frac{\alpha}{2}}$ with $n - 1$ degrees of freedom.

Step 4 Use Formula (2) to determine the lower and upper bounds of the confidence interval.

Step 5 Interpret the result.

Technology Approach

Step 2 Use a statistical spreadsheet or graphing calculator with advanced statistical features to obtain the confidence interval. We will use MINITAB to construct the confidence interval. The steps for constructing confidence intervals using the TI-83/84 Plus graphing calculators, MINITAB, Excel, and StatCrunch are given in the Technology Step-by-Step on pages 419–420.

Step 3 Interpret the result.

Solution

Step 1 The data are obtained from a simple random sample. In addition, there are likely thousands of 2007 Ford Taurus vehicles on the road, so the sample size is small relative to the population size. Figure 15 shows a normal probability plot and boxplot for the data in Table 3. All the data lie within the bounds of the normal probability plot, indicating the data could come from a population that is normally distributed. The boxplot does not reveal any outliers. The requirements for constructing the confidence interval are satisfied.

Figure 15

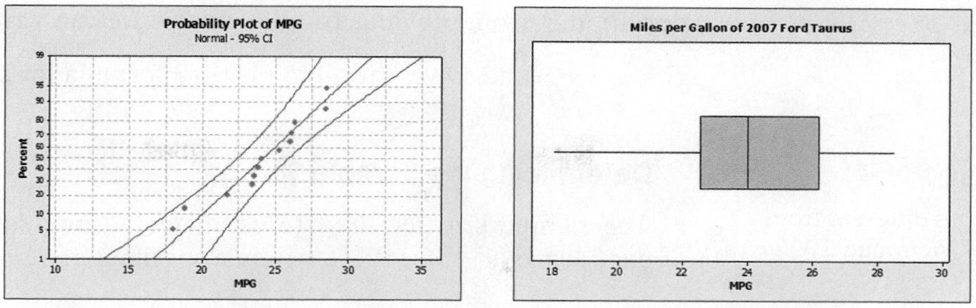

(a) (b)

By-Hand Solution

Step 2 We determined the sample mean in Example 1 to be $\bar{x} = 24.13$ mpg. Using a calculator, the sample standard deviation is $s = 3.21$ mpg.

Step 3 Because we want a 95% confidence interval, we have $\alpha = 1 - 0.95 = 0.05$. The sample size is $n = 13$. So we find $t_{\frac{\alpha}{2}} = t_{\frac{0.05}{2}} = t_{0.025}$ with $13 - 1 = 12$ degrees of freedom. Table VI shows that $t_{0.025} = 2.179$.

Step 4 Substituting into Formula (2), we obtain:

Lower bound:

$$\bar{x} - t_{\frac{\alpha}{2}} \cdot \frac{s}{\sqrt{n}} = 24.13 - 2.179 \cdot \frac{3.21}{\sqrt{13}} = 22.19$$

Upper bound:

$$\bar{x} + t_{\frac{\alpha}{2}} \cdot \frac{s}{\sqrt{n}} = 24.13 + 2.179 \cdot \frac{3.21}{\sqrt{13}} = 26.07$$

Step 5 We are 95% confident that the mean miles per gallon of all 2007 Ford Taurus cars is between 22.19 and 26.07 mpg.

Technology Solution

Step 2 Figure 16 shows the results from MINITAB.

Figure 16

One-Sample T: MPG

```
Variable  N     Mean  StDev  SE Mean          95% CI
MPG      13  24.1308 3.2082   0.8898  (22.1921, 26.0694)
```

MINITAB presents confidence intervals in the form (*lower bound, upper bound*). The lower bound is 22.19 and the upper bound is 26.07.

Step 3 We are 95% confident that the mean miles per gallon of all 2007 Ford Taurus cars is between 22.19 and 26.07 mpg.

Notice that $t_{0.025} = 2.179$ for 12 degrees of freedom, while $z_{0.025} = 1.96$. The t-distribution gives a larger critical value, so the width of the interval is wider. Remember, this larger critical value is necessary to account for the increased variability due to using s as an estimate of σ.

Remember, 95% confidence refers to our confidence in the method. If we obtained 100 samples of size $n = 13$ from the population of 2007 Ford Tauruses, we would expect about 95 of the samples to result in confidence intervals that include μ. We do not know whether the interval in Example 4 includes μ or does not include μ.

Note to Instructor

Consider assigning the "Constructing a Confidence Interval from a Non-normal Distribution" activity from the Student Activity Workbook.

What should we do if the requirements to compute a t-interval are not met? We could increase the sample size beyond 30 observations, or we could try to use *nonparametric procedures*. **Nonparametric procedures** typically do not require normality, and the methods are resistant to outliers. A third option is to use resampling methods, such as bootstrapping. Nonparametric procedures and resampling methods are not presented in this text.

5 Find the Sample Size Needed to Estimate the Population Mean within a Given Margin of Error

The margin of error in constructing a confidence interval about the population mean is $E = t_{\frac{\alpha}{2}} \cdot \frac{s}{\sqrt{n}}$. Solving this for n, we obtain $n = \left(\frac{t_{\frac{\alpha}{2}} \cdot s}{E}\right)^2$. The problem with this formula is that the critical value $t_{\frac{\alpha}{2}}$ requires that we know the sample size to determine the degrees of freedom, $n - 1$. Obviously, if we do not know n we cannot know the degrees of freedom. The solution to this problem lies in the fact that the t-distribution approaches the standard normal z-distribution as the sample size increases. To convince yourself of this, look at the last few rows of Table VI and compare them to the corresponding z-scores for 95% or 99% confidence. Now, if we use z in place of t, and a sample standard

Note the value of s needs to come from a pilot study or prior study.

deviation, s, from previous or pilot studies we can write the margin of error formula as $E = z_{\frac{\alpha}{2}} \cdot \frac{s}{\sqrt{n}}$ and solve it for n to obtain a formula for determining sample size.

! CAUTION

Rounding *up* is different from rounding *off*. We round 5.32 *up* to 6 and *off* to 5.

Note to Instructor

Ask students to identify the reason we round up rather than round off.

Determining the Sample Size *n*

The sample size required to estimate the population mean, μ, with a level of confidence $(1 - \alpha) \cdot 100\%$ within a specified margin of error, E, is given by

$$n = \left(\frac{z_{\frac{\alpha}{2}} \cdot s}{E}\right)^2 \quad (3)$$

where n is rounded up to the nearest whole number.

EXAMPLE 5 Determining Sample Size

Problem We again consider the problem of estimating the miles per gallon of a 2007 Ford Taurus. How large a sample is required to estimate the mean miles per gallon within 0.5 mile per gallon with 95% confidence?

Approach Use Formula (3) with $z_{\frac{\alpha}{2}} = z_{0.025} = 1.96$, $s = 3.21$, and $E = 0.5$ to find the required sample size.

Solution We substitute the values of z, s, and E into Formula (3) and obtain

$$n = \left(\frac{z_{\frac{\alpha}{2}} \cdot s}{E}\right)^2 = \left(\frac{1.96 \cdot 3.21}{0.5}\right)^2 = 158.34$$

! CAUTION

Don't forget to round up when determining sample size.

We round 158.34 up to 159. A sample size of $n = 159$ results in an interval estimate of the population mean miles per gallon of a 2007 Ford Taurus with a margin of error of 0.5 mile per gallon with 95% confidence.

Now Work Problem 45

9.2 ASSESS YOUR UNDERSTANDING

VOCABULARY AND SKILL BUILDING

1. As the number of degrees of freedom in the *t*-distribution increases, the spread of the distribution decreases (increases/decreases).

2. *True or False*: The *t*-distribution is centered at μ. False

3. The notation t_α is the *t*-value such that the area under the *t*-distribution to the right of t_α is α.

4. *True or False*: The value of $t_{0.10}$ with 5 degrees of freedom is greater than the value of $t_{0.10}$ with 10 degrees of freedom. True

5. *True or False*: To construct a confidence interval about the mean, the population from which the sample is drawn must be approximately normal. False

6. The procedure for constructing a confidence interval about a mean is robust, which means minor departures from normality do not affect the accuracy of the interval.

NW 7. (a) Find the *t*-value such that the area in the right tail is 0.10 with 25 degrees of freedom. 1.316

(b) Find the *t*-value such that the area in the right tail is 0.05 with 30 degrees of freedom. 1.697

(c) Find the *t*-value such that the area left of the *t*-value is 0.01 with 18 degrees of freedom. [*Hint:* Use symmetry.] −2.552

(d) Find the critical *t*-value that corresponds to 90% confidence. Assume 20 degrees of freedom. 1.725

8. (a) Find the *t*-value such that the area in the right tail is 0.02 with 19 degrees of freedom. 2.205

(b) Find the *t*-value such that the area in the right tail is 0.10 with 32 degrees of freedom. 1.309

(c) Find the *t*-value such that the area left of the *t*-value is 0.05 with 6 degrees of freedom. [*Hint:* Use symmetry.] −1.943

(d) Find the critical *t*-value that corresponds to 95% confidence. Assume 16 degrees of freedom. 2.120

In Problems 9–14, a simple random sample of size n < 30 has been obtained. From the normal probability plot and boxplot, judge whether a t-interval should be constructed.

9. No

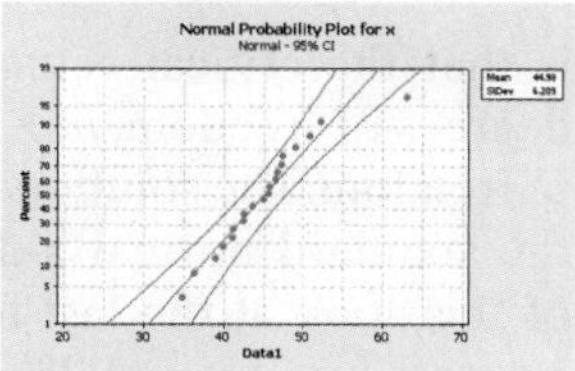

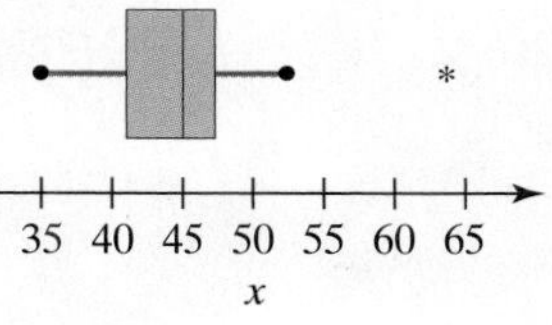

10. No

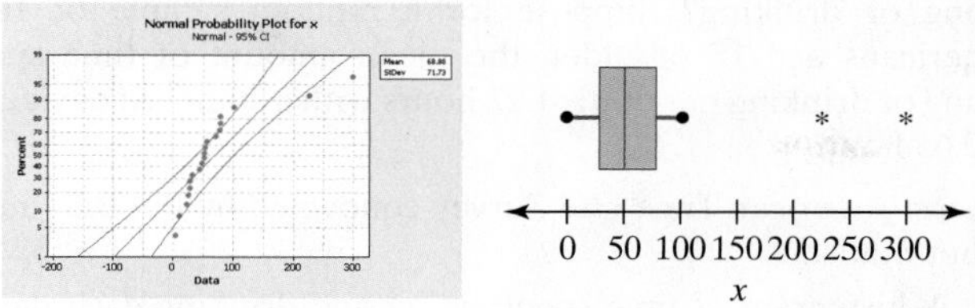

11. No

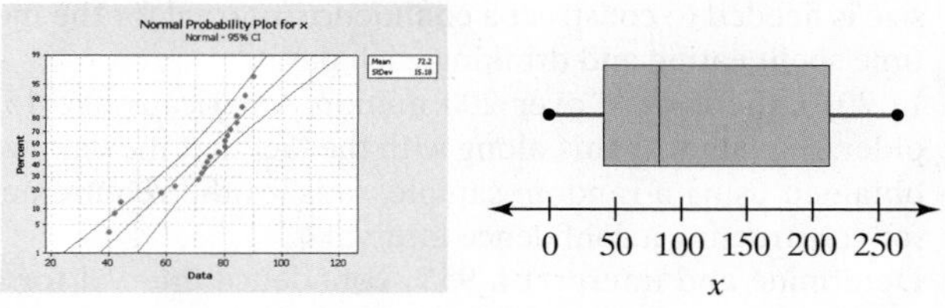

12. No

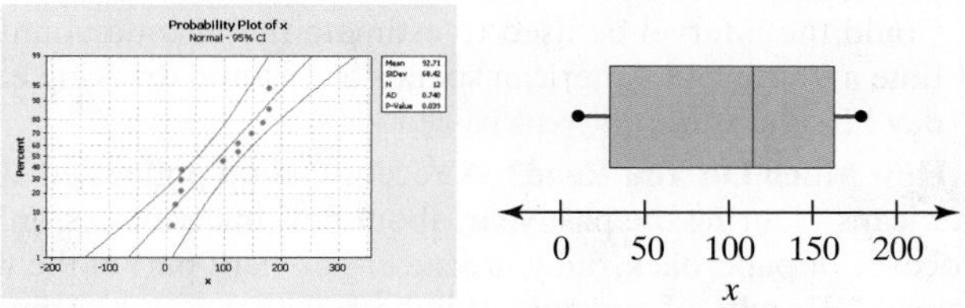

13. Yes

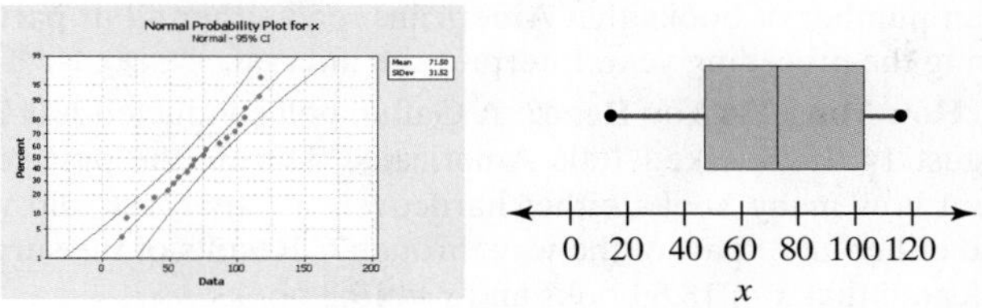

14. Yes

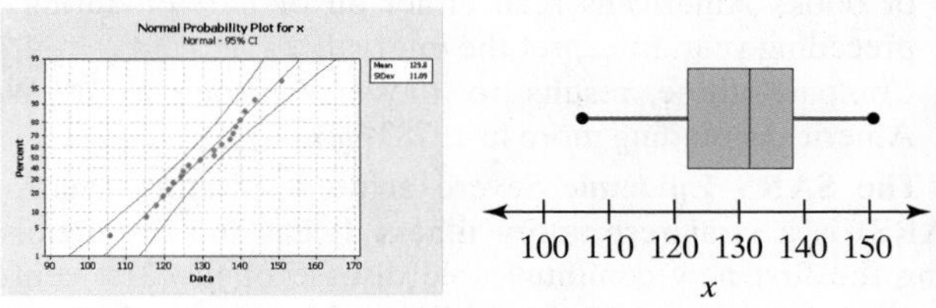

In Problems 15–18, determine the point estimate of the population mean and margin of error for each confidence interval.

15. Lower bound: 18, upper bound: 24 $\bar{x} = 21$, $E = 3$

16. Lower bound: 20, upper bound: 30 $\bar{x} = 25$, $E = 5$

17. Lower bound: 5, upper bound: 23 $\bar{x} = 14$, $E = 9$

18. Lower bound: 15, upper bound: 35 $\bar{x} = 25$, $E = 10$

19. A simple random sample of size n is drawn from a population that is normally distributed. The sample mean, $\bar{x}$, is found to be 108, and the sample standard deviation, s, is found to be 10.

(a) Construct a 96% confidence interval for μ if the sample size, n, is 25. (103.7, 112.3)

(b) Construct a 96% confidence interval for μ if the sample size, n, is 10. How does decreasing the sample size affect the margin of error, E? (100.4, 115.6); increases

(c) Construct a 90% confidence interval for μ if the sample size, n, is 25. Compare the results to those obtained in part (a). How does decreasing the level of confidence affect the size of the margin of error, E? (104.6, 111.4); decreases

(d) Could we have computed the confidence intervals in parts (a)–(c) if the population had not been normally distributed? Why? No

20. A simple random sample of size n is drawn from a population that is normally distributed. The sample mean, $\bar{x}$, is found to be 50, and the sample standard deviation, s, is found to be 8.

(a) Construct a 98% confidence interval for μ if the sample size, n, is 20. (45.5, 54.5)

(b) Construct a 98% confidence interval for μ if the sample size, n, is 15. How does decreasing the sample size affect the margin of error, E? (44.6, 55.4); increases

(c) Construct a 95% confidence interval for μ if the sample size, n, is 20. Compare the results to those obtained in part (a). How does decreasing the level of confidence affect the margin of error, E? (46.3, 53.7); decreases

(d) Could we have computed the confidence intervals in parts (a)–(c) if the population had not been normally distributed? Why? No

21. A simple random sample of size n is drawn. The sample mean, $\bar{x}$, is found to be 18.4, and the sample standard deviation, s, is found to be 4.5.

(a) Construct a 95% confidence interval for μ if the sample size, n, is 35. (16.85, 19.95)

(b) Construct a 95% confidence interval for μ if the sample size, n, is 50. How does increasing the sample size affect the margin of error, E? (17.12, 19.68); decreases

(c) Construct a 99% confidence interval for μ if the sample size, n, is 35. Compare the results to those obtained in part (a). How does increasing the level of confidence affect the margin of error, E? (16.32, 20.48); increases

(d) If the sample size is $n = 15$, what conditions must be satisfied to compute the confidence interval? Population must be normal.

22. A simple random sample of size n is drawn. The sample mean, $\bar{x}$, is found to be 35.1, and the sample standard deviation, s, is found to be 8.7.

(a) Construct a 90% confidence interval for μ if the sample size, n, is 40. (32.78, 37.42)

(b) Construct a 90% confidence interval for μ if the sample size, n, is 100. How does increasing the sample size affect the margin of error, E? (33.66, 36.54); decreases

(c) Construct a 98% confidence interval for μ if the sample size, n, is 40. Compare the results to those obtained in part (a). How does increasing the level of confidence affect the margin of error, E? (31.76, 38.44); increases

(d) If the sample size is $n = 18$, what conditions must be satisfied to compute the confidence interval? Population must be normal.

APPLYING THE CONCEPTS

23. You Explain It! Hours Worked In a survey conducted by the Gallup organization, 1100 adult Americans were asked how many hours they worked in the previous week. Based on the results, a 95% confidence interval for mean number of hours worked was lower bound: 42.7 and upper bound: 44.5. Which of the following represents a reasonable interpretation of the result? For those that are not reasonable, explain the flaw.

(a) There is a 95% probability the mean number of hours worked by adult Americans in the previous week was between 42.7 hours and 44.5 hours.

(b) We are 95% confident that the mean number of hours worked by adult Americans in the previous week was between 42.7 hours and 44.5 hours. Correct

(c) 95% of adult Americans worked between 42.7 hours and 44.5 hours last week.

(d) We are 95% confident that the mean number of hours worked by adults in Idaho in the previous week was between 42.7 hours and 44.5 hours.

24. You Explain It! Sleeping A 90% confidence interval for the number of hours that full-time college students sleep during a weekday is lower bound: 7.8 hours and upper bound: 8.8 hours. Which of the following represents a reasonable interpretation of the result? For those that are not reasonable, explain the flaw. (d) is correct

(a) 90% of full-time college students sleep between 7.8 hours and 8.8 hours.

(b) We are 90% confident that the mean number of hours of sleep that full-time college students get any day of the week is between 7.8 hours and 8.8 hours.

(c) There is a 90% probability that the mean hours of sleep that full-time college students get during a weekday is between 7.8 hours and 8.8 hours.

(d) We are 90% confident that the mean hours of sleep that full-time college students get during a weekday is between 7.8 hours and 8.8 hours.

25. You Explain It! Drive-Through Service Time The trade magazine QSR routinely checks the drive-through service times of fast-food restaurants. A 90% confidence interval that results from examining 607 customers in Taco Bell's drive-through has a lower bound of 161.5 seconds and an upper bound of 164.7 seconds. What does this mean?

26. You Explain It! MySpace.com According to Nielsen/NetRatings, the mean amount of time spent on MySpace.com per user per month in July 2007 was 171.0 minutes. A 95% confidence interval for the mean amount of time spent on MySpace.com monthly has a lower bound of 151.4 minutes and an upper bound of 190.6 minutes. What does this mean?

27. Hours Worked Revisited For the "Hours Worked" survey conducted by Gallup in Problem 23, provide two recommendations for increasing the precision of the interval.

28. Sleeping Revisited Refer to the "Sleeping" results from Problem 24. What could be done to increase the precision of the confidence interval?

29. Blood Alcohol Concentration A random sample of 51 fatal crashes in 2009 in which the driver had a positive blood alcohol concentration (BAC) from the National Highway Traffic Safety Administration results in a mean BAC of 0.167 grams per deciliter (g/dL) with a standard deviation of 0.010 g/dL.

(a) A histogram of blood alcohol concentrations in fatal accidents shows that BACs are highly skewed right. Explain why a large sample size is needed to construct a confidence interval for the mean BAC of fatal crashes with a positive BAC.

(b) In 2009, there were approximately 25,000 fatal crashes in which the driver had a positive BAC. Explain why this, along with the fact that the data were obtained using a simple random sample, satisfies the requirements for constructing a confidence interval.

(c) Determine and interpret a 90% confidence interval for the mean BAC in fatal crashes in which the driver had a positive BAC. (0.1647, 0.1693)

(d) All 50 states and the District of Columbia use a BAC of 0.08 g/dL as the legal intoxication level. Is it possible that the mean BAC of all drivers involved in fatal accidents who are found to have positive BAC values is less than the legal intoxication level? Explain. Yes, but not likely

30. Hungry or Thirsty? How much time do Americans spend eating or drinking? Suppose for a random sample of 1001 Americans age 15 or older, the mean amount of time spent eating or drinking per day is 1.22 hours with a standard deviation of 0.65 hour.

Source: American Time Use Survey conducted by the Bureau of Labor Statistics

(a) A histogram of time spent eating and drinking each day is skewed right. Use this result to explain why a large sample size is needed to construct a confidence interval for the mean time spent eating and drinking each day.

(b) In 2010, there were over 200 million Americans age 15 or older. Explain why this, along with the fact that the data were obtained using a random sample, satisfies the requirements for constructing a confidence interval.

(c) Determine and interpret a 95% confidence interval for the mean amount of time Americans age 15 or older spend eating and drinking each day. (1.180, 1.260)

(d) Could the interval be used to estimate the mean amount of time a 9-year-old American spends eating and drinking each day? Explain. No, different population

31. How Much Do You Read? A recent Gallup poll asked 1006 Americans, "During the past year, about how many books, either hardcover or paperback, did you read either all or part of the way through?" Results of the survey indicated that $\bar{x} = 13.4$ books and $s = 16.6$ books. Construct a 99% confidence interval for the mean number of books that Americans read either all or part of during the preceding year. Interpret the interval. (12.05, 14.75)

32. How Much Do You Read? A Gallup poll conducted July 21–August 14, 1978, asked 1006 Americans, "During the past year, about how many books, either hardcover or paperback, did you read either all or part of the way through?" Results of the survey indicated that $\bar{x} = 18.8$ books and $s = 19.8$ books.

(a) Construct a 99% confidence interval for the mean number of books Americans read either all or part of during the preceding year. Interpret the interval. (17.19, 20.41)

(b) Compare these results to those of Problem 31. Were Americans reading more in 1978? Yes

33. The SARS Epidemic Severe acute respiratory syndrome (SARS) is a viral respiratory illness. It has the distinction of being the first new communicable disease of the 21st century. Based on interviews with 81 SARS patients, researchers found that the mean incubation period was 4.6 days, with a standard deviation of 15.9 days. Based on this information, construct a 95% confidence interval for the mean incubation period of the SARS virus. Interpret the interval. (1.08, 8.12)

Source: Gabriel M. Leung et al., "The Epidemiology of Severe Acute Respiratory Syndrome in the 2003 Hong Kong Epidemic: An Analysis of All 1755 Patients," *Annals of Internal Medicine* 141:662–673, 2004

34. Tensile Strength Tensile strength is the amount of stress a material can withstand before it breaks. Researchers wanted to determine the tensile strength of a resin cement used in bonding crowns to teeth. The researchers bonded crowns to 72 extracted teeth. Using a tensile resistance test, they found the mean tensile strength of the resin cement to be 242.2 newtons (N), with a standard deviation of 70.6 N. Based on this information, construct a 90% confidence interval for the mean tensile strength of the resin cement. (228.33, 256.07)

Source: Simonides Consani et al., "Effect of Cement Types on the Tensile Strength of Metallic Crowns Submitted to Thermocycling," *Brazilian Dental Journal* 14(3), 2003

35. 4 GB Flash Memory Card After scanning the UPC code of a 4 GB flash memory card using his smartphone, Michael Sullivan received the following prices for the goods at a variety of online retailers. Treat these data as a simple random sample of all online retailers.

12.25	13.49	13.76	14.75	14.99
14.99	15.27	15.95	17.88	20.49

Source: ScanLife

(a) Determine a point estimate for the population mean price of the memory card. $15.382

(b) Use the normal probability plot and boxplot shown next to assist in verifying the requirements for constructing a confidence interval for the mean price.

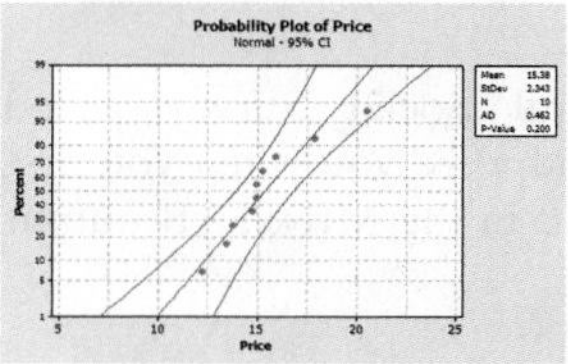

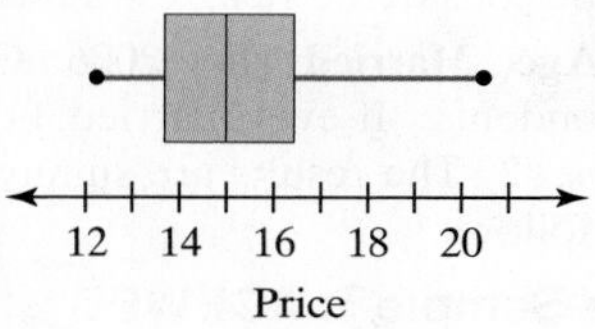

(c) Construct and interpret a 95% confidence interval to estimate the mean price of a 4 GB flash memory card. (13.706, 17.058)

(d) Construct and interpret a 99% confidence interval to estimate the mean price of a 4 GB flash memory card. (12.974, 17.790)

(e) What happens to the interval as the level of confidence is increased? Explain why this is a logical result. Width increases

36. Travel Taxes Travelers pay taxes for flying, car rentals, and hotels. The following data represent the total travel tax for a 3-day business trip in eight randomly selected cities. *Note:* Chicago travel taxes are the highest in the country at $101.27.

67.81	78.69	68.99	84.36
80.24	86.14	101.27	99.29

(a) Determine a point estimate for the population mean travel tax. $83.349

(b) Use the normal probability plot and boxplot shown next to assist in verifying the requirements for constructing a confidence interval for the mean travel tax.

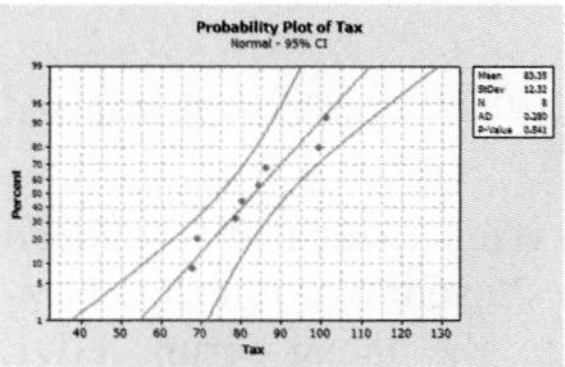

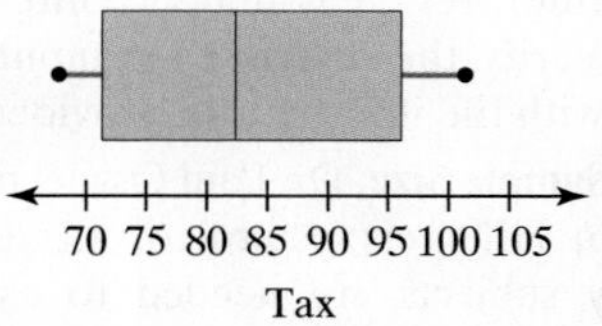

(c) Construct and interpret a 95% confidence interval to estimate the mean tax paid for a 3-day business trip. (73.044, 93.654)

(d) What would you recommend to a researcher who wants to increase the precision of the interval, but does not have access to additional data? Decrease level of confidence

37. Crash Test Results for "Mini" Cars The Insurance Institute for Highway Safety (IIHS) routinely conducts crash tests on vehicles to determine the cost of repairs. The following data represent the vehicle repair costs for 2009-model mini- and micro-cars resulting from front-full and rear-full crash tests at 6 miles per hour. Treat these data as a simple random sample of 14 low-impact crashes. Construct and interpret a 90% confidence interval for the mean repair cost of a low-impact bumper crash on a mini- or micro-car. Use the normal probability plot and boxplot to assist in verifying the model requirements. (1612.5, 2667.4)

Vehicle	Front Full	Rear Full
Smart Fortwo	$1480	$631
Chevrolet Aveo	$1071	$1370
Mini Cooper	$2291	$929
Toyota Yaris	$1688	$3345
Honda Fit	$1124	$3648
Hyundai Accent	$3476	$2057
Kia Rio	$3701	$3148

Source: IIHS News Release, June 2009

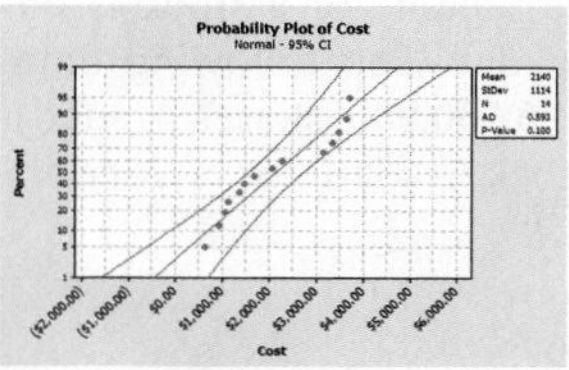

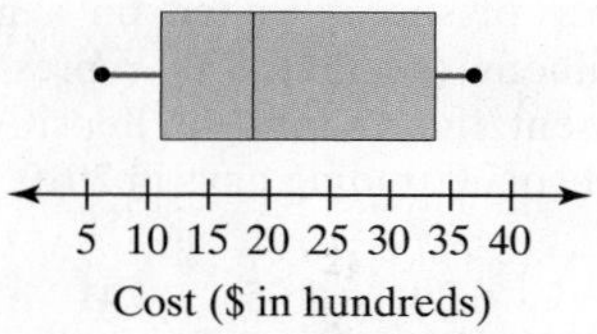

38. Crawling Babies The following data represent the age (in weeks) at which babies first crawl based on a survey of 12 mothers conducted by Essential Baby. Construct and interpret a 95% confidence interval for the mean age at which a baby first crawls. Use the normal probability plot and boxplot to assist in verifying the model requirements. (31.9, 44.6)

52	30	44	35	39	26
47	37	56	26	39	28

Source: www.essentialbaby.com

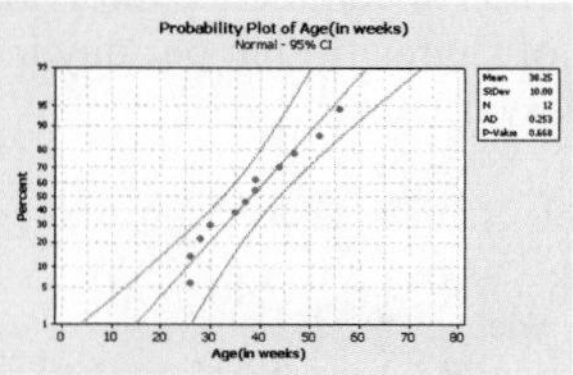

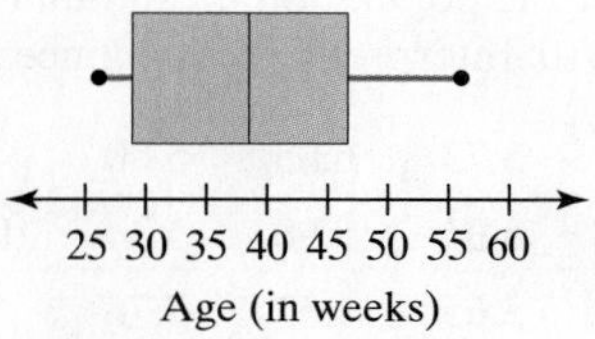

39. Harley-Davidson Stock Volume The trade volume of a stock is the number of shares traded on a given day. The following data, in millions (so that 2.45 represents 2,450,000 shares traded), represent the volume of Harley-Davidson stock traded for a random sample of 40 trading days in 2010. (a) 2.337 million

2.45	2.10	7.11	2.91	1.92	1.45	2.31	1.41
1.62	4.48	2.30	1.42	3.26	2.82	1.66	2.30
1.58	1.91	1.67	2.66	1.47	1.14	3.06	3.09
2.83	1.77	1.50	6.19	2.84	1.94	2.02	1.71
1.87	1.83	2.03	2.62	1.81	1.89	1.64	0.89

Source: TD Ameritrade

(a) Use the data to compute a point estimate for the population mean number of shares traded per day in 2010.

(b) Construct a 90% confidence interval for the population mean number of shares traded per day in 2010. Interpret the confidence interval. (2.013, 2.661)

(c) A second random sample of 40 days in 2010 resulted in the data shown next. Construct another 90% confidence interval for the population mean number of shares traded per day in 2010. Interpret the confidence interval. (1.978, 2.412)

2.07	2.39	1.24	2.02	2.23	1.67	2.06	2.74
5.19	2.38	3.32	2.44	2.34	2.74	1.37	1.60
1.71	1.64	2.20	1.43	1.48	2.05	3.75	3.30
2.70	2.44	1.67	1.38	3.12	1.69	1.79	2.05
3.59	1.79	2.20	1.54	0.84	2.19	1.69	1.77

(d) Explain why the confidence intervals obtained in parts (b) and (c) are different.

40. PepsiCo Stock Volume The trade volume of a stock is the number of shares traded on a given day. The following data, in millions (so that 6.16 represents 6,160,000 shares traded), represent the volume of PepsiCo stock traded for a random sample of 40 trading days in 2010.

6.16	6.39	5.05	4.41	4.16	4.00	2.37	7.71
4.98	4.02	4.95	4.97	7.54	6.22	4.84	7.29
5.55	4.35	4.42	5.07	8.88	4.64	4.13	3.94
4.28	6.69	3.25	4.80	7.56	6.96	6.67	5.04
7.28	5.32	4.92	6.92	6.10	6.71	6.23	2.42

Source: TD Ameritrade

(a) Use the data to compute a point estimate for the population mean number of shares traded per day in 2010. 5.430 million

(b) Construct a 95% confidence interval for the population mean number of shares traded per day in 2010. Interpret the confidence interval. (4.957, 5.903)

(c) A second random sample of 40 days in 2010 resulted in the data shown next. Construct another 95% confidence interval for the population mean number of shares traded per day in 2010. Interpret the confidence interval. (5.298, 6.322)

6.12	5.73	6.85	5.00	4.89	3.79	5.75	6.04
4.49	6.34	5.90	5.44	10.96	4.54	5.46	6.58
8.57	3.65	4.52	7.76	5.27	4.85	4.81	6.74
3.65	4.80	3.39	5.99	7.65	8.13	6.69	4.37
6.89	5.08	8.37	5.68	4.96	5.14	7.84	3.71

(d) Explain why the confidence intervals obtained in parts (b) and (c) are different.

41. Sullivan Survey: Cell Phone Bills Treat the data obtained in the Sullivan Statistics Survey as a simple random sample of adult Americans. One question asked in the survey was "If you own a cell phone, what was your cell phone bill last month? Express answers to the penny." Retrieve the results of this question.

(a) Draw a histogram of the data and comment on the shape. Skewed right

(b) Draw a boxplot of the data. Are there any outliers? Yes

(c) Based on the results to parts (a) and (b), explain why a large sample size might be desirable to construct a confidence interval for the mean monthly cell phone bill.

(d) Use statistical software to determine the point estimate of the mean monthly cell phone bill. \$104.972

(e) Use statistical software to construct a 95% confidence interval for the mean monthly cell phone bill. (95.896, 114.048)

42. Sullivan Survey: What Is Rich? Treat the data obtained in the Sullivan Statistics Survey as a simple random sample of adult Americans. One question asked in the survey was "In your opinion, what minimum annual income for an individual qualifies an individual to be considered rich?" Retrieve the results of this question.

(a) Draw a histogram of the data. Is there anything unusual about the graph? Explain.

(b) Draw a boxplot of the data. Are there any outliers?

(c) Use statistical software to determine the point estimate of the mean income adult Americans consider rich. \$381,407

(d) Use statistical software to construct a 95% confidence interval for the mean income that qualifies an individual to be considered rich. (342426, 420389)

43. Age Married The 2006 General Social Survey asked respondents, "If ever married, how old were you when you first married?" The results are summarized in the MINITAB output that follows:

One-Sample T: AGEWED

```
Variable      N    Mean  StDev  SE Mean       95.0% CI
AGEWED    26540  22.150  4.885    0.030  (22.091, 22.209)
```

(a) Use the summary to determine the point estimate of the population mean and margin of error for the confidence interval. $\bar{x} = 22.150$, $E = 0.059$

(b) Interpret the confidence interval.

(c) Verify the results by computing a 95% confidence interval with the information provided.

44. Sexual Relations A question on the 2006 General Social Survey was this: "About how many times did you engage in intercourse during the month?" The question was only asked of participants who had previously indicated that they had engaged in sexual intercourse during the past month. The results are summarized in the MINITAB output that follows:

One-Sample T: SEXFREQ2

```
Variable    N  Mean   StDev  SE Mean     95.0% CI
SEXFREQ2  357  7.678  6.843    0.362  (6.966, 8.390)
```

(a) Use the summary to determine the point estimate of the population mean and margin of error for the confidence interval. $\bar{x} = 7.678$, $E = 0.712$

(b) Interpret the confidence interval.

(c) Verify the results by computing a 95% confidence interval with the information provided.

NW **45. Sample Size** Dr. Paul Oswiecmiski wants to estimate the mean serum HDL cholesterol of all 20- to 29-year-old females. How many subjects are needed to estimate the mean serum HDL cholesterol of all 20- to 29-year-old females within 2 points with 99% confidence assuming that $s = 13.4$ based on earlier studies? Suppose that Dr. Oswiecmiski would be content with 95% confidence. How does the decrease in confidence affect the sample size required? 298; 173; decreases

46. Sample Size Dr. Paul Oswiecmiski wants to estimate the mean serum HDL cholesterol of all 20- to 29-year-old males. How many subjects are needed to estimate the mean serum HDL cholesterol of all 20- to 29-year-old males within 1.5 points with 90% confidence, assuming that $s = 12.5$ based on earlier studies? Suppose that Dr. Oswiecmiski would prefer 95% confidence. How does the increase in confidence affect the sample size required? 188; 267; increases

47. Reading A recent Gallup poll asked Americans to disclose the number of books they read during the previous year. Initial survey results indicate that $s = 16.6$ books.

(a) How many subjects are needed to estimate the number of books Americans read the previous year within four books with 95% confidence? 67

(b) How many subjects are needed to estimate the number of books Americans read the previous year within two books with 95% confidence? 265

(c) What effect does doubling the required accuracy have on the sample size? Sample size quadruples

(d) How many subjects are needed to estimate the number of books Americans read the previous year within four books with 99% confidence? Compare this result to part (a). How does increasing the level of confidence in the estimate affect sample size? Why is this reasonable? 115

48. Television A researcher wanted to determine the mean number of hours per week (Sunday through Saturday) the typical person watches television. Results from the Sullivan Statistics Survey indicate that $s = 7.5$ hours.

(a) How many people are needed to estimate the number of hours people watch television per week within 2 hours with 95% confidence? 55

(b) How many people are needed to estimate the number of hours people watch television per week within 1 hour with 95% confidence? 217

(c) What effect does doubling the required accuracy have on the sample size? Sample size quadruples

(d) How many people are needed to estimate the number of hours people watch television per week within 2 hours with 90% confidence? Compare this result to part (a). How does decreasing the level of confidence in the estimate affect sample size? Why is this reasonable? 39

49. Resistance and Robustness The data sets represent simple random samples from a population whose mean is 100.

Data Set I

106	122	91	127	88
74	77	108		

Data Set II

106	122	91	127	88
74	77	108	87	88
111	86	113	115	97
122	99	86	83	102

Data Set III

106	122	91	127	88
74	77	108	87	88
111	86	113	115	97
122	99	86	83	102
88	111	118	91	102
80	86	106	91	116

(a) Compute the sample mean of each data set.

(b) For each data set, construct a 95% confidence interval about the population mean.

(c) What effect does the sample size n have on the width of the interval?

For parts (d)–(e), suppose that the data value 106 was accidentally recorded as 016.

(d) For each data set, construct a 95% confidence interval about the population mean using the incorrectly entered data.

(e) Which intervals, if any, still capture the population mean, 100? What concept does this illustrate?

50. Effect of Outliers The following small data set represents a simple random sample from a population whose mean is 50.

43	63	53	50	58	44
53	53	52	41	50	43

(a) A normal probability plot indicates that the data could come from a population that is normally distributed with no outliers. Compute a 95% confidence interval for this data set. (46.1, 54.4)

(b) Suppose that the observation, 41, is inadvertently entered into the computer as 14. Verify that this observation is an outlier.

(c) Construct a 95% confidence interval on the data set with the outlier. What effect does the outlier have on the confidence interval? (40.2, 55.8)

(d) Consider the following data set, which represents a simple random sample of size 36 from a population whose mean is 50. Verify that the sample mean for the large data set is the same as the sample mean for the small data set.

(e) (47.7, 52.8); decreases width of interval

43	63	53	50	58	44
53	53	52	41	50	43
47	65	56	58	41	52
49	56	57	50	38	42
59	54	57	41	63	37
46	54	42	48	53	41

(e) Compute a 95% confidence interval for the large data set. Compare the results to part (a). What effect does increasing the sample size have on the confidence interval?

(f) Suppose that the last observation, 41, is inadvertently entered as 14. Verify that this observation is an outlier.

(g) Compute a 95% confidence interval for the large data set with the outlier. Compare the results to part (e). What effect does an outlier have on a confidence interval when the data set is large? (46.3, 52.7)

51. Simulation: Normal Distribution IQ scores based on the Wechsler Intelligence Scale for Children (WISC) are known to be normally distributed with $\mu = 100$ and $\sigma = 15$.

(a) Use StatCrunch, MINITAB, or some other statistical software to simulate obtaining 100 simple random samples of size $n = 5$ from this population.

(b) Obtain the sample mean and sample standard deviation for each of the 100 samples.

(c) Construct 95% t-intervals for each of the 100 samples.

(d) How many of the intervals do you expect to include the population mean? How many of the intervals actually include the population mean?

52. Simulation: Exponential Distribution The *exponential probability distribution* can be used to model waiting time in line or the lifetime of electronic components. Its density function is skewed right. Suppose the wait-time in a line can be modeled by the exponential distribution with $\mu = \sigma = 5$ minutes.

(a) Use StatCrunch, MINITAB, or some other statistical software to generate 100 random samples of size $n = 4$ from this population.

(b) Construct 95% *t*-intervals for each of the 100 samples found in part (a).

(c) How many of the intervals do you expect to include the population mean? How many of the intervals actually contain the population mean? Explain what your results mean.

(d) Repeat parts (a)–(c) for samples of size $n = 15$ and $n = 25$. Explain what your results mean.

53. Putting It Together: Smoking Cessation Study Researchers Havar Brendryen and Pal Kraft conducted a study in which 396 subjects were randomly assigned to either an experimental smoking cessation program or control group. The experimental program consisted of the Internet and phone-based Happy Ending Intervention, which lasted 54 weeks and consisted of more than 400 contacts by e-mail, Web pages, interactive voice response, and short message service (SMS) technology. The control group received a self-help booklet. Both groups were offered free nicotine replacement therapy. Abstinence was defined as "not even a puff of smoke, for the last 7 days," and assessed by means of Internet surveys or telephone interviews. The response variable was abstinence after 12 months. Of the participants in the experimental program, 22.3% reported abstinence; of the participants in the control group, 13.1% reported abstinence. *Source:* "Happy Ending: A Randomized Controlled Trial of a Digital MultiMedia Smoking Cessation Intervention." Havar Brendryen and Pal Kraft. *Addiction* 103(3):478–484, 2008. 53. (a) Completely randomized design

(a) What type of experimental design is this?

(b) What is the treatment? How many levels does it have?

(c) What is the response variable? Whether the smoker quits or not

(d) What are the statistics reported by the authors?

(e) According to Wikipedia.com, an **odds ratio** is the ratio of the odds of an event occurring in one group to the odds of it occurring in another group. These groups might be men and women, an experimental group and a control group, or any other dichotomous classification. If the probabilities of the event in each of the groups are p (first group) and q (second group), then the odds ratio is

$$\frac{\dfrac{p}{(1-p)}}{\dfrac{q}{(1-q)}} = \frac{p(1-q)}{q(1-p)}$$

An odds ratio of 1 indicates that the condition or event under study is equally likely in both groups. An odds ratio greater than 1 indicates that the condition or event is more likely in the first group. And an odds ratio less than 1 indicates that the condition or event is less likely in the first group. The odds ratio must be greater than or equal to zero. As the odds of the first group approach zero, the odds ratio approaches zero. As the odds of the second group approach zero, the odds ratio approaches positive infinity. Verify that the odds ratio for this study is 1.90. What does this mean?

(f) The authors of the study reported a 95% confidence interval for the odds ratio to be *lower bound:* 1.12 and *upper bound* 3.26. Interpret this result.

(g) Write a conclusion that generalizes the results of this study to the population of all smokers.

53. (d) 22.3% abstinent in the experimental group; 13.1% abstinent in the control group

54. Putting It Together: How Many Drinks? A question on the General Social Survey was "When you drink, how many drinks do you have?" The results are shown next.

Number of Drinks	Frequency
1	119
2	66
3	27
4	12
5	8
6	5
7	4
8	1
9	0
10	0
11	0
12	1

(a) Draw a histogram of the data and comment on the shape of the distribution. Skewed right

(b) Determine the mean and standard deviation for number of drinks. $\bar{x} = 2.0$; $s = 1.6$

(c) What is the mode number of drinks? One drink

(d) What is the probability a randomly selected individual consumes two drinks? 0.2716

(e) Would it be unusual to observe an individual who consumes at least eight drinks? Why?

(f) What shape will the distribution of the sample mean have? Why? Approximately normal; Central Limit Theorem

(g) Construct a 95% confidence interval for the mean number of drinks. Interpret this interval. (1.8, 2.2)

EXPLAINING THE CONCEPTS

55. Explain why the *t*-distribution has less spread as the number of degrees of freedom increases.

56. The procedures for constructing a *t*-interval are *robust*. Explain what this means.

57. Explain what is meant by *degrees of freedom*.

58. The mean age of the 43 presidents of the United States (as of 2011) on the day of inauguration is 54.6 years, with a standard deviation of 6.3 years. A researcher constructed a 95% confidence interval for the mean age of presidents on inauguration day. He wrote that he was 95% confident that the mean age of the president on inauguration day is between 52.7 and 56.5 years of age. Is there anything wrong with the researcher's analysis? Explain.

59. Suppose you have two populations: Population A—All students at Illinois State University ($N = 21{,}000$) and Population B—All residents of the city of Homer Glen, IL ($N = 21{,}000$). You want to estimate the mean age of each population using two separate samples each of size $n = 75$. If you construct a 95% confidence interval for each population mean, will the margin of error for population A be larger, the same, or smaller than the margin of error for population B? Justify your reasoning. A smaller than B

60. Population A has standard deviation $\sigma_A = 5$, and population B has standard deviation $\sigma_B = 10$. How many times larger than Population A's sample size does Population B's need to be to estimate μ with the same margin of error? [*Hint:* Compute n_B/n_A]. 4 times

Consumer Reports® Consumer Reports Tests Tires

Consumer Reports' specialized auto-test facility is the largest, most sophisticated consumer-based auto-testing facility in the world. Located on 327 acres in East Haddam, Connecticut, the facility is staffed by a team of experienced engineers and test personnel who buy and test more than 40 new cars, SUVs, minivans, and light trucks each year. For each vehicle, Consumer Reports conducts more than 46 individual tests, ranging from emergency handling, acceleration, and braking to fuel-economy measurements, noise-level evaluations, and bumper-impact tests.

As part of testing vehicles, Consumer Reports tests tires. Our tire evaluations include dry and wet braking from 60 mph, braking on ice, snow traction on a flat surface, snow traction on a snow hill, emergency handling, routine cornering, ride comfort, rolling resistance, and noise. All the test data are recorded using an optical instrument that provides precise speed and distance measurements.

The following table contains the dry brake stopping distance (in feet) data for one brand of tires recently tested.

Measurement	Distance
1	131.8
2	123.2
3	132.9
4	139.8
5	140.3
6	128.3
7	129.3
8	129.5
9	134.0

(a) A normal probability plot of the dry brake distance data is shown. What does this plot suggest about the distribution of the brake data?

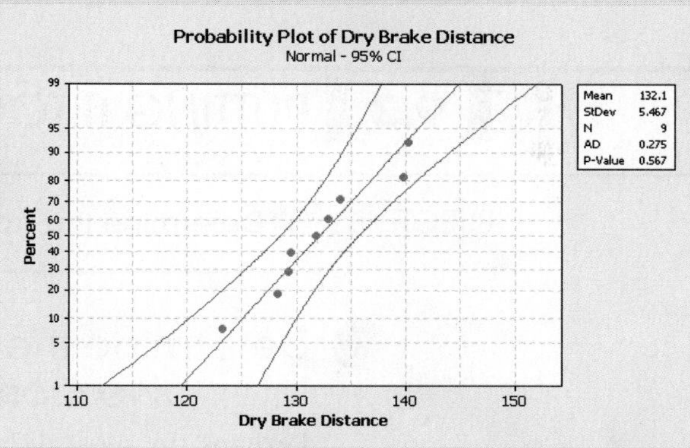

(b) Does the data set contain any outliers?

(c) Use these data to construct a 95% confidence interval for the mean dry braking distance for this brand of tires. Write a statement that explains the meaning of this confidence interval to the readers of *Consumer Reports* magazine.

***Note to Readers:** In many cases, our test protocol and analytical methods are more complicated than described in these examples. The data and discussions have been modified to make the material more appropriate for the audience.*

Technology Step-By-Step

Confidence Intervals for μ

TI-83/84 Plus

1. If necessary, enter raw data in L1.
2. Press STAT, highlight TESTS, and select `8:TInterval`.
3. If the data are raw, highlight DATA. Make sure `List` is set to L1 and `Freq` to 1. If summary statistics are known, highlight STATS and enter the summary statistics.
4. Enter the confidence level following `C-Level:`.
5. Highlight `Calculate`; press ENTER.

MINITAB

1. If you have raw data, enter them in column C1.
2. Select the **Stat** menu, highlight **Basic Statistics**, then highlight **1-Sample *t*. . . .**

3. If you have raw data, enter C1 in the cell marked "Samples in columns". If you have summarized data, select the "Summarized data" radio button and enter the summarized data. Select **Options...** and enter a confidence level. Click OK twice.

Excel
1. Load the XLSTAT Add-in.
2. Enter the raw data in Column A.
3. Select the **XLSTAT** menu, highlight **Parametric tests**. Select **One-sample t-test and z-test**.
4. Place the cursor in the Data cell. Highlight the raw data in the spreadsheet. Be sure the box for Student's t test is checked and the radio button for One sample is selected. Click the Options tab. For a 90% confidence interval, let the Significance level (%) equal 10; for a 95% confidence interval, let the Significance level (%) equal 5, and so on. Click OK.

StatCrunch
1. If you have raw data, enter them into the spreadsheet. Name the column variable.
2. Select **Stat**, highlight **T Statistics**, select **One sample**, and then choose either **with data** or **with summary**.
3. If you chose **with data**, select the column that has the observations, then click Next>. If you chose **with summary**, enter the mean, standard deviation, and sample size. Click Next>.
4. Choose the confidence interval radio button. Enter the level of confidence. Click Calculate.

9.3 PUTTING IT TOGETHER: WHICH PROCEDURE DO I USE?

OBJECTIVE 1 Determine the appropriate confidence interval to construct

1 Determine the Appropriate Confidence Interval to Construct

Perhaps the most difficult aspect of constructing a confidence interval is determining which type to construct. To assist in your decision making, we present Figure 17.

Figure 17

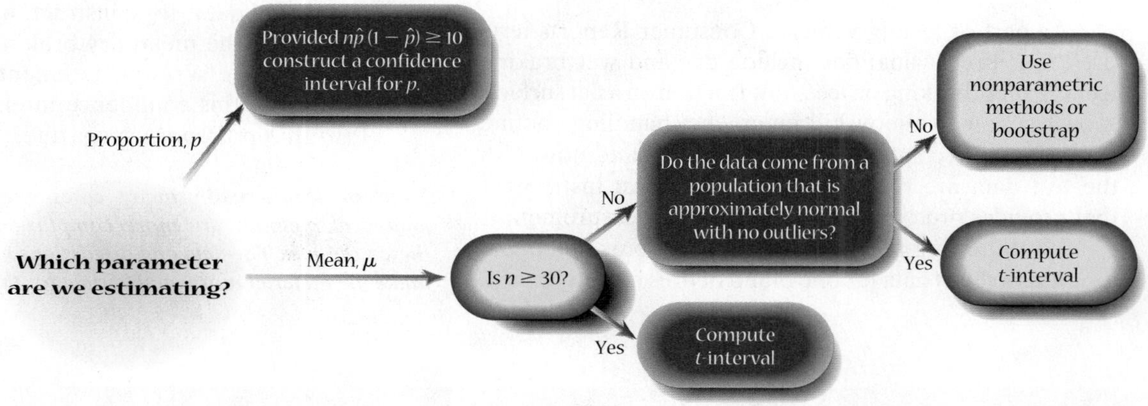

EXAMPLE 1 Constructing a Confidence Interval: Which Method Do I Use?

TABLE 4		
323.9	326.8	370.6
450.7	368.8	423.8
398.8	417.5	
382.7	343.1	

Problem Robert wishes to estimate the mean number of miles that his Buick Lacrosse can be driven on a full tank of gas. He fills up his car with regular unleaded gasoline from the same gas station 10 times and records the number of miles that he drives until his low-tank indicator light comes on. He obtains the data shown in Table 4. Construct a 95% confidence interval for the mean number of miles driven on a full tank of gas.

Approach Follow the flow chart given in Figure 17.

Solution We are asked to construct a 95% confidence interval for the *mean* number of miles driven. We will treat the data as a simple random sample from a large population. Because the sample size is small, we verify that the data come from a population that is normally distributed with no outliers by drawing a normal probability plot and boxplot. See Figure 18. The normal probability plot shows the data could come from a population that is normally distributed, and the boxplot shows there are no outliers. We may proceed with constructing the confidence interval for the population mean.

Figure 18

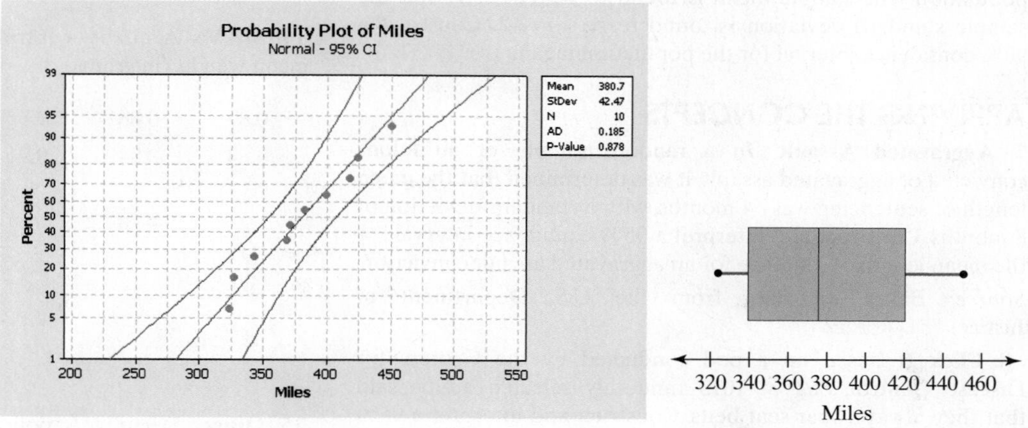

By-Hand Solution

From the sample data in Table 5, we have $n = 10$, $\bar{x} = 380.67$, and $s = 42.47$. For a 95% confidence interval with $n - 1 = 10 - 1 = 9$ degrees of freedom, we have

$$t_{\frac{\alpha}{2}} = t_{\frac{0.05}{2}} = t_{0.025} = 2.262$$

Lower bound:

$$\bar{x} - t_{\frac{\alpha}{2}} \cdot \frac{s}{\sqrt{n}} = 380.67 - 2.262 \cdot \frac{42.47}{\sqrt{10}} = 350.29$$

Upper bound:

$$\bar{x} + t_{\frac{\alpha}{2}} \cdot \frac{s}{\sqrt{n}} = 380.67 + 2.262 \cdot \frac{42.47}{\sqrt{10}} = 411.05$$

Technology Solution

Figure 19 shows the results from StatCrunch.

Figure 19

95% confidence interval results:
μ : mean of Variable

Variable	Sample Mean	Std. Err.	DF	L. Limit	U. Limit
Miles	380.67	13.429769	9	350.28976	411.05023

So

Lower bound: 350.29 Upper bound: 411.05

Interpretation We are 95% confident that the population mean miles driven on a full tank of gas is between 350.29 and 411.05.

9.3 ASSESS YOUR UNDERSTANDING

SKILL BUILDING

In Problems 1–8, construct the appropriate confidence interval.

1. A simple random sample of size $n = 300$ individuals who are currently employed is asked if they work at home at least once per week. Of the 300 employed individuals surveyed, 35 responded that they did work at home at least once per week. Construct a 99% confidence interval for the population proportion of employed individuals who work at home at least once per week. (0.069, 0.165)

2. A simple random sample of size $n = 785$ adults was asked if they follow college football. Of the 785 surveyed, 275 responded that they did follow college football. Construct a 95% confidence interval for the population proportion of adults who follow college football. (0.317, 0.383)

3. A simple random sample of size $n = 12$ is drawn from a population that is normally distributed. The sample mean is found to be $\bar{x} = 45$, and the sample standard deviation is found to be $s = 14$. Construct a 90% confidence interval for the population mean. (37.74, 52.26)

4. A simple random sample of size $n = 17$ is drawn from a population that is normally distributed. The sample mean is found to be $\bar{x} = 3.25$, and the sample standard deviation is found to be $s = 1.17$. Construct a 95% confidence interval for the population mean. (2.65, 3.85)

5. A simple random sample of size $n = 40$ is drawn from a population. The sample mean is found to be $\bar{x} = 120.5$, and the sample standard deviation is found to be $s = 12.9$. Construct a 99% confidence interval for the population mean. (114.98, 126.02)

6. A simple random sample of size $n = 210$ is drawn from a population. The sample mean is found to be $\bar{x} = 20.1$, and the sample standard deviation is found to be $s = 3.2$. Construct a 90% confidence interval for the population mean. (19.73, 20.47)

APPLYING THE CONCEPTS

7. Aggravated Assault In a random sample of 40 felons convicted of aggravated assault, it was determined that the mean length of sentencing was 54 months, with a standard deviation of 8 months. Construct and interpret a 95% confidence interval for the mean length of sentence for an aggravated assault conviction. *Source:* Based on data from the U.S. Department of Justice. (51.4, 56.6)

8. Click It Based on a poll conducted by the Centers for Disease Control, 862 of 1013 randomly selected adults said that they always wear seat belts. Construct and interpret a 95% confidence interval for the proportion of adults who always wear seat belts. (0.829, 0.873)

9. Estate Tax Returns In a random sample of 100 estate tax returns that was audited by the Internal Revenue Service, it was determined that the mean amount of additional tax owed was \$3421 with a standard deviation of \$2583. Construct and interpret a 90% confidence interval for the mean additional amount of tax owed for estate tax returns. (\$2992.2, \$3849.9)

10. Muzzle Velocity Fifty rounds of a new type of ammunition were fired from a test weapon, and the muzzle velocity of the projectile was measured. The sample had a mean muzzle velocity of 863 meters per second and a standard deviation of 2.7 meters per second. Construct and interpret a 99% confidence interval for the mean muzzle velocity. (861.98, 864.02)

11. Worried about Retirement? In a survey of 1008 adult Americans the Gallup organization asked, "When you retire, do you think you will have enough money to live comfortably or not?" Of the 1008 surveyed, 526 stated that they were worried about having enough money to live comfortably in retirement. Construct a 90% confidence interval for the proportion of adult Americans who are worried about having enough money to live comfortably in retirement. (0.496, 0.548)

12. Theme Park Spending In a random sample of 40 visitors to a certain theme park, it was determined that the mean amount of money spent per person at the park (including ticket price) was \$93.43 per day with a standard deviation of \$15. Construct and interpret a 99% confidence interval for the mean amount spent daily per person at the theme park. (87.007, 99.853)

In Problems 13–16, decide if a 95% t-interval about the population mean can be constructed. If it can, do so. If it cannot be constructed, state the reason why. For convenience, a normal probability plot and boxplot are given.

13. Gestation Period The following data represent the gestation period of a simple random sample of $n = 12$ live births. (262.4, 273.1)

266	270	277	278	258	275
261	260	270	269	252	277

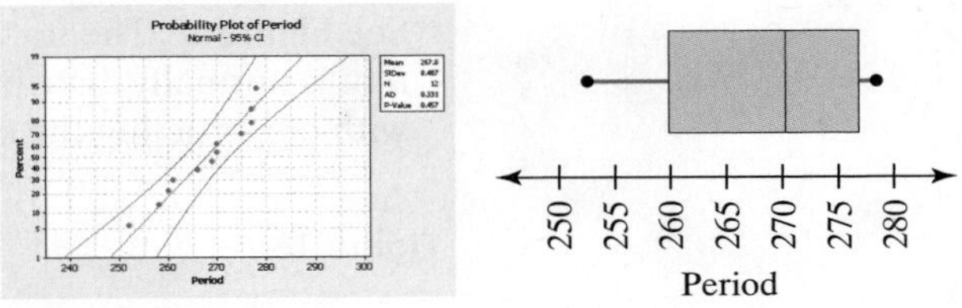

14. M&Ms A quality-control engineer wanted to estimate the mean weight (in grams) of a plain M&M candy. (0.851, 0.894)

0.87	0.88	0.82	0.90	0.86	0.86
0.84	0.84	0.91	0.94	0.88	0.87

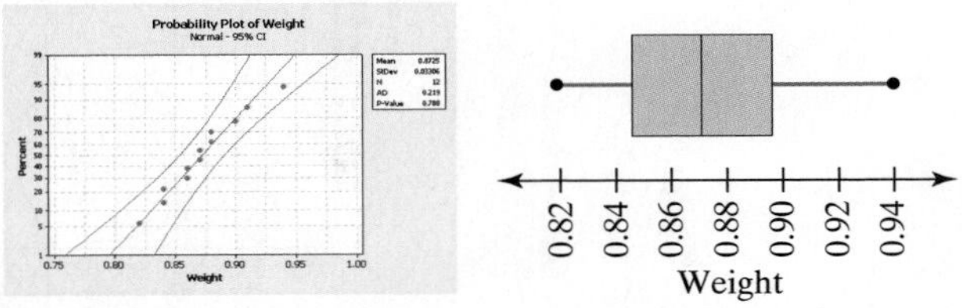

15. Officer Friendly A police officer hides behind a billboard to catch speeders. The following data represent the number of minutes he waits before first observing a car that is exceeding the speed limit by more than 10 miles per hour on 10 randomly selected days: No, outlier

1.0	5.4	0.8	10.7	0.5
0.9	3.9	0.4	2.5	3.9

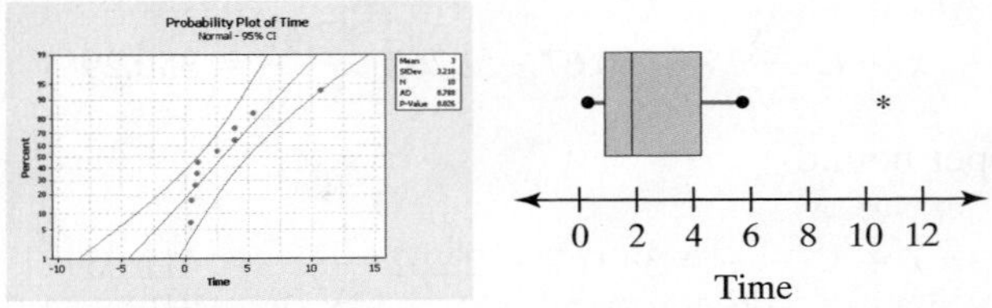

16. Law Graduate Salaries A random sample of recent graduates of law school was obtained in which the graduates were asked to report their starting salary. The data, based on results reported by the National Association for Law Placement, are as follows: No; nonnormal data

54,400	115,000	132,000	45,000	137,500
60,500	56,250	63,500	125,000	47,250
47,000	160,000	112,500	78,000	58,000
142,000	46,500	57,000	55,000	115,000

Source: NALP, July 2010.

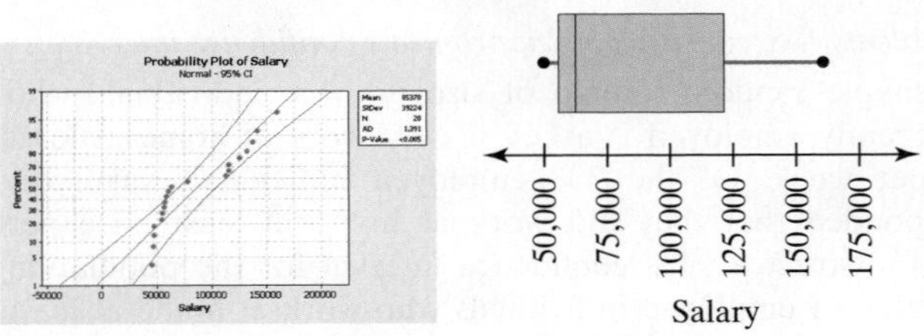

CHAPTER 9 REVIEW

Summary

In this chapter, we discussed estimation methods. We estimated the values of the parameters p and μ. We started by estimating the value of a population proportion, p. A confidence interval is an interval of numbers for an unknown parameter that is reported with a level of confidence. The level of confidence represents the proportion of intervals that will contain the parameter if a large number of different samples is obtained and is denoted $(1-\alpha)\cdot 100\%$. A $(1-\alpha)\cdot 100\%$ confidence interval for the population proportion p is given by $\hat{p} \pm z_{\alpha/2}\cdot\sqrt{\frac{\hat{p}(1-\hat{p})}{n}}$, provided the data are obtained using simple random sampling or through a randomized experiment, $n\hat{p}(1-\hat{p}) \geq 10$, and the sample size is no more than 5% of the population size (independence requirement).

In Section 9.2 we learned how to estimate the population mean, μ. To construct this interval, we required that the sample come from a population that is normally distributed or the sample size is large (so that the distribution of $\bar{x}$ is approximately normal). We also required that the sample size be no more than 5% of the population size (independence requirement) and that the data be obtained using simple random sampling or through a randomized experiment. Because the population standard deviation is likely unknown (since we do not know μ, how could we expect to know σ?), we use Student's t-distribution with $n-1$ degrees of freedom to construct a confidence interval for the population mean. A $(1-\alpha)\cdot 100\%$ confidence interval for the population mean, μ, is given by $\bar{x} \pm t_{\alpha/2}\cdot\frac{s}{\sqrt{n}}$ where $t_{\alpha/2}$ has $n-1$ degrees of freedom.

Vocabulary

Point estimate (p. 391)
Confidence interval (p. 392)
Level of confidence (p. 392)
Margin of error (p. 393)
Critical value (p. 395)
Student's t-distribution (p. 406)
t-Interval (p. 410)
Robust (p. 410)
Nonparametric procedures (p. 411)

Formulas

Confidence Intervals

- A $(1-\alpha)\cdot 100\%$ confidence interval for p is $\hat{p} \pm z_{\frac{\alpha}{2}}\cdot\sqrt{\frac{\hat{p}(1-\hat{p})}{n}}$, provided that $n\hat{p}(1-\hat{p}) \geq 10$ and $n \leq 0.05N$.
- A $(1-\alpha)\cdot 100\%$ confidence interval for μ is $\bar{x} \pm t_{\frac{\alpha}{2}}\cdot\frac{s}{\sqrt{n}}$, where $t_{\alpha/2}$ has $n-1$ degrees of freedom, provided that the population from which the sample was drawn is normal or that the sample size is large ($n \geq 30$) and $n \leq 0.05N$.

Sample Size

- To estimate the population proportion within a margin of error E at a $(1-\alpha)\cdot 100\%$ level of confidence requires a sample of size $n = \hat{p}(1-\hat{p})\left(\frac{z_{\frac{\alpha}{2}}}{E}\right)^2$ (rounded up to the next integer), where $\hat{p}$ is a prior estimate of the population proportion.
- To estimate the population proportion within a margin of error E at a $(1-\alpha)\cdot 100\%$ level of confidence requires a sample of size $n = 0.25\left(\frac{z_{\frac{\alpha}{2}}}{E}\right)^2$ (rounded up to the next integer) when no prior estimate is available.
- To estimate the population mean within a margin of error E at a $(1-\alpha)\cdot 100\%$ level of confidence requires a sample of size $n = \left(\frac{z_{\frac{\alpha}{2}}\cdot s}{E}\right)^2$ (rounded up to the next integer).

Objectives

Section	You should be able to . . .	Examples	Review Exercises
9.1	1 Obtain a point estimate for the population proportion (p. 391)	1	15(a)
	2 Construct and interpret a confidence interval for the population proportion (p. 391)	3, 4	15(b)
	3 Determine the sample size necessary for estimating a population proportion within a specified margin of error (p. 399)	6	15(c), 15(d)
9.2	1 Obtain a point estimate for the population mean (p. 405)	1	14(a)
	2 State properties of Student's t-distribution (p. 405)	2	5, 6, 7
	3 Determine t-values (p. 408)	3	1
	4 Construct and interpret a confidence interval for a population mean (p. 409)	4	8, 9, 10(b), 11(b), 12(b), 12(d), 13(b), 13(c), 14(c)
	5 Find the sample size needed to estimate the population mean within a given margin of error (p. 411)	5	10(c)
9.3	1 Determine the appropriate confidence interval to construct (p. 420)	1	8–15

Review Exercises

1. Find the critical t-value for constructing a confidence interval for a population mean at the given level of confidence for the given sample size, n.

(a) 99% confidence; $n = 18$ 2.898

(b) 90% confidence; $n = 27$ 1.706

2. IQ Scores Many of the examples and exercises in the text have dealt with IQ scores. We now know that IQ scores based on the Stanford–Binet IQ test are normally distributed with a mean of 100 and standard deviation 15. If you were to obtain 100 different simple random samples of size 20 from the population of all adult humans and determine 95% confidence intervals for each of them, how many of the intervals would you expect to include 100? What causes a particular interval to not include 100? 95; chance in sampling

3. What does the 95% represent in a 95% confidence interval?

4. For what proportion of samples will a 90% confidence interval for a population mean not capture the true population mean? 10%

5. The area under the t-distribution with 18 degrees of freedom to the right of $t = 1.56$ is 0.0681. What is the area under the t-distribution with 18 degrees of freedom to the left of $t = -1.56$? Why? 0.0681

6. Which is larger, the area under the t-distribution with 10 degrees of freedom to the right of $t = 2.32$ or the area under the standard normal distribution to the right of $z = 2.32$? Why? t-distribution

7. State the properties of Student's t-distribution.

8. A simple random sample of size n is drawn from a population. The sample mean, $\bar{x}$, is 54.8 and the sample standard deviation is 10.5.

(a) Construct the 90% confidence interval for the population mean if the sample size, n, is 30. (51.54, 58.06)

(b) Construct the 90% confidence interval for the population mean if the sample size, n, is 51. How does increasing the sample size affect the width of the interval? (52.34, 57.26); decreases

(c) Construct the 99% confidence interval for the population mean if the sample size, n, is 30. Compare the results to those obtained in part (a). How does increasing the level of confidence affect the confidence interval? (49.52, 60.08); increases width

9. A simple random sample of size n is drawn from a population that is known to be normally distributed. The sample mean, $\bar{x}$, is determined to be 104.3 and the sample standard deviation, s, is determined to be 15.9. (c) (95.49; 113.11); increases width

(a) Construct the 90% confidence interval for the population mean if the sample size, n, is 15. (97.07, 111.53)

(b) Construct the 90% confidence interval for the population mean if the sample size, n, is 25. How does increasing the sample size affect the width of the interval? (98.86, 109.74); decreases

(c) Construct the 95% confidence interval for the population mean if the sample size, n, is 15. Compare the results to those obtained in part (a). How does increasing the level of confidence affect the confidence interval?

10. Long Life? In a survey of 35 adult Americans, it was found that the mean age (in years) that people would like to live to is 87.9 with a standard deviation of 15.5. An analysis of the raw data indicates the distribution is skewed left. (b) (82.58, 93.22)

(a) Explain why a large sample size is necessary to construct a confidence interval for the mean age that people would like to live. Skewed left

(b) Construct and interpret a 95% confidence interval for the mean.

4. 95% of samples result in intervals that include the unknown parameter.

(c) How many adult Americans would need to be surveyed to estimate the mean age that people would like to live to within 2 years with 95% confidence? 231 11. (a) Skewed right

11. E-mail One question asked in the General Social Survey was this: "How many e-mails do you send in a day?" The results of 928 respondents indicate that the mean number of e-mails sent in a day is 10.4, with a standard deviation of 28.5.

(a) Given the fact that 1 standard deviation to the left of the mean results in a negative number of e-mails being sent, what shape would you expect the distribution of e-mails sent to have?

(b) Construct and interpret a 90% confidence interval for the mean number of e-mails sent per day. (8.86, 11.94)

12. Caffeinated Sports Drinks Researchers conducted an experiment to determine the effectiveness of a commercial caffeinated carbohydrate–electrolyte sports drink compared with a placebo. Sixteen highly trained cyclists each completed two trials of prolonged cycling in a warm environment, one while receiving the sports drink and another while receiving a placebo. For a given trial, one beverage treatment was administered throughout a 2-hour variable-intensity cycling bout followed by a 15-minute performance ride. Total work (in kilojoules) performed during the final 15 minutes was used to measure performance. The beverage order for individual subjects was randomly assigned with a period of at least five days separating the trials. Assume that the researchers verified the normality of the population of total work performed for each treatment. *Source*: Kirk J. Cureton, Gordon L. Warren, et al., "Caffeinated Sports Drink: Ergogenic Effects and Possible Mechanisms." *International Journal of Sport Nutrition and Exercise Metabolism* 17(1):35–55, 2007

(a) Why do you think the sample size was small ($n = 16$) for this experiment?

(b) For the sports-drink treatment, the mean total work performed during the performance ride for the $n = 16$ riders was 218 kilojoules, with standard deviation 31 kilojoules. Construct and interpret a 95% confidence interval for the population mean total work performed. (201.5, 234.5)

(c) Is it possible for the population mean total work performed for the sports-drink treatment to be less than 198 kilojoules? Do you think this is likely? Yes; no

(d) For the placebo treatment, the mean total work performed during the performance ride for the $n = 16$ riders was 178 kilojoules, with standard deviation 31 kilojoules. Construct and interpret a 95% confidence interval for the population mean total work performed. (161.5, 194.5)

(e) Is it possible for the population mean total work performed for the placebo treatment to be more than 198 kilojoules? Do you think this is likely? Yes; no

(f) The researchers concluded that the caffeinated carbohydrate–electrolyte sports drink substantially enhanced physical performance during prolonged exercise compared with the placebo. Do your findings in parts (b) and (d) support the researchers' conclusion? Explain. Yes

13. Family Size A random sample of 60 married couples who have been married 7 years was asked the number of children they have. The results of the survey are as follows:

0	0	0	3	3	3	1	3	2	2	3	1
3	2	4	0	3	3	3	1	0	2	3	3
1	4	2	3	1	3	3	5	0	2	3	0
4	4	2	2	3	2	2	2	2	3	4	3
2	2	1	4	3	2	4	2	1	2	3	2

Note: $\bar{x} = 2.27$, $s = 1.22$.

(a) What is the shape of the distribution of the sample mean? Why? Normal

(b) Compute a 95% confidence interval for the mean number of children of all couples who have been married 7 years. Interpret this interval. (1.95, 2.59)

(c) Compute a 99% confidence interval for the mean number of children of all couples who have been married 7 years. Interpret this interval. (1.85, 2.69)

14. Diameter of Douglas Fir Trees The diameter of the Douglas fir tree is measured at a height of 1.37 meters. The following data represent the diameter in centimeters of a random sample of 12 Douglas firs in the western Washington Cascades.

156	190	147	173	159	181
162	130	101	147	113	109

Source: L. Winter. "Live Tree and Tree-Ring Records to Reconstruct the Structural Development of an Old-Growth Douglas Fir/Western Hemlock Stand in the Western Washington Cascades." Corvallis, OR: Forest Science Data Bank, 2005.

(a) Obtain a point estimate for the mean and standard deviation diameter of a Douglas fir tree in the western Washington Cascades. $\bar{x} = 147.3$, $s = 28.8$

(b) Because the sample size is small, we must verify that the data come from a population that is normally distributed and that the data do not contain any outliers. The figures show the normal probability plot and boxplot. Are the conditions for constructing a confidence interval for the population mean diameter satisfied? Yes

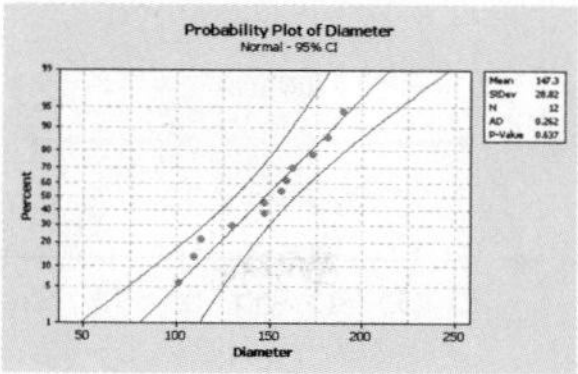

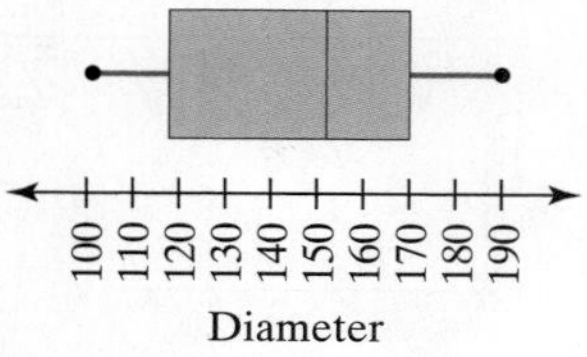

(c) Construct a 95% confidence interval for the mean diameter of a Douglas fir tree in the western Washington Cascades. (129.0, 165.6)

15. Hypertension In a random sample of 678 adult males 20 to 34 years of age, it was determined that 58 of them have hypertension (high blood pressure).

Source: The Centers for Disease Control.

(a) Obtain a point estimate for the proportion of adult males 20 to 34 years of age who have hypertension. 0.086

(b) Construct a 95% confidence interval for the proportion of adult males 20 to 34 years of age who have hypertension. Interpret the confidence interval. (0.065, 0.107)

(c) You wish to conduct your own study to determine the proportion of adult males 20 to 34 years old who have hypertension. What sample size would be needed for the estimate to be within 3 percentage points with 95% confidence if you use the point estimate obtained in part (a)? 336

(d) You wish to conduct your own study to determine the proportion of adult males 20 to 34 years old who have hypertension. What sample size would be needed for the estimate to be within 3 percentage points with 95% confidence if you don't have a prior estimate? 1068

Problems in the chapter test are labeled by section.objective. For example, 2.3 means Section 2, Objective 3.

CHAPTER TEST

2.2 **1.** State the properties of Student's t-distribution.

2.3 **2.** Find the critical t-value for constructing a confidence interval about a population mean at the given level of confidence for the given sample size, n.

(a) 96% confidence; $n = 26$ 2.167

(b) 98% confidence; $n = 18$ 2.567

2.4 **3.** Determine the point estimate of the population mean and margin of error if the confidence interval has lower bound: 125.8 and upper bound: 152.6. $\bar{x} = 139.2$, $E = 13.4$

2.4 **4.** A question on the 2006 General Social Survey was this: "How many family members do you know that are in prison?" The results of 499 respondents indicate that the mean number of family members in jail is 1.22, with a standard deviation of 0.59.

(a) What shape would you expect the distribution of this variable to have? Why? Skewed right

(b) Construct and interpret a 99% confidence interval for the mean number of family members in jail. (1.151, 1.289)

2.4 **5.** A random sample of 50 recent college graduates results in a mean time to graduate of 4.58 years, with a standard deviation of 1.10 years.

Source: Based on data from *The Toolbox Revisited* by Clifford Adelman, U.S. Department of Education

(a) Compute and interpret a 90% confidence interval for time to graduate with a bachelor's degree. (4.319, 4.841)

(b) Does this evidence contradict the widely held belief that it takes 4 years to complete a bachelor's degree? Why? Yes

6. The campus at Joliet Junior College has a lake. A student used a Secchi disk to measure the clarity of the lake's water by lowering the disk into the water and measuring the distance below the water surface at which the disk is no longer visible. The following measurements (in inches) were taken on the lake at various points in time over the course of a year.

82	64	62	66	68	43
38	26	68	56	54	66

Source: Virginia Piekarski, Joliet Junior College

2.1 **(a)** Use the data to compute a point estimate for the population mean and population standard deviation.

(b) Because the sample size is small, we must verify that the data are normally distributed and do not contain any outliers. The figures on the next page show the normal probability plot and boxplot. Are the conditions for constructing a confidence interval about μ satisfied? Yes

6.(a) $\bar{x} = 57.8$, $s = 15.4$

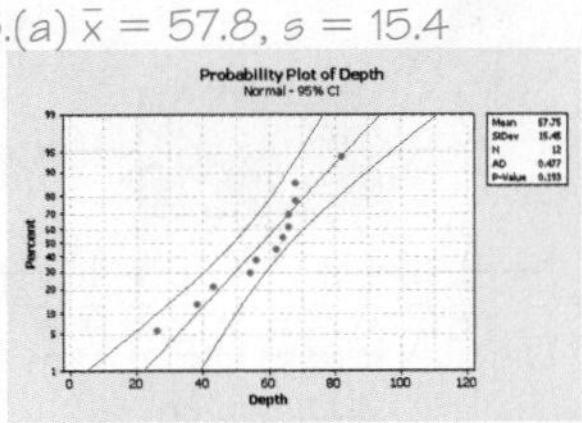

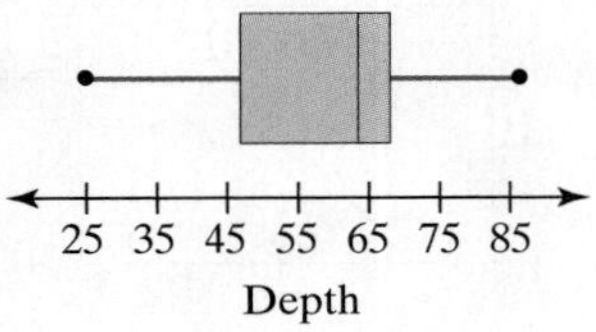

2.4 **(c)** Construct a 95% confidence interval for the mean Secchi disk measurement. Interpret this interval. (48.0, 67.6)

2.4 **(d)** Construct a 99% confidence interval for the mean Secchi disk measurement. Interpret this interval. (44.0, 71.6)

7. From a random sample of 1201 Americans, it was discovered that 1139 of them lived in neighborhoods with acceptable levels of carbon monoxide. *Source:* Environmental Protection Agency.

1.1 **(a)** Obtain a point estimate for the proportion of Americans who live in neighborhoods with acceptable levels of carbon monoxide. 0.948

1.2 **(b)** Construct a 99% confidence interval for the proportion of Americans who live in neighborhoods with acceptable levels of carbon monoxide. (0.932, 0.964)

1.3 **(c)** You wish to conduct your own study to determine the proportion of Americans who live in neighborhoods with acceptable levels of carbon monoxide. What sample size would be needed for the estimate to be within 1.5 percentage points with 90% confidence if you use the estimate obtained in part (a)? 593

1.3 **(d)** You wish to conduct your own study to determine the proportion of Americans who live in neighborhoods with acceptable levels of carbon monoxide. What sample size would be needed for the estimate to be within 1.5 percentage points with 90% confidence if you do not have a prior estimate? 3007

8. Wimbledon Match Lengths A tennis enthusiast wants to estimate the mean length of men's singles matches held during the Wimbledon tennis tournament. From the Wimbledon history archives, he randomly selects 40 matches played during the tournament since the year 1968 (when professional players were first allowed to participate). The lengths of the 40 selected matches, in minutes, follow:

110	76	84	231	122	115	87	137
101	119	138	132	136	111	194	92
198	153	256	146	149	103	116	163
182	132	123	178	140	151	115	107
202	128	60	89	94	95	89	182

Source: www.wimbledon.org

2.1 **(a)** Obtain a point estimate of the population mean length of men's singles matches during Wimbledon. 133.4

(b) A frequency histogram of the data is shown next. Explain why a large sample is necessary to construct a confidence interval for the population mean length of men's singles matches during Wimbledon.

Wimbledon Match Lengths

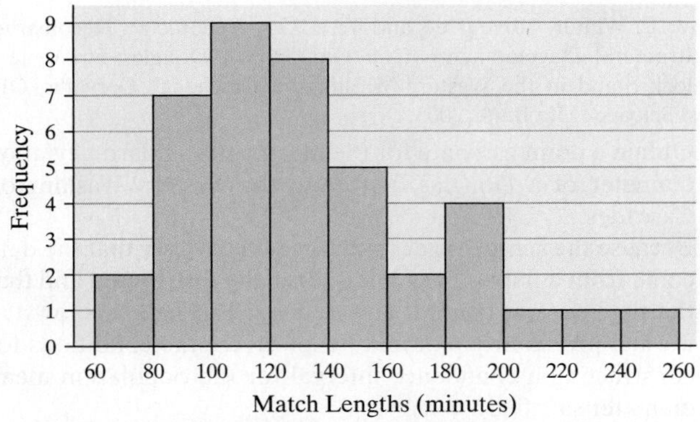

2.4 **(c)** Construct and interpret a 90% confidence interval for the population mean length of men's singles matches during Wimbledon. (114.9, 151.9)

2.4 **(d)** Construct and interpret a 95% confidence interval for the population mean length of men's singles matches during Wimbledon. (119.6, 147.2)

(e) What effect does increasing the level of confidence have on the interval? width increases

(f) Do the confidence intervals computed in parts (c) and (d) represent an estimate for the population mean length of men's singles matches during all professional tennis tournaments? Why? No

Making an Informed Decision

How Much Should I Spend for this House?

One of the biggest purchases we make in our lifetimes is for a home. Questions that we all ask are these:

- How much should I spend for a particular home?
- How many bathrooms are there?
- How long should I expect a home to be on the market?
- What is the cost per square foot?

The purpose of this project is to help you make an informed decision about housing values. This will help to ensure you receive a good deal when purchasing a home.

(a) Go to a real estate Web site such as www.realtor.com or www.zillow.com and enter the particular zip code you are interested in moving to. Randomly select at least 30 homes for sale and record the following information:

- Asking price
- Square footage
- Number of days on the market
- Cost per square foot (asking price divided by square footage)

(b) For each of the variables identified, determine a 95% confidence interval. Interpret the interval.

(c) Now randomly select 30 recently sold homes and determine the percentage discount from the asking price. This is determined by computing $\frac{\text{asking price} - \text{closing price}}{\text{asking price}}$.

(d) Determine a 95% confidence interval for percentage discount. Interpret the interval.

(e) For the type of house you are considering (such as a 2400 square foot 3-bedroom/2-bath home), identify at least 20 homes that are for sale in the neighborhood you are considering. Compute a 95% confidence interval for the asking price of this type of home.

(f) Write a report that details how much you should expect to pay for the type of house you are considering.

The Chapter 9 Case Study is located on the CD that accompanies this text.

10 Hypothesis Tests Regarding a Parameter

Making an Informed Decision

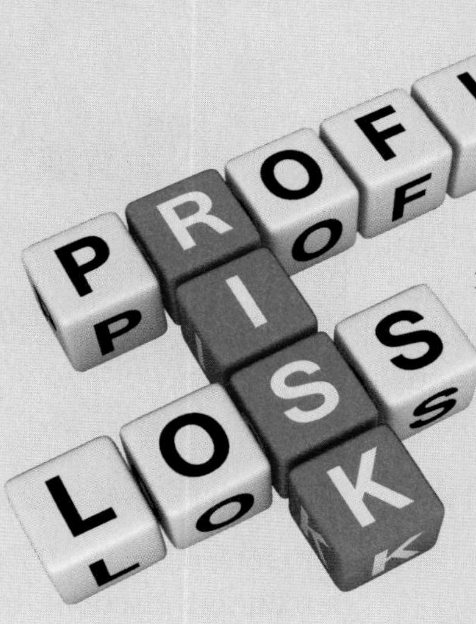

Suppose you have just received a $1000 bonus at your job. Rather than waste the money on frivolous items, you decide to invest the money so you can use it later to buy a home. You have many investment options. Your family and friends who have some experience investing recommend mutual funds. Which fund should you choose? See the Decisions project on page 466.

PUTTING IT TOGETHER

In Chapter 9, we mentioned there are two types of inferential statistics: (1) estimation and (2) hypothesis testing. We have already discussed procedures for estimating the population proportion, the population mean, and the population standard deviation.

We now focus our attention on hypothesis testing. Hypothesis testing is used to test statements regarding a characteristic of one or more populations. In this chapter, we will test hypotheses regarding a single population parameter. The hypotheses that we test concern the population proportion, the population mean, and the population standard deviation.

10.1 THE LANGUAGE OF HYPOTHESIS TESTING

Preparing for This Section Before getting started, review the following:

- Parameter versus statistic (Section 1.1, p. 5)
- Simple random sampling (Section 1.3, pp. 23–26)
- Table 9 (Section 6.2, p. 313)
- Sampling distribution of $\bar{x}$ (Section 8.1, pp. 367–375)

OBJECTIVES
1. Determine the null and alternative hypotheses
2. Explain Type I and Type II errors
3. State conclusions to hypothesis tests

We begin with an example.

EXAMPLE 1 Is Your Friend Cheating?

Problem A friend of yours wants to play a simple coin-flipping game. If the coin comes up heads, you win; if it comes up tails, your friend wins. Suppose the outcome of five plays of the game is T, T, T, T, T. Is your friend cheating?

Approach To decide whether your friend is cheating, determine the likelihood of obtaining five tails in a row. You can do this by assuming the coin is fair so that $P(\text{tail}) = P(\text{head}) = {}^1/_2$ and the flips of the coin are independent. Next ask, "Is it unusual to obtain five tails in a row with a fair coin?"

Solution We will determine the probability of getting five tails in a row, assuming that the coin is fair. The flips of the coin are independent, so

$$\begin{aligned} P(\text{five tails in a row}) &= P(\text{T and T and T and T and T}) \\ &= P(\text{T})\cdot P(\text{T})\cdot P(\text{T})\cdot P(\text{T})\cdot P(\text{T}) \\ &= \frac{1}{2}\cdot\frac{1}{2}\cdot\frac{1}{2}\cdot\frac{1}{2}\cdot\frac{1}{2} \\ &= \left(\frac{1}{2}\right)^5 \\ &= 0.03125 \end{aligned}$$

If we flipped a *fair* coin 5 times, 100 different times, we would expect about 3 of the 100 experiments to result in all tails. So what we observed is possible but not likely. You can make one of two conclusions:

1. Your friend is not cheating and happens to be lucky.
2. Your friend is not using a fair coin (that is, the probability of obtaining a tail on one flip is greater than ${}^1/_2$) and is cheating.

Is your friend cheating, or did you just happen to experience an unusual result from a fair coin?

This is at the heart of *hypothesis testing*. We make an assumption about reality (in this case, the probability of obtaining a tail is ${}^1/_2$). We then look at (or gather) sample evidence to determine whether it contradicts our assumption.

Note to Instructor
If you like, you can print out and distribute the Preparing for This Section quiz located in the Instructor's Resource Center. The purpose of the quiz is to verify that the students have the prerequisite knowledge for the section.

Note to Instructor
Before starting this section, divide your students into groups. Each group should define the following (along with the symbolic representation): population mean, sample mean, population standard deviation, sample standard deviation, and standard error of the mean.

Note to Instructor
We intentionally do not answer the question as to whether the friend actually is cheating. This can form a basis for classroom discussion. Survey the class to determine who is willing to accuse his or her friend of cheating. Also, address the fact that, in reality, we will not know for sure if the friend is (or is not) cheating.

1 Determine the Null and Alternative Hypotheses

According to *dictionary.com*, a **hypothesis** is a proposition assumed as a premise in an argument. The word hypothesis comes from the Greek word *hypotithenai*, which means "to suppose." The definition of *hypothesis* in statistics is given next.

DEFINITION

A **hypothesis** is a statement regarding a characteristic of one or more populations.

In this chapter, we look at hypotheses regarding a single population parameter. Consider the following:

(A) According to a Gallup poll conducted in 2008, 80% of Americans felt satisfied with the way things were going in their personal lives. A researcher wonders if the percentage of satisfied Americans is different today (a statement regarding a population proportion).

(B) The packaging on a light bulb states that the bulb will last 500 hours under normal use. A consumer advocate would like to know if the mean lifetime of a bulb is less than 500 hours (a statement regarding the population mean).

(C) The standard deviation of the rate of return for a certain class of mutual funds is 0.08 percent. A mutual fund manager believes the standard deviation of the rate of return for his fund is less than 0.08 percent (a statement regarding the population standard deviation).

CAUTION
If population data are available, there is no need for inferential statistics.

We test these types of statements using sample data because it is usually impossible or impractical to gain access to the entire population. The procedure (or process) we use to test such statements is called *hypothesis testing*.

DEFINITION

Hypothesis testing is a procedure, based on sample evidence and probability, used to test statements regarding a characteristic of one or more populations.

The basic steps in conducting a hypothesis test are these:

Steps in Hypothesis Testing

1. Make a statement regarding the nature of the population.
2. Collect evidence (sample data) to test the statement.
3. Analyze the data to assess the plausibility of the statement.

Note to Instructor
Emphasize that sample data cannot prove that a hypothesis is true.

Because we use sample data to test hypotheses, we cannot state with 100% certainty that the statement is true; we can only determine whether the sample data support the statement or not. In fact, because the statement can be either true or false, hypothesis testing is based on two types of hypotheses. In this chapter, the hypotheses will be statements regarding the value of a population parameter.

DEFINITIONS

The **null hypothesis**, denoted H_0 (read "H-naught"), is a statement to be tested. The null hypothesis is a statement of no change, no effect, or no difference and is assumed true until evidence indicates otherwise.

The **alternative hypothesis**, denoted H_1 (read "H-one"), is a statement that we are trying to find evidence to support.

In this chapter, there are three ways to set up the null and alternative hypotheses.

1. Equal hypothesis versus not equal hypothesis **(two-tailed test)**
   H_0: parameter = some value
   H_1: parameter $\neq$ some value
2. Equal versus less than **(left-tailed test)**
   H_0: parameter = some value
   H_1: parameter $<$ some value
3. Equal versus greater than **(right-tailed test)**
   H_0: parameter = some value
   H_1: parameter $>$ some value

In Other Words
The null hypothesis is a statement of *status quo* or *no difference* and always contains a statement of equality. The null hypothesis is assumed to be true until we have evidence to the contrary. We seek evidence that supports the statement in the alternative hypothesis.

Left- and right-tailed tests are referred to as **one-tailed tests**. Notice that in the left-tailed test the direction of the inequality sign in the alternative hypothesis points to the left ($<$), while in the right-tailed test the direction of the inequality sign in the alternative hypothesis points to the right ($>$). In all three tests, the null hypothesis contains a statement of equality.

Refer to the three hypotheses made on the previous page. In Situation A, the null hypothesis is expressed using the notation H_0: $p = 0.80$. This is a statement of *status quo* or no difference. The Latin phrase *status quo* means "the existing state or condition." So, the statement in the null hypothesis means that American opinions have not changed from 2008. We are trying to show that the proportion is different today, so the alternative hypothesis is H_1: $p \neq 0.80$. In Situation B, the null hypothesis is H_0: $\mu = 500$. This is a statement of no difference between the population mean and the lifetime stated on the label. We are trying to show that the mean lifetime is less than 500 hours, so the alternative hypothesis is H_1: $\mu < 500$. In Situation C, the null hypothesis is H_0: $\sigma = 0.08$. This is a statement of no difference between the population standard deviation rate of return of the manager's mutual fund and all mutual funds. The alternative hypothesis is H_1: $\sigma < 0.08$. Do you see why?

The statement we are trying to gather evidence for, which is dictated by the researcher before any data are collected, determines the structure of the alternative hypothesis (two-tailed, left-tailed, or right-tailed). For example, the label on a can of soda states that the can contains 12 ounces of liquid. A consumer advocate would be concerned only if the mean contents are less than 12 ounces, so the alternative hypothesis is H_1: $\mu < 12$. However, a quality-control engineer for the soda manufacturer would be concerned if there is too little or too much soda in the can, so the alternative hypothesis would be H_1: $\mu \neq 12$. In both cases, however, the null hypothesis is a statement of no difference between the manufacturer's assertion on the label and the actual mean contents of the can, so the null hypothesis is H_0: $\mu = 12$.

EXAMPLE 2 Forming Hypotheses

In-Class Discussion

Ask students to explain why the alternative in Example 2(a) is $p > 0.02$, rather than $p \neq 0.02$. Ask similar questions for (b) and (c). When would a researcher use a $\neq$ alternative instead of $>$ or $<$? Answer: When he or she is not sure of the direction of the alternative.

Problem Determine the null and alternative hypotheses. State whether the test is two-tailed, left-tailed, or right-tailed.

(a) The Medco pharmaceutical company has just developed a new antibiotic for children. Two percent of children taking competing antibiotics experience headaches as a side effect. A researcher for the Food and Drug Administration wishes to know if the percentage of children taking the new antibiotic who experience headaches as a side effect is more than 2%.

(b) The *Blue Book* value of a used 3-year-old Chevy Corvette Z06 is $56,130. Grant wonders if the mean price of a used 3-year-old Chevy Corvette Z06 in the Miami metropolitan area is different from $56,130.

(c) The standard deviation of the contents in a 64-ounce bottle of detergent using an old filling machine is 0.23 ounce. The manufacturer wants to know if a new filling machine has less variability.

In Other Words

Structuring the null and alternative hypotheses:
1. Identify the parameter to be tested.
2. Determine the status quo value of the parameter.
3. Determine the statement that reflects what we are trying to gather evidence for.

Approach In each case, we must determine the parameter to be tested, the statement of no change or no difference (status quo), and the statement we are attempting to gather evidence for.

Solution

(a) The hypothesis deals with a population proportion, p. If the new drug is no different from competing drugs, the proportion of individuals taking it who experience a headache will be 0.02; so the null hypothesis is H_0: $p = 0.02$. We want to determine if the proportion of individuals who experience a headache is more than 0.02, so the alternative hypothesis is H_1: $p > 0.02$. This is a right-tailed test because the alternative hypothesis contains a $>$ symbol.

(b) The hypothesis deals with a population mean, μ. If the mean price of a 3-year-old Corvette Z06 in Miami is no different from the *Blue Book* price, then the population mean in Miami will be $56,130, so the null hypothesis is H_0: $\mu = 56{,}130$. Grant wants

In Other Words
Look for key phrases when forming the alternative hypothesis. For example, *more than* means >; *different from* means ≠; *less than* means <; and so on. See Table 9 on page 313 for a list of key phrases and the symbols they translate into.

Now Work Problem 17(a)

to know if the mean price is different from \$56,130, so the alternative hypothesis is H_1: $\mu \neq 56{,}130$. This is a two-tailed test because the alternative hypothesis contains a ≠ symbol.

(c) The hypothesis deals with a population standard deviation, σ. If the new machine is no different from the old one, the standard deviation of the amount in the bottles filled by the new machine will be 0.23 ounce, so the null hypothesis is H_0: $\sigma = 0.23$. The company wants to know if the new machine has *less* variability than the old machine, so the alternative hypothesis is H_1: $\sigma < 0.23$. This is a left-tailed test because the alternative hypothesis contains a < symbol.

2 Explain Type I and Type II Errors

In Other Words
When you are testing a hypothesis, there is always the possibility that your conclusion will be wrong. To make matters worse, you won't know whether you are wrong or not! Don't fret, however; we have tools to help manage these incorrect conclusions.

As stated earlier, we use sample data to decide whether or not to reject the statement in the null hypothesis. Because this decision is based on incomplete (sample) information, there is always the possibility of making an incorrect decision. In fact, there are four possible outcomes from hypothesis testing.

Note to Instructor
Discuss the idea of a false positive or false negative as it relates to Type I and Type II errors.

Four Outcomes from Hypothesis Testing

1. Reject the null hypothesis when the alternative hypothesis is true. This decision would be correct.
2. Do not reject the null hypothesis when the null hypothesis is true. This decision would be correct.
3. Reject the null hypothesis when the null hypothesis is true. This decision would be incorrect. This type of error is called a **Type I error**.
4. Do not reject the null hypothesis when the alternative hypothesis is true. This decision would be incorrect. This type of error is called a **Type II error**.

Figure 1 illustrates the two types of errors that can be made in hypothesis testing.

Figure 1

		Reality	
		H_0 Is True	H_1 Is True
Conclusion	Do Not Reject H_0	Correct Conclusion	Type II Error
	Reject H_0	Type I Error	Correct Conclusion

Note to Instructor
Discuss the difference between "beyond all reasonable doubt" and "beyond all doubt," and how this relates to hypothesis testing.

We illustrate the idea of Type I and Type II errors by looking at hypothesis testing from the point of view of a criminal trial. In any trial, the defendant is assumed to be innocent. (We give the defendant the benefit of the doubt.) The district attorney must collect and present evidence proving that the defendant is guilty beyond all reasonable doubt.

Because we are seeking evidence for guilt, it becomes the alternative hypothesis. Innocence is assumed, so it is the null hypothesis.

H_0: the defendant is innocent

H_1: the defendant is guilty

In a trial, the jury obtains information (sample data). It then deliberates about the evidence (the data analysis). Finally, it either convicts the defendant (rejects the null hypothesis) or declares the defendant not guilty (fails to reject the null hypothesis).

Note that the defendant is never declared innocent. That is, the null hypothesis is never declared true. The two correct decisions are to declare an innocent person not guilty or declare a guilty person to be guilty. The two incorrect decisions are to convict

In Other Words
A Type I error is like putting an innocent person in jail. A Type II error is like letting a guilty person go free.

an innocent person (a Type I error) or to let a guilty person go free (a Type II error). It is helpful to think in this way when trying to remember the difference between a Type I and a Type II error.

EXAMPLE 3 Type I and Type II Errors

Problem The Medco pharmaceutical company has just developed a new antibiotic. Two percent of children taking competing antibiotics experience headaches as a side effect. A researcher for the Food and Drug Administration wishes to know if the percentage of children taking the new antibiotic who experience a headache as a side effect is more than 2%. The researcher conducts a hypothesis test with H_0: $p = 0.02$ and H_1: $p > 0.02$. Explain what it would mean to make a (a) Type I error and (b) Type II error.

Approach A Type I error occurs if we reject the null hypothesis when it is true. A Type II error occurs if we do not reject the null hypothesis when the alternative hypothesis is true.

Solution

(a) A Type I error is made if the sample evidence leads the researcher to believe that $p > 0.02$ (that is, we reject the null hypothesis) when, in fact, the proportion of children who experience a headache is not greater than 0.02.

(b) A Type II error is made if the researcher does not reject the null hypothesis that the proportion of children experiencing a headache is equal to 0.02 when, in fact, the proportion of children who experience a headache is more than 0.02. In other words, the sample evidence led the researcher to believe $p = 0.02$ when in fact the true proportion is some value larger than 0.02.

Now Work Problems 17(b) and (c)

The Probability of Making a Type I or Type II Error

Recall from Chapter 9 that we never know whether a confidence interval contains the unknown parameter. We only know the likelihood that a confidence interval captures the parameter. Similarly, we never know whether the conclusion of a hypothesis test is correct. However, just as we place a level of confidence in the construction of a confidence interval, we can determine the probability of making errors when testing hypotheses. The following notation is commonplace:

$$\alpha = P(\text{Type I error}) = P(\text{rejecting } H_0 \text{ when } H_0 \text{ is true})$$
$$\beta = P(\text{Type II error}) = P(\text{not rejecting } H_0 \text{ when } H_1 \text{ is true})$$

The symbol β is the Greek letter beta (pronounced "BAY tah"). The probability of making a Type I error, α, is chosen by the researcher *before* the sample data are collected. This probability is referred to as the *level of significance*.

DEFINITION The **level of significance**, α, is the probability of making a Type I error.

The choice of the level of significance depends on the consequences of making a Type I error. If the consequences are severe, the level of significance should be small (say, $\alpha = 0.01$). However, if the consequences are not severe, a higher level of significance can be chosen (say $\alpha = 0.05$ or $\alpha = 0.10$).

Why is the level of significance not always set at $\alpha = 0.01$? Reducing the probability of making a Type I error increases the probability of making a Type II error, β. Using our court analogy, a jury is instructed that the prosecution must provide proof of guilt "beyond all reasonable doubt." This implies that we are choosing to make α small so that the probability of convicting an innocent person is very small. The consequence of the small α, however, is a large β, which means many guilty defendants will go free. For now, we are content to recognize the inverse relation between α and β (as one goes up the other goes down).

In Other Words
As the probability of a Type I error increases, the probability of a Type II error decreases, and vice versa.

3 State Conclusions to Hypothesis Tests

CAUTION

We never *accept* the null hypothesis, because, without having access to the entire population, we don't know the exact value of the parameter stated in the null hypothesis. Rather, we say that we do not reject the null hypothesis. This is just like the court system. We never declare a defendant innocent, but rather say the defendant is not guilty.

Once the decision whether or not to reject the null hypothesis is made, the researcher must state his or her conclusion. It is important to recognize that we never *accept* the null hypothesis. Again, the court system analogy helps to illustrate the idea. The null hypothesis is H_0: innocent. When the evidence presented to the jury is not enough to convict beyond all reasonable doubt, the jury's verdict is "not guilty."

Notice that the verdict does not state that the null hypothesis of innocence is true; it states that there is not enough evidence to conclude guilt. This is a huge difference. Being told that you are not guilty is very different from being told that you are innocent!

So, sample evidence can never prove the null hypothesis to be true. By not rejecting the null hypothesis, we are saying that the evidence indicates the null hypothesis *could* be true. That is, there is not enough evidence to reject our assumption that the null hypothesis is true.

EXAMPLE 4 Stating the Conclusion

Problem The Medco pharmaceutical company has just developed a new antibiotic. Two percent of children taking competing antibiotics experience a headache as a side effect. A researcher for the Food and Drug Administration believes that the proportion of children taking the new antibiotic who experience a headache as a side effect is more than 0.02. From Example 2(a), we know the null hypothesis is H_0: $p = 0.02$ and the alternative hypothesis is H_1: $p > 0.02$.

Suppose that the sample evidence indicates that

(a) the null hypothesis is rejected. State the conclusion.

(b) the null hypothesis is not rejected. State the conclusion.

Approach When the null hypothesis is rejected, we say that there is sufficient evidence to support the statement in the alternative hypothesis. When the null hypothesis is not rejected, we say that there is not sufficient evidence to support the statement in the alternative hypothesis. We never say that the null hypothesis is true!

Solution

(a) The statement in the alternative hypothesis is that the proportion of children taking the new antibiotic who experience a headache as a side effect is more than 0.02. Because the null hypothesis ($p = 0.02$) is rejected, there is sufficient evidence to conclude that the proportion of children who experience a headache as a side effect is more than 0.02.

(b) Because the null hypothesis is not rejected, there is not sufficient evidence to say that the proportion of children who experience a headache as a side effect is more than 0.02.

Now Work Problem 25

10.1 ASSESS YOUR UNDERSTANDING

VOCABULARY AND SKILL BUILDING

1. A hypothesis is a statement regarding a characteristic of one or more populations.

2. Hypothesis testing is a procedure, based on sample evidence and probability, used to test statements regarding a characteristic of one or more populations.

3. The null hypothesis is a statement of no change, no effect, or no difference.

4. The alternative hypothesis is a statement we are trying to find evidence to support.

5. If we reject the null hypothesis when the statement in the null hypothesis is true, we have made a Type I error.

6. If we do not reject the null hypothesis when the statement in the alternative hypothesis is true, we have made a Type II error.

7. The level of significance is the probability of making a Type I error.

8. *True or False*: Sample evidence can prove a null hypothesis is true. False

In Problems 9–14, the null and alternative hypotheses are given. Determine whether the hypothesis test is left-tailed, right-tailed, or two-tailed. What parameter is being tested?

9. H_0: $\mu = 5$ Right-tailed, μ
H_1: $\mu > 5$

10. H_0: $p = 0.2$ Left-tailed, p
H_1: $p < 0.2$

16. H_0: μ = \$17,072; H_1: $\mu \neq$ \$17,072 19. H_0: $\sigma = 0.7$ psi; H_1: $\sigma < 0.7$ psi 37. (a) H_0: $p = 0.067$; H_1: $p < 0.067$

11. H_0: $\sigma = 4.2$ Two-tailed, σ
H_1: $\sigma \neq 4.2$

12. H_0: $p = 0.76$ Right-tailed, p
H_1: $p > 0.76$

13. H_0: $\mu = 120$ Left-tailed, μ
H_1: $\mu < 120$

14. H_0: $\sigma = 7.8$ Two-tailed, σ
H_1: $\sigma \neq 7.8$

In Problems 15–22, (a) determine the null and alternative hypotheses, (b) explain what it would mean to make a Type I error, and (c) explain what it would mean to make a Type II error.

15. Teenage Mothers According to the U.S. Census Bureau, 10.5% of registered births in the United States in 2007 were to teenage mothers. A sociologist believes that this percentage has increased since then. H_0: $p = 0.105$; H_1: $p > 0.105$

16. Charitable Contributions According to the Center on Philanthropy at Indiana University, the mean charitable contribution per household among households with income of \$1 million or more in the United States in 2005 was \$17,072. A researcher believes that the level of giving has changed since then.

NW **17. Single-Family Home Price** According to the National Association of Home Builders, the mean price of an existing single-family home in 2009 was \$218,600. A real estate broker believes that because of the recent credit crunch, the mean price has decreased since then. H_0: μ = \$218,600; H_1: μ < \$218,600

18. Fair Packaging and Labeling Federal law requires that a jar of peanut butter that is labeled as containing 32 ounces must contain at least 32 ounces. A consumer advocate feels that a certain peanut butter manufacturer is shorting customers by underfilling the jars. H_0: $\mu = 32$ ounces; H_1: $\mu < 32$ ounces

19. Valve Pressure The standard deviation in the pressure required to open a certain valve is known to be $\sigma = 0.7$ psi. Due to changes in the manufacturing process, the quality-control manager feels that the pressure variability has been reduced.

20. Overweight According to the Centers for Disease Control and Prevention, 19.6% of children aged 6 to 11 years are overweight. A school nurse thinks that the percentage of 6- to 11-year-olds who are overweight is higher in her school district.

21. Cell Phone Service According to the *CTIA–The Wireless Association*, the mean monthly cell phone bill was \$47.47 in 2010. A researcher suspects that the mean monthly cell phone bill is different today. H_0: μ = \$47.47; H_1: $\mu \neq$ \$47.47

22. SAT Math Scores In 2010, the standard deviation SAT score on the Critical Reading Test for all students taking the exam was 112. A teacher believes that, due to changes to high school curricula, the standard deviation of SAT math scores has decreased. H_0: $\sigma = 112$; H_1: $\sigma < 112$

20. H_0: $p = 0.196$; H_1: $p > 0.196$

In Problems 23–34, state the conclusion based on the results of the test.

23. For the hypotheses in Problem 15, the null hypothesis is rejected.

24. For the hypotheses in Problem 16, the null hypothesis is not rejected.

NW **25.** For the hypotheses in Problem 17, the null hypothesis is not rejected.

26. For the hypotheses in Problem 18, the null hypothesis is rejected.

27. For the hypotheses in Problem 19, the null hypothesis is not rejected.

28. For the hypotheses in Problem 20, the null hypothesis is not rejected.

29. For the hypotheses in Problem 21, the null hypothesis is rejected.

30. For the hypotheses in Problem 22, the null hypothesis is not rejected.

31. For the hypotheses in Problem 15, the null hypothesis is not rejected.

32. For the hypotheses in Problem 16, the null hypothesis is rejected.

33. For the hypotheses in Problem 17, the null hypothesis is rejected.

34. For the hypotheses in Problem 18, the null hypothesis is not rejected.

APPLYING THE CONCEPTS

35. Popcorn Consumption According to popcorn.org, the mean consumption of popcorn annually by Americans is 54 quarts. The marketing division of popcorn.org unleashes an aggressive campaign designed to get Americans to consume even more popcorn. (c) Type I error; 0.05

(a) Determine the null and alternative hypotheses that would be used to test the effectiveness of the marketing campaign. H_0: $\mu = 54$ quarts; H_1: $\mu > 54$ quarts

(b) A sample of 800 Americans provides enough evidence to conclude that the marketing campaign was effective. Provide a statement that should be put out by the marketing department.

(c) Suppose, in fact, that the mean annual consumption of popcorn after the marketing campaign is 53.4 quarts. Has a Type I or Type II error been made by the marketing department? If they tested the hypothesis at the $\alpha = 0.05$ level of significance, what is the probability of making a Type I error?

36. Test Preparation The mean score on the SAT Math Reasoning exam is 516. A test preparation company states that the mean score of students who take its course is higher than 516.

(a) Determine the null and alternative hypotheses.

(b) If sample data indicate that the null hypothesis should not be rejected, state the conclusion of the company.

(c) Suppose, in fact, that the mean score of students taking the preparatory course is 522. Has a Type I or Type II error been made? If we tested this hypothesis at the $\alpha = 0.01$ level, what is the probability of committing a Type I error? Type II; 0.01

(d) If we wanted to decrease the probability of making a Type II error, would we need to increase or decrease the level of significance? Increase (a) H_0: $\mu = 516$; H_1: $\mu > 516$

37. Marijuana Use According to the Centers for Disease Control and Prevention, in 2008, 6.7% of 12- to 17-year-olds had used marijuana in the previous 6 months. The Drug Abuse and Resistance Education (DARE) program underwent several major changes to keep up with technology and issues facing students in the 21st century. After the changes, a school resource officer (SRO) thinks that the proportion of 12- to 17-year-olds who have used marijuana in the past 6 months has decreased.

(a) Determine the null and alternative hypotheses.

(b) If sample data indicate that the null hypothesis should not be rejected, state the conclusion of the SRO.

(c) Suppose, in fact, that the proportion of 12- to 17-year-olds who have used marijuana in the past 6 months is 6.4%. Was a Type I or Type II error committed? Type II

38. Migraines According to the Centers for Disease Control, 15.2% of American adults experience migraine headaches. Stress is a major contributor to the frequency and intensity of headaches. A massage therapist feels that she has a technique that can reduce the frequency and intensity of migraine headaches.

(a) Determine the null and alternative hypotheses that would be used to test the effectiveness of the massage therapist's techniques. H_0: $p = 0.152$; H_1: $p < 0.152$

(b) A sample of 500 American adults who participated in the massage therapist's program results in data that indicate that the null hypothesis should be rejected. Provide a statement that supports the massage therapist's program.

(c) Suppose, in fact, that the percentage of patients in the program who experience migraine headaches is 15.3%. Was a Type I or Type II error committed? Type I error

39. Consumer Reports The following is an excerpt from a *Consumer Reports* article.

The platinum Gasaver makes some impressive claims. The device, \$188 for two, is guaranteed to increase gas mileage by 22% says the manufacturer, National Fuelsaver. Also, the company quotes "the government" as concluding, "Independent testing shows greater fuel savings with Gasaver than the 22 percent claimed by the developer." Readers have told us they want to know more about it.

The Environmental Protection Agency (EPA), after its lab tests of the Platinum Gasaver, concluded, "Users of the device would not be expected to realize either an emission or fuel economy benefit." The Federal Trade Commission says, "No government agency endorses gas-saving products for cars."

Determine the null and alternative hypotheses that the EPA used to draw the conclusion stated in the second paragraph.

40. Prolong Engine Treatment The manufacturer of Prolong Engine Treatment claims that if you add one 12-ounce bottle of its \$20 product your engine will be protected from excessive wear. An infomercial claims that a woman drove 4 hours without oil, thanks to Prolong. *Consumer Reports* magazine tested engines in which they added Prolong to the motor oil, ran the engines, drained the oil, and then determined the time until the engines seized.

(a) Determine the null and alternative hypotheses that *Consumer Reports* will test. H_0: $\mu = 4$ hours; H_1: $\mu < 4$ hours

(b) Both engines took exactly 13 minutes to seize. What conclusion might *Consumer Reports* draw based on this evidence?

39. H_0: $\mu = 0$; H_1: $\mu > 0$, where μ is the mean increase   40. (b) Prolong's claim is not true

41. Refer to Problem 18. Researchers must choose the level of significance based on the consequences of making a Type I error. In your opinion, is a Type I error or Type II error more serious? Why? On the basis of your answer, decide on a level of significance, α. Be sure to support your opinion.

EXPLAINING THE CONCEPTS

42. If the consequences of making a Type I error are severe, would you choose the level of significance, α, to equal 0.01, 0.05, or 0.10? Why? 0.01

43. What happens to the probability of making a Type II error, β, as the level of significance, α, decreases? Why? Increases

44. The following is a quotation from Sir Ronald A. Fisher, a famous statistician.

> *For the logical fallacy of believing that a hypothesis has been proved true, merely because it is not contradicted by the available facts, has no more right to insinuate itself in statistics than in other kinds of scientific reasoning.... It would, therefore, add greatly to the clarity with which the tests of significance are regarded if it were generally understood that tests of significance, when used accurately, are capable of rejecting or invalidating hypotheses, in so far as they are contradicted by the data; but that they are never capable of establishing them as certainly true....*

In your own words, explain what this quotation means.

45. In your own words, explain the difference between "beyond all reasonable doubt" and "beyond all doubt." Use these phrases to explain why we never "accept" the statement in the null hypothesis.

10.2 HYPOTHESIS TESTS FOR A POPULATION PROPORTION

Preparing for This Section Before getting started, review the following:

- Using probabilities to identify unusual events (Section 5.1, p. 235)
- z_α notation (Section 7.2, pp. 344–345)
- Sampling distribution of the sample proportion (Section 8.2, pp. 379–384)
- Computing normal probabilities (Section 7.2, pp. 338–342)
- Binomial probability distribution (Section 6.2, pp. 309–319)

OBJECTIVES

1. Explain the logic of hypothesis testing
2. Test hypotheses about a population proportion
3. Test hypotheses about a population proportion using the binomial probability distribution

1 Explain the Logic of Hypothesis Testing

Recall that the best point estimate of p, the proportion of the population with a certain characteristic, is given by

$$\hat{p} = \frac{x}{n}$$

where x is the number of individuals in the sample with the specified characteristic and n is the sample size. We learned in Section 8.2 that the sampling distribution of $\hat{p}$ is approximately normal, with mean $\mu_{\hat{p}} = p$ and standard deviation $\sigma_{\hat{p}} = \sqrt{\frac{p(1-p)}{n}}$, provided that the following requirements are satisfied.

1. The sample is a simple random sample.
2. $np(1 - p) \geq 10$
3. The sampled values are independent of each other ($n \leq 0.05N$).

We will present three methods for testing hypotheses. The first method is called the classical (traditional) approach, the second method is the P-value approach, and the third method uses confidence intervals. Your instructor may choose to cover one, two, or all three approaches to hypothesis testing.

First, we lay out a scenario that will be used to understand both the classical and P- value approaches. Suppose a politician wants to know if a majority (more than 50%) of her constituents are in favor of a certain policy. We are therefore testing the following hypotheses:

$$H_0: p = 0.5 \quad \text{versus} \quad H_1: p > 0.5$$

The politician hires a polling firm to obtain a random sample of 1000 registered voters in her district and finds that 534 are in favor of the policy, so $\hat{p} = \frac{534}{1000} = 0.534$. Do these results suggest that among *all* registered voters more than 50% favor the policy? Or is it possible that the true proportion of registered voters who favor the policy is some proportion less than 0.5 and we just happened to survey a majority in favor of the policy? In other words, would it be unusual to obtain a sample proportion of 0.534 or higher from a population whose proportion is 0.5? What is convincing, or *statistically significant*, evidence?

DEFINITION

When observed results are unlikely under the assumption that the null hypothesis is true, we say the result is **statistically significant** and we reject the null hypothesis.

To determine if a sample proportion of 0.534 is statistically significant, we build a probability model. After all, a second random sample of 1000 registered voters will likely result in a different sample proportion, and we want to describe this variability so we can determine if the results we obtained are unusual. Since $np(1 - p) = 1000(0.5)(1 - 0.5) = 250 \geq 10$ and the sample size ($n = 1000$) is sufficiently smaller than the population size (provided there are at least $N = 20{,}000$ registered voters in the politician's district), we can use a normal model to describe the variability in $\hat{p}$. The mean of the distribution of $\hat{p}$ is $\mu_{\hat{p}} = 0.5$ (since we assume the statement in the null hypothesis is true) and the standard deviation of the distribution of $\hat{p}$ is $\sigma_{\hat{p}} = \sqrt{\frac{p(1-p)}{n}} = \sqrt{\frac{0.5(1-0.5)}{1000}} \approx 0.016$. Figure 2 shows the sampling distribution of the sample proportion for the "politician" example.

Figure 2

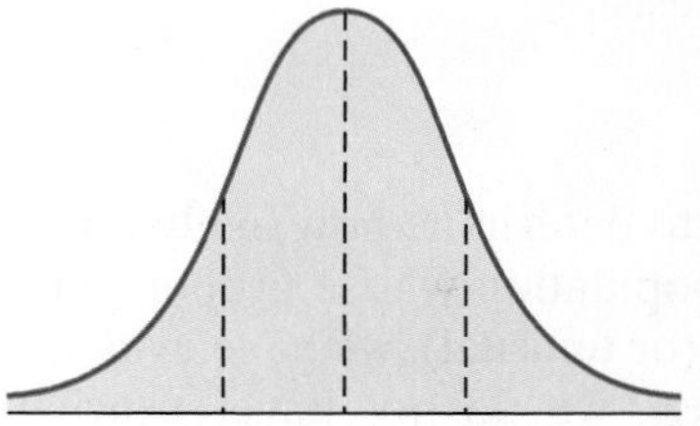

Now that we have a model that describes the distribution of the sample proportion, we can use it to look at the logic of the classical and P-value approaches to test if a majority of the politician's constituents are in favor of the policy.

The Logic of the Classical Approach

We may consider the sample evidence to be statistically significant (or sufficient) if the sample proportion is too many standard deviations, say 2, above the assumed population proportion of 0.5.

Recall that $z = \frac{\hat{p} - \mu_{\hat{p}}}{\sigma_{\hat{p}}}$ represents the number of standard deviations that $\hat{p}$ is from the population proportion, p. Our simple random sample of 1000 registered voters results in a sample proportion of 0.534, so under the assumption that the null hypothesis is true we have

$$z = \frac{\hat{p} - \mu_{\hat{p}}}{\sigma_{\hat{p}}} = \frac{0.534 - 0.5}{\sqrt{\frac{0.5(1-0.5)}{1000}}} = 2.15$$

The sample proportion is 2.15 standard deviations above the hypothesized population proportion of 0.5, which is more than 2 standard deviations (that is, "too far") above the hypothesized population proportion. So we will reject the null hypothesis. There is statistically significant (sufficient) evidence to conclude that a majority of registered voters are in favor of the policy.

Why does it make sense to reject the null hypothesis if the sample proportion is more than 2 standard deviations away from the hypothesized proportion? The area under the standard normal curve to the right of $z = 2$ is 0.0228, as shown in Figure 3.

Figure 3

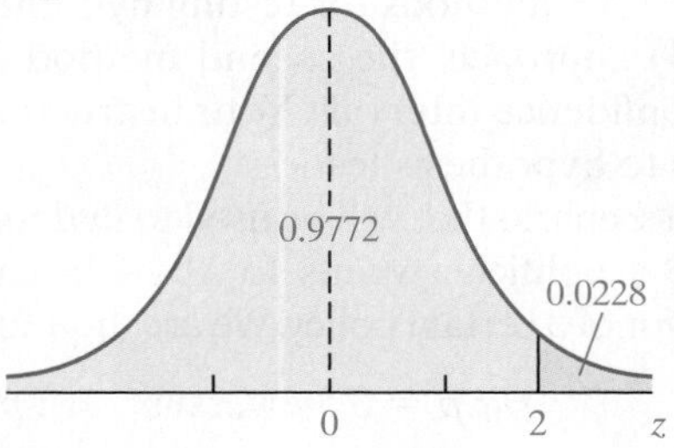

Figure 4

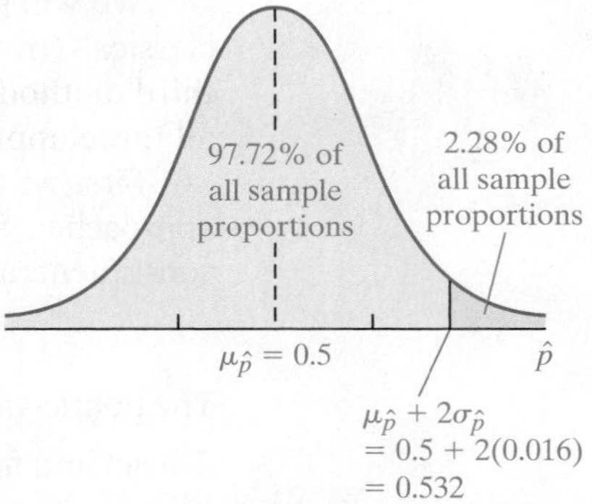

Figure 4 shows that, if the null hypothesis is true (that is, if the population proportion is 0.5), then 97.72% of all sample proportions will be 0.532 or less, and only 2.28% of the sample proportions will be more than 0.532 (0.532 is 2 standard deviations above the hypothesized proportion of 0.5). If a sample proportion lies in the blue region, we are inclined to believe it came from a population whose proportion is greater than 0.5, rather than believe that the population proportion equals 0.5 and our sample just happened to result in a proportion of registered voters much higher than 0.5.

Notice that our criterion for rejecting the null hypothesis will lead to making a Type I error (rejecting a true null hypothesis) 2.28% of the time. This is because 2.28% of all sample proportions are more than 0.532, even though the population proportion is 0.5.

This discussion illustrates the following point.

> **Hypothesis Testing Using the Classical Approach**
>
> If the sample proportion is too many standard deviations from the proportion stated in the null hypothesis, we reject the null hypothesis.

The Logic of the *P*-Value Approach

A second criterion we may use for testing hypotheses is to determine how likely it is to obtain a sample proportion of 0.534 or higher from a population whose proportion is 0.5. If a sample proportion of 0.534 or higher is unlikely (or unusual), we have evidence against the statement in the null hypothesis. Otherwise, we do not have sufficient evidence against the statement in the null hypothesis.

We can compute the probability of obtaining a sample proportion of 0.534 or higher from a population whose proportion is 0.5 using the normal model. See Figure 5.

Figure 5

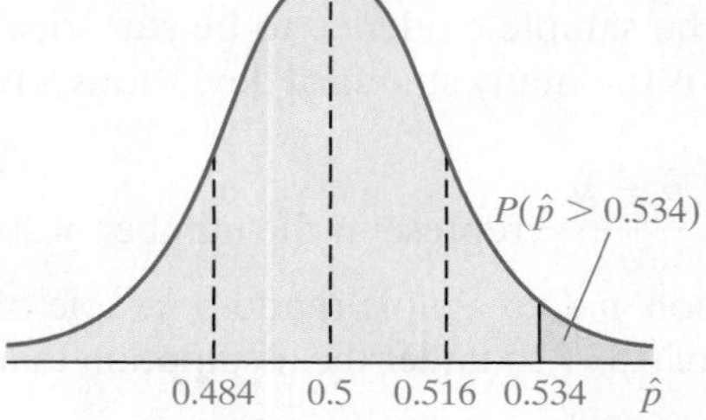

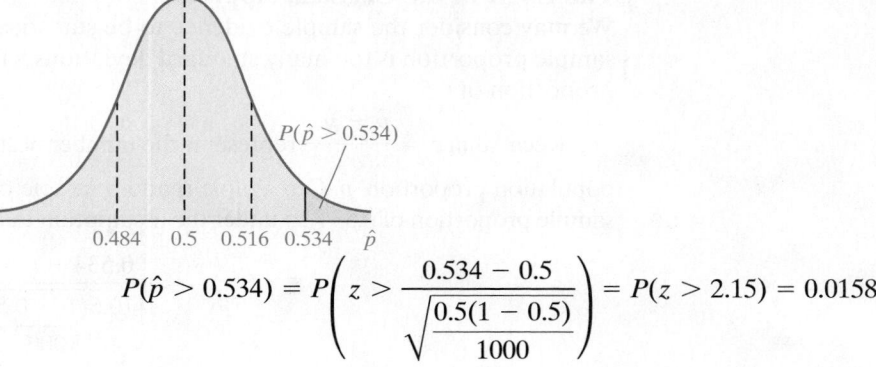

$$P(\hat{p} > 0.534) = P\left(z > \frac{0.534 - 0.5}{\sqrt{\frac{0.5(1-0.5)}{1000}}}\right) = P(z > 2.15) = 0.0158$$

The value 0.0158 is called the *P-value*, which means about 2 samples in 100 will give a sample proportion as high or higher than the one we obtained *if* the population proportion really is 0.5. Because these results are unusual, we take this as evidence against the statement in the null hypothesis.

DEFINITION

A ***P*-value** is the probability of observing a sample statistic as extreme or more extreme than the one observed under the assumption that the statement in the null hypothesis is true. Put another way, the *P*-value is the likelihood or probability that a sample will result in a statistic such as the one obtained if the null hypothesis is true.

This discussion illustrates the idea behind hypothesis testing using the *P*-value approach.

Note to Instructor
Consider assigning the "Interpreting *P*-values" activity from the Student Activity Workbook.

Hypothesis Testing Using the *P*-Value Approach

If the probability of getting a sample proportion as extreme or more extreme than the one obtained is small under the assumption the statement in the null hypothesis is true, reject the null hypothesis.

Figure 6 illustrates the situation for both the classical and *P*-value approaches. The distribution in blue shows the distribution of the sample proportion assuming the statement in the null hypothesis is true. The sample proportion of 0.534 is too far from the assumed population proportion of 0.5. Therefore, we reject the null hypothesis that $p = 0.5$ and conclude that $p > 0.5$, as indicated by the distribution in red. We do not know what the population proportion of registered voters who are in favor of the policy is, but we have evidence to say it is greater than 0.5 (a majority).

Figure 6

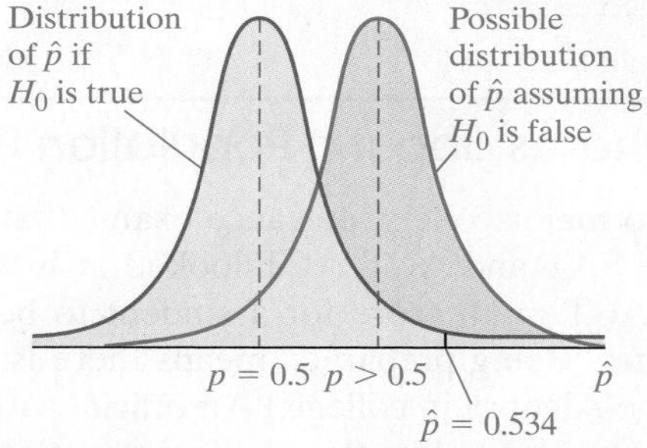

2 Test Hypotheses about a Population Proportion

We now formalize the procedure for testing hypotheses regarding a population proportion.

Testing Hypotheses Regarding a Population Proportion, *p*

Use Steps 1–5 provided that

- The sample is obtained by simple random sampling or the data result from a randomized experiment.
- $np_0(1 - p_0) \geq 10$.
- The sampled values are independent of each other.

Step 1 Determine the null and alternative hypotheses. The hypotheses can be structured in one of three ways:

Two-Tailed	Left-Tailed	Right-Tailed
$H_0: p = p_0$	$H_0: p = p_0$	$H_0: p = p_0$
$H_1: p \neq p_0$	$H_1: p < p_0$	$H_1: p > p_0$

Note: p_0 is the assumed value of the population proportion.

Step 2 Select a level of significance α, depending on the seriousness of making a Type I error.

Classical Approach

Step 3 Compute the **test statistic**

$$z_0 = \frac{\hat{p} - p_0}{\sqrt{\frac{p_0(1 - p_0)}{n}}}$$

P-Value Approach

By Hand Step 3 Compute the **test statistic**

$$z_0 = \frac{\hat{p} - p_0}{\sqrt{\frac{p_0(1 - p_0)}{n}}}$$

Use Table V to determine the critical value.

	Two-Tailed	Left-Tailed	Right-Tailed
Critical value	$-z_{\frac{\alpha}{2}}$ and $z_{\frac{\alpha}{2}}$	$-z_{\alpha}$	z_{α}

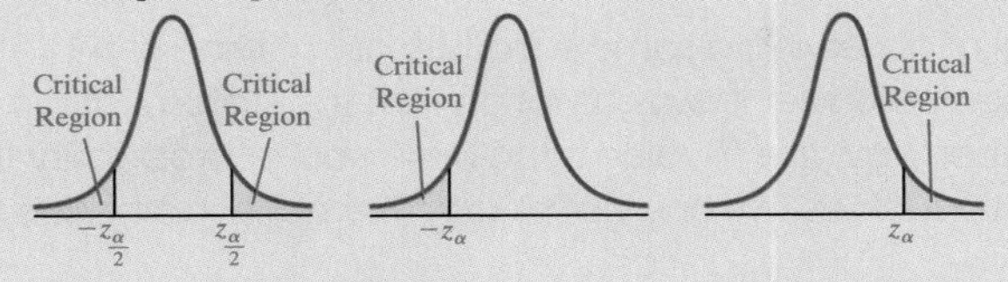

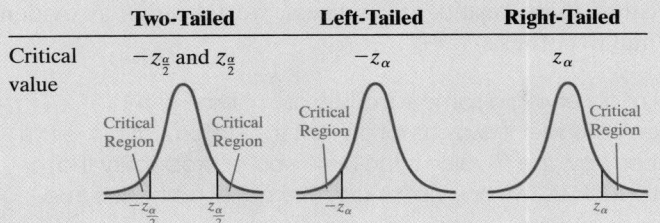

Step 4 Compare the critical value with the test statistic.

Two-Tailed	Left-Tailed	Right-Tailed
If $z_0 < -z_{\frac{\alpha}{2}}$ or $z_0 > z_{\frac{\alpha}{2}}$, reject the null hypothesis.	If $z_0 < -z_{\alpha}$, reject the null hypothesis.	If $z_0 > z_{\alpha}$, reject the null hypothesis.

Use Table V to determine the P-value.

Two-Tailed	Left-Tailed	Right-Tailed

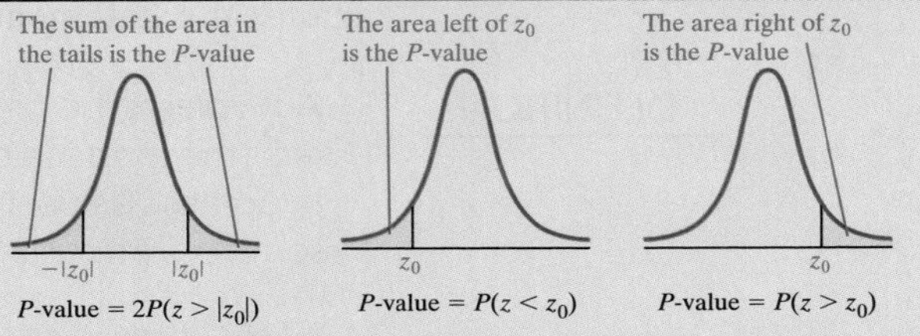

Technology Step 3 Use a statistical spreadsheet or calculator with statistical capabilities to obtain the P-value. The directions for obtaining the P-value using the TI-83/84 Plus graphing calculator, MINITAB, Excel, and StatCrunch are in the Technology Step-by-Step on page 448.

Step 4 If P-value $< \alpha$, reject the null hypothesis.

Step 5 State the conclusion.

Note to Instructor
Consider assigning the "Testing a Claim with Skittles I" activity from the Student Activity Workbook.

Notice in Step 3 that we are using p_0 (the proportion stated in the null hypothesis) in computing the standard error rather than $\hat{p}$, as we did in constructing confidence intervals about p. This is because H_0 is assumed to be true when performing a hypothesis test, so the assumed mean of the distribution of $\hat{p}$ is $\mu_{\hat{p}} = p_0$ and the assumed standard error is $\sigma_{\hat{p}} = \sqrt{\dfrac{p_0(1 - p_0)}{n}}$.

EXAMPLE 1 Testing Hypotheses about a Population Proportion: Left-Tailed Test

Problem The two major college entrance exams that a majority of colleges accept for admission are the SAT and ACT. ACT looked at historical records and established 22 as the minimum ACT math score for a student to be considered prepared for college mathematics. [**Note:** "Being prepared" means there is a 75% probability of successfully completing College Algebra in college.] An official with the Illinois State Department of Education wonders whether less than half of the students in her state are prepared for College Algebra. She obtains a simple random sample of 500 records of students who have taken the ACT and finds that 219 are prepared for college mathematics (that is, scored at least 22 on the ACT math test). Does this represent significant evidence that less than half of Illinois students are prepared for college mathematics upon graduation from a high school? Use the $\alpha = 0.05$ level of significance. *Source:* ACT High School Profile Report.

Approach This problem deals with a hypothesis test of a proportion. We want to determine if the sample evidence shows that less than half of the students are prepared for college mathematics. Symbolically, we represent this as $p < \frac{1}{2}$ or $p < 0.5$.

Verify the three requirements to perform the hypothesis test: the sample must be a simple random sample, $np_0(1 - p_0) \geq 10$, and the sample size cannot be more than 5% of the population size (for independence). Then we follow Steps 1 through 5.

Solution We assume that $p = 0.5$. The sample is a simple random sample. Also, $np_0(1 - p_0) = 500(0.5)(1 - 0.5) = 125 > 10$. Provided that there are over 10,000 students in the state, the sample size is less than 5% of the population size. Assuming that this is the case, the requirements are satisfied. We now proceed with Steps 1 through 5.

Step 1 The burden of proof lies in showing $p < 0.5$. We assume there is no difference between the proportion of students *ready* for college math and the proportion of students *not ready* for college math. Therefore, the statement in the null hypothesis is that $p = 0.5$. So we have

$$H_0: p = 0.5 \quad \text{versus} \quad H_1: p < 0.5$$

Step 2 The level of significance is $\alpha = 0.05$.

Classical Approach

Step 3 The assumed value of the population proportion is $p_0 = 0.5$. The sample proportion is $\hat{p} = \frac{x}{n} = \frac{219}{500} = 0.438$. We want to know if it is unusual to obtain a sample proportion of 0.438 or less from a population whose proportion is assumed to be 0.5.

The test statistic is

$$z_0 = \frac{\hat{p} - p_0}{\sqrt{\frac{p_0(1-p_0)}{n}}} = \frac{0.438 - 0.5}{\sqrt{\frac{0.5(1-0.5)}{500}}} = -2.77$$

Because this is a left-tailed test, we determine the critical value at the $\alpha = 0.05$ level of significance to be $-z_{0.05} = -1.645$. The critical region is shown in Figure 7.

Figure 7

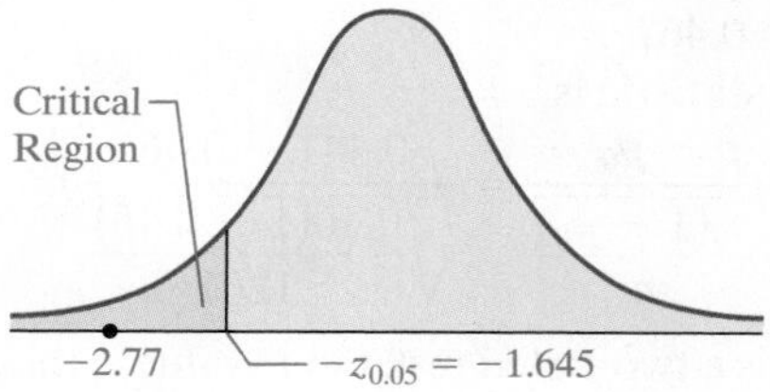

Step 4 The test statistic is $z_0 = -2.77$. We label this point in Figure 7. Because the test statistic is less than the critical value $(-2.77 < -1.645)$, we reject the null hypothesis.

P-Value Approach

By Hand Step 3 The assumed value of the population proportion is $p_0 = 0.5$. The sample proportion is $\hat{p} = \frac{x}{n} = \frac{219}{500} = 0.438$. We want to know how likely it is to obtain a sample proportion of 0.438 or less from a population whose proportion is assumed to be 0.5.

The test statistic is

$$z_0 = \frac{\hat{p} - p_0}{\sqrt{\frac{p_0(1-p_0)}{n}}} = \frac{0.438 - 0.5}{\sqrt{\frac{0.5(1-0.5)}{500}}} = -2.77$$

Because this is a left-tailed test, the *P*-value is the area under the standard normal distribution to the left of the test statistic, $z_0 = -2.77$, as shown in Figure 8. So, $P\text{-value} = P(z < z_0) = P(z < -2.77) = 0.0028$.

Figure 8

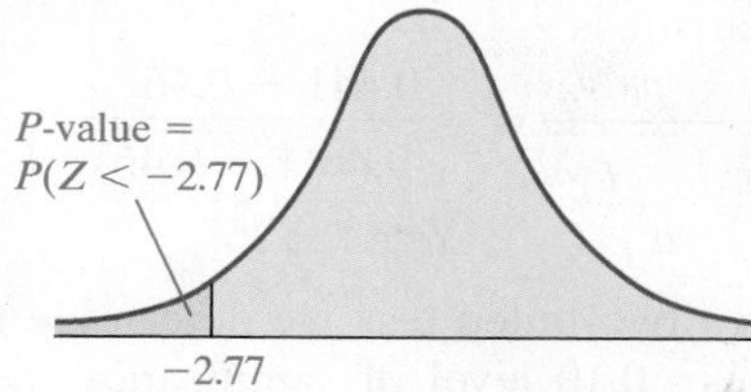

Technology Step 3 Using MINITAB, we find the *P*-value is 0.003. See Figure 9.

Figure 9

```
Test and CI for One Proportion
Test of p = 0.5 vs p < 0.5

                                        95%
                                       Upper
Sample    X    N  Sample p             Bound  Z-Value  P-Value
1       219  500  0.438000          0.474496    -2.77    0.003
```

Step 4 The *P*-value of 0.003 means that *if* the null hypothesis that $p = 0.5$ is true, we expect 219 or fewer successes in 500 trials in less than 1 sample in 100! The observed results are unusual, indeed. Because the *P*-value is less than the level of significance, $\alpha = 0.05$ $(0.003 < 0.05)$, we reject the null hypothesis.

Step 5 There is sufficient evidence at the $\alpha = 0.05$ level of significance to conclude that fewer than half of the Illinois students are prepared for college mathematics. In other words, the data suggest less than a majority of the students in the state of Illinois are prepared for college mathematics.

Now Work Problem 15

EXAMPLE 2 Testing Hypotheses about a Population Proportion: Two-Tailed Test

Problem When asked, "What do you think is more important—to protect the right of Americans to own guns or to control gun ownership?" 46% of all Americans said protecting the right to own guns is more important. The Pew Research Center surveyed 1267 randomly selected Americans with at least a bachelor's degree and found that 559 believed that protecting the right to own guns is more important. Does this result suggest the proportion of Americans with at least a bachelor's degree feel differently than the general American population when it comes to gun control? Use the $\alpha = 0.1$ level of significance.

Approach This problem deals with a hypothesis test of a proportion. Verify the three requirements to perform the hypothesis test. Then follow Steps 1–5.

Solution We want to know if the proportion of Americans with at least a bachelor's degree who believe protecting the right of Americans to own guns is more important is *different from* 0.46. To conduct the test, we assume the sample comes from a population with $p = 0.46$. The sample is a simple random sample. Also, $np_0(1 - p_0) = 1267(0.46)(1 - 0.46) = 314.7 \geq 10$. Because there are well over 10 million Americans with at least a bachelor's degree, the sample size is less than 5% of the population. We may now proceed with Steps 1 through 5.

Step 1 We want to know whether the proportion is *different* from 0.46, which can be written $p \neq 0.46$, so this is a two-tailed test.

$$H_0: p = 0.46 \quad \text{versus} \quad H_1: p \neq 0.46$$

Step 2 The level of significance is $\alpha = 0.1$.

Classical Approach

Step 3 We assume the sample comes from a population with $p_0 = 0.46$. The sample proportion is $\hat{p} = \frac{x}{n} = \frac{559}{1267} = 0.441$. Is obtaining a sample proportion of 0.441 from a population whose proportion is 0.46 likely, or is it unusual?

The test statistic is

$$z_0 = \frac{\hat{p} - p_0}{\sqrt{\frac{p_0(1 - p_0)}{n}}} = \frac{0.441 - 0.46}{\sqrt{\frac{0.46(1 - 0.46)}{1267}}} = -1.36$$

Because this is a two-tailed test, we determine the critical values at the $\alpha = 0.10$ level of significance to be $-z_{0.1/2} = -z_{0.05} = -1.645$ and $z_{0.1/2} = z_{0.05} = 1.645$. The critical regions are shown in Figure 10.

Figure 10

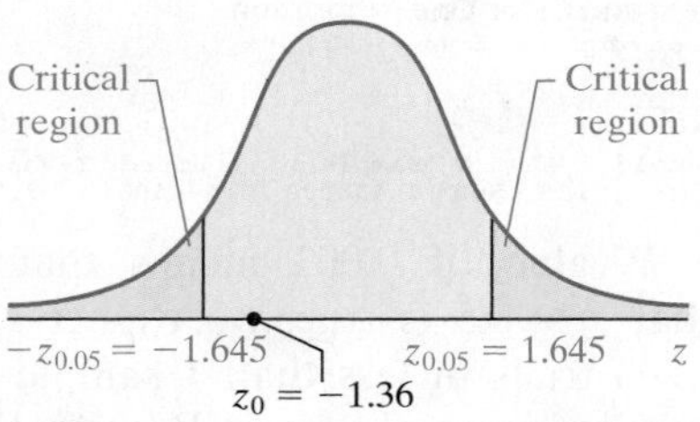

Step 4 The test statistic is $z_0 = -1.36$. We label this point in Figure 10. Because the test statistic does not lie in the critical region, we do not reject the null hypothesis.

P-Value Approach

By Hand Step 3 We assume the sample comes from a population with $p_0 = 0.46$. The sample proportion is $\hat{p} = \frac{x}{n} = \frac{559}{1267} = 0.441$. What is the likelihood of obtaining a sample proportion of 0.441 from a population whose proportion is 0.46?

The test statistic is

$$z_0 = \frac{\hat{p} - p_0}{\sqrt{\frac{p_0(1 - p_0)}{n}}} = \frac{0.441 - 0.46}{\sqrt{\frac{0.46(1 - 0.46)}{1267}}} = -1.36$$

Because this is a two-tailed test, the *P*-value is the area under the standard normal distribution to the left of $-|z_0| = -1.36$ and to the right of $|z_0| = 1.36$, as shown in Figure 11.

Figure 11

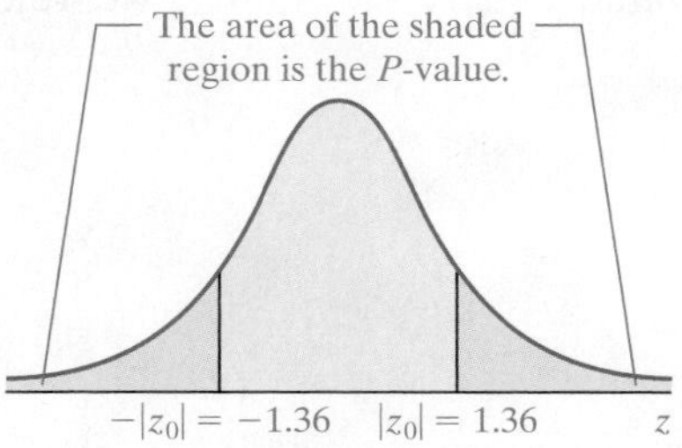

$$\begin{aligned} P\text{-value} &= P(Z < -|z_0|) + P(Z > |z_0|) \\ &= 2P(Z < -1.36) \\ &= 2(0.0869) \\ &= 0.1738 \end{aligned}$$

Technology Step 3 Using StatCrunch, we find the *P*-value is 0.1794. See Figure 12.

Figure 12

Hypothesis test results:
p : proportion of successes for population
H_0 : p = 0.46
H_A : p ≠ 0.46

Proportion	Count	Total	Sample Prop.	Std. Err.	Z-Stat	P-value
p	559	1267	0.4411997	0.014001917	-1.3426958	0.1794

Step 4 The *P*-value of 0.1738 [Technology: 0.1794] means that *if* the null hypothesis that $p = 0.46$ is true, we expect the type of results we observed (or more extreme results) in about 17 or 18 out of 100 samples. The observed results are not unusual. Because the *P*-value is greater than the level of significance, $\alpha = 0.1$ $(0.1738 > 0.1)$, we do not reject the null hypothesis.

Step 5 There is not sufficient evidence at the $\alpha = 0.1$ level of significance to conclude that Americans with at least a bachelor's degree feel differently than the general American population when it comes to gun control.

CAUTION

In Example 2, we do not have enough evidence to reject the statement in the null hypothesis. In other words, it is not unusual to obtain a sample proportion of 0.441 from a population whose proportion is 0.46. However, this does not imply that we are accepting the statement in the null hypothesis (that is, we are not saying that the proportion equals 0.46). We are only saying we do not have enough evidence to conclude that the proportion is different from 0.46. Be sure that you understand the difference between "accepting" and "not rejecting." It is similar to the difference between being declared "innocent" versus "not guilty."

Also, be sure you understand that the P-value is the probability of obtaining a sample mean as extreme or more extreme than the one observed *if* the statement in the null hypothesis is true. The P-value does not represent the probability that the null hypothesis is true. The statement in the null hypothesis is either true or false, we just don't know which.

In practice, the level of significance is not reported using the P-value approach. Instead, only the P-value is given, and the reader of the study must interpret its value and judge its significance.

Now Work Problem 21

Test a Hypothesis Using a Confidence Interval

Recall, the level of confidence, $(1 - \alpha) \cdot 100\%$, in a confidence interval represents the percentage of intervals that will contain the unknown parameter if repeated samples are obtained.

Two-Tailed Hypothesis Testing Using Confidence Intervals

When testing H_0: $p = p_0$ versus H_1: $p \neq p_0$, if a $(1 - \alpha) \cdot 100\%$ confidence interval contains p_0, we do not reject the null hypothesis. However, if the confidence interval does not contain p_0, we conclude that $p \neq p_0$ at the level of significance, α.

EXAMPLE 3 Testing a Hypothesis Using a Confidence Interval

Problem A June 2007 study conducted by Students Against Destructive Decisions (SADD) revealed that 37% of teens 16 to 17 years of age text while driving. Does a 2009 study by Princeton Survey Research Associates International, which found 272 of 800 randomly selected 16- to 17-year-olds had texted while driving provide evidence that the proportion of teens who text while driving has changed since 2007? Use a 95% confidence interval to answer the question.

Approach The 95% confidence interval was obtained in Example 4, page 397, Section 9.1. If the interval does not include 0.37, reject the null hypothesis H_0: $p = 0.37$ in favor of H_1: $p \neq 0.37$.

Solution The 95% confidence interval for p based on the Princeton Survey has a lower bound of 0.307 and an upper bound of 0.373. Because 0.37 is within the bounds of the confidence interval, there is not sufficient evidence to conclude that the proportion of teens who text while driving has changed since 2007.

Now Work Problem 23

3 Test Hypotheses about a Population Proportion Using the Binomial Probability Distribution

Note to Instructor

This section is optional and may be skipped without loss of continuity.

For the sampling distribution of $\hat{p}$ to be approximately normal, we require that $np(1 - p)$ be at least 10. What if this requirement is not satisfied? In Section 6.2, we used the binomial probability formula to identify unusual events. We stated that an event was unusual if the probability of observing the event was less than 0.05. This criterion is based on the P-value approach to testing hypotheses; the probability that we computed was the P-value. We use this same approach to test hypotheses regarding a population proportion for small samples.

EXAMPLE 4 Hypothesis Test for a Population Proportion: Small Sample Size

Problem According to the U.S. Department of Agriculture, 48.9% of males aged 20 to 39 years consume the recommended daily requirement of calcium. After an aggressive "Got Milk" advertising campaign, the USDA conducts a survey of 35 randomly selected males aged 20 to 39 and finds that 21 of them consume the recommended daily allowance (RDA) of calcium. At the $\alpha = 0.10$ level of significance, is there evidence to conclude that the percentage of males aged 20 to 39 who consume the RDA of calcium has increased?

Approach We use the following steps:

Step 1 Determine the null and alternative hypotheses.

Step 2 Check whether $np_0(1 - p_0)$ is greater than or equal to 10, where p_0 is the proportion stated in the null hypothesis. If it is, then the sampling distribution of $\hat{p}$ is approximately normal and we can use the steps on pages 439–440. Otherwise, we use Steps 3 and 4, presented next.

Step 3 Compute the *P*-value. For right-tailed tests, the *P*-value is the probability of obtaining x or more successes. For left-tailed tests, the *P*-value is the probability of obtaining x or fewer successes.* The *P*-value is always computed with the proportion given in the null hypothesis. Remember, we assume that the null is true until we have evidence to the contrary.

Step 4 If the *P*-value is less than the level of significance, α, reject the null hypothesis.

Solution

Step 1 The status quo or no change proportion of 20- to 39-year-old males who consume the recommended daily requirement of calcium is 0.489. We wish to know whether the advertising campaign increased this proportion. Therefore,

$$H_0: p = 0.489 \quad \text{and} \quad H_1: p > 0.489$$

Step 2 From the null hypothesis, we have $p_0 = 0.489$. There were $n = 35$ individuals surveyed, so $np_0(1 - p_0) = 35(0.489)(1 - 0.489) = 8.75$. Because $np_0(1 - p_0) < 10$, the sampling distribution of $\hat{p}$ is not approximately normal.

Step 3 Let the random variable X represent the number of individuals who consume the daily requirement of calcium. We have $x = 21$ successes in $n = 35$ trials, so $\hat{p} = \frac{21}{35} = 0.6$. We want to judge whether the larger proportion is due to an increase in the population proportion or to sampling error. We obtained $x = 21$ successes in the survey and this is a right-tailed test, so the *P*-value is $P(X \geq 21)$.

$$P\text{-value} = P(X \geq 21) = 1 - P(X < 21) = 1 - P(X \leq 20)$$

Figure 13

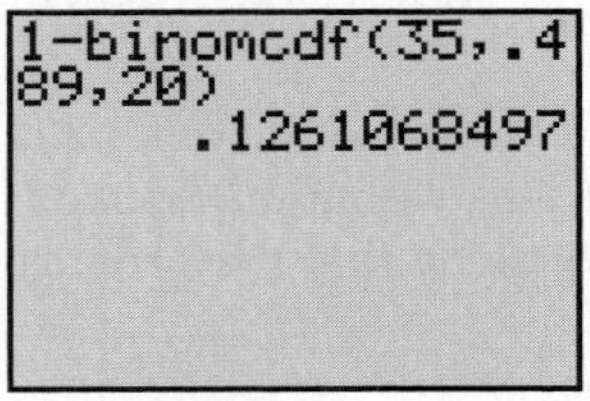

We will compute this *P*-value using a TI-84 Plus graphing calculator, with $n = 35$ and $p = 0.489$. Figure 13 shows the results.

The *P*-value is 0.1261. MINITAB, StatCrunch, and Excel will compute exact *P*-values using this approach as well.

Step 4 The *P*-value is greater than the level of significance $(0.1261 > 0.10)$, so we do not reject H_0. There is insufficient evidence (at the $\alpha = 0.1$ level of significance) to conclude that the proportion of 20- to 39-year-old males who consume the recommended daily allowance of calcium has increased.

Now Work Problem 27

*We will not address *P*-values for two-tailed hypothesis tests. For those who are interested, the *P*-value is 2 times the probability of obtaining x or more successes if $\hat{p} > p$ and 2 times the probability of obtaining x or fewer successes if $\hat{p} < p$.

15. H_0: $p = 0.019$ vs. H_1: $p > 0.019$; P-value $= 0.2578$ 16. Do not reject H_0; H_0: $p = 0.94$, H_1: $p > 0.94$, $z_0 = 0.69$, P-value $= 0.2451$

10.2 ASSESS YOUR UNDERSTANDING

VOCABULARY AND SKILL BUILDING

1. When observed results are unlikely under the assumption that the null hypothesis is true, we say the result is ____statistically significant____ and we reject the null hypothesis.

2. *True or False*: When testing a hypothesis using the Classical Approach, if the sample proportion is too many standard deviations from the proportion stated in the null hypothesis, we reject the null hypothesis. True 3. False

3. *True or False*: When testing a hypothesis using the *P*-value Approach, if the *P*-value is large, we reject the null hypothesis.

4. Determine the critical value for a right-tailed test regarding a population proportion at the $\alpha = 0.01$ level of significance. 2.33

5. Determine the critical value for a left-tailed test regarding a population proportion at the $\alpha = 0.1$ level of significance. −1.28

6. Determine the critical value for a two-tailed test regarding a population proportion at the $\alpha = 0.05$ level of significance. ±1.96

In Problems 7–12, test the hypothesis using (a) the classical approach and (b) the P-value approach. Be sure to verify the requirements of the test.

7. H_0: $p = 0.3$ versus H_1: $p > 0.3$
$n = 200$; $x = 75$; $\alpha = 0.05$ P-value $= 0.0104$

8. H_0: $p = 0.6$ versus H_1: $p < 0.6$
$n = 250$; $x = 124$; $\alpha = 0.01$ P-value $= 0.0004$

9. H_0: $p = 0.55$ versus H_1: $p < 0.55$
$n = 150$; $x = 78$; $\alpha = 0.1$ P-value $= 0.2296$

10. H_0: $p = 0.25$ versus H_1: $p < 0.25$
$n = 400$; $x = 96$; $\alpha = 0.1$ P-value $= 0.3228$

11. H_0: $p = 0.9$ versus H_1: $p \neq 0.9$
$n = 500$; $x = 440$; $\alpha = 0.05$ P-value $= 0.1362$

12. H_0: $p = 0.4$ versus H_1: $p \neq 0.4$
$n = 1000$; $x = 420$; $\alpha = 0.01$ P-value $= 0.1970$

13. You Explain It! Stock Analyst Some have argued that throwing darts at the stock pages to decide which companies to invest in could be a successful stock-picking strategy. Suppose a researcher decides to test this theory and randomly chooses 100 companies to invest in. After 1 year, 53 of the companies were considered winners; that is, they outperformed other companies in the same investment class. To assess whether the dart-picking strategy resulted in a majority of winners, the researcher tested H_0: $p = 0.5$ versus H_1: $p > 0.5$ and obtained a *P*-value of 0.2743. Explain what this *P*-value means and write a conclusion for the researcher. Do not reject H_0

14. You Explain It! ESP Suppose an acquaintance claims to have the ability to determine the birth month of randomly selected individuals. To test such a claim, you randomly select 80 individuals and ask the acquaintance to state the birth month of the individual. If the individual has the ability to determine birth month, then the proportion of correct birth months should exceed $\frac{1}{12}$, the rate one would expect from simply guessing.

(a) State the null and alternative hypotheses for this experiment.

(b) Suppose the individual was able to guess 9 correct birth months. The *P*-value for such results is 0.1726. Explain what this *P*-value means and write a conclusion for the test.

14. (a) H_0: $p = \frac{1}{12}$ vs. H_1: $p > \frac{1}{12}$ (b) Do not reject H_0

APPLYING THE CONCEPTS

NW **15. Lipitor** The drug Lipitor is meant to reduce total cholesterol and LDL cholesterol. In clinical trials, 19 out of 863 patients taking 10 mg of Lipitor daily complained of flulike symptoms. Suppose that it is known that 1.9% of patients taking competing drugs complain of flulike symptoms. Is there evidence to conclude that more than 1.9% of Lipitor users experience flulike symptoms as a side effect at the $\alpha = 0.01$ level of significance?

16. Nexium Nexium is a drug that can be used to reduce the acid produced by the body and heal damage to the esophagus due to acid reflux. The manufacturer of Nexium claims that more than 94% of patients taking Nexium are healed within 8 weeks. In clinical trials, 213 of 224 patients suffering from acid reflux disease were healed after 8 weeks. Test the manufacturer's claim at the $\alpha = 0.01$ level of significance.

17. Worried about Retirement? In April 2009, the Gallup organization surveyed 676 adults aged 18 and older and found that 352 believed they would not have enough money to live comfortably in retirement. Does the sample evidence suggest that a majority of adults in the United States believe they will not have enough money in retirement? Use the $\alpha = 0.05$ level of significance.

18. Ready for College? There are two major college entrance exams that a majority of colleges accept for admission, the SAT and ACT. ACT looked at historical records and established 21 as the minimum score on the ACT reading portion of the exam for a student to be considered prepared for social science in college.
Note: "Being prepared" means there is a 75% probability of successfully completing a social science in college.

An official with the Illinois State Department of Education wonders whether a majority of the students in her state are prepared to take social science. She obtains a simple random sample of 500 records of students who have taken the ACT and finds that 269 are prepared for social science in college (that is, scored at least 21 on the reading portion of the ACT). Does this represent significant evidence that a majority of the students in the state of Illinois are prepared for social science in college upon graduation? Use the $\alpha = 0.05$ level of significance. *Source:* ACT High School Profile Report. Reject H_0

19. Critical Job Skills In August 2003, 56% of employed adults in the United States reported that basic mathematical skills were critical or very important to their job. The supervisor of the job placement office at a 4-year college thinks this percentage has increased due to increased use of technology in the workplace. He takes a random sample of 480 employed adults and finds that 297 of them feel that basic mathematical skills are critical or very important to their job. Is there sufficient evidence to conclude that the percentage of employed adults who feel basic mathematical skills are critical or very important to their job has increased at the $\alpha = 0.05$ level of significance? Reject H_0 20. Do not reject H_0

20. Eating Together In December 2001, 38% of adults with children under the age of 18 reported that their family ate dinner together 7 nights a week. In a recent poll, 403 of 1122 adults with children under the age of 18 reported that their family ate dinner together 7 nights a week. Has the proportion of families with children under the age of 18 who eat dinner together 7 nights a week decreased? Use the $\alpha = 0.05$ significance level.

17. Do not reject H_0; H_0: $p = 0.5$, H_1: $p > 0.5$; P-value $= 0.1379$

NW **21. Taught Enough Math?** In 1994, 52% of parents of children in high school felt it was a serious problem that high school students were not being taught enough math and science. A recent survey found that 256 of 800 parents of children in high school felt it was a serious problem that high school students were not being taught enough math and science. Do parents feel differently today than they did in 1994? Use the $\alpha = 0.05$ level of significance.? Reject H_0
Source: Based on "Reality Check: Are Parents and Students Ready for More Math and Science?" *Public Agenda,* 2006.

22. Living Alone? In 2000, 58% of females aged 15 years of age and older lived alone, according to the U.S. Census Bureau. A sociologist tests whether this percentage is different today by conducting a random sample of 500 females aged 15 years of age and older and finds that 285 are living alone. Is there sufficient evidence at the $\alpha = 0.1$ level of significance to conclude the proportion has changed since 2000? Do not reject H_0

NW **23. Quality of Education** In August 2002, 47% of parents who had children in grades K–12 were satisfied with the quality of education the students receive. In September 2010, the Gallup organization conducted a poll of 1013 parents who have children in grades K–12 and asked if they were satisfied with the quality of education the students receive. Of the 1013 surveyed, 437 indicated that they were satisfied. Construct a 95% confidence interval to assess whether this represents evidence that parents' attitudes toward the quality of education in the United States has changed since August 2002. (0.401, 0.461); reject H_0

24. Infidelity According to menstuff.org, 22% of married men have "strayed" at least once during their married lives.

(a) Describe how you might go about administering a survey to assess the accuracy of this statement.

(b) A survey of 500 married men results in 122 indicating that they have "strayed" at least once during their married life. Construct a 95% confidence interval for the population proportion of married men who have strayed. Use this interval to assess the accuracy of the statement made by menstuff.org. (0.206, 0.282); do not reject H_0

25. Talk to the Animals In a survey conducted by the American Animal Hospital Association, 37% of respondents stated that they talk to their pets on the answering machine or telephone. A veterinarian found this result hard to believe, so he randomly selected 150 pet owners and discovered that 54 of them spoke to their pet on the answering machine or telephone. Does the veterinarian have the right to be skeptical? Use a 0.05 level of significance. No

26. Eating Salad According to a survey conducted by the Association for Dressings and Sauces (this is an actual association!), 85% of American adults eat salad at least once a week. A nutritionist suspects that the percentage is higher than this. She conducts a survey of 200 American adults and finds that 171 of them eat salad at least once a week. Conduct the appropriate test that addresses the nutritionist's suspicions. Use a 0.1 level of significance. H_0: $p = 0.85$ vs. H_1: $p > 0.85$; P-value = 0.4207

NW **27. Small-Sample Hypothesis Test** Professors Honey Kirk and Diane Lerma of Palo Alto College developed a "learning community curriculum that blended the developmental mathematics and the reading curriculum with a structured emphasis on study skills." In a typical developmental mathematics course at Palo Alto College, 50% of the students complete the course with a letter grade of A, B, or C. In the experimental course, of the 16 students enrolled, 11 completed the course with a letter grade of A, B, or C. Do you believe the experimental course was effective at the $\alpha = 0.05$ level of significance? *Source:* Kirk, Honey & Lerma, Diane, "Reading Your Way to Success in Mathematics: A Paired Course of Developmental Mathematics and Reading." *MathAMATYC Educator,* Vol.1. No. 2, 2010. P-value = 0.1051

28. P-value = 0.2887 29. P-value = 0.0976

28. Small-Sample Hypothesis Test In 1997, 4% of mothers smoked more than 21 cigarettes during their pregnancy. An obstetrician believes that the percentage of mothers who smoke 21 cigarettes or more is less than 4% today. She randomly selects 120 pregnant mothers and finds that 3 of them smoked 21 or more cigarettes during pregnancy. Does the sample data support the obstetrician's belief? Use the $\alpha = 0.05$ level of significance.

29. Small-Sample Hypothesis Test According to the U.S. Census Bureau, in 2009, 2.1% of Americans worked at home. An economist believes that the percentage of Americans working at home has increased since then. He randomly selects 150 working Americans and finds that 6 of them work at home. Do a higher proportion of Americans work at home? Use the $\alpha = 0.05$ level of significance.

30. Small-Sample Hypothesis Test According to the U.S. Census Bureau, in 2009, 7.8% of Americans had a travel time to work of more than 60 minutes. An urban economist believes that the percentage of Americans who have a travel time to work of more than 60 minutes has increased since then. She randomly selects 80 working Americans and finds that 11 of them have a travel time to work that is more than 60 minutes. Test the urban economist's belief at the $\alpha = 0.1$ level of significance. P-value = 0.0461

31. Statistics in the Media One of the more popular statistics reported in the media is the president's job approval rating. The approval rating is reported as the proportion of Americans who approve of the job that the sitting president is doing and is typically based on a random sample of registered voters.

(a) This proportion tends to fluctuate from week to week. Name some reasons for the fluctuation in the statistic.

(b) A recent article had the headline "Obama Ratings Rise." This headline was written because a December 2010 poll showed President Obama's approval rating to be 0.48 (48%). A poll the following January based on 1500 randomly selected Americans showed that 747 approved of the job Obama was doing. Do the results of the January poll indicate that the proportion of Americans who approve of the job Obama is doing is significantly higher than December's level? Explain.

32. Statistics in the Media In November 2009, 65% (0.65) of Americans favored the death penalty for a person convicted of murder. In November 2010, 1025 adult Americans were asked by the Gallup organization, "Are you in favor of the death penalty for a person convicted of murder?" Of the 1025 adults surveyed, 653 responded yes. The headline in the article reporting the survey results stated, "Fewer Americans Favor the Death Penalty." Use a test of significance to support or refute this headline. Refute

33. Sullivan Statistics Survey: Political Philosophy According to Gallup, 21% of Americans consider themselves to be liberal. The Sullivan Statistics Survey asked respondents to disclose their political philosophy: Conservative, Liberal, Moderate. Treat the results of the Sullivan Statistics Survey as a random sample of adult Americans. Do the survey results suggest the proportion is higher than that reported by Gallup? Use an $\alpha = 0.1$ level of significance. Yes, it appears a higher proportion are liberal.

34. Sullivan Statistics Survey: Smokers According to the Centers for Disease Control, in 2008, 21% of adult Americans age 18 or older were current smokers. Treat the results of the Sullivan Statistics Survey as a random sample of adult Americans. Do the survey results suggest that the proportion of adult Americans who are current smokers has declined? Use an $\alpha = 0.05$ level of significance. Yes; P-value = 0.0017

35. Are Spreads Accurate? For every NFL game there is a team that is expected to win by a certain number of points. In betting parlance, this is called the spread. For example, if the Chicago Bears are expected to beat the Green Bay Packers by 3 points, a sports bettor would say, "Chicago is minus three." So, if the Bears lose to Green Bay, or do not win by more than 3 points, a bet on Chicago would be a loser. If point spreads are accurate, we would expect about half of all games played to result in the favored team winning (beating the spread) and about half of all games to result in the team favored to not beat the spread. The following data represent the results of 45 randomly selected games where a 0 indicates the favored team did not beat the spread and a 1 indicates the favored team beat the spread. Do the data suggest that sport books establish accurate spreads?

0	0	0	0	0
1	0	0	1	0
0	0	0	1	0
1	1	0	0	1
0	0	1	1	1
0	0	1	1	0
1	0	0	1	0
0	1	1	0	1
0	0	1	1	1

Source: http://www.vegasinsider.com

36. Accept versus Do Not Reject In the United States, historically, 40% of registered voters are Republican. Suppose you obtain a simple random sample of 320 registered voters and find 142 registered Republicans.

(a) Consider the hypotheses $H_0: p = 0.4$ versus $H_1: p > 0.4$. Explain what the researcher would be testing. Perform the test at the $\alpha = 0.05$ level of significance. Write a conclusion for the test. Do not reject

(b) Consider the hypotheses $H_0: p = 0.41$ versus $H_1: p > 0.41$. Explain what the researcher would be testing. Perform the test at the $\alpha = 0.05$ level of significance. Write a conclusion for the test. Do not reject

(c) Consider the hypotheses $H_0: p = 0.42$ versus $H_1: p > 0.42$. Explain what the researcher would be testing. Perform the test at the $\alpha = 0.05$ level of significance. Write a conclusion for the test. Do not reject

(d) Based on the results of parts (a)–(c), write a few sentences that explain the difference between "accepting" the statement in the null hypothesis versus "not rejecting" the statement in the null hypothesis.

37. Interesting Results Suppose you wish to find out the answer to the age-old question, "Do Americans prefer Coke or Pepsi?" You conduct a blind taste test in which individuals are randomly asked to drink one of the colas first, followed by the other cola, and then asked to disclose which drink they prefer. Results of your taste test indicate that 53 of 100 individuals prefer Pepsi.

(a) Conduct a hypothesis test (preferably using technology) $H_0: p = p_0$ versus $H_1: p \neq p_0$ for $p_0 = 0.42, 0.43, 0.44, \ldots, 0.64$ at the $\alpha = 0.05$ level of significance. For which values of p_0 do you not reject the null hypothesis? What do each of the values of p_0 represent? 0.44 to 0.62, inclusive

(b) Construct a 95% confidence interval for the proportion of individuals who prefer Pepsi. (0.432, 0.628)

(c) Suppose you changed the level of significance in conducting the hypothesis test to $\alpha = 0.01$? What would happen to the range of values of p_0 for which the null hypothesis is not rejected? Why does this make sense? Increases

38. Simulation Simulate drawing 100 simple random samples of size $n = 40$ from a population whose proportion is 0.3.

(a) Test the null hypothesis $H_0: p = 0.3$ versus $H_1: p \neq 0.3$ for each simulated sample.

(b) If we test the hypothesis at the $\alpha = 0.1$ level of significance, how many of the 100 samples would you expect to result in a Type I error? 10

(c) Count the number of samples that lead to a rejection of the null hypothesis. Is it close to the expected value determined in part (b)? (d) We know $p = 0.3$

(d) How do we know that a rejection of the null hypothesis results in making a Type I error in this situation?

39. Simulation Simulate drawing 100 simple random samples of size $n = 15$ from a population whose proportion is 0.2.

(a) Test the null hypothesis $H_0: p = 0.2$ versus $H_1: p \neq 0.2$ for each simulated sample.

(b) If we test the hypothesis at the $\alpha = 0.1$ level of significance, how many of the 100 samples would you expect to result in a Type I error? 10

(c) Count the number of samples that lead to a rejection of the null hypothesis. Is it close to the expected value determined in part (b)? What might account for any discrepancies?

(d) How do we know that a rejection of the null hypothesis results in making a Type I error in this situation?

40. Putting It Together: Lupus Based on historical birthing records, the proportion of males born worldwide is 0.51. In other words, the commonly held belief that boys are just as likely as girls is false. Systematic lupus erythematosus (SLE), or lupus for short, is a disease in which one's immune system attacks healthy cells and tissue by mistake. It is well known that lupus tends to exist more in females than in males. Researchers wondered, however, if families with a child who had lupus had a lower ratio of males to females than the general population. If this were true, it would suggest that something happens during conception that causes males to be conceived at a lower rate when the SLE gene is present. To determine if this hypothesis is true, the researchers obtained records of families with a child who had SLE. A total of 23 males and 79 females were found to have SLE. The 23 males with SLE had a total of 23 male siblings and 22 female siblings. The 79 females with SLE had a total of 69 male siblings and 80 female siblings. *Source:* L.N. Moorthy, M.G.E. Peterson, K.B. Onel, and T.J.A. Lehman. "Do Children with Lupus Have Fewer Male Siblings" *Lupus* 2008 17:128–131, 2008.

(a) Explain why this is an observational study.

(b) Is the study retrospective or prospective? Why?

(c) There are a total of $23 + 69 = 92$ male siblings in the study. How many female siblings are in the study? 102

(d) Draw a relative frequency bar graph of gender of the siblings.

(e) Find a point estimate for the proportion of male siblings in families where one of the children has SLE. 0.474

(f) Does the sample evidence suggest that the proportion of male siblings in families where one of the children has SLE is less than 0.51, the accepted proportion of males born in the general population? Use the $\alpha = 0.05$ level of significance. Do not reject H_0 (g) (0.404, 0.544)

(g) Construct a 95% confidence interval for the proportion of male siblings in a family where one of the children has SLE.

41. Putting It Together: Naughty or Nice? Yale University graduate student J. Kiley Hamlin conducted an experiment in which 16 ten-month-old babies were asked to watch a climber

35. Yes; do not reject H_0; P-value = 0.297

character attempt to ascend a hill. On two occasions, the baby witnesses the character fail to make the climb. On the third attempt, the baby witnesses either a helper toy push the character up the hill or a hinderer toy prevent the character from making the ascent. The helper and hinderer toys were shown to each baby in a random fashion for a fixed amount of time. The baby was then placed in front of each toy and allowed to choose which toy he or she wished to play with. In 14 of the 16 cases, the baby chose the helper toy. *Source:* J. Kiley Hamlin et al., "Social Evaluation by Preverbal Infants." *Nature*, Nov. 2007.

(a) Why is it important to randomly expose the baby to the helper or hinderer toy first? Avoid bias

(b) What would be the appropriate null and alternative hypotheses if the researcher is attempting to show that babies prefer helpers over hinderers? H_0: $p = 0.5$ vs. H_1: $p > 0.5$

(c) Use the binomial probability formula to determine the P-value for this test. 0.0021

(d) In testing 12 six-month-old babies, all 12 preferred the helper toy. The P-value was reported as 0.0002. Interpret this result.

EXPLAINING THE CONCEPTS

42. Explain what a P-value is. What is the criterion for rejecting the null hypothesis using the P-value approach?

43. Suppose we are testing the hypothesis H_0: $p = 0.3$ versus H_1: $p > 0.3$ and we find the P-value to be 0.23. Explain what this means. Would you reject the null hypothesis? Why?

44. Suppose we are testing the hypothesis H_0: $p = 0.65$ versus H_1: $p \neq 0.65$ and we find the P-value to be 0.02. Explain what this means. Would you reject the null hypothesis? Why?

45. Discuss the advantages and disadvantages of using the Classical Approach to hypothesis testing. Discuss the advantages and disadvantages of using the P-value approach to hypothesis testing.

46. The headline reporting the results of a poll conducted by the Gallup organization stated "Majority of Americans at Personal Best in the Morning." The results indicated that a survey of 1100 Americans resulted in 55% stating they were at their personal best in the morning. The poll's results were reported with a margin of error of 3%. Explain why the Gallup organization's headline is accurate.

47. Explain what "statistical significance" means.

Technology Step-By-Step

Hypothesis Tests Regarding a Population Proportion

TI-83/84 Plus

1. Press STAT, highlight TESTS, and select `5:1-PropZTest`.
2. For the value of p_0, enter the value of the population proportion stated in the null hypothesis.
3. Enter the number of successes, x, and the sample size, n.
4. Select the direction of the alternative hypothesis.
5. Highlight **Calculate** or **Draw**, and press ENTER.

MINITAB

1. If you have raw data, enter them in C1, using 0 for failure and 1 for success.
2. Select the **Stat** menu, highlight **Basic Statistics**, then highlight **1-Proportion**.
3. If you have raw data, select the "Samples in columns" radio button and enter C1. If you have summarized statistics, select "Summarized data." Enter the number of trials and the number of successes.
4. Enter the value of the proportion stated in the null hypothesis. Click Options. Enter the direction of the alternative hypothesis. If $np_0(1 - p_0) \geq 10$, check the box marked "Use test and interval based on normal distribution." Click OK twice.

Excel

1. Load the XLSTAT Add-In.
2. Select the XLSTAT menu and select **Parametric Tests**. From the drop-down menu, select **z-test for one proportion**.
3. In the cell marked Frequency, enter the number of successes. In the cell marked Sample size, enter the number of trials. In the cell marked Test proportion, enter the proportion stated in the null hypothesis. Check the Frequency radio button. Choose the appropriate direction for the alternative hypothesis. Be sure Hypothesize difference (D): is set to zero. Enter the level of significance. Click OK.

StatCrunch

1. If you have raw data, enter them into the spreadsheet. Name the column variable.
2. Select **Stat**, highlight **Proportions**, select **One sample**, and then choose either **with data** or **with summary**.
3. If you chose **with data**, select the column that has the observations, choose which outcome represents a success, then click Next>. If you chose **with summary**, enter the number of successes and the number of trials. Click Next>.
4. Choose the hypothesis test radio button. Enter the value of the proportion stated in the null hypothesis and choose the direction of the alternative hypothesis from the pull-down menu. Click Calculate.

10.3 HYPOTHESIS TESTS FOR A POPULATION MEAN

Preparing for This Section Before getting started, review the following:

- Sampling distribution of $\bar{x}$ (Section 8.1, pp. 367–375)
- The t-distribution (Section 9.2, pp. 405–409)
- Using probabilities to identify unusual results (Section 5.1, p. 235)
- Confidence intervals for a mean (Section 9.2, pp. 409–411)

OBJECTIVES

1. **Test hypotheses about a mean**
2. **Understand the difference between statistical significance and practical significance**

1 Test Hypotheses about a Mean

In Section 8.1 we learned that the distribution of $\bar{x}$ is approximately normally distributed with mean $\mu_{\bar{x}} = \mu$ and standard deviation $\sigma_{\bar{x}} = \dfrac{\sigma}{\sqrt{n}}$ provided the population from which the sample was drawn is normally distributed or the sample size is sufficiently large (because of the Central Limit Theorem). So $z = \dfrac{\bar{x} - \mu}{\dfrac{\sigma}{\sqrt{n}}}$ follows a standard normal distribution. However, it is unreasonable to expect to know σ without knowing μ. This problem was resolved by William Gosset, who determined that $t = \dfrac{\bar{x} - \mu}{\dfrac{s}{\sqrt{n}}}$ follows Student's t-distribution with $n - 1$ degrees of freedom. We use this distribution to perform hypothesis tests on a mean.

Testing hypotheses about a mean follows the same logic as testing a hypothesis about a population proportion. The only difference is that we use Student's t-distribution, rather than the normal distribution.

Testing Hypotheses Regarding a Population Mean

To test hypotheses regarding the population mean, we use the following steps, provided that

- The sample is obtained using simple random sampling or from a randomized experiment.
- The sample has no outliers, and the population from which the sample is drawn is normally distributed or the sample size, n, is large ($n \geq 30$).
- The sampled values are independent of each other.

Step 1 Determine the null and alternative hypotheses. The hypotheses can be structured in one of three ways:

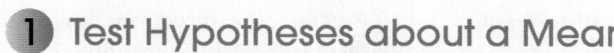

Two-Tailed	Left-Tailed	Right-Tailed
H_0: $\mu = \mu_0$	H_0: $\mu = \mu_0$	H_0: $\mu = \mu_0$
H_1: $\mu \neq \mu_0$	H_1: $\mu < \mu_0$	H_1: $\mu > \mu_0$

Note: μ_0 is the assumed value of the population mean.

Step 2 Select a level of significance, α, depending on the seriousness of making a Type I error.

Classical Approach

Step 3 Compute the **test statistic**

$$t_0 = \frac{\bar{x} - \mu_0}{\dfrac{s}{\sqrt{n}}}$$

which follows Student's t-distribution with $n - 1$ degrees of freedom.

P-Value Approach

By Hand Step 3 Compute the **test statistic**

$$t_0 = \frac{\bar{x} - \mu_0}{\dfrac{s}{\sqrt{n}}}$$

which follows Student's t-distribution with $n - 1$ degrees of freedom.

Use Table VI to determine the critical value.

	Two-Tailed	Left-Tailed	Right-Tailed
Critical value(s)	$-t_{\frac{\alpha}{2}}$ and $t_{\frac{\alpha}{2}}$	$-t_{\alpha}$	t_{α}

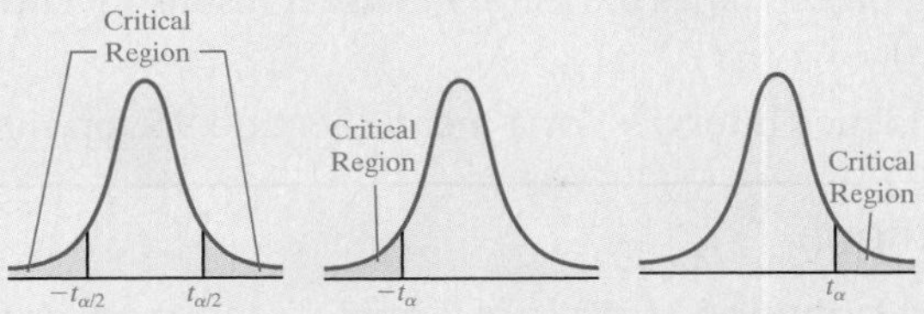

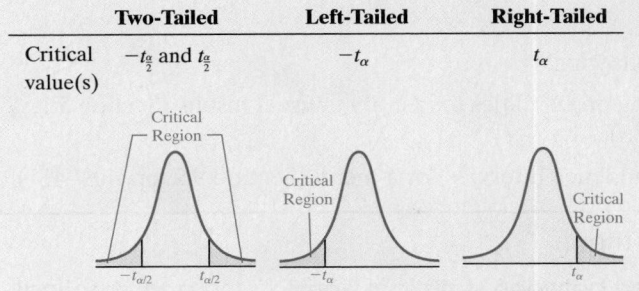

Step 4 Compare the critical value to the test statistic.

Two-Tailed	Left-Tailed	Right-Tailed
If $t_0 < -t_{\frac{\alpha}{2}}$ or $t_0 > t_{\frac{\alpha}{2}}$, reject the null hypothesis.	If $t_0 < -t_{\alpha}$, reject the null hypothesis.	If $t_0 > t_{\alpha}$, reject the null hypothesis.

Use Table VI to approximate the *P*-value.

Two-Tailed	Left-Tailed	Right-Tailed

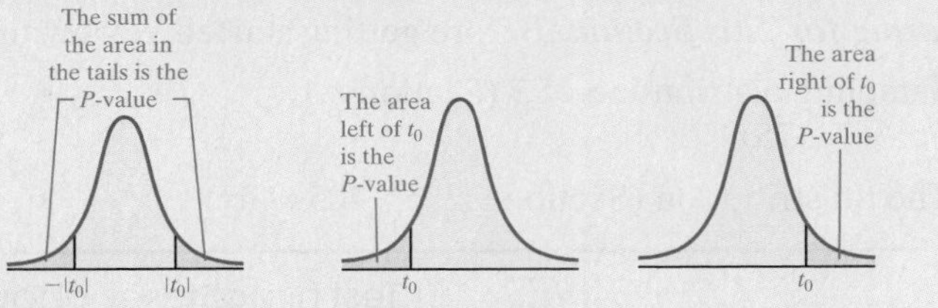

P-value $= 2P(t > |t_0|)$	*P*-value $= P(t < t_0)$	*P*-value $= P(t > t_0)$

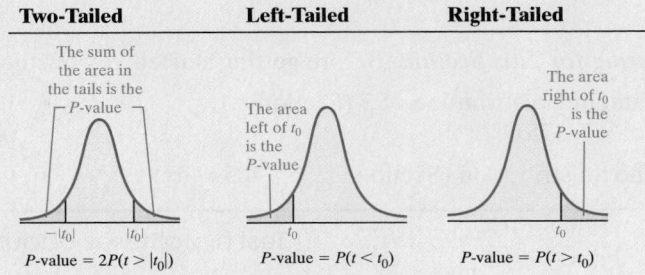

Technology Step 3 Use a statistical spreadsheet or calculator with statistical capabilities to obtain the *P*-value. The directions for obtaining the *P*-value using the TI-83/84 Plus graphing calculator, MINITAB, Excel, and StatCrunch, are in the Technology Step-by-Step on page 460.

Step 4 If the *P*-value $< \alpha$, reject the null hypothesis.

Step 5 State the conclusion.

Notice that the procedure just presented requires either that the population from which the sample was drawn be normal or that the sample size be large ($n \geq 30$). The procedure is robust, so minor departures from normality will not adversely affect the results of the test. However, if the data include outliers, the procedure should not be used.

We will verify these assumptions by constructing normal probability plots (to assess normality) and boxplots (to discover whether there are outliers). If the normal probability plot indicates that the data do not come from a normal population or if the boxplot reveals outliers, nonparametric tests should be performed.

Before we look at a couple of examples, it is important to understand that we cannot find exact *P*-values using the *t*-distribution table (Table VI) because the table provides *t*-values only for certain areas. However, we can use the table to calculate lower and upper bounds on the *P*-value. To find exact *P*-values, we use statistical software or a graphing calculator with advanced statistical features.

Note to Instructor
Consider assigning the "Testing a Claim with Skittles II" activity from the Student Activity Workbook.

EXAMPLE 1 Testing a Hypothesis about a Population Mean: Large Sample

Problem The mean height of American males is 69.5 inches. The heights of the 43 male U.S. presidents* (Washington through Obama) have a mean 70.78 inches and a standard deviation of 2.77 inches. Treating the 43 presidents as a simple random sample, determine if there is evidence to suggest that U.S. presidents are taller than the average American male. Use the $\alpha = 0.05$ level of significance.

Approach Assume that all U.S. presidents come from a population whose height is 69.5 inches (that is, there is no difference between heights of U.S. presidents and the general American male population). Then determine the likelihood of obtaining a sample mean of 70.78 inches or higher from a population whose mean is 69.5 inches. If the result is unlikely, reject the assumption stated in the null hypothesis in favor of the more likely notion that the mean height of U.S. presidents is greater than 69.5 inches. However, if obtaining a sample mean of 70.78 inches from a population whose mean is assumed to be 69.5 inches is not unusual, do not reject the null hypothesis (and attribute the difference to sampling error). Assume the population of potential U.S. presidents is large (for independence). Because the sample size is large, the distribution of $\bar{x}$ is approximately normal. Follow Steps 1 through 5.

*Grover Cleveland was elected to two non-consecutive terms, so there have technically been 44 presidents of the United States.

Solution

Step 1 We want to know if U.S. presidents are taller than the typical American male who is 69.5 inches. We assume there is no difference between the height of a typical American male and U.S. presidents, so we have

$$H_0: \mu = 69.5 \text{ inches} \quad \text{versus} \quad H_1: \mu > 69.5 \text{ inches}$$

Step 2 The level of significance is $\alpha = 0.05$.

Classical Approach

Step 3 The sample mean is $\bar{x} = 70.78$ inches and the sample standard deviation is $s = 2.77$ inches.

The test statistic is

$$t_0 = \frac{\bar{x} - \mu_0}{\frac{s}{\sqrt{n}}} = \frac{70.78 - 69.5}{\frac{2.77}{\sqrt{43}}} = 3.030$$

Because this is a right-tailed test, we determine the critical value at the $\alpha = 0.05$ level of significance with $43 - 1 = 42$ degrees of freedom to be $t_{0.05} = 1.684$ (using 40 degrees of freedom since this is closest to 42). The critical region is shown in Figure 14.

Figure 14

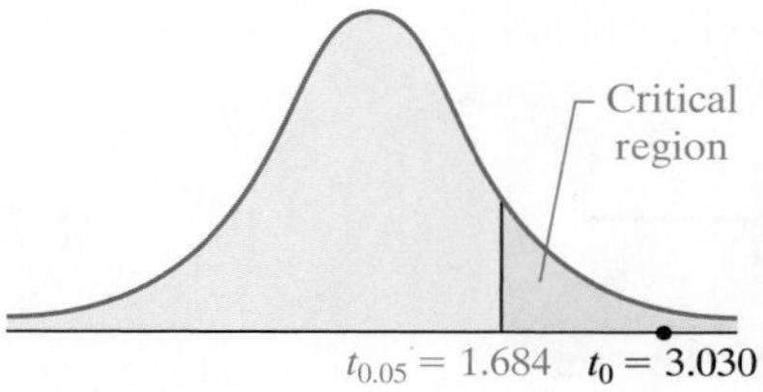

Step 4 The test statistic is $t_0 = 3.030$. We label this point in Figure 14. Because the test statistic lies in the critical region, we reject the null hypothesis.

P-Value Approach

By Hand Step 3 The sample mean is $\bar{x} = 70.78$ inches and the sample standard deviation is $s = 2.77$ inches.

The test statistic is

$$t_0 = \frac{\bar{x} - \mu_0}{\frac{s}{\sqrt{n}}} = \frac{70.78 - 69.5}{\frac{2.77}{\sqrt{43}}} = 3.030$$

Because this is a right-tailed test, the *P*-value is the area under the *t*-distribution with 42 degrees of freedom to the right of $t_0 = 3.030$ as shown in Figure 15.

Figure 15

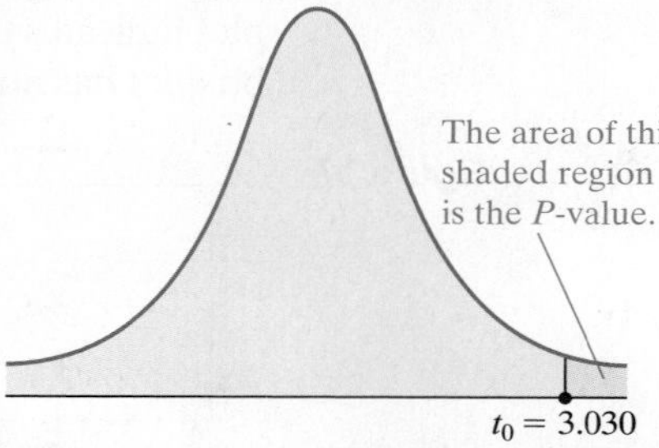

Using Table VI, we find the row that corresponds to 40 degrees of freedom (we use 40 degrees of freedom because it is closest to the actual degrees of freedom, $43 - 1 = 42$). The value 3.030 lies between 2.971 and 3.307. The value of 2.971 has an area of 0.0025 to the right under the *t*-distribution with 40 degrees of freedom. The area under the *t*-distribution with 40 degrees of freedom to the right of 3.307 is 0.001.

Because 3.030 is between 2.971 and 3.307, the *P*-value is between 0.001 and 0.0025. So

$$0.001 < P\text{-value} < 0.0025$$

Technology Step 3 Using a TI-84 Plus graphing calculator, we find the *P*-value is 0.0021. See Figure 16.

Figure 16

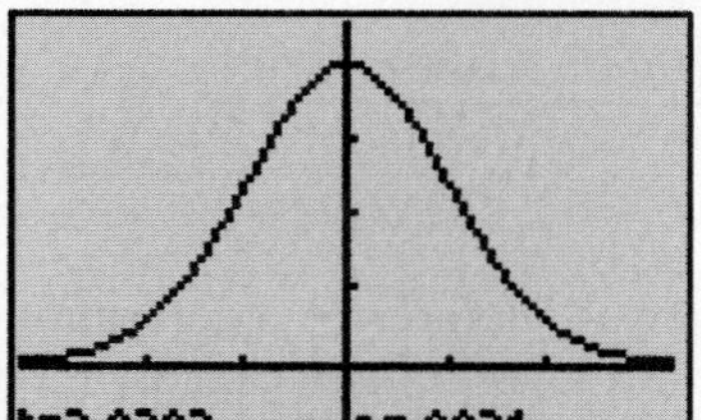

Step 4 The *P*-value of 0.0021 [by hand: $0.001 < P$-value < 0.0025] means that, *if* the null hypothesis that $\mu = 69.5$ inches is true, we expect a sample mean of 70.78 inches or higher in about 2 out of 1000 samples. The results we obtained do not seem to be consistent with the assumption that the mean height of this population is 69.5 inches. Put another way, because the *P*-value is less than the level of significance, $\alpha = 0.05$ $(0.0021 < 0.05)$, we reject the null hypothesis.

Step 5 There is sufficient evidence at the $\alpha = 0.05$ level of significance to conclude that U.S. presidents are taller than the typical American male.

Now Work Problem 13

EXAMPLE 2 Testing a Hypothesis about a Population Mean: Small Sample

Problem The "fun size" of a Snickers bar is supposed to weigh 20 grams. Because the penalty for selling candy bars under their advertised weight is severe, the manufacturer calibrates the machine so the mean weight is 20.1 grams. The quality-control engineer at M&M–Mars, the Snickers manufacturer, is concerned about the calibration. He obtains a random sample of 11 candy bars, weighs them, and obtains the data in Table 1. Should the machine be shut down and calibrated? Because shutting down the plant is very expensive, he decides to conduct the test at the $\alpha = 0.01$ level of significance.

TABLE 1

19.68	20.66	19.56
19.98	20.65	19.61
20.55	20.36	21.02
21.50	19.74	

Source: Michael Carlisle, student at Joliet Junior College

Approach Assume that the machine is calibrated correctly. So there is no difference between the actual mean weight and the calibrated weight of the candy. We want to know whether the machine is incorrectly calibrated, which would result in a mean weight that is too high or too low. Therefore, this is a two-tailed test.

Before performing the hypothesis test, verify that the data come from a population that is normally distributed with no outliers. Construct a normal probability plot and boxplot to verify these requirements. Then proceed to follow Steps 1 through 5.

Solution Figure 17 displays the normal probability plot and boxplot. The normal probability plot indicates that the data could come from a population that is approximately normal. The boxplot has no outliers. We can proceed with the hypothesis test.

Figure 17

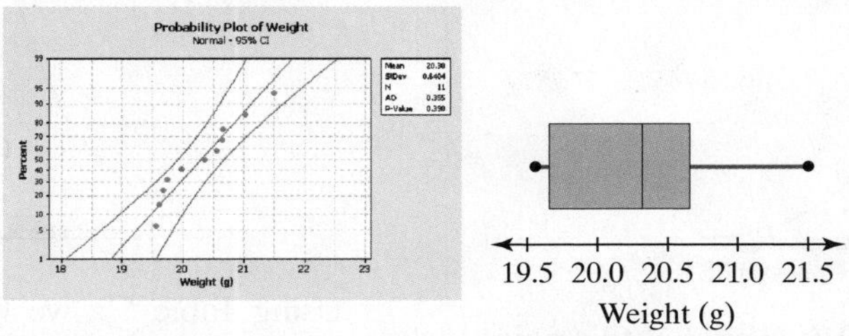

Step 1 The engineer wishes to determine whether the Snickers have a mean weight of 20.1 grams or not. The hypotheses can be written

$$H_0: \mu = 20.1 \quad \text{versus} \quad H_1: \mu \neq 20.1$$

This is a two-tailed test.

Step 2 The level of significance is $\alpha = 0.01$.

Classical Approach

Step 3 From the data in Table 1, the sample mean is $\bar{x} = 20.301$ ounces and the sample standard deviation is $s = 0.64$ ounce.

The test statistic is

$$t_0 = \frac{\bar{x} - \mu_0}{\frac{s}{\sqrt{n}}} = \frac{20.301 - 20.1}{\frac{0.64}{\sqrt{11}}} = 1.042$$

Because this is a two-tailed test, we determine the critical values at the $\alpha = 0.01$ level of significance with $11 - 1 = 10$ degrees of freedom to be $-t_{0.01/2} = -t_{0.005} = -3.169$ and $t_{0.01/2} = t_{0.005} = 3.169$. The critical regions are shown in Figure 18.

Figure 18

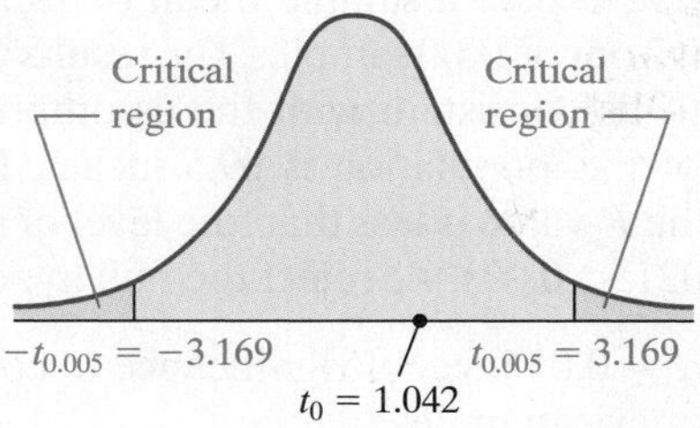

P-Value Approach

By Hand Step 3 From the data in Table 1, the sample mean is $\bar{x} = 20.301$ ounces and the sample standard deviation is $s = 0.64$ ounce.

The test statistic is

$$t_0 = \frac{\bar{x} - \mu_0}{\frac{s}{\sqrt{n}}} = \frac{20.301 - 20.1}{\frac{0.64}{\sqrt{11}}} = 1.042$$

Because this is a two-tailed test, the *P*-value is the area under the *t*-distribution with $n - 1 = 11 - 1 = 10$ degrees of freedom to the left of $-t_0 = -1.042$ and to the right of $t_0 = 1.042$, as shown in Figure 19. That is, $P\text{-value} = P(t < -1.042) + P(t > 1.042) = 2P(t > 1.042)$, with 10 degrees of freedom.

Figure 19

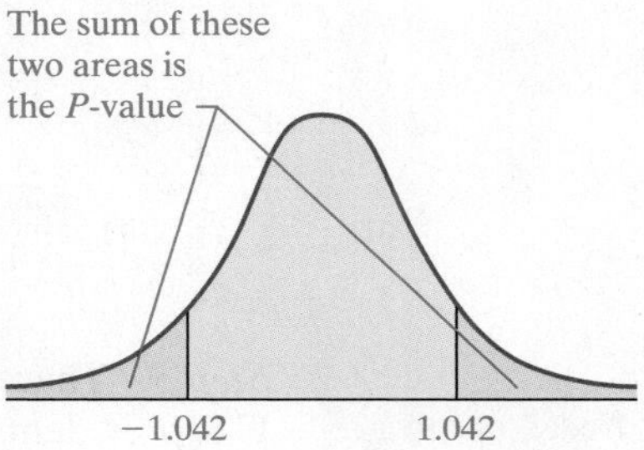

Step 4 The test statistic is $t_0 = 1.042$. Because the test statistic does not lie in the critical region, we do not reject the null hypothesis.

Using Table VI, we find the row that corresponds to 10 degrees of freedom. The value 1.042 lies between 0.879 and 1.093. The value of 0.879 has an area of 0.20 to the right under the t-distribution. The area under the t-distribution to the right of 1.093 is 0.15.

Because 1.042 is between 0.879 and 1.093, the P-value is between 2(0.15) and 2(0.20). So

$$0.30 < P\text{-value} < 0.40$$

Technology Step 3 Using MINITAB, we find that the exact P-value is 0.323.

Step 4 The P-value of 0.323 [by-hand: $0.30 < P$-value < 0.40] means that, *if* the null hypothesis that $\mu = 20.1$ ounces is true, we expect about 32 out of 100 samples to result in a sample mean as extreme or more extreme than the one obtained. The result we obtained is not unusual, so we do not reject the null hypothesis.

Step 5 There is not sufficient evidence to conclude that the Snickers have a mean weight different from 20.1 grams at the $\alpha = 0.01$ level of significance. The machine should not be shut down.

Now Work Problem 21

2 Understand the Difference between Statistical Significance and Practical Significance

In Other Words
Results are statistically significant if the difference between the observed result and the statement made in the null hypothesis is unlikely to occur due to chance alone.

When a large sample size is used in a hypothesis test, the results could be statistically significant even though the difference between the sample statistic and mean stated in the null hypothesis may have no *practical significance.*

DEFINITION

Practical significance refers to the idea that, while small differences between the statistic and parameter stated in the null hypothesis are statistically significant, the difference may not be large enough to cause concern or be considered important.

EXAMPLE 3 Statistical versus Practical Significance

Problem According to the American Community Survey, the mean travel time to work in Collin County, Texas, in 2008 was 27.3 minutes. The Department of Transportation reprogrammed all the traffic lights in Collin County in an attempt to reduce travel time. To determine if there is evidence that travel time has decreased as a result of the reprogramming, the Department of Transportation obtains a random sample of 2500 commuters, records their travel time to work, and finds a sample mean of 27.0 minutes with a standard deviation of 8.5 minutes. Does this result suggest that travel time has decreased at the $\alpha = 0.05$ level of significance?

Approach We will use both the classical and P-value approach to test the hypothesis.

Solution

Step 1 The Department of Transportation wants to know if the mean travel time to work has decreased from 27.3 minutes. From this, we have

$$H_0: \mu = 27.3 \text{ minutes} \quad \text{versus} \quad H_1: \mu < 27.3 \text{ minutes}$$

Step 2 The level of significance is $\alpha = 0.05$.

Step 3 The test statistic is

$$t_0 = \frac{\bar{x} - \mu_0}{\frac{s}{\sqrt{n}}} = \frac{27.0 - 27.3}{\frac{8.5}{\sqrt{2500}}} = -1.765$$

Classical Approach

Step 3(continued) Because this is a left-tailed test, the critical value with $\alpha = 0.05$ and $2500 - 1 = 2499$ degrees of freedom is $-t_{0.05} \approx -1.645$ (use the last row of Table VI when the degrees of freedom is greater than 1000).

Step 4 Because the test statistic is less than the critical value (the test statistic falls in the critical region), we reject the null hypothesis.

P-Value Approach

Step 3 (continued) Because this is a left-tailed test, the P-value is P-value $= P(t_0 < -1.765)$. From Table VI, we find the approximate P-value is $0.025 < P\text{-value} < 0.05$ [Technology: P-value $= 0.0389$].

Step 4 Because the P-value is less than the level of significance, $\alpha = 0.05$, we reject the null hypothesis.

Step 5 There is sufficient evidence at the $\alpha = 0.05$ level of significance to conclude the mean travel time to work has decreased.

While the difference between 27.0 minutes and 27.3 minutes is statistically significant, it has no practical meaning. After all, is 0.3 minute (18 seconds) really going to make anyone feel better about his or her commute to work?

CAUTION

Beware of studies with large sample sizes that claim statistical significance because the differences may not have any practical meaning.

The reason that the results from Example 3 were statistically significant had to do with the large sample size. The moral of the story is this:

> Large sample sizes can lead to results that are statistically significant, while the difference between the statistic and parameter in the null hypothesis is not enough to be considered practically significant.

5. (b) $-t_{0.005} = -2.819$; $t_{0.005} = 2.819$ (e) (99.39, 110.21); do not reject H_0

10.3 ASSESS YOUR UNDERSTANDING

SKILL BUILDING

1. **(a)** Determine the critical value for a right-tailed test of a population mean at the $\alpha = 0.01$ level of significance with 15 degrees of freedom. 2.602

(b) Determine the critical value for a left-tailed test of a population mean at the $\alpha = 0.05$ level of significance based on a sample size of $n = 20$. -1.729

(c) Determine the critical values for a two-tailed test of a population mean at the $\alpha = 0.05$ level of significance based on a sample size of $n = 13$. ± 2.179

2. **(a)** Determine the critical value for a right-tailed test of a population mean at the $\alpha = 0.1$ level of significance with 22 degrees of freedom. 1.321

(b) Determine the critical value for a left-tailed test of a population mean at the $\alpha = 0.01$ level of significance based on a sample size of $n = 40$. -2.426

(c) Determine the critical values for a two-tailed test of a population mean at the $\alpha = 0.01$ level of significance based on a sample size of $n = 33$. ± 2.738

3. To test H_0: $\mu = 50$ versus H_1: $\mu < 50$, a simple random sample of size $n = 24$ is obtained from a population that is known to be normally distributed. (a) $t_0 = -1.379$ (b) $-t_{0.05} = -1.714$

(a) If $\bar{x} = 47.1$ and $s = 10.3$, compute the test statistic.

(b) If the researcher decides to test this hypothesis at the $\alpha = 0.05$ level of significance, determine the critical value.

(c) Draw a t-distribution that depicts the critical region.

(d) Will the researcher reject the null hypothesis? Why? No

4. To test H_0: $\mu = 40$ versus H_1: $\mu > 40$, a simple random sample of size $n = 25$ is obtained from a population that is known to be normally distributed.

(a) If $\bar{x} = 42.3$ and $s = 4.3$, compute the test statistic. $t_0 = 2.674$

(b) If the researcher decides to test this hypothesis at the $\alpha = 0.1$ level of significance, determine the critical value. $t_{0.1} = 1.318$

(c) Draw a t-distribution that depicts the critical region.

(d) Will the researcher reject the null hypothesis? Why? Yes

5. To test H_0: $\mu = 100$ versus H_1: $\mu \neq 100$, a simple random sample of size $n = 23$ is obtained from a population that is known to be normally distributed.

(a) If $\bar{x} = 104.8$ and $s = 9.2$, compute the test statistic. $t_0 = 2.502$

(b) If the researcher decides to test this hypothesis at the $\alpha = 0.01$ level of significance, determine the critical values.

(c) Draw a t-distribution that depicts the critical region.

(d) Will the researcher reject the null hypothesis? Why? No

(e) Construct a 99% confidence interval to test the hypothesis.

6. To test H_0: $\mu = 80$ versus H_1: $\mu < 80$, a simple random sample of size $n = 22$ is obtained from a population that is known to be normally distributed. (a) $t_0 = -1.711$ (b) $-t_{0.02} = -2.189$

(a) If $\bar{x} = 76.9$ and $s = 8.5$, compute the test statistic.

(b) If the researcher decides to test this hypothesis at the $\alpha = 0.02$ level of significance, determine the critical value.

(c) Draw a t-distribution that depicts the critical region.

(d) Will the researcher reject the null hypothesis? Why? No

7. To test H_0: $\mu = 20$ versus H_1: $\mu < 20$, a simple random sample of size $n = 18$ is obtained from a population that is known to be normally distributed.

(a) If $\bar{x} = 18.3$ and $s = 4.3$, compute the test statistic. $t_0 = -1.677$

(b) Draw a t-distribution with the area that represents the P-value shaded.

(c) Approximate and interpret the P-value. 0.0559

(d) If the researcher decides to test this hypothesis at the $\alpha = 0.05$ level of significance, will the researcher reject the null hypothesis? Why? No

8. To test H_0: $\mu = 4.5$ versus H_1: $\mu > 4.5$, a simple random sample of size $n = 13$ is obtained from a population that is known to be normally distributed.

(a) If $\bar{x} = 4.9$ and $s = 1.3$, compute the test statistic. $t_0 = 1.109$

(b) Draw a *t*-distribution with the area that represents the *P*-value shaded.

(c) Approximate and interpret the *P*-value. 0.1445

(d) If the researcher decides to test this hypothesis at the $\alpha = 0.1$ level of significance, will the researcher reject the null hypothesis? Why? No

9. To test H_0: $\mu = 105$ versus H_1: $\mu \neq 105$, a simple random sample of size $n = 35$ is obtained.

(a) Does the population have to be normally distributed to test this hypothesis by using the methods presented in this section? Why? No (b) $t_0 = -3.108$

(b) If $\bar{x} = 101.9$ and $s = 5.9$, compute the test statistic.

(c) Draw a *t*-distribution with the area that represents the *P*-value shaded.

(d) Approximate and interpret the *P*-value. 0.0038

(e) If the researcher decides to test this hypothesis at the $\alpha = 0.01$ level of significance, will the researcher reject the null hypothesis? Why? Yes

10. To test H_0: $\mu = 45$ versus H_1: $\mu \neq 45$, a simple random sample of size $n = 40$ is obtained.

(a) Does the population have to be normally distributed to test this hypothesis by using the methods presented in this section? Why? No

(b) If $\bar{x} = 48.3$ and $s = 8.5$, compute the test statistic. $t_0 = 2.455$

(c) Draw a *t*-distribution with the area that represents the *P*-value shaded.

(d) Determine and interpret the *P*-value. 0.0186

(e) If the researcher decides to test this hypothesis at the $\alpha = 0.01$ level of significance, will the researcher reject the null hypothesis? Why? No

(f) Construct a 99% confidence interval to test the hypothesis. (44.66, 51.94); do not reject H_0

APPLYING THE CONCEPTS

11. You Explain It! ATM Withdrawals According to the Crown ATM Network, the mean ATM withdrawal is \$67. PayEase, Inc., manufacturers an ATM that allows one to pay bills (electric, water, parking tickets, and so on), as well as withdraw money. A review of 40 withdrawals shows the mean withdrawal is \$73 from a PayEase ATM machine. Do people withdraw more money from a PayEase ATM machine?

(a) Determine the appropriate null and alternative hypotheses to answer the question. H_0: $\mu = 67$; H_1: $\mu > 67$

(b) Suppose the *P*-value for this test is 0.02. Explain what this value represents.

(c) Write a conclusion for this hypothesis test assuming an $\alpha = 0.05$ level of significance.

12. You Explain It! Are Women Getting Taller? In 1990, the mean height of women 20 years of age or older was 63.7 inches based on data obtained from the Centers for Disease Control and Prevention's *Advance Data Report*, No. 347. Suppose that a random sample of 45 women who are 20 years of age or older today results in a mean height of 63.9 inches.

(a) State the appropriate null and alternative hypotheses to assess whether women are taller today. H_0: $\mu = 63.7$; H_1: $\mu > 63.7$

(b) Suppose the *P*-value for this test is 0.35. Explain what this value represents.

(c) Write a conclusion for this hypothesis test assuming an $\alpha = 0.10$ level of significance.

NW **13. Ready for College?** The ACT is a college entrance exam. In addition to administering this exam, researchers at ACT gauge high school students' readiness for college-level subjects. For example, ACT has determined that a score of 22 on the mathematics portion of the ACT suggests that a student is ready for college-level mathematics. To achieve this goal, ACT recommends that students take a core curriculum of math courses in high school. This core is 1 year of credit each in Algebra I, Algebra II, and Geometry. Suppose a random sample of 200 students who completed this core set of courses results in a mean ACT math score of 22.6 with a standard deviation of 3.9. Do these results suggest that students who complete the core curriculum are ready for college-level mathematics? That is, are they scoring above 22 on the math portion of the ACT? (a) H_0: $\mu = 22$; H_1: $\mu > 22$

(a) State the appropriate null and alternative hypotheses.

(b) Verify that the requirements to perform the test using the *t*-distribution are satisfied. (c) Reject H_0; *P*-value = 0.0154

(c) Use the classical or *P*-value approach at the $\alpha = 0.05$ level of significance to test the hypotheses in part (a).

(d) Write a conclusion based on your results to part (c).

14. SAT Verbal Scores Do students who learned English as well as another language simultaneously score worse on the SAT Critical Reading exam than the general population of test takers? The mean score among all test takers on the SAT Critical Reading exam is 501. A random sample of 100 test takers who learned English as well as another language simultaneously had a mean SAT Critical Reading score of 485 with a standard deviation of 116. Do these results suggest that students who learn English as well as another language simultaneously score worse on the SAT Critical Reading exam? (a) H_0: $\mu = 501$; H_1: $\mu < 501$

(a) State the appropriate null and alternative hypotheses.

(b) Verify that the requirements to perform the test using the *t*-distribution are satisfied. (c) Reject H_0: *P*-value = 0.0855

(c) Use the classical or *P*-value approach at the $\alpha = 0.1$ level of significance to test the hypotheses in part (a).

(d) Write a conclusion based on your results to part (c).

15. Effects of Alcohol on the Brain In a study published in the *American Journal of Psychiatry* (157:737–744, May 2000), researchers wanted to measure the effect of alcohol on the development of the hippocampal region in adolescents. The hippocampus is the portion of the brain responsible for long-term memory storage. The researchers randomly selected 12 adolescents with alcohol use disorders. They wanted to determine whether the hippocampal volumes in the alcoholic adolescents were less than the normal volume of 9.02 cubic centimeters (cm^3). An analysis of the sample data revealed that the hippocampal volume is approximately normal with $\bar{x} = 8.10$ and $s = 0.7$. Conduct the appropriate test at the $\alpha = 0.01$ level of significance. Reject H_0

16. Effects of Plastic Resin Para-nonylphenol is found in polyvinyl chloride (PVC) used in the food processing and packaging industries. Researchers wanted to determine the effect this substance had on the organ weight of first-generation mice when both parents were exposed to 50 micrograms per liter (μg/L) of para-nonylphenol in drinking water for 4 weeks. After 4 weeks, the mice were bred. After 100 days, the offspring of the exposed parents were sacrificed and the kidney weights were determined. The mean kidney weight of the 12 offspring was found to be 396.9 milligrams (mg), with a standard deviation of 45.4 mg. Is there significant evidence to conclude that the kidney weight of the offspring whose parents were exposed to 50 μg/L of para-nonylphenol in drinking water for 4 weeks is greater than 355.7 mg, the mean weight of kidneys in normal 100-day old mice at the $\alpha = 0.05$ level of significance? *Source:* Vendula Kyselova et al.,

"Effects of *p*-nonylphenol and resveratrol on body and organ weight and in vivo fertility of outbred CD-1 mice," *Reproductive Biology and Endocrinology*, 2003. Reject H_0

17. Credit Scores A Fair Isaac Corporation (FICO) score is used by credit agencies (such as mortgage companies and banks) to assess the creditworthiness of individuals. Its value ranges from 300 to 850. An individual with a FICO score over 700 is considered to be a quality credit risk. According to Fair Isaac Corporation, the mean FICO score is 703.5. A credit analyst wondered whether high-income individuals (incomes in excess of \$100,000 per year) had higher credit scores. He obtained a random sample of 40 high-income individuals and found the sample mean credit score to be 714.2 with a standard deviation of 83.2. Conduct the appropriate test to determine if high-income individuals have higher FICO scores at the $\alpha = 0.05$ level of significance. Do not reject H_0

18. TVaholics According to the American Time Use Survey, the typical American spends 154.8 minutes (2.58 hours) per day watching television. Do Internet users spend less time each day watching television? A survey of 50 Internet users results in a mean time watching television per day of 128.7 minutes, with a standard deviation of 46.5 minutes. Conduct the appropriate test to determine if Internet users spend less time watching television at the $\alpha = 0.05$ level of significance. *Source:* Norman H. Nie and D. Sunshine Hillygus. "Where Does Internet Time Come From? A Reconnaissance." *IT & Society,* 1(2) Reject H_0 19. (35.44, 42.36)

19. Age of Death-Row Inmates In 2002, the mean age of an inmate on death row was 40.7 years, according to data obtained from the U.S. Department of Justice. A sociologist wondered whether the mean age of a death-row inmate has changed since then. She randomly selects 32 death-row inmates and finds that their mean age is 38.9, with a standard deviation of 9.6. Construct a 95% confidence interval about the mean age. What does the interval imply?

20. Energy Consumption In 2001, the mean household expenditure for energy was \$1493, according to data obtained from the U.S. Energy Information Administration. An economist wanted to know whether this amount has changed significantly from its 2001 level. In a random sample of 35 households, he found the mean expenditure (in 2001 dollars) for energy during the most recent year to be \$1618, with standard deviation \$321. Construct a 95% confidence interval about the mean energy expenditure. What does the interval imply? (1507.7, 1728.3)

NW **21. Waiting in Line** The mean waiting time at the drive-through of a fast-food restaurant from the time an order is placed to the time the order is received is 84.3 seconds. A manager devises a new drive-through system that he believes will decrease wait time. He initiates the new system at his restaurant and measures the wait time for 10 randomly selected orders. The wait times are provided in the table.

108.5	67.4	58.0	75.9	65.1
80.4	95.5	86.3	70.9	72.0

(a) Because the sample size is small, the manager must verify that wait time is normally distributed and the sample does not contain any outliers. The normal probability plot and boxplot are shown. Are the conditions for testing the hypothesis satisfied? Yes

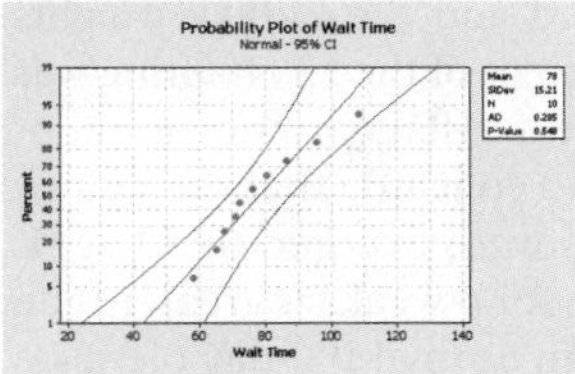

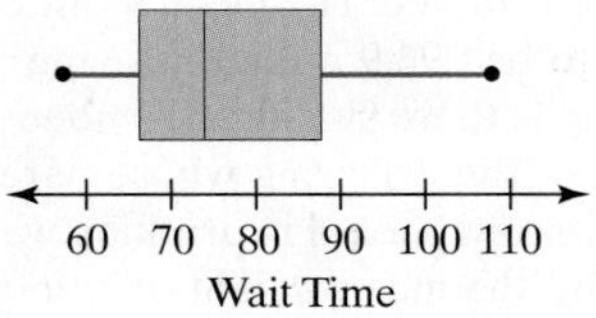

(b) Is the new system effective? Use the $\alpha = 0.1$ level of significance. No; $t_0 = -1.310$; do not reject H_0

22. Reading Rates Michael Sullivan, son of the author, decided to enroll in a reading course that allegedly increases reading speed and comprehension. Prior to enrolling in the class, Michael read 198 words per minute (wpm). The following data represent the words per minute read for 10 different passages read after the course.

206	217	197	199	210
210	197	212	227	209

(a) Because the sample size is small, we must verify that reading speed is normally distributed and the sample does not contain any outliers. The normal probability plot and boxplot are shown. Are the conditions for testing the hypothesis satisfied? Yes

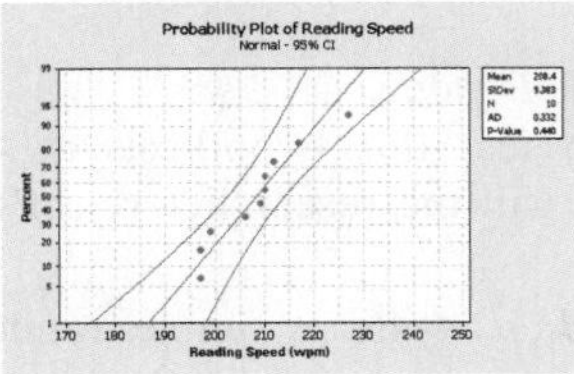

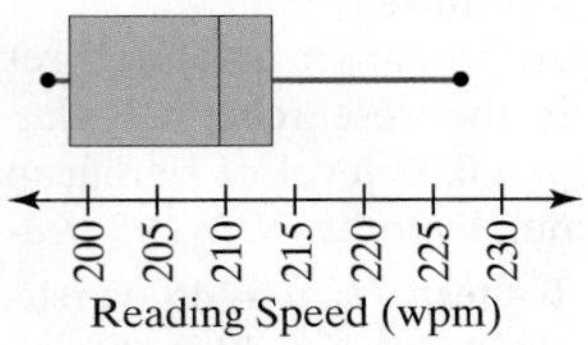

(b) Was the class effective? Use the $\alpha = 0.10$ level of significance. Yes; $t_0 = 3.499$; reject H_0

23. Calcium in Rainwater Calcium is essential to tree growth because it promotes the formation of wood and maintains cell walls. In 1990, the concentration of calcium in precipitation in Chautauqua, New York, was 0.11 milligram per liter (mg/L). A random sample of 10 precipitation dates in 2010 results in the following data:

0.065	0.087	0.070	0.262	0.126
0.183	0.120	0.234	0.313	0.108

Source: National Atmospheric Deposition Program

(a) Because the sample size is small, we must verify that calcium concentrations are normally distributed and the sample does not have any outliers. The normal probability plot and boxplot are shown. Are the conditions for conducting the hypothesis test satisfied? Yes

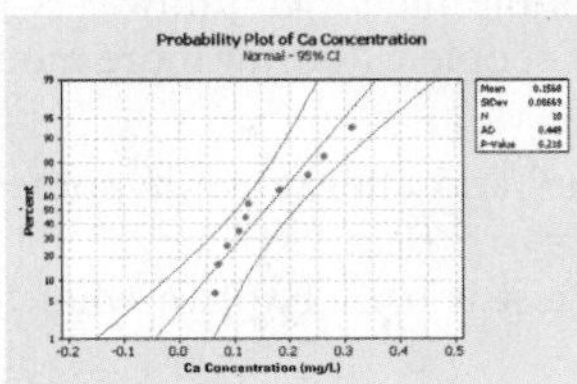

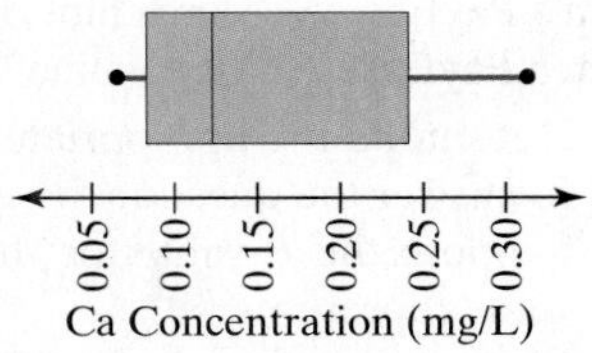

(b) Does the sample evidence suggest that calcium concentrations have changed since 1990? Use the $\alpha = 0.05$ level of significance. No; do not reject H_0

24. Filling Bottles A certain brand of apple juice is supposed to have 64 ounces of juice. Because the penalty for underfilling bottles is severe, the target mean amount of juice is 64.05 ounces. However, the filling machine is not precise, and the exact amount of juice varies from bottle to bottle. The quality-control manager wishes to verify that the mean amount of juice in each bottle is 64.05 ounces so that she can be sure that the machine is not over- or underfilling. She randomly samples 22 bottles of juice, measures the content, and obtains the following data:

64.05	64.05	64.03	63.97	63.95	64.02
64.01	63.99	64.00	64.01	64.06	63.94
63.98	64.05	63.95	64.01	64.08	64.01
63.95	63.97	64.10	63.98		

(a) Because the sample size is small, she must verify that the amount of juice is normally distributed and the sample does not contain any outliers. The normal probability plot and boxplot are shown. Are the conditions for testing the hypothesis satisfied? Yes

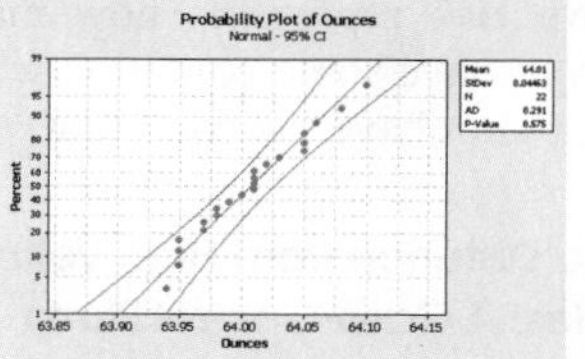

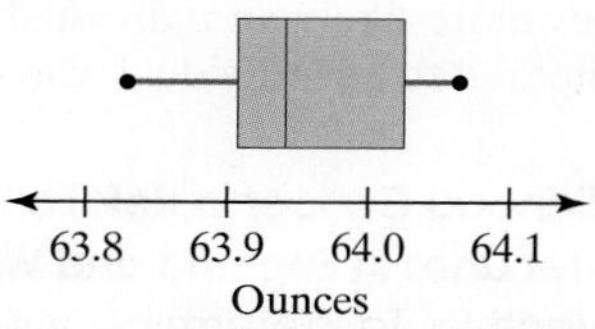

(b) Should the assembly line be shut down so that the machine can be recalibrated? Use a 0.01 level of significance. Yes

(c) Explain why a level of significance of $\alpha = 0.01$ might be more reasonable than $\alpha = 0.1$. [*Hint:* Consider the consequences of incorrectly rejecting the null hypothesis.]

25. Volume of Apple Stock In 2007, Apple stock had a mean daily volume of 35.1 million shares, according to Yahoo!Finance. A random sample of 40 trading days in 2010 resulted in a sample mean of 23.6 million shares with a standard deviation of 11.7 million shares. (b) Yes

(a) Based on the histogram and boxplot shown (from StatCrunch), why is a large sample necessary to conduct a hypothesis test about the mean? Skewed right with outliers

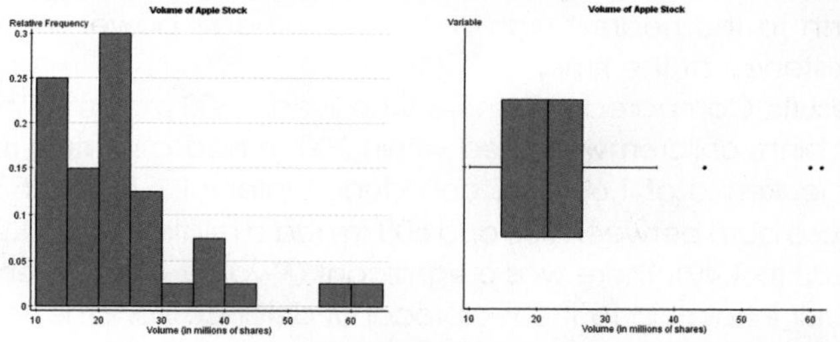

(b) Does the evidence suggest that the volume of Apple stock has changed since 2007? Use the $\alpha = 0.05$ level of significance.

26. Volume of Google Stock Google became a publicly traded company in August 2004. Initially, the stock traded over 10 million shares each day! Since the initial offering, the volume of stock traded daily has decreased substantially. In 2007, the mean daily volume in Google stock was 5.44 million shares, according to Yahoo!Finance. A random sample of 35 trading days in 2010 resulted in a sample mean of 3.28 million shares with a standard deviation of 1.68 million shares.

(a) Based on the histogram and boxplot shown (from StatCrunch), why is a large sample necessary to conduct a hypothesis test about the mean? Skewed right with outliers

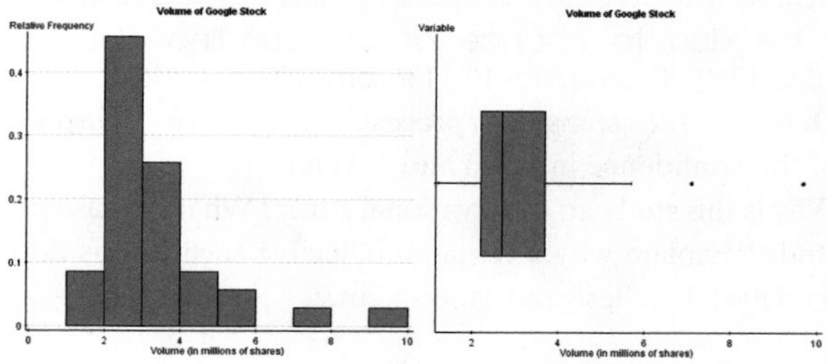

(b) Does the evidence suggest that the volume of Google stock has changed since 2007? Use the $\alpha = 0.05$ level of significance. Yes

27. Using Confidence Intervals to Test Hypotheses Test the hypotheses in Problem 23 by constructing a 99% confidence interval. (0.0677, 0.2459); do not reject H_0

28. Using Confidence Intervals to Test Hypotheses Test the hypotheses in Problem 24 by constructing a 95% confidence interval. (63.987, 64.027); reject H_0

29. Using Confidence Intervals to Test Hypotheses Test the hypotheses in Problem 25 by constructing a 95% confidence interval. (19.858, 27.342); reject H_0

30. Using Confidence Intervals to Test Hypotheses Test the hypotheses in Problem 26 by constructing a 95% confidence interval. (2.703, 3.857); reject H_0

31. Statistical Significance versus Practical Significance A math teacher claims that she has developed a review course that increases the scores of students on the math portion of the SAT exam. Based on data from the College Board, SAT scores are normally distributed with $\mu = 515$. The teacher obtains a random sample of 1800 students, puts them through the review class, and finds that the mean SAT math score of the 1800 students is 519 with a standard deviation of 111.

(a) State the null and alternative hypotheses. (b) Reject H_0

(b) Test the hypothesis at the $\alpha = 0.10$ level of significance. Is a mean SAT math score of 519 significantly higher than 515?

(c) Do you think that a mean SAT math score of 519 versus 515 will affect the decision of a school admissions administrator? In other words, does the increase in the score have any practical significance?

(d) Test the hypothesis at the $\alpha = 0.10$ level of significance with $n = 400$ students. Assume the same sample statistics. Is a sample mean of 519 significantly more than 515? What do you conclude about the impact of large samples on the *P*-value ? Do not reject H_0

32. Statistical Significance versus Practical Significance The manufacturer of a daily dietary supplement claims that its product will help people lose weight. The company obtains a random sample of 950 adult males aged 20 to 74 who take the supplement and finds their mean weight loss after 8 weeks to be 0.9 pound with standard deviation weight loss of 7.2 pounds. (a) H_0: $\mu = 0$ pound; H_1: $\mu > 0$ pound

(a) State the null and alternative hypotheses.

(b) Test the hypothesis at the $\alpha = 0.1$ level of significance. Is a mean weight loss of 0.9 pound significant?

(c) Do you think that a mean weight loss of 0.9 pound is worth the expense and commitment of a daily dietary supplement? In other words, does the weight loss have any practical significance? (b) $t_0 = 3.85$; P-value < 0.0001; reject H_0

(d) Test the hypothesis at the $\alpha = 0.1$ level of significance with $n = 40$ subjects. Assume the same sample statistics. Is a sample mean weight loss of 0.9 pound significantly more than 0 pound? What do you conclude about the impact of large samples on the *P*-value?

33. Sullivan Statistics Survey and Credit Card Debt According to the credit reporting agency Transunion, the mean credit card debt in the United States among individuals with credit cards for the period between April and June of 2010 was \$4951. Treating the results of the StatCrunch survey as a random sample of U.S. residents, determine whether there is evidence to suggest that credit card debt is lower than \$4951. Use the $\alpha = 0.05$ level of significance. Reject H_0

34. Sullivan Statistics Survey and Televisions According to the Nielsen's Television Audience Report, the mean number of televisions per household in 2009 was 2.9. Treating the results of the StatCrunch survey as a random sample of U.S. residents, determine whether there is evidence to suggest the number of televisions per household has risen since then. Use the $\alpha = 0.05$ level of significance. (b) Skewed right; yes; yes, large sample size

(a) Retrieve the results of the number of televisions per household from the Sullivan Statistics Survey. What is the mean and standard deviation number of televisions per household in the survey? $\bar{x} = 3.2$; $s = 1.7$

(b) Draw a boxplot of the data. Describe the shape of the distribution. Are there any outliers? Do you believe it is reasonable to use the normal model to describe the distribution of the sample mean? Why?

(c) Conduct the appropriate test to determine if the results of the survey suggest the number of televisions per household has increased since 2009. Reject H_0; P-value = 0.0126

35. Accept versus Do Not Reject The mean IQ score of humans is 100. Suppose the director of Institutional Research at Joliet Junior College (JJC) obtains a simple random sample of 40 JJC students and finds the mean IQ is 103.4 with a standard deviation of 13.2.

(a) Consider the hypotheses H_0: $\mu = 100$ versus H_1: $\mu > 100$. Explain what the director of Institutional Research is testing. Perform the test at the $\alpha = 0.05$ level of significance. Write a conclusion for the test. Do not reject H_0

(b) Consider the hypotheses H_0: $\mu = 101$ versus H_1: $\mu > 101$. Explain what the director of Institutional Research is testing. Perform the test at the $\alpha = 0.05$ level of significance. Write a conclusion for the test. Do not reject H_0

(c) Consider the hypotheses H_0: $\mu = 102$ versus H_1: $\mu > 102$. Explain what the director of Institutional Research is testing. Perform the test at the $\alpha = 0.05$ level of significance. Write a conclusion for the test. Do not reject H_0

(d) Based on the results of parts (a)–(c), write a few sentences that explain the difference between "accepting" the statement in the null hypothesis versus "not rejecting" the statement in the null hypothesis.

36. Simulation Simulate drawing 100 simple random samples of size $n = 15$ from a population that is normally distributed with mean 100 and standard deviation 15.

(a) Test the null hypothesis H_0: $\mu = 100$ versus H_1: $\mu \neq 100$ for each of the 100 simple random samples.

(b) If we test this hypothesis at the $\alpha = 0.05$ level of significance, how many of the 100 samples would you expect to result in a Type I error? 5

(c) Count the number of samples that lead to a rejection of the null hypothesis. Is it close to the expected value determined in part (b)?

(d) Describe how we know that a rejection of the null hypothesis results in making a Type I error in this situation.

37. Simulation The *exponential probability distribution* can be used to model waiting time in line or the lifetime of electronic components. Its density function is skewed right. Suppose the wait-time in a line can be modeled by the exponential distribution with $\mu = \sigma = 5$ minutes.

(a) Simulate obtaining 100 simple random samples of size $n = 10$ from the population described. That is, simulate obtaining a simple random sample of 10 individuals waiting in a line where the wait time is expected to be 5 minutes.

(b) Test the null hypothesis H_0: $\mu = 5$ versus the alternative H_1: $\mu \neq 5$ for each of the 100 simulated simple random samples.

(c) If we test this hypothesis at the $\alpha = 0.05$ level of significance, how many of the 100 samples would you expect to result in a Type I error? 5

(d) Count the number of samples that lead to a rejection of the null hypothesis. Is it close to the expected value determined in part (c)? What might account for any discrepancies?

38. Putting It Together: Analyzing a Study An abstract in a journal article is a short synopsis of the study. The following abstract is from an article in the *British Medical Journal* (BMJ). The article uses *relative risk* in the analysis, which is common in health-related studies. **Relative risk** represents how many times more likely an individual is to have some condition when compared to an individual who does not have the condition.

Childhood Cancer in Relation to Distance from High Voltage Power Lines in England and Wales: A Case-Control Study

Objective To determine whether there is an association between distance of home address at birth from high voltage power lines and the incidence of leukemia and other cancers in children in England and Wales.

Design Case-control study.

Setting Cancer registry and National Grid records.

Subjects Records of 29,081 children with cancer, including 9,700 with leukemia. Children were aged 0–14 years and born in England and Wales, 1962–95. Controls were individually matched for sex, approximate date of birth, and birth registration district. No active participation was required.

Main outcome measures Distance from home address at birth to the nearest high voltage overhead power line in existence at the time.

Results Compared with those who lived >600 m from a line at birth, children who lived within 200 m had a relative risk of leukemia of 1.69 (95% confidence interval 1.13 to 2.53); those born between 200 and 600 m had a relative risk of 1.23 (1.02 to 1.49). There was a significant (P-value < 0.01) trend in risk in relation to the reciprocal of distance from the line. No excess risk in relation to proximity to lines was found for other childhood cancers.

Conclusions There is an association between childhood leukemia and proximity of home address at birth to high voltage power lines, and the apparent risk extends to a greater distance than would have been expected from previous studies. About 4% of children in England and Wales live within 600 m of high voltage lines at birth. If the association is causal, about 1% of childhood leukemia in England and Wales would be attributable to these lines, though this estimate has considerable statistical uncertainty. There is no accepted biological mechanism to explain the epidemiological results; indeed, the relation may be due to chance or confounding. *Source*: *BMJ* 2005;330:1290 (4 June), doi:10.1136/bmj.330.7503.1290

(a) Describe the statistical process. Include an interpretation of the confidence interval and P-value.

(b) Why is this study an observational study? What is a case-control study? Explain why a research objective such as this does not lend itself to a designed experiment.

EXPLAINING THE CONCEPT

39. What's the Problem? The head of institutional research at a university believed that the mean age of full-time students was declining. In 1995, the mean age of a full-time student was known to be 27.4 years. After looking at the enrollment records of all 4934 full-time students in the current semester, he found that the mean age was 27.1 years, with a standard deviation of 7.3 years. He conducted a hypothesis of H_0: $\mu = 27.4$ years versus H_1: $\mu < 27.4$ years and obtained a P-value of 0.0019. He concluded that the mean age of full-time students did decline. Is there anything wrong with his research?

40. The procedures for testing a hypothesis regarding a population mean are robust. What does this mean?

41. Explain the difference between *statistical significance* and *practical significance*.

42. Wanna Live Longer? Become a Chief Justice The life expectancy of a male during the course of the past 100 years is approximately 27,725 days. Go to Wikipedia.com and download the data that represent the lifespan of chief justices of Canada for those who have died. Conduct a test to determine whether the evidence suggests that chief justices of Canada live longer than the general population of males. Suggest a reason why the conclusion drawn may be flawed.

Consumer Reports® Eyeglass Lenses

Eyeglasses are part medical device and part fashion statement, a marriage that has always made them a tough buy. Aside from the thousands of different frames the consumer has to choose from, various lens materials and coatings can add to the durability, and the cost, of a pair of eyeglasses. One manufacturer even goes so far as to claim that its lenses are "the most scratch-resistant plastic lenses ever made." With a claim like that, we had to test the lenses.

One test involved tumbling the lenses in a drum containing scrub pads of grit of varying size and hardness. Afterward, readings of the lenses' haze were taken on a spectrometer to determine how scratched they had become. To evaluate their scratch resistance, we measured the difference between the haze reading before and after tumbling.

The photo illustrates the difference between an uncoated lens (on the left) and the manufacturer's "scratch-resistant" lens (on the right).

The table to the right contains the haze measurements both before and after the scratch resistance test for this manufacturer. Haze difference is measured by subtracting the before score from the after score. In other words, haze difference is computed as After – Before.

Before	After	Difference
0.18	0.72	0.54
0.16	0.85	0.69
0.20	0.71	0.51
0.17	0.42	0.25
0.21	0.76	0.55
0.21	0.51	0.30

(a) Suppose it is known that the closest competitor to the manufacturer's lens has a mean haze difference of 0.6. Does the evidence indicate that this manufacturer's lenses are more scratch resistant?

(b) Write a paragraph for the readers of *Consumer Reports* magazine that explains your findings.

Note to Readers: *In many cases, our test protocol and analytical methods are more complicated than described in these examples. The data and discussions have been modified to make the material more appropriate for the audience.*

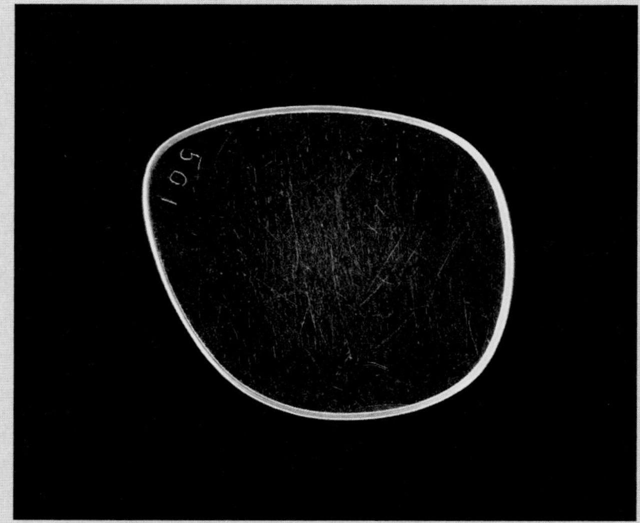

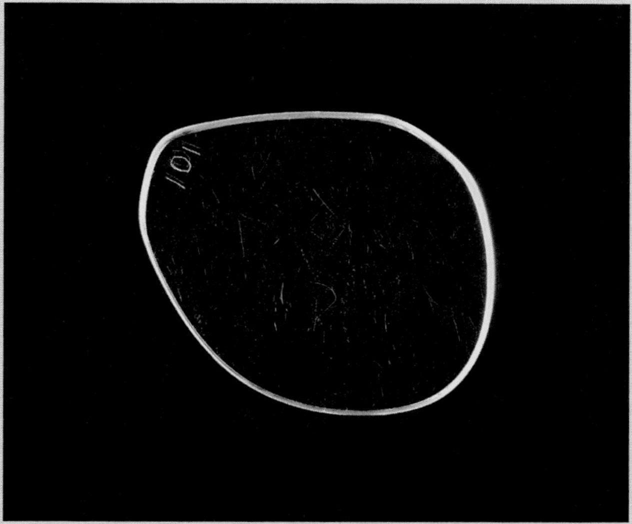

Source: © 2001 by Consumers Union of U.S., Inc., Yonkers, NY 10703-1057, a nonprofit organization. Reprinted with permission from the June 2001 issue of CONSUMER REPORTS® for educational purposes only. No commercial use or photocopying permitted. To learn more about Consumers Union, log onto www.ConsumersReports.org.

Technology Step-By-Step

Hypothesis Tests Regarding μ

TI-83/84 Plus

1. If necessary, enter raw data in L1.
2. Press STAT, highlight TESTS, and select `2:T-Test`.
3. If the data are raw, highlight DATA; make sure that List is set to L1 and Freq is set to 1. If summary statistics are known, highlight STATS and enter the summary statistics. For the value of μ_0, enter the value of the mean stated in the null hypothesis.
4. Select the direction of the alternative hypothesis.
5. Highlight **Calculate** or **Draw** and press ENTER. The TI-83/84 gives the *P*-value.

MINITAB

1. Enter raw data in column C1.
2. Select the **Stat** menu, highlight **Basic Statistics**, then highlight **1-Sample t . . .** .
3. If you have raw data, enter C1 in the cell marked "Samples in columns". If you have summary statistics, select the "Summarized data" radio button. Enter the value of the sample size, sample mean, and sample standard deviation. Check the box for "Perform hypothesis test" and enter the hypothesized mean (this is the value of the mean stated in the null hypothesis). Click Options and choose the direction of the alternative hypothesis. Click OK twice.

Excel

1. Enter raw data into Column A.
2. Load the XLSTAT Add-in, if necessary.
3. Select the XLSTAT menu and highlight Parametric tests. Select One-sample t-test and z-test.
4. Place the cursor in the Data: cell and then highlight the data in the spreadsheet. Check Student's *t*-test.
5. Click the Options tab. Choose the appropriate direction of the alternative hypothesis. Enter the mean stated in the null hypothesis in the Theoretical mean: cell. Enter the level of significance required for a confidence interval. For example, enter 10 for a 90% confidence interval.

StatCrunch

1. If you have raw data, enter them into the spreadsheet. Name the column variable.
2. Select **Stat**, highlight **T Statistics**, select **One sample**, and then choose either **with data** or **with summary**.
3. If you chose **with data**, select the column that has the observations, then click Next>. If you chose **with summary**, enter the mean, standard deviation, and sample size. Click Next>.
4. Choose the hypothesis test radio button. Enter the value of the mean stated in the null hypothesis and choose the direction of the alternative hypothesis from the pull-down menu. Click Calculate.

10.4 PUTTING IT TOGETHER: WHICH METHOD DO I USE?

OBJECTIVE 1 Determine the appropriate hypothesis test to perform

1 Determine the Appropriate Hypothesis Test to Perform

Perhaps the most difficult aspect of testing hypotheses is determining which hypothesis test to conduct. To assist in the decision making, we present Figure 20, which shows which approach to take in testing hypotheses for the three parameters discussed in this chapter.

Figure 20

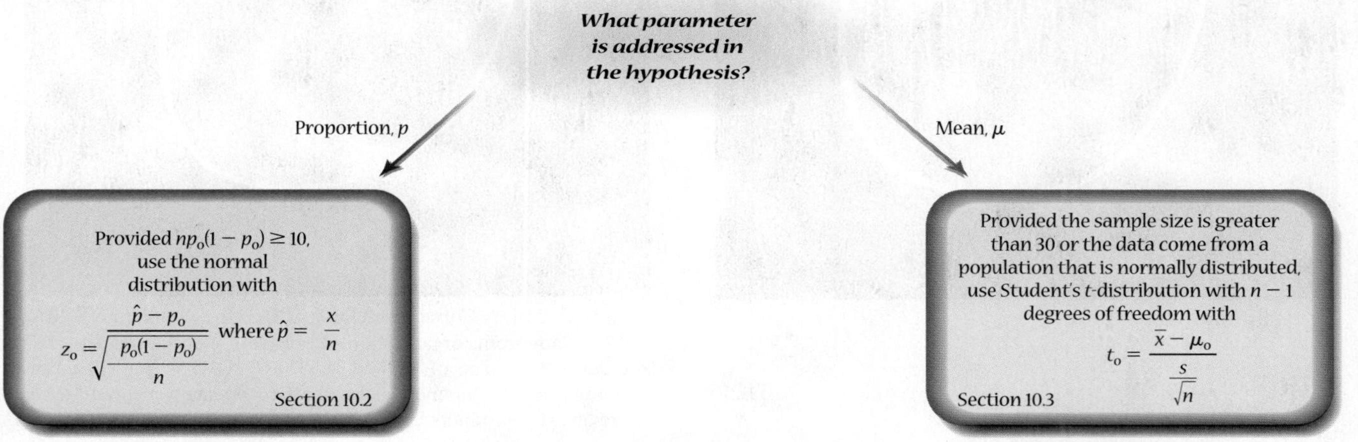

What parameter is addressed in the hypothesis?
Proportion, p
Mean, μ
Provided $np_0(1-p_0) \geq 10$, use the normal distribution with
$z_0 = \dfrac{\hat{p}-p_0}{\sqrt{\dfrac{p_0(1-p_0)}{n}}}$ where $\hat{p} = \dfrac{x}{n}$
Section 10.2
Provided the sample size is greater than 30 or the data come from a population that is normally distributed, use Student's t-distribution with $n-1$ degrees of freedom with
$t_0 = \dfrac{\bar{x}-\mu_0}{\dfrac{s}{\sqrt{n}}}$
Section 10.3

2. H_0: $p = 0.5$, H_1: $p > 0.5$, $z_0 = 2.12$, P-value $= 0.0170$; reject H_0 3. H_0: $\mu = 25$, H_1: $\mu \neq 25$, $t_0 = -0.738$, P-value $= 0.4729$; do not reject H_0

10.4 ASSESS YOUR UNDERSTANDING

SKILL BUILDING

1. A simple random sample of size $n = 19$ is drawn from a population that is normally distributed. The sample mean is found to be 0.8, and the sample standard deviation is found to be 0.4. Test whether the population mean is less than 1.0 at the $\alpha = 0.01$ level of significance. P-value $= 0.0214$; do not reject H_0

2. A simple random sample of size $n = 200$ individuals with a valid driver's license is asked if they drive an American-made automobile. Of the 200 individuals surveyed, 115 responded that they drive an American-made automobile. Determine if a majority of those with a valid driver's license drive an American-made automobile at the $\alpha = 0.05$ level of significance.

3. A simple random sample of size $n = 15$ is drawn from a population that is normally distributed. The sample mean is found to be 23.8, and the sample standard deviation is found to be 6.3. Is the population mean different from 25 at the $\alpha = 0.01$ level of significance?

4. A simple random sample of size $n = 65$ is drawn from a population. The sample mean is found to be 583.1, and the sample standard deviation is found to be 114.9. Is the population mean different from 600 at the $\alpha = 0.1$ level of significance?

5. A simple random sample of size $n = 40$ is drawn from a population. The sample mean is found to be 108.5, and the sample standard deviation is found to be 17.9. Is the population mean greater than 100 at the $\alpha = 0.05$ level of significance?

6. A simple random sample of size $n = 320$ adults was asked their favorite ice cream flavor. Of the 320 individuals surveyed, 58 responded that they preferred mint chocolate chip. Do less than 25% of adults prefer mint chocolate chip ice cream? Use the $\alpha = 0.01$ level of significance.

APPLYING THE CONCEPTS

7. Smarter Kids? Does playing Mozart for unborn babies result in children with higher IQs? A psychologist obtains a random sample of 20 mothers in the first trimester of their pregnancy. The mothers are asked to play Mozart in the house at least 30 minutes each day until they give birth. After 5 years, the child is administered an IQ test. We know that IQs are normally distributed with a mean of 100. If the IQs of the 20 children in the study result in a sample mean of 104.2, and a sample standard deviation of 14.7, is there evidence that the children have higher IQs? Use the $\alpha = 0.05$ level of significance.

8. The Atomic Bomb In October 1945, the Gallup organization asked 1487 randomly sampled Americans, "Do you think we can develop a way to protect ourselves from atomic bombs in case other countries tried to use them against us?" with 788 responding yes. Did a majority of Americans feel the United States could develop a way to protect itself from atomic bombs in 1945? Use the $\alpha = 0.05$ level of significance.

9. Tattoos In 2001, 23% of American university undergraduate students had at least one tattoo. A health practitioner suspects that the percent has changed since then. She obtains a random sample of 1026 university undergraduates and finds that 254 have at least one tattoo. Is this sufficient evidence to conclude that the proportion is different from 0.23 at the $\alpha = 0.1$ level of significance?

10. Number of Credit Cards Among individuals who have credit cards in 2010, the mean number of cards is 3.5 according to the Federal Reserve Bank of Boston. Treat the individuals who have credit cards in the Sullivan Statistics Survey as a simple random sample of credit card holders. The $n = 160$ individuals have a mean of 3.3 cards and a standard deviation of 2.3 cards. Do the results of the survey imply that the mean number of cards per individual is less than 3.5? Use the $\alpha = 0.05$ level of significance. No; do not reject H_0

11. Toner Cartridge The manufacturer of a toner cartridge claims the mean number of printouts is 10,000 for each cartridge. A consumer advocate is concerned that the actual mean number of printouts is lower. He selects a random sample of 14 such cartridges and obtains the following number of printouts:

9,600	10,300	9,000	10,750	9,490	9,080	9,655
9,520	10,070	9,999	10,470	8,920	9,964	10,330

(a) Because the sample size is small, he must verify that the number of printouts is normally distributed and the sample does not contain any outliers. The normal probability plot and boxplot are shown. Are the conditions for testing the hypothesis satisfied? Yes

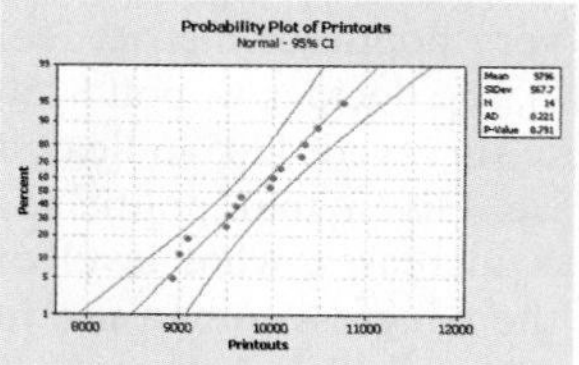

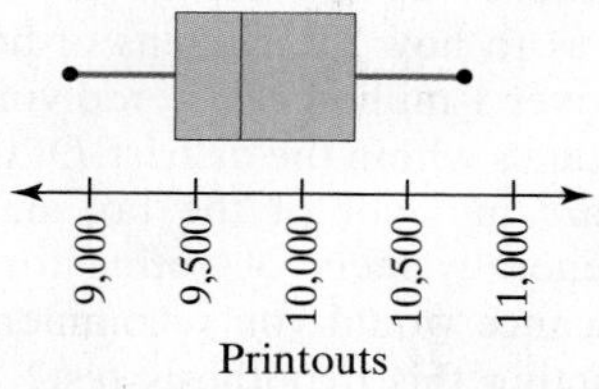

(b) Are the consumer advocate's concerns founded? Use the $\alpha = 0.05$ level of significance.

12. Vehicle Emission Inspection A certain vehicle emission inspection station advertises that the wait time for customers is less than 8 minutes. A local resident is skeptical and collects a random sample of 49 wait times for customers at the testing station. He finds that the sample mean is 7.34 minutes, with a standard deviation of 3.2 minutes. Does the sample evidence support the resident's skepticism? Use the $\alpha = 0.01$ level of significance. Do not reject H_0: $\mu = 8$ vs. H_1: $\mu < 8$

13. Lights Out With a previous contractor, the mean time to replace a streetlight was 3.2 days. A city councilwoman thinks that the new contractor is not getting the streetlights replaced as quickly. She selects a random sample of 12 streetlight service calls and obtains the following times to replacement (in days).

6.2	7.1	5.4	5.5	7.5	2.6
4.3	2.9	3.7	0.7	5.6	1.7

(a) Because the sample size is small, she must verify that replacement time is normally distributed and the sample does not contain any outliers. The normal probability plot and boxplot are shown. Are the conditions for testing the hypothesis satisfied? Yes

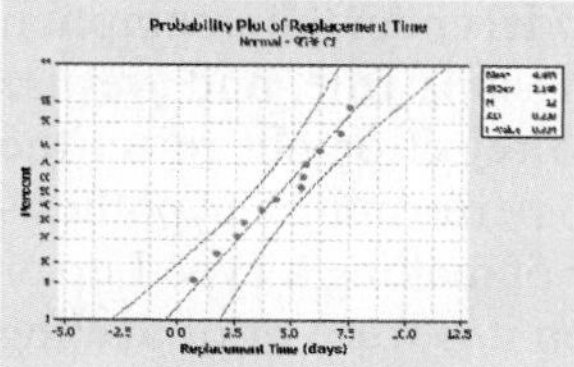

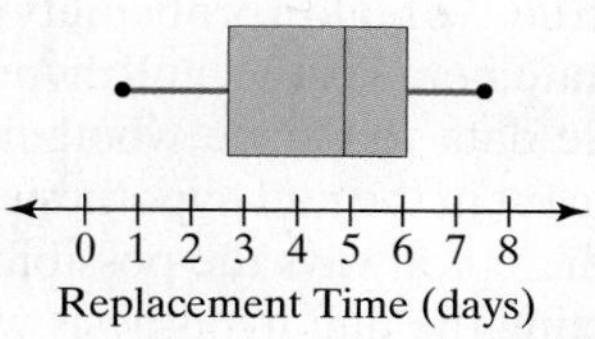

6. H_0: $p = 0.25$, H_1: $p < 0.25$, $z_0 = -2.84$, P-value $= 0.0023$; reject H_0 7. H_0: $\mu = 100$, H_1: $\mu > 100$, $t_0 = 1.28$, P-value $= 0.1084$; do not reject H_0
8. H_0: $p = 0.5$, H_1: $p > 0.5$, $z_0 = 2.31$, P-value $= 0.0104$; reject H_0 9. H_0: $p = 0.23$, H_1: $p \neq 0.23$, $z_0 = 1.37$, P-value $= 0.1706$; do not reject H_0

(b) Is there enough evidence to support the councilwoman's belief at the $\alpha = 0.05$ level of significance?

14. Text while Driving According to the research firm Toluna, the proportion of individuals who text while driving is 0.26. Suppose a random sample of 60 individuals are asked to disclose if they text while driving. Results of the survey are shown next, where 0 indicates no and 1 indicates yes. Do the data contradict the results of Toluna? Use the $\alpha = 0.05$ level of significance.

0	0	0	0	0	0	1	0	0	1
0	0	1	1	1	0	1	1	1	0
1	0	0	0	0	0	0	1	0	1
1	0	1	0	1	0	0	0	0	0
0	1	1	0	0	0	0	0	0	1
0	1	1	0	1	0	0	0	0	1

15. Political Decision Politicians often form their positions on various policies through polling. Suppose the U.S. Congress is considering passage of a tax increase to pay down the national debt. National polls suggest the general population is equally split on the matter. A congresswoman wants to poll her constituency on this controversial tax increase. To get a good sense as to how the citizens of her very populous district feel (well over 1 million registered voters), she decides to poll 8250 individuals within the district. Of those surveyed, 4205 indicated they are in favor of the tax increase. Given that politicians are generally leery of voting for tax increases, what level of significance would you recommend the congresswoman use in conducting this hypothesis test? Do the results of the survey represent statistically significant evidence a majority of the district favor the tax increase? What would you recommend to the congresswoman?

16. Quality Control Suppose the mean wait-time for a telephone reservation agent at a large airline is 43 seconds. A manager with the airline is concerned that business may be lost due to customers having to wait too long for an agent. To address this concern, the manager develops new airline reservation policies that are intended to reduce the amount of time an agent needs to spend with each customer. A random sample of 250 customers results in a sample mean wait-time of 42.3 seconds with a standard deviation of 4.2 seconds. Using an $\alpha = 0.05$ level of significance, do you believe the new policies were effective? Do you think the results have any practical significance? Yes, reject H_0: $\mu = 43$; no

17. Putting It Together: Ideal Number of Children The Gallup organization conducted a survey and asked, "What do you think is the ideal number of children for a family to have?" The results of the survey are shown in the table.

Ideal Number of Children	Frequency
0	15
1	31
2	525
3	256
4	66
5	10
6	4
7	3
8	1
9	0
10	3
11	1

(a) Construct a relative frequency histogram for the ideal number of children. Comment on the shape of the distribution. Skewed right (c) $\bar{x} = 2.47$; $s = 1.02$

(b) What is the mode ideal number of children? 2

(c) Determine the mean and standard deviation number of children. Round your answers to the nearest hundredth.

(d) Explain why a large sample size is needed to perform any inference regarding this population. Skewed right

(e) In May 1997, the ideal number of children was considered to be 2.64. Do the results of this poll indicate that people's beliefs as to the ideal number of children have changed? Use $\alpha = 0.05$. Yes, reject H_0

11. (b) H_0: $\mu = 10{,}000$, H_1: $\mu < 10{,}000$, $t_0 = -1.343$, P-value $= 0.1012$, do not reject H_0
13. (b) H_0: $\mu = 3.2$, H_1: $\mu > 3.2$, $t_0 = 1.989$, P-value $= 0.0361$; reject H_0 14. H_0: $p = 0.026$ vs H_1: $p \neq 0.26$; do not reject H_0
15. Likely $\alpha = 0.01$ or 0.05: it depends on α since P-value $= 0.039$

CHAPTER 10 REVIEW

Summary

In this chapter, we discussed hypothesis testing. A statement is made regarding a population parameter, which leads to a null, H_0, and alternative hypothesis, H_1. The null hypothesis is a statement of "no change" or "no difference" and assumed to be true. We build a probability model under the assumption the statement in the null hypothesis is true, and we use sample data to decide whether to reject or not reject the statement in the null hypothesis. In performing a hypothesis test, there is always the possibility of making a Type I error (rejecting the null hypothesis when it is true) or of making a Type II error (not rejecting the null hypothesis when it is false). The probability of making a Type I error is equal to the level of significance, α, of the test. We discussed hypothesis tests on the parameters p and μ in this chapter.

The first test introduced was hypothesis tests about a population proportion p. Provided certain requirements were satisfied (simple random sample or randomized experiment, independence, and a large sample size), we were able to use the normal model to assess statements made in the null hypothesis.

Then we discussed hypothesis testing on the mean. Here we also required a simple random sample (or randomized experiment) and independence, but we also required that either the sample come from a population that is normally distributed with no outliers or a large ($n \geq 30$) sample size. When dealing with small sample sizes, we tested the normality requirement with a normal probability plot and the outlier requirement with a boxplot.

Both hypothesis tests were performed using both the classical method and the *P*-value approach. The *P*-value approach to testing hypotheses has appeal because the rejection rule is always to reject the null hypothesis if the *P*-value is less than the level of significance, α.

Vocabulary

Hypothesis (p. 430)
Hypothesis testing (p. 430)
Null hypothesis (p. 430)
Alternative hypothesis (p. 430)
Two-tailed test (p. 430)
Left-tailed test (p. 430)
Right-tailed test (p. 430)
One-tailed test (p. 431)
Type I error (p. 432)
Type II error (p. 432)
Level of significance (p. 433)
Statistically significant (p. 437)
P-value (p. 439)
Test statistic (pp. 439, 449)
Practical significance (p. 453)

Formulas

Test Statistics

- $z_0 = \dfrac{\hat{p} - p_0}{\sqrt{\dfrac{p_0(1 - p_0)}{n}}}$ follows the standard normal distribution if $np_0(1 - p_0) \geq 10$ and $n \leq 0.05N$
- $t_0 = \dfrac{\bar{x} - \mu_0}{\dfrac{s}{\sqrt{n}}}$ follows Student's *t*-distribution with $n - 1$ degrees of freedom if the population from which the sample was drawn is normal or if the sample size is large ($n \geq 30$).

Objectives

Section	You should be able to . . .	Examples	Review Exercises
10.1	1 Determine the null and alternative hypotheses (p. 429)	2	1(a), 2(a)
	2 Explain Type I and Type II errors (p. 432)	3	1(b), 1(c), 2(b), 2(c), 3, 4, 11(e)
	3 State conclusions to hypothesis tests (p. 434)	4	1(d), 1(e), 2(d), 2(e)
10.2	1 Explain the logic of hypothesis testing (p. 436)	pp. 436–439	19, 21, 22
	2 Test hypotheses about a population proportion (p. 439)	1, 2, 3	7, 8, 11, 12, 15, 16
	3 Test hypotheses about a population proportion using the binomial probability distribution (p. 443)	4	17
10.3	1 Test hypotheses about a mean (p. 449)	1, 2	5, 6, 11, 12, 13, 14, 18
	2 Understand the difference between statistical significance and practical significance (p. 453)	3	16, 18
10.4	1 Determine the appropriate hypothesis test to perform (p. 460)		5–18

Review Exercises

For Problems 1 and 2, (a) determine the null and alternative hypotheses, (b) explain what it would mean to make a Type I error, (c) explain what it would mean to make a Type II error, (d) state the conclusion that would be reached if the null hypothesis is not rejected, and (e) state the conclusion that would be reached if the null hypothesis is rejected.

1. Credit-Card Debt According to creditcard.com, the mean outstanding credit-card debt of college undergraduates was \$3173 in 2010. A researcher believes that this amount has decreased since then.

2. More Credit-Card Debt Among all credit cards issued, the proportion of cards that result in default was 0.13 in 2010. A credit analyst with Visa believes this proportion is different today.

3. A test is conducted at the $\alpha = 0.05$ level of significance. What is the probability of a Type I error? 0.05

4. β is computed to be 0.113. What is the probability of a Type II error? What is the power of the test? How would you interpret the power of the test? 0.113; 0.887

5. To test H_0: $\mu = 100$ versus H_1: $\mu > 100$, a simple random sample of size $n = 35$ is obtained from an unknown distribution. The sample mean is 104.3 and the sample standard deviation is 12.4.

(a) To use the *t*-distribution, why must the sample size be large?

(b) Use the classical or *P*-value approach to decide whether to reject the statement in the null hypothesis at the $\alpha = 0.05$ level of significance. Reject H_0; *P*-value = 0.0240

6. To test H_0: $\mu = 50$ versus H_1: $\mu \neq 50$, a simple random sample of size $n = 15$ is obtained from a population that is normally distributed. The sample mean is 48.1 and the sample standard deviation is 4.1.

(a) Why is it likely that the population from which the sample was drawn is normally distributed? Small sample size

(b) Use the classical or *P*-value approach to decide whether to reject the statement in the null hypothesis at the $\alpha = 0.05$ level of significance. Do not reject H_0; *P*-value = 0.0943

In Problems 7 and 8, test the hypothesis at the $\alpha = 0.05$ level of significance, using (a) the classical approach and (b) the P-value approach. Be sure to verify the requirements of the test.

7. $H_0: p = 0.6$ versus $H_1: p > 0.6$
$n = 250; x = 165$ Reject H_0

8. $H_0: p = 0.35$ versus $H_1: p \neq 0.35$
$n = 420; x = 138$ Do not reject H_0

9. Sneeze According to work done by Nick Wilson of Otago University Wellington, the proportion of individuals who cover their mouth when sneezing is 0.733. As part of a school project, Mary decides to confirm the work of Professor Wilson by observing 100 randomly selected individuals sneeze and finds that 78 covered their mouth when sneezing.

(a) What are the null and alternative hypotheses for Mary's project? $H_0: p = 0.733$ vs. $H_1: p \neq 0.733$

(b) Verify the requirements that allow use of the normal model to test the hypothesis are satisfied.

(c) Does the sample evidence contradict Professor Wilson's findings? No; P-value = 0.2892

10. Emergency Room The proportion of patients who visit the emergency room (ER) and die within the year is 0.05. *Source:* SuperFreakonomics. Suppose a hospital administrator is concerned that his ER has a higher proportion of patients who die within the year. In a random sample of 250 patients who have visited the ER in the past year, 17 have died. Should the administrator be concerned? A little; P-value = 0.0951

11. Linear Rotary Bearing A linear rotary bearing is designed so that the distance between the retaining rings is 0.875 inch. The quality-control manager suspects that the manufacturing process needs to be recalibrated because the mean distance between the retaining rings is greater than 0.875 inch. In a random sample of 36 bearings, he finds the sample mean distance between the retaining rings is 0.876 inch with standard deviation 0.005 inch.

(a) Are the requirements for conducting a hypothesis test satisfied? Yes (b) $H_0: \mu = 0.875$ vs. $H_1: \mu > 0.875$

(b) State the null and alternative hypotheses.

(c) The quality-control manager decides to use an $\alpha = 0.01$ level of significance. Why do you think this level of significance was chosen? The consequences of making a Type I error

(d) Does the evidence suggest the machine be recalibrated? No

(e) What does it mean for the quality-control engineer to make a Type I error? A Type II error?

12. Normal Temperature Carl Reinhold August Wunderlich said that the mean temperature of humans is 98.6°F. Researchers Philip Mackowiak, Steven Wasserman, and Myron Levine [*JAMA*, Sept. 23–30 1992; 268(12):1578–80] thought that the mean temperature of humans is less than 98.6°F. They measured the temperature of 148 healthy adults 1 to 4 times daily for 3 days, obtaining 700 measurements. The sample data resulted in a sample mean of 98.2°F and a sample standard deviation of 0.7°F. Test whether the mean temperature of humans is less than 98.6°F at the $\alpha = 0.01$ level of significance. Reject H_0; P-value < 0.0001

13. Conforming Golf Balls The U.S. Golf Association requires that golf balls have a diameter that is 1.68 inches. To determine if Maxfli XS golf balls conform to USGA standards, a random sample of Maxfli XS golf balls was selected. Their diameters are shown in the table.

1.683	1.677	1.681
1.685	1.678	1.686
1.684	1.684	1.673
1.685	1.682	1.674

Source: Michael McCraith, Joliet Junior College

(a) Because the sample size is small, the engineer must verify that the diameter is normally distributed and the sample does not contain any outliers. The normal probability plot and boxplot are shown. Are the conditions for testing the hypothesis satisfied? Yes (b) (1.6781, 1.6839); do not reject H_0

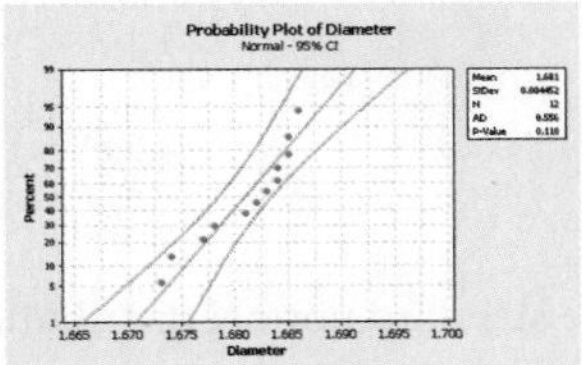

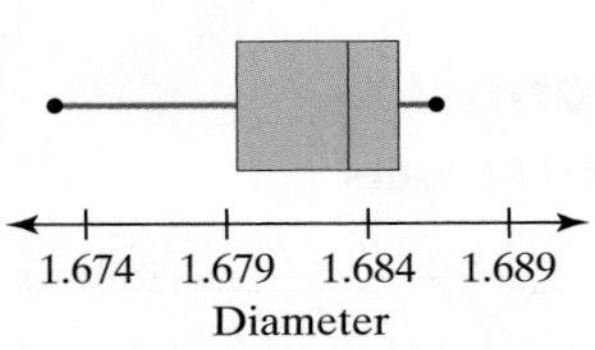

(b) Construct a 95% confidence interval to judge whether the golf balls conform to USGA standards. Be sure to state the null and alternative hypothesis and write a conclusion.

14. Studying Enough? It is suggested by college mathematics instructors that students spend 2 hours outside class studying for every hour in class. So, for a 4-credit-hour math class, students should spend at least 8 hours (480 minutes) studying each week. The given data, from Michael Sullivan's College Algebra class, represent the time spent on task recorded in MyMathLab (in minutes) for randomly selected students during the third week of the semester. Determine if the evidence suggests students may not, in fact, be following the advice. That is, does the evidence suggest students are studying less than 480 minutes each week? Use $\alpha = 0.05$ level of significance. *Note*: A normal probability plot and boxplot indicate that the data come from a population that is normally distributed with no outliers.

504	267	220	322	538	542
428	481	413	302	602	

Source: MyMathLab

15. Sleeping Patterns of Pregnant Women A random sample of 150 pregnant women indicated that 81 napped at least twice per week. Do a majority of pregnant women nap at least twice a week? Use the $\alpha = 0.05$ level of significance. *Source:* National Sleep Foundation Do not reject H_0

16. Grim Report Throughout the country, the proportion of first-time, first-year community college students who return for their second year of studies is 0.52 according to the Community College Survey of Student Engagement. Suppose a community college institutes new policies geared toward increasing student retention. The first year this policy was in place there were 2843 first-time, first-year students. Of these students, 1516 returned for their second year of studies. Treat these students as a random sample of all first-time, first-year students. Do a statistically significant higher proportion of students return for their second year under this policy? Use the $\alpha = 0.1$ level of significance.

14. Do not reject H_0; P-value = 0.0730

Would you say the results are practically significant? In other words, do you believe the results are significant enough that other community colleges might consider emulating these same policies? Statistically significant

17. Teen Prayer In 1995, 40% of adolescents stated they prayed daily. A researcher wanted to know whether this percentage has risen since then. He surveys 40 adolescents and finds that 18 pray on a daily basis. Is this evidence that the proportion of adolescents who pray daily has increased at the $\alpha = 0.05$ level of significance? No

18. A New Teaching Method A large university has a college algebra enrollment of 5000 students each semester. Because of space limitations, the university decides to offer its college algebra courses in a self-study format in which students learn independently, but have access to tutors and other help in a lab setting. Historically, students in traditional college algebra scored 73.2 points on the final exam, and the coordinator of this course is concerned that test scores are going to decrease in the new format. At the end of the first semester using the new delivery system, 3851 students took the final exams and had a mean score of 72.8 and a standard deviation of 12.3. Treating these students as a simple random sample of all students, determine whether or not the scores decreased significantly at the $\alpha = 0.05$ level of significance. Do you think that the decrease in scores has any practical significance?

19. Explain the difference between "accepting" and "not rejecting" a null hypothesis. 18. Reject H_0; no practical significance

20. According to the American Time Use Survey, the mean number of hours each day Americans age 15 and older spend eating and drinking is 1.22. A researcher wanted to know if Americans age 15 to 19 spent less time eating and drinking. After surveying 50 Americans age 15 to 19 and running the appropriate hypothesis test, she obtained a *P*-value of 0.0329. State the null and alternative hypothesis this researcher used and interpret the *P*-value. H_0: $\mu = 1.22$ vs. H_1: $\mu < 1.22$

21. Explain the procedure for testing a hypothesis using the Classical Approach. What is the criterion for judging whether to reject the null hypothesis?

22. Explain the procedure for testing a hypothesis using the *P*-value Approach. What is the criterion for judging whether to reject the null hypothesis?

Problems in the chapter test are labeled by section.objective. For example, 2.3 means Section 2, Objective 3.

CHAPTER TEST

1. According to the American Time Use Survey, adult Americans spent 42.6 minutes per day on phone calls and answering or writing email in 2006.

1.1 **(a)** Suppose that we want to judge whether the amount of daily time spent on phone calls and answering or writing email has increased. Write the appropriate null and alternative hypothesis. H_0: $\mu = 42.6$; H_1: $\mu > 42.6$

1.3 **(b)** The sample data indicated that the null hypothesis should be rejected. Write a conclusion.

1.2 **(c)** Explain what it would mean if we made a Type I error in conducting the test from part (a).

1.2 **(d)** Explain what it would mean if we made a Type II error in conducting the test from part (a).

2. The trade magazine *QSR* routinely examines fast-food drive-through service times. Recent research by the magazine indicates that the mean time a car spends in a McDonald's drive-through is 167.1 seconds. A McDonald's manager in Salt Lake City feels that she has instituted a drive-through policy that results in lower drive-through service times. A random sample of 70 cars results in a mean service time of 163.9 seconds with standard deviation 15.3 seconds. Determine whether the policy is effective in reducing drive-through service times.

1.1 **(a)** State the null and alternative hypotheses.

(b) Because the cost of instituting the policy is quite high, the quality-control researcher at McDonald's chooses to test the hypothesis using an $\alpha = 0.01$ level of significance. Why is this a good idea?

3.1 **(c)** Conduct the appropriate test to determine if the policy is effective. Do not reject H_0

3.1 **3.** Perhaps you have been asked this question: "Did you get your 8 hours of sleep last night?" In a recent survey of 151 postpartum women, the folks at the National Sleep Foundation found that the mean sleep time was 7.8 hours, with a standard deviation of 1.4 hours. Does the evidence suggest that postpartum women do not get enough sleep? Use $\alpha = 0.05$ level of significance. Reject H_0

2. (a) H_0: $\mu = 167.1$; H_1: $\mu < 167.1$

3.1 **4.** The outside diameter of a manufactured part must be 1.3825 inches, according to customer specifications. The data shown represent a random sample of 10 parts. Use a 95% confidence interval to judge whether the part has been manufactured to specifications.

Note: A normal probability plot and boxplot indicate that the data come from a population that is normally distributed with no outliers. (1.3824, 1.3828); do not reject H_0

1.3821	1.3830	1.3823	1.3829	1.3830
1.3829	1.3826	1.3825	1.3823	1.3824

Source: Dennis Johnson, student at Joliet Junior College

2.2 **5.** In many parliamentary procedures, a supermajority is defined as an excess of 60% of voting members. In a poll conducted by the Gallup organization on May 10, 1939, 1561 adult Americans were asked, "Do you think the United States will have to fight Japan within your lifetime?" Of the 1561 respondents, 954 said no. Does this constitute sufficient evidence that a supermajority of Americans did not feel the United States would have to fight Japan within their lifetimes? Do not reject H_0

3.2 **6.** A Zone diet is one with a 40%–30%–30% distribution of carbohydrate, protein, and fat, respectively, and is based on the book *Enter the Zone*. In a study conducted by researchers Christopher Gardner and associates, 79 subjects were administered the Zone diet. After 12 months, the mean weight loss was 1.6 kg, with a standard deviation of 5.4 kg. Do these results suggest that the weight loss was statistically significantly greater than zero at the 0.05 level of significance?

Do you believe the weight loss has any practical significance? Why? *Source:* Christopher D. Gardner, Alexandre Kiazand, and Sofiya Alhassan, et al. "Comparison of the Atkins, Zone, Ornish, and LEARN Diets for Change in Weight and Related Risk Factors among Overweight Premenopausal Women. The A to Z Weight Loss Study: A Randomized Trial." *Journal of the American Medical Association,* March 2007. Reject H_0; not practical

2.3 **7.** According to the Pew Research Center, the proportion of the American population who use only a cellular telephone (no land line) is 0.37. Jason conducts a survey of thirty 20- to 24-year-olds who live on their own and finds that 16 do not have a land line to their home. Does this provide sufficient evidence to conclude that the proportion of 20- to 24-year-olds who live on their own and don't have a land line is greater than 0.37? Use an $\alpha = 0.10$ level of significance. Reject H_0

Making an Informed Decision

Selecting a Mutual Fund

Suppose you have just received a $1000 bonus at your job. Rather than waste the money on frivolous items, you decide to invest the money so that you can apply it toward the purchase of a home one day. Many investment options are available. Your family and friends, who have some experience in investing, recommend mutual funds. Which mutual funds should you choose?

Thousands of mutual funds are available to invest in. According to Wikipedia, "a **mutual fund** is a professionally managed type of collective investment scheme that pools money from many investors and invests typically in investment securities (stocks, bonds, and so on)."

(a) Research the various classifications (Growth, Value, and so on) of mutual funds. Decide on a particular mutual fund classification.

(b) Go to www.morningstar.com. Morningstar is a mutual fund rating agency that ranks mutual funds according to a star rating. The 5-star rating system divides the mutual funds into percentile classes. A mutual fund with a 5-star rating is in the top 20% of all mutual funds in the category. Choose a mutual fund that has at least a 4-star rating and has been around for at least 5 years.

(c) Research the historical monthly rates of return of the mutual fund you selected in part (b). You will use two criteria in selecting a mutual fund. First, the mean rate of return of the fund over the past 48 months must exceed 7%. Second, the proportion of the past 48 months where the rate of return is positive must exceed 0.7. Treat the selected months as a random sample of rates of return. Conduct the appropriate tests to see if the mutual fund you selected meets your criteria.

The Chapter 10 Case Study is located on the CD that accompanies this text.

11 Inferences on Two Samples

OUTLINE

Making an Informed Decision

You have decided to purchase a car. A couple areas of concern for you are: 1. What kind of gas mileage does the car get? 2. Will the car hold its value? See the Decisions Project on page 514.

PUTTING IT TOGETHER

In Chapters 9 and 10 we discussed inferences regarding a single population parameter. The inferential methods presented in those chapters will be modified slightly in this chapter so that we can compare two population parameters.

The first section presents inferential methods for comparing two population proportions. The first order of business is to decide whether the data are obtained from an independent or dependent sample—simply put, we determine if the observations in one sample are somehow related to the observations in the other. We then discuss methods for comparing two proportions from both an independent and dependent sample.

Section 11.2 presents inferential methods used to handle matched-pairs designs (Section 1.6, p. 49) when the response variable is quantitative. For example, we might want to know whether the reaction time in an individual's dominant hand is different from the reaction time in the nondominant hand. To conduct this test, we might randomly choose the individual's hand to begin with and measure the reaction time in each hand. We could then determine if the reaction time is significantly different.

Section 11.3 presents inferential methods used to handle completely randomized designs when there are two levels of treatment and the response variable is quantitative (Section 1.6, pp. 47–49). For example, we might randomly divide 100 volunteers who have a common cold into two groups, a control group and an experimental group. The control group would receive a placebo and the experimental group would receive a specific amount of some experimental drug. The response variable might be time until the cold symptoms go away.

We wrap up the chapter with a Putting It Together section. One of the more difficult aspects of inference is determining which inferential method to use. This section helps develop this skill.

11.1 INFERENCE ABOUT TWO POPULATION PROPORTIONS

Preparing for This Section Before getting started, review the following:

- Completely randomized design (Section 1.6, pp 47–49)
- Matched-pairs design (Section 1.6, p. 49)
- Estimating a population proportion (Section 9.1, pp. 391–401)
- Hypothesis tests about a population proportion (Section 10.2, pp. 436–444)
- Statistical versus practical significance (Section 10.3, pp. 453–454)

OBJECTIVES

1 Distinguish between independent and dependent sampling

2 Test hypotheses regarding two proportions from independent samples

3 Construct and interpret confidence intervals for the difference between two population proportions

4 Test hypotheses regarding two proportions from dependent samples

5 Determine the sample size necessary for estimating the difference between two population proportions

1 Distinguish between Independent and Dependent Sampling

Let's consider two scenarios:

Note to Instructor

If you like, you can print out and distribute the Preparing for This Section quiz located in the Instructor's Resource Center. The purpose of this quiz is to verify the students have the prerequisite knowledge for the section.

Scenario 1: Among competing acne medications, does one perform better than the other? To answer this question, researchers applied Medication A to one part of the subject's face and Medication B to a different part of the subject's face to determine the proportion of subjects whose acne cleared up. The part of the face that received Medication A was randomly determined.

Scenario 2: Do individuals who make fast-food purchases with a credit card tend to spend more than those who pay with cash? To answer this question, a marketing manager randomly selects 30 credit-card receipts and 30 cash receipts to determine if the credit-card receipts have a significantly higher dollar amount, on average.

Is there a difference in the approach taken to select the individuals in each study? Yes! In scenario 1, once an individual is selected, one part of his or her face is "matched-up" with a second part of the face. In scenario 2, the receipts selected from the credit-card group have nothing at all to do with the receipts selected from the cash group.

DEFINITIONS

A sampling method is **independent** when the individuals selected for one sample do not dictate which individuals are to be in a second sample. A sampling method is **dependent** when the individuals selected to be in one sample are used to determine the individuals in the second sample. Dependent samples are often referred to as **matched-pairs** samples. It is possible for an individual to be matched against him- or herself.

So, the sampling method in scenario 1 is dependent (or a matched-pairs sample), while the sampling method in scenario 2 is independent.

EXAMPLE 1 Distinguishing between Independent and Dependent Sampling

Problem Decide whether the sampling method is independent or dependent. Then determine whether the response variable is qualitative or quantitative.

(a) Joliet Junior College decided to implement a course redesign of its developmental mathematics program. Students either enrolled in a traditional lecture format course or a lab-based format in which lectures and homework are done using video and the course management system MyMathLab. There were 1200 students enrolled in the traditional lecture format and 300 enrolled in the lab-based format. Once the course ended, the researchers determined whether the student passed the course with an A, B, or C. The goal of the study was to determine whether the proportion of students who passed the lab-based format exceeded that of the lecture format.

(b) Do women tend to select a spouse who has an IQ higher than their own? To answer this question, researchers randomly selected 20 women and their husbands. They measured the IQ of each husband–wife team to determine if there is a significant difference in IQ.

Approach Determine whether the individuals in one group were used to determine the individuals in the other group. If so, the sampling method is dependent. If not, the sampling method is independent. Finally, consider the response variable in the study. Is it qualitative with two outcomes? If so, inferential methods based on proportions are appropriate. Is it quantitative? If so, inferential methods based on means may be appropriate.

Solution

(a) The sampling method is independent because the individuals in the lecture format are not related to the individuals in the lab-based format. The response variable is whether the student passed the course or not. Because there are two outcomes, pass or do not pass, the researchers can compare the proportion of students passing the lecture course to those passing the lab-based course.

(b) The sampling method is dependent because once a wife is selected her husband is automatically enrolled in the study. That is, the wife–husband team is "matched-up." The response variable, IQ, is quantitative.

Now Work Problem 3

In this section, we discuss inference based on proportions for both independent and dependent samples.

2 Test Hypotheses Regarding Two Proportions from Independent Samples

In Sections 9.1 and 10.2, we discussed inference regarding a single population proportion. We now discuss inference for comparing two proportions. We begin with inference comparing two proportions from independent samples.

For example, in clinical trials of the drug Nasonex, a drug that is meant to relieve allergy symptoms, 26% of patients receiving 200 micrograms (μg) of Nasonex reported a headache as a side effect, while 22% of patients receiving a placebo reported a headache as a side effect. Researchers want to determine whether the proportion of patients receiving Nasonex and complaining of headaches is significantly higher than the proportion of patients receiving the placebo and complaining of headaches.

To conduct inference about two population proportions from independent samples, we must first determine the sampling distribution of the difference of two proportions. Recall that the point estimate of a population proportion, p, is given by $\hat{p} = \frac{x}{n}$, where x is the number of the n individuals in the sample that have a specific characteristic. In addition, recall that the sampling distribution of $\hat{p}$ is approximately normal with mean $\mu_{\hat{p}} = p$ and standard deviation $\sigma_{\hat{p}} = \sqrt{\frac{p(1-p)}{n}}$, provided that $np(1-p) \geq 10$ and $n \leq 0.05N$, so $Z = \dfrac{\hat{p} - p}{\sqrt{\dfrac{p(1-p)}{n}}}$ is approximately normal with mean 0 and standard deviation 1. Using this information along with the idea of independent sampling from two populations, we obtain the sampling distribution of the difference between two proportions.

Sampling Distribution of the Difference between Two Proportions (Independent Sample)

Suppose a simple random sample of size n_1 is taken from a population where x_1 of the individuals have a specified characteristic, and a simple random sample of size n_2 is independently taken from a different population where x_2 of the individuals have a specified characteristic. The sampling distribution of $\hat{p}_1 - \hat{p}_2$, where $\hat{p}_1 = \frac{x_1}{n_1}$ and $\hat{p}_2 = \frac{x_2}{n_2}$, is approximately normal, with mean $\mu_{\hat{p}_1-\hat{p}_2} = p_1 - p_2$ and standard deviation $\sigma_{\hat{p}_1-\hat{p}_2} = \sqrt{\frac{p_1(1-p_1)}{n_1} + \frac{p_2(1-p_2)}{n_2}}$, provided that $n_1\hat{p}_1(1-\hat{p}_1) \geq 10$ and $n_2\hat{p}_2(1-\hat{p}_2) \geq 10$ and each sample size is no more than 5% of the population size. The standardized version of $\hat{p}_1 - \hat{p}_2$ is then written as

$$Z = \frac{(\hat{p}_1 - \hat{p}_2) - (p_1 - p_2)}{\sqrt{\frac{p_1(1-p_1)}{n_1} + \frac{p_2(1-p_2)}{n_2}}}$$

which has an approximate standard normal distribution.

Now that we know the approximate sampling distribution of $\hat{p}_1 - \hat{p}_2$, we can introduce a procedure that can be used to test hypotheses regarding two population proportions. We first consider the test statistic. Following the discussion for testing hypotheses on a single proportion, it seems reasonable that the test statistic for the difference of two population proportions would be

$$z_0 = \frac{(\hat{p}_1 - \hat{p}_2) - (p_1 - p_2)}{\sqrt{\frac{p_1(1-p_1)}{n_1} + \frac{p_2(1-p_2)}{n_2}}} \qquad \textbf{(1)}$$

When comparing two population proportions, the null hypothesis is a statement of "no difference" (as always), so H_0: $p_1 = p_2$. Because the null hypothesis is assumed to be true, the test assumes that $p_1 = p_2$, or $p_1 - p_2 = 0$. We also assume that both p_1 and p_2 equal p, where p is the common population proportion. If we substitute this value of p into Equation (1), we obtain

$$z_0 = \frac{(\hat{p}_1 - \hat{p}_2) - (p_1 - p_2)}{\sqrt{\frac{p_1(1-p_1)}{n_1} + \frac{p_2(1-p_2)}{n_2}}} = \frac{\hat{p}_1 - \hat{p}_2 - 0}{\sqrt{\frac{p(1-p)}{n_1} + \frac{p(1-p)}{n_2}}} = \frac{\hat{p}_1 - \hat{p}_2}{\sqrt{p(1-p)}\sqrt{\frac{1}{n_1} + \frac{1}{n_2}}} \qquad \textbf{(2)}$$

In Other Words
The pooled estimate of p is obtained by summing the number of individuals in the sample that have a certain characteristic and dividing this result by the sum of the two sample sizes.

We need a point estimate of p because it is unknown. The best point estimate of p is called the **pooled estimate of *p***, denoted $\hat{p}$, where

$$\hat{p} = \frac{x_1 + x_2}{n_1 + n_2}$$

Substituting the pooled estimate of p into Equation (2), we obtain

$$z_0 = \frac{\hat{p}_1 - \hat{p}_2}{\sigma_{\hat{p}_1 - \hat{p}_2}} = \frac{\hat{p}_1 - \hat{p}_2}{\sqrt{\hat{p}(1-\hat{p})}\sqrt{\frac{1}{n_1} + \frac{1}{n_2}}}$$

This test statistic will be used to test hypotheses regarding two population proportions.

Hypothesis Test Regarding the Difference between Two Population Proportions

To test hypotheses regarding two population proportions, p_1 and p_2, we can use the steps that follow, provided that

- the samples are independently obtained using simple random sampling or through a randomized experiment,
- $n_1\hat{p}_1(1-\hat{p}_1) \geq 10$ and $n_2\hat{p}_2(1-\hat{p}_2) \geq 10$, and
- $n_1 \leq 0.05N_1$ and $n_2 \leq 0.05N_2$ (the sample size is no more than 5% of the population size); this requirement ensures the independence necessary for a binomial experiment.

Step 1 Determine the null and alternative hypotheses. The hypotheses can be structured in one of three ways:

Two-Tailed	Left-Tailed	Right-Tailed
H_0: $p_1 = p_2$	H_0: $p_1 = p_2$	H_0: $p_1 = p_2$
H_1: $p_1 \neq p_2$	H_1: $p_1 < p_2$	H_1: $p_1 > p_2$

Note: p_1 is the population proportion for population 1, and p_2 is the population proportion for population 2.

Step 2 Select a level of significance, α, depending on the seriousness of making a Type I error.

Classical Approach

Step 3 Compute the **test statistic**

$$z_0 = \frac{\hat{p}_1 - \hat{p}_2}{\sqrt{\hat{p}(1-\hat{p})}\sqrt{\dfrac{1}{n_1} + \dfrac{1}{n_2}}}, \text{ where } \hat{p} = \frac{x_1 + x_2}{n_1 + n_2}$$

Use Table V to determine the critical value.

	Two-Tailed	Left-Tailed	Right-Tailed
Critical value	$-z_{\frac{\alpha}{2}}$ **and** $z_{\frac{\alpha}{2}}$	$-z_\alpha$	z_α

Critical region

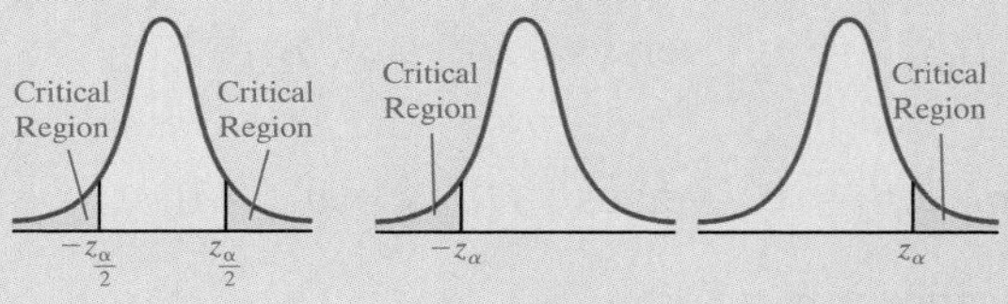

Step 4 Compare the critical value to the test statistic.

Two-Tailed	Left-Tailed	Right-Tailed
If $z_0 < -z_{\frac{\alpha}{2}}$ or $z_0 > z_{\frac{\alpha}{2}}$, reject the null hypothesis.	If $z_0 < -z_\alpha$, reject the null hypothesis.	If $z_0 > z_\alpha$, reject the null hypothesis.

P-Value Approach

By Hand Step 3 Compute the **test statistic**

$$z_0 = \frac{\hat{p}_1 - \hat{p}_2}{\sqrt{\hat{p}(1-\hat{p})}\sqrt{\dfrac{1}{n_1} + \dfrac{1}{n_2}}}, \text{ where } \hat{p} = \frac{x_1 + x_2}{n_1 + n_2}$$

Use Table V to determine the *P*-value.

Two-Tailed	Left-Tailed	Right-Tailed

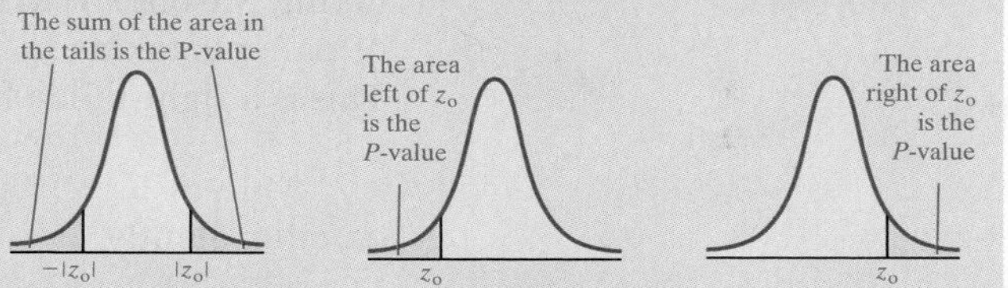

P-value $= 2P(z > |z_0|)$ P-value $= P(z < z_0)$ P-value $= P(z > z_0)$

Technology Step 3 Use a statistical spreadsheet or calculator with statistical capabilities to obtain the *P*-value. The directions for obtaining the *P*-value using the TI-83/84 Plus graphing calculator, Excel, MINITAB, and StatCrunch are in the Technology Step-by-Step on page 482.

Step 4 If *P*-value $< \alpha$, reject the null hypothesis.

Step 5 State the conclusion.

EXAMPLE 2 Testing a Hypothesis Regarding Two Population Proportions

Problem In clinical trials of Nasonex, 3774 adult and adolescent allergy patients (patients 12 years and older) were randomly divided into two groups. The patients in group 1 (experimental group) received 200 μg of Nasonex, while the patients in group 2 (control group) received a placebo. Of the 2103 patients in the experimental group, 547 reported headaches as a side effect. Of the 1671 patients in the control group, 368 reported headaches as a side effect. Is there significant evidence to conclude that the proportion of Nasonex users that experienced headaches as a side effect is greater than the proportion in the control group at the $\alpha = 0.05$ level of significance?

Approach Note that this is a completely randomized design. The response variable is whether or not the patient reports a headache. The treatments are the drugs: Nasonex or a placebo. The subjects are the 3774 adult and adolescent allergy patients.

We are attempting to determine if the evidence suggests that the proportion of patients who report a headache and are receiving Nasonex is greater than the proportion of patients who report a headache and are receiving a placebo. We will call the group that received Nasonex sample 1 and the group that received a placebo sample 2.

We must verify the requirements to perform the hypothesis test. That is, the sample must be a simple random sample or the result of a randomized experiment and $n_1\hat{p}_1(1-\hat{p}_1) \geq 10$ and $n_2\hat{p}_2(1-\hat{p}_2) \geq 10$. In addition, the sample size cannot be more than 5% of the population size. Then we follow the preceding Steps 1 through 5.

Solution First we verify that the requirements are satisfied.

1. The samples are independent. The subjects were assigned to the treatment randomly.
2. We have $x_1 = 547$, $n_1 = 2103$, $x_2 = 368$, and $n_2 = 1671$, so

$$\hat{p}_1 = \frac{x_1}{n_1} = \frac{547}{2103} = 0.260 \text{ and } \hat{p}_2 = \frac{x_2}{n_2} = \frac{368}{1671} = 0.220. \text{ Therefore,}$$

$$n_1\hat{p}_1(1-\hat{p}_1) = 2103(0.260)(1-0.260) = 404.6172 \geq 10$$

$$n_2\hat{p}_2(1-\hat{p}_2) = 1671(0.220)(1-0.220) = 286.7436 \geq 10$$

3. More than 10 million Americans 12 years old or older are allergy sufferers, so both sample sizes are less than 5% of the population size.

All three requirements are satisfied, so we now proceed to follow Steps 1 through 5.

Step 1 We want to know whether the proportion of patients taking Nasonex who experience a headache is greater than the proportion of patients taking the placebo who experience a headache. Letting p_1 represent the population proportion of patients taking Nasonex who experience a headache and p_2 represent the population proportion of patients taking the placebo who experience a headache, we want to know if $p_1 > p_2$. This is a right-tailed hypothesis with

$$H_0: p_1 = p_2 \quad \text{versus} \quad H_1: p_1 > p_2$$

or, equivalently,

$$H_0: p_1 - p_2 = 0 \quad \text{versus} \quad H_1: p_1 - p_2 > 0$$

Step 2 The level of significance is $\alpha = 0.05$.

Classical Approach

Step 3 From verifying requirement 2, we have $\hat{p}_1 = 0.260$ and $\hat{p}_2 = 0.220$. To find the test statistic, we first compute the pooled estimate of p:

$$\hat{p} = \frac{x_1 + x_2}{n_1 + n_2} = \frac{547 + 368}{2103 + 1671} = 0.242$$

The test statistic is

$$z_0 = \frac{\hat{p}_1 - \hat{p}_2}{\sqrt{\hat{p}(1-\hat{p})}\sqrt{\frac{1}{n_1} + \frac{1}{n_2}}} = \frac{0.260 - 0.220}{\sqrt{0.242(1-0.242)}\sqrt{\frac{1}{2103} + \frac{1}{1671}}} = 2.85$$

Because this is a right-tailed test, we determine the critical value at the $\alpha = 0.05$ level of significance to be $z_{0.05} = 1.645$. The critical region is shown in Figure 1.

Figure 1

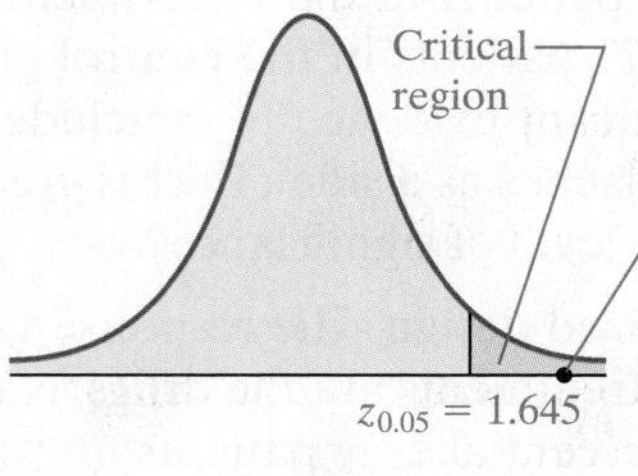

Step 4 The test statistic is $z_0 = 2.85$. We label this point in Figure 1. Because the test statistic is greater than the critical value ($2.85 > 1.645$), we reject the null hypothesis.

P-Value Approach

By Hand Step 3 From verifying requirement 2, we have $\hat{p}_1 = 0.260$ and $\hat{p}_2 = 0.220$. To find the test statistic, we first compute the pooled estimate of p:

$$\hat{p} = \frac{x_1 + x_2}{n_1 + n_2} = \frac{547 + 368}{2103 + 1671} = 0.242$$

The test statistic is

$$z_0 = \frac{\hat{p}_1 - \hat{p}_2}{\sqrt{\hat{p}(1-\hat{p})}\sqrt{\frac{1}{n_1} + \frac{1}{n_2}}} = \frac{0.260 - 0.220}{\sqrt{0.242(1-0.242)}\sqrt{\frac{1}{2103} + \frac{1}{1671}}} = 2.85$$

Because this is a right-tailed test, the *P*-value is the area under the standard normal distribution to the right of the test statistic, $z_0 = 2.85$, as shown in Figure 2.

Figure 2

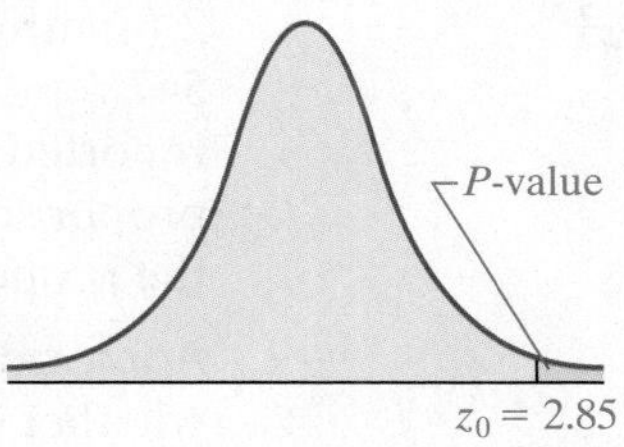

$$P\text{-value} = P(z_0 > 2.85) = 0.0022$$

Technology Step 3 Using MINITAB, we find the *P*-value is 0.002. See Figure 3.

Figure 3

Test and CI for Two Proportions

```
Sample      X     N   Sample p
1         547  2103   0.260105
2         368  1671   0.220227

Difference = p (1) - p (2)
Estimate for difference: 0.0398772
90% CI for difference: (0.0169504, 0.0628040)
Test for difference = 0 (vs > 0): Z = 2.86 P-Value = 0.002
```

Step 4 The *P*-value of 0.002 means that *if* the null hypothesis that $p_1 - p_2 = 0$ (or $p_1 = p_2$) is true, we expect 2 samples in 1000 to yield the results we obtained! The observed results are unusual, indeed. Because the *P*-value is less than the level of significance, $\alpha = 0.05$ $(0.002 < 0.05)$, we reject the null hypothesis.

Step 5 There is sufficient evidence at the $\alpha = 0.05$ level of significance to conclude the proportion of individuals 12 years and older taking 200 μg of Nasonex who experience headaches is greater than the proportion of individuals 12 years and older taking a placebo who experience headaches.

! CAUTION

In any statistical study, be sure to consider practical significance. Many statistically significant results can be produced simply by increasing the sample size.

Looking back at the results of Example 1, we notice that the proportion of individuals taking 200 μg of Nasonex who experience headaches is *statistically significantly* greater than the proportion of individuals 12 years and older taking a placebo who experience headaches. However, we need to ask ourselves a pressing question. Would you not take an allergy medication because 26% of patients experienced a headache taking the medication versus 22% who experienced a headache taking a placebo? Most people would be willing to accept the additional risk of a headache to relieve their allergy symptoms. While the difference of 4% is statistically significant, it does not have any *practical significance*.

Now Work Problem 19

3 Construct and Interpret Confidence Intervals for the Difference between Two Population Proportions

The sampling distribution of the difference of two proportions, $\hat{p}_1 - \hat{p}_2$, from independent samples can also be used to construct confidence intervals for the difference of two proportions.

Constructing a $(1 - \alpha) \cdot 100\%$ Confidence Interval for the Difference between Two Population Proportions (Independent Samples)

To construct a $(1 - \alpha) \cdot 100\%$ confidence interval for the difference between two population proportions from independent samples, the following requirements must be satisfied:

1. The samples are obtained independently, using simple random sampling or from a randomized experiment.
2. $n_1 \hat{p}_1(1 - \hat{p}_1) \geq 10$ and $n_2 \hat{p}_2(1 - \hat{p}_2) \geq 10$.
3. $n_1 \leq 0.05N_1$ and $n_2 \leq 0.05N_2$ (the sample size is no more than 5% of the population size); this ensures the independence necessary for a binomial experiment.

Provided that these requirements are met, a $(1 - \alpha) \cdot 100\%$ confidence interval for $p_1 - p_2$ is given by

$$\text{Lower bound: } (\hat{p}_1 - \hat{p}_2) - z_{\frac{\alpha}{2}} \cdot \sqrt{\frac{\hat{p}_1(1 - \hat{p}_1)}{n_1} + \frac{\hat{p}_2(1 - \hat{p}_2)}{n_2}}$$

$$\text{Upper bound: } (\hat{p}_1 - \hat{p}_2) + z_{\frac{\alpha}{2}} \cdot \sqrt{\frac{\hat{p}_1(1 - \hat{p}_1)}{n_1} + \frac{\hat{p}_2(1 - \hat{p}_2)}{n_2}} \quad (3)$$

Notice that we do not pool the sample proportions. This is because we are not making any assumptions regarding their equality, as we did in hypothesis testing.

EXAMPLE 3 Constructing a Confidence Interval for the Difference between Two Population Proportions

Problem The Gallup organization surveyed 1100 adult Americans on May 6–9, 2002, and conducted an independent survey of 1100 adult Americans on May 3–6, 2010. In both surveys they asked the following: "Right now, do you think the state of moral values in the country as a whole is getting better or getting worse?" On May 3–6, 2010, 836 of the 1100 surveyed responded that the state of moral values is getting worse; on May 6–9, 2002, 737 of the 1100 surveyed responded that the state of moral values is getting worse. Construct and interpret a 90% confidence interval for the difference between the two population proportions.

Approach We can compute a 90% confidence interval for the two population proportions provided that the stated requirements are satisfied. We then construct the interval by hand using Formula (3) or using technology.

Solution We have to verify the requirements for constructing a confidence interval for the difference between two population proportions.

1. The sample were obtained independently through a random sample.
2. For the May 3–6, 2010, survey (sample 1), we have $n_1 = 1100$ and $x_1 = 836$, so $\hat{p}_1 = \dfrac{x_1}{n_1} = \dfrac{836}{1100} = 0.76$. For the May 6–9, 2002, survey (sample 2), we have $n_2 = 1100$ and $x_2 = 737$, so $\hat{p}_2 = \dfrac{x_2}{n_2} = \dfrac{737}{1100} = 0.67$. Therefore,
$$n_1\hat{p}_1(1-\hat{p}_1) = 1100\,(0.76)\,(1-0.76) = 200.64 \geq 10$$
$$n_2\hat{p}_2(1-\hat{p}_2) = 1100\,(0.67)\,(1-0.67) = 243.21 \geq 10$$
3. The population of adult Americans exceeded 100 million in 2002 and 2010, so the sample size is definitely less than 5% of the population size.

By-Hand Solution

Substituting into Formula (3) with $\hat{p}_1 = 0.76$, $n_1 = 1100$, $\hat{p}_2 = 0.67$ and $n_2 = 1100$, we obtain the lower and upper bounds on the confidence interval:

$$\text{Lower bound: } (\hat{p}_1 - \hat{p}_2) - z_{\frac{\alpha}{2}} \cdot \sqrt{\frac{\hat{p}_1(1-\hat{p}_1)}{n_1} + \frac{\hat{p}_2(1-\hat{p}_2)}{n_2}}$$
$$= (0.76 - 0.67) - 1.645 \cdot \sqrt{\frac{0.76(1-0.76)}{1100} + \frac{0.67(1-0.67)}{1100}}$$
$$= 0.09 - 0.03$$
$$= 0.06$$

$$\text{Upper bound: } (\hat{p}_1 - \hat{p}_2) + z_{\frac{\alpha}{2}} \cdot \sqrt{\frac{\hat{p}_1(1-\hat{p}_1)}{n_1} + \frac{\hat{p}_2(1-\hat{p}_2)}{n_2}}$$
$$= (0.76 - 0.67) + 1.645 \cdot \sqrt{\frac{0.76(1-0.76)}{1100} + \frac{0.67(1-0.67)}{1100}}$$
$$= 0.09 + 0.03$$
$$= 0.12$$

Technology Solution

Figure 4 shows the 90% confidence interval using a TI-84 Plus graphing calculator

Figure 4

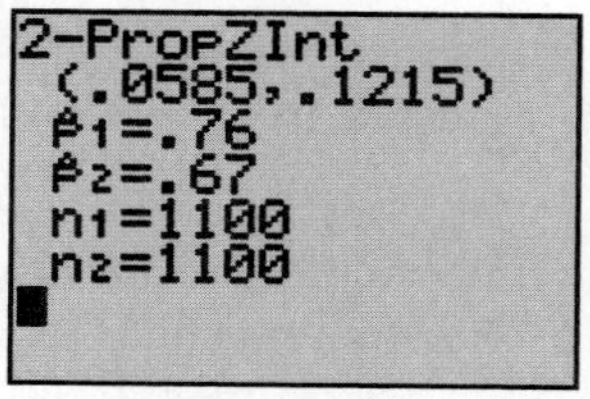

In Figure 4, the lower bound is 0.0585. The upper bound is 0.1215.

Interpretation We are 90% confident that the difference between the proportion of adult Americans who believed that the state of moral values in the country as a whole was getting worse from 2002 to 2010 is between 0.06 and 0.12. To put this statement into everyday language, we might say that we are 90% confident that the percentage of adult

Americans who believe that the state of moral values in the country as a whole was getting worse increased between 6% and 12% from 2002 to 2010. Because this interval does not contain 0, we might conclude that a higher proportion of the country believed that the state of moral values was getting worse in the United States in 2010 than in 2002.

Now Work Problem 23

4 Test Hypotheses Regarding Two Proportions from Dependent Samples

We stated that dependent samples were samples in which the individuals selected to participate in the study were somehow related. Objectives 2 and 3 in this section compared two proportions obtained from independent samples. But what if we want to compare two proportions with matched-pairs data (i.e., dependent samples)? In this case, we can use **McNemar's Test**.

To understand the idea behind the McNemar's Test, we present a hypothetical situation. Suppose we want to determine whether there is a difference between two ointments meant to treat poison ivy. Rather than randomly divide a group of individuals with poison ivy into two groups, where group 1 gets ointment A and group 2 gets ointment B and compare the proportion of individuals who heal in each group, we might instead apply ointment A on one arm and ointment B on the other arm of each individual and record whether the poison ivy cleared up. The individuals in each group are not independent, since each ointment is applied to the same individual. How might we determine whether the proportion of healed poison ivy sufferers differs between the two treatments? To answer this question, let's say the results of the experiment are as given in Table 1.

TABLE 1

		Ointment A	
		Healed (success)	**Did not heal (failure)**
Ointment B	**Healed (success)**	293	43
	Did not heal (failure)	31	103

Just as we did when comparing two population proportions from independent samples, we assume that the proportion of subjects healed with ointment A equals the proportion of subjects healed with ointment B (there is no healing difference in the ointments). So the null hypothesis is H_0: $p_A = p_B$. There are a total of $293 + 43 + 31 + 103 = 470$ subjects in the study. In this experiment, the sample proportion of subjects who healed with ointment A is $\hat{p}_A = \dfrac{293 + 31}{470} = 0.689$, and the sample proportion of subjects who healed with ointment B is $\hat{p}_B = \dfrac{293 + 43}{470} = 0.715$. McNemar's Test will be used to determine if the difference in sample proportions is due to sampling error, or if the differences are significant enough to conclude that the proportions are different, so the alternative hypothesis is H_0: $p_A \neq p_B$.

Testing a Hypothesis Regarding the Difference of Two Proportions: Dependent Samples

To test hypotheses regarding two population proportions, p_1 and p_2, where the samples are dependent, arrange the data in a contingency table as follows:

		Treatment A	
		Success	**Failure**
Treatment B	**Success**	f_{11}	f_{12}
	Failure	f_{21}	f_{22}

We can use the steps that follow provided that

1. the samples are dependent and are obtained randomly and
2. the total number of observations where the outcomes differ must be greater than or equal to 10. That is, $f_{12} + f_{21} \geq 10$.

Step 1 Determine the null and alternative hypotheses.

H_0: the proportions between the two populations are equal ($p_1 = p_2$)

H_1: the proportions between the two populations differ ($p_1 \neq p_2$)

Step 2 Select a level of significance, α, depending on the seriousness of making a Type I error.

Step 3 Compute the test statistic*

$$z_0 = \frac{|f_{12} - f_{21}| - 1}{\sqrt{f_{12} + f_{21}}}$$

Classical Approach

Step 3 (continued) Use Table V to determine the critical value. This is a two-tailed test. However, z_0 is always positive, so we only need to find the right critical value, $z_{\frac{\alpha}{2}}$.

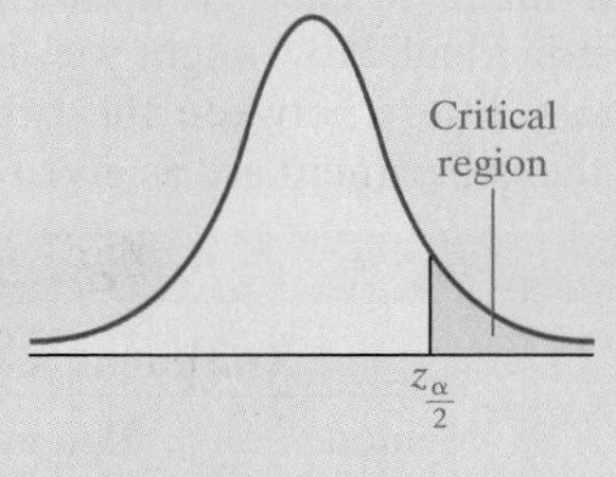

Step 4 If $z_0 > z_{\frac{\alpha}{2}}$, reject the null hypothesis.

P-Value Approach

Step 3 (continued) Use Table V to determine the *P*-value. Because z_0 is always positive, we find the area right of z_0 and then double this area (since this is a two-tailed test).

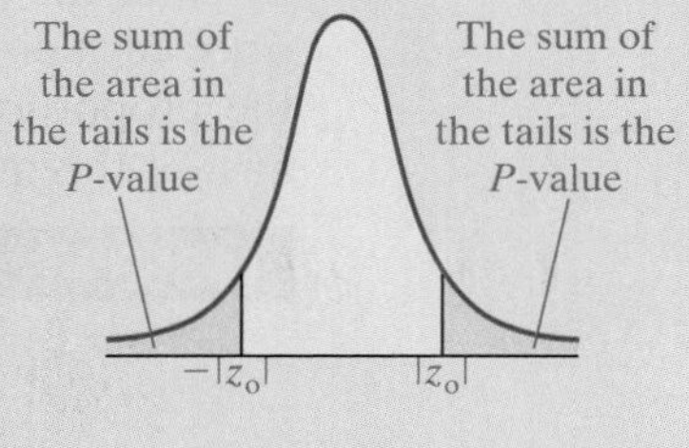

Step 4 If the *P*-value $< \alpha$, reject the null hypothesis.

Step 5 State the conclusion.

*We will not discuss the underlying theory behind the test statistic as it is beyond the scope of this course.

EXAMPLE 4 Analyzing the Difference of Two Proportions from Matched-Pairs Data

Problem A recent General Social Survey asked the following two questions of a random sample of 1492 adult Americans under the hypothetical scenario that the government suspected that a terrorist act was about to happen:

- Do you believe the authorities should have the right to tap people's telephone conversations?
- Do you believe the authorities should have the right to stop and search people on the street at random?

Using Technology

At the time of this printing, none of the technologies presented in this text offer McNemar's test.

The results of the survey are shown in Table 2.

TABLE 2

		Random Stop: Agree	Random Stop: Disagree
Tap Phone	**Agree**	494	335
	Disagree	126	537

Do the proportions who agree with each scenario differ significantly? Use the $\alpha = 0.05$ level of significance.

Approach The sample proportion of individuals who believe that the authorities should be able to tap phones is $\hat{p}_T = \frac{494 + 335}{1492} = 0.556$. The sample proportion of individuals who believe that the authorities should be able to randomly stop and search an individual on the street is $\hat{p}_R = \dfrac{494 + 126}{1492} = 0.416$. We want to determine whether the difference in sample proportions is due to sampling error or to the fact that the population proportions differ.

The samples are dependent and were obtained randomly. The total number of individuals who agree with one scenario, but disagree with the other, is $335 + 126 = 461$, which is greater than 10. We can proceed with McNemar's Test.

Solution

Step 1 The hypotheses are as follows:

H_0: the proportions between the two populations are equal ($p_T = p_R$)
H_1: the proportions between the two populations differ ($p_T \neq p_R$)

Step 2 The level of significance is $\alpha = 0.05$.

Step 3 The test statistic is

$$z_0 = \frac{|f_{12} - f_{21}| - 1}{\sqrt{f_{12} + f_{21}}} = \frac{|335 - 126| - 1}{\sqrt{335 + 126}} = 9.69$$

Classical Approach

Step 3 (continued) The critical value with an $\alpha = 0.05$ level of significance is $z_{\frac{\alpha}{2}} = z_{0.025} = 1.96$. The critical region is displayed in Figure 5.

Figure 5

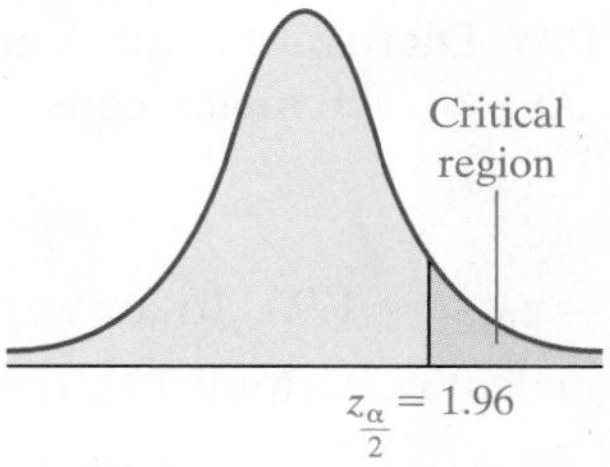

Step 4 Because $z_0 > z_{\frac{\alpha}{2}}$ (the test statistic lies in the critical region), we reject the null hypothesis.

P-Value Approach

Step 3 (continued) The *P*-value is two times the area under the standard normal distribution to the right of the test statistic, $z_0 = 9.69$. The test statistic is so large that the *P*-value < 0.0001.

Step 4 Because *P*-value $< \alpha$, we reject the null hypothesis.

Step 5 There is sufficient evidence to conclude that there is a difference in the proportion of adult Americans who believe it is okay to phone tap versus stopping and searching people on the street in the event that the government believed a terrorist plot was about to happen. In fact, looking at the sample proportions, it seems clear that more people are willing to allow phone tapping than they are to allow stopping and searching on the street.

Now Work Problem 33

5 Determine the Sample Size Necessary for Estimating the Difference between Two Population Proportions

In Section 9.1, we introduced a method for determining the sample size, n, required to estimate a single population proportion within a specified margin of error, E, with a specified level of confidence. This formula was obtained by solving the margin of error, $E = z_{\frac{\alpha}{2}} \cdot \sqrt{\dfrac{\hat{p}(1 - \hat{p})}{n}}$, for n. We can follow the same approach to determine the sample size when we want to estimate two population proportions. Notice that the margin of error, E, in Formula (3) is given by $E = z_{\frac{\alpha}{2}} \cdot \sqrt{\dfrac{\hat{p}_1(1 - \hat{p}_1)}{n_1} + \dfrac{\hat{p}_2(1 - \hat{p}_2)}{n_2}}$. Assuming that $n_1 = n_2 = n$, we can solve this expression for $n = n_1 = n_2$ and obtain the result on the next page.

CAUTION
When doing sample size calculations, always round up.

Sample Size for Estimating $p_1 - p_2$

The sample size required to obtain a $(1 - \alpha) \cdot 100\%$ confidence interval with a margin of error, E, is given by

$$n = n_1 = n_2 = [\hat{p}_1(1 - \hat{p}_1) + \hat{p}_2(1 - \hat{p}_2)]\left(\frac{z_{\frac{\alpha}{2}}}{E}\right)^2 \qquad (4)$$

rounded up to the next integer, if prior estimates of p_1 and p_2, $\hat{p}_1$ and $\hat{p}_2$, are available. If prior estimates of p_1 and p_2 are unavailable, the sample size is

$$n = n_1 = n_2 = 0.5\left(\frac{z_{\frac{\alpha}{2}}}{E}\right)^2 \qquad (5)$$

rounded up to the next integer. The margin of error should always be expressed as a decimal when using Formulas (4) and (5).

Note to Instructor
The 0.5 in Formula (5) results from adding 0.25 and 0.25, the maximum value of $p(1 - p)$.

EXAMPLE 5 Determining Sample Size

Problem A nutritionist wishes to estimate the difference between the proportion of males and females who consume the USDA's recommended daily intake of calcium. What sample size should be obtained if she wishes the estimate to be within 3 percentage points with 95% confidence, assuming that

(a) she uses the results of the USDA's 1994–1996 Diet and Health Knowledge Survey, according to which 51.1% of males and 75.2% of females consume the USDA's recommended daily intake of calcium, and

(b) she does not use any prior estimates?

Approach We have $E = 0.03$ and $z_{\frac{\alpha}{2}} = z_{\frac{0.05}{2}} = z_{0.025} = 1.96$. To answer part (a), we let $\hat{p}_1 = 0.511$ (for males) and $\hat{p}_2 = 0.752$ (for females) in Formula (4). To answer part (b), we use Formula (5).

Solution

(a) Substituting $E = 0.03$, $z_{0.025} = 1.96$, $\hat{p}_1 = 0.511$, and $\hat{p}_2 = 0.752$ into Formula (4), we obtain

$$n_1 = n_2 = [\hat{p}_1(1 - \hat{p}_1) + \hat{p}_2(1 - \hat{p}_2)]\left(\frac{z_{\frac{\alpha}{2}}}{E}\right)^2$$

$$= [0.511(1 - 0.511) + 0.752(1 - 0.752)]\left(\frac{1.96}{0.03}\right)^2$$

$$= 1862.6$$

We round this value up to 1863. The nutritionist must survey 1863 randomly selected males and 1863 randomly selected females.

(b) Substituting $E = 0.03$ and $z_{0.025} = 1.96$ into Formula (5), we obtain

$$n_1 = n_2 = 0.5\left(\frac{z_{\frac{\alpha}{2}}}{E}\right)^2 = 0.5\left(\frac{1.96}{0.03}\right)^2 = 2134.2$$

We round this value up to 2135. The nutritionist must survey 2135 randomly selected males and 2135 randomly selected females.

Now Work Problem 39

We can see that having prior estimates of the population proportions reduces the number of individuals that need to be surveyed.

In Other Words
If possible, obtain a prior estimate of $\hat{p}$ when doing sample size computations.

11.1 ASSESS YOUR UNDERSTANDING

VOCABULARY AND SKILL BUILDING

1. A sampling method is ___independent___ when the individuals selected for one sample do not dictate which individuals are selected to be in a second sample.

2. A sampling method is ___dependent___ when the individuals selected for one sample are used to determine the individuals in the second sample.

In Problems 3–8, determine whether the sampling is dependent or independent. Indicate whether the response variable is qualitative or quantitative.

NW **3.** A sociologist wishes to compare the annual salaries of married couples in which both spouses work and determines each spouse's annual salary. Dependent; quantitative

4. A researcher wishes to determine the effects of alcohol on people's reaction time to a stimulus. She randomly divides 100 people aged 21 or older into two groups. Group 1 is asked to drink 3 ounces of alcohol, while group 2 drinks a placebo. Both drinks taste the same, so the individuals in the study do not know which group they belong to. Thirty minutes after consuming the drink, the subjects in each group perform a series of tests meant to measure reaction time. Independent; quantitative

5. In May 2002, the Gallup Organization asked 1050 randomly selected adult Americans age 18 or older, "Do you believe it is morally acceptable or morally wrong [rotated] to conduct medical research using stem cells obtained from human embryos?" The same question was asked of 1050 randomly selected adult Americans in May 2010. Independent; qualitative

6. A political scientist wants to know how a random sample of 18- to 25-year-olds feel about Democrats and Republicans in Congress. She obtains a random sample of 1030 registered voters 18 to 25 years of age and asks, "Do you have favorable/unfavorable [rotated] opinion of the Democratic/Republican [rotated] party?" Each individual was asked to disclose his or her opinion about each party. Dependent; qualitative

7. An educator wants to determine whether a new curriculum significantly improves standardized test scores for third grade students. She randomly divides 80 third-graders into two groups. Group 1 is taught using the new curriculum, while group 2 is taught using the traditional curriculum. At the end of the school year, both groups are given the standardized test and the mean scores are compared. Independent; quantitative

8. A psychologist wants to know whether subjects respond faster to a go/no go stimulus or a choice stimulus. With the go/no go stimulus, subjects must respond to a particular stimulus by pressing a button and disregard other stimuli. In the choice stimulus, the subjects respond differently depending on the stimulus. The psychologist randomly selects 20 subjects, and each subject is presented a series of go/no go stimuli and choice stimuli. The mean reaction time to each stimulus is compared. Dependent; quantitative

SKILL BUILDING

In Problems 9–12, conduct each test at the $\alpha = 0.05$ level of significance by determining (a) the null and alternative hypotheses, (b) the test statistic, (c) the critical value, and (d) the P-value. Assume that the samples were obtained independently using simple random sampling.

9. Test whether $p_1 > p_2$. Sample data: $x_1 = 368, n_1 = 541, x_2 = 351, n_2 = 593$ Reject H_0

10. Test whether $p_1 < p_2$. Sample data: $x_1 = 109, n_1 = 475, x_2 = 78, n_2 = 325$ Do not reject H_0

11. Test whether $p_1 \neq p_2$. Sample data: $x_1 = 28, n_1 = 254, x_2 = 36, n_2 = 301$ Do not reject H_0

12. Test whether $p_1 \neq p_2$. Sample data: $x_1 = 804, n_1 = 874, x_2 = 902, n_2 = 954$ Reject H_0

In Problems 13–16, construct a confidence interval for $p_1 - p_2$ at the given level of confidence. 13. (−0.075, 0.015)

13. $x_1 = 368, n_1 = 541, x_2 = 421, n_2 = 593$, 90% confidence

14. $x_1 = 109, n_1 = 475, x_2 = 78, n_2 = 325$, 99% confidence

15. $x_1 = 28, n_1 = 254, x_2 = 36, n_2 = 301$, 95% confidence

16. $x_1 = 804, n_1 = 874, x_2 = 892, n_2 = 954$, 95% confidence

14. (−0.090, 0.068) 15. (−0.063, 0.043) 16. (−0.039, 0.009)

In Problems 17 and 18, test whether the population proportions differ at the $\alpha = 0.05$ level of significance by determining (a) the null and alternative hypotheses, (b) the test statistic, (c) the critical value, and (d) the P-value. Assume that the samples are dependent and were obtained randomly. 17. Do not reject H_0

17.

		Treatment A	
		Success	**Failure**
Treatment B	**Success**	45	19
	Failure	14	23

18.

		Treatment A	
		Success	**Failure**
Treatment B	**Success**	84	21
	Failure	11	37

18. Do not reject H_0

APPLYING THE CONCEPTS

NW **19. Prevnar** The drug Prevnar is a vaccine meant to prevent certain types of bacterial meningitis. It is typically administered to infants starting around 2 months of age. In randomized, double-blind clinical trials of Prevnar, infants were randomly divided into two groups. Subjects in group 1 received Prevnar, while subjects in group 2 received a control vaccine. After the first dose, 107 of 710 subjects in the experimental group (group 1) experienced fever as a side effect. After the first dose, 67 of 611 of the subjects in the control group (group 2) experienced fever as a side effect. Does the evidence suggest that a higher proportion of subjects in group 1 experienced fever as a side effect than subjects in group 2 at the $\alpha = 0.05$ level of significance? Yes; reject H_0; P-value = 0.0139

20. Prevnar The drug Prevnar is a vaccine meant to prevent certain types of bacterial meningitis. It is typically administered to infants starting around 2 months of age. In randomized, double-blind clinical trials of Prevnar, infants were randomly divided into two groups. Subjects in group 1 received Prevnar, while subjects in group 2 received a control vaccine. After the second dose, 137 of 452 subjects in the experimental group (group 1) experienced drowsiness as a side effect. After the second dose, 31 of 99 subjects in the control group (group 2) experienced drowsiness as a side effect. Does the evidence suggest that a lower proportion of subjects in group 1 experienced drowsiness as a side effect than subjects in group 2 at the $\alpha = 0.05$ level of significance? Do not reject H_0; P-value = 0.4207

21. Abstain from Alcohol In October 1947, the Gallup organization surveyed 1100 adult Americans and asked, "Are you a total abstainer from, or do you on occasion consume, alcoholic beverages?" Of the 1100 adults surveyed, 407 indicated that they were total abstainers. In July 2010, the same question was asked of 1100 adult Americans and 333 indicated that they were total abstainers. Has the proportion of adult Americans who totally abstain from alcohol changed? Use the $\alpha = 0.05$ level of significance. Yes; reject H_0; P-value = 0.0008

22. Views on the Death Penalty The Pew Research Group conducted a poll in which they asked, "Are you in favor of, or opposed to, executing persons as a general policy when the crime was committed while under the age of 18?" Of the 580 Catholics surveyed, 180 indicated they favored capital punishment; of the 600 seculars (those who do not associate with a religion) surveyed, 238 favored capital punishment. Is there a significant difference in the proportion of individuals in these groups in favor of capital punishment for persons under the age of 18? Use the $\alpha = 0.01$ level of significance. Yes; reject H_0; P-value = 0.0018

NW **23. Tattoos** The Harris Poll conducted a survey in which they asked, "How many tattoos do you currently have on your body?" Of the 1205 males surveyed, 181 responded that they had at least one tattoo. Of the 1097 females surveyed, 143 responded that they had at least one tattoo. Construct a 95% confidence interval to judge whether the proportion of males that have at least one tattoo differs significantly from the proportion of females that have at least one tattoo. Interpret the interval. (−0.008, 0.048); do not reject H_0

24. Body Mass Index The body mass index (BMI) of an individual is one measure that is used to judge whether an individual is overweight or not. A BMI between 20 and 25 indicates that one is at a normal weight. In a survey of 750 men and 750 women, the Gallup organization found that 203 men and 270 women were normal weight. Construct a 90% confidence interval to gauge whether there is a difference in the proportion of men and women who are normal weight. Interpret the interval. (−0.128, −0.050); reject H_0

25. Side Effects In clinical trials of the allergy medicine Clarinex (5 mg), it was reported that 50 out of 1655 individuals in the Clarinex group and 31 out of 1652 individuals in the placebo group experienced dry mouth as a side effect of their respective treatments. *Source*: www.clarinex.com 25. (b) No

(a) Is the proportion of individuals experiencing dry mouth greater for those taking Clarinex than for those taking a placebo at the $\alpha = 0.05$ level of significance? Reject H_0

(b) Is the difference between the groups practically significant?

26. Practical versus Statistical Significance In clinical trials for treatment of a skin disorder, 642 of 2105 patients receiving the current standard treatment were cured of the disorder and 697 of 2115 patients receiving a new proposed treatment were cured of the disorder.

(a) Does the new procedure cure a higher percentage of patients at the $\alpha = 0.05$ level of significance? Reject H_0

(b) Do you think that the difference in success rates is practically significant? What factors might influence your decision?

27. Iraq War In March 2003, the Pew Research Group surveyed 1508 adult Americans and asked, "Do you believe the United States made the right or wrong decision to use military force in Iraq?" Of the 1508 adult Americans surveyed, 1086 stated the United States made the right decision. In August 2010, the Pew Research Group asked the same question of 1508 adult Americans and found that 618 believed the United States made the right decision.

(a) In the survey question, the choices "right" and "wrong" were randomly rotated. Why?

(b) Construct and interpret a 90% confidence interval for the difference between the two population proportions, $p_{2003} - p_{2010}$. (0.282, 0.338)

28. Course Redesign In many colleges and universities around the country, educators are changing their approach to instruction from a "teacher/lecture-centered model" to a "student-centered model" where students learn in a laboratory environment in which students can proceed at a pace suitable to their learning needs and lecture is de-emphasized. In one school where this model was being introduced, of the 743 students who enrolled in the traditional lecture model, 364 passed; of the 567 in the student-centered model, 335 passed.

(a) What is the response variable in this study? What is the explanatory variable? Pass or not; delivery method

(b) Does the evidence suggest that the student-centered model results in a higher pass rate than the traditional model? Use the $\alpha = 0.05$ level of significance. Yes; reject H_0

29. Sullivan Statistics Survey: Deficit Reduction In the Sullivan Statistics Survey, respondents were asked, "Would you be willing to pay higher taxes if the tax revenue went directly toward deficit reduction?" Treat the respondents as a simple random sample of adult Americans.

(a) What proportion of the males who took the survey is willing to pay higher taxes to reduce the deficit? What proportion of the females who took the survey is willing to pay higher taxes to reduce the deficit? 0.317; 0.216

(b) Is there significant evidence to suggest the proportions of males and females who are willing to pay higher taxes to reduce the deficit differs at the $\alpha = 0.05$ level of significance? Do not reject H_0

30. Sullivan Statistics Survey: Facebook In the Sullivan Statistics Survey, respondents were asked to disclose whether they have a Facebook account. Treat the respondents as a simple random sample of adult Americans.

(a) What proportion of the males who took the survey has a Facebook account? What proportion of the females who took the survey has a Facebook account? 0.695; 0.845

(b) Is there significant evidence to suggest a higher proportion of females than males has a Facebook account at the $\alpha = 0.05$ level of significance? Yes; reject H_0

31. Political Grammar Psychologists Teenie Matlock and Caitlin Fausey asked students to read two sentences about hypothetical politicians. Ninety-eight students read, "Last year, Mark was having an affair with his assistant and was taking hush money from a prominent constituent." Let's call this sentence A. Ninety-four other students read, "Last year, Mark had an affair with his assistant and took hush money from a prominent constituent." We will call this sentence B. *Source:* Fausey, C.M., and Matlock, T. Can Grammar Win Elections? *Political Psychology*, no. doi: 10.1111/j. 1467-9221.2010.00802.x

(a) What are the specific differences in the way the two sentences are phrased?

(b) In the study, 71 of the 98 students who read sentence A and 49 of the 98 students who read sentence B felt the politician would not be re-elected. Do these results suggest that the sentence structure makes a difference in deciding whether the politician would be re-elected? Yes; reject H_0: $p_1 = p_2$

(c) Research "imperfect aspect" and "perfect aspect." Does this help explain any differences in the results of the survey?

32. Web Page Design Suppose John has an online company that sells custom rims for cars. John has designed two different Web pages that he wants to use to sell his rims online. However, he cannot decide which page to go with, so he decides to collect data to see which site results in a higher proportion of sales. He hires a firm that has the ability to randomly assign one of his two Web page designs to potential customers. With Web page design I, John secures a sale from 54 out of 523 hits to the page. With Web page design II, John secures a sale from 62 out of 512 hits to the page.

(a) What is the response variable in this study? What is the explanatory variable? Secure sale or not; Web page design

(b) Based on these results, which Web page, if any, should John go with? Why? *Note:* This problem is based on the type of research done by Adobe Test & Target. Do not reject H_0

NW **33. Hazardous Activities** In a survey of 3029 adult Americans, the Harris Poll asked people whether they smoked cigarettes and whether they always wear a seat belt in a car. The table shows the results of the survey. For each activity, we define a success as finding an individual who participates in the hazardous activity.

	No Seat Belt (success)	Seat Belt (failure)
Smoke (success)	67	448
Do not smoke (failure)	327	2187

(a) Why is this a dependent sample?

(b) Is there a significant difference in the proportion of individuals who smoke and the proportion of individuals who do not wear a seat belt? In other words, is there a significant difference between the proportion of individuals who engage in hazardous activities? Use the $\alpha = 0.05$ level of significance. Reject H_0

34. Income Taxes The Gallup organization conducted a survey in which they asked 1020 adult Americans whether they felt low-income people paid their fair share of taxes. Then they asked whether they felt high-income people paid their fair share of taxes. For each income group, a success is identifying an individual who feels the person pays his or her fair share of taxes. Is there a significant difference in the proportion of adult Americans who feel high-income people pay their fair share of taxes and the proportion who feel low-income people pay their fair share of taxes? Use the $\alpha = 0.05$ level of significance. Reject H_0

		Low-Income	
		Fair Share (success)	**Not Fair Share (failure)**
High-Income	**Fair Share (success)**	73	146
	Not Fair Share (failure)	274	548

35. Voice-Recognition Systems Have you ever been frustrated by computer telephone systems that do not understand your voice commands? Quite a bit of effort goes into designing these systems to minimize voice-recognition errors. Researchers at the Oregon Graduate Institute of Science and Technology developed a new method of voice recognition (called a remapped network) that was thought to be an improvement over an existing neural network. The data shown are based on results of their research. Does the evidence suggest that the remapped network has a different proportion of errors than the neural network? Use the $\alpha = 0.05$ level of significance. Reject H_0

		Remapped Network	
		Recognized Word (success)	**Did Not Recognize Word (failure)**
Neural Network	**Recognized Word (success)**	9326	385
	Did Not Recognize Word (failure)	456	29

Source: Wei, Wei, Leen, Todd, Barnard, and Etienne, "A Fast Histogram-Based Postprocessor That Improves Posterior Probability Estimates." *Neural Computation* 11:1235–1248.

36. Poison Ivy Look back at the data in Table 1 comparing the effectiveness of two ointments on page 475. Conduct the appropriate test to determine if one ointment has a different effectiveness than the other. Use the $\alpha = 0.05$ level of significance. Do not reject H_0

37. Own a Gun? In October 2010, the Gallup organization surveyed 1134 American adults and found that 441 had a gun in the home. In October 2009, the Gallup organization had surveyed 1134 American adults and found that 458 had a gun in the home. Suppose that a newspaper article has a headline that reads, "Fewer Guns in the Home." Is this an accurate headline? Why? No

38. Accupril Accupril, a medication supplied by Pfizer Pharmaceuticals, is meant to control hypertension. In clinical trials of Accupril, 2142 subjects were divided into two groups. The 1563 subjects in group 1 (the experimental group) received Accupril. The 579 subjects in group 2 (the control group) received a placebo. Of the 1563 subjects in the experimental group, 61 experienced dizziness as a side effect. Of the 579 subjects in the control group, 15 experienced dizziness as a side effect. To test whether the proportion experiencing dizziness in the experimental group is greater than that in the control group, the researchers entered the data into MINITAB statistical software and obtained the following results:

Test and Confidence Interval for Two Proportions

```
Sample     X      N  Sample p
1         61   1563  0.039028
2         15    579  0.025907

Estimate for p(1) - p(2): 0.0131208
95% CI for p(1) - p(2): (-0.00299150, 0.0292330)
Test for p(1) - p(2) = 0 (vs > 0): Z = 1.46 P-Value = 0.072
```

What conclusion can be drawn from the clinical trials?

NW **39. Determining Sample Size** A physical therapist wants to determine the difference in the proportion of men and women who participate in regular, sustained physical activity. What sample size should be obtained if she wishes the estimate to be within 3 percentage points with 95% confidence, assuming that

(a) she uses the 1998 estimates of 21.9% male and 19.7% female from the U.S. National Center for Chronic Disease Prevention and Health Promotion? 1406

(b) she does not use any prior estimates? 2135

40. Determining Sample Size An educator wants to determine the difference between the proportion of males and females who have completed 4 or more years of college. What sample size should be obtained if she wishes the estimate to be within 2 percentage points with 90% confidence, assuming that

(a) she uses the 1999 estimates of 27.5% male and 23.1% female from the U.S. Census Bureau? 2551

(b) she does not use any prior estimates? 3383

41. Putting It Together: Salk Vaccine On April 12, 1955, Dr. Jonas Salk released the results of clinical trials for his vaccine to prevent polio. In these clinical trials, 400,000 children were randomly divided in two groups. The subjects in group 1 (the experimental group) were given the vaccine, while the subjects in group 2 (the control group) were given a placebo. Of the 200,000 children in the experimental group, 33 developed polio. Of the 200,000 children in the control group, 115 developed polio.

(a) What type of experimental design is this?

(b) What is the response variable?

(c) What are the treatments? Placebo or vaccine

(d) What is a placebo? Innocuous medication

(e) Why is such a large number of subjects needed for this study? Low incidence rate of polio

(f) Does it appear to be the case that the vaccine was effective? Yes; reject H_0

EXPLAINING THE CONCEPTS

42. Why do we use a pooled estimate of the population proportion when testing a hypothesis about two proportions? Why do we not use a pooled estimate of the population proportion when constructing a confidence interval for the difference of two proportions?

43. Explain the difference between an independent and dependent sample.

41. (a) Completely randomized design (b) Whether the subject contracted polio or not

Technology Step-By-Step

Inference for Two Population Proportions

TI-83/84 Plus

Hypothesis Tests

1. Press `STAT`, highlight TESTS, and select `6:2-PropZTest ...`.
2. Enter the values of x_1, n_1, x_2, and n_2.
3. Highlight the appropriate relation between p_1 and p_2 in the alternative hypothesis.
4. Highlight Calculate or Draw and press `ENTER`. Calculate gives the test statistic and *P*-value. Draw will draw the *Z*-distribution with the *P*-value shaded.

Confidence Intervals

Follow the same steps given for hypothesis tests, except select `B:2-PropZInt...`. Also, select a confidence level (such as 95% = 0.95).

MINITAB

1. Enter the raw data into columns C1 and C2, if necessary.
2. Select the **Stat** menu, highlight **Basic Statistics**, then highlight **2 Proportions ...** .
3. If you have raw data, click "Samples in different columns" and enter C1 for first sample and C2 for second sample. If you have summary statistics, select "Summarized data." Enter the number of successes in the "events" cell and the number of trials in the "trials" cell for each sample.
4. Click Options... and enter the level of confidence desired, the "test difference" (usually 0), and the direction of the alternative hypothesis. Click OK twice.

Excel

Hypothesis Tests or Confidence Intervals

1. Load the XLSTAT Add-in. Select the XLSTAT menu, highlight Parametric tests. From the pull-down menu, select z-test for two proportions.
2. Enter the number of successes for sample 1 in the Frequency 1: cell; enter the sample size for sample 1 in the Sample size 1: cell; and so on. Make sure Data format: is set to Frequencies. Select the correct alternative hypothesis. Enter the Hypothesized difference (D) (usually 0), and select the Significance level (%). For a 95% confidence interval, enter 5. Click OK.

StatCrunch

Hypothesis Tests or Confidence Intervals

1. If you have raw data, enter them into the spreadsheet. Name each column variable.
2. Select **Stat**, highlight **Proportions**, select **Two sample**, and then choose either **with data** or **with summary**.
3. If you chose **with data**, select the column that has the observations, choose which outcome represents a success for each sample, then click Next>. If you chose **with summary**, enter the number of successes and the number of trials for each sample. Click Next>.
4. If you choose the hypothesis test radio button, enter the value of the proportion stated in the null hypothesis and choose the direction of the alternative hypothesis from the pull-down menu. If you choose the confidence interval radio button, enter the level of confidence. Click Calculate.

11.2 INFERENCE ABOUT TWO MEANS: DEPENDENT SAMPLES

Preparing for This Section Before getting started, review the following:

- Matched-pairs design (Section 1.6, p. 49)
- Confidence intervals about μ (Section 9.2, pp. 409–411)
- Hypothesis tests about μ (Section 10.3, pp. 449–453)
- Type I and Type II errors (Section 10.1, pp. 432–433)

OBJECTIVES

1 Test hypotheses regarding matched-pairs data

2 Construct and interpret confidence intervals about the population mean difference of matched-pairs data

Note to Instructor
If you like, you can print out and distribute the Preparing for This Section quiz located in the Instructor's Resource Center. The purpose of this quiz is to verify the students have the prerequisite knowledge for the section.

In this section, we discuss inference on the difference of two means for dependent sampling. We will address inference when the sampling is independent in Section 11.3.

1 Test Hypotheses Regarding Matched-Pairs Data

Inference on matched-pairs data is very similar to inference regarding a population mean. Recall that, if the population from which the sample was drawn is normally distributed or the sample size is large ($n \geq 30$), we said that

$$t = \frac{\bar{x} - \mu}{\frac{s}{\sqrt{n}}}$$

follows Student's t-distribution with $n - 1$ degrees of freedom.

When analyzing matched-pairs data, we compute the difference in each matched pair and then perform inference on the differenced data using the methods of Section 9.2 or 10.3.

In Other Words
Statistical inference methods on matched-pairs data use the same methods as inference on a single population mean, except that the *differences* are analyzed.

Testing Hypotheses Regarding the Difference of Two Means Using a Matched-Pairs Design

To test hypotheses regarding the mean difference of matched-pairs data, we can use the following steps, provided that

- the sample is obtained using simple random sampling or through a randomized experiment,
- the sample data are matched pairs,
- the differences are normally distributed with no outliers or the sample size, n, is large ($n \geq 30$).
- The sampled values are independent (sample size is no more than 5% of population size).

Step 1 Determine the null and alternative hypotheses. The hypotheses can be structured in one of three ways, where μ_d is the population mean difference of the matched-pairs data.

Two-Tailed	Left-Tailed	Right-Tailed
H_0: $\mu_d = 0$	H_0: $\mu_d = 0$	H_0: $\mu_d = 0$
H_1: $\mu_d \neq 0$	H_1: $\mu_d < 0$	H_1: $\mu_d > 0$

Step 2 Select a level of significance, α, depending on the seriousness of making a Type I error.

Classical Approach

Step 3 Compute the **test statistic**

$$t_0 = \frac{\bar{d} - 0}{\frac{s_d}{\sqrt{n}}} = \frac{\bar{d}}{\frac{s_d}{\sqrt{n}}}$$

which follows Student's t-distribution with $n - 1$ degrees of freedom. The values of $\bar{d}$ and s_d are the mean and standard deviation of the differenced data. Use Table VI to determine the critical value.

	Two-Tailed	Left-Tailed	Right-Tailed
Critical value	$-t_{\frac{\alpha}{2}}$ and $-t_{\frac{\alpha}{2}}$	$-t_{\alpha}$	t_{α}
Critical region			

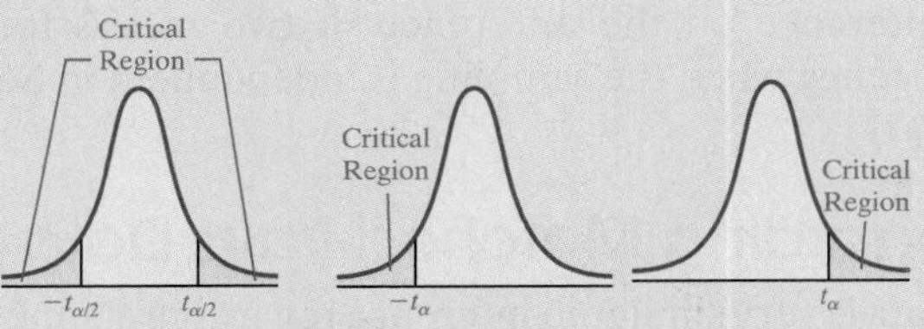

Step 4 Compare the critical value to the test statistic.

Two-Tailed	Left-Tailed	Right-Tailed
If $t_0 < -t_{\frac{\alpha}{2}}$ or $t_0 > t_{\frac{\alpha}{2}}$, reject the null hypothesis.	If $t_0 < -t_{\alpha}$, reject the null hypothesis.	If $t_0 > t_{\alpha}$, reject the null hypothesis.

P-Value Approach

By Hand Step 3 Compute the **test statistic**

$$t_0 = \frac{\bar{d} - 0}{\frac{s_d}{\sqrt{n}}} = \frac{\bar{d}}{\frac{s_d}{\sqrt{n}}}$$

which follows Student's t-distribution with $n - 1$ degrees of freedom. The values of $\bar{d}$ and s_d are the mean and standard deviation of the differenced data. Use Table VI to approximate the P-value.

Two-Tailed	Left-Tailed	Right-Tailed

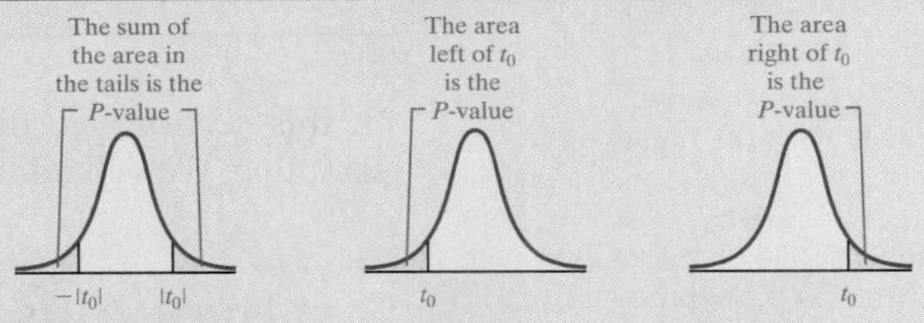

Two-Tailed	Left-Tailed	Right-Tailed
P-value $= 2P(t > \lvert t_0 \rvert)$	P-value $= P(t < t_0)$	P-value $= P(t > t_0)$

Technology Step 3 Use a statistical spreadsheet or calculator with statistical capabilities to obtain the P-value. The directions for obtaining the P-value using the TI-83/84 Plus graphing calculator, MINITAB, Excel and StatCrunch, are in the Technology Step-by-Step on pages 492–493.

Step 4 If P-value $< \alpha$, reject the null hypothesis

Step 5 State the conclusion.

The procedures just presented are **robust**, which means that minor departures from normality will not adversely affect the results of the test. If the data have outliers, however, the procedure should not be used.

We verify the assumption that the differenced data come from a population that is normally distributed by constructing normal probability plots. We use boxplots to determine whether there are outliers. If the normal probability plot indicates that the differenced data are not normally distributed or the boxplot reveals outliers, nonparametric tests should be performed.

EXAMPLE 1 Testing Hypotheses Regarding Matched-Pairs Data

Problem Professor Andy Neill measured the time (in seconds) required to catch a falling meter stick for 12 randomly selected students' dominant hand and nondominant hand. Professor Neill wants to know if the reaction time in an individual's dominant hand is less than the reaction time in his or her nondominant hand. A coin flip is used to determine whether reaction time is measured using the dominant or nondominant hand first. Conduct the test at the $\alpha = 0.05$ level of significance. The data obtained are presented in Table 3.

TABLE 3

Student	Dominant Hand, X_i	Nondominant Hand, Y_i
1	0.177	0.179
2	0.210	0.202
3	0.186	0.208
4	0.189	0.184
5	0.198	0.215
6	0.194	0.193
7	0.160	0.194
8	0.163	0.160
9	0.166	0.209
10	0.152	0.164
11	0.190	0.210
12	0.172	0.197

Source: Professor Andy Neill, Joliet Junior College

Note to Instructor

Remind students of some of the key phrases in the statement we are gathering evidence for that help them to determine whether the test is right-tailed, left-tailed, or two-tailed. Examples include "less than," "more than," "no different."

Approach This is a matched-pairs design because the variable is measured on the same subject for both the dominant and nondominant hand, the treatments in this experiment. We compute the difference between the dominant time and the nondominant time. So, for the first student we compute $X_1 - Y_1$, for the second student we compute $X_2 - Y_2$, and so on. If the reaction time in the dominant hand is less than the reaction time in the nondominant hand, we would expect the values of $X_i - Y_i$ to be negative. We assume that there is no difference and seek evidence that leads us to believe that there is a difference.

Before we perform the hypothesis test, we must verify that the differences come from a population that is approximately normally distributed with no outliers because the sample size is small. We will construct a normal probability plot and boxplot of the differenced data to verify these requirements. We then proceed to follow Steps 1 through 5.

Note to Instructor

Emphasize the importance of constructing a table such as Table 4. Not only does it help organize the information, but it can be used to help students see the direction of the alternative hypothesis.

Solution We compute the differences as $d_i = X_i - Y_i$ = time of dominant hand for ith student minus time of nondominant hand for ith student. We expect these differences to be negative, so we wish to determine if $\mu_d < 0$. Table 4 displays the differences.

CAUTION

The way that we define the difference determines the direction of the alternative hypothesis in one-tailed tests. In Example 1, we expect $X_i < Y_i$, so the difference $X_i - Y_i$ is expected to be negative. Therefore, the alternative hypothesis is $H_1: \mu_d < 0$, and we have a left-tailed test. However, if we computed the differences as $Y_i - X_i$, we would expect the differences to be positive, and we have a right-tailed test!

TABLE 4

Student	Dominant Hand, X_i	Nondominant Hand, Y_i	Difference, d_i
1	0.177	0.179	0.177 − 0.179 = −0.002
2	0.210	0.202	0.210 − 0.202 = 0.008
3	0.186	0.208	−0.022
4	0.189	0.184	0.005
5	0.198	0.215	−0.017
6	0.194	0.193	0.001
7	0.160	0.194	−0.034
8	0.163	0.160	0.003
9	0.166	0.209	−0.043
10	0.152	0.164	−0.012
11	0.190	0.210	−0.020
12	0.172	0.197	−0.025
			$\sum d_i = -0.158$

We compute the mean and standard deviation of the differences and obtain $\overline{d} = -0.0132$ rounded to four decimal places and $s_d = 0.0164$ rounded to four decimal places. We must verify that the data come from a population that is approximately normal with no outliers. Figure 6 shows the normal probability plot and boxplot of the differenced data.

Figure 6

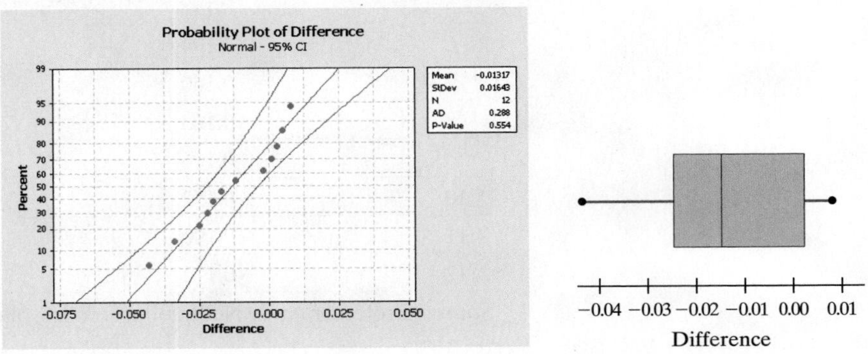

The normal probability plot is roughly linear and the boxplot does not show any outliers. We can proceed with the hypothesis test.

Step 1 Professor Neill wants to know if the reaction time in the dominant hand is less than the reaction time in the nondominant hand. We express this as $\mu_d < 0$. We have

$$H_0: \mu_d = 0 \quad \text{versus} \quad H_1: \mu_d < 0$$

This test is left-tailed.

Step 2 The level of significance is $\alpha = 0.05$.

Classical Approach

Step 3 The sample mean is $\overline{d} = -0.0132$ second and the sample standard deviation is $s_d = 0.0164$ second.

The test statistic is

$$t_0 = \frac{\overline{d}_0}{\frac{s_d}{\sqrt{n}}} = \frac{-0.0132}{\frac{0.0164}{\sqrt{12}}} = -2.788$$

Because this is a left-tailed test, we determine the critical value at the $\alpha = 0.05$ level of significance with $12 - 1 = 11$ degrees of freedom to be $-t_{0.05} = -1.796$. The critical region is shown in Figure 7.

Figure 7

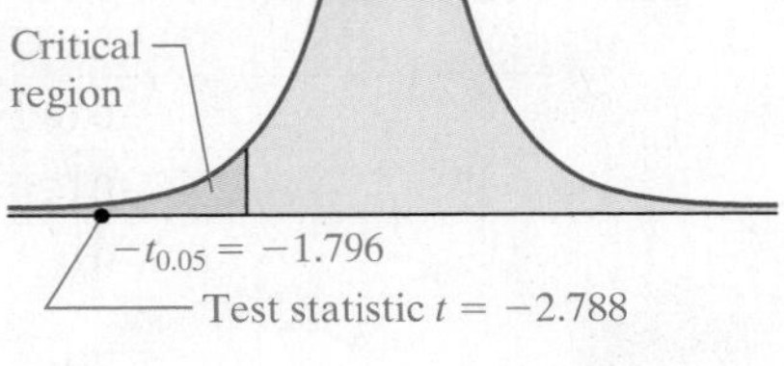

P-Value Approach

By Hand Step 3 The sample mean is $\overline{d} = -0.0132$ second and the sample standard deviation is $s_d = 0.0164$ second.

The test statistic is

$$t_0 = \frac{\overline{d}_0}{\frac{s_d}{\sqrt{n}}} = \frac{-0.0132}{\frac{0.0164}{\sqrt{12}}} = -2.788$$

Because this is a left-tailed test, the *P*-value is the area under the *t*-distribution with $12 - 1 = 11$ degrees of freedom to the left of the test statistic, $t_0 = -2.788$, as shown in Figure 8(a). That is, *P*-value $= P(t < t_0) = P(t < -2.788)$ with 11 degrees of freedom.

Because of the symmetry of the *t*-distribution, the area under the *t*-distribution to the left of -2.788 equals the area under the *t*-distribution to the right of 2.788. So the *P*-value $= P(t_0 < -2.788) = P(t_0 > 2.788)$. See Figure 8(b).

Figure 8

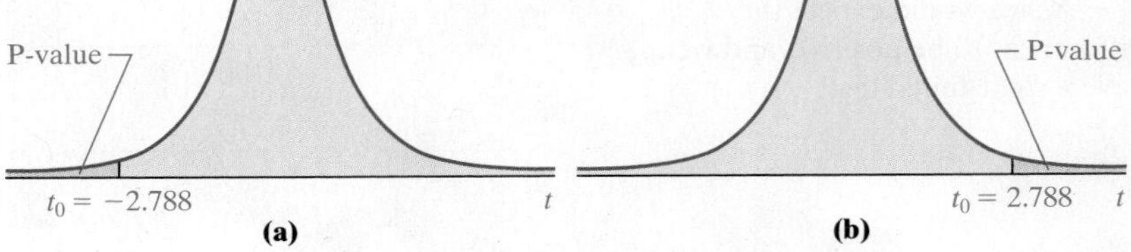

Step 4 The test statistic, $t_0 = -2.788$, is labeled in Figure 7. Because the test statistic lies in the critical region, we reject the null hypothesis.

Using Table VI, we find the row that corresponds to 11 degrees of freedom. The value 2.788 lies between 2.718 and 3.106. The value of 2.718 has an area of 0.01 to the right under the t-distribution with 11 degrees of freedom. The value of 3.106 has an area of 0.005 to the right under the t-distribution with 11 degrees of freedom.

Because 2.788 is between 2.718 and 3.106, the P-value is between 0.005 and 0.01. So $0.005 < P\text{-value} < 0.01$.

Technology Step 3 Using StatCrunch, we find the P-value is 0.009. See Figure 9.

Figure 9

Hypothesis test results:

$\mu_1 - \mu_2$: mean of the paired difference between Dominant and Nondominant

$H_0 : \mu_1 - \mu_2 = 0$

$H_A : \mu_1 - \mu_2 < 0$

Difference	Sample Diff.	Std. Err.	DF	T-Stat	P-value
Dominant - Nondominant	-0.013166667	0.0047431504	11	-2.7759328	0.009

Differences stored in column, Differences.

Step 4 The P-value of 0.009 [by hand: $0.005 < P\text{-value} < 0.01$] means that *if* the null hypothesis that mean difference is zero is true, we expect a sample mean of -0.0132 second or lower in about 9 out of 1000 samples. The results we obtained do not seem to be consistent with the assumption the mean difference in reaction time between the dominant and nondominant hand is 0 second. Simply put, because the P-value is less than the level of significance, $\alpha = 0.05$ ($0.009 < 0.05$), Professor Neill rejects the null hypothesis.

Step 5 There is sufficient evidence at the $\alpha = 0.05$ level of significance to conclude that the reaction time in the dominant hand is less than the reaction time in the nondominant hand.

Now Work Problem 7(a) and (b)

2 Construct and Interpret Confidence Intervals about the Population Mean Difference of Matched-Pairs Data

We can also create a confidence interval for the population mean difference, μ_d, using the sample mean difference, $\bar{d}$, the sample standard deviation difference, s_d, the sample size, and $t_{\frac{\alpha}{2}}$. Remember, a confidence interval about a population mean is given in the following form:

Point estimate $\pm$ margin of error

Based on the preceding formula, we compute the confidence interval for μ_d as follows:

Confidence Interval for Matched-Pairs Data

A $(1 - \alpha) \cdot 100\%$ confidence interval for μ_d is given by

$$\text{Lower bound: } \bar{d} - t_{\frac{\alpha}{2}} \cdot \frac{s_d}{\sqrt{n}} \qquad \text{Upper bound: } \bar{d} + t_{\frac{\alpha}{2}} \cdot \frac{s_d}{\sqrt{n}} \tag{1}$$

The critical value $t_{\alpha/2}$ is determined using $n - 1$ degrees of freedom. The values of $\bar{d}$ and s_d are the mean and standard deviation of the differenced data.

Note: The interval is exact when the population is normally distributed and approximately correct for nonnormal populations, provided that n is large.

EXAMPLE 2 Constructing a Confidence Interval for Matched-Pairs Data

Problem Using the data from Table 4 on page 485, construct a 95% confidence interval estimate of the mean difference, μ_d.

By Hand Approach

Step 1 Compute the differenced data. Because the sample size is small, we must verify that the differenced data come from a population that is approximately normal with no outliers.

Step 2 Compute the sample mean difference, $\bar{d}$, and the sample standard deviation difference, s_d.

Step 3 Determine the critical value, $t_{\frac{\alpha}{2}}$, with $\alpha = 0.05$ and $n - 1$ degrees of freedom.

Step 4 Use Formula (1) to determine the lower and upper bounds.

Step 5 Interpret the results.

By-Hand Solution

Step 1 We computed the differenced data and verified that they come from a population that is approximately normally distributed with no outliers in Example 1.

Step 2 We computed the sample mean difference, $\bar{d}$, to be -0.0132 and the sample standard deviation of the difference, s_d, to be 0.0164 in Example 1.

Step 3 Using Table VI with $\alpha = 0.05$ and $12 - 1 = 11$ degrees of freedom, we find $t_{\frac{\alpha}{2}} = t_{0.025} = 2.201$.

Step 4 Substituting into Formula (1), we find

$$\text{Lower bound: } \bar{d} - t_{\frac{\alpha}{2}} \cdot \frac{s_d}{\sqrt{n}} = -0.0132 - 2.201 \cdot \frac{0.0164}{\sqrt{12}} = -0.0236$$

$$\text{Upper bound: } \bar{d} + t_{\frac{\alpha}{2}} \cdot \frac{s_d}{\sqrt{n}} = -0.0132 + 2.201 \cdot \frac{0.0164}{\sqrt{12}} = -0.0028$$

Step 5 We are 95% confident the mean difference between the dominant hand's reaction time and the nondominant hand's reaction time is between -0.0236 and -0.0028 second. In other words, we are 95% confident the dominant hand has a mean reaction time that is somewhere between 0.0028 second and 0.0236 second faster than the nondominant hand. Because the confidence interval does not contain zero, the evidence suggests the reaction time of a person's dominant hand is different from the reaction time of the nondominant hand.

Technology Approach

Step 1 Compute the differenced data. Because the sample size is small, verify the differenced data come from a population that is approximately normal with no outliers.

Step 2 Use a statistical spreadsheet or graphing calculator with advanced statistical features to obtain the confidence interval. We will use a TI-84 Plus to construct the confidence interval. The steps for constructing confidence intervals using StatCrunch, MINITAB. Excel, and the TI-83/84 graphing calculators are given in the Technology Step-by-Step on pages 492–493.

Step 3 Interpret the result.

Technology Solution

Step 1 Figure 10 shows the results from a TI-84 Plus graphing calculator.

Figure 10

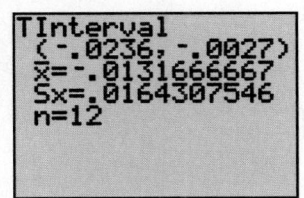

```
TInterval
 (-.0236,-.0027)
 x̄=-.0131666667
 Sx=.0164307546
 n=12
```

Step 2 We are 95% confident the mean difference between the dominant hand's reaction time and the nondominant hand's reaction time is between -0.0236 and -0.0027 second. In other words, we are 95% confident the dominant hand has a mean reaction time that is somewhere between 0.0027 second and 0.0236 second faster than the nondominant hand. Because the confidence interval does not contain zero, the evidence suggests the reaction time of the dominant hand is different from the reaction time of the nondominant hand.

Now Work Problem 7(c)

11.2 ASSESS YOUR UNDERSTANDING

SKILL BUILDING

1. A researcher wants to show the mean from population 1 is less than the mean from population 2 in matched-pairs data. If the observations from sample 1 are X_i and the observations from sample 2 are Y_i, and $d_i = X_i - Y_i$, then the null hypothesis is H_0: $\mu_d = 0$ and the alternative hypothesis is H_1: μ_d __<__ 0.

2. A researcher wants to show the mean from population 1 is less than the mean from population 2 in matched-pairs data. If the observations from sample 1 are X_i and the observations from sample 2 are Y_i and $d_i = Y_i - X_i$, then the null hypothesis is H_0: $\mu_d = 0$ and the alternative hypothesis is H_1: μ_d __>__ 0.

In Problems 3 and 4, assume that the differences are normally distributed.

3.

Observation	1	2	3	4	5	6	7
X_i	7.6	7.6	7.4	5.7	8.3	6.6	5.6
Y_i	8.1	6.6	10.7	9.4	7.8	9.0	8.5

(a) Determine $d_i = X_i - Y_i$ for each pair of data.
(b) Compute $\bar{d}$ and s_d. $\bar{d} = -1.614$, $s_d = 1.915$
(c) Test if $\mu_d < 0$ at the $\alpha = 0.05$ level of significance. Reject H_0

(d) Compute a 95% confidence interval about the population mean difference μ_d. $(-3.39, 0.16)$

4.

Observation	1	2	3	4	5	6	7	8
X_i	19.4	18.3	22.1	20.7	19.2	11.8	20.1	18.6
Y_i	19.8	16.8	21.1	22.0	21.5	18.7	15.0	23.9

(a) Determine $d_i = X_i - Y_i$ for each pair of data.
(b) Compute $\bar{d}$ and s_d. $\bar{d} = -1.075$, $s_d = 3.833$
(c) Test if $\mu_d \neq 0$ at the $\alpha = 0.01$ level of significance.
(d) Compute a 99% confidence interval about the population mean difference μ_d. $(-5.82, 3.67)$ (c) Do not reject H_0

APPLYING THE CONCEPTS

5. Naughty or Nice? Yale University graduate student J. Kiley Hamlin conducted an experiment in which 16 ten-month-old babies were asked to watch a climber character attempt to ascend a hill. On two occasions, the baby witnesses the character fail to make the climb. On the third attempt, the baby witnesses either a helper toy push the character up the hill, or a hinderer toy preventing the character from making the ascent. The helper and hinderer toys were shown to each baby in a random fashion for a fixed amount of time. In Problem 41 from Section 10.2, we learned that, after watching both the helper and hinderer toy in action, 14 of 16 ten-month-old babies preferred to play with the helper toy when given a choice as to which toy to play with. A second part of this experiment showed the climber approach the helper toy, which is not a surprising action, and then alternatively the climber approached the hinderer toy, which is a surprising action. The amount of time the ten-month-old watched the event was recorded. The mean difference in time spent watching the climber approach the hinderer toy versus watching the climber approach the helper toy was 1.14 seconds with a standard deviation of 1.75 second.

Source: J. Kiley Hamlin et al., "Social Evaluation by Preverbal Infants," Nature, Nov. 2007.

(a) State the null and alternative hypothesis to determine if babies tend to look at the hinderer toy longer than the helper toy. H_0: $\mu_d = 0$ vs. H_1: $\mu_d > 0$
(b) Assuming the differences are normally distributed with no outliers, test if the difference in the amount of time the baby will watch the hinderer toy versus the helper toy is greater than 0 at the 0.05 level of significance. Reject H_0; P-value $= 0.0099$
(c) What do you think the results of this experiment imply about 10-month-olds' ability to assess surprising behavior?

6. Caffeine-Enhanced Workout? Since its removal from the banned substances list in 2004 by the World Anti-Doping Agency, caffeine has been used by athletes with the expectancy that it enhances their workout and performance. Many studies have been conducted to assess the effect of caffeine on athletes, but few look at the role it plays in sedentary females. Researchers at the University of Western Australia conducted a test in which they determined the rate of energy expenditure (kilojoules) on 10 healthy, sedentary females who were nonregular caffeine users. Each female was randomly assigned either a placebo or caffeine pill (6 mg/kg) 60 minutes prior to exercise. The subject rode an exercise bicycle for 15 minutes at 65% of their maximum heart rate, and the energy expenditure was measured. The process was repeated on a separate day for the remaining treatment. The mean difference in energy expenditure (caffeine–placebo) was 18 kJ with a standard deviation of 19 kJ.

Source: Wallman, Karen E. "Effect of Caffeine on Exercise Performance in Sedentary Females," *Journal of Sports Science and Medicine* (2010) 9, 183–189 6 (a) H_0: $\mu_d = 0$ vs. H_2: $\mu_d > 0$

(a) State the null and alternative hypothesis to determine if caffeine increases energy expenditure.
(b) Assuming the differences are normally distributed, determine if caffeine appears to increase energy expenditure at the $\alpha = 0.05$ level of significance. Reject H_0; P-value $= 0.0075$

NW **7. Muzzle Velocity** The following data represent the muzzle velocity (in feet per second) of rounds fired from a 155-mm gun. For each round, two measurements of the velocity were recorded using two different measuring devices, with the following data obtained:

Observation	1	2	3	4	5	6
A	793.8	793.1	792.4	794.0	791.4	792.4
B	793.2	793.3	792.6	793.8	791.6	791.6

Observation	7	8	9	10	11	12
A	791.7	792.3	789.6	794.4	790.9	793.5
B	791.6	792.4	788.5	794.7	791.3	793.5

Source: Ronald Christenson and Larry Blackwood. "Tests for Precision and Accuracy of Multiple Measuring Devices." *Technometrics*, 35(4):411–421, 1993.

(a) Why are these matched-pairs data?
(b) Is there a difference in the measurement of the muzzle velocity between device A and device B at the $\alpha = 0.01$ level of significance? Do not reject H_0
Note: A normal probability plot and boxplot of the data indicate that the differences are approximately normally distributed with no outliers.
(c) Construct a 99% confidence interval about the population mean difference. Interpret your results. $(-0.31, 0.54)$
(d) Draw a boxplot of the differenced data. Does this visual evidence support the results obtained in part (b)?

8. Reaction Time In an experiment conducted online at the University of Mississippi, study participants are asked to react to a stimulus. In one experiment, the participant must press a key on seeing a blue screen. Reaction time (in seconds) to press the key is measured. The same person is then asked to press a key on seeing a red screen, again with reaction time measured. The results for six randomly sampled study participants are as follows:

Participant	1	2	3	4	5	6
Blue	0.582	0.481	0.841	0.267	0.685	0.450
Red	0.408	0.407	0.542	0.402	0.456	0.533

Source: PsychExperiments at the University of Mississippi

(a) Why are these matched-pairs data?
(b) In this study, the color that the student was first asked to react to was randomly selected. Why is this a good idea in this experiment?
(c) Is the reaction time to the blue stimulus different from the reaction time to the red stimulus at the $\alpha = 0.01$ level of significance? Do not reject H_0
Note: A normal probability plot and boxplot of the data indicate that the differences are approximately normally distributed with no outliers.

(d) Construct a 99% confidence interval about the population mean difference. Interpret your results. (−0.3789, 0.1929)

(e) Draw a boxplot of the differenced data. Does this visual evidence support the results obtained in part (b)?

9. SUV versus Car It is a commonly held belief that SUVs are safer than cars. If an SUV and car are in a collision, does the SUV sustain less damage (as suggested by the cost of repair)? The Insurance Institute for Highway Safety crashed SUVs into cars. The SUV was moving 10 miles per hour and the front of the SUV crashed into the rear of the car.

SUV into Car	SUV Damage	Car Damage
Honda CR-V into Honda Civic	1721	1274
Toyota RAV4 into Toyota Corolla	1434	2327
Hyundai Tucson into Kia Forte	850	3223
Volkswagen Tiguan into Volkswagen Golf	2329	2058
Jeep Patriot into Dodge Caliber	1415	3095
Ford Escape into Ford Focus	1470	3386
Nissan Rogue into Nissan Sentra	2884	4560

Source: Insurance Institute for Highway Safety

(a) Why are these matched-pairs data?

(b) Draw a boxplot of the differenced data. Does the visual evidence support the belief that SUVs have a lower repair cost?

(c) Do the data suggest the repair cost for the car is higher? Use an $\alpha = 0.05$ level of significance. Yes; P-value = 0.0181

Note: A normal probability plot indicates the differenced data are approximately normal with no outliers.

10. Secchi Disk A Secchi disk is an 8-inch-diameter weighted disk that is painted black and white and attached to a rope. The disk is lowered into water and the depth (in inches) at which it is no longer visible is recorded. The measurement is an indication of water clarity. An environmental biologist is interested in determining whether the water clarity of the lake at Joliet Junior College is improving. She takes measurements at the same location on eight dates during the course of a year and repeats the measurements on the same dates 5 years later. She obtains the following results:

Observation	1	2	3	4	5	6	7	8
Date	5/11	6/7	6/24	7/8	7/27	8/31	9/30	10/12
Initial depth, X_i	38	58	65	74	56	36	56	52
Depth 5 years later, Y_i	52	60	72	72	54	48	58	60

Source: Virginia Piekarski, Joliet Junior College

(a) Why is it important to take the measurements on the same date?

(b) Does the evidence suggest that the clarity of the lake is improving at the $\alpha = 0.05$ level of significance? Reject H_0

Note: A normal probability plot and boxplot of the data indicate that the differences are approximately normally distributed with no outliers.

(c) Draw a boxplot of the differenced data. Does this visual evidence support the results obtained in part (b)?

11. Getting Taller? To test the belief that sons are taller than their fathers, a student randomly selects 13 fathers who have adult male children. She records the height of both the father and son in inches and obtains the following data. Are sons taller than their fathers? Use the $\alpha = 0.1$ level of significance.

Note: A normal probability plot and boxplot of the data indicate that the differences are approximately normally distributed with no outliers. Do not reject H_0

	1	2	3	4	5	6	7
Height of father, X_i	70.3	67.1	70.9	66.8	72.8	70.4	71.8
Height of son, Y_i	74.1	69.2	66.9	69.2	68.9	70.2	70.4

	8	9	10	11	12	13
Height of father, X_i	70.1	69.9	70.8	70.2	70.4	72.4
Height of son, Y_i	69.3	75.8	72.3	69.2	68.6	73.9

Source: Anna Behounek, student at Joliet Junior College

12. Waiting in Line A quality-control manager at an amusement park feels that the amount of time that people spend waiting in line for the American Eagle roller coaster is too long. To determine if a new loading/unloading procedure is effective in reducing wait time in line, he measures the amount of time (in minutes) people are waiting in line on 7 days. After implementing the new procedure, he again measures the amount of time (in minutes) people are waiting in line on 7 days and obtains the following data. To make a reasonable comparison, he chooses days when the weather conditions are similar. Is the new loading/unloading procedure effective in reducing wait time at the $\alpha = 0.05$ level of significance? Do not reject H_0

Note: A normal probability plot and boxplot of the data indicate that the differences are approximately normally distributed with no outliers.

Day:	Mon (2 P.M.)	Tues (2 P.M.)	Wed (2 P.M.)	Thurs (2 P.M.)	Fri (2 P.M.)
Wait time before, X_i	11.6	25.9	20.0	38.2	57.3
Wait time after, Y_i	10.7	28.3	19.2	35.9	59.2

Day:	Sat (11 A.M.)	Sat (4 P.M.)	Sun (12 noon)	Sun (4 P.M.)
Wait time before, X_i	32.1	81.8	57.1	62.8
Wait time after, Y_i	31.8	75.3	54.9	62.0

13. Hardness Testing The manufacturer of hardness testing equipment uses steel-ball indenters to penetrate metal that is being tested. However, the manufacturer thinks it would be better to use a diamond indenter so that all types of metal can be tested. Because of differences between the two types of indenters, it is suspected that the two methods will produce different hardness readings. The metal specimens to be tested are large enough so that two indentions can be made. Therefore, the manufacturer uses both indenters on each specimen and compares the hardness readings. Construct a 95% confidence interval to judge whether the two indenters result in different measurements.

Specimen	1	2	3	4	5	6	7	8	9
Steel ball	50	57	61	71	68	54	65	51	53
Diamond	52	56	61	74	69	55	68	51	56

Note: A normal probability plot and boxplot of the data indicate that the differences are approximately normally distributed with no outliers. (0.1, 2.5); Reject H_0

14. Car Rentals The following data represent the daily rental for a compact automobile charged by two car rental companies, Thrifty and Hertz, in 10 locations. Test whether Thrifty is less expensive than Hertz at the $\alpha = 0.1$ level of significance.

Note: A normal probability plot and boxplot of the data indicate that the differences are approximately normally distributed with no outliers. Do not reject H_0

City	Thrifty	Hertz
Chicago	21.81	18.99
Los Angeles	29.89	48.99
Houston	17.90	19.99
Orlando	27.98	35.99
Boston	24.61	25.60
Seattle	21.96	22.99
Pittsburgh	20.90	19.99
Phoenix	47.75	36.99
New Orleans	33.81	26.99
Minneapolis	33.49	20.99

Source: Yahoo!Travel

15. DUI Simulator To illustrate the effects of driving under the influence (DUI) of alcohol, a police officer brought a DUI simulator to a local high school. Student reaction time in an emergency was measured with unimpaired vision and also while wearing a pair of special goggles to simulate the effects of alcohol on vision. For a random sample of nine teenagers, the time (in seconds) required to bring the vehicle to a stop from a speed of 60 miles per hour was recorded.

Subject	1	2	3	4	5	6	7	8	9
Normal, X_i	4.47	4.24	4.58	4.65	4.31	4.80	4.55	5.00	4.79
Impaired, Y_i	5.77	5.67	5.51	5.32	5.83	5.49	5.23	5.61	5.63

(a) Whether the student had unimpaired vision or wore goggles first was randomly selected. Why is this a good idea in designing the experiment?

(b) Use a 95% confidence interval to test if there is a difference in braking time with impaired vision and normal vision where the differences are computed as "impaired minus normal."

Note: A normal probability plot and boxplot of the data indicate that the differences are approximately normally distributed with no outliers. (0.688, 1.238)

16. Braking Distance An automotive researcher wanted to estimate the difference in distance required to come to a complete stop while traveling 40 miles per hour on wet versus dry pavement. Because car type plays a role, the researcher used eight different cars with the same driver and tires. The braking distance (in feet) on both wet and dry pavement is shown in the table in the next column. Construct a 95% confidence interval for the mean difference in braking distance on wet versus dry pavement where the differences are computed as "wet minus dry." Interpret the interval. (29.55, 35.85)

Note: A normal probability plot and boxplot of the data indicate that the differences are approximately normally distributed with no outliers.

Car	1	2	3	4	5	6	7	8
Wet	106.9	100.9	108.8	111.8	105.0	105.6	110.6	107.9
Dry	71.8	68.8	74.1	73.4	75.9	75.2	75.7	81.0

17. Does Octane Matter? Octane is a measure of how much the fuel can be compressed before it spontaneously ignites. Some people believe that higher-octane fuels result in better gas mileage for their cars. To test this claim, a researcher randomly selected 11 individuals (and their cars) to participate in the study. Each participant received 10 gallons of gas and drove his or her car on a closed course that simulated both city and highway driving. The number of miles driven until the car ran out of gas was recorded. A coin flip was used to determine whether the car was filled up with 87-octane or 92-octane fuel first, and the driver did not know which type of fuel was in the tank. The results are in the following table:

Driver:	1	2	3	4	5	6
Miles on 87 octane	234	257	243	215	114	287
Miles on 92 octane	237	238	229	224	119	297

Driver:	7	8	9	10	11
Miles on 87 octane	315	229	192	204	547
Miles on 92 octane	351	241	186	209	562

(a) Why is it important that the matching be done by driver and car?

(b) Why is it important to conduct the study on a closed track?

(c) The normal probability plots for miles on 87 octane and miles on 92 octane are shown. Are either of these variables normally distributed? No

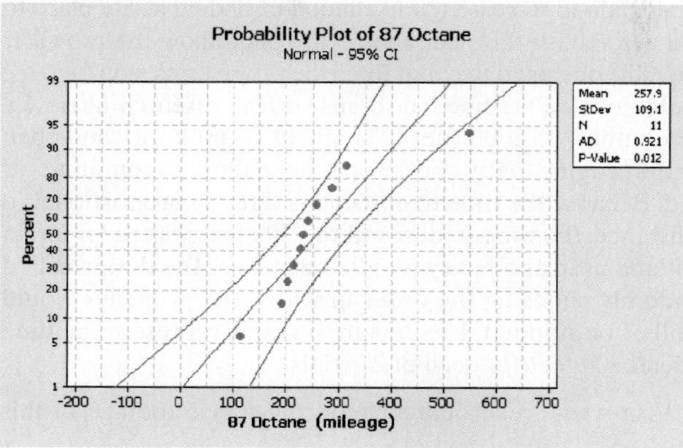

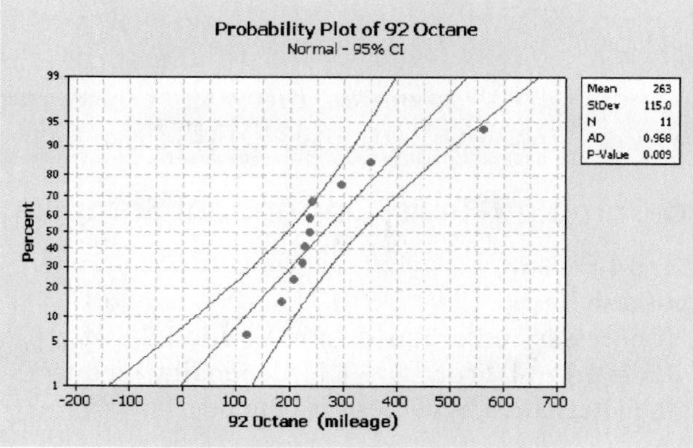

(d) The differences are computed as 92 octane minus 87 octane. The normal probability plot of the differences is shown. Is there reason to believe that the differences are normally distributed? Conclude that the differences can be normally distributed even though the original data are not. Yes

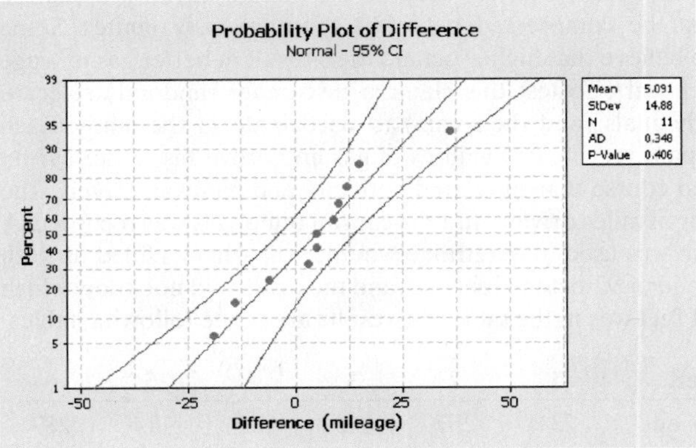

(e) The researchers used MINITAB to determine whether the mileage from 92 octane is greater than the mileage from 87 octane. The results are as follows:

Paired T-Test and CI: 92 Octane, 87 Octane

```
Paired T for 92 Octane - 87 Octane

              N      Mean     StDev   SE Mean
92 Octane    11   263.000   115.041    34.686
87 Octane    11   257.909   109.138    32.906
Difference   11   5.09091  14.87585   4.48524

95% lower bound for mean difference: -3.03841
T-Test of mean difference = 0 (vs > 0): T-Value = 1.14 P-Value = 0.141
```

What do you conclude? Why? Fail to reject H_0; P-value is too large.

18. Putting It Together: Glide Testing You are a passenger in a single-propeller-driven aircraft that experiences engine failure in the middle of a flight. The pilot wants to maximize the distance that the plane can glide to increase the likelihood of finding a safe place to land. To accomplish this goal, should the pilot allow the propeller to "windmill" or should the pilot force the propeller to stop?

To obtain the data needed to answer the research question, a pilot climbed to 8000 feet at a speed of 60 knots and then killed the engine with the propeller either windmilling or stopped. Because the time to descend is directly proportional to glide distance, the time to descend to 7200 feet was recorded in seconds and used as a proxy for glide distance. The design called for randomly choosing the order in which the propeller would windmill or be stopped. The data in the table represent the time to descend 800 feet for each of 27 trials.

Note: Visit www.aceaerobaticschool.com to see footage of this scenario.

Trial	Windmilling	Stopped	Trial	Windmilling	Stopped
1	73.4	82.3	15	64.2	82.5
2	68.9	75.8	16	67.5	81.1
3	74.1	75.7	17	71.2	72.3
4	71.7	71.7	18	75.6	77.7
5	74.2	68.8	19	73.1	82.6
6	63.5	74.2	20	77.4	79.5
7	64.4	78.0	21	77.0	82.3
8	60.9	68.5	22	77.8	79.5
9	79.5	90.6	23	77.0	79.7
10	74.5	81.9	24	72.3	73.4
11	76.5	72.9	25	69.2	76.0
12	70.3	75.7	26	63.9	74.2
13	71.3	77.6	27	70.3	79.0
14	72.7	174.3			

Source: Catherine Elizabeth Cavagnaro. "Glide Testing: A Paired Samples Experiment." *Stats* 46, Fall 2006.

(a) The trials took place over the course of a few days. However, for each trial, the pilot conducted both windmilling and stopped propeller one right after the other to minimize any impact of a change in weather conditions. Knowing this, explain why this is matched-pair data.

(b) Why does the researcher randomly determine whether to windmill or stop the propeller first for each trial?

(c) Explain why blinding is not possible for this experiment.

(d) What is the response variable in the study? What are the treatments? (e) An outlier

(e) Compute the difference as "difference = stopped − windmilling." Draw a boxplot of the differenced data. What do you notice?

(f) From part (b), you should notice that trial 14 results in an outlier. Because our sample size is small, this outlier will have a major effect on any results. The author of the article indicated that it was possibly a situation in which there was an updraft of wind, causing the plane to take quite a bit longer than normal to fall 800 feet. Explain why this explanation makes it reasonable to eliminate trial 14 from the analysis.

(g) Redraw a boxplot of the data with trial 14 eliminated. Based on the shape of the boxplot, do you believe it is reasonable to proceed with a matched-pair *t*-test? Yes

(h) The researchers wanted to determine if stopping the propeller resulted in a longer glide distance. Based on this goal, determine the null and alternative hypotheses. H_0: $\mu_d = 0$ vs. H_1: $\mu_d > 0$

(i) Conduct the appropriate test to answer the researcher's question.

(j) Write a few sentences outlining your recommendations to pilots who experience engine failure. (i) Reject H_0

Technology Step-By-Step

Two-Sample *t*-Tests, Dependent Sampling

TI-83/84 Plus

Hypothesis Tests

1. If necessary, enter raw data in L1 and L2. Let L3 = L1 − L2 (or L2 − L1), depending on how the alternative hypothesis is defined.
2. Press STAT, highlight TESTS, and select `2:T-Test`.
3. If the data are raw, highlight DATA, making sure that List is set to L3 with frequency set to 1. If summary statistics are known, highlight STATS and enter the summary statistics.

4. Highlight the appropriate relation in the alternative hypothesis.
5. Highlight Calculate or Draw and press `ENTER`. Calculate gives the test statistic and *P*-value. Draw will draw the *t*-distribution with the *P*-value shaded.

Confidence Intervals
Follow the same steps given for hypothesis tests, except select `8: TInterval`. Also, select a confidence level (such as 95% = 0.95).

MINITAB

1. If necessary, enter raw data in columns C1 and C2.
2. Select the **Stat** menu, highlight **Basic Statistics**, and then select **Paired-t . . .** .
3. If you have raw data, enter C1 in the cell marked "First Sample" and enter C2 in the cell marked "Second Sample." If you have summarized data, click the "Summarized data" radio button and enter the summary statistics. Click Options . . . , select the direction of the alternative hypothesis and select a confidence level. Click OK twice.

Excel

1. Enter the raw data into Columns A and B.
2. Select the Formulas menu. Select More Functions. Highlight Statistical, and select TTtest from the drop-down menu.
3. Place the cursor in Array1. Highlight the data in Column A. Place the cursor in Array2. Highlight the data in Column B. Place the cursor in the Tails cell. Enter the number corresponding to the test you desire (1 for a one-tailed distribution; 2 for a two-tailed distribution). Place the cursor in the Type cell. Enter 1 for a paired t-test.

StatCrunch

1. If necessary, enter the raw data into the first two columns of the spreadsheet. Name each column variable.
2. Select **Stat**, highlight **T Statistics**, select **Paired**.
3. Select the column that contains the data for Sample 1. Select the column that contains the data for Sample 2. Note that the differences are computed Sample1 – Sample 2. Click Next>.
4. If you choose the hypothesis test radio button, enter the value of the mean stated in the null hypothesis and choose the direction of the alternative hypothesis from the pull-down menu. If you choose the confidence interval radio button, enter the level of confidence. Click Calculate.

11.3 INFERENCE ABOUT TWO MEANS: INDEPENDENT SAMPLES

Preparing for This Section Before getting started, review the following:

- The Completely Randomized Design (Section 1.6, pp. 47–49)
- Confidence intervals about μ (Section 9.2, pp. 409–411)
- Hypothesis tests about μ (Section 10.3, pp. 449–453)
- Type I and Type II errors (Section 10.1, pp. 432–433)

OBJECTIVES

1 Test hypotheses regarding the difference of two independent means

2 Construct and interpret confidence intervals regarding the difference of two independent means

Note to Instructor
If you like, you can print out and distribute the Preparing for This Section quiz located in the Instructor's Resource Center. The purpose of the quiz is to verify that the students have the prerequisite knowledge for the section.

Note to Instructor
Students should be familiar with the concept of hypothesis testing by now, so the pace can be a little quicker.

We now turn our attention to inferential methods for comparing means from two independent samples. For example, we might wish to know whether a new experimental drug relieves symptoms attributable to the common cold. The response variable might be the time until the cold symptoms go away. If the drug is effective, the mean time until the cold symptoms go away should be less for individuals taking the drug than for those not taking the drug. If we let μ_1 represent the mean time until cold symptoms go away for the individuals taking the drug, and μ_2 represent the mean time until cold symptoms go away for individuals taking a placebo, the null and alternative hypotheses will be

$$H_0: \mu_1 = \mu_2 \quad \text{versus} \quad H_1: \mu_1 < \mu_2$$

Note to Instructor

The computations in this section become quite tedious. You might consider emphasizing technology solutions. This allows for more emphasis on the *P*-value approach to hypothesis testing.

Note to Instructor

We do not discuss comparing the difference between two means using the pooled standard deviation. This is because the test requires that the two independent samples come from populations with the same variance. Verifying the requirement of equal population variances suggests using the *F*-test. Numerous statisticians (including George Box) have shown that the *F*-test is extremely sensitive to departures from normality. In fact, Box states, "It would seem logical to replace the usual analysis ... which uses a pooled estimate ... by the alternative criterion proposed by Welch." (Source: "Nonnormality and Tests on Variances." *Biometrica* 40: 318–340)

Note to Instructor

The actual degrees of freedom is

$$df = \frac{\left(\frac{s_1^2}{n_1} + \frac{s_2^2}{n_2}\right)^2}{\frac{1}{n_1 - 1}\cdot\left(\frac{s_1^2}{n_1}\right)^2 + \frac{1}{n_2 - 1}\cdot\left(\frac{s_2^2}{n_2}\right)^2}$$

This formula is so messy that we recommend using the smaller of $n_1 - 1$ or $n_2 - 1$ degrees of freedom when performing by-hand computation.

or, equivalently,

$$H_0: \mu_1 - \mu_2 = 0 \quad \text{versus} \quad H_1: \mu_1 - \mu_2 < 0$$

To conduct this test, we might randomly divide 500 volunteers who have a common cold into two groups: an experimental group (group 1) and a control group (group 2). The control group will receive a placebo and the experimental group will receive a predetermined amount of the experimental drug. Next, determine the time until the cold symptoms go away. Compute $\bar{x}_1$, the sample mean time until cold symptoms go away in the experimental group, and $\bar{x}_2$, the sample mean time until cold symptoms go away in the control group. Now we determine whether the difference in the sample means, $\bar{x}_1 - \bar{x}_2$, is significantly less than 0, the assumed difference stated in the null hypothesis. To do this, we need to know the sampling distribution of $\bar{x}_1 - \bar{x}_2$.

It is unreasonable to expect to know information regarding σ_1 and σ_2 without knowing information regarding the population means. Therefore, we must develop a sampling distribution for the difference of two means when the population standard deviations are unknown.

The comparison of two means with unequal (and unknown) population variances is called the Behrens–Fisher problem. While an exact method for performing inference on the equality of two means with unequal population standard deviations does not exist, an approximate solution is available. The approach that we use is known as **Welch's approximate *t***, in honor of English statistician Bernard Lewis Welch (1911–1989).

Sampling Distribution of the Difference of Two Means: Independent Samples with Population Standard Deviations Unknown (Welch's *t*)

Suppose that a simple random sample of size n_1 is taken from a population with unknown mean μ_1 and unknown standard deviation σ_1. In addition, a simple random sample of size n_2 is taken from a second population with unknown mean μ_2 and unknown standard deviation σ_2. If the two populations are normally distributed or the sample sizes are sufficiently large ($n_1 \geq 30$ and $n_2 \geq 30$), then

$$t = \frac{(\bar{x}_1 - \bar{x}_2) - (\mu_1 - \mu_2)}{\sqrt{\frac{s_1^2}{n_1} + \frac{s_2^2}{n_2}}} \qquad (1)$$

approximately follows Student's *t*-distribution with the smaller of $n_1 - 1$ or $n_2 - 1$ degrees of freedom, where $\bar{x}_1$ is the sample mean and s_1 is the sample standard deviation from population 1, and $\bar{x}_2$ is the sample mean and s_2 is the sample standard deviation from population 2.

1 Test Hypotheses Regarding the Difference of Two Independent Means

Now that we know the approximate sampling distribution of $\bar{x}_1 - \bar{x}_2$, we can introduce a procedure that can be used to test hypotheses regarding two population means.

Testing Hypotheses Regarding the Difference of Two Means

To test hypotheses regarding two population means, μ_1 and μ_2, with unknown population standard deviations, we can use the following steps, provided that

- the samples are obtained using simple random sampling or through a randomized experiment;
- the samples are independent;
- the populations from which the samples are drawn are normally distributed or the sample sizes are large ($n_1 \geq 30$ and $n_2 \geq 30$);
- for each sample, the sample size is no more than 5% of the population size.

Step 1 Determine the null and alternative hypotheses. The hypotheses are structured in one of three ways:

Two-Tailed	Left-Tailed	Right-Tailed
H_0: $\mu_1 = \mu_2$	H_0: $\mu_1 = \mu_2$	H_0: $\mu_1 = \mu_2$
H_1: $\mu_1 \neq \mu_2$	H_1: $\mu_1 < \mu_2$	H_1: $\mu_1 > \mu_2$

Note: μ_1 is the population mean for population 1, and μ_2 is the population mean for population 2.

Step 2 Select a level of significance α, depending on the seriousness of making a Type I error.

Classical Approach

Step 3 Compute the **test statistic**

$$t_0 = \frac{(\bar{x}_1 - \bar{x}_2) - (\mu_1 - \mu_2)}{\sqrt{\dfrac{s_1^2}{n_1} + \dfrac{s_2^2}{n_2}}}$$

which approximately follows Student's t-distribution. Use Table VI to determine the critical value using the smaller of $n_1 - 1$ or $n_2 - 1$ degrees of freedom.

	Two-Tailed	Left-Tailed	Right-Tailed
Critical value(s)	$-t_{\frac{\alpha}{2}}$ and $t_{\frac{\alpha}{2}}$	$-t_{\alpha}$	t_{α}
Critical region			

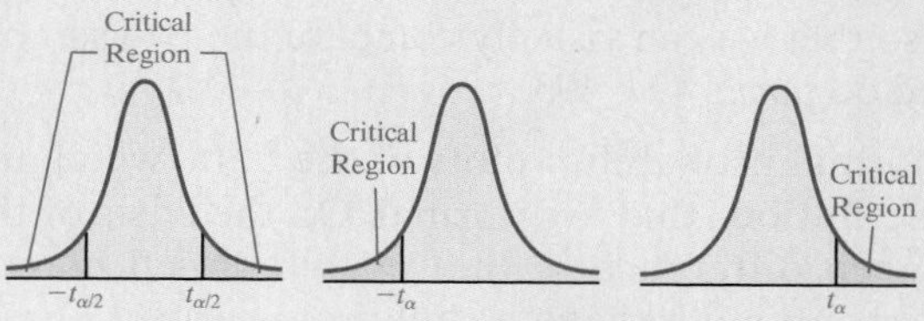

Step 4 Compare the critical value to the test statistic.

Two-Tailed	Left-Tailed	Right-Tailed
If $t_0 < -t_{\frac{\alpha}{2}}$ or $t_0 > t_{\frac{\alpha}{2}}$, reject the null hypothesis.	If $t_0 < -t_{\alpha}$, reject the null hypothesis.	If $t_0 > t_{\alpha}$, reject the null hypothesis.

P-Value Approach

By Hand Step 3 Compute the **test statistic**

$$t_0 = \frac{(\bar{x}_1 - \bar{x}_2) - (\mu_1 - \mu_2)}{\sqrt{\dfrac{s_1^2}{n_1} + \dfrac{s_2^2}{n_2}}}$$

which approximately follows Student's t-distribution. Use Table VI to approximate the P-value using the smaller of $n_1 - 1$ or $n_2 - 1$ degrees of freedom.

Two-Tailed	Left-Tailed	Right-Tailed

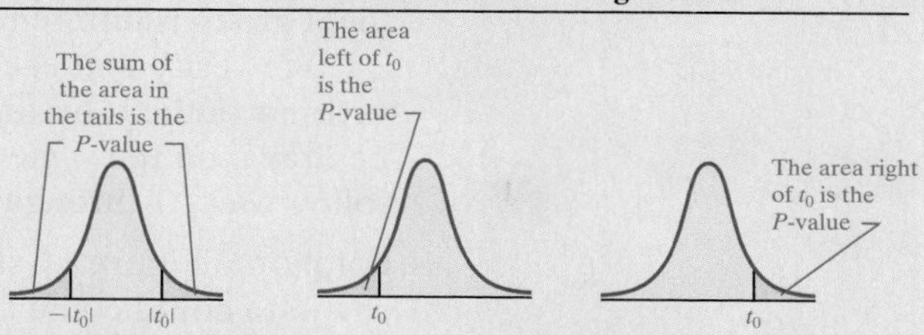

P-value $= 2P(t > |t_0|)$ $\quad$ P-value $= P(t < t_0)$ $\quad$ P-value $= P(t > t_0)$

Technology Step 3 Use a statistical spreadsheet or calculator with statistical capabilities to obtain the P-value. The directions for obtaining the P-value using the TI-83/84 Plus graphing calculator, Excel, MINITAB, and StatCrunch are in the Technology Step-by-Step on page 505.

Step 4 If P-value $< \alpha$, reject the null hypothesis.

Step 5 State the conclusion.

The procedure just presented is robust, so minor departures from normality will not adversely affect the results of the test. If the data have outliers, however, the procedure should not be used.

We verify these requirements by constructing normal probability plots (to assess normality) and boxplots (to determine whether there are outliers). If the normal probability plots indicate that the data come from populations that are not normally distributed or the boxplots reveals outliers, then nonparametric tests should be performed.

EXAMPLE 1 Testing Hypotheses Regarding Two Means

Problem In the Spacelab Life Sciences 2 payload, 14 male rats were sent to space. Upon their return, the red blood cell mass (in milliliters) of the rats was determined. A control group of 14 male rats was held under the same conditions (except for space flight) as the space rats, and their red blood cell mass was also determined when the space rats returned. The project, led by Dr. Paul X. Callahan, resulted in the data listed in

Table 5. Does the evidence suggest that the flight animals have a different red blood cell mass from the control animals at the $\alpha = 0.05$ level of significance?

TABLE 5

Flight				Control			
8.59	8.64	7.43	7.21	8.65	6.99	8.40	9.66
6.87	7.89	9.79	6.85	7.62	7.44	8.55	8.70
7.00	8.80	9.30	8.03	7.33	8.58	9.88	9.94
6.39	7.54			7.14	9.14		

Source: NASA Life Sciences Data Archive

Approach This experiment is a completely randomized design with response variable red blood cell mass. The treatment is space flight, which is set at two levels: space flight or no space flight. The experimental units are the 28 rats. The expectation is that all other variables that may affect red blood cell mass are accounted for by holding both groups of rats in the same condition (other than space flight) and through random assignment.

We are attempting to determine if the evidence suggests that space flight affects red blood cell mass. We assume no difference, so we assume the mean red blood cell mass of the flight group equals that of the control group. We want to show that the mean of the flight group is different from the mean of the control group.

We verify that each sample comes from a population that is approximately normal with no outliers by drawing normal probability plots and boxplots. The boxplots will be drawn on the same graph so that we can visually compare the two samples. We then follow Steps 1 through 5, listed on pages 494–495.

Solution Figure 11 shows normal probability plots of the data, which indicate that the data could come from populations that are normal. On the basis of the boxplots, it seems that there is not much difference in the red blood cell mass of the two samples, although the flight group might have a slightly lower red blood cell mass. We have to determine if this difference is significant or due to random sampling error (chance).

Figure 11

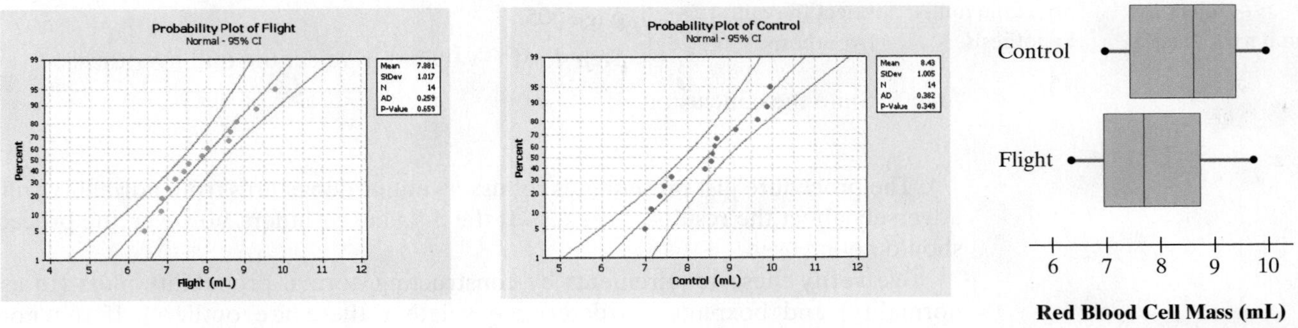

Step 1 We want to know whether the flight animals have a different red blood cell mass from the control animals. Let μ_1 represent the mean red blood cell mass of the flight animals and μ_2 represent the mean red blood cell mass of the control animals. We are attempting to gather evidence that shows $\mu_1 \neq \mu_2$, and we have the hypotheses

$$H_0: \mu_1 = \mu_2 \quad \text{versus} \quad H_1: \mu_1 \neq \mu_2 \qquad \text{or} \qquad H_0: \mu_1 - \mu_2 = 0 \quad \text{versus} \quad H_1: \mu_1 - \mu_2 \neq 0$$

Step 2 The level of significance $\alpha = 0.05$.

Classical Approach

Step 3 The statistics for sample 1 (the flight rats) are $n_1 = 14, \bar{x}_1 = 7.881$, and $s_1 = 1.017$.

The statistics for sample 2 (the control rats) are $n_2 = 14, \bar{x}_2 = 8.430$, and $s_2 = 1.005$.

The test statistic is

$$t_0 = \frac{(\bar{x}_1 - \bar{x}_2) - (\mu_1 - \mu_2)}{\sqrt{\frac{s_1^2}{n_1} + \frac{s_2^2}{n_2}}}$$

$$= \frac{(7.881 - 8.430) - 0}{\sqrt{\frac{1.017^2}{14} + \frac{1.005^2}{14}}}$$

$$= \frac{-0.549}{0.3821288115}$$

$$= -1.437$$

Step 4 The test statistic is $t_0 = -1.437$. We label this point in Figure 12.

This is a two-tailed test with $\alpha = 0.05$. Since the sample sizes of the experimental group and control group are both 14, we have $n_1 - 1 = 14 - 1 = 13$ degrees of freedom. The critical values are $t_{\frac{\alpha}{2}} = t_{\frac{0.05}{2}} = t_{0.025} = 2.160$ and $-t_{0.025} = -2.160$. The critical region is displayed in Figure 12.

Figure 12

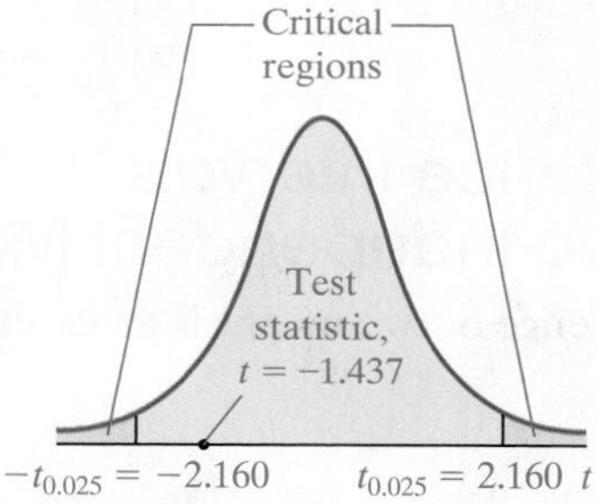

Because the test statistic does not lie within a critical region, we do not reject the null hypothesis.

P-Value Approach

By Hand Step 3 The statistics for sample 1 (the flight rats) are $n_1 = 14, \bar{x}_1 = 7.881$, and $s_1 = 1.017$. The statistics for sample 2 (the control rats) are $n_2 = 14, \bar{x}_2 = 8.430$, and $s_2 = 1.005$.

The test statistic is

$$t_0 = \frac{(\bar{x}_1 - \bar{x}_2) - (\mu_1 - \mu_2)}{\sqrt{\frac{s_1^2}{n_1} + \frac{s_2^2}{n_2}}} = \frac{(7.881 - 8.430) - 0}{\sqrt{\frac{1.017^2}{14} + \frac{1.005^2}{14}}}$$

$$= \frac{-0.549}{0.3821288115}$$

$$= -1.437$$

Because this is a two-tailed test, the *P*-value is the area under the *t*-distribution to the left of $t_0 = -1.437$ plus the area under the *t*-distribution to the right of $t_0 = 1.437$. See Figure 13.

Figure 13

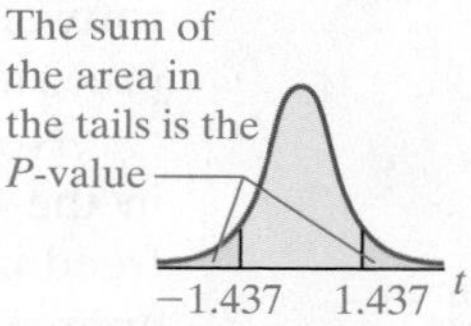

Since the sample size of the experimental group and control group are both 14, we have $n_1 - 1 = 14 - 1 = 13$ degrees of freedom. Because of symmetry, we use Table VI to estimate the area under the *t*-distribution to the right of $t_0 = 1.437$ and double it.

$$P\text{-value} = P(t_0 < -1.437 \text{ or } t_0 > 1.437) = 2P(t_0 > 1.437)$$

Using Table VI, we find the row that corresponds to 13 degrees of freedom. The value 1.437 lies between 1.350 and 1.771. The area under the *t*-distribution with 13 degrees of freedom to the right of 1.350 is 0.10. The area under the *t*-distribution with 13 degrees of freedom to the right of 1.771 is 0.05. After doubling these values, we have

$$0.10 < P\text{-value} < 0.20$$

Technology Step 3 Using Excel, we find the *P*-value is 0.1627. See Figure 14.

Figure 14

t-Test: *Two-Sample Assuming Unequal Variances*

	Flight	*Control*
Mean	7.880714286	8.43
Variance	1.035207143	1.010969231
Observations	14	14
Hypothesized Mean Difference	0	
df	26	
t Stat	−1.436781704	
P(T<=t) one-tail	0.081352709	
t Critical one-tail	1.705616341	
P(T<=t) two-tail	0.162705419	
t Critical two-tail	2.055530786	

Step 4 The *P*-value of 0.1627 [by hand: 0.10 < *P*-value < 0.20] means that *if* the null hypothesis that the mean difference of zero is true, we expect results similar to the ones obtained in about 16 out of 100 samples. The results we obtained are not unusual if the null hypothesis is true. Simply put, because the *P*-value is greater than the level of significance (0.1627 > 0.05), we do not reject the null hypothesis.

Step 5 There is not sufficient evidence to conclude that the flight animals have a different red blood cell mass from the control animals at the $\alpha = 0.05$ level of significance.

The degrees of freedom used to determine the critical value(s) presented in Example 1 are conservative. Results that are more accurate can be obtained by using the following degrees of freedom:

$$\text{df} = \frac{\left(\dfrac{s_1^2}{n_1} + \dfrac{s_2^2}{n_2}\right)^2}{\dfrac{\left(\dfrac{s_1^2}{n_1}\right)^2}{n_1 - 1} + \dfrac{\left(\dfrac{s_2^2}{n_2}\right)^2}{n_2 - 1}} \qquad \textbf{(2)}$$

When using Formula (2) to compute degrees of freedom, round down to the nearest integer to use Table VI. For hand inference, it is recommended that we use the smaller of $n_1 - 1$ or $n_2 - 1$ as the degrees of freedom to ease computation. However, computer software will use Formula (2) when computing the degrees of freedom for increased precision in determining the *P*-value.

Notice that the degrees of freedom in the technology solution are 26* versus 13 in the conservative solution done by hand in Example 1. With the lower degrees of freedom, the critical t is larger (2.160 with 13 degrees of freedom versus 2.056 with approximately 26 degrees of freedom). The larger critical value increases the number of standard deviations the difference in the sample means must be from the hypothesized mean difference before the null hypothesis is rejected. Therefore, in using the smaller of $n_1 - 1$ or $n_2 - 1$ degrees of freedom, we need more substantial evidence to reject the null hypothesis. This requirement decreases the probability of a Type I error (rejecting the null hypothesis when the null hypothesis is true) below the actual level of α chosen by the researcher. This is what we mean when we say that the method of using the lesser of $n_1 - 1$ and $n_2 - 1$ as a proxy for degrees of freedom is conservative compared with using Formula (2).

CAUTION

The degrees of freedom in by-hand solutions will not equal the degrees of freedom in technology solutions unless you use Formula (2) to compute degrees of freedom.

Now Work Problem 13

2 Construct and Interpret Confidence Intervals Regarding the Difference of Two Independent Means

Constructing a confidence interval for the difference of two means is an extension of the results presented in Section 9.2.

Constructing a $(1 - \alpha) \cdot 100\%$ Confidence Interval for the Difference of Two Means

A simple random sample of size n_1 is taken from a population with unknown mean μ_1 and unknown standard deviation σ_1. Also, a simple random sample of size n_2 is taken from a population with unknown mean μ_2 and unknown standard deviation σ_2. If the two populations are normally distributed or the sample sizes are sufficiently large ($n_1 \geq 30$ and $n_2 \geq 30$), a $(1 - \alpha) \cdot 100\%$ confidence interval about $\mu_1 - \mu_2$ is given by

$$\text{Lower bound: } (\bar{x}_1 - \bar{x}_2) - t_{\frac{\alpha}{2}} \cdot \sqrt{\frac{s_1^2}{n_1} + \frac{s_2^2}{n_2}}$$

and **(3)**

$$\text{Upper bound: } (\bar{x}_1 - \bar{x}_2) + t_{\frac{\alpha}{2}} \cdot \sqrt{\frac{s_1^2}{n_1} + \frac{s_2^2}{n_2}}$$

where $t_{\frac{\alpha}{2}}$ is computed using the smaller of $n_1 - 1$ or $n_2 - 1$ degrees of freedom or Formula (2).

*Actually, the degrees of freedom are 25.996, but Excel rounded to 26.

EXAMPLE 2 Constructing a Confidence Interval for the Difference of Two Means

Problem Construct a 95% confidence interval for $\mu_1 - \mu_2$ using the data presented in Table 5 on page 496.

Approach The normal probability plots and boxplot (Figure 11) indicate that the data are approximately normal with no outliers. We compute the confidence interval with $\alpha = 0.05$ using Formula (3) or using technology.

By-Hand Solution

We have already found the sample statistics in Example 1. In addition, we found $t_{\frac{\alpha}{2}} = t_{0.025}$ with 13 degrees of freedom to be 2.160. Substituting into Formula (3), we obtain the following results:

Lower bound: $(\bar{x}_1 - \bar{x}_2) - t_{\frac{\alpha}{2}} \cdot \sqrt{\dfrac{s_1^2}{n_1} + \dfrac{s_2^2}{n_2}}$

$$= (7.881 - 8.430) - 2.160 \cdot \sqrt{\frac{1.017^2}{14} + \frac{1.005^2}{14}}$$
$$= -0.549 - 0.825$$
$$= -1.374$$

Upper bound: $(\bar{x}_1 - \bar{x}_2) + t_{\frac{\alpha}{2}} \cdot \sqrt{\dfrac{s_1^2}{n_1} + \dfrac{s_2^2}{n_2}}$

$$= (7.881 - 8.430) + 2.160 \cdot \sqrt{\frac{1.017^2}{14} + \frac{1.005^2}{14}}$$
$$= -0.549 + 0.825$$
$$= 0.276$$

Technology Solution

Figure 15 shows the results from MINITAB.

Figure 15

Two-Sample T-Test and CI: Flight, Control

```
Two-sample T for Flight vs Control

         N  Mean  StDev  SE Mean
Flight  14  7.88   1.02     0.27
Control 14  8.43   1.01     0.27

Difference = mu (Flight) - mu (Control)
Estimate for difference:  -0.549
95% CI for difference:  (-1.337, 0.238)
T-Test of difference = 0 (vs not =): T-Value = -1.44  P-Value = 0.163  DF = 25
```

Interpretation We are 95% confident the mean difference between the red blood cell mass of the flight animals and control animals is between −1.374 [Technology: −1.337] mL and 0.276 [Technology: 0.238] mL. The confidence interval contains zero, so there is not sufficient evidence to conclude there is a difference in the red blood cell mass of the flight group and the control group. That is, space flight does not seem to affect red blood cell mass significantly.

Now Work Problem 21

⚠ CAUTION

We would use the pooled two-sample *t*-test when the two samples come from populations that have the same variance. *Pooling* refers to finding a weighted average of the two sample variances from the independent samples. It is difficult to verify that two population variances might be equal based on sample data, so we will always use Welch's *t* when comparing two means.

What about the Pooled Two-Sample *t*-Tests?

Perhaps you have noticed that statistical software and graphing calculators with advanced statistical features provide an option for two types of two-sample *t*-tests: one that assumes equal population variances (pooling) and one that does not assume equal population variances. Welch's *t*-statistic does not assume that the population variances are equal and can be used whether the population variances are equal or not. The test that assumes equal population variances is referred to as the *pooled t-statistic*.

The **pooled *t*-statistic** is computed by finding a weighted average of the sample variances and uses this average in the computation of the test statistic. The advantage of this test statistic is that it exactly follows Student's *t*-distribution with $n_1 + n_2 - 2$ degrees of freedom.

The disadvantage of the test statistic is that it requires that the population variances be equal. How is this requirement to be verified? While a test for determining the equality of variances does exist (*F*-test, on CD that accompanies this text), the test *requires* that each population be normally distributed. However, the *F*-test is not robust. Any minor departures from normality will make the results of the *F*-test unreliable. It has been recommended by many statisticians* that a preliminary *F*-test to check the requirement of equality of variance not be performed. In fact, George Box once said, "To make preliminary tests on variances is rather like putting to sea in a rowing boat to find out whether conditions are sufficiently calm for an ocean liner to leave port!"

*Moser and Stevens, "Homogeneity of Variance in the Two-Sample Means Test." *American Statistician* 46(1).

Because the formal F-test for testing the equality of variances is so volatile, we are content to use Welch's t. Welch's t-test is more conservative than the pooled t. The price that must be paid for the conservative approach is that the probability of a Type II error is higher with Welch's t than with the pooled t when the population variances are equal. However, the two tests typically provide the same conclusion, even if the assumption of equal population standard deviations seems reasonable.

11.3 ASSESS YOUR UNDERSTANDING

SKILL BUILDING*

In Problems 1–6, assume that the populations are normally distributed.

1. (a) Test whether $\mu_1 \neq \mu_2$ at the $\alpha = 0.05$ level of significance for the given sample data. Do not reject H_0 (b) $(-1.53, 3.73)$
(b) Construct a 95% confidence interval about $\mu_1 - \mu_2$.

	Population 1	Population 2
n	15	15
$\bar{x}$	15.3	14.2
s	3.2	3.5

2. (a) Test whether $\mu_1 \neq \mu_2$ at the $\alpha = 0.05$ level of significance for the given sample data. Reject H_0
(b) Construct a 95% confidence interval about $\mu_1 - \mu_2$.

	Population 1	Population 2
n	20	20
$\bar{x}$	111	104
s	8.6	9.2

3. (a) Test whether $\mu_1 > \mu_2$ at the $\alpha = 0.1$ level of significance for the given sample data. Reject H_0
(b) Construct a 90% confidence interval about $\mu_1 - \mu_2$

	Population 1	Population 2
n	25	18
$\bar{x}$	50.2	42.0
s	6.4	9.9

4. (a) Test whether $\mu_1 < \mu_2$ at the $\alpha = 0.05$ level of significance for the given sample data. Reject H_0
(b) Construct a 95% confidence interval about $\mu_1 - \mu_2$.

	Population 1	Population 2
n	40	32
$\bar{x}$	94.2	115.2
s	15.9	23.0

2. (b) (1.11, 12.89) 3. (b) (3.57, 12.83) 4. (b) $(-30.75, -11.25)$

5. Test whether $\mu_1 < \mu_2$ at the $\alpha = 0.02$ level of significance for the given sample data. Reject H_0

	Population 1	Population 2
n	32	25
$\bar{x}$	103.4	114.2
s	12.3	13.2

6. Test whether $\mu_1 > \mu_2$ at the $\alpha = 0.05$ level of significance for the given sample data. Do not reject H_0

	Population 1	Population 2
n	23	13
$\bar{x}$	43.1	41.0
s	4.5	5.1

APPLYING THE CONCEPTS

7. Elapsed Time to Earn a Bachelor's Degree Clifford Adelman, a researcher with the Department of Education, followed a cohort of students who graduated from high school in 1992. He monitored the progress the students made toward completing a bachelor's degree. One aspect of his research was to determine whether students who first attended community college took longer to attain a bachelor's degree than those who immediately attended and remained at a 4-year institution. The data in the table summarize the results of his study.

	Community College to 4-Year Transfer	No Transfer
n	268	1145
Sample mean time to graduate in years	5.43	4.43
Sample standard deviation time to graduate in years	1.162	1.015

Source: Clifford Adelman, *The Toolbox Revisited*. United States Department of Education, 2006.

(a) Does the evidence suggest that community college transfer students take longer to attain a bachelor's degree? Use an $\alpha = 0.01$ level of significance. Yes; reject H_0
(b) Construct a 95% confidence interval for $\mu_{\text{community college}} - \mu_{\text{no transfer}}$ to approximate the mean additional time it takes to complete a bachelor's degree if you begin in community college. (0.818, 1.182)

*The by-hand confidence intervals in the back of the text were computed using the smaller of $n_1 - 1$ or $n_2 - 1$ degrees of freedom.

(c) Do the results of parts (a) and (b) imply that community college causes you to take extra time to earn a bachelor's degree? Cite some reasons that you think might contribute to the extra time to graduate.

8. Treating Bipolar Mania Researchers conducted a randomized, double-blind study to measure the effects of the drug olanzapine on patients diagnosed with bipolar disorder. A total of 115 patients with a DSM-IV diagnosis of bipolar disorder were randomly divided into two groups. Group 1 ($n_1 = 55$) received 5 to 20 mg per day of olanzapine, while group 2 ($n_2 = 60$) received a placebo. The effectiveness of the drug was measured using the Young–Mania rating scale total score with the net improvement in the score recorded. The results are presented in the table. Does the evidence suggest that the experimental group experienced a larger mean improvement than the control group at the $\alpha = 0.01$ level of significance? Reject H_0

	Experimental Group	Control Group
n	55	60
Mean improvement	14.8	8.1
Sample standard deviation	12.5	12.7

Source: "Efficacy of Olanzapine in Acute Bipolar Mania," *Archives of General Psychiatry*, 59(9), pp. 841–848.

9. Walking in the Airport, Part I Do people walk faster in the airport when they are departing (getting on a plane) or when they are arriving (getting off a plane)? Researcher Seth B. Young measured the walking speed of travelers in San Francisco International Airport and Cleveland Hopkins International Airport. His findings are summarized in the table.

Direction of Travels	Departure	Arrival
Mean speed (feet per minute)	260	269
Standard deviation (feet per minute)	53	34
Sample size	35	35

Source: Seth B. Young. "Evaluation of Pedestrian Walking Speeds in Airport Terminals." *Transportation Research Record*. Paper 99-0824.

(a) Is this an observational study or a designed experiment? Why? Observational

(b) Explain why it is reasonable to use Welch's t-test.

(c) Do individuals walk at different speeds depending on whether they are departing or arriving at the $\alpha = 0.05$ level of significance? Do not reject H_0

10. Walking in the Airport, Part II Do business travelers walk at a different pace than leisure travelers? Researcher Seth B. Young measured the walking speed of business and leisure travelers in San Francisco International Airport and Cleveland Hopkins International Airport. His findings are summarized in the table.

Type of Traveler	Business	Leisure
Mean speed (feet per minute)	272	261
Standard deviation (feet per minute)	43	47
Sample size	20	20

Source: Seth B. Young. "Evaluation of Pedestrian Walking Speeds in Airport Terminals." *Transportation Research Record*, Paper 99-0824.

10. (a) Observational

(a) Is this an observational study or a designed experiment? Why?

(b) What must be true regarding the populations to use Welch's t-test to compare the means? Normally distributed

(c) Assuming that the requirements listed in part (b) are satisfied, determine whether business travelers walk at a different speed from leisure travelers at the $\alpha = 0.05$ level of significance. Do not reject H_0

11. Priming Two Dutch researchers conducted a study in which two groups of students were asked to answer 42 questions from Trivial Pursuit. The students in group 1 were asked to spend 5 minutes thinking about what it would mean to be a professor, while the students in group 2 were asked to think about soccer hooligans. The 200 students in group 1 had a mean score of 23.4 with a standard deviation of 4.1, while the 200 students in group 2 had a mean score of 17.9 with a standard deviation of 3.9. *Source:* Based on the research of Dijksterhuis, Ap, and Ad van Knippenberg. "The relation between perception and behavior, or how to win a game of Trivial Pursuit." *Journal of Personality and Social Psychology* 74.4 (1998): 865+. *Academic OneFile.* Web. 5 July 2010.

(a) Determine the 95% confidence interval for the difference in scores, $\mu_1 - \mu_2$. Interpret the interval. (4.71, 6.29)

(b) What does this say about priming?

12. Government Waste In a Gallup poll conducted August 31–September 2, 2009, 513 national adults aged 18 years of age or older who consider themselves to be Republican were asked, "Of every tax dollar that goes to the federal government in Washington, D.C., how many cents of each dollar would you say are wasted?" The mean wasted was found to be 54 cents with a standard deviation of 2.9 cents. The same question was asked of 513 national adults aged 18 years of age or older who consider themselves to be Democrat. The mean wasted was found to be 41 cents with a standard deviation of 2.6 cents. Construct a 95% confidence interval for the mean difference in government waste, $\mu_R - \mu_D$. Interpret the interval. (12.66, 13.34)

NW **13. Ramp Metering** Ramp metering is a traffic engineering idea that requires cars entering a freeway to stop for a certain period of time before joining the traffic flow. The theory is that ramp metering controls the number of cars on the freeway and the number of cars accessing the freeway, resulting in a freer flow of cars, which ultimately results in faster travel times. To test whether ramp metering is effective in reducing travel times, engineers in Minneapolis, Minnesota, conducted an experiment in which a section of freeway had ramp meters installed on the on-ramps. The response variable for the study was speed of the vehicles. A random sample of 15 cars on the highway for a Monday at 6 P.M. with the ramp meters on and a second random sample of 15 cars on a different Monday at 6 P.M. with the meters off resulted in the following speeds (in miles per hour).

Ramp Meters On		
28	48	56
38	31	25
43	46	50
35	55	40
42	26	47

Ramp Meters Off		
24	26	42
34	37	31
47	38	17
29	23	40
37	52	41

(a) Draw side-by-side boxplots of each data set. Does there appear to be a difference in the speeds? Are there any outliers?

(b) Are the ramp meters effective in maintaining a higher speed on the freeway? Use the $\alpha = 0.10$ level of significance.

Note: Normal probability plots indicate the data could come from a population that is normally distributed. Yes; P-value = 0.0489

14. Measuring Reaction Time Researchers at the University of Mississippi wanted to determine whether the reaction time (in seconds) of males differed from that of females to a go/no go stimulus. The researchers randomly selected 20 females and 15 males to participate in the study. The go/no go stimulus required the student to respond to a particular stimulus and not to respond to other stimuli. The results are as follows:

Female Students				Male Students		
0.588	0.652	0.442	0.293	0.375	0.256	0.427
0.340	0.636	0.391	0.367	0.654	0.563	0.405
0.377	0.646	0.403	0.377	0.374	0.465	0.402
0.380	0.403	0.617	0.434	0.373	0.488	0.337
0.443	0.481	0.613	0.274	0.224	0.477	0.655

Source: PsychExperiments at the University of Mississippi

(a) Is it reasonable to use Welch's t-test? Why Yes

Note: Normal probability plots indicate that the data are approximately normal and boxplots indicate that there are no outliers.

(b) Test whether there is a difference in the reaction times of males and females at the $\alpha = 0.05$ level of significance. Do not reject H_0

(c) Draw boxplots of each data set using the same scale. Does this visual evidence support the results obtained in part (b)?

15. Bacteria in Hospital Carpeting Researchers wanted to determine if carpeted rooms contained more bacteria than uncarpeted rooms. To determine the amount of bacteria in a room, researchers pumped the air from the room over a Petri dish at the rate of 1 cubic foot per minute for eight carpeted rooms and eight uncarpeted rooms. Colonies of bacteria were allowed to form in the 16 Petri dishes. The results are presented in the table. A normal probability plot and boxplot indicate that the data are approximately normally distributed with no outliers. Do carpeted rooms have more bacteria than uncarpeted rooms at the $\alpha = 0.05$ level of significance? Do not reject H_0

Carpeted Rooms (bacteria/cubic foot)		Uncarpeted Rooms (bacteria/cubic foot)	
11.8	10.8	12.1	12.0
8.2	10.1	8.3	11.1
7.1	14.6	3.8	10.1
13.0	14.0	7.2	13.7

Source: William G. Walter and Angie Stober. "Microbial Air Sampling in a Carpeted Hospital." *Journal of Environmental Health*, 30 (1968), p. 405.

16. Visual versus Textual Learners Researchers wanted to know whether there was a difference in comprehension among students learning a computer program based on the style of the text. They randomly divided 36 students into two groups of 18 each. The researchers verified that the 36 students were similar in terms of educational level, age, and so on. Group 1 individuals learned the software using a visual manual (*multimodal instruction*), while group 2 individuals learned the software using a textual manual (*unimodal instruction*). The following data represent scores that the students received on an exam given to them after they studied from the manuals.

Visual Manual		Textual Manual	
51.08	60.35	64.55	56.54
57.03	76.60	57.60	39.91
44.85	70.77	68.59	65.31
75.21	70.15	50.75	51.95
56.87	47.60	49.63	49.07
75.28	46.59	43.58	48.83
57.07	81.23	57.40	72.40
80.30	67.30	49.48	42.01
52.20	60.82	49.57	61.16

Source: Mark Gellevij et al. "Multimodal versus Unimodal Instruction in a Complex Learning Context." *Journal of Experimental Education* 70(3):215–239, 2002.

16. (a) Completely randomized design

(a) What type of experimental design is this?

(b) What are the treatments? visual vs. textual manual

(c) A normal probability plot and boxplot indicate it is reasonable to use Welch's t-test. Is there a difference in test scores at the $\alpha = 0.05$ level of significance? Reject H_0

17. Does the Designated Hitter Help? In baseball, the American League allows a designated hitter (DH) to bat for the pitcher, who is typically a weak hitter. In the National League, the pitcher must bat. The common belief is that this results in American League teams scoring more runs. In interleague play, when American League teams visit National League teams, the American League pitcher must bat. So, if the DH does result in more runs, we would expect that American League teams will score fewer runs when visiting National League parks. To test this claim, a random sample of runs scored by American League teams without their DH is given in the following table and with their DH in the table on the following page. Does the designated hitter result in more runs scored at the $\alpha = 0.05$ level of significance?

Note: $\bar{x}_{NL} = 4.3$, $s_{NL} = 2.6$, $\bar{x}_{AL} = 6.0$, $s_{AL} = 3.5$. Reject H_0

National League Park (without DH)				
1	5	5	4	7
2	6	2	9	2
8	8	2	10	4
4	3	4	1	9
3	5	1	3	3
3	5	2	7	2

American League Park (with DH)				
6	2	3	6	8
1	3	7	6	4
4	12	5	6	13
6	9	5	6	7
4	3	2	5	5
6	14	14	7	0

Source: espn.com

18. Rhythm & Blues versus Alternatives A music industry producer wondered whether there is a difference in lengths (in seconds) of rhythm & blues songs versus alternative songs. He obtained a random sample of each music category and documented song lengths. The results are in the following table. Test whether the length of rhythm & blues songs is different from the length of alternative songs at the $\alpha = 0.1$ level of significance.

Note: $\bar{x}_{RB} = 242.7$, $s_{RB} = 26.9$, $\bar{x}_{ALT} = 238.3$, $s_{ALT} = 28.9$. Do not reject H_0

Rhythm & Blues (in seconds)				
267	244	233	293	231
224	271	246	258	255
281	256	236	231	224
203	258	237	228	217
205	217	227	211	235
241	211	257	321	264

Alternative (in seconds)				
246	279	226	255	249
225	216	197	216	232
256	307	237	216	187
258	253	223	264	255
227	274	192	213	272
226	251	202	278	216

Source: www.yahoo.com/music

19. Sullivan Statistics Survey: Ideal Number of Children One question on the Sullivan Statistics Survey asked, "What do you think is the ideal number of children for a family to have?" Do the results of the survey suggest there is a difference between males and females in regard to this question? Use the $\alpha = 0.05$ level of significance. Reject H_0

20. Sullivan Statistics Survey: Watching Television Do males tend to watch more television? Use the results of the Sullivan Statistics Survey, which asked, "How many hours did you watch television last week (Sunday though Saturday)?" Do the results suggest males watch more television each week than females? Use the $\alpha = 0.05$ level of significance. Reject H_0

NW **21. Kids and Leisure** Young children require a lot of time. This time commitment cuts into a parent's leisure time. A sociologist wanted to estimate the difference in the amount of daily leisure time (in hours) of adults who do not have children under the age of 18 years and the amount of daily leisure time (in hours) of adults who have children under the age of 18 years. A random sample of 40 adults with no children under the age of 18 years results in a mean daily leisure time of 5.62 hours, with a standard deviation of 2.43 hours. A random sample of 40 adults with children under the age of 18 years results in a mean daily leisure time of 4.10 hours, with a standard deviation of 1.82 hours. Construct and interpret a 90% confidence interval for the mean difference in leisure time between adults with no children and adults with children. *Source:* American Time Use Survey (0.71, 2.33)

22. Aluminum Bottles The aluminum bottle, first introduced in 1991 by CCL Container for mainly personal and household items such as lotions, has become popular with beverage manufacturers. Besides being lightweight and requiring less packaging, the aluminum bottle is reported to cool faster and stay cold longer than typical glass bottles. A small brewery tests this claim and obtains the following information regarding the time (in minutes) required to chill a bottle of beer from room temperature (75°F) to serving temperature (45°F). Construct and interpret a 90% confidence interval for the mean difference in cooling time for clear glass versus aluminum. (38.08, 44.72)

	Clear Glass	Aluminum
Sample size	42	35
Mean time to chill	133.8	92.4
Sample standard deviation	9.9	7.3

23. Comparing Step Pulses A physical therapist wanted to know whether the mean step pulse of men was less than the mean step pulse of women. She randomly selected 51 men and 70 women to participate in the study. Each subject was required to step up and down onto a 6-inch platform for 3 minutes. The pulse of each subject (in beats per minute) was then recorded. After the data were entered into MINITAB, the following results were obtained (a) H_0: $\mu_{men} = \mu_{women}$ vs. H_1: $\mu_{men} < \mu_{women}$

Two Sample T-Test and Confidence Interval

```
Two sample T for Men vs Women
        N      Mean      StDev      SE Mean
Men     51     112.3     11.3       1.6
Women   70     118.3     14.2       1.7

95% CI for mu Men - mu Women: (-10.7, -1.5)
T-Test mu Men = mu Women (vs <):T = -2.61 P = 0.0051  DF = 118
```

(a) State the null and alternative hypotheses.

(b) Identify the P-value and state the researcher's conclusion if the level of significance was $\alpha = 0.01$. 0.0051; reject H_0

(c) What is the 95% confidence interval for the mean difference in pulse rates of men versus women? Interpret this interval. (−10.7, − 1.5)

24. Comparing Flexibility A physical therapist believes that women are more flexible than men. She measures the flexibility of 31 randomly selected women and 45 randomly selected men by determining the number of inches subjects could reach while sitting on the floor with their legs straight out and back perpendicular to the ground. The more flexible an individual is, the higher the measured flexibility will be. After entering the data into MINITAB, she obtained the results on the next page. H_0: $\mu_{men} = \mu_{women}$ vs. H_1: $\mu_{men} < \mu_{women}$

Two Sample T-Test and Confidence Interval

```
Two sample T for Men vs Women

         N      Mean     StDev    SE Mean
Men     45     18.64      3.29       0.49
Women   31     20.99      2.07       0.37

95% CI for mu Men − mu Women: (−3.58, −1.12)
T-Test mu Men = mu Women (vs <):T = −3.82 P = 0.0001 DF = 73
```

(a) State the null and alternative hypotheses.

(b) Identify the *P*-value and state the researcher's conclusion if the level of significance was $\alpha = 0.01$. 0.0001; reject H_0

(c) What is the 95% confidence interval for the mean difference in flexibility of men versus women? Interpret this interval. (−3.58, −1.12)

25. Putting It Together: Online Homework Professor Stephen Zuro of Joliet Junior College wanted to determine whether an online homework system improved scores on a final exam. In the fall semester, he taught a precalculus class using the online homework system (which meant students did their homework online and received instant feedback about their answers along with helpful guidance). In the spring semester, he taught a precalculus class without the homework system (which meant students were responsible for doing their homework the old-fashioned way—paper and pencil). Professor Zuro made sure to teach the two courses identically (same text, syllabus, tests, meeting time, meeting location, and so on). The table summarizes the results of the two classes on their final exam.

	Fall Semester	Spring Semester
Number of students	27	25
Mean final exam score	73.6	67.9
Standard deviation final exam score	10.3	12.4

(a) What type of experimental design is this?

(b) What is the response variable? What are the treatments in the study? Final exam; homework delivery

(c) What factors are controlled in the experiment?

(d) In many experiments, the researcher will recruit volunteers and randomly assign the individuals to a treatment group. In what regard was this done for this experiment?

(e) Did the students perform better on the final exam in the fall semester? Use an $\alpha = 0.05$ level of significance. Yes

(f) Can you think of any factors that may confound the results? Could Professor Zuro have done anything about these confounding factors?

EXPLAINING THE CONCEPTS

26. Explain why using the smaller of $n_1 - 1$ or $n_2 - 1$ degrees of freedom to determine the critical t instead of Formula (2) is conservative.

25. (a) Completely randomized design (c) Teacher, location, time, text, syllabus, tests (f) Quality of students entering class; warm weather in spring

Consumer Reports® The High Cost of Convenience

Consumer Reports was interested in comparing a name-brand paper towel with a new version packaged in a box. The towels in the box, which cost nearly twice as much as the traditional roll, are marketed for their convenience. Given the difference in cost, one might wonder if the boxed version performs better than the traditional roll. To help answer this question, technicians at Consumers Union subjected both types of towels to five physical tests: absorption time in water, absorption time in oil, absorption capacity in water, absorption capacity in oil, and wet strength. For brevity, we will discuss only the results of the absorption time in water test.

The absorption time in water was defined as the amount of time necessary for a single sheet to absorb a predetermined amount of water. To compare the absorption times of the two types of towels, we tested six randomly selected sheets of paper towels. To avoid potential sources of bias, the individual sheets were taken from different samples of the products, and the tests were conducted in a randomly chosen order.

Consumer Reports wanted to determine whether the water absorption time for the boxed version is less than the water absorption time for the traditional roll.

(a) Write the null and alternative hypotheses, letting μ_{box} represent the mean absorption time for the boxed version and μ_{roll} represent the mean absorption time for the roll version.

(b) Normal probability plots of the water absorption times for the two products are shown next. Based on the normal probability plots, is it reasonable to conduct a two-sample hypothesis test?

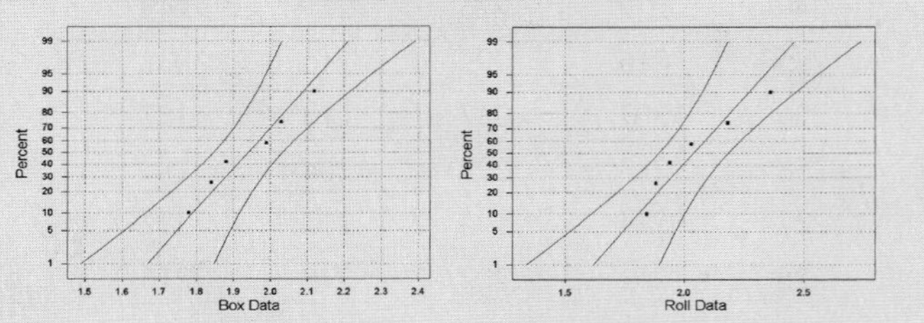

(c) A boxplot of the water absorption times for the two products follows:

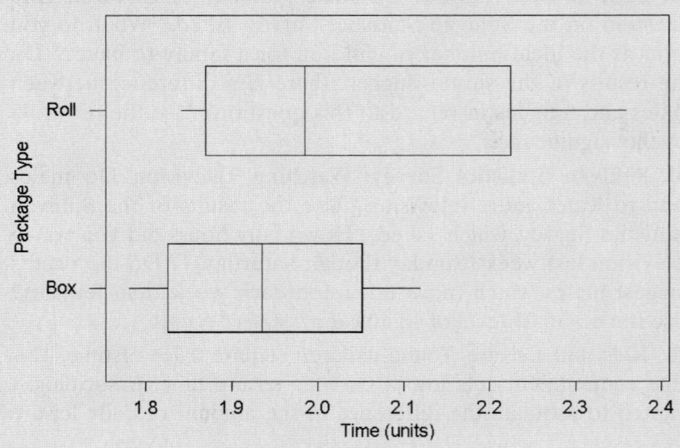

Does the data set have any outliers? Based on the boxplots, do you think that the absorption times for the boxed version are lower than the absorption times for the roll?

(d) To conduct the test, we used MINITAB to perform a two-sample *t*-test. The results are as shown. Using the MINITAB output, determine the value of the test statistic. What is the *P*-value of the test? Although they are not discussed here, the other physical tests provided similar results. Write an article that states your conclusion and any recommendations that you would make regarding the purchase of the two products.

Two-Sample T-Test and CI: Absorption Time In Water, CU

```
Two-sample   T    for Absorption      Time    In Water
CU-Text      N            Mean       StDev     SE Mean
Box          6          0.9717      0.0538       0.022
Roll         6          1.0200      0.0942       0.038

Difference = mu (Box) - mu (Roll)
Estimate for difference: -0.0483
95% upper bound for difference: 0.0320
T-Test of difference = 0 (vs <):
T-Value = -1.09 P-Value = 0.150 DF = 10
Both use Pooled StDev = 0.0767
```

Note to Readers: *In many cases, our test protocol and analytical methods are more complicated than described in these examples. The data and discussions have been modified to make the material more appropriate for the audience.*

Technology Step-By-Step

Two-Sample *t*-Tests, Independent Sampling

TI-83/84 Plus

Hypothesis Tests

1. If necessary, enter raw data in L1 and L2.
2. Press STAT, highlight TESTS, and select 4:2-SampTTest ... .
3. If the data are raw, highlight Data, making sure that List1 is set to L1 and List2 is set to L2, with frequencies set to 1. If summary statistics are known, highlight STATS and enter the summary statistics.
4. Highlight the appropriate relation between μ_1 and μ_2 in the alternative hypothesis. Set Pooled to NO.
5. Highlight Calculate or Draw and press ENTER. Calculate gives the test statistic and *P*-value. Draw will draw the *t*-distribution with the *P*-value shaded.

Confidence Intervals

Follow the steps given for hypothesis tests, except select Ø: 2-SampTInt. Also, select a confidence level (such as 95% = 0.95).

MINITAB

1. If necessary, enter raw data in columns C1 and C2.
2. Select the **Stat** menu, highlight **Basic Statistics**, then highlight **2-Sample t** ... .
3. If you have raw data, select "Samples in different columns." Enter C1 in the cell marked "First" and enter C2 in the cell marked "Second." If you have summarized data, select "Summarized data." Enter the summary statistics in the appropriate cell. Click Options .... Select the direction of the alternative hypothesis, enter the "test difference" (usually zero), and select a confidence level. Click OK twice.

Excel

1. Enter the raw data into Columns A and B.
2. Select the Formulas menu. Select More Functions. Highlight Statistical, and select Ttest from the drop-down menu.
3. Place the cursor in Array1. Highlight the data in Column A. Place the cursor in Array2. Highlight the data in Column B. Place the cursor in the Tails cell. Enter the number corresponding to the test you desire (1 for a one-tailed distribution; 2 for a two-tailed distribution). Place the cursor in the Type cell. Enter 3 for a two-sample unequal variance test.

StatCrunch

1. If necessary, enter the raw data into the first two columns of the spreadsheet. Name the column variables.
2. Select **Stat**, highlight **T Statistics**, select **Two sample**, and then choose either **with data** or **with summary**.
3. Select the column that contains the data for Sample 1. Select the column that contains the data for Sample 2. Note that the differences are computed Sample 1 − Sample 2. Uncheck the box "Pool variances." Click Next>.
4. If you choose the hypothesis test radio button, enter the value of the mean stated in the null hypothesis and choose the direction of the alternative hypothesis from the pull-down menu. If you choose the confidence interval radio button, enter the level of confidence. Click Calculate.

11.4 PUTTING IT TOGETHER: WHICH METHOD DO I USE?

OBJECTIVE **1 Determine the appropriate hypothesis test to perform**

1 Determine the Appropriate Hypothesis Test to Perform

Again, the ability to recognize the type of test to perform is one of the most important aspects of statistical analysis. To help decide which test to use when conducting inference on two samples, we provide the flow chart in Figure 16. Use it to assist you in the problems that follow.

Figure 16

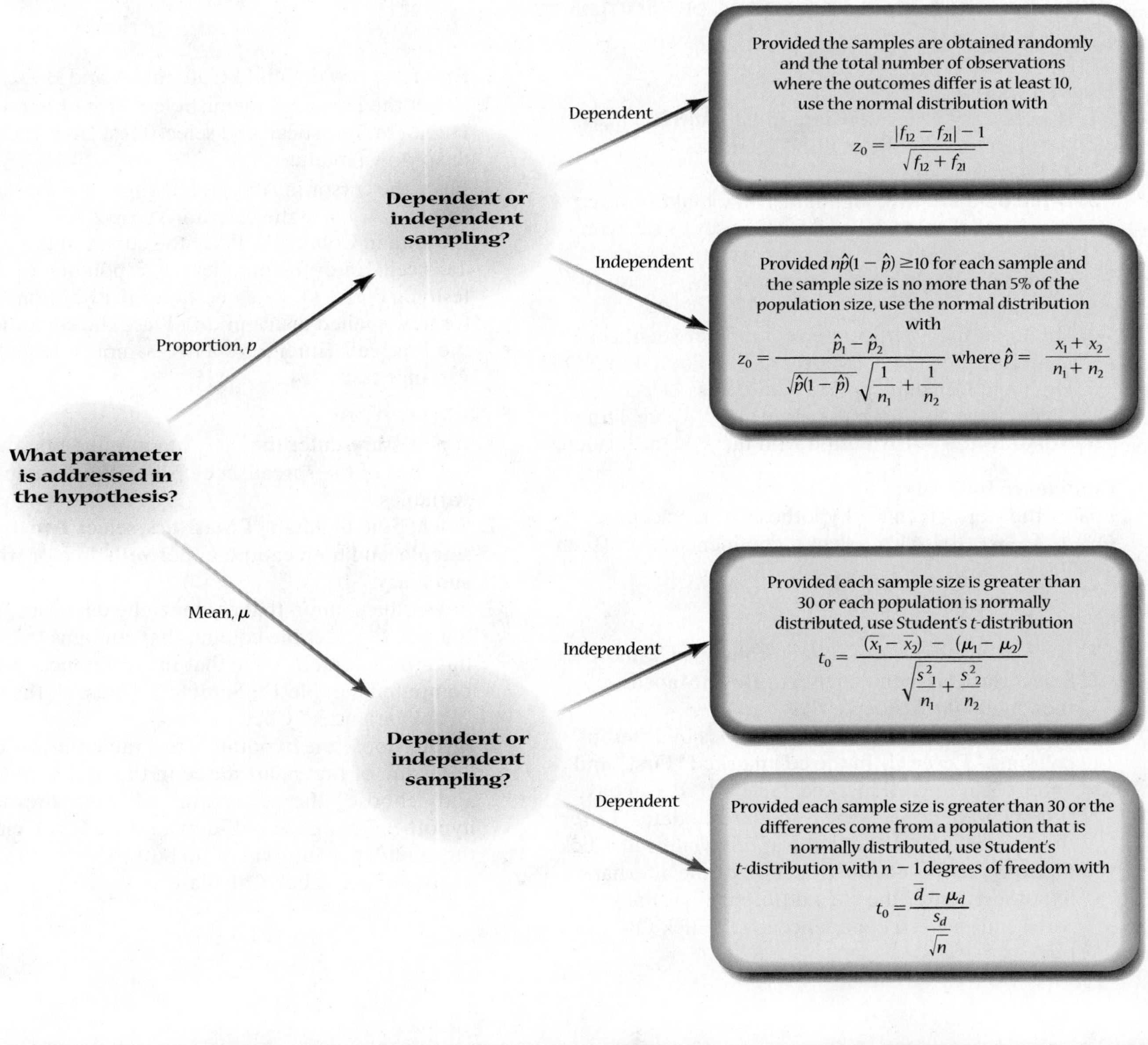
What parameter is addressed in the hypothesis?
Proportion, p
Mean, μ
Dependent or independent sampling?
Dependent
Provided the samples are obtained randomly and the total number of observations where the outcomes differ is at least 10, use the normal distribution with
$z_0 = \dfrac{|f_{12} - f_{21}| - 1}{\sqrt{f_{12} + f_{21}}}$
Independent
Provided $n\hat{p}(1 - \hat{p}) \geq 10$ for each sample and the sample size is no more than 5% of the population size, use the normal distribution with
$z_0 = \dfrac{\hat{p}_1 - \hat{p}_2}{\sqrt{\hat{p}(1-\hat{p})}\sqrt{\dfrac{1}{n_1} + \dfrac{1}{n_2}}}$ where $\hat{p} = \dfrac{x_1 + x_2}{n_1 + n_2}$
Dependent or independent sampling?
Independent
Provided each sample size is greater than 30 or each population is normally distributed, use Student's t-distribution
$t_0 = \dfrac{(\bar{x}_1 - \bar{x}_2) - (\mu_1 - \mu_2)}{\sqrt{\dfrac{s_1^2}{n_1} + \dfrac{s_2^2}{n_2}}}$
Dependent
Provided each sample size is greater than 30 or the differences come from a population that is normally distributed, use Student's t-distribution with $n - 1$ degrees of freedom with
$t_0 = \dfrac{\bar{d} - \mu_d}{\dfrac{s_d}{\sqrt{n}}}$

11.4 ASSESS YOUR UNDERSTANDING

SKILL BUILDING

In Problems 1–10, perform the appropriate hypothesis test.

1. A researcher wanted to determine the effectiveness of a new cream in the treatment of warts. She identified 138 individuals who had two warts. She applied cream A on one wart and cream B on the second wart. Test whether the proportion of successes with cream A is different from cream B at the $\alpha = 0.05$ level of significance. Do not reject H_0

		Treatment A	
		Success	**Failure**
Treatment B	**Success**	63	9
	Failure	13	53

2. A random sample of $n_1 = 120$ individuals results in $x_1 = 43$ successes. An independent sample of $n_2 = 130$ individuals results in $x_2 = 56$ successes. Does this represent sufficient evidence to conclude that $p_1 \neq p_2$ at the $\alpha = 0.01$ level of significance? Do not reject H_0

3. A random sample of size $n = 13$ obtained from a population that is normally distributed results in a sample mean of 45.3 and sample standard deviation of 12.4. An independent sample of size $n = 18$ obtained from a population that is normally distributed results in a sample mean of 52.1 and sample standard deviation of 14.7. Does this constitute sufficient evidence to conclude that the population means differ at the $\alpha = 0.05$ level of significance? Do not reject H_0

4. A random sample of $n_1 = 135$ individuals results in $x_1 = 40$ successes. An independent sample of $n_2 = 150$ individuals results in $x_2 = 60$ successes. Does this represent sufficient evidence to conclude that $p_1 < p_2$ at the $\alpha = 0.05$ level of significance? Reject H_0

5. A random sample of size $n = 41$ results in a sample mean of 125.3 and a sample standard deviation of 8.5. An independent sample of size $n = 50$ results in a sample mean of 130.8 and sample standard deviation of 7.3. Does this constitute sufficient evidence to conclude that the population means differ at the $\alpha = 0.01$ level of significance? Reject H_0

6. The following data represent the measure of a variable before and after a treatment.

Individual	**1**	**2**	**3**	**4**	**5**
Before, X_i	93	102	90	112	107
After, Y_i	95	100	95	115	107

Does the sample evidence suggest that the treatment is effective in increasing the value of the response variable? Use the $\alpha = 0.05$ level of significance. Do not reject H_0

Note: Assume that the differenced data come from a population that is normally distributed with no outliers.

7. The following data represent the measure of a variable before and after a treatment.

Individual	**1**	**2**	**3**	**4**	**5**
Before, X_i	40	32	53	48	38
After, Y_i	38	33	49	48	33

Does the sample evidence suggest that the treatment is effective in decreasing the value of the response variable? Use the $\alpha = 0.10$ level of significance. Reject H_0

Note: Assume that the differenced data come from a population that is normally distributed with no outliers.

8. Conduct the appropriate test to determine if the population proportions for the two treatments differ at the $\alpha = 0.05$ level of significance. Do not reject H_0

Note: The samples are dependent and obtained randomly.

		Treatment A	
		Success	**Failure**
Treatment B	**Success**	392	45
	Failure	58	103

APPLYING THE CONCEPTS

9. Collision Claims Automobile collision insurance is used to pay for any claims made against the driver in the event of an accident. This type of insurance will typically pay to repair any assets that your vehicle damages.

(a) Collision claims tend to be skewed right. Why do you think this is the case?

(b) A random sample of 40 collision claims of 30- to 59-year-old drivers results in a mean claim of \$3669 with a standard deviation of \$2029. An independent random sample of 40 collision claims of 20- to 24-year-old drivers results in a mean claim of \$4586 with a standard deviation of \$2302. Using the concept of hypothesis testing, provide an argument that justifies charging a higher insurance premium to 20- to 24-year-old drivers. *Source:* Based on data obtained from the Insurance Institute for Highway Safety. Reject H_0

10. TIMS Report and Kumon TIMS is an acronym for the Third International Mathematics and Science Study. Kumon promotes a method of studying mathematics that it claims develops mathematical ability. Do data support this claim? In one particular question on the TIMS exam, a random sample of 400 non-Kumon students resulted in 73 getting the correct answer. For the same question, a random sample of 400 Kumon students resulted in 130 getting the correct answer. Perform the appropriate test to substantiate Kumon's claims. Are there any confounding factors regarding the claim? *Source*: TIMS and PROM/SE Assessment of Kumon Students: What the Results Indicate, Kumon North America. Reject H_0

11. Health and Happiness In a General Social Survey, adult Americans were asked if they were happy or unhappy, and they were asked whether they were healthy or unhealthy. The table shows the results of the survey. Are healthy people also happy people? Use the $\alpha = 0.05$ level of significance. Reject H_0

	Healthy (Success)	**Not Healthy (Failure)**
Happy (success)	2499	123
Not happy (failure)	70	59

12. Cash or Credit? Do people tend to spend more money on fast-food when they use a credit card? The following data represent a random sample of credit-card and cash purchases.

Credit				
16.78	23.89	13.89	15.54	10.35
12.76	18.32	20.67	18.36	19.16
Cash				
10.76	6.26	18.98	11.36	6.78
21.76	8.90	15.64	13.78	9.21

Source: Brian Ortiz, student at Joliet Junior College

(a) Draw boxplots of each data set using the same scale. What do the boxplots imply for cash versus credit?

(b) Test whether the sample evidence suggests that people spend more when using a credit card. Use the $\alpha = 0.01$ level of significance.
Note: Normal probability plots indicate that each sample could come from a population that is normally distributed. Do not reject H_0

(c) Suppose that you were looking to gather evidence to convince your manager that an effort needs to be made to boost credit-card sales. Would it be legitimate to change the level to $\alpha = 0.05$ after seeing the results from part (b)? Why? No

13. Walmart versus Target Is there a difference in the pricing at Walmart versus Target for health and beauty supplies? To answer this question, a student randomly selected 10 identical products at each store and recorded the price. Assuming that the conditions for conducting the test are satisfied, determine if there is a price difference between Walmart and Target for health and beauty supplies. Use the $\alpha = 0.05$ level of significance. Do not reject H_0

Product	Price at Walmart ($)	Price at Target ($)
Herbal Essence	2.94	2.94
Dial body wash	3.16	3.79
Listerine Whitening	4.74	4.74
Colgate White	2.84	2.49
Mens Speed Stick	1.72	1.97
Women Dove deodorant	1.72	1.72
Benadryl Allergy	3.77	3.99
Gillette razors	7.44	7.99
Q-Tips	3.77	3.64
Nice 'n Easy color blend	5.98	5.99

Source: Vicki Wnek, student at Joliet Junior College

14. Predicting Election Outcomes Researchers Alexander Todorov and associates conducted an experiment in which 695 individuals were shown black and white photographs of individuals running for Congress (either the U.S. Senate or House of Representatives). In each instance, the individuals were exposed to the photograph of both the winner and runner-up (in random order) for 1 second. The individuals were then asked to decide who they believed was more competent (and, therefore, more likely to receive their vote). Of the 695 individuals exposed to the photos, 469 correctly predicted the winner of the race. Do the results suggest that a quick 1-second view of a black and white photo represents enough information to judge the winner of an election (based on perceived level of competence of the individual) more often than not? Use the $\alpha = 0.05$ level of significance. *Source:* Todorov, Mandisodza, Goren, Hall, "Inferences of Competence from Faces Predict Election Outcomes." *Science* Vol. 308. Reject H_0; P-value < 0.0001

15. Gas Prices in Chicago In January 2011, the national mean price per gallon (in dollars) of regular unleaded gasoline was 3.101. The following data represent a random sample of 21 gas stations in Chicago. Is gas in Chicago more expensive than the nation? Reject H_0; P-value $= 0.0003$

Note: A normal probability plot and boxplot indicate the data could come from a normal population with no outliers.

3.00	3.06	3.07	3.09	3.12	3.12	3.13
3.15	3.15	3.16	3.17	3.18	3.19	3.19
3.20	3.20	3.21	3.22	3.24	3.25	3.25

Source: gasbuddy.com

16. Bribe 'em with Chocolate In a study published in the journal *Teaching of Psychology*, the article "Fudging the Numbers: Distributing Chocolate Influences Student Evaluations of an Undergraduate Course" states that distributing chocolate to students prior to teacher evaluations increases results. The authors randomly divided three sections of a course taught by the same instructor into two groups. Fifty of the students were given chocolate by an individual not associated with the course and 50 of the students were not given chocolate. The mean score from students who received chocolate was 4.2, while the mean score for the nonchocolate group was 3.9. Suppose that the sample standard deviation of both the chocolate and nonchocolate group was 0.8. Does chocolate appear to improve teacher evaluations? Use the $\alpha = 0.1$ level of significance. Yes; reject H_0

17. Unwed Women Having Children The Pew Research Group asked the following question of individuals who earned in excess of $100,000 per year and those who earned less than $100,000 per year: "Do you believe that it is morally wrong for unwed women to have children?" Of the 1205 individuals who earned in excess of $100,000 per year, 710 said yes; of the 1310 individuals who earned less than $100,000 per year, 695 said yes. Construct a 95% confidence interval to determine if there is a difference in the proportion of individuals who believe it is morally wrong for unwed women to have children. (0.019, 0.097)

18. Volume of Stock The daily volume of a stock represents the total number of shares traded in the stock. The following data represent the daily volume (in millions) of General Electric (GE) Corporation stock and Pfizer stock for 13 randomly selected days in 2010. (a) Differences normal with no outliers

(a) What conditions must be satisfied to conduct the appropriate test to determine if the daily volume of General Electric Corporation stock is greater than that of Pfizer?

(b) Assuming that the conditions from part (a) are satisfied, determine if the daily volume of General Electric Corporation stock is greater than that of Pfizer. Use the $\alpha = 0.05$ level of significance. Reject H_0; P-value $= 0.006$

Date	Volume of GE (millions)	Volume of Pfizer (millions)
10/25	53.6	67.3
11/3	65.8	50.5
11/5	69.8	57.5
11/11	46.6	44.2
11/17	36.3	37.8
11/23	55.9	39.7
11/29	56.5	39.1
12/1	68.9	44.8
12/6	58.8	53.3
12/9	39.1	31.7
12/13	67.9	47.2
12/22	43.0	35.7
12/30	28.9	29.8

Source: Yahoo!Finance

19. Comparing Rates of Return You want to invest some money in a domestic (only U.S. stocks) mutual fund and have narrowed your choice down to value funds or growth funds. Value funds tend to invest in companies that appear to be inexpensive relative to the stock market; growth funds tend to invest in companies that are expected to grow their revenues substantially over time. To help make your decision about which of the two fund types to invest in, you decide to obtain a random sample of 3-year rates of return for 10 different value funds and 10 different growth funds.

Value Funds				
9.54	8.76	12.53	9.52	8.71
6.09	7.63	6.02	6.02	11.71
Growth Funds				
7.57	8.37	8.63	9.02	8.36
7.95	9.33	7.53	6.93	8.37

Source: Morningstar.com

(a) We want to compare two means. Because the sample sizes are small, the sample data must come from populations that are normally distributed with no outliers. The normal probability plots for both sets of data are shown. Do the plots indicate that it is reasonable to believe that the sample data come from a population that is normally distributed? Yes

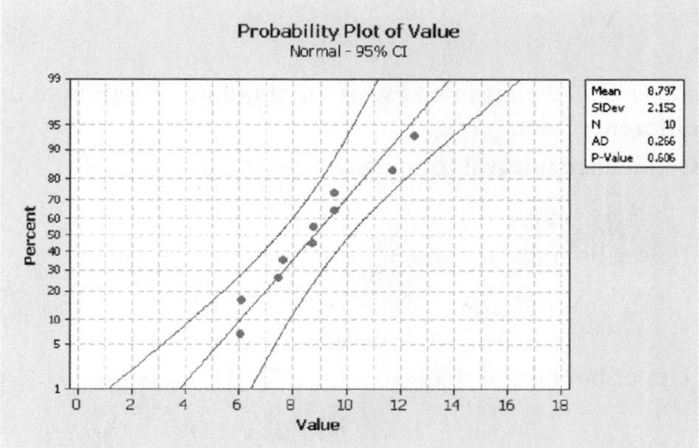

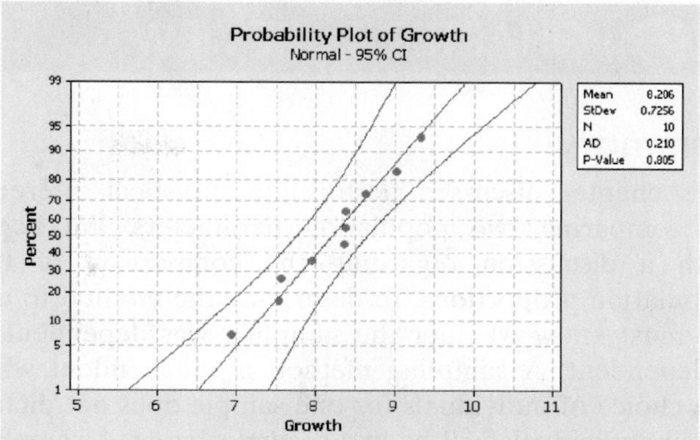

(b) To judge whether the sample data have any outliers and to visualize any differences between the two sample data sets, draw side-by-side boxplots of the data. Are there any outliers? No

(c) Conduct the appropriate test to determine if there is any difference in the rate of return between value funds and growth funds. Use the $\alpha = 0.05$ level of significance. Do not reject H_0

20. Which Stock? You want to invest in a stock and have narrowed your choices down to either Citibank (C) or Wells Fargo (WFC). To help you decide which stock to invest in, you decide to compare weekly rates of return for the two stocks. Which would be a better sampling plan: (a) randomly choose 15 weeks and determine the rate of return of Citibank and then independently randomly choose 15 weeks and determine the rate of return of Wells Fargo or (b) randomly choose 15 weeks and determine the rate of return of both companies and compare the rate of return. For both scenarios, explain the inferential method you would use and justify your sampling plan. Matched-pairs design

EXPLAINING THE CONCEPTS

In Problems 21–26, for each study, explain which statistical procedure (estimating a single proportion; estimating a single mean; hypothesis test for a single proportion; hypothesis test for a single mean; hypothesis test or estimation of two proportions, dependent or independent; hypothesis test or estimation of two means, dependent or independent) would most likely be used for the research objective given. Assume all model requirements for conducting the appropriate procedure have been satisfied.

21. Is the mean IQ of the students in Professor Dang's statistics class higher than that of the general population, 100?

22. Do adult males who take a single aspirin daily experience a lower rate of heart attacks than adult males who do not take aspirin daily? Hypothesis test for two proportions – independent sample

23. Does Marriott Courtyard charge more than Holiday Inn Express for a one-night stay? Matched-pairs t-test on difference of means

24. What is the typical amount of time 20- to 24-year-old males spend brushing their teeth (each time they brush)?

25. What proportion of registered voters is in favor of a tax increase to reduce the federal debt? Confidence interval for a single proportion

26. Does drinking 2 cups of water before a meal assist with weight loss? Two-sample t-test of independent means

21. Hypothesis test for a single mean 24. Confidence interval for a single mean

CHAPTER 11 REVIEW

Summary

This chapter discussed performing statistical inference by comparing two population parameters. We began with a discussion regarding the comparison of two population proportions. To determine the method to use, we must know whether the sampling was dependent or independent. A sampling method is independent when the choice of individuals for one sample does not dictate which individuals will be in a second sample. A sampling method is dependent when the individuals selected for one sample are used to determine the individuals in the second sample.

Section 11.1 continued by considering statistical inference for comparing two population proportions from independent samples. To perform these tests, $n\hat{p}(1-\hat{p})$ must be greater than or equal to 10 for each population, and each sample size can be no more than 5% of the population size. The distribution of $\hat{p}_1 - \hat{p}_2$ is approximately normal, with mean $p_1 - p_2$ and standard deviation $\sqrt{\frac{p_1(1-p_1)}{n_1} + \frac{p_2(1-p_2)}{n_2}}$. If the samples are dependent, we use McNemar's Test.

For dependent sampling, we use the paired t-test to perform statistical inference on two means. For independent sampling, we use Welch's approximate t for inference on two means. For both tests, the population must be normally distributed or the sample sizes must be large.

To help determine which test to use, we included the flow chart in Figure 16.

Vocabulary

Independent (p. 468)
Dependent (p. 468)
Matched pairs (p. 468)
Pooled estimate of p (p. 470)
McNemar's Test (p. 475)
Robust (p. 484)
Welch's approximate t (p. 494)
Pooled t-statistic (p. 499)

Formulas

- Test statistic comparing two population proportions (independent sampling):

$$z_0 = \frac{(\hat{p}_1 - \hat{p}_2) - (p_1 - p_2)}{\sqrt{\hat{p}(1-\hat{p})}\sqrt{\frac{1}{n_1} + \frac{1}{n_2}}}$$

where $\hat{p} = \frac{x_1 + x_2}{n_1 + n_2}$

- Confidence interval for the difference of two proportions (independent sampling):

Lower bound: $(\hat{p}_1 - \hat{p}_2) - z_{\frac{\alpha}{2}} \cdot \sqrt{\frac{\hat{p}_1(1-\hat{p}_1)}{n_1} + \frac{\hat{p}_2(1-\hat{p}_2)}{n_2}}$

Upper bound: $(\hat{p}_1 - \hat{p}_2) + z_{\frac{\alpha}{2}} \cdot \sqrt{\frac{\hat{p}_1(1-\hat{p}_1)}{n_1} + \frac{\hat{p}_2(1-\hat{p}_2)}{n_2}}$

- Test statistic comparing two population proportions (dependent sampling):

$$z_0 = \frac{|f_{12} - f_{21}| - 1}{\sqrt{f_{12} + f_{21}}}$$

- Sample size for estimating $p_1 - p_2$:

$$n = n_1 = n_2 = [\hat{p}_1(1-\hat{p}_1) + \hat{p}_2(1-\hat{p}_2)]\left(\frac{z_{\alpha/2}}{E}\right)^2$$

$$n = n_1 = n_2 = 0.5\left(\frac{z_{\alpha/2}}{E}\right)^2$$

- Test statistic for matched-pairs data:

$$t_0 = \frac{\bar{d} - \mu_d}{\frac{s_d}{\sqrt{n}}}$$

where $\bar{d}$ is the mean and s_d is the standard deviation of the differenced data

- Confidence interval for matched-pairs data:

Lower bound: $\bar{d} - t_{\frac{\alpha}{2}} \cdot \frac{s_d}{\sqrt{n}}$

Upper bound: $\bar{d} + t_{\frac{\alpha}{2}} \cdot \frac{s_d}{\sqrt{n}}$

- Test statistic comparing two means (independent sampling):

$$t_0 = \frac{(\bar{x}_1 - \bar{x}_2) - (\mu_1 - \mu_2)}{\sqrt{\frac{s_1^2}{n_1} + \frac{s_2^2}{n_2}}}$$

- Confidence interval for the difference of two means (independent samples):

Lower bound: $(\bar{x}_1 - \bar{x}_2) - t_{\frac{\alpha}{2}} \cdot \sqrt{\frac{s_1^2}{n_1} + \frac{s_2^2}{n_2}}$

Upper bound: $(\bar{x}_1 - \bar{x}_2) + t_{\frac{\alpha}{2}} \cdot \sqrt{\frac{s_1^2}{n_1} + \frac{s_2^2}{n_2}}$

Objectives

Section	You should be able to ...	Examples	Review Exercises
11.1	1 Distinguish between independent and dependent sampling (p. 468)	1	1, 2
	2 Test hypotheses regarding two proportions from independent samples (p. 469)	2	6, 9(a)
	3 Construct and interpret confidence intervals for the difference between two population proportions (p. 473)	3	9(b)
	4 Test hypotheses regarding two proportions from dependent samples (p. 475)	4	10
	5 Determine the sample size necessary for estimating the difference between two population proportions (p. 477)	5	11
11.2	1 Test hypotheses regarding matched-pairs data (p. 483)	1	3(c), 7(b)
	2 Construct and interpret confidence intervals about the population mean difference of matched-pairs data (p. 487)	2	3(d), 12
11.3	1 Test hypotheses regarding the difference of two independent means (p. 494)	1	4(a), 5(a), 8(b)
	2 Construct and interpret confidence intervals regarding the difference of two independent means (p. 498)	2	4(b), 13
11.4	1 Determine the appropriate hypothesis test to perform (p. 506)		3–10, 12, 13

Review Exercises

In Problems 1 and 2, determine if the sampling is dependent or independent. Indicate whether the response variable is qualitative or quantitative.

1. A researcher wants to know if the mean length of stay in for-profit hospitals is different from the mean length of stay in not-for-profit hospitals. He randomly selected 20 individuals in the for-profit hospital and matched them with 20 individuals in the not-for-profit hospital by diagnosis. Dependent; quantitative

2. An urban economist believes that commute times to work in the South are less than commute times to work in the Midwest. He randomly selects 40 employed individuals in the South and 40 employed individuals in the Midwest and determines their commute times. Independent; quantitative

In Problem 3, assume that the paired differences come from a population that is normally distributed.

3.

Observation	1	2	3	4	5	6
X_i	34.2	32.1	39.5	41.8	45.1	38.4
Y_i	34.9	31.5	39.5	41.9	45.5	38.8

(a) Compute $d_i = X_i - Y_i$ for each pair of data.
(b) Compute $\bar{d}$ and s_d. $\bar{d} = -0.167$, $s_d = 0.450$
(c) Test the hypothesis that $\mu_d < 0$ at the $\alpha = 0.05$ level of significance. Do not reject H_0
(d) Compute a 98% confidence interval for the population mean difference μ_d. $(-0.79, 0.45)$

In Problems 4 and 5, assume that the populations are normally distributed and that independent sampling occurred.

4.

	Population 1	Population 2
n	13	8
$\bar{x}$	32.4	28.2
s	4.5	3.8

(a) Test the hypothesis that $\mu_1 \neq \mu_2$ at the $\alpha = 0.1$ level of significance for the given sample data. Reject H_0
(b) Construct a 90% confidence interval for $\mu_1 - \mu_2$. $(0.73, 7.67)$

5. Test the hypothesis that $\mu_1 > \mu_2$ at the $\alpha = 0.01$ level of significance for the given sample data. Do not reject H_0

	Population 1	Population 2
n	45	41
$\bar{x}$	48.2	45.2
s	8.4	10.3

6. A random sample of $n_1 = 555$ individuals results in $x_1 = 451$ successes. An independent sample of $n_2 = 600$ individuals results in $x_2 = 510$ successes. Does this represent sufficient evidence to conclude that $p_1 \neq p_2$ at the $\alpha = 0.05$ level of significance? Do not reject H_0

7. **Height versus Arm Span** A statistics student heard that an individual's arm span is equal to the individual's height. To test this hypothesis, the student used a random sample of 10 students and obtained the following data.

Student:	1	2	3	4	5
Height (inches)	59.5	69	77	59.5	74.5
Arm span (inches)	62	65.5	76	63	74
Student:	**6**	**7**	**8**	**9**	**10**
Height (inches)	63	61.5	67.5	73	69
Arm span (inches)	66	61	69	70	71

Source: John Climent, Cecil Community College

(a) Is the sampling method dependent or independent? Why? Dependent

(b) Does the sample evidence contradict the belief that an individual's height and arm span are the same at the $\alpha = 0.05$ level of significance? Do not reject H_0

Note: A normal probability plot indicates that the data and differenced data are normally distributed. A boxplot indicates that the data and differenced data have no outliers.

8. **McDonald's versus Wendy's** A student wanted to determine whether the wait time in the drive-through at McDonald's differed from that at Wendy's. She used a random sample of 30 cars at McDonald's and 27 cars at Wendy's and obtained these results:

Wait Time at McDonald's Drive-Through (seconds)

151.09	227.38	111.84	131.21	128.75
191.60	126.91	137.90	195.44	246.59
141.78	127.35	121.21	101.03	95.09
122.06	122.62	100.04	71.37	153.34
140.44	126.62	116.72	131.69	100.94
115.66	147.28	81.43	86.31	156.34

Wait Time at Wendy's Drive-Through (seconds)

281.90	71.02	204.29	128.59	133.56
187.53	199.86	190.91	110.55	110.64
196.84	233.65	171.01	182.54	183.79
284.48	363.34	270.82	390.50	471.62
123.66	174.43	385.90	386.71	155.53
203.62	119.61			

Source: Catherine M. Simmons, student at Joliet Junior College

Note: The sample size for Wendy's is less than 30. However, the data do not contain any outliers, so the Central Limit Theorem can be used. (a) Independent

(a) Is the sampling method dependent or independent?

(b) Is there a difference in wait times at each restaurant's drive-through? Use the $\alpha = 0.1$ level of significance. Reject H_0

(c) Draw boxplots of each data set using the same scale. Does this visual evidence support the results obtained in part (b)? Yes

9. **Treatment for Osteoporosis** Osteoporosis is a condition in which people experience decreased bone mass and an increase in the risk of bone fracture. Actonel is a drug that helps combat osteoporosis in postmenopausal women. In clinical trials, 1374 postmenopausal women were randomly divided into experimental and control groups. The subjects in the experimental group were administered 5 milligrams (mg) of Actonel, while the subjects in the control group were administered a placebo. The number of women who experienced a bone fracture over the course of 1 year was recorded. Of the 696 women in the experimental group, 27 experienced a fracture during the course of the year. Of the 678 women in the control group, 49 experienced a fracture during the course of the year.

(a) Test the hypothesis that a lower proportion of women in the experimental group experienced a bone fracture than the women in the control group at the $\alpha = 0.01$ level of significance. Reject H_0 (b) $(-0.06, -0.01)$

(b) Construct a 95% confidence interval for the difference between the two population proportions, $p_{exp} - p_{\text{control}}$.

(c) What type of experimental design is this? What are the treatments? Completely randomized design; placebo and Actonel

(d) The experiment was double-blind. What does this mean?

10. **Obligations to Vote and Serve** In the General Social Survey, individuals were asked whether civic duty included voting and whether it included serving on a jury. The results of the survey are shown in the table. Is there a difference in the proportion of individuals who feel jury duty is a civic duty and the proportion of individuals who feel voting is a civic duty? Use the $\alpha = 0.05$ level of significance. Do not reject H_0

		Jury	
		Duty (success)	**Not Duty (failure)**
Voting	Duty (success)	1322	65
	Not duty (failure)	45	17

11. **Determining Sample Size** A nutritionist wants to estimate the difference between the percentage of men and women who have high cholesterol. What sample size should be obtained if she wishes the estimate to be within 2 percentage points with 90% confidence, assuming that

(a) she uses the 1994 estimates of 18.8% male and 20.5% female from the National Center for Health Statistics? 2136

(b) she does not use any prior estimates? 3383

12. **Height versus Arm Span** Construct and interpret a 95% confidence interval for the population mean difference between height and arm span using the data from Problem 7. What does the interval lead us to conclude regarding any differences between height and arm span? $(-1.37, 2.17)$

13. **McDonald's versus Wendy's** Construct and interpret a 95% confidence interval about $\mu_M - \mu_W$ using the data from Problem 8. How might a marketing executive with McDonald's use this information? $(-128.868, -42.218)$

Problems in the chapter test are labeled by section.objective. For example, 2.3 means Section 2, Objective 3.

CHAPTER TEST

In Problems 1 and 2, determine whether the sampling method is independent or dependent.

1.1 **1.** A stock analyst wants to know if there is a difference between the mean rate of return from energy stocks and that from financial stocks. He randomly selects 13 energy stocks and computes the rate of return for the past year. He randomly selects 13 financial stocks and computes the rate of return for the past year. Independent

1.1 **2.** A prison warden wants to know if men receive longer sentences for crimes than women. He randomly samples 30 men and matches them with 30 women by type of crime committed and records their lengths of sentence. Dependent

In Problem 3, assume that the paired differences come from a population that is normally distributed.

3.

Observation	1	2	3	4	5	6	7
X_i	18.5	21.8	19.4	22.9	18.3	20.2	23.1
Y_i	18.3	22.3	19.2	22.3	18.9	20.7	23.9

(a) Compute $d_i = X_i - Y_i$ for each pair of data.

(b) Compute $\bar{d}$ and s_d. $\bar{d} = -0.2$, $s_d = 0.526$

2.1 **(c)** Test the hypothesis that $\mu_d \neq 0$ at the $\alpha = 0.01$ level of significance. Do not reject H_0

2.2 **(d)** Compute a 95% confidence interval for the population mean difference μ_d. $(-0.69, 0.29)$ 4. (b) $(-12.44, 0.04)$

In Problems 4 and 5, assume that the populations are normally distributed and that independent sampling occurred.

4.

	Population 1	Population 2
n	24	27
$\bar{x}$	104.2	110.4
s	12.3	8.7

3.1 **(a)** Test the hypothesis that $\mu_1 \neq \mu_2$ at the $\alpha = 0.1$ level of significance for the given sample data. Reject H_0

3.2 **(b)** Construct a 95% confidence interval for $\mu_1 - \mu_2$.

3.1 **5.** Test the hypothesis that $\mu_1 < \mu_2$ at the $\alpha = 0.05$ level of significance for the given sample data. Do not reject H_0

	Population 1	Population 2
n	13	8
$\bar{x}$	96.6	98.3
s	3.2	2.5

6. A random sample of $n_1 = 650$ individuals results in $x_1 = 156$ successes. An independent sample of $n_2 = 550$ individuals results in $x_2 = 143$ successes. Does this represent sufficient evidence to conclude that $p_1 < p_2$ at the $\alpha = 0.05$ level of significance? Do not reject H_0

7. A researcher wants to know whether the acidity of rain (pH) near Houston, Texas, is significantly different from that near Chicago, Illinois. He randomly selects 12 rain dates in Texas and 14 rain dates in Illinois and obtains the following data:

Texas

4.69	5.10	5.22	4.46	4.93	4.65
5.22	4.76	4.25	5.14	4.11	4.71

Illinois

4.40	4.69	4.22	4.64	4.54	4.35	4.69
4.40	4.75	4.63	4.45	4.49	4.36	4.52

Source: National Atmospheric Deposition Program

1.1 **(a)** Is the sampling method dependent or independent? Why? Independent

(b) Because the sample sizes are small, what must be true regarding the populations from which the samples were drawn? Normal

(c) Draw side-by-side boxplots of the data. What does the visual evidence imply about the pH of rain in the two states?

3.1 **(d)** Does the evidence suggest that there is a difference in the pH of rain in Chicago and Houston? Use the $\alpha = 0.05$ level of significance. Yes

8. In a study conducted to determine the role that sleep disorders play in academic performance, researcher Jane Gaultney conducted a survey of 1845 college students. The students completed a survey to determine if they had a sleep disorder (such as narcolepsy, insomnia, or restless leg syndrome). Of the 503 students with a sleep disorder, the mean grade point average was 2.65 with a standard deviation of 0.87. Of the 1342 students without a sleep disorder, the mean grade point average was 2.82 with a standard deviation of 0.83. *Source:* SLEEP 2010: Associated Professional Sleep Societies 24th Annual Meeting (b) Reject H_0; P-value = 0.0001

(a) What is the response variable in this study? What is the explanatory variable? GPA; sleep disorder or not

3.1 **(b)** Is there evidence to suggest sleep disorders adversely affect one's GPA at the $\alpha = 0.05$ level of significance?

2.1 **9.** In Problem 9 from Section 11.2 we analyzed data in which an SUV crashed into the rear bumper of a car. Now we are going to reverse roles and allow the car traveling 10 miles per hour to collide into the rear bumper of an SUV. The data are below. Do the given data suggest the repair cost of the car is higher? Use the $\alpha = 0.1$ level of significance. Reject H_0; P-value = 0.051

Car into SUV	SUV Damage	Car Damage
Kia Forte into Hyundai Tucson	2091	1510
Dodge Caliber into Jeep Patriot	1338	2559
Honda Civic into Honda CR-V	1053	4921
Volkswagen Golf into Volkswagen Tiguan	1872	4555
Nissan Sentra into Nissan Rogue	1428	5114
Ford Focus into Ford Escape	2208	5203
Toyota Corolla into Toyota RAV4	6015	3852

Source: Insurance Institute for Highway Safety

10. Zoloft is a drug used to treat obsessive-compulsive disorder (OCD). In randomized, double-blind clinical trials, 926 patients diagnosed with OCD were randomly divided into two groups. Subjects in group 1 (experimental group) received 200 milligrams per day (mg/day) of Zoloft, while subjects in group 2 (control group) received a placebo. Of the 553 subjects in the experimental group, 77 experienced dry mouth as a side effect.

10. (a) Completely randomized design (b) Whether the subject gets dry mouth or not 14. (1.03, 1.17); reject H_0

Of the 373 subjects in the control group, 34 experienced dry mouth as a side effect.

(a) What type of experimental design is this?

(b) What is the response variable?

1.2 **(c)** Do a higher proportion of subjects experience dry mouth who are taking Zoloft versus the proportion taking the placebo? Use the $\alpha = 0.05$ level of significance. Yes

1.3 **11.** Does hypnotism result in a different success rate for men and women who are trying to quit smoking? Researchers at *Science* magazine analyzed studies involving 5600 male and female smokers. Of the 2800 females, 644 quit smoking; of the 2800 males, 840 quit smoking. Construct a 90% confidence interval for the difference in proportion of males and females, $p_M - p_F$, and use the interval to judge whether there is a difference in the proportions. (0.051, 0.089); reject H_0

1.4 **12.** The General Social Survey asked the following two questions of randomly selected individuals.

- Do you favor or oppose the death penalty for persons convicted of murder?
- Should it be possible for a woman to obtain a legal abortion?

The results of the survey are given in the table. Is there a difference in the proportion who favor the death penalty and favor abortion? Use $\alpha = 0.05$ level of significance. Reject H_0

	Favor Death Penalty	Oppose Death Penalty
Favor abortion	7956	2549
Oppose abortion	11685	4272

1.5 **13.** A researcher wants to estimate the difference between the percentage of individuals without a high school diploma who smoke and the percentage of individuals with bachelor's degrees who smoke. What sample size should be obtained if she wishes the estimate to be within 4 percentage points with 95% confidence, assuming that

(a) she uses the 1999 estimates of 32.2% of those without a high school diploma and 11.1% of those with a bachelor's degree from the National Center for Health Statistics? 762

(b) she does not use any prior estimates? 1201

3.2 **14.** It is commonplace to gain weight after quitting smoking. Does the drug Naltrexone help limit weight gain when individuals quit smoking? To determine the effectiveness of this drug, 147 subjects who smoked 20 or more cigarettes daily were randomly divided into two groups. Everyone received a 21-milligram (mg) transdermal nicotine patch (to curb nicotine cravings while trying to quit smoking). Seventy-two subjects received a placebo, while 75 received 25 mg of Naltrexone. After 6 weeks, the placebo subjects had a mean weight gain of 1.9 kg, with a standard deviation of 0.22 kg; the Naltrexone subjects had a mean weight gain of 0.8 kg with a standard deviation of 0.21 kg. Construct a 95% confidence interval for the mean difference in weight gain for the two groups. Based on this interval, do you believe that Naltrexone is effective in controlling weight gain following smoking cessation? Do the results have any practical significance? *Source*: Stephanie O'Malley et al. "A Controlled Trial of Naltrexone Augmentation of Nicotine Replacement Therapy for Smoking Cessation." *Archives of Internal Medicine*, Vol. 166, 667–674

Making an Informed Decision

Which Car Should I Buy?

You have decided to purchase a car and have narrowed your choice down to two cars. However, you have two areas of concern. First, you want to purchase the car that gets the better gas mileage. Second, you want to purchase the car that holds its value better. To help make an informed decision, you decide to collect some data and run some tests.

(a) Decide on two cars that are similar that you would consider purchasing.

(b) Go to www.fueleconomy.gov and obtain data on the fuel economy of each car you are considering. Treat the data as a random sample of all cars.

(c) Draw side-by-side boxplots of the fuel economy to verify there are no outliers and to verify it is reasonable to conclude the data come from a population that is normally distributed (if your sample size is small).

(d) Conduct the appropriate test to determine if there is a significant difference in the gas mileage of the two cars.

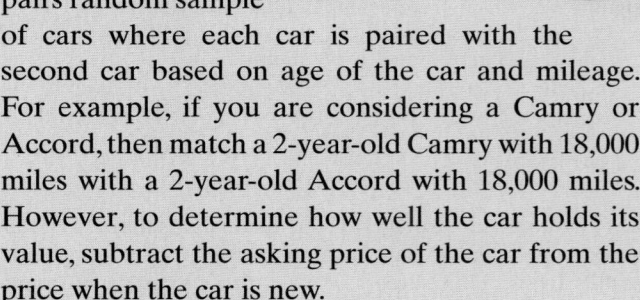

(e) Go to an online Web site that lists used cars for sale. Obtain a matched-pairs random sample of cars where each car is paired with the second car based on age of the car and mileage. For example, if you are considering a Camry or Accord, then match a 2-year-old Camry with 18,000 miles with a 2-year-old Accord with 18,000 miles. However, to determine how well the car holds its value, subtract the asking price of the car from the price when the car is new.

(f) Conduct the appropriate test to determine if one car holds its value better than the other car.

(g) Write a report detailing which car you would purchase.

The Chapter 11 Case Study is located on the CD that accompanies this text.

12 Additional Inferential Procedures

OUTLINE

Making an Informed Decision

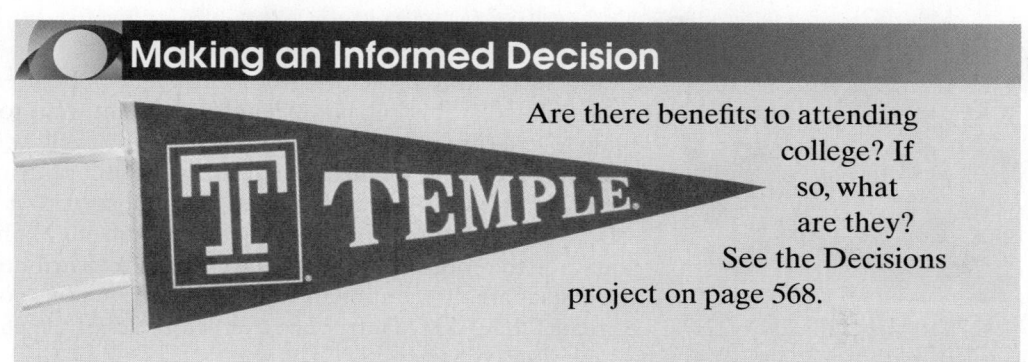

Are there benefits to attending college? If so, what are they? See the Decisions project on page 568.

PUTTING IT TOGETHER

In Chapters 9 through 11, we introduced statistical methods that can be used to test hypotheses regarding a population parameter such as p or μ.

Often, however, rather than being interested in testing a hypothesis regarding a parameter of a probability distribution, we are interested in testing a hypothesis regarding the entire probability distribution. For example, we might wish to test if the distribution of colors in a bag of plain M&M candies is 13% brown, 14% yellow, 13% red, 20% orange, 24% blue, and 16% green. We introduce methods for testing hypotheses such as this in Section 12.1.

In Section 12.2, we discuss a method that can be used to determine whether two qualitative variables are independent based on a sample. If they are not independent, the value of one variable affects the value of the other variable, so the variables are somehow related. We conclude Section 12.2 by introducing tests for homogeneity. This procedure is used to compare proportions from two or more populations. It is an extension of the two-sample z-test for proportions from independent samples discussed in Section 11.1.

In Chapter 4, we learned methods for describing the relation between two quantitative variables-bivariate data.

In Section 12.3, we test whether a linear relation exists between two quantitative variables based on methods presented in Chapter 10.

In Section 12.4, we construct confidence intervals about the predicted value of the response variable.

12.1 GOODNESS-OF-FIT TEST

Preparing for This Section Before getting started, review the following:

- Mutually exclusive (Section 5.2, p. 247)
- Expected value (Section 6.1, pp. 303–304)
- Mean of a binomial random variable (Section 6.2, pp. 316–317)

OBJECTIVE 1 Perform a goodness-of-fit test

1 Perform a Goodness-of-Fit Test

In this section, we present a procedure that can be used to test hypotheses regarding a probability distribution. For example, we might want to test whether the distribution of plain M&M candies in a bag is 13% brown, 14% yellow, 13% red, 20% orange, 24% blue, and 16% green. Or we might want to test whether the number of hits a player gets in his next four at-bats follows a binomial distribution with $n = 4$ and $p = 0.298$.

We use symbol χ^2, chi-square, pronounced "kigh-square" (to rhyme with "sky-square"), to represent values of the chi-square distribution. We can find critical values of the chi-square distribution in Table VII in Appendix A of the text. Before discussing how to read Table VII, we introduce characteristics of the chi-square distribution.

Note to Instructor

If you like, you can print out and distribute the Preparing for This Section quiz located in the Instructor's Resource Center. The purpose of the quiz is to verify that the students have the prerequisite knowledge for the section.

Characteristics of the Chi-Square Distribution

1. It is not symmetric.
2. The shape of the chi-square distribution depends on the degrees of freedom, just like Student's t-distribution.
3. As the number of degrees of freedom increases, the chi-square distribution becomes more nearly symmetric. See Figure 1.
4. The values of χ^2 are nonnegative (greater than or equal to 0).

Figure 1

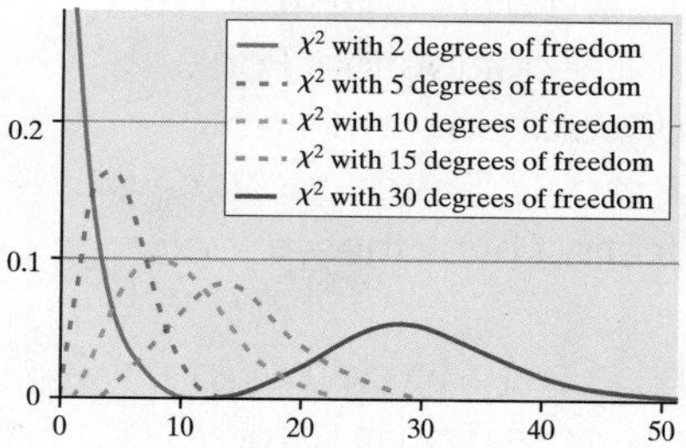

Table VII is structured similarly to Table VI for the t-distribution. The left column represents the degrees of freedom, and the top row represents the area under the chi-square distribution to the right of the critical value. We use the notation χ^2_α to denote the critical χ^2-value such that the area under the chi-square distribution to the right of χ^2_α is α.

EXAMPLE 1 Finding Critical Values for the Chi-Square Distribution

Problem Find the critical values that separate the middle 90% of the chi-square distribution from the 5% area in each tail, assuming 15 degrees of freedom.

Approach We perform the following steps to obtain the critical values.

Step 1 Draw a chi-square distribution with the critical values and areas labeled.

Step 2 Use Table VII to find the critical values.

Solution

Step 1 Figure 2 shows the chi-square distribution with 15 degrees of freedom and the unknown critical values labeled. The area to the right of the right critical value is 0.05. We denote this critical value $\chi^2_{0.05}$. The area to the right of the left critical value is $1 - 0.05 = 0.95$. We denote this critical value $\chi^2_{0.95}$.

Figure 2

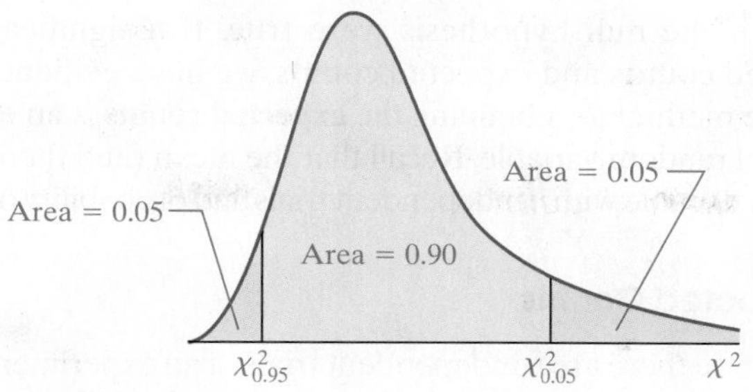

Step 2 Figure 3 shows a partial representation of Table VII. The row containing 15 degrees of freedom is boxed. The columns corresponding to an area to the right of 0.95 and 0.05 are also boxed. The critical values are $\chi^2_{0.95} = 7.261$ and $\chi^2_{0.05} = 24.996$.

Figure 3

Degrees of Freedom	Area to the Right of the Critical Value									
	0.995	0.99	0.975	0.95	0.90	0.10	0.05	0.025	0.01	0.005
1	—	—	0.001	0.004	0.016	2.706	3.841	5.024	6.635	7.879
2	0.010	0.020	0.051	0.103	0.211	4.605	5.991	7.378	9.210	10.597
3	0.072	0.115	0.216	0.352	0.584	6.251	7.815	9.348	11.345	12.838
12	3.074	3.571	4.404	5.226	6.304	18.549	21.026	23.337	26.217	28.299
13	3.565	4.107	5.009	5.892	7.042	19.812	22.362	24.736	27.688	29.819
14	4.075	4.660	5.629	6.571	7.790	21.064	23.685	26.119	29.141	31.319
15	4.601	5.229	6.262	7.261	8.547	22.307	24.996	27.488	30.578	32.801
16	5.142	5.812	6.908	7.962	9.312	23.542	26.296	28.845	32.000	34.267
17	5.697	6.408	7.564	8.672	10.085	24.769	27.587	30.191	33.409	35.718
18	6.365	7.215	8.231	9.288	10.265	25.200	28.601	31.595	24.265	36.456

In studying Table VII, we notice that the degrees of freedom are numbered 1 to 30, inclusive, then 40, 50, 60, . . . , 100. If the number of degrees of freedom is not in the table, choose the degrees of freedom closest to that desired. If the degrees of freedom are exactly between two values, find the mean of the values. For example, to find the critical value corresponding to 75 degrees of freedom, compute the mean of the critical values corresponding to 70 and 80 degrees of freedom.

Now that we understand the chi-square distribution, we can discuss the *goodness-of-fit* test.

DEFINITION

A **goodness-of-fit test** is an inferential procedure used to determine whether a frequency distribution follows a specific distribution.

As an example, we might want to test if a die is fair. This would mean the probability of each outcome is $\frac{1}{6}$ when a die is cast. Because we give the die the benefit of the doubt (that is, assume the die is fair), the null hypothesis is:

$$H_0: p_1 = p_2 = p_3 = p_4 = p_5 = p_6 = \frac{1}{6}$$

As another example, according to the U.S. Census Bureau in 2000, 19.0% of the population of the United States resided in the Northeast, 22.9% in the Midwest, 35.6% in the South, and 22.5% in the West. We might want to test if the distribution of U.S. residents is the same today as it was in 2000. Since the null hypothesis is a statement of "no change," we have

H_0: The distribution of residents in the U.S. is the same today as it was in 2000.

The idea behind testing these types of hypotheses is to compare the actual number of observations for each category of data with the number of observations we would expect if the null hypothesis were true. If a significant difference exists between the observed counts and expected counts, we have evidence against the null hypothesis.

The method for obtaining the **expected counts** is an extension of the expected value of a binomial random variable. Recall that the mean (and therefore expected value) of a binomial random variable with n independent trials and probability of success, p, is given by $E = \mu = np$.

In Other Words
The expected count for each category is the number of trials of the experiment times the probability of success in the category.

Expected Counts

Suppose there are n independent trials of an experiment with $k \geq 3$ mutually exclusive possible outcomes. Let p_1 represent the probability of observing the first outcome and E_1 represent the expected count of the first outcome; p_2 represent the probability of observing the second outcome and E_2 represent the expected count of the second outcome; and so on. The expected counts for each possible outcome are given by

$$E_i = \mu_i = np_i \quad \text{for} \quad i = 1, 2, \ldots, k$$

EXAMPLE 2 Finding Expected Counts

TABLE 1 DISTRIBUTION OF POPULATION IN THE U.S. IN 2000

Region	Percent
Northeast	19.0
Midwest	22.9
South	35.6
West	22.5

Source: U.S. Census Bureau

Problem An urban economist wishes to determine whether the distribution of residents in the United States is the same today as it was in 2000. See Table 1. If the economist randomly selects 1500 households in the United States, compute the expected number of households in each region, assuming that the distribution of households has not changed since 2000.

Approach

Step 1 Determine the probabilities for each outcome.

Step 2 There are $n = 1500$ trials (the 1500 households surveyed) of the experiment. We expect $np_{\text{Northeast}}$ of the households surveyed to reside in the Northeast, np_{Midwest} of the households to reside in the Midwest, and so on.

Solution

Step 1 The probabilities are the relative frequencies from the 2000 distribution: $p_{\text{Northeast}} = 0.190$, $p_{\text{Midwest}} = 0.229$, $p_{\text{South}} = 0.356$, and $p_{\text{West}} = 0.225$.

Step 2 The expected counts for each location are as follows:

Expected count of Northeast: $np_{\text{Northeast}} = 1500(0.190) = 285$
Expected count of Midwest: $np_{\text{Midwest}} = 1500(0.229) = 343.5$
Expected count of South: $np_{\text{South}} = 1500(0.356) = 534$
Expected count of West: $np_{\text{West}} = 1500(0.225) = 337.5$

Of the 1500 households surveyed, the economist expects to have 285 households in the Northeast, 343.5 households in the Midwest, 534 households in the South, and 337.5 households in the West if the distribution of residents of the United States is the same today as it was in 2000.

Now Work Problem 5

To conduct a hypothesis test, we compare the observed counts with the expected counts. If the observed counts are significantly different from the expected counts, we have evidence against the null hypothesis. To perform this test, we need a test statistic and sampling distribution.

Note to Instructor
Consider assigning the "Goodness-of-Fit with M&Ms" activity from the Student Activity Workbook.

CAUTION
Goodness-of-fit tests are used to test hypotheses regarding the distribution of a variable based on a single population. If you wish to compare two or more populations, you must use the tests for homogeneity presented in Section 12.2.

Test Statistic for Goodness-of-Fit Tests

Let O_i represent the observed counts of category i, E_i represent the expected counts of category i, k represent the number of categories, and n represent the number of independent trials of an experiment. Then the formula

$$\chi^2 = \sum \frac{(O_i - E_i)^2}{E_i} \qquad i = 1, 2, \ldots, k$$

approximately follows the chi-square distribution with $k - 1$ degrees of freedom, provided that

1. all expected frequencies are greater than or equal to 1 (all $E_i \geq 1$) and
2. no more than 20% of the expected frequencies are less than 5.

Note: $E_i = np_i$ for $i = 1, 2, \ldots, k$.

In Example 2, there were $k = 4$ categories (Northeast, Midwest, South, and West).

Now that we know the distribution of goodness-of-fit tests, we can present a method for testing hypotheses regarding the distribution of a random variable.

The Goodness-of-Fit Test

To test hypotheses regarding a distribution, use the steps that follow.

Step 1 Determine the null and alternative hypotheses:

H_0: The random variable follows a certain distribution.
H_1: The random variable does not follow the distribution in the null hypothesis.

Step 2 Decide on a level of significance, α, depending on the seriousness of making a Type I error.

Step 3

(a) Calculate the expected counts, E_i, for each of the k categories: $E_i = np_i$ for $i = 1, 2, \ldots, k$, where n is the number of trials and p_i is the probability of the ith category, assuming that the null hypothesis is true.

(b) Verify that the requirements for the goodness-of-fit test are satisfied.

1. All expected counts are greater than or equal to 1 (all $E_i \geq 1$).
2. No more than 20% of the expected counts are less than 5.

CAUTION

If the requirements in Step 3(b) are not satisfied, one option is to combine two or more low-frequency categories into a single category.

Classical Approach

Step 3 (continued)

(c) Compute the **test statistic**

$$\chi_0^2 = \sum \frac{(O_i - E_i)^2}{E_i}$$

Note: O_i is the observed count for the ith category.

Step 4 Determine the critical value. All goodness-of-fit tests are right-tailed tests, so the critical value is χ^2_α with $k - 1$ degrees of freedom. See Figure 4.

Figure 4

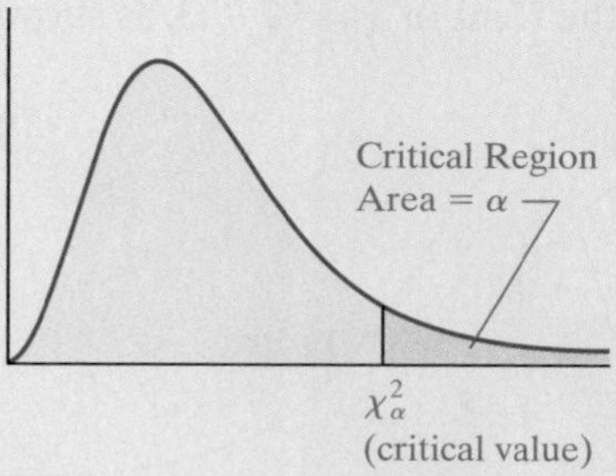

Compare the critical value to the statistic. If $\chi_0^2 > \chi^2_\alpha$, reject the null hypothesis.

P-Value Approach

By Hand Step 3 (continued)

(c) Compute the **test statistic**

$$\chi_0^2 = \sum \frac{(O_i - E_i)^2}{E_i}$$

Note: O_i is the observed count for the ith category.

(d) Use Table VII to approximate the *P*-value by determining the area under the chi-square distribution with $k - 1$ degrees of freedom to the right of the test statistic. See Figure 5.

Figure 5

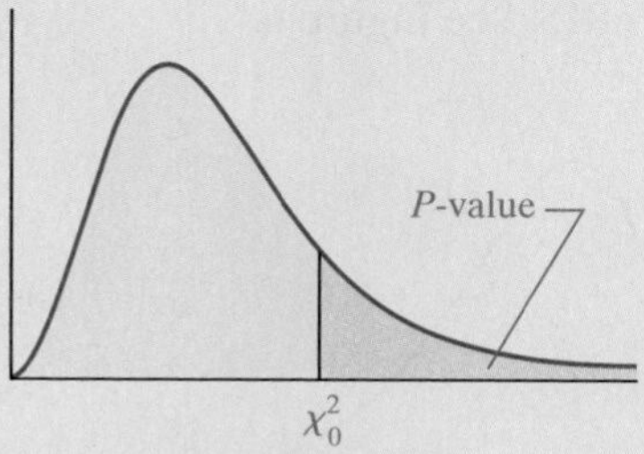

Technology Step 3 (continued)

(c) Use a statistical spreadsheet or calculator with statistical capabilities to obtain the *P*-value. The directions for obtaining the *P*-value using the TI-84 Plus graphing calculator, MINITAB, Excel, and StatCrunch are in the Technology Step-by-Step on page 527.

Step 4 If *P*-value $< \alpha$, reject the null hypothesis.

Step 5 State the conclusion.

EXAMPLE 3 Conducting a Goodness-of-Fit Test

Problem An urban economist wonders if the distribution of U.S. residents in the United States is different today than it was in 2000. In 2000, 19.0% of the population of the United States resided in the Northeast, 22.9% in the Midwest, 35.6% in the South, and 22.5% in the West (based on data obtained from the Census Bureau). The economist randomly selects 1500 households in the United States and obtains the frequency distribution shown in Table 2. **Note:** The data in Table 2 are based on the results of the 2010 Census.

TABLE 2

Region	Frequency
Northeast	269
Midwest	327
South	554
West	350

Does the evidence suggest that the distribution has changed since 2000 at the $\alpha = 0.05$ level of significance?

Approach We follow Steps 1 through 5 just listed.

Solution

Step 1 Here, the null hypothesis, a statement of "no difference," means no difference between 2000 and today. We need the evidence (sample data) to show that the distribution is different today.

H_0: The distribution of residents of the United States is the same today as it was in 2000.

H_1: The distribution of residents of the United States is different today from what it was in 2000.

Step 2 The level of significance is $\alpha = 0.05$.

Step 3

(a) We computed the expected counts in Example 2. The observed and expected counts are in Table 3.

TABLE 3

Region	Observed Counts	Expected Counts
Northeast	269	285
Midwest	327	343.5
South	554	534
West	350	337.5

(b) Since all expected counts are greater than or equal to 5, the requirements for the goodness-of-fit test are satisfied.

Classical Approach

Step 3 (continued)

(c) The test statistic is

$$\chi_0^2 = \sum \frac{(O_i - E_i)^2}{E_i}$$

$$= \frac{(269-285)^2}{285} + \frac{(327-343.5)^2}{343.5} + \frac{(554-534)^2}{534} + \frac{(350-337.5)^2}{337.5}$$

$$= 2.903$$

Step 4 There are $k = 4$ categories, so we find the critical value using $4 - 1 = 3$ degrees of freedom. The critical value is $\chi^2_{0.05} = 7.815$. See Figure 6.

Figure 6

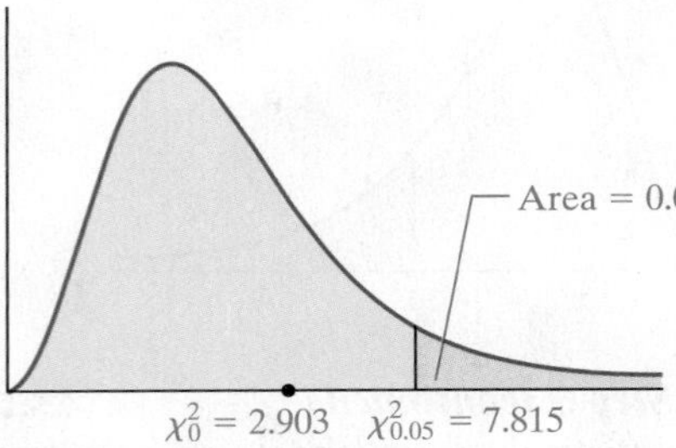

Because the test statistic, 2.903, is less then the critical value, 7.815, we do not reject the null hypothesis.

P-Value Approach

By Hand Step 3 (continued)

(c) The test statistic is

$$\chi_0^2 = \sum \frac{(O_i - E_i)^2}{E_i}$$

$$= \frac{(269-285)^2}{285} + \frac{(327-343.5)^2}{343.5} + \frac{(554-534)^2}{534} + \frac{(350-337.5)^2}{337.5}$$

$$= 2.903$$

(d) There are $k = 4$ categories. The P-value is the area under the chi-square distribution with $4 - 1 = 3$ degrees of freedom to the right of $\chi_0^2 = 2.903$, as shown in Figure 7.

Figure 7

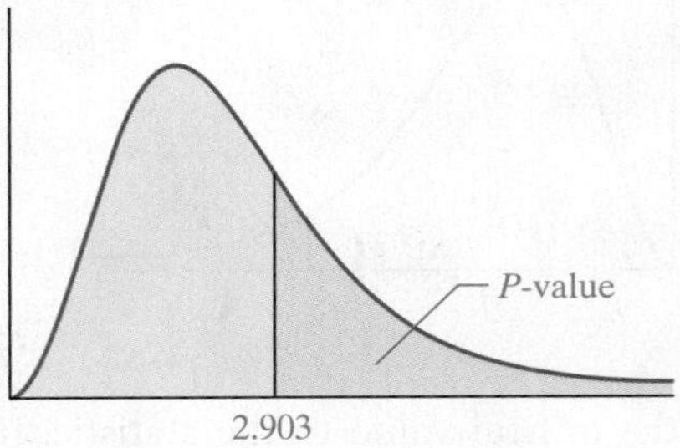

Using Table VII, we find the row that corresponds to 3 degrees of freedom. The value of 2.903 lies to the left of 6.251. The area under the chi-square distribution (with 3 degrees of freedom) to the right of 6.251 is 0.10. Because 2.903 is to the left of 6.251, the P-value is greater than 0.10. So P-value > 0.10.

Historical Note

The goodness-of-fit test was invented by Karl Pearson (the Pearson of correlation coefficient fame). Pearson believed that statistics should be done by determining the distribution of a random variable. Such a determination could be made only by looking at large numbers of data. This philosophy caused Pearson to "butt heads" with Ronald Fisher, because Fisher believed in analyzing small samples.

Technology Step 3 (continued)

(c) Figure 8 shows the result of the Goodness-of-Fit test from StatCrunch. The *P*-value is reported as 0.4068.

Figure 8 **Chi-Square goodness-of-fit results:**

Observed: Observed

Expected: Expected

N	DF	Chi-Square	P-Value
1500	3	2.9028487	0.4068

Step 4 Because the *P*-value is greater than the level of significance (Tech: $0.4068 > 0.05$), we do not reject the null hypothesis.

Step 5 There is not sufficient evidence at the $\alpha = 0.05$ level of significance to conclude that the distribution of the United States residents today is different from the distribution in 2000.

If we compare the observed and expected counts, we see that a shift in population is occurring (even though it is not a statistically significant shift). The Northeast and Midwest have observed counts below what is expected under the assumption of no population shift, while the South and West have population counts above what is expected. While the results do not have any statistical significance, there may be practical significance. See Problem 25 for a follow up to this analysis.

EXAMPLE 4 Conducting a Goodness-of-Fit Test

Problem An obstetrician wants to know whether the proportions of children born on each day of the week are the same. She randomly selects 500 birth records and obtains the data shown in Table 4 (based on data obtained from *Vital Statistics of the United States*, 2008).

TABLE 4

Day of Week	Frequency
Sunday	46
Monday	76
Tuesday	83
Wednesday	81
Thursday	81
Friday	80
Saturday	53

Is there reason to believe that the day on which a child is born occurs with equal frequency at the $\alpha = 0.01$ level of significance?

Approach Follow Steps 1 through 5 presented on page 519.

Solution

Step 1 The null hypothesis is a statement of "no difference," so we assume that the day on which a child is born occurs with equal frequency. If 1 represents Sunday, 2 represents Monday, and so on, we have

$$H_0: p_1 = p_2 = p_3 = p_4 = p_5 = p_6 = p_7 = \frac{1}{7}$$

H_1: At least one of the proportions is different from the others.

Step 2 The level of significance is $\alpha = 0.01$.

Step 3

(a) The expected count for each category (day of the week), assuming the null hypothesis is true, is

$$500\left(\frac{1}{7}\right) \approx 71.4$$

(b) Since all expected counts are greater than or equal to 5, the requirements for the goodness-of-fit test are satisfied.

(c) The test statistic is

$$\chi_0^2 = \frac{(46 - 500/7)^2}{500/7} + \frac{(76 - 500/7)^2}{500/7} + \frac{(83 - 500/7)^2}{500/7} + \frac{(81 - 500/7)^2}{500/7}$$

$$+ \frac{(81 - 500/7)^2}{500/7} + \frac{(80 - 500/7)^2}{500/7} + \frac{(53 - 500/7)^2}{500/7} = 19.568$$

Classical Approach

Step 4 There are $k = 7$ categories, so we find the critical value using $7 - 1 = 6$ degrees of freedom. The critical value is $\chi^2_{0.01} = 16.812$. See Figure 9.

Figure 9

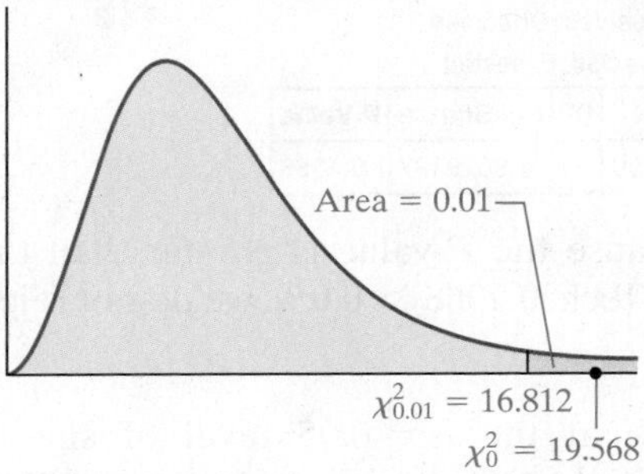

Because the test statistic, 19.568, is greater than the critical value, 16.812, we reject the null hypothesis.

P-Value Approach

Step 3 (continued)

(d) There are $k = 7$ categories. The P-value is the area under the chi-square distribution with $7 - 1 = 6$ degrees of freedom to the right of $\chi^2_0 = 19.568$, as shown in Figure 10.

Figure 10

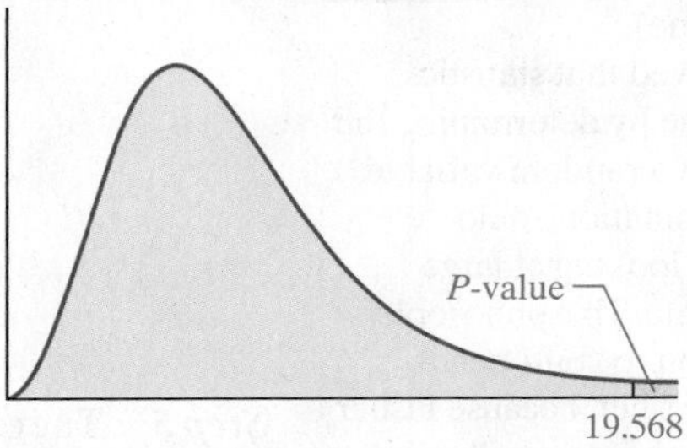

Using Table VII, we find the row that corresponds to 6 degrees of freedom. The value of 19.568 is greater than 18.548, which has an area under the chi-square distribution of 0.005 to the right, so the P-value is less than 0.005 (P-value < 0.005). Using technology, the exact P-value is 0.0033. Because the P-value is less than the level of significance, $\alpha = 0.01$, we reject the null hypothesis.

Step 5 There is sufficient evidence at the $\alpha = 0.01$ level of significance to reject the belief that the day of the week on which a child is born does not occur with equal frequency.

Now Work Problem 19

12.1 ASSESS YOUR UNDERSTANDING

VOCABULARY AND SKILL BUILDING

1. *True or False*: The shape of the chi-square distribution depends on the degrees of freedom. True

2. A goodness-of-fit test is an inferential procedure used to determine whether a frequency distribution follows a specific distribution.

3. Suppose there are n independent trials of an experiment with $k > 3$ mutually exclusive outcomes, where p_i represents the probability of observing the ith outcome. The expected counts for each possible outcome are given by $E_i =$ np_i.

4. What are the two requirements that must be satisfied to perform a goodness-of-fit test? All $E_i \geq 1$; no more than 20% of expected frequencies less than 5

In Problems 5 and 6, determine the expected counts for each outcome.

NW **5.**

$n = 500$				
p_i	**0.2**	**0.1**	**0.45**	**0.25**
Expected counts	100	50	225	125

6.

$n = 700$				
p_i	**0.15**	**0.3**	**0.35**	**0.20**
Expected counts	105	210	245	140

In Problems 7–10, determine (a) the χ^2 test statistic, (b) the degrees of freedom, (c) the critical value using $\alpha = 0.05$, and (d) test the hypothesis at the $\alpha = 0.05$ level of significance.

7. H_0: $p_A = p_B = p_C = p_D = \frac{1}{4}$

H_1: At least one of the proportions is different from the others. Do not reject H_0

Outcome	A	B	C	D
Observed	30	20	28	22
Expected	25	25	25	25

8. H_0: $p_A = p_B = p_C = p_D = p_E = \frac{1}{5}$

H_1: At least one of the proportions is different from the others. Do not reject H_0

Outcome	A	B	C	D	E
Observed	38	45	41	33	43
Expected	40	40	40	40	40

9. H_0: The random variable X is binomial with $n = 4, p = 0.8$

H_1: The random variable X is not binomial with $n = 4$, $p = 0.8$ Reject H_0

X	0	1	2	3	4
Observed	1	38	132	440	389
Expected	1.6	25.6	153.6	409.6	409.6

10. H_0: The random variable X is binomial with $n = 4, p = 0.3$

H_1: The random variable X is not binomial with $n = 4$, $p = 0.3$ Reject H_0

X	0	1	2	3	4
Observed	260	400	280	50	10
Expected	240.1	411.6	264.6	75.6	8.1

APPLYING THE CONCEPTS

NW **11. Plain M&Ms** According to the manufacturer of M&Ms, 13% of the plain M&Ms in a bag should be brown, 14% yellow, 13% red, 24% blue, 20% orange, and 16% green. A student randomly selected a bag of plain M&Ms. He counted the number of M&Ms that were each color and obtained the results shown in the table. Test whether plain M&Ms follow the distribution stated by M&M/Mars at the $\alpha = 0.05$ level of significance. Reject H_0

Color	Frequency
Brown	61
Yellow	64
Red	54
Blue	61
Orange	96
Green	64

12. Peanut M&Ms According to the manufacturer of M&Ms, 12% of the peanut M&Ms in a bag should be brown, 15% yellow, 12% red, 23% blue, 23% orange, and 15% green. A student randomly selected a bag of peanut M&Ms. He counted the number of M&Ms that were each color and obtained the results shown in the table. Test whether peanut M&Ms follow the distribution stated by M&M/Mars at the $\alpha = 0.05$ level of significance. Do not reject H_0

Color	Frequency
Brown	53
Yellow	66
Red	38
Blue	96
Orange	88
Green	59

13. Benford's Law, Part I Our number system consists of the digits 0, 1, 2, 3, 4, 5, 6, 7, 8, and 9. The first significant digit in any number must be 1, 2, 3, 4, 5, 6, 7, 8, or 9 because we do not write numbers such as 12 as 012. Although we may think that each digit appears with equal frequency so that each digit has a $\frac{1}{9}$ probability of being the first significant digit, this is not true. In 1881, Simon Newcomb discovered that first digits do not occur with equal frequency. This same result was discovered again in 1938 by physicist Frank Benford. After studying much data, he was able to assign probabilities of occurrence to the first digit in a number as shown.

Digit	1	2	3	4	5
Probability	0.301	0.176	0.125	0.097	0.079
Digit	6	7	8	9	
Probability	0.067	0.058	0.051	0.046	

Source: T. P. Hill, "The First Digit Phenomenon," *American Scientist*, July–August, 1998.

The probability distribution is now known as Benford's Law and plays a major role in identifying fraudulent data on tax returns and accounting books. For example, the following distribution represents the first digits in 200 allegedly fraudulent checks written to a bogus company by an employee attempting to embezzle funds from his employer.

First digit	1	2	3	4	5	6	7	8	9
Frequency	36	32	28	26	23	17	15	16	7

Source: State of Arizona vs. Wayne James Nelson

(a) Because these data are meant to prove that someone is guilty of fraud, what would be an appropriate level of significance when performing a goodness-of-fit test?

(b) Using the level of significance chosen in part (a), test whether the first digits in the allegedly fraudulent checks obey Benford's Law. Reject H_0

(c) Based on the results of part (b), do you think that the employee is guilty of embezzlement? Yes

14. Benford's Law, Part II Refer to Problem 13. The following distribution lists the first digit of the surface area (in square miles) of 335 rivers. Is there evidence at the $\alpha = 0.05$ level of significance to support the belief that the distribution follows Benford's Law? Yes

First digit	1	2	3	4	5	6	7	8	9
Frequency	104	55	36	38	24	29	18	14	17

Source: Eric W. Weisstein, Benford's Law, from *MathWorld*—A Wolfram Web Resource.

15. Always Wear a Helmet The National Highway Traffic Safety Administration publishes reports about motorcycle fatalities and helmet use. The distribution shows the proportion of fatalities by location of injury for motorcycle accidents.

Location of injury	Multiple Locations	Head	Neck	Thorax	Abdomen/ Lumbar/Spine
Proportion	0.57	0.31	0.03	0.06	0.03

The following data show the location of injury and fatalities for 2068 riders not wearing a helmet.

Location of injury	Multiple Locations	Head	Neck	Thorax	Abdomen/ Lumbar/Spine
Number	1036	864	38	83	47

(a) Does the distribution of fatal injuries for riders not wearing a helmet follow the distribution for all riders? Use the $\alpha = 0.05$ level of significance. No; reject H_0

(b) Compare the observed and expected counts for each category. What does this information tell you?

16. Weapon of Choice Nationally, the distribution of weapons used in robberies is as shown in the table.

Weapon	Gun	Knife	Strong-arm	Other
Proportion	0.42	0.09	0.40	0.09

Source: Federal Bureau of Investigation

The data on the following page represent the weapon of choice in 1652 robberies on school property.

Weapon	Gun	Knife	Strong-arm	Other
Proportion	329	122	857	344

(a) Does the distribution of weapon choice in robberies in schools follow the national distribution? Use the $\alpha = 0.05$ level of significance. No; reject H_0

(b) Compare the observed and expected counts for each category. What does this information tell you?

17. Does It Matter Where I Sit? Does the location of your seat in a classroom play a role in attendance or grade? To answer this question, Professors Katherine Perkins and Carl Wieman randomly assigned 400 students* in a general education physics course to one of four groups. *Source:* Perkins, Katherine K. and Wieman, Carl E, "The Surprising Impact of Seat Location on Student Performance" *The Physics Teacher*, Vol. 43, Jan. 2005.

The 100 students in group 1 sat 0 to 4 meters from the front of the class, the 100 students in group 2 sat 4 to 6.5 meters from the front, the 100 students in group 3 sat 6.5 to 9 meters from the front, and the 100 students in group 4 sat 9 to 12 meters from the front.

(a) For the first half of the semester, the attendance for the whole class averaged 83%. So, if there is no effect due to seat location, we would expect 83% of students in each group to attend. The data show the attendance history for each group. How many students in each group attended, on average? Is there a significant difference among the groups in attendance patterns? Use the $\alpha = 0.05$ level of significance. 84, 84, 84, 81; no

Group	1	2	3	4
Attendance	0.84	0.84	0.84	0.81

(b) For the second half of the semester, the groups were rotated so that group 1 students moved to the back of class and group 4 students moved to the front. The same switch took place between groups 2 and 3. The attendance for the second half of the semester averaged 80%. The data show the attendance records for the original groups (group 1 is now in back, group 2 is 6.5 to 9 meters from the front, and so on). How many students in each group attended, on average? Is there a significant difference in attendance patterns? Use the $\alpha = 0.05$ level of significance. Do you find anything curious about these data? 84, 81, 78, 76; no

Group	1	2	3	4
Attendance	0.84	0.81	0.78	0.76

(c) At the end of the semester, the proportion of students in the top 20% of the class was determined. Of the students in group 1, 25% were in the top 20%; of the students in group 2, 20% were in the top 20%; of the students in group 3, 15% were in the top 20%; of the students in group 4, 19% were in the top 20%. How many students would we expect to be in the top 20% of the class if seat location plays no role in grades? Is there a significant difference in the number of students in the top 20% of the class by group? 20 in each group; no

*The number of students was increased so that goodness-of-fit procedures could be used.

(d) In earlier sections, we discussed results that were statistically significant, but did not have any practical significance. Discuss the practical significance of these results. In other words, given the choice, would you prefer sitting in the front or back? Front

18. Racial Profiling On January 1, 2004, it became mandatory for all police departments in Illinois to record data pertaining to race from every traffic stop. The village of Mundelein, Illinois, has been collecting data since 2000. Rather than using census data to determine the racial distribution of the village, they thought it better to use data based on who is using the roads in Mundelein. So they collected data on at-fault drivers involved in car accidents in the village (the implicit assumption here is that race is independent of fault in a crash) and obtained the following distribution of race for users of roads in Mundelein.

Race	White	African American	Hispanic	Asian
Proportion	0.719	0.028	0.207	0.046

Source: Village of Mundelein, Illinois

The following data represent the races of all 9868 drivers who were stopped for a moving violation in the village of Mundelein in a recent year.

Race	White	African American	Hispanic	Asian
Proportion	7079	273	2025	491

Source: Village of Mundelein, Illinois

(a) Does the distribution of race in traffic stops reflect the distribution of drivers in Mundelein? In other words, is there any evidence of racial profiling in Mundelein? Use the $\alpha = 0.05$ level of significance. Yes; no discrimination

(b) Compare observed and expected counts for each category. What does this information tell you?

NW **19. Birthdays of Players in 2010 NHL Draft** In 2008, Malcolm Gladwell released his book *Outliers*. In the book, Gladwell claims that more hockey players are born in January through March than in October through December. The following data show the number of players selected in the 2010 National Hockey League draft according to their birth month. Is there evidence to suggest that hockey players' birthdates are not uniformly distributed throughout the year? Use the $\alpha = 0.05$ level of significance. Reject H_0

Birth Month	Frequency
January–March	63
April–June	56
July–September	28
October–December	34

Source: http://freezethepuck.wordpress.com

20. Bicycle Deaths A researcher wanted to determine whether bicycle deaths were uniformly distributed over the days of the week. She randomly selected 200 deaths that involved a bicycle, recorded the day of the week on which the death occurred, and obtained the following results (the data are based on information obtained from the Insurance Institute for Highway Safety).

Day of the Week	Frequency	Day of the Week	Frequency
Sunday	16	Thursday	34
Monday	35	Friday	41
Tuesday	16	Saturday	30
Wednesday	28		

Is there reason to believe that bicycle fatalities occur with equal frequency with respect to day of the week at the $\alpha = 0.05$ level of significance? Reject H_0

21. Pedestrian Deaths A researcher wanted to determine whether pedestrian deaths were uniformly distributed over the days of the week. She randomly selected 300 pedestrian deaths, recorded the day of the week on which the death occurred, and obtained the following results (the data are based on information obtained from the Insurance Institute for Highway Safety).

Day of the Week	Frequency	Day of the Week	Frequency
Sunday	39	Thursday	41
Monday	40	Friday	49
Tuesday	30	Saturday	61
Wednesday	40		

Test the belief that the day of the week on which a fatality happens involving a pedestrian occurs with equal frequency at the $\alpha = 0.05$ level of significance. Reject H_0

22. Is the Die Loaded? A player in a craps game suspects that one of the dice being used in the game is loaded. A loaded die is one in which all the possibilities (1, 2, 3, 4, 5, and 6) are not equally likely. The player throws the die 400 times, records the outcome after each throw, and obtains the following results:

Outcome	Frequency	Outcome	Frequency
1	62	4	62
2	76	5	57
3	76	6	67

(a) Do you think that the die is loaded? Use the $\alpha = 0.01$ level of significance. Do not reject H_0

(b) Why do you think the player might conduct the test at the $\alpha = 0.01$ level of significance rather than, say, the $\alpha = 0.1$ level of significance?

23. Home Schooling A school social worker wants to determine if the grade distribution of home-schooled children is different in her district than nationally. The U.S. National Center for Education Statistics provided her with the following data, which represent the relative frequency of home-schooled children by grade level.

Grade	Relative Frequency
K	0.076
1–3	0.253
4–5	0.158
6–8	0.235
9–12	0.278

She obtains a sample of 25 home-schooled children within her district that yields the following data:

Grade	Frequency
K	6
1–3	9
4–5	3
6–8	4
9–12	3

(a) Because of the low cell counts, combine cells into three categories K–3, 4–8, and 9–12.

(b) Is the grade distribution of home-schooled children different in her district from the national grade distribution at the $\alpha = 0.05$ level of significance? Reject H_0

24. Golden Benford The Fibonacci sequence is a famous sequence of numbers whose elements commonly occur in nature. The terms in the Fibonacci sequence are 1, 1, 2, 3, 5, 8, 13, 21, ... The ratio of consecutive terms approaches the *golden ratio*, $\Phi = \frac{1 + \sqrt{5}}{2}$. The distribution of the first digit of the first 85 terms in the Fibonacci sequence, is as shown in the following table:

Digit	1	2	3	4	5	6	7	8	9
Frequency	25	16	11	7	7	5	4	6	4

Is there evidence to support the belief that the first digit of the Fibonacci numbers follows the Benford distribution (shown in Problem 13) at the $\alpha = 0.05$ level of significance? Do not reject H_0

Note: Although it is technically necessary to consolidate cells, we will not. 25. (d) Higher sample sizes require less significant evidence.

25. Population Revisited In Example 3 we found that there was not enough evidence to support the conclusion that the distribution of the population in the United States was shifting. The following table shows the results of a survey of $n = 5000$ households.

Region	Frequency
Northeast	900
Midwest	1089
South	1846
West	1165

Source: Based on results of the 2010 U.S. Census

(a) Refer to the distribution of households in 2000 from Example 3. Determine the expected number of households in each region under the assumption the population distribution has not changed since 2000. (b) The same

(b) Determine the proportion of households in each region based on the results of the survey. Compare these proportions to those in Table 2 from Example 3. What do you notice?

(c) Does the sample evidence above suggest that the distribution of residents in the United States has changed since 2000? Yes, reject H_0

(d) Discuss the role sample size can play in determining whether the statement in the null hypothesis is rejected.

26. Testing the Random-Number Generator Statistical software and graphing calculators with advanced statistical features use random-number generators to create random numbers conforming to a specified distribution.

(a) Use a random-number generator to create a list of 500 trials of a binomial experiment with $n = 5$ and $p = 0.2$.

(b) What proportion of the numbers generated should be 0? 1? 2? 3? 4? 5?

(c) Test whether the random-number generator is generating random outcomes of a binomial experiment with $n = 5$ and $p = 0.2$ by performing a chi-square goodness-of-fit test at the $\alpha = 0.01$ level of significance.

In Section 10.2, we tested hypotheses regarding a population proportion using a z-test. However, we can also use the chi-square goodness-of-fit test to test hypotheses with $k = 2$ possible outcomes. In Problems 27 and 28, we test hypotheses with the use of both methods.

27. Low Birth Weight According to the U.S. Census Bureau, 7.1% of all babies born are of low birth weight (<5 lb, 8 oz). An obstetrician wanted to know whether mothers between the ages of 35 and 39 years give birth to a higher percentage of low-birth-weight babies. She randomly selected 240 births for which the mother was 35 to 39 years old and found 22 low-birth-weight babies. (b) Do not reject H_0

(a) If the proportion of low-birth-weight babies for mothers in this age group is 0.071, compute the expected number of low-birth-weight births to 35- to 39-year-old mothers. What is the expected number of births to mothers 35 to 39 years old that are not low birth weight? 17.04; 222.96

(b) Answer the obstetrician's question at the $\alpha = 0.05$ level of significance using the chi-square goodness-of-fit test.

(c) Answer the question by using the approach presented in Section 10.2. Do not reject H_0

28. Living Alone? In 2000, 25.8% of Americans 15 years of age or older lived alone, according to the Census Bureau. A sociologist, who believes that this percentage is greater today, conducts a random sample of 400 Americans 15 years of age or older and finds that 164 are living alone.

(a) If the proportion of Americans aged 15 years or older living alone is 0.258, compute the following expected numbers: Americans 15 years of age or older who live alone; Americans 15 years of age or older who do not live alone. 103.2; 296.8

(b) Test the sociologist's belief at the $\alpha = 0.05$ level of significance using the goodness-of-fit test. Reject H_0

(c) Test the belief by using the approach presented in Section 10.2. Reject H_0

29. Putting It Together: The V-2 Rocket in London In Thomas Pynchon's book *Gravity Rainbow*, the characters discuss whether the Poisson probabilistic model can be used to describe the locations that Germany's feared V-2 rocket would land in. They divided London into 0.25-km^2 regions. They then counted the number of rockets that landed in each region, with the following results:

Number of rocket hits	0	1	2	3	4	5	6	7
Observed number of regions	229	211	93	35	7	0	0	1

Source: Lawrence Lesser. "Even More Fun Learning Statistics." *Stats: The Magazine for Students of Statistics*, Issue 49.

(a) Estimate the mean number of rocket hits in a region by computing $\mu = \sum xP(x)$. Round your answer to four decimal places. 0.9323

(b) Explain why the requirements for conducting a goodness-of-fit test are not satisfied. All expected counts should be ≥ 1

(c) After consolidating the table, we obtain the following distribution for rocket hits. Using the Poisson probability model, $P(x) = \frac{\mu^x}{x!}e^{-\mu}$, where μ is the mean from part (a), we can obtain the probability distribution for the number of rocket hits. Find the probability of 0 hits in a region. Then find the probability of 1 hit, 2 hits, 3 hits, and 4 or more hits. 0.3936, 0.3670, 0.1711, 0.0532, 0.0151

Number of rocket hits	0	1	2	3	4 or more
Observed number of regions	229	211	93	35	8

(d) A total of $n = 576$ rockets was fired. Determine the expected number of regions hit by computing "expected number of regions" $= np$, where p is the probability of observing that particular number of hits in the region.

(e) Conduct a goodness-of-fit test for the distribution using the $\alpha = 0.05$ level of significance. Do the rockets appear to be modeled by a Poisson random variable? Yes

30. Putting It Together: Weldon's Dice On February 2, 1894, Frank Raphael Weldon wrote a letter to Francis Galton that included the results of 26,306 rolls of 12 dice. Weldon recorded the results such that a roll of a 5 or 6 resulted in a success, while a roll of 1, 2, 3, or 4 was a failure. The number of successes in each roll of the 12 dice are recorded in the table.

Number of Successes	Frequency	Number of Successes	Frequency
0	185	7	1331
1	1149	8	403
2	3265	9	105
3	5475	10	14
4	6114	11	4
5	5194	12	0
6	3067		

Source: Chance Magazine, Vol. 22, No. 4, 2009

(a) What is the probability of rolling a 5 or 6 when throwing a six-sided fair die? (d) Reject H_0; P-value < 0.0001

(b) Treating the probability determined in part (a) as the probability of success, compute the theoretical probability of 0, 1, 2, . . . , 12 successes in throwing 12 dice.

(c) Use the probabilities found in part (b) to determine the expected frequency in observing 0, 1, 2, . . . , 12 successes after throwing the 12 dice 26,306 times.

(d) Conduct a goodness-of-fit test to determine if the number of successes follows a binomial probability distribution. **Note:** Combine 11 and 12 into a single bin.

EXPLAINING THE CONCEPTS

30. (a) $\frac{1}{3}$

31. Why is goodness of fit a good choice for the title of the procedures used in this section?

32. Explain why chi-square goodness-of-fit tests are always right tailed.

33. If the expected count of a category is less than 1, what can be done to the categories so that a goodness-of-fit test can still be performed?

Technology Step-By-Step

Goodness-of-Fit Test

TI-84 Plus*

1. Enter the observed counts in L1 and enter the expected counts in L2.
2. Press STAT, highlight TESTS, and select D:χ^2-GOF-Test....
3. Enter L1 after Observed:, and enter L2 after Expected:. Enter the appropriate degrees of freedom following df:. Highlight either Calculate or Draw and press ENTER.

MINITAB

1. Enter the observed counts in column C1. Enter expected proportions or counts, assuming that the null hypothesis is true, in column C2, if necessary.
2. Select the **Stat** menu, highlight **Tables**, then highlight **Chi-square Goodness-of-Fit Test (One Variable)....**
3. Select the Observed Counts radio button and enter C1 in the cell. If you are testing equal proportions, select this radio button. If you entered expected proportions in C2, select the "Specific proportions" radio button and enter C2. If you entered expected counts in C2, select the "Proportions specified by historical counts" radio button and enter C2. Click OK.

*The TI-83 and older TI-84 Plus graphing calculators do not have this capability.

Excel

1. Load the XLSTAT Add-in.
2. Enter the category names in column A. Enter the proportions used to formulate expected counts in column B. Enter the observed counts in column C.
3. Select **Parametric tests**, highlight Multinomial goodness of fit.
4. Place the cursor in the Frequencies cell. Highlight the data in column C. Place the cursor in the Expected proportions cell. Highlight the data in column B. Be sure the proportions radio button is selected. Check the Column labels box. Check the Chi-square test box. Enter a level of significance. Click OK.

StatCrunch

1. Enter the observed counts in the first column. Enter the expected counts in the second column. Name the columns observed and expected.
2. Select **Stat**, highlight **Goodness-of-fit**, then highlight **Chi-Square test**.
3. Select the column that contains the observed counts and select the column that contains the expected counts. Click Calculate.

12.2 TESTS FOR INDEPENDENCE AND THE HOMOGENEITY OF PROPORTIONS

Preparing for This Section Before getting started, review the following:

- The language of hypothesis tests (Section 10.1, pp. 429–434)
- Independent events (Section 5.3, pp. 259–261)
- Contingency Tables and Association (Section 4.4, pp. 214–221)
- Mean of a binomial random variable (Section 6.2, pp. 316–317)
- Testing a hypothesis about two population proportions (Section 11.1, pp. 468–478)

OBJECTIVES

1 Perform a test for independence

2 Perform a test for homogeneity of proportions

Note to Instructor

If you like, you can print out and distribute the Preparing for This Section quiz located in the Instructor's Resource Center. The purpose of the quiz is to verify that the students have the prerequisite knowledge for the section.

In Section 4.4 we discussed the association between two variables by examining the relative frequency marginal distributions in a contingency table. In this section, we develop methods for performing statistical inference on two categorical variables to determine whether there is any association between the two variables. We call the method the *chi-square test for independence*.

1 Perform a Test for Independence

We begin with a definition.

DEFINITION

The **chi-square test for independence** is used to determine whether there is an association between a row variable and column variable in a contingency table constructed from sample data. The null hypothesis is that the variables are not associated; in other words, they are independent. The alternative hypothesis is that the variables are associated, or dependent.

In Other Words
In a chi-square independence test, the null hypothesis is always
H_0: The variables are independent
The alternative hypothesis is always
H_1: The variables are not independent

The idea behind testing these types of hypotheses is to compare actual counts to the counts we would expect if the null hypothesis were true (the variables are independent). If a significant difference between the actual counts and expected counts exists, we take this as evidence against the null hypothesis.

To obtain the expected counts, we compute the number of observations expected within each cell under the assumption the null hypothesis is true. Recall, if two events E and F are independent, then $P(E \text{ and } F) = P(E) \cdot P(F)$. We can use the Multiplication Rule for Independent Events to obtain the expected proportion of observations within each cell under the assumption of independence. We then multiply this result by n, the sample size, to obtain the expected count within each cell.*

EXAMPLE 1 Determining the Expected Counts in a Test for Independence

Note to Instructor
Consider assigning the "Independent?" activity from the Student Activity Workbook.

Problem Is there a relationship between marital status and happiness? The data in Table 5 show the marital status and happiness of individuals who participated in the General Social Survey. Compute the expected counts within each cell, assuming that marital status and happiness are independent.

TABLE 5

		Marital Status			
		Married	**Widowed**	**Divorced/ Separated**	**Never Married**
Happiness	**Very Happy**	600	63	112	144
	Pretty Happy	720	142	355	459
	Not Too Happy	93	51	119	127

Approach

Step 1 Compute the row and column totals.

Step 2 Compute the relative marginal frequencies for the row variable and column variable.

Step 3 Use the Multiplication Rule for Independent Events to compute the expected proportion of observations within each cell assuming independence.

Step 4 Multiply the proportions by 2985, the sample size, to obtain the expected counts within each cell.

*Recall that the expected value of a binomial random variable for n independent trials of a binomial experiment with probability of success p is given by $E = \mu = np$.

Solution

Step 1 The row totals (blue) and column totals (red) are presented in Table 6.

TABLE 6

		Marital Status				
		Married	**Widowed**	**Divorced/Separated**	**Never Married**	**Row Totals**
Happiness	**Very Happy**	600	63	112	144	919
	Pretty Happy	720	142	355	459	1676
	Not Too Happy	93	51	119	127	390
	Column Totals	1413	256	586	730	2985

Step 2 The relative marginal frequencies for the row variable (happiness) and column variable (marital status) are presented in Table 7.

TABLE 7

		Marital Status				
		Married	**Widowed**	**Divorced/Separated**	**Never Married**	**Relative Frequency**
Happiness	**Very Happy**	600	63	112	144	$\frac{919}{2985} \approx 0.308$
	Pretty Happy	720	142	355	459	$\frac{1676}{2985} \approx 0.561$
	Not Too Happy	93	51	119	127	$\frac{390}{2985} \approx 0.131$
	Relative Frequency	$\frac{1413}{2985} \approx 0.473$	$\frac{256}{2985} \approx 0.086$	$\frac{586}{2985} \approx 0.196$	$\frac{730}{2985} \approx 0.245$	1

Step 3 We assume the variables are independent and use the Multiplication Rule for Independent Events to compute the expected proportions for each cell. For example, the proportion of individuals who are "very happy" and "married" would be

$$\begin{pmatrix}\text{Proportion "very happy"} \\ \text{and "married"}\end{pmatrix} = (\text{proportion "very happy"}) \cdot (\text{proportion "married"})$$
$$= \left(\frac{919}{2985}\right)\left(\frac{1413}{2985}\right)$$
$$= 0.145737$$

Table 8 shows the expected proportion in each cell, assuming independence.

TABLE 8

		Marital Status			
		Married	**Widowed**	**Divorced/Separated**	**Never Married**
Happiness	**Very Happy**	0.145737	0.026404	0.060440	0.075292
	Pretty Happy	0.265783	0.048153	0.110226	0.137312
	Not Too Happy	0.061847	0.011205	0.025649	0.031952

Step 4 In Table 9, we multiply the expected proportions in Table 8 by 2985, the sample size, to obtain the expected counts.

TABLE 9

		Marital Status			
		Married	**Widowed**	**Divorced/Separated**	**Never Married**
Happiness	**Very Happy**	2985(0.145737) = 435.025	2985(0.026404) = 78.816	2985(0.060440) = 180.413	2985(0.075292) = 224.747
	Pretty Happy	793.362	143.737	329.025	409.876
	Not Too Happy	184.613	33.447	76.562	95.377

If happiness and marital status are independent, we would expect a random sample of 2985 individuals to contain about 435 who are "very happy" and "married."

The technique used in Example 1 to find the expected counts might seem rather tedious. It certainly would be more pleasant if we could determine a shortcut formula to obtain the expected counts. Consider the expected count for "very happy" and "married." This expected count was obtained by multiplying the proportion of individuals who are "very happy," the proportion of individuals who are "married," and the number of individuals in the sample. That is,

$$\begin{aligned}\text{Expected count} &= (\text{proportion "very happy"})(\text{proportion "married"})(\text{sample size})\\ &= \frac{919}{2985}\cdot\frac{1413}{2985}\cdot 2985\\ &= \frac{919\cdot 1413}{2985} \quad \text{Cancel the 2985s}\\ &= \frac{(\text{row total for happiness})(\text{column total for marital status})}{\text{table total}}\end{aligned}$$

This leads to the following general result:

Expected Frequencies in a Chi-Square Test for Independence

To find the expected frequency in a cell when performing a chi-square independence test, multiply the cell's row total by its column total and divide this result by the table total. That is,

$$\text{Expected frequency} = \frac{(\text{row total})(\text{column total})}{\text{table total}} \qquad \textbf{(1)}$$

For example, the expected frequency for "very happy and married" is

$$\text{Expected frequency} = \frac{(\text{row total})(\text{column total})}{\text{table total}} = \frac{(919)(1413)}{2985} = 435.024$$

Now Work Problem 7(a)

This result is close to that obtained in Table 9 (the difference exists because of rounding error; in fact, 435.024 is more accurate).

We need a test statistic and sampling distribution to see whether the expected and observed counts are significantly different.

Test Statistic for the Test of Independence

Let O_i represent the observed number of counts in the ith cell and E_i represent the expected number of counts in the ith cell. Then

$$\chi^2 = \sum \frac{(O_i - E_i)^2}{E_i}$$

approximately follows the chi-square distribution with $(r - 1)(c - 1)$ degrees of freedom, where r is the number of rows and c is the number of columns in the contingency table, provided that (1) all expected frequencies are greater than or equal to 1 and (2) no more than 20% of the expected frequencies are less than 5.

In Example 1, there were $r = 3$ rows and $c = 4$ columns.

We now present a method for testing hypotheses regarding the association between two variables in a contingency table.

Chi-Square Test for Independence

To test the association between (or independence of) two variables in a contingency table, we use the steps that follow:

Step 1 Determine the null and alternative hypotheses.

H_0: The row variable and column variable are independent.
H_1: The row variable and column variable are dependent.

Step 2 Choose a level of significance, α, depending on the seriousness of making a Type I error.

Step 3
(a) Calculate the expected frequencies (counts) for each cell in the contingency table using Formula (1).
(b) Verify that the requirements for the chi-square test for independence are satisfied:

1. All expected frequencies are greater than or equal to 1 (all $E_i \geq 1$).
2. No more than 20% of the expected frequencies are less than 5.

Classical Approach

Step 3 (continued)
(c) Compute the **test statistic**

$$\chi_0^2 = \sum \frac{(O_i - E_i)^2}{E_i}$$

Note: O_i is the observed frequency for the ith cell.

Step 4 Determine the critical value. All chi-square tests for independence are right-tailed tests, so the critical value is χ^2_α with $(r - 1)(c - 1)$ degrees of freedom, where r is the number of rows and c is the number of columns in the contingency table. See Figure 11.

Figure 11

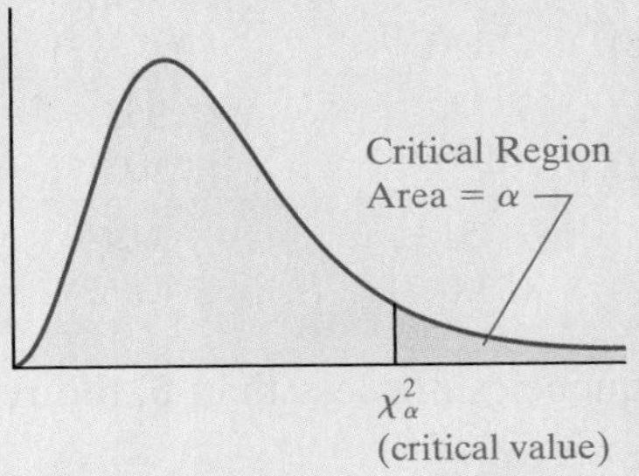

Compare the critical value to the test statistic. If $\chi_0^2 > \chi^2_\alpha$, reject the null hypothesis.

P-Value Approach

By Hand Step 3 (continued)
(c) Compute the **test statistic**

$$\chi_0^2 = \sum \frac{(O_i - E_i)^2}{E_i}$$

Note: O_i is the observed frequency for the ith cell.

(d) Use Table VII to determine an approximate P-value by determining the area under the chi-square distribution with $(r - 1)(c - 1)$ degrees of freedom to the right of the test statistic, where r is the number of rows and c is the number of columns in the contingency table. See Figure 12.

Figure 12

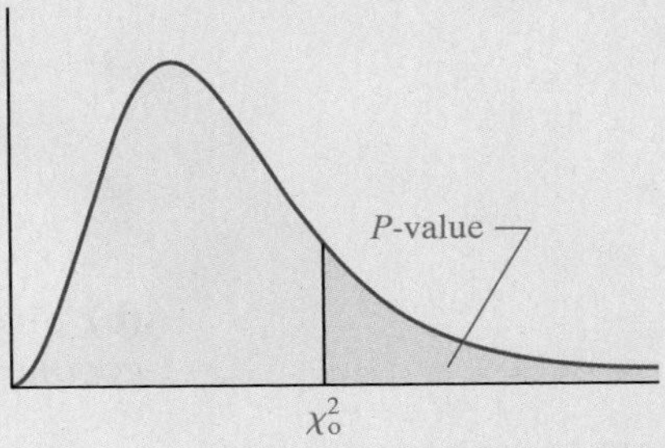

Technology Step 3 (continued)
(c) Use a statistical spreadsheet or calculator with statistical capabilities to obtain the P-value. The directions for obtaining the P-value using the TI-83/84 Plus graphing calculator, MINITAB, Excel, and StatCrunch are in the Technology Step-by-Step on page 542.

Step 4 If P-value $< \alpha$, reject the null hypothesis.

Step 5 State the conclusion.

EXAMPLE 2 Performing a Chi-Square Test for Independence

Problem Does the sample evidence suggest that one's happiness depends on one's marital status? We present the data from Table 5 in Example 1 again in Table 10 to answer this question. Use the $\alpha = 0.05$ level of significance.

TABLE 10

		Marital Status			
		Married	Widowed	Divorced/Separated	Never Married
Happiness	Very Happy	600	63	112	144
	Pretty Happy	720	142	355	459
	Not Too Happy	93	51	119	127

Approach We follow Steps 1 through 5 just given.

Solution

Step 1 We wish to determine whether happiness and marital status are dependent or independent. The null hypothesis is a statement of "no effect," so we state the hypotheses as follows:

H_0: Happiness and marital status are independent (not related)

H_1: Happiness and marital status are dependent (related)

Step 2 The level of significance is $\alpha = 0.05$.

Step 3

(a) The expected frequencies were determined in Example 1. Table 11 shows the observed frequencies, with the expected frequencies in parentheses.

TABLE 11

		Marital Status			
		Married	Widowed	Divorced/Separated	Never Married
Happiness	Very Happy	600 (435.025)	63 (78.816)	112 (180.413)	144 (224.747)
	Pretty Happy	720 (793.362)	142 (143.737)	355 (329.025)	459 (409.876)
	Not Too Happy	93 (184.613)	51 (33.447)	119 (76.562)	127 (95.377)

(b) Since none of the expected frequencies are less than 5, the requirements for the goodness-of-fit test are satisfied.

Classical Approach

Step 3 (continued)

(c) $$\chi_0^2 = \frac{(600 - 435.025)^2}{435.025} + \frac{(63 - 78.816)^2}{78.816} + \frac{(112 - 180.413)^2}{180.413} + \cdots + \frac{(119 - 76.562)^2}{76.562} + \frac{(127 - 95.377)^2}{95.377}$$

$$= 224.116$$

Step 4 There are $r = 3$ rows and $c = 4$ columns, so we find the critical value using $(r - 1)(c - 1) = (3 - 1)(4 - 1) = 6$ degrees of freedom. The critical value is $\chi^2_{0.05} = 12.592$. See Figure 13.

P-Value Approach

By Hand Step 3 (continued)

(c) $$\chi_0^2 = \frac{(600 - 435.025)^2}{435.025} + \frac{(63 - 78.816)^2}{78.816} + \frac{(112 - 180.413)^2}{180.413} + \cdots + \frac{(119 - 76.562)^2}{76.562} + \frac{(127 - 95.377)^2}{95.377}$$

$$= 224.116$$

(d) There are $r = 3$ rows and $c = 4$ columns, so we find the P-value using $(r - 1)(c - 1) = (3 - 1)(4 - 1) = 6$ degrees of freedom. The P-value is the area under the chi-square distribution with 6 degrees of freedom to the right of $\chi_0^2 = 224.116$.

Figure 13

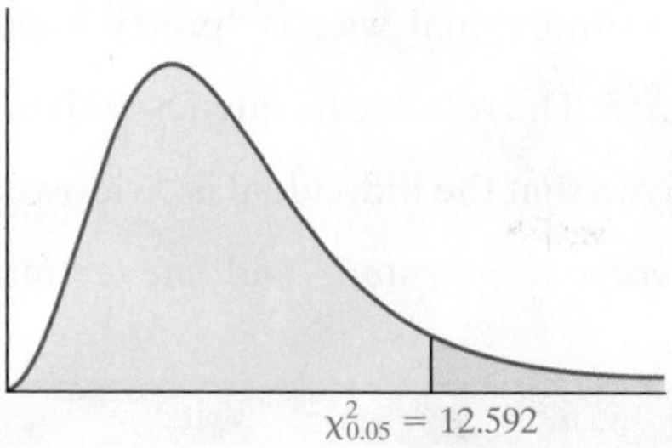

Because the test statistic, 224.116, is greater than the critical value, $\chi^2_{0.05} = 12.592$, we reject the null hypothesis.

Using Table VII, we find the row that corresponds to 6 degrees of freedom. The value of 224.116 is greater than 18.548. The area under the chi-square distribution to the right of 18.548 is 0.005. Because 224.116 is greater than 18.548, the *P*-value is less than 0.005, so we have *P*-value < 0.005.

Technology Step 3 **(*continued*)**

(c) Figure 14 shows the *P*-value obtained from a TI-84 Plus graphing calculator using the Calculate feature. The *P*-value is reported as 1.38×10^{-45}, which is very close to 0.

Figure 14

Step 4 Because the *P*-value is less than the level of significance, we reject the null hypothesis.

Step 5 There is sufficient evidence, at the $\alpha = 0.05$ level of significance, to conclude that happiness and marital status are dependent. We conclude that happiness and marital status are related to each other.

Now Work Problems 7(b)–(e)

To see the relation between happiness and marital status, we draw bar graphs of the conditional distributions of happiness by marital status. Recall that a conditional distribution lists the relative frequency of each category of a variable, given a specific value of the other variable in a contingency table. For example, we can calculate the relative frequency of "very happy," given that an individual is "married." We repeat this for each remaining category of marital status.

EXAMPLE 3 Constructing a Conditional Distribution and Bar Graph

Problem Find the conditional distribution of happiness by marital status for the data in Table 10. Then draw a bar graph that represents the conditional distribution of happiness by marital status.

Approach First, compute the relative frequency for happiness, given that the individual is "married." Then compute the relative frequency for happiness, given that the individual is "widowed," and so on. For each marital status, we will draw four bars side by side. The horizontal axis represents level of happiness, and the vertical axis represents the relative frequency of happiness for each marital status.

Solution We start with the individuals who are "married." The relative frequency with which we observe an individual who is "very happy," given that the individual is "married," is $\frac{600}{1413} = 0.425$. The relative frequency with which we observe an individual who is "pretty happy," given that the individual is "married," is $\frac{720}{1413} = 0.510$. The relative frequency with which we observe an individual who is "not too happy," given that the individual is "married," is $\frac{93}{1413} = 0.066$.

We now compute the relative frequency for each level of happiness, given that the individual is "widowed." The relative frequency with which we observe an individual who is "very happy," given that the individual is "widowed," is $\frac{63}{256} = 0.246$. The relative frequency with which we observe an individual who is "pretty happy," given that the individual is "widowed," is $\frac{142}{256} = 0.555$. The relative frequency with which we observe an individual who is "not too happy," given that the individual is "widowed," is $\frac{51}{256} = 0.199$.

We repeat the process for "divorced/separated" and "never married" and obtain Table 12.

TABLE 12

		Marital Status			
		Married	**Widowed**	**Divorced/Separated**	**Never Married**
Happiness	**Very Happy**	$\frac{600}{1413} = 0.425$	$\frac{63}{256} = 0.246$	$\frac{112}{586} = 0.191$	$\frac{144}{730} = 0.197$
	Pretty Happy	$\frac{720}{1413} = 0.510$	$\frac{142}{256} = 0.555$	$\frac{355}{586} = 0.606$	$\frac{459}{730} = 0.629$
	Not Too Happy	$\frac{93}{1413} = 0.066$	$\frac{51}{256} = 0.199$	$\frac{119}{586} = 0.203$	$\frac{127}{730} = 0.174$

From the conditional distribution by marital status, the association between happiness and marital status should be apparent. The proportion of individuals who are "very happy" is highest in the "married" category. In addition, the proportion of individuals who are "not too happy" is lowest in the "married" category.

Figure 15 shows the bar graph of the conditional distribution. The blue bars represent the proportion of individuals who are "married" for each level of happiness, the green bars represent the proportion of individuals who are "widowed" for each level of happiness, and the purple bars represent the proportion of individuals who are "divorced/separated" for each level of happiness. The yellow bars represent the individuals who "never married,"

Figure 15

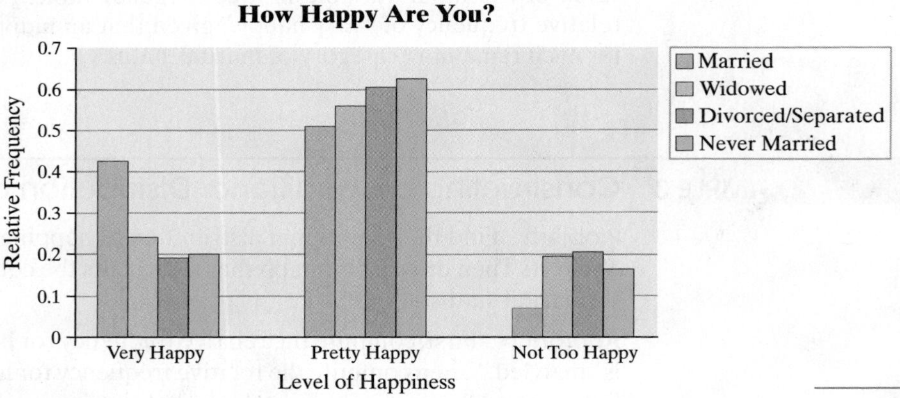

2 Perform a Test for Homogeneity of Proportions

In Other Words
The chi-square test for homogeneity of proportions is used to compare proportions from two or more populations.

We now discuss a second type of chi-square test that can be used to compare the population proportions from two or more independent samples. The test is an extension of the two-sample Z-test introduced in Section 11.1, where we compared two population proportions from independent samples.

DEFINITION

In a **chi-square test for homogeneity of proportions,** we test whether different populations have the same proportion of individuals with some characteristic.

For example, we might look at the proportion of individuals who experience headaches as a side effect for a placebo group (group 1) and for one experimental group that receives 50 milligrams (mg) per day of a medication (group 2) and another that receives 100 mg per day (group 3). We assume that the proportion of individuals who experience a headache as a side effect is the same in each population (because the null hypothesis is a statement of "no difference"). So our hypotheses are

H_0: $p_1 = p_2 = p_3$

H_1: At least one of the population proportions is different from the others.

The procedures for performing a test of homogeneity are identical to those for a test of independence.

EXAMPLE 4 A Test for Homogeneity of Proportions

Problem Zocor is a drug manufactured by Merck and Co. that is meant to reduce the level of LDL (bad) cholesterol and increase the level of HDL (good) cholesterol. In clinical trials of the drug, patients were randomly divided into three groups. Group 1 received Zocor, group 2 received a placebo, and group 3 received cholestyramine, a cholesterol-lowering drug currently available. Table 13 contains the number of patients in each group who did and did not experience abdominal pain as a side effect.

TABLE 13

	Group 1 (Zocor)	Group 2 (placebo)	Group 3 (cholestyramine)
Number of people who experienced abdominal pain	51	5	16
Number of people who did not experience abdominal pain	1532	152	163

Source: Merck and Co.

Is there evidence to indicate that the proportion of subjects in each group who experienced abdominal pain is different at the $\alpha = 0.01$ level of significance?

Approach We will follow Steps 1 through 5 on page 531.

Solution

Step 1 The null hypothesis is a statement of "no difference," so the proportion of subjects in each group who experienced abdominal pain are equal. We state the hypotheses as follows:

H_0: $p_1 = p_2 = p_3$

H_1: At least one of the proportions is different from the others.

Here, p_1, p_2, and p_3 are the proportions in groups 1, 2, and 3, respectively.

Step 2 The level of significance is $\alpha = 0.01$.

Step 3

(a) The expected frequency of subjects who experienced abdominal pain in group 1 is the product of the row total of individuals who experienced abdominal pain and the column total of individuals in group 1, divided by the total number of subjects in the study. Table 14 on the next page contains the row and column totals, the observed frequencies, and the expected frequencies (in parentheses). So

$$E = \frac{(51 + 5 + 16)(51 + 1532)}{51 + 5 + 16 + 1532 + 152 + 163} = \frac{72 \cdot 1583}{1919} = 59.393$$

(b) Since none of the expected frequencies are less than 5, the requirements for the test of homogeneity of proportions are satisfied.

TABLE 14

	Observed (and Expected) Frequencies			
	Group 1 (Zocor)	**Group 2 (placebo)**	**Group 3 (cholestyramine)**	**Row Totals**
Number of people who experienced abdominal pain	51 (59.393)	5 (5.891)	16 (6.716)	72
Number of people who did not experience abdominal pain	1532 (1523.607)	152 (151.109)	163 (172.284)	1847
Column totals	1583	157	179	1919

Classical Approach

Step 3 (continued)

(c) The test statistic is

$$\chi_0^2 = \frac{(51-59.393)^2}{59.393} + \frac{(5-5.891)^2}{5.891} + \frac{(16-6.716)^2}{6.716} + \frac{(1532-1523.607)^2}{1523.607} + \frac{(152-151.109)^2}{151.109} + \frac{(163-172.284)^2}{172.284} = 14.707$$

Step 4 There are $r = 2$ rows and $c = 3$ columns, so we find the critical value using $(2-1)(3-1) = 2$ degrees of freedom. The critical value is $\chi^2_{0.01} = 9.210$. See Figure 16.

Figure 16

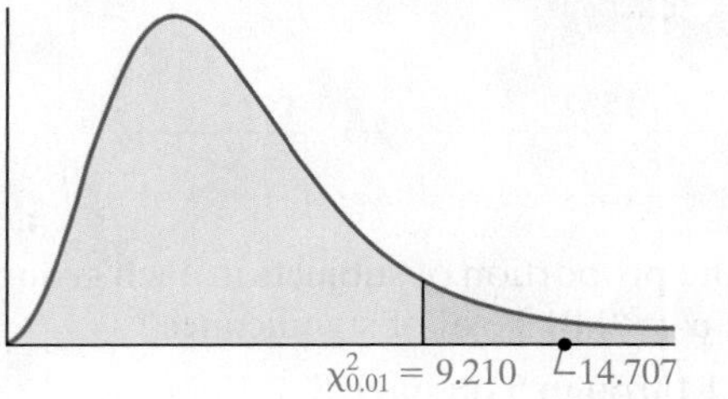

Because the test statistic, 14.707, is greater than the critical value, 9.210, we reject the null hypothesis.

P-Value Approach

By Hand Step 3 (continued)

(c) The test statistic is

$$\chi_0^2 = \frac{(51-59.393)^2}{59.393} + \frac{(5-5.891)^2}{5.891} + \frac{(16-6.716)^2}{6.716} + \frac{(1532-1523.607)^2}{1523.607} + \frac{(152-151.109)^2}{151.109} + \frac{(163-172.284)^2}{172.284} = 14.707$$

(d) There are $r = 2$ rows and $c = 3$ columns, so we find the *P*-value using $(2-1)(3-1) = 2$ degrees of freedom. The *P*-value is the area under the chi-square distribution with 2 degrees of freedom to the right of $\chi_0^2 = 14.707$, as shown in Figure 17.

Figure 17

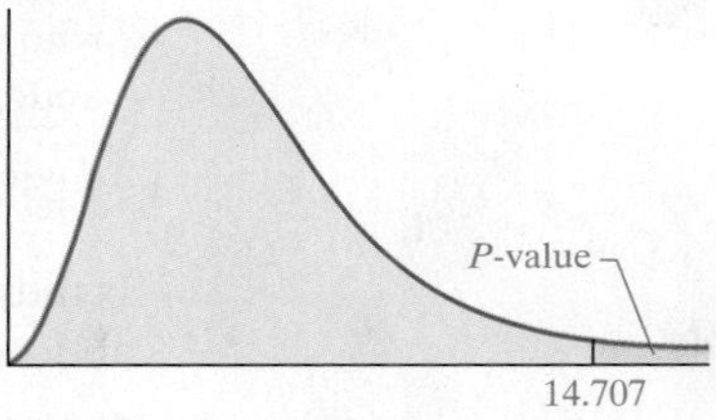

Using Table VII, in the row corresponding to 2 degrees of freedom, the area under the chi-square distribution with 2 degrees of freedom, to the right of 10.597, is 0.005. Because 14.707 is to the right of 10.597, the *P*-value is less than 0.005. So *P*-value < 0.005.

Technology Step 3 (continued)

(c) Figure 18 shows the *P*-value obtained from StatCrunch. The *P*-value is reported as 0.0006.

Figure 18

Contingency table results:

Rows: var1

Columns: None

	Group 1	Group 2	Group 3	Total
Pain	51	5	16	72
No Pain	1532	152	163	1847
Total	1583	157	179	1919

Chi-Square test:

Statistic	DF	Value	P-value
Chi-square	2	14.706513	0.0006

Step 4 Because the *P*-value is less than the level of significance, $\alpha = 0.01$, we reject the null hypothesis.

CAUTION

If we reject the null hypothesis in a chi-square test for homogeneity, we are saying there is sufficient evidence to believe that at least one proportion is different from the others. However, it does not tell us which proportions differ.

Step 5 There is sufficient evidence at the $\alpha = 0.01$ level of significance to reject the null hypothesis that the proportion of subjects in each group who experience abdominal pain are equal. We conclude that at least one of the three groups experiences abdominal pain at a rate different from the other two groups.

Figure 19 shows the bar graph. From the graph, it is apparent that a higher proportion of patients taking cholestyramine experience abdominal pain as a side effect.

Figure 19

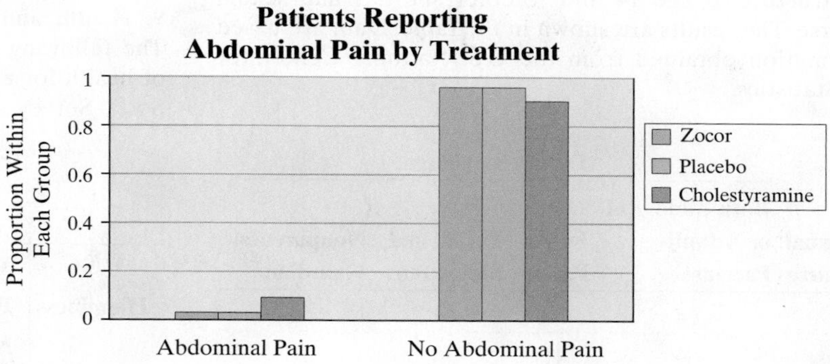

Now Work Problem 15

Recall that the requirements for performing a chi-square test are that all expected frequencies are greater than 1 and that at most 20% of the expected frequencies can be less than 5. If these requirements are not satisfied, the researcher has one of two options: (1) combine two or more columns (or rows) to increase the expected frequencies or (2) increase the sample size.

12.2 ASSESS YOUR UNDERSTANDING

VOCABULARY AND SKILL BUILDING

1. *True or False*: The expected frequencies in a chi-square test for independence are found using the formula

$$\text{Expected frequency} = \frac{(\text{row total})(\text{column total})}{\text{table total}}$$ True

2. In a chi-square test for homogeneity of proportions, we test whether different populations have the same proportion of individuals with some characteristic.

3. The following table contains observed values and expected values in parentheses for two categorical variables, X and Y, where variable X has three categories and variable Y has two categories:

	X_1	X_2	X_3
Y_1	34 (36.26)	43 (44.63)	52 (48.11)
Y_2	18 (15.74)	21 (19.37)	17 (20.89)

(a) Compute the value of the chi-square test statistic. 1.701

(b) Test the hypothesis that X and Y are independent at the $\alpha = 0.05$ level of significance. Do not reject H_0

4. The table in the next column contains observed values and expected values in parentheses for two categorical variables, X and Y, where variable X has three categories and variable Y has two categories.

	X_1	X_2	X_3
Y_1	87 (75.12)	74 (80.43)	34 (39.46)
Y_2	12 (23.88)	32 (25.57)	18 (12.54)

(a) Compute the value of the chi-square test statistic. 13.053

(b) Test the hypothesis that X and Y are independent at the $\alpha = 0.05$ level of significance. Reject H_0

5. The following table contains the number of successes and failures for three categories of a variable.

	Category 1	Category 2	Category 3
Success	76	84	69
Failure	44	41	49

Test whether the proportions are equal for each category at the $\alpha = 0.01$ level of significance. Do not reject H_0; P-value $= 0.370$

6. The following table contains the number of successes and failures for three categories of a variable.

	Category 1	Category 2	Category 3
Success	204	199	214
Failure	96	121	98

Test whether the proportions are equal for each category at the $\alpha = 0.01$ level of significance. Do not reject H_0; P-value = 0.171

APPLYING THE CONCEPTS

NW **7. Family Structure and Sexual Activity** A sociologist wants to discover whether the sexual activity of females between the ages of 15 and 19 years of age and family structure are associated. She randomly selects 380 females between the ages of 15 and 19 years of age and asks each to disclose her family structure at age 14 and whether she has had sexual intercourse. The results are shown in the table. Data are based on information obtained from the U.S. National Center for Health Statistics.

	Family Structure			
Had Sexual Intercourse	**Both Biological or Adoptive Parents**	**Single Parent**	**Parent and Stepparent**	**Nonparental Guardian**
Yes	64	59	44	32
No	86	41	36	18

(a) Compute the expected values of each cell under the assumption of independence.
(b) Verify that the requirements for performing a chi-square test of independence are satisfied.
(c) Compute the chi-square test statistic. 10.357
(d) Test whether family structure and sexual activity of 15- to 19-year-old females are independent at the $\alpha = 0.05$ level of significance. Reject H_0
(e) Compare the observed frequencies with the expected frequencies. Which cell contributed most to the test statistic? Was the expected frequency greater than or less than the observed frequency? What does this information tell you?
(f) Construct a conditional distribution by family structure and draw a bar graph. Does this evidence support your conclusion in part (d)?

8. Prenatal Care An obstetrician wants to learn whether the amount of prenatal care and the wantedness of the pregnancy are associated. He randomly selects 939 women who had recently given birth and asks them to disclose whether their pregnancy was intended, unintended, or mistimed. In addition, they were to disclose when they started receiving prenatal care, if ever. The results of the survey are as follows:

	Months Pregnant before Prenatal Care Began		
Wantedness of Pregnancy	**Less Than 3 Months**	**3 to 5 Months**	**More Than 5 Months (or never)**
Intended	593	26	33
Unintended	64	8	11
Mistimed	169	19	16

(a) Compute the expected values of each cell under the assumption of independence.
(b) Verify that the requirements for performing a chi-square test of independence are satisfied.
(c) Compute the chi-square test statistic. 21.357
(d) Test whether prenatal care and the wantedness of pregnancy are independent at the $\alpha = 0.05$ level of significance. Reject H_0
(e) Compare the observed frequencies with the expected frequencies. Which cell contributed most to the test statistic? Was the expected frequency greater than or less than the observed frequency? What does this information tell you?
(f) Construct a conditional distribution by wantedness of the pregnancy and draw a bar graph. Does this evidence support your conclusion in part (d)?

9. Health and Happiness Are health and happiness related? The following data represent the level of happiness and level of health for a random sample of individuals from the General Social Survey.

		Health			
		Excellent	**Good**	**Fair**	**Poor**
Happiness	**Very Happy**	271	261	82	20
	Pretty Happy	247	567	231	53
	Not Too Happy	33	103	92	36

Source: General Social Survey

(a) Does the evidence suggest that health and happiness are related? Use the $\alpha = 0.05$ level of significance.
(b) Construct a conditional distribution of happiness by level of health and draw a bar graph. (a) Yes; they are related
(c) Write a few sentences that explain the relation, if any, between health and happiness.

10. Health and Education Does amount of education play a role in the healthiness of an individual? The following data represent the level of health and the highest degree earned for a random sample of individuals from the General Social Survey. (c) Age, since younger folks are less likely to not have a high school diploma

		Health			
		Excellent	**Good**	**Fair**	**Poor**
Education	**Less than High School**	72	202	199	62
	High School	465	877	358	108
	Junior College	80	138	49	11
	Bachelor	229	276	64	12
	Graduate	130	147	32	2

Source: General Social Survey

(a) Does the evidence suggest that health and education are related? Use the $\alpha = 0.05$ level of significance.
(b) Construct a conditional distribution of health by level of education and draw a bar graph. (a) Yes; they are related
(c) Write a few sentences that explain the relation, if any, between health and education. Can you think of any lurking variables that help to explain the relation between these two variables?

11. Profile of Smokers The following data represent the smoking status by level of education for residents of the United States 18 years old or older from a random sample of 1054 residents. (a) Do not reject H_0

	Smoking Status		
Number of Years of Education	Current	Former	Never
<12	178	88	208
12	137	69	143
13–15	44	25	44
16 or more	34	33	51

Source: National Health Interview Survey

(a) Test whether smoking status and level of education are independent at the $\alpha = 0.05$ level of significance.

(b) Construct a conditional distribution of smoking status by number of years of education, and draw a bar graph. Does this evidence support your conclusion in part (a)?

12. Pro Life or Pro Choice A recent Gallup organization poll asked male and female Americans whether they were pro life or pro choice when it comes to abortion issues. The results of the survey are as follows: (a) Do not reject H_0

	Pro Life/Pro Choice	
Gender	Pro Life	Pro Choice
Men	196	199
Women	239	249

(a) Test whether an individual's opinion regarding abortion is independent of gender at the $\alpha = 0.1$ level of significance.

(b) Construct a conditional distribution of abortion opinion by gender and draw a bar graph. Does this evidence support your conclusion in part (a)?

13. Equal Opportunity Do you believe everyone has an equal opportunity to obtain a quality education in the United States? The results of this General Social Survey question are presented next by level of education. (a) No; not equal

	Highest Degree				
	Less Than High School	High School	Junior College	Bachelor	Graduate
Yes	302	551	29	100	46
No	83	200	24	71	31

Source: General Social Survey

(a) Does the evidence suggest that the proportion of individuals who feel everyone has an equal opportunity to obtain a quality education in the United States is equal for each level of education? Use the $\alpha = 0.05$ level of significance.

(b) Construct a conditional distribution of opinion by level of education and draw a bar graph of the conditional distribution. What role does education appear to play in beliefs about access to quality education?

14. Celebrex Celebrex, a drug manufactured by Pfizer, Inc., is used to relieve symptoms associated with osteoarthritis and rheumatoid arthritis in adults. In clinical trials of the medication, some subjects reported dizziness as a side effect. The researchers wanted to discover whether the proportion of subjects taking Celebrex who reported dizziness as a side effect differed significantly from that for other treatment groups. The following data were collected.

	Drug				
Side Effect	Celebrex	Placebo	Naproxen	Diclofenac	Ibuprofen
Dizziness	83	32	36	5	8
No dizziness	4063	1832	1330	382	337

Source: Pfizer, Inc.

(a) Test whether the proportion of subjects within each treatment group who experienced dizziness are the same at the $\alpha = 0.01$ level of significance. Do not reject

(b) Construct a conditional distribution of side effect by treatment and draw a bar graph. Does this evidence support your conclusion in part (a)?

NW **15. What's in a Word?** In a recent survey conducted by the Pew Research Center for the People & the Press, a random sample of adults 18 years of age or older living in the continental United States was asked their reaction to the word *socialism*. In addition, the individuals were asked to disclose which political party they most associate with. Results of the survey are given in the table. (a) Yes, reject H_0

	Democrat	Independent	Republican
Positive	220	144	62
Negative	279	410	351

Source: Pew Research

(a) Does the evidence suggest a different proportion of individuals within each political affiliation reacts positively to the word *socialism*? Use the $\alpha = 0.05$ level of significance.

(b) Construct a conditional distribution of reaction by political party.

(c) Write a summary about the "partisan divide" regarding reaction to the word *socialism*.

16. What's in a Word? Part II In a recent survey conducted by the Pew Research Center for the People & the Press, a random sample of adults 18 years of age or older living in the continental United States was asked their reaction to the word *capitalism*. In addition, the individuals were asked to disclose which political party they most associate with. Results of the survey are given in the table.

	Democrat	Independent	Republican
Positive	235	288	256
Negative	264	266	157

Source: Pew Research

(a) Does the evidence suggest a different proportion of individuals within each political affiliation reacts positively to the word *capitalism*? Use the $\alpha = 0.05$ level of significance. Yes, reject H_0

(b) Construct a conditional distribution of reaction by political party.

(c) Write a summary about the "partisan divide" regarding reaction to the word *capitalism*.

(d) Compare the results of this problem with that of Problem 15. Write a short report detailing the findings of the two survey questions.

17. Dropping a Course A survey of 52 randomly selected students who dropped a course in the current semester was conducted at a community college. The goal of the survey was to learn why students drop courses. The following data were collected: "Personal" drop reasons include financial, transportation, family issues, health issues, and lack of child care. "Course" drop reasons include reducing one's load, being unprepared for the course, the course was not what was expected, dissatisfaction with teaching, and not getting the desired grade. "Work" drop reasons include an increase in hours, a change in shift, and obtaining full-time employment. The results of the survey are as follows:

Gender	Drop Reason	Gender	Drop Reason
Male	Personal	Male	Work
Female	Personal	Male	Work
Male	Work	Female	Course
Male	Personal	Male	Work
Male	Course	Female	Course
Male	Course	Female	Course
Female	Course	Female	Course
Female	Course	Male	Work
Male	Course	Male	Personal
Female	Course	Male	Course
Male	Personal	Female	Course
Male	Work	Female	Course
Male	Work	Male	Course
Male	Course	Female	Course
Male	Course	Male	Work
Male	Work	Male	Course
Female	Personal	Female	Work
Male	Course	Male	Personal
Female	Work	Male	Work
Male	Work	Female	Course
Male	Work	Male	Course
Female	Course	Male	Personal
Female	Personal	Female	Course
Female	Personal	Female	Work
Female	Personal	Male	Work

(a) Construct a contingency table for the two variables.
(b) Test whether gender is independent of drop reason at the $\alpha = 0.1$ level of significance. Reject H_0
(c) Construct a conditional distribution of drop reason by gender and draw a bar graph. Does this evidence support your conclusion in part (b)?

18. Political Affiliation A political scientist wanted to learn whether there is any association between the education level of a registered voter and his or her political party affiliation. He randomly selected 46 registered voters and obtained the following data:

Education	Political Party	Education	Political Party
Grade school	Democrat	High school	Democrat
College	Republican	College	Republican
High school	Democrat	College	Republican
High school	Republican	Grade school	Democrat
High school	Democrat	High school	Republican
Grade school	Democrat	High school	Democrat
College	Republican	High school	Democrat
Grade school	Democrat	College	Republican
High school	Democrat	High school	Republican
High school	Democrat	Grade school	Democrat
Grade school	Democrat	High school	Democrat
College	Republican	College	Democrat
Grade school	Democrat	College	Republican
College	Democrat	High school	Republican
College	Democrat	College	Democrat
Grade school	Republican	College	Democrat
College	Republican	High school	Democrat
Grade school	Republican	College	Republican
College	Republican	College	Democrat
High school	Democrat	High school	Republican
College	Democrat	College	Republican
College	Republican	High school	Republican
College	Democrat	College	Democrat

(a) Construct a contingency table for the two variables.
(b) Test whether level of education is independent of political affiliation at the $\alpha = 0.1$ level of significance. Do not reject H_0
(c) Construct a conditional distribution of political party by level of education and draw a bar graph. Does this evidence support your conclusion in part (b)?

19. Sullivan Statistics Survey In the Sullivan Statistics Survey, respondents were asked to disclose their political affiliation (Democrat, Independent, Republican) and also answer the following question: "Would you be willing to pay higher taxes if the tax revenue went directly toward deficit reduction?" Create a contingency table and determine whether the results suggest there is an association between political affiliation and willingness to pay higher taxes to directly reduce the federal debt. Use the $\alpha = 0.05$ level of significance. Do not reject H_0

20. Sullivan Statistics Survey In the Sullivan Statistics Survey, respondents were asked to disclose their political philosophy (Conservative, Moderate, Liberal) and also answer the following question: "Is a language other than English the primary language spoken in your home?" Create a contingency table and determine whether the results suggest there is an association between political philosophy and whether a language other than English is primarily spoken at home. Use the $\alpha = 0.05$ level of significance. Do not reject H_0

21. Putting It Together: Women, Aspirin, and Heart Attacks In a famous study by the Physicians Health Study Group from Harvard University from the late 1980s, 22,000 healthy male physicians were randomly divided into two groups; half the physicians took aspirin every other day, and the others were given a placebo. Of the physicians in the aspirin group, 104 heart attacks occurred; of the physicians in the placebo group, 189 heart attacks occurred. The results were statistically significant, which led to the advice that males should take an aspirin every other day in the interest of reducing the chance of having a heart attack. Does the same advice apply to women?

In a randomized, placebo-controlled study, 39,876 healthy women 45 years of age or older were randomly divided into two groups. The women in group 1 received 100 mg of aspirin every other day; the women in group 2 received a placebo every other day. The women were monitored for 10 years to determine if they experienced a cardiovascular event (such as heart attack or stroke). Of the 19,934 in the aspirin group, 477 experienced a heart attack. Of the 19,942 women in the placebo group, 522 experienced a heart attack. *Source:* Paul M. Ridker et al. "A Randomized Trial of Low-Dose Aspirin in the Primary Prevention of Cardiovascular Disease in Women." *New England Journal of Medicine* 352:1293–1304.

(a) What is the population being studied? What is the sample?
(b) What is the response variable? Is it qualitative or quantitative? Heart attack or not; qualitative
(c) What are the treatments? Aspirin, placebo
(d) What type of experimental design is this?
(e) How does randomization deal with the explanatory variables that were not controlled in the study?
(f) Determine whether the proportion of cardiovascular events in each treatment group is different using a two-sample Z-test for comparing two proportions. Use the $\alpha = 0.05$ level of significance. What is the test statistic?
(g) Determine whether the proportion of cardiovascular events in each treatment group is different using a chi-square test for homogeneity of proportions. Use the $\alpha = 0.05$ level of significance. What is the test statistic?
(h) Square the test statistic from part (f) and compare it to the test statistic from part (g). What do you conclude? $z_0^2 = \chi_0^2$

EXPLAINING THE CONCEPTS

22. Explain the differences between the chi-square test for independence and the chi-square test for homogeneity. What are the similarities?

23. Why does the test for homogeneity follow the same procedures as the test for independence?

21. (a) Healthy women $\geq$ 45 years old; 39,876 women 21. (d) Completely randomized design 21. (f) Do not reject H_0; $z_0 = -1.44$
21. (g) $\chi_0^2 = 2.061$; do not reject H_0

Consumer Reports® Dirty Birds?

Hungry for a cheap, low-fat alternative to beef, Americans are eating more chicken than ever. Although precise figures are impossible to obtain, the U.S. Centers for Disease Control and Prevention reported that the number of cases of outbreaks of illness caused by chicken rose threefold between 1988 and 1992. Salmonella bacteria were the most common cause of these outbreaks.

In a study for *Consumer Reports*, we purchased 1000 fresh, whole broiler chickens at grocery stores in 36 cities across the United States over a 5-week period. Our shoppers packed the birds in coolers and shipped them overnight to the lab. There, tests were conducted to determine the presence of salmonella and campylobacter, another chicken-related bug. The results of the study for salmonella were as follows:

	Salmonella		
Brand	**Present**	**Absent**	**Total**
A	8	192	**200**
B	17	183	**200**
C	27	173	**200**
D	14	186	**200**
E	20	180	**200**
Total	**86**	**914**	**1000**

Assuming that the chickens represent a random sample from each brand included in the study, use the information presented in the table to answer the following:

(a) Calculate the proportion of incidence for each brand shown in the table.
(b) Compute a 95% confidence interval for the incidence of salmonella for brand C.
(c) Using a chi-square test of homogeneity of proportions, is there evidence that the five brands have the same incidence rate for salmonella?
(d) Brands A and D are major competitors in the same market. The manufacturer of brand A claims to have improved its cleanliness and claims that it is substantially cleaner than brand D. Is there evidence to support this contention?
(e) Write a paragraph for the readers of *Consumer Reports* magazine that explains your conclusions.

Note to Readers: *In many cases, our test protocol and analytical methods are more complicated than described in these examples. The data and discussions have been modified to make the material more appropriate for the audience.*

Technology Step-By-Step

Chi-Square Tests

TI-83/84 Plus

1. Access the MATRIX menu. Highlight the EDIT menu, and select `1:[A]`.
2. Enter the number of rows and columns of the contingency table (matrix).
3. Enter the cell entries for the observed matrix, and press `2nd QUIT`. Repeat Steps 1–3 for the expected values, but enter the expected frequencies in matrix B.
4. Press `STAT`, highlight the TESTS menu, and select `C:`χ^2` - Test`.
5. With the cursor after Observed:, enter matrix [A] by accessing the MATRIX menu, highlighting NAMES, and selecting `1:[A]`.
6. With the cursor after Expected:, enter matrix [B] by accessing the MATRIX menu, highlighting NAMES, and selecting `2:[B]`.
7. Highlight Calculate or Draw, and press `ENTER`.

MINITAB

1. Enter the data into the MINITAB spreadsheet.
2. Select the **Stat** menu, highlight **Tables**, and select **Chi-Square Test (Two-Way Table in Worksheet)** ....
3. Select the columns that contain the data, and click OK.

Excel

1. Load the XLSTAT Add-in.
2. Enter the data in a contingency table. Column A should be the row variable. For example, for the data in Table 5, column A is level of happiness. Each subsequent column is the counts of each category of the column variable. For the data in Table 5, enter the counts for each marital status. Title each column (including the first column indicating the row variable).
3. Select **Describing data**;, highlight **Contingency table**.
4. Place the cursor in the Contingency table cell. Highlight the table in the spreadsheet. Check the box Labels included. Click the Options tab.
5. Check the box Chi-square test. Choose a level of significance. Click OK.

StatCrunch

1. If the data are already in a contingency table, enter them into the spreadsheet. The first column is the row variable. For example, for the data in Table 5, the first column is level of happiness. Each subsequent column is the counts of each category of the column variable. For the data in Table 5, enter the counts for each marital status. Title each column (including the first column indicating the row variable). If the data are not in a contingency table, enter each variable in a column and name the column variable.
2. Select **Stat**, highlight **Tables**, select **Contingency**, then highlight **with data** or **with summary**.
3. Select the column variable(s). Then select the row variable. For example, the data in Table 5 has four column variables ("Married," and so on) and the row label is "Happiness." Click Next>.
4. Decide what values you want displayed. Click Calculate.

12.3 TESTING THE SIGNIFICANCE OF THE LEAST-SQUARES REGRESSION MODEL

Preparing for This Section Before getting started, review the following:

- Scatter diagrams; correlation (Section 4.1, pp. 178–186)
- Least-squares regression (Section 4.2, pp. 194–202)
- Sampling distribution of the sample mean $\bar{x}$ (Section 8.1, pp. 367–375)
- Testing a hypothesis about μ (Section 10.3, pp. 449–453)
- Confidence intervals about a mean (Section 9.2, pp. 409–411)

OBJECTIVES

1. State the requirements of the least-squares regression model
2. Compute the standard error of the estimate
3. Verify that the residuals are normally distributed
4. Conduct inference on the slope
5. Construct a confidence interval about the slope of the least-squares regression model

Note to Instructor

If you like, you can print out and distribute the Preparing for This Section quiz located in the Instructor's Resource Center. The purpose of the quiz is to verify that the students have the prerequisite knowledge for the section.

As a quick review of the topics discussed in Chapter 4, we present the following example:

EXAMPLE 1 Least-Squares Regression

Note to Instructor

You might want to continue using the data collected in Chapter 4 for Sections 12.3 and 12.4.

Problem A family doctor is interested in examining the relationship between a patient's age and total cholesterol. He randomly selects 14 of his female patients and obtains the data presented in Table 15. The data are based on results obtained from the National Center for Health Statistics. Draw a scatter diagram, compute the correlation coefficient, and find the least-squares regression equation and the coefficient of determination.

TABLE 15

Age, x	Total Cholesterol, y	Age, x	Total Cholesterol, y
25	180	42	183
25	195	48	204
28	186	51	221
32	180	51	243
32	210	58	208
32	197	62	228
38	239	65	269

Approach We will use a TI-84 Plus graphing calculator.

Solution Figure 20 displays the scatter diagram. Figure 21 displays the output. The linear correlation coefficient is 0.718. The least-squares regression equation for these data is $\hat{y} = 1.3991x + 151.3537$, where $\hat{y}$ represents the predicted total cholesterol for a female whose age is x.

The coefficient of determination, R^2, is 0.515, so 51.5% of the variation in total cholesterol is explained by the regression line. Figure 22 shows a graph of the least-squares regression equation on the scatter diagram.

Figure 20

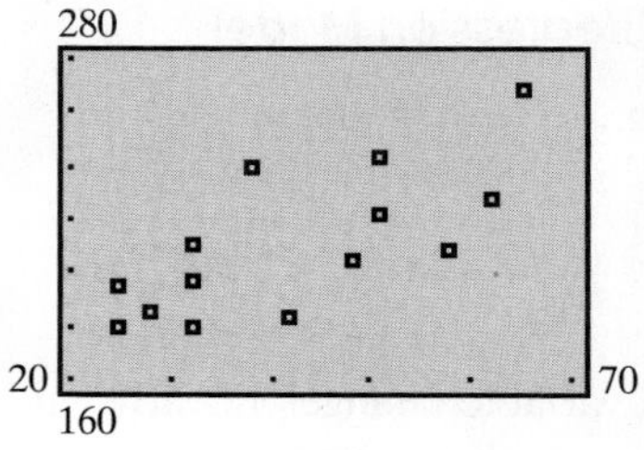

Figure 21

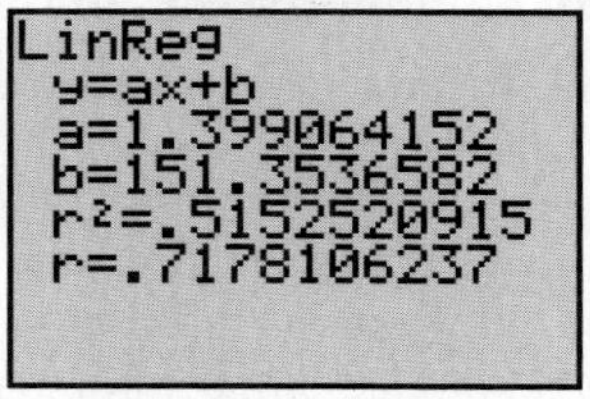

Figure 22

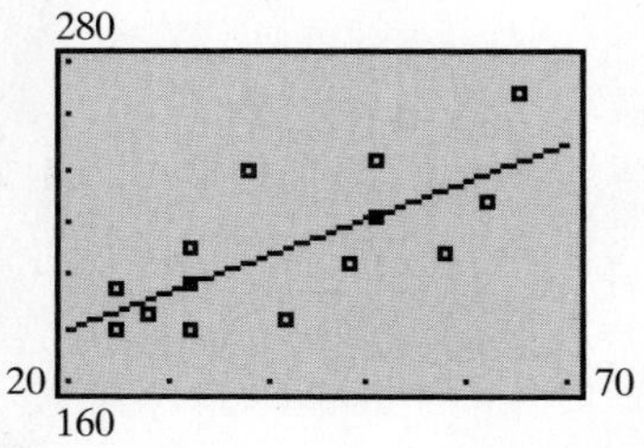

The information obtained in Example 1 is descriptive in nature. Notice that the descriptions are both graphical (as in the scatter diagram) and numerical (as in the correlation coefficient, the least-squares regression equation, and the coefficient of determination).

1 State the Requirements of the Least-Squares Regression Model

In the least-squares regression equation $\hat{y} = b_1x + b_0$, the values for the slope, b_1, and intercept, b_0, are statistics, just as the sample mean, $\bar{x}$, and sample standard deviation, s, are statistics. The statistics b_0 and b_1 are estimates for the population intercept, β_0, and the population slope, β_1. The true linear relation between the explanatory variable, x, and the response variable, y, is given by $y = \beta_1x + \beta_0$.

In Other Words
Because b_0 and b_1 are statistics, they have sampling distributions.

Because b_0 and b_1 are statistics, their values vary from sample to sample, so a sampling distribution is associated with each. We use this sampling distribution to perform inference on b_0 and b_1. For example, we might want to test whether β_1 is different from 0. If we have sufficient evidence to this effect, we conclude that there is a linear relation between the explanatory variable, x, and response variable, y.

To find the sampling distributions of b_0 and b_1, we have some requirements of the population from which the bivariate data (x_i, y_i) were sampled. Just as in Section 8.1 when we discussed the sampling distribution of $\bar{x}$, we start by asking what would happen if we took many samples for a given value of the explanatory variable, x. For example, in Table 1 we notice that our sample included three women aged 32 years with different corresponding values of y: 180, 210, and 197. This means that y varies for a given value of x, so there is a distribution of total cholesterol levels for $x = 32$ years. If we looked at *all* women aged 32, we could find the population mean total cholesterol for *all* 32-year-old women, denoted $\mu_{y|32}$. The notation $\mu_{y|32}$ is read "the mean value of the response variable y given that the value of the explanatory variable is 32." We could repeat this process for any other age. In general, different ages have a different population mean total cholesterol. This brings us to our first requirement regarding inference on the least-squares regression model.

In Other Words
When doing inference on the least-squares regression model, we require (1) for any explanatory variable, x, the mean of the response variable, y, depends on the value of x through a linear equation, and (2) the response variable, y, is normally distributed with a constant standard deviation, σ. The mean increases/decreases at a constant rate depending on the slope, while the standard deviation remains constant.

Requirement 1 for Inference on the Least-Squares Regression Model

For any particular value of the explanatory variable x (such as 32 in Example 1), the mean of the corresponding responses in the population depends linearly on x. That is,

$$\mu_{y|x} = \beta_1x + \beta_0$$

for some numbers β_0 and β_1, where $\mu_{y|x}$ represents the population mean response when the value of the explanatory variable is x.

We also have a requirement regarding the distribution of the response variable for any particular value of the explanatory variable.

Requirement 2 for Inference on the Least-Squares Regression Model

The response variable is normally distributed with mean $\mu_{y|x} = \beta_1x + \beta_0$ and standard deviation σ.

This requirement states that the mean of the response variable changes linearly, but the standard deviation remains constant, and the distribution of the response variable is normal. For example, a sample of the total cholesterol of many 32-year-old females would be normal with mean $\mu_{y|32} = \beta_1(32) + \beta_0$ and standard deviation σ. For 43-year-old females, the distribution would be normal with mean $\mu_{y|43} = \beta_1(43) + \beta_0$ and standard deviation σ. See Figure 23.

Figure 23

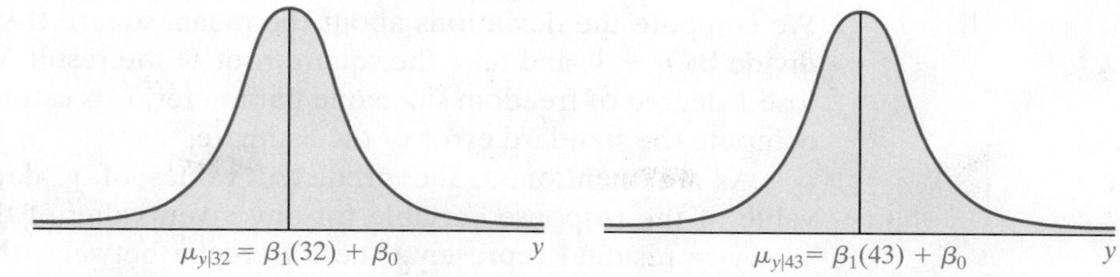

In Other Words
The larger σ is, the more spread out the data are around the regression line.

A large value of σ, the population standard deviation, indicates that the data are widely dispersed about the regression line, and a small value of σ indicates that the data lie fairly close to the regression line. Figure 24 illustrates these ideas. The regression line represents the mean value of each normal distribution at a specified value of x. The standard deviation of each distribution is σ.

Figure 24

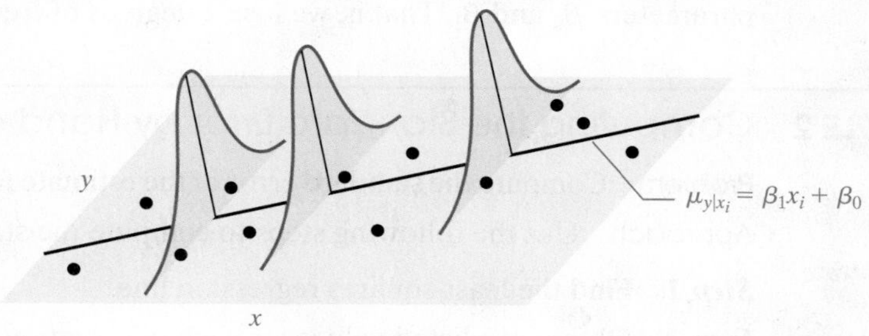

Of course, not all the observed values of the response variable lie on the true regression line $\mu_{y|x} = \beta_1 x + \beta_0$. The difference between the observed and predicted value of the response variable is an error term or residual, ε_i. We now present the least-squares regression model.

DEFINITION

The **least-squares regression model** is given by

$$y_i = \beta_1 x_i + \beta_0 + \varepsilon_i \qquad (1)$$

where

y_i is the value of the response variable for the ith individual

β_0 and β_1 are the parameters to be estimated based on sample data

x_i is the value of the explanatory variable for the ith individual

ε_i is a random error term with mean 0 and standard deviation $\sigma_{\varepsilon_i} = \sigma$, the error terms are independent

$i = 1, \ldots, n$, where n is the sample size (number of ordered pairs in the data set)

Because the expected value, or mean, of y_i is $\beta_1 x_i + \beta_0$ and the expression on the left side of Equation (1) equals the expression on the right side, the expected value, or mean, of the error term, ε_i, is 0.

Now Work Problem 13(a)

2 Compute the Standard Error of the Estimate

In Section 4.2, we learned how to estimate β_0 and β_1. We now present the method for obtaining the estimate of σ, the standard deviation of the response variable y for any given value of x. The unbiased estimator of σ is called the *standard error of the estimate*.

Recall the formula for the sample standard deviation from Section 3.2:

$$s = \sqrt{\frac{\Sigma(x_i - \bar{x})^2}{n - 1}}$$

We compute the deviations about the mean, square them, add the squared deviations, divide by $n - 1$, and take the square root of the result. We divide by $n - 1$ because we lose 1 degree of freedom since one parameter, $\bar{x}$, is estimated. The same logic is used to compute the standard error of the estimate.

As we mentioned, the predicted values of y, denoted $\hat{y}_i$, represent the mean value of the response variable for any given value of the explanatory variable, x_i. So $y_i - \hat{y}_i$ = residual represents the difference between the observed value, y_i, and the mean value, $\hat{y}_i$. This calculation is used to compute the standard error of the estimate.

DEFINITION

The **standard error of the estimate**, s_e, is found using the formula

$$s_e = \sqrt{\frac{\Sigma(y_i - \hat{y}_i)^2}{n-2}} = \sqrt{\frac{\Sigma \text{residuals}^2}{n-2}} \quad (2)$$

We divide by $n - 2$ because in a least-squares regression we have estimated two parameters, β_0 and β_1. That is, we lose 2 degrees of freedom.

EXAMPLE 2 Computing the Standard Error by Hand

Note to Instructor

This example is presented to illustrate how a standard error of the estimate is found using Formula (2). In practice, standard errors are found using technology.

Problem Compute the standard error of the estimate for the data in Table 15 on page 543.

Approach Use the following steps to compute the standard error of the estimate.

Step 1 Find the least-squares regression line.

Step 2 Obtain predicted values for each observation in the data set.

Step 3 Compute the residuals for each observation in the data set.

Step 4 Compute Σ residuals^2.

Step 5 Compute the standard error of the estimate using Formula (2).

Solution

Step 1 In Example 1, the least-squares regression was $\hat{y} = 1.3991x + 151.3537$.

Step 2 Column 3 of Table 16 shows the predicted values for the $n = 14$ observations.

Step 3 Column 4 of Table 16 shows the residuals for the 14 observations.

TABLE 16

Age, x	Total Cholesterol, y	$\hat{y} = 1.3991x + 151.3537$	Residuals, $y - \hat{y}$	Residuals^2, $(y - \hat{y})^2$
25	180	186.33	−6.33	40.0689
25	195	186.33	8.67	75.1689
28	186	190.53	−4.53	20.5209
32	180	196.12	−16.12	259.8544
32	210	196.12	13.88	192.6544
32	197	196.12	0.88	0.7744
38	239	204.52	34.48	1188.8704
42	183	210.12	−27.12	735.4944
48	204	218.51	−14.51	210.5401
51	221	222.71	−1.71	2.9241
51	243	222.71	20.29	411.6841
58	208	232.50	−24.50	600.2500
62	228	238.10	−10.10	102.0100
65	269	242.30	26.70	712.8900
				Σresiduals^2 = 4553.705

CAUTION

Be sure to divide by $n - 2$ when computing the standard error of the estimate.

Step 4 Sum the squared residuals in column 5 to find the sum of squared errors:

$$\sum \text{residuals}^2 = 4553.705$$

Step 5 Use Formula (2) to compute the standard error of the estimate.

$$s_e = \sqrt{\frac{\sum \text{residuals}^2}{n-2}} = \sqrt{\frac{4553.705}{14-2}} = 19.48$$

EXAMPLE 3 Obtaining the Standard Error of the Estimate Using Technology

Problem Obtain the standard error of the estimate for the data in Table 15 using statistical software.

Approach Use Excel to obtain the standard error. The steps for obtaining the standard error of the estimate using TI-83/84 Plus graphing calculators, MINITAB, Excel, and StatCrunch are given in the Technology Step-by-Step on page 557.

Solution Figure 25 shows the partial output from Excel. Notice that the results agree with the by-hand computation.

Figure 25

Regression Statistics	
Multiple R	0.7178106
R Square	0.5152521
Adjusted R Square	0.4748564
Standard Error	19.480535
Observations	14

Now Work Problem 13(b)

3 Verify That the Residuals Are Normally Distributed

CAUTION

The residuals must be normally distributed to perform inference on the least-squares regression line.

The least-squares regression model $y_i = \beta_1 x_i + \beta_0 + \varepsilon_i$ requires the response variable, y_i, to be normally distributed. Because $\beta_1 x_i + \beta_0$ is constant for any x_i, if y_i is normal, then the residuals, ε_i, must be normal. To perform statistical inference on the regression line, we verify that the residuals are normally distributed by examining a normal probability plot.

EXAMPLE 4 Verifying That the Residuals Are Normally Distributed

Problem Verify that the residuals obtained in Table 16 from Example 2 are normally distributed.

Approach Construct a normal probability plot to assess normality. If the normal probability plot is roughly linear, the residuals are said to be normal.

Solution Figure 26 contains the normal probability plot obtained from MINITAB.

Figure 26

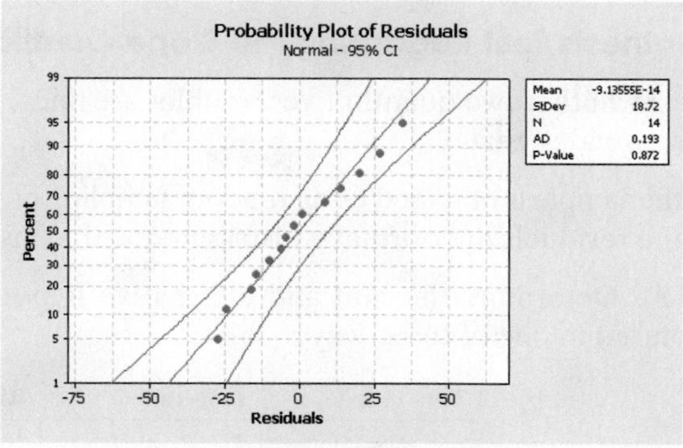

Because the points follow a linear pattern (all the points lie within the bounds created by MINITAB), the residuals are normally distributed. We can perform inference on the least-squares regression equation.

Note to Instructor

Consider assigning the "Using a Randomization Test for Correlation" activity from the Student Activity Workbook.

Now Work Problem 13(c)

4 Conduct Inference on the Slope

At this point, we know how to estimate the intercept and slope of the least-squares regression model. We can also compute the standard error of the estimate, s_e, which is an estimate of σ, the standard deviation of the response variable about the true

In Other Words
Remember, the null hypothesis is a statement of "no effect." So the null hypothesis H_0: $\beta_1 = 0$ means there is no linear relation between the explanatory and response variables.

least-squares regression model, and we know how to assess the normality of the residuals. We will now use this information to test whether a linear relation exists between the explanatory and the response variables.

We want to answer the following question: Do the sample data provide sufficient evidence to conclude that a linear relation exists between the two variables? If there is no linear relation between the response and explanatory variables, the slope of the true regression line will be zero. Do you know why? A slope of zero means that information about the explanatory variable, x, does not change our estimate of the value of the response variable, y.

Using the notation of hypothesis testing, we can perform one of three tests:

Two-Tailed	Left-Tailed	Right-Tailed
H_0: $\beta_1 = 0$	H_0: $\beta_1 = 0$	H_0: $\beta_1 = 0$
H_1: $\beta_1 \neq 0$	H_1: $\beta_1 < 0$	H_1: $\beta_1 > 0$

The null hypothesis is $\beta_1 = 0$, the statement of "no effect." We want to find evidence of a relation in the alternative hypothesis. The two-tailed test determines whether a linear relation exists between two variables without regard to the sign of the slope. The left-tailed test determines whether the slope of the true regression line is negative. The right-tailed test determines whether the slope of the true regression line is positive.

CAUTION
Before testing H_0: $\beta_1 = 0$, be sure to draw a residual plot to verify that a linear model is appropriate.

To test any one of these hypotheses, we need to know the sampling distribution of b_1. It turns out that, when certain conditions are met,

$$t = \frac{b_1 - \beta_1}{\dfrac{s_e}{\sqrt{\Sigma(x_i - \bar{x})^2}}} = \frac{b_1 - \beta_1}{s_{b_1}}$$

Note Because $s_x = \sqrt{\dfrac{\Sigma(x_i - \bar{x})^2}{n - 1}}$, the standard deviation of b_1 can be calculated using

$$s_{b_1} = \frac{s_e}{\sqrt{n - 1}\, s_x}$$ ◀

follows Student's t-distribution with $n - 2$ degrees of freedom, where n is the number of observations, b_1 is the estimate of the slope of the regression line β_1, and s_{b_1} is the sample standard deviation of b_1.

Note that

$$s_{b_1} = \frac{s_e}{\sqrt{\Sigma(x_i - \bar{x})^2}}$$

Hypothesis Test Regarding the Slope Coefficient, β_1

To test whether two quantitative variables are linearly related, we use the following steps provided that

1. the sample is obtained using random sampling or from a randomized experiment.
2. the residuals are normally distributed with constant error variance.

Step 1 Determine the null and alternative hypotheses. The hypotheses can be structured in one of three ways:

Two-Tailed	Left-Tailed	Right-Tailed
H_0: $\beta_1 = 0$	H_0: $\beta_1 = 0$	H_0: $\beta_1 = 0$
H_1: $\beta_1 \neq 0$	H_1: $\beta_1 < 0$	H_1: $\beta_1 > 0$

Note to Instructor
Remind students that the procedures presented here are similar to those presented for testing hypotheses about μ with σ unknown.

Step 2 Select a level of significance, α, depending on the seriousness of making a Type I error.

Classical Approach
Step 3 Compute the **test statistic**

$$t_0 = \frac{b_1 - \beta_1}{s_{b_1}} = \frac{b_1}{s_{b_1}}$$

P-Value Approach
By-Hand Step 3 Compute the **test statistic**

$$t_0 = \frac{b_1 - \beta_1}{s_{b_1}} = \frac{b_1}{s_{b_1}}$$

which follows Student's t-distribution with $n - 2$ degrees of freedom. Use Table VI to determine the critical value.

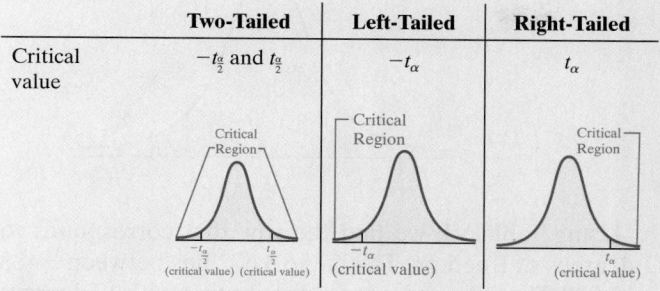

	Two-Tailed	Left-Tailed	Right-Tailed
Critical value	$-t_{\frac{\alpha}{2}}$ and $t_{\frac{\alpha}{2}}$	$-t_{\alpha}$	t_{α}

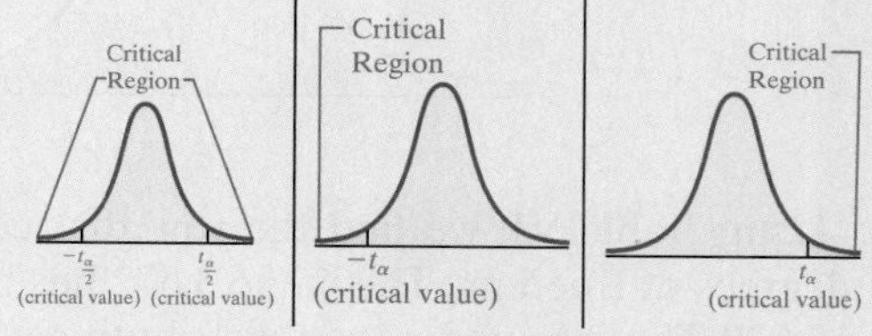

Step 4 Compare the critical value to the test statistic.

Two-Tailed	Left-Tailed	Right-Tailed
If $t_0 < -t_{\frac{\alpha}{2}}$ or $t_0 > t_{\frac{\alpha}{2}}$, reject the null hypothesis.	If $t_0 < -t_{\alpha}$, reject the null hypothesis.	If $t_0 > t_{\alpha}$, reject the null hypothesis.

which follows Student's t-distribution with $n - 2$ degrees of freedom. Use Table VI to approximate the P-value.

Two-Tailed	Left-Tailed	Right-Tailed

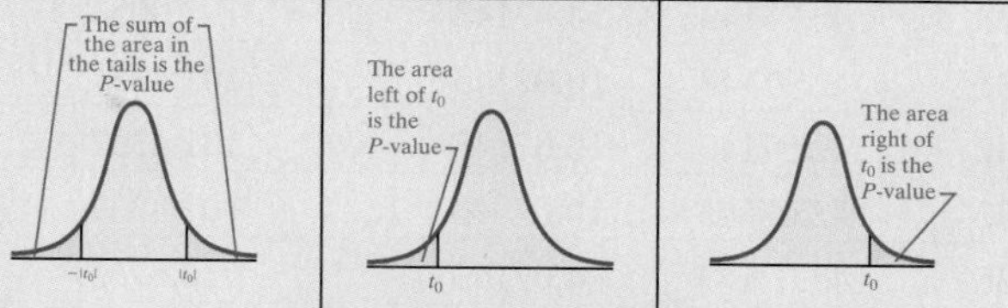

Two-Tailed	Left-Tailed	Right-Tailed
P-value $= 2P(t > \lvert t_0 \rvert)$	P-value $= P(t < t_0)$	P-value $= P(t > t_0)$

Technology Step 3 Use a statistical spreadsheet or calculator with statistical capabilities to obtain the P-value. The directions for obtaining the P-value using the TI-83/84 Plus graphing calculator, MINITAB, Excel, and StatCrunch are in the Technology Step-by-Step on page 557.

Step 4 If P-value $< \alpha$, reject the null hypothesis.

Step 5 State the conclusion.

Because these procedures are **robust**, minor departures from normality will not adversely affect the results of the test. In fact, for large samples ($n \geq 30$), inferential procedures regarding b_1 can be used even with significant departures from normality.

EXAMPLE 5 Testing for a Linear Relation

Problem Test whether a linear relation exists between age and total cholesterol at the $\alpha = 0.05$ level of significance using the data in Table 15 from Example 1.

Approach Verify that the requirements to perform the inference are satisfied. Then follow Steps 1 through 5.

Solution In Example 1, we were told that the individuals were randomly selected. In Example 4, we confirmed that the residuals were normally distributed.

We can now follow Steps 1 through 5.

Step 1 We want to know if there is a linear relation between age and total cholesterol without regard to the sign of the slope. This is a two-tailed test and we have

$$H_0: \beta_1 = 0 \quad \text{versus} \quad H_1: \beta_1 \neq 0$$

Step 2 The level of significance is $\alpha = 0.05$.

CAUTION

In Step 3, use unrounded values of the sample mean in the computation of $\Sigma(x_i - \bar{x})^2$ to avoid round-off error.

Classical Approach

Step 3 We obtained an estimate of β_1 in Example 1 to be $b_1 = 1.3991$, and we computed the standard error, $s_e = 19.48$, in Example 2. To determine the standard deviation of b_1, we compute $\Sigma(x_i - \bar{x})^2$, where the x_i are the values of the explanatory variable, age, and $\bar{x}$ is the sample mean. We compute this value in Table 17 on the following page.

P-Value Approach

By-Hand Step 3 From Step 3 of the Classical Approach, we have that the test statistic is $t_0 = 3.572$.

Because this is a two-tailed test, the P-value is the sum of the area under the t-distribution with $14 - 2 = 12$ degrees of freedom to the left of $-t_0 = -3.572$, and to the right of $t_0 = 3.572$, as shown in Figure 28. That is,

TABLE 17

Age, x	$\bar{x}$	$x_i - \bar{x}$	$(x_i - \bar{x})^2$
25	42.07143	−17.07143	291.4337
25	42.07143	−17.07143	291.4337
28	42.07143	−14.07143	198.0051
32	42.07143	−10.07143	101.4337
32	42.07143	−10.07143	101.4337
32	42.07143	−10.07143	101.4337
38	42.07143	−4.07143	16.5765
42	42.07143	−0.07143	0.0051
48	42.07143	5.92857	35.1479
51	42.07143	8.92857	79.7194
51	42.07143	8.92857	79.7194
58	42.07143	15.92857	253.7193
62	42.07143	19.92857	397.1479
65	42.07143	22.92857	525.7193
			$\Sigma(x_i - \bar{x})^2 = 2472.9284$

We have

$$s_{b_1} = \frac{s_e}{\sqrt{\Sigma(x_i - \bar{x})^2}} = \frac{19.48}{\sqrt{2472.9284}} = 0.3917$$

The test statistic is

$$t_0 = \frac{b_1}{s_{b_1}} = \frac{1.3991}{0.3917} = 3.572$$

Because this is a two-tailed test, we determine the critical t-values at the $\alpha = 0.05$ level of significance with $n - 2 = 14 - 2 = 12$ degrees of freedom to be $-t_{0.05/2} = -t_{0.025} = -2.179$ and $t_{0.05/2} = t_{0.025} = 2.179$. The critical regions are displayed in Figure 27.

Figure 27

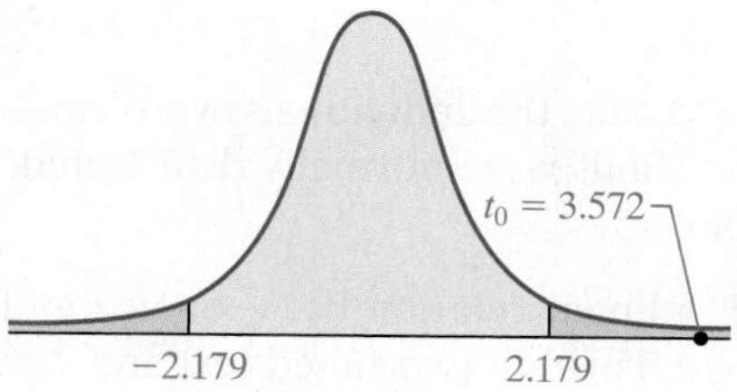

Step 4 The test statistic is $t_0 = 3.572$. We label this point in Figure 27. Because the test statistic is greater than the critical value $t_{0.025} = 2.179$, we reject the null hypothesis.

P-value $= P(t < -3.572) + P(t > 3.572) = 2P(t > 3.572)$, with 12 degrees of freedom.

Figure 28

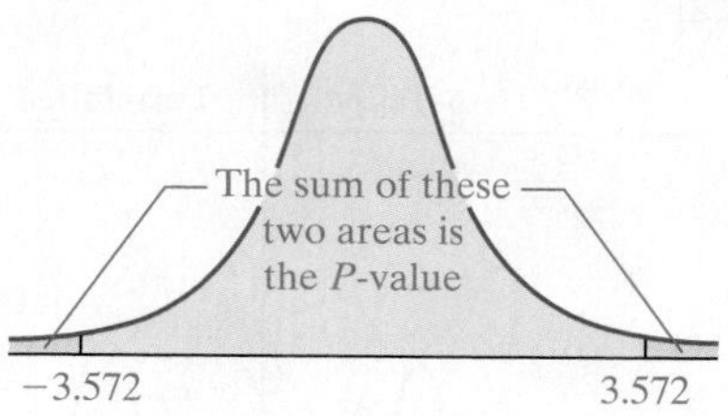

Using Table VI, we find the row that corresponds to 12 degrees of freedom. The value 3.572 lies between 3.428 and 3.930. The area under the t-distribution with 12 degrees of freedom to the right of 3.428 is 0.0025. The area under the t-distribution with 12 degrees of freedom to the right of 3.930 is 0.001.

Because 3.572 is between 3.428 and 3.930, the P-value is between 2(0.001) and 2(0.0025). So,

$$0.002 < P\text{-value} < 0.005.$$

Using Technology Step 3 Using MINITAB, we find the P-value is 0.004. See Figure 29.

Figure 29

Regression Analysis

```
The regression equation is
total cholesterol = 151 + 1.40 age

Predictor        Coef     StDev        T        P
Constant       151.35     17.28     8.76    0.000
Age            1.3991    0.3917     3.57    0.004

S = 19.48       R-Sq = 51.5%      R-Sq(adj) = 47.5%

Analysis of Variance

Source              Df       SS       MS        F        P
Regression           1   4840.5   4840.5    12.76    0.004
Residual Error      12   4553.9    379.5
Total               13   9394.4
```

Step 4 The P-value of 0.004 suggests that about 4 samples in 1000 would yield a slope estimate that is as extreme as or more extreme than the one obtained if the null hypothesis of no linear relation were true. Because the P-value is less than the level of significance, $\alpha = 0.05$, we reject the null hypothesis.

CAUTION

If we do not reject H_0, then we use the sample mean of y to predict the value of the response for any value of the explanatory variable.

Step 5 There is sufficient evidence at the $\alpha = 0.05$ level of significance to conclude that a linear relation exists between age and total cholesterol.

Now Work Problems 13(d) and 13(e)

5 Construct a Confidence Interval about the Slope of the Least-Squares Regression Model

We can also obtain confidence intervals for the slope of the least-squares regression line. The procedure is identical to that for obtaining confidence intervals for a mean. As was the case with confidence intervals for a population mean, the confidence interval for the slope of the least-squares regression line is of the form

$$\text{Point estimate} \pm \text{margin of error}$$

Confidence Intervals for the Slope of the Regression Line

A $(1 - \alpha) \cdot 100\%$ confidence interval for the slope of the true regression line, β_1, is given by the following formulas:

$$\text{Lower bound: } b_1 - t_{\alpha/2} \cdot \frac{s_e}{\sqrt{\Sigma(x_i - \bar{x})^2}}$$

$$\text{Upper bound: } b_1 + t_{\alpha/2} \cdot \frac{s_e}{\sqrt{\Sigma(x_i - \bar{x})^2}} \quad (3)$$

Here, $t_{\alpha/2}$ is computed with $n - 2$ degrees of freedom.

Note: This interval can be computed only if the data are randomly obtained, the residuals are normally distributed, and there is constant error variance.

EXAMPLE 6 Constructing a Confidence Interval for the Slope of the True Regression Line

Problem Determine a 95% confidence interval for the slope of the true regression line for the data presented in Table 15 in Example 1.

By-Hand Approach

Step 1 Determine the least-squares regression line.

Step 2 Verify that the requirements for inference on the regression line are satisfied.

Step 3 Compute s_e.

Step 4 Determine the critical value $t_{\alpha/2}$ with $n - 2$ degrees of freedom.

Step 5 Compute the bounds on the $(1 - \alpha) \cdot 100\%$ confidence interval for β_1 using Formula (3).

Step 6 Interpret the result by stating, "We are 95% confident that β_1 is between *lower bound* and *upper bound*."

By-Hand Solution

Step 1 The least-squares regression line was determined in Example 1 and is $\hat{y} = 1.3991x + 151.3537$.

Step 2 The requirements were verified in Examples 1–5.

Step 3 We computed s_e in Example 2, obtaining $s_e = 19.48$.

Step 4 Because we wish to determine a 95% confidence interval, we have $\alpha = 0.05$. Therefore, we need to find $t_{0.05/2} = t_{0.025}$ with $14 - 2 = 12$ degrees of freedom. Referring to Table VI, we find that $t_{0.025} = 2.179$.

Technology Approach

Step 1 Use a statistical spreadsheet or graphing calculator with advanced statistical features to obtain the confidence interval. We will use StatCrunch. The steps for constructing confidence intervals using StatCrunch, the TI-83/84 Plus graphing calculators, MINITAB, and Excel are given in the Technology Step-by-Step on page 557.

Step 2 Interpret the result.

Technology Solution

Step 1 Figure 30 shows the results obtained from StatCrunch.

Figure 30

Simple linear regression results:
Dependent Variable: Cholesterol
Independent Variable: Age
Cholesterol = 151.35365 + 1.3990642 Age
Sample size: 14
R (correlation coefficient) = 0.7178
R-sq = 0.5152521
Estimate of error standard deviation: 19.480536

Parameter estimates:

Parameter	Estimate	Std. Err.	DF	95% L. Limit	95% U. Limit
Intercept	151.35365	17.28376	12	113.69558	189.01173
Slope	1.3990642	0.39173746	12	0.5455416	2.2525868

Step 5 We use Formula (3) to find the lower and upper bounds.

$$\text{Lower bound: } b_1 - t_{\alpha/2} \cdot \frac{s_e}{\sqrt{\Sigma(x_i - \bar{x})^2}} = 1.3991 - 2.179 \cdot \frac{19.48}{\sqrt{2472.9284}} = 1.3991 - 0.8536 = 0.5455$$

$$\text{Upper bound: } b_1 + t_{\alpha/2} \cdot \frac{s_e}{\sqrt{\Sigma(x_i - \bar{x})^2}} = 1.3991 + 2.179 \cdot \frac{19.48}{\sqrt{2472.9284}} = 1.3991 + 0.8536 = 2.2527$$

Step 6 We are 95% confident that the mean increase in cholesterol for each additional year of life is somewhere between 0.5455 and 2.2527. Because the 95% confidence interval does not include 0, we reject H_0: $\beta_1 = 0$.

The lower bound (95% L. Limit) is 0.5455 and the upper bound (95% U. Limit) is 2.2526.

Step 2 We are 95% confident that the mean increase in cholesterol for each additional year of life is between 0.5455 and 2.2526. Because the confidence interval does not contain 0, we reject H_0: $\beta_1 = 0$.

Now Work Problem 13(f)

CAUTION

It is best that the values of the explanatory variable be spread out when doing regression analysis.

In looking carefully at the formula for the standard deviation of b_1, we should notice that the larger the value of $\Sigma(x_i - \bar{x})^2$ is, the smaller the value of s_{b_1}. This result implies that whenever we are finding a least-squares regression line we should attempt to make the values of the explanatory variable, x, as evenly spread out as possible so that b_1, our estimate of β_1, is as precise as possible.

Inference on the Linear Correlation Coefficient

Perhaps you are wondering why we have not presented hypothesis tests regarding the linear correlation coefficient in this section. Recall, in Chapter 4 we introduced a quick method for testing the significance of the correlation coefficient, even though we did not have a full appreciation of statistical inference. At this point we intentionally avoid discussion of inference on the correlation coefficient for two basic reasons: (1) The hypothesis test on the slope and a hypothesis test on the linear correlation coefficient will yield the same conclusion, and (2) inferential methods on the linear correlation coefficient, ρ, require that the y's at any given x be normally distributed and that the x's at any given y be normally distributed. That is, testing a hypothesis such as H_0: $\rho = 0$ versus H_1: $\rho \neq 0$ requires that the two variables follow a **bivariate normal distribution** or be **jointly normally distributed**. Verifying this requirement is a difficult task. Although a normal probability plot of the x_i's and a separate normal probability plot of the y_i's generally mean that the joint distribution is normal, it is not guaranteed. For these two reasons, we will be content in verifying the linearity of the data by performing inference on the slope coefficient only.

12.3 ASSESS YOUR UNDERSTANDING

VOCABULARY AND SKILL BUILDING

1. Suppose a least-squares regression line is given by $\hat{y} = 4.302x - 3.293$. What is the mean value of the response variable if $x = 20$? 82.7

2. *True or False*: In a least-squares regression, the response variable is normally distributed with mean $\mu_{y|x}$ and standard deviation σ. True

3. In the least-squares regression model, $y_i = \beta_1 x_i + \beta_0 + \varepsilon_i$, ε_i is a random error term with mean 0 and standard deviation $\sigma_{\varepsilon_i} = \sigma$

4. If H_0: $\beta_1 = 0$ is not rejected, what is the best estimate for the value of the response variable for any value of the explanatory variable? $\bar{y}$

In Problems 5–10, use the results of Problems 7–12, respectively, from Section 4.2 to answer the following questions:

(a) What are the estimates of β_0 and β_1?

(b) Compute the standard error, the point estimate for σ.

(c) Assuming the residuals are normally distributed, determine s_{b_1}.

(d) Assuming the residuals are normally distributed, test H_0: $\beta_1 = 0$ versus H_1: $\beta_1 \neq 0$ at the $\alpha = 0.05$ level of significance.

5.

x	3	4	5	7	8
y	4	6	7	12	14

6.

x	3	5	7	9	11
y	0	2	3	6	9

7.

x	−2	−1	0	1	2
y	−4	0	1	4	5

8.

x	−2	−1	0	1	2
y	7	6	3	2	0

9.

x	20	30	40	50	60
y	100	95	91	83	70

10.

x	5	10	15	20	25
y	2	4	7	11	18

APPLYING THE CONCEPTS

11. An Unhealthy Commute The following data represent commute times (in minutes) and a score on a well-being survey.

Commute Time (minutes), *x*	Gallup-Healthways Well-Being Index Composite Score, *y*
5	69.2
15	68.3
25	67.5
35	67.1
50	66.4
72	66.1
105	63.9

Source: The Gallup Organization

Use the results from Problem 17 in Section 4.2 to answer the following questions: (a) $b_0 = 69.0296$; $b_1 = -0.0479$

(a) Treating commute time as the explanatory variable, *x*, determine the estimates of β_0 and β_1.

(b) Compute the standard error of the estimate, s_e. 0.3680

(c) A normal probability plot of the residuals indicates it is reasonable to conclude the residuals are normally distributed. Determine s_{b_1}. 0.0043

(d) Test whether a linear relation exists between commute time and well-being index composite score at the $\alpha = 0.05$ level of significance. Reject H_0; *P*-value = 0.0001

(e) Construct a 95% confidence interval about the slope of the true least-squares regression line. (−0.0589, −0.0369)

12. Credit Scores An economist wants to determine the relation between one's FICO score, *x*, and the interest rate of a 36-month auto loan, *y*. The data represent the interest rate (in percent) a bank might offer on a 36-month auto loan for various FICO scores.

Credit Score, *x*	Interest Rate (percent), *y*
545	18.982
595	17.967
640	12.218
675	8.612
705	6.680
750	5.150

Source: www.myfico.com

Use the results from Problem 18 in Section 4.2 to answer the following questions: (d) Reject H_0; *P*-value = 0.0009

(a) Treating credit score as the explanatory variable, *x*, determine the estimates of β_0 and β_1. $b_0 = 61.3687$; $b_1 = -0.0764$

(b) Compute the standard error of the estimate, s_e. 1.4241

(c) A normal probability plot of the residuals indicates it is reasonable to conclude the residuals are normally distributed. Determine s_{b_1}. 0.0085

(d) Test whether a linear relation exists between credit score and interest rate at the $\alpha = 0.05$ level of significance.

(e) Construct a 95% confidence interval about the slope of the true least-squares regression line. (−0.1001, −0.0527)

NW **13. Height versus Head Circumference** A pediatrician wants to determine the relation that may exist between a child's height and head circumference. She randomly selects 11 children from her practice, measures their heights and head circumferences, and obtains the following data:

Height (inches), *x*	Head Circumference (inches), *y*	Height (inches), *x*	Head Circumference (inches), *y*
27.75	17.5	26.5	17.3
24.5	17.1	27	17.5
25.5	17.1	26.75	17.3
26	17.3	26.75	17.5
25	16.9	27.5	17.5
27.75	17.6		

Source: Denise Slucki, student at Joliet Junior College

Use the results from Problem 19 in Section 4.2 to answer the following questions:

(a) Treating height as the explanatory variable, *x*, determine the estimates of β_0 and β_1. $b_0 = 12.4932$, $b_1 = 0.1827$

(b) Compute the standard error of the estimate, s_e. 0.0954

(c) Determine whether the residuals are normally distributed. Yes

(d) If the residuals are normally distributed, determine s_{b_1}. 0.0276

(e) If the residuals are normally distributed, test whether a linear relation exists between height and head circumference at the $\alpha = 0.01$ level of significance. Reject H_0

(f) If the residuals are normally distributed, construct a 95% confidence interval about the slope of the true least-squares regression line. (0.1204, 0.2451) (g) 17.34 inches

(g) A child comes in for a physical, and the nurse determines his height to be 26.5 inches. However, the child is being rather uncooperative, so the nurse is unable to measure the head circumference of the child. What would be a good estimate of this child's head circumference? Why is this a good estimate?

14. Bone Length Research performed at NASA and led by Dr. Emily R. Morey-Holton measured the lengths of the right humerus and right tibia in 11 rats that were sent into space on Spacelab Life Sciences 2. The following data were collected:

Right Humerus (mm), *x*	Right Tibia (mm), *y*	Right Humerus (mm), *x*	Right Tibia (mm), *y*
24.80	36.05	25.90	37.38
24.59	35.57	26.11	37.96
24.59	35.57	26.63	37.46
24.29	34.58	26.31	37.75
23.81	34.20	26.84	38.50
24.87	34.73		

Source: NASA Life Sciences Data Archive

Use the results from Problem 22 in Section 4.2 to answer the following questions: (a) $b_0 = 1.1140$; $b_1 = 1.3902$

(a) Treating the length of the right humerus as the explanatory variable, *x*, determine the estimates of β_0 and β_1.

(b) Compute the standard error of the estimate. 0.4944

(c) Determine whether the residuals are normally distributed. Yes

(d) If the residuals are normally distributed, determine s_{b_1}. 0.1501

(e) If the residuals are normally distributed, test whether a linear relation exists between the length of the right humerus, *x*, and the length of the right tibia, y, at the $\alpha = 0.01$ level of significance. Reject H_0

(f) If the residuals are normally distributed, construct a 99% confidence interval for the slope of the true least-squares regression line. (0.9024, 1.8780)

(g) What is the mean length of the right tibia on a rat whose right humerus is 25.93 mm? 37.162 mm

15. Concrete As concrete cures, it gains strength. The following data represent the 7-day and 28-day strength (in pounds per square inch) of a certain type of concrete:

7-Day Strength, x	28-Day Strength, y	7-Day Strength, x	28-Day Strength, y
2300	4070	2480	4120
3390	5220	3380	5020
2430	4640	2660	4890
2890	4620	2620	4190
3330	4850	3340	4630

(a) $b_0 = 2675.6$, $b_1 = 0.6764$

(a) Treating the 7-day strength as the explanatory variable, x, determine the estimates of β_0 and β_1. (d) 0.2055

(b) Compute the standard error of the estimate. 271.04

(c) Determine whether the residuals are normally distributed. Yes

(d) If the residuals are normally distributed, determine s_{b_1}.

(e) If the residuals are normally distributed, test whether a linear relation exists between 7-day strength and 28-day strength at the $\alpha = 0.05$ level of significance. Reject H_0

(f) If the residuals are normally distributed, construct a 95% confidence interval for the slope of the true least-squares regression line. (0.2025, 1.1503)

(g) What is the estimated mean 28-day strength of this concrete if the 7-day strength is 3000 psi? 4704.8 psi

16. Tar and Nicotine Every year the Federal Trade Commission (FTC) must report tar and nicotine levels in cigarettes to Congress. The FTC obtains the tar and nicotine levels in over 1200 brands of cigarettes. A random sample from those reported to Congress is given in the following table: (a) $b_0 = 0.2088$; $b_1 = 0.0575$

Brand	Tar (mg), x	Nicotine (mg), y
Barclay 100	5	0.4
Benson and Hedges King	16	1.1
Camel Regular	24	1.7
Chesterfield King	24	1.4
Doral	8	0.5
Kent Golden Lights	9	0.8
Kool Menthol	9	0.8
Lucky Strike	24	1.5
Marlboro Gold	15	1.2
Newport Menthol	18	1.3
Salem Menthol	17	1.3
Virginia Slims Ultra Light	5	0.5
Winston Light	10	0.8

Source: Federal Trade Commission

(a) Treating the amount of tar as the explanatory variable, x, determine the estimates of β_0 and β_1. (d) 0.0046

(b) Compute the standard error of the estimate. 0.1121

(c) Determine whether the residuals are normally distributed. Yes

(d) If the residuals are normally distributed, determine s_{b_1}.

(e) If the residuals are normally distributed, test whether a linear relation exists between the amount of tar, x, and the amount of nicotine, y, at the $\alpha = 0.1$ level of significance. Reject H_0

(f) If the residuals are normally distributed, construct a 90% confidence interval for the slope of the true least-squares regression line. (0.0492, 0.0658)

(g) What is the mean amount of nicotine in a cigarette that has 12 milligrams of tar? 0.90 mg

17. United Technologies versus the S&P 500 United Technologies is a conglomerate that includes companies such as Otis Elevators and Carrier Heating and Cooling. The ticker symbol of the company is UTX. The following data represent the rate of return of UTX stock for 11 months, compared with the rate of return of the Standard and Poor's Index of 500 stocks. Both are in percent. (a) $b_0 = 0.1200$, $b_1 = 1.0997$

Month	Rate of Return of S&P 500, x	Rate of Return in United Technologies, y
Apr-10	1.48	1.82
May-10	−8.20	−9.57
Jun-10	−5.39	−3.67
Jul-10	6.88	9.53
Aug-10	−4.74	−7.72
Sept-10	8.76	9.24
Oct-10	3.69	4.97
Nov-10	−0.23	1.24
Dec-10	6.53	4.59
Jan-11	2.26	3.27
Feb-11	3.20	3.28

Source: TD Ameritrade

(a) Treating the rate of return of the S&P 500 as the explanatory variable, x, determine the estimates of β_0 and β_1.

(b) Assuming the residuals are normally distributed, test whether a linear relation exists between the rate of return of the S&P 500, x, and the rate of return for United Technologies stock, y, at the $\alpha = 0.1$ level of significance. Reject H_0

(c) Assuming the residuals are normally distributed, construct a 90% confidence interval for the slope of the true least-squares regression line. (0.9192, 1.2802)

(d) What is the mean rate of return for United Technologies stock if the rate of return of the S&P 500 is 3.25%? 3.694%

18. American Black Bears The American black bear (*Ursus americanus*) is one of eight bear species in the world. It is the smallest North American bear and the most common bear species on the planet. In 1969, Dr. Michael R. Pelton of the University of Tennessee initiated a long-term study of the population in Great Smoky Mountains National Park. One aspect of the study was to develop a model that could be used to predict a bear's weight (since it is not practical to weigh bears in the field). One variable that is thought to be related to weight is the length of the bear. The following data represent the lengths and weights of 12 American black bears.

Total Length (cm), x	Weight (kg), y
139.0	110
138.0	60
139.0	90
120.5	60
149.0	85
141.0	100
141.0	95
150.0	85
166.0	155
151.5	140
129.5	105
150.0	110

Source: fieldtripearth.org

Use the results from Problem 20 in Section 4.2 to answer the following questions:

(a) Treating total length as the explanatory variable, x, determine the estimates of β_0 and β_1. $b_0 = -142.4700$, $b_1 = 1.6942$

(b) Assuming the residuals are normally distributed, test whether a linear relation exists between total length and weight at the $\alpha = 0.05$ level of significance. Reject H_0

(c) Assuming the residuals are normally distributed, construct a 95% confidence interval for the slope of the true least-squares regression line. (0.4897, 2.8989)

(d) What is the mean weight of American black bears of length 146.0 cm? 104.9 kg

19. CEO Performance (Refer to Problem 31 in Section 4.1) The following data represent the total compensation for 10 randomly selected chief executive officers (CEOs) and the company's stock performance in 2009.

Company	Compensation (millions of dollars)	Stock Return (%)
Kraft Foods	26.35	5.91
Sara Lee	12.48	30.39
Boeing	19.44	31.72
Middleby	13.37	79.76
Exelon	12.21	−8.40
Northern Trust	11.89	2.69
Abbott Laboratories	26.21	4.53
Archer Daniels Midland	14.95	10.80
McDonald's	17.57	4.01
Baxter International	14.36	11.76

Source: Chicago Tribune, May 23, 2010

19. (a) $b_0 = 33.2350$; $b_1 = -0.9428$

(a) Treating compensation as the explanatory variable, x, determine the estimates of β_0 and β_1.

(b) Assuming the residuals are normally distributed, test whether a linear relation exists between compensation and stock return at the $\alpha = 0.05$ level of significance. Do not reject H_0

(c) Assuming the residuals are normally distributed, construct a 95% confidence interval for the slope of the true least-squares regression line. (−4.5924 , 2.7067)

(d) Based on your results to parts (b) and (c), would you recommend using the least-squares regression line to predict the stock return of a company based on the CEO's compensation? Why? What would be a good estimate of the stock return based on the data in the table? No; $\bar{y} = 17.317\%$

20. Calories versus Sugar The following data represent the number of calories per serving and the number of grams of sugar per serving for a random sample of high-protein and moderate-protein energy bars.

Calories, x	Sugar, y	Calories, x	Sugar, y
180	10	270	20
200	18	320	2
210	14	110	10
220	20	180	12
220	0	200	22
230	28	220	24
240	2	230	24

Source: Consumer Reports

(a) Draw a scatter diagram of the data, treating calories as the explanatory variable. What type of relation, if any, appears to exist between calories and sugar? No relation

(b) Determine the least-squares regression equation from the sample data. $\hat{y} = 17.8675 - 0.0146x$

(c) Compute the standard error of the estimate. 9.3749

(d) Determine whether the residuals are normally distributed.

(e) Determine s_{b_1}. 0.0549

(f) If the residuals are normally distributed, test whether a linear relation exists between calories and sugar content at the $\alpha = 0.01$ level of significance. Do not reject H_0

(g) If the residuals are normally distributed, construct a 95% confidence interval about the slope of the true least-squares regression line. (−0.1343, 0.1051)

(h) For a randomly selected energy bar, would you recommend using the least-squares regression line obtained in part (b) to predict the sugar content of the energy bar? Why? What would be a good estimate for the sugar content of the energy bar? No; $\bar{y} = 14.7$ grams

21. Age versus HDL Cholesterol A doctor wanted to determine whether there is a relation between a male's age and his HDL (so-called good) cholesterol. He randomly selected 17 of his patients and determined their HDL cholesterol. He obtained the data on the following page:

Age, x	HDL Cholesterol, y	Age, x	HDL Cholesterol, y
38	57	38	44
42	54	66	62
46	34	30	53
32	56	51	36
55	35	27	45
52	40	52	38
61	42	49	55
61	38	39	28
26	47		

Source: Data based on information obtained from the National Center for Health Statistics

(a) Draw a scatter diagram of the data, treating age as the explanatory variable. What type of relation, if any, appears to exist between age and HDL cholesterol? No relation

(b) Determine the least-squares regression equation from the sample data. $\hat{y} = 50.7841 - 0.1298x$

(c) Assuming the residuals are normally distributed, test whether a linear relation exists between age and HDL cholesterol levels at the $\alpha = 0.01$ level of significance. Do not reject H_0

(d) Assuming the residuals are normally distributed, construct a 95% confidence interval for the slope of the true least-squares regression line. $(-0.5605, 0.3008)$

(e) For a 42-year-old male patient who visits the doctor's office, would you recommend using the least-squares regression line obtained in part (b) to predict the HDL cholesterol of this patient? Why? What would be a good estimate for the HDL cholesterol of this patient? No; $\bar{y} = 44.9$

22. The output shown was obtained from MINITAB.

```
The regression equation is
y = 12.4 + 1.40 x

Predictor      Coef     StDev        T       P
Constant     12.396     1.381     8.97   0.000
x            1.3962    0.1245    11.21   0.000

S = 2.167     R-Sq = 91.3%   R-Sq(adj)  = 90.6%
```

(a) The least-squares regression equation is $\hat{y} = 1.3962x + 12.396$. What is the predicted value of y at $x = 10$? 26.36

(b) What is the mean of y at $x = 10$? 26.36

(c) The standard error, s_e, is 2.167. What is an estimate of the standard deviation of y at $x = 10$? 2.167

(d) If the requirements for inference on the least-squares regression model are satisfied, what is the distribution of y at $x = 10$? Normal; $\mu \approx 26.36, \sigma \approx 2.167$

23. Influential Observations Zillow.com is a site that can be used to assess the value of homes in your neighborhood. The organization provides a list of homes for sale as well as a Zestimate, which is the price Zillow believes the home will sell for. The following data represent the Zestimate and sale price (in thousands of dollars) of a random sample of recently sold homes in Charleston, South Carolina.

Zestimate	Sale Price
362	370
309	315
365.5	371.9
215	218
184	186.5
252.5	260
247.5	250.8
244	251

Source: zillow.com

(a) Draw a scatter diagram of the data, treating the Zestimate as the explanatory variable and sale price as the response variable.

(b) Determine the least-squares regression line. Test whether there is a relation between the Zestimate and sale price at the $\alpha = 0.05$ level of significance. $\hat{y} = 1.0228x - 0.7590$; reject H_0

(c) A home with a Zestimate of \$370,000 recently sold for \$150,000. Determine the least-squares regression line with this home included. Test whether there is a relation between the Zestimate and sale price at the $\alpha = 0.05$ level of significance. Do you think this observation is influential? $\hat{y} = 0.5220x + 115.8094$; do not reject H_0; yes

EXPLAINING THE CONCEPTS

24. Why is it important to perform graphical as well as analytical analysis when analyzing relations between two quantitative variables?

25. What do the y-coordinates on the least-squares regression line represent?

26. Why is it desirable to have the explanatory variables spread out to test a hypothesis regarding β_1 or to construct confidence intervals about β_1?

27. Why don't we conduct inference on the linear correlation coefficient?

Technology Step-By-Step

Testing the Least-Squares Regression Model

TI-83/84 Plus

Hypothesis Test on the Slope

1. Enter the explanatory variable in L1 and the response variable in L2.
2. Press STAT, highlight TESTS, and select `F:LinRegTTest...`.
3. Be sure that Xlist is L1 and Ylist is L2. Make sure that `Freq:` is set to 1. Select the direction of the alternative hypothesis. Place the cursor on Calculate and press ENTER.

Confidence Interval for the Slope

1. Enter the explanatory variable in L1 and the response variable in L2.
2. Press STAT, highlight TESTS, and select `G: LinRegTint ....`
3. Be sure that Xlist is L1 and Ylist is L2. Make sure the `Freq:` is set to 1. Select the confidence level. Highlight Calculate. Press ENTER.

MINITAB

1. With the explanatory variable in C1 and the response variable in C2, select the **Stat** menu and highlight **Regression**. Highlight and select **Regression ....**
2. Select the explanatory variable (MINITAB calls them predictors) and response variable and click OK.

Excel

1. Be sure the Data Analysis ToolPak is activated. This is done by selecting File, then selecting Options. Highlight Add-Ins. In the Manage: pull-down menu, choose Excel Add-ins and click Go ... Check the Analysis ToolPak and click Okay.
2. Enter the explanatory variable in column A and the response variable in column B.
3. Select the Data menu and then select **Data Analysis ....**
4. Select the **Regression** option.
5. With the cursor in the Y-range cell, highlight the range of cells that contains the response variable. With the cursor in the X-range cell, highlight the range of cells that contains the explanatory variable. Click OK.

StatCrunch

Hypothesis Test on the Slope

1. Enter the explanatory variable in column var1 and the response variable in column var2.
2. Select Stat>Regression>Simple Linear. Choose var1 for the X-variable, choose var2 for the Y-variable. Click Next.
3. Select the Hypothesis Tests radio button. Choose the appropriate values in the null hypothesis for both the intercept and slope. Choose the direction of the alternative hypothesis. Click Calculate.

Confidence Interval for the Slope

1. Enter the explanatory variable in column var1 and the response variable in column var2.
2. Select Stat>Regression>Simple Linear. Choose var1 for the X-variable, choose var2 for the Y-variable. Click Next.
3. Select the Confidence Intervals radio button. Choose the confidence level. Click Calculate.

12.4 CONFIDENCE AND PREDICTION INTERVALS

Preparing for This Section Before getting started, review the following:

- Confidence intervals about μ (Section 9.2, pp. 409–411)

OBJECTIVES

1 Construct confidence intervals for a mean response

2 Construct prediction intervals for an individual response

Note to Instructor

If you like, you can print out and distribute the Preparing for This Section quiz located in the Instructor's Resource Center. The purpose of the quiz is to verify that the students have the prerequisite knowledge for the section.

We know how to obtain the least-squares regression equation of best fit from data. We also know how to use the least-squares regression equation to obtain a predicted value. For example, the least-squares regression equation for the cholesterol data introduced in Example 1 from Section 12.3 is

$$\hat{y} = 1.3991x + 151.3537$$

where $\hat{y}$ represents the predicted total cholesterol for a female whose age is x. The predicted value of total cholesterol for a given age x actually has two interpretations:

1. It represents the mean total cholesterol for all females whose age is x.
2. It represents the predicted total cholesterol for a randomly selected female whose age is x.

Note to Instructor
Given the tedious calculations in this section, it is recommended that by-hand solutions be de-emphasized. Let software do the work so that students can concentrate on the results.

So, if we let $x = 42$ in the least-squares regression equation $\hat{y} = 1.3991x + 151.3537$, we obtain $\hat{y} = 1.3991(42) + 151.3537 = 210.1$. We can interpret this result in one of two ways:

1. The mean total cholesterol for all 42-year-old females is 210.1.
2. Our estimate of the total cholesterol for a randomly selected 42-year-old female is 210.1.

Of course, there is a margin of error in making predictions, so we construct intervals about any predicted value to describe its accuracy. The type of interval constructed will depend on whether we are predicting a mean total cholesterol for all 42-year-old females or the total cholesterol for an individual 42-year-old female. In other words, the margin of error is going to be different for predicting the mean total cholesterol for all females who are 42 years old versus the total cholesterol for one individual. Which prediction (the mean or the individual) do you think will have a wider confidence interval? It seems logical that the distribution of means should have less variability (and therefore a lower margin of error) than the distribution of individuals. After all, in the distribution of means, high total cholesterols can be offset by low total cholesterols.

DEFINITIONS

Confidence intervals for a mean response are intervals constructed about the predicted value of *y*, at a given level of *x*, that are used to measure the accuracy of the mean response of all the individuals in the population.

Prediction intervals for an individual response are intervals constructed about the predicted value of *y* that are used to measure the accuracy of a single individual's predicted value.

In Other Words
Confidence intervals are intervals for the mean of the population. Prediction intervals are intervals for an individual from the population.

If we use the least-squares regression equation to predict the mean total cholesterol for all 42-year-old females, we construct a confidence interval for a mean response. If we use the least-squares regression equation to predict the total cholesterol for a single 42-year-old female, we construct a prediction interval for an individual response.

1 Construct Confidence Intervals for a Mean Response

The structure of a confidence interval is the same as it was in Section 9.1. The interval is of the form

Point estimate ± margin of error

The following formula can be used to construct a confidence interval about $\hat{y}$.

Confidence Interval for the Mean Response of *y*, $\hat{y}$

A $(1-\alpha)\cdot 100\%$ confidence interval for $\hat{y}$, the mean response of *y* for a specified value of *x*, is given by

$$\text{Lower bound: } \hat{y} - t_{\alpha/2}\cdot s_e\sqrt{\frac{1}{n} + \frac{(x^* - \bar{x})^2}{\Sigma(x_i - \bar{x})^2}}$$

$$\text{Upper bound: } \hat{y} + t_{\alpha/2}\cdot s_e\sqrt{\frac{1}{n} + \frac{(x^* - \bar{x})^2}{\Sigma(x_i - \bar{x})^2}} \quad (1)$$

where x^* is the given value of the explanatory variable, n is the number of observations, and $t_{\alpha/2}$ is the critical value with $n-2$ degrees of freedom.

Note The interval may be constructed provided the residuals are normally distributed or the sample size is large. ◀

EXAMPLE 1 Constructing a Confidence Interval for a Mean Response by Hand

Problem Construct a 95% confidence interval for the predicted mean total cholesterol of all 42-year-old females using the data in Table 15 on page 543.

Approach Determine a confidence interval for the predicted mean total cholesterol at $x^* = 42$ using Formula (1), since our estimate is for the mean cholesterol of all 42-year-old females.

Solution The least-squares regression equation is $\hat{y} = 1.3991x + 151.3537$. To find the predicted mean total cholesterol of all 42-year-olds, let $x^* = 42$ in the regression equation and obtain $\hat{y} = 1.3991(42) + 151.3537 = 210.1$. From Example 2 in Section 12.3, we found that $s_e = 19.48$, and from Example 5 in Section 12.3, we found that $\Sigma(x_i - \bar{x})^2 = 2472.9284$ and $\bar{x} = 42.07143$. The critical t value, $t_{\alpha/2} = t_{0.025}$, with $n - 2 = 14 - 2 = 12$ degrees of freedom is 2.179. The 95% confidence interval for the predicted mean total cholesterol for all 42-year-old females is therefore

$$\text{Lower bound: } \hat{y} - t_{\alpha/2} \cdot s_e \cdot \sqrt{\frac{1}{n} + \frac{(x^* - \bar{x})^2}{\Sigma(x_i - \bar{x})^2}} = 210.1 - 2.179 \cdot 19.48 \cdot \sqrt{\frac{1}{14} + \frac{(42 - 42.07143)^2}{2472.9284}} = 198.8$$

$$\text{Upper bound: } \hat{y} + t_{\alpha/2} \cdot s_e \cdot \sqrt{\frac{1}{n} + \frac{(x^* - \bar{x})^2}{\Sigma(x_i - \bar{x})^2}} = 210.1 + 2.179 \cdot 19.48 \cdot \sqrt{\frac{1}{14} + \frac{(42 - 42.07143)^2}{2472.9284}} = 221.4$$

We are 95% confident that the mean total cholesterol of all 42-year-old females is between 198.8 and 221.4.

Now Work Problems 3(a) and (b)

2 Construct Prediction Intervals for an Individual Response

The procedure for obtaining a prediction interval for an individual response is similar to that for finding a confidence interval for a mean response. The only difference is the standard error. More variability is associated with individuals than with means. Therefore, the computation of the interval must account for this increased variability. Again, the form of the interval is

Point estimate $\pm$ margin of error

In Other Words
Prediction intervals are wider than confidence intervals because it is tougher to guess the value for an individual than the mean of a population.

The following formula can be used to construct a prediction interval about $\hat{y}$.

Prediction Interval for an Individual Response about $\hat{y}$

A $(1 - \alpha) \cdot 100\%$ prediction interval for $\hat{y}$, the individual response of y, is given by

$$\text{Lower bound: } \hat{y} - t_{\alpha/2} \cdot s_e \sqrt{1 + \frac{1}{n} + \frac{(x^* - \bar{x})^2}{\Sigma(x_i - \bar{x})^2}}$$

$$\text{Upper bound: } \hat{y} + t_{\alpha/2} \cdot s_e \sqrt{1 + \frac{1}{n} + \frac{(x^* - \bar{x})^2}{\Sigma(x_i - \bar{x})^2}} \qquad \textbf{(2)}$$

where x^* is the given value of the explanatory variable, n is the number of observations, and $t_{\alpha/2}$ is the critical value with $n - 2$ degrees of freedom.

Note The interval may be constructed provided the residuals are normally distributed or the sample size is large. ◀

Notice that the only difference between Formulas (1) and (2) is the "1 + " under the radical in Formula (2).

EXAMPLE 2 Constructing a Prediction Interval for an Individual Response by Hand

Problem Construct a 95% prediction interval for the predicted total cholesterol of a 42-year-old female.

Approach Determine the predicted total cholesterol at $x^* = 42$ and use Formula (2), since our estimate is for a particular 42-year-old female.

Solution The least-squares regression equation is $\hat{y} = 1.3991x + 151.3537$. To find the predicted total cholesterol of a 42-year-old, let $x^* = 42$ in the regression equation and obtain $\hat{y} = 1.3991(42) + 151.3537 = 210.1$. From Example 2 in Section 12.3, we found that $s_e = 19.48$; from Example 5 in Section 12.3 we found that $\sum(x_i - \bar{x})^2 = 2472.9284$ and $\bar{x} = 42.07143$. We find $t_{\alpha/2} = t_{0.025}$ with $n - 2 = 14 - 2 = 12$ degrees of freedom to be 2.179.

The 95% prediction interval for the predicted total cholesterol for a 42-year-old female is

$$\text{Lower bound: } \hat{y} - t_{\alpha/2}\cdot s_e\sqrt{1 + \frac{1}{n} + \frac{(x^* - \bar{x})^2}{\sum(x_i - \bar{x})^2}} = 210.1 - 2.179\cdot 19.48\cdot\sqrt{1 + \frac{1}{14} + \frac{(42 - 42.07143)^2}{2472.9284}} = 166.2$$

$$\text{Upper bound: } \hat{y} + t_{\alpha/2}\cdot s_e\sqrt{1 + \frac{1}{n} + \frac{(x^* - \bar{x})^2}{\sum(x_i - \bar{x})^2}} = 210.1 + 2.179\cdot 19.48\cdot\sqrt{1 + \frac{1}{14} + \frac{(42 - 42.07143)^2}{2472.9284}} = 254.0$$

We are 95% confident that the total cholesterol of a randomly selected 42-year-old female is between 166.2 and 254.0.

Now Work Problems 3(c) and (d)

Notice that the interval about the individual (prediction interval for an individual response) is wider than the interval about the mean (confidence interval for a mean response). The reason for this should be clear: More variability is associated with individuals than with groups of individuals. That is, it is more difficult to predict a single 42-year-old female's total cholesterol than it is to predict the mean total cholesterol for all 42-year-old females.

EXAMPLE 3 Confidence and Prediction Intervals Using Technology

Using Technology
The bounds for confidence and prediction intervals obtained using statistical software may differ from bounds computed by hand due to rounding error.

Problem Construct a 95% confidence interval for the predicted mean total cholesterol of all 42-year-old females using statistical software. Construct a 95% prediction interval for the predicted total cholesterol for a 42-year-old female using statistical software.

Approach We will use MINITAB to obtain the intervals. The steps for obtaining confidence and prediction intervals using MINITAB, Excel, and StatCrunch are given in the Technology Step-by-Step on page 562.

Solution Figure 31 shows the results obtained from MINITAB.

Figure 31 **Predicted Values**

```
    Fit    StDev Fit        95.0% CI              95.0% PI
 210.11         5.21   ( 198.77, 221.46)    ( 166.18, 254.05)
```

12.4 ASSESS YOUR UNDERSTANDING

VOCABULARY AND SKILL BUILDING

1. Intervals constructed about the predicted value of y, at a given level of x, that are used to measure the accuracy of the mean response of all individuals in the population are called _confidence_ intervals for a(n) _mean_ response.

2. Intervals constructed about the predicted value of y, at a given level of x, that are used to measure the accuracy of a single individual's prediction are called _prediction_ intervals for a(n) _individual_ response.

In Problems 3–6, use the results of Problems 5–8 in Section 12.3.

NW **3.** Using the sample data from Problem 5 in Section 12.3,

(a) Predict the mean value of y if $x = 7$. 11.8

(b) Construct a 95% confidence interval for the mean value of y if $x = 7$. (10.8, 12.8)

(c) Predict the value of y if $x = 7$. 11.8

(d) Construct a 95% prediction interval for the value of y if $x = 7$. (9.9, 13.7)

(e) Explain the difference between the prediction in parts (a) and (c).

4. Using the sample data from Problem 6 in Section 12.3,

(a) Predict the mean value of y if $x = 8$. 5.1

(b) Construct a 95% confidence interval for the mean value of y if $x = 8$. (4.0, 6.2)

(c) Predict the value of y if $x = 8$. 5.1

(d) Construct a 95% prediction interval for the value of y if $x = 8$. (2.5, 7.7)

(e) Explain the difference between the prediction in parts (a) and (c).

5. Using the sample data from Problem 7 in Section 12.3,

(a) Predict the mean value of y if $x = 1.4$. 4.3

(b) Construct a 95% confidence interval for the mean value of y if $x = 1.4$. (2.5, 6.1)

(c) Predict the value of y if $x = 1.4$. 4.3

(d) Construct a 95% prediction interval for the value of y if $x = 1.4$. (0.9, 7.7)

6. Using the sample data from Problem 8 in Section 12.3,

(a) Predict the mean value of y if $x = 1.8$. 0.4

(b) Construct a 90% confidence interval for the mean value of y if $x = 1.8$. (−0.8, 1.6)

(c) Predict the value of y if $x = 1.8$. 0.4

(d) Construct a 90% prediction interval for the value of y if $x = 1.8$. (−1.6, 2.4)

APPLYING THE CONCEPTS

7. An Unhealthy Commute Use the results of Problem 11 from Section 12.3 to answer the following questions:

(a) Predict the mean well-being index composite score of all individuals whose commute time is 20 minutes. 68.07

(b) Construct a 90% confidence interval for the mean well-being index composite score of all individuals whose commute time is 20 minutes. (67.723, 68.420)

(c) Predict the well-being index composite score of Jane, whose commute time is 20 minutes. 68.07

(d) Construct a 90% prediction interval for the well-being index composite score of Jane, whose commute time is 20 minutes. (67.252, 68.891)

(e) Explain the difference between the predictions made in parts (a) and (c).

8. Credit Scores Use the results of Problem 12 from Section 12.3 to answer the following questions:

(a) Predict the mean interest rate of all individuals whose credit score is 730. 5.619% (b) (3.729, 7.509)

(b) Construct a 90% confidence interval for the mean interest rate of all individuals whose credit score is 730.

(c) Predict the interest rate of Kaleigh, whose credit score is 730. 5.619%

(d) Construct a 90% prediction interval for the interest rate of Kaleigh, whose credit score is 730. (2.043, 9.195)

(e) Explain the difference between the prediction made in parts (a) and (c).

9. Height versus Head Circumference Use the results of Problem 13 from Section 12.3 to answer the following questions:

(a) Predict the mean head circumference of children who are 25.75 inches tall. 17.20 inches

(b) Construct a 95% confidence interval for the mean head circumference of children who are 25.75 inches tall. (17.12, 17.28)

(c) Predict the head circumference of a randomly selected child who is 25.75 inches tall. 17.20 inches

(d) Construct a 95% prediction interval for the head circumference of a child who is 25.75 inches tall. (16.97, 17.43)

(e) Explain the difference between the predictions in parts (a) and (c).

10. Bone Length Use the results of Problem 14 in Section 12.3 to answer the following questions:

(a) Predict the mean length of the right tibia of all rats whose right humerus is 25.83 mm. 37.023 mm

(b) Construct a 95% confidence interval for the mean length found in part (a). (36.647, 37.399)

(c) Predict the length of the right tibia of a randomly selected rat whose right humerus is 25.83 mm. 37.023 mm

(d) Construct a 95% prediction interval for the length found in part (c). (35.843, 38.203)

(e) Explain why the predicted lengths found in parts (a) and (c) are the same, yet the intervals constructed in parts (b) and (d) are different.

11. Concrete Use the results of Problem 15 from Section 12.3 to answer the following questions:

(a) Predict the mean 28-day strength of concrete whose 7-day strength is 2550 psi. 4400.4 psi

(b) Construct a 95% confidence interval for the mean 28-day strength of concrete whose 7-day strength is 2550 psi. (4147.8, 4653.1)

(c) Predict the 28-day strength of concrete whose 7-day strength is 2550 psi. 4400.4 psi

(d) Construct a 95% prediction interval for the 28-day strength of concrete whose 7-day strength is 2550 psi.

(e) Explain the difference between the predictions in parts (a) and (c). (d) (3726.3, 5074.6)

12. Tar and Nicotine Use the results of Problem 16 in Section 12.3 to answer the following questions:

(a) Predict the mean nicotine content of all cigarettes whose tar content is 12 mg. 0.90 mg

(b) Construct a 95% confidence interval for the tar content found in part (a). (0.83, 0.97)

(c) Predict the nicotine content of a randomly selected cigarette whose tar content is 12 mg. 0.90 mg

(d) Construct a 95% prediction interval for the nicotine content found in part (c). (0.64, 1.16)

(e) Explain why the predicted nicotine contents found in parts (a) and (c) are the same, yet the intervals constructed in parts (b) and (d) are different.

13. United Technologies versus the S&P 500 Use the results of Problem 17 in Section 12.3 to answer the following questions:

(a) What is the mean rate of return for United Technologies stock if the rate of return of the S&P 500 is 4.2%? 4.739%

(b) Construct a 90% confidence interval for the mean rate of return found in part (a). (3.662, 5.815)

(c) Predict the rate of return on United Technologies stock if the rate of return on the S&P 500 for a randomly selected month is 4.2%. 4.739%

(d) Construct a 90% prediction interval for the rate of return found in part (c). (1.441, 8.037)

(e) Explain why the predicted rates of return found in parts (a) and (c) are the same, yet the intervals constructed in parts (b) and (d) are different.

14. American Black Bears Use the results of Problem 18 from Section 12.3 to answer the following questions:

(a) Predict the mean weight of American black bears with a total length of 154.5 cm. 119.3 kg

(b) Construct a 95% confidence interval for the mean weight of American black bears with a total length of 154.5 cm.

(c) Predict the weight of a randomly selected American black bear that is 154.5 cm long. 119.3 kg

(d) Construct a 95% prediction interval for the weight of an American black bear that is 154.5 cm long. (68.9, 169.6)

(e) Explain why the predicted weights in parts (a) and (c) are the same, yet the intervals constructed in parts (b) and (d) are different.

14. (b) (99.9, 138.7)

15. CEO Performance Use the results of Problem 19 from Section 12.3 to answer the following:

(a) Explain why it does not make sense to construct confidence or prediction intervals based on the least-squares regression equation. Did not reject H_0: $\beta_1 = 0$

(b) Construct a 95% confidence interval for the mean stock return. $(-0.679, 35.313)$

16. Calories versus Sugar Use the results of Problem 20 from Section 12.3 to answer the following:

(a) Explain why it does not make sense to construct confidence or prediction intervals based on the least-squares regression equation. Did not reject H_0: $\beta_1 = 0$

(b) Construct a 95% confidence interval for the mean sugar content of energy bars. (9.5, 19.9)

17. Putting It Together: 3D Television Prices One factor that influences the cost of a 3D television is its size. The following data represent the size and price for a random sample of 3D televisions of varying brands and models.

Brand/Model	Size (in.)	Price ($)
Sony Bravia KDL-40HX800	40	1168
Samsung UN40C7000WF	40	1170
Samsung UN46C7000	46	1494
Sony Bravia 46HX800	46	1500
Samsung UN46C8000	46	1559
Sharp LC52LE925UN	52	2700
Samsung UN55C7000WF	55	2600
Sony Bravia XBR-60LX900	60	3890
Panasonic Viera TC-P65VT25	65	4478

Source: *Best Buy*

(a) Draw a scatter diagram of the data using size as the explanatory variable.

(b) Determine the linear correlation coefficient between the size and price. 0.979

(c) Does a linear relation exist between size and price? Yes

(d) Find the least-squares regression line treating size as the explanatory variable. $\hat{y} = -4599.2 + 137.67x$

(e) Interpret the slope.

(f) Is it reasonable to interpret the intercept? Explain. No

(g) What proportion of variability in price is explained by the variability in size? 95.7%

(h) Determine estimates for β_0 and β_1.

(i) Compute the standard error of the estimate. 269.0488

(j) Determine whether the residuals are normally distributed.

(k) Determine s_{b_1}. 10.9656 (j) Yes

(l) Assuming residuals are normally distributed, test whether a linear relation exists between size and price at the $\alpha = 0.05$ level of significance. Reject H_0

(m) Assuming residuals are normally distributed, construct a 95% confidence interval for the slope of the true least-squares regression line. (111.7416, 163.6007)

(n) Predict the mean price of 52-inch 3D televisions. $2560

(o) Construct a 95% confidence interval about the mean price of 52-inch televisions. ($2341.4, $2778.0)

(p) Is the price of the 52-inch Sharp 3D television above or below the average price for 52-inch 3D televisions? Above

(q) Predict the price of a randomly selected 52-inch 3D television. $2560

(r) Construct a 95% prediction interval for the price a 52-inch 3D television. ($1887.0, $3232.3)

(s) In part (g), you found the proportion of variability in price that is explained by the variability in size. What lurking variables might also have an effect on price?

(h) $b_0 = -4599.2217$, $b_1 = 137.6711$

Technology Step-By-Step

Confidence and Prediction Intervals

TI-83/84 Plus

The TI-83/84 Plus graphing calculators do not compute confidence or prediction intervals.

MINITAB

1. With the predictor variable in C1 and the response variable in C2, select the **Stat** menu and highlight **Regression**. Highlight and select **Regression . . . .**
2. Select the explanatory (predictor) and response variables.
3. Click the Options ... button.
4. In the cell marked "Prediction intervals for new observations," enter the value of x^*. Select a confidence level. Click OK twice.

Excel

1. Enter the values of the explanatory variable in Column A and the corresponding values of the response variable in Column B.
2. Select the XLSTAT menu. Choose the Modeling Data menu and select Linear Regression.
3. With the cursor in the Y/Dependent variables quantitative cell, highlight the data in Column B. With the cursor in the X/Explanatory variables quantitative cell, highlight the data in Column A.
4. Enter the value of the explanatory variable for which you wish to make predictions in a cell. Select the Prediction menu. Check the Prediction box. With the cursor in the X/Explanatory variable quantitative cell, highlight the cell that contains the value of the explanatory variable. Click OK.

StatCrunch

Follow the steps given in Section 12.3 for testing the significance of the least-squares regression model. At Step 3, click Next> instead of Calculate. Check the box "Predict Y for X=" and enter the value of the explanatory variable. Choose a level of significance and click Calculate. Or, if you like, click Next> and then select "Plot the fitted line" and check the confidence and prediction interval boxes. Then click Calculate.

CHAPTER 12 REVIEW

Summary

In this chapter, we introduced chi-square methods and inference on the least-squares regression line.

The first chi-square method involved tests for goodness-of-fit. We used the chi-square distribution to test whether a random variable followed a certain distribution. This is done by comparing the expected values based on the distribution of the random variable to the observed values.

In Section 12.2 we introduced chi-square methods that allowed us to perform tests for independence and homogeneity. In a test for independence, the researcher obtains random data for two variables and tests whether the variables are associated. The null hypothesis in these tests is always that the variables are not associated (independent). The test statistic compares the expected values if the variables were independent to those observed. If the expected and observed values differ significantly, we reject the null hypothesis and conclude that there is evidence to support the belief that the variables are not independent (they are associated). We draw bar graphs of the marginal distributions to help us see the association, if any.

The last chi-square test was the test for homogeneity of proportions. This test is similar to the test for independence, except we are testing whether the proportion of individuals from different populations with a certain characteristic is equal ($p_1 = p_2 = \cdots = p_k$).

The last two sections of this chapter dealt with inferential techniques that can be used on the least-squares regression model $y_i = \beta_0 + \beta_1 x_i + \varepsilon_i$.

In Section 12.3, we used sample data to obtain estimates of an intercept and slope. The residuals are required to be normally distributed, with mean 0 and constant standard deviation σ. The residuals for each observation should be independent. We verified these requirements through residual plots and a normal probability plot of the residuals. Provided that these requirements are satisfied, we can test hypotheses regarding the slope to determine whether or not the relation between the explanatory and response variables is linear.

In Section 12.4, we learned how to construct confidence and prediction intervals for a predicted value. We constructed confidence intervals for a mean response and prediction intervals for an individual response.

Vocabulary

Goodness-of-fit test (p. 517)
Expected counts (pp. 518, 530)
Test statistic (pp. 519, 530)
Chi-square test for independence (p. 528)
Chi-square test for homogeneity of proportions (p. 534)
Least-squares regression model (p. 545)
Standard error of the estimate (p. 546)
Robust (p. 549)
Bivariate normal distribution (p. 552)
Jointly normally distributed (p. 552)
Confidence interval for a mean response (p. 558)
Prediction interval for an individual response (p. 558)

Formulas

Expected Counts in a Goodness-of-Fit Test

$E_i = \mu_i = np_i \quad \text{for} \quad i = 1, 2, \ldots, k$

Chi-Square Test Statistic

$$\chi^2 = \sum \frac{(O_i - E_i)^2}{E_i} \qquad i = 1, 2, \ldots, k$$

Expected Frequencies in a Test for Independence or Homogeneity

$$\text{Expected frequency} = \frac{(\text{row total})(\text{column total})}{\text{table total}}$$

Standard Error of the Estimate

$$s_e = \sqrt{\frac{\Sigma(y_i - \hat{y}_i)^2}{n-2}} = \sqrt{\frac{\Sigma \text{residuals}^2}{n-2}}$$

Standard Error of b_1

$$s_{b_1} = \frac{s_e}{\sqrt{\Sigma(x_i - \bar{x})^2}}$$

Confidence Intervals for the Slope of the Regression Line

A $(1-\alpha) \cdot 100\%$ confidence interval for the slope of the true regression line, β_1, is given by the following formulas:

$$\text{Lower bound: } b_1 - t_{\alpha/2} \cdot \frac{s_e}{\sqrt{\Sigma(x_i - \bar{x})^2}} = b_1 - t_{\alpha/2} \cdot s_{b_1}$$

$$\text{Upper bound: } b_1 + t_{\alpha/2} \cdot \frac{s_e}{\sqrt{\Sigma(x_i - \bar{x})^2}} = b_1 + t_{\alpha/2} \cdot s_{b_1}$$

Here, $t_{\alpha/2}$ is computed with $n - 2$ degrees of freedom.

Confidence Interval about the Mean Response of $\hat{y}$

A $(1-\alpha) \cdot 100\%$ confidence interval about the mean response of y, $\hat{y}$, is given by the following formulas:

$$\text{Lower bound: } \hat{y} - t_{\alpha/2} \cdot s_e \sqrt{\frac{1}{n} + \frac{(x^* - \bar{x})^2}{\Sigma(x_i - \bar{x})^2}}$$

$$\text{Upper bound: } \hat{y} + t_{\alpha/2} \cdot s_e \sqrt{\frac{1}{n} + \frac{(x^* - \bar{x})^2}{\Sigma(x_i - \bar{x})^2}}$$

Here, x^* is the given value of the explanatory variable, and $t_{\alpha/2}$ is the critical value with $n - 2$ degrees of freedom.

Prediction Interval about an Individual Response, $\hat{y}$
A $(1 - \alpha) \cdot 100\%$ prediction interval for the individual response of y, $\hat{y}$, is given by

Lower bound: $\hat{y} - t_{\alpha/2} \cdot s_e \sqrt{1 + \dfrac{1}{n} + \dfrac{(x^* - \bar{x})^2}{\Sigma(x_i - \bar{x})^2}}$

Upper bound: $\hat{y} + t_{\alpha/2} \cdot s_e \sqrt{1 + \dfrac{1}{n} + \dfrac{(x^* - \bar{x})^2}{\Sigma(x_i - \bar{x})^2}}$

where x^* is the given value of the explanatory variable and $t_{\alpha/2}$ is the critical value with $n - 2$ degrees of freedom.

Objectives

Section	You should be able to ...	Examples	Review Exercises
12.1	1 Perform a goodness-of-fit test (p. 516)	2–4	1 and 2
12.2	1 Perform a test for independence (p. 528)	1–3	3 and 4
	2 Perform a test for homogeneity of proportions (p. 534)	4	5
12.3	1 State the requirements of the least-squares regression model (p. 544)	pp. 544–545	6
	2 Compute the standard error of the estimate (p. 545)	2 and 3	7(b), 8(b)
	3 Verify that the residuals are normally distributed (p. 547)	4	7(c), 8(c)
	4 Conduct inference on the slope (p. 547)	5	7(e), 8(e), 9(b)
	5 Construct a confidence interval about the slope of the least-squares regression model (p. 551)	6	7(f), 8(f)
12.4	1 Construct confidence intervals for a mean response (p. 558)	1 and 3	7(g), 8(g)
	2 Construct prediction intervals for an individual response (p. 559)	2 and 3	7(i), 8(i)

Review Exercises

1. Roulette Wheel A pit boss suspects that a roulette wheel is out of balance. A roulette wheel has 18 black slots, 18 red slots, and 2 green slots. The pit boss spins the wheel 500 times and records the following frequencies: Do not reject H_0

Outcome	Frequency
Black	233
Red	237
Green	30

Is the wheel out of balance? Use the $\alpha = 0.05$ level of significance.

2. World Series Are the teams that play in the World Series evenly matched? To win a World Series, a team must win 4 games. If the teams are evenly matched, we would expect the number of games played in the World Series to follow the distribution shown in the first two columns of the following table. The third column represents the actual number of games played in each World Series from 1930 to 2010. Do the data support the distribution that would exist if the teams are evenly matched and the outcome of each game is independent? Use the $\alpha = 0.05$ level of significance. Do not reject H_0

Number of Games	Probability	Observed Frequency
4	0.125	15
5	0.25	17
6	0.3125	18
7	0.3125	30

Source: Major League Baseball

3. *Titanic* With 20% of men, 74% of women, and 52% of children surviving the infamous *Titanic* disaster, it is clear that the saying "women and children first" was followed. But what, if any, role did the class of service play in the survival of passengers? The data shown represent the survival status of passengers by class of service.

		Class		
		First	Second	Third
Survival Status	Survived	203	118	178
	Did Not Survive	122	167	528

(a) Is class of service independent of survival rate? Use the $\alpha = 0.05$ level of significance. No

(b) Construct a conditional distribution of survival status by class of service and draw a bar graph. What does this summary tell you?

4. Premature Birth and Education Does the length of term of pregnancy play a role in the level of education of the baby? Researchers in Norway followed over 1 million births between 1967 and 1988 and looked at the educational attainment of the children. The following data are based on the results of their research. Note that a full-term pregnancy is 38 weeks. Is gestational period independent of completing a high school diploma? Use the $\alpha = 0.05$ level of significance. No; dependent

		Gestational Period (weeks)				
		22–27	28–32	33–36	37–42	43+
Less Than High School Degree	Yes	14	34	140	1010	81
	No	26	65	343	3032	208

Source: Chicago Tribune, March 26, 2008.

5. Roosevelt versus Landon One of the most famous presidential elections (from a statistician's point of view) is the 1936 contest between incumbent Franklin D. Roosevelt (FDR) and Republican challenger Alf Landon. The notoriety of the election comes from the fact that polling done by *Literary Digest* suggested that Landon would win by a 3 to 2 margin. However, Roosevelt actually crushed Landon in the general election.

After the election, author and editor David Lawrence studied the vote. Lawrence asked the following question: "To what extent was the campaign a reflection of a new trend in American politics, a trend in which the federal government's paternalistic interest in the citizen brought an amazing reward to the party in power?" As part of FDR's New Deal policies to help get the United States out of the Great Depression, the federal government created the Agricultural Adjustment Administration (AAA). The AAA tried to force higher prices for commodities by paying farmers not to farm and not to bring cattle to market.

To determine whether farm subsidies may have played a role in the election results, Lawrence looked at election results in 2052 counties. He segmented the counties based on AAA funding between 1934 and 1935 as follows:

- High-funded AAA counties received $500,000 or more in AAA money
- Medium-funded AAA counties received between $100,000 and $500,000 in AAA money
- Low-funded AAA counties received some AAA money, but less than $100,000
- No AAA-funded counties received no funds at all

Treat the following data as a random sample of voters within each county type. The results are based on the election results in the various counties.

	High-Funded	Medium-Funded	Low-Funded	No Funding
Roosevelt	745	641	513	411
Landon	498	484	437	465

Source: Folsom, Burton, "New Deal or Raw Deal?" Simon & Schuster, 2008.

(a) Do the data suggest that the level of funding received by counties through the AAA is associated with the candidate? Use the $\alpha = 0.05$ level of significance. Yes, reject H_0

(b) Construct a conditional distribution of candidate by level of AAA funding and draw a bar graph.

6. What is the simple least-squares regression model? What are the requirements to perform inference on a simple least-squares regression line? How do we verify that these requirements are met?

7. Seat Choice and GPA A biology professor wants to investigate the relation between the seat location chosen by a student on the first day of class and the student's cumulative grade point average. He randomly selected an introductory biology class and obtained the following information for the 38 students in the class.

Row Chosen, x	GPA, y	Row Chosen, x	GPA, y
1	4.00	5	3.22
2	3.35	5	3.36
2	3.50	5	3.58
2	3.67	5	3.67
2	3.75	5	3.69
3	3.37	5	3.72
3	3.62	5	3.84
4	2.35	6	2.35
4	2.71	6	2.63
4	3.75	6	3.15
5	3.10	6	3.69
6	3.71	7	3.90
7	2.88	8	2.30
7	2.93	8	2.54
7	3.00	8	2.61
7	3.21	9	2.71
7	3.53	9	3.74
7	3.74	9	3.75
7	3.75	11	1.71

Source: S. Kalinowski and Taper M. "The Effect of Seat Location on Exam Grades and Student Perceptions in an Introductory Biology Class." *Journal of College Science Teaching,* 36(4):54–57, 2007.

(a) $b_0 = 3.8589$, $b_1 = -0.1049$, 3.334

(a) Treating row as the explanatory variable, determine the estimates of β_0 and β_1. What is the mean GPA of students who choose a seat in the fifth row?

(b) Compute the standard error of the estimate, s_e. 0.5102 (c) Yes

(c) Determine whether the residuals are normally distributed.

(d) If the residuals are normally distributed, determine s_{b_1}. 0.0366

(e) If the residuals are normally distributed, test whether a linear relation exists between the explanatory variable, row choice, and response variable, GPA, at the $\alpha = 0.05$ level of significance. Reject H_0

(f) If the residuals are normally distributed, construct a 95% confidence interval for the slope of the true least-squares regression line. $(-0.1791, -0.0307)$

(g) Construct a 95% confidence interval for the mean GPA of students who choose a seat in the fifth row. (3.159, 3.509)

(h) Predict the GPA of a randomly selected student who chooses a seat in the fifth row. 3.334

(i) Construct a 95% prediction interval for the GPA found in part (h). (2.285, 4.384)

(j) Explain why the predicted GPAs found in parts (a) and (h) are the same, yet the intervals are different.

8. Apartments The following data represent the square footage and rents for apartments in Queens, New York.

Square Footage, x	Rent per Month ($), y
500	650
588	1215
1000	2000
688	1655
825	1250
1259	2700
650	1200
560	1250
1073	2350
1452	3300
1305	3100

Source: apartments.com

(a) What are the estimates of β_0 and β_1? What is the mean rent of a 900-square-foot apartment in Queens? (c) yes

(b) Compute the standard error of the estimate, s_e. 229.547

(c) Determine whether the residuals are normally distributed.

(d) If the residuals are normally distributed, determine s_{b_1}.

(e) If the residuals are normally distributed, test whether a linear relation exists between the explanatory variable, x, and response variable, y, at the $\alpha = 0.05$ level of significance. Reject H_0

(f) If the residuals are normally distributed, construct a 95% confidence interval for the slope of the true least-squares regression line. (2.0416, 3.0214) (d) 0.2166

(g) Construct a 90% confidence interval for the mean rent of all 900-square-foot apartments in Queens. ($1752.20, $2006.00)

(h) Predict the rent of a particular 900-square-foot apartment in Queens. $1879.15

(i) Construct a 90% prediction interval for the rent of a particular 900-square-foot apartment in Queens.

(j) Explain why the predicted rents found in parts (a) and (h) are the same, yet the intervals are different.

(a) $b_0 = -399.2$, $b_1 = 2.5315$; $1879.15 (i) ($1439.60, $2318.60)

Problems in the chapter test are labeled by section.objective. For example, 2.3 means Section 2, Objective 3.

CHAPTER TEST

1.1 **1.** A pit boss is concerned that a pair of dice being used in a craps game is not fair. The distribution of the expected sum of two fair dice is as follows:

Sum of Two Dice	Probability	Sum of Two Dice	Probability
2	$\frac{1}{36}$	8	$\frac{5}{36}$
3	$\frac{2}{36}$	9	$\frac{4}{36}$
4	$\frac{3}{36}$	10	$\frac{3}{36}$
5	$\frac{4}{36}$	11	$\frac{2}{36}$
6	$\frac{5}{36}$	12	$\frac{1}{36}$
7	$\frac{6}{36}$		

The pit boss rolls the dice 400 times and records the sum of the dice. The table shows the results. Do you think the dice are fair? Use the $\alpha = 0.01$ level of significance. Do not reject H_0

Sum of Two Dice	Frequency	Sum of Two Dice	Frequency
2	16	8	59
3	23	9	45
4	31	10	34
5	41	11	19
6	62	12	11
7	59		

1.1 **2.** A researcher wanted to determine if the distribution of educational attainment of Americans today is different from the distribution in 2000. The distribution of educational attainment in 2000 was as follows:

Education	Relative Frequency
Not a high school graduate	0.158
High school graduate	0.331
Some college	0.176
Associate's degree	0.078
Bachelor's degree	0.170
Advanced degree	0.087

Source: Statistical Abstract of the United States.

The researcher randomly selects 500 Americans, learns their levels of education, and obtains the data shown in the table. Do the data suggest that the distribution of educational attainment has changed since 2000? Use the $\alpha = 0.1$ level of significance. Educational attainment has not changed.

Education	Frequency
Not a high school graduate	72
High school graduate	159
Some college	85
Associate's degree	44
Bachelor's degree	92
Advanced degree	48

2.2 **3.** In a poll conducted by Harris Poll, a random sample of adult Americans was asked, "How important are moral values when deciding how to vote?" The results of the survey by disclosed political affiliation are shown in the table.

		Political Affiliation		
		Republican	**Independent**	**Democrat**
Morality	**Important**	644	662	670
	Not important	56	155	147

(a) Do the sample data suggest that the proportion of adults who feel morality is important differ based on political affiliation? Use the $\alpha = 0.05$ level of significance.

(b) Construct a conditional distribution of morality by party affiliation and draw a bar graph. What does this summary tell you? (a) Yes; proportions differ

2.2 **4.** The General Social Survey regularly asks individuals to disclose their religious affiliation. The following data represent the religious affiliation of young adults, aged 18 to 29, in the 1970s, 1980s, 1990s, and 2000s. Do the data suggest different proportions of 18- to 29-year-olds have been affiliated with religion in the past four decades? Use the $\alpha = 0.05$ level of significance. Yes, reject H_0

	1970s	1980s	1990s	2000s
Affiliated	2395	3022	2121	624
Unaffiliated (no religion)	327	412	404	2087

Source: General Social Survey

2.1 **5.** Many municipalities are passing legislation that forbids smoking in restaurants and bars. Bar owners claim that these laws hurt their business. Are their concerns legitimate? The following data represent the smoking status and frequency of visits to bars from the General Social Survey. Do smokers tend to spend more time in bars? Use the $\alpha = 0.05$ level of significance. Yes

	Almost Daily	Several Times a Week	Several Times a Month	Once a Month	Several Times a Year	Once a Year	Never
Smoker	80	409	294	362	433	336	1265
Nonsmoker	57	350	379	471	573	568	3297

3.1 **6.** State the requirements to perform inference on a simple least-squares regression line.

7. Crickets make a chirping noise by sliding their wings rapidly over each other. Perhaps you have noticed that the number of chirps seems to increase with the temperature. The following table lists the temperature (in degrees Fahrenheit, °F) and the number of chirps per second for the striped ground cricket. (a) $b_0 = -0.309$, $b_1 = 0.2119$; 16.69

Temperature, x	Chirps per Second, y	Temperature, x	Chirps per Second, y
88.6	20.0	71.6	16.0
93.3	19.8	84.3	18.4
80.6	17.1	75.2	15.5
69.7	14.7	82.0	17.1
69.4	15.4	83.3	16.2
79.6	15.0	82.6	17.2
80.6	16.0	83.5	17.0
76.3	14.4		

Source: George W. Pierce. *The Songs of Insects*, Cambridge, MA: Harvard University Press, 1949, pp. 12–21.

7.(c) Yes (d) 0.0387

(a) What are the estimates of β_0 and β_1? What is the mean number of chirps when the temperature is 80.2°F?

3.2 **(b)** Compute the standard error of the estimate, s_e. 0.9715

3.3 **(c)** Determine whether the residuals are normally distributed.

(d) If the residuals are normally distributed, determine s_{b_1}.

3.4 **(e)** If the residuals are normally distributed, test whether a linear relation exists between the explanatory variable, x, and response variable, y, at the $\alpha = 0.05$ level of significance. Reject H_0

3.5 **(f)** If the residuals are normally distributed, construct a 95% confidence interval for the slope of the true least-squares regression line. (0.1283, 0.2955)

4.1 **(g)** Construct a 90% confidence interval for the mean number of chirps found in part (a). (16.24, 17.13)

(h) Predict the number of chirps on a day when the temperature is 80.2°F. 16.69

4.2 **(i)** Construct a 90% prediction interval for the number of chirps found in part (h). (14.91, 18.46)

(j) Explain why the predicted number of chirps found in parts (a) and (h) are the same, yet the intervals are different.

8. The following data represent the height (inches) of boys between the ages of 2 and 10 years.

Age, x	Boy Height, y	Age, x	Boy Height, y	Age, x	Boy Height, y
2	36.1	5	45.6	8	48.3
2	34.2	5	44.8	8	50.9
2	31.1	5	44.6	9	52.2
3	36.3	6	49.8	9	51.3
3	39.5	7	43.2	10	55.6
4	41.5	7	47.9	10	59.5
4	38.6	8	51.4		

Source: National Center for Health Statistics

(a) Treating age as the explanatory variable, determine the estimates of β_0 and β_1. What is the mean height of a 7-year-old boy? $b_0 = 29.705$; $b_1 = 2.6351$; 48.15 inches

3.2 **(b)** Compute the standard error of the estimate, s_e. 2.450

3.4 **(c)** Assuming the residuals are normally distributed, test whether a linear relation exists between the explanatory variable, age, and response variable, height, at the $\alpha = 0.05$ level of significance. Reject H_0

3.5 **(d)** Assuming the residuals are normally distributed, construct a 95% confidence interval for the slope of the true least-squares regression line. (2.2008, 3.0694)

4.1 **(e)** Construct a 90% confidence interval for the mean height found in part (a). (47.11, 49.19)

(f) Predict the height of a 7-year-old boy. 48.15 inches

4.2 **(g)** Construct a 90% prediction interval for the height found in part (f). (43.78, 52.52)

(h) Explain why the predicted heights found in parts (a) and (f) are the same, yet the intervals are different.

9. A researcher believes that as age increases the grip strength (pounds per square inch, psi) of an individual's dominant hand decreases. From a random sample of 17 females, he obtains the following data.

Age, x	Grip Strength, y	Age, x	Grip Strength, y
15	65	34	45
16	60	37	58
28	58	41	70
61	60	43	73
53	46	49	45
43	66	53	60
16	56	61	56
25	75	68	30
28	46		

Source: Kevin McCarthy, student at Joliet Junior College

(a) Treating age as the explanatory variable, determine the estimates of β_0 and β_1. $b_0 = 67.388$; $b_1 = -0.2632$

1.4 **(b)** Assuming the residuals are normally distributed, test whether a linear relation exists between the explanatory variable, age, and response variable, grip strength, at the $\alpha = 0.05$ level of significance. Do not reject H_0

(c) Based on your answer to (b), what would be a good estimate of the grip strength of a randomly selected 42-year-old female? 57 psi

Making an Informed Decision

Benefits of College

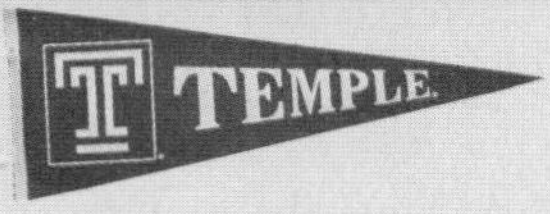

Are there benefits to attending college? If so, what are they? In this project, we will identify some of the perks that a college education provides. Obtain a random sample of at least 50 people aged 21 years or older and administer the following survey.

Please answer the following questions:

1. What is the highest level of education you have attained?

______Have not completed high school

______High school graduate

______College graduate

2. What is your employment status?

______Employed

______Unemployed, but actively seeking work

______Unemployed, but not actively seeking work

3. If you are employed, what is your annual income?

______Less than $20,000

______$20,000–$39,999

______$40,000–$60,000

______More than $60,000

4. If you are employed, which statement best describes the level of satisfaction you have with your career? Answer this question only if you are employed.

______Satisfied—I enjoy my job and am happy with my career.

______Somewhat satisfied—Work is work, but I am not unhappy with my career.

______Somewhat dissatisfied—I do not enjoy my work, but I also have no intention of leaving.

______Dissatisfied—Going to work is painful. I would quit tomorrow if I could.

(a) Use the results of the survey to create a contingency table for each of the following categories:

- Level of education/employment status
- Level of education/annual income
- Level of education/job satisfaction
- Annual income/job satisfaction

(b) Perform a chi-square test for independence on each contingency table from part (a).

(c) Draw bar graphs for each contingency table from part (a).

(d) Write a report that details your findings.

The Chapter 12 Case Study is located on the CD that accompanies this text.

Appendix A Tables

TABLE I

Random Numbers

Row Number	01–05	06–10	11–15	16–20	21–25	26–30	31–35	36–40	41–45	46–50
	Column Number									
01	89392	23212	74483	36590	25956	36544	68518	40805	09980	00467
02	61458	17639	96252	95649	73727	33912	72896	66218	52341	97141
03	11452	74197	81962	48443	90360	26480	73231	37740	26628	44690
04	27575	04429	31308	02241	01698	19191	18948	78871	36030	23980
05	36829	59109	88976	46845	28329	47460	88944	08264	00843	84592
06	81902	93458	42161	26099	09419	89073	82849	09160	61845	40906
07	59761	55212	33360	68751	86737	79743	85262	31887	37879	17525
08	46827	25906	64708	20307	78423	15910	86548	08763	47050	18513
09	24040	66449	32353	83668	13874	86741	81312	54185	78824	00718
10	98144	96372	50277	15571	82261	66628	31457	00377	63423	55141
11	14228	17930	30118	00438	49666	65189	62869	31304	17117	71489
12	55366	51057	90065	14791	62426	02957	85518	28822	30588	32798
13	96101	30646	35526	90389	73634	79304	96635	06626	94683	16696
14	38152	55474	30153	26525	83647	31988	82182	98377	33802	80471
15	85007	18416	24661	95581	45868	15662	28906	36392	07617	50248
16	85544	15890	80011	18160	33468	84106	40603	01315	74664	20553
17	10446	20699	98370	17684	16932	80449	92654	02084	19985	59321
18	67237	45509	17638	65115	29757	80705	82686	48565	72612	61760
19	23026	89817	05403	82209	30573	47501	00135	33955	50250	72592
20	67411	58542	18678	46491	13219	84084	27783	34508	55158	78742

TABLE II

Critical Values for Correlation Coefficient

n	
3	0.997
4	0.950
5	0.878
6	0.811
7	0.754
8	0.707
9	0.666
10	0.632
11	0.602
12	0.576
13	0.553
14	0.532
15	0.514
16	0.497
17	0.482
18	0.468
19	0.456
20	0.444
21	0.433
22	0.423
23	0.413
24	0.404
25	0.396
26	0.388
27	0.381
28	0.374
29	0.367
30	0.361

TABLE III

Binomial Probability Distribution

This table computes the probability of obtaining x successes in n trials of a binomial experiment with probability of success p.

		p																			
n	x	0.01	0.05	0.10	0.15	0.20	0.25	0.30	0.35	0.40	0.45	0.50	0.55	0.60	0.65	0.70	0.75	0.80	0.85	0.90	0.95
2	0	0.9801	0.9025	0.8100	0.7225	0.6400	0.5625	0.4900	0.4225	0.3600	0.3025	0.2500	0.2025	0.1600	0.1225	0.0900	0.0625	0.0400	0.0225	0.0100	0.0025
	1	0.0198	0.0950	0.1800	0.2550	0.3200	0.3750	0.4200	0.4550	0.4800	0.4950	0.5000	0.4950	0.4800	0.4550	0.4200	0.3750	0.3200	0.2550	0.1800	0.0950
	2	0.0001	0.0025	0.0100	0.0225	0.0400	0.0625	0.0900	0.1225	0.1600	0.2025	0.2500	0.3025	0.3600	0.4225	0.4900	0.5625	0.6400	0.7225	0.8100	0.9025
3	0	0.9703	0.8574	0.7290	0.6141	0.5120	0.4219	0.3430	0.2746	0.2160	0.1664	0.1250	0.0911	0.0640	0.0429	0.0270	0.0156	0.0080	0.0034	0.0010	0.0001
	1	0.0294	0.1354	0.2430	0.3251	0.3840	0.4219	0.4410	0.4436	0.4320	0.4084	0.3750	0.3341	0.2880	0.2389	0.1890	0.1406	0.0960	0.0574	0.0270	0.0071
	2	0.0003	0.0071	0.0270	0.0574	0.0960	0.1406	0.1890	0.2389	0.2880	0.3341	0.3750	0.4084	0.4320	0.4436	0.4410	0.4219	0.3840	0.3251	0.2430	0.1354
	3	0.0000+	0.0001	0.0010	0.0034	0.0080	0.0156	0.0270	0.0429	0.0640	0.0911	0.1250	0.1664	0.2160	0.2746	0.3430	0.4219	0.5120	0.6141	0.7290	0.8574
4	0	0.9606	0.8145	0.6561	0.5220	0.4096	0.3164	0.2401	0.1785	0.1296	0.0915	0.0625	0.0410	0.0256	0.0150	0.0081	0.0039	0.0016	0.0005	0.0001	0.0000+
	1	0.0388	0.1715	0.2916	0.3685	0.4096	0.4219	0.4116	0.3845	0.3456	0.2995	0.2500	0.2005	0.1536	0.1115	0.0756	0.0469	0.0256	0.0115	0.0036	0.0005
	2	0.0006	0.0135	0.0486	0.0975	0.1536	0.2109	0.2646	0.3105	0.3456	0.3675	0.3750	0.3675	0.3456	0.3105	0.2646	0.2109	0.1536	0.0975	0.0486	0.0135
	3	0.0000+	0.0005	0.0036	0.0115	0.0256	0.0469	0.0756	0.1115	0.1536	0.2005	0.2500	0.2995	0.3456	0.3845	0.4116	0.4219	0.4096	0.3685	0.2916	0.1715
	4	0.0000+	0.0000+	0.0001	0.0005	0.0016	0.0039	0.0081	0.0150	0.0256	0.0410	0.0625	0.0915	0.1296	0.1785	0.2401	0.3164	0.4096	0.5220	0.6561	0.8145
5	0	0.9510	0.7738	0.5905	0.4437	0.3277	0.2373	0.1681	0.1160	0.0778	0.0503	0.0313	0.0185	0.0102	0.0053	0.0024	0.0010	0.0003	0.0001	0.0000+	0.0000+
	1	0.0480	0.2036	0.3281	0.3915	0.4096	0.3955	0.3602	0.3124	0.2592	0.2059	0.1563	0.1128	0.0768	0.0488	0.0284	0.0146	0.0064	0.0022	0.0005	0.0000+
	2	0.0010	0.0214	0.0729	0.1382	0.2048	0.2637	0.3087	0.3364	0.3456	0.3369	0.3125	0.2757	0.2304	0.1811	0.1323	0.0879	0.0512	0.0244	0.0081	0.0011
	3	0.0000+	0.0011	0.0081	0.0244	0.0512	0.0879	0.1323	0.1811	0.2304	0.2757	0.3125	0.3369	0.3456	0.3364	0.3087	0.2637	0.2048	0.1382	0.0729	0.0214
	4	0.0000+	0.0000+	0.0005	0.0022	0.0064	0.0146	0.0284	0.0488	0.0768	0.1128	0.1563	0.2059	0.2592	0.3124	0.3602	0.3955	0.4096	0.3915	0.3281	0.2036
	5	0.0000+	0.0000+	0.0000+	0.0001	0.0003	0.0010	0.0024	0.0053	0.0102	0.0185	0.0313	0.0503	0.0778	0.1160	0.1681	0.2373	0.3277	0.4437	0.5905	0.7738
6	0	0.9415	0.7351	0.5314	0.3771	0.2621	0.1780	0.1176	0.0754	0.0467	0.0277	0.0156	0.0083	0.0041	0.0018	0.0007	0.0002	0.0001	0.0000+	0.0000+	0.0000+
	1	0.0571	0.2321	0.3543	0.3993	0.3932	0.3560	0.3025	0.2437	0.1866	0.1359	0.0938	0.0609	0.0369	0.0205	0.0102	0.0044	0.0015	0.0004	0.0001	0.0000+
	2	0.0014	0.0305	0.0984	0.1762	0.2458	0.2966	0.3241	0.3280	0.3110	0.2780	0.2344	0.1861	0.1382	0.0951	0.0595	0.0330	0.0154	0.0055	0.0012	0.0001
	3	0.0000+	0.0021	0.0146	0.0415	0.0819	0.1318	0.1852	0.2355	0.2765	0.3032	0.3125	0.3032	0.2765	0.2355	0.1852	0.1318	0.0819	0.0415	0.0146	0.0021
	4	0.0000+	0.0001	0.0012	0.0055	0.0154	0.0330	0.0595	0.0951	0.1382	0.1861	0.2344	0.2780	0.3110	0.3280	0.3241	0.2966	0.2458	0.1762	0.0984	0.0305
	5	0.0000+	0.0000+	0.0001	0.0004	0.0015	0.0044	0.0102	0.0205	0.0369	0.0609	0.0938	0.1359	0.1866	0.2437	0.3025	0.3560	0.3932	0.3993	0.3543	0.2321
	6	0.0000+	0.0000+	0.0000+	0.0000+	0.0001	0.0002	0.0007	0.0018	0.0041	0.0083	0.0156	0.0277	0.0467	0.0754	0.1176	0.1780	0.2621	0.3771	0.5314	0.7351
7	0	0.9321	0.6983	0.4783	0.3206	0.2097	0.1335	0.0824	0.0490	0.0280	0.0152	0.0078	0.0037	0.0016	0.0006	0.0002	0.0001	0.0000+	0.0000+	0.0000+	0.0000+
	1	0.0659	0.2573	0.3720	0.3960	0.3670	0.3115	0.2471	0.1848	0.1306	0.0872	0.0547	0.0320	0.0172	0.0084	0.0036	0.0013	0.0004	0.0001	0.0000+	0.0000+
	2	0.0020	0.0406	0.1240	0.2097	0.2753	0.3115	0.3177	0.2985	0.2613	0.2140	0.1641	0.1172	0.0774	0.0466	0.0250	0.0115	0.0043	0.0012	0.0002	0.0000+
	3	0.0000+	0.0036	0.0230	0.0617	0.1147	0.1730	0.2269	0.2679	0.2903	0.2918	0.2734	0.2388	0.1935	0.1442	0.0972	0.0577	0.0287	0.0109	0.0026	0.0002
	4	0.0000+	0.0002	0.0026	0.0109	0.0287	0.0577	0.0972	0.1442	0.1935	0.2388	0.2734	0.2918	0.2903	0.2679	0.2269	0.1730	0.1147	0.0617	0.0230	0.0036
	5	0.0000+	0.0000+	0.0002	0.0012	0.0043	0.0115	0.0250	0.0466	0.0774	0.1172	0.1641	0.2140	0.2613	0.2985	0.3177	0.3115	0.2753	0.2097	0.1240	0.0406
	6	0.0000+	0.0000+	0.0000+	0.0001	0.0004	0.0013	0.0036	0.0084	0.0172	0.0320	0.0547	0.0872	0.1306	0.1848	0.2471	0.3115	0.3670	0.3960	0.3720	0.2573
	7	0.0000+	0.0000+	0.0000+	0.0000+	0.0000+	0.0001	0.0002	0.0006	0.0016	0.0037	0.0078	0.0152	0.0280	0.0490	0.0824	0.1335	0.2097	0.3206	0.4783	0.6983

Note: 0.0000+ means the probability is 0.0000 rounded to four decimal places. However, the probability is *not* zero.

TABLE III (*continued*)

		p																			
n	*x*	0.01	0.05	0.10	0.15	0.20	0.25	0.30	0.35	0.40	0.45	0.50	0.55	0.60	0.65	0.70	0.75	0.80	0.85	0.90	0.95
8	0	0.9227	0.6634	0.4305	0.2725	0.1678	0.1001	0.0576	0.0319	0.0168	0.0084	0.0039	0.0017	0.0007	0.0002	0.0001	0.0000+	0.0000+	0.0000+	0.0000+	0.0000+
	1	0.0746	0.2793	0.3826	0.3847	0.3355	0.2670	0.1977	0.1373	0.0896	0.0548	0.0313	0.0164	0.0079	0.0033	0.0012	0.0004	0.0001	0.0000+	0.0000+	0.0000+
	2	0.0026	0.0515	0.1488	0.2376	0.2936	0.3115	0.2965	0.2587	0.2090	0.1569	0.1094	0.0703	0.0413	0.0217	0.0100	0.0038	0.0011	0.0002	0.0000+	0.0000+
	3	0.0001	0.0054	0.0331	0.0839	0.1468	0.2076	0.2541	0.2786	0.2787	0.2568	0.2188	0.1719	0.1239	0.0808	0.0467	0.0231	0.0092	0.0026	0.0004	0.0000+
	4	0.0000+	0.0004	0.0046	0.0185	0.0459	0.0865	0.1361	0.1875	0.2322	0.2627	0.2734	0.2627	0.2322	0.1875	0.1361	0.0865	0.0459	0.0185	0.0046	0.0004
	5	0.0000+	0.0000+	0.0004	0.0026	0.0092	0.0231	0.0467	0.0808	0.1239	0.1719	0.2188	0.2568	0.2787	0.2786	0.2541	0.2076	0.1468	0.0839	0.0331	0.0054
	6	0.0000+	0.0000+	0.0000+	0.0002	0.0011	0.0038	0.0100	0.0217	0.0413	0.0703	0.1094	0.1569	0.2090	0.2587	0.2965	0.3115	0.2936	0.2376	0.1488	0.0515
	7	0.0000+	0.0000+	0.0000+	0.0000+	0.0001	0.0004	0.0012	0.0033	0.0079	0.0164	0.0313	0.0548	0.0896	0.1373	0.1977	0.2670	0.3355	0.3847	0.3826	0.2793
	8	0.0000+	0.0000+	0.0000+	0.0000+	0.0000+	0.0000+	0.0001	0.0002	0.0007	0.0017	0.0039	0.0084	0.0168	0.0319	0.0576	0.1001	0.1678	0.2725	0.4305	0.6634
9	0	0.9135	0.6302	0.3874	0.2316	0.1342	0.0751	0.0404	0.0207	0.0101	0.0046	0.0020	0.0008	0.0003	0.0001	0.0000+	0.0000+	0.0000+	0.0000+	0.0000+	0.0000+
	1	0.0830	0.2985	0.3874	0.3679	0.3020	0.2253	0.1556	0.1004	0.0605	0.0339	0.0176	0.0083	0.0035	0.0013	0.0004	0.0001	0.0000+	0.0000+	0.0000+	0.0000+
	2	0.0034	0.0629	0.1722	0.2597	0.3020	0.3003	0.2668	0.2162	0.1612	0.1110	0.0703	0.0407	0.0212	0.0098	0.0039	0.0012	0.0003	0.0000+	0.0000+	0.0000+
	3	0.0001	0.0077	0.0446	0.1069	0.1762	0.2336	0.2668	0.2716	0.2508	0.2119	0.1641	0.1160	0.0743	0.0424	0.0210	0.0087	0.0028	0.0006	0.0001	0.0000+
	4	0.0000+	0.0006	0.0074	0.0283	0.0661	0.1168	0.1715	0.2194	0.2508	0.2600	0.2461	0.2128	0.1672	0.1181	0.0735	0.0389	0.0165	0.0050	0.0008	0.0000+
	5	0.0000+	0.0000+	0.0008	0.0050	0.0165	0.0389	0.0735	0.1181	0.1672	0.2128	0.2461	0.2600	0.2508	0.2194	0.1715	0.1168	0.0661	0.0283	0.0074	0.0006
	6	0.0000+	0.0000+	0.0001	0.0006	0.0028	0.0087	0.0210	0.0424	0.0743	0.1160	0.1641	0.2119	0.2508	0.2716	0.2668	0.2336	0.1762	0.1069	0.0446	0.0077
	7	0.0000+	0.0000+	0.0000+	0.0000+	0.0003	0.0012	0.0039	0.0098	0.0212	0.0407	0.0703	0.1110	0.1612	0.2162	0.2668	0.3003	0.3020	0.2597	0.1722	0.0629
	8	0.0000+	0.0000+	0.0000+	0.0000+	0.0000+	0.0001	0.0004	0.0013	0.0035	0.0083	0.0176	0.0339	0.0605	0.1004	0.1556	0.2253	0.3020	0.3679	0.3874	0.2985
	9	0.0000+	0.0000+	0.0000+	0.0000+	0.0000+	0.0000+	0.0000+	0.0001	0.0003	0.0008	0.0020	0.0046	0.0101	0.0207	0.0404	0.0751	0.1342	0.2316	0.3874	0.6302
10	0	0.9044	0.5987	0.3487	0.1969	0.1074	0.0563	0.0282	0.0135	0.0060	0.0025	0.0010	0.0003	0.0001	0.0000+	0.0000+	0.0000+	0.0000+	0.0000+	0.0000+	0.0000+
	1	0.0914	0.3151	0.3874	0.3474	0.2684	0.1877	0.1211	0.0725	0.0403	0.0207	0.0098	0.0042	0.0016	0.0005	0.0001	0.0000+	0.0000+	0.0000+	0.0000+	0.0000+
	2	0.0042	0.0746	0.1937	0.2759	0.3020	0.2816	0.2335	0.1757	0.1209	0.0763	0.0439	0.0229	0.0106	0.0043	0.0014	0.0004	0.0001	0.0000+	0.0000+	0.0000+
	3	0.0001	0.0105	0.0574	0.1298	0.2013	0.2503	0.2668	0.2522	0.2150	0.1665	0.1172	0.0746	0.0425	0.0212	0.0090	0.0031	0.0008	0.0001	0.0000+	0.0000+
	4	0.0000+	0.0010	0.0112	0.0401	0.0881	0.1460	0.2001	0.2377	0.2508	0.2384	0.2051	0.1596	0.1115	0.0689	0.0368	0.0162	0.0055	0.0012	0.0001	0.0000+
	5	0.0000+	0.0001	0.0015	0.0085	0.0264	0.0584	0.1029	0.1536	0.2007	0.2340	0.2461	0.2340	0.2007	0.1536	0.1029	0.0584	0.0264	0.0085	0.0015	0.0001
	6	0.0000+	0.0000+	0.0001	0.0012	0.0055	0.0162	0.0368	0.0689	0.1115	0.1596	0.2051	0.2384	0.2508	0.2377	0.2001	0.1460	0.0881	0.0401	0.0112	0.0010
	7	0.0000+	0.0000+	0.0000+	0.0001	0.0008	0.0031	0.0090	0.0212	0.0425	0.0746	0.1172	0.1665	0.2150	0.2522	0.2668	0.2503	0.2013	0.1298	0.0574	0.0105
	8	0.0000+	0.0000+	0.0000+	0.0000+	0.0001	0.0004	0.0014	0.0043	0.0106	0.0229	0.0439	0.0763	0.1209	0.1757	0.2335	0.2816	0.3020	0.2759	0.1937	0.0746
	9	0.0000+	0.0000+	0.0000+	0.0000+	0.0000+	0.0000+	0.0001	0.0005	0.0016	0.0042	0.0098	0.0207	0.0403	0.0725	0.1211	0.1877	0.2684	0.3474	0.3874	0.3151
	10	0.0000+	0.0000+	0.0000+	0.0000+	0.0000+	0.0000+	0.0000+	0.0000+	0.0001	0.0003	0.0010	0.0025	0.0060	0.0135	0.0282	0.0563	0.1074	0.1969	0.3487	0.5987

Note: 0.0000+ means the probability is 0.0000 rounded to four decimal places. However, the probability is *not* zero.

TABLE III (*continued*)

		p																			
n	***x***	**0.01**	**0.05**	**0.10**	**0.15**	**0.20**	**0.25**	**0.30**	**0.35**	**0.40**	**0.45**	**0.50**	**0.55**	**0.60**	**0.65**	**0.70**	**0.75**	**0.80**	**0.85**	**0.90**	**0.95**
11	0	0.8953	0.5688	0.3138	0.1673	0.0859	0.0422	0.0198	0.0088	0.0036	0.0014	0.0005	0.0002	0.0000+	0.0000+	0.0000+	0.0000+	0.0000+	0.0000+	0.0000+	0.0000+
	1	0.0995	0.3293	0.3835	0.3248	0.2362	0.1549	0.0932	0.0518	0.0266	0.0125	0.0054	0.0021	0.0007	0.0002	0.0000+	0.0000+	0.0000+	0.0000+	0.0000+	0.0000+
	2	0.0050	0.0867	0.2131	0.2866	0.2953	0.2581	0.1998	0.1395	0.0887	0.0513	0.0269	0.0126	0.0052	0.0018	0.0005	0.0001	0.0000+	0.0000+	0.0000+	0.0000+
	3	0.0002	0.0137	0.0710	0.1517	0.2215	0.2581	0.2568	0.2254	0.1774	0.1259	0.0806	0.0462	0.0234	0.0102	0.0037	0.0011	0.0002	0.0000+	0.0000+	0.0000+
	4	0.0000+	0.0014	0.0158	0.0536	0.1107	0.1721	0.2201	0.2428	0.2365	0.2060	0.1611	0.1128	0.0701	0.0379	0.0173	0.0064	0.0017	0.0003	0.0000+	0.0000+
	5	0.0000+	0.0001	0.0025	0.0132	0.0388	0.0803	0.1321	0.1830	0.2207	0.2360	0.2256	0.1931	0.1471	0.0985	0.0566	0.0268	0.0097	0.0023	0.0003	0.0000+
	6	0.0000+	0.0000+	0.0003	0.0023	0.0097	0.0268	0.0566	0.0985	0.1471	0.1931	0.2256	0.2360	0.2207	0.1830	0.1321	0.0803	0.0388	0.0132	0.0025	0.0001
	7	0.0000+	0.0000+	0.0000+	0.0003	0.0017	0.0064	0.0173	0.0379	0.0701	0.1128	0.1611	0.2060	0.2365	0.2428	0.2201	0.1721	0.1107	0.0536	0.0158	0.0014
	8	0.0000+	0.0000+	0.0000+	0.0000+	0.0002	0.0011	0.0037	0.0102	0.0234	0.0462	0.0806	0.1259	0.1774	0.2254	0.2568	0.2581	0.2215	0.1517	0.0710	0.0137
	9	0.0000+	0.0000+	0.0000+	0.0000+	0.0000+	0.0001	0.0005	0.0018	0.0052	0.0126	0.0269	0.0513	0.0887	0.1395	0.1998	0.2581	0.2953	0.2866	0.2131	0.0867
	10	0.0000+	0.0000+	0.0000+	0.0000+	0.0000+	0.0000+	0.0000+	0.0002	0.0007	0.0021	0.0054	0.0125	0.0266	0.0518	0.0932	0.1549	0.2362	0.3248	0.3835	0.3293
	11	0.0000+	0.0000+	0.0000+	0.0000+	0.0000+	0.0000+	0.0000+	0.0000+	0.0000+	0.0002	0.0005	0.0014	0.0036	0.0088	0.0198	0.0422	0.0859	0.1673	0.3138	0.5688
12	0	0.8864	0.5404	0.2824	0.1422	0.0687	0.0317	0.0138	0.0057	0.0022	0.0008	0.0002	0.0001	0.0000+	0.0000+	0.0000+	0.0000+	0.0000+	0.0000+	0.0000+	0.0000+
	1	0.1074	0.3413	0.3766	0.3012	0.2062	0.1267	0.0712	0.0368	0.0174	0.0075	0.0029	0.0010	0.0003	0.0001	0.0000+	0.0000+	0.0000+	0.0000+	0.0000+	0.0000+
	2	0.0060	0.0988	0.2301	0.2924	0.2835	0.2323	0.1678	0.1088	0.0639	0.0339	0.0161	0.0068	0.0025	0.0008	0.0002	0.0000+	0.0000+	0.0000+	0.0000+	0.0000+
	3	0.0002	0.0173	0.0852	0.1720	0.2362	0.2581	0.2397	0.1954	0.1419	0.0923	0.0537	0.0277	0.0125	0.0048	0.0015	0.0004	0.0001	0.0000+	0.0000+	0.0000+
	4	0.0000+	0.0021	0.0213	0.0683	0.1329	0.1936	0.2311	0.2367	0.2128	0.1700	0.1208	0.0762	0.0420	0.0199	0.0078	0.0024	0.0005	0.0001	0.0000+	0.0000+
	5	0.0000+	0.0002	0.0038	0.0193	0.0532	0.1032	0.1585	0.2039	0.2270	0.2225	0.1934	0.1489	0.1009	0.0591	0.0291	0.0115	0.0033	0.0006	0.0000+	0.0000+
	6	0.0000+	0.0000+	0.0005	0.0040	0.0155	0.0401	0.0792	0.1281	0.1766	0.2124	0.2256	0.2124	0.1766	0.1281	0.0792	0.0401	0.0155	0.0040	0.0005	0.0000+
	7	0.0000+	0.0000+	0.0000+	0.0006	0.0033	0.0115	0.0291	0.0591	0.1009	0.1489	0.1934	0.2225	0.2270	0.2039	0.1585	0.1032	0.0532	0.0193	0.0038	0.0002
	8	0.0000+	0.0000+	0.0000+	0.0001	0.0005	0.0024	0.0078	0.0199	0.0420	0.0762	0.1208	0.1700	0.2128	0.2367	0.2311	0.1936	0.1329	0.0683	0.0213	0.0021
	9	0.0000+	0.0000+	0.0000+	0.0000+	0.0001	0.0004	0.0015	0.0048	0.0125	0.0277	0.0537	0.0923	0.1419	0.1954	0.2397	0.2581	0.2362	0.1720	0.0852	0.0173
	10	0.0000+	0.0000+	0.0000+	0.0000+	0.0000+	0.0000+	0.0002	0.0008	0.0025	0.0068	0.0161	0.0339	0.0639	0.1088	0.1678	0.2323	0.2835	0.2924	0.2301	0.0988
	11	0.0000+	0.0000+	0.0000+	0.0000+	0.0000+	0.0000+	0.0000+	0.0001	0.0003	0.0010	0.0029	0.0075	0.0174	0.0368	0.0712	0.1267	0.2062	0.3012	0.3766	0.3413
	12	0.0000+	0.0000+	0.0000+	0.0000+	0.0000+	0.0000+	0.0000+	0.0000+	0.0000+	0.0001	0.0002	0.0008	0.0022	0.0057	0.0138	0.0317	0.0687	0.1422	0.2824	0.5404

Note: 0.0000+ means the probability is 0.0000 rounded to four decimal places. However, the probability is *not* zero.

TABLE III (*continued*)

		p																			
n	***x***	**0.01**	**0.05**	**0.10**	**0.15**	**0.20**	**0.25**	**0.30**	**0.35**	**0.40**	**0.45**	**0.50**	**0.55**	**0.60**	**0.65**	**0.70**	**0.75**	**0.80**	**0.85**	**0.90**	**0.95**
15	0	0.8601	0.4633	0.2059	0.0874	0.0352	0.0134	0.0047	0.0016	0.0005	0.0001	0.0000+	0.0000+	0.0000+	0.0000+	0.0000+	0.0000+	0.0000+	0.0000+	0.0000+	0.0000+
	1	0.1303	0.3658	0.3432	0.2312	0.1319	0.0668	0.0305	0.0126	0.0047	0.0016	0.0005	0.0001	0.0000+	0.0000+	0.0000+	0.0000+	0.0000+	0.0000+	0.0000+	0.0000+
	2	0.0092	0.1348	0.2669	0.2856	0.2309	0.1559	0.0916	0.0476	0.0219	0.0090	0.0032	0.0010	0.0003	0.0001	0.0000+	0.0000+	0.0000+	0.0000+	0.0000+	0.0000+
	3	0.0004	0.0307	0.1285	0.2184	0.2501	0.2252	0.1700	0.1110	0.0634	0.0318	0.0139	0.0052	0.0016	0.0004	0.0001	0.0000+	0.0000+	0.0000+	0.0000+	0.0000+
	4	0.0000+	0.0049	0.0428	0.1156	0.1876	0.2252	0.2186	0.1792	0.1268	0.0780	0.0417	0.0191	0.0074	0.0024	0.0006	0.0001	0.0000+	0.0000+	0.0000+	0.0000+
	5	0.0000+	0.0006	0.0105	0.0449	0.1032	0.1651	0.2061	0.2123	0.1859	0.1404	0.0916	0.0515	0.0245	0.0096	0.0030	0.0007	0.0001	0.0000+	0.0000+	0.0000+
	6	0.0000+	0.0000+	0.0019	0.0132	0.0430	0.0917	0.1472	0.1906	0.2066	0.1914	0.1527	0.1048	0.0612	0.0298	0.0116	0.0034	0.0007	0.0001	0.0000+	0.0000+
	7	0.0000+	0.0000+	0.0003	0.0030	0.0138	0.0393	0.0811	0.1319	0.1771	0.2013	0.1964	0.1647	0.1181	0.0710	0.0348	0.0131	0.0035	0.0005	0.0000+	0.0000+
	8	0.0000+	0.0000+	0.0000+	0.0005	0.0035	0.0131	0.0348	0.0710	0.1181	0.1647	0.1964	0.2013	0.1771	0.1319	0.0811	0.0393	0.0138	0.0030	0.0003	0.0000+
	9	0.0000+	0.0000+	0.0000+	0.0001	0.0007	0.0034	0.0116	0.0298	0.0612	0.1048	0.1527	0.1914	0.2066	0.1906	0.1472	0.0917	0.0430	0.0132	0.0019	0.0000+
	10	0.0000+	0.0000+	0.0000+	0.0000+	0.0001	0.0007	0.0030	0.0096	0.0245	0.0515	0.0916	0.1404	0.1859	0.2123	0.2061	0.1651	0.1032	0.0449	0.0105	0.0006
	11	0.0000+	0.0000+	0.0000+	0.0000+	0.0000+	0.0001	0.0006	0.0024	0.0074	0.0191	0.0417	0.0780	0.1268	0.1792	0.2186	0.2252	0.1876	0.1156	0.0428	0.0049
	12	0.0000+	0.0000+	0.0000+	0.0000+	0.0000+	0.0000+	0.0001	0.0004	0.0016	0.0052	0.0139	0.0318	0.0634	0.1110	0.1700	0.2252	0.2501	0.2184	0.1285	0.0307
	13	0.0000+	0.0000+	0.0000+	0.0000+	0.0000+	0.0000+	0.0000+	0.0001	0.0003	0.0010	0.0032	0.0090	0.0219	0.0476	0.0916	0.1559	0.2309	0.2856	0.2669	0.1348
	14	0.0000+	0.0000+	0.0000+	0.0000+	0.0000+	0.0000+	0.0000+	0.0000+	0.0000+	0.0001	0.0005	0.0016	0.0047	0.0126	0.0305	0.0668	0.1319	0.2312	0.3432	0.3658
	15	0.0000+	0.0000+	0.0000+	0.0000+	0.0000+	0.0000+	0.0000+	0.0000+	0.0000+	0.0000+	0.0000+	0.0001	0.0005	0.0016	0.0047	0.0134	0.0352	0.0874	0.2059	0.4633
20	0	0.8179	0.3585	0.1216	0.0388	0.0115	0.0032	0.0008	0.0002	0.0000+	0.0000+	0.0000+	0.0000+	0.0000+	0.0000+	0.0000+	0.0000+	0.0000+	0.0000+	0.0000+	0.0000+
	1	0.1652	0.3774	0.2702	0.1368	0.0576	0.0211	0.0068	0.0020	0.0005	0.0001	0.0000+	0.0000+	0.0000+	0.0000+	0.0000+	0.0000+	0.0000+	0.0000+	0.0000+	0.0000+
	2	0.0159	0.1887	0.2852	0.2293	0.1369	0.0669	0.0278	0.0100	0.0031	0.0008	0.0002	0.0000+	0.0000+	0.0000+	0.0000+	0.0000+	0.0000+	0.0000+	0.0000+	0.0000+
	3	0.0010	0.0596	0.1901	0.2428	0.2054	0.1339	0.0716	0.0323	0.0123	0.0040	0.0011	0.0002	0.0000+	0.0000+	0.0000+	0.0000+	0.0000+	0.0000+	0.0000+	0.0000+
	4	0.0000+	0.0133	0.0898	0.1821	0.2182	0.1897	0.1304	0.0738	0.0350	0.0139	0.0046	0.0013	0.0003	0.0000+	0.0000+	0.0000+	0.0000+	0.0000+	0.0000+	0.0000+
	5	0.0000+	0.0022	0.0319	0.1028	0.1746	0.2023	0.1789	0.1272	0.0746	0.0365	0.0148	0.0049	0.0013	0.0003	0.0000+	0.0000+	0.0000+	0.0000+	0.0000+	0.0000+
	6	0.0000+	0.0003	0.0089	0.0454	0.1091	0.1686	0.1916	0.1712	0.1244	0.0746	0.0370	0.0150	0.0049	0.0012	0.0002	0.0000+	0.0000+	0.0000+	0.0000+	0.0000+
	7	0.0000+	0.0000+	0.0020	0.0160	0.0545	0.1124	0.1643	0.1844	0.1659	0.1221	0.0739	0.0366	0.0146	0.0045	0.0010	0.0002	0.0000+	0.0000+	0.0000+	0.0000+
	8	0.0000+	0.0000+	0.0004	0.0046	0.0222	0.0609	0.1144	0.1614	0.1797	0.1623	0.1201	0.0727	0.0355	0.0136	0.0039	0.0008	0.0001	0.0000+	0.0000+	0.0000+
	9	0.0000+	0.0000+	0.0001	0.0011	0.0074	0.0271	0.0654	0.1158	0.1597	0.1771	0.1602	0.1185	0.0710	0.0336	0.0120	0.0030	0.0005	0.0000+	0.0000+	0.0000+
	10	0.0000+	0.0000+	0.0000+	0.0002	0.0020	0.0099	0.0308	0.0686	0.1171	0.1593	0.1762	0.1593	0.1171	0.0686	0.0308	0.0099	0.0020	0.0002	0.0000+	0.0000+
	11	0.0000+	0.0000+	0.0000+	0.0000+	0.0005	0.0030	0.0120	0.0336	0.0710	0.1185	0.1602	0.1771	0.1597	0.1158	0.0654	0.0271	0.0074	0.0011	0.0001	0.0000+
	12	0.0000+	0.0000+	0.0000+	0.0000+	0.0001	0.0008	0.0039	0.0136	0.0355	0.0727	0.1201	0.1623	0.1797	0.1614	0.1144	0.0609	0.0222	0.0046	0.0004	0.0000+
	13	0.0000+	0.0000+	0.0000+	0.0000+	0.0000+	0.0002	0.0010	0.0045	0.0146	0.0366	0.0739	0.1221	0.1659	0.1844	0.1643	0.1124	0.0545	0.0160	0.0020	0.0000+
	14	0.0000+	0.0000+	0.0000+	0.0000+	0.0000+	0.0000+	0.0002	0.0012	0.0049	0.0150	0.0370	0.0746	0.1244	0.1712	0.1916	0.1686	0.1091	0.0454	0.0089	0.0003
	15	0.0000+	0.0000+	0.0000+	0.0000+	0.0000+	0.0000+	0.0000+	0.0003	0.0013	0.0049	0.0148	0.0365	0.0746	0.1272	0.1789	0.2023	0.1746	0.1028	0.0319	0.0022
	16	0.0000+	0.0000+	0.0000+	0.0000+	0.0000+	0.0000+	0.0000+	0.0000+	0.0003	0.0013	0.0046	0.0139	0.0350	0.0738	0.1304	0.1897	0.2182	0.1821	0.0898	0.0133
	17	0.0000+	0.0000+	0.0000+	0.0000+	0.0000+	0.0000+	0.0000+	0.0000+	0.0000+	0.0002	0.0011	0.0040	0.0123	0.0323	0.0716	0.1339	0.2054	0.2428	0.1901	0.0596
	18	0.0000+	0.0000+	0.0000+	0.0000+	0.0000+	0.0000+	0.0000+	0.0000+	0.0000+	0.0000+	0.0002	0.0008	0.0031	0.0100	0.0278	0.0669	0.1369	0.2293	0.2852	0.1887
	19	0.0000+	0.0000+	0.0000+	0.0000+	0.0000+	0.0000+	0.0000+	0.0000+	0.0000+	0.0000+	0.0000+	0.0001	0.0005	0.0020	0.0068	0.0211	0.0576	0.1368	0.2702	0.3774
	20	0.0000+	0.0000+	0.0000+	0.0000+	0.0000+	0.0000+	0.0000+	0.0000+	0.0000+	0.0000+	0.0000+	0.0000+	0.0000+	0.0002	0.0008	0.0032	0.0115	0.0388	0.1216	0.3585

Note: 0.0000+ means the probability is 0.0000 rounded to four decimal places. However, the probability is *not* zero.

TABLE IV

Cumulative Binomial Probability Distribution

This table computes the cumulative probability of obtaining x successes in n trials of a binomial experiment with probability of success p.

		p																			
n	x	0.01	0.05	0.10	0.15	0.20	0.25	0.30	0.35	0.40	0.45	0.50	0.55	0.60	0.65	0.70	0.75	0.80	0.85	0.90	0.95
2	0	0.9801	0.9025	0.8100	0.7225	0.6400	0.5625	0.4900	0.4225	0.3600	0.3025	0.2500	0.2025	0.1600	0.1225	0.0900	0.0625	0.0400	0.0225	0.0100	0.0025
	1	0.9999	0.9975	0.9900	0.9775	0.9600	0.9375	0.9100	0.8775	0.8400	0.7975	0.7500	0.6975	0.6400	0.5775	0.5100	0.4375	0.3600	0.2775	0.1900	0.0975
	2	1	1	1	1	1	1	1	1	1	1	1	1	1	1	1	1	1	1	1	1
3	0	0.9703	0.8574	0.7290	0.6141	0.5120	0.4219	0.3430	0.2746	0.2160	0.1664	0.1250	0.0911	0.0640	0.0429	0.0270	0.0156	0.0080	0.0034	0.0010	0.0001
	1	0.9997	0.9928	0.9720	0.9393	0.8960	0.8438	0.7840	0.7183	0.6480	0.5748	0.5000	0.4253	0.3520	0.2818	0.2160	0.1563	0.1040	0.0608	0.0280	0.0073
	2	1.0000–	0.9999	0.9990	0.9966	0.9920	0.9844	0.9730	0.9571	0.9360	0.9089	0.8750	0.8336	0.7840	0.7254	0.6570	0.5781	0.4880	0.3859	0.2710	0.1426
	3	1	1	1	1	1	1	1	1	1	1	1	1	1	1	1	1	1	1	1	1
4	0	0.9606	0.8145	0.6561	0.5220	0.4096	0.3164	0.2401	0.1785	0.1296	0.0915	0.0625	0.0410	0.0256	0.0150	0.0081	0.0039	0.0016	0.0005	0.0001	0.0000+
	1	0.9994	0.9860	0.9477	0.8905	0.8192	0.7383	0.6517	0.5630	0.4752	0.3910	0.3125	0.2415	0.1792	0.1265	0.0837	0.0508	0.0272	0.0120	0.0037	0.0005
	2	1.0000–	0.9995	0.9963	0.9880	0.9728	0.9492	0.9163	0.8735	0.8208	0.7585	0.6875	0.6090	0.5248	0.4370	0.3483	0.2617	0.1808	0.1095	0.0523	0.0140
	3	1.0000–	1.0000–	0.9999	0.9995	0.9984	0.9961	0.9919	0.9850	0.9744	0.9590	0.9375	0.9085	0.8704	0.8215	0.7599	0.6836	0.5904	0.4780	0.3439	0.1855
	4	1	1	1	1	1	1	1	1	1	1	1	1	1	1	1	1	1	1	1	1
5	0	0.9510	0.7738	0.5905	0.4437	0.3277	0.2373	0.1681	0.1160	0.0778	0.0503	0.0313	0.0185	0.0102	0.0053	0.0024	0.0010	0.0003	0.0001	0.0000+	0.0000+
	1	0.9990	0.9774	0.9185	0.8352	0.7373	0.6328	0.5282	0.4284	0.3370	0.2562	0.1875	0.1312	0.0870	0.0540	0.0308	0.0156	0.0067	0.0022	0.0005	0.0000+
	2	1.0000–	0.9988	0.9914	0.9734	0.9421	0.8965	0.8369	0.7648	0.6826	0.5931	0.5000	0.4069	0.3174	0.2352	0.1631	0.1035	0.0579	0.0266	0.0086	0.0012
	3	1.0000–	1.0000–	0.9995	0.9978	0.9933	0.9844	0.9692	0.9460	0.9130	0.8688	0.8125	0.7438	0.6630	0.5716	0.4718	0.3672	0.2627	0.1648	0.0815	0.0226
	4	1.0000–	1.0000–	1.0000–	0.9999	0.9997	0.9990	0.9976	0.9947	0.9898	0.9815	0.9688	0.9497	0.9222	0.8840	0.8319	0.7627	0.6723	0.5563	0.4095	0.2262
	5	1	1	1	1	1	1	1	1	1	1	1	1	1	1	1	1	1	1	1	1
6	0	0.9415	0.7351	0.5314	0.3771	0.2621	0.1780	0.1176	0.0754	0.0467	0.0277	0.0156	0.0083	0.0041	0.0018	0.0007	0.0002	0.0001	0.0000+	0.0000+	0.0000+
	1	0.9985	0.9672	0.8857	0.7765	0.6554	0.5339	0.4202	0.3191	0.2333	0.1636	0.1094	0.0692	0.0410	0.0223	0.0109	0.0046	0.0016	0.0004	0.0001	0.0000+
	2	1.0000–	0.9978	0.9842	0.9527	0.9011	0.8306	0.7443	0.6471	0.5443	0.4415	0.3438	0.2553	0.1792	0.1174	0.0705	0.0376	0.0170	0.0059	0.0013	0.0001
	3	1.0000–	0.9999	0.9987	0.9941	0.9830	0.9624	0.9295	0.8826	0.8208	0.7447	0.6563	0.5585	0.4557	0.3529	0.2557	0.1694	0.0989	0.0473	0.0159	0.0022
	4	1.0000–	1.0000–	0.9999	0.9996	0.9984	0.9954	0.9891	0.9777	0.9590	0.9308	0.8906	0.8364	0.7667	0.6809	0.5798	0.4661	0.3446	0.2235	0.1143	0.0328
	5	1.0000–	1.0000–	1.0000–	1.0000–	0.9999	0.9998	0.9993	0.9982	0.9959	0.9917	0.9844	0.9723	0.9533	0.9246	0.8824	0.8220	0.7379	0.6229	0.4686	0.2649
	6	1	1	1	1	1	1	1	1	1	1	1	1	1	1	1	1	1	1	1	1
7	0	0.9321	0.6983	0.4783	0.3206	0.2097	0.1335	0.0824	0.0490	0.0280	0.0152	0.0078	0.0037	0.0016	0.0006	0.0002	0.0001	0.0000+	0.0000+	0.0000+	0.0000+
	1	0.9980	0.9556	0.8503	0.7166	0.5767	0.4449	0.3294	0.2338	0.1586	0.1024	0.0625	0.0357	0.0188	0.0090	0.0038	0.0013	0.0004	0.0001	0.0000+	0.0000+
	2	1.0000–	0.9962	0.9743	0.9262	0.8520	0.7564	0.6471	0.5323	0.4199	0.3164	0.2266	0.1529	0.0963	0.0556	0.0288	0.0129	0.0047	0.0012	0.0002	0.0000+
	3	1.0000–	0.9998	0.9973	0.9879	0.9667	0.9294	0.8740	0.8002	0.7102	0.6083	0.5000	0.3917	0.2898	0.1998	0.1260	0.0706	0.0333	0.0121	0.0027	0.0002
	4	1.0000–	1.0000–	0.9998	0.9988	0.9953	0.9871	0.9712	0.9444	0.9037	0.8471	0.7734	0.6836	0.5801	0.4677	0.3529	0.2436	0.1480	0.0738	0.0257	0.0038
	5	1.0000–	1.0000–	1.0000–	0.9999	0.9996	0.9987	0.9962	0.9910	0.9812	0.9643	0.9375	0.8976	0.8414	0.7662	0.6706	0.5551	0.4233	0.2834	0.1497	0.0444
	6	1.0000–	1.0000–	1.0000–	1.0000–	1.0000-	0.9999	0.9998	0.9994	0.9984	0.9963	0.9922	0.9848	0.9720	0.9510	0.9176	0.8665	0.7903	0.6794	0.5217	0.3017
	7	1	1	1	1	1	1	1	1	1	1	1	1	1	1	1	1	1	1	1	1

Note: 0.0000+ means the probability is 0.0000 rounded to four decimal places. However, the probability is *not* zero.
1.0000– means the probability is 1.0000 rounded to four decimal places. However, the probability is *not* one.

TABLE IV (*continued*)

		p																			
n	*x*	0.01	0.05	0.10	0.15	0.20	0.25	0.30	0.35	0.40	0.45	0.50	0.55	0.60	0.65	0.70	0.75	0.80	0.85	0.90	0.95
8	0	0.9227	0.6634	0.4305	0.2725	0.1678	0.1001	0.0576	0.0319	0.0168	0.0084	0.0039	0.0017	0.0007	0.0002	0.0001	0.0000+	0.0000+	0.0000+	0.0000+	0.0000+
	1	0.9973	0.9428	0.8131	0.6572	0.5033	0.3671	0.2553	0.1691	0.1064	0.0632	0.0352	0.0181	0.0085	0.0036	0.0013	0.0004	0.0001	0.0000+	0.0000+	0.0000+
	2	0.9999	0.9942	0.9619	0.8948	0.7969	0.6785	0.5518	0.4278	0.3154	0.2201	0.1445	0.0885	0.0498	0.0253	0.0113	0.0042	0.0012	0.0002	0.0000+	0.0000+
	3	1.0000-	0.9996	0.9950	0.9786	0.9437	0.8862	0.8059	0.7064	0.5941	0.4770	0.3633	0.2604	0.1737	0.1061	0.0580	0.0273	0.0104	0.0029	0.0004	0.0000+
	4	1.0000–	1.0000–	0.9996	0.9971	0.9896	0.9727	0.9420	0.8389	0.8263	0.7396	0.6367	0.5230	0.4059	0.2936	0.1941	0.1138	0.0563	0.0214	0.0050	0.0004
	5	1.0000–	1.0000–	1.0000–	0.9998	0.9988	0.9958	0.9887	0.9747	0.9502	0.9115	0.8555	0.7799	0.6846	0.5722	0.4482	0.3215	0.2031	0.1052	0.0381	0.0058
	6	1.0000–	1.0000–	1.0000–	1.0000–	0.9999	0.9996	0.9987	0.9964	0.9915	0.9819	0.9648	0.9368	0.8936	0.8309	0.7447	0.6329	0.4967	0.3428	0.1869	0.0572
	7	1.0000–	1.0000–	1.0000–	1.0000–	1.0000-	1.0000–	0.9999	0.9998	0.9993	0.9983	0.9961	0.9916	0.9832	0.9681	0.9424	0.8999	0.8322	0.7275	0.5695	0.3366
	8	1	1	1	1	1	1	1	1	1	1	1	1	1	1	1	1	1	1	1	1
9	0	0.9135	0.6302	0.3874	0.2316	0.1342	0.0751	0.0404	0.0207	0.0101	0.0046	0.0020	0.0008	0.0003	0.0001	0.0000+	0.0000+	0.0000+	0.0000+	0.0000+	0.0000+
	1	0.9966	0.9288	0.7748	0.5995	0.4362	0.3003	0.1960	0.1211	0.0705	0.0385	0.0195	0.0091	0.0038	0.0014	0.0004	0.0001	0.0000+	0.0000+	0.0000+	0.0000+
	2	0.9999	0.9916	0.9470	0.8591	0.7382	0.6007	0.4628	0.3373	0.2318	0.1495	0.0898	0.0498	0.0250	0.0112	0.0043	0.0013	0.0003	0.0000+	0.0000+	0.0000+
	3	1.0000–	0.9994	0.9917	0.9661	0.9144	0.8343	0.7297	0.6089	0.4826	0.3614	0.2539	0.1658	0.0994	0.0536	0.0253	0.0100	0.0031	0.0006	0.0001	0.0000+
	4	1.0000–	1.0000–	0.9991	0.9944	0.9804	0.9511	0.9012	0.8283	0.7334	0.6214	0.5000	0.3786	0.2666	0.1717	0.0988	0.0489	0.0196	0.0056	0.0009	0.0000+
	5	1.0000–	1.0000–	0.9999	0.9994	0.9969	0.9900	0.9747	0.9464	0.9006	0.8342	0.7461	0.6386	0.5174	0.3911	0.2703	0.1657	0.0856	0.0339	0.0083	0.0006
	6	1.0000–	1.0000–	1.0000–	1.0000–	0.9997	0.9987	0.9957	0.9888	0.9750	0.9502	0.9102	0.8505	0.7682	0.6627	0.5372	0.3993	0.2618	0.1409	0.0530	0.0084
	7	1.0000–	1.0000–	1.0000–	1.0000–	1.0000–	0.9999	0.9996	0.9986	0.9962	0.9909	0.9805	0.9615	0.9295	0.8789	0.8040	0.6997	0.5638	0.4005	0.2252	0.0712
	8	1.0000–	1.0000–	1.0000–	1.0000–	1.0000–	1.0000–	1.0000–	0.9999	0.9997	0.9992	0.9980	0.9954	0.9899	0.9793	0.9596	0.9249	0.8658	0.7684	0.6126	0.3698
	9	1	1	1	1	1	1	1	1	1	1	1	1	1	1	1	1	1	1	1	1
10	0	0.9044	0.5987	0.3487	0.1969	0.1074	0.0563	0.0282	0.0135	0.0060	0.0025	0.0010	0.0003	0.0001	0.0000+	0.0000+	0.0000+	0.0000+	0.0000+	0.0000+	0.0000+
	1	0.9957	0.9139	0.7361	0.5443	0.3758	0.2440	0.1493	0.0860	0.0464	0.0233	0.0107	0.0045	0.0017	0.0005	0.0001	0.0000+	0.0000+	0.0000+	0.0000+	0.0000+
	2	0.9999	0.9885	0.9298	0.8202	0.6778	0.5256	0.3828	0.2616	0.1673	0.0996	0.0547	0.0274	0.0123	0.0048	0.0016	0.0004	0.0001	0.0000+	0.0000+	0.0000+
	3	1.0000–	0.9990	0.9872	0.9500	0.8791	0.7759	0.6496	0.5138	0.3823	0.2660	0.1719	0.1020	0.0548	0.0260	0.0106	0.0035	0.0009	0.0001	0.0000+	0.0000+
	4	1.0000–	0.9999	0.9984	0.9901	0.9672	0.9219	0.8497	0.7515	0.6331	0.5044	0.3770	0.2616	0.1662	0.0949	0.0473	0.0197	0.0064	0.0014	0.0001	0.0000+
	5	1.0000–	1.0000–	0.9999	0.9986	0.9936	0.9803	0.9527	0.9051	0.8338	0.7384	0.6230	0.4956	0.3669	0.2485	0.1503	0.0781	0.0328	0.0099	0.0016	0.0001
	6	1.0000–	1.0000–	1.0000–	0.9999	0.9991	0.9965	0.9894	0.9740	0.9452	0.8980	0.8281	0.7340	0.6177	0.4862	0.3504	0.2241	0.1209	0.0500	0.0128	0.0010
	7	1.0000–	1.0000–	1.0000–	1.0000–	0.9999	0.9996	0.9984	0.9952	0.9877	0.9726	0.9453	0.9004	0.8327	0.7384	0.6172	0.4744	0.3222	0.1798	0.0702	0.0115
	8	1.0000–	1.0000–	1.0000–	1.0000–	1.0000–	1.0000–	0.9999	0.9995	0.9983	0.9955	0.9893	0.9767	0.9536	0.9140	0.8507	0.7560	0.6242	0.4557	0.2639	0.0861
	9	1.0000–	1.0000–	1.0000–	1.0000–	1.0000–	1.0000–	1.0000–	1.0000–	0.9999	0.9997	0.9990	0.9975	0.9940	0.9865	0.9718	0.9437	0.8926	0.8031	0.6513	0.4013
	10	1	1	1	1	1	1	1	1	1	1	1	1	1	1	1	1	1	1	1	1

Note: 0.0000+ means the probability is 0.0000 rounded to four decimal places. However, the probability is *not* zero.
1.0000– means the probability is 1.0000 rounded to four decimal places. However, the probability is *not* one.

TABLE IV (*continued*)

		p																			
n	*x*	**0.01**	**0.05**	**0.10**	**0.15**	**0.20**	**0.25**	**0.30**	**0.35**	**0.40**	**0.45**	**0.50**	**0.55**	**0.60**	**0.65**	**0.70**	**0.75**	**0.80**	**0.85**	**0.90**	**0.95**
11	0	0.8953	0.5688	0.3138	0.1673	0.0859	0.0422	0.0198	0.0088	0.0036	0.0014	0.0005	0.0002	0.0000+	0.0000+	0.0000+	0.0000+	0.0000+	0.0000+	0.0000+	0.0000+
	1	0.9948	0.8981	0.6974	0.4922	0.3221	0.1971	0.1130	0.0606	0.0302	0.0139	0.0059	0.0022	0.0007	0.0002	0.0000+	0.0000+	0.0000+	0.0000+	0.0000+	0.0000+
	2	0.9998	0.9848	0.9104	0.7788	0.6174	0.4552	0.3127	0.2001	0.1189	0.0652	0.0327	0.0148	0.0059	0.0020	0.0006	0.0001	0.0000+	0.0000+	0.0000+	0.0000+
	3	1.0000–	0.9984	0.9815	0.9306	0.8389	0.7133	0.5696	0.4256	0.2963	0.1911	0.1133	0.0610	0.0293	0.0122	0.0043	0.0012	0.0002	0.0000+	0.0000+	0.0000+
	4	1.0000–	0.9999	0.9972	0.9841	0.9496	0.8854	0.7897	0.6683	0.5326	0.3971	0.2744	0.1738	0.0994	0.0501	0.0216	0.0076	0.0020	0.0003	0.0000+	0.0000+
	5	1.0000–	1.0000–	0.9997	0.9973	0.9883	0.9657	0.9218	0.8513	0.7535	0.6331	0.5000	0.3669	0.2465	0.1487	0.0782	0.0343	0.0117	0.0027	0.0003	0.0000+
	6	1.0000–	1.0000–	1.0000–	0.9997	0.9980	0.9924	0.9784	0.9499	0.9006	0.8262	0.7256	0.6029	0.4672	0.3317	0.2103	0.1146	0.0504	0.0159	0.0028	0.0001
	7	1.0000–	1.0000–	1.0000–	1.0000–	0.9998	0.9988	0.9957	0.9878	0.9707	0.9390	0.8867	0.8089	0.7037	0.5744	0.4304	0.2867	0.1611	0.0694	0.0185	0.0016
	8	1.0000–	1.0000–	1.0000–	1.0000–	1.0000–	0.9999	0.9994	0.9980	0.9941	0.9852	0.9673	0.9348	0.8811	0.7999	0.6873	0.5448	0.3826	0.2212	0.0896	0.0152
	9	1.0000–	1.0000–	1.0000–	1.0000–	1.0000–	1.0000–	1.0000–	0.9998	0.9993	0.9976	0.9941	0.9861	0.9698	0.9394	0.8870	0.8029	0.6779	0.5078	0.3026	0.1019
	10	1.0000–	1.0000–	1.0000–	1.0000–	1.0000–	1.0000–	1.0000–	1.0000–	1.0000-	0.9996	0.9995	0.9986	0.9964	0.9912	0.9802	0.9578	0.9141	0.8327	0.6862	0.4312
	11	1	1	1	1	1	1	1	1	1	1	1	1	1	1	1	1	1	1	1	1
12	0	0.8864	0.5404	0.2824	0.1422	0.0687	0.0317	0.0138	0.0057	0.0022	0.0008	0.0002	0.0001	0.0000+	0.0000+	0.0000+	0.0000+	0.0000+	0.0000+	0.0000+	0.0000+
	1	0.9938	0.8816	0.6590	0.4435	0.2749	0.1584	0.0850	0.0424	0.0196	0.0083	0.0032	0.0011	0.0003	0.0001	0.0000+	0.0000+	0.0000+	0.0000+	0.0000+	0.0000+
	2	0.9998	0.9804	0.8891	0.7358	0.5583	0.3907	0.2528	0.1513	0.0834	0.0421	0.0193	0.0079	0.0028	0.0008	0.0002	0.0000+	0.0000+	0.0000+	0.0000+	0.0000+
	3	1.0000–	0.9978	0.9744	0.9078	0.7946	0.6488	0.4925	0.3467	0.2253	0.1345	0.0730	0.0356	0.0153	0.0056	0.0017	0.0004	0.0001	0.0000+	0.0000+	0.0000+
	4	1.0000–	0.9998	0.9957	0.9761	0.9274	0.8424	0.7237	0.5833	0.4382	0.3044	0.1938	0.1117	0.0573	0.0255	0.0095	0.0028	0.0006	0.0001	0.0000+	0.0000+
	5	1.0000–	1.0000–	0.9995	0.9954	0.9806	0.9456	0.8822	0.7873	0.6652	0.5269	0.3872	0.2607	0.1582	0.0846	0.0386	0.0143	0.0039	0.0007	0.0001	0.0000+
	6	1.0000–	1.0000–	0.9999	0.9993	0.9961	0.9857	0.9614	0.9154	0.8418	0.7393	0.6128	0.4731	0.3348	0.2127	0.1178	0.0544	0.0194	0.0046	0.0005	0.0000+
	7	1.0000–	1.0000–	1.0000–	0.9999	0.9994	0.9972	0.9905	0.9745	0.9427	0.8883	0.8062	0.6956	0.5618	0.4167	0.2763	0.1576	0.0726	0.0239	0.0043	0.0002
	8	1.0000–	1.0000–	1.0000–	1.0000–	0.9999	0.9996	0.9983	0.9944	0.9847	0.9644	0.9270	0.8655	0.7747	0.6533	0.5075	0.3512	0.2054	0.0922	0.0256	0.0022
	9	1.0000–	1.0000–	1.0000–	1.0000–	1.0000–	1.0000–	0.9998	0.9992	0.9972	0.9921	0.9807	0.9579	0.9166	0.8487	0.7472	0.6093	0.4417	0.2642	0.1109	0.0196
	10	1.0000–	1.0000–	1.0000–	1.0000–	1.0000–	1.0000–	1.0000–	0.9999	0.9997	0.9989	0.9968	0.9917	0.9804	0.9576	0.9150	0.8416	0.7251	0.5565	0.3410	0.1184
	11	1.0000–	1.0000–	1.0000–	1.0000–	1.0000–	1.0000–	1.0000–	1.0000–	1.0000–	0.9999	0.9998	0.9992	0.9978	0.9943	0.9862	0.9683	0.9313	0.8578	0.7176	0.4596
	12	1	1	1	1	1	1	1	1	1	1	1	1	1	1	1	1	1	1	1	1

Note: 0.0000+ means the probability is 0.0000 rounded to four decimal places. However, the probability is *not* zero.
1.0000– means the probability is 1.0000 rounded to four decimal places. However, the probability is *not* one.

TABLE IV (*continued*)

		p																			
n	***x***	**0.01**	**0.05**	**0.10**	**0.15**	**0.20**	**0.25**	**0.30**	**0.35**	**0.40**	**0.45**	**0.50**	**0.55**	**0.60**	**0.65**	**0.70**	**0.75**	**0.80**	**0.85**	**0.90**	**0.95**
15	0	0.8601	0.4633	0.2059	0.0874	0.0352	0.0134	0.0047	0.0016	0.0005	0.0001	0.0000+	0.0000+	0.0000+	0.0000+	0.0000+	0.0000+	0.0000+	0.0000+	0.0000+	0.0000+
	1	0.9904	0.8290	0.5490	0.3186	0.1671	0.0802	0.0353	0.0142	0.0052	0.0017	0.0005	0.0001	0.0000+	0.0000+	0.0000+	0.0000+	0.0000+	0.0000+	0.0000+	0.0000+
	2	0.9996	0.9638	0.8159	0.6042	0.3980	0.2361	0.1268	0.0617	0.0271	0.0107	0.0037	0.0011	0.0003	0.0001	0.0000+	0.0000+	0.0000+	0.0000+	0.0000+	0.0000+
	3	1.0000–	0.9945	0.9444	0.8227	0.6482	0.4613	0.2969	0.1727	0.0905	0.0424	0.0176	0.0063	0.0019	0.0005	0.0001	0.0000+	0.0000+	0.0000+	0.0000+	0.0000+
	4	1.0000–	0.9994	0.9873	0.9383	0.8358	0.6865	0.5155	0.3519	0.2173	0.1204	0.0592	0.0255	0.0093	0.0028	0.0007	0.0001	0.0000+	0.0000+	0.0000+	0.0000+
	5	1.0000–	0.9999	0.9978	0.9832	0.9389	0.8518	0.7216	0.5643	0.4032	0.2608	0.1509	0.0769	0.0338	0.0124	0.0037	0.0008	0.0001	0.0000+	0.0000+	0.0000+
	6	1.0000–	1.0000–	0.9997	0.9964	0.9819	0.9434	0.8689	0.7548	0.6098	0.4522	0.3036	0.1818	0.0950	0.0422	0.0152	0.0042	0.0008	0.0001	0.0000+	0.0000+
	7	1.0000–	1.0000–	1.0000–	0.9994	0.9958	0.9827	0.9500	0.8868	0.7869	0.6535	0.5000	0.3465	0.2131	0.1132	0.0500	0.0173	0.0042	0.0006	0.0000+	0.0000+
	8	1.0000–	1.0000–	1.0000–	0.9999	0.9992	0.9958	0.9848	0.9578	0.9050	0.8182	0.6964	0.5478	0.3902	0.2452	0.1311	0.0566	0.0181	0.0036	0.0003	0.0000+
	9	1.0000–	1.0000–	1.0000–	1.0000–	0.9999	0.9992	0.9963	0.9876	0.9662	0.9231	0.8491	0.7392	0.5968	0.4357	0.2784	0.1484	0.0611	0.0168	0.0022	0.0001
	10	1.0000–	1.0000–	1.0000–	1.0000–	1.0000–	0.9999	0.9993	0.9972	0.9907	0.9745	0.9408	0.8796	0.7827	0.6481	0.4845	0.3135	0.1642	0.0617	0.0127	0.0006
	11	1.0000–	1.0000–	1.0000–	1.0000–	1.0000–	1.0000–	0.9999	0.9995	0.9981	0.9937	0.9824	0.9576	0.9095	0.8273	0.7031	0.5387	0.3518	0.1773	0.0556	0.0055
	12	1.0000–	1.0000–	1.0000–	1.0000–	1.0000–	1.0000–	1.0000–	0.9999	0.9997	0.9989	0.9963	0.9893	0.9729	0.9383	0.8732	0.7639	0.6020	0.3958	0.1841	0.0362
	13	1.0000–	1.0000–	1.0000–	1.0000–	1.0000–	1.0000–	1.0000–	1.0000–	1.0000–	0.9999	0.9995	0.9983	0.9948	0.9858	0.9647	0.9198	0.8329	0.6814	0.4510	0.1710
	14	1.0000–	1.0000–	1.0000–	1.0000–	1.0000–	1.0000–	1.0000–	1.0000–	1.0000–	1.0000–	1.0000–	0.9999	0.9995	0.9984	0.9953	0.9866	0.9648	0.9126	0.7941	0.5367
	15	1	1	1	1	1	1	1	1	1	1	1	1	1	1	1	1	1	1	1	1
20	0	0.8179	0.3585	0.1216	0.0388	0.0115	0.0032	0.0008	0.0002	0.0000+	0.0000+	0.0000+	0.0000+	0.0000+	0.0000+	0.0000+	0.0000+	0.0000+	0.0000+	0.0000+	0.0000+
	1	0.9831	0.7358	0.3917	0.1756	0.0692	0.0243	0.0076	0.0021	0.0005	0.0001	0.0000+	0.0000+	0.0000+	0.0000+	0.0000+	0.0000+	0.0000+	0.0000+	0.0000+	0.0000+
	2	0.9990	0.9245	0.6769	0.4049	0.2061	0.0913	0.0355	0.0121	0.0036	0.0009	0.0002	0.0000+	0.0000+	0.0000+	0.0000+	0.0000+	0.0000+	0.0000+	0.0000+	0.0000+
	3	1.0000–	0.9841	0.8670	0.6477	0.4114	0.2252	0.1071	0.0444	0.0160	0.0049	0.0013	0.0003	0.0000+	0.0000+	0.0000+	0.0000+	0.0000+	0.0000+	0.0000+	0.0000+
	4	1.0000–	0.9974	0.9568	0.8298	0.6296	0.4148	0.2375	0.1182	0.0510	0.0189	0.0059	0.0015	0.0003	0.0000+	0.0000+	0.0000+	0.0000+	0.0000+	0.0000+	0.0000+
	5	1.0000–	0.9997	0.9887	0.9327	0.8042	0.6172	0.4164	0.2454	0.1256	0.0553	0.0207	0.0064	0.0016	0.0003	0.0000+	0.0000+	0.0000+	0.0000+	0.0000+	0.0000+
	6	1.0000–	1.0000–	0.9976	0.9781	0.9133	0.7858	0.6080	0.4166	0.2500	0.1299	0.0577	0.0214	0.0065	0.0015	0.0003	0.0000+	0.0000+	0.0000+	0.0000+	0.0000+
	7	1.0000–	1.0000–	0.9996	0.9941	0.9679	0.8982	0.7723	0.6010	0.4159	0.2520	0.1316	0.0580	0.0210	0.0060	0.0013	0.0002	0.0000+	0.0000+	0.0000+	0.0000+
	8	1.0000–	1.0000–	0.9999	0.9987	0.9900	0.9591	0.8867	0.7624	0.5956	0.4143	0.2517	0.1308	0.0565	0.0196	0.0051	0.0009	0.0001	0.0000+	0.0000+	0.0000+
	9	1.0000–	1.0000–	1.0000–	0.9998	0.9974	0.9861	0.9520	0.8782	0.7553	0.5914	0.4119	0.2493	0.1275	0.0532	0.0171	0.0039	0.0006	0.0000+	0.0000+	0.0000+
	10	1.0000–	1.0000–	1.0000–	1.0000–	0.9994	0.9961	0.9829	0.9468	0.8725	0.7507	0.5881	0.4086	0.2447	0.1218	0.0480	0.0139	0.0026	0.0002	0.0000+	0.0000+
	11	1.0000–	1.0000–	1.0000–	1.0000–	0.9999	0.9991	0.9949	0.9804	0.9435	0.8692	0.7483	0.5857	0.4044	0.2376	0.1133	0.0409	0.0100	0.0013	0.0001	0.0000+
	12	1.0000–	1.0000–	1.0000–	1.0000–	1.0000–	0.9998	0.9987	0.9940	0.9790	0.9420	0.8684	0.7480	0.5841	0.3990	0.2277	0.1018	0.0321	0.0059	0.0004	0.0000+
	13	1.0000–	1.0000–	1.0000–	1.0000–	1.0000–	1.0000–	0.9997	0.9985	0.9935	0.9786	0.9423	0.8701	0.7500	0.5834	0.3920	0.2142	0.0867	0.0219	0.0024	0.0000+
	14	1.0000–	1.0000–	1.0000–	1.0000–	1.0000–	1.0000–	1.0000–	0.9997	0.9984	0.9936	0.9793	0.9447	0.8744	0.7546	0.5836	0.3828	0.1958	0.0673	0.0113	0.0003
	15	1.0000–	1.0000–	1.0000–	1.0000–	1.0000–	1.0000–	1.0000–	1.0000–	0.9997	0.9985	0.9941	0.9811	0.9490	0.8818	0.7625	0.5852	0.3704	0.1702	0.0432	0.0026
	16	1.0000–	1.0000–	1.0000–	1.0000–	1.0000–	1.0000–	1.0000–	1.0000–	1.0000–	0.9997	0.9987	0.9951	0.9840	0.9556	0.8929	0.7748	0.5886	0.3523	0.1330	0.0159
	17	1.0000–	1.0000–	1.0000–	1.0000–	1.0000–	1.0000–	1.0000–	1.0000–	1.0000–	1.0000–	0.9998	0.9991	0.9964	0.9879	0.9645	0.9087	0.7939	0.5951	0.3231	0.0755
	18	1.0000–	1.0000–	1.0000–	1.0000–	1.0000–	1.0000–	1.0000–	1.0000–	1.0000–	1.0000–	1.0000–	0.9999	0.9995	0.9979	0.9924	0.9757	0.9308	0.8244	0.6083	0.2642
	19	1.0000–	1.0000–	1.0000–	1.0000-	1.0000–	1.0000–	1.0000–	1.0000–	1.0000–	1.0000–	1.0000–	1.0000–	1.0000–	0.9998	0.9992	0.9968	0.9885	0.9612	0.8784	0.6415
	20	1	1	1	1	1	1	1	1	1	1	1	1	1	1	1	1	1	1	1	1

Note: 0.0000+ means the probability is 0.0000 rounded to four decimal places. However, the probability is *not* zero.
1.0000– means the probability is 1.0000 rounded to four decimal places. However, the probability is *not* one.

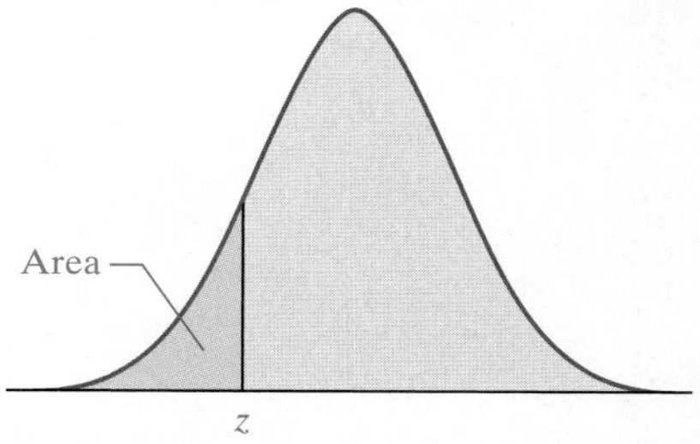

TABLE V

Standard Normal Distribution

z	.00	.01	.02	.03	.04	.05	.06	.07	.08	.09
−3.4	0.0003	0.0003	0.0003	0.0003	0.0003	0.0003	0.0003	0.0003	0.0003	0.0002
−3.3	0.0005	0.0005	0.0005	0.0004	0.0004	0.0004	0.0004	0.0004	0.0004	0.0003
−3.2	0.0007	0.0007	0.0006	0.0006	0.0006	0.0006	0.0006	0.0005	0.0005	0.0005
−3.1	0.0010	0.0009	0.0009	0.0009	0.0008	0.0008	0.0008	0.0008	0.0007	0.0007
−3.0	0.0013	0.0013	0.0013	0.0012	0.0012	0.0011	0.0011	0.0011	0.0010	0.0010
−2.9	0.0019	0.0018	0.0018	0.0017	0.0016	0.0016	0.0015	0.0015	0.0014	0.0014
−2.8	0.0026	0.0025	0.0024	0.0023	0.0023	0.0022	0.0021	0.0021	0.0020	0.0019
−2.7	0.0035	0.0034	0.0033	0.0032	0.0031	0.0030	0.0029	0.0028	0.0027	0.0026
−2.6	0.0047	0.0045	0.0044	0.0043	0.0041	0.0040	0.0039	0.0038	0.0037	0.0036
−2.5	0.0062	0.0060	0.0059	0.0057	0.0055	0.0054	0.0052	0.0051	0.0049	0.0048
−2.4	0.0082	0.0080	0.0078	0.0075	0.0073	0.0071	0.0069	0.0068	0.0066	0.0064
−2.3	0.0107	0.0104	0.0102	0.0099	0.0096	0.0094	0.0091	0.0089	0.0087	0.0084
−2.2	0.0139	0.0136	0.0132	0.0129	0.0125	0.0122	0.0119	0.0116	0.0113	0.0110
−2.1	0.0179	0.0174	0.0170	0.0166	0.0162	0.0158	0.0154	0.0150	0.0146	0.0143
−2.0	0.0228	0.0222	0.0217	0.0212	0.0207	0.0202	0.0197	0.0192	0.0188	0.0183
−1.9	0.0287	0.0281	0.0274	0.0268	0.0262	0.0256	0.0250	0.0244	0.0239	0.0233
−1.8	0.0359	0.0351	0.0344	0.0336	0.0329	0.0322	0.0314	0.0307	0.0301	0.0294
−1.7	0.0446	0.0436	0.0427	0.0418	0.0409	0.0401	0.0392	0.0384	0.0375	0.0367
−1.6	0.0548	0.0537	0.0526	0.0516	0.0505	0.0495	0.0485	0.0475	0.0465	0.0455
−1.5	0.0668	0.0655	0.0643	0.0630	0.0618	0.0606	0.0594	0.0582	0.0571	0.0559
−1.4	0.0808	0.0793	0.0778	0.0764	0.0749	0.0735	0.0721	0.0708	0.0694	0.0681
−1.3	0.0968	0.0951	0.0934	0.0918	0.0901	0.0885	0.0869	0.0853	0.0838	0.0823
−1.2	0.1151	0.1131	0.1112	0.1093	0.1075	0.1056	0.1038	0.1020	0.1003	0.0985
−1.1	0.1357	0.1335	0.1314	0.1292	0.1271	0.1251	0.1230	0.1210	0.1190	0.1170
−1.0	0.1587	0.1562	0.1539	0.1515	0.1492	0.1469	0.1446	0.1423	0.1401	0.1379
−0.9	0.1841	0.1814	0.1788	0.1762	0.1736	0.1711	0.1685	0.1660	0.1635	0.1611
−0.8	0.2119	0.2090	0.2061	0.2033	0.2005	0.1977	0.1949	0.1922	0.1894	0.1867
−0.7	0.2420	0.2389	0.2358	0.2327	0.2296	0.2266	0.2236	0.2206	0.2177	0.2148
−0.6	0.2743	0.2709	0.2676	0.2643	0.2611	0.2578	0.2546	0.2514	0.2483	0.2451
−0.5	0.3085	0.3050	0.3015	0.2981	0.2946	0.2912	0.2877	0.2843	0.2810	0.2776
−0.4	0.3446	0.3409	0.3372	0.3336	0.3300	0.3264	0.3228	0.3192	0.3156	0.3121
−0.3	0.3821	0.3783	0.3745	0.3707	0.3669	0.3632	0.3594	0.3557	0.3520	0.3483
−0.2	0.4207	0.4168	0.4129	0.4090	0.4052	0.4013	0.3974	0.3936	0.3897	0.3859
−0.1	0.4602	0.4562	0.4522	0.4483	0.4443	0.4404	0.4364	0.4325	0.4286	0.4247
−0.0	0.5000	0.4960	0.4920	0.4880	0.4840	0.4801	0.4761	0.4721	0.4681	0.4641

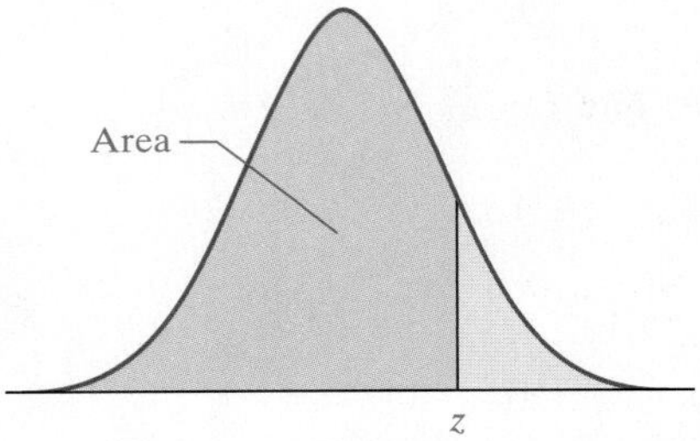

TABLE V *(continued)*

					Standard Normal Distribution					
z	**.00**	**.01**	**.02**	**.03**	**.04**	**.05**	**.06**	**.07**	**.08**	**.09**
0.0	0.5000	0.5040	0.5080	0.5120	0.5160	0.5199	0.5239	0.5279	0.5319	0.5359
0.1	0.5398	0.5438	0.5478	0.5517	0.5557	0.5596	0.5636	0.5675	0.5714	0.5753
0.2	0.5793	0.5832	0.5871	0.5910	0.5948	0.5987	0.6026	0.6064	0.6103	0.6141
0.3	0.6179	0.6217	0.6255	0.6293	0.6331	0.6368	0.6406	0.6443	0.6480	0.6517
0.4	0.6554	0.6591	0.6628	0.6664	0.6700	0.6736	0.6772	0.6808	0.6844	0.6879
0.5	0.6915	0.6950	0.6985	0.7019	0.7054	0.7088	0.7123	0.7157	0.7190	0.7224
0.6	0.7257	0.7291	0.7324	0.7357	0.7389	0.7422	0.7454	0.7486	0.7517	0.7549
0.7	0.7580	0.7611	0.7642	0.7673	0.7704	0.7734	0.7764	0.7794	0.7823	0.7852
0.8	0.7881	0.7910	0.7939	0.7967	0.7995	0.8023	0.8051	0.8078	0.8106	0.8133
0.9	0.8159	0.8186	0.8212	0.8238	0.8264	0.8289	0.8315	0.8340	0.8365	0.8389
1.0	0.8413	0.8438	0.8461	0.8485	0.8508	0.8531	0.8554	0.8577	0.8599	0.8621
1.1	0.8643	0.8665	0.8686	0.8708	0.8729	0.8749	0.8770	0.8790	0.8810	0.8830
1.2	0.8849	0.8869	0.8888	0.8907	0.8925	0.8944	0.8962	0.8980	0.8997	0.9015
1.3	0.9032	0.9049	0.9066	0.9082	0.9099	0.9115	0.9131	0.9147	0.9162	0.9177
1.4	0.9192	0.9207	0.9222	0.9236	0.9251	0.9265	0.9279	0.9292	0.9306	0.9319
1.5	0.9332	0.9345	0.9357	0.9370	0.9382	0.9394	0.9406	0.9418	0.9429	0.9441
1.6	0.9452	0.9463	0.9474	0.9484	0.9495	0.9505	0.9515	0.9525	0.9535	0.9545
1.7	0.9554	0.9564	0.9573	0.9582	0.9591	0.9599	0.9608	0.9616	0.9625	0.9633
1.8	0.9641	0.9649	0.9656	0.9664	0.9671	0.9678	0.9686	0.9693	0.9699	0.9706
1.9	0.9713	0.9719	0.9726	0.9732	0.9738	0.9744	0.9750	0.9756	0.9761	0.9767
2.0	0.9772	0.9778	0.9783	0.9788	0.9793	0.9798	0.9803	0.9808	0.9812	0.9817
2.1	0.9821	0.9826	0.9830	0.9834	0.9838	0.9842	0.9846	0.9850	0.9854	0.9857
2.2	0.9861	0.9864	0.9868	0.9871	0.9875	0.9878	0.9881	0.9884	0.9887	0.9890
2.3	0.9893	0.9896	0.9898	0.9901	0.9904	0.9906	0.9909	0.9911	0.9913	0.9916
2.4	0.9918	0.9920	0.9922	0.9925	0.9927	0.9929	0.9931	0.9932	0.9934	0.9936
2.5	0.9938	0.9940	0.9941	0.9943	0.9945	0.9946	0.9948	0.9949	0.9951	0.9952
2.6	0.9953	0.9955	0.9956	0.9957	0.9959	0.9960	0.9961	0.9962	0.9963	0.9964
2.7	0.9965	0.9966	0.9967	0.9968	0.9969	0.9970	0.9971	0.9972	0.9973	0.9974
2.8	0.9974	0.9975	0.9976	0.9977	0.9977	0.9978	0.9979	0.9979	0.9980	0.9981
2.9	0.9981	0.9982	0.9982	0.9983	0.9984	0.9984	0.9985	0.9985	0.9986	0.9986
3.0	0.9987	0.9987	0.9987	0.9988	0.9988	0.9989	0.9989	0.9989	0.9990	0.9990
3.1	0.9990	0.9991	0.9991	0.9991	0.9992	0.9992	0.9992	0.9992	0.9993	0.9993
3.2	0.9993	0.9993	0.9994	0.9994	0.9994	0.9994	0.9994	0.9995	0.9995	0.9995
3.3	0.9995	0.9995	0.9995	0.9996	0.9996	0.9996	0.9996	0.9996	0.9996	0.9997
3.4	0.9997	0.9997	0.9997	0.9997	0.9997	0.9997	0.9997	0.9997	0.9997	0.9998

(b) Confidence Interval Critical Values, $z_{\alpha/2}$

Level of Confidence	Critical Value, $z_{\alpha/2}$
0.90 or 90%	1.645
0.95 or 95%	1.96
0.98 or 98%	2.33
0.99 or 99%	2.575

(c) Hypothesis Testing Critical Values

Level of Significance, α	Left-Tailed	Right-Tailed	Two-Tailed
0.10	−1.28	1.28	±1.645
0.05	−1.645	1.645	±1.96
0.01	−2.33	2.33	±2.575

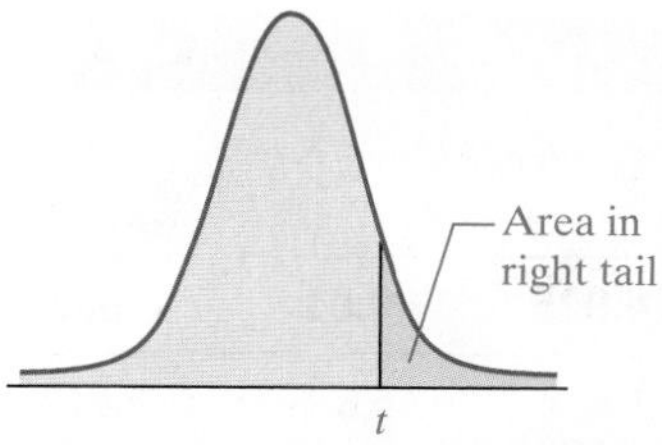

TABLE VI

t-Distribution
Area in Right Tail

df	0.25	0.20	0.15	0.10	0.05	0.025	0.02	0.01	0.005	0.0025	0.001	0.0005
1	1.000	1.376	1.963	3.078	6.314	12.706	15.894	31.821	63.657	127.321	318.309	636.619
2	0.816	1.061	1.386	1.886	2.920	4.303	4.849	6.965	9.925	14.089	22.327	31.599
3	0.765	0.978	1.250	1.638	2.353	3.182	3.482	4.541	5.841	7.453	10.215	12.924
4	0.741	0.941	1.190	1.533	2.132	2.776	2.999	3.747	4.604	5.598	7.173	8.610
5	0.727	0.920	1.156	1.476	2.015	2.571	2.757	3.365	4.032	4.773	5.893	6.869
6	0.718	0.906	1.134	1.440	1.943	2.447	2.612	3.143	3.707	4.317	5.208	5.959
7	0.711	0.896	1.119	1.415	1.895	2.365	2.517	2.998	3.499	4.029	4.785	5.408
8	0.706	0.889	1.108	1.397	1.860	2.306	2.449	2.896	3.355	3.833	4.501	5.041
9	0.703	0.883	1.100	1.383	1.833	2.262	2.398	2.821	3.250	3.690	4.297	4.781
10	0.700	0.879	1.093	1.372	1.812	2.228	2.359	2.764	3.169	3.581	4.144	4.587
11	0.697	0.876	1.088	1.363	1.796	2.201	2.328	2.718	3.106	3.497	4.025	4.437
12	0.695	0.873	1.083	1.356	1.782	2.179	2.303	2.681	3.055	3.428	3.930	4.318
13	0.694	0.870	1.079	1.350	1.771	2.160	2.282	2.650	3.012	3.372	3.852	4.221
14	0.692	0.868	1.076	1.345	1.761	2.145	2.264	2.624	2.977	3.326	3.787	4.140
15	0.691	0.866	1.074	1.341	1.753	2.131	2.249	2.602	2.947	3.286	3.733	4.073
16	0.690	0.865	1.071	1.337	1.746	2.120	2.235	2.583	2.921	3.252	3.686	4.015
17	0.689	0.863	1.069	1.333	1.740	2.110	2.224	2.567	2.898	3.222	3.646	3.965
18	0.688	0.862	1.067	1.330	1.734	2.101	2.214	2.552	2.878	3.197	3.610	3.922
19	0.688	0.861	1.066	1.328	1.729	2.093	2.205	2.539	2.861	3.174	3.579	3.883
20	0.687	0.860	1.064	1.325	1.725	2.086	2.197	2.528	2.845	3.153	3.552	3.850
21	0.686	0.859	1.063	1.323	1.721	2.080	2.189	2.518	2.831	3.135	3.527	3.819
22	0.686	0.858	1.061	1.321	1.717	2.074	2.183	2.508	2.819	3.119	3.505	3.792
23	0.685	0.858	1.060	1.319	1.714	2.069	2.177	2.500	2.807	3.104	3.485	3.768
24	0.685	0.857	1.059	1.318	1.711	2.064	2.172	2.492	2.797	3.091	3.467	3.745
25	0.684	0.856	1.058	1.316	1.708	2.060	2.167	2.485	2.787	3.078	3.450	3.725
26	0.684	0.856	1.058	1.315	1.706	2.056	2.162	2.479	2.779	3.067	3.435	3.707
27	0.684	0.855	1.057	1.314	1.703	2.052	2.158	2.473	2.771	3.057	3.421	3.690
28	0.683	0.855	1.056	1.313	1.701	2.048	2.154	2.467	2.763	3.047	3.408	3.674
29	0.683	0.854	1.055	1.311	1.699	2.045	2.150	2.462	2.756	3.038	3.396	3.659
30	0.683	0.854	1.055	1.310	1.697	2.042	2.147	2.457	2.750	3.030	3.385	3.646
31	0.682	0.853	1.054	1.309	1.696	2.040	2.144	2.453	2.744	3.022	3.375	3.633
32	0.682	0.853	1.054	1.309	1.694	2.037	2.141	2.449	2.738	3.015	3.365	3.622
33	0.682	0.853	1.053	1.308	1.692	2.035	2.138	2.445	2.733	3.008	3.356	3.611
34	0.682	0.852	1.052	1.307	1.691	2.032	2.136	2.441	2.728	3.002	3.348	3.601
35	0.682	0.852	1.052	1.306	1.690	2.030	2.133	2.438	2.724	2.996	3.340	3.591
36	0.681	0.852	1.052	1.306	1.688	2.028	2.131	2.434	2.719	2.990	3.333	3.582
37	0.681	0.851	1.051	1.305	1.687	2.026	2.129	2.431	2.715	2.985	3.326	3.574
38	0.681	0.851	1.051	1.304	1.686	2.024	2.127	2.429	2.712	2.980	3.319	3.566
39	0.681	0.851	1.050	1.304	1.685	2.023	2.125	2.426	2.708	2.976	3.313	3.558
40	0.681	0.851	1.050	1.303	1.684	2.021	2.123	2.423	2.704	2.971	3.307	3.551
50	0.679	0.849	1.047	1.299	1.676	2.009	2.109	2.403	2.678	2.937	3.261	3.496
60	0.679	0.848	1.045	1.296	1.671	2.000	2.099	2.390	2.660	2.915	3.232	3.460
70	0.678	0.847	1.044	1.294	1.667	1.994	2.093	2.381	2.648	2.899	3.211	3.435
80	0.678	0.846	1.043	1.292	1.664	1.990	2.088	2.374	2.639	2.887	3.195	3.416
90	0.677	0.846	1.042	1.291	1.662	1.987	2.084	2.368	2.632	2.878	3.183	3.402
100	0.677	0.845	1.042	1.290	1.660	1.984	2.081	2.364	2.626	2.871	3.174	3.390
1000	0.675	0.842	1.037	1.282	1.646	1.962	2.056	2.330	2.581	2.813	3.098	3.300
z	0.674	0.842	1.036	1.282	1.645	1.960	2.054	2.326	2.576	2.807	3.090	3.291

TABLE VII

Chi-Square (χ^2) Distribution

Area to the Right of Critical Value

Degrees of Freedom	0.995	0.99	0.975	0.95	0.90	0.10	0.05	0.025	0.01	0.005
1	—	—	0.001	0.004	0.016	2.706	3.841	5.024	6.635	7.879
2	0.010	0.020	0.051	0.103	0.211	4.605	5.991	7.378	9.210	10.597
3	0.072	0.115	0.216	0.352	0.584	6.251	7.815	9.348	11.345	12.838
4	0.207	0.297	0.484	0.711	1.064	7.779	9.488	11.143	13.277	14.860
5	0.412	0.554	0.831	1.145	1.610	9.236	11.070	12.833	15.086	16.750
6	0.676	0.872	1.237	1.635	2.204	10.645	12.592	14.449	16.812	18.548
7	0.989	1.239	1.690	2.167	2.833	12.017	14.067	16.013	18.475	20.278
8	1.344	1.646	2.180	2.733	3.490	13.362	15.507	17.535	20.090	21.955
9	1.735	2.088	2.700	3.325	4.168	14.684	16.919	19.023	21.666	23.589
10	2.156	2.558	3.247	3.940	4.865	15.987	18.307	20.483	23.209	25.188
11	2.603	3.053	3.816	4.575	5.578	17.275	19.675	21.920	24.725	26.757
12	3.074	3.571	4.404	5.226	6.304	18.549	21.026	23.337	26.217	28.300
13	3.565	4.107	5.009	5.892	7.042	19.812	22.362	24.736	27.688	29.819
14	4.075	4.660	5.629	6.571	7.790	21.064	23.685	26.119	29.141	31.319
15	4.601	5.229	6.262	7.261	8.547	22.307	24.996	27.488	30.578	32.801
16	5.142	5.812	6.908	7.962	9.312	23.542	26.296	28.845	32.000	34.267
17	5.697	6.408	7.564	8.672	10.085	24.769	27.587	30.191	33.409	35.718
18	6.265	7.015	8.231	9.390	10.865	25.989	28.869	31.526	34.805	37.156
19	6.844	7.633	8.907	10.117	11.651	27.204	30.144	32.852	36.191	38.582
20	7.434	8.260	9.591	10.851	12.443	28.412	31.410	34.170	37.566	39.997
21	8.034	8.897	10.283	11.591	13.240	29.615	32.671	35.479	38.932	41.401
22	8.643	9.542	10.982	12.338	14.041	30.813	33.924	36.781	40.289	42.796
23	9.260	10.196	11.689	13.091	14.848	32.007	35.172	38.076	41.638	44.181
24	9.886	10.856	12.401	13.848	15.659	33.196	36.415	39.364	42.980	45.559
25	10.520	11.524	13.120	14.611	16.473	34.382	37.652	40.646	44.314	46.928
26	11.160	12.198	13.844	15.379	17.292	35.563	38.885	41.923	45.642	48.290
27	11.808	12.879	14.573	16.151	18.114	36.741	40.113	43.195	46.963	49.645
28	12.461	13.565	15.308	16.928	18.939	37.916	41.337	44.461	48.278	50.993
29	13.121	14.256	16.047	17.708	19.768	39.087	42.557	45.722	49.588	52.336
30	13.787	14.953	16.791	18.493	20.599	40.256	43.773	46.979	50.892	53.672
40	20.707	22.164	24.433	26.509	29.051	51.805	55.758	59.342	63.691	66.766
50	27.991	29.707	32.357	34.764	37.689	63.167	67.505	71.420	76.154	79.490
60	35.534	37.485	40.482	43.188	46.459	74.397	79.082	83.298	88.379	91.952
70	43.275	45.442	48.758	51.739	55.329	85.527	90.531	95.023	100.425	104.215
80	51.172	53.540	57.153	60.391	64.278	96.578	101.879	106.629	112.329	116.321
90	59.196	61.754	65.647	69.126	73.291	107.565	113.145	118.136	124.116	128.299
100	67.328	70.065	74.222	77.929	82.358	118.498	124.342	129.561	135.807	140.169

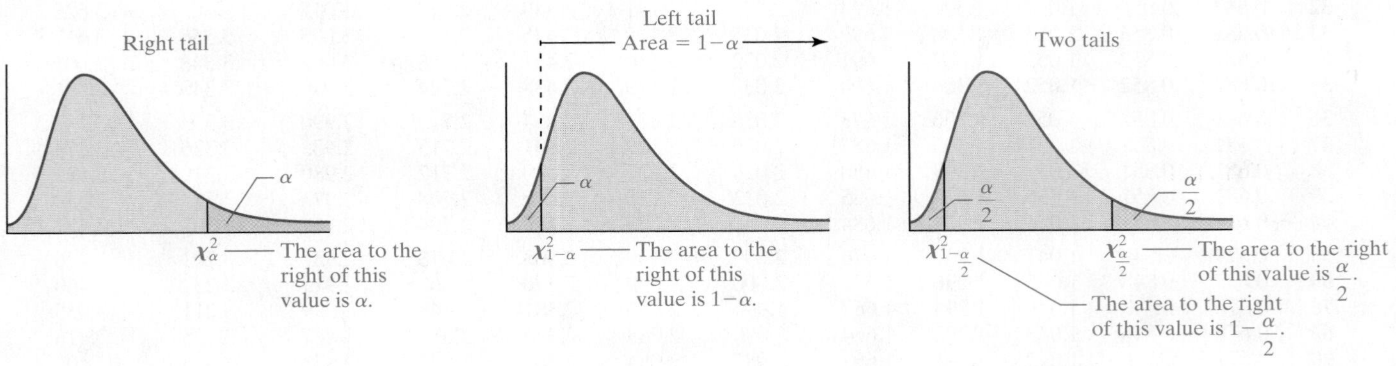

Right tail
α
χ^2_α
The area to the right of this value is α.
Left tail
Area = $1-\alpha$
α
$\chi^2_{1-\alpha}$
The area to the right of this value is $1-\alpha$.
Two tails
$\frac{\alpha}{2}$
$\frac{\alpha}{2}$
$\chi^2_{1-\frac{\alpha}{2}}$
$\chi^2_{\frac{\alpha}{2}}$
The area to the right of this value is $\frac{\alpha}{2}$.
The area to the right of this value is $1-\frac{\alpha}{2}$.

Answers

CHAPTER 1 Data Collection

1.1 Assess Your Understanding (page 11)

1. Statistics is the science of collecting, organizing, summarizing, and analyzing information to draw a conclusion and answer questions. In addition, statistics is about providing a measure of confidence in any conclusions.

2. The group to be studied as defined by the research objective is the population. Any subset of the population is a sample.

3. individual **4.** Descriptive; inferential **5.** statistic; parameter **6.** Variables **7.** Parameter **8.** Parameter **9.** Statistic **10.** Statistic **11.** Parameter **12.** Parameter **13.** Statistic **14.** Statistic **15.** Qualitative **16.** Quantitative **17.** Quantitative **18.** Qualitative **19.** Quantitative **20.** Quantitative **21.** Qualitative **22.** Qualitative **23.** Discrete **24.** Continuous **25.** Continuous **26.** Discrete **27.** Continuous **28.** Continuous **29.** Dis crete **30.** Continuous **31.** Nominal **32.** Ordinal **33.** Ratio **34.** Interval **35.** Ordinal **36.** Nominal **37.** Ratio **38.** Interval

39. Population: teenagers 13 to 17 years of age who live in the United States. Sample: 1028 teenagers 13 to 17 years of age who live in the United States

40. Population: all Coca-Cola bottles filled on October 15. Sample: 50 Coca-Cola bottles filled on October 15

41. Population: entire soybean crop. Sample: 100 plants selected

42. Population: all United States households. Sample: 50,000 households surveyed

43. Population: women 27 to 44 years of age with hypertension. Sample: 7373 women 27 to 44 years of age with hypertension

44. Population: full-time students enrolled at the community college. Sample: the 128 full-time students surveyed

45. Individuals: Motorola Droid X, Motorola Droid 2, Apple iPhone 4, Samsung Epic 4G, Samsung Captivate
Variables: weight, service provider, depth
Data for weight: 5.47, 5.96, 4.8, 5.5, 4.5 (ounces)
Data for service provider: Verizon, Verizon, ATT, Sprint, ATT
Data for depth: 0.39, 0.53, 0.37, 0.6, 0.39 (inches)
The variable *weight* is continuous; the variable *service provider* is qualitative; the variable *depth* is continuous.

46. Individuals: 3 Series, 5 Series, 6 Series, 7 Series, X3, Z4 Roadster
Variables: body style, weight, number of seats
Data for body style: coupe, sedan, convertible, sedan, sport utility, coupe
Data for weight: 3362, 4056, 4277, 4564, 4012, 3505
Data for number of seats: 4, 5, 4, 5, 5, 2
The variable *body style* is qualitative; the variable *weight* is continuous; the variable *number of seats* is discrete.

47. Individuals: Alabama, Colorado, Indiana, North Carolina, Wisconsin
Variables: minimum age for driver's license (unrestricted), mandatory belt use seating positions, maximum allowable speed limit on rural interstates in 2011
Data for minimum age for driver's license: 17, 17, 18, 16, 18
Data for mandatory belt use seating positions: front, front, all, all, all
Data for maximum allowable speed limit on rural interstates in 2011: 70, 75, 70, 70, 65 (mph)
The variable *minimum age for driver's license* is continuous; the variable *mandatory belt use seating positions* is qualitative; the variable *maximum allowable speed limit on rural interstates in 2011* is continuous.

48. Individuals: Apple iPod Touch, Zune HD, SanDisk Sansa Clip+, Sony X-Series Walkman, Apple iPod Nano
Variables: rating, memory, audio playback time
Data for rating: outstanding, excellent, excellent, excellent, very good
Data for memory: 32, 32, 4, 16, 8 (GB)
Data for audio playback time: 40, 33, 15, 33, 24 (hours)
The variable *rating* is qualitative; the variable *memory* is continuous; the variable *audio playback time* is continuous.

49. (a) To determine if adolescents 18–21 who smoke have a lower IQ than nonsmokers
(b) All adolescents 18–21; the 20,211 18-year-old Israeli male military recruits.
(c) The average IQ of smokers was 94; the average IQ of nonsmokers was 101.
(d) Lower IQ individuals are more likely to choose to smoke.

50. (a) To determine if application of duct tape is as effective as cryotherapy in the treatment of common warts
(b) People with warts; the 51 patients with warts
(c) 85% of the patients in group 1 and 60% of the patients in group 2 had complete resolution of their warts.
(d) Duct tape is significantly more effective in treating warts than cryotherapy.

51. (a) To determine the proportion of adult Americans who believe the federal government wastes 51 cents or more of every dollar
(b) American adults aged 18 years or older
(c) 1026 American adults aged 18 years or older
(d) Of the 1026 individuals surveyed, 35% indicated that 51 cents or more is wasted.
(e) Gallup is 95% certain that the percentage of all adult Americans who believe the federal government wastes 51 cents or more of every dollar received is between 31% and 39%.

52. (a) To determine the proportion of employees in the United States who participate in an employer-sponsored automatic payroll deduction for a 401(k) plan to save for retirement
(b) All employees in the United States
(c) 1172 employees in the United States
(d) Of the 1172 employees surveyed, 27% indicated they were currently participating in an automatic payroll deduction for a 401(k) plan to save for retirement.
(e) The Principal Financial Group is 95% certain that the percentage of employees in the United States who participate in an employer-sponsored automatic payroll deduction for a 401(k) plan to save for retirement is between 23% and 31%.

53. Nominal: ordinal, the level of measurement changes because the goal of the research has changed. Rather than the number being used to identify the player, it is now also used to explain the caliber of the player, with a higher number implying a lower caliber of player.

54. (a) Nominal **(b)** Ordinal **(c)** Ratio

55. (a) To determine the role that TV-watching by children younger than 3 plays in future attention problems of the children
(b) All children under 3 years of age
(c) 967 children
(d) For every hour that kids under 3 watched violent child-oriented entertainment, their risk doubled for attention problems 5 years later.
(e) Children under the age of 3 should not watch television in general. However, if they do watch television, the show should be of the educational variety. Shows that are violent double the risk of attention problems 5 years later for every hour per day the child watches. Even nonviolent (and noneducational) television shows result in a substantial risk for attention problems.

56. Qualitative variables describe characteristics of individuals. Quantitative variables provide numerical counts or measures of individuals.

57. A discrete variable is a quantitative variable that has a finite or countable number of possible values. A discrete variable cannot take on every possible value between any two possible values. Continuous variables are also quantitative variables, but there are an infinite number of possible values that are not countable. A continuous variable may take on every possible value between any two values.

58. A variable is at the nominal level of measurement if the values of the variable provide a naming scheme in which the values of the variable cannot be ranked or put in a specific order. A variable is at the ordinal level of measurement if it has the characteristics of the nominal level of measurement and the naming scheme allows the values of the variable to be ranked or placed in a specific order. A variable is at the interval level of measurement if it has the properties of the ordinal level of measurement and the difference in the values of the variable has meaning. A value of zero does not mean the absence of the quantity. Arithmetic operations such as addition and subtraction can be performed on the values of the variable. A variable at the ratio level of measurement has the properties of the interval level, and the ratio of the values of the variable has meaning. A value of zero at the ratio level means the absence of the quantity. Arithmetic operations such as multiplication and division can be performed on the values of the variable.

59. This means that the values of the variable change from individual to individual. In addition, certain variables can change over time for certain individuals. Because data vary, two different statistical analyses of the same variable can lead to different results.

60. (1) Identify the research objective, (2) collect the data needed to answer the question(s) posed in the research objective, (3) describe the data, (4) perform inference (extend the results of the sample to the population and report a level of confidence in the results).

61. No. We measure age to as much accuracy as we wish.

1.2 Assess Your Understanding (page 19)

1. The explanatory variable is the variable that affects the value of the response variable. In research, we want to see how changes in the value of the explanatory variable affect the value of the response variable.

2. An observational study measures the value of the response variable without manipulating or influencing the value of the explanatory variable. A designed experiment attempts to control the values of the explanatory variables and see how varying the value of certain explanatory variables affects the value of the response variable. In a designed experiment, the individuals in the study are typically divided into groups, and each group is given a specific value of the explanatory variable. A designed experiment allows the researcher to claim causation; an observational study only allows the researcher to talk about association.

3. Confounding exists in a study when the effects of two or more explanatory variables are not separated. So any relation that appears to exist between a certain explanatory variable and the response variable may be due to some other variable or variables not accounted for in the study. A lurking variable is a variable not accounted for in a study, but one that affects the value of the response variable.

4. It depends. Sometimes there are ethical reasons why an experiment cannot be conducted. Other times the researcher may want to conduct an observational study first to validate a belief before investing time and money in an experiment. Certainly, a designed experiment is the superior analytical tool if ethics, time, and money are not an issue.

5. Cross-sectional studies collect information at a specific point in time (or over a very short period of time). Case-control studies are retrospective (they look back in time). Also, individuals that have a certain characteristic (such as cancer) in a case-control study are matched with those that do not have the characteristic. Case-control studies are typically superior to cross-sectional studies.

6. A cohort study identifies the individuals to participate and then follows them over a period of time. During this period, information about the individuals is gathered, but there is no attempt to influence the individuals. Cohort studies are superior to case-control studies because cohort studies do not require recall to obtain the data.

7. There is a perceived benefit to obtaining a flu shot, so there are ethical issues in intentionally denying certain seniors access.

8. A retrospective study looks at data from the past either through recall or records. A prospective study gathers data over time by following the individuals in the study and recording data as they occur.

9. Observational study **10.** Experiment

11. Experiment **12.** Observational study

13. Observational study **14.** Experiment

15. Experiment **16.** Observational study

17. **(a)** Cohort
(b) Whether the individual has heart disease or not; whether the individual is happy or not
(c) Confounding due to lurking variables

18. **(a)** Cross-sectional
(b) Whether the woman has nonmelanoma skin cancer or not; amount of caffeinated coffee consumed
(c) The adjustment is necessary to avoid confounding due to lurking variables.

19. **(a)** The researchers administered a questionnaire to obtain their results, so there is no control of the explanatory variable. This is a cross-sectional study.
(b) Body mass index; whether a TV is in the bedroom or not
(c) Answers will vary. Some lurking variables might be the amount of exercise per week and eating habits.
(d) The researchers made an effort to avoid confounding by accounting for potential lurking variables.
(e) No. This is an observational study, so all we can say is that a television in the bedroom is associated with a higher body mass index.

20. **(a)** The researchers simply observed the individuals over time. This is a cohort study.
(b) Weight gain; whether the individual is married/cohabitating or not
(c) Answers will vary. Some possibilities include having children or the number of times the individual eats out per week.
(d) No. This is an observational study, so all we can say is that being married or cohabiting is associated with weight gain.

21. Answers will vary. This is a prospective, cohort observational study. Some possible lurking variables include smoking habits, eating habits, exercise, and family history of cancer. The study concluded that there might be an increased risk of certain blood cancers in people with prolonged exposure to electromagnetic fields. The author of the article reminds us that this is an observational study, so there is no control of variables that may affect the likelihood of getting certain cancers. In addition, the author states that we should do things in our lives that promote health.

22. This is a cross-sectional study. Cultural differences, parents' education level

23. **(a)** To determine whether lung cancer is associated with exposure to tobacco smoke within the household.
(b) It is case-controlled because there is a group of individuals with lung cancer who never smoked being compared to a group of individuals without lung cancer who never smoked. It is retrospective because the data looked at historical records based on interview.
(c) Whether the individual has lung cancer or not; qualitative
(d) Number of smoker-years; quantitative
(e) Answers will vary. Some possibilities include household income or amount of exposure to tobacco outside the home.
(f) Approximately 17% of lung cancers among nonsmokers can be attributed to high levels of exposure to cigarette smoke during childhood and adolescence. No, we cannot conclude that exposure to smoke causes lung cancer; however, we can conclude that it is associated with lung cancer.
(g) Yes, but the researcher would need to use lab animals, such as rats, not human subjects.

1.3 Assess Your Understanding (page 27)

1. The frame is a list of the individuals in the population we are studying.

2. A simple random sample is a sample of size n from a population of size N, where every possible sample of size n has an equally likely chance of occurring.

3. Once an individual is selected, he or she cannot be selected again.

4. Random sampling is a technique that uses chance to select individuals from a population to be in a sample. It is used because it maximizes the likelihood that the individuals in the sample are representative of the individuals in the population. In convenience sampling, the individuals in the sample likely do not represent the individuals in the population because chance was not used to select the individuals.

5. Answers will vary. One option would be to write each name on a sheet of paper and choose the names out of a hat. A second option would be to number the books from 1 to 9 and randomly select three numbers.

6. Answers will vary. One option would be to write each player's name on a sheet of paper and choose the names out of a hat. A second option would be to number the players from 1 to 10 and randomly select two numbers.

7. **(a)** 616, 630; 616, 631; 616, 632; 616, 645; 616, 649; 616, 650; 630, 631; 630, 632; 630, 645; 630, 649; 630, 650; 631, 632; 631, 645; 631, 649; 631, 650; 632, 645; 632, 649; 632, 650; 645, 649; 645, 650; 649, 650

(b) There is a 1 in 21 chance the pair of courses will be EPR 630 and EPR 645.

8. **(a)** 1, 2; 1, 3; 1, 4; 1, 5; 1, 6; 1, 7; 2, 3; 2, 4; 2, 5; 2, 6; 2, 7; 3, 4; 3, 5; 3, 6; 3, 7; 4, 5; 4, 6; 4, 7; 5, 6; 5, 7; 6, 7
(b) There is a 1 in 21 chance the pair *The United Nations* and *Amnesty International* will be selected.

9. **(a)** 83, 67, 84, 38, 22, 24, 36, 58, 34
(b) Answers may vary depending on the type of technology used.

10. **(a)** 2869, 5518, 6635, 2182, 0603, 2654, 2686, 0135, 4080, 6621, 3774, 0826, 0916, 3188, 0876, 5418, 0037, 3130, 2882, 0662
(b) Answers may vary depending on the type of technology used.

11. **(a)** Answers will vary. **(b)** Answers will vary.

12. **(a)** Answers will vary. **(b)** Answers will vary.

13. **(a)** The list provided by the administration serves as the frame. Number the students on the list from 1 through 19,935. Using a random-number generator, set a seed (or select a starting point if using Table I in Appendix A). Generate 25 different numbers randomly. The students corresponding to these numbers will be the 25 students in the sample.
(b) Answers will vary.

14. **(a)** The list provided by the mayor will serve as the frame. Number the residents on the list from 1 through 5832. Using a random-number generator, set a seed or select a starting point if using Table I in Appendix A. Generate 20 different numbers randomly. The residents corresponding to these numbers will be the 20 residents in the sample.
(b) Answers will vary.

15. Answers will vary. However, the members should be numbered from 1 to 32. Then, using the table of random numbers or a random-number generator, four different numbers should be selected. The names corresponding to these numbers will represent the simple random sample.

16. Answers will vary. However, the employees should be numbered from 1 to 29. Then, using the table of random numbers or a random-number generator, five different numbers should be selected. The names corresponding to these numbers will represent the simple random sample.

1.4 Assess Your Understanding (page 36)

1. If the population can be divided into homogeneous, nonoverlapping groups

2. Systematic

3. Convenience samples are not random samples. Individuals who participate are often self-selected, so the results are not likely to be representative of the population.

4. cluster	**5.** stratified	**6.** False
7. False	**8.** True	**9.** True
10. False	**11.** Systematic	**12.** Cluster
13. Cluster	**14.** Stratified	**15.** Simple random
16. Convenience	**17.** Cluster	**18.** Stratified
19. Convenience	**20.** Systematic	**21.** Stratified

22. Simple random

23. 16, 41, 66, 91, 116, 141, 166, 191, 216, 241, 266, 291, 316, 341, 366, 391, 416, 441, 466, 491

24. 763, 185, 377, 304, 626, 392, 315, 084, 565, 508

25. Answers will vary. To obtain the sample, number the Democrats 1 to 16 and obtain a simple random sample of size 2. Then number the Republicans 1 to 16 and obtain a simple random sample of size 2. Be sure to use a different starting point in Table I or a different seed for each stratum.

26. Answers will vary.

27. **(a)** 90
(b) Randomly select a number between 1 and 90. Suppose that we randomly select 15; then the individuals in the survey will be 15, 105, 195, 285, . . ., 4425.

28. **(a)** 7269
(b) Randomly select a number between 1 and 7269. Suppose that we randomly select 2000; then the individuals in the survey will be 2000, 9269, 16538, . . ., 939701.

29. SRS: number from 1 to 1280. Randomly select 128 students to survey
Stratified: Randomly select four students from each section to survey.
Cluster: Randomly select four sections; survey all students in these four sections.
Answers will vary.

30. No. The "clusters" were not randomly selected.

31. Answers will vary. A good choice might be stratified sampling with the strata being commuters and noncommuters.

32. Answers will vary. One option would be cluster sampling. Each cluster would be a class. Randomly select clusters and then survey all the students in the selected classes.

33. Answers will vary. One option would be cluster sampling. The clusters could be the city blocks. Randomly select clusters and then survey all the households on the selected city blocks.

34. Answers will vary. Probably the most logical choice is systematic sampling.

35. Answers will vary. Simple random sampling will work fine here, especially because a list of 6600 individuals who meet the needs of our study already exists (the frame).

36. Answers will vary. Simple random sampling will work because a list of all households in the population exists. Just number the households 1 to *N* and use a random-number generator to obtain the households in the survey.

37. **(a)** Registered voters who have voted in the past few elections.
(b) Because each individual has an equally likely chance of being selected, there is a chance that one group may be over- or underrepresented.
(c) By using a stratified sample, the strategist can obtain a simple random sample within each strata so that the number of individuals in the sample is proportionate to the number of individuals in the population.

38. Random sampling means that the individuals chosen to be in the sample are selected by chance. This approach minimizes the chance that one part of the population is under- or overrepresented in the sample. There is no guarantee, however, that the sample will provide accurate information about the population.

1.5 Assess Your Understanding (page 42)

1. A closed question has fixed choices for answers, whereas an open question is a free-response question. Closed questions are easier to analyze, but limit the responses. Open questions allow respondents to state exactly how they feel, but are harder to analyze due to the variety of answers and possible misinterpretation of answers.

2. A certain segment of the population is not represented in the sample proportionally to its size in the population.

3. Bias means that the results of the sample are not representative of the population. Three types of bias: sampling bias, nonresponse bias, response bias. Sampling bias could mean that the sampling was not done using random sampling, but rather through a convenience sample. Nonresponse bias could be the result of an inability to contact an individual selected to be in a sample. Response bias could be the result of misunderstanding a question on a survey. A census could have bias through misinterpreted questions on a survey.

4. Nonsampling error is the error that results from undercoverage, nonresponse bias, response bias, or data-entry errors. Essentially, it is the error that results from the process of obtaining the data. Sampling error is the error that results because a sample is being used to estimate information about a population.

5. **(a)** Sampling bias due to undercoverage since the first 60 customers may not be representative of the customer population.
(b) Since a complete frame is not possible, systematic random sampling could be used to make the sample more representative of the customer population.

6. **(a)** Sampling bias since only homes in the southwest corner of the village are selected. These households may have different demographics than those in the other parts of the village.
(b) Perhaps a cluster sample could be used, with the clusters being city blocks.

7. **(a)** Response bias due to a poorly worded question.
(b) The survey should begin by stating the current penalty for selling a gun illegally. The question might be rewritten as "Do you approve or disapprove of harsher penalties for individuals who sell guns illegally?" The words *approve* and *disapprove* should be rotated from individual to individual.

8. **(a)** Response bias due to a poorly worded question
(b) The question could be rephrased as "On average, how many hours of sleep do you get each night?"

9. **(a)** Nonresponse bias; if the survey is only written in English, non-English speaking homes will not complete the survey, resulting in undercoverage

(b) The survey can be improved through face-to-face or telephone interviews.

10. **(a)** Nonresponse bias; there is a very low response rate.
(b) It is likely that face-to-face interviews may need to take place, or the survey needs to have an incentive.

11. **(a)** Sampling bias due to undercoverage, since the readers of the magazine may not be representative of all Australian women, and interviewer error, since advertisements and images in the magazine could affect the women's view of themselves.
(b) A well-designed sampling plan (not in a magazine), such as a cluster sample, could make the sample more representative of the intended population.

12. **(a)** Sampling bias due to a bad sampling plan (convenience sampling) and possible response bias due to misrepresented answer
(b) The teacher could use cluster sampling to obtain students for the sample; then each student would be weighed to get an accurate weight measurement.

13. **(a)** Response bias due to a poorly worded question
(b) The question should be reworded so that it doesn't imply the opinion of the editors. One possibility might be "Do you believe that a marriage can be maintained after an extramarital relation?"

14. **(a)** Sampling bias due to a poor choice of a frame
(b) The company could use cluster sampling and obtain a list of faculty from the human resources department at selected colleges.

15. **(a)** Response bias because the students are not likely to be truthful when the teacher is administering the survey
(b) The survey should be administered by an impartial party so that the students will be more likely to respond truthfully.

16. **(a)** Response bias because the respondents aren't likely to give truthful responses
(b) Send a trained interviewer to the houses.

17. No; the survey still suffers from undercoverage (sampling bias), nonresponse bias, and potentially response bias.

18. The General Social Survey uses random sampling to obtain the individuals who take the survey, so the results of their survey are more likely to be representative of the population than a Web survey in which individuals typically self-select to be in the survey.

19. The ordering of the questions is likely to affect the survey results. Perhaps question B should be asked first. Another possibility is to rotate the questions randomly.

20. The ordering of the questions is likely to affect the survey results. The questions should be rotated randomly. *Prohibit* is a strong word. People don't like to be prohibited from doing things. If the word must be used, it should be offset by the word *allow*, and the use of the words *prohibit* and *allow* should be rotated within the question.

21. The company is using a reward in the form of the $5.00 payment and an incentive by telling the readers that his or her input will make a difference.

22. The choices need to be rotated so that any response bias due to the ordering of the questions is minimized.

23. The frame is anyone with a landline phone. Any household without a landline phone, households on the do-not-call registry, and homeless individuals are excluded. This could result in sampling bias due to undercoverage.

24. Answers will vary. If households that have caller ID have a trait that is not part of those households that do not have caller ID, then the survey would have nonresponse bias.

25. Definitely, especially if households that are on the do-not-call registry have a trait that is not part of those households that are not on the do-not-call registry.

26. There is a higher chance that an individual at least 70 years of age will be at home.

27. Poorly trained interviewers; interviewer bias, surveyed too many female voters.

33. Sampling bias: using an incorrect frame led to undercoverage. Nonresponse bias: the low response rate.

35. **(a)** All cars that travel on the road in question
(b) Speed **(c)** Quantitative **(d)** Ratio
(e) No. It is impossible to get a list of all the cars that travel on the road.
(f) Yes, systematic sampling makes the most sense.
(g) Answers will vary. One bias is sampling bias. If the city council wants to use the cars of residents who live in the neighborhood to gauge the prevailing speed, then individuals who are not part of the population were in the sample, so the sample is not representative of the population.

36. Frames are obtained periodically, whereas populations are constantly changing.

37. Callbacks, incentives

38. Better survey results. Trained interviewers can elicit responses to difficult questions.

39. The researcher can learn common answers.

40. Pro: higher chance of making contact with individuals. Con: people upset being interrupted during dinner.

41. Better survey results. A low response rate may mean that some segments of the population are underrepresented or that only individuals with strong opinions have participated.

42. Changing the order helps prevent bias due to previous-question answers or situations where respondents are more likely to pick earlier choices.

43. The question is ambiguous since CD could mean compact disc or certificate of deposit. The question could be improved by not using the abbreviation.

44. Offering rewards or incentives encourages individuals to respond to the survey, which increases response rates.

1.6 Assess Your Understanding (page 50)

1. **(a)** A person, object, or some other well-defined item upon which a treatment is applied
(b) Any combination of the values of the factors (explanatory variables)
(c) A quantitative or qualitative variable that represents the variable of interest
(d) The variable whose effect on the response variable is to be assessed by the experimenter
(e) An innocuous medication, such as a sugar tablet, that looks, tastes, and smells like the experimental medication
(f) The effect of two factors (explanatory variables) on the response variable cannot be distinguished.

2. Replication is the application of the treatment to more than one experimental unit.

3. In a single-blind experiment, the subject does not know which treatment is received. In a double-blind experiment, neither the subject nor the researcher in contact with the subject knows which treatment is received.

4. completely randomized; matched pairs

5. False **6.** True

7. **(a)** The placebo is the flavored-water drink that looks and tastes like the sports drinks. The placebo serves as the baseline against which to compare the results when the noncaffeinated and caffeinated sports drinks are administered.
(b) The cyclists and the researcher administering the treatments do not know when the cyclists have been given the caffeinated sports drink, the noncaffeinated sports drink, or the placebo.
(c) Randomization is used to determine the order of the treatments for each subject.
(d) Population: all athletes. Sample: 16 highly trained cyclists
(e) Treatments: caffeinated sports drink, noncaffeinated sports drink, or flavored-water placebo
(f) Total work
(g) A repeated-measures design takes measurements on the same subjects using multiple treatments. A matched-pairs design is a special case of the repeated-measures design that uses two treatments.

8. **(a)** The placebo is a drug that looks and tastes like topiramate. The placebo serves as the baseline against which to compare the results when topiramate is administered.
(b) Neither the subject nor the researcher in contact with the subject knows whether the placebo or topiramate is being administered.
(c) The subjects were randomly assigned to either the topiramate group or the placebo group.
(d) Population: all men and women aged 18 to 65 years diagnosed with alcohol dependence. Sample: 371 men and women aged 18 to 65 years diagnosed with alcohol dependence.

(e) Treatments: 300 mg of topiramate or a placebo daily
(f) Percentage of heavy drinking days

9. (a) Score on achievement test
(b) Method of teaching, grade level, intelligence, school district, teacher. Fixed: grade level, school district, teacher. Set at a predetermined level: method of teaching
(c) New teaching method and traditional method; 2
(d) Random assignment **(e)** Group 2
(f) Completely randomized design
(g) 500 first-grade students in District 203
(h)

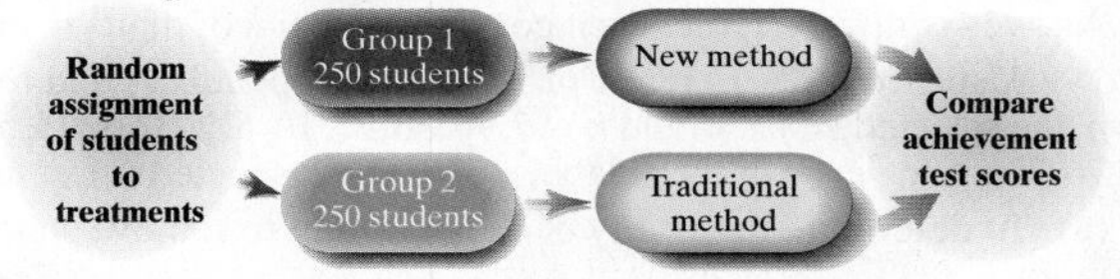

10. (a) Proportion of subjects with a cold
(b) Gender, age, geographic location, overall health, drug intervention. Fixed: gender, age, location. Set at a predetermined level: drug intervention
(c) Experimental drug and placebo; 2
(d) Random assignment
(e) Completely randomized design
(f) 300 males
(g)

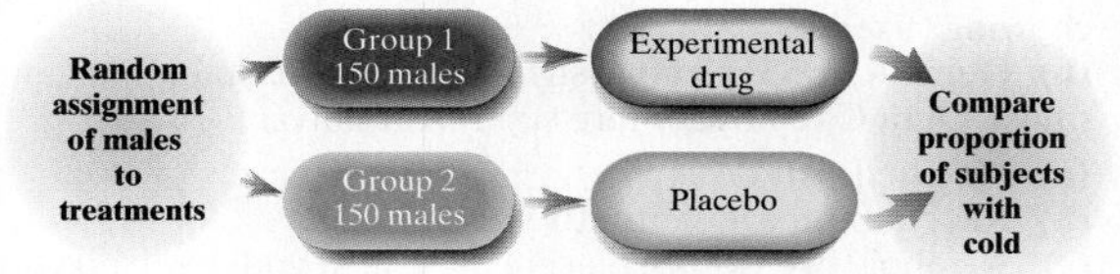

11. (a) Matched pair **(b)** Whiteness level
(c) Crest Whitestrips Premium with brushing and flossing versus brushing and flossing alone
(d) Answers will vary. One possible variable would be diet. Certain foods and tobacco products are more likely to stain teeth. This could affect the whiteness level.
(e) Answers will vary. One possible answer is that using twins helps control for genetic factors (like weak teeth) that may affect the results of the study.

12. (a) Matched pair
(b) Difference in test scores
(c) Math course

13. (a) Completely randomized design
(b) Adults with insomnia
(c) Wake time after sleep onset (WASO)
(d) CBT, RT, placebo
(e) 75 adults with insomnia
(f)

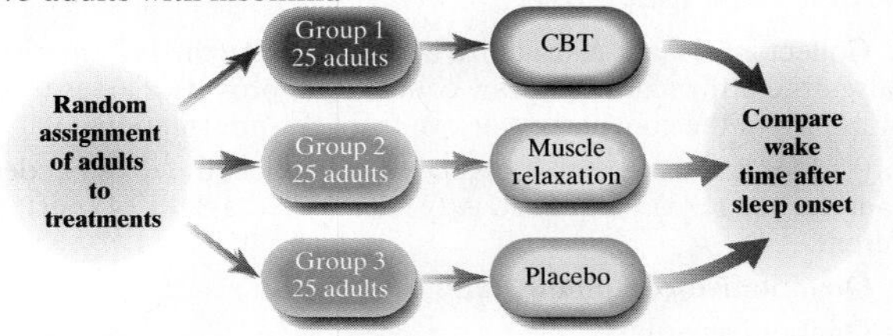

14. (a) Completely randomized design
(b) Adult outpatients diagnosed as having major depression and having a baseline Hamilton Rating Scale for Depression (HAM-D) score of at least 20.
(c) Change in the HAM-D over the treatment period
(d) Type of drug: St. John's wort extract or placebo
(e) 200 outpatients diagnosed with depression
(f) The placebo group
(g)

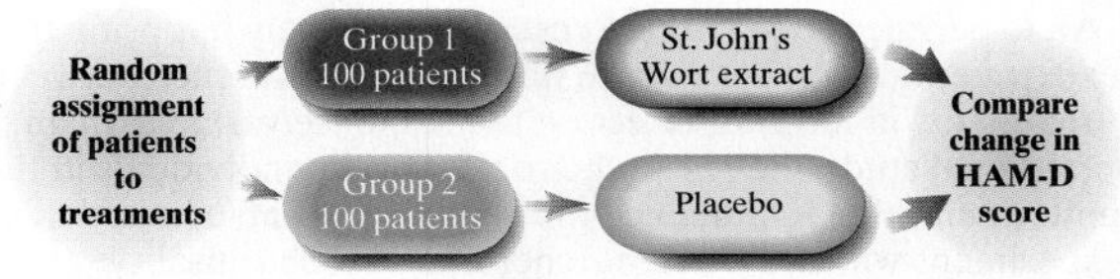

15. (a) Completely randomized design
(b) Adults older than 60 years in good health
(c) Score on a standardized test of learning and memory
(d) Drug: 40 mg of ginkgo 3 times per day or a matching placebo
(e) 98 men and 132 women older than 60 in good health
(f) The placebo group
(g)

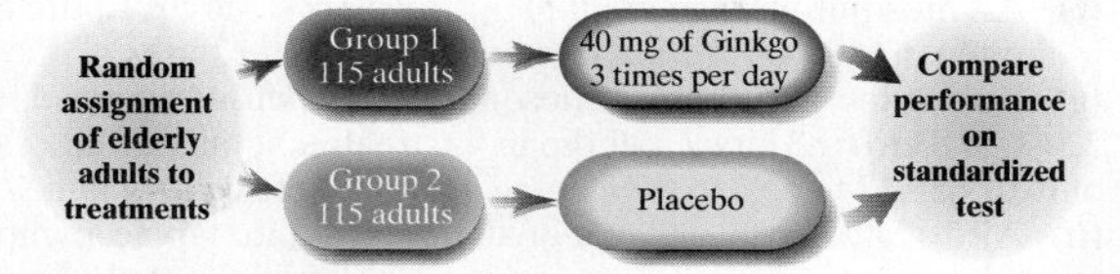

16. (a) Completely randomized design
(b) Obese individuals
(c) Volume of stomach; quantitative
(d) 2508-kJ diet versus regular diet
(e) The 23 obese patients
(f)

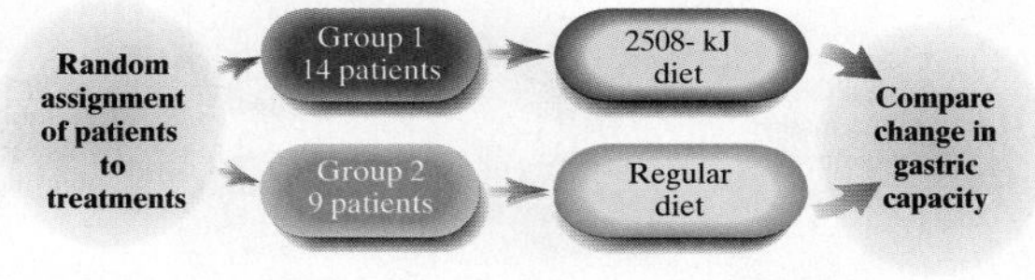

17. (a) Matched-pairs design
(b) Distance yardstick falls
(c) Dominant versus nondominant hand
(d) 15 students
(e) To eliminate bias due to starting on dominant or nondominant first for each trial
(f)

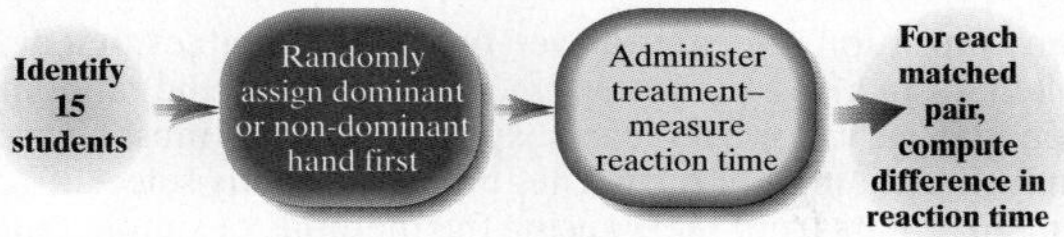

18. (a) Matched-pairs design
(b) Distance ball hit
(c) Shaft type: graphite shaft versus steel shaft
(d) 10 golfers
(e) To eliminate bias due to type of shaft used first
(f)

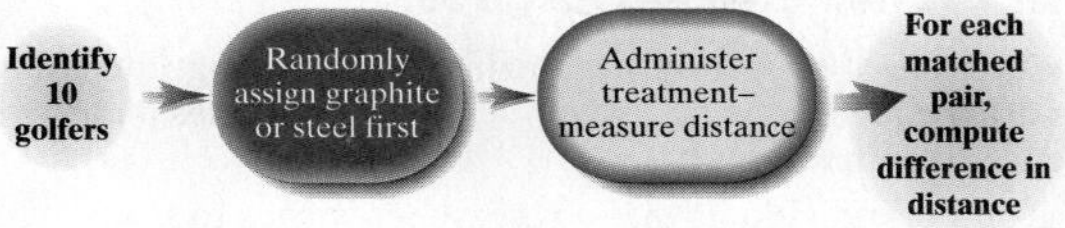

19. Answers will vary.

20. (a) Completely randomized design
(b) Answers will vary.

21. Answers will vary. Completely randomized design is likely best.

22. Answers will vary. Completely randomized design is likely best.

23. Answers will vary. Matched-pairs design is likely best (match by type of exterior finish).

24. Answers will vary. Matched-pairs design is likely best (match by car model).

25. (a) Blood pressure
(b) Daily consumption of salt, daily consumption of fruits and vegetables, body's ability to process salt
(c) Salt: controlled; fruits/vegetables: controlled, body: cannot be controlled. To deal with variability in body types, randomly assign experimental units to each treatment group.
(d) Answers will vary. Three might be a good choice; one level below RDA, one equal to RDA, one above RDA.

28. Answers will vary. For the completely randomized design, the researcher would randomly assign each subject to either drink Coke or Pepsi. The response variable would be the proportion of subjects who prefer Coke versus the proportion of subjects who prefer Pepsi. The subject would be blinded; however, the researcher would not, so this is a single-blind experiment. For the matched-pairs design, the researcher would randomly determine whether each subject drinks Coke first or Pepsi first. The response variable would be either the proportion of subjects who prefer Coke or the proportion of subjects who prefer Pepsi. This would also be a single-blind experiment. The matched-pairs design is likely superior.

29. (a) To determine if nymphs of *Brachytron pretense* will control mosquitoes
(b) Completely randomized design
(c) Mosquito larvae density; quantitative; discrete, since the larvae are counted
(d) Introduction of nymphs of *Brachytron pretense* into water tanks containing mosquito larvae; nymphs added or no nymphs added

(e) Temperature, amount of rainfall, fish, other larvae, sunlight
(f) All mosquito larvae in all breeding places; the mosquito larvae in the ten 300-liter outdoor, open concrete water tanks
(g) During the study period, mosquito larvae density changed from 7.34 to 0.83 to 6.83 larvae per dip in the treatment tanks, while changing only from 7.12 to 6.83 to 6.79 larvae per dip in the control tanks.
(h) All 10 tanks were cleaned of all nonmosquito larvae, nymphs, and fish so that only mosquito larvae were left in the tanks. Five tanks were treated with 10 nymphs of *Brachytron pretense*, while five tanks were left untreated, serving as the control. In other words, the contents of the tanks were as identical as possible, except for the treatment.
(i)

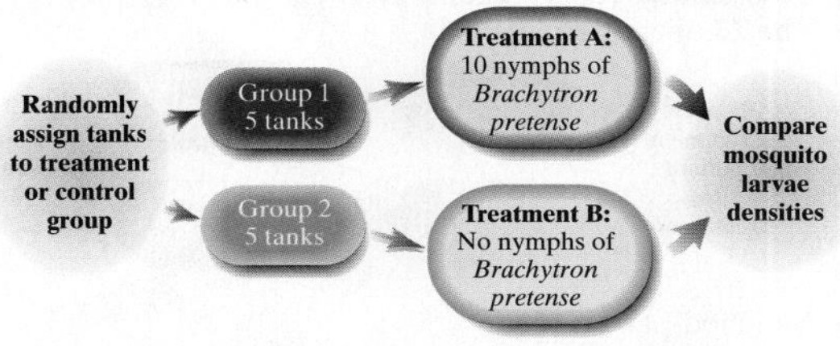

(j) Nymphs of *Brachytron pretense* can be used effectively as a strong, ecologically friendly control of mosquitoes and mosquito-borne diseases.

30. Control groups are needed in a designed experiment to serve as a baseline against which other treatments can be compared.

31. Randomization is meant to even out those variables that are not controlled for in a designed experiment. Answers to the randomization question may vary; however, each experimental unit must be assigned randomly. For example, a researcher might randomly select 30 experimental units from the 90 using the methods of simple random sampling and assign them to treatment 1. Then the researcher could randomly select another 30 experimental units from the remaining 60 and assign them to treatment 2. The remaining experimental units would go to treatment 3.

Chapter 1 Review Exercises (page 56)

1. The science of collecting, organizing, summarizing, and analyzing data to draw conclusions or answer questions; provides a measure of confidence to conclusions.

2. A group of individuals that a researcher wishes to study

3. A subset of the population

4. Measures the value of the response variable without attempting to influence the value of either the response or explanatory variables.

5. Applies a treatment to the individuals in the study to isolate the effect of the treatment on the response variable.

6. (1) *Cross-sectional studies:* collect information about individuals at a specific point in time or over a very short period of time. (2) *Case-control studies:* look back in time and match individuals possessing certain characteristic with those that do not. (3) *Cohort studies:* collect information about a group of individuals over a period of time.

7. (1) Identify the research objective, (2) collect the data needed to answer the research questions, (3) describe the data, (4) perform inference

8. (1) *Sampling bias* occurs when the techniques used to select individuals to be in the sample favor one part of the population over another. (2) *Nonresponse bias* occurs when the individuals selected to be in the sample that do not respond to the survey have different opinions from those that do respond. (3) *Response bias* exists when the answers on a survey do not reflect the true feelings of the respondent.

9. *Nonsampling errors* are errors that result from undercoverage, nonresponse bias, response bias, or data-entry errors. *Sampling errors* are errors that result from using a sample to estimate information about a population. They result because samples contain incomplete information regarding a population.

10. (1) Identify the problem to be solved. (2) Determine the factors that affect the response variable. (3) Determine the number of experimental units. (4) Determine the level of each factor. (5) Conduct the experiment. (6) Test the claim.

11. Quantitative; discrete
12. Quantitative; continuous
13. Qualitative
14. Statistic
15. Parameter
16. Interval
17. Nominal
18. Ordinal
19. Ratio
20. Observational study
21. Experiment
22. Cohort study
23. Convenience sample
24. Cluster sample
25. Stratified sample
26. Systematic sample

27. **(a)** Sampling bias; undercoverage or nonrepresentative sample due to poor sampling frame
(b) Response bias; interviewer error
(c) Data-entry error

28. Answers will vary.

29. Answers will vary.

30. Answers will vary. Label each goggle with pairs of digits from 00 to 99. Using row 12, column 1 of Table I in Appendix A and reading down, the selected labels would be 55, 96, 38, 85, 10, 67, 23, 39, 45, 57, 82, 90, and 76. The goggles with these labels would be inspected for defects.

31. **(a)** To determine the ability of chewing gum to remove stains from teeth.
(b) Designed experiment, because treatments were intentionally imposed on the experimental units (teeth) to determine their effect on a response variable (percentage of stain removed)
(c) Completely randomized design
(d) Percentage of stain removed
(e) Type of stain remover (gum or saliva); qualitative
(f) The 64 stained teeth (bovine incisors)
(g) The amount of time chewing (fixed at 120 minutes); method of chewing (fixed by simulator)
(h) Gums A and B remove significantly more stain than gum C or saliva. Gum C removes more stain than saliva.

32. **(a)** Matched-pair design
(b) Reaction time; quantitative
(c) Alcohol (two drinks: placebo and 40% vodka mixed with orange juice)
(d) Food consumption; caffeine intake
(e) Weight; gender
(f) To act as a placebo to control for psychosomatic effects of alcohol
(g) Alcohol delays reaction time significantly in seniors for low levels of alcohol consumption. The study applies to healthy seniors who are not regular drinkers.

33. Answers will vary.

34. Answers will vary.

35. In a completely randomized design, the experimental units are randomly assigned to one of the treatments. The value of the response variable is compared for each treatment. In a matched-pairs design, experimental units are matched up on the basis of some common characteristic (such as husband–wife or twins). The difference in the matched-up experimental units is analyzed.

Chapter 1 Test (page 59)

1. Collect information, organize and summarize the information, analyze the information to draw conclusions, provide a measure of confidence in the conclusions drawn from the information.

2. (1) Identify the research objective, (2) collect the data needed to answer the research questions, (3) describe the data, (4) perform inference

3. Quantitative, continuous, ratio

4. Qualitative, ordinal

5. Quantitative, discrete, ratio

6. Experiment, battery life

7. Observational study; fan opinion on presence of asterisk on record ball

8. A *cross-sectional study* collects data at a specific point in time or over a short period of time; a *cohort study* collects data over a period of time, sometimes over a long period of time; a *case-controlled study* is retrospective, looking back in time to collect data.

9. An experiment involves the researcher actively imposing treatments on experimental units in order to observe any difference between the treatments in terms of effect on the response variable. In an observational study, the researcher observes the individuals in the study without attempting to influence the response variable in any way. Only an experiment will allow a researcher to establish causality.

10. A control group is necessary for a baseline comparison. Comparing other treatments to the control group allows the researcher to identify which, if any, of the other treatments are superior to the current treatment (or no treatment at all). Blinding is important to eliminate bias due to the individual or experimenter knowing which treatment is being applied.

11. (1) Identify the problem to be solved, (2) determine the factors that affect the response variable, (3) determine the number of experimental units, (4) determine the level of each factor, (5) conduct the experiment, (6) test the claim.

12. Number the franchise locations 1 to 15. Use Table I in Appendix A or a random-number generator to determine four unique numbers. The franchise locations corresponding to these numbers are the franchises in the sample. Results will vary.

13. Obtain a simple random sample for each stratum. Be sure to use a different starting point in Table I in Appendix A or a different seed for each stratum. Results will vary.

14. Number the blocks from 1 to 2500 and obtain a simple random sample of size 10. The blocks corresponding to these numbers represent the blocks analyzed. Analyze all trees on each of the selected blocks. Results will vary.

15. Ideally, k would be $600/14 = 42$ (rounded down). Randomly select a number between 1 and 42. This represents the first slot machine inspected. Then inspect every 42nd machine thereafter. Results will vary.

16. In a completely randomized design, the experimental units are randomly assigned to one of the treatments. The value of the response variable is compared for each treatment.

17. (a) Sampling bias (voluntary response)
(b) Nonresponse bias
(c) Response bias (poorly worded question)
(d) Sampling bias (undercoverage)

18. (a) Lymphocyte count
(b) Space flight
(c) Matched pairs
(d) Four flight members
(e)

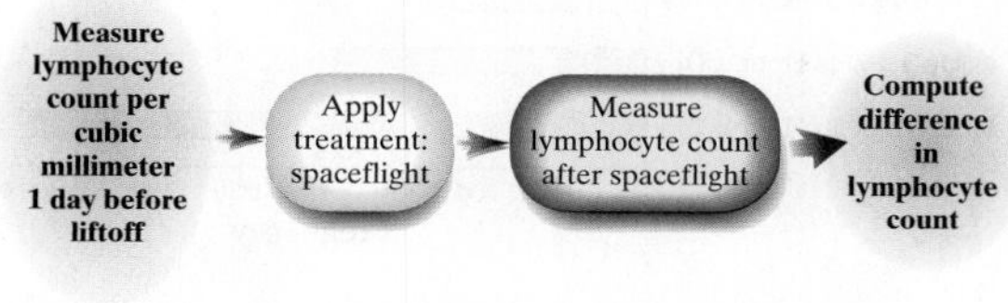

19. (a) Completely randomized design
(b) Improvement in skin irritation
(c) Topical cream; 0.5%, 1.0%, 0%
(d) Neither the subjects nor the person applying the treatments were aware of which treatment was being given.
(e) Placebo group (0% cream)
(f) 225 patients with skin irritation
(g)

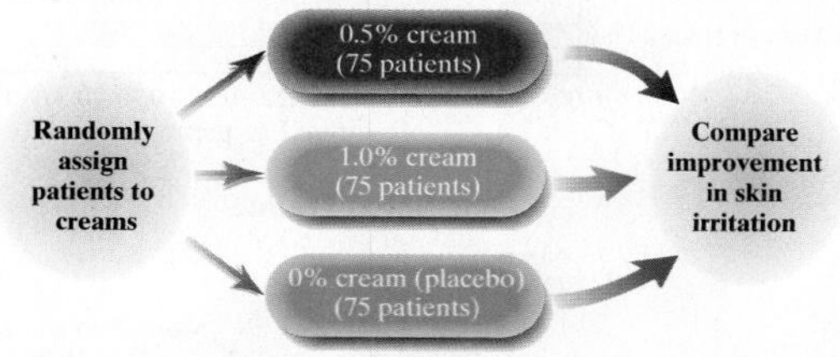

20. (a) Subjects were observed over a long period of time and certain characteristics were recorded. The response variable was recorded at the end of the study.
(b) Bone mineral density; weekly cola consumption
(c) Quantitative
(d) The researchers observed values of variables that could potentially impact bone mineral density (besides cola consumption) so their effect could be isolated from the variable of interest.
(e) Smoking status; alcohol consumption, physical activity, calcium intake.
(f) Women who consumed at least one cola per day (on average) had a bone mineral density that was significantly lower at the femoral neck than those who consumed less than one cola per day. No, they are associated.

CHAPTER 2 Summarizing Data in Tables and Graphs

2.1 Assess Your Understanding (page 69)

1. Raw data are data that are not organized.

2. number; proportion (or percent)

3. 1 (although rounding may cause the result to vary slightly)

4. See definition on page 65. A Pareto chart is a bar graph whose bars are drawn in decreasing order of frequency or relative frequency.

5. (a) Washing your hands; 61%
(b) Drinking orange juice; 2%
(c) 25%

6. (a) 9.5% **(b)** 10.2% **(c)** 338,000

7. (a) China **(b)** 50 million **(c)** 350 million
(d) Should use relative frequency since China's population is much higher, it is likely to have a higher frequency just due to population size.

8. (a) 29,830,000 whites were living in poverty.
(b) 22.9% of those living in poverty were Hispanic.
(c) The graph could be misleading because it does not account for the different population sizes of each ethnicity.

9. (a) 69% **(b)** 55.2 million **(c)** Inferential

10. (a) 5% **(b)** 2.6 million

11. (a) 0.42; 0.61 **(b)** 55 +
(c) 18–34 **(d)** As age increases, so does likelihood to buy American

12. (a) 0.46; 0.41 **(b)** Thinner
(c) Younger **(d)** Smarter

13. (a)

Response	Relative Frequency
Never	0.0262
Rarely	0.0678
Sometimes	0.1156
Most of the time	0.2632
Always	0.5272

(b) 52.7% **(c)** 9.4%
(d)

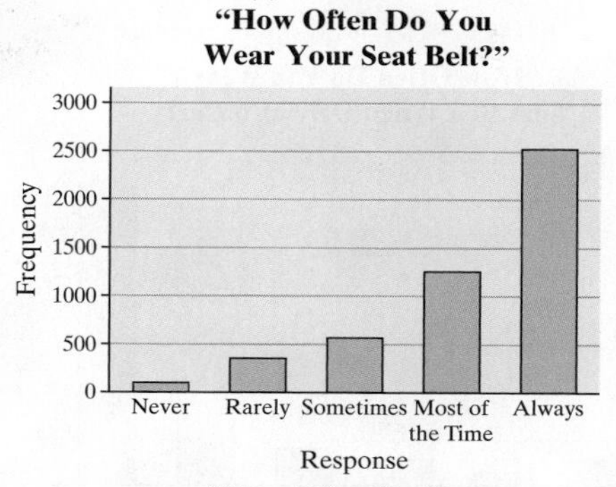

(e)

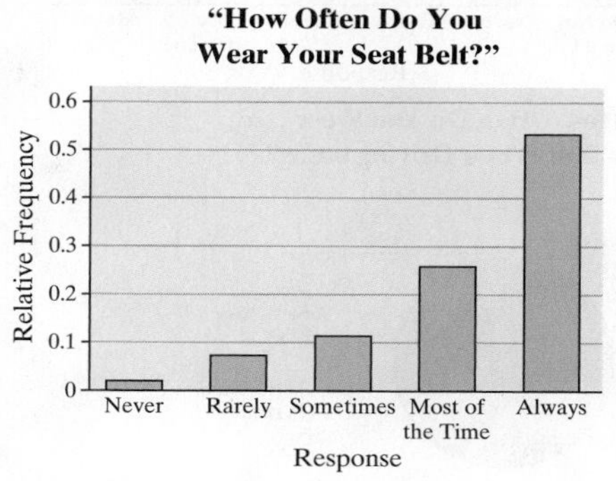

(f)

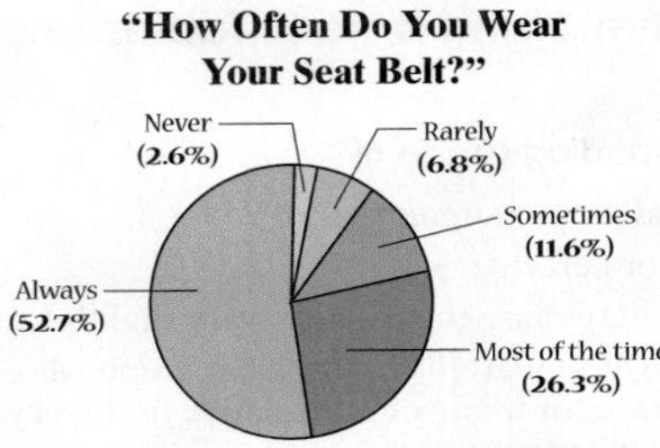

(g) This is an inferential statement because it is taking a result of the sample and generalizing it to the population "all college students."

14. (a)

Response	Relative Frequency
I do not drive a car	0.0522
Never	0.0247
Rarely	0.0522
Sometimes	0.0723
Most of the time	0.1501
Always	0.6484

(b) 64.84% **(c)** 7.69%

(d)

(e)

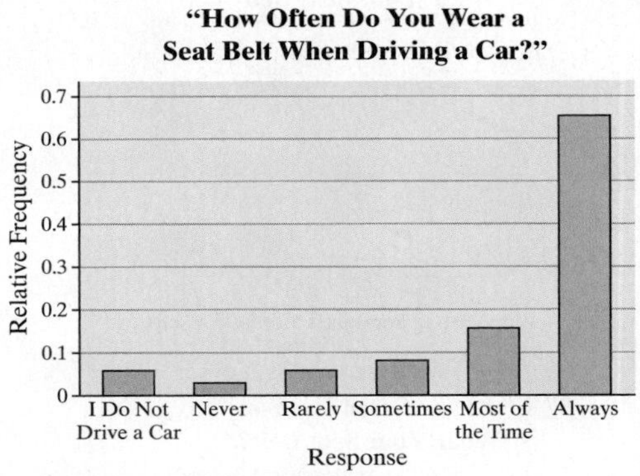

(f)

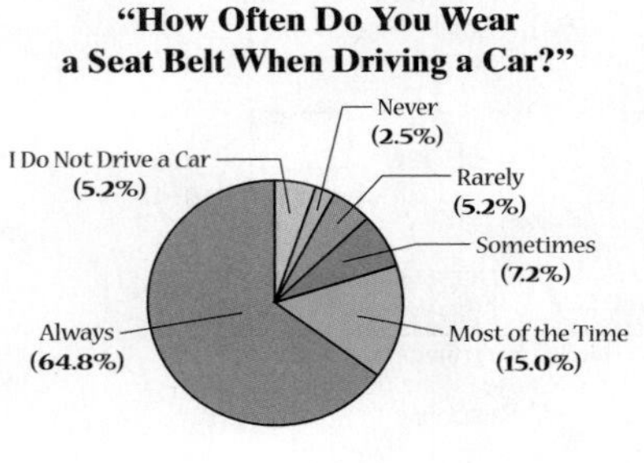

(g)

Response	Relative Frequency
Never	0.0261
Rarely	0.0551
Sometimes	0.0763
Most of the time	0.1584
Always	0.6841

It appears individual's seat belt use does not vary much whether they are a driver or passenger.

(h) This is a descriptive statement since it is a summary of the data collected.

15. (a)

Response	Relative Frequency
More than 1 hour a day	0.3678
Up to 1 hour a day	0.1873
A few times a week	0.1288
A few times a month or less	0.0790
Never	0.2371

(b) 0.2371 (about 24%)

(c)

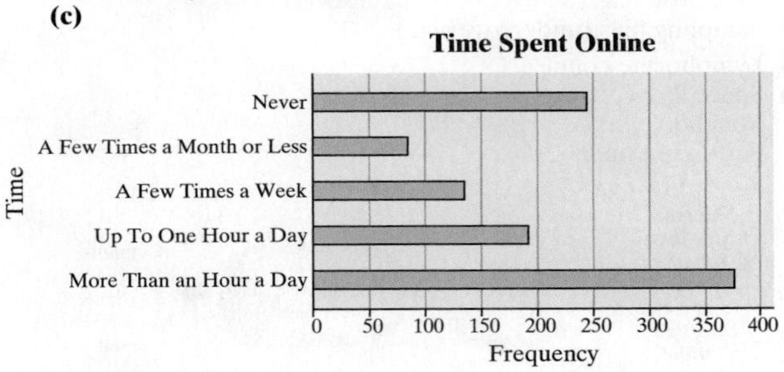

(d)

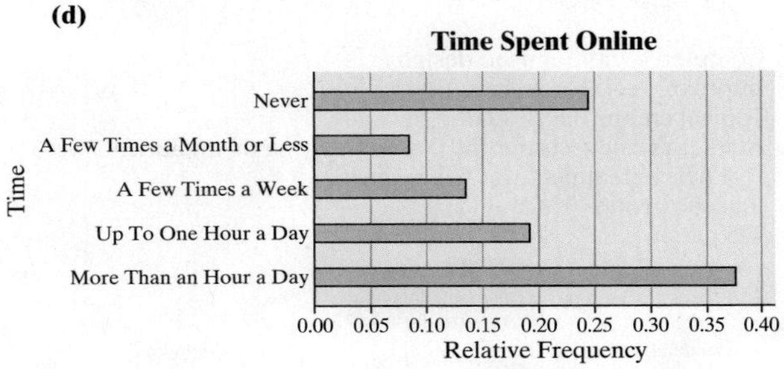

(e)

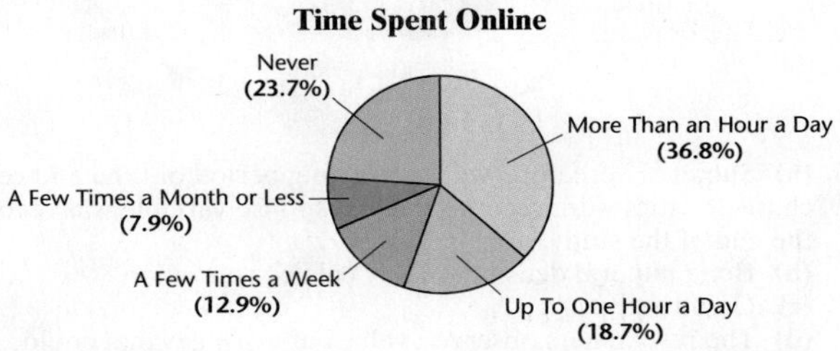

(f) No level of confidence is provided along with the estimate.

16. (a)

Response	Relative Frequency
Several times a week	0.1977
Once or twice a week	0.3916
A few times a month	0.2495
Very rarely	0.1516
Never	0.0096

(b) 0.3916

(c)

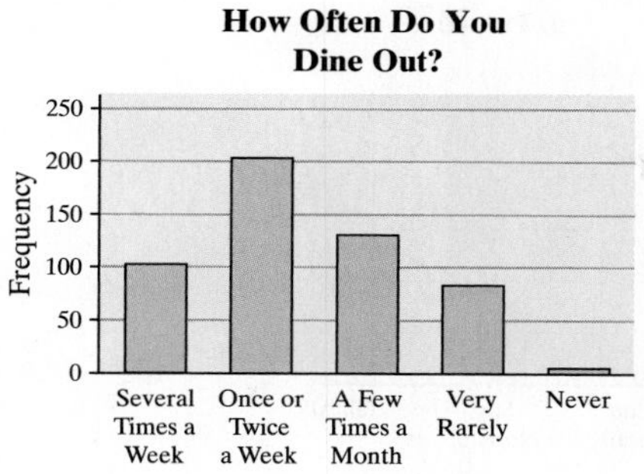

(d)

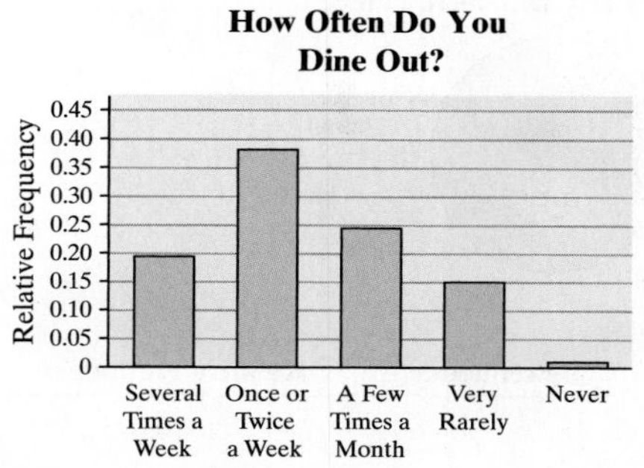

17. (a), (b)

Number of Texts	Adults	Teens
None	0.0894	0.0207
1 to 10	0.5052	0.2201
11 to 20	0.1286	0.1100
21 to 50	0.1286	0.1802
51 to 100	0.0692	0.1802
101+	0.0790	0.2887

(c)

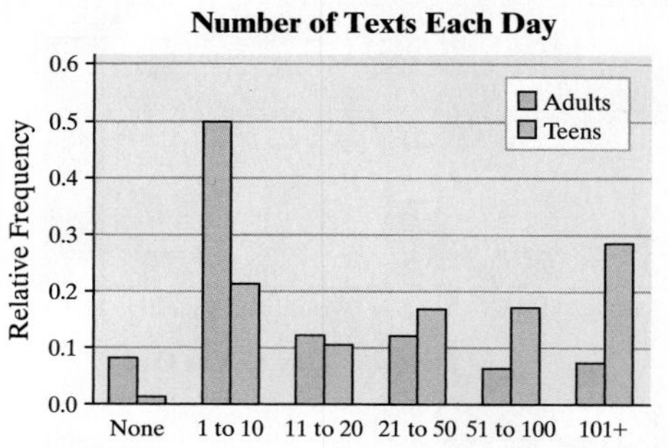

(d) Adults are much more likely to do fewer texts per day, while teens are much more likely to do more texting per day.

18. (a), (b)

Educational Attainment	Males	Females
Not a high school graduate	0.1407	0.1275
High school graduate	0.3122	0.3108
Some college, no degree	0.1672	0.1765
Associate's degree	0.0794	0.0961
Bachelor's degree	0.1905	0.1922
Advanced degree	0.1101	0.0971

(c)

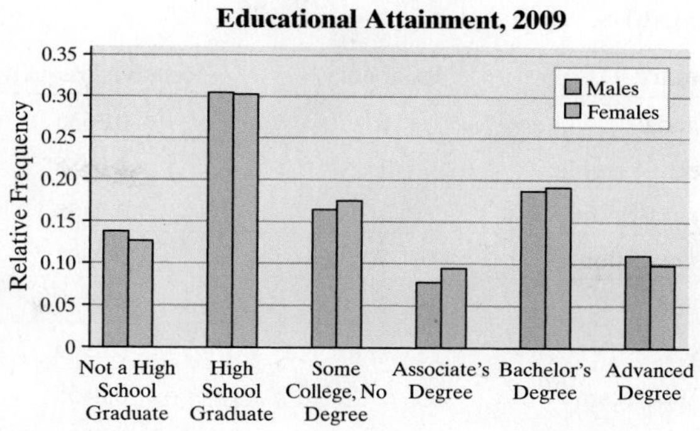

(d) Answers will vary.

19. (a)

Dream Job	Males	Females
Professional Athlete	0.4040	0.18
Actor/Actress	0.2626	0.37
President of the United States	0.1313	0.13
Rock Star	0.1313	0.13
Not Sure	0.0707	0.19

(b)

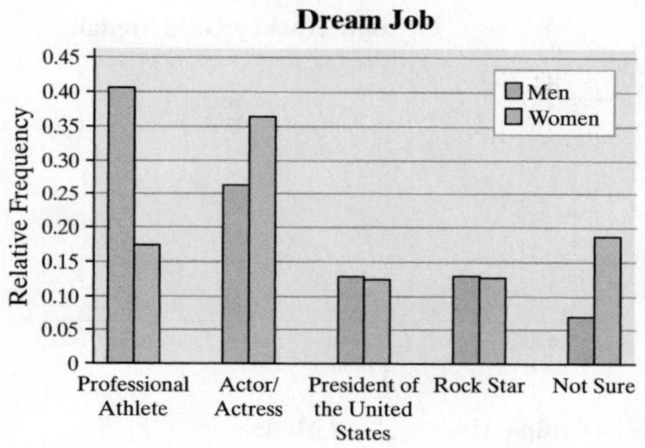

(c) Answers will vary.

20. (a)

Color	Luxury Cars	Sports Cars
White	0.25	0.10
Black	0.22	0.15
Silver	0.16	0.18
Gray	0.12	0.15
Blue	0.07	0.13
Red	0.07	0.15
Gold	0.06	0.05
Green	0.03	0.02
Brown	0.02	0.07

(b)

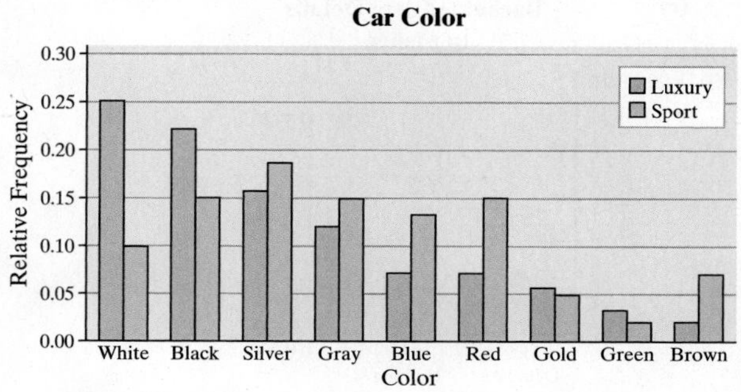

(c) Answers will vary.

21. (a), (b)

Country	Frequency	Relative Frequency
Canada	8	0.3636
Czech Republic	1	0.0455
Great Britain	1	0.0455
Soviet Union	7	0.3182
Sweden	2	0.0909
U.S.A.	2	0.0909
Unified Team	1	0.0455

(c) **Olympic Hockey Gold Medals**

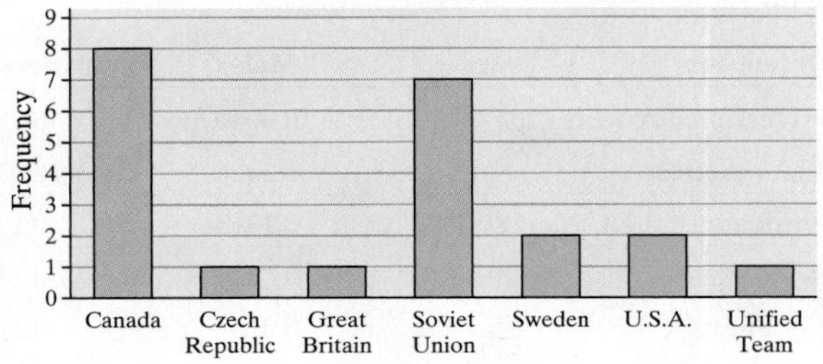

(d) **Olympic Hockey Gold Medals**

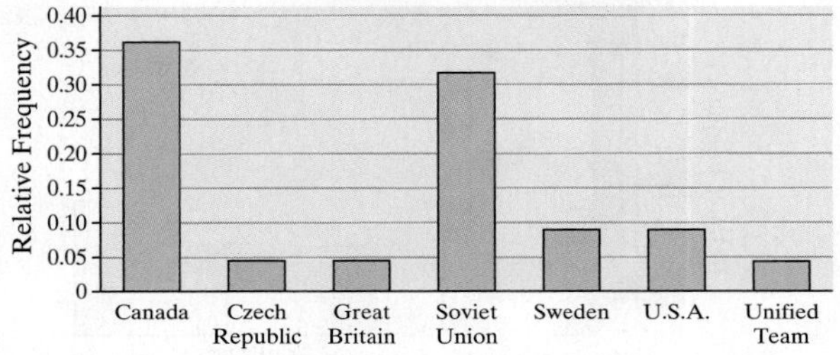

(e) **Olympic Hockey Gold Medals**

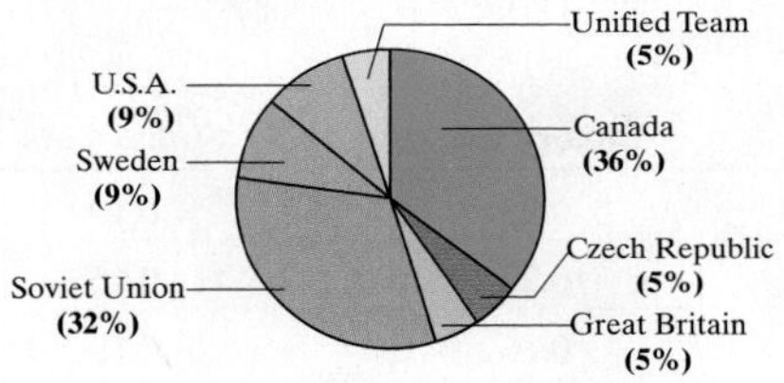

22. (a), (b)

Response	Frequency	Relative Frequency
Edit details	7	0.28
Say nothing	4	0.16
Tell all	14	0.56

(c) **Bachelor Party Details to Fiancé**

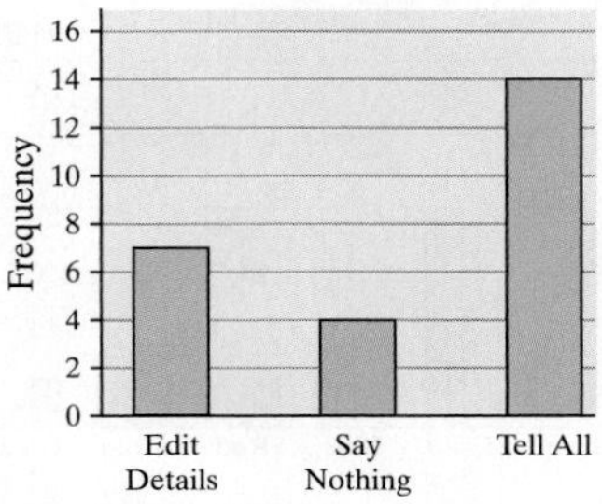

(d) **Bachelor Party Details to Fiancé**

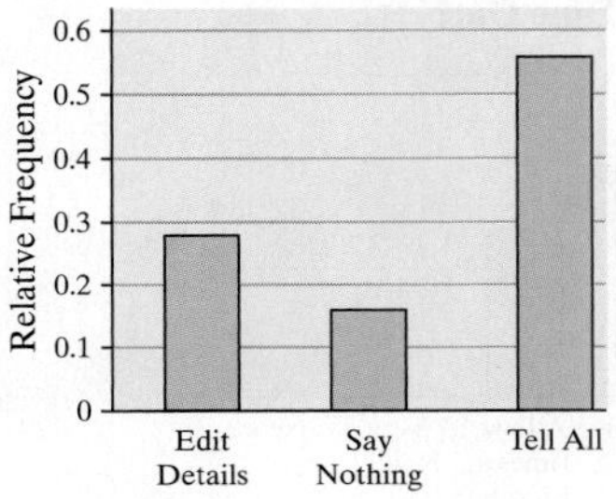

(e) **Bachelor Party Details to Fiancé**

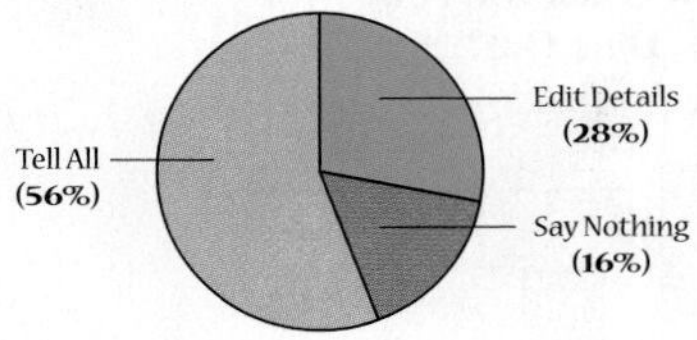

23. (a), (b)

Day	Frequency	Relative Frequency
Sunday	3	0.075
Monday	2	0.05
Tuesday	5	0.125
Wednesday	6	0.15
Thursday	2	0.05
Friday	14	0.35
Saturday	8	0.2

(c) Answers will vary. Monday would likely be the worst bet, and Thursday may be the best choice.

(d) **Favorite Day to Eat Out**

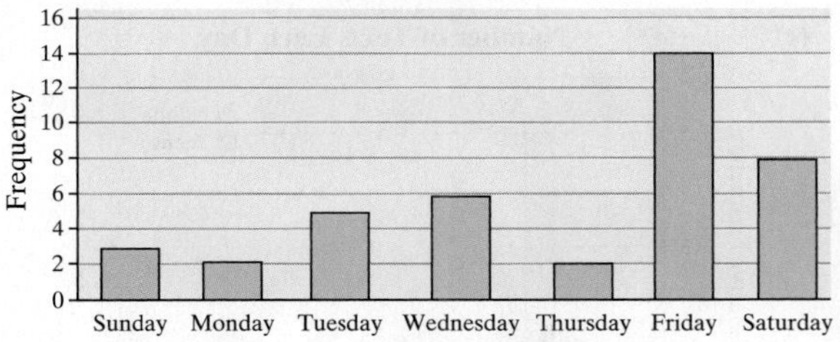

(e) **Favorite Day to Eat Out**

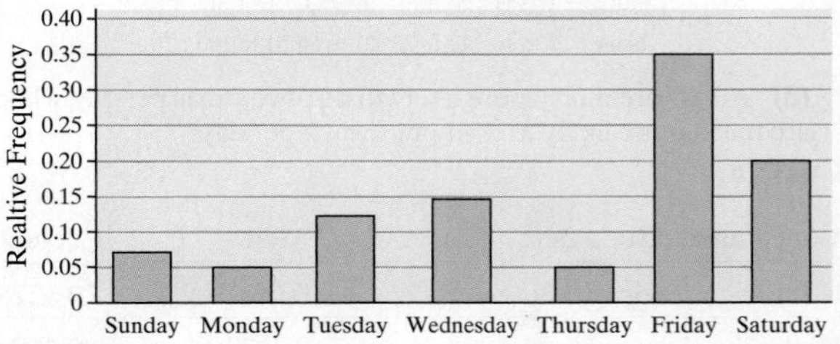

(f) **Favorite Day to Eat Out**

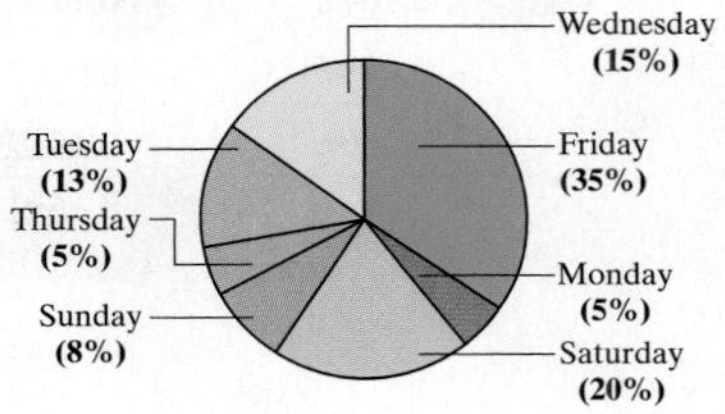

24. (a), (b)

Blood Type	Frequency	Relative Frequency
A	18	0.36
AB	4	0.08
B	6	0.12
O	22	0.44

(c) O
(d) AB
(e) 44%; inferential
(f) Answers will vary.
(g)

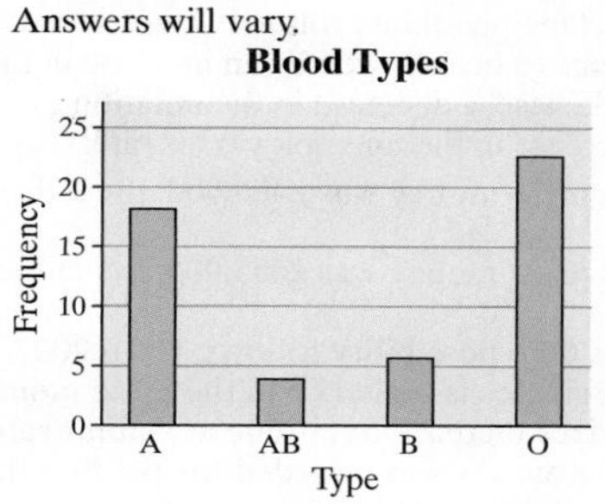

(h)

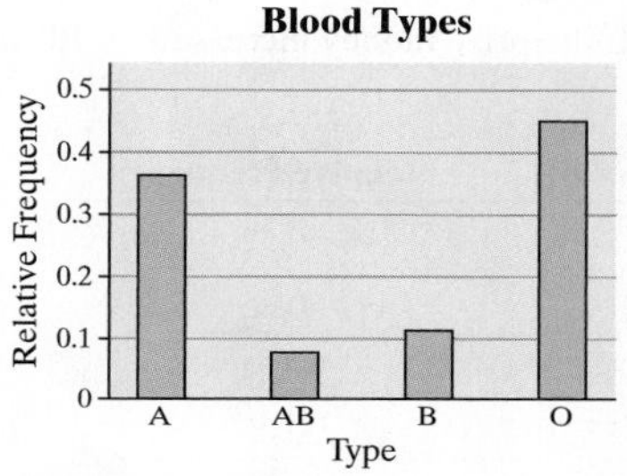

(i)

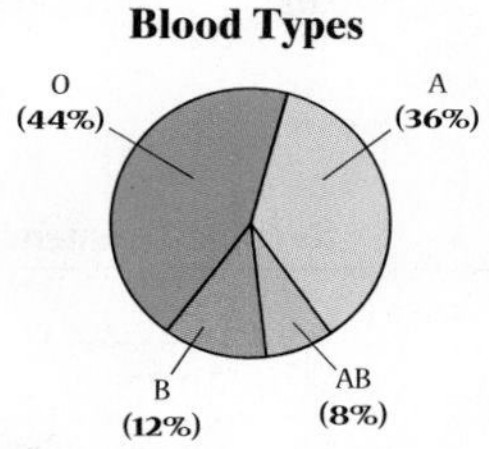

25. (a), (b)

Language Studied	Frequency	Relative Frequency
Chinese	3	0.100
French	3	0.100
German	3	0.100
Italian	2	0.067
Japanese	2	0.067
Latin	2	0.067
Russian	1	0.033
Spanish	14	0.467

(c)

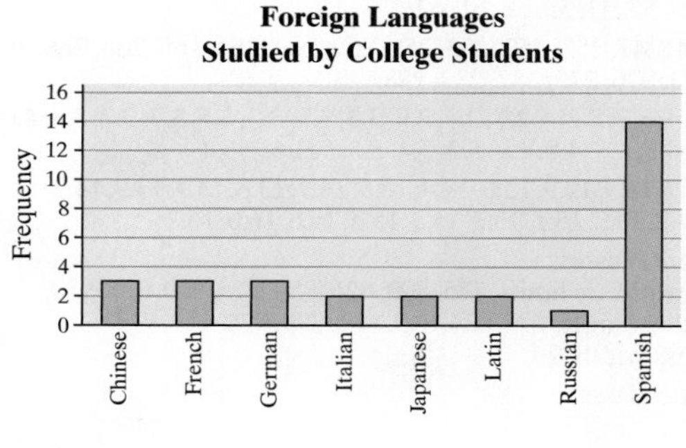

(d)

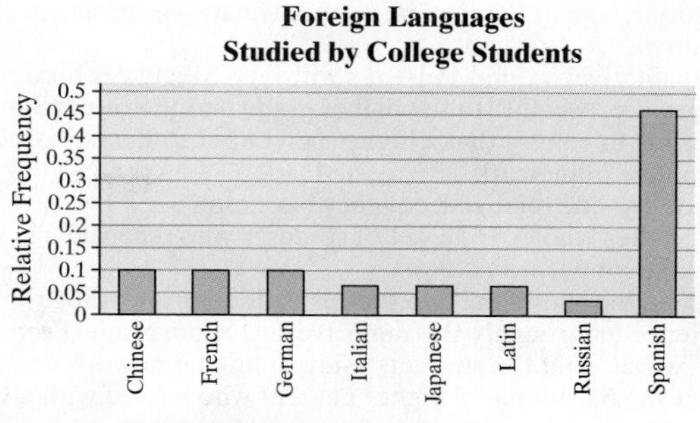

(e)

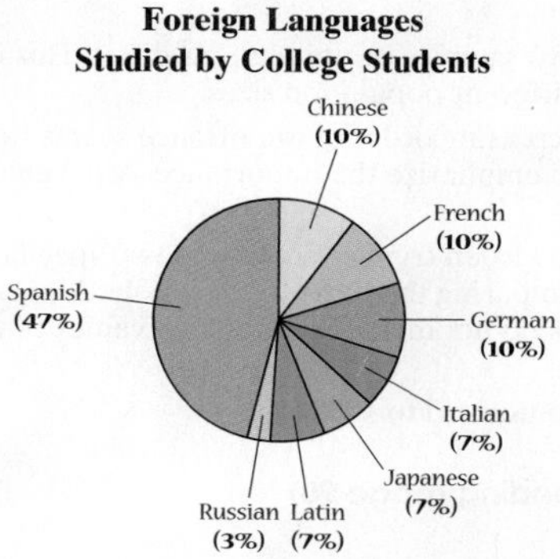

26. (a)

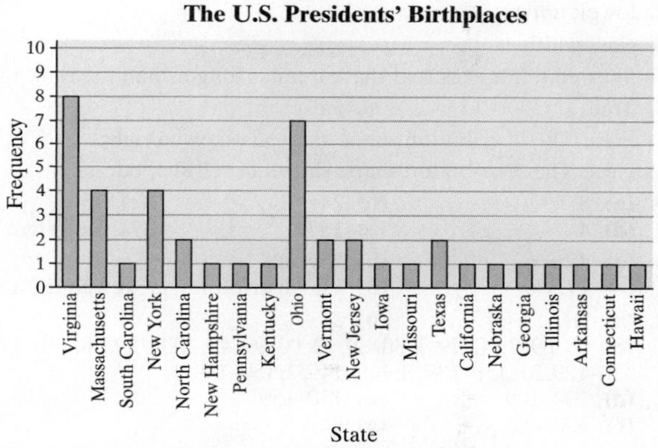

(b) More presidents were born in Virginia than in any other state.
(c) Virginia is one of the original 13 colonies.

27. (a) Yes, because there are parts (each continent) and a whole (entire land area).

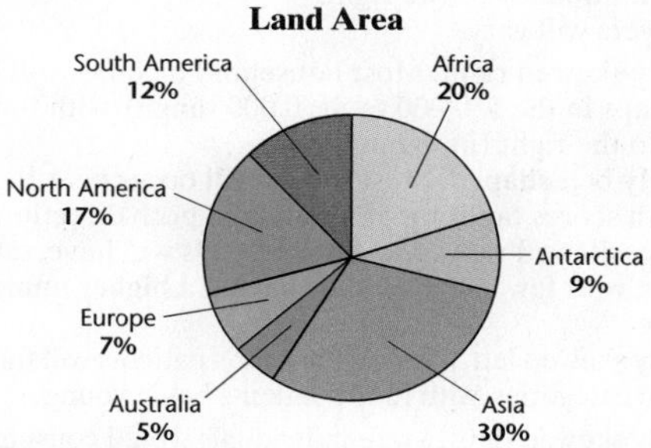

(b) No, because there is no whole to compare the parts to.

28. Answers will vary.

29. Answers will vary.

30. (a) To determine if online homework improves student learning over traditional pencil-and-paper homework.
(b) Experiment
(c) Answers will vary. Some examples are same teacher, same semester, same course.
(d) There could be differences between the classes. The instructor may give more instruction to one class than the other. The instructor is not blinded, so he or she may treat one group differently from the other.
(e) *Number of students*: quantitative, discrete; *average age*: quantitative, continuous; *average exam score*: quantitative,

continuous; *type of homework*: qualitative; *college experience*: qualitative
(f) Qualitative; ordinal. Answers will vary. Likely yes because it gives more "weight" to the higher grade and the researcher is attempting to convey that a higher percent of students passed using online homework.
(g) Side-by-side relative frequency bar graph
(h) Yes; the "whole" is the set of students who received a grade for the course for each class type.
(i) The table shows the two groups with no prior college experience had roughly the same average exam grade. From the bar graph, we see that the students using online homework had a lower percent for As, but had a higher percent who passed with a C or better.

31. When the size of the two samples or populations differ. This is done to eliminate the effect of different population sizes.

32. Answers may vary. Decreasing order of importance seems to be a good choice if the goal is to emphasize the importance. A pie chart does not allow for order.

33. A bar graph is preferred when trying to compare two specific values. Pie charts are useful for comparing the parts to the whole. A pie chart cannot be drawn if the data do not include all possible values of the qualitative variable.

34. No. The percentages do not add to 100%.

2.2 Assess Your Understanding (page 90)

1. classes
2. lower; upper
3. class width
4. Skewed left means that the left tail is longer than the right tail.
5. True **6.** False
7. False. The distribution shape shown is skewed right.
8. False. The distribution shape shown is bell shaped.
9. (a) 8 **(b)** 2 **(c)** 15
(d) 4 **(e)** 15% **(f)** Bell shaped
10. (a) 4 cars **(b)** 9 weeks
(c) 17.3% **(d)** The distribution is skewed right.
11. (a) 200 **(b)** 10
(c) 60–69, 2; 70–79, 3; 80–89, 13; 90–99, 42; 100–109, 58; 110–119, 40; 120–129, 31; 130–139, 8; 140–149, 2; 150–159, 1
(d) 100–109 **(e)** 150–159
(f) 5.5% **(g)** No
12. (a) Class width is 200.
(b) Classes: 0–199; 200–399; 400–599; 600–799; 800–999; 1000–1199; 1200–1399; 1400–1599.
(c) Highest frequency is in class 0–199.
(d) Distribution is skewed right.
(e) Answers will vary.
13. (a) Likely skewed right. Most household incomes will be to the left (perhaps in the $50,000 to $150,000 range), with fewer higher incomes to the right (in the millions).
(b) Likely bell-shaped. Most scores will occur near the middle range, with scores tapering off equally in both directions.
(c) Likely skewed right. Most households will have, say, 1 to 4 occupants, with fewer households having a higher number of occupants.
(d) Likely skewed left. Most Alzheimer's patients will fall in older-aged categories, with fewer patients being younger.
14. (a) Likely skewed right. More individuals would consume fewer alcoholic drinks per week, while fewer individuals would consume more alcoholic drinks per week.
(b) Likely uniform. There will be approximately an equal number of students in each age category.
(c) Likely skewed left. Most hearing-aid patients will fall in older-aged categories, with fewer patients being younger.
(d) Likely bell-shaped. Most heights will occur, say, in the 66- to 70-inch range, with heights tapering off equally in both directions.
15. (a) 70% **(b)** 40%; 2006
(c) Approximately 73%; 2009
(d) Decrease of about 43%
(e) About an increase of about 87.5%

16. (a) About 8.8 million motor vehicles were produced in the United States in 1991.
(b) About 13.0 million motor vehicles were produced in the United States in 1999.
(c) The number of vehicles produced increased by about 47.7%.
(d) The number of vehicles produced decreased by about 56%.
17. (a) For 1992, the unemployment rate was about 7.5% and the inflation rate was about 3.0%.
(b) For 2009, the unemployment rate was about 9.2% and the inflation rate was about −0.4%.
(c) For 1992, the misery index was about 10.5%. For 2009, the misery index was about 8.8%.
(d) Answers may vary. One possibility follows: An increase in the inflation rate seems to be followed by an increase in the unemployment rate. Likewise, a decrease in the inflation rate seems to be followed by a decrease in the unemployment rate.
18. (a) In 1996, the men's prize money was £400,000; the ladies' prize money was £350,000.
(b) In 2006, the men's prize money was £655,000; the ladies' prize money was £625,000.
(c) Answers may vary. One possibility follows: Until 2007, the prize money for men's singles is higher than the prize money for ladies' singles. Both prizes increase over time at similar rates.
(d) In 2007, equal prize money was awarded for the first time. The prize money for each was £700,000.
(e) From 2010 to 2011, the prize money increased by 10%.
19. (a)

Number of Children under 5	Relative Frequency
0	0.32
1	0.36
2	0.24
3	0.06
4	0.02

(b) 24% **(c)** 60%
20. (a)

Number of Free Throws until a Miss	Relative Frequency
1	0.32
2	0.22
3	0.18
4	0.14
5	0.04
6	0.06
7	0
8	0.02
9	0
10	0.02

(b) 14% of the time she first missed on the fourth try.
(c) 2% of the time she first missed on the tenth try.
(d) 10% of the time she made at least five in a row.
21. 10, 11, 14, 21, 24, 24, 27, 29, 33, 35, 35, 35, 37, 37, 38, 40, 40, 41, 42, 46, 46, 48, 49, 49, 53, 53, 55, 58, 61, 62
22. 240, 244, 247, 252, 252, 253, 259, 259, 263, 264, 265, 268, 268, 269, 270, 271, 271, 273, 276, 276, 282, 283, 288
23. 1.2, 1.4, 1.6, 2.1, 2.4, 2.7, 2.7, 2.9, 3.3, 3.3, 3.3, 3.5, 3.7, 3.7, 3.8, 4.0, 4.1, 4.1, 4.3, 4.6, 4.6, 4.8, 4.8, 4.9, 5.3, 5.4, 5.5, 5.8, 6.2, 6.4
24. 12.3, 12.7, 12.9, 12.9, 13.0, 13.4, 13.5, 13.7, 13.8, 13.9, 13.9, 14.2, 14.4, 14.4, 14.7, 14.7, 14.8, 14.9, 15.1, 15.2, 15.2, 15.5, 15.6, 16.0, 16.3
25. (a) Eight classes
(b) Lower class limits: 775, 800, 825, 850, 875, 900, 925, 950; upper class limits; 799, 824, 849, 874, 899, 924, 949, 974
(c) Class width: 25
26. (a) Nine classes

(b) Lower class limits: 0, 1.0, 2.0, 3.0, 4.0, 5.0, 6.0, 7.0, 8.0; upper class limits: 0.9, 1.9, 2.9, 3.9, 4.9, 5.9, 6.9, 7.9, 8.9
(c) Class width: 1.0

27. (a) Seven classes
(b) Lower class limits: 15, 20, 25, 30, 35, 40, 45; upper class limits: 19, 24, 29, 34, 39, 44, 49
(c) Class width: 5 years

28. (a) Six classes
(b) Lower class limits: 0, 5000, 10000, 15000, 20000, 25000; upper class limits: 4999, 9999, 14999, 19999, 24999, 29999
(c) Class width: 5000

29. (a)

Tuition	Relative Frequency
775–799	0.1982
800–824	0.6126
825–849	0.1351
850–874	0.0450
875–899	0
900–924	0
925–949	0
950–974	0.0090

(b) **Tuition at California Community Colleges**

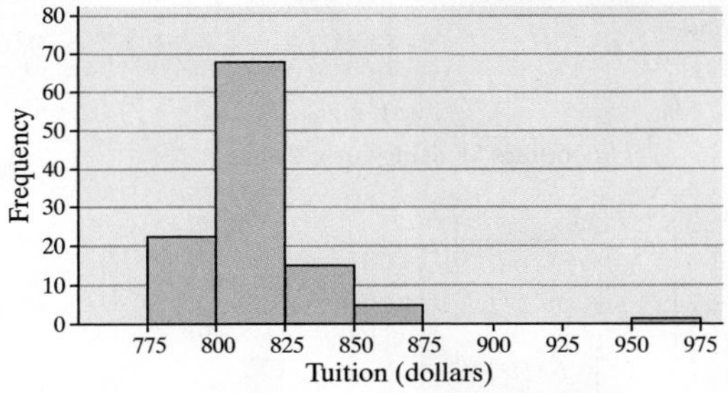

(c) **Tuition at California Community Colleges**

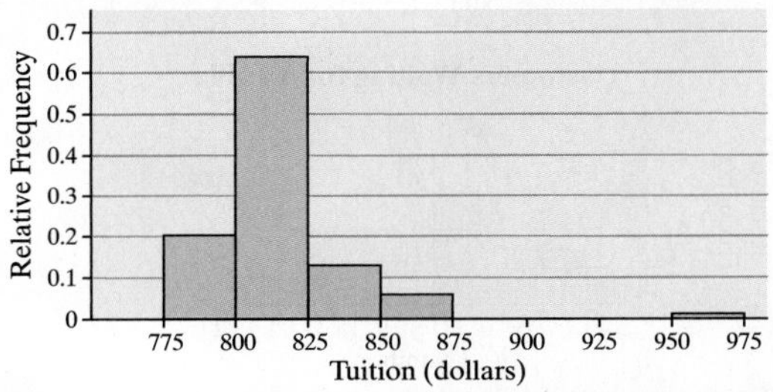

19.82% of California community colleges have tuition below $800. 5.4% of California community colleges have tuition above $850.

30. (a)

Magnitude	Relative Frequency
0–0.9	0.0014
1.0–1.9	0.0014
2.0–2.9	0.2074
3.0–3.9	0.2159
4.0–4.9	0.4715
5.0–5.9	0.0927
6.0–6.9	0.0084
7.0–7.9	0.0012
8.0–8.9	0.0001

(b) **Worldwide Earthquakes, 2010**

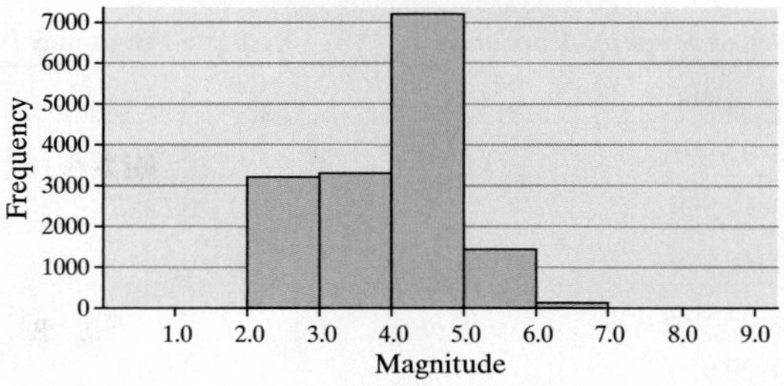

(c) **Worldwide Earthquakes, 2010**

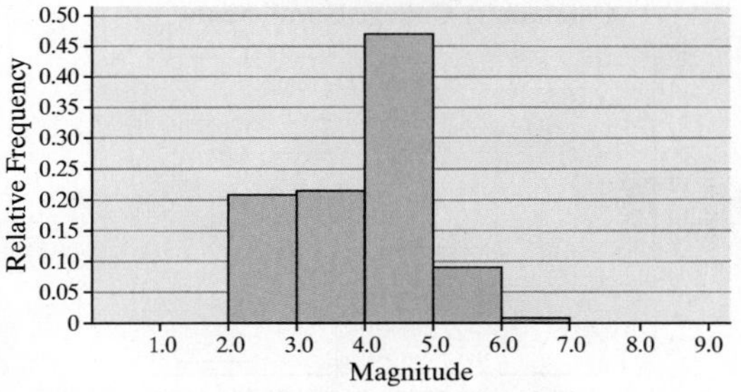

47.15% of the earthquakes measured from 4.0 to 4.9 in magnitude; 89.77% of the earthquakes measured 4.9 in magnitude or less.

31. (a)

Age	Relative Frequency
15–19	0.1032
20–24	0.2512
25–29	0.2803
30–34	0.2232
35–39	0.1160
40–44	0.0244
45–49	0.0017

(b) **Live Births, 2010**

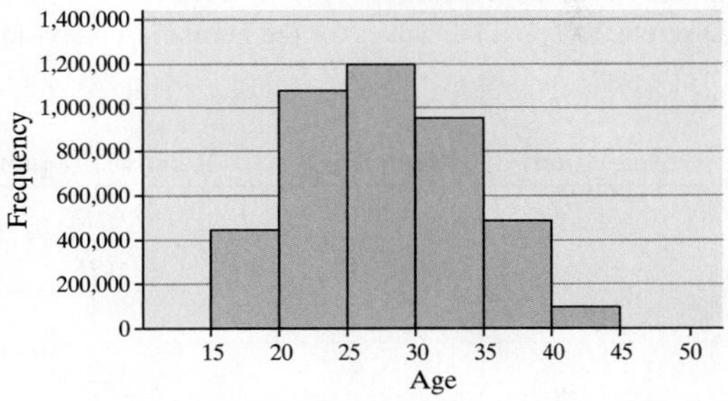

(c) **Live Births, 2010**

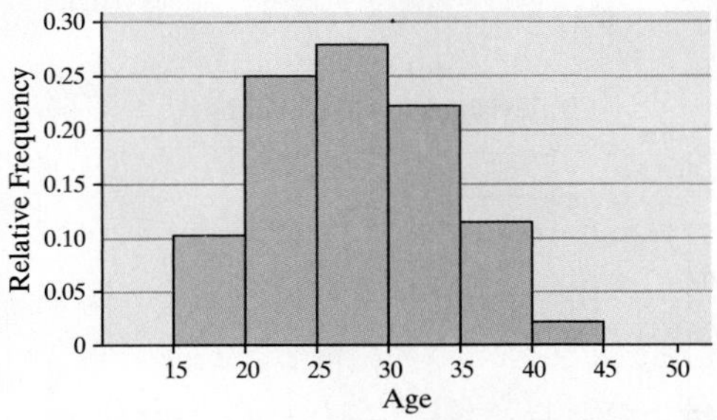

2.44% of births were to women 40 to 44 years of age; 35.44% of births were to women 24 years of age or younger.

32. (a)

Number of Students Enrolled	Relative Frequency
0–4,999	0.3542
5,000–9,999	0.3750
10,000–14,999	0.1458
15,000–19,999	0.1042
20,000–24,999	0
25,000–29,999	0.0208

(b) **Community College Enrollments**

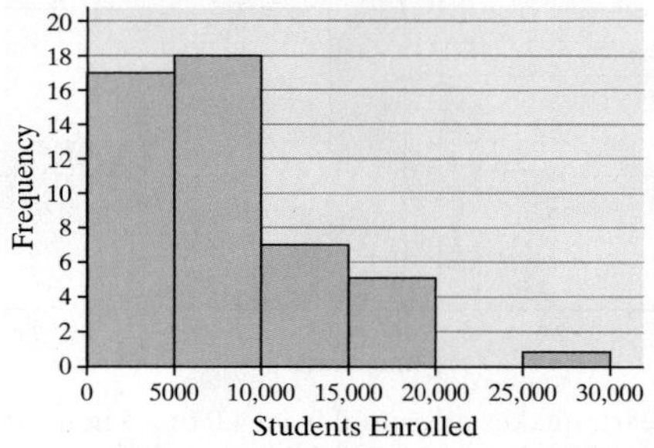

(c) **Community College Enrollments**

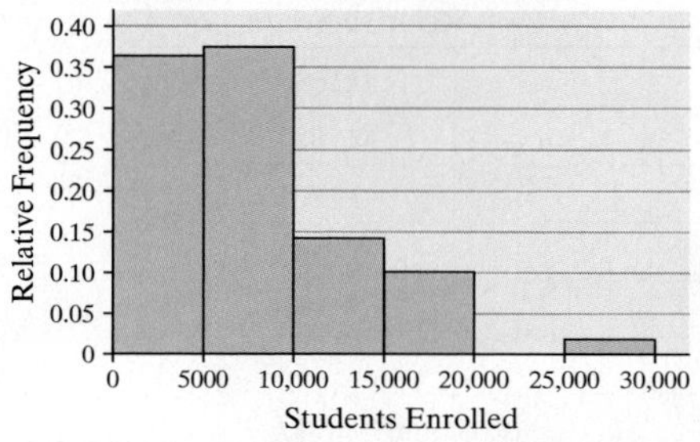

37.5% of public community colleges in Illinois enrolled between 5,000 and 9,999 students; 12.5% of public community colleges in Illinois enrolled 15,000 or more students.

33. (a) Discrete. The possible values for the number of televisions are countable.

(b), (c)

Number of Televisions	Frequency	Relative Frequency
0	1	0.025
1	14	0.35
2	14	0.35
3	8	0.2
4	2	0.05
5	1	0.025

(d) 20% **(e)** 7.5%

(f) **Televisions in Household**

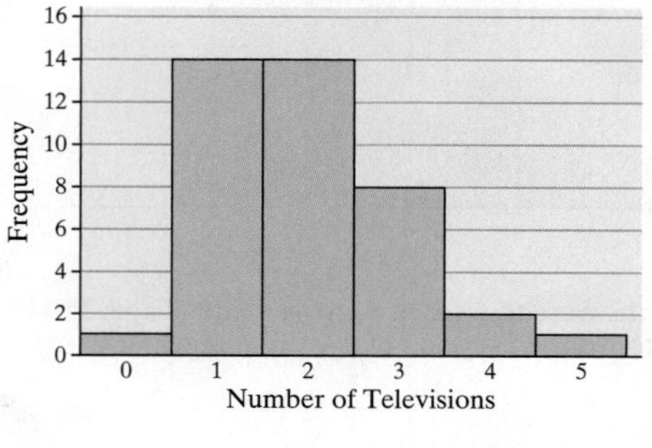

(g) **Televisions in Household**

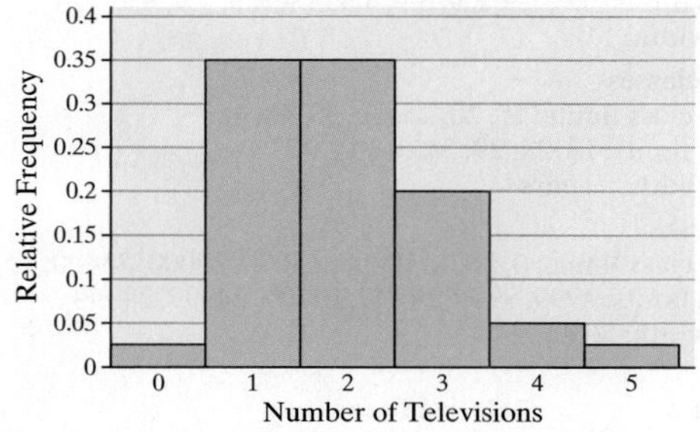

(h) Skewed right

34. (a) Discrete. The possible values for the number of customers are countable.

(b), (c)

Number of Customers	Frequency	Relative Frequency	Number of Customers	Frequency	Relative Frequency
3	2	0.05	9	4	0.1
4	3	0.075	10	4	0.1
5	3	0.075	11	4	0.1
6	5	0.125	12	0	0
7	4	0.1	13	2	0.05
8	8	0.2	14	1	0.025

(d) 27.5% **(e)** 20%

(f) **Customers Waiting for a Table**

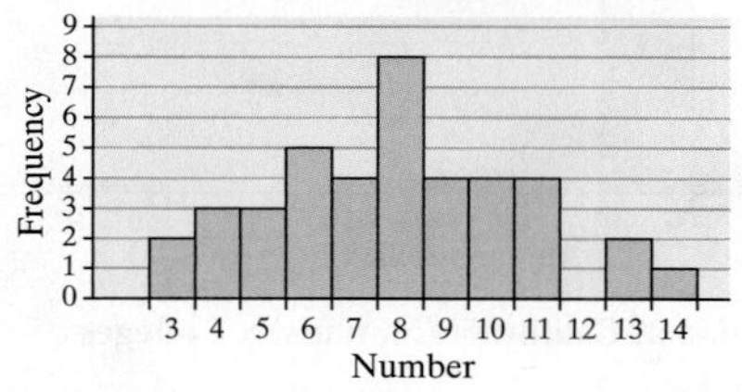

(g) **Customers Waiting for a Table**

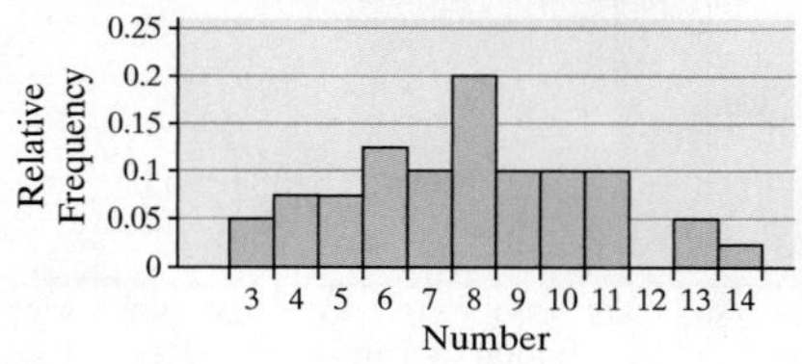

(h) Symmetric

35. (a), (b)

2009 PER CAPITA DISPOSABLE INCOME BY STATE		
Class	**Frequency**	**Relative Frequency**
30,000–35,999	21	0.4118
36,000–41,999	18	0.3529
42,000–47,999	7	0.1373
48,000–53,999	3	0.0588
54,000–59,999	1	0.0196
60,000–65,999	0	0
66,000–71,999	1	0.0196

(c)

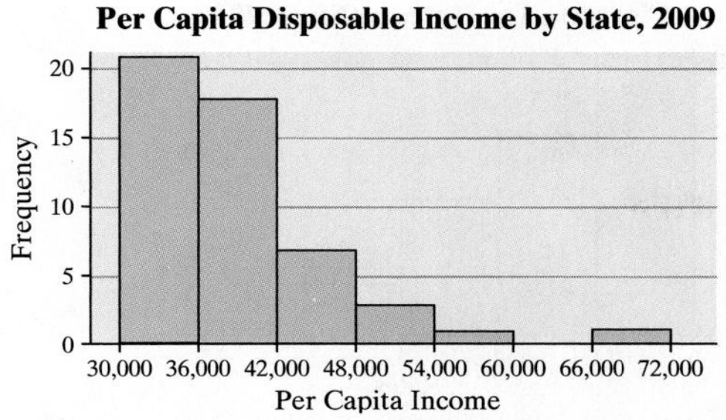

(d)

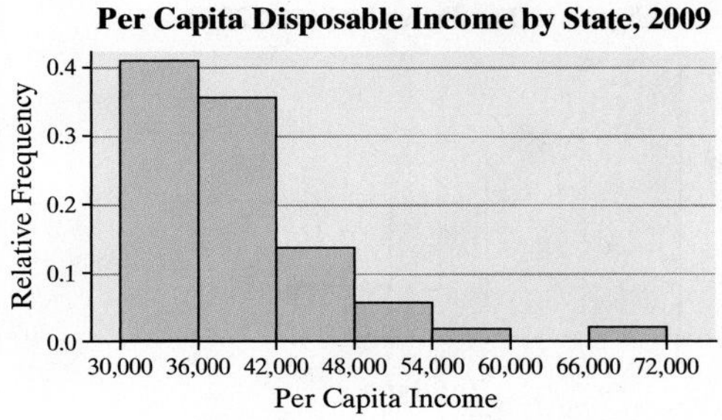

(e) The distribution is skewed right.

(f)

Class	Frequency	Relative Frequency
30,000–32,999	9	0.1765
33,000–35,999	12	0.2353
36,000–38,999	10	0.1961
39,000–41,999	8	0.1569
42,000–44,999	5	0.0980
45,000–47,999	2	0.0392
48,000–50,999	3	0.0588
51,000–53,999	0	0
54,000–56,999	1	0.0196
57,000–59,999	0	0
60,000–62,999	0	0
63,000–65,999	0	0
66,000–68,999	1	0.0196

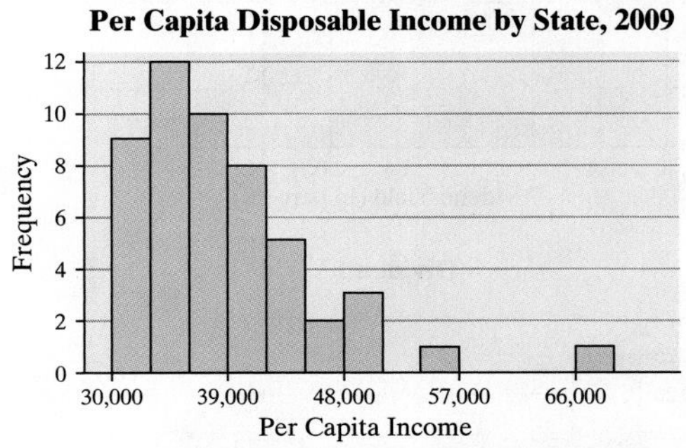

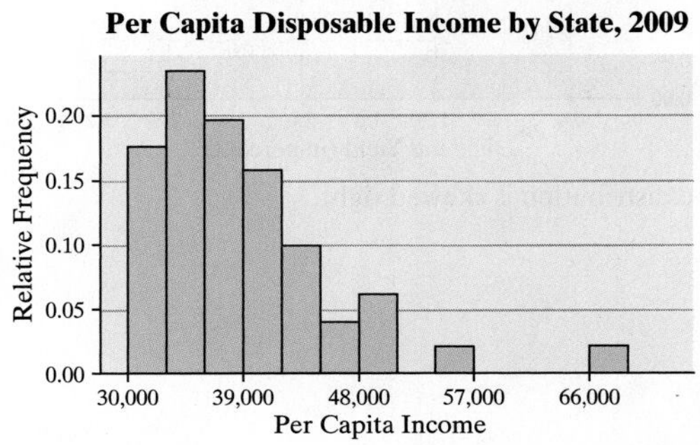

The distribution is skewed right.

(g) Answers will vary.

36. (a), (b)

2009 UNINSURED RATES BY STATE

Class	Frequency	Relative Frequency
4–5.9	1	0.0196
6–7.9	0	0
8–9.9	5	0.0980
10–11.9	9	0.1765
12–13.9	6	0.1176
14–15.9	7	0.1373
16–17.9	5	0.0980
18–19.9	11	0.2157
20–21.9	5	0.0980
22–23.9	1	0.0196
24–25.9	1	0.0196

(c)

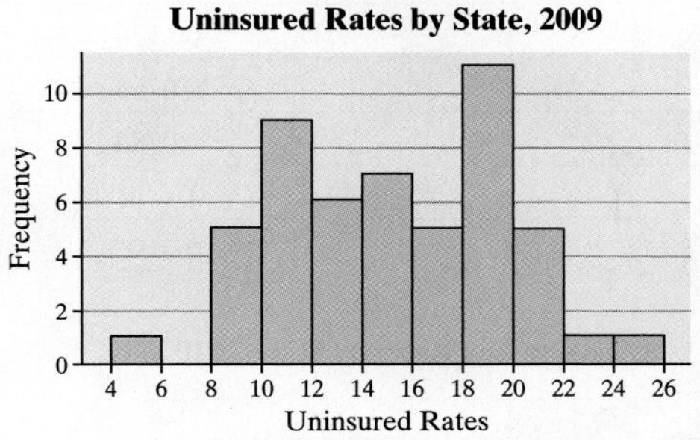

(d)

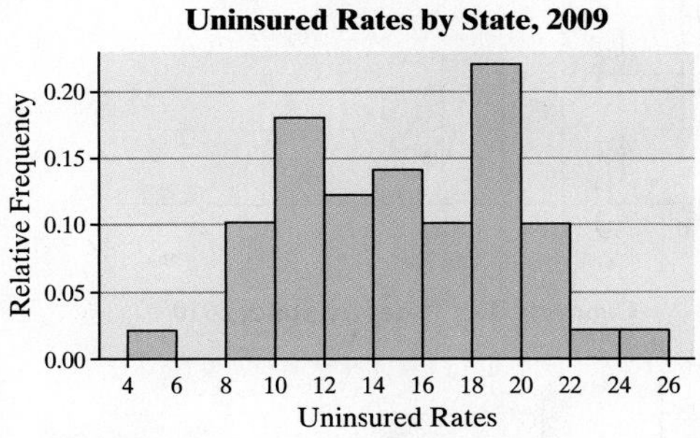

(e) The distribution is symmetric.

(f)

2009 UNINSURED RATES BY STATE

Class	Frequency	Relative Frequency
4–7.9	1	0.0196
8–11.9	14	0.2745
12–15.9	13	0.2549
16–19.9	16	0.3137
20–23.9	6	0.1176
24–27.9	1	0.0196

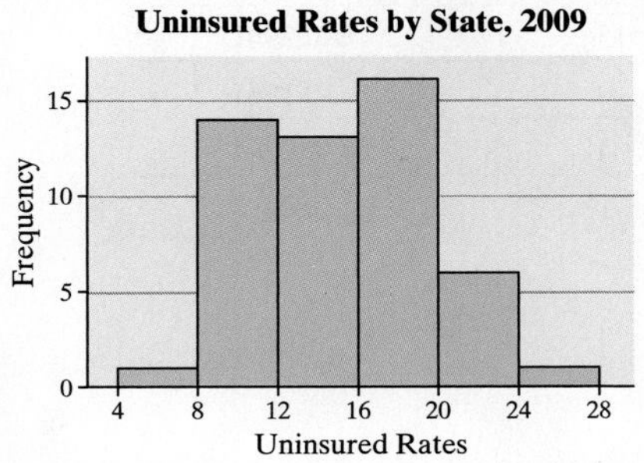

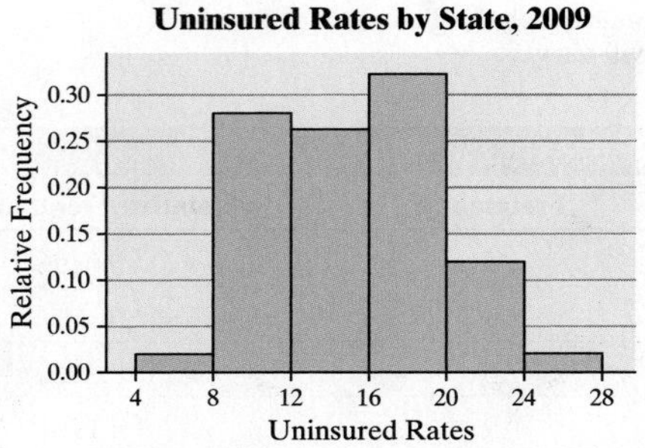

The shape of the distribution is symmetric.

(g) Answers will vary.

37. (a), (b)

Class	Frequency	Relative Frequency
0–0.49	7	0.1373
0.5–0.99	14	0.2745
1–1.49	7	0.1373
1.5–1.99	8	0.1569
2–2.49	6	0.1176
2.5–2.99	4	0.0784
3–3.49	4	0.0784
3.5–3.99	0	0
4–4.49	1	0.0196

(c)

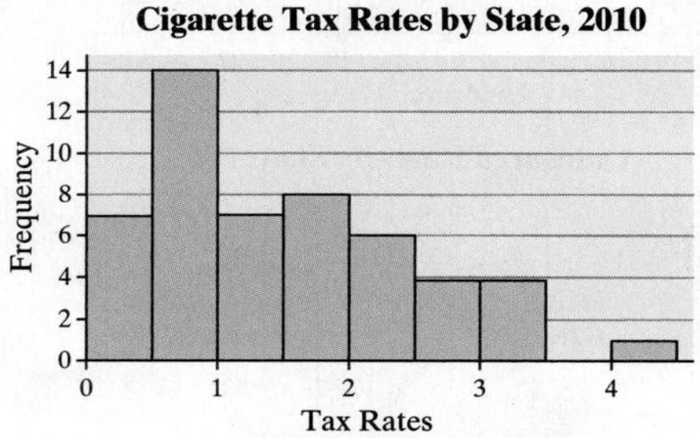

(d)

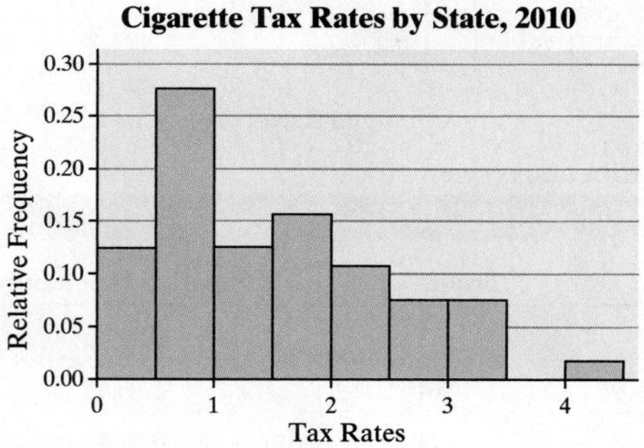

(e) Skewed right

(f)

Class	Frequency	Relative Frequency
0–0.99	21	0.4118
1–1.99	15	0.2941
2–2.99	10	0.1961
3–3.99	4	0.0784
4–4.99	1	0.0196

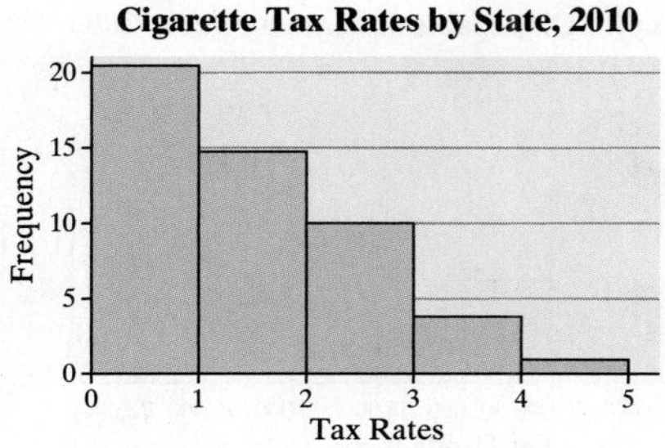

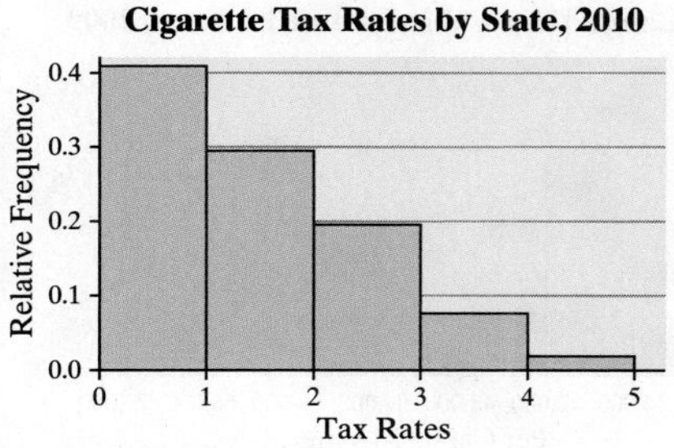

Skewed right

(g) Answers will vary.

38. (a), (b)

DIVIDEND YIELD

Class Interval	Number of Stocks	Relative Frequency
0–0.39	7	0.2500
0.40–0.79	4	0.1429
0.80–1.19	5	0.1786
1.20–1.59	2	0.0714
1.60–1.99	3	0.1071
2.0–2.39	4	0.1429
2.4–2.79	2	0.0714
2.8–3.19	1	0.0357

(c)

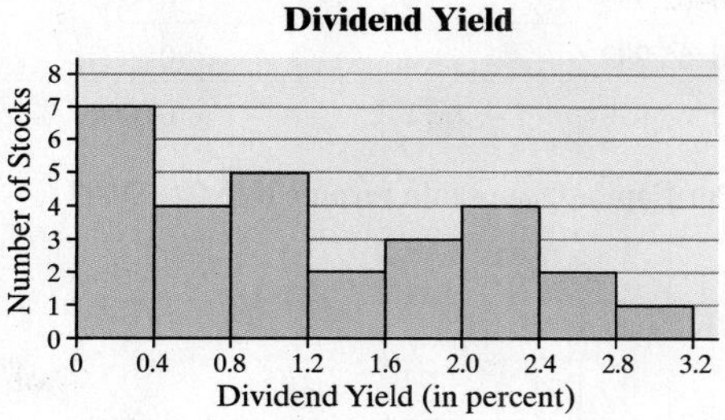

(d)

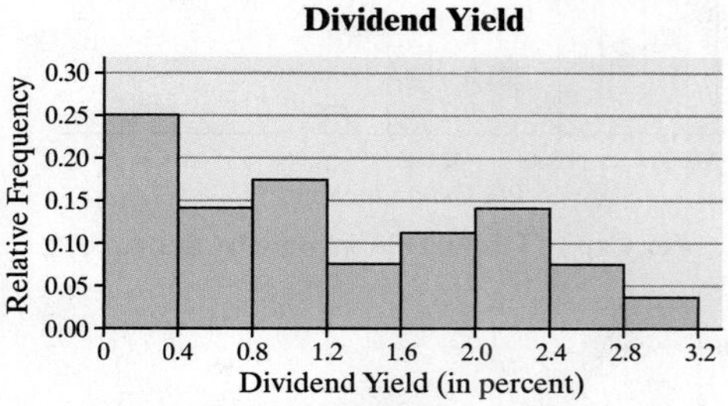

(e) The distribution is skewed right.

(f)

DIVIDEND YIELD

Class	Number of Stocks	Relative Frequency
0.0–0.79	11	0.3929
0.8–1.59	7	0.2500
1.6–2.39	7	0.2500
2.4–3.19	3	0.1071

Dividend Yield

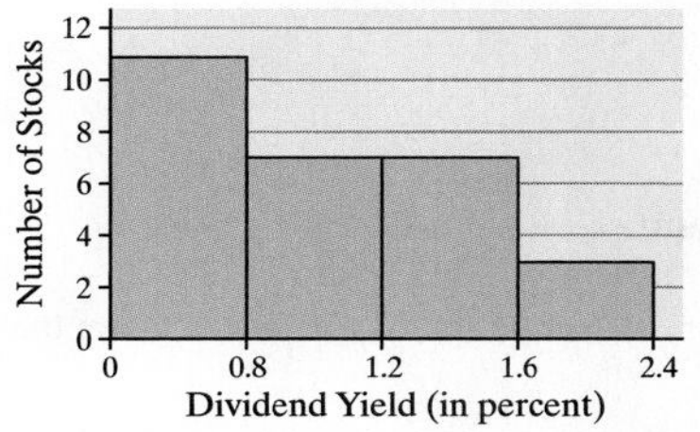

Dividend Yield

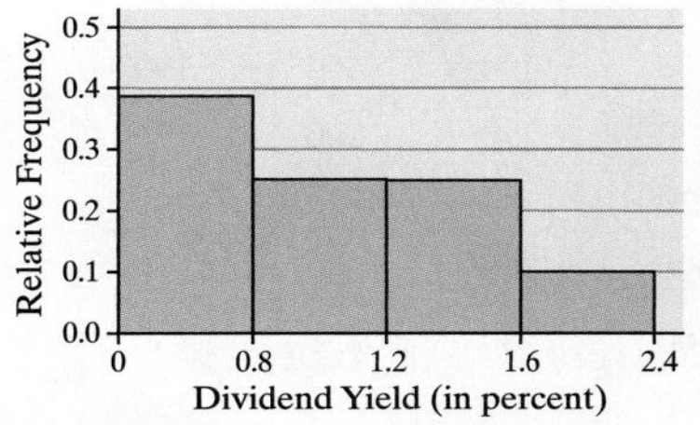

The distribution is skewed right.

(g) Answers will vary.

39. Answers may vary. One possible answer follows:

(a) Lower class limit of first class: 100; class width: 100

(b), (c)

Class	Frequency	Relative Frequency
100–199	4	0.0784
200–299	17	0.3333
300–399	7	0.1373
400–499	11	0.2157
500–599	3	0.0588
600–699	7	0.1373
700–799	1	0.0196
800–899	0	0
900–999	0	0
1000–1099	0	0
1100–1199	0	0
1200–1299	0	0
1300–1399	1	0.0196

(d) **Violent Crimes per 100,000 Population by State, 2009**

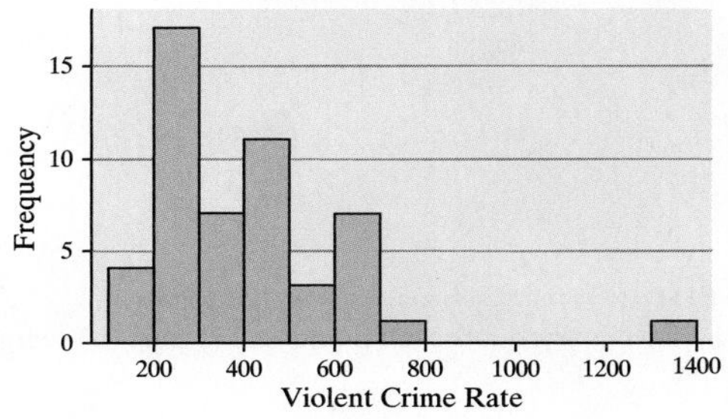

(e) **Violent Crimes per 100,000 Population by State, 2009**

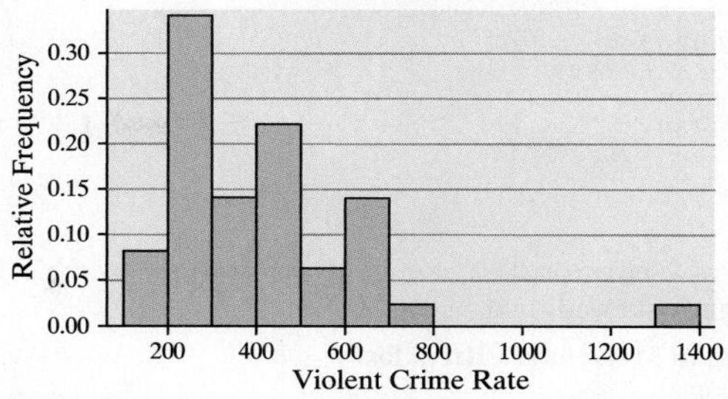

(f) Skewed right

40. Answers may vary. One possible answer follows:

(a) Lower class limit of first class: 6; class width: 3

(b), (c)

DAILY VOLUME OF ALTRIA STOCK (IN MILLIONS)

Class Intervals	Frequency	Relative Frequency
6–8.99	15	0.4286
9–11.99	9	0.2571
12–14.99	4	0.1143
15–17.99	4	0.1143
18–20.99	2	0.0571
21–23.99	1	0.0286

(d) **Daily Volume of Altria Stock**

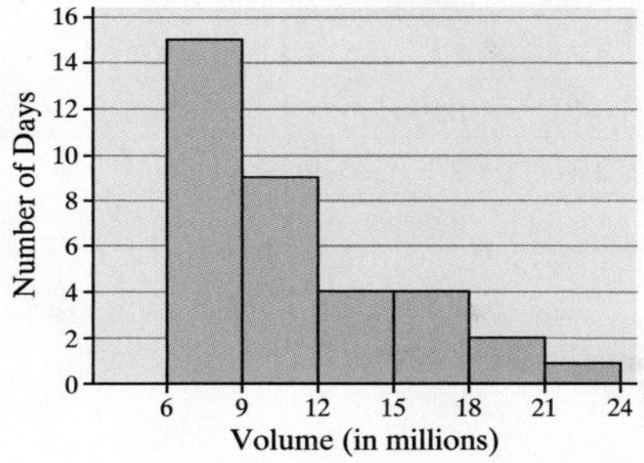

(e) **Daily Volume of Altria Stock**

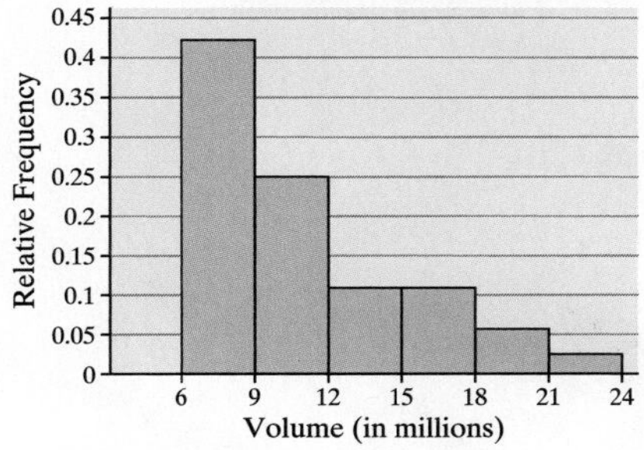

(f) Skewed right.

41. (a) **President Ages at Inauguration**

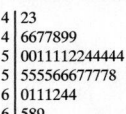

```
4 | 23
4 | 6677899
5 | 0011112244444
5 | 555566677778
6 | 0111244
6 | 589
```

Legend: 4 | 2 represents 42 years.

(b) Bell shaped

42. (a) **Divorce Rates by State, 2006**

2	1 2 3
2	5 6 7 8 9 9 9
3	0 0 0 2 3 3
3	5 5 5 6 6 6 8 8 9 9 9
4	0 1 1 3 3 4 4
4	5 7 7 8 9
5	1 1 3 4
5	7
6	
6	7

Legend: 2 | 1 represents 2.1 divorces per 1000 population.

(b) Slightly skewed right.

43. (a) **Fat in McDonald's Breakfast**

0	39
1	1266
2	1224577
3	0012267
4	6
5	159

Legend: 5 | 1 represents 51 grams of fat.

(b) Bell shaped

44. (a) **Gasoline Mileages**

2	223
2	55567889999
3	00000111111112222233333333333334444444444444
3	5555555556666666666666778
4	0223

Legend: 2 | 2 represents 22 miles per gallon.

(b) Bell shaped

45. (a)

17.3	10.5	8.7	9.4	8.8	6.7	6.5
12.3	9.6	8.9	13.1	8.8	7.5	15.4
14.5	7.5	8.1	8.6	7.8	10.2	25.3
14.6	10.4	7.7	8.6	7.6	9.0	
14.6	9.4	8.1	8.8	8.1	7.6	
13.2	10.0	12.3	7.1	9.8	6.1	
15.7	7.8	13.9	9.2	10.5	14.4	
17.2	8.6	10.7	6.9	10.0	7.7	

Electric Rates by State, 2010

6	1579
7	155667788
8	11166678889
9	024468
10	0024557
11	
12	33
13	129
14	4566
15	47
16	
17	23
18	
19	
20	
21	
22	
23	
24	
25	3

Legend: 6 | 1 represents 6.1 cents per kWh.

(b) Skewed right

(c) 25.33 cents/kW-h; answers will vary.

46. (a)

68	100	94	222	121	121	97
118	86	96	131	94	112	170
91	89	87	123	193	80	93
59	92	124	126	59	202	87
118	119	75	71	90	89	113
180	80	108	138	86	162	85
119	98	49	106	85	33	91
89	111					

Home Appreciation from 1991 to 2010

3	3
4	9
5	99
6	8
7	15
8	00556677999
9	0112344678
10	068
11	1238899
12	11346
13	18
14	
15	
16	2
17	0
18	0
19	3
20	2
21	
22	2

Legend: 3 | 3 represents 33 percent price increase.

(b) Skewed right

(c) Answers may vary. A histogram may be better given the spread in data.

47. (a)

450	1350	400	280	380	670	300
630	610	260	490	400	190	260
410	430	620	250	200	670	230
520	270	120	280	330	490	
470	230	590	700	500	210	
340	500	460	160	250	130	
300	330	500	310	380	230	
640	280	240	620	250	330	

(b) **Violent Crime Rates by State, 2009**

1	2369
2	013334555667888
3	001333488
4	001356799
5	00029
6	1223477
7	0
8	
9	
10	
11	
12	
13	5

Legend: 1 | 2 represents 120 violent crimes per 100,000 population

(c) **Violent Crime Rates by State, 2009**

1	23
1	69
2	013334
2	555667888
3	0013334
3	88
4	0013
4	56799
5	0002
5	9
6	12234
6	77
7	0
7	
8	
8	
9	
9	
10	
10	
11	
11	
12	
12	
13	
13	5

Legend: 1 | 2 represents 120 violent crimes per 100,000 population

(d) Answers will vary, but the stem-and-leaf in part (b) seems like a better graph.

48. (a) Ages of Academy Award Winners

Best Actor		Best Actress
9	2	1566899
98877766220	3	012233333455689
876555332200	4	1125599
43210	5	
200	6	11
6	7	4
	8	0

Legend: 2 | 1 represents 21 years of age.

(b) Answers will vary.

49. (a) Home Run Distances

McGwire		Bonds
	32	00
	33	
10	34	7
00	35	0
9000	36	00015
70000	37	005555
85500000	38	000005
80000	39	00146
900	40	000045
00000	41	0000000000155677
5300000	42	000000009
0000000	43	00000556
000	44	00002
820000	45	04
100	46	
8000	47	
0	48	8
	49	
0	50	
00	51	
7	52	
	53	
	54	
0	55	

Legend: 0 | 34 | 7 represents 340 feet for McGwire and 347 feet for Bonds.

(b) Answers will vary.

53. Televisions in Household

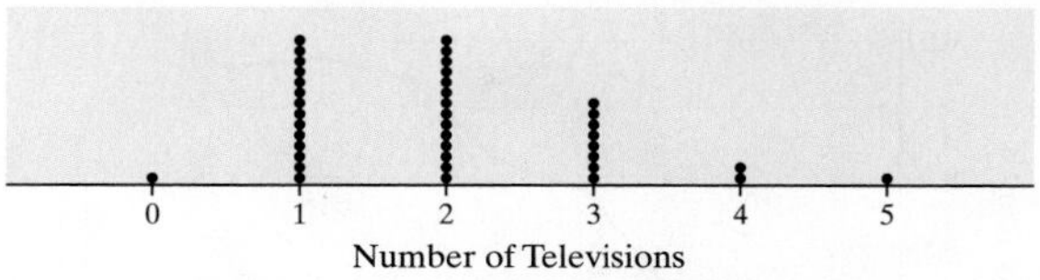

54. Customers Waiting for a Table

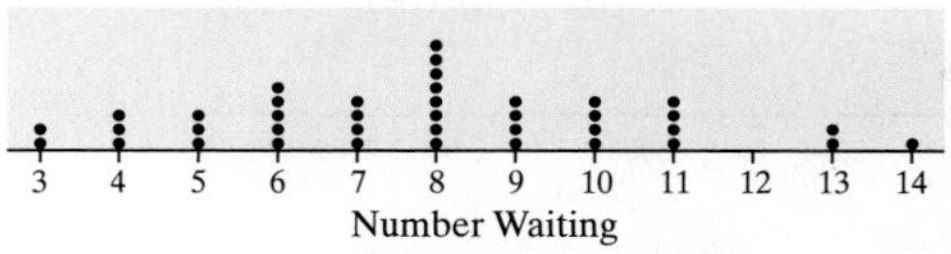

55. Walt Disney Company, 2010

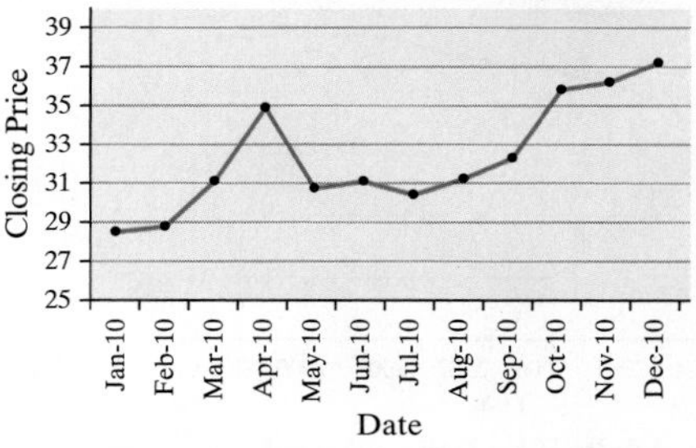

Disney stock increased 30.7%.

56. Google Inc. Stock

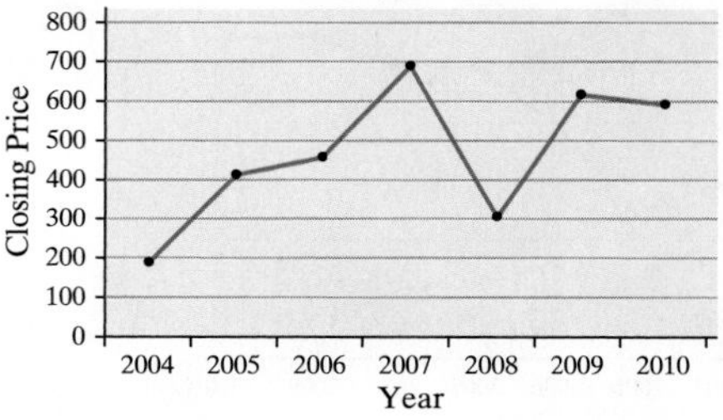

Google stock decreased 4.2%.

57. Debt as a Percent of Gross Domestic Product

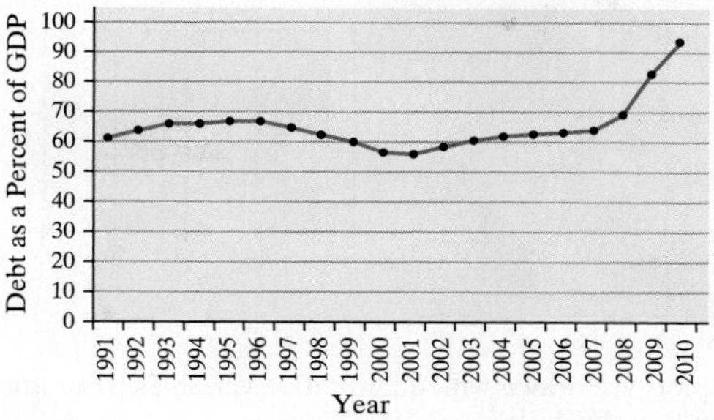

During the late 1990s, debt as a percent of GDP was decreasing, it was increasing slightly during the early to mid-2000s, and it has increased substantially from 2007 to 2010.

58. Percent of 18- to 24-Year-Olds Enrolled in College

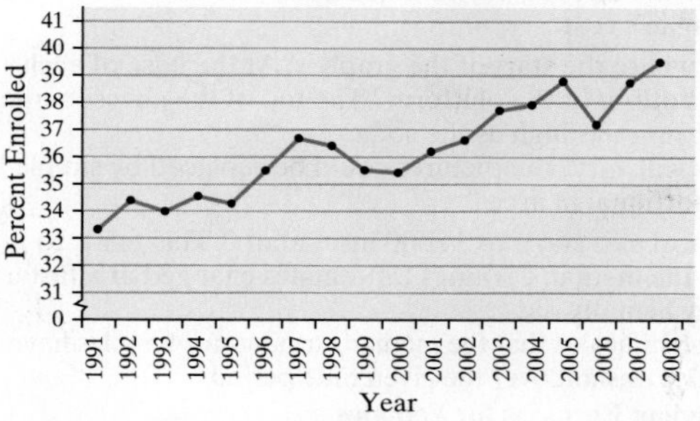

The percent of 18- to 24-year-olds enrolled in college has been steadily increasing since 2000 (except from 2005 to 2006).

59. Answers will vary.

60. Age: Histogram or stem-and-leaf plot; Income: histogram or stem-and-leaf plot; Marital Status: bar graph or pie chart; Number of vehicles: histogram, stem-and-leaf plot, or dot plot

61. Answers will vary.

62. Classes shouldn't overlap so there is no confusion as to which class an observation belongs.

63. Histograms are useful for large data sets or data sets with a large amount of spread. Stem-and-leaf plots are nice because the raw data can easily be retrieved. A disadvantage of stem-and-leaf plots is that the steps in constructing the plots must sometimes be modified.

64. There is no such thing as a correct class width, however some choices are better than others.

65. Relative frequencies should be used when comparing two data sets with different sample sizes.

66. Yes.

67. Skewed Right

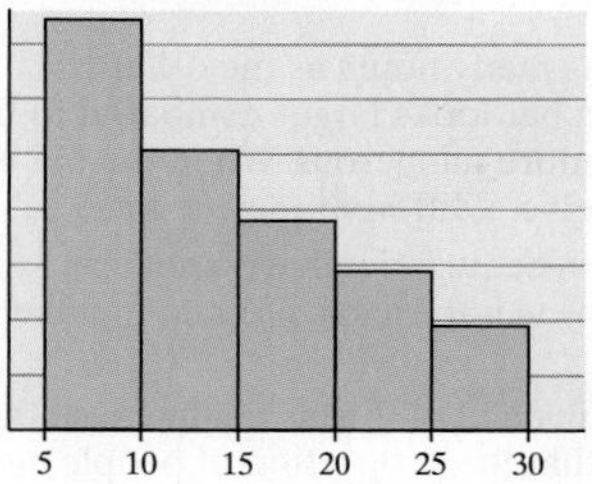

Skewed Left

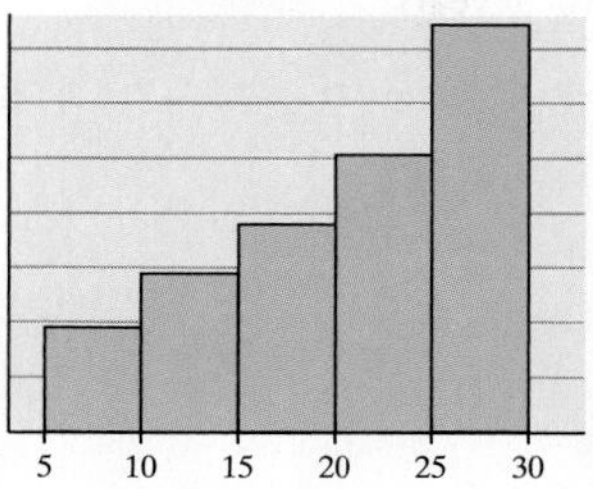

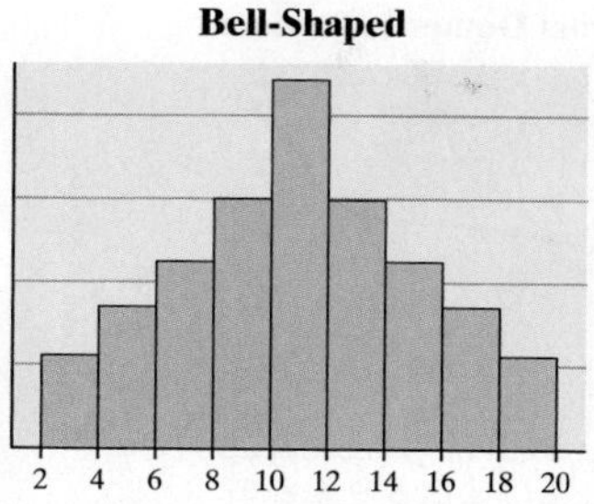

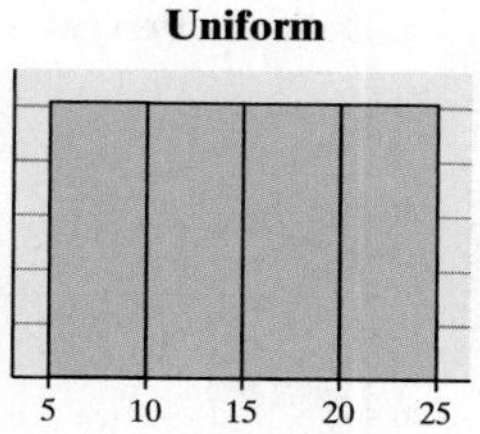

68. Time-series plots are drawn with quantitative variables. They are drawn to see trends in the data.

2.3 Assess Your Understanding (page 106)

1. The lengths of the bars are not proportional. For example, the bar representing the cost of Clinton's inauguration should be slightly more than 9 times the one for Carter's cost and twice as long as the bar representing Reagan's cost.

2. **(a)** Unclear where the start of the graph is: At the base of each figure or the bottom of the platform? The top of the cheeseburger should be 2.2 times as high as the soda.
(b) Answers will vary. The pictures could be replaced by simple bars that are proportional in area.

3. **(a)** The vertical axis starts at 34,500 instead of 0. This tends to indicate that the median earnings for females changed at a faster rate than they actually did.
(b) This graph indicates that the median earnings for females have remained fairly constant over the given time period.

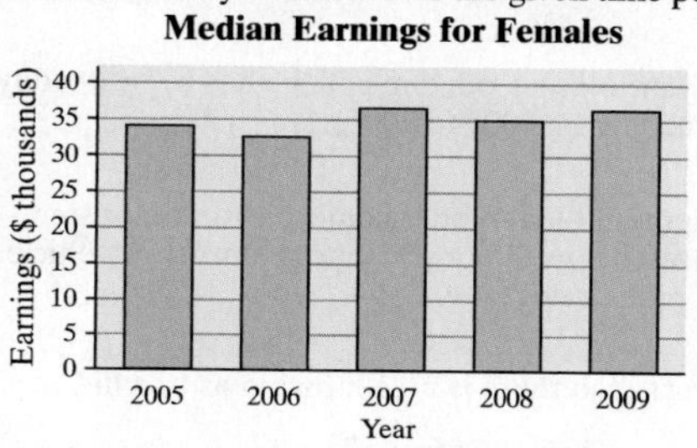

4. **(a)** The vertical axis starts at 4 instead of 0. Readers may think the percent of those employed aged 55 to 64 years who are union members is much higher than for those aged 25 to 34 years.
(b)

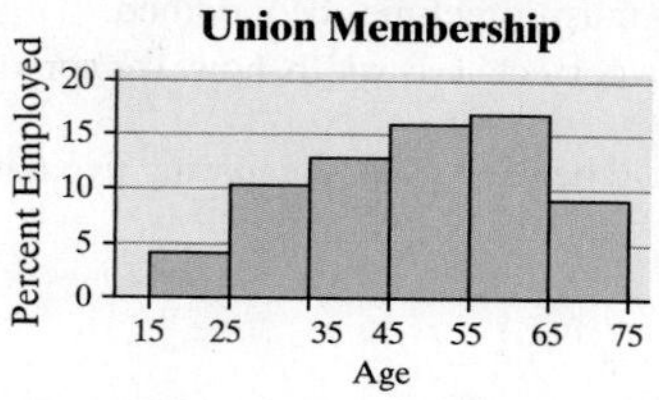

5. The bar for 12p–6p covers twice as many hours as the other bars. By combining two 3-hour periods, this bar looks larger compared to the others, making afternoon hours look more dangerous. When the bar is split into two periods, the graph may give a different impression.

6. The graph is comparing counts for two categories that do not cover the same number of years. A better comparison is the incidence rate (number of accidents per 100,000 licensed drivers).

7. **(a)** The vertical axis starts at 0.1 instead of 0. This might cause the reader to conclude, for example, that the proportion of people aged 25 to 34 who are not covered by health insurance is more than twice the proportion for those aged 45 to 54 years.
(b)

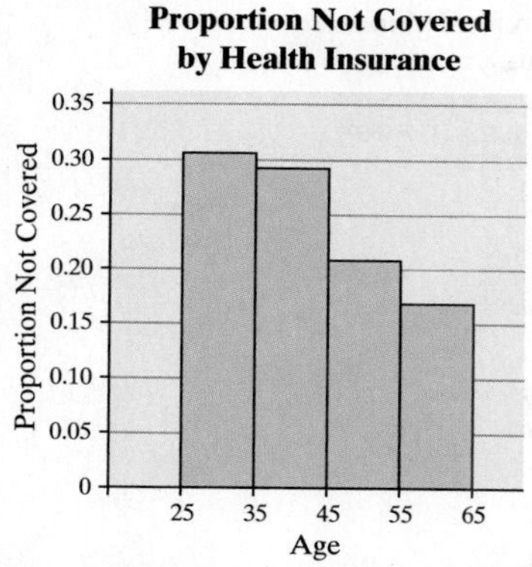

8. **(a)** The vertical axis starts at 50 without indicating a gap.
(b) It may be trying to convey that new home construction increased significantly in the Midwest between 2000 and 2004, then declined at roughly twice the rate between 2004 and 2009.
(c) The graph does support this view. The sharp drop in 2006 indicates a market cooling and less demand for new construction. No.

9. This graph is misleading because it does not take into account the size of the population of each state. Certainly, Vermont is going to pay less in total taxes than California simply because its population is so much lower. The moral of the story here is that many variables should be considered on per capita (per person) basis. For example, this graph should be drawn to represent taxes paid per capita (per person).

10. **(a)** Roughly 97 times larger
(b) About 73 days

11. **(a)** The bar for housing should be a little more than twice the length of the bar for transportation, but it is not.
(b) Adjust the graph so that the lengths of the bars are proportional.

12. **(a)**

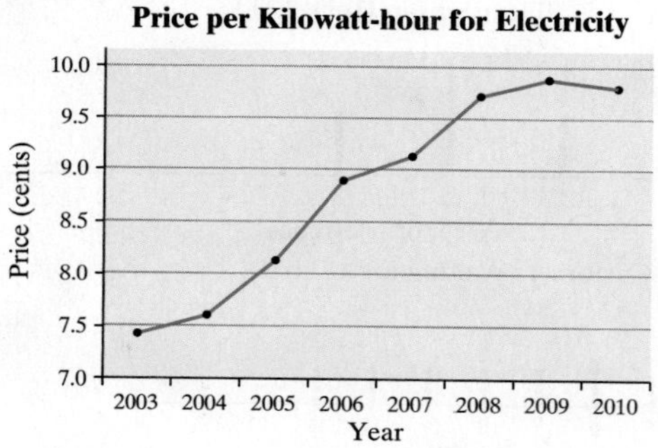

(b)

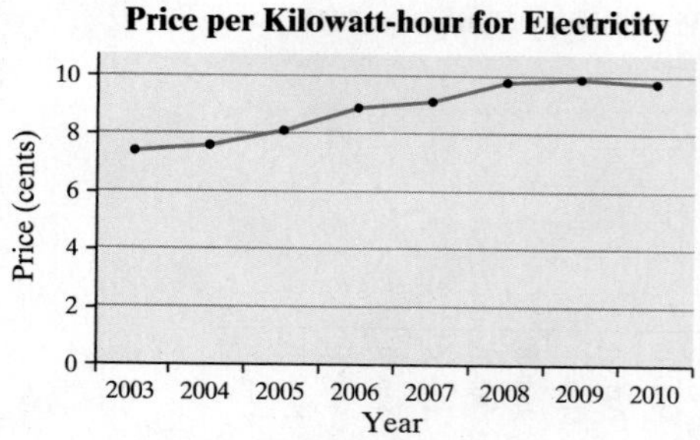

13. **(a)**

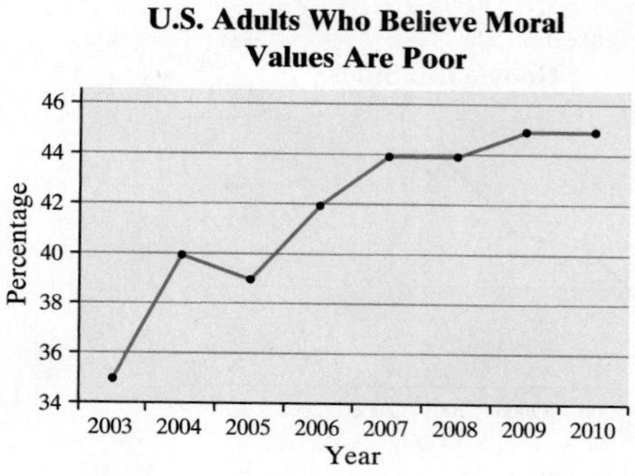

(b) **U.S. Adults Who Believe Moral Values Are Poor**

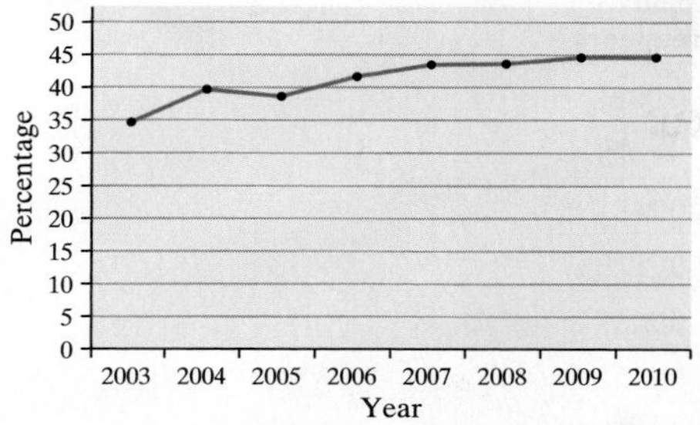

14. The graph does not support the safety manager's claim. The vertical scale starts at 0.17 instead of 0, so the difference between the bars is distorted. While there has been a decrease, it appears that the decrease is roughly 10% of the 1992 rate.

15. (a) The politician's view:

Health Care as a Percent of GDP

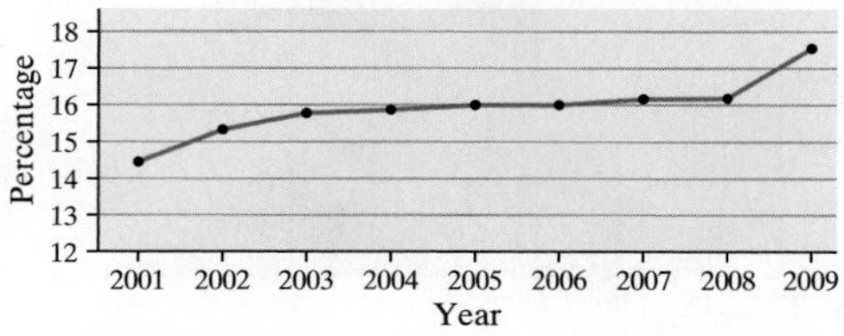

(b) The health care industry's view:

Health Care as a Percent of GDP

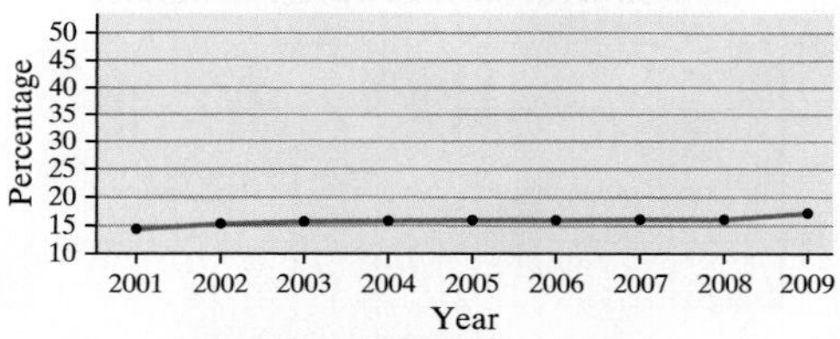

(c) A view that is not misleading:

Health Care as a Percent of GDP

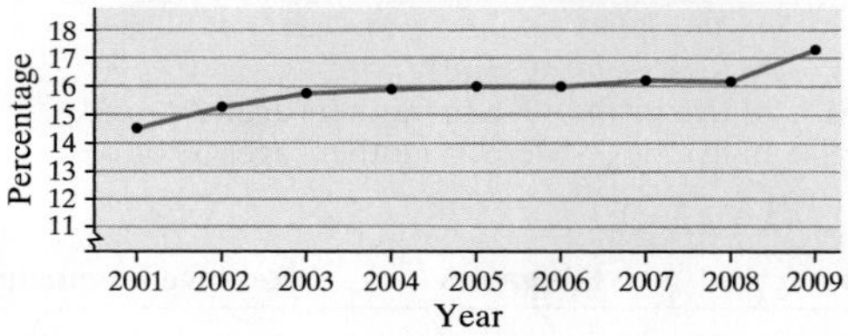

16. (a) Graphic that is not misleading:

Unleaded Gasoline Cost

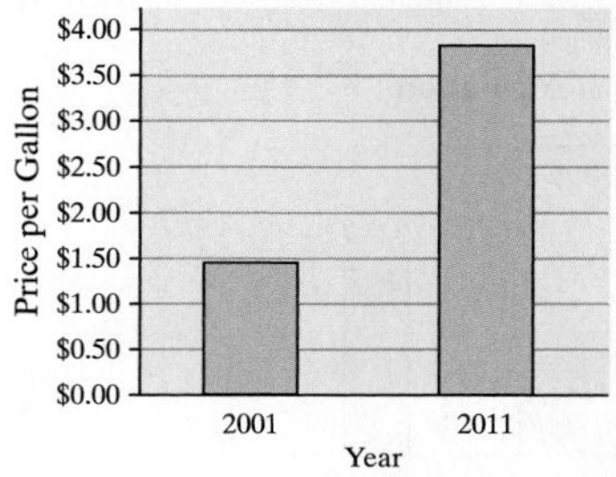

(b) Graphic that is misleading (graphics may vary):

Unleaded Gasoline Cost

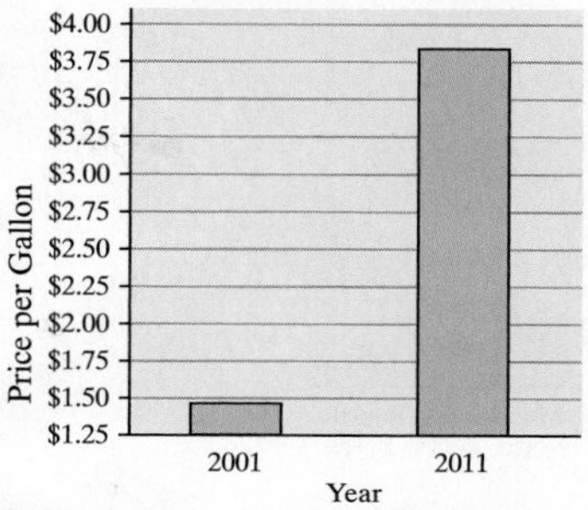

17. (a) Graphic that is not misleading:

Overweight Adults in U.S.

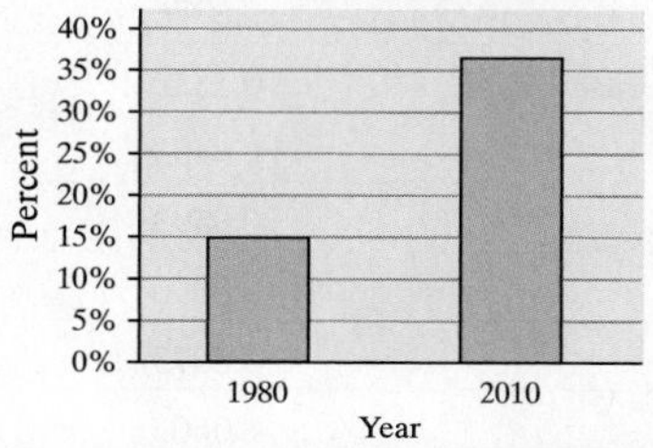

(b) Graphic that is misleading (graphics may vary):

Overweight Adults in U.S.

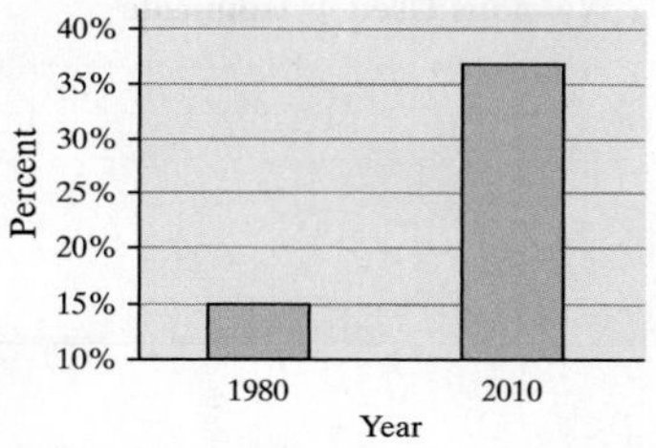

18. (a) A bar graph.
(b) A reader cannot tell whether the graph ends at the top of the nipple on the baby bottle or at the end of the milk.
(c) **Ideal Number of Children**

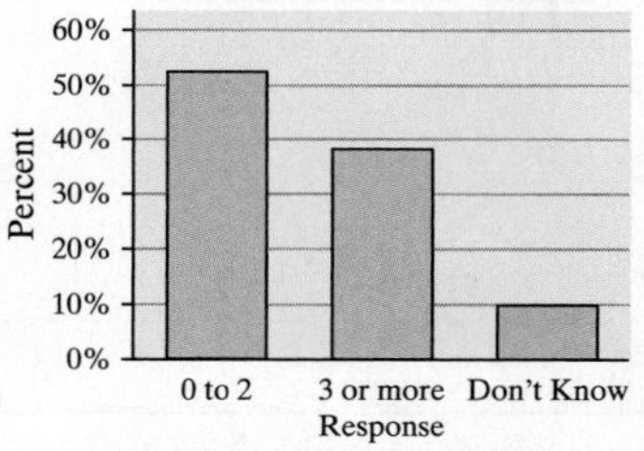

19. This is a histogram and the bars do not touch. In addition, there are no labels on the axes and no title.

20. (a) Cornell tuition (quantitative, discrete, interval level); Cornell ranking (qualitative, ordinal level)
(b) The graph was likely generated from existing data sources.
(c) Time series.
(d) Answers may vary. The graph appears to show that the cost to attend Cornell is increasing while its ranking is decreasing. The graph is misleading, because the ranking graph may imply that ranking is getting worse when in fact a lower value means a better ranking.
(e) No horizontal or vertical scale is provided; the horizontal scale is inconsistent; the vertical scale is inconsistent between graphs.

Chapter 2 Review Exercises (page 110)

1. (a) 2216 participants
(b) 0.653

(c) **Convincing Voice in Purchasing a Car**

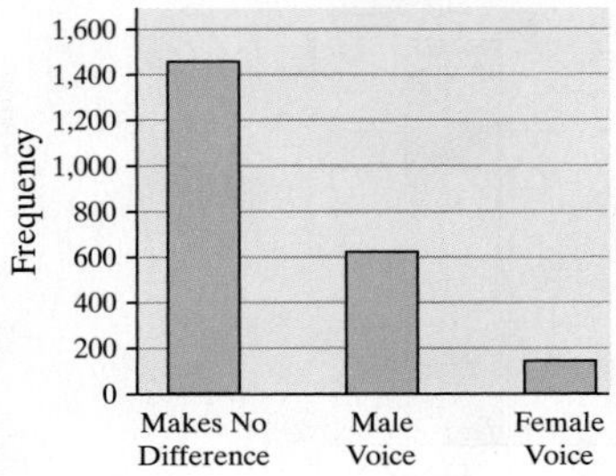

2. (a)

Type of Weapon	Relative Frequency
Firearms	0.6776
Knives or cutting instruments	0.1352
Blunt objects	0.0453
Personal weapons	0.0593
Strangulation	0.0090
Fire	0.0073
Other weapon	0.0663

(b) 4.5% of homicides were committed using a blunt object.

(c) **Weapons Used in Homicide**

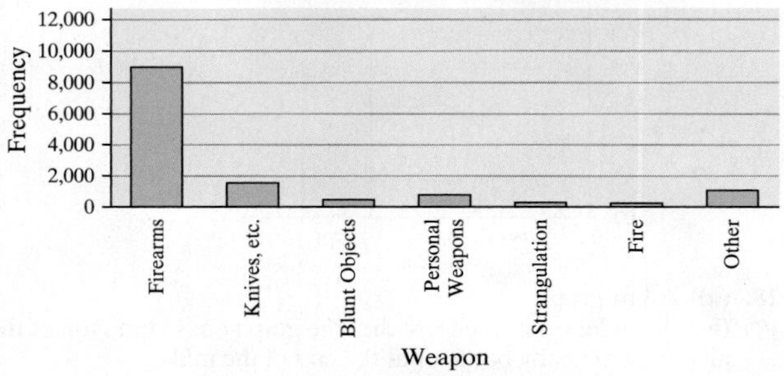

(d) **Weapons Used in Homicide**

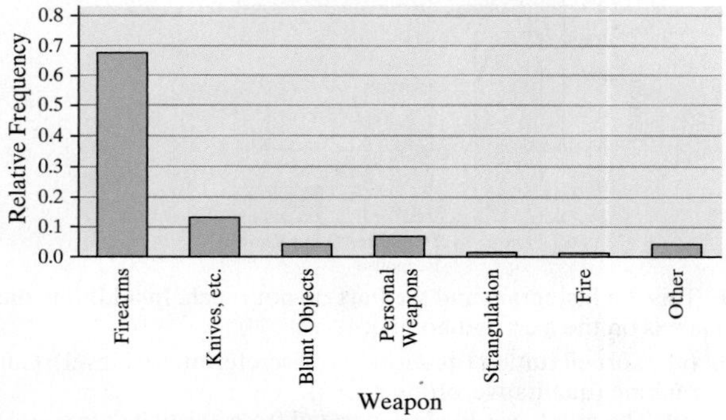

(e) **Weapons Used in Homicide**

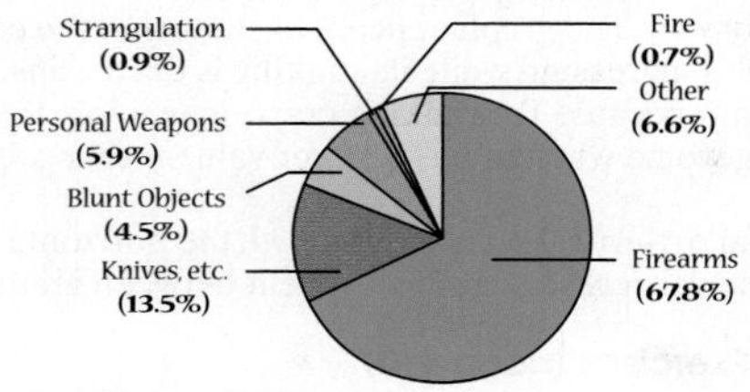

3. (a)

Age of Mother	Relative Frequency
10–14	0.0014
15–19	0.1025
20–24	0.2481
25–29	0.2820
30–34	0.2257
35–39	0.1152
40–44	0.0250

(b) **Live Births in the U.S. by Age of Mother**

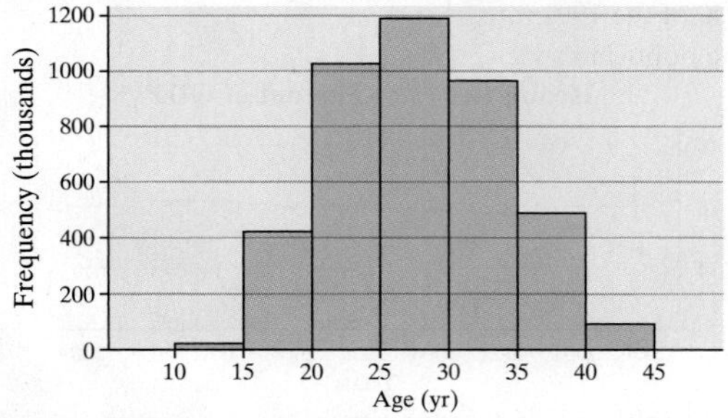

The distribution is roughly bell shaped.

(c) **Live Births in the U.S. by Age of Mother**

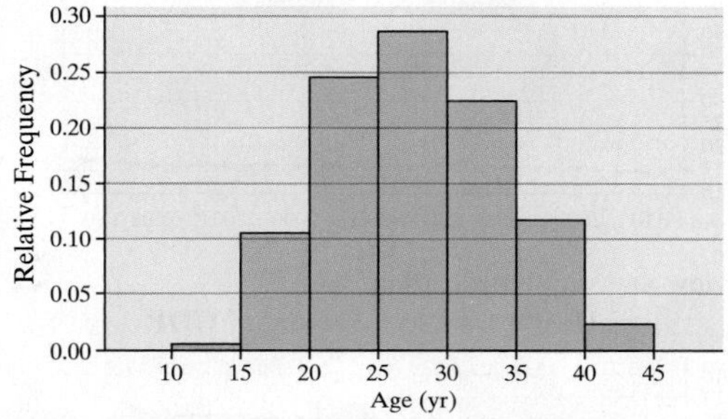

(d) 24.81% of live births were to mothers aged 20 to 24.

(e) 36.59% of live births were to mothers ages 30 or older.

4. (a), (b)

Affiliation	Frequency	Relative Frequency
Democrat	46	0.46
Independent	16	0.16
Republican	38	0.38

(c) **Political Affiliation**

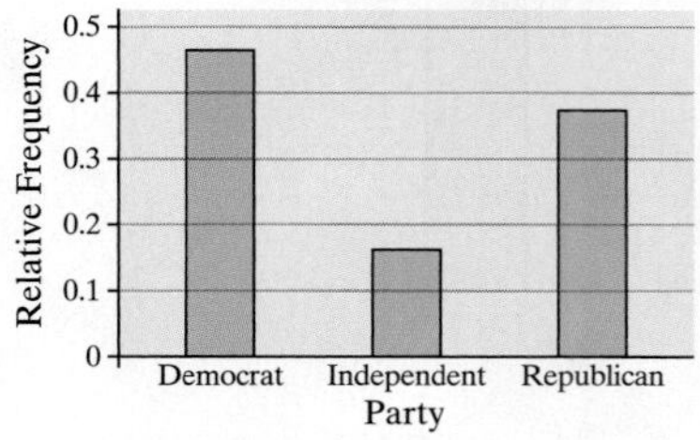

(d) **Political Affiliation**

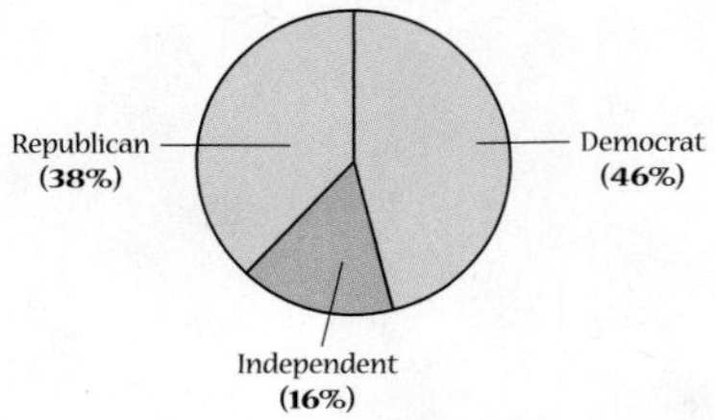

(e) Democrat appears to be the most common affiliation.

5. (a), (b)

Number of Children	Frequency	Relative Frequency
0	7	0.1167
1	7	0.1167
2	18	0.3000
3	20	0.3333
4	7	0.1167
5	1	0.0167

(c) **Number of Children for Couples Married 7 Years**

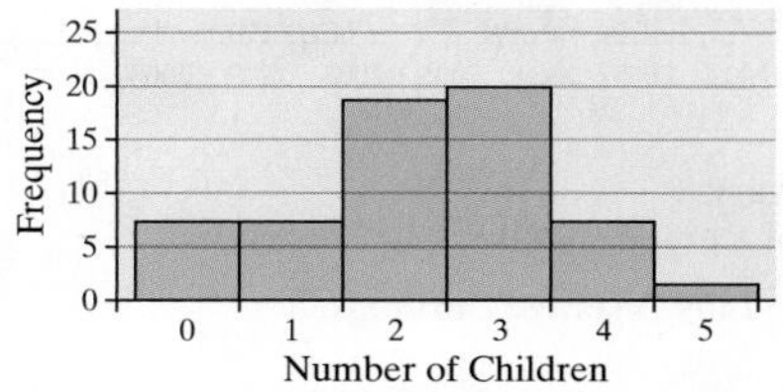

The distribution is symmetric.

(d) **Number of Children for Couples Married 7 Years**

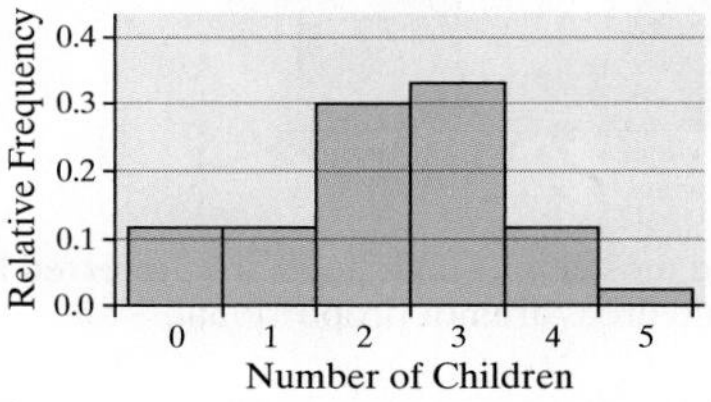

(e) 30% of the couples has two children.

(f) 76.7% of the couples has at least two children.

(g)

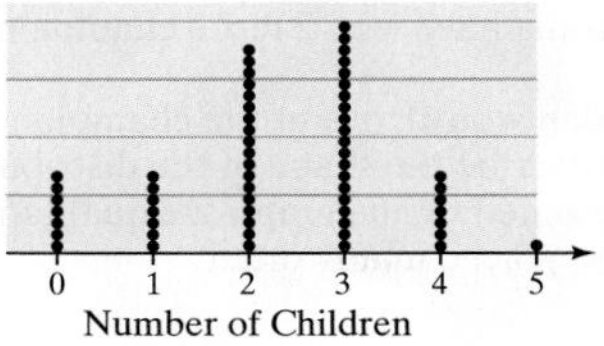

6. (a), (b)

HOME OWNERSHIP RATE BY STATE

Home Ownership Rate	Frequency	Relative Frequency
40–44.9	1	0.0196
45–49.9	0	0.0000
50–54.9	1	0.0196
55–59.9	2	0.0392
60–64.9	2	0.0392
65–69.9	19	0.3725
70–74.9	21	0.4118
75–79.9	5	0.0980

(c) **Home Ownership Rates by State, 2009**

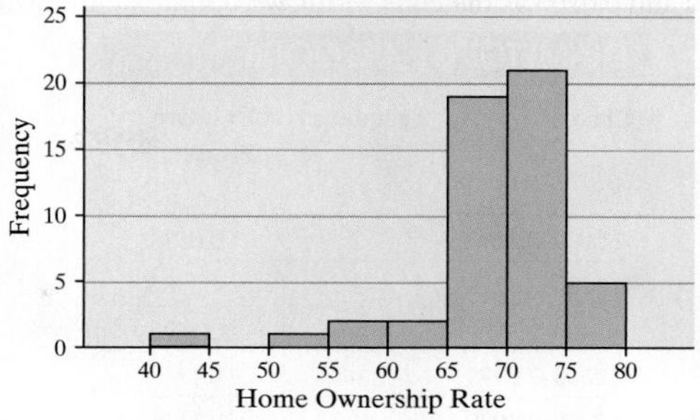

(d) **Home Ownership Rates by State, 2009**

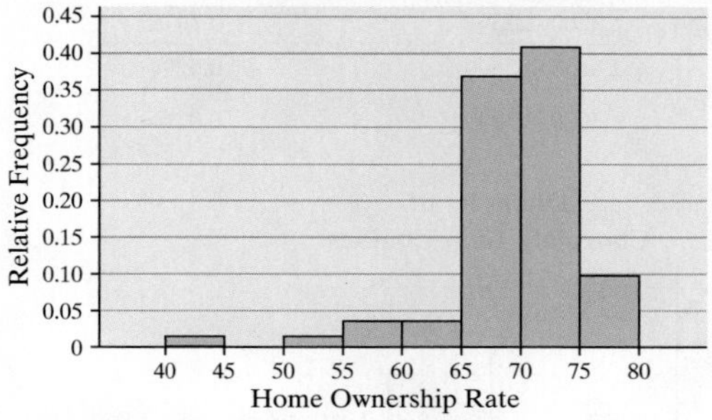

(e) The distribution is skewed left.

(f)

HOME OWNERSHIP RATE BY STATE

Home Ownership Rate	Frequency	Relative Frequency
40–49.9	1	0.0196
50–59.9	3	0.0588
60–69.9	21	0.4118
70–79.9	26	0.5098

Home Ownership Rates by State, 2009

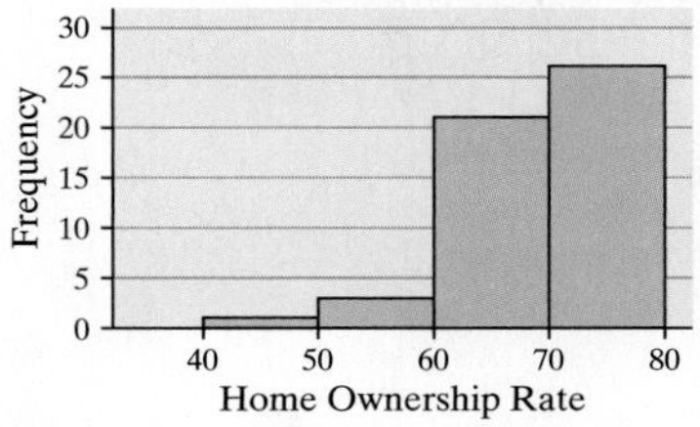

Home Ownership Rates by State, 2009

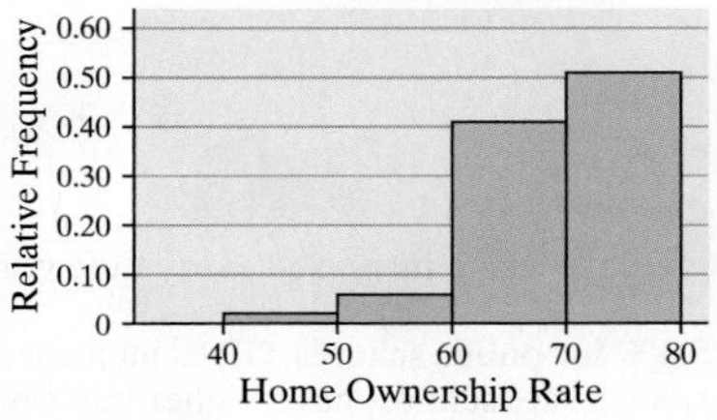

7. (a), (b) Answers will vary. Using 2.2000 as the lower class limit of the first class and 0.0200 as the class width, we obtain the following:

DIAMETER OF A COOKIE

Class	Frequency	Relative Frequency
2.2000–2.2199	2	0.0588
2.2200–2.2399	3	0.0882
2.2400–2.2599	5	0.1471
2.2600–2.2799	6	0.1765
2.2800–2.2999	4	0.1176
2.3000–2.3199	7	0.2059
2.3200–2.3399	5	0.1471
2.3400–2.3599	1	0.0294
2.3600–2.3799	1	0.0294

(c)

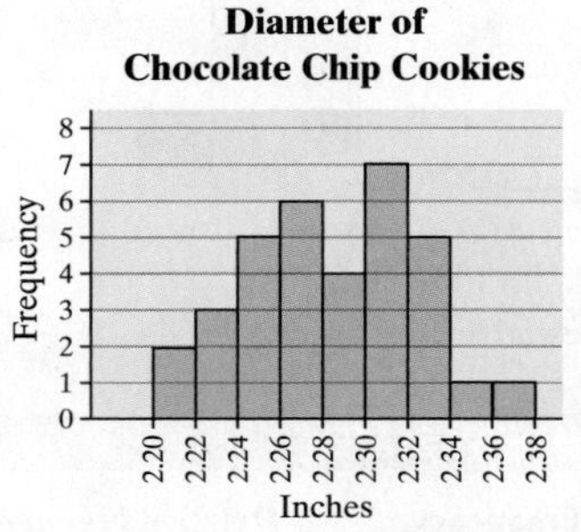

The distribution is roughly symmetric.

(d)

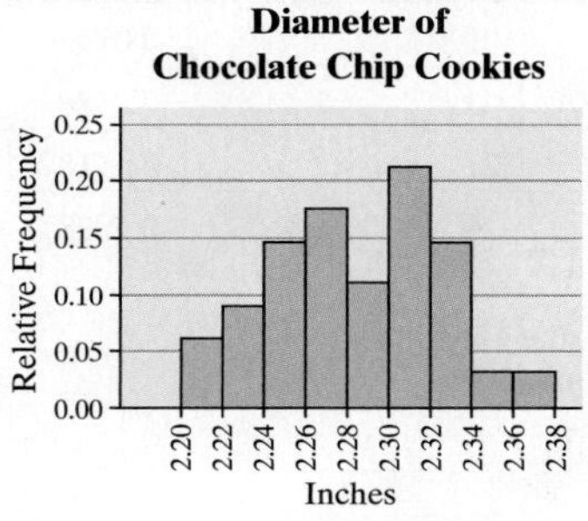

8. **Hours Spent Online**

13 | 467
14 | 05578
15 | 1236
16 | 456
17 | 113449
18 | 066889
19 | 2
20 | 168
21 | 119
22 | 29
23 | 48
24 | 4
25 | 7

Legend: 13 | 4 = average 13.4 hours per week.

The distribution is skewed right.

9. (a) Yes. Grade point averages have increased every time period for all schools.
(b) GPAs increased 5.6% for public schools. GPAs increased 6.8% for private schools. Private schools have higher inflation both because the GPAs are higher, and they are increasing faster.
(c) The graph is misleading because it starts at 2.6 on the vertical axis.

10. (a)

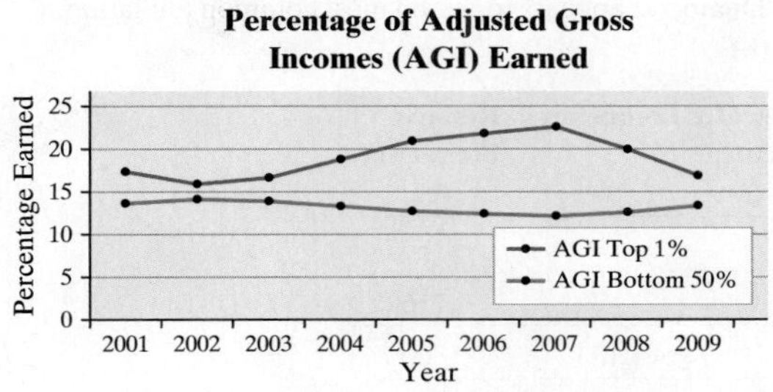

(b)

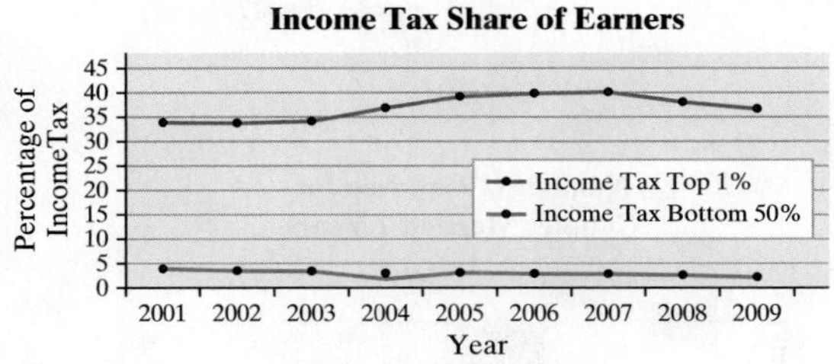

11. (a) Answers will vary.
(b) An example of a graph that does not mislead:

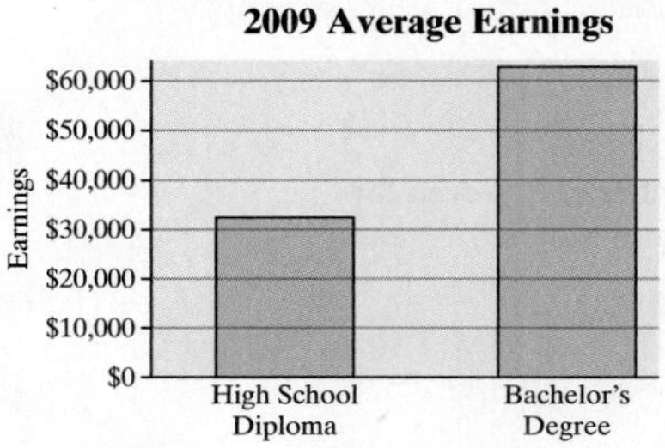

12. (a) Flats are preferred most; extra-high heels are preferred least.
(b) The bar heights and areas are not proportional.

Chapter 2 Test (page 113)

1. (a) Representatives of the United States have won the most championships. They have won 15 championships.
(b) Representatives of Australia have won 2 more championships than Germany.
(c) Representatives of Sweden won 18.6% of the championships.
(d) It is not appropriate to describe the shape of the distribution as skewed right. The data represented by the graph are qualitative, so the bars in the graph could be placed in any order.

2. (a)

Response	Frequency	Relative Frequency
New tolls	412	0.4100
Increase gas tax	181	0.1801
No new roads	412	0.4100

(b) About 18.01% of respondents indicated they would like to see an increase in gas taxes.

(c)

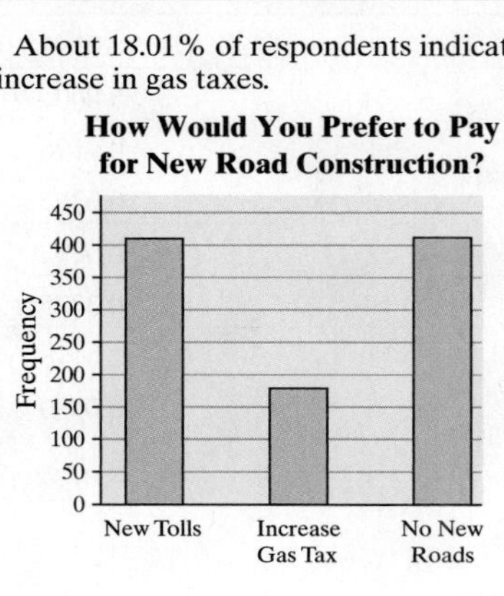

(d) **How Would You Prefer to Pay for New Road Construction?**

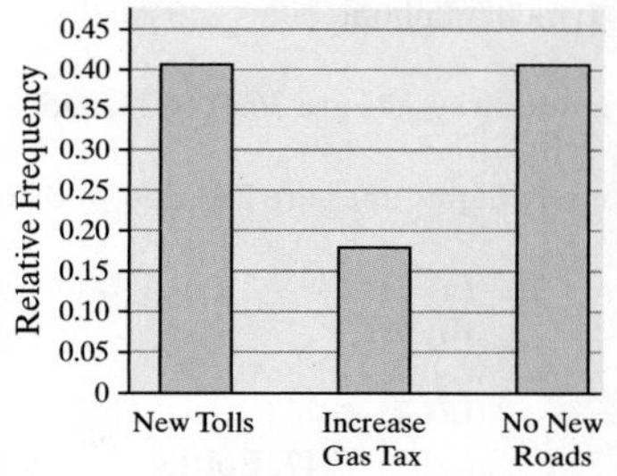

(e) **How Would You Prefer to Pay for New Road Construction?**

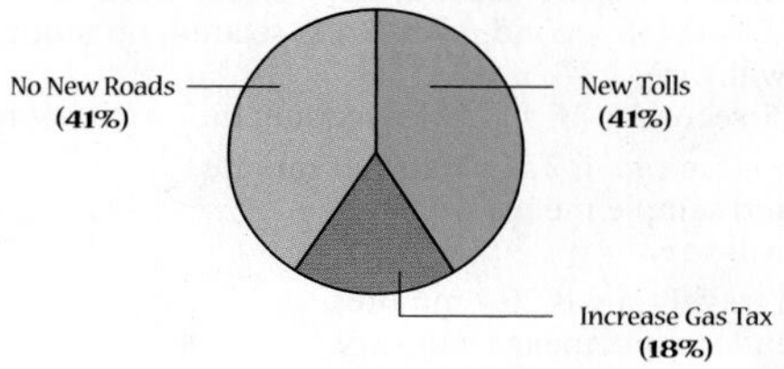

3. (a), (b)

Educational Attainment	Frequency	Relative Frequency
No high school diploma	9	0.18
High school graduate	16	0.32
Some college	9	0.18
Associate's degree	4	0.08
Bachelor's degree	8	0.16
Advanced degree	4	0.08

(c) **Educational Attainment of Commuters**

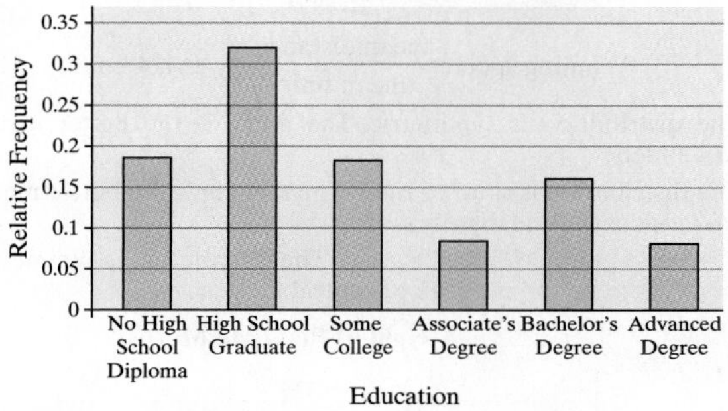

(d) Educational Attainment of Commuters

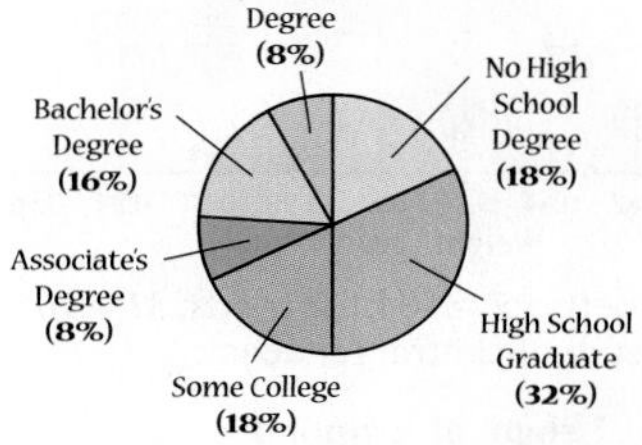

(e) High school graduate is the most common educational level.

4. (a), (b)

Number of Customers	Frequency	Relative Frequency
1	5	0.10
2	7	0.14
3	12	0.24
4	6	0.12
5	8	0.16
6	5	0.10
7	2	0.04
8	4	0.08
9	1	0.02

(c) **Number of Cars Arriving at McDonald's**

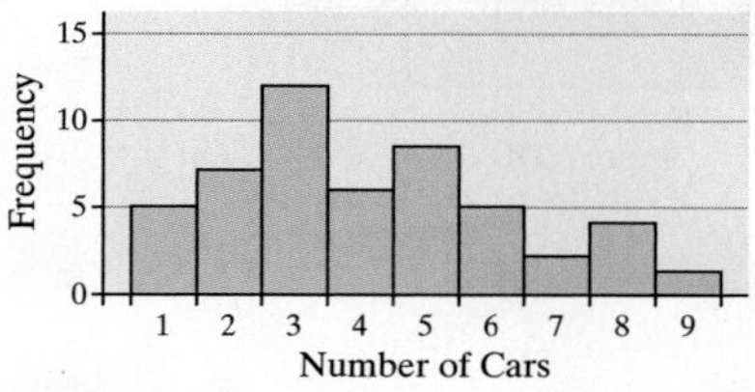

The distribution is skewed right.

(d) **Number of Cars Arriving at McDonald's**

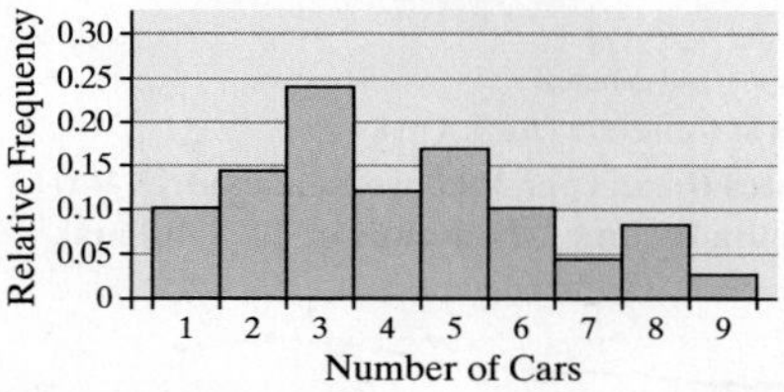

(e) 24% of weeks, three cars arrived between 11:50 A.M. and noon.
(f) 76% of weeks, at least three cars arrived between 11:50 A.M. and noon.

(g)

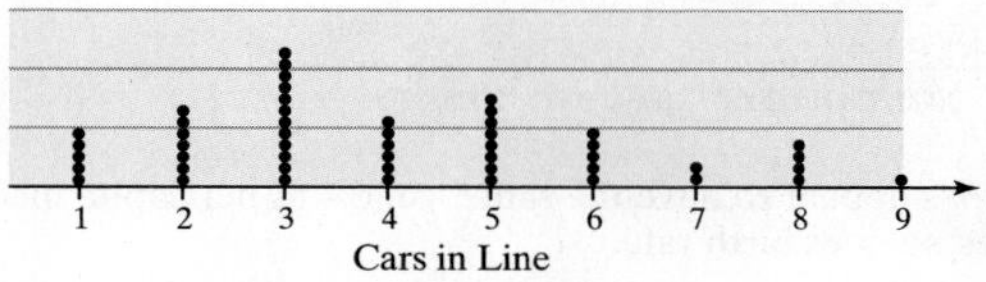

5. Answers may vary. One possibility follows:

(a), (b) Using a lower class limit of the first class of 20 and a class width of 10:

Class	Frequency	Relative Frequency
20–29	1	0.025
30–39	6	0.15
40–49	10	0.25
50–59	14	0.35
60–69	6	0.15
70–79	3	0.075

(c) **Serum HDL of 20–29 Year Olds**

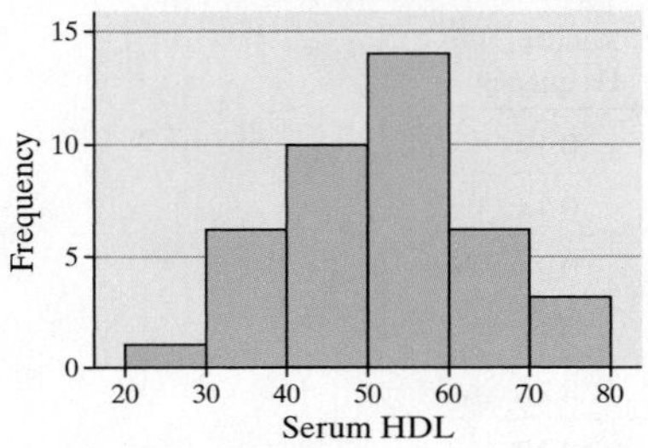

(d) **Serum HDL of 20–29 Year Olds**

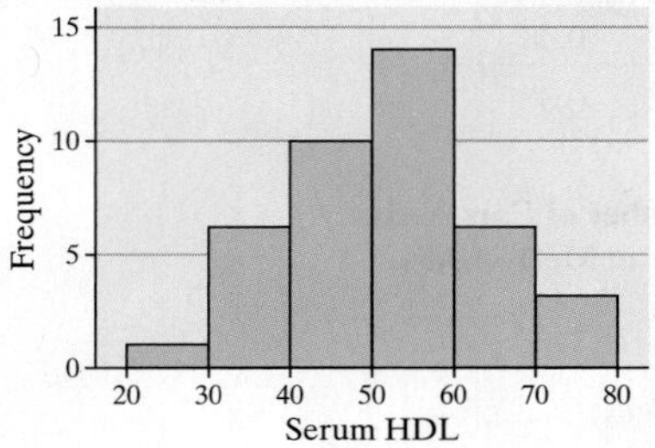

(e) Bell shaped

6. (a) **Time Spent on Homework**

4	0567
5	26
6	13
7	01338
8	59
9	1369
10	3899
11	0018
12	556

Legend: 4 | 0 represents 40 minutes.

The distribution is symmetric (uniform).

7. **Fertility Rates (births per 1000 women aged 15–44) and per Capita Income (thousands of 2008 dollars)**

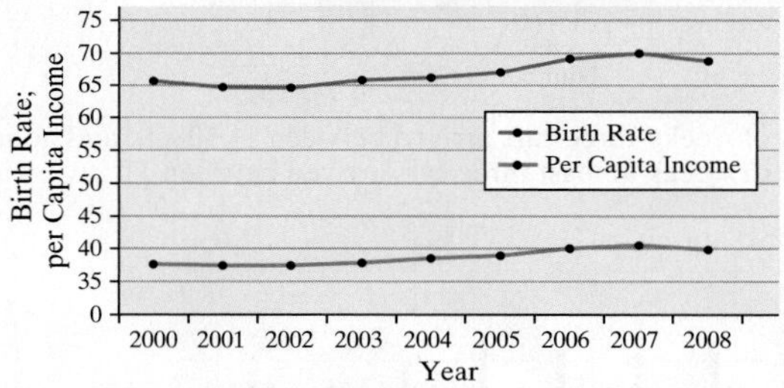

The graphs appear to have the same trend—as per capita income increases, so does birth rate.

8. Answers will vary.

CHAPTER 3 Numerically Summarizing Data

3.1 Assess Your Understanding (page 124)

1. A statistic is resistant if it is not sensitive to extreme values. The median is resistant because it is a positional measure of central tendency, and increasing the largest value or decreasing the smallest value does not affect the position of the center. The mean is not resistant because it is a function of the sum of the values of data. Changing the magnitude of one value changes the sum of the values.

2. $67,530 is the mean household income.

3. HUD uses the median because the data are skewed. Explanations will vary.

4. The mean will likely be larger. Explanations will vary.

5. The median is between the 5000th and the 5001st ordered values.

6. False

7. $\bar{x} = 11$ **8.** $\bar{x} = 82$

9. $\mu = 9$ **10.** $\mu = 15$

11. Mean price per ad slot was $3.01 million.

12. The missing value is 32.

13. Mean cost is $2025.25; median cost is $2209; there is no mode cost.

14. Mean phone bill is $41.41; median phone bill is $40.76; there is no mode phone bill.

15. The mean, median, and mode strengths are 3670, 3830, and 4090 pounds per square inch, respectively.

16. The mean, median, and mode flight times are 266, 266, and 260 minutes, respectively.

17. (a) mean > median **(b)** mean = median **(c)** mean < median Justification will vary.

18. (a) IV **(b)** III **(c)** II **(d)** I

19. (a) Tap: $\bar{x} = 7.50$; $M = 7.485$; mode = 7.47. Bottled: $\bar{x} = 5.194$; $M = 5.22$; mode = 5.26 **(b)** $\bar{x} = 7.05$; $M = 7.485$; the median is resistant.

20. (a) Blue stimulus: $\bar{x} = 0.551$ second, $M = 0.5315$ second; no mode. Red stimulus: $\bar{x} = 0.458$ second, $M = 0.432$ second, no mode. **(b)** Answers will vary. **(c)** $\bar{x} = 1.8125$ seconds; $M = 0.5315$ second; the median is resistant.

21. (a) The mean pulse rate is 72.2 beats per minute. **(b)** Samples and sample means will vary. **(c)** Answers will vary.

22. (a) The mean travel time is 26.4 minutes. **(b)** Samples and sample means will vary. **(c)** Answers will vary.

23. (a) 536,237 thousand metric tons **(b)** Per capita is better because it adjusts CO_2 emissions for population. After all, countries with more people will, in general, have higher CO_2 emissions. **(c)** Mean = 2.693 thousand metric tons; median = 2.660 thousand metric tons; mean

24. (a) Mean winning time = 86.572 hours
Median winning time = 86.251 hours
(b) Mean winning distance = 3498.7 km
Median winning distance = 3453 km
(c) Mean winning margin = 5.667 min
Median winning margin = 6.317 min
(d) Mean winning speed: $\bar{x} = 40.420$ km/h

$$\text{Winning speed: } \frac{\sum \text{distance}}{\sum \text{time}} = 40.414 \text{ km/h}$$

$$\text{Winning speed: } \frac{\text{mean distance}}{\text{mean time}} = 40.414 \text{ km/h}$$

25. The distribution is symmetric. The mean is the better measure of central tendency.

26. The distribution is skewed right. The median is the better measure of central tendency of the distribution.

27. $\bar{x} = 0.875$ gram; $M = 0.875$ gram. The distribution is symmetric, so the mean is the better measure of central tendency.

Weight of Plain M&Ms

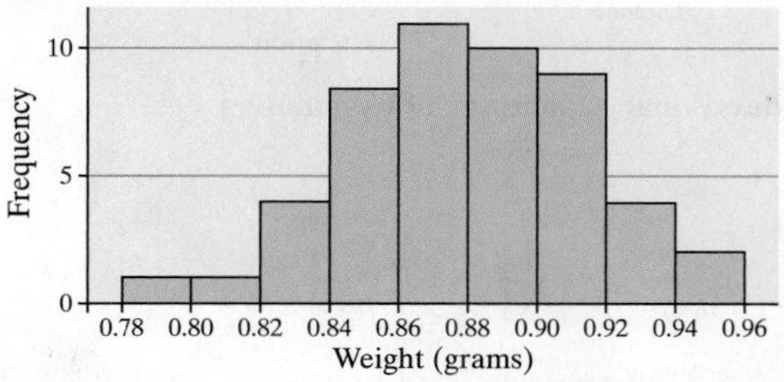

28. The distribution is symmetric; $\bar{x} = 104.1$ seconds; $M = 104$ seconds. The mean is the better measure of central tendency.

Length of Eruptions

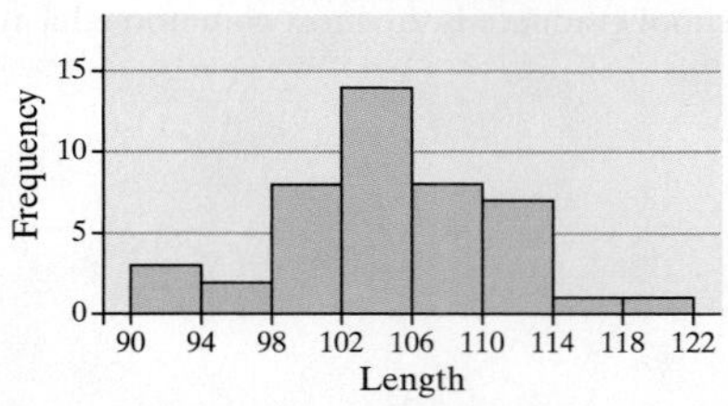

29. The distribution is skewed left; $\bar{x} = 22$ hours; $M = 25$ hours. The median is the better measure of central tendency.

Hours Worked per Week

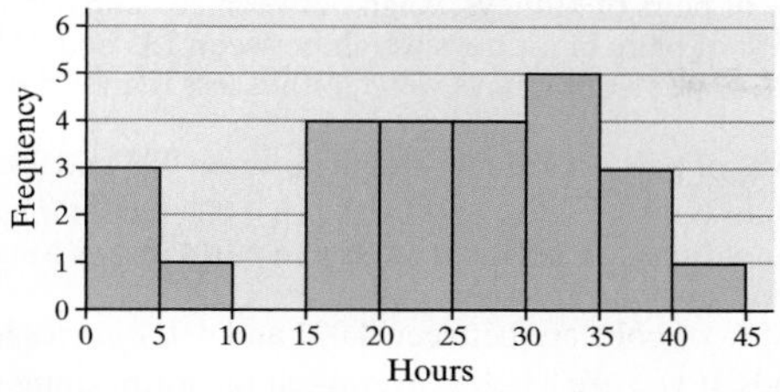

30. The distribution is skewed right; $\bar{x} = \$1392.83$; $M = \$1177.50$. The median is the better measure of central tendency.

Car Dealer's Profit

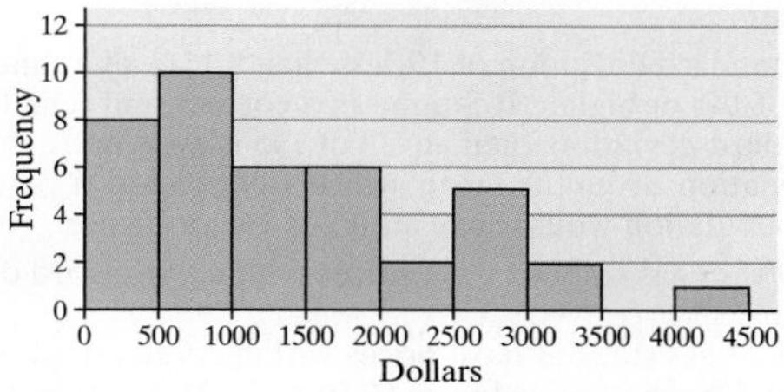

31. (a) Moderate **(b)** Yes, to avoid response bias

32. The mode diagnosis of admission is gunshot wound.

33. Sample of size 5: All data recorded correctly: $\bar{x} = 99.8$; $M = 100$; 106 recorded as 160: $\bar{x} = 110.6$; $M = 100$

Sample of size 12: All data recorded correctly: $\bar{x} = 100.4$; $M = 101$; 106 recorded as 160: $\bar{x} = 104.9$; $M = 101$

Sample of size 30: All data recorded correctly: $\bar{x} = 100.6$; $M = 99$; 106 recorded as 160: $\bar{x} = 102.4$; $M = 99$

For each sample size, the mean becomes larger, but the median remains constant. As the sample size increases, the effect of the misrecorded data on the mean decreases.

34. 67.8 inches

35. The unreadable score is 44.

36. Although the median survival time is only 11 months, the histogram tells us that those who survive the first 20 months end up with a fairly high survival rate. After all, once past the first 20 months, 50% of patients survive at least 80 months. So the trick is to fight hard and get through the first 20 months.

37. Answers will vary. **38.** Answers will vary.

39. (a) Mean = \$50,000; median = \$50,000; mode = \$50,000
(b) New data set: 32.5, 32.5, 47.5, 52.5, 52.5, 52.5, 57.5, 57.5, 62.5, 77.5; mean = \$52,500; median = \$52,500; mode = \$52,500. All three measures increased by \$2500.
(c) New data set: 31.5, 31.5, 47.25, 52.5, 52.5, 52.5, 57.75, 57.75, 63, 78.75; mean = \$52,500; median = \$52,500; mode = \$52,500. All three measures increased by 5%.
(d) New data set: 30, 30, 45, 50, 50, 50, 55, 55, 60, 100; mean = \$52,500; median = \$50,000; mode = \$50,000.
The mean increased by \$2500, but the median and the mode remained at \$50,000.

40. (a) $\bar{x} = 75.2$ **(b)** $M = 71$
(c) The median is the better measure of central tendency since the distribution is skewed right.
(d) $\bar{x} = 79.2$
(e) Adding 4 to each score increases the mean by 4.

41. The trimmed mean is 0.875. Explanations will vary.

42. Midrange = 0.87. Midrange is not resistant; it only considers extreme data points.

43. (a) Discrete
(b) Skewed right

Number of Days High School Students Consumed Alcohol in the Past Week

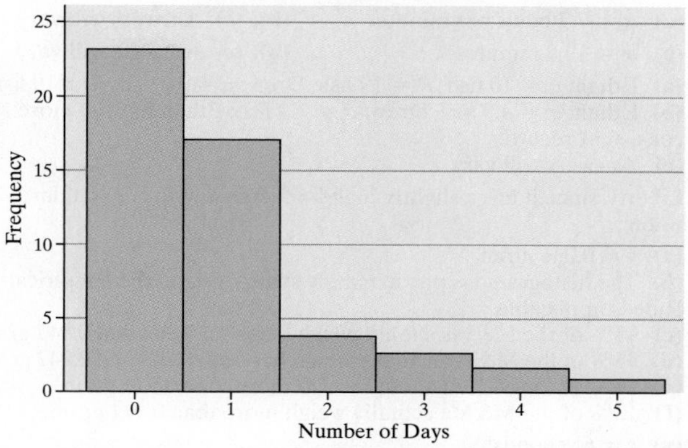

(c) Since the data are skewed right, we would expect the mean to be greater than the median.
(d) Mean: 0.94; median: 1; the mean can be less than the median in skewed-right data. Therefore, using the rule *mean greater than median implies the data are skewed right* does not always work.
(e) 0
(f) Yes. It is difficult to get truthful responses to this type of question. Carlos would need to ensure that the identity of the respondents is anonymous.

44. (a) The mean will be less than 723 because in left-skewed distributions, the mean is usually less than the median.
(b) 50%

45. The median is resistant because it is a positional measure of central tendency, and increasing the largest value or decreasing the smallest value does not affect the position of the center. The mean is not resistant because it is a function of the sum of the values of data. Changing the magnitude of one value changes the sum of the values.

46. No. Each state has a different population size. This must be taken into account.

47. (a) Median
(b) Skewed right
(c) There are a few households with very high net worth.

48. The salary distribution is skewed right, so the players' negotiator would want to use the median salary; the owners' negotiator would use the mean salary to refute the players' claim.

49. The distribution is skewed right, so the median amount of money lost is less than the mean amount lost.

50. (a) Median; the distribution of home prices tends to be skewed.
(b) Mode; the data are qualitative.
(c) Mean; the data are quantitative and symmetric.
(d) Median; the data are quantitative and skewed.
(e) Median; NFL salaries are skewed right.
(f) Mode; the data are qualitative.

3.2 Assess Your Understanding (page 140)

1. zero

2. Mean; mean; spread **3.** True

4. True **5.** $s^2 = 36$; $s = 6$

6. $s^2 = 100$; $s = 10$ **7.** $\sigma^2 = 16$; $\sigma = 4$

8. $\sigma^2 = 64$; $\sigma = 8$ **9.** $s^2 = 196$; $s = 14$

10. $\sigma^2 = 25$; $\sigma = 5$

11. $R = \$1537$; $s^2 = 507{,}013.6$ dollars^2; $s = \$712.0$

12. $R = \$13.92$; $s^2 = 22.584$ dollars^2; $s = \$4.752$

13. $R = 1150$ psi; $s = 459.6$ psi

14. $R = 25$ minutes; $s = 8.4$ minutes

15. The data go from 30 to 75; in (a) they are clustered between 40 and 60.

16. (a) III **(b)** I **(c)** IV **(d)** II

17. (a) Tap: $R = 0.59$; bottled: $R = 0.26$; tap water has more dispersion.
(b) Tap: $s = 0.154$; bottled: 0.081; tap water has more dispersion.

18. **(a)** Blue: $R = 0.574$ second; red: $R = 0.140$ second. The response time to the blue stimulus has more dispersion.
(b) Blue: $s = 0.1994$ second; red: $s = 0.0647$ second. The response time to blue has more dispersion.

19. **(a)** $\sigma = 7.7$ beats per minute **(b), (c)** Answers will vary.

20. **(a)** $\sigma = 12.8$ minutes **(b), (c)** Answers will vary.

21. **(a)** Ethan: $\mu = 10$ fish, $R = 19$ fish; Drew: $\mu = 10$ fish, $R = 19$ fish
(b) Ethan: $\sigma = 4.9$ fish, Drew: $\sigma = 7.9$ fish; Ethan has the more consistent record.
(c) Answers will vary.

22. Liberty, since it has a slightly higher median and lower standard deviation.

23. **(a)** $s = 0.036$ gram
(b) The histogram is approximately symmetric, so the Empirical Rule is applicable.
(c) 95% of the M&Ms should weigh between 0.803 and 0.947 gram.
(d) 96% of the M&Ms actually weigh between 0.803 and 0.947 gram.
(e) 16% of the M&Ms should weigh more than 0.911 gram.
(f) 12% of the M&Ms actually weigh more than 0.911 gram.

24. **(a)** $s = 6$ seconds
(b) The histogram is approximately symmetric, so the Empirical Rule is applicable.
(c) 95% of the eruptions should last between 92 and 116 seconds.
(d) 93% of the observed eruptions actually lasted between 92 and 116 seconds.
(e) 16% of the eruptions should last less than 98 seconds.
(f) 11% of the observed eruptions actually lasted fewer than 98 seconds.

25.

	Car 1	Car 2
Sample mean	$\bar{x} = 223.5$ mi	$\bar{x} = 237.2$ mi
Median	$M = 223$ mi	$M = 230$ mi
Mode	None	None
Range	$R = 93$ mi	$R = 166$ mi
Sample variance	$s^2 = 475.1$ mi^2	$s^2 = 2406.9$ mi^2
Sample standard deviation	$s = 21.8$ mi	$s = 49.1$ mi

Answers will vary.

26.

	Rates of Return	
	Fund A	Fund B
Sample mean	$\bar{x} = 3.05\%$	$\bar{x} = 3.41\%$
Median	$M = 3.05\%$	$M = 3.65\%$
Mode	None	4.3%
Range	$R = 10.9\%$	$R = 19.6\%$
Sample variance	$s^2 = 8.95(\%)^2$	$s^2 = 31.23(\%)^2$
Sample standard deviation	$s = 2.99\%$	$s = 5.59\%$

Answers will vary.

27. **(a)** Consumer goods stocks: $\bar{x} = 9.805\%$, $M = 10.11\%$; energy stocks: $\bar{x} = 11.679\%$, $M = 10.76\%$. Energy stocks have the higher mean and median rate of return.
(b) Consumer goods stocks: $s = 8.993\%$; energy stocks: $s = 9.340\%$. Energy stocks are riskier, so the investor is paying for the higher return. Probably worth it.

28. Chicago: $R = 39°F$, $\sigma = 9.7°F$; San Diego: $R = 16°F$, $\sigma = 4.4°F$; Chicago has more dispersion.

29. **(a)** 95% of people have an IQ score between 70 and 130.
(b) 5% of people have an IQ score either less than 70 or greater than 130.
(c) 2.5% of people have an IQ score greater than 130.

30. **(a)** 68% of SAT math scores are between 401 and 629.
(b) 32% of SAT math scores are either less than 401 or greater than 629.
(c) 2.5% of SAT math scores are greater than 743.

31. **(a)** 95% of pairs of kidneys weigh between 265 and 385 grams.
(b) 99.7% of pairs of kidneys weigh between 235 and 415 grams.
(c) 0.3% of pairs of kidneys weigh either less than 235 or more than 415 grams.
(d) 81.5% of pairs of kidneys weigh between 295 and 385 grams.

32. **(a)** 68% of bolts are between 3.993 and 4.007 inches long.
(b) 95% of bolts are between 3.986 and 4.014 inches long.
(c) 5% of the bolts are discarded.
(d) 15.85% of bolts are between 4.007 and 4.021 inches long.

33. It depends. If you are a below average student (meaning you expect to have a mean score below 80%), you are better off with Professor Alpha, since about 97.5% of students will score 70% or better in the class. If you are an above average student, you would go with Professor Omega, since you likely want an A, and about 16% of the class will score 90% or higher.

34. With a standard deviation of 15, less than 0.15% of humans would have an IQ of 145 or higher. If Summers is correct, and females have a lower standard deviation, then an IQ of 145 is even more than three standard deviations from the mean, which means a lower percentage of the female population would have an IQ of 145 or higher.

35. **(a)** 88.9% of gas stations have prices within 3 standard deviations of the mean.
(b) 84% of gas stations have prices within 2.5 standard deviations of the mean. Gasoline priced from $2.91 to $3.21 is within 2.5 standard deviations of the mean.
(c) At least 75% of gas stations have prices between $2.94 and $3.18.

36. **(a)** At least 75% of commuters in Boston have a commute time within 2 standard deviations of the mean.
(b) At least 55.6% of commuters have a commute time within 1.5 standard deviations of the mean. They commute between 15.15 and 39.45 minutes to work.
(c) At least 88.9% of commuters commute between 3 and 51.6 minutes to work.

37. There is more variation among individuals than among means.

38. **(a)** $R = \$45$, $\sigma^2 = 160$, $\sigma = \$12.6$
(b) Option 1: $R = \$45$, $\sigma^2 = 160$, $\sigma = \$12.6$
(c) Option 2: $R = \$47.25$, $\sigma^2 = 176.4$, $\sigma = \$13.3$
(d) Option 3: $R = \$70$, $\sigma^2 = 341.3$, $\sigma = \$18.5$

39. Sample of size 5: correct $s = 5.3$, incorrect $s = 27.9$
Sample of size 12: correct $s = 14.7$, incorrect $s = 22.7$
Sample of size 30: correct $s = 15.9$, incorrect $s = 19.2$
As the sample size increases, the effect of the misrecorded observation on standard deviation decreases.

40. $s = 0$. If all values in a data set are identical, there is zero variance.

41. **(a)** 6.11 cm **(b)** 5.67 cm **(c)** 5.59 cm
(d) Standard deviation is lower for each group than it is for the groups combined.

42. MAD = $544.25, $s = \$712.05$

43. **(a)** Skewness = 3; distribution is skewed right.
(b) Skewness = 0; distribution is perfectly symmetric.
(c) Skewness = −2.5; distribution is skewed left.
(d) Skewness = 0; distribution is symmetric.
(e) Skewness = 0.05; distribution is symmetric.

44. **(a)** Average rate of return = 14.9%, risk level = 14.7%
(b) To minimize risk, invest 30% in foreign stock.
(c) Answers will vary.
(d) At least 75% of returns are between −12.8% and 44.4%. At least 88.9% of returns are between −27.1% and 58.7%.

45. **(a)** Bond: $\bar{x} = 2.375\%$, $s = 0.669\%$; stock: $\bar{x} = 8.0125\%$, $s = 0.903\%$
(b) Stocks have more spread (because they are riskier investments).
(c) Bond: 0.0625; stock: 0.625
(d) Bond: 0.28, stock: 0.11; based on the coefficient of variation, bonds have more spread. Bonds have 0.28 standard deviation per unit mean, while stocks have 0.11 standard deviation per unit mean.
(e) Inches: $\bar{x} = 70$ inches, $s = 2.5$ inches; centimeters: $\bar{x} = 177.8$ cm; $s = 6.368$ cm; CV = 0.036 for both data sets. When converting units of measure, the coefficient of variation is unchanged.

46. Answers will vary.

47. Answers will vary.

48. No. It is not appropriate to compare standard deviations for two units of measure. Assuming the same variable is being measured, each should be reported in the same unit of measure (such as converting the inches to centimeters).

49. Degrees of freedom refers to the number of data values that are free to be any value while requiring the entire data set to have a specified mean. For example, if a data set is composed of 10 observations, 9 of the observations are free to be any value, while the tenth must be a specific value to obtain a specific mean.

50. No. The range, standard deviation, and variance are all sensitive to extreme observations.

51. A statistic is biased if it consistenty under- or overestimates the value of the corresponding parameter.

52. The range only uses two observations from a data set, whereas the standard deviation uses all the observations.

53. There is more spread among heights when gender is not accounted for. Think about the range of heights from the shortest female to the tallest male (in general) versus the range of heights from the shortest female to the tallest female and the shortest male to the tallest male.

54. Standard deviation measures spread by determining the mean distance to the typical observation.

Data Set 1:

x	$\bar{x}$	$x_i - \bar{x}$	$(x_i - \bar{x})^2$
3	4	−1	1
4	4	0	0
5	4	1	1

$\Sigma(x_i - \bar{x})^2 = 2$

$$s = \sqrt{\frac{2}{3-1}} = 1$$

Data Set 2:

x	$\bar{x}$	$x_i - \bar{x}$	$(x_i - \bar{x})^2$
0	4	−4	16
4	4	0	0
8	4	4	16

$\Sigma(x_i - \bar{x})^2 = 32$

$$s = \sqrt{\frac{32}{3-1}} = 4$$

Data set 2 has the higher standard deviation because the observations are farther from the mean, on average.

55. The IQ of residents in your home town would have a higher standard deviation because the college campus likely has certain admission requirements which make the individuals more homogeneous as far as intellect goes.

56. 15, 15, 15, 15, 15, 15, 15, 15

57.

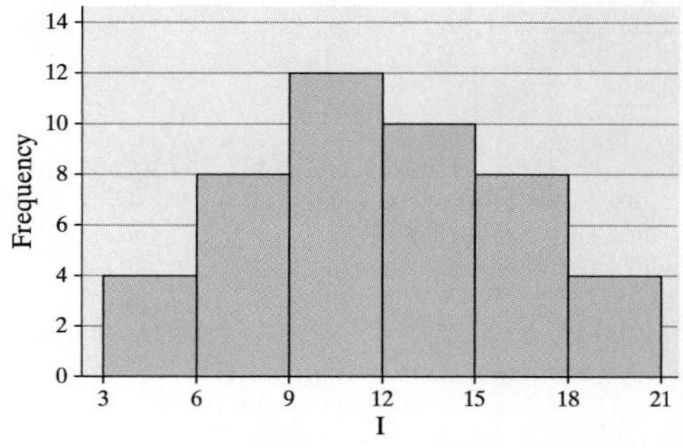

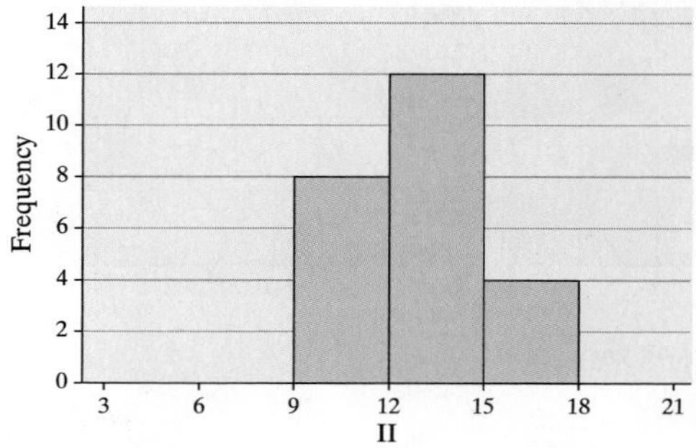

Histogram I has the larger standard deviation.

58. Even though the mean wait time increased, patrons were happy because there was less variability in wait time (so fastpass decreases standard deviation wait times). This suggests that people get less upset at long lines than they do at not having their expectations (as to how long they will need to wait in line) satisfied.

3.3 Assess Your Understanding (page 151)

1. $\mu = 3289.5$ g, $\sigma = 657.2$ g
2. $\bar{x} = 2419$ ft^2, $s = 907.0$ ft^2
3. $\bar{x} = 70.6$°F, $s = 3.5$°F
4. $\mu = 29.9$ years, $\sigma = 20.3$ years
5. **(a)** $\mu = 32.3$ years, $\sigma = 5.7$ years
(b)

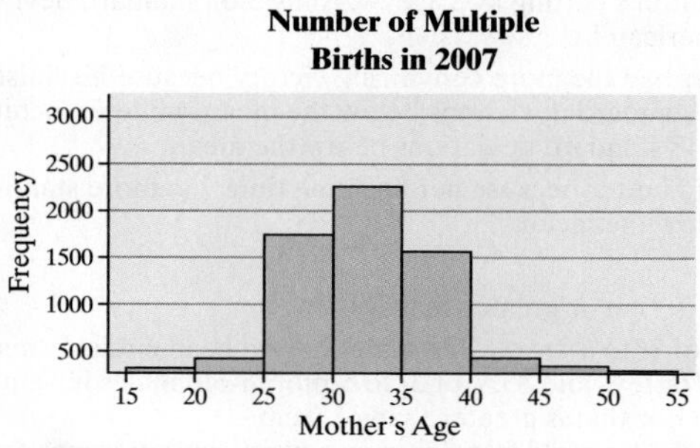

(c) 95% of mothers of multiple births are between 20.9 and 43.7 years of age.

6. **(a)** $\mu = 520.2$, $\sigma = 117.3$
(b)

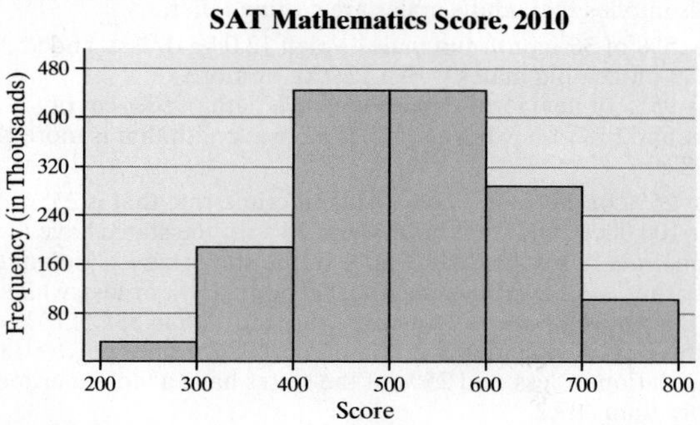

(c) 95% of the SAT math scores are between 285.6 and 754.8.

7. Grouped data: $\mu = \$1.505$, $\sigma = \$0.982$; raw data: $\mu = \$1.447$, $\sigma = \$0.935$
8. Grouped data: $\bar{x} \approx 1.214\%$, $s \approx 0.865\%$; raw data: $\bar{x} = 1.129\%$, $s = 0.910\%$
9. GPA = 3.27
10. Course average = 87.15%
11. Cost per pound = \$2.97
12. Cost per pound = \$3.38
13. **(a)** Males: $\mu = 36.2$ years, $\sigma = 22.0$ years
(b) Females: $\mu = 39.6$ years, $\sigma = 23.9$ years
(c) Females have the higher mean age.
(d) Females have more dispersion in age.
14. **(a)** 1980: $\mu = 25.5$ years, $\sigma = 5.4$ years
(b) 2007: $\mu = 27.9$ years, $\sigma = 6.4$ years
(c) 2007 has the higher mean age of new mothers.
(d) 2007 has more dispersion in the age of new mothers.
15. $M = 3367.9$ g
16. $M = 2298.3$ ft^2
17. $M = 70.4$°F
18. $M = 25.4$ years
19. Modal class: 3,000–3,999 g
20. Modal class: 1,500–1,999 ft^2

3.4 Assess Your Understanding (page 159)

1. z-score
2. kth percentile

3. Quartiles

4. interquartile range

5. −0.30; −0.43; the 40-week gestation baby weighs less relative to the gestation period.

6. 0.61; 0.85; the 34-week gestation baby weighs less relative to the gestation period.

7. The man is relatively taller.

8. The woman is relatively taller.

9. Felix Hernandez had the better year because his ERA was 2.14 standard deviations below the Americen League mean ERA, while Johnson's ERA was only 1.78 standard deviations below the National League's mean ERA.

10. Williams had the better year relative to his peers, because his batting average was 3.82 standard deviations above the mean 1941 batting average. Hamilton's batting average was only 3.01 standard deviations above the American League's mean.

11. Will Power had the more convincing victory because his finishing time was 1.76 standard deviations below the mean, while Franchitti's victory was 1.48 standard deviations below the mean.

12. Zandra did better because her finishing time was more standard deviations below the mean.

13. 239

14. Less than 7.9 cm or greater than 8.1 cm

15. **(a)** 15% of 3- to 5-month-old males have a head circumference that is 41.0 cm or less, and 85% of 3- to 5-month-old males have a head circumference that is greater than 41.0 cm.
(b) 90% of 2-year-old females have a waist circumference that is 52.7 cm or less, and 10% of 2-year-old females have a waist circumference that is more than 52.7 cm.
(c) The heights at each percentile decrease as the age increases. This implies that adults males are getting taller.

16. **(a)** 5% of 36-month-old males weigh 12.0 kg or less, and 95% of 36-month-old males weigh 12.0 kg or more.
(b) 95% of newborn females have a length of 53.8 cm or less, and 5% of newborn females have a length that is more than 53.8 cm.

17. **(a)** 25% of the states have a violent crime rate that is 255.3 crimes per 100,000 population or less, and 75% of the states have a violent crime rate more than 255.3. 50% of the states have a violent crime rate that is 335.5 crimes per 100,000 population or less, while 50% of the states have a violent crime rate more than 335.5. 75% of the states have a violent crime rate that is 497.2 crimes per 100,000 population or less, and 25% of the states have a violent crime rate more than 497.2.
(b) 241.9 crimes per 100,000 population; the middle 50% of all observations have a range of 241.9 crimes per 100,000 population.
(c) Yes
(d) Skewed right. The difference between Q_1 and Q_2 is quite a bit less than the difference between Q_2 and Q_3. In addition, the outlier in the right tail of the distribution implies that the distribution is skewed right.

18. **(a)** 25% of the sections, the student spends 42 minutes or less on homework for this section, and 75% of the time, the student spends more than 42 minutes. 50% of the time, the student spends 51.5 minutes or less on homework for this section, and 50% spend more than 51.5 minutes. 75% of the time, the student spends 72.5 minutes or less on homework for this section, and 25% of the time, the student spends more than 72.5 minutes.
(b) 30.5 minutes; the middle 50% of time spent has a range of 30.5 minutes of time spent on homework.
(c) Yes
(d) Skewed right. The difference between Q_1 and Q_2 is quite a bit less than the difference between Q_2 and Q_3.

19. **(a)** 50th percentile
(b) 90th percentile
(c) 105

20. **(a)** 28th percentile
(b) 96th percentile
(c) 500

21. **(a)** $z = -0.73$. The individual whose car got 36.3 miles per gallon was 0.73 standard deviations below the mean.
(b) By hand, TI-83 or 84, StatCrunch: $Q_1 = 36.85$ mpg, $Q_2 = 38.35$ mpg, $Q_3 = 41.0$ mpg; MINITAB: $Q_1 = 36.575$ mpg, $Q_2 = 38.35$ mpg, $Q_3 = 41.2$ mpg
(c) By hand, TI-83 or 84, StatCrunch: IQR = 4.15 mpg; MINITAB: IQR = 4.625 mpg
(d) By hand, TI-83 or 84, StatCrunch: lower fence = 30.625 mpg, upper fence = 47.225 mpg. Yes, 47.5 mpg is an outlier, MINITAB: lower fence = 29.6375 mpg, upper fence = 48.1375 mpg. There are no outliers using MINITAB's quartiles.

22. **(a)** $z = -1.21$. Blackie's hemoglobin level is 1.21 standard deviations below the mean.
(b) By hand, TI-83/84, StatCrunch: $Q_1 = 9.15$ g/dL, $Q_2 = 9.95$ g/dL, $Q_3 = 11.1$ g/dL; MINITAB: $Q_1 = 9.025$ g/dL, $Q_2 = 9.950$ g/dL, $Q_3 = 11.15$ g/dL
(c) By hand, TI-83/84, StatCrunch: IQR = 1.95 g/dL; MINITAB: IQR = 2.125 g/dL
(d) By hand, TI-83/84, StatCrunch: lower fence = 6.225 g/dL, upper fence = 14.025 g/dL; MINITAB: lower fence = 5.8375 g/dL, upper fence = 14.3375 g/dL; the only outlier is 5.7 g/dL.

23. **(a)** By hand, TI-83/84: Q_1: −0.075, Q_2: 0.02, Q_3: 0.075; StatCrunch: Q_1: −0.07, Q_2: 0.02, Q_3: 0.07; MINITAB: Q_1: −0.07, Q_2: 0.02, Q_3: 0.075. Using the by-hand quartiles, 25% of the monthly returns are less than or equal to the first quartile, −0.075, and about 75% of the monthly returns are greater than −0.075; 50% of the monthly returns are less than or equal to the second quartile, 0.02, and about 50% of the monthly returns are greater than 0.02; about 75% of the monthly returns are less than or equal to the third quartile, 0.075, and about 25% of the monthly returns are greater than 0.075.
(b) 0.30 is an outlier.

24. **(a)** By hand, TI-83/84, StatCrunch: Q_1: 6.12, Q_2: 8.46, Q_3: 10.06; MINITAB: Q_1: 6.02, Q_2: 8.46, Q_3: 10.14. Using the by-hand quartiles, 25% of the countries have per capita CO_2 emissions that are less than or equal to 6.12, and about 75% of the countries have per capita CO_2 emissions that exceed 6.12. About 50% of the countries have per capita CO_2 emissions that are less than or equal to the second quartile, 8.46, and about 50% of the countries have per capita CO_2 emissions that exceed 8.46. About 75% of the countries have per capita CO_2 emissions less than or equal to 10.06, and about 25% of the countries have per capita CO_2 emissions that exceed 10.06.
(b) No

25. By hand, TI-83/84, StatCrunch: The cutoff point is 574 minutes. MINITAB: The cutoff point is 578 minutes. If more minutes are used, the customer is contacted.

26. By hand, TI-83/84, StatCrunch: Daily charges must exceed $219 before the customer is contacted. MINITAB: Daily charges must exceed $229 before the customer is contacted.

27. **(a)** $12,777 is an outlier.
(b) **Students' Weekly Income**

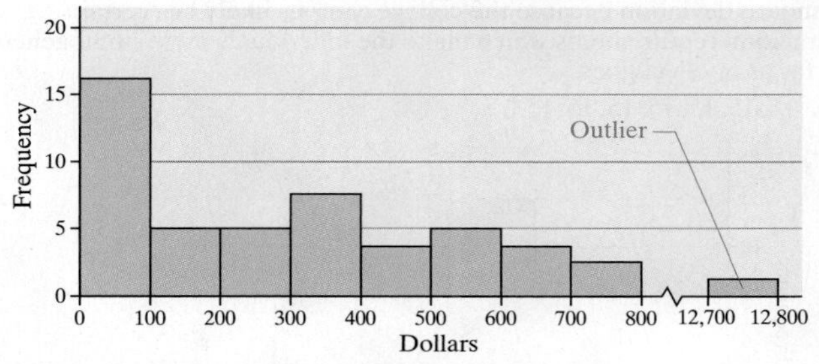

(c) Answers will vary.

28. **(a)** $115 and $1000 are outliers.
(b) **Students' Weekly Expenditures**

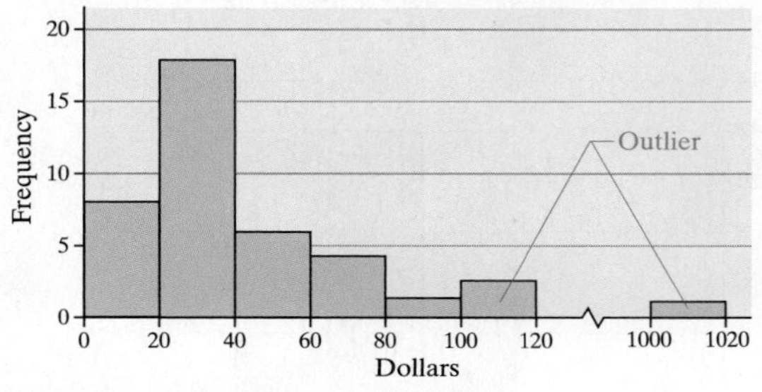

(c) Answers will vary.

29. Mean of the z-scores is 0.0; standard deviation of the z-scores is 1.0.

Student	z-Score
Perpectual Bempah	0.49
Megan Brooks	−1.58
Jeff Honeycutt	−1.58
Clarice Jefferson	1.14
Crystal Kurtenbach	−0.03
Janette Lantka	1.01
Kevin McCarthy	1.01
Tommy Ohm	−0.55
Kathy Wojdyla	0.10

30. Mean of the z-scores is 0.0; standard deviation of the z-scores is 1.0.

Student	z-Score	Student	z-Score
Amanda	0.98	Scot	1.45
Amber	−0.42	Erica	−1.20
Tim	−1.36	Tiffany	−1.13
Mike	0.44	Glenn	0.98
Nicole	0.28		

31. (a) $s = 58.0$ minutes; by hand, TI-83/84: IQR $= 56.5$ minutes; MINITAB: IQR $= 58.8$ minutes
(b) $s = 115.0$ minutes; by hand, TI-83/84: IQR $= 56.5$ minutes; MINITAB: IQR $= 58.8$ minutes. The standard deviation almost doubles in value, while the interquartile range is not affected. The standard deviation is not resistant to extreme observations, but the interquartile range is resistant.

32. Answers will vary.

33. Answers will vary. The kth percentile separates the lower k percent of the data from the upper $(100 - k)$ percent of the data.

34. Since the percentile of a score is rounded to the nearest integer, it is possible for two different scores to have the same percentile.

35. A five-star fund is in the top 10% of the funds. That is, it is above the bottom 90%, but within the top 10% of the ranked funds.

36. No; when an outlier is discovered, it should be investigated to find its cause.

37. One qualifies for Mensa if one's intelligence is in the top 2% of people.

38. Comparing z-scores allows a unitless comparison of the number of standard deviations an observation is from the mean.

39. The interquartile range is preferred when the data are skewed or have outliers. An advantage of standard deviation is that it uses all the observations in its computation.

40. The first quartile is the 25th percentile, which means that 25% of the observations are less than or equal to the value and 75% of the observations are greater than the value. The second quartile is the 50th percentile, which means that 50% of the observations are less than or equal to the value and 50% of the observations are greater than the value. The third quartile is the 75th percentile, which means that 75% of the observations are less than or equal to the value and 25% of the observations are greater than the value.

3.5 Assess Your Understanding (page 168)

1. The five-number summary consists of the minimum value in the data set, the first quartile, median, third quartile, and the maximum value in the data set.

2. Right

3. (a) Skewed right
(b) 0, 1, 3, 6, 16

4. (a) Symmetric
(b) −1, 2, 5, 8, 11

5. (a) 40
(b) 52
(c) y
(d) Symmetric
(e) Skewed right

6. (a) 16
(b) 22
(c) y
(d) Yes; 30
(e) Skewed left

7.

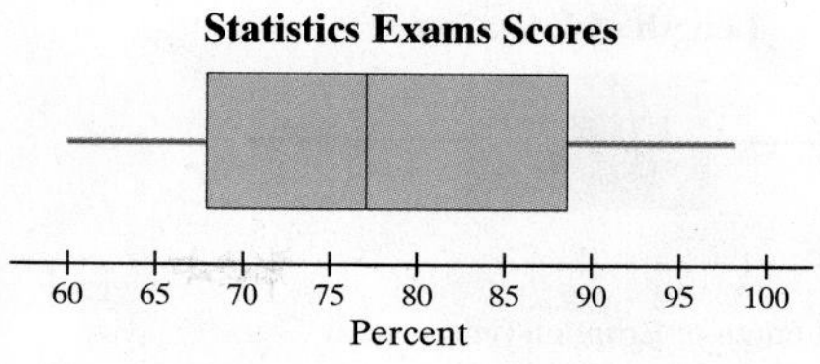

8.

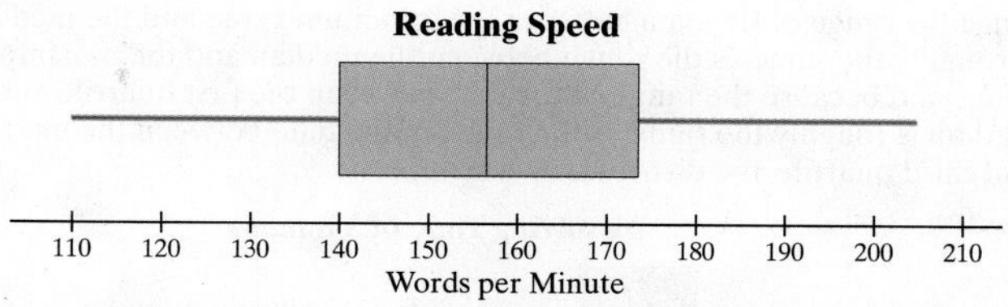

9. (a) By hand, TI-83 or 84, StatCrunch: 42, 50.5, 54.5, 57.5, 69; MINITAB: 42, 50.25, 54.5, 57.75, 69
(b)

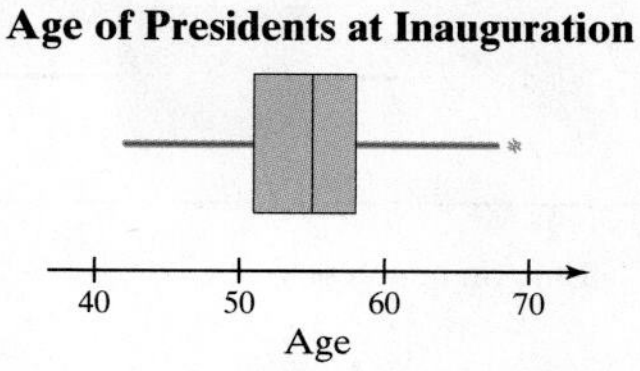

(c) Symmetric with an outlier.

10. (a) 7.2, 9, 10, 11.2, 16.4
(b)

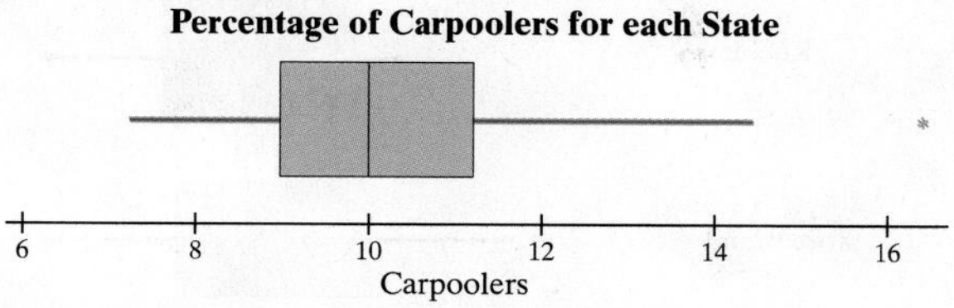

(c) Skewed right since the median is left of center in the box, and the distance from the median to the minimum value is less than the distance from the median to the maximum value.

11. (a)

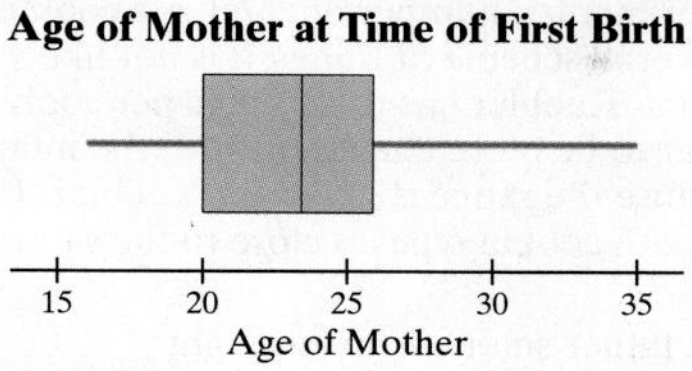

(b) Slightly skewed right

12. (a)

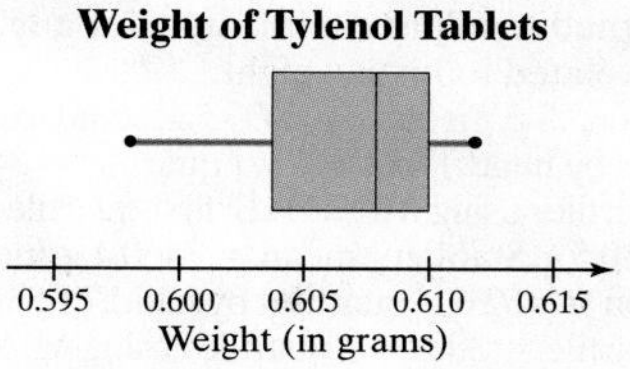

(b) Slightly skewed left

13.

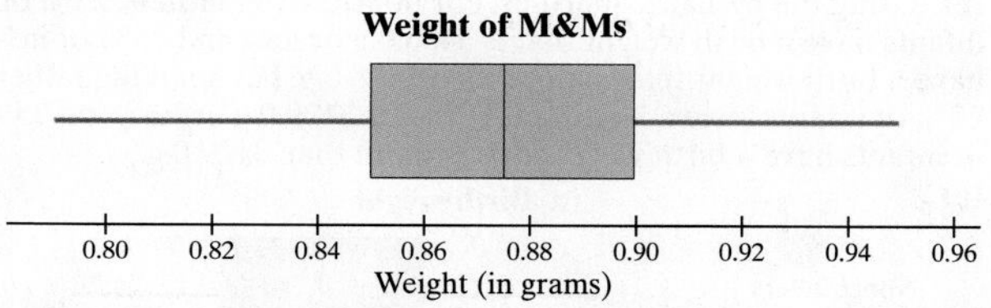

Since the range of the data between the minimum value and the median is roughly the same as the range between the median and the maximum value, and because the range of the data between the first quartile and median is the same as the range of the data between the median and third quartile, the distribution is symmetric.

14.

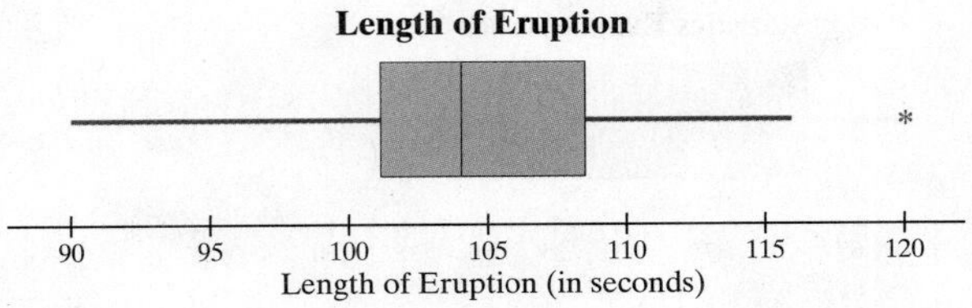

Since the range of the data between the minimum value and the median is roughly the same as the range between the median and the maximum value, and because the range of the data between the first quartile and median is roughly the same as the range of the data between the median and third quartile, the distribution is symmetric.

15. (a)

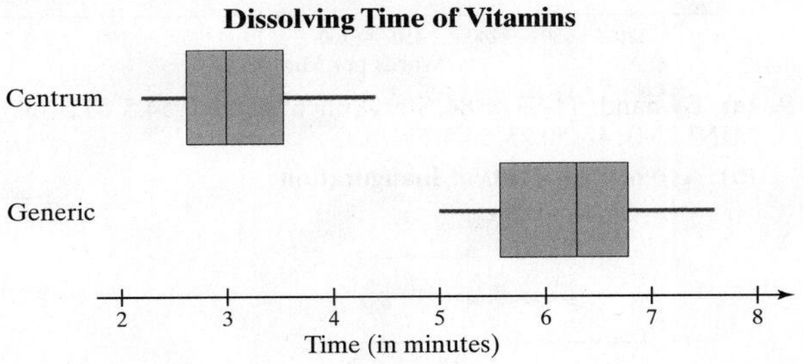

(b) Generic
(c) Centrum

16. (a)

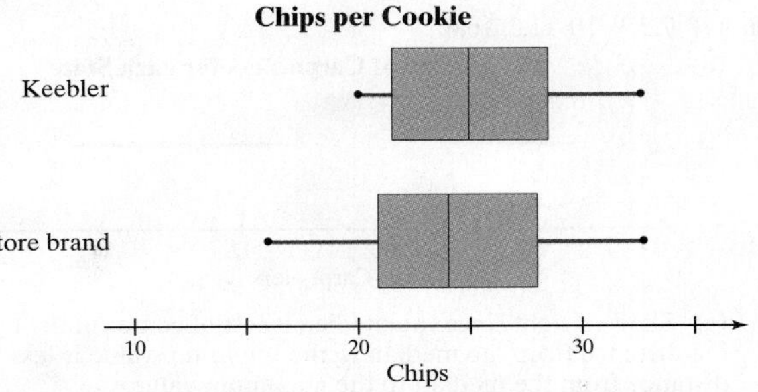

(b) Keebler has a higher median number of chips per cookie based on this sample. In the overall scheme of things, it is not likely the case that we could say that Keebler has more chips per cookie.
(c) Keebler does appear to be more consistent with the number of chips per cookie because the range is lower for Keebler. The interquartile range for both cookie types is close to the same.

17. (a) Observational study
(b) Whether or not the father smoked; birth weight
(c) Eating habits, exercise habits, whether the mother received prenatal care
(d) The researchers attempted to adjust their results for any variables that may also be related to birth weight.
(e) Nonsmokers: mean = 3665.5 g; median = 3693.5 g; standard deviation = 356.0 g; quartiles by hand, TI-83/84: first quartile = 3436.0 g, third quartile = 3976.0 g; quartiles using MINITAB: first quartile = 3432.8 g, third quartile = 3980.5 g. Smokers: mean = 3460.4 g, median = 3475.0 g, standard deviation = 452.6 g; quartiles by hand, TI-83/84: first quartile = 3129.0 g, third quartile = 3807.0 g; quartiles using MINITAB: first quartile = 3113.3 g, third quartile = 3828.3 g
(f) Using the by-hand quartiles: For nonsmoking fathers, 25% of infants have a birth weight that is 3436.0 g or less, and 75% of infants have a birth weight that is more than 3436.0 g. For smoking fathers, 25% of infants have a birth weight that is 3129.0 g or less, and 75% of infants have a birth weight that is more than 3129.0 g.
(g)

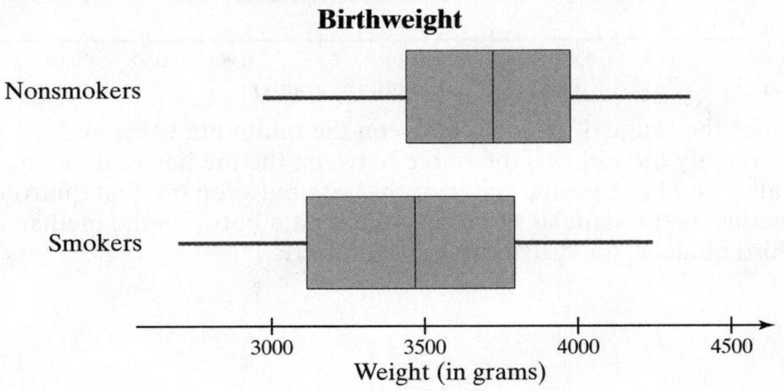

18. Boxplot II likely has the higher standard deviation because the interquartile range is larger in boxplot II.

19. Using the boxplot: If the median is left of center in the box, and the right whisker is longer than the left whisker, the distribution is skewed right. If the median is in the center of the box, and the left and right whiskers are roughly the same length, the distribution is symmetric. If the median is right of center in the box, and the left whisker is longer than the right whisker, the distribution is skewed left.

Using the quartiles: If the distance from the median to the first quartile is less than the distance from the median to the third quartile, or the distance from the median to the minimum value in the data set is less than the distance from the median to the maximum value in the data set, then the distribution is skewed right. If the distance from the median to the first quartile is the same as the distance from the median to the third quartile, or the distance from the median to the minimum value in the data set is the same as the distance from the median to the maximum value in the data set, the distribution is symmetric. If the distance from the median to the first quartile is more than the distance from the median to the third quartile, or the distance from the median to the minimum value in the data set is more than the distance from the median to the maximum value in the data set, the distribution is skewed left.

Chapter 3 Review Exercises (page 172)

1. (a) Mean = 792.51 m/sec, median = 792.40 m/sec
(b) Range = 4.8 m/sec, $s^2 = 2.03$, $s = 1.42$ m/sec

2. (a) $\bar{x} = \$10,178.9$, $M = \$9980$
(b) Range: $R = \$8550$, $s = \$3074.9$, IQR = \$5954.5; using MINITAB: IQR = \$5954
(c) $\bar{x} = \$13,178.9$, $M = \$9980$; range: $R = \$35,550$, $s = \$10,797.5$, IQR = \$5954.5 [using MINITAB: \$5954]. The median and interquartile range are resistant.

3. (a) $\mu = 57.8$ years, $M = 58.0$ years, bimodal: 56 and 62
(b) Range = 25 years, $\sigma = 7.0$ years
(c) Answers will vary.

4. (a) Skewed right

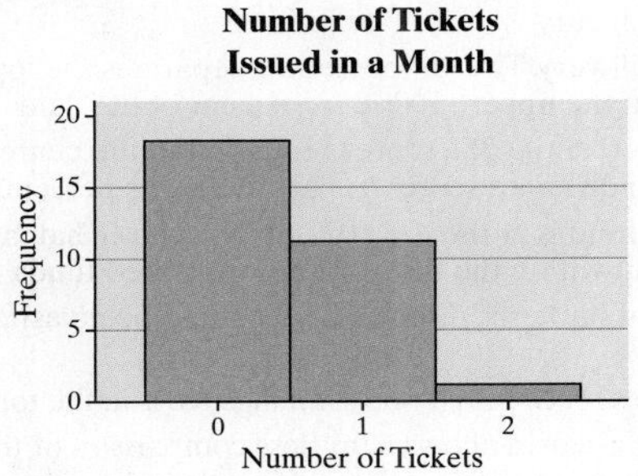

(b) Mean greater than median.
(c) $\bar{x} = 0.4$, $M = 0$
(d) 0

5. (a) 441; 759
(b) 95% of the light bulbs have a life between 494 and 706 hours.
(c) 81.5% of the light bulbs have a life between 547 and 706 hours.
(d) The firm can expect to replace 0.15% of the light bulbs.
(e) At least 84% of the light bulbs have a life within 2.5 standard deviations of the mean.
(f) At least 75% of the light bulbs have a life between 494 and 706 hours.

6. (a) $\bar{x} = 27.7$ minutes **(b)** $s = 19.1$ minutes

7. 3.33

8. Female, since her weight is more standard deviations above the mean

9. (a) Two-seam fastball **(b)** Two-seam fastball
(c) Four-seam fastball **(d)** 88 mph
(e) Symmetric **(f)** Skewed right

10. (a) $\mu = 2358.75$ words; $M = 2144$ words
(b) Quartiles by hand, TI-83/84, StatCrunch: $Q_1 = 1390$, $Q_2 = 2144$, $Q_3 = 2942$; quartiles by MINITAB: $Q_1 = 1373$, $Q_2 = 2144$, $Q_3 = 2960$. Using the by-hand quartiles: 25% of the inaugural addresses had 1390 words or less, 75% of the inaugural addresses had more than 1390 words; 50% of the inaugural addresses had 2144 words or less, 50% of the inaugural addresses

had more than 2144 words; 75% of the inaugural addresses had 2942 words or less, 25% of the inaugural addresses had more than 2942 words.
(c) By hand, TI-83/84, StatCrunch: 135, 1390, 2144, 2942, 8445; MINITAB: 135, 1373, 2144, 2960, 8445
(d) $\sigma = 1393.2$ words; by hand, TI-83/84: IQR $= 1552$; MINITAB: IQR $= 1587$
(e) Yes; 5433 and 8445 are outliers
(f) **Number of Words in Inaugural Addresses**

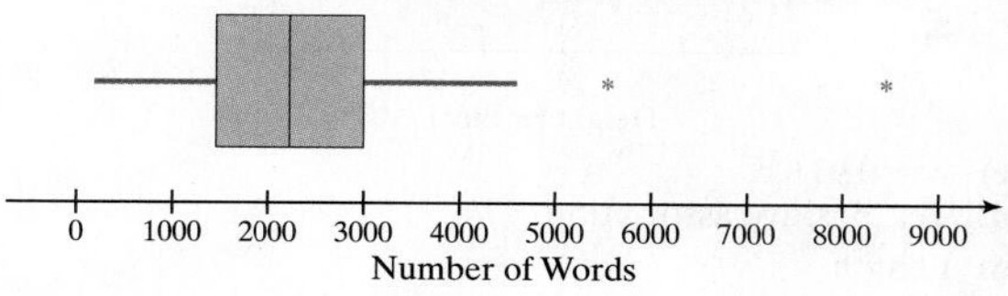

(g) Skewed right since the median is slightly left of center in the box and the right whisker is longer than the left whisker (even without considering the outlier).
(h) The median is the better measure since the outliers inflate the value of the mean.
(i) The interquartile range is the better measure since the outliers inflate the value of the standard deviation.

11. 85% of 19-year-old females have a height that is 67.1 inches or less, and 15% of 19-year-old females have a height that is more than 67.1 inches.

12. The median is used for three measures since it is likely the case that one of the three measures is extreme relative to the other two, thus substantially affecting the value of the mean. Since the median is resistant to extreme values, it is the better measure of central tendency.

Chapter 3 Test (page 174)

1. (a) $\bar{x} = 80$ min
(b) $M = 79.5$ min
(c) $\bar{x} = 192.5$ min, $M = 79.5$ min; the median is resistant.

2. From motor vehicles **3.** 63 min

4. (a) 23.8 min
(b) 41 min; the middle 50% of all study times has a range of 41 min.
(c) The interquartile range is resistant; the standard deviation is not resistant.

5. (a) 3282; 5322
(b) 95% of the cartridges print between 3622 and 4982 pages.
(c) The firm can expect to replace 2.5% of the cartridges.
(d) At least 55.6% of the cartridges have a page count within 1.5 standard deviations of the mean.
(e) At least 88.9% of the cartridges print between 3282 and 5322 pages.

6. (a) 74.9 minutes **7.** \$2.17
(b) 14.7 minutes

8. (a) Material A: $\bar{x} = 6.404$ million cycles
Material B: $\bar{x} = 11.332$ million cycles
(b) Material A: $M = 5.785$ million cycles
Material B: $M = 8.925$ million cycles
(c) Material A: $s = 2.626$ million cycles
Material B: $s = 5.900$ million cycles
Material B is more dispersed.
(d) Material A (in million cycles): 3.17, 4.52, 5.785, 8.01, 11.92
Material B (in million cycles): 5.78, 6.84, 8.925, 14.71, 24.37
(e) **Bearing Failures**

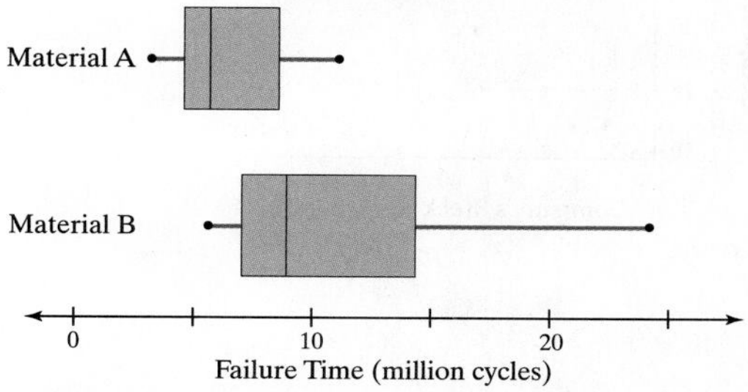

Answers will vary.
(f) The distributions are skewed right.

9. Quartiles by hand, TI-83/84 (in grams): $Q_1 = 5.58$, $Q_2 = 5.60$, $Q_3 = 5.67$; quartiles by MINITAB (in grams): $Q_1 = 5.58$, $Q_2 = 5.60$, $Q_3 = 5.6625$. Using the by-hand quartiles: 25% of quarters have a weight that is 5.58 g or less, 75% of the quarters have a weight more than 5.58 g; 50% of the quarters have a weight that is 5.60 g or less, 50% of the quarters have a weight more than 5.60 g; 75% of the quarters have a weight that is 5.67 g or less, 25% of the quarters have a weight that is more than 5.67 g. The quarter whose weight is 5.84 g is an outlier.

10. Armando should report his ACT math score since it is more standard deviations above the mean.

11. 15% of 10-year-old males have a height that is 53.5 inches or less, and 85% of 10-year-old males have a height that is more than 53.5 inches.

12. The median will be less than the mean for income data, so you should report the median.

13. (a) Report the mean since the distribution is symmetric.
(b) Histogram I has more dispersion. The range of classes is larger.

CHAPTER 4 Describing the Relation between Two Variables

4.1 Assess Your Understanding (page 186)

1. Univariate data measure the value of a single variable for each individual in the study. Bivariate data measure values of two variables for each individual.

2. response **3.** scatter diagram

4. Two variables that are linearly related are positively associated if increases in the explanatory variable tend to be associated with increases in the response variable. Two variables that are linearly related are negatively associated if increases in the explanatory variable tend to be associated with decreases in the response variable.

5. -1 **6.** False
7. lurking **8.** False
9. Nonlinear **10.** Linear, negative
11. Linear, positive **12.** Nonlinear
13. (a) III **(b)** IV
(c) II **(d)** I
14. (a) IV **(b)** III
(c) I **(d)** II

15. (a) Linear; positive association
(b) The point (48, 56000) appears to stick out. Reasons may vary. One possibility is a high concentration of government jobs that require a bachelor's degree but pay less than the private sector in a region with a high cost of living.
(c) The correlation coefficient is not resistant.

16. (a) No linear relation
(b) The point (61000, 21) appears to stick out. One possible reason is the religious beliefs of the residents.
(c) No linear relation

17. (a)

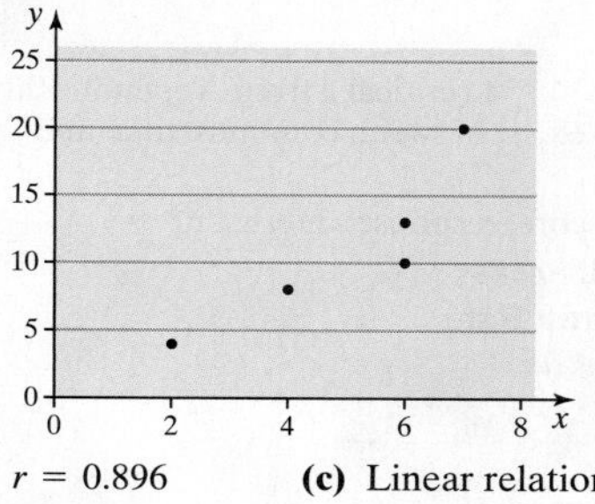

(b) $r = 0.896$ **(c)** Linear relation

18. (a)

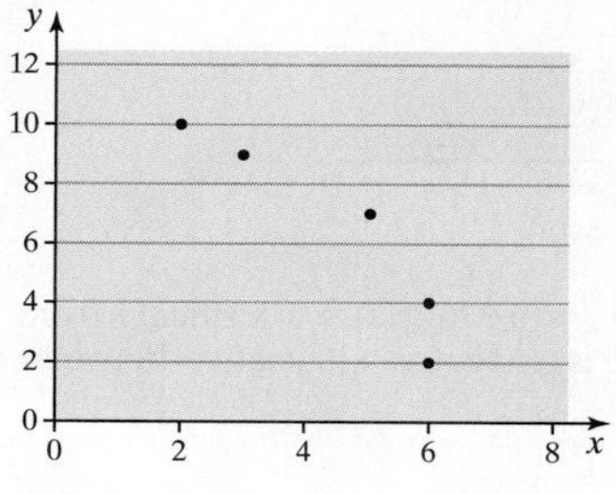

(b) $r = -0.933$ **(c)** Linear relation

19. (a)

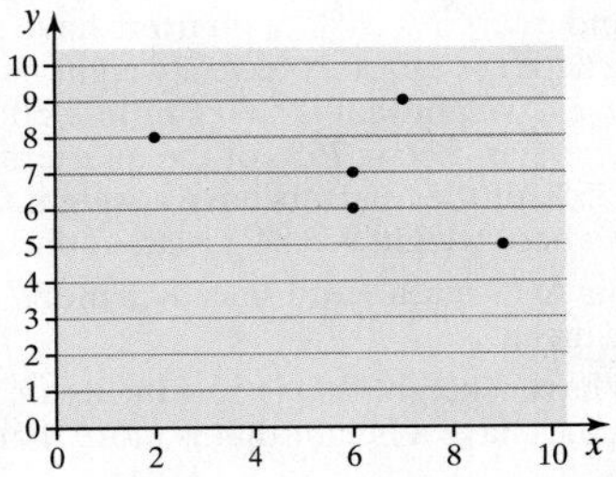

(b) $r = -0.496$ **(c)** No linear relation

20. (a)

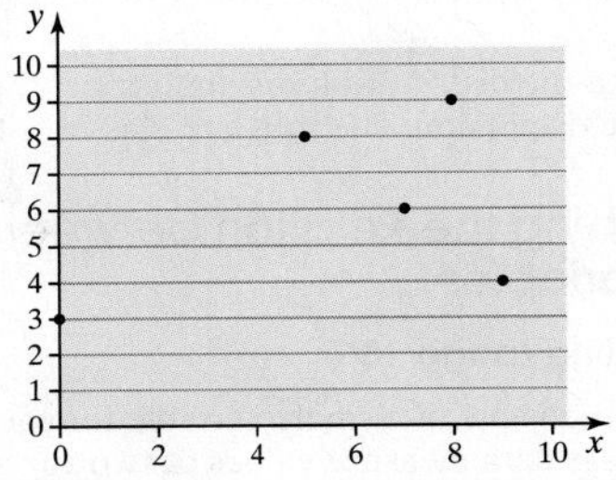

(b) $r = 0.440$ **(c)** No linear relation

21. (a) Positive **(b)** Negative
(c) Negative **(d)** Negative
(e) No correlation

22. (a) Negative **(b)** Positive
(c) Positive **(d)** No correlation
(e) Negative

23. Yes; $0.79 > 0.361$ (critical r for $n = 30$), so countries in which students answered a greater percentage of items in the background questionnaire tended to have higher mean scores on the TIMMS exam.

24. Yes; $|r| = 0.52 > 0.361$ (critical r for $n = 30$), so countries in which a greater percentage of students skipped class at least once in the last month tended to have lower mean scores on the TIMMS exam.

25. (a) Explanatory: commute time; response: well-being score
(b)

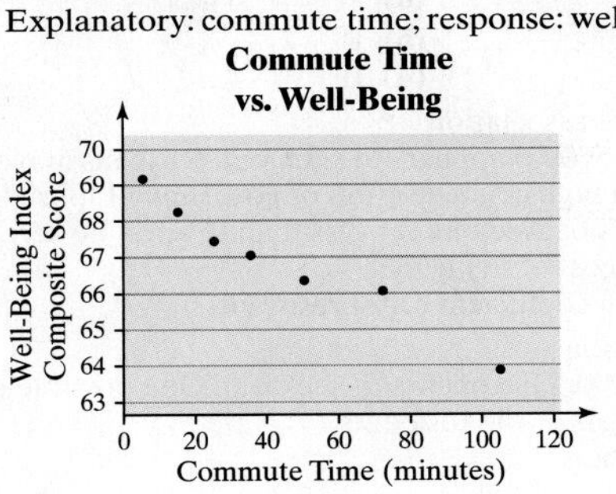

(c) -0.981
(d) $|-0.981| = 0.981 > 0.754$ (critical r from Appendix Table II), so a negative association exists between commute time and well-being index score.

26. (a) Explanatory: credit score; response: interest rate
(b)

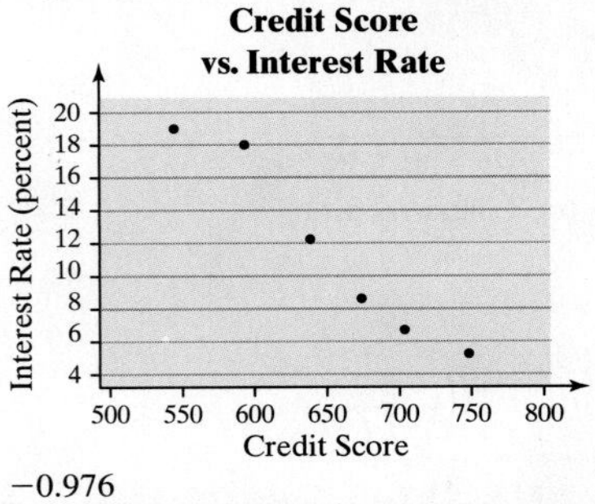

(c) -0.976
(d) Yes, because $|-0.976| = 0.976 > 0.811$ (critical r from Appendix Table II). There is a negative association between credit score and interest rate.

27. (a) Explanatory: height; response: head circumference
(b)

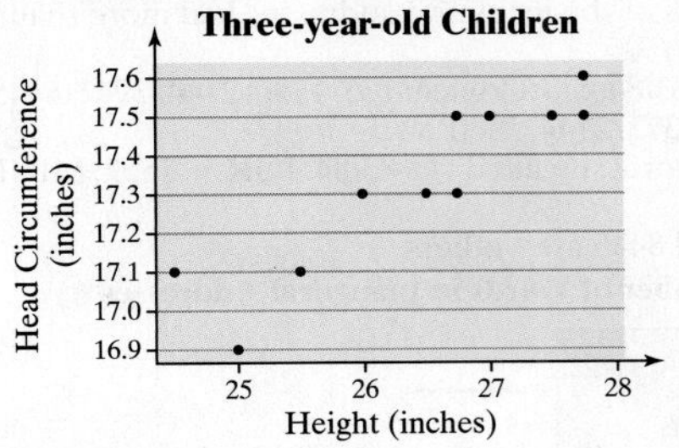

(c) $r = 0.911$
(d) Yes; positive association

28. (a) Length
(b)

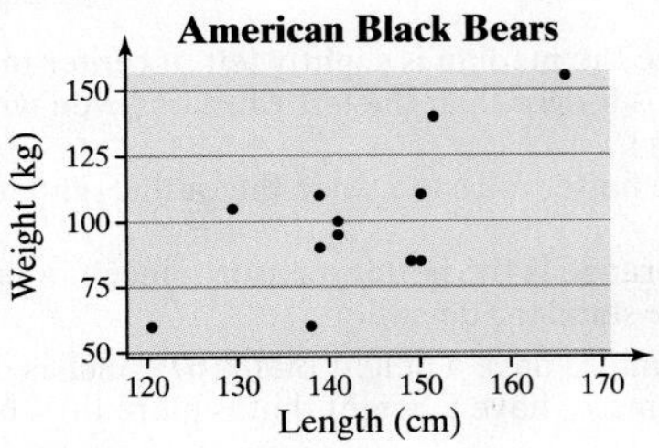

(c) $r = 0.704$
(d) Yes; positive association

29. (a) Explanatory: weight; response: miles per gallon
(b)

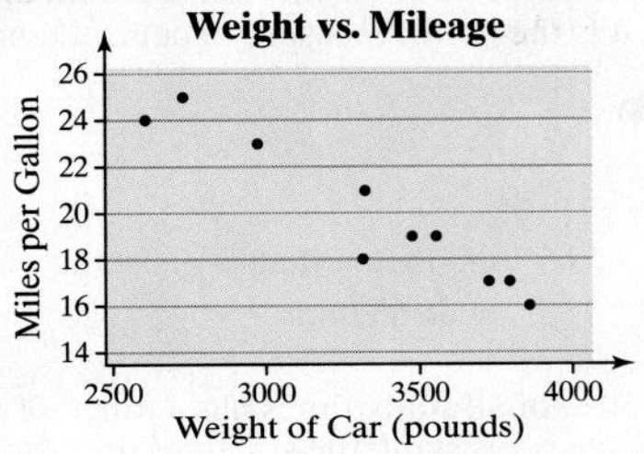

(c) $r = -0.960$ **(d)** Yes; negative association

30. (a)

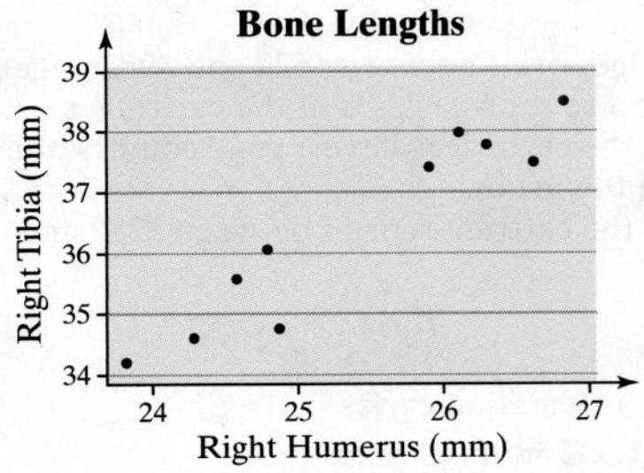

(b) $r = 0.951$ **(c)** Yes; positive association
(d) Converting units has no effect on the correlation coefficient.

31. (a) Stock return
(b)

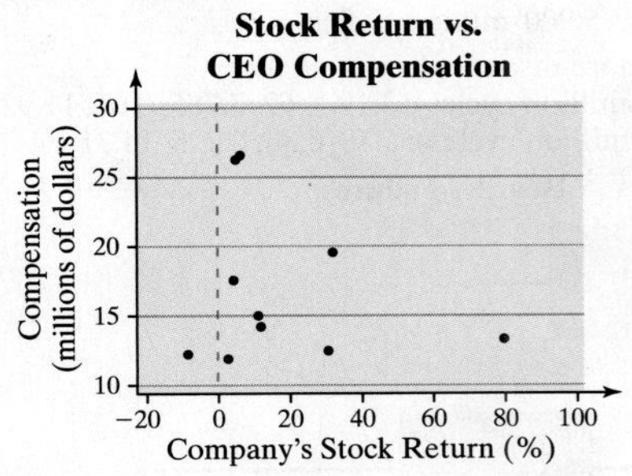

(c) -0.206 **(d)** No; no

32. (a)

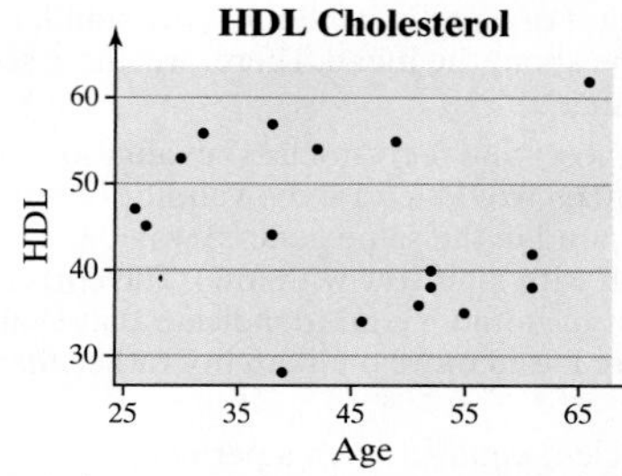

No relation appears to exist between age and HDL cholesterol.
(b) −0.164 **(c)** No

33. (a)

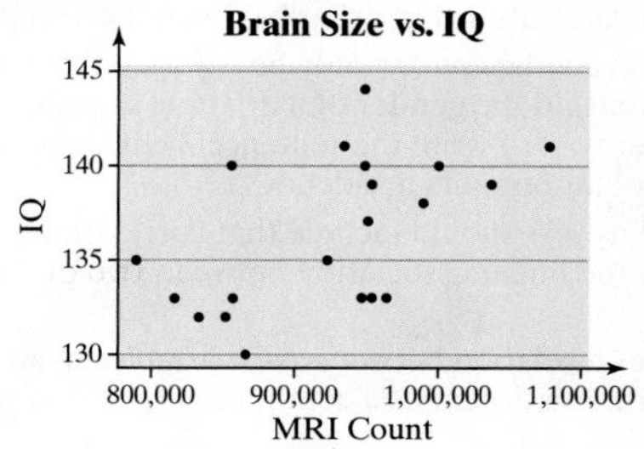

(b) $r = 0.548$. A positive association exists between MRI count and IQ.
(c)

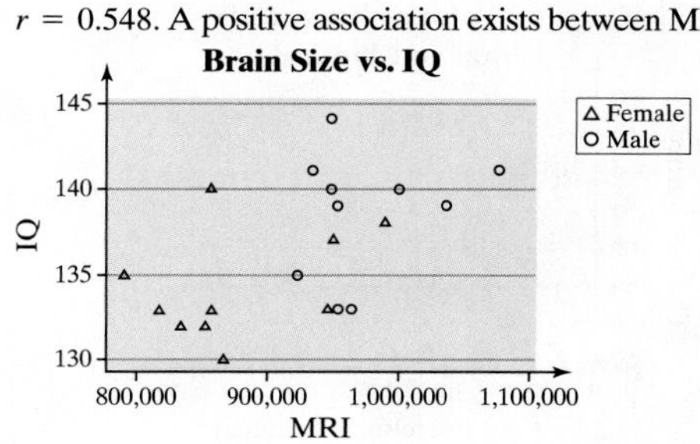

The females have lower MRI counts. Looking at each gender's plot, we see that the relation that appeared to exist between brain size and IQ disappears.

(d) Females: $r = 0.359$; males: $r = 0.236$. No linear relation exists between brain size and IQ.

34. (a)

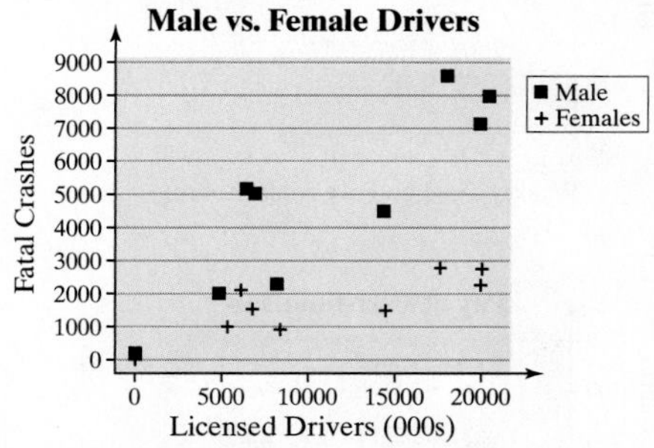

(b) Yes; males tend to have a higher fatal crash rate.
(c) Males: 0.883
(d) Females: 0.836
(e) Males have a slightly stronger linear relation between number of licensed drivers and number of crashes than females. Reasons will vary.

35. (a)

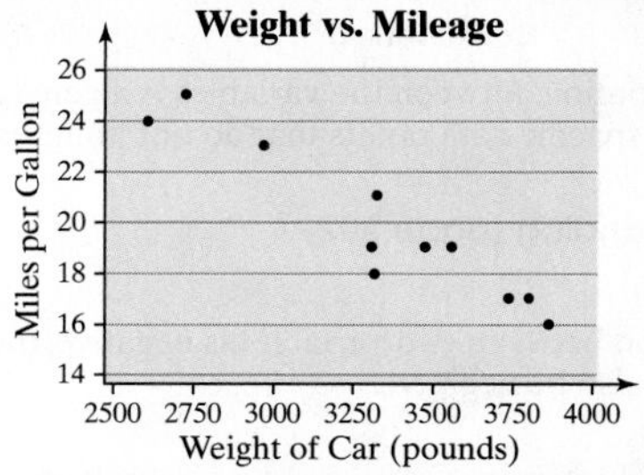

(b) Correlation coefficient (with Taurus included): $r = -0.954$
(c) The results are reasonable because the Taurus follows the overall pattern of the data.

(d)

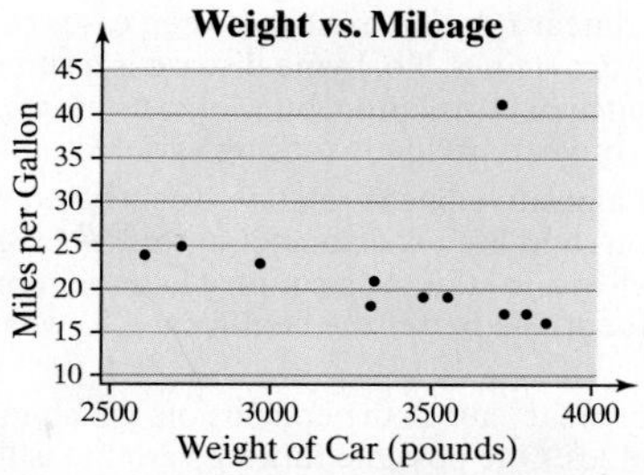

(e) Correlation coefficient (with Fusion included): $r = -0.195$
(f) The Fusion is a hybrid car; the other cars are not hybrids.

36. (a)

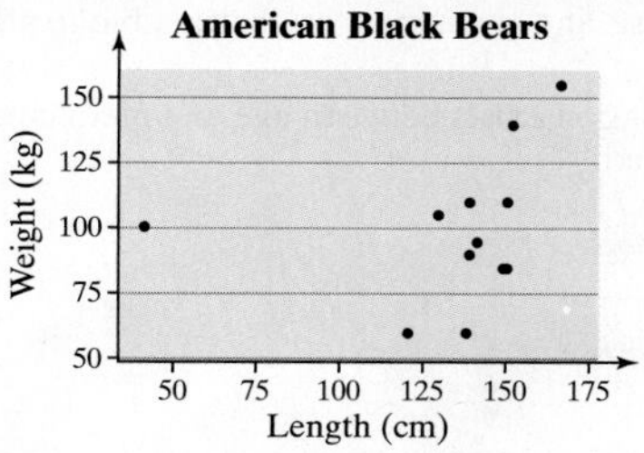

(b) $r = 0.254$
(c) The incorrectly entered data value is far away from the rest of the points. The incorrectly entered data value decreases the value of the correlation coefficient because the correlation coefficient is not resistant.

37. (a) 1: 0.816; 2: 0.817; 3: 0.816; 4: 0.817
(b)

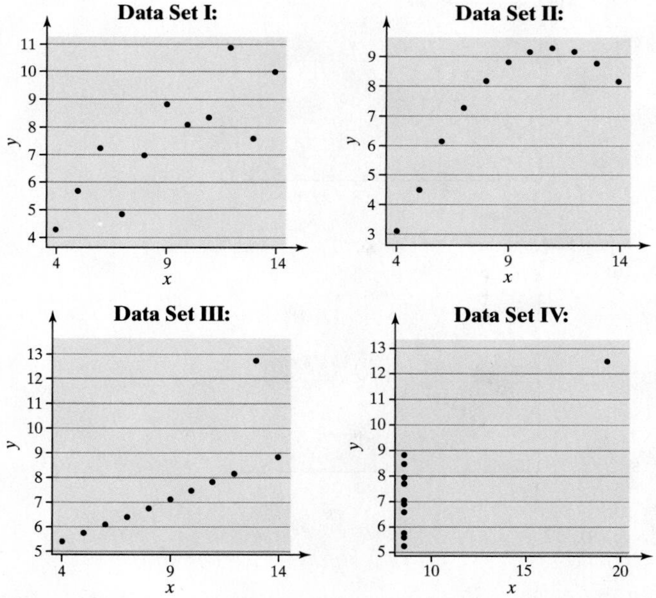

38. Answers may vary. Compare correlation coefficients and scatter diagrams to choose the one that appears to have the strongest association. Team ERA has the strongest correlation.

39. To have the lowest correlation between the two stocks, invest in Dell and Exxon Mobil: $r = -0.044$. If your goal is to have one stock go up when the other goes down, invest in Dell and TECO Energy: $r = -0.177$.

40. (a)

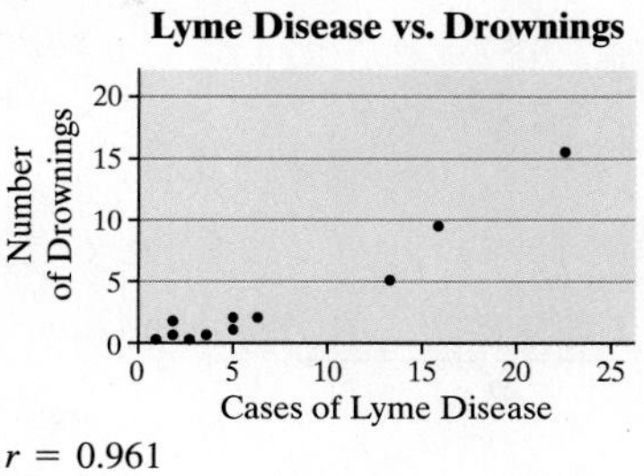

(b) $r = 0.961$

(c) A strong, positive, linear relation exists between cases of Lyme disease and number of drownings. No, Lyme disease is a summer disease. This is an instance of correlation, but not causation. Temperature and time of year are likely lurking variables.

41. $r = 0.599$ implies that a positive linear relation exists between the number of television stations and life expectancy, but this is correlation, not causation. The more television stations a country has, the more affluent it is. The more affluent, the better the health care, so wealth is a likely lurking variable.

42. The investigator is "not clear" about the conclusion, which indicates there may be lurking variables. One possible lurking variable is the health consciousness of the mother.

43. No; a likely lurking variable is the economy. In a strong economy, crime rates tend to decrease, and consumers are better able to afford cell phones.

44. Although no *linear* relation exists between age and median income, the two variables are related.

45. (a)

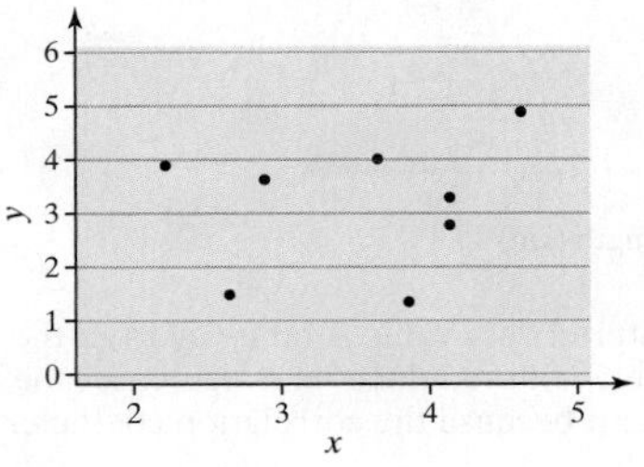

$r = 0.228$

(b)

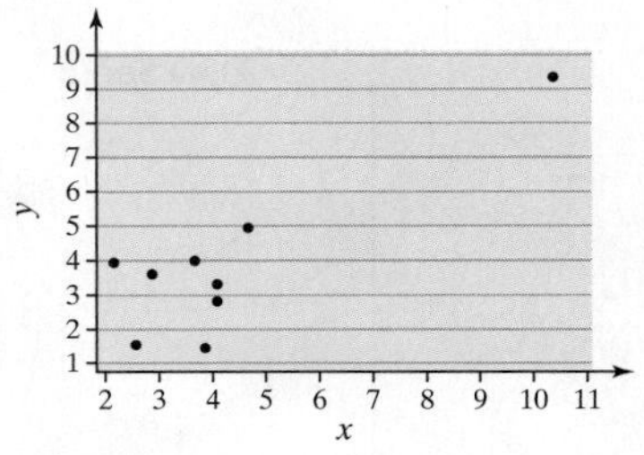

$r = 0.860$

46. (a)

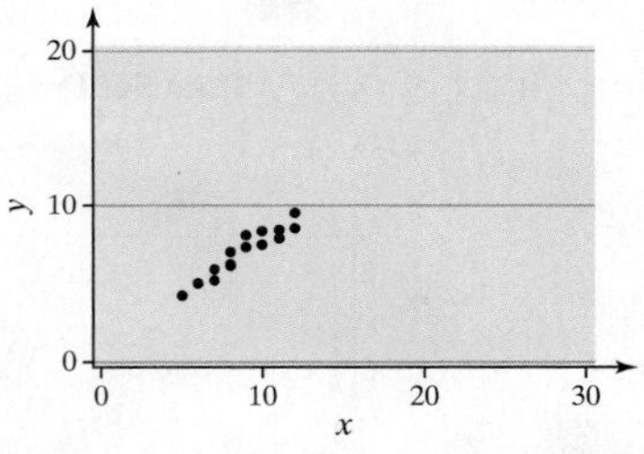

(b) 0.952

(c)

$2x$	10	12	14	14	16	16	16	16
$2y$	8.4	10	10.4	11.8	12	12.4	12.2	13.8
$2x$	18	18	20	20	22	22	24	24
$2y$	14.4	16	16.6	14.8	16.8	15.6	17	19

(d)

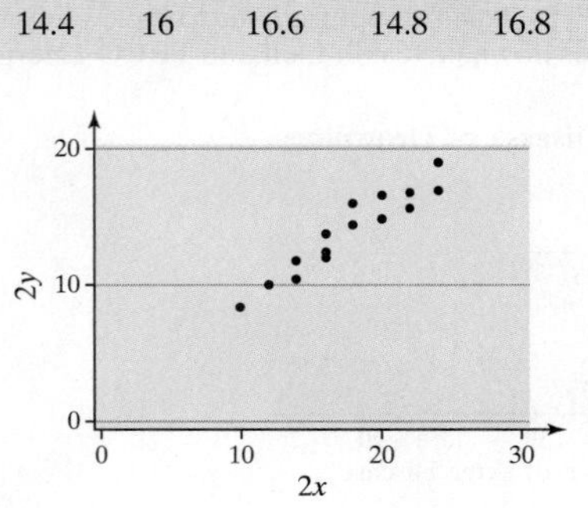

(e) 0.952

(f) By doubling the values of x and y, we double the standard deviations and deviations about the mean. Therefore, the z-scores for each point are unchanged.

47. Answers may vary. For those who feel "in-class" evaluations are meaningful, a correlation of 0.68 would lend some validity, because it indicates that students respond in the same general way on RateMyProfessors.com (high with high, low with low). The correlations between quality and easiness or hotness tend to indicate that evaluations at RateMyProfessors.com are based more on likability rather than actual quality of teaching.

48. If the correlation coefficient equals 1, then a perfect positive linear relation exists between the variables, and the points of the scatter diagram lie exactly on a straight line with a positive slope.

49. If $r = 0$, then no linear relationship exists between the variables.

50. The linear correlation coefficient can only be calculated from bivariate quantitative data, and the gender of a driver is a qualitative variable. A possible better way to write the sentence: Gender is associated with the rate of automobile accidents.

51. Answers will vary. Answers should include that correlation measures the strength of the linear association between two quantitative variables.

52. Correlation describes a relation between two variables in an observational study. Causation describes a conditional (if–then) relation in an experimental study.

53.

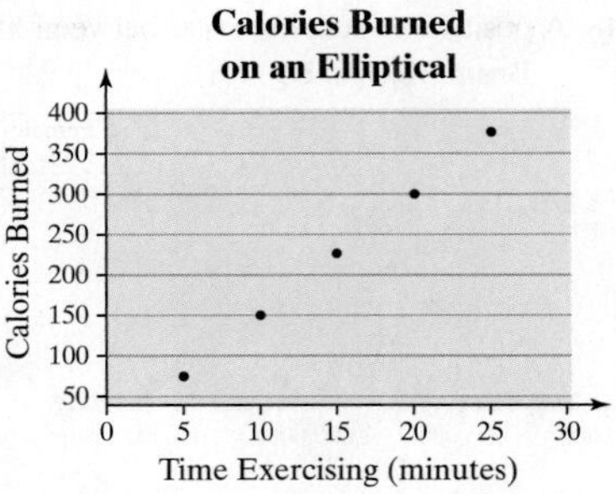

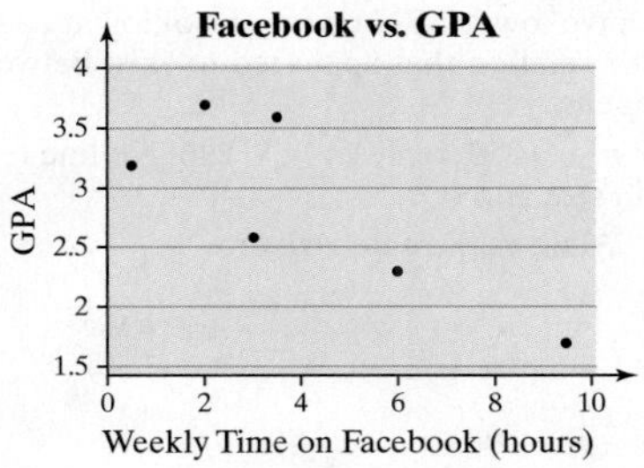

54. Deterministic

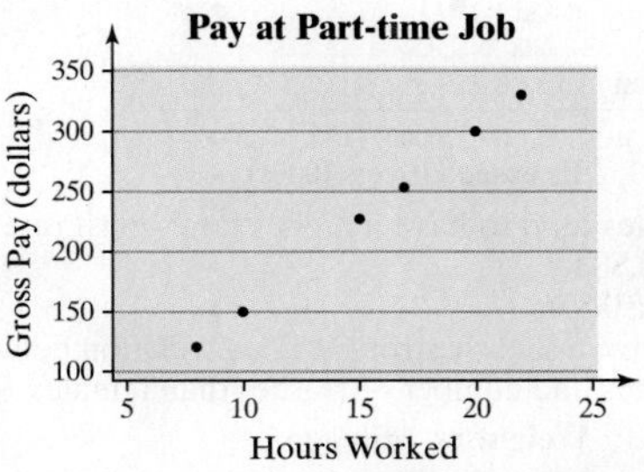

55. No, the negative association between the variables is a general trend in the data. There may be specific data points that do not fit in that trend.

4.2 Assess Your Understanding (page 202)

1. residual

2. If the linear correlation between two variables is negative, the slope of the regression line will also be negative.

3. True

4. If $r = 0$, then the slope of the linear regression line will also be zero, and the line will be $\hat{y} = \bar{y}$ since all regression lines contain the point $(\bar{x}, \bar{y})$.

5. (a)

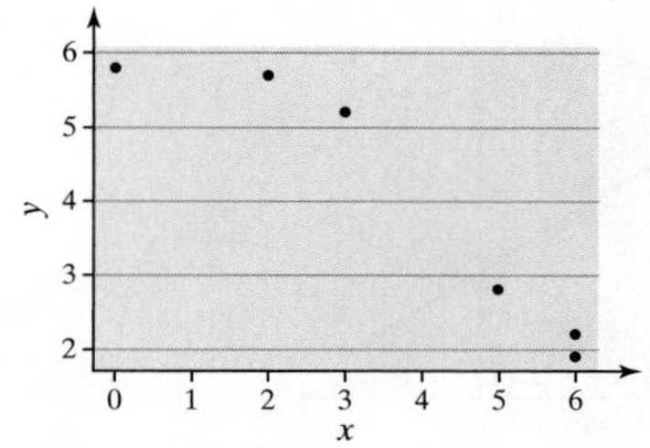

(b) $\hat{y} = -0.7136x + 6.5498$

(c)

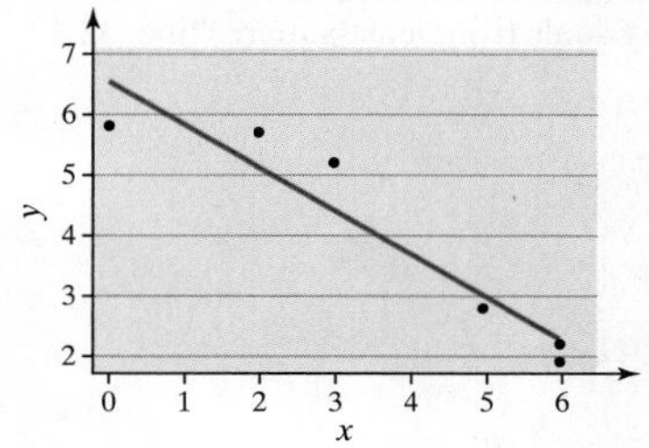

6. (a)

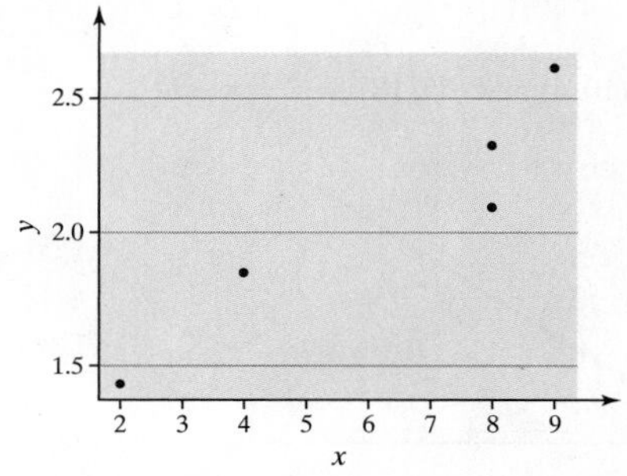

(b) $\hat{y} = 0.1457x + 1.1370$

(c)

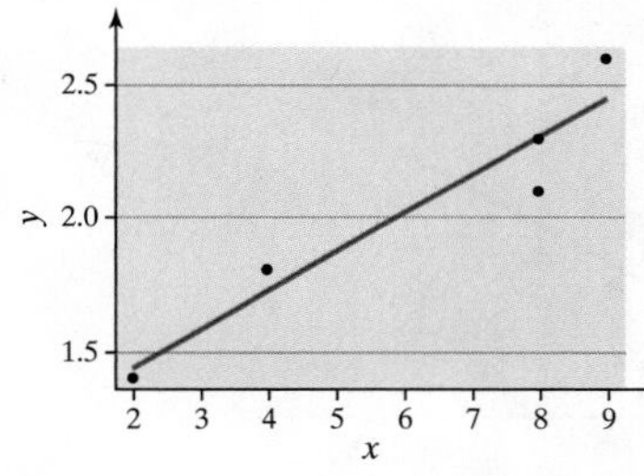

7. (a)

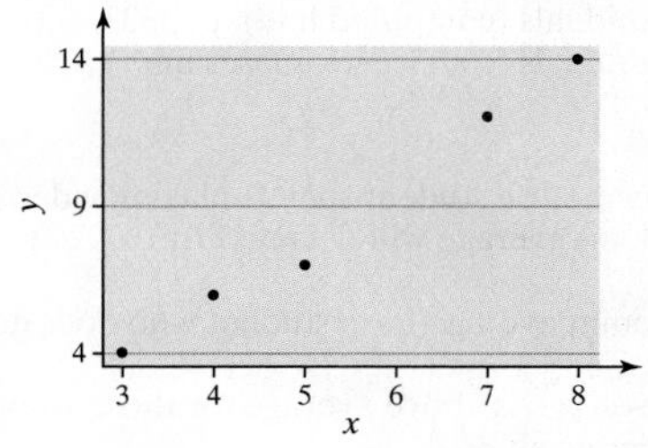

(b) Using points (3, 4) and (8, 14): $\hat{y} = 2x - 2$

(c)

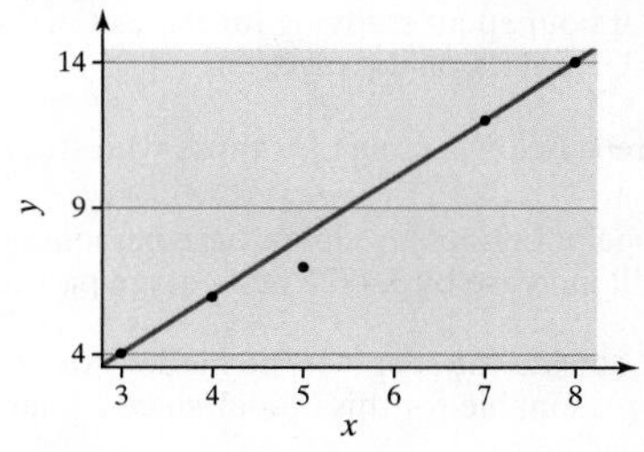

(d) $\hat{y} = 2.0233x - 2.3256$

(e)

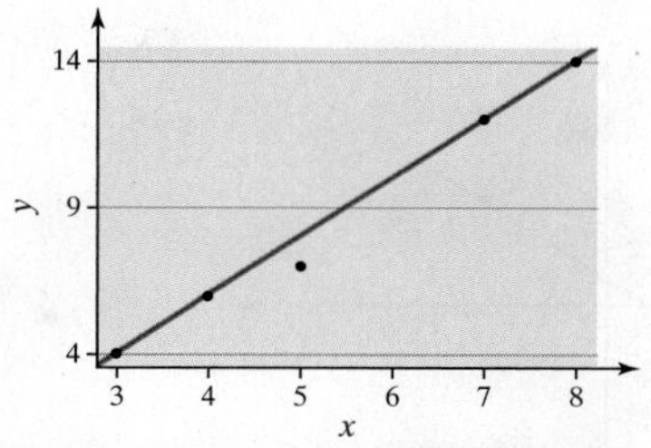

(f) Sum of squared residuals (computed line): 1

(g) Sum of squared residuals (least-squares line): 0.7907

(h) Answers will vary.

8. (a)

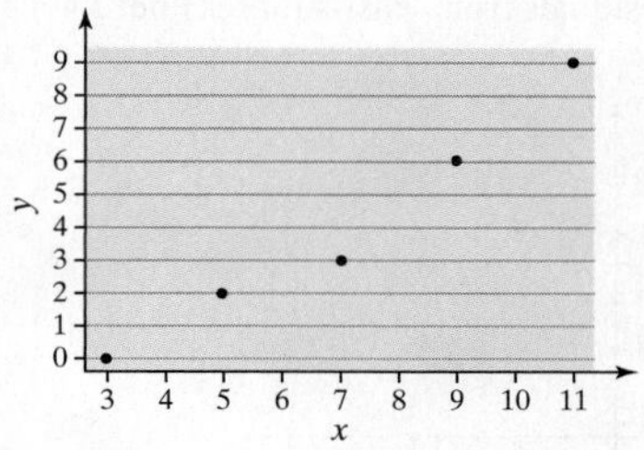

(b) Using points (3, 0) and (11, 9): $\hat{y} = \frac{9}{8}x - \frac{27}{8}$

(c)

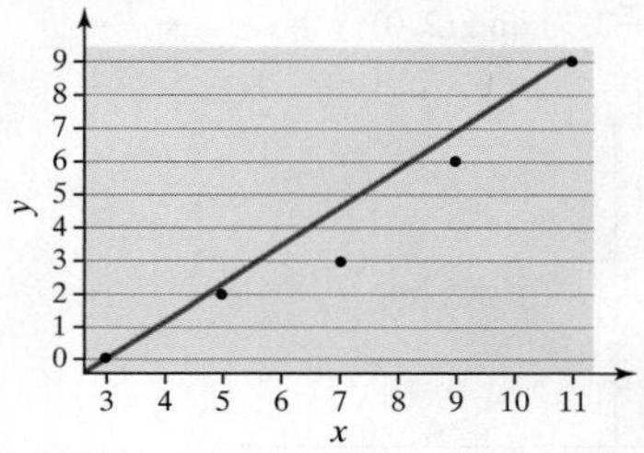

(d) $\hat{y} = 1.1x - 3.7$

(e)

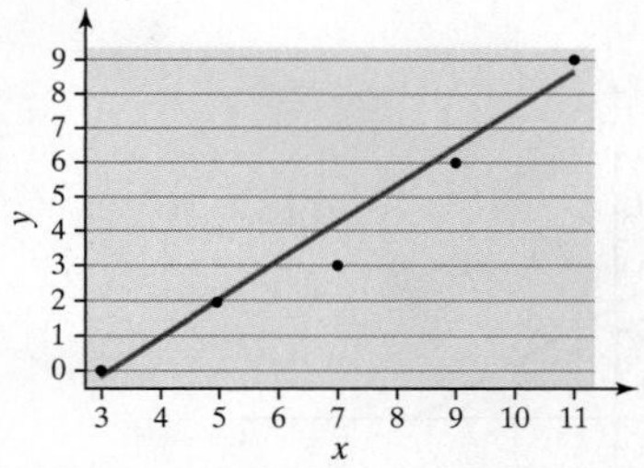

(f) Sum of squared residuals (computed line): 2.875

(g) Sum of squared residuals (least-squares line): 1.6

(h) Answers will vary.

9. (a)

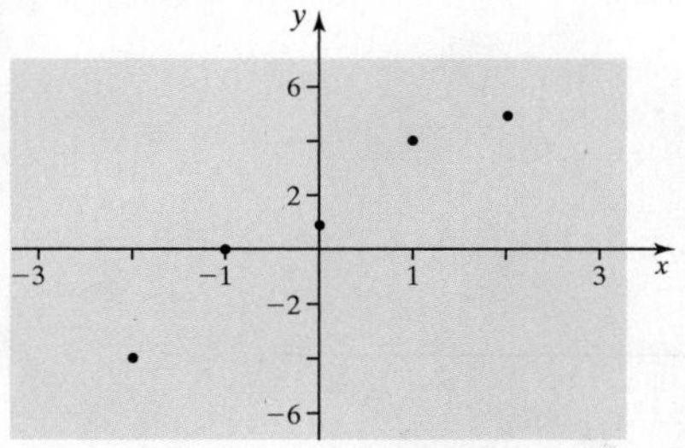

(b) Using points (−2, −4) and (2, 5): $\hat{y} = \frac{9}{4}x + \frac{1}{2} = 2.25x + 0.5$

(c)

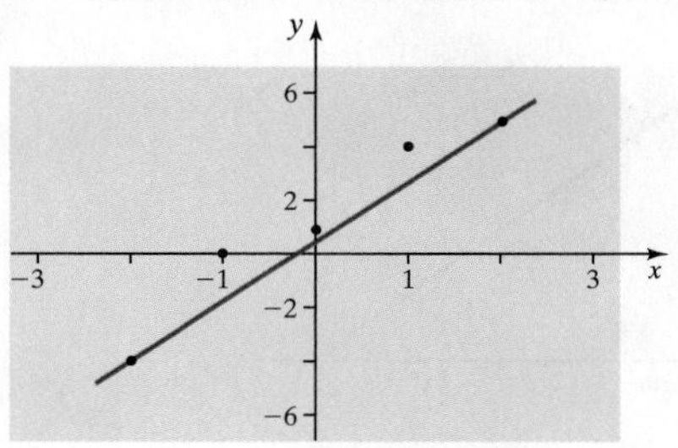

(d) $\hat{y} = 2.2x + 1.2$

(e)

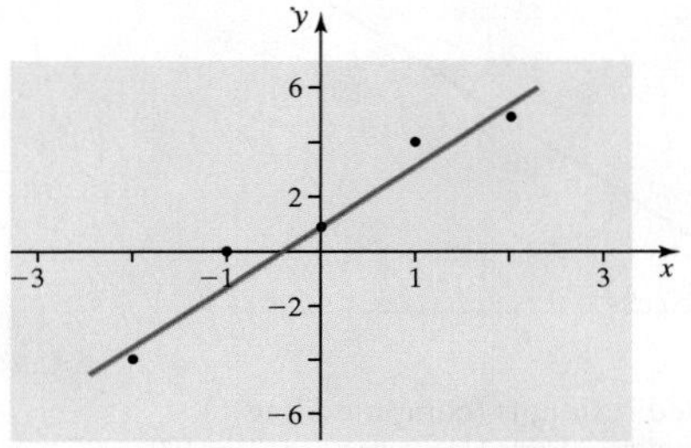

(f) Sum of squared residuals (computed line): 4.875

(g) Sum of squared residuals from least-squares line: 2.4

(h) Answers will vary.

10. (a)

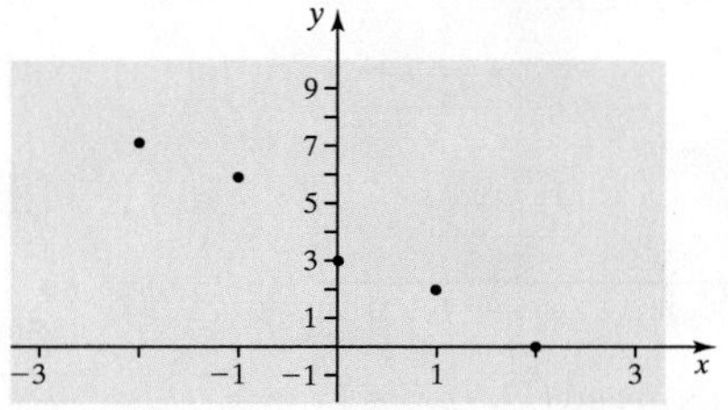

(b) Using the points $(-2, 7)$ and $(2, 0)$: $\hat{y} = -\frac{7}{4}x + \frac{7}{2} = -1.75x + 3.5$

(c)

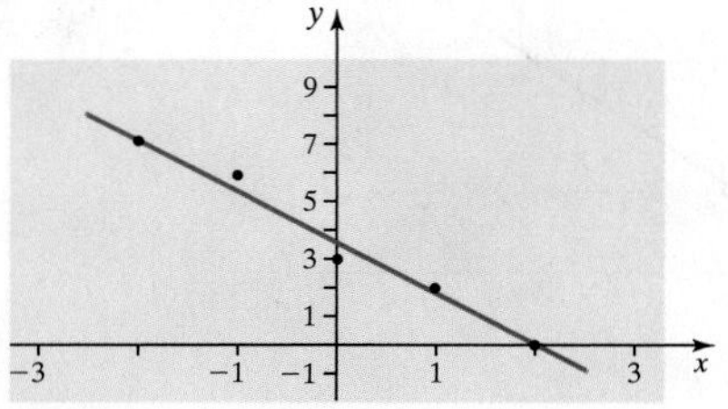

(d) $\hat{y} = -1.8x + 3.6$

(e)

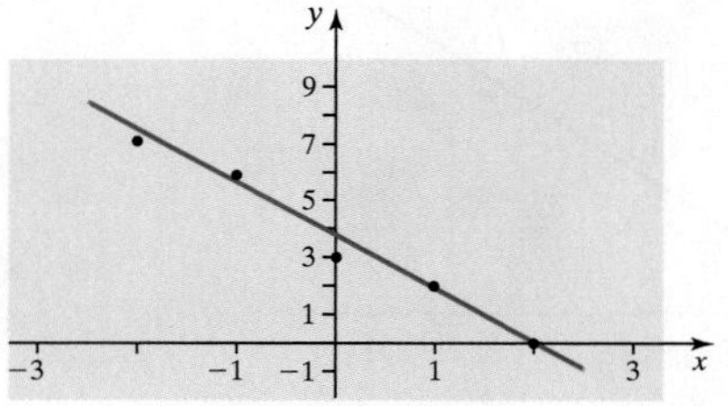

(f) Sum of squared residuals (computed line): 0.875

(g) Sum of squared residuals from least-squares line: 0.8

(h) Answers will vary.

11. (a)

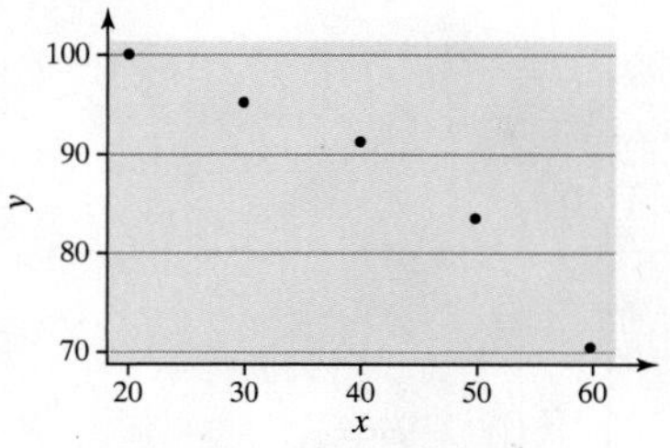

(b) Using points $(30, 95)$ and $(60, 70)$: $\hat{y} = -\frac{5}{6}x + 120$

(c)

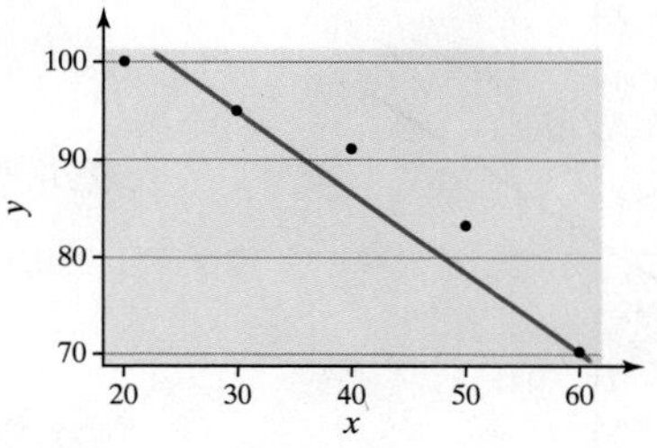

(d) $\hat{y} = -0.72x + 116.6$

(e)

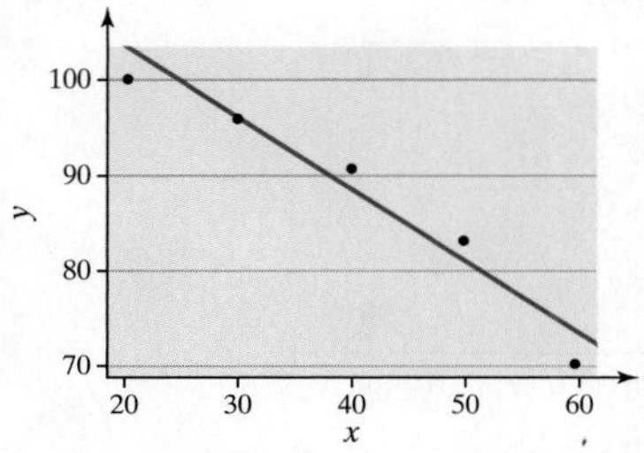

(f) Sum of squared residuals (computed line): 51.6667

(g) Sum of squared residuals from least-squares line: 32.4

(h) Answers will vary.

12. (a)

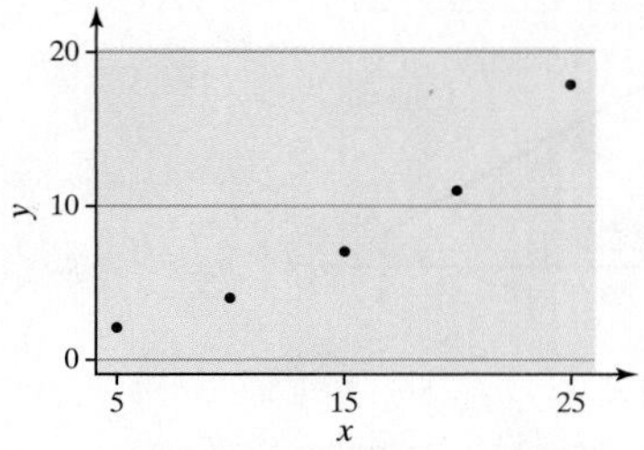

(b) Using points $(10, 4)$ and $(25, 18)$: $\hat{y} = \frac{14}{15}x - \frac{16}{3}$

(c)

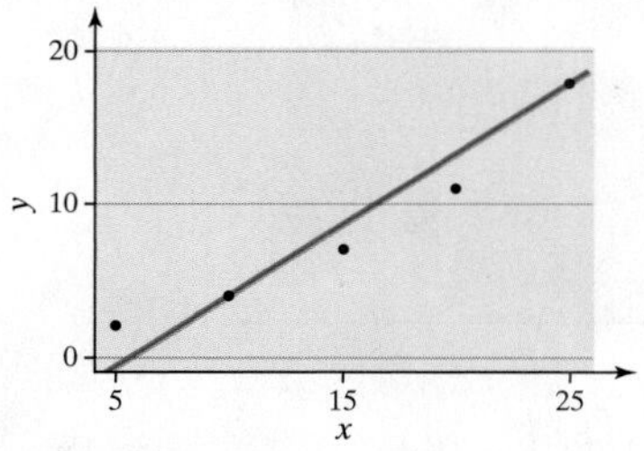

(d) $\hat{y} = 0.78x - 3.3$

(e)

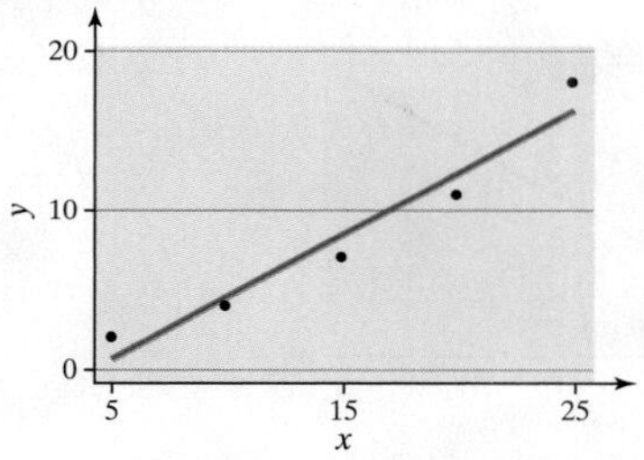

(f) Sum of squared residuals (computed line): 15.3333

(g) Sum of squared residuals from least-squares line: 9.1

(h) Answers will vary.

13. (a) 2.51

(b) For each additional hour a student spends playing video games in a week, the grade-point average will decrease by 0.0526 points, on average.

(c) The mean grade-point average for a student who does not play video games is 2.9342.

(d) The grade-point average is above average for those who play video games 7 hours per week.

14. (a) 65.7

(b) For each additional hour spent studying for the exam, the exam score increased by 6.3333 points, on average.

(c) 53.0

(d) The student's score is below average for those who studied for 5 hours.

15. (a) For each percentage point increase in on-base percentage, the winning percentage will increase by 3.4722 percentage points, on average.

(b) The y-intercept is outside the scope of the model. An on-base percentage of 0 is not reasonable for this model, since a team cannot win if players do not reach base.

(c) No; 0.250 is outside the scope of the model.

(d) The residual would be 0.0828. This residual indicates that San Francisco's winning percentage is above average for teams with an on-base percentage of 0.321.

16. **(a)** For each hundred thousand megawatts of energy prodece, the carbon dioxide emissions will increase by 0.7676 hundred thousand tons, on average.
(b) No; we expect a country to produce at least some energy. We would expect the y-intercept to be 0, since there would be no energy production to generate carbon dioxide emissions.
(c) No; the value is outside the scope of the model.
(d) The residual is 670 hundred thousand tons. This indicates that the carbon dioxide emission for China is above average for countries producing 3260 hundred thousand megawatts of energy.

17. **(a)** $\hat{y} = -0.0479x + 69.0296$
(b) Slope: for each 1-minute increase in commute time, the index score decreases by 0.0479, on average; y-intercept: The average index score for a person with a 0-minute commute is 69.0296. A person who works from home will have a 0-minute commute, so the y-intercept has a meaningful interpretation.
(c) 67.6
(d) Barbara's score is less than the mean score for people with a 20-minute commute, 68.1, so she is less well off.

18. **(a)** $\hat{y} = -0.0764x + 61.3687$
(b) Slope: For each 1-point increase in credit score, the interest rate decreases by 0.0764, on average; y-intercept: A credit score of 0 is not possible, so the y-intercept has no meaningful interpretation.
(c) 6.1315%
(d) The average rate for people with a credit score of 680 is 9.4167%. The 8.3% interest rate is a good offer for Bob since it is lower than the mean.

19. **(a)** $\hat{y} = 0.1827x + 12.4932$
(b) If height increases by 1 inch, head circumference increases by about 0.1827 inch, on average. It is not appropriate to interpret the y-intercept. It is outside the scope of the model.
(c) $\hat{y} = 17.06$ inches
(d) Residual $= -0.16$ inch; below
(e)

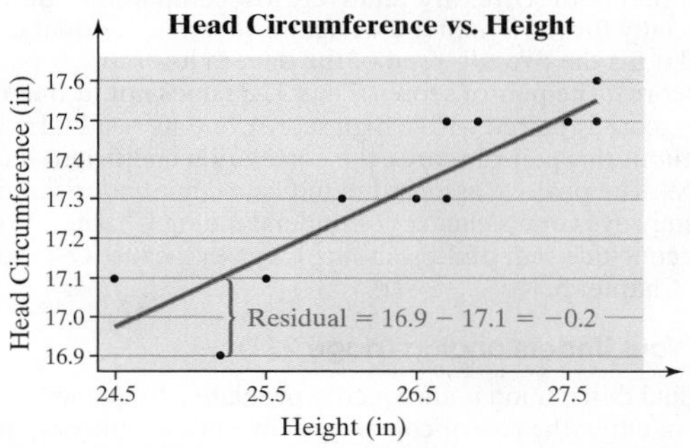

(f) For children who are 26.75 inches tall, head circumference varies.
(g) No; 32 inches is outside the scope of the model.

20. **(a)** $\hat{y} = 1.6942x - 142.4709$
(b) For each centimeter increase in length, the weight of the bear will increase by 1.6942 kilograms, on average. It is not appropriate to interpret the y-intercept, because a length of 0 centimeters for a bear does not make sense.
(c) The predicted weight is 110.0 kg.
(d) The residual is -25.0 kg. This bear's weight is below average for 149.0 cm bears.

21. **(a)** $\hat{y} = -0.0069x + 42.9068$
(b) For every pound added to the weight of the car, gas mileage in the city will decrease by 0.0069 mile per gallon, on average. It is not appropriate to interpret the y-intercept.
(c) $\hat{y} = 18.0668$ when $x = 3600$, so the Regal mileage is only slightly below average.
(d) It is not reasonable to use this least-squares regression to predict the miles per gallon of a Toyota Prius because a Prius is a different type of car (hybrid).

22. **(a)** $\hat{y} = 1.3902x + 1.1140$
(b) If the humerus increases in length by 1 mm, the length of the tibia increases by about 1.3902 mm, on average. It does not make sense to interpret the y-intercept.
(c) Residual $= 0.548$ mm; above
(d)

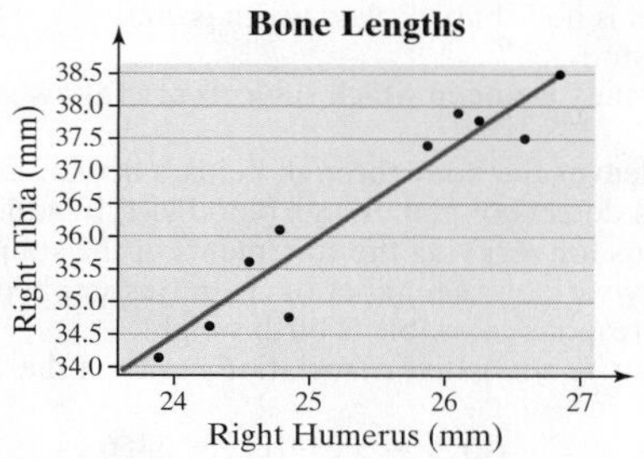

(e) $\hat{y} = 36.300$ mm

23. **(a)** $\hat{y} = -0.0029x + 0.8861$
(b) For each additional cola consumed per week, bone mineral density will decrease by 0.0029 g/cm2, on average.
(c) For a woman who does not drink cola, the mean bone mineral density will be 0.8861 g/cm2.
(d) The predicted bone mineral density is 0.8745 g/cm2.
(e) This bone mineral density is below average for women who consume 4 cans of cola per week.
(f) No; 2 cans of cola per day equates to 14 cans per week, which is outside the scope of the model.

24. **(a)** $\hat{y} = -2.8273x + 88.7327$ **(b)** For every additional absence, the student's final grade drops 2.8273 points, on average. The average final grade of students who miss no classes is 88.7327.
(c) $\hat{y} = 74.60$; residual is -0.70; the final grade is below average for 5 absences.
(d)

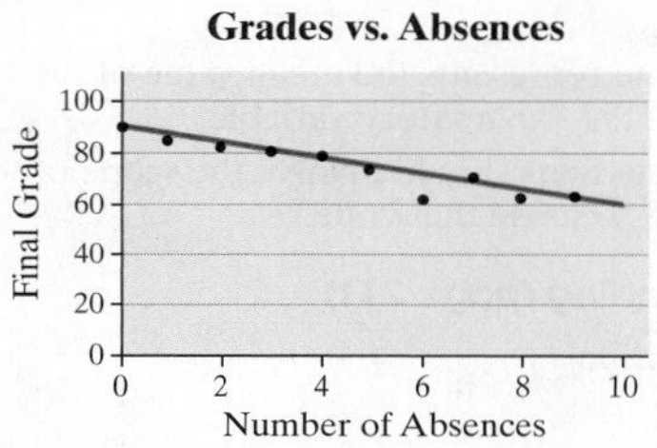

(e) No; 15 absences is outside the scope of the model.

25. In both cases, $\hat{y} = \bar{y} = 17.3\%$.

26. **(a)** $\hat{y} = 0.00002x + 119.1662$ **(b)** The slope is close to zero.
(c) MRI count 1,000,000: $\hat{y} = \bar{y} = 134.3$; MRI count 830,000: $\hat{y} = \bar{y} = 134.3$

27. **(a)** Males: $\hat{y} = 0.3428x + 998.4488$
Females: $\hat{y} = 0.1045x + 514.1520$
(b) Males: If the number of licensed drivers increases by 1 (thousand), then the number of fatal crashes increases by 0.3428, on average. Females: If the number of licensed drivers increases by 1 (thousand), then the number of fatal crashes increases by 0.1045, on average. Since females tend to be involved in fewer fatal crashes, an insurance company may use this information to argue for higher rates for male customers.
(c) Above average; above average; below average. An insurance company may use this information to argue for higher rates for younger drivers and lower rates for older drivers. The same relationship holds for females.

28. **(a)** Square footage
(b)

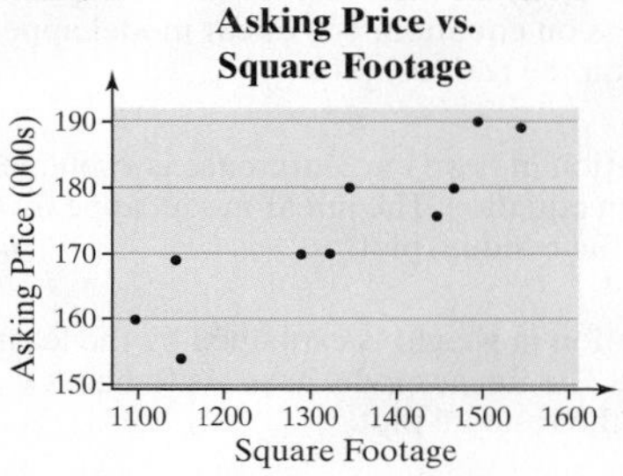

(c) $r = 0.916$ **(d)** Yes **(e)** $\hat{y} = 0.0686x + 83.2366$
(f) For each square foot added to the area, the asking price of the house will increase by $68.60 (that is, 0.0686 thousand dollars).
(g) It is not reasonable to interpret the intercept.
(h) Above average; factors that could affect the price include location and updates such as thermal windows or new siding.

29. **(a)** The distribution is bell shaped; class width is 200.
(b) Observational study
(c) A prospective study is one in which subjects are followed forward in time.
(d) Since cotinine leaves the body through fluids, a urinalysis is a less intrusive way to detect cotinine than a blood test. In addition, this provides a means for verifying the statements of the subjects.
(e) The explanatory variable is number of cigarettes smoked during third trimester: the response variable is birth weight.
(f) There appears to be a negative association between the variables.
(g) $r = -0.355$ **(h)** $\hat{y} = -31.014x + 3456.04$
(i) For each additional cigarette smoked, birth weight decreases by 31.014 grams, on average.
(j) The mean birth weight of a baby whose mother smokes but does not smoke in the third trimester is 3456.04 grams.
(k) No; 10 cigarettes per day equates to roughly 900 in the third trimester, which is outside the scope of the model.
(l) No; an observational study cannot establish causation.
(m) Some lurking variables could be genetic factors or the general health of the mother.

30. A residual is the difference between the observed value of y and the predicted value of *y*. If the residual is positive, the observed value is above average for the given value of the explanatory variable.

31. Values of the explanatory variable that are much larger or much smaller than those observed are considered *outside the scope of the model.* It is dangerous to make such predictions because we do not know the behavior of the data for which we have no observations.

32. Answers will vary.

33. Each point's *y*-coordinate represents the mean value of the response variable for a given value of the explanatory variable.

34. Answers may vary. Discussions should involve the scope of the model and the idea of being "outside the scope."

4.3 Assess Your Understanding (page 211)

1. coefficient of determination

2. explained; unexplained

3. **(a)** III **(b)** II
(c) IV **(d)** I

4. **(a)** $R^2 = 10.24\%$; 10.24% of the variance in the response variable is explained by the least-squares regression line.
(b) $R^2 = 1.69\%$; 1.69% of the variance in the response variable is explained by the least-squares regression line.
(c) $R^2 = 16\%$; 16% of the variance in the response variable is explained by the least-squares regression line.
(d) $R^2 = 86.49\%$; 86.49% of the variance in the response variable is explained by the least-squares regression line.

5. 83.0% of the variation in the length of eruption is explained by the least-squares regression equation.

6. 57.5% of the variation in 28-day strength is explained by the least-squares regression equation.

7. **(a)** $R^2 = 96.1\%$
(b) 96.1% of the variation in the well-being index composite score can be explained by the least-squares regression equation. The linear model appears to be appropriate, based on the residual plot.

8. **(a)** $R^2 = 95.2\%$
(b) 95.2% of the variation in the interest rate can be explained by the least-squares regression equation. The linear model appears to be appropriate, based on the residual plot.

9. **(a)** $R^2 = 83.0\%$
(b) 83.0% of the variation in head circumference is explained by the least-squares regression equation. The linear model appears to be appropriate, based on the residual plot.

10. **(a)** $R^2 = 49.5\%$
(b) 49.5% of the variation in weight is explained by the least-squares regression line. The linear model appears to be appropriate, based on the residual plot.

11. **(a)** $R^2 = 92.1\%$
(b) 92.1% of the variance in gas mileage is explained by the linear model. The least-squares regression model appears to be appropriate.

12. **(a)** $R^2 = 90.5\%$
(b) 90.5% of the variation in the length of the right tibia is explained by the least-squares regression line. The least-squares regression model appears to be appropriate.

13. The coefficient of determination with the Viper included is $R^2 = 58.0\%$. Adding the Viper reduces the amount of variability explained by the model by approximately 34%.

14. $R^2 = 71.7\%$; the value increases.

15. **(a)**

GE vs. S&P 500

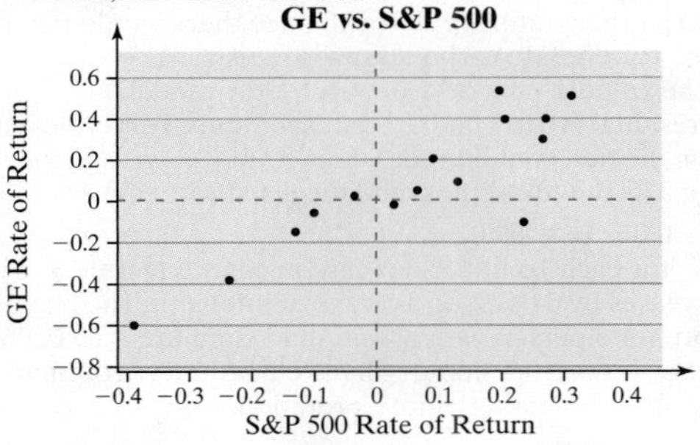

(b) $r = 0.884$
(c) Yes, since $0.884 > 0.514$ (from Appendix Table II)
(d) $\hat{y} = 1.4020x - 0.0012$
(e) 0.1390
(f) Below
(g) For each percentage point increase in the rate of return for the S&P 500, the rate of return of GE stock will increase by about 1.40 percentage points, on average.
(h) The y-intercept indicates that the rate of return for GE stock will be −0.0012 when there is no change to the S&P 500.
(i) $R^2 = 78.2\%$

16. The correlation coefficient is $r = 0.6893$, which shows a moderate linear relationship. The linear regression equation is $\hat{y} = 0.7712x + 13.8386$. The slope indicates that for a 1-point increase in the exam score for Chapter 2 there is a 0.77 point increase in the exam score for Chapter 3, on average. The pair of scores (33.3, 45.7) is an outlier in that both scores are relatively low compared to the other scores, especially for the Chapter 2 exam; however, its residual is not unusual and it fits the overall trend of the data (a low score is paired with a low score). The pair of scores (78.0, 37.3) does not fit the overall trend (a low score is paired with a high score), and its residual is also unusual; without this pair of scores, the correlation coefficient increases to $r = 0.7889$. The positive association indicates that understanding Chapter 2 improves one's chances of understanding Chapter 3 , though we may not conclude that understanding Chapter 2 causes one to understand Chapter 3.

4.4 Assess Your Understanding (page 221)

1. A marginal distribution is a frequency or relative frequency distribution of either the row or column variable in a contingency table. A conditional distribution is the relative frequency of each category of one variable, given a specific value of the other variable in a contingency table.

2. Yes; the conditional distribution by level of education is different from the conditional distribution by employment status.

3. Correlation is used with quantitative variables; association is used with categorical variables.

4. Simpson's Paradox represents a situation in which an association between two variables changes direction or goes away when a third variable is introduced.

5. **(a)**

	x_1	x_2	x_3	Marginal Distribution
y_1	20	25	30	75
y_2	30	25	50	105
Marginal Distribution	50	50	80	180

(b)

	x_1	x_2	x_3	Relative Frequency Marginal Distribution
y_1	20	25	30	0.417
y_2	30	25	50	0.583
Relative Frequency Marginal Distribution	0.278	0.278	0.444	1

(c)

	x_1	x_2	x_3
y_1	0.400	0.500	0.375
y_2	0.600	0.500	0.625
Total	1	1	1

(d) **Conditional Distribution**

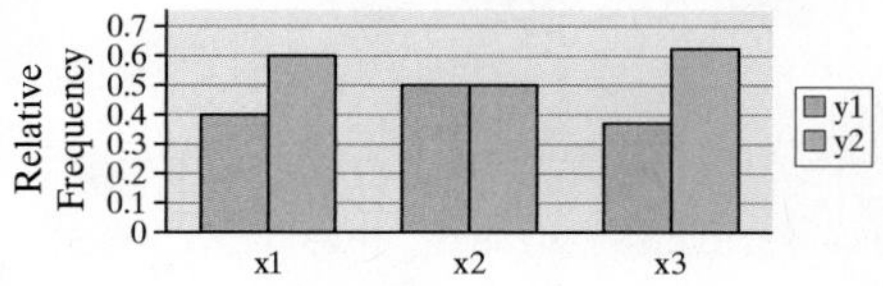

6. (a)

	x_1	x_2	x_3	Marginal Distribution
y_1	35	25	20	80
y_2	65	75	80	220
Marginal Distribution	100	100	100	300

(b)

	x_1	x_2	x_3	Relative Frequency Marginal Distribution
y_1	35	25	20	0.267
y_2	65	75	80	0.733
Relative Frequency Marginal Distribution	0.333	0.333	0.333	1

(c)

	x_1	x_2	x_3
y_1	0.350	0.250	0.200
y_2	0.650	0.750	0.800
Total	1	1	1

(d) **Conditional Distribution**

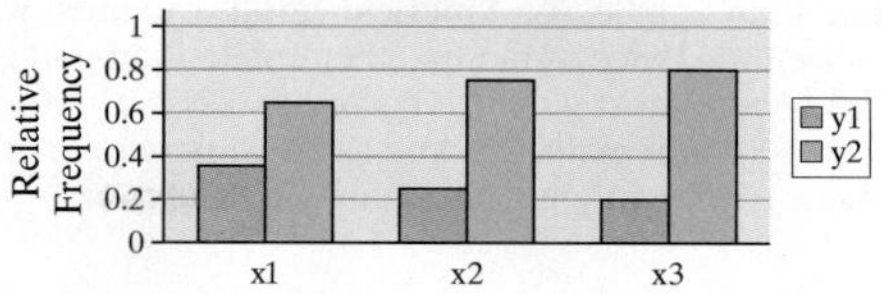

7. (a) 2160 adult Americans were surveyed; 536 were 55 and older.
(b)

Likely to Buy	Age 18–34	35–44	45–54	55+	Relative Frequency Marginal Distribution
More likely	238	329	360	402	0.615
Less likely	22	6	22	16	0.031
Neither	282	201	164	118	0.354
Relative Frequency Marginal Distribution	0.251	0.248	0.253	0.248	1

(c) 0.615
(d)

Likely to Buy	Age 18–34	35–44	45–54	55+
More likely	0.439	0.614	0.659	0.750
Less likely	0.041	0.011	0.040	0.030
Neither	0.520	0.375	0.300	0.220
Total	1	1	1	1

(e) **Likelihood to Buy "Made in America"**

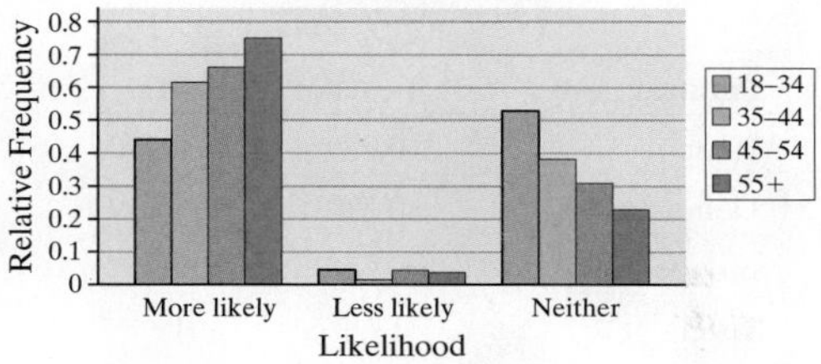

(f) The number of people more likely to buy a product because it is made in America increases with age. On the other hand, age does not seem to be a significant factor in whether a person is less likely to buy a product because it is made in America.

8. (a) 2162 adult Americans were surveyed; 1120 males were surveyed.

8. (b)

Gender	Trait Richer	Thinner	Smarter	Younger	None of These	Relative Frequency Marginal Distribution
Male	520	158	159	181	102	0.518
Female	425	300	144	81	92	0.482
Relative Frequency Marginal Distribution	0.437	0.212	0.140	0.121	0.090	1

(c) 0.437
(d)

Gender	Trait Richer	Thinner	Smarter	Younger	None of These	Total
Male	0.464	0.141	0.142	0.162	0.091	1
Female	0.408	0.288	0.138	0.078	0.088	1

(e) **Which Would You Like to Be?**

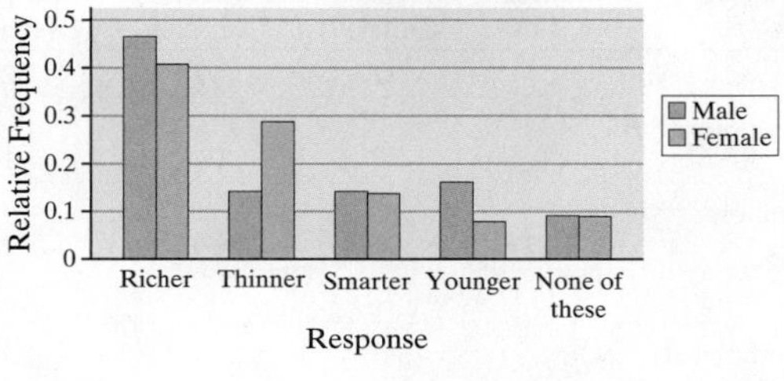

(f) An American adult who most wants to be richer is slightly more likely to be male than female. An American adult who most wants to be thinner is more than twice as likely to be female than male, while an American adult who most wants to be younger is more than twice as likely to be male than female. An American adult who most wants to be smarter is nearly equally likely to be male or female.

9. (a)

Political Party	Gender: Female	Male	Frequency Marginal Distribution
Republican	105	115	220
Democrat	150	103	253
Independent	150	179	329
Frequency Marginal Distribution	405	397	802

(b)

Political Party	Gender: Female	Male	Relative Frequency Marginal Distribution
Republican	105	115	0.274
Democrat	150	103	0.315
Independent	150	179	0.410
Relative Frequency Marginal Distribution	0.505	0.495	1

(c) 0.410

(d)

Political Party	Gender: Female	Male
Republican	0.259	0.290
Democrat	0.370	0.259
Independent	0.370	0.451
Total	1	1

(e)

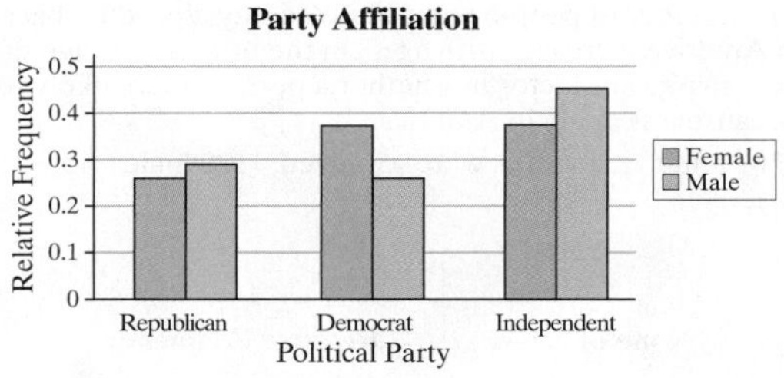

(f) Yes; males are more likely to be Independents and less likely to be Democrats.

10. (a)

Opinion on Availability of Abortion	Education Level: High School or Less	Some College	College Graduate	Frequency Marginal Distribution
Generally available	90	72	113	275
Allowed, but more limited	51	60	77	188
Illegal, with few exceptions	125	94	69	288
Never permitted	51	14	17	82
Frequency Marginal Distribution	317	240	276	833

(b)

Opinion on Availability of Abortion	Education Level: High School or Less	Some College	College Graduate	Relative Frequency Marginal Distribution
Generally available	90	72	113	0.330
Allowed, but more limited	51	60	77	0.226
Illegal, with few exceptions	125	94	69	0.346
Never permitted	51	14	17	0.098
Relative Frequency Marginal Distribution	0.381	0.288	0.331	1

(c) 0.062

(d)

Opinion on Availability of Abortion	Education Level: High School or Less	Some College	College Graduate
Generally available	0.284	0.300	0.409
Allowed, but more limited	0.161	0.250	0.279
Illegal, with few exceptions	0.394	0.392	0.250
Never permitted	0.161	0.058	0.062
Total	1	1	1

(e)

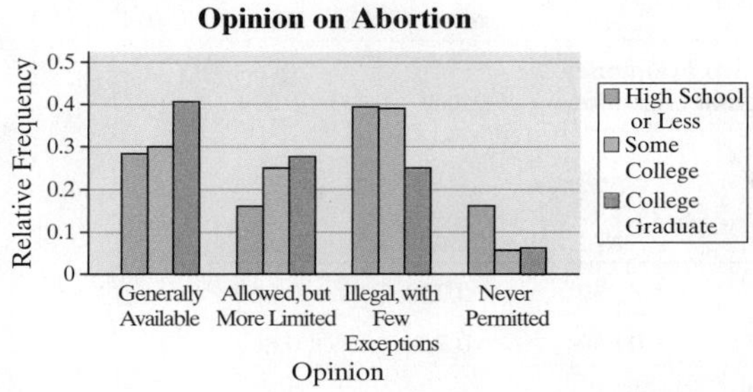

(f) Yes; as education level increases, respondents are more likely to feel that abortion should be available.

11.

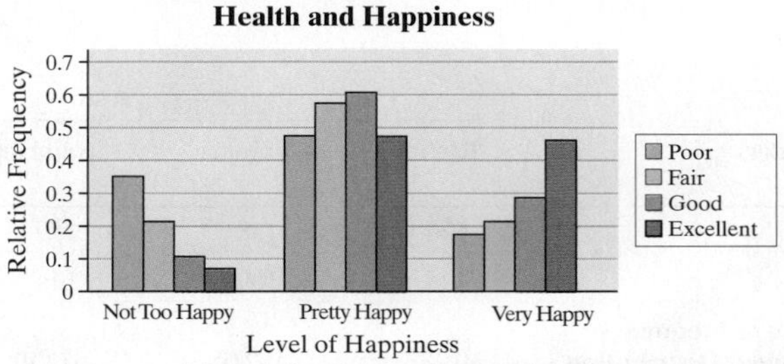

Based on the conditional distribution by health, we can see that healthier people tend to be happier. As health increases, the percent who are very happy increases, while the percent who are not happy decreases.

12.

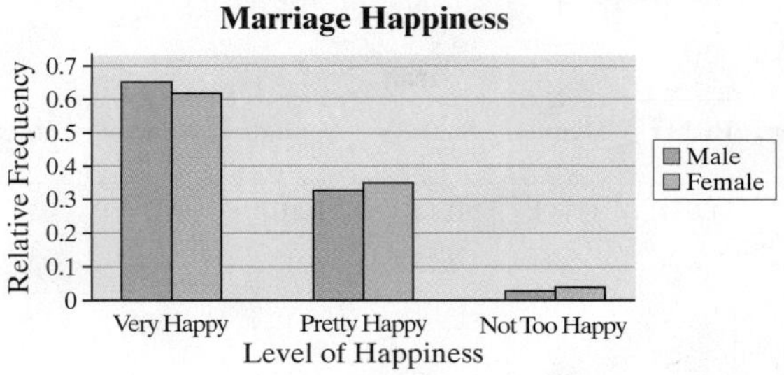

Based on the conditional distribution, there does not appear to be a significant association between gender and marriage happiness.

13. **(a)** Smokers: 0.239; nonsmokers: 0.314; this implies that it is healthier to smoke.
(b) Smokers: 0.036; Nonsmokers: 0.016
(c) Proportion deceased after 20 years by smoking status and age

	Age						
	18–24	25–34	35–44	45–54	55–64	65–74	75 or Older
Smoker	0.036	0.024	0.128	0.208	0.443	0.806	1
Nonsmoker	0.016	0.032	0.058	0.154	0.331	0.783	1

(d)

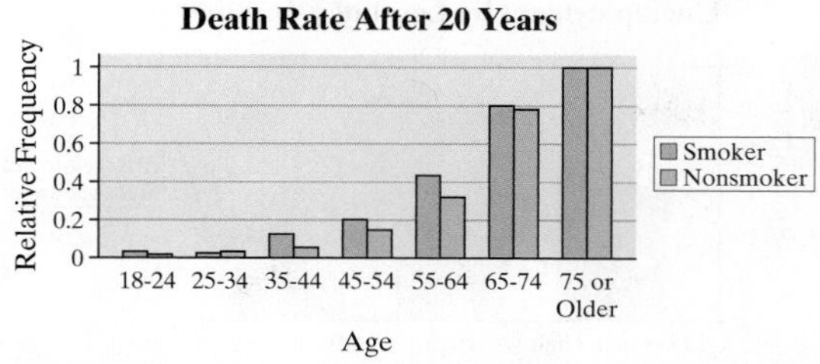

(e) Answers may vary. When taking age into account, the direction of association changed. In almost all age groups, smokers had a higher death rate than nonsmokers. The most notable exception is for the 25 to 34 age group, the largest age group for the nonsmokers. A possible explanation could be rigorous physical activity (e.g., rock climbing) that nonsmokers are more likely to participate in than smokers.

14. **(a)** Treatment B; treatment A was effective 78% of the time, whereas treatment B was effective 82.6% of the time.
(b) Treatment A: 0.931; treatment B: 0.867
(c)

Stone Size	Treatment A	Treatment B
Small	0.931	0.867
Large	0.780	0.688

(d)

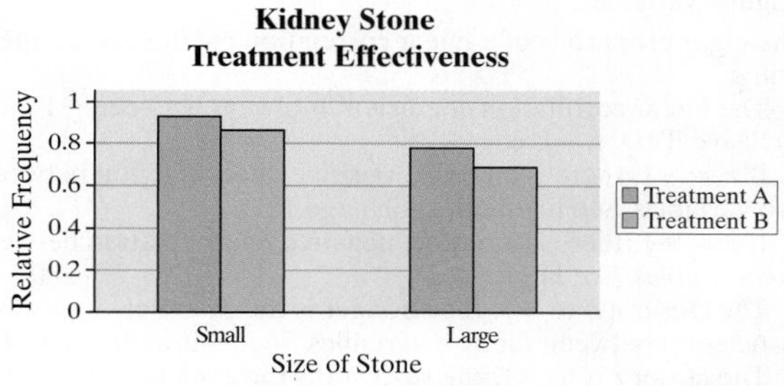

(e) Answers may vary. The direction of the association reversed after taking the size of the stone into account. For each size of stone (small or large), treatment A worked better than treatment B.

Chapter 4 Review Exercises (page 226)

1. **(a)** If the home team is favored by 3 points, the winning margin predicted by the regression equation is 3.009 points.
(b) If the visiting team is favored by 7 points, the winning margin (for the visiting team) predicted by the regression equation is 7.061 points.
(c) For each 1-point increase in the spread, the winning margin increases by 1.007 points, on average.
(d) If the spread is 0, the home team is expected to lose by 0.012 point, on average.
(e) 39% of the variation in winning margins can be explained by the least-squares regression equation.

2. **(a)** Fat content
(b)

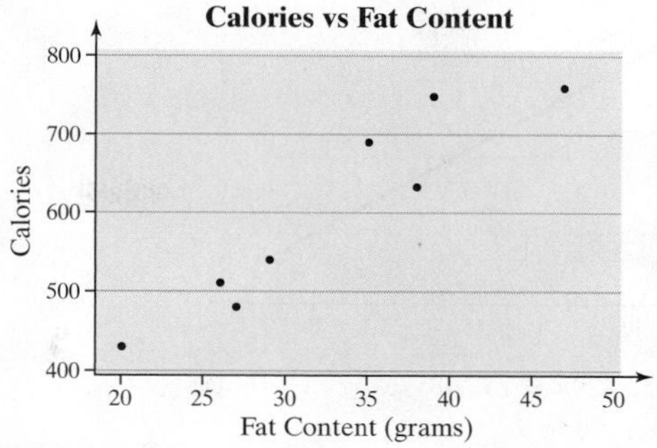

(c) $r = 0.944$
(d) Yes; a strong linear relation exists between fat content and calories in fast-food restaurant sandwiches.

3. **(a)**

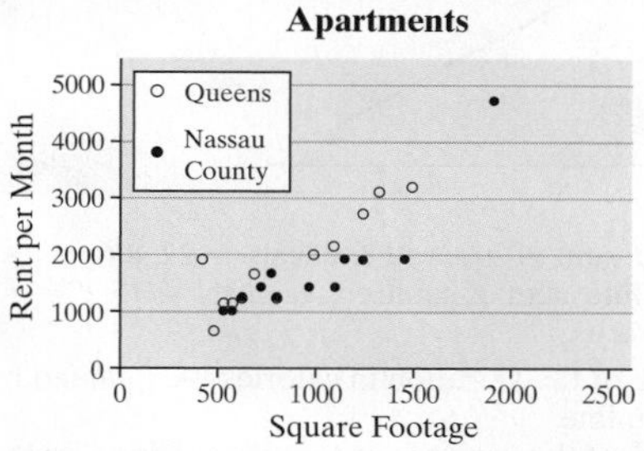

(b) Queens: $r = 0.909$; Nassau County: $r = 0.867$
(c) Both locations appear to have a positive linear association between square footage and monthly rent.
(d) For small apartments (those less than 1000 square feet in area), there seems to be no difference in rent between Queens and Nassau County. In larger apartments, Queens seems to have higher rents than Nassau County.

4. **(a)** $\hat{y} = 13.7334x + 150.9469$
(b)

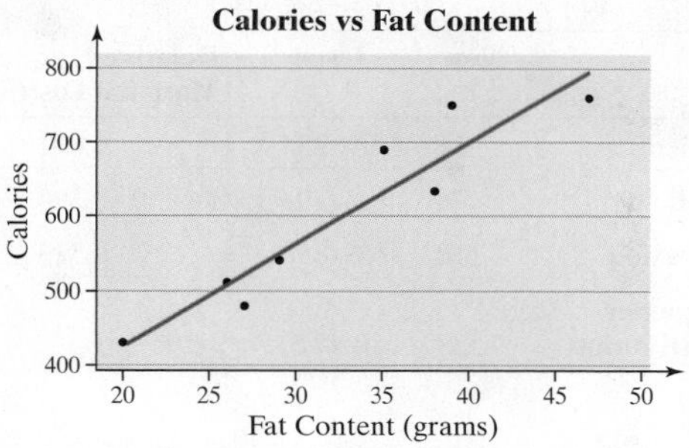

(c) The slope indicates that each additional gram of fat in a sandwich adds approximately 13.73 calories, on average. The y-intercept indicates that a sandwich with no fat will contain about 151 calories.
(d) 562.9 calories
(e) Below average (the average value is 727.7 calories)

5. **(a)** $\hat{y} = 2.2091x - 34.3148$
(b) The slope of the least-squares regression line indicates that, for each additional square foot of floor area, the rent increases by \$2.21, on average. It is not appropriate to interpret the y-intercept since it is not possible to have an apartment with 0 square footage.
(c) This apartment's rent is below average.

6. **(a)**

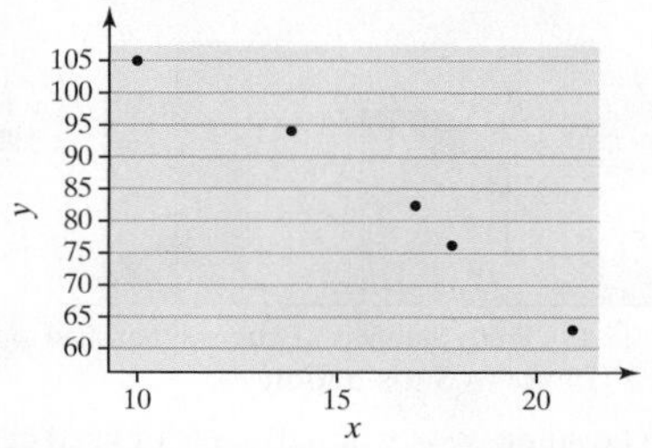

(b) Using points (10, 105) and (18, 76), $\hat{y} = -\frac{29}{8}x + \frac{565}{4}$.

(c)

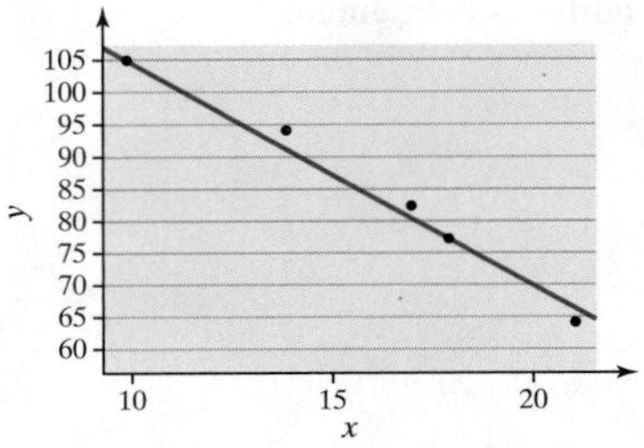

(d) $\hat{y} = -3.8429x + 145.4857$

(e)

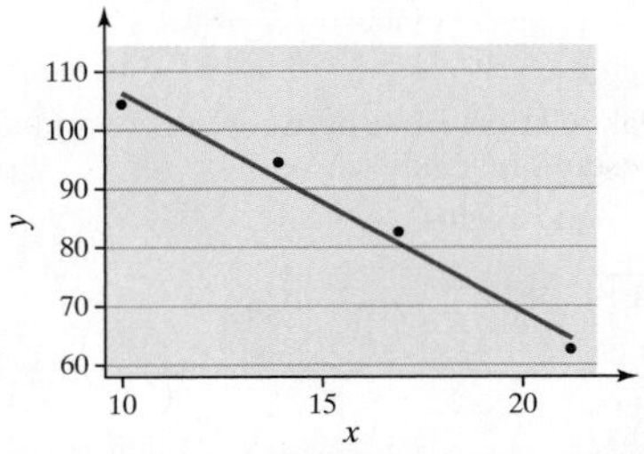

(f) Computed line: sum of squared residuals = 22.406
(g) Least-squares line: sum of squared residuals = 16.271
(h) Answers will vary.

7. $R^2 = 89.1\%$; 89.1% of the variation in calories is explained by the least-squares regression line.

8. $R^2 = 82.7\%$; 82.7% of the variance in rent is explained by the least-squares regression model.

9. No; correlation does not imply causation. Florida has a large number of tourists in warmer months, times when more people will be in the water to cool off. The larger number of people in the water splashing around leads to a larger number of shark attacks.

10. (a) 203
(b)

Satisfaction	Car Type: New	Car Type: Used	Relative Frequency Marginal Distribution
Not too satisfied	11	25	0.091
Pretty satisfied	78	79	0.396
Extremely satisfied	118	85	0.513
Relative Frequency Marginal Distribution	0.523	0.477	1

(c) 0.513
(d)

Satisfaction	Car Type: New	Car Type: Used
Not too satisfied	0.053	0.132
Pretty satisfied	0.377	0.418
Extremely satisfied	0.570	0.450
Total	1	1

(e)

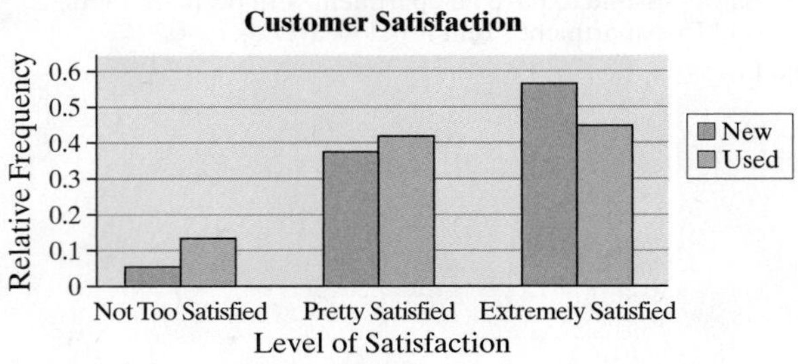

(f) There appears to be some association. Buyers of used cars are more likely to be dissatisfied and are less likely to be extremely satisfied than buyers of new cars.

11. (a) In 1982, the unemployment rate was approximately 10.3%. In 2009, the unemployment rate was approximately 10.0%. The 1982 recession appears to be worse.
(b) The unemployment rates are displayed in the table.

Recession	Level of Education: Less than High School	High School	Bachelor's Degree or Higher
Recession of 1982	16.1%	10.2%	3.8%
Recession of 2009	16.7%	11.8%	4.8%

(c)

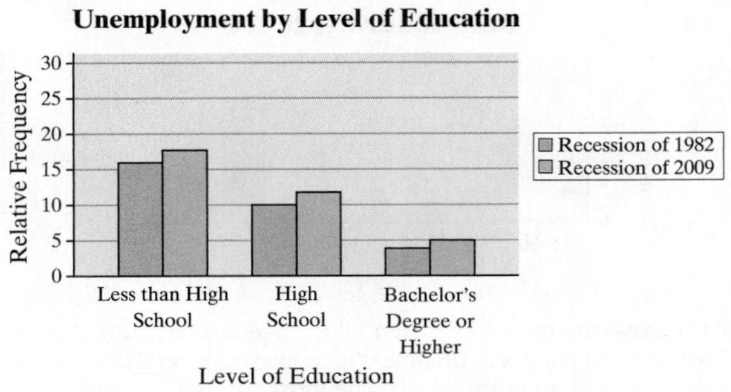

(d) Answer will vary. The discussion should include the observation that, although the overall unemployment rate was higher in 1982, the unemployment rate within each level of education was higher in 2009.

12. (a) A positive linear relation appears to exist between number of marriages and number unemployed.
(b) Population is highly correlated with both the number of marriages and the number unemployed. The size of the population affects both variables.
(c) No association exists between the two variables.
(d) Answers may vary. A strong correlation between two variables may be due to a third variable that is highly correlated with the two original variables.

13. The eight properties of a linear correlation coefficient are the following:
1. The linear correlation coefficient is always between −1 and 1, inclusive. That is, $-1 \le r \le 1$.
2. If $r = +1$, there is a perfect positive linear relation between the two variables. See Figure 4(a) on page 181.
3. If $r = -1$, there is a perfect negative linear relation between the two variables. See Figure 4(d).
4. The closer r is to +1, the stronger is the evidence of positive association between the two variables. See Figures 4(b) and 4(c).
5. The closer r is to −1, the stronger is the evidence of negative association between the two variables. See Figures 4(e) and 4(f).
6. If r is close to 0, there is no evidence of a *linear* relation between the two variables. Because the linear correlation coefficient is a measure of the strength of the linear relation, r close to 0 does not imply no relation, just no linear relation. See Figures 4(g) and 4(h).
7. The linear correlation coefficient is a unitless measure of association. So the unit of measure for x and y plays no role in the interpretation of r.
8. The correlation coefficient is not resistant.

14. (a) Answers will vary.
(b) The slope can be interpreted as "the school day decreases by 0.01 hour for each 1% increase in percent low income, on average." The y-intercept can be interpreted as the length of the school day when 0% of the population is low income.
(c) $\hat{y} = 6.91$ hours
(d)–(f) Answers will vary.

Chapter 4 Test (page 229)

1. (a) Temperature

(b)

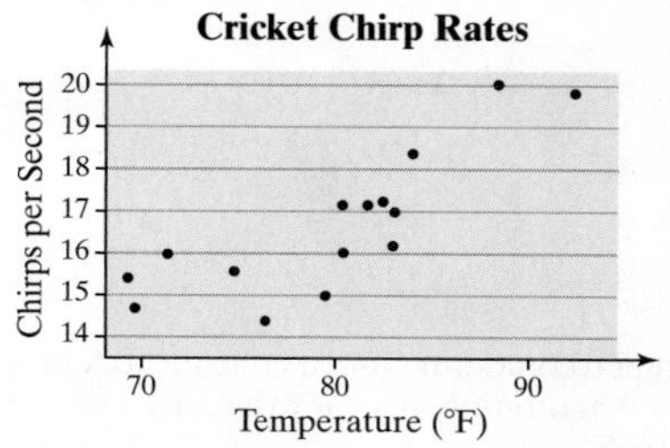

(c) $r = 0.835$

(d) Yes, a positive linear relation exists between temperature and chirps per second.

(e) $\hat{y} = 0.2119x - 0.3091$

(f) If the temperature increases 1°F, the number of chirps per second increases by 0.2119, on average. Since there are no observations near 0°F, it does not make sense to interpret the y-intercept.

(g) At 83.3°F, $\hat{y} = 17.3$ chirps per second.

(h) Below average

(i) No; outside the scope of the model

(j) $R^2 = 69.7\%$; 69.7% of the variation in number of chirps per second is explained by the least-squares regression line.

2. Correlation does not imply causation. It is possible that a lurking variable, such as income level or educational level, is affecting both the explanatory and response variables.

3. (a)

	Belief				
Education Level	**Yes, Definitely**	**Yes, Probably**	**No, Probably Not**	**No, Definitely Not**	**Relative Frequency Marginal Distribution**
Less than high school	316	66	21	9	0.173
High school	956	296	122	65	0.606
Bachelor's	267	131	62	64	0.221
Relative Frequency Marginal Distribution	0.648	0.208	0.086	0.058	1

(b) 0.648

(c)

	Belief				
Education Level	**Yes, Definitely**	**Yes, Probably**	**No, Probably Not**	**No, Definitely Not**	**Total**
Less than high school	0.767	0.160	0.051	0.022	1
High school	0.664	0.206	0.085	0.045	1
Bachelor's	0.510	0.250	0.118	0.122	1

(d)

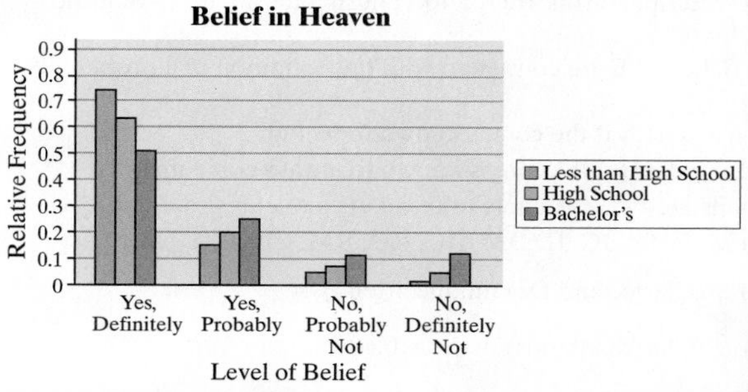

(e) Yes; as education level increases, the percent who definitely believe in Heaven decreases (i.e., doubt in Heaven increases).

4. (a)

	College Applicants		
	Accepted	**Denied**	**Total**
Male	0.158	0.842	1
Female	0.310	0.690	1

(b) 0.158 of the males who applied was accepted. 0.310 of the females who applied was accepted.

(c) Conclusion: a higher proportion of females was accepted.

(d) 0.150 of the males applying to the business school was accepted. 0.143 of the females applying to the business school was accepted.

(e) 0.40 of the males applying to the social work school was accepted. 0.364 of the females applying to the social work school was accepted.

(f) Answers will vary. A larger number of males applied to the business school, which has an overall lower acceptance rate than the social work school, so more male applicants were declined.

5. The data would have a perfect negative linear relation. A scatter diagram would show all the observations being collinear (falling on the same line) with a negative slope.

6. If the slope of the least-squares regression line is negative, the correlation between the explanatory and response variables is also negative.

7. If a linear correlation coefficient is close to zero, this means that there is no linear relation between the explanatory and response variable. This does not mean there is no relation, just no *linear* relation.

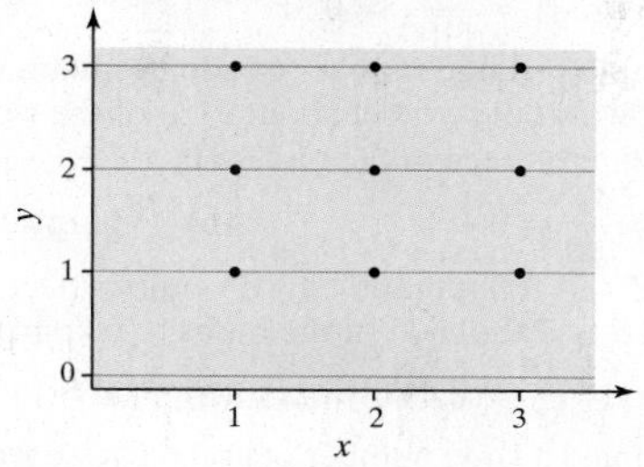

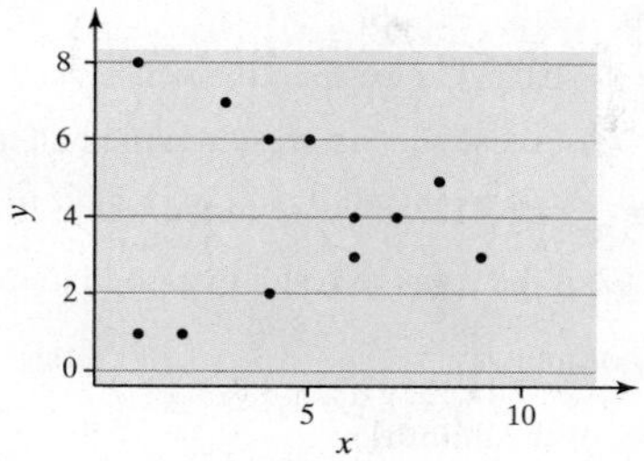

CHAPTER 5 Probability

5.1 Assess Your Understanding (page 242)

1. The probability of an impossible event is zero. No; when a probability is based on an empirical experiment, a probability of zero does not mean the event cannot occur.

2. An event is unusual if it has a low probability of occurring. The choice of a cutoff should consider the context of the problem.

3. True

4. True

5. experiment

6. event

7. Rule 1: All probabilities in the model are greater than or equal to zero and less than or equal to one.

Rule 2: The sum of the probabilities in the model is 1.

The outcome "blue" is an impossible event since P(blue) = 0.

8. Rule 1: All probabilities in the model are greater than or equal to zero and less than or equal to one.

Rule 2: The sum of the probabilities in the model is 1.

All the M&Ms in the bag are yellow.

9. This is not a probability model because P(green) < 0.

10. This is not a probability model because the sum of the probabilities is not 1.

11. The numbers 0, 0.01, 0.35, and 1 could be probabilities.

12. The numbers $\frac{1}{2}, \frac{3}{4}, \frac{2}{3}$, and 0 could be probabilities.

13. The probability of 0.42 means that approximately 42 out of every 100 dealt hands will contain two cards of the same value and three cards of different value. No, probability refers to long-term behavior, not short-term.

14. The probability of 0.44 means that approximately 44 out of every 100 dealt hands will contain two cards of the same value and five cards of different value. No, probability refers to long-term behavior, not short-term.

15. The empirical probability is 0.95.

16. The empirical probability is 0.80.

17. $P(2) \neq \frac{1}{11}$ since the outcomes are not equally likely.

18. No; blood types are not equally likely.

19. $S = \{1H, 1T, 2H, 2T, 3H, 3T, 4H, 4T, 5H, 5T, 6H, 6T\}$

20. $S = \{SSS, SSF, SFS, FSS, SFF, FSF, FFS, FFF\}$

21. 0.428 **22.** 0.372 **23.** $P(E) = \frac{3}{10} = 0.3$

24. $P(F) = \frac{2}{5} = 0.4$ **25.** $P(E) = \frac{2}{5} = 0.4$ **26.** $P(F) = \frac{1}{2} = 0.5$

27. (a) $P(\text{plays sports}) = \frac{288}{500} = 0.576$
(b) If we sampled 1000 high school students, we would expect that about 576 of the students play organized sports.

28. (a) $P(\text{volunteered}) = \frac{341}{1100} = 0.31$
(b) If we sampled a large number of adult females (18 years of age or older), we would expect about 31% of the women have volunteered at least once in the past year.

29. (a) $P(\text{red}) = \frac{40}{100} = 0.4$ **(b)** $P(\text{purple}) = \frac{25}{100} = 0.25$
(c) If we sampled 100 tulip bulbs, we would expect about 40 of the bulbs to be red and about 25 of the bulbs to be purple.

30. (a) $P(\text{Titleist}) = \frac{35}{80} = 0.4375$ **(b)** $P(\text{Top-Flite}) = \frac{20}{80} = 0.25$
(c) If we sampled a large number of golf balls, we would expect about 43.75% of the balls to be Titleist and about 25% to be Top-Flite.

31. (a) $S = \{0, 00, 1, 2, 3, 4, \ldots, 35, 36\}$
(b) $P(8) = \frac{1}{38} = 0.0263$, if we spun the wheel 1000 times, we would expect about 26 of those times to result in the ball landing in slot 8.
(c) $P(\text{odd}) = \frac{18}{38} = 0.4737$, if we spun the wheel 100 times, we would expect about 47 of the spins to result in an odd number.

32. (a) $P(\text{1st day of month}) = \frac{12}{365}$
(b) $P(\text{31st day of the month}) = \frac{7}{365}$
(c) $P(\text{born in December}) = \frac{31}{365}$
(d) $P(\text{born on November 8}) = \frac{1}{365}$
(e) No; it is unlikely that you would guess her birthday.
(f) No; outcomes are not equally likely.

33. (a) $\{SS, Ss, sS, ss\}$
(b) $P(ss) = \frac{1}{4}$; there is a 25% probability that a randomly selected offspring will have sickle-cell anemia.
(c) $P(\text{Ss or sS}) = \frac{1}{2} = 0.5$; there is 50% probability that a randomly selected offspring will be a carrier of sickle-cell anemia.

34. (a) $\{SS, Ss, sS, ss\}$
(b) $P(ss) = \frac{1}{4} = 0.25$; there is a 25% probability that a randomly selected offspring will not have Huntington's disease.
(c) $P(SS, Ss, sS) = \frac{3}{4} = 0.75$; there is a 75% probability that a randomly selected offspring will have Huntington's disease.

35. (a)

Response	Probability
Never	0.026
Rarely	0.068
Sometimes	0.116
Most of the time	0.263
Always	0.527

(b) It would be unusual to randomly find a college student who never wears a seatbelt when riding in a car driven by someone else, because $P(\text{never}) < 0.05$.

36. (a)

Response	Probability
Never	0.026
Rarely	0.055
Sometimes	0.076
Most of the time	0.158
Always	0.684

(b) It would be unusual to randomly find a college student who never wears a seatbelt while driving, because $P(\text{never}) < 0.05$.

37. (a)

Type of Larceny Theft	Probability
Pocket picking	0.006
Purse snatching	0.009
Shoplifting	0.207
From motor vehicles	0.341
Motor vehicle accessories	0.140
Bicycles	0.065
From buildings	0.223
From coin-operated machines	0.008

(b) Purse snatching larcenies are unusual.
(c) Bicycle larcenies are not unusual.

38. (a)

Age	Probability
15–19	0.016
20–24	0.073
25–29	0.252
30–34	0.352
35–39	0.240
40–44	0.051
45–54	0.016

(b) Multiple births are unusual for 15- to 19-year-old mothers.
(c) Multiple births are not too unusual for 40- to 44-year-old mothers.

39. A, B, C, and F are consistent with the definition of a probability model.

40. Use model A if the coin is known to be fair.

41. Use model B if the coin is known to always come up tails.

42. If tails are twice as likely to come up, model F should be used.

43. (a) $S = \{JR, JC, JD, JM, RC, RD, RM, CD, CM, DM\}$
(b) $P(\text{Clarice and Dominique attend}) = \frac{1}{10} = 0.10$
(c) $P(\text{Clarice attends}) = \frac{4}{10} = 0.40$
(d) $P(\text{John stays home}) = \frac{6}{10} = 0.60$

44. (a) {Screamin' Eagle–The Boss, Screamin' Eagle–Mine Train, Screamin' Eagle–Batman, Screamin' Eagle–Mr. Freeze, Screamin' Eagle–Ninja, Screamin' Eagle–Big Spin, Screamin' Eagle–Evel Knievel, Screamin' Eagle–Xcalibur, Screamin' Eagle–Sky Screamer, The Boss–Mine Train, The Boss–Batman, The Boss–Mr. Freeze, The Boss–Ninja, The Boss–Big Spin, The Boss–Evel Knievel, The Boss–Xcalibur, The Boss–Sky Screamer, Mine Train–Batman, Mine Train–Mr. Freeze, Mine Train–Ninja, Mine Train–Big Spin, Mine Train–Evel Knievel, Mine Train-Xcalibur, Mine Train–Sky Screamer, Batman–Mr. Freeze, Batman–Ninja, Batman–Big Spin, Batman–Evel Knievel, Batman–Xcalibur, Batman–Sky Screamer, Mr. Freeze–Ninja, Mr. Freeze–Big Spin, Mr. Freeze–Evel Knievel, Mr. Freeze–Xcalibur, Mr. Freeze–Sky Screamer, Ninja–Big Spin, Ninja–Evel Knievel, Ninja–Xcalibur, Ninja–Sky Screamer, Big Spin–Evel Knievel, Big Spin–Xcalibur, Big Spin–Sky Screamer, Evel Knievel–Xcalibur, Evel Knievel–Sky Screamer, Xcalibur–Sky Screamer}

(b) $P(\text{Mr. Freeze and Evel Knievel}) = \frac{1}{45} = 0.022$

(c) $P(\text{Screamin' Eagle}) = \frac{9}{45} = 0.2$

(d) $P(\text{two wooden coasters}) = \frac{3}{45} = 0.067$

(e) $P(\text{no wooden coasters}) = \frac{21}{45} = 0.467$

45. (a) $P(\text{right field}) = \frac{24}{73} = 0.329$

(b) $P(\text{left field}) = \frac{2}{73} = 0.027$

(c) It was unusual for Barry Bonds to hit a home run to left field; the probability is less than 5%.

46. (a) Answers will vary. **(b)** Answers will vary.

(c) $P(3) = \frac{1}{6}$

47. Answers will vary.

48. (a) Classical method is used.
(b) Empirical method is used.
(c) Subjective method is used.
(d) Empirical method is used.

49. The dice appear to be loaded since the outcomes are not equally likely.

50. Answers will vary.

51. $P(\text{income is greater than } \$58{,}500) = \frac{1}{2} = 0.5$

52. $P(\text{SAT math score} \geq 700) = 0.75$

53. Answers will vary.

54. (a) Qualitative
(b) Because the data are qualitative and multiple responses are possible, a bar chart is the appropriate display.

Viagra Side Effects

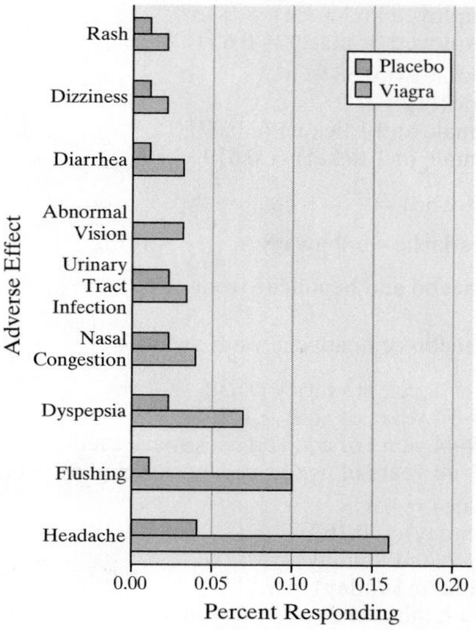

(c) For the Viagra group, $P(\text{flushing}) = \frac{73}{734} = 0.099$; this is not unusual.

(d) For the placebo group, $P(\text{flushing}) = \frac{7}{725} = 0.010$; this is somewhat unusual.
(e) Since it is unusual for someone in the placebo group to experience flushing, we would conclude that the individual received the Viagra treatment.
(f) This is a completely randomized design.

55. The Law of Large Numbers states that, as the number of repetitions of a probability experiment increases (long term), the proportion with which a certain outcome is observed (relative frequency) gets closer to the probability of the outcome. The games at a gambling casino are designed to benefit the casino in the long run; the risk to the casino is minimal because of the large number of gamblers.

56. Outcomes are equally likely when each outcome has the same probability of occurring.

57. An event is unusual if it has a low probability of occurring. The same cutoff should not always be used to identify unusual events. Selecting a cutoff is subjective and should take into account the consequences of incorrectly identifying an event as unusual.

58. Historically, rain has occurred on 70% of the days with otherwise similar conditions. It does not mean that it will rain 70% of the day. It could rain all day or it might not rain at all. Since the probability of rain is relatively high, it might not be a good day to plan on an outdoor activity.

59. Empirical probability is based on the outcomes of a probability experiment and is the relative frequency of the event. Classical probability is based on counting techniques and is equal to the ratio of the number of ways an event can occur to the number of possible outcomes of the experiment.

60. At the beginning of the game, there is a 0.25 probability of selecting the envelope with \$100. So the probability your envelope contains \$100 is 0.25. Once the host discards two envelopes that are known not to contain the \$100, you should switch, because the probability the envelope in the host's hands has \$100 is 0.75. This is because the host knows which envelope contains the \$100, so the original probability that you did not select the \$100 envelope does not change.

5.2 Assess Your Understanding (page 254)

1. Two events are disjoint (mutually exclusive) if they have no outcomes in common.

2. $P(E) + P(F)$

3. $P(E) + P(F) - P(E \text{ and } F)$

4. Two events E and E^C are complementary if $P(E \text{ and } E^C) = 0$ and if $P(E \text{ or } E^c) = 1$.

5. E and $F = \{5, 6, 7\}$; E and F are not mutually exclusive.

6. F and $G = \{9\}$; F and G are not mutually exclusive.

7. F or $G = \{5, 6, 7, 8, 9, 10, 11, 12\}$; $P(F \text{ or } G) = \frac{2}{3}$

8. E or $H = \{2, 3, 4, 5, 6, 7\}$; $P(E \text{ or } H) = \frac{1}{2}$

9. There are no outcomes in event "E and G." Events E and G are mutually exclusive.

10. There are no outcomes in event "F and H." Events F and H are mutually exclusive.

11. $E^c = \{1, 8, 9, 10, 11, 12\}$; $P(E^c) = \frac{1}{2}$

12. $F^c = \{1, 2, 3, 4, 10, 11, 12\}$; $P(F^c) = \frac{7}{12}$

13. $P(E \text{ or } F) = 0.55$ **14.** $P(E \text{ and } F) = 0.10$

15. $P(E \text{ or } F) = 0.70$ **16.** $P(E \text{ and } F) = 0$

17. $P(E^c) = 0.75$ **18.** $P(F^c) = 0.55$

19. $P(F) = 0.30$ **20.** $P(E) = 0.50$

21. $P(\text{Titleist or Maxfli}) = \frac{17}{20} = 0.85$

22. $P(\text{Maxfli or Top-Flite}) = \frac{11}{20} = 0.55$

23. $P(\text{not a Titleist}) = \frac{11}{20} = 0.55$

24. $P(\text{not a Top-Flite}) = \frac{17}{20} = 0.85$

25. (a) All the probabilities are nonnegative; the sum of the probabilities equals 1.
(b) $P(\text{rifle or shotgun}) = 0.057$. If 1000 murders in 2009 were randomly selected, we would expect 57 of them to be the result of a rifle or shotgun.

(c) $P(\text{handgun, rifle, or shotgun}) = 0.53$. If 100 murders in 2009 were randomly selected, we would expect 53 of them to be the result of a handgun, rifle, or shotgun.
(d) $P(\text{not a gun}) = 0.329$. There is a 32.9% chance of randomly selecting a murder that was not committed with a gun.
(e) A murder with a shotgun is unusual.

26. (a) All the probabilities are nonnegative; the sum of the probabilities equal 1.
(b) $P(\text{earning a physical or life sciences degree}) = 0.290$. There is a 29% probability that a randomly selected doctoral candidate received a degree in either the physical or life sciences.
(c) $P(\text{doctorate in physical, life, or computer sciences or mathematics}) = 0.354$. There is a 35.4% probability that a randomly selected doctoral candidate received a degree in the physical, life, or computer sciences or in mathematics.
(d) $P(\text{not in mathematics}) = 0.969$. The probability is 96.9% that a randomly selected doctoral candidate did not receive a degree in mathematics.
(e) It is unusual to earn a doctoral degree in mathematics.

27. No; for example, on one draw of a card from a standard deck, let E = diamond, F = club, and G = red card.

28. $P(A \text{ or } B \text{ or } C) = P(A) + P(B) + P(C) - P(A \text{ and } B) - P(A \text{ and } C) - P(B \text{ and } C) + 2P(A \text{ and } B \text{ and } C)$

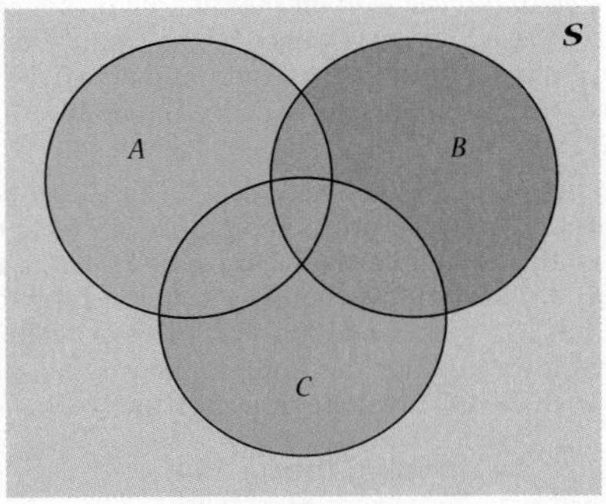

29. (a) $P(\text{30- to 39-year-old mother}) = 0.592$. If we randomly select 1000 mothers involved in a multiple birth we'd expect about 592 to be between 30 and 39 years old.
(b) $P(\text{not 30 to 39 years old}) = 0.408$. There is a 40.8% probability that a mother involved in a multiple birth was either younger than 30 or older than 39.
(c) $P(\text{younger than 45 years}) = 0.984$. The probability that a randomly selected mother involved in a multiple birth was younger than 45 years old is 98.4%.
(d) $P(\text{at least 20 years old}) = 0.984$. There is a 98.4% probability that a randomly selected mother involved with a multiple birth was at least 20 years old.

30. (a) All the probabilities are nonnegative; the sum of the probabilities equals 1.
(b) $P(\text{4 or more rooms}) = 0.896$. If we randomly select 1000 U.S. housing units, we'd expect about 896 to have 4 or more rooms.
(c) $P(\text{fewer than 8 rooms}) = 0.844$. There is an 84.4% probability that a randomly selected house will have fewer than 8 rooms.
(d) $P(\text{from 4 to 6 rooms}) = 0.617$. There is a 61.7% probability that a randomly selected house will have 4, 5, or 6 rooms.
(e) $P(\text{at least 2 rooms}) = 0.995$. The probability is 99.5% that a randomly selected house will have at least 2 rooms.

31. (a) $P(\text{heart or club}) = \frac{1}{2} = 0.5$
(b) $P(\text{heart or club or diamond}) = \frac{3}{4} = 0.75$
(c) $P(\text{ace or heart}) = \frac{4}{13} = 0.308$

32. (a) $P(\text{two or three}) = \frac{2}{13} = 0.154$
(b) $P(\text{two or three or four}) = \frac{3}{13} = 0.231$
(c) $P(\text{two or club}) = \frac{4}{13} = 0.308$

33. (a) $P(\text{birthday is not November 8}) = \frac{364}{365} = 0.997$
(b) $P(\text{birthday is not 1st of month}) = \frac{353}{365} = 0.967$
(c) $P(\text{birthday is not 31st of month}) = \frac{358}{365} = 0.981$
(d) $P(\text{birthday is not in December}) = \frac{334}{365} = 0.915$

34. (a) $P(\text{green or red}) = \frac{10}{19} = 0.526$
(b) $P(\text{not green}) = \frac{18}{19} = 0.947$

35. No; some people have both vision and hearing problems, but we do not know the proportion.

36. No; some people visit the doctor for both a blood pressure check and urinalysis, but we do not know the proportion.

37. (a) $P(\text{between 6 and 10 years old}) = \frac{5}{24} = 0.208$; not unusual
(b) $P(\text{more than 5 years old}) = \frac{17}{24} = 0.708$
(c) $P(\text{less than 1 year old}) = \frac{1}{24} = 0.042$; yes, this is unusual

38. (a) $P(\text{only English or only Spanish is spoken}) = 0.93$
(b) $P(\text{language other than only English or only Spanish}) = 0.07$
(c) $P(\text{not only English is spoken}) = 0.19$
(d) No; the sum of the probabilities would be greater than 1, and there would be no probability model.

39. (a) $P(\text{worker drives or takes public transportation}) = 0.915$. There is a 91.5% probability that a randomly selected worker either drives or takes public transportation to work.
(b) $P(\text{worker neither drives nor takes public transportation}) = 0.085$. There is an 8.5% probability that a randomly selected worker neither drives nor takes public transportation to work.
(c) $P(\text{worker does not drive}) = 0.133$. The probability is 13.3% that a randomly selected worker does not drive to work.
(d) No; the probability a person drives or walks or takes public transportation would be 106.5%, which is greater than 1.

40. (a) $P(\text{both spouses work}) = \frac{1149}{1700} = 0.676$
(b) $P(\text{1 child under age 18}) = \frac{353}{1700} = 0.208$
(c) $P(\text{2 or more children under age 18 and both spouses work}) = \frac{37}{170} = 0.218$
(d) $P(\text{no children or only husband works}) = \frac{1041}{1700} = 0.612$
(e) $P(\text{only wife works}) = \frac{63}{850} = 0.074$; no, this would not be unusual

41. (a) $P(\text{died from cancer}) = 0.007$
(b) $P(\text{current smoker}) = 0.057$
(c) $P(\text{died from cancer and was current cigar smoker}) = 0.001$
(d) $P(\text{died from cancer or was current cigar smoker}) = 0.064$

42. (a) $P(\text{employed}) = 0.284$
(b) $P(\text{male}) = 0.507$
(c) $P(\text{employed and male}) = 0.137$
(d) $P(\text{employed or male}) = 0.654$

43. (a) $P(\text{female}) = 0.584$
(b) $P(\text{1 ticket}) = 0.107$
(c) $P(\text{female and 1 ticket}) = 0.071$
(d) $P(\text{female or 1 ticket}) = 0.619$

44. (a) $P(\text{placebo}) = \frac{2}{5} = 0.40$
(b) $P(\text{headache went away}) = \frac{94}{125} = 0.752$
(c) $P(\text{placebo and headache went away}) = \frac{28}{125} = 0.224$
(d) $P(\text{placebo or headache went away}) = \frac{116}{125} = 0.928$

45. (a) $P(\text{uses social media}) = 0.638$
(b) $P(\text{45–54 years of age}) = 0.264$
(c) $P(\text{35–44 years of age and uses social media}) = 0.168$
(d) $P(\text{35–44 years of age or uses social media}) = 0.706$

46. (a) $P(\text{male}) = 0.658$
(b) $P(\text{Sunday}) = 0.167$
(c) $P(\text{male and Sunday}) = 0.109$
(d) $P(\text{male or Sunday}) = 0.715$
(e) Yes, a fatality on Wednesday involving a female driver is unusual.

47. (a) Crash type, system, and number of crashes

(b) Crash type: qualitative; system: qualitative; number of crashes: quantitative, discrete

(c)

Crash Type	Current System	Red-Light Cameras
Reported injury	0.26	0.24
Reported property damage only	0.35	0.36
Unreported injury	0.07	0.07
Unreported property damage only	0.32	0.33
Total	1	1

(d)

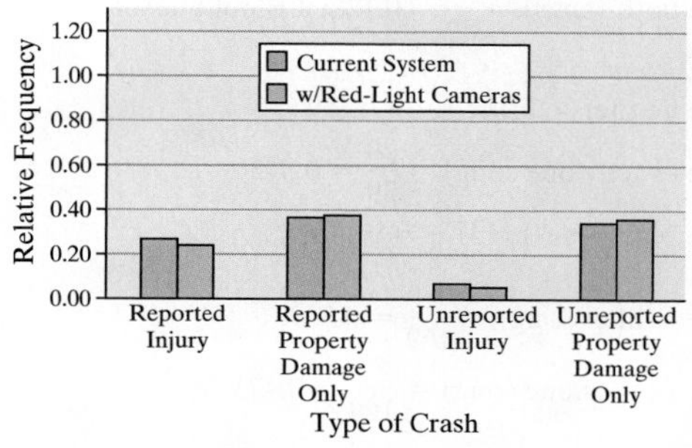

(e) Current system: $\frac{1121}{13} \approx 86.2$ crashes

With cameras: $\frac{922}{13} \approx 70.9$ crashes

(f) Not possible; we would need to know the number of crashes at each intersection.

(g) Since the mean number of crashes is less with the cameras, it appears that the program will be beneficial.

(h) $P(\text{reported injuries}) = \frac{289}{1121} = 0.258$

(i) $P(\text{only property damage}) = \frac{641}{922} = 0.695$

(j) When accounting for the cause of the crash (rear end vs. red-light running), the camera system does not reduce all types of accidents. Under the camera system, red-light running crashes decreased, but rear-end crashes increased.

(k) Recommendations may vary. The benefits of the decrease in red-light running crashes must be weighed against the negative of increased rear-end crashes. Seriousness of injuries and amount of property damage may need to be considered.

48. (a)

Score	Relative Frequency
30–39	0.025
40–49	0.025
50–59	0.05
60–69	0.125
70–79	0.325
80–89	0.275
90–99	0.175
Total	1

(b)

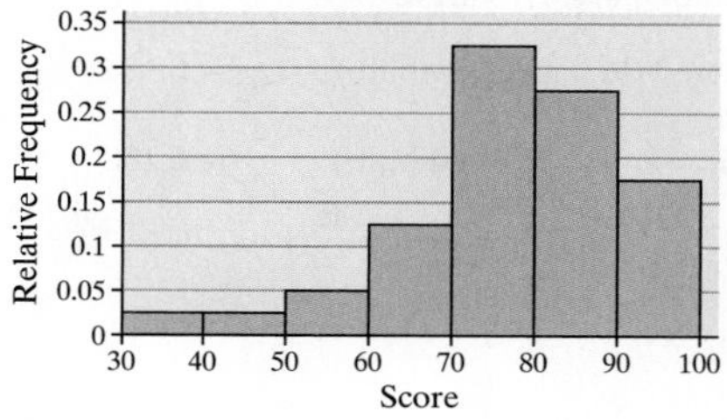

(c) Mean: 77; median: 77

(d) The distribution is skewed slightly to the left.

(e) Standard deviation: 13.06; interquartile range: 15

(f) $P(\text{less than } 70) = 0.225$

(g) $P(80 \text{ or higher}) = 0.45$

(h) $P(\text{less than } 30) = 0$

5.3 Assess Your Understanding (page 262)

1. independent **2.** Multiplication **3.** Addition **4.** False **5.** $P(E) \cdot P(F)$ **6.** 0

7. (a) Dependent **(b)** Dependent **(c)** Independent

8. (a) Independent **(b)** Independent **(c)** Dependent

9. $P(E \text{ and } F) = 0.18$

10. $P(E \text{ and } F) = 0.63$

11. $P(5 \text{ heads}) = \frac{1}{32} = 0.03125$; if we flipped a coin 5 times, one hundred different times, we would expect to observe 5 heads in a row about 3 times.

12. $P(\text{tossing 4 ones in a row}) = \frac{1}{6^4} = 0.0008$. If a die is tossed, 0.08% of the time all 4 tosses will be 1.

13. $P(\text{two left-handed people are chosen}) = 0.0169$

$P(\text{at least one person chosen is right-handed}) = 0.9831$

14. (a) Knowing that Shawn won one of the lotteries would not affect his chance of winning the other. **(b)** 0.0000000000000279

15. (a) $P(\text{all five are negative}) = 0.9752$ **(b)** $P(\text{at least one is positive}) = 0.0248$

16. (a) $P(\text{all 100 last}) = 0.6058$ **(b)** $P(\text{at least one burns out}) = 0.3942$

17. (a) $P(\text{two will live to 41 years}) = 0.99515$ **(b)** $P(\text{five will live to 41 years}) = 0.98791$ **(c)** $P(\text{at least one of five dies}) = 0.01209$; it would be unusual that at least one of the five dies before age 41.

18. (a) $P(\text{two will live to 41 years}) = 0.99710$ **(b)** $P(\text{five will live to 41 years}) = 0.99277$ **(c)** $P(\text{at least one of five dies}) = 0.00723$; it would be unusual that at least one of the five dies before age 41.

19. (a) $P(\text{two of two have mental illness}) = 0.09$ **(b)** $P(\text{six of six have mental illness}) = 0.000729$ **(c)** $P(\text{at least one of six has mental illness}) = 0.882$ **(d)** No, it would not be unusual for none of the four to have mental illness.

20. (a) $P(\text{two inspectors do not identify low-quality timber}) = 0.04$ **(b)** Three inspectors should be hired to keep the probability of failing to identify low-quality timber at less than 1%. **(c)** In repeated inspections of timbers, we expect both inspectors will fail to identify a low-quality timber about 4 times out of 100.

21. (a) $P(\text{one failure}) = 0.15$, not unusual; $P(\text{two failure}) = 0.0225$, unusual **(b)** $P(\text{succeed}) = 1 - P(\text{fail}) = 1 - 0.0225 = 0.9775$ **(c)** 5 components

22. (a) $P(\text{12 positive tests}) = 0.8864$ **(b)** $P(\text{at least one negative test}) = 0.1136$

23. (a) $P(\text{batter makes 10 consecutive outs}) = 0.02825$; If we randomly selected 100 different at-bats of 10, we would expect about 3 to result in a streak of 10 consecutive outs. **(b)** A cold streak would be unusual. **(c)** $P(\text{5 consecutive outs and then base hit}) = 0.0504$

24. $P(\text{makes eight consecutive free shots}) = 0.032$; it is unusual for the player to make eight consecutive free-throw shots.

25. (a) $P(\text{two strikes in a row}) = 0.09$ **(b)** $P(\text{turkey}) = 0.027$ **(c)** $P(\text{3 strikes followed by nonstrike}) = 0.0189$

26. (a) $P(\text{four Nascar fans}) = 0.1212$ **(b)** $P(\text{at least one non-Nascar fan}) = 0.8788$ **(c)** $P(\text{no one likes Nascar}) = 0.0283$ **(d)** $P(\text{at least one likes Nascar}) = 0.9717$

27. (a) $P(\text{all three have driven under the influence of alcohol}) = 0.0244$
(b) $P(\text{at least one has not driven under the influence of alcohol}) = 0.9756$
(c) $P(\text{none has driven under the influence of alcohol}) = 0.3579$
(d) $P(\text{at least one has driven under the influence of alcohol}) = 0.6421$

28. $P(\text{at least } 1) = 0.9999$; answers will vary.

29. $P(\text{audited and owns dog}) = 0.025$

30. $P(\text{girl and in excess of 40 pounds}) = 0.099$

31. No, it would not be unusual since the probability of all three stocks increasing by at least 10% is about 0.077.

32. (a) $P(\text{male and bets on professional sports}) = 0.0823$
(b) $P(\text{male or bets on professional sports}) = 0.5717$
(c) The independence assumption is not correct.
(d) $P(\text{male or bets on professional sports}) = 0.548$

33. (a) $\left(\frac{1}{2}\right)^{24} \approx 5.96 \times 10^{-8}$
(b) $\left(\frac{1}{2}\right)^{36} \approx 1.46 \times 10^{-11}$

5.4 Assess Your Understanding (page 270)

1. F occurring; E has occurred

2. No

3. $P(F \mid E) = 0.75$

4. $P(F \mid E) = 0.525$

5. $P(F \mid E) = 0.568$

6. $P(F \mid E) = 0.411$

7. $P(E \text{ and } F) = 0.32$

8. $P(E \text{ and } F) = 0.24$

9. The events are not independent.

10. The events are not independent.

11. $P(\text{club}) = \frac{1}{4}$; $P(\text{club} \mid \text{black card}) = \frac{1}{2}$

12. $P(\text{king}) = \frac{1}{13}$; $P(\text{king} \mid \text{heart}) = \frac{1}{13}$; no; independent

13. $P(\text{rainy} \mid \text{cloudy}) = \frac{0.21}{0.37} = 0.568$

14. $P(\text{cancer death} \mid \text{25 to 34 years old}) = \frac{0.0015}{0.0171} = 0.088$

15. $P(\text{unemployed} \mid \text{dropout}) = \frac{0.021}{0.080} = 0.263$

16. $P(> \$100{,}000 \mid \text{live in Northeast}) = \frac{0.054}{0.179} = 0.302$

17. (a) $P(\text{35–44} \mid \text{more likely}) = \frac{329}{1329} = 0.248$
(b) $P(\text{more likely} \mid \text{35–44}) = \frac{329}{536} = 0.614$
(c) No; they are less likely to buy American; 0.439 for 18- to 34-year-olds compared to 0.615 in general.

18. (a) $P(\text{0 tickets} \mid \text{female}) = \frac{97}{115} = 0.843$
(b) $P(\text{female} \mid \text{0 tickets}) = \frac{97}{168} = 0.577$
(c) Not really; $P(\text{0 tickets} \mid \text{female}) = 0.843$ and $P(\text{0 tickets} \mid \text{male}) = 0.866$

19. (a) $P(\text{driver} \mid \text{female}) = \frac{11{,}856}{18{,}219} = 0.651$
(b) $P(\text{female} \mid \text{passenger}) = \frac{6363}{12{,}816} = 0.496$
(c) Male; $P(\text{male} \mid \text{driver}) = \frac{32{,}873}{44{,}729} = 0.735$

20. (a) $P(\text{female} \mid \text{Sunday}) = \frac{4325}{12{,}547} = 0.345$
(b) $P(\text{Sunday} \mid \text{female}) = \frac{4325}{25{,}759} = 0.168$
(c) No; for any given day of the week, $P(\text{male} \mid \text{day})$ is between 0.65 and 0.67, so the probability that a fatality is male is essentially the same for every day of the week.

21. $P(\text{both TVs work}) = 0.4$; $P(\text{at least one TV does not work}) = 0.6$

22. $P(\text{two women are chosen}) = \frac{2}{7} = 0.286$

23. (a) $P(\text{first card is a king and the second card is a king}) = \frac{1}{221} = 0.005$
(b) $P(\text{first card is a king and the second card is a king}) = \frac{1}{169} = 0.006$

24. (a) $P(\text{first card is a club and the second card is a club}) = \frac{1}{17} = 0.059$
(b) $P(\text{first card is a club and the second card is a club}) = \frac{1}{16} = 0.0625$

25. $P(\text{Dave and then Neta are chosen}) = \frac{1}{20} = 0.05$

26. $P(\text{Yolanda hosts, then Lorrie hosts the parties}) = \frac{1}{20} = 0.05$

27. (a) $P(\text{like both songs}) = \frac{5}{39} = 0.128$; it is not unusual to like both songs.
(b) $P(\text{like neither song}) = \frac{14}{39} = 0.359$
(c) $P(\text{like exactly one song}) = \frac{20}{39} = 0.513$
(d) $P(\text{like both songs}) = \frac{25}{169} = 0.148$;
$P(\text{like neither song}) = \frac{64}{169} = 0.379$;
$P(\text{like exactly one song}) = \frac{80}{169} = 0.473$

28. (a) $P(\text{both are diet soda}) = \frac{1}{22} = 0.0455$
(b) $P(\text{both are regular soda}) = \frac{6}{11} = 0.545$; it is not unusual to choose two regular sodas.
(c) $P(\text{one regular and one diet soda}) = \frac{9}{22} = 0.409$

29.

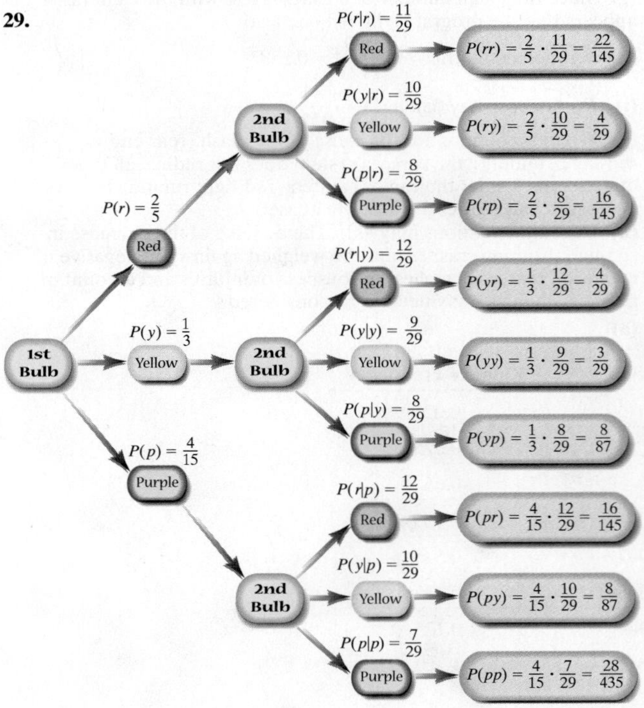

(a) $P(\text{two red bulbs}) = \frac{22}{145} = 0.152$
(b) $P(\text{first a red and then a yellow bulb}) = \frac{4}{29} = 0.138$
(c) $P(\text{first a yellow and then a red bulb}) = \frac{4}{29} = 0.138$
(d) $P(\text{a red bulb and a yellow bulb}) = \frac{8}{29} = 0.276$

30.

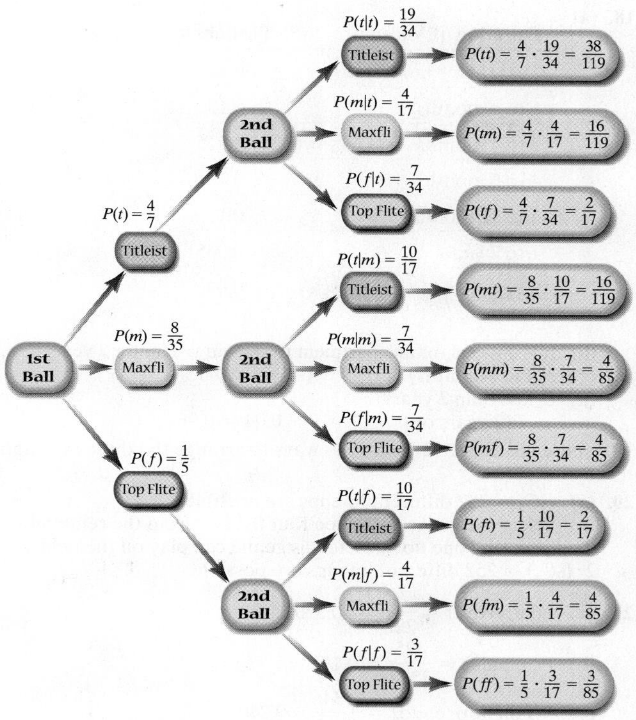

(a) $P(\text{two Titleists}) = \dfrac{38}{119} = 0.319$
(b) $P(\text{first a Titleist and then a Maxfli}) = \dfrac{16}{119} = 0.134$
(c) $P(\text{first a Maxfli and then a Titleist}) = \dfrac{16}{119} = 0.134$
(d) $P(\text{a Maxfli and a Titleist}) = \dfrac{32}{119} = 0.269$

31. $P(\text{female and smokes}) = 0.090$; it would not be unusual to randomly select a female who smokes.
32. $P(\text{male and holds multiple jobs}) = 0.023$; it would be unusual to randomly select an employed male who has more than one job.
33. (a) $P(\text{10 people each have a different birthday}) = 0.883$
(b) $P(\text{at least two of the ten people have the same birthday}) = 0.117$
34. $P(\text{at least 2 people in a group of 23 share the same birthday}) = 0.507$
35. (a) Yes; $P(\text{male}) = \dfrac{1}{2} = P(\text{male} \mid \text{0 activities}) = \dfrac{1}{2}$
(b) No; $P(\text{female}) = \dfrac{1}{2} \neq P(\text{female} \mid \text{5+ activities}) = \dfrac{71}{109} = 0.651$
(c) Yes; $P(\text{1–2 activities and 3–4 activities}) = 0$
(d) No; $P(\text{male and 1–2 activities}) = 0.2025 \neq 0$
36. (a) No; $P(\text{Republican}) = 0.55 \neq P(\text{Republican} \mid 30-44) = 0.470$
(b) Yes: $P(\text{Democrat}) = 0.45 = P(\text{Democrat} \mid 65+) = 0.45$
(c) Yes; $P(\text{17–29 and 45–64}) = 0$
(d) No; $P(\text{Republican and 45–64}) = 0.269 \neq 0$
37. (a) $P(\text{being dealt five clubs}) = 0.000495$
(b) $P(\text{being dealt a flush}) = 0.002$
38. $P(\text{being dealt a royal flush}) = 0.00000154$
39. (a) $P(\text{two defective chips}) = 0.0000245$
(b) Assuming independence: $P(\text{two defective chips}) = 0.000025$
40. (a) $P(\text{first is Roger Cummings; second is Rick Whittingham}) = 2.37 \times 10^{-8}$
(b) $P(\text{first is Roger Cummings; second is Rick Whittingham}) = 2.37 \times 10^{-8}$
41. $P(\text{45–54 years old}) = \dfrac{546}{2160} = 0.253$; $P(\text{45–54 years old} \mid \text{more likely}) = \dfrac{360}{1329} = 0.271$; the events are not independent.
42. $P(\text{female}) = \dfrac{115}{197} = 0.584$; $P(\text{female} \mid \text{1 ticket}) = \dfrac{14}{21} = 0.667$; the events are not independent.
43. $P(\text{female}) = \dfrac{18{,}219}{57{,}545} = 0.317$; $P(\text{female} \mid \text{driver}) = \dfrac{11{,}856}{44{,}729} = 0.265$; the events are not independent.
44. $P(\text{male}) = \dfrac{49{,}571}{75{,}330} = 0.658$; $P(\text{male} \mid \text{Wednesday}) = \dfrac{5782}{8793} = 0.658$; the events are independent.

5.5 Assess Your Understanding (page 283)

1. permutation
2. combination
3. True
4. $n \cdot (n-1) \cdot \cdots \cdot 3 \cdot 2 \cdot 1$; 1
5. $5! = 120$
6. $7! = 5040$
7. $10! = 3{,}628{,}800$
8. $12! = 479{,}001{,}600$
9. $0! = 1$
10. $1! = 1$
11. ${}_6P_2 = 30$
12. ${}_7P_2 = 42$
13. ${}_4P_4 = 24$
14. ${}_7P_7 = 5040$
15. ${}_5P_0 = 1$
16. ${}_4P_0 = 1$
17. ${}_8P_3 = 336$
18. ${}_9P_4 = 3024$
19. ${}_8C_3 = 56$
20. ${}_9C_2 = 36$
21. ${}_{10}C_2 = 45$
22. ${}_{12}C_3 = 220$
23. ${}_{52}C_1 = 52$
24. ${}_{40}C_{40} = 1$
25. ${}_{48}C_3 = 17{,}296$
26. ${}_{30}C_4 = 27{,}405$
27. *ab, ac, ad, ae, ba, bc, bd, be, ca, cb, cd, ce, da, db, dc, de, ea, eb, ec, ed*; ${}_5P_2 = 20$
28. *ab, ac, ad, ba, bc, bd, ca, cb, cd, da, db, dc*; ${}_4P_2 = 12$
29. *ab, ac, ad, ae, bc, bd, be, cd, ce, de*; ${}_5C_2 = 10$
30. *ab, ac, ad, bc, bd, cd*; ${}_4C_2 = 6$
31. He can wear 24 different shirt-and-tie combinations.
32. She can wear 15 different outfits.
33. Dan can arrange the songs $12! = 479{,}001{,}600$ ways.
34. Fifteen students can be lined up $15! = 1.30767 \times 10^{12}$ ways.
35. The salesperson can take $8! = 40{,}320$ different routes.
36. The 10 songs can be played $10! = 3{,}628{,}800$ ways.
37. At most 18,278 companies can be listed on the NYSE.
38. At most 12,338,352 companies can be listed on the NASDAQ.
39. (a) 10,000 different codes are possible.
(b) $P(\text{correct code is guessed}) = \dfrac{1}{10{,}000}$
40. (a) 10^9 different Social Security numbers are possible.
(b) $P(\text{guessing the president's Social Security number}) = \dfrac{1}{10^9}$
41. $26^8 = 2.09 \times 10^{11}$ different user names are possible.
42. $10 \cdot 26^7 = 8.03 \times 10^{10}$ additional user names are possible.
43. (a) There are $50^3 = 125{,}000$ lock combinations.
(b) $P(\text{guessing the correct combination}) = \dfrac{1}{50^3} = \dfrac{1}{125{,}000}$
44. There are $26 \cdot 10^5 = 2{,}600{,}000$ different license plates.
45. The top three cars can finish in ${}_{40}P_3 = 59{,}280$ ways.
46. The top two horses can finish in ${}_{10}P_2 = 90$ ways.
47. The officers can be chosen in ${}_{20}P_4 = 116{,}280$ ways.
48. ${}_{50}P_4 = 5{,}527{,}200$ different leadership structures are possible.
49. There are ${}_{25}P_4 = 303{,}600$ possible outcomes.
50. There are ${}_{21}C_9 = 293{,}930$ possible committee structures.
51. There are ${}_{50}C_5 = 2{,}118{,}760$ possible simple random samples of size 5.
52. There are ${}_{100}C_7 = 1.60076 \times 10^{10}$ possible simple random samples of size 7.
53. ${}_6C_2 = 15$ different birth and gender orders are possible.
54. ${}_8C_3 = 56$ different birth and gender orders are possible.
55. $\dfrac{10!}{3! \cdot 2! \cdot 2! \cdot 3!} = 25{,}200$ different sequences are possible.
56. $\dfrac{12!}{1! \cdot 4! \cdot 3! \cdot 4!} = 138{,}600$ different sequences are possible.
57. The trees can be planted $\dfrac{11!}{4! \cdot 5! \cdot 2!} = 6930$ different ways.
58. $\dfrac{9!}{3! \cdot 4!} = 2520$ different batting orders are possible.
59. $P(\text{winning}) = \dfrac{1}{{}_{39}C_5} = \dfrac{1}{575{,}757}$

60. $P(\text{winning}) = \dfrac{1}{{}_{56}C_5 \cdot 46} = 0.0000000057$

61. (a) $P(\text{jury has only students}) = \dfrac{1}{153} = 0.0065$

(b) $P(\text{jury has only faculty}) = \dfrac{1}{34} = 0.0294$

(c) $P(\text{jury has two students and three faculty}) = \dfrac{20}{51} = 0.3922$

62. (a) $P(\text{committee is all Democrats}) = 0.0127$
(b) $P(\text{committee is all Republicans}) = 0.0028$
(c) P (committee has three Democrats and four Republicans) $= 0.2442$

63. $P(\text{shipment is rejected}) = 0.1283$

64. $P(\text{selecting two 60-watt light bulbs}) = 0.3517$

65. (a) $P(\text{you like 2 of 4 songs}) = 0.3916$
(b) $P(\text{you like 3 of 4 songs}) = 0.1119$
(c) $P(\text{you like all 4 songs}) = 0.0070$

66. (a) $P(\text{2 of the 3 cans are diet soda}) = 0.1227$
(b) $P(\text{1 of the 3 cans is diet soda}) = 0.4909$
(c) $P(\text{all 3 cans are diet soda}) = 0.0045$

67. (a) Five cards can be selected from a deck ${}_{52}C_5 = 2{,}598{,}960$ ways.
(b) Three of the same card can be chosen $13 \cdot {}_4C_3 = 52$ ways.
(c) The remaining two cards can be chosen ${}_{12}C_2 \cdot {}_4C_1 \cdot {}_4C_1 = 1056$ ways.
(d) $P(\text{three of a kind}) = \dfrac{52 \cdot 1056}{2{,}598{,}960} = 0.0211$

68. (a) Five cards can be selected from a deck ${}_{52}C_5 = 2{,}598{,}960$ ways.
(b) Two of the same card can be chosen $13 \cdot {}_4C_2 = 78$ ways.
(c) The remaining three cards can be chosen ${}_{12}C_3 \cdot {}_4C_1 \cdot {}_4C_1 \cdot {}_4C_1 = 14{,}080$ ways.
(d) $P(\text{two of a kind}) = \dfrac{78 \cdot 14{,}080}{2{,}598{,}960} = 0.4226$

69. $P(\text{all 4 modems tested work}) = 0.4912$

70. $P(\text{all 5 TVs tested work}) = 0.7291$

71. (a) $21 \cdot 5 \cdot 21 \cdot 21 \cdot 5 \cdot 21 \cdot 10 \cdot 10 = 486{,}202{,}500$ passwords are possible.
(b) $42 \cdot 10 \cdot 42 \cdot 42 \cdot 10 \cdot 42 \cdot 10 \cdot 10 = 420^4 \approx 3.11 \times 10^{10}$ passwords are possible.

5.6 Assess Your Understanding (page 289)

1. A permutation is an arrangement in which order matters; a combination is an arrangement in which order does not matter.

2. The empirical method assigns probabilities using relative frequencies.

3. AND is generally associated with multiplication; OR is generally associated with addition.

4. $P(\text{seven}) \approx \dfrac{350}{1000} = 0.35$

5. $P(E) = \dfrac{4}{10} = 0.4$

6. $P(F) = \dfrac{3}{10} = 0.3$

7. *abc, acb, abd, adb, abe, aeb, acd, adc, ace, aec, ade, aed, bac, bca, bad, bda, bae, bea, bcd, bdc, bce, bec, bde, bed, cde, ced, cab, cba, cad, cda, cae, cea, cbd, cdb, cde, ced, dab, dba, dac, dca, dae, dea, dbc, dcb, dbe, deb, dce, dec, eab, eba, eac, eca, ead, eda, ebc, ecb, ebd, edb, ecd, edc*

8. $P(E \text{ or } F) = 0.7 + 0.2 = 0.9$

9. $P(E \text{ or } F) = 0.7 + 0.2 - 0.15 = 0.75$

10. $\dfrac{6!2!}{4!} = 60$

11. ${}_7P_3 = 210$

12. ${}_9C_4 = 126$

13. $P(E \text{ and } F) = P(E) \cdot P(F) = 0.4$

14. $P(F \mid E) = \dfrac{P(E \text{ and } F)}{P(E)} = \dfrac{4}{9} = 0.444$

15. $P(E \text{ and } F) = P(E) \cdot P(F \mid E) = 0.27$

16. *abc, abd, abe, acd, ace, ade, bcd, bce, bde, cde*

17. $P(\text{plays soccer}) = \dfrac{22}{500} = 0.044$

18. (a)

Duration of Vacancy	Probability
Less than 1 month	0.21
1 to 2 months	0.19
2 to 4 months	0.225
4 to 6 months	0.15
6 to 12 months	0.12
1 to 2 years	0.065
2 years or more	0.04

(b) It is unusual for an apartment to remain vacant for 2 years or more.
(c) $P(\text{1 to 4 months}) = 0.19 + 0.225 = 0.415$
(d) $P(\text{less than 2 years}) = 1 - P(\text{2 years or more}) = 1 - 0.04 = 0.96$

19. There are $3 \cdot 3 \cdot 2 \cdot 2 \cdot 1 \cdot 1 = 36$ ways to arrange the three men and three women.

20. (a) ${}_{10}C_5 = 252$ different lineups are possible.
(b) Select the goalie first, then four fielders from the remaining 9 players (the one not selected as goalie can play on the field). $2 \cdot ({}_9C_4) = 252$ different lineups are possible.

21. (a) $P(\text{survived}) = \dfrac{711}{2224} = 0.320$

(b) $P(\text{female}) = \dfrac{425}{2224} = 0.191$

(c) $P(\text{female or child}) = \dfrac{534}{2224} = 0.240$

(d) $P(\text{female and survived}) = \dfrac{316}{2224} = 0.142$

(e) $P(\text{female or survived}) = \dfrac{820}{2224} = 0.369$

(f) $P(\text{survived} \mid \text{female}) = \dfrac{316}{425} = 0.744$

(g) $P(\text{survived} \mid \text{child}) = \dfrac{57}{109} = 0.523$

(h) $P(\text{survived} \mid \text{male}) = \dfrac{338}{1690} = 0.2$

(i) Yes, the survival rate was much higher for women and children.

(j) $P(\text{both females survived}) = \dfrac{316}{425} \cdot \dfrac{315}{424} = 0.552$

22. (a) $P(\text{all 4 users}) = (0.17)^4 = 0.00084$
(b) $P(\text{at least 1 user}) = 1 - P(\text{no users}) = 1 - (0.83)^4 = 0.525$

23. Shawn can fill out the report in ${}_{12}C_3 = 220$ different ways.

24. (a) $P(\text{junior}) = \dfrac{112}{449} = 0.249$

(b) $P(\text{senior} \mid \text{NHS}) = \dfrac{37}{87} = 0.425$

25. (a) $P(\text{win both}) = \dfrac{1}{5.2 \times 10^6} \cdot \dfrac{1}{705{,}600} = 0.00000000000027$

(b) $P(\text{win Jubilee twice}) = \left(\dfrac{1}{705{,}600}\right)^2 = 0.000000000002$

26. (a) $6! = 720$ different arrangements are possible using all 6 letters.
(b) ${}_6P_4 = 360$ different arrangements are possible using only 4 letters.
(c) $P(\text{six-letter word}) = \dfrac{3}{720} = \dfrac{1}{240} = 0.0042$

27. $P(\text{parent owns} \mid \text{teenager owns}) = \dfrac{0.43}{0.79} = 0.544$

28. Jim is using subjective probability.

29. ${}_{12}C_8 = 495$ different sets of questions can be answered.

30. Todd could put together ${}_{12}P_9 = 79{,}833{,}600$ different exercise routines.

31. $2 \cdot 2 \cdot 3 \cdot 8 \cdot 2 = 192$ different cars are possible.

32. (a) $P(\text{on Lingo board}) = \dfrac{15}{21} = \dfrac{5}{7} = 0.714$

(b) $P(\text{stopper}) = \dfrac{3}{21} = \dfrac{1}{7} = 0.143$

(c) P(LINGO on first) = 0 (there is no way to get 5 in a row with only 1 ball)
(d) P(LINGO on 2nd) $= \frac{6}{21} \cdot \frac{1}{20} = \frac{1}{70} = 0.0143$

Chapter 5 Review Exercises (page 293)

1. (a) Possible probabilities are 0, 0.75, 0.41.
(b) Possible probabilities are $\frac{2}{5}, \frac{1}{3}, \frac{6}{7}$.

2. $P(E) = \frac{1}{5} = 0.2$ **3.** $P(F) = \frac{2}{5} = 0.4$

4. $P(E) = \frac{3}{5} = 0.6$ **5.** $P(E^c) = \frac{4}{5} = 0.8$

6. $P(E \text{ or } F) = 0.89$ **7.** $P(E \text{ or } F) = 0.48$

8. $P(E \text{ and } F) = 0.09$

9. Events E and F are not independent because $P(E \text{ and } F) \neq P(E) \cdot P(F)$.

10. $P(E \text{ and } F) = 0.2655$ **11.** $P(E \mid F) = 0.5$

12. (a) $7! = 5040$ **(b)** $0! = 1$ **(c)** ${}_9C_4 = 126$
(d) ${}_{10}C_3 = 120$ **(e)** ${}_9P_2 = 72$ **(f)** ${}_{12}P_4 = 11{,}880$

13. (a) $P(\text{green}) = \frac{1}{19} = 0.0526$; If the wheel is spun 100 times, we would expect about 5 spins to end with the ball in a green slot.
(b) $P(\text{green or red}) = \frac{10}{19} = 0.5263$; If the wheel is spun 100 times, we would expect about 53 spins to end with the ball in either a green slot or a red slot.
(c) $P(\text{00 or red}) = \frac{19}{38} = 0.5$; If the wheel is spun 100 times, we would expect about 50 spins to end with the ball either in 00 or in a red slot.
(d) $P(\text{31 and black}) = 0$; this is called an impossible event.

14. (a) $P(\text{fatality was alcohol related}) = \frac{9817}{33{,}722} = 0.291$
(b) $P(\text{fatality was not alcohol related}) = \frac{23{,}905}{33{,}722} = 0.709$
(c) P(both fatalities were alcohol related) = 0.085
(d) P(neither fatality was alcohol related) = 0.503
(e) P(at least one fatality was alcohol related) = 0.497

15. (a)

Age	Probability
18–79	0.121
80–89	0.252
90–99	0.253
100 or older	0.373

(b) It is not unusual for an individual to want to live between 18 and 79 years.

16. (a) P(baby was postterm) = 0.056
(b) P(baby weighed 3000 to 3999 grams) = 0.656
(c) P(baby weighed 3000 to 3999 grams and was postterm) = 0.041
(d) P(baby weighed 3000 to 3999 grams or was postterm) = 0.672
(e) P(baby weighed < 1000 grams and was postterm) = 0.000007; this event is not impossible.
(f) P(baby weighed 3000 to 3999 grams | baby was postterm) = 0.724
(g) The events "postterm baby" and "weighs 3000 to 3999 grams" are not independent.

17. (a) P(trusts) = 0.18
(b) P(does not trust) = 0.82
(c) Yes, P(all three trust) = 0.006
(d) P(at least one of three does not trust) = 0.994
(e) No, P(all five do not trust) = 0.371
(f) P(at least one of five trusts) = 0.629

18. P(matching the three winning numbers) = 0.001

19. P(matching the four winning numbers) = 0.0001

20. P(drawing three aces) = 0.00018

21. $26^2 \cdot 10^4 = 6{,}760{,}000$ different license plates can be formed.

22. The students can be seated in ${}_{10}P_4 = 5040$ different arrangements.

23. There are $\frac{10!}{4! \cdot 3! \cdot 2!} = 12{,}600$ different vertical arrangements of the flags.

24. There are ${}_{55}C_8 = 1{,}217{,}566{,}350$ possible simple random samples.

25. $P(\text{winning Pick 5}) = \frac{1}{{}_{35}C_5} = \frac{1}{324{,}632} = 0.000003$

26. (a) P(three Merlot) = 0.0455
(b) P(two Merlot) = 0.3182
(c) P(no Merlot) = 0.1591

27. Answers will vary, but should be reasonably close to $\frac{1}{38}$ for part (a) and $\frac{1}{19}$ for part (b).

28. Answers will vary. Subjective probability is based on personal experience or intuition (e.g., "There is a 70% chance that the Packers will make it to the NFL playoffs in 2012.")

29. (a) There are 13 clubs in the deck.
(b) Thirty-seven cards remain in the deck. Forty-one cards are not known by you. Eight of the unknown cards are clubs.
(c) $P(\text{next card dealt is a club}) = \frac{8}{41}$
(d) P(two clubs in a row) = 0.0341
(e) No

30. (a) $P(\text{home run to left field}) = \frac{34}{70} = 0.486$; there is a 48.6% probability that a randomly selected home run by McGwire went to left field.
(b) P(home run to right field) = 0
(c) No; it was not impossible for McGwire to hit a home run to right field. He just never did it.

31. Someone winning a lottery twice is not that unlikely considering millions of people play lotteries who have already won a lottery (sometimes more than one) each week, and many lotteries have multiple drawings each week.

32. (a) $P(\text{Bryce}) = \frac{119}{1009} = 0.118$; not unusual
(b) $P(\text{Gourmet}) = \frac{264}{1009} = 0.262$
(c) $P(\text{Mallory} \mid \text{Single Cup}) = \frac{3}{25} = 0.12$
(d) $P(\text{Bryce} \mid \text{Gourmet}) = \frac{3}{88} = 0.034$; yes, this is unusual.
(e) While it is not unusual for Bryce to sell a case, it is unusual for him to sell a Gourmet case.
(f) No; $P(\text{Mallory}) = \frac{186}{1009} \neq P(\text{Mallory} \mid \text{Filter}) = \frac{1}{3}$.
(g) No; $P(\text{Paige and Gourmet}) = \frac{42}{1009} \neq 0$.

Chapter 5 Test (page 295)

1. Possible probabilities are 0.23, 0, $\frac{3}{4}$.

2. $P(\text{Jason}) = \frac{1}{5}$ **3.** $P(\text{Chris or Elaine}) = \frac{2}{5}$ **4.** $P(E^c) = \frac{4}{5}$

5. (a) $P(E \text{ or } F) = P(E) + P(F) = 0.59$
(b) $P(E \text{ and } F) = P(E) \cdot P(F) = 0.0814$

6. (a) $P(E \text{ and } F) = P(E) \cdot P(F \mid E) = 0.105$
(b) $P(E \text{ or } F) = P(E) + P(F) - P(E \text{ and } F) = 0.495$
(c) $P(E \mid F) = \frac{P(E \text{ and } F)}{P(F)} = \frac{7}{30} = 0.233$
(d) No; $P(E) = 0.15 \neq P(E \mid F) = 0.233$

7. (a) $8! = 40{,}320$ **(b)** ${}_{12}C_6 = 924$
(c) ${}_{14}P_8 = 121{,}080{,}960$

8. (a) $P(7 \text{ or } 11) = \frac{8}{36} = \frac{2}{9} = 0.222$; If the die are thrown 100 times, we would expect the player will win on the first roll about 22 times.
(b) $P(2, 3, \text{or } 12) = \frac{4}{36} = \frac{1}{9} = 0.111$; If the die are thrown 100 times, we would expect that the player will lose on the first roll about 11 times.

9. $P(\text{structure}) = 0.32$; $P(\text{not in a structure}) = 1 - P(\text{structure}) = 0.68$

10. (a) All the probabilities are greater than or equal to zero and less than or equal to one, and the sum of the probabilities is 1.
(b) P(a peanut butter cookie) = 0.24
(c) P(next box sold is mint, caramel, or shortbread) = 0.53
(d) P(next box sold is not mint) = 0.75

11. (a) $P(\text{ideal is 2}) = \frac{155}{297} = 0.522$

(b) $P(\text{female and ideal is 2}) = \frac{87}{297} = 0.293$

(c) $P(\text{female or ideal is 2}) = \frac{256}{297} = 0.862$

(d) $P(\text{ideal is 2} \mid \text{female}) = \frac{87}{188} = 0.463$

(e) $P(\text{male} \mid \text{ideal is 4}) = \frac{8}{36} = 0.222$

12. (a) $P(\text{win two in a row}) = 0.336$
(b) $P(\text{win seven in a row}) = 0.022$
(c) $P(\text{lose at least one of next seven}) = 1 - P(\text{win seven in a row}) = 0.978$

13. $P(\text{shipment accepted}) = 0.8$

14. There are $6! = 720$ different arrangements of the letters LINCEY.

15. ${}_{29}C_5 = 118{,}755$ different subcommittees can be formed.

16. $P(\text{winning Cash 5}) = \frac{1}{{}_{43}C_5} = \frac{1}{962{,}598} = 0.00000104$

17. $26 \cdot 36^7 = 2.04 \times 10^{12}$ different passwords are possible.

18. It would take 679,156 seconds (about 7.9 days) to generate all the passwords.

19. Subjective probability was used. It is not possible to repeat probability experiments to estimate the probability of life on Mars.

20. $\frac{15!}{2! \cdot 4! \cdot 4! \cdot 5!} = 9{,}459{,}450$ different sequences are possible.

21. $P(\text{guessing correctly}) = \frac{9}{40} = 0.225$

CHAPTER 6 Discrete Probability Distributions

6.1 Assess Your Understanding (page 305)

1. A random variable is a numerical measure of the outcome of a probability experiment.

2. A discrete random variable has either a finite number of values or a countable number of values. A continuous random variable has an infinite number of values that can be represented as an interval on a number line.

3. Each probability must be between 0 and 1, inclusive, and the sum of the probabilities must equal 1.

4. Answers will vary. One possibility: The mean of a discrete random variable can be thought of as the mean outcome when a probability experiment is repeated a large number of times.

5. (a) Discrete, $x = 0, 1, 2, \ldots, 20$ (b) Continuous, $t > 0$
(c) Discrete, $x = 0, 1, 2, \ldots$ (d) Continuous, $s \geq 0$

6. (a) Continuous, $t > 0$ (b) Continuous, $w > 0$
(c) Discrete, $x = 1, 2, \ldots$ (d) Discrete, $x = 0, 1, 2, \ldots, 20$

7. (a) Continuous, $r \geq 0$ (b) Discrete, $x = 0, 1, 2, 3, \ldots$
(c) Discrete, $x = 0, 1, 2, 3, \ldots$ (d) Continuous, $t > 0$

8. (a) Discrete, $x = 0, 1, 2, 3, \ldots$ (b) Continuous, $d > 0$
(c) Discrete, $x = 0, 1, 2, 3, \ldots$ (d) Continuous, $a > 0$

9. Yes, it is a probability distribution.

10. Yes, it is a probability distribution.

11. No, $P(50) < 0$.

12. Yes, it is a probability distribution.

13. No, $\Sigma P(x) \neq 1$

14. No, $\Sigma P(x) \neq 1$

15. $P(4) = 0.3$

16. $P(2) = 0.15$

17. (a) Each probability is between 0 and 1, inclusive, and the sum of the probabilities equals 1.

(b) **Televisions per Household**

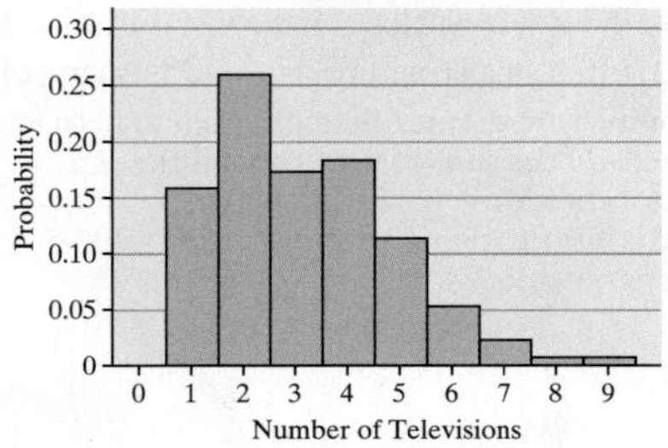

(c) $\mu_X = 3.2$ televisions; if we surveyed many households, we would expect the mean number of televisions per household to be 3.2.
(d) $\sigma_X = 1.7$ televisions
(e) $P(3) = 0.176$
(f) $P(3 \text{ or } 4) = 0.362$
(g) $P(0) = 0$; no, this is not an impossible event.

18. (a) Each probability is between 0 and 1, inclusive, and the sum of the probabilities equals 1.

(b) **Parental Involvement in School (child grades 6–8)**

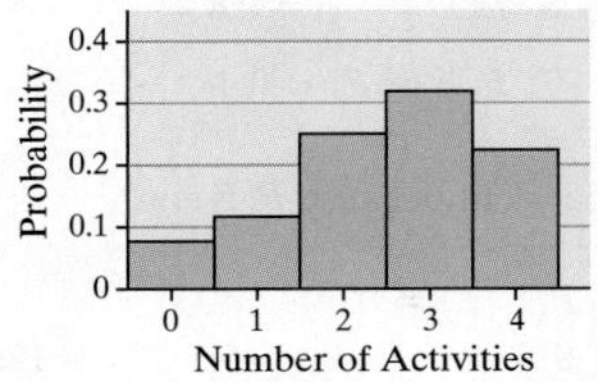

(c) $\mu_X = 2.5$ activities; on average, parents of 6th to 8th graders are involved in 2.5 activities.
(d) $\sigma_X = 1.2$ activities
(e) $P(3) = 0.322$
(f) $P(3 \text{ or } 4) = 0.552$

19. (a) Each probability is between 0 and 1, inclusive, and the sum of the probabilities equals 1.

(b) **Ichiro's Hit Parade**

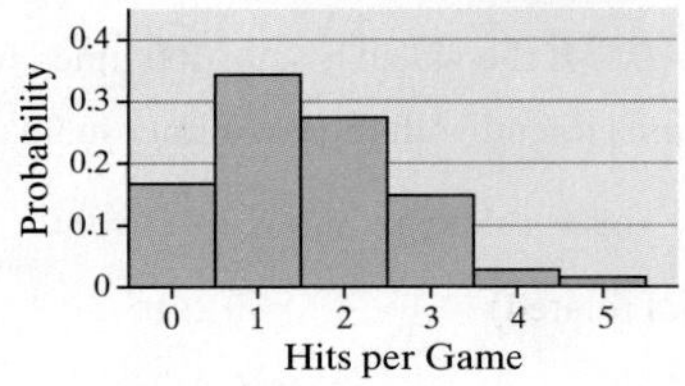

(c) $\mu_X = 1.6$ hits; over many games, Ichiro is expected to average about 1.6 hits per game.
(d) $\sigma_X = 1.2$ hits
(e) $P(2) = 0.2857$
(f) $P(X > 1) = 0.4969$

20. (a) All probabilities are between 0 and 1, inclusive, and the sum of the probabilities is 1.

(b) **Waiting in Line**

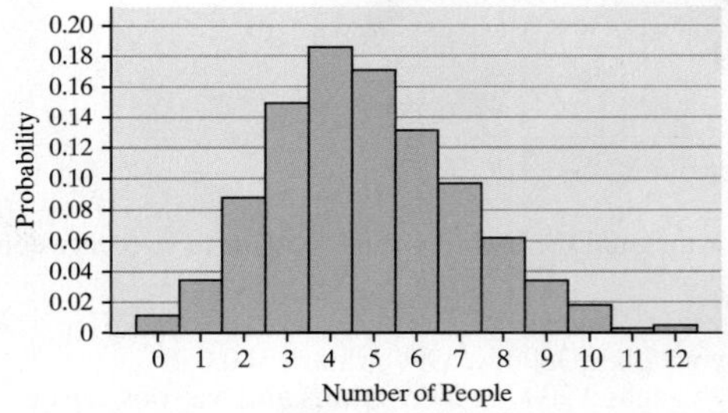

(c) $\mu_X = 4.9$ people; in the long run, the average number of people waiting in line during lunch is 4.9.
(d) $\sigma_X = 2.2$ people
(e) $P(8) = 0.063$
(f) $P(X \geq 10) = 0.029$; yes, this would be unusual

21. (a)

x (games played)	$P(x)$
4	0.1954
5	0.2069
6	0.2184
7	0.3793

(b)

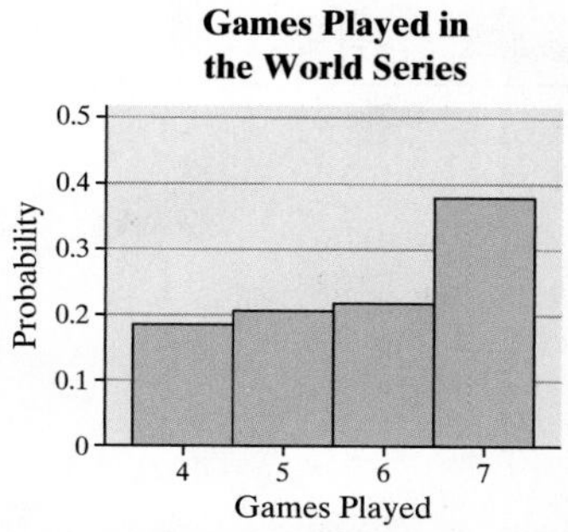

(c) $\mu_X = 5.8$ games; the World Series, if played many times, would be expected to last about 5.8 games, on average.

(d) $\sigma_X = 1.1$ games

22. (a)

x (number of children)	P(x)
0	0.0111
1	0.0333
2	0.5778
3	0.2778
4	0.0778
5	0.0189
6	0.0033

(b)

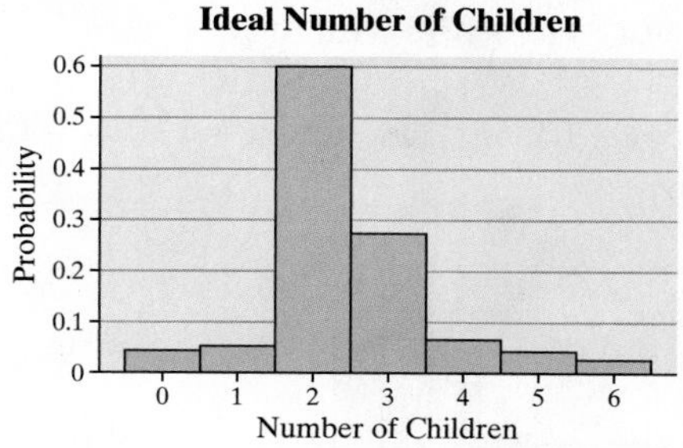

(c) $\mu_X = 2.4$; the mean ideal number of children for adult Americans is 2.4.

(d) $\sigma_X = 0.8$

23. (a)

x (stars)	P(x)
1	0.1160
2	0.0983
3	0.1777
4	0.1645
5	0.4435

(b)

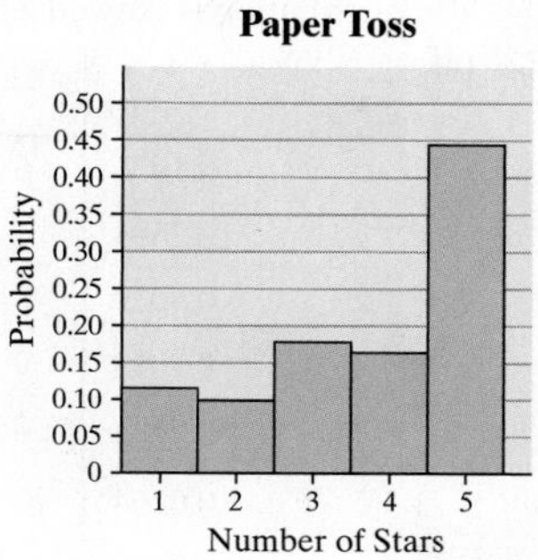

(c) $\mu_X = 3.7$; if we surveyed many Paper Toss players, the mean rating would be 3.7.

(d) $\sigma_X = 1.4$

24. (a)

x (tickets)	P(x)
0	0.8535
1	0.1061
2	0.0202
3	0.0202

(b)

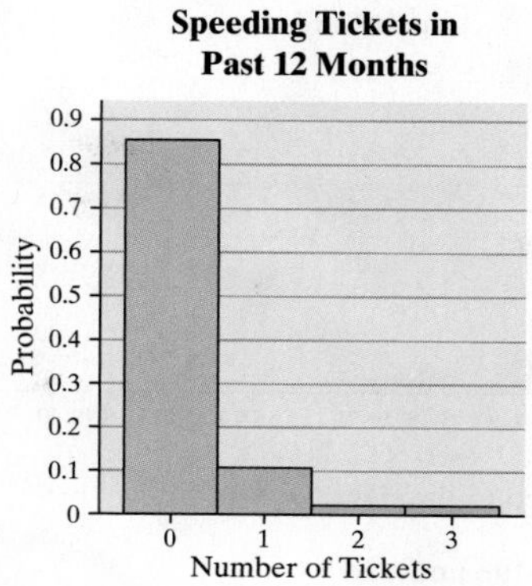

(c) $\mu_X = 0.2$; if we surveyed many drivers, the mean number of speeding tickets in the past 12 months would be 0.2.

(d) $\sigma_X = 0.6$

25. (a) $P(4) = 0.099$ **(b)** $P(4 \text{ or } 5) = 0.153$
(c) $P(X \geq 6) = 0.125$
(d) $\mu_X = 2.9$ children; we would expect the mother to have had 2.9 children, on average.

26. (a) $P(5) = 0.233$ **(b)** $P(5 \text{ or } 6) = 0.341$
(c) $P(7, 8, \text{or } 9) = 0.055$
(d) $\mu_X = 4.3$ rooms; we would expect a rental unit to have 4.3 rooms, on average.

27. $E(X) = \$86.00$; the insurance company expects to make an average profit of \$86.00 on every 20-year-old female it insures for 1 year.

28. $E(X) = \$33.50$; the insurance company expects to earn an average profit of \$33.50 on every 20-year-old male it insures for 1 year.

29. The expected profit is \$12,000.

30. The expected profit is \$15,000.

31. $E(X) = -\$0.26$; if you played 1000 times, you would expect to lose about \$260.

32. $E(X) = -\$0.42$; if the lottery is played many times, a player expects to lose \$0.42 per ticket.

33. (a) The expected cash prize is \$0.30. After paying \$1.00 to play, your expected profit is $-\$0.70$.
(b) A grand prize of \$118,000,000 has an expected profit greater than zero.
(c) The size of the grand prize does not affect the chance of winning provided the probabilities remain constant.

34. (a) A student who guesses will expect zero points.
(b) Answers will vary.

35. Answers will vary. The simulations illustrate the Law of Large Numbers.

36. Answers will vary. The simulations illustrate the Law of Large Numbers.

37. (a) 3.3 credit cards **(b)** 2.3 credit cards
(c)

x (credit cards)	P(x)
1	0.14375
2	0.275
3	0.26875
4	0.1125
5	0.08125
6	0.04375
7	0.025
8	0.01875
9	0.0125
10	0.0125
20	0.00625

(d)

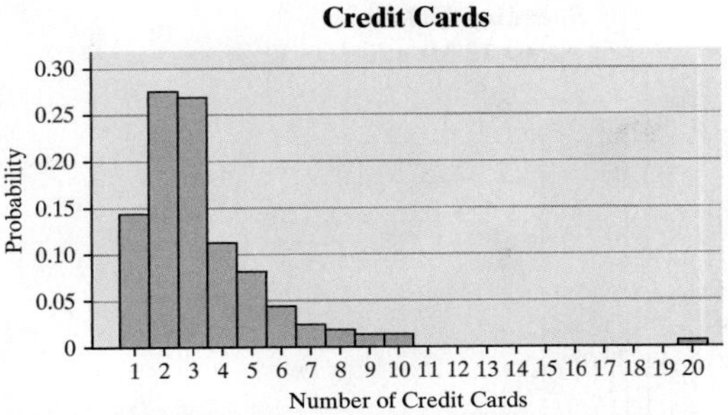

The distribution is skewed to the right.

(e) $\mu_X = 3.3; \sigma_X = 2.3$

(f) 0.05; this result is a little unusual.

(g) $P(\text{two with exactly two credit cards}) = 0.0744$. If we surveyed two individuals 100 different times, we would expect about 7 of the surveys to result in two people with two credit cards.

6.2 Assess Your Understanding (page 320)

1. trial **2.** success; failure **3.** True **4.** $\leq$ **5.** np **6.** $np(1-p) \geq 10$

7. Not binomial, because the random variable is continuous

8. Not binomial, because the random variable is continuous

9. Binomial **10.** Binomial

11. Not binomial, because the trials are not independent

12. Binomial

13. Not binomial, because the number of trials is not fixed

14. Not binomial, because the number of trials is not fixed

15. Binomial

16. Not binomial, because the trials are not independent

17. $P(3) = 0.2150$ **18.** $P(12) = 0.2184$ **19.** $P(38) = 0.0532$

20. $P(3) = 0.0607$ **21.** $P(3) = 0.2786$ **22.** $P(17) = 0.0123$

23. $P(X \leq 3) = 0.9144$ **24.** $P(X < 5) = 0.0949$

25. $P(X > 3) = 0.5$ **26.** $P(X \geq 12) = 0.8867$

27. $P(X \leq 4) = 0.5833$ **28.** $P(X \geq 8) = 0.7133$

29. (a)

x	$P(x)$	x	$P(x)$
0	0.1176	4	0.0595
1	0.3025	5	0.0102
2	0.3241	6	0.0007
3	0.1852		

(b) $\mu_X = 1.8; \sigma_X = 1.1$ **(c)** $\mu_X = 1.8; \sigma_X = 1.1$

(d)

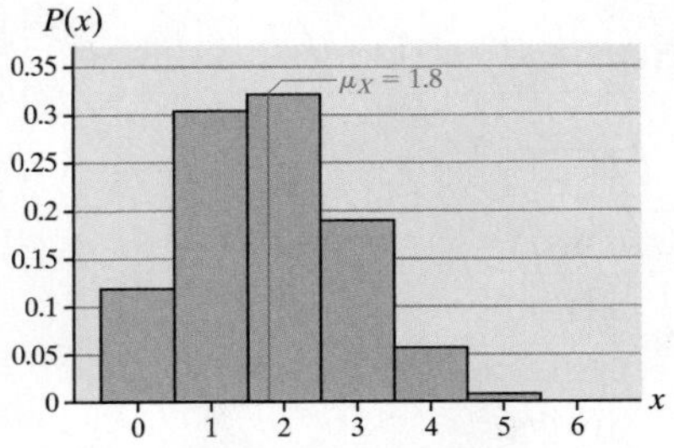

The distribution is skewed right.

30. (a)

x	$P(x)$	x	$P(x)$
0	0.0039	5	0.2188
1	0.0313	6	0.1094
2	0.1094	7	0.0313
3	0.2188	8	0.0039
4	0.2734		

(b) $\mu_X = 4; \sigma_X = 1.4$ **(c)** $\mu_X = 4; \sigma_X = 1.4$

(d)

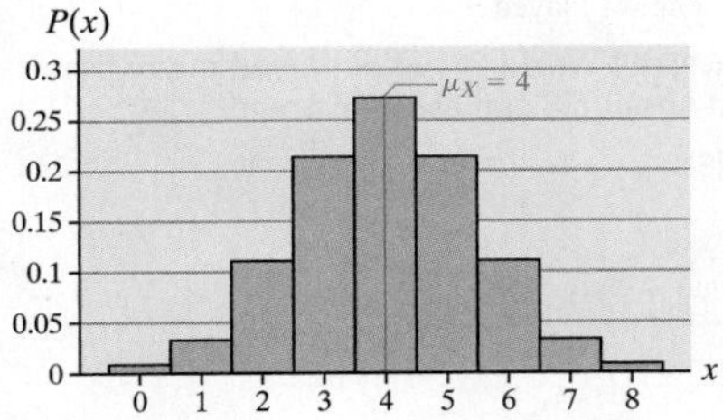

The distribution is symmetric.

31. (a)

x	$P(x)$	x	$P(x)$
0	0.0000	5	0.1168
1	0.0001	6	0.2336
2	0.0012	7	0.3003
3	0.0087	8	0.2253
4	0.0389	9	0.0751

(b) $\mu_X = 6.75; \sigma_X = 1.3$ **(c)** $\mu_X = 6.75; \sigma_X = 1.3$

(d)

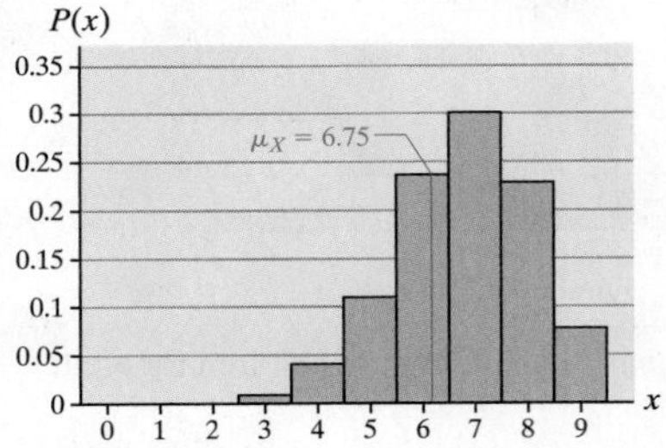

The distribution is skewed left.

32. (a)

x	$P(x)$	x	$P(x)$
0	0.1074	6	0.0055
1	0.2684	7	0.0008
2	0.3020	8	0.0001
3	0.2013	9	0.0000
4	0.0881	10	0.0000
5	0.0264		

(b) $\mu_X = 2; \sigma_X = 1.3$ **(c)** $\mu_X = 2; \sigma_X = 1.3$

(d)

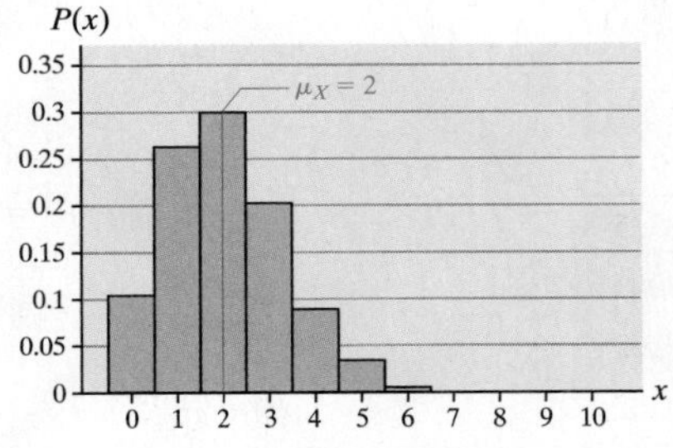

The distribution is skewed right.

33. (a)

x	$P(x)$	x	$P(x)$
0	0.0010	6	0.2051
1	0.0098	7	0.1172
2	0.0439	8	0.0439
3	0.1172	9	0.0098
4	0.2051	10	0.0010
5	0.2461		

(b) $\mu_X = 5; \sigma_X = 1.6$ **(c)** $\mu_X = 5; \sigma_X = 1.6$

(d)

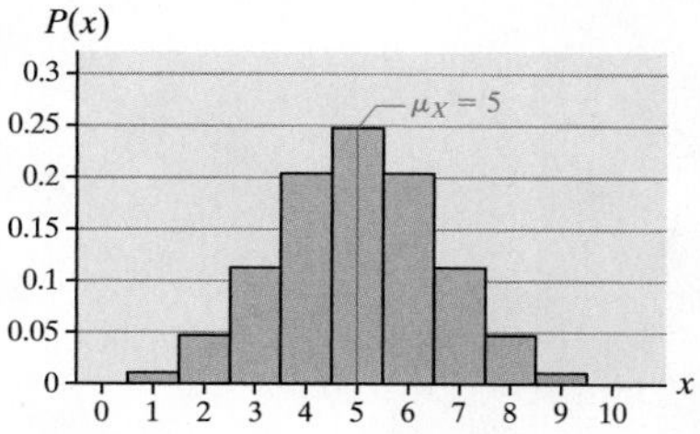

The distribution is symmetric.

34. (a)

x	$P(x)$	x	$P(x)$
0	0.0000	5	0.0661
1	0.0000	6	0.1762
2	0.0003	7	0.3020
3	0.0028	8	0.3020
4	0.0165	9	0.1342

(b) $\mu_X = 7.2; \sigma_X = 1.2$ **(c)** $\mu_X = 7.2; \sigma_X = 1.2$

(d)

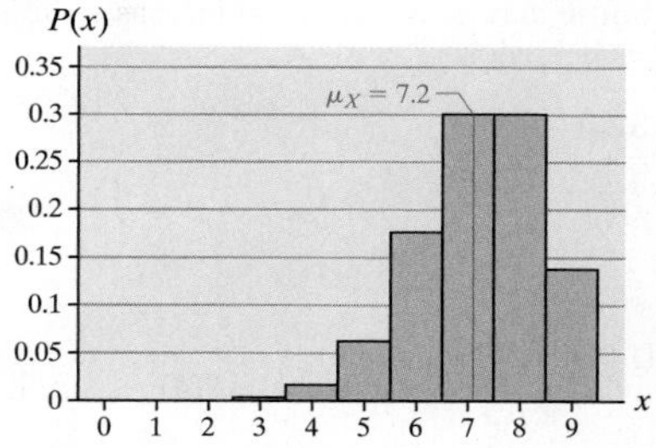

The distribution is skewed left.

35. (a) This is a binomial experiment because:
1. It is performed a fixed number of times, $n = 15$.
2. The trials are independent.
3. For each trial, there are two possible mutually exclusive outcomes: on time and not on time.
4. The probability of "on time" is fixed at $p = 0.80$.
(b) $P(10) = 0.1032$; in 100 trials of this experiment, we expect about 10 trials to result in exactly 10 flights being on time.
(c) $P(X < 10) = 0.0611$; in 100 trials of this experiment, we expect about 6 trials to result in fewer than 10 flights being on time.
(d) $P(X \geq 10) = 0.9389$; in 100 trials of this experiment, we expect about 94 trials to result in at least 10 flights being on time.
(e) $P(8 \leq X \leq 10) = 0.16$; in 100 trials of this experiment, we expect about 16 trials to result in between 8 and 10 flights, inclusive, being on time.

36. (a) This is a binomial experiment because:
1. It is performed a fixed number of times, $n = 10$.
2. The trials are independent.
3. For each trial, there are two possible mutually exclusive outcomes: started smoking before turning 21 years old, started smoking at or after 21 years old.
4. The probability of "starting to smoke before 21 years of age" is fixed at $p = 0.90$.
(b) $P(8) = 0.1937$; in 100 trials of this experiment, we expect about 19 trials to result in exactly 8 adult smokers who started smoking before age 21.
(c) $P(X < 8) = 0.0702$; in 100 trials of this experiment, we expect about 7 trials to result in fewer than 8 adult smokers who started smoking before age 21.
(d) $P(X \geq 8) = 0.9298$; in 100 trials of this experiment, we expect about 93 trials to result in at least 8 adult smokers who started smoking before age 21.
(e) $P(7 \leq X \leq 9) = 0.6385$; in 100 trials of this experiment, we expect about 64 trials to result in between 7 and 9 adult smokers, inclusive, who started smoking before age 21.

37. (a) $P(15) = 0.0520$; in 100 trials of this experiment, we expect about 5 trials to result in exactly 15 adult Americans who feel the state of morals is poor.
(b) $P(X \leq 10) = 0.3843$; in 100 trials of this experiment, we expect about 38 trials to result in no more than 10 adult Americans who feel the state of morals is poor.
(c) $P(X > 16) = 0.0174$; in 100 trials of this experiment, we expect about 2 trials to result in more than 16 adult Americans who feel the state of morals is poor.
(d) $P(13 \text{ or } 14) = 0.2103$; in 100 trials of this experiment, we expect about 21 trials to result in 13 or 14 adult Americans who feel the state of morals is poor.
(e) Yes; $P(X \geq 20) = 0.0004$

38. (a) $P(3) = 0.0596$ **(b)** $P(X \leq 3) = 0.9841$
(c) $P(1 \leq X \leq 4) = 0.6389$
(d) It would be unusual to find 4 or more patients who experienced insomnia as a side effect because $P(X \geq 4) = 0.0159 < 0.05$.

39. (a) $P(4) = 0.1655$ **(b)** $P(X < 3) = 0.4752$
(c) Yes; the probability is 0.0272.

40. (a) $P(2) = 0.1240$ **(b)** $P(X < 3) = 0.9691$
(c) Yes; $P(X > 4) = 0.0005$

41. (a) 0.1667 **(b)** $P(X \leq 2) = 0.0421$
(c) The number of Hispanics on the jury is unusually low, given the composition of the population from which it came.

42. $P(X \geq 17) = 0.0348$; in 100 trials of this experiment, we expect about 3 trials to result in at least 17 red cars.

43. (a) $\mu_X = 80$ flights; $\sigma_X = 4$ flights
(b) We expect that, in a random sample of 100 flights from Orlando to Los Angeles, 80 will be on time.
(c) It would not be unusual to have 75 on-time flights because 75 is within 2 standard deviations of the mean.

44. (a) $\mu_X = 180; \sigma_X = 4.2$
(b) In a random sample of 200 adult smokers, we expect 180 to report that they started smoking before turning 21 years old.
(c) No, because 185 is within 2 standard deviations of the mean.

45. (a) $\mu_X = 225; \sigma_X = 11.1$
(b) In a random sample of 500 adult Americans, we expect 225 to believe that the overall state of moral values in the United States is poor.
(c) No, $\mu - 2\sigma_X < 240 < \mu + 2\sigma_X$

46. (a) $E(X) = 12$ patients with insomnia
(b) It would be unusual to observe 20 patients with insomnia, because 20 is more than 2 standard deviations above the mean.

47. We would expect 824 out of 1030 parents to spank their children. The results suggest that parents' attitudes have changed since $781 < \mu_X - 2\sigma_X = 824 - 2(12.8) = 798.4$.

48. We would expect 121 out of 1100 adult Americans to have confidence in the federal goverment. Since $84 < \mu_X - 2\sigma_X = 121 - 2(10.4) = 100.2$, it seems that American adults may have less confidence in the federal government at the time of the survey than they did in 2000.

49. Yes; it would be unusual, because 600 is more than 2 standard deviations above the mean.

50. It would not be unusual to observe 86 patients who experience headaches, because 86 is within 2 standard deviations of the mean.

51. We would expect $500{,}000(0.56) = 280{,}000$ of the stops to be pedestrians who are nonwhite. Because $500{,}000(0.56)(1 - 0.56) = 123{,}200 \geq 10$, we can use the Empirical Rule to identify cutoff points for unusual results. The standard deviation number of stops is 351. If the number of stops of nonwhite pedestrians exceeds $280{,}000 + 2(351) = 280{,}702$, we would say the result is unusual. The actual number of stops is $500{,}000(0.89) = 445{,}000$, which is definitely unusual. A potential criticism of this analysis is the use of 0.44 as the proportion of whites, since the actual proportion of whites may be different due to individuals commuting back and forth to the city.

52. (a), (b) Answers will vary.
(c) $P(29) = 0.3340$
(d) Answers will vary.
(e) $P(X \le 27) = 0.0217$
(f) Simulated mean will vary. $E(X) = 29.4$ males.
(g) Simulated standard deviation will vary. $\sigma_X = 0.8$.
(h) Answers will vary.

53. (a) You would select 20 high school students.
(b) You would select 33 high school students.

54. (a) You would select 38 residents 25 years and older.
(b) You would select 65 residents 25 years and older.

55. An experiment is binomial provided
1. The experiment consists of a fixed number, n, of trials.
2. The trials are independent.
3. Each trial has two possible mutually exclusive outcomes: success and failure.
4. The probability of success, p, remains constant for each trial of the experiment.

56. Success means the outcome you are measuring.

57. As n increases, the binomial distribution becomes more bell shaped.

58. When n is small, the shape of the binomial distribution is determined by p. If p is close to zero, the distribution is skewed right; if p is close to 0.5, the distribution is approximately symmetric; and if p is close to 1, the distribution is skewed left.

59. When the binomial distribution is approximately bell shaped, about 95% of the outcomes are in the interval from $\mu - 2\sigma$ to $\mu + 2\sigma$. The Empirical Rule can be used when $np(1 - p) \ge 10$.

Chapter 6 Review Exercises (page 324)

1. (a) Discrete, $s = 0, 1, 2, \ldots$ **(b)** Continuous, $s \ge 0$
(c) Continuous, $h \ge 0$ **(d)** Discrete, $x = 0, 1, 2, \ldots$

2. (a) It is not a probability distribution because $\Sigma P(x) \ne 1$.
(b) It is a probability distribution.

3. (a)

x	$P(x)$
4	0.2778
5	0.2361
6	0.2639
7	0.2222

(b)

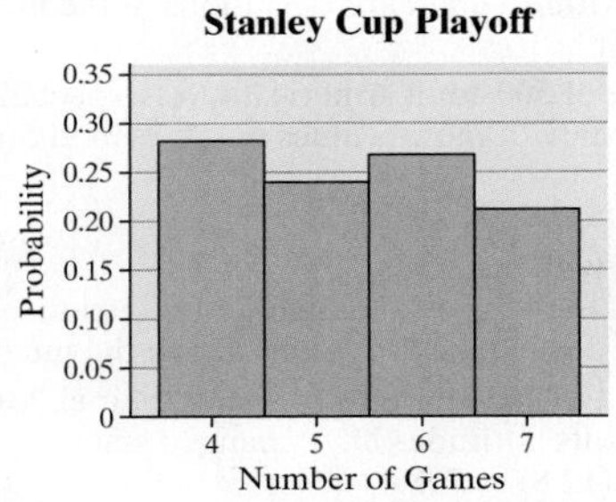

(c) $\mu_X = 5.4$ games; on average, we expect the Stanley Cup playoff to require 5.4 games.
(d) $\sigma_X = 1.1$ games

4. (a) $E(X) = -\$0.12$ **(b)** \$16.80

5. (a) Binomial experiment
(b) Not a binomial experiment because the number of trials is not fixed.

6. (a) $P(1) = 0.3151$ **(b)** $P(X < 2) = 0.6424$
(c) $P(X \ge 2) = 0.3576$ **(d)** $P(X \le 2) = 0.9885$
(e) No; $P(X > 3) = 0.0608$ **(f)** $\mu_X = 50; \sigma_X = 6.9$
(g) When $n = 800$, $\mu_X = 40$ and $\sigma_X = 6.2$, so 51 lies within two standard deviations of the mean. The hospital should not be investigated.

7. (a) $P(10) = 0.1859$
(b) $P(X < 5) = 0.0093$
(c) $P(X \ge 5) = 0.9907$
(d) $P(7 \le X \le 12) = 0.8779$ (tech: 0.8778)
(e) $\mu_X = 120$ women; $\sigma_X = 6.9$ women
(f) It would not be unusual to have 110 females in a sample of 200 believe that the driving age should be 18, because 110 is within 2 standard deviations of the mean.

8. (a)

x	$P(x)$	x	$P(x)$
0	0.00002	5	0.20764
1	0.00037	6	0.31146
2	0.00385	7	0.26697
3	0.02307	8	0.10011
4	0.08652		

(b) $\mu_X = 6; \sigma_X = 1.2$
(c)

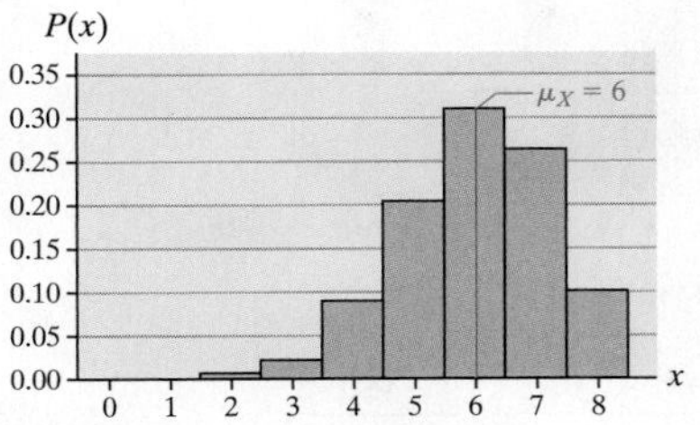

The distribution is skewed left.

9. As a rule of thumb, if X is binomially distributed, the Empirical Rule can be used when $np(1 - p) \ge 10$.

10. We can sample without replacement and use the binomial probability distribution to approximate probabilities when the sample size is small in relation to the population size. As a rule of thumb, if the sample size is less than 5% of the population size, the trials can be considered nearly independent.

11. $P(X \ge 12) = 0.03$, so the result of the survey is unusual. This suggests that emotional abuse may be a factor that increases the likelihood of self-injurious behavior.

Chapter 6 Test (page 326)

1. (a) Discrete; $r = 0, 1, 2, \ldots, 365$
(b) Continuous; $m > 0$
(c) Discrete; $x = 0, 1, 2, \ldots$
(d) Continuous; $w > 0$

2. (a) It is a probability distribution.
(b) It is not a probability distribution because $P(4) = -0.11$, which is negative.

3. (a)

x	$P(x)$
3	0.43
4	0.27
5	0.30

(b)

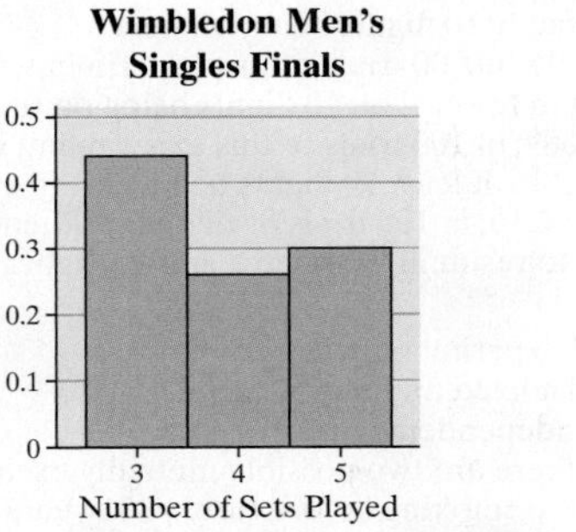

(c) $\mu_X = 3.9$ sets. On average, we expect the Wimbledon men's singles final match for the championship to require 3.9 sets of play.
(d) $\sigma_X = 0.8$ sets

4. $E(X) = 72.50$; the insurance company expects to earn an average profit of \$72.50 for each 35-year-old male it insures for 1 year for \$100,000.

5. An experiment is binomial provided:
1. The experiment consists of a fixed number, n, of trials.
2. The trials are independent.
3. Each trial has two possible mutually exclusive outcomes: success and failure.
4. The probability of success, p, remains constant for each trial of the experiment.

6. (a) Not a binomial experiment because the trials are not independent and the number of trials is not fixed
(b) Binomial experiment

7. (a) $P(15) = 0.1746$; in 100 trials of this experiment, we expect about 17 trials to result in exactly 15 married people who hide purchases from their mates.
(b) $P(X \geq 19) = 0.0692$; in 100 trials of this experiment, we expect about 7 trials to result in at least 19 married people who hide purchases from their mates.
(c) $P(X < 19) = 0.9308$; in 100 trials of this experiment, we expect about 93 trials to result in fewer than 19 married people who hide purchases from their mates.
(d) $P(15 \leq X \leq 17) = 0.5981$; in 100 trials of this experiment, we expect about 60 trials to result in between 15 and 17 married people, inclusive, who hide purchases from their mates.

8. (a) We would expect 600 out of 1200 adult Americans to say they pay too much tax.
(b) We can use the Empirical Rule to identify unusual events since $np(1-p) = 300 \geq 10$.
(c) Yes; these results do contradict the belief since 640 is more than two standard deviations above the mean.

9. (a)

x	$P(x)$
0	0.3277
1	0.4096
2	0.2048
3	0.0512
4	0.0064
5	0.0003

(b) $\mu_X = 1$; $\sigma_X = 0.9$

(c)

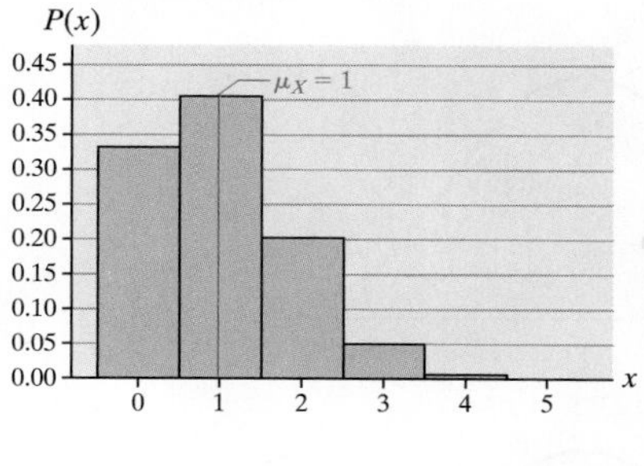

CHAPTER 7 The Normal Probability Distribution

7.1 Assess Your Understanding (page 335)

1. probability density function

2. model

3. True

4. $\frac{1}{2}$

5. $\mu - \sigma$; $\mu + \sigma$

6. probability; proportion

7. This graph is not symmetric; it cannot represent a normal density function.

8. The graph can represent a normal density function.

9. This graph is not always greater than zero; it cannot represent a normal density function.

10. This graph increases as the value of X becomes very large or very small; it cannot represent a normal density function.

11. The graph can represent a normal density function.

12. This graph is not bell-shaped; it cannot represent a normal density function.

13. (a) $P(5 \leq X \leq 10) = \frac{1}{6}$ **(b)** 12

14. (a) $P(15 \leq X \leq 25) = \frac{1}{3}$ **(b)** 27

15. $P(X \geq 20) = \frac{1}{3}$

16. $P(X \leq 5) = \frac{1}{6}$

17. (a)

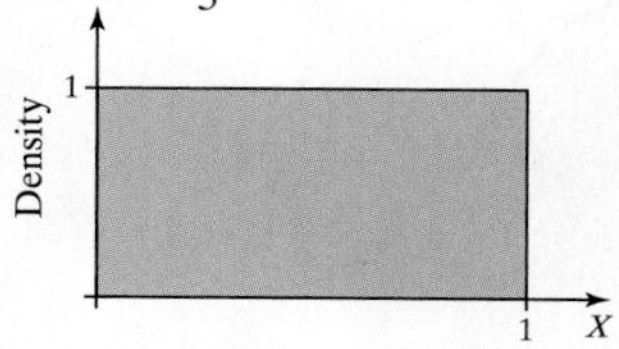

(b) $P(0 \leq X \leq 0.2) = 0.2$
(c) $P(0.25 \leq X \leq 0.6) = 0.35$
(d) $P(X > 0.95) = 0.05$
(e) Answers will vary.

18. (a)

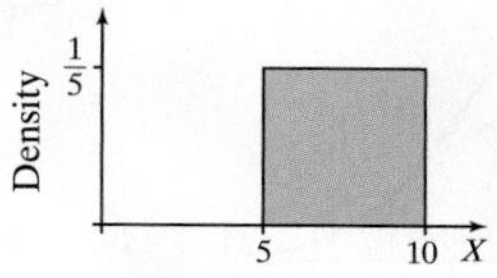

(b) $P(6 \leq X \leq 8) = \frac{2}{5} = 0.4$
(c) $P(5 \leq X \leq 8) = \frac{3}{5} = 0.6$
(d) $P(X \leq 6) = \frac{1}{5} = 0.2$

19. Normal

20. Not normal

21. Not normal

22. Normal

23. Graph A: $\mu = 10, \sigma = 2$; graph B: $\mu = 10, \sigma = 3$. A larger standard deviation makes the graph lower and more spread out.

24. Graph A: $\mu = 8, \sigma = 2$; graph B: $\mu = 14, \sigma = 2$. A larger mean shifts the graph to the right.

25. $\mu = 2, \sigma = 3$

26. $\mu = 5, \sigma = 2$

27. $\mu = 100, \sigma = 15$

28. $\mu = 530, \sigma = 100$

29.

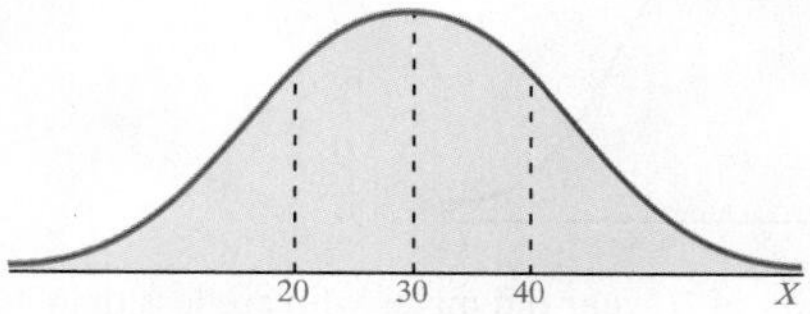

30.

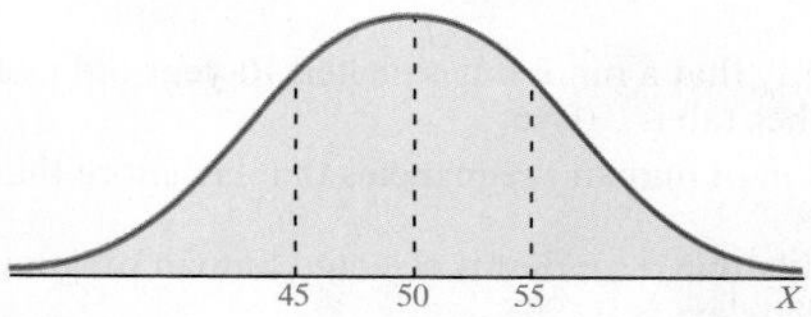

31. (a)

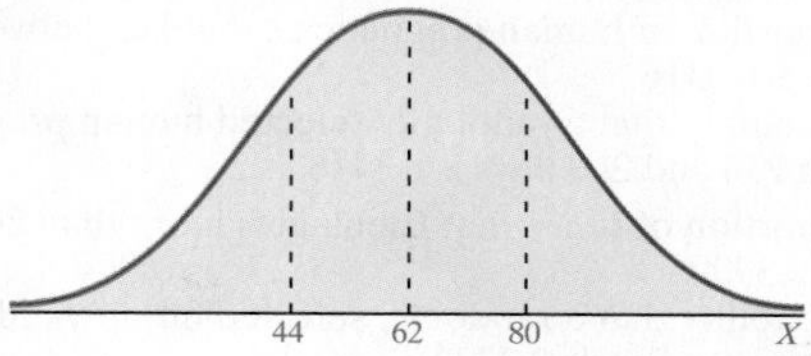

(b)

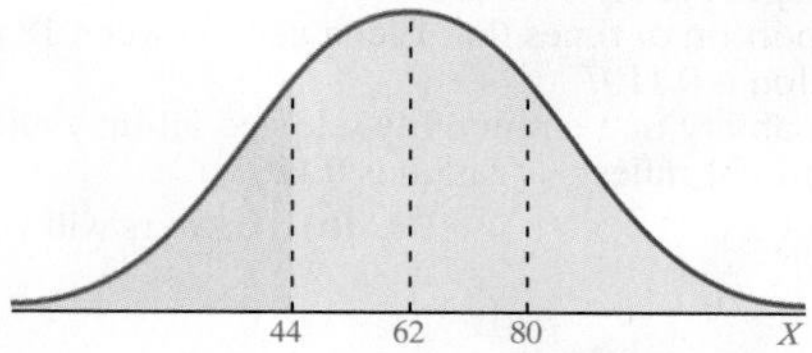

(c) (i) 15.87% of the cell phone plans in the United States are less than \$44.00 per month.

(ii) The probability is 0.1587 that a randomly selected cell phone plan in the United States is less than \$44.00 per month.

32. (a)

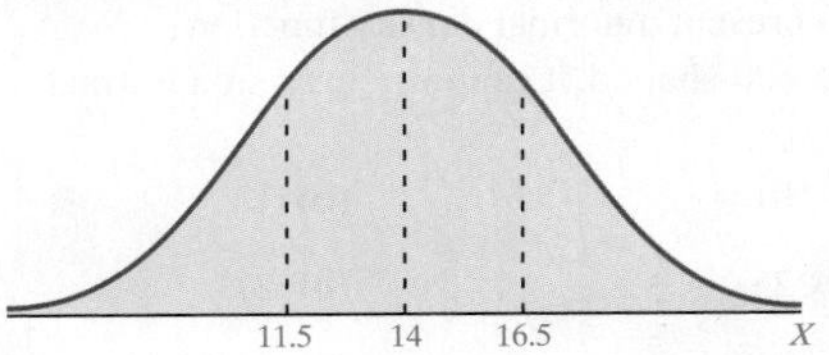

(b)

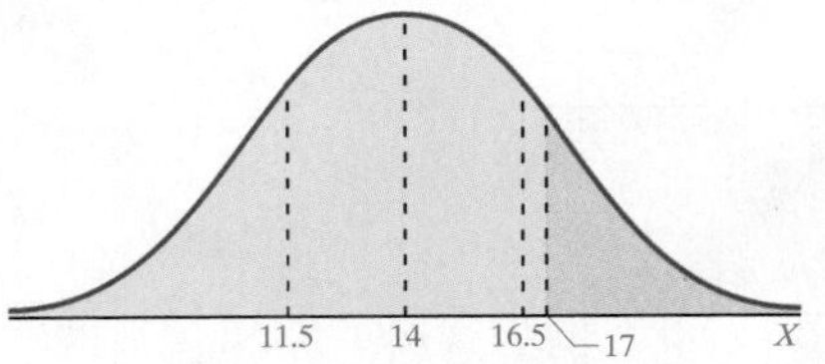

(c) (i) 11.51% of all refrigerators are kept for more than 17 years.
(ii) The probability is 0.1151 that a randomly selected refrigerator is more than 17 years old.

33. (a)

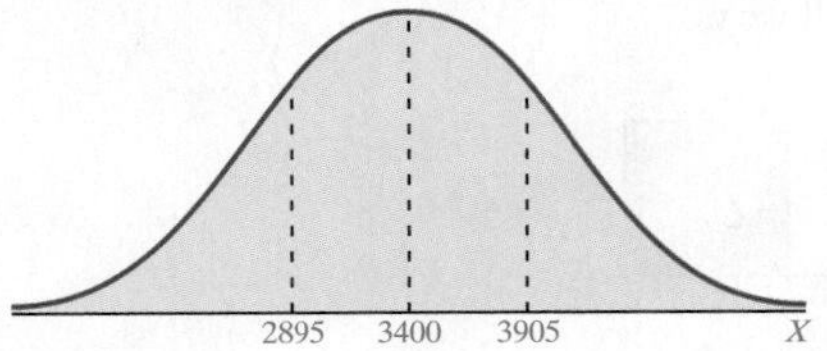

(b)

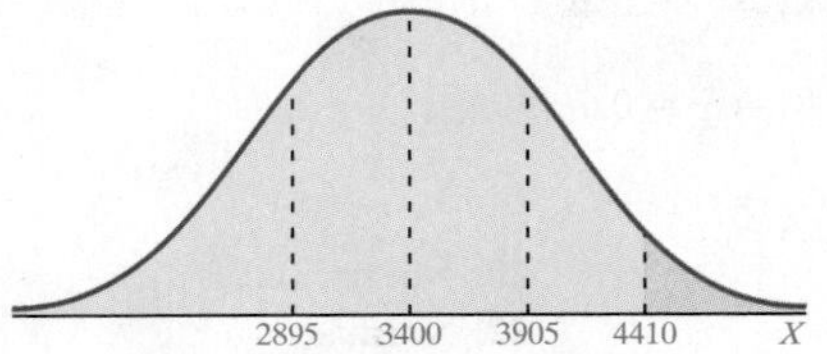

(c) (i) 2.28% of all full-term babies have a birth weight of more than 4410 grams.
(ii) The probability is 0.0228 that the birth weight of a randomly chosen full-term baby is more than 4410 grams.

34. (a), (b)

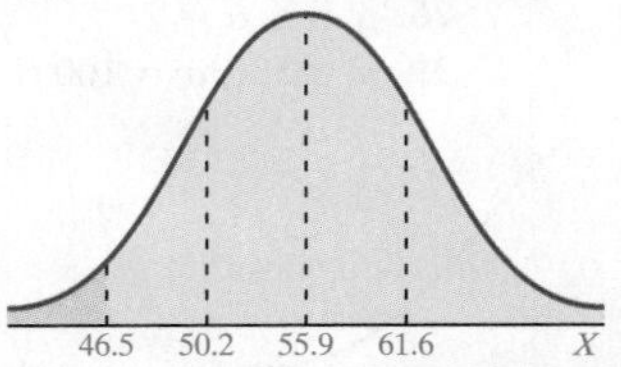

(c) (i) The proportion of 10-year-old males who are less than 46.5 inches tall is 0.0496.
(ii) The probability that a randomly selected 10-year-old male is less than 46.5 inches tall is 0.0496.

35. (a) (i) The proportion of human pregnancies that last more than 280 days is 0.1908.
(ii) The probability that a randomly selected human pregnancy lasts more than 280 days is 0.1908.
(b) (i) The proportion of human pregnancies that last between 230 and 260 days is 0.3416.
(ii) The probability that a randomly selected human pregnancy lasts between 230 and 260 days is 0.3416.

36. (a) (i) The proportion of times that Elena gets more than 26 miles per gallon is 0.3309.
(ii) The probability that a randomly selected fill-up yields at least 26 miles per gallon is 0.3309.
(b) (i) The proportion of times that Elena gets between 18 and 21 miles per gallon is 0.1107.
(ii) The probability that a randomly selected fill-up yields between 18 and 21 miles per gallon is 0.1107.

37. (b) Answers will vary. **38. (b)** Answers will vary.

7.2 Assess Your Understanding (page 345)

1. standard normal distribution
2. α **3.** 0.3085 **4.** 0.4207
5. (a) Area = 0.0071 **(b)** Area = 0.3336
(c) Area = 0.9115 **(d)** Area = 0.9998
6. (a) Area = 0.0002 **(b)** Area = 0.0233
(c) Area = 0.8212 **(d)** Area = 0.9981
7. (a) Area = 0.9987 **(b)** Area = 0.9441
(c) Area = 0.0375 **(d)** Area = 0.0009
8. (a) Area = 0.9998 **(b)** Area = 0.7088
(c) Area = 0.0129 **(d)** Area = 0.0003
9. (a) Area = 0.9586 **(b)** Area = 0.2088
(c) Area = 0.8479
10. (a) Area = 0.9892 **(b)** Area = 0.4525
(c) Area = 0.9749
11. (a) Area = 0.0456 [Tech: 0.0455] **(b)** Area = 0.0646
(c) Area = 0.5203 [Tech: 0.5202]
12. (a) Area = 0.0032 [Tech: 0.0033] **(b)** Area = 0.0476
(c) Area = 0.2987 [Tech: 0.2988]
13. $z = -1.28$ **14.** $z = -0.84$ **15.** $z = 0.67$
16. $z = 0.39$ **17.** $z_1 = -2.575$; $z_2 = 2.575$
18. $z_1 = -1.88$; $z_2 = 1.88$ **19.** $z_{0.01} = 2.33$
20. $z_{0.02} = 2.05$ **21.** $z_{0.025} = 1.96$ **22.** $z_{0.15} = 1.04$

23.

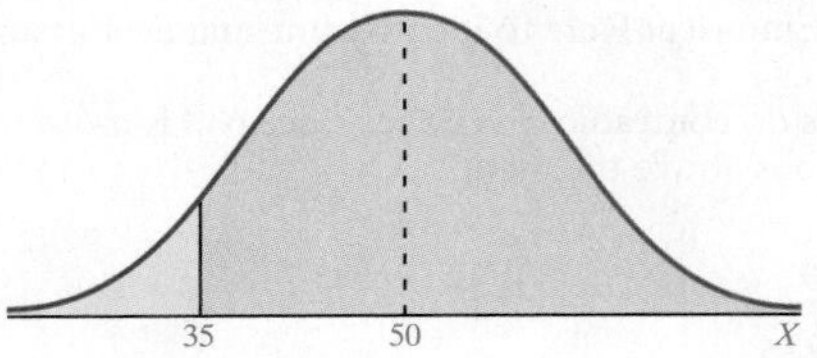

$P(X > 35) = 0.9838$
Tech: $P(X > 35) = 0.9839$

24.

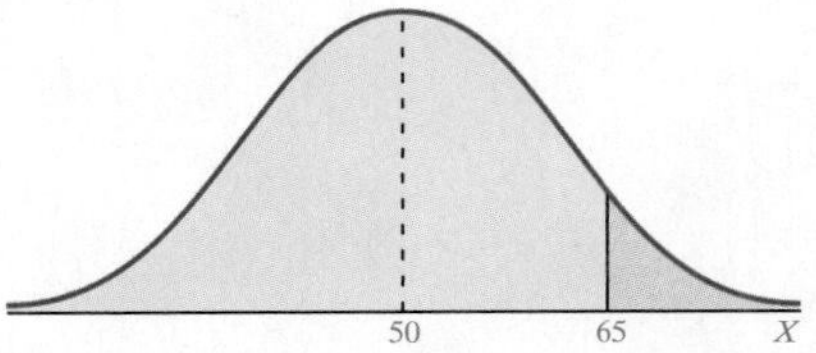

$P(X > 65) = 0.0162$
Tech: $P(X > 65) = 0.0161$

25.

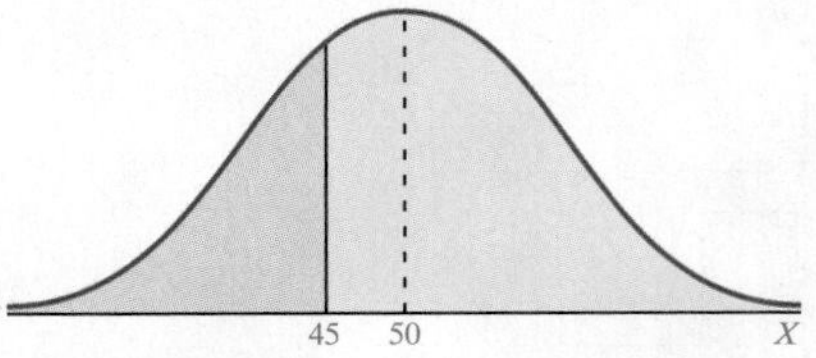

$P(X \leq 45) = 0.2389$
Tech: $P(X \leq 45) = 0.2375$

26.

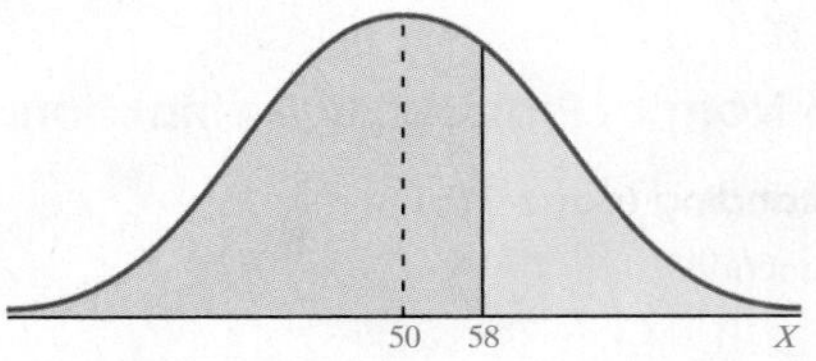

$P(X \leq 58) = 0.8729$
Tech: $P(X \leq 58) = 0.8735$

27.

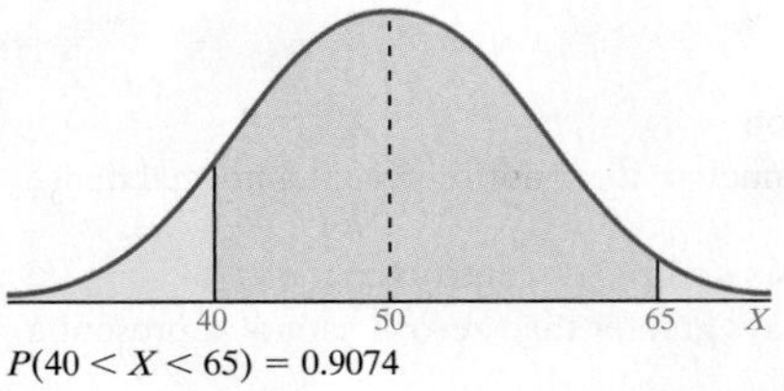

$P(40 < X < 65) = 0.9074$

28.

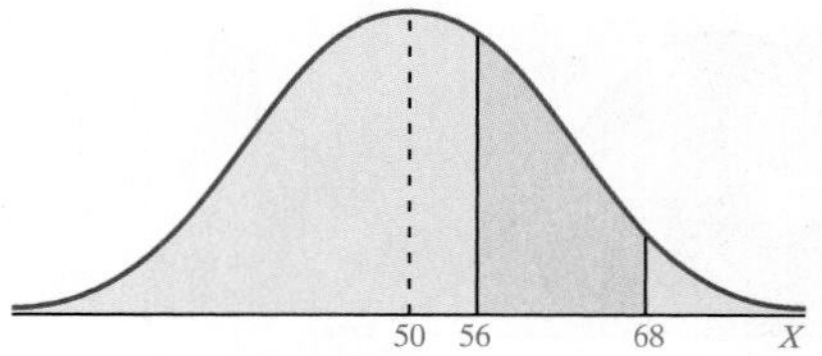

$P(56 < X < 68) = 0.1898$
Tech: $P(56 < X < 68) = 0.1906$

29.

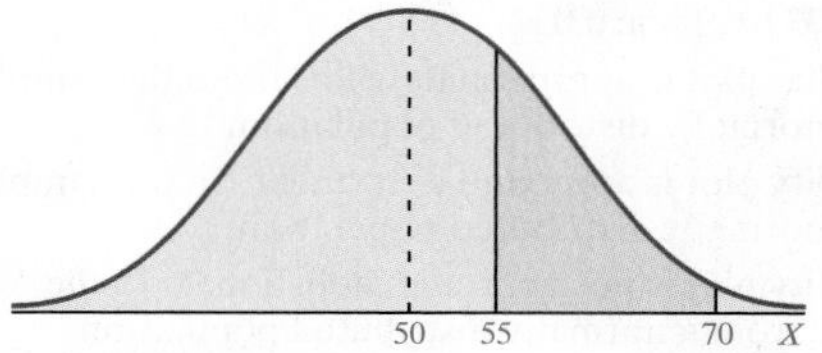

$P(55 \leq X \leq 70) = 0.2368$
Tech: $P(55 \leq X \leq 70) = 0.2354$

30.

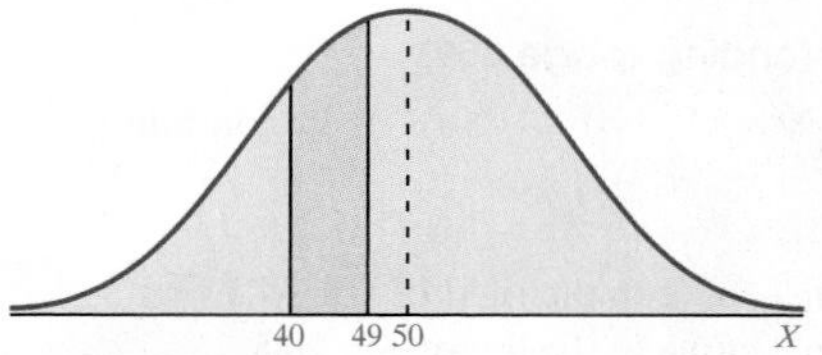

$P(40 \leq X \leq 49) = 0.3679$
Tech: $P(40 \leq X \leq 49) = 0.3666$

31.

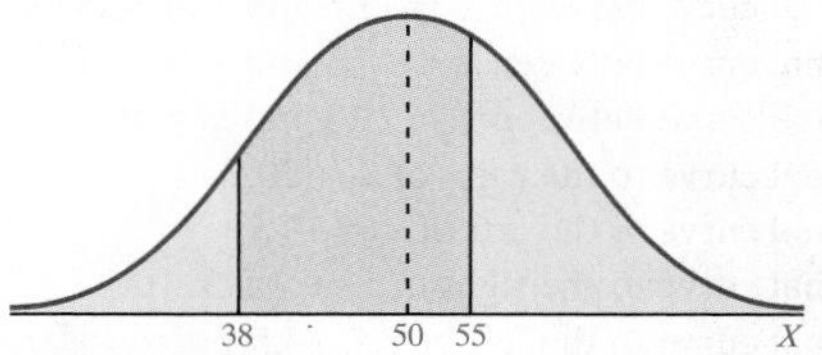

$P(38 < X \leq 55) = 0.7175$
Tech: $P(38 < X \leq 55) = 0.7192$

32.

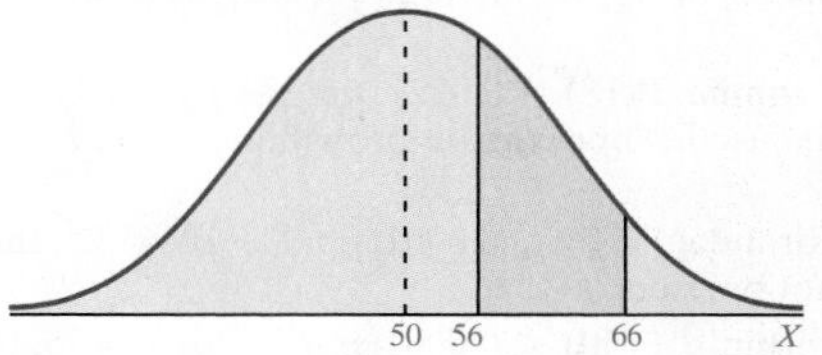

$P(56 \leq X < 66) = 0.1839$
Tech: $P(56 \leq X < 66) = 0.1845$

33. $x = 40.62$ (Tech: 40.61) is at the 9th percentile.
34. $x = 58.96$ (Tech: 58.97) is at the 90th percentile.
35. $x = 56.16$ (Tech: 56.15) is at the 81st percentile.
36. $x = 47.83$ (Tech: 47.86) is at the 38th percentile.
37. **(a)** $P(X < 20) = 0.1587$
(b) $P(X > 22) = 0.1587$
(c) $P(19 \leq X \leq 21) = 0.4772$
(d) Yes; $P(X < 18) = 0.0013$. About 1 egg in 1000 hatches in less than 18 days.
38. **(a)** $P(X < 100) = 0.1492$ (Tech: 0.1488)
(b) $P(X > 140) = 0.2643$ (Tech: 0.2660)
(c) $P(110 \leq X \leq 130) = 0.3189$ (Tech: 0.3165)
(d) Yes; $P(X > 200) = 0.0009$, so less than 1 student in 1000 can read more than 200 words per minute.
39. **(a)** $P(1000 \leq X \leq 1400) = 0.8658$ (Tech: 0.8657)
(b) $P(X < 1000) = 0.0132$
(c) 0.7019 (Tech: 0.7004) of the bags have more than 1200 chocolate chips.
(d) 0.1230 (Tech: 0.1228) of the bags have fewer than 1125 chocolate chips.
(e) A bag that contains 1475 chocolate chips is at the 96th percentile.
(f) A bag that contains 1050 chocolate chips is at the 4th percentile.
40. **(a)** $P(X < 100) = 0.0918$ (Tech: 0.0922)
(b) $P(X > 160) = 0.2296$ (Tech: 0.2292)
(c) $P(120 \leq X \leq 180) = 0.6625$ (Tech: 0.6620)
(d) $P(X > 180) = 0.0764$ (Tech: 0.0762). No; about 8 cars in 100 will spend more than 3 minutes in the drive-through.
41. **(a)** 0.4013 of pregnancies last more than 270 days.
(b) 0.1587 of pregnancies last fewer than 250 days.
(c) 0.7590 (Tech: 0.7571) of pregnancies last between 240 and 280 days.
(d) $P(X > 280) = 0.1894$ (Tech: 0.1908)
(e) $P(X \leq 245) = 0.0951$ (Tech: 0.0947)
(f) Yes; 0.0043 of births are very preterm. So about 4 births in 1000 births are very preterm.
42. **(a)** 0.1894 (Tech: 0.1902) of the light bulbs last less than the advertised time.
(b) 0.0401 (Tech: 0.0397) of the light bulbs last more than 1650 hours.
(c) $P(1625 \leq X \leq 1725) = 0.0923$ (Tech: 0.0931)
(d) $P(X > 1400) = 0.9957$ (Tech: 0.9958)
43. **(a)** 0.0764 (Tech: 0.0766) of the rods have a length of less than 24.9 cm.
(b) 0.0324 (Tech: 0.0321) of the rods will be discarded.
(c) The plant manager expects to discard 162 (Tech: 161) of the 5000 rods manufactured.
(d) To meet the order, the plant manager should manufacture 11,804 (Tech: 11,808) rods.
44. **(a)** 0.0668 of the ball bearings have a diameter of more than 5.03 mm.
(b) 0.0124 of the ball bearings will be discarded.
(c) Each day the plant manager expects to discard 372 of the 30,000 ball bearings manufactured.
(d) To meet the order, the plant manufacturer should manufacture 57,711 ball bearings.
45. **(a)** $P(X \geq 5) = 0.3228$ (Tech: 0.3232)
(b) $P(X \leq -2) = 0.4286$ (Tech: 0.4272)
(c) The favored team is equally likely to win or lose relative to the spread. Yes; a mean of 0 implies the spreads are accurate.
46. **(a)** $P(X \geq 5) = 0.2912$ (Tech: 0.2910)
(b) $P(X \leq -2) = 0.4641$ (Tech: 0.4635)
(c) $P(X > 0) = 0.4641$ (Tech: 0.4635); the favored team is more likely to lose than to win relative to the spread, so the spreads are not accurate. There is possible point shaving.
47. **(a)** The 17th percentile for incubation time is 20 days.
(b) From 19 to 23 days make up the middle 95% of incubation times of the eggs.
48. **(a)** The 90th percentile reading speed is 156 words per minute.
(b) The cutoffs for unusual reading times are 78 and 172 words per minute.
49. **(a)** The 30th percentile for the number of chips in an 18-ounce bag is 1201 (Tech: 1200) chips.
(b) The middle 99% of the bags contain between 958 and 1566 chocolate chips.
50. Wendy's should offer a free meal to any customer who must wait more than 206 seconds.
51. **(a)** 11.51% of customers receive the service for half-price.
(b) So that no more than 3% receives the discount, the guaranteed time limit should be 22 minutes.
52. **(a)**

Birth Weight (g)	Relative Frequency
0–499	< 0.0001
500–999	0.0001
1000–1499	0.0005
1500–1999	0.0028
2000–2499	0.0276
2500–2999	0.1702
3000–3499	0.4148
3500–3999	0.2954
4000–4499	0.0765
4500–4999	0.0110
5000–5499	0.0012

(b)

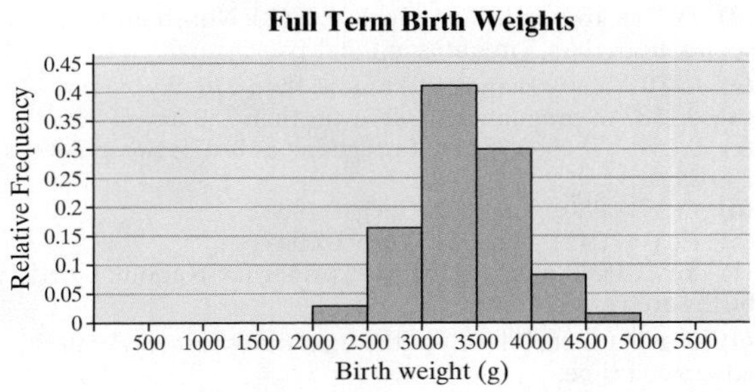

The distribution is fairly symmetric and bell shaped.

(c) $\mu = 3375$ g, $\sigma = 493$ g

(d)

Birth Weight (g)	Proportion Using Normal Model (Using Technology)
0–499	< 0.0001
500–999	< 0.0001
1000–1499	0.0001
1500–1999	0.0026
2000–2499	0.0352
2500–2999	0.1849
3000–3499	0.3759
3500–3999	0.2971
4000–4499	0.0911
4500–4999	0.0108
5000–5499	0.0005

(e) The normal model appears to be effective in describing the birth weights of babies.

53. The area under a normal curve can be interpreted as probability, proportion, or percentile.

54. Reporting the probability as < 0.0001 accurately describes the event as possible but highly unlikely. Reporting the probability as 0.0000 might be incorrectly interpreted to mean that the event is impossible.

55. Reporting the probability as > 0.9999 accurately describes the event as highly likely, but not certain. Reporting the probability as 1.0000 might be incorrectly interpreted to mean that the event is certain.

56. You did better on the SAT. On the ACT, you scored in the 83rd percentile. On the SAT, you scored in the 85th percentile.

7.3 Assess Your Understanding (page 353)

1. normal probability plot

2. True

3. The sample data do not come from a normally distributed population.

4. The sample data come from a normally distributed population.

5. The sample data do not come from a normally distributed population.

6. The sample data do not come from a normally distributed population.

7. The sample data come from a normally distributed population.

8. The sample data come from a normally distributed population.

9. (a) The sample data come from a normally distributed population.
(b) $\bar{x} = 1247.4$ chips, $s = 101.0$ chips
(c)

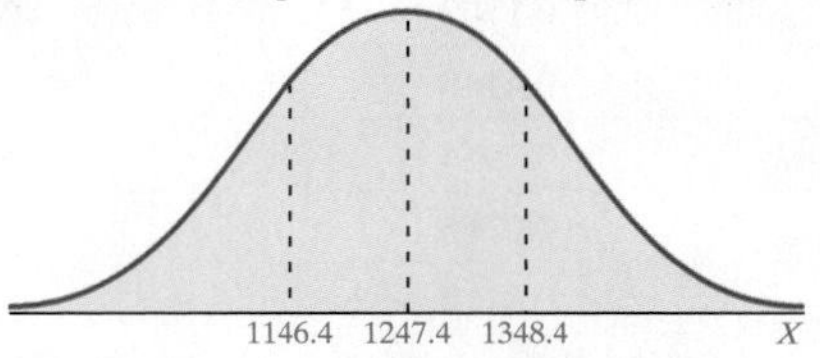

(d) $P(X \geq 1000) = 0.9929$ (Tech: 0.9928)
(e) $P(1200 \leq X \leq 1400) = 0.6153$ (Tech: 0.6152)

10. (a) The sample data come from a normally distributed population.
(b) $\bar{x} = 20.90$ hours, $s = 10.52$ hours
(c)

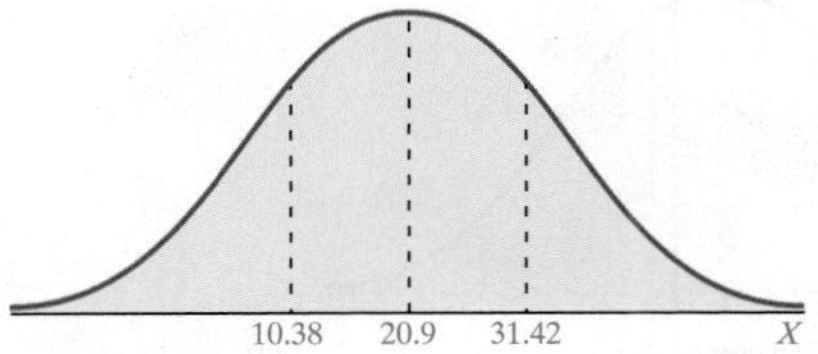

(d) $P(20 \leq X \leq 35) = 0.4458$ (Tech: 0.4440)
(e) $P(X > 40) = 0.0344$ (Tech: 0.0347)

11. The normal probability plot is approximately linear. So the sample data could come from a normally distributed population.

12. The normal probability plot is approximately linear. So the sample data could come from a normally distributed population.

13. The normal probability plot is not approximately linear. So the sample data do not come from a normally distributed population.

14. The normal probability plot is not approximately linear. So the sample data do not come from a normally distributed population.

7.4 Assess Your Understanding (page 359)

1. $np(1 - p) \geq 10$; np; $\sqrt{np(1 - p)}$ **2.** continuity

3. $P(X \leq 4.5)$

4. $P(2.5 \leq X \leq 10.5)$

5. Area under the normal curve to the right of $x = 39.5$

6. Area under the normal curve to the left of $x = 20.5$

7. Area under the normal curve between $x = 7.5$ and $x = 8.5$

8. Area under the normal curve between $x = 11.5$ and $x = 12.5$

9. Area under the normal curve between $x = 17.5$ and $x = 24.5$

10. Area under the normal curve between $x = 29.5$ and $x = 40.5$

11. Area under the normal curve to the right of $x = 20.5$

12. Area under the normal curve to the left of $x = 39.5$

13. Area under the normal curve to the right of $x = 500.5$

14. Area under the normal curve to the left of $x = 34.5$

15. Using the binomial formula, $P(20) = 0.0616$; $np(1 - p) = 14.4$, the normal distribution can be used. Approximate probability is 0.0618. (Tech: 0.0603)

16. Using the binomial formula, $P(18) = 0.0221$; $np(1 - p) = 10.2$, the normal distribution can be used. Approximate probability is 0.0220. (Tech: 0.0216)

17. Using the binomial formula, $P(30) < 0.0001$; $np(1 - p) = 7.5$, the normal distribution cannot be used.

18. Using the binomial formula, $P(50) < 0.0001$; $np(1 - p) = 4.75$, the normal distribution cannot be used.

19. Using the binomial formula, $P(60) = 0.0677$; $np(1 - p) = 14.1$, the normal distribution can be used. Approximate probability is 0.0630. (Tech: 0.0645)

20. Using the binomial formula, $P(70) = 0.0970$; $np(1 - p) = 13.6$, the normal distribution can be used. Approximate probability is 0.0926. (Tech: 0.0932)

21. (a) $P(130) \approx 0.0444$ (Tech: 0.0431)
(b) $P(X \geq 130) \approx 0.9332$ (Tech: 0.9328)
(c) $P(X < 125) \approx 0.0021$
(d) $P(125 \leq X \leq 135) \approx 0.5536$ (Tech: 0.5520)

22. (a) $P(80) \approx 0.1034$ (Tech: 0.0995)
(b) $P(X \geq 80) \approx 0.5517$ (Tech: 0.5497)
(c) $P(X < 70) \approx 0.0043$
(d) $P(70 \leq X \leq 90) \approx 0.9914$ (Tech: 0.9913)

23. (a) $P(250) \approx 0.0029$ (Tech: 0.0029)
(b) $P(X \leq 220) \approx 0.3446$ (Tech: 0.3429)
(c) $P(X > 250) \approx 0.0110$ (Tech: 0.0109)
(d) $P(220 \leq X \leq 250) \approx 0.6769$ (Tech: 0.6785)
(e) $P(X \geq 260) \approx 0.0010$ (Tech: 0.0010); yes; this result is unusual since the probability is less than 0.05.

24. (a) $P(100) \approx 0.0018$ (Tech: 0.0018)
(b) $P(X < 75) \approx 0.2327$ (Tech: 0.2324)
(c) Yes; the probability is 0.0039.

25. (a) $P(X \geq 130) \approx 0.0028$
(b) Yes, the result is unusual. Less than 3 samples in 1000 will result in 130 or more living at home if the true percentage is 55%.

26. (a) $P(X \geq 110) \approx 0.0066$ (Tech: 0.0065)
(b) Yes, the result is unusual. Less than 7 samples in 1000 will result in 110 or more living at home if the true percentage is 46%.

27. (a) $P(X \geq 75) \approx 0.0007$
(b) Yes; less than 1 sample in 1000 will result in 75 or more respondents preferring a male if the true percentage is 37%.

28. (a) $P(X \geq 20) \approx 0.1190$ (Tech: 0.1191)
(b) No; the result is not unusual.

Chapter 7 Review Exercises (page 362)

1. (a) $\mu = 60$ **(b)** $\sigma = 10$
(c) (i) The proportion of values for the random variable to the right of $x = 75$ is 0.0668.
(ii) The probability that a randomly selected value is greater than $x = 75$ is 0.0668.
(d) (i) The proportion of values for the random variable between $x = 50$ and $x = 75$ is 0.7745.
(ii) The probability that a randomly selected value is between $x = 50$ and $x = 75$ is 0.7745.

2.

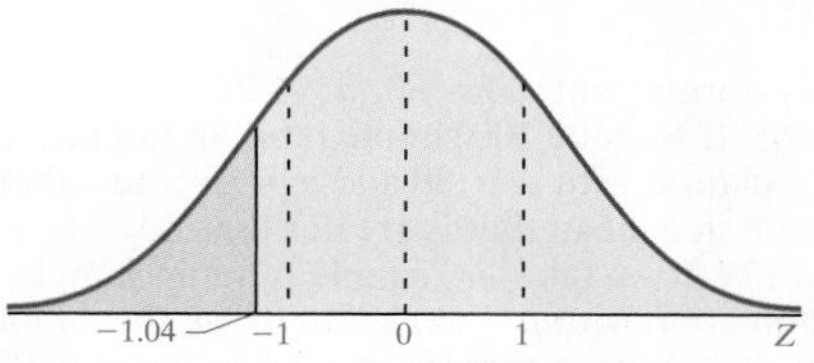

Area under the normal curve to the left of -1.04 is 0.1492.

3.

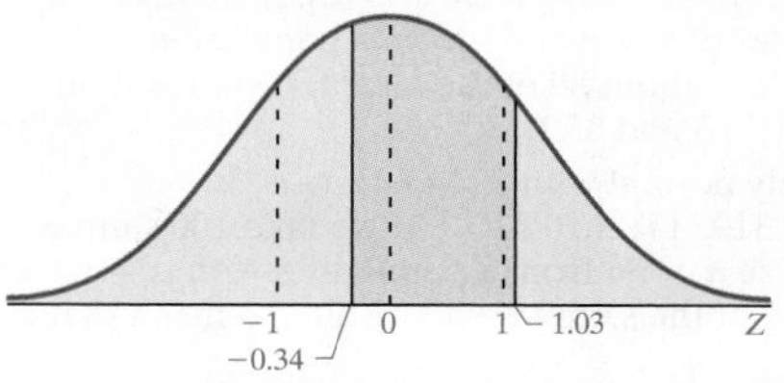

Area under the normal curve between -0.34 and 1.03 is 0.4816.

4. $z = 0.04$

5. $z_1 = -1.75$ and $z_2 = 1.75$

6. $z_{0.20} = 0.84$

7.

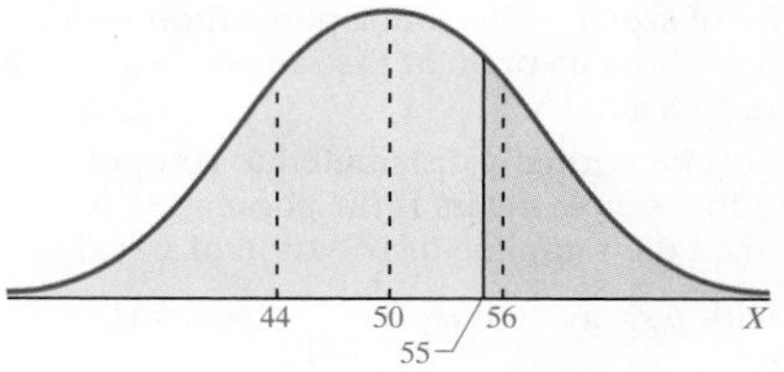

$P(X > 55) = 0.2033$ (Tech: 0.2023)

8.

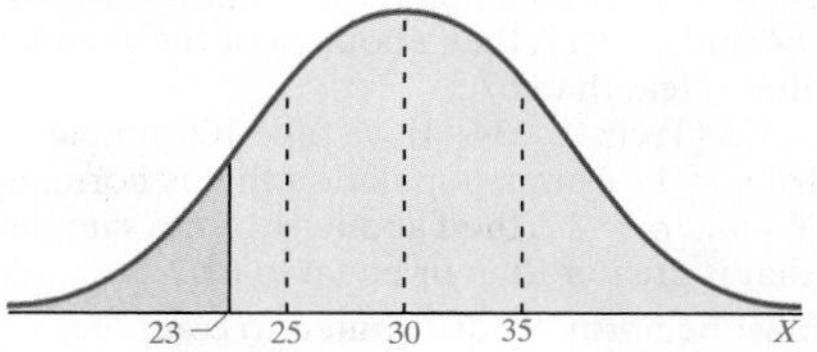

$P(X \leq 23) = 0.0808$

9.

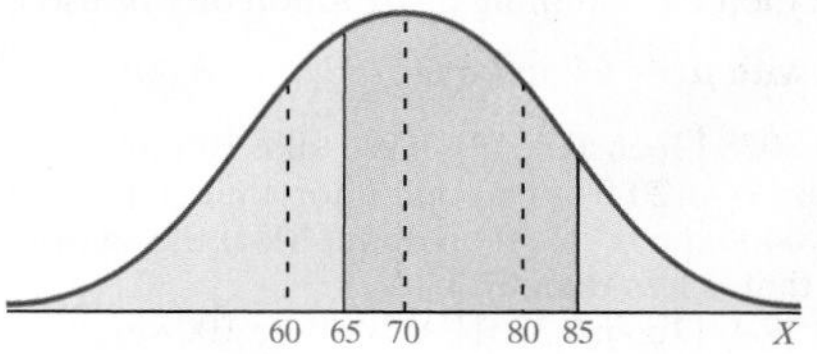

$P(65 < X < 85) = 0.6247$

10. (a) 0.1271 (Tech: 0.1279) of the tires last at least 75,000 miles.
(b) 0.0116 (Tech: 0.0115) of the tires last at most 60,000 miles.
(c) $P(65{,}000 \leq X \leq 80{,}000) = 0.8613$ (Tech: 0.8606)
(d) The company should advertise 60,980 (Tech: 60,964) miles as its mileage warranty.

11. (a) The probability is 0.0475 (Tech: 0.0478) that the test taker scores above 125.
(b) The probability is 0.2514 (Tech: 0.2525) that the test taker scores below 90.
(c) 0.2476 (Tech: 0.2487) of the test takers score between 110 and 140.
(d) $P(X > 150) = 0.0004$
(e) A score of 131 places a child at the 98th percentile.
(f) Normal children score between 71 and 129 points.

12. (a) 0.0119 (Tech: 0.0120) of the baseballs produced are too heavy for use.
(b) 0.0384 (Tech: 0.0380) of the baseballs produced are too light to use.
(c) 0.9497 (Tech: 0.9500) of the baseballs produced are within acceptable weight limits.
(d) 8424 (Tech: 8421) should be manufactured.

13. (a) $np(1 - p) = 62.1 > 10$, so the normal distribution can be used to approximate the binomial probabilities.
(b) $P(125) \approx 0.0213$ (Tech: 0.0226) Interpretation: Approximately 2 of every 100 random samples of 250 adult Americans will result in exactly 125 who state that they have read at least 6 books within the past year.
(c) $P(X < 120) \approx 0.7157$ (Tech: 0.7160) Interpretation: Approximately 72 of every 100 random samples of 250 adult Americans will result in fewer than 120 who state that they have read at least 6 books within the past year.
(d) $P(X \geq 140) \approx 0.0009$ Interpretation: Approximately 1 of every 1000 random samples of 250 adult Americans will result in 140 or more who state that they have read at least 6 books within the past year.
(e) $P(100 \leq X \leq 120) \approx 0.7336$ (Tech: 0.7328) Interpretation: Approximately 73 of every 100 random samples of 250 adult Americans will result in between 100 and 120, inclusive, who state that they have read at least 6 books within the past year.

14. The sample appears to be from a normally distributed population.

15. The sample is not from a normal population.

16. Not normal

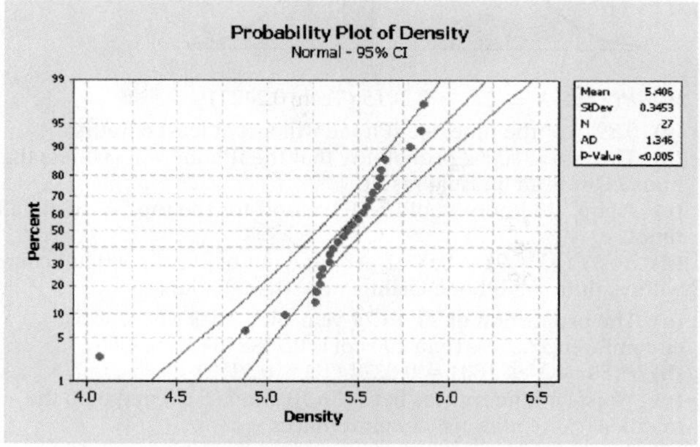

17. (a) $P(X \leq 30) = 0.0010$
(b) Yes; this contradicts the *USA Today* "Snapshot." About 1 sample in 1000 will result in 30 or fewer who do their most creative thinking while driving, if the true percentage is 20%.

18. (a)

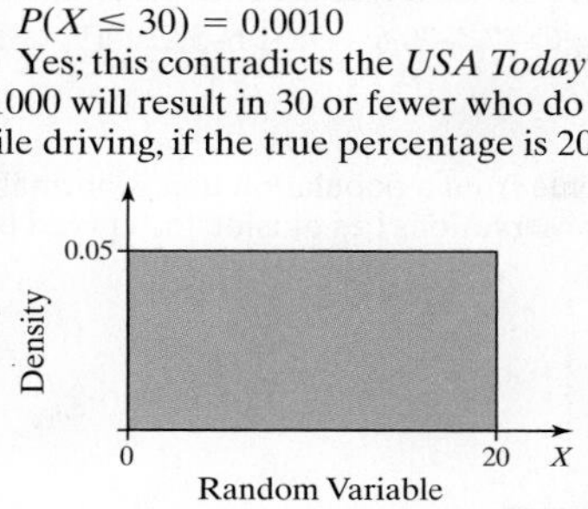

(b) $P(0 \leq X \leq 5) = 0.25$ **(c)** $P(10 \leq X \leq 18) = 0.4$

19. A normal curve has the following properties:
1. It is symmetric about its mean μ.
2. Its highest point occurs at μ.
3. It has inflection points at $\mu - \sigma$ and $\mu + \sigma$.
4. The area under the curve is 1.
5. The area under the curve to the right of μ equals the area under the curve to the left of μ. Both equal $\frac{1}{2}$.
6. As the value of X increases, the graph approaches but never equals zero. When the value of X decreases, the graph approaches but never equals zero.

7. The Empirical Rule: Approximately 68% of the area under the standard normal curve is between $\mu - \sigma$ and $\mu + \sigma$. Approximately 95% of the area under the standard normal curve is between $\mu - 2\sigma$ and $\mu + 2\sigma$. Approximately 99.7% of the area under the standard normal curve is between $\mu - 3\sigma$ and $\mu + 3\sigma$.

20. The graph plots actual observations against expected z-scores, assuming that the data are normal. If the plot is not linear, then we have evidence that the data are not normal.

Chapter 7 Test (page 363)

1. (a) $\mu = 7$ **(b)** $\sigma = 2$
(c) (i) The proportion of values for the random variable to the left of $x = 10$ is 0.9332.
(ii) The probability that a randomly selected value is less than $x = 10$ is 0.9332.
(d) (i) The proportion of values for the random variable between $x = 5$ and $x = 8$ is 0.5328.
(ii) The probability that a randomly selected value is between $x = 5$ and $x = 8$ is 0.5328.

2.

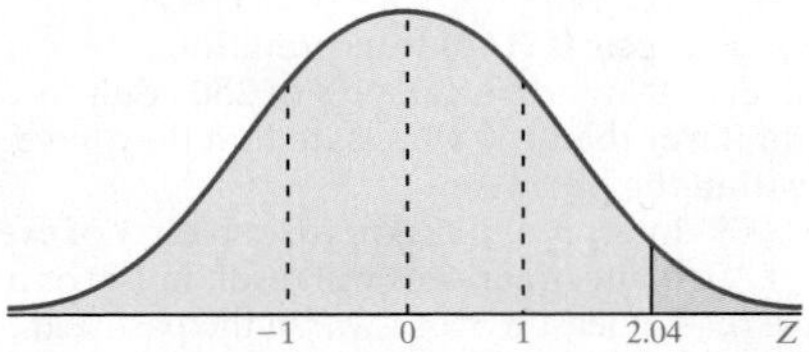

Area under the normal curve to the right of 2.04 is 0.0207.

3. $z_1 = -1.555$; $z_2 = 1.555$ **4.** $z_{0.04} = 1.75$

5. (a)

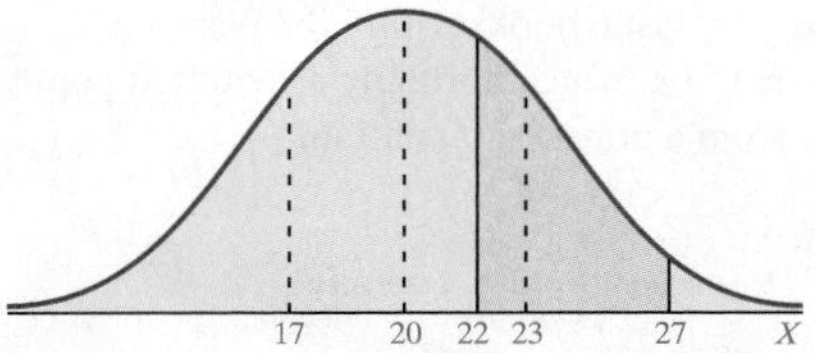

(b) $P(22 \le X \le 27) = 0.2415$ (Tech: 0.2427)

6. (a) 0.8944 of the time, the iPhone will last at least 6 hours.
(b) There is a 0.0062 probability that the iPhone will last less than 5 hours. This is an unusual result.
(c) About 8.3 hours would be the cutoff for the top 5% of all talk times.
(d) Yes; $P(X > 9) = 0.0062$. About 6 out of every 1000 full charges will result in the iPhone lasting more than 9 hours.

7. (a) The proportion of 20- to 29-year-old males whose waist circumference is less than 100 cm is 0.7088 (Tech: 0.7080).
(b) $P(80 \le X \le 100) = 0.5274$ (Tech: 0.5272)
(c) Waist circumferences between 70 and 115 cm make up the middle 90% of all waist circumferences.
(d) A waist circumference of 75 cm is at the 10th percentile.

8. A: ≥76.4; B: 70.7–76.3; C: 57.3–70.6; D: 51.6–57.2; E: <51.6

9. (a) $P(100) \approx 0.0025$
(b) $P(X < 60) \approx 0.0062$

10. The data likely do not come from a population that is normally distributed since one of the observations lies outside the curved bounds.

11. (a)

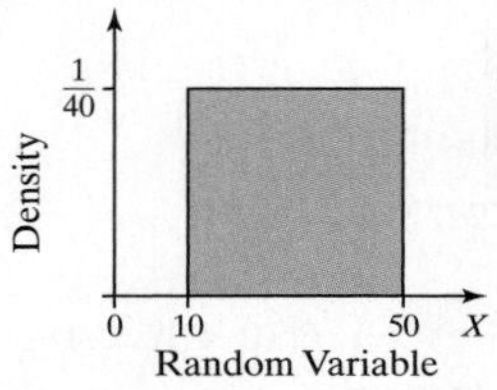

(b) $P(20 \le X \le 30) = 0.25$
(c) $P(X < 15) = 0.125$

CHAPTER 8 Sampling Distributions

8.1 Assess Your Understanding (page 376)

1. sampling distribution **2.** $\mu; \dfrac{\sigma}{\sqrt{n}}$
3. standard error; mean **4.** True
5. False **6.** False

7. The sampling distribution of $\bar{x}$ is normal with $\mu_{\bar{x}} = 30$ and $\sigma_{\bar{x}} = \dfrac{8}{\sqrt{10}} \approx 2.530$.

8. The population does not need to be normally distributed because the sample is sufficiently large, $n = 40 \ge 30$. The sampling distribution of $\bar{x}$ is approximately normal with $\mu_{\bar{x}} = 50$, $\sigma_{\bar{x}} = \dfrac{4}{\sqrt{40}} = \dfrac{2}{\sqrt{10}} \approx 0.632$.

9. $\mu_{\bar{x}} = 80, \sigma_{\bar{x}} = 2$ **10.** $\mu_{\bar{x}} = 64, \sigma_{\bar{x}} = 3$

11. $\mu_{\bar{x}} = 52, \sigma_{\bar{x}} = \dfrac{10}{\sqrt{21}} \approx 2.182$

12. $\mu_{\bar{x}} = 27, \sigma_{\bar{x}} = \dfrac{6}{\sqrt{15}} \approx 1.549$

13. (a) $\mu_{\bar{x}} = 500$ **(b)** $\sigma_{\bar{x}} = 20$
(c) The population must be normally distributed.
(d) $\sigma = 80$

14. (a) $\mu_{\bar{x}} = 12$ **(b)** $\sigma_{\bar{x}} = 0.05$
(c) The population must be normally distributed.
(d) $\sigma = 0.15$

15. (a) $\bar{x}$ is approximately normal with $\mu_{\bar{x}} = 80$, $\sigma_{\bar{x}} = 2$.
(b) $P(\bar{x} > 83) = 0.0668$. If we take 100 simple random samples of size $n = 49$ from a population with $\mu = 80$ and $\sigma = 14$, then about 7 of the samples will result in a mean that is greater than 83.
(c) $P(\bar{x} \le 75.8) = 0.0179$. If we take 100 simple random samples of size $n = 49$ from a population with $\mu = 80$ and $\sigma = 14$, then about 2 of the samples will result in a mean that is less than or equal to 75.8.
(d) $P(78.3 < \bar{x} < 85.1) = 0.7969$ [Tech: 0.7970]. If we take 100 simple random samples of size $n = 49$ from a population with $\mu = 80$ and $\sigma = 14$, then about 80 of the samples will result in a mean that is between 78.3 and 85.1.

16. (a) $\bar{x}$ is approximately normal with $\mu_{\bar{x}} = 64$, $\sigma_{\bar{x}} = 3$.
(b) $P(\bar{x} < 62.6) = 0.3192$ [Tech: 0.3204]. If we take 100 simple random samples of size $n = 36$ from a population with $\mu = 64$ and $\sigma = 18$, then about 32 of the samples will result in a mean that is less than 62.6.
(c) $P(\bar{x} \ge 68.7) = 0.0582$ [Tech: 0.0586]. If we take 100 simple random samples of size $n = 36$ from a population with $\mu = 64$ and $\sigma = 18$, then about 6 of the samples will result in a mean that is greater than or equal to 68.7.
(d) $P(59.8 < \bar{x} < 65.9) = 0.6549$ [Tech: 0.6560]. If we take 100 simple random samples of size $n = 36$ from a population with $\mu = 64$ and $\sigma = 18$, then about 65 or 66 of the samples will result in a mean that is between 59.8 and 65.9.

17. (a) The population must be normally distributed to compute probabilities involving the sample mean. If the population is normally distributed, then the sampling distribution of $\bar{x}$ is also normally distributed with $\mu_{\bar{x}} = 64$ and $\sigma_{\bar{x}} = \dfrac{17}{\sqrt{12}} \approx 4.907$.
(b) $P(\bar{x} < 67.3) = 0.7486$ [Tech: 0.7493]. If we take 100 simple random samples of size $n = 12$ from a population that is normally distributed with $\mu = 64$ and $\sigma = 17$, then about 75 of the samples will result in a mean that is less than 67.3.
(c) $P(\bar{x} \ge 65.2) = 0.4052$ [Tech: 0.4034]. If we take 100 simple random samples of size $n = 12$ from a population that is normally distributed with $\mu = 64$ and $\sigma = 17$, then about 41 of the samples will result in a mean that is greater than or equal to 65.2.

18. (a) The population must be normally distributed to compute probabilities involving the sample mean. If the population is normally distributed, then the sampling distribution of $\bar{x}$ is also normally distributed with $\mu_{\bar{x}} = 64$ and $\sigma_{\bar{x}} = \dfrac{17}{\sqrt{20}} \approx 3.801$.
(b) $P(\bar{x} < 67.3) = 0.8078$ [Tech: 0.8073]. If we take 100 simple random samples of size $n = 20$ from a population that is normally distributed with $\mu = 64$ and $\sigma = 17$, then about 81 of the samples will result in a mean that is less than 67.3.
(c) $P(\bar{x} \ge 65.2) = 0.3745$ [Tech: 0.3761]. If we take 100 simple random samples of size $n = 20$ from a population that is normally distributed with $\mu = 64$ and $\sigma = 17$, then about 37 of the samples will result in a mean that is greater than or equal to 65.2.
(d) Increasing the sample size increases $P(\bar{x} < 67.3)$ but decreases $P(\bar{x} > 65.2)$. This happens because $\sigma_{\bar{x}}$ decreases as n increases.

19. (a) $P(X < 260) = 0.3520$ [Tech: 0.3538]. If we randomly select 100 human pregnancies, then about 35 of the pregnancies will last less than 260 days.

(b) The sampling distribution of $\bar{x}$ is normal with $\mu_{\bar{x}} = 266$ and $\sigma_{\bar{x}} = \dfrac{16}{\sqrt{20}} \approx 3.578$.
(c) $P(\bar{x} \leq 260) = 0.0465$ [Tech: 0.0468]. If we take 100 simple random samples of size $n = 20$ human pregnancies, then about 5 of the samples will result in a mean gestation period of 260 days or less.
(d) $P(\bar{x} \leq 260) = 0.0040$. If we take 1000 simple random samples of size $n = 50$ human pregnancies, then about 4 of the samples will result in a mean gestation period of 260 days or less.
(e) This result would be unusual, so the sample likely came from a population whose mean gestation period is less than 266 days.
(f) $P(256 \leq \bar{x} \leq 276) = 0.9844$ [Tech: 0.9845]. If we take 100 simple random samples of size $n = 15$ human pregnancies, then about 98 of the samples will result in a mean gestation period between 256 and 276 days, inclusive.

20. **(a)** $P(X < 40) = 0.1894$ [Tech: 0.1892]. If we select a simple random sample of $n = 100$ males ages 20 to 29, then about 19 of the males will have an upper leg length that is less than 40 cm.
(b) $P(\bar{x} < 40) = 0.0041$. If we take 1000 simple random samples of size $n = 9$ males ages 20 to 29, then about 4 of the samples will result in a mean upper leg length that is less than 40 cm.
(c) $P(\bar{x} < 40) = 0.0011$. If we take 1000 simple random samples of size $n = 12$ males ages 20 to 29, then about 1 of the samples will result in a mean upper leg length that is less than 40 cm.
(d) Increasing the sample size decreases $P(\bar{x} < 40)$. This happens because $\sigma_{\bar{x}}$ decreases as n increases.
(e) Yes; this result is unusual. $P(\bar{x} \geq 46) = 0.0170$.

21. **(a)** $P(X > 95) = 0.3085$. If we select a simple random sample of $n = 100$ second grade students, then about 31 of the students will read more than 95 words per minute.
(b) $P(\bar{x} > 95) = 0.0418$ [Tech: 0.0416]. If we take 100 simple random samples of size $n = 12$ second grade students, then about 4 of the samples will result in a mean reading rate that is more than 95 words per minute.
(c) $P(\bar{x} > 95) = 0.0071$ [Tech: 0.0072]. If we take 1000 simple random samples of size $n = 24$ second grade students, then about 7 of the samples will result in a mean reading rate that is more than 95 words per minute.
(d) Increasing the sample size decreases $P(\bar{x} > 95)$. This happens because $\sigma_{\bar{x}}$ decreases as n increases.
(e) A mean reading rate of 92.8 wpm is not unusual since $P(\bar{x} \geq 92.8) = 0.1056$ [Tech: 0.1052]. This means that the new reading program is not abundantly more effective than the old program.
(f) There is a 5% chance that the mean reading speed of a random sample of 20 second-grade students will exceed 93.9 words per minute [Tech: 93.7].

22. **(a)** $P(X > 95) = 0.3192$ [Tech: 0.3190]. If we select a simple random sample of $n = 100$ time intervals between eruptions, then about 32 of the intervals will be longer than 95 minutes.
(b) $P(\bar{x} > 95) = 0.0179$ [Tech: 0.0177]. If we take 100 simple random samples of size $n = 20$ time intervals between eruptions, then about 2 of the samples will result in a mean longer than 95 minutes.
(c) $P(\bar{x} > 95) = 0.0049$ [Tech: 0.0050]. If we take 1000 simple random samples of size $n = 30$ time intervals between eruptions, then about 5 of the samples will result in a mean longer than 95 minutes.
(d) Increasing the sample size reduces $P(\bar{x} > 95)$. This happens because $\sigma_{\bar{x}}$ decreases as n increases.
(e) This result would be unusual, so it might indicate that the mean time between eruptions is actually greater than 85 minutes.
(f) The likelihood that the mean length of time between eruptions exceeds 88.8 minutes is 0.20.

23. **(a)** $P(X > 0) = 0.5675$ [Tech: 0.5694]. If we select a simple random sample of $n = 100$ months, then about 57 of the months will have positive rates of return.
(b) $P(\bar{x} > 0) = 0.7291$ [Tech: 0.7277]. If we take 100 simple random samples of size $n = 12$ months, then about 73 of the samples will result in a mean monthly rate of return that is positive.
(c) $P(\bar{x} > 0) = 0.8051$ [Tech: 0.8043]. If we take 100 simple random samples of size $n = 24$ months, then about 81 of the samples will result in a mean monthly rate of return that is positive.
(d) $P(\bar{x} > 0) = 0.8531$ [Tech: 0.8530]. If we take 100 simple random samples of size $n = 36$ months, then about 85 of the samples will result in a mean monthly rate of return that is positive.
(e) The likelihood of earning a positive rate of return increases as the investment time horizon increases.

24. **(a)** $P(X > 34) = 0.2843$ [Tech: 0.2839]. If we select a simple random sample of $n = 100$ Cobalts, then about 28 of the Cobalts will get more than 34 miles per gallon.
(b) $P(\bar{x} > 34) = 0.0351$ [Tech: 0.0354]. If we take 100 simple random samples of size $n = 10$ Cobalts, then about 4 of the samples will result in a mean mileage that exceeds 34 miles per gallon.
(c) $P(\bar{x} > 34) = 0.0052$ [Tech: 0.0053]. If we take 1000 simple random samples of size $n = 20$ Cobalts, then about 5 of the samples will result in a mean mileage that exceeds 34 miles per gallon. This result would be unusual.

25. **(a)** A sample size of at least 30 is needed to compute the probabilities.
(b) $P(\bar{x} < 10) = 0.0028$. If we take 1000 simple random samples of size $n = 40$ oil changes, then about 3 of the samples will result in a mean time of less than 10 minutes.
(c) There is a 10% chance of being at or below a mean oil-change time of 10.8 minutes.

26. **(a)** A sample size of at least 30 is needed to compute the probabilities.
(b) $P(\bar{x} \leq 56.8) = 0.1131$ [Tech: 0.1137]. If we take 100 simple random samples of size $n = 40$ cars, then about 11 of the samples will result in a mean time of 56.8 seconds or less spent at the window. This result is not unusual, so the new system is not abundantly more effective than the old system.
(c) There is a 15% chance the mean time will be at or below 57.4 minutes.

27. **(a)** Since we have a large sample ($n = 50 \geq 30$) the Central Limit Theorem allows us to say that the sampling distribution of the mean is approximately normal.
(b) $\mu_{\bar{x}} = 3$, $\sigma_{\bar{x}} = \dfrac{\sqrt{3}}{\sqrt{50}} = \sqrt{\dfrac{3}{50}} \approx 0.245$
(c) $P(\bar{x} \geq 3.6) = 0.0071$ [Tech: 0.0072]. If we take 1000 simple random samples of size $n = 50$ ten-gram portions of peanut butter, then about 7 of the samples will result in a mean of at least 3.6 insect fragments. This result is unusual. We might conclude that the sample comes from a population with a mean higher than 3 insect fragments per ten-gram portion.

28. **(a)** Since we have a large sample ($n = 40 \geq 30$), the Central Limit Theorem allows us to say that the sampling distribution of the mean is approximately normal.
(b) $\mu_{\bar{x}} = 20$, $\sigma_{\bar{x}} = \dfrac{\sqrt{20}}{\sqrt{40}} = \sqrt{\dfrac{1}{2}} \approx 0.707$
(c) $P(\bar{x} \geq 22.1) = 0.0015$. If we take 1000 simple random samples of size $n = 40$ one-hour time periods between 12:00 noon and 1:00 P.M., then about 2 of the samples will result in a mean of at least 22.1 cars arriving at the drive-through. This result is unusual. We might conclude that business has increased and that the rate of arrival is now greater than 20 cars per hour between 12:00 noon and 1:00 P.M.

29. **(a)** No; the variable "weekly time spent watching television" is likely skewed right.
(b) $\bar{x}$ is approximately normal with $\mu_{\bar{x}} = 2.35$ and $\sigma_{\bar{x}} = \dfrac{1.93}{\sqrt{40}} \approx 0.305$.
(c) $P(2 \leq \bar{x} \leq 3) = 0.8583$ [Tech: 0.8577]. If we take 100 simple random samples of size $n = 40$ adult Americans, then about 86 of the samples will result in a mean time between 2 and 3 hours watching television on a weekday.
(d) $P(\bar{x} \leq 1.89) = 0.0793$. If we take 100 simple random samples of size $n = 35$ adult Americans, then about 8 of the samples will result in a mean time of 1.89 hours or less watching television on a weekday. This result is not unusual, so this evidence is insufficient to conclude that avid Internet users watch less television.

30. **(a)** No; the variable "ATM withdrawal" is likely skewed right.
(b) $\bar{x}$ is approximately normal with $\mu_{\bar{x}} = 67$ and $\sigma_{\bar{x}} = \dfrac{35}{\sqrt{50}} \approx 4.950$.
(c) $P(70 \leq \bar{x} \leq 75) = 0.2183$ [Tech: 0.2192]. If we take 100 simple random samples of size $n = 50$ ATM withdrawals, then about 22 of the samples will result in a mean withdrawal amount between \$70 and \$75.

31. **(a)** $\mu = 46.3$ years old
(b) Samples: (37, 38); (37, 45); (37, 50); (37, 48); (37, 60); (38, 45); (38, 50); (38, 48); (38, 60); (45, 50); (45, 48); (45, 60); (50, 48); (50, 60); (48, 60)

(c)

$\bar{x}$	Probability	$\bar{x}$	Probability
37.5	$\frac{1}{15}$	46.5	$\frac{1}{15}$
41	$\frac{1}{15}$	47.5	$\frac{1}{15}$
41.5	$\frac{1}{15}$	48.5	$\frac{1}{15}$
42.5	$\frac{1}{15}$	49	$\frac{2}{15}$
43	$\frac{1}{15}$	52.5	$\frac{1}{15}$
43.5	$\frac{1}{15}$	54	$\frac{1}{15}$
44	$\frac{1}{15}$	55	$\frac{1}{15}$

(d) $\mu_{\bar{x}} = 46.3$ years old
(e) $P(43.3 \le \bar{x} \le 49.3) = \frac{7}{15} = 0.467$
(f)

Samples	
37, 38, 45	38, 45, 50
37, 38, 50	38, 45, 48
37, 38, 48	38, 45, 60
37, 38, 60	38, 50, 48
37, 45, 50	38, 50, 60
37, 45, 48	38, 48, 60
37, 45, 60	45, 50, 48
37, 50, 48	45, 50, 60
37, 50, 60	45, 48, 60
37, 48, 60	50, 48, 60

Sampling Distribution	
$\bar{x}$	Probability
40	0.05
41	0.05
41.7	0.05
43.3	0.05
43.7	0.05
44	0.05
44.3	0.05
45	0.10
45.3	0.05
47.3	0.05
47.7	0.10
48.3	0.05
48.7	0.05
49	0.05
49.3	0.05
51	0.05
51.7	0.05
52.7	0.05

$\mu_{\bar{x}} = 46.3$ years old;
$P(43.3 \le \bar{x} \le 49.3) = 0.7$

As the sample size increases, the probability of obtaining a sample mean age within 3 years of the population mean age increases.

32. (a) $\mu = 128$ minutes
(b)

Samples	
132, 112	112, 131
132, 151	151, 122
132, 122	151, 120
132, 120	151, 131
132, 131	122, 120
112, 151	122, 131
112, 122	120, 131
112, 120	

(c)

Sampling Distribution	
$\bar{x}$	Probability
116	0.0667
117	0.0667
121	0.0667
121.5	0.0667
122	0.0667
125.5	0.0667
126	0.0667
126.5	0.0667
127	0.0667
131.5	0.1333
135.5	0.0667
136.5	0.0667
141	0.0667
141.5	0.0667

(d) $\mu_{\bar{x}} = 128$ minutes **(e)** $P(123 \le \bar{x} \le 133) = 0.4$
(f)

Samples	
132, 112, 151	112, 151, 122
132, 112, 122	112, 151, 120
132, 112, 120	112, 151, 131
132, 112, 131	112, 122, 120
132, 151, 122	112, 122, 131
132, 151, 120	112, 120, 131
132, 151, 131	151, 122, 120
132, 122, 120	151, 122, 131
132, 122, 131	151, 120, 131
132, 120, 131	122, 120, 131

Sampling Distribution	
$\bar{x}$	Probability
118	0.05
121	0.05
121.3	0.05
121.7	0.05
122	0.05
124.3	0.05
124.7	0.05
125	0.05
127.7	0.10
128.3	0.10
131	0.05
131.3	0.05
131.7	0.05
134	0.05
134.3	0.05
134.7	0.05
135	0.05
138	0.05

$\mu_{\bar{x}} = 128$ minutes; $P(123 \le \bar{x} \le 133) = 0.5$
As the sample size increases, the probability of obtaining a sample mean running time within 5 minutes of the population mean running time increases.

33. (a)

x	$P(x)$
35	0.0263
−1	0.9737

(b) $\mu = -\$0.05$, $\sigma = \$5.76$
(c) $\bar{x}$ is approximately normal with $\mu_{\bar{x}} = -\$0.05$ and
$\sigma_{\bar{x}} = \frac{5.76}{\sqrt{100}} = \$0.576$.
(d) $P(\bar{x} > 0) = 0.4641$ [Tech: 0.4654]
(e) $P(\bar{x} > 0) = 0.4522$ [Tech: 0.4511]
(f) $P(\bar{x} > 0) = 0.3936$ [Tech: 0.3918]
(g) The probability of being ahead decreases as the number of games played increases.

34. A sampling distribution is a probability distribution for all possible values of a statistic computed from a sample of size n.

35. The Central Limit Theorem states that, regardless of the distribution of the population, the sampling distribution of the sample means becomes approximately normal as the sample size, n, increases.

36. An infinite population is a population with countless members. The finite population correction factor is $\sqrt{\frac{N-n}{N-1}}$. If the sample, n, is less than 5% of the population size, N, the finite population correction factor can be ignored. When the sample size is small relative to the population, the value of the finite population correction factor is close to 1. For example, if $N = 1{,}000{,}000$ and $n = 30$, the finite population correction factor is 0.9999855.

37. (b); The distribution for the larger sample size has the smaller standard deviation.

38. (b), (a), (c); Distribution (b) appears to be approximately normal, so any sample size will suffice. Of distributions (a) and (c), distribution (c) is more skewed and will require a larger sample size in order for the distribution of sample means to be approximately normal.

39. (a) We would expect that Jack's distribution would be skewed left but not as much as the original distribution. Diane's distribution should be bell shaped and symmetric, that is, approximately normal. **(b)** We would expect both distributions to have a mean of 50. **(c)** We expect Jack's distribution to have standard deviation $\frac{10}{\sqrt{3}} \approx 5.8$. We expect Diane's distribution to have standard deviation $\frac{10}{\sqrt{30}} \approx 1.8$.

8.2 Assess Your Understanding (page 384)

1. 0.44

2. sample proportion; $\frac{x}{n}$

3. False

4. True

5. The sampling distribution of $\hat{p}$ is approximately normal when $n \le 0.05N$ and $np(1-p) \ge 10$.

6. The standard deviation of $\hat{p}$ decreases as the sample size increases. If the sample size is increased by a factor of 4, the standard deviation is reduced by a factor of 2.

7. The sampling distribution of $\hat{p}$ is approximately normal with $\mu_{\hat{p}} = 0.4$ and $\sigma_{\hat{p}} = \sqrt{\frac{0.4(0.6)}{500}} \approx 0.022$.

8. The sampling distribution of $\hat{p}$ is approximately normal with $\mu_{\hat{p}} = 0.7$ and $\sigma_{\hat{p}} = \sqrt{\frac{0.7(0.3)}{300}} \approx 0.026$.

9. The sampling distribution of $\hat{p}$ is approximately normal with $\mu_{\hat{p}} = 0.103$ and $\sigma_{\hat{p}} = \sqrt{\frac{0.103(0.897)}{1000}} \approx 0.010$.

10. The sampling distribution of $\hat{p}$ is approximately normal with $\mu_{\hat{p}} = 0.84$ and $\sigma_{\hat{p}} = \sqrt{\frac{0.84(0.16)}{1010}} \approx 0.012$.

11. (a) The sampling distribution of $\hat{p}$ is approximately normal with $\mu_{\hat{p}} = 0.8$ and $\sigma_{\hat{p}} = \sqrt{\frac{0.8(0.2)}{75}} \approx 0.046$.
(b) $P(\hat{p} \ge 0.84) = 0.1922$ [Tech: 0.1932]. About 19 out of 100 random samples of size $n = 75$ will result in 63 or more individuals (that is, 84% or more) with the characteristic.
(c) $P(\hat{p} \le 0.68) = 0.0047$. About 5 out of 1000 random samples of size $n = 75$ will result in 51 or fewer individuals (that is, 68% or less) with the characteristic.

12. (a) The sampling distribution of $\hat{p}$ is approximately normal with $\mu_{\hat{p}} = 0.65$ and $\sigma_{\hat{p}} = \sqrt{\frac{0.65(0.35)}{200}} \approx 0.034$.
(b) $P(\hat{p} \ge 0.68) = 0.1867$ [Tech: 0.1869]. About 19 out of 100 random samples of size $n = 200$ will result in 136 or more individuals (that is, 68% or more) with the characteristic.
(c) $P(\hat{p} \le 0.59) = 0.0375$ [Tech: 0.0376]. About 4 out of 100 random samples of size $n = 200$ will result in 118 or fewer individuals (that is, 59% or less) with the characteristic.

13. (a) The sampling distribution of $\hat{p}$ is approximately normal with $\mu_{\hat{p}} = 0.35$ and $\sigma_{\hat{p}} = \sqrt{\frac{0.35(0.65)}{1000}} \approx 0.015$.
(b) $P(\hat{p} \ge 0.39) = 0.0040$. About 4 out of 1000 random samples of size $n = 1000$ will result in 390 or more individuals (that is, 39% or more) with the characteristic.
(c) $P(\hat{p} \le 0.32) = 0.0233$ [Tech: 0.0234]. About 2 out of 100 random samples of size $n = 1000$ will result in 320 or fewer individuals (that is, 32% or less) with the characteristic.

14. (a) The sampling distribution of $\hat{p}$ is approximately normal with $\mu_{\hat{p}} = 0.42$ and $\sigma_{\hat{p}} = \sqrt{\frac{0.42(0.58)}{1460}} \approx 0.013$.
(b) $P(\hat{p} \ge 0.45) = 0.0102$ [Tech:0.0101]. About 1 out of 100 random samples of size $n = 1460$ will result in 657 or more individuals (that is, 45% or more) with the characteristic.
(c) $P(\hat{p} \le 0.4) = 0.0606$ [Tech: 0.0608]. About 6 out of 100 random samples of size $n = 1460$ will result in 584 or fewer individuals (that is, 40% or less) with the characteristic.

15. (a) The sampling distribution of $\hat{p}$ is approximately normal with $\mu_{\hat{p}} = 0.47$ and $\sigma_{\hat{p}} = \sqrt{\frac{0.47(0.53)}{200}} \approx 0.035$.
(b) $P(\hat{p} > 0.5) = 0.1977$ [Tech: 0.1976]. About 20 out of 100 random samples of size $n = 200$ Americans will result in more than 100 individuals (that is, more than 50%) who can order a meal in a foreign language.
(c) $P(\hat{p} \le 0.4) = 0.0239$ [Tech: 0.0237]. About 2 out of 100 random samples of size $n = 200$ Americans will result in 80 or fewer individuals (that is, 40% or less) who can order a meal in a foreign language. This result is unusual.

16. (a) The sampling distribution of $\hat{p}$ is approximately normal with $\mu_{\hat{p}} = 0.82$ and $\sigma_{\hat{p}} = \sqrt{\frac{0.82(0.18)}{100}} \approx 0.038$.
(b) $P(\hat{p} \ge 0.85) = 0.2177$ [Tech: 0.2174]. About 22 out of 100 random samples of size $n = 100$ Americans will result in at least 85 (that is, at least 85%) who are satisfied with their lives.
(c) $P(\hat{p} \le 0.75) = 0.0344$ [Tech: 0.0342]. About 3 out of 100 random samples of size $n = 100$ Americans will result in 75 or fewer individuals (that is, 75% or less) who are satisfied with their lives. This result is unusual.

17. (a) The sampling distribution of $\hat{p}$ is approximately normal with $\mu_{\hat{p}} = 0.39$ and $\sigma_{\hat{p}} = \sqrt{\frac{0.39(0.61)}{500}} \approx 0.022$.
(b) $P(\hat{p} < 0.38) = 0.3228$ [Tech: 0.3233). About 32 out of 100 random samples of size $n = 500$ adult Americans will result in fewer than 190 individuals (that is, less than 38%) who believe that marriage is obsolete.
(c) $P(0.40 < \hat{p} < 0.45) = 0.3198$ [Tech: 0.3203]. About 32 out of 100 random samples of size $n = 500$ adult Americans will result in between 200 and 225 individuals (that is, between 40% and 45%) who believe that marriage is obsolete.
(d) $P(\hat{p} \ge 0.42) = 0.0838$ [Tech: 0.0845]. About 8 out of 100 random samples of size $n = 500$ adult Americans will result in 210 or more individuals (that is, 42% or more) who believe that marriage is obsolete. This result is not unusual.

18. (a) The sampling distribution of $\hat{p}$ is approximately normal with $\mu_{\hat{p}} = 0.29$ and $\sigma_{\hat{p}} = \sqrt{\frac{0.29(0.71)}{500}} \approx 0.020$.
(b) $P(\hat{p} > 0.3) = 0.3121$ [Tech: 0.3111]. About 31 out of 100 random samples of size $n = 500$ adults will result in more than 150 individuals (that is, more than 30%) who do not own a credit card.
(c) $P(0.25 < \hat{p} < 0.30) = 0.6635$ [Tech: 0.6646]. About 66 out of 100 random samples of size $n = 500$ adults will result in between 125 and 150 individuals (that is, between 25% and 30%) who do not own a credit card.
(d) $P(\hat{p} \le 0.25) = 0.0244$ [Tech: 0.0244]. About 2 out of 100 random samples of size $n = 500$ adults will result in 125 or fewer individuals (that is, 25% or less) who do not own a credit card. This result is unusual.

19. $P(X \ge 121) = P(\hat{p} \ge 0.11) = 0.1335$ [Tech: 0.1345]. This result is not unusual, so this evidence is insufficient to conclude that the proportion of Americans who are afraid to fly has increased above 0.10. In other words, the results obtained could be due to sampling error and the true proportion is still 0.10.

20. $P(X \ge 52) = P(\hat{p} \ge 0.208) = 0.1251$ [Tech: 0.1246]. The result is not unusual, so this evidence is insufficient to conclude that the proportion of women 40–44 years of age who have not given birth has increased above 0.18. In other words, the results obtained could be due to sampling error and the true proportion is still 0.18.

21. $P(X \geq 164) = P(\hat{p} \geq 0.529) = 0.0853$ [Tech: 0.0847]. When the final election results will show 49% of voters supporting an increase in funding for education, approximately 9 out of 100 random samples of 310 voters will result in 52.9% or more who support the increase. This result is not unusual, so it would not be unusual for a wrong call to be made in an election if exit polling alone was considered. The exit polling could be biased in favor of an increase in funding for education, since a voter who voted against it in the privacy of the voting booth might not want to admit it to a pollster.

22. The probability that the engineer accepts the shipment is approximately 0.01. The acceptance policy is sound.

23. (a) 62 more adult Americans must be polled to make $np(1 - p) \geq 10$.
(b) 13 more adult Americans must be polled if $p = 0.2$.

24. (a) 12 more teenagers must be sampled if $p = 0.9$.
(b) 111 more teenagers must be sampled if $p = 0.95$.

25. A sample of size $n = 20$ households represents more than 5% of the population size $N = 100$ households in the association. Thus, the results from individuals in the sample are not independent of one another.

26. (a) $\hat{p} = \dfrac{410}{500} = 0.82$
(b) $\sigma_{\hat{p}} = 0.017$

Chapter 8 Review Exercises (page 387)

1. A sampling distribution is a probability distribution for all possible values of a statistic computed from a sample of size n.

2. The sampling distribution of $\bar{x}$ is exactly normal when the underlying population distribution is normal. The sampling distribution of $\bar{x}$ is approximately normal when the sample size is large, usually greater than 30, regardless of how the population is distributed.

3. The sampling distribution of $\hat{p}$ is approximately normal when $np(1 - p) \geq 10$, provided that $n \leq 0.05N$.

4. $\mu_{\bar{x}} = \mu$, $\sigma_{\bar{x}} = \dfrac{\sigma}{\sqrt{n}}$, and $\mu_{\hat{p}} = p$, $\sigma_{\hat{p}} = \sqrt{\dfrac{p(1-p)}{n}}$

5. (a) $P(x > 2625) = 0.3085$. If we select a simple random sample of $n = 100$ pregnant women, then about 31 will have energy needs of more than 2625 kcal/day. This result is not unusual.
(b) $\bar{x}$ is normal with $\mu_{\bar{x}} = 2600$ kcal and $\sigma_{\bar{x}} = \dfrac{50}{\sqrt{20}} = \dfrac{25}{\sqrt{5}} \approx$ 11.180 kcal.
(c) $P(\bar{x} > 2625) = 0.0125$ [Tech: 0.0127]. If we take 100 simple random samples of size $n = 20$ pregnant women, then about 1 of the samples will result in a mean energy need of more than 2625 kcal/day. This result is unusual.

6. (a) $\bar{x}$ is approximately normal with $\mu_{\bar{x}} = 0.75$ inch and $\sigma_{\bar{x}} = \dfrac{0.004}{\sqrt{30}} \approx 0.001$ inch.
(b) $P(\bar{x} < 0.748) + P(\bar{x} > 0.752) = 0.0062$. There is a 0.0062 probability that the inspector will conclude that the machine needs adjustment when, in fact, it does not need adjustment.

7. (a) No, the variable "number of televisions" is likely skewed right.
(b) $\bar{x} = 2.55$ televisions
(c) $P(\bar{x} \geq 2.55) = 0.0778$ [Tech: 0.0777]. If we take 100 simple random samples of size $n = 40$ households, then about 8 of the samples will result in a mean of 2.55 televisions or more. This result is not unusual, so it does not contradict the results reported by A. C. Nielsen.

8. (a) The sampling distribution of $\hat{p}$ is approximately normal with $\mu_{\hat{p}} = 0.72$ and $\sigma_{\hat{p}} = \sqrt{\dfrac{0.72(0.28)}{600}} \approx 0.018$.
(b) $P(\hat{p} \leq 0.70) = 0.1379$ [Tech: 0.1376]. About 14 out of 100 random samples of size $n = 600$ 18- to 29-year-olds will result in no more than 70% who would prefer to start their own business.
(c) Yes; it would be a little unusual for 450 of the 600 randomly selected 18- to 29-year-olds to prefer to start their own business. $P(X \geq 450) = P(\hat{p} \geq 0.75) = 0.0505$ [Tech: 0.0509].

9. $P(X \geq 60) = P(\hat{p} \geq 0.12) = 0.0681$ [Tech: 0.0680]. This result is not that unusual. There is some evidence to suggest that the proportion of adults 25 years of age or older with advanced degrees has increased above 10%.

10. (a) The sampling distribution of $\hat{p}$ is approximately normal with $\mu_{\hat{p}} = 0.280$ and $\sigma_{\hat{p}} = \sqrt{\dfrac{0.28(0.72)}{500}} \approx 0.020$.
(b) $P(\hat{p} \geq 0.310) = 0.0681$ [Tech: 0.0676]. It would not be unusual for a career 0.280 hitter to have a season in which he hits 0.310.
(c) $P(\hat{p} \leq 0.255) = 0.1056$ [Tech: 0.1066]. It would not be unusual for a career 0.280 hitter to have a season in which he hits 0.255.
(d) Batting averages between 0.260 and 0.300 lie within 1 standard deviation of the mean of the sampling distribution.
(e) It is unlikely that a career 0.280 hitter hits 0.280 each season, so he will have seasons where he bats below 0.280 and seasons where he bats above 0.280, and batting averages as low as 0.260 and as high as 0.300 are not unusual [$P(\hat{p} \leq 0.260) \approx 0.16$ and $P(\hat{p} \geq 0.300) \approx 0.16$]. Based on a single season, we cannot conclude that a player who hit 0.260 is worse than a player who hit 0.300 because neither result would be unusual for players who had identical career batting averages of 0.280.

Chapter 8 Test (page 388)

1. Regardless of the shape of the population, the sampling distribution of $\bar{x}$ becomes approximately normal as the sample size n increases.

2. $\mu_{\bar{x}} = 50$, $\sigma_{\bar{x}} = \dfrac{24}{\sqrt{36}} = 4$

3. (a) $P(X > 100) = 0.3859$ [Tech: 0.3875]. If we select a simple random sample of $n = 100$ batteries of this type, then about 39 batteries would last more than 100 minutes. This result is not unusual.
(b) $\bar{x}$ is normally distributed with $\mu_{\bar{x}} = 90$ minutes and $\sigma_{\bar{x}} = \dfrac{35}{\sqrt{10}} \approx 11.068$ minutes.
(c) $P(\bar{x} > 100) = 0.1841$ [Tech: 0.1831]. If we take 100 simple random samples of size $n = 10$ batteries of this type, then about 18 of the samples will result in a mean charge life of more than 100 minutes. This result is not unusual.
(d) $P(\bar{x} > 100) = 0.0764$ [Tech: 0.0766]. If we take 100 simple random samples of size $n = 25$ batteries of this type, then about 8 of the samples will result in a mean charge life of more than 100 minutes.
(e) The probabilities are different because a change in n causes a change in $\sigma_{\bar{x}}$.

4. (a) $\bar{x}$ is approximately normally distributed with $\mu_{\bar{x}} = 20$ liters and $\sigma_{\bar{x}} = \dfrac{0.05}{\sqrt{45}} \approx 0.007$ liter.
(b) $P(\bar{x} < 1.98) + P(\bar{x} > 2.02) = 0.0074$ [Tech: 0.0073]. There is a 0.0074 probability that the quality-control manager will shut down the machine even though it is correctly calibrated.

5. (a) The sampling distribution of $\hat{p}$ is approximately normal with $\mu_{\hat{p}} = 0.224$ and $\sigma_{\hat{p}} = \sqrt{\dfrac{0.224(0.776)}{300}} \approx 0.024$.
(b) $P(X \geq 50) = P(\hat{p} \geq 0.1667) = 0.9913$ [Tech: 0.9914]. About 99 out of 100 random samples of size $n = 300$ adults will result in at least 50 adults (that is, at least 16.7%) who are smokers.
(c) Yes; it would be unusual for 18% or less of 300 randomly selected adults to be smokers. $P(\hat{p} \leq 0.18) = 0.0336$ [Tech: 0.0338].

6. (a) For the sample proportion to be normal, the sample size must be large enough to meet the condition $np(1 - p) \geq 10$. Since $p = 0.01$, we have

$$n(0.01)(1 - 0.01) \geq 10$$
$$0.0099n \geq 10$$
$$n \geq \frac{10}{0.0099} \approx 1010.1$$

Thus, the sample size must be at least 1011 to satisfy the condition.
(b) No; it would not be unusual for a random sample of 1500 Americans to result in fewer than 10 with peanut or tree nut allergies. $P(X \leq 9) = P(\hat{p} \leq 0.006) = 0.0594$ [Tech: 0.0597].

7. $P(X \geq 82) = P(\hat{p} \geq 0.082) = 0.0681$ [Tech: 0.0685]. This result is not unusual, so this evidence is insufficient to conclude that the proportion of households with a net worth in excess of \$1 million has increased above 7%.

CHAPTER 9 Estimating the Value of a Parameter

9.1 Assess Your Understanding (page 401)

1. point estimate
2. level of confidence; $(1 - \alpha)100\%$
3. False
4. critical value

5. increases

6. decreases

7. $z_{\alpha/2} = z_{0.05} = 1.645$

8. $z_{\alpha/2} = z_{0.005} = 2.575$

9. $z_{\alpha/2} = z_{0.01} = 2.33$

10. $z_{\alpha/2} = z_{0.04} = 1.75$

11. $\hat{p} = 0.225, E = 0.024, x = 270$

12. $\hat{p} = 0.0625, E = 0.0115, x = 70$

13. $\hat{p} = 0.4855, E = 0.0235, x = 816$

14. $\hat{p} = 0.862, E = 0.009, x = 9251$

15. Lower bound: 0.146, upper bound: 0.254

16. Lower bound: 0.319, upper bound: 0.481

17. Lower bound: 0.191, upper bound: 0.289

18. Lower bound: 0.306 [Tech: 0.307], upper bound: 0.360

19. Lower bound: 0.759 [Tech: 0.758], upper bound: 0.805

20. Lower bound: 0.567 [Tech: 0.566], upper bound: 0.633 [Tech: 0.634]

21. **(a)** Flawed; no interval has been provided about the population proportion.
(b) Flawed; this interpretation indicates that the level of confidence is varying.
(c) Correct
(d) Flawed; this interpretation suggests that this interval sets the standard for all the other intervals, which is not true.

22. **(a)** Correct
(b) Flawed; this interpretation indicates that the level of confidence is varying.
(c) Flawed; this interpretation suggests that this interval sets the standard for all the other intervals, which is not true.
(d) Flawed; no interval has been provided about the population proportion.

23. We are 95% confident that the population proportion of adult Americans who dread Valentine's Day is between 0.135 and 0.225.

24. We are 95% confident that the population proportion of adult Americans who consider their commute to work very or somewhat stressful is between 0.20 and 0.28.

25. **(a)** $\hat{p} = 0.150$
(b) $n\hat{p}(1 - \hat{p}) = 460.40 \geq 10$, and the sample is less than 5% of the population.
(c) Lower bound: 0.140, upper bound: 0.160
(d) We are 90% confident that the proportion of adult Americans 18 years and older who have used their smartphones to make a purchase is between 0.140 and 0.160.

26. **(a)** $\hat{p} = 0.430$
(b) $n\hat{p}(1 - \hat{p}) = 282.60 \geq 10$, and the sample is less than 5% of the population.
(c) Lower bound: 0.401, upper bound: 0.459
(d) We are 95% confident that the proportion of workers and retirees in the United States 25 years of age and older who have less than $10,000 in savings is between 0.401 and 0.459.

27. **(a)** $\hat{p} = 0.519$
(b) $n\hat{p}(1 - \hat{p}) = 250.39 \geq 10$, and the sample is less than 5% of the population.
(c) Lower bound: 0.488, upper bound: 0.550 [Tech: (0.489, 0.550)]
(d) Yes; it is possible that the population proportion is more than 60%, because it is possible that the true proportion is not captured in the confidence interval. It is not likely.
(e) Lower bound: 0.450, upper bound: 0.512 [Tech: (0.450, 0.511)]

28. **(a)** $\hat{p} = 0.75$
(b) $n\hat{p}(1 - \hat{p}) = 192 \geq 10$, and the sample is less than 5% of the population.
(c) Lower bound: 0.715, upper bound: 0.785
(d) Yes; it is possible that the population proportion is below 70%, because it is possible that the true proportion is not captured in the confidence interval. It is not likely.
(e) Lower bound: 0.215, upper bound: 0.285

29. **(a)** $\hat{p} = 0.540$
(b) $n\hat{p}(1 - \hat{p}) = 434.20 \geq 10$, and the sample is less than 5% of the population.
(c) Lower bound: 0.520, upper bound: 0.560
(d) Lower bound: 0.509, upper bound: 0.571
(e) Increasing the level of confidence widens the interval.

30. **(a)** $\hat{p} = 0.470$
(b) $n\hat{p}(1 - \hat{p}) = 261.56 \geq 10$, and the sample is less than 5% of the population.
(c) Lower bound: 0.440, upper bound: 0.500 [Tech: (0.439, 0.500)]
(d) Lower bound: 0.430, upper bound: 0.510 [Tech: (0.430, 0.509)]
(e) Increasing the level of confidence widens the interval.

31. Lower bound: 0.205, upper bound: 0.307

32. Lower bound: 0.084, upper bound: 0.178 [Tech: (0.084, 0.177)]

33. **(a)** Using $\hat{p} = 0.635, n = 1708$.
(b) Using $\hat{p} = 0.5, n = 1842$.

34. **(a)** Using $\hat{p} = 0.669, n = 1499$.
(b) Using $\hat{p} = 0.5, n = 1692$.

35. **(a)** Using $\hat{p} = 0.15, n = 1731$.
(b) Using $\hat{p} = 0.5, n = 3394$.

36. **(a)** Using $\hat{p} = 0.34, n = 1269$.
(b) Using $\hat{p} = 0.5, n = 1414$.

37. **(a)** Using $\hat{p} = 0.53, n = 1064$.
(b) Using $\hat{p} = 0.5, n = 1068$.
(c) The results are close because $0.53(1 - 0.53) = 0.2491$ is very close to 0.25.

38. **(a)** Using $\hat{p} = 0.55, n = 419$.
(b) Using $\hat{p} = 0.5, n = 423$.
(c) The results are close because $0.55(1 - 0.55) = 0.2475$ is very close to 0.25.

39. At least $n = 984$ people were surveyed.

40. At least $n = 773$ people were surveyed.

41. Answers will vary.

42. **(a)** Answers will vary.
(b) Answers will vary.
(c) Answers will vary.
(d) Answers will vary.
(e) Answers will vary. Expect 95% of the intervals to contain the population proportion.

43. Lower bound: 0.018, upper bound: 0.316

44. Since $\hat{p} = 0$, the upper and lower bounds of the confidence interval using the normal model are both zero. Using Agresti and Coull's method, lower bound: −0.040, upper bound: 0.326. We are 95% confident that the proportion of adults who walk to work is between 0 and 0.326.

45. **(a)** $\hat{p} = 0.920$
(b) $n\hat{p}(1 - \hat{p}) = 73.6 \geq 10$, and the sample is less than 5% of the population.
(c) Lower bound: 0.903, upper bound: 0.937
(d) Yes; it is possible that the proportion is less than 0.85, because it is possible that the true proportion is not captured in the confidence interval. It is not likely.
(e) $\hat{p} = 0.770$.
(f) $n\hat{p}(1 - \hat{p}) = 1075.8 \geq 10$, and the sample is less than 5% of the population.
(g) Lower bound: 0.759, upper bound: 0.781
(h) Yes; it is possible that the proportion is greater than 0.85, because it is possible that the true proportion is not captured in the confidence interval. It is not likely.
(i) The proportion who say that they wash their hands is greater than the proportion who actually do. Explanations why may vary. One possibility is that people lie about their hand-washing habits out of embarrassment.

46. A 95% confidence interval means that the method works for 95% of all samples. That is, the interval will include the unknown parameter 95% of the time.

47. When the sample size n is multiplied by 4, the margin of error E is multiplied by $\frac{1}{\sqrt{4}} = \frac{1}{2}$.

48. They use the margin of error formula with $\hat{p} = 0.5$.

49. Matthew's estimate will have the smaller margin of error since $\frac{2.575}{\sqrt{400}} < \frac{1.96}{\sqrt{100}}$.

50. Mariya's interval is wrong. The upper and lower bounds are not the same distance from the point estimate.

51. The sample is not random. The U.S. Congress is not representative of the human race as a whole.

9.2 Assess Your Understanding (page 412)

1. decreases

2. False; the t-distribution is centered at 0.

3. α

4. True

5. False; the population does not need to be normally distributed if the sample size is sufficiently large.

6. robust

7. **(a)** $t_{0.10} = 1.316$
(b) $t_{0.05} = 1.697$
(c) $t_{0.99} = -2.552$
(d) $t_{0.05} = 1.725$

8. **(a)** $t_{0.02} = 2.205$
(b) $t_{0.10} = 1.309$
(c) $t_{0.95} = -1.943$
(d) $t_{0.025} = 2.120$

9. No; the data are not normal and contain an outlier.

10. No; the data are not normal and contain outliers.

11. No; the data are not normal.

12. No; the data are not normal.

13. Yes; the data appear normal, and there are no outliers.

14. Yes; the data appear normal, and there are no outliers.

15. $\bar{x} = 21$, $E = 3$

16. $\bar{x} = 25$, $E = 5$

17. $\bar{x} = 14$, $E = 9$

18. $\bar{x} = 25$, $E = 10$

19. **(a)** Lower bound: 103.7, upper bound: 112.3
(b) Lower bound: 100.4, upper bound: 115.6; decreasing the sample size increases the margin of error.
(c) Lower bound: 104.6, upper bound: 111.4; decreasing the level of confidence decreases the margin of error.
(d) No; the sample sizes were too small.

20. **(a)** Lower bound: 45.5, upper bound: 54.5
(b) Lower bound: 44.6, upper bound: 55.4; decreasing the sample size increases the margin of error.
(c) Lower bound: 46.3, upper bound: 53.7; decreasing the level of confidence decreases the margin of error.
(d) No; the sample sizes were too small.

21. **(a)** Lower bound: 16.85, upper bound: 19.95
(b) Lower bound: 17.12, upper bound: 19.68; increasing the sample size decreases the margin of error.
(c) Lower bound: 16.32, upper bound: 20.48 [Tech: (16.33, 20.48)]; increasing the level of confidence increases the margin of error.
(d) If $n = 15$, the population must be normal.

22. **(a)** Lower bound: 32.78, upper bound: 37.42
(b) Lower bound: 33.66, upper bound: 36.54; increasing the sample size decreases the margin of error.
(c) Lower bound: 31.76, upper bound: 38.44; increasing the level of confidence increases the margin of error.
(d) If $n = 18$, the population must be normal.

23. **(a)** Flawed; this interpretation implies that the population mean varies rather than the interval.
(b) Correct
(c) Flawed; this interpretation makes an implication about individuals rather than the mean.
(d) Flawed; the interpretation should be about the mean number of hours worked by adult Americans, not about adults in Idaho.

24. **(a)** Flawed; this interpretation makes an implication about individuals rather than the mean.
(b) Flawed; the interpretation should be about the mean number of hours of sleep during a weekday, not any day of the week.
(c) Flawed; this interpretation implies that the population mean varies rather than the interval.
(d) Correct

25. We are 90% confident that the mean drive-through service time of Taco Bell restaurants is between 161.5 and 164.7 seconds.

26. We are 95% confident that the mean amount of time spent on MySpace.com per user per month is between 151.4 and 190.6 minutes.

27. (1) Increase the sample size, and (2) decrease the level of confidence to narrow the confidence interval.

28. (1) Increase the sample size, and (2) decrease the level of confidence to narrow the confidence interval.

29. **(a)** Since the distribution of blood alcohol concentrations is not normally distributed (highly skewed right), the sample must be large so that the distribution of the sample mean will be approximately normal.
(b) The sample size is less than 5% of the population.
(c) Lower bound: 0.1647, upper bound: 0.1693; we are 90% confident that the mean BAC in fatal crashes where the driver had a positive BAC is between 0.1647 and 0.1693 g/dL.
(d) Yes; it is possible that the mean BAC is less than 0.08 g/dL, because it is possible that the true mean is not captured in the confidence interval, but it is not likely.

30. **(a)** Since the distribution of time spent eating and drinking each day is not normally distributed (skewed right), the sample must be large so that the distribution of the sample mean will be approximately normal.
(b) The sample size is less than 5% of the population.
(c) Lower bound: 1.180, upper bound: 1.260; we are 95% confident that the mean amount of time Americans age 15 or older spend eating and drinking each day is between 1.180 and 1.260 hours.
(d) No; only Americans age 15 or older were sampled. The results cannot be generalized to other age groups.

31. Lower bound: 12.05 books, upper bound: 14.75 books; we can be 99% confident that the mean number of books read by Americans in the past year was between 12.05 and 14.75.

32. **(a)** Lower bound: 17.19 books, upper bound: 20.41 books; we can be 99% confident that the mean number of books read by Americans during 1978 was between 17.19 and 20.41.
(b) Americans were reading more in 1978.

33. Lower bound: 1.08 days, upper bound: 8.12 days; we can be 95% confident that the mean incubation period of patients with SARS is between 1.08 and 8.12 days.

34. Lower bound: 228.33N, upper bound: 256.07N; researchers are 90% confident that the mean tensile strength of the resin cement is between 228.33 and 256.07 newtons.

35. **(a)** $\bar{x} = \$15.382$
(b) We can reasonably assume that the sample size is small relative to the population size. All the data lie within the bounds of the normal probability plot. The boxplot does not reveal any outliers.
(c) Lower bound: 13.707, upper bound: 17.057 [Tech: (13.706, 17.058)]
(d) Lower bound: 12.975, upper bound: 17.789 [Tech: (12.974, 17.790)]
(e) As the level of confidence increases, the width of the interval increases. A wider interval is more likely to include the population mean than a smaller subinterval.

36. **(a)** $\bar{x} = \$83.349$
(b) The sample size is small relative to the population size. All the data lie within the bounds of the normal probability plot. The boxplot does not reveal any outliers.
(c) Lower bound: 73.044, upper bound: 93.654 [Tech: (73.046, 93.652)]
(d) To increase the precision of the interval without additional data, decrease the level of confidence.

37. Lower bound: 1612.5, upper bound: 2667.4. All the data lie within the bounds of the normal probability plot. The boxplot does not reveal any outliers.

38. Lower bound: 31.9, upper bound: 44.6. All the data lie within the bounds of the normal probability plot. The boxplot does not reveal any outliers.

39. **(a)** $\bar{x} = 2.337$ million shares
(b) Lower bound: 2.013, upper bound: 2.661; we are 90% confident that the mean number of shares of Harley-Davidson stock traded per day in 2010 was between 2.013 and 2.661 million shares.
(c) Lower bound: 1.978, upper bound: 2.412; we are 90% confident that the mean number of shares of Harley-Davidson stock traded per day in 2010 was between 1.978 and 2.412 million shares.
(d) The confidence intervals are different because of variation in sampling. The samples have different means and standard deviations that lead to different confidence intervals.

40. **(a)** $\bar{x} = 5.430$ million shares
(b) Lower bound: 4.957 [Tech: 4.956], upper bound: 5.903; we are 95% confident that the mean number of shares of PepsiCo stock traded per day in 2010 was between 4.957 and 5.903 million shares.
(c) Lower bound: 5.298, upper bound: 6.322 [Tech: (5.298, 6.321)]; we are 95% confident that the mean number of shares traded per

day in 2010 was between 5.298 and 6.322 million shares.
(d) The confidence intervals are different because of variation in sampling. The samples have different means and standard deviations that lead to different confidence intervals.

41. (a) **Cell Phone Bills**

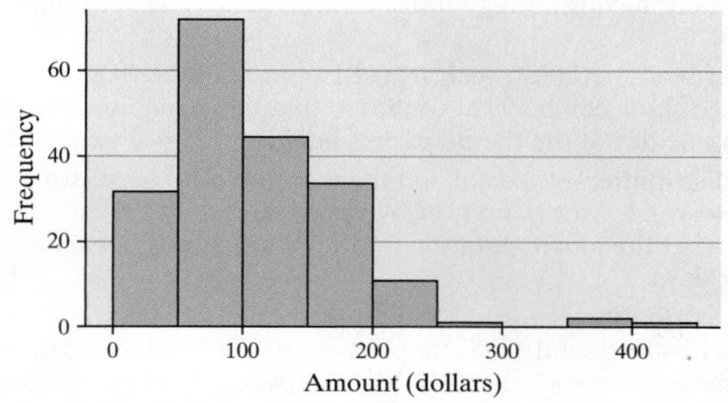

The distribution of cell phone bills is skewed right.
(b) **Cell Phone Bills**

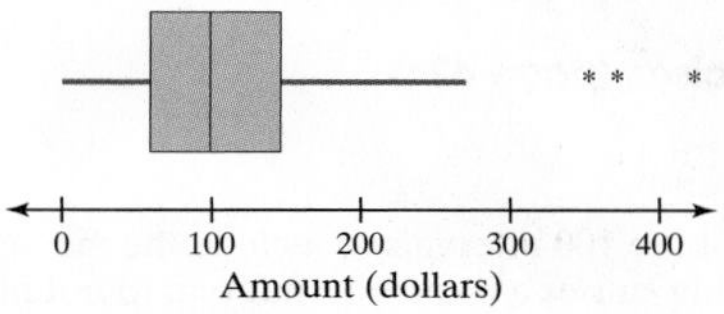

Yes, there are outliers.
(c) Since the distribution of cell phone bills is not normally distributed (skewed right with outliers), the sample must be large so that the distribution of the sample mean will be approximately normal.
(d) $\bar{x} = \$104.972$
(e) Lower bound: \$95.896, upper bound: \$114.048

42. (a) **What Is Rich?**

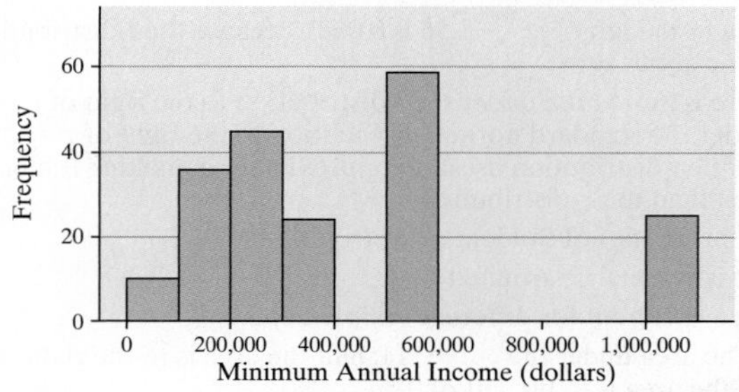

The graph is unusual because there are large gaps between the bars and while we might expect data concerning salaries to be skewed to the right, the salaries do not form a tail.
(b) **What Is Rich?**

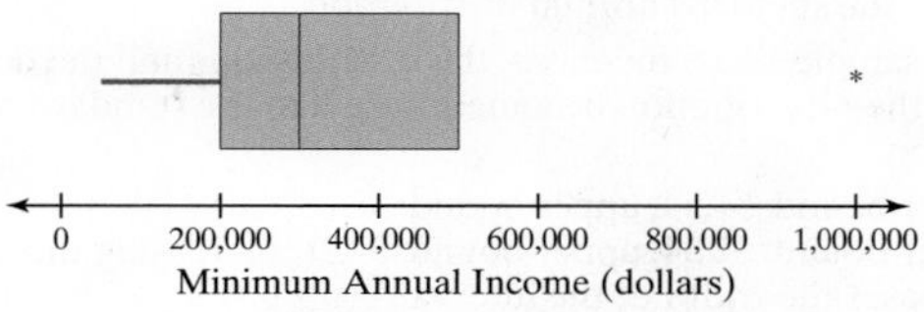

Yes, according to the boxplot, \$1,000,000 is an outlier. However, there are 25 occurrences of \$1,000,000 in the data set. This "outlier" comprises over 6% of the data and is not so unusual.
(c) $\bar{x} = \$381{,}407$
(d) Lower bound: \$342,426, upper bound: \$420,389

43. (a) $\bar{x} = 22.150$ years, $E = 0.059$ year
(b) We are 95% confident that the mean age of people when first married is between 22.091 and 22.209 years.
(c) Lower bound: $22.150 - 1.962 \cdot \dfrac{4.885}{\sqrt{26{,}540}} \approx 22.091$

Upper bound: $22.150 + 1.962 \cdot \dfrac{4.885}{\sqrt{26{,}540}} \approx 22.209$

44. (a) $\bar{x} = 7.678$, $E = 0.712$
(b) We are 95% confident that, of people who engaged in sexual intercourse during the past month, the mean number of times they engaged in intercourse during that month was between 6.966 and 8.390 times.
(c) Lower bound: $7.678 - 1.984 \cdot \dfrac{6.843}{\sqrt{357}} \approx 6.959$

Upper bound: $7.678 + 1.984 \cdot \dfrac{6.843}{\sqrt{357}} \approx 8.397$

45. For a 99% confidence level, $n = 298$ patients; for a 95% confidence level, $n = 173$ patients. Decreasing the confidence level decreases the sample size needed.

46. For a 90% confidence level, $n = 188$ subjects are needed; for a 95% confidence level, $n = 267$ subjects are needed. Increasing the confidence level increases the sample size needed.

47. (a) To estimate within four books with 95% confidence, $n = 67$ subjects are needed.
(b) To estimate within two books with 95% confidence, $n = 265$ subjects are needed.
(c) Doubling the required accuracy quadruples the sample size.
(d) To estimate within four books with 99% confidence, $n = 115$ subjects are needed. Increasing the level of confidence increases the sample size. For a fixed margin of error, greater confidence can be achieved with a larger sample size.

48. (a) To estimate within 2 hours with 95% confidence, $n = 55$ people are needed.
(b) To estimate within 1 hour with 95% confidence, $n = 217$ people are needed.
(c) Doubling the required accuracy quadruples the sample size.
(d) To estimate within 2 hours with 90% confidence, $n = 39$ people are needed. Decreasing the level of confidence decreases the sample size. For a fixed margin of error, a smaller sample size will result in a lower level of confidence.

49. (a) Set I: $\bar{x} \approx 99.1$; set II: $\bar{x} \approx 99.1$; set III: $\bar{x} \approx 99.0$
(b) Set I: Lower bound: 82.6, upper bound: 115.6 [Tech: 115.7]
Set II: Lower bound: 91.7, upper bound: 106.5
Set III: Lower bound: 93.5, upper bound: 104.5 [Tech: 104.6]
(c) As the size of the sample increases, the width of the confidence interval decreases.
(d) Set I: Lower bound: 58.6, upper bound: 117.2
Set II: Lower bound: 83.2, upper bound: 106.0
Set III: Lower bound: 88.1, upper bound: 103.9
(e) Each interval contains the population mean. The procedure for constructing the confidence interval is robust. This also illustrates the Law of Large Numbers, and Central Limit Theorem.

50. (a) Lower bound: 46.1, upper bound: 54.4
(b) 14 is less than the lower fence; $14 < Q_1 - 1.5(\text{IQR}) = 29.25$.
(c) Lower bound: 40.2; upper bound: 55.8; the outlier shifts the confidence interval to the left.
(d) $\bar{x} = 50.25$
(e) Lower bound: 47.7; upper bound: 52.8; increasing the sample size reduces the width of the interval.
(f) 14 is less than the lower fence; $14 < Q_1 - 1.5(\text{IQR}) = 23.5$.
(g) Lower bound: 46.3; upper bound: 52.7; the outlier shifts the confidence interval only slightly to the left.

51. (a) Answers will vary.
(b) Answers will vary.
(c) Answers will vary.
(d) Answers will vary. Expect 95% of the intervals to contain the population mean.

52. (a) Answers will vary.
(b) Answers will vary.
(c) Answers will vary. Expect fewer than 95% of the intervals to contain the population mean.
(d) Answers will vary. Since the data come from a population that is not normally distributed, the procedure for constructing the confidence interval requires that the sample size be large.

53. (a) Completely randomized design
(b) The treatment is the smoking cessation program. There are 2 levels.
(c) The response variable is whether or not the smoker had 'even a puff' from a cigarette in the past 7 days.
(d) The statistics reported are 22.3% of participants in the experimental group reported abstinence and 13.1% of participants in the control group reported abstinence.
(e) $\dfrac{p(1-q)}{q(1-p)} = \dfrac{0.223(1-0.131)}{0.131(1-0.223)} \approx 1.90$; this means that reported

abstinence is almost twice as likely in the experimental group than in the control group.
(f) The authors are 95% confident that the population odds ratio is between 1.12 and 3.26.
(g) Answers will vary. One possibility: smoking cessation is more likely when the Happy Ending Intervention program is used rather than the control method.

54. (a)

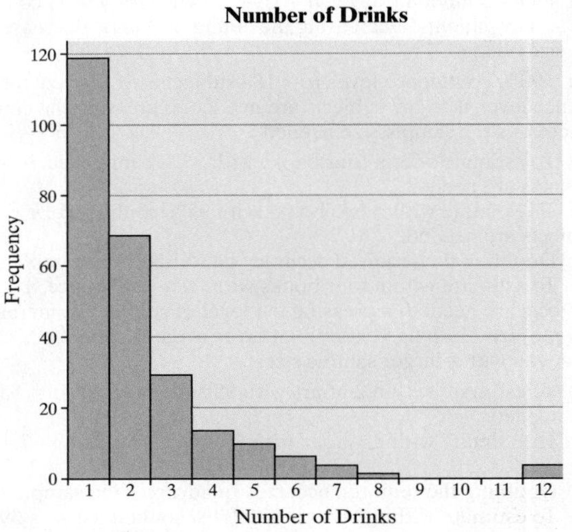

The distribution is skewed right.
(b) $\bar{x} = 2.0$ drinks, $s = 1.6$ drinks
(c) Mode = 1 drink
(d) $P(2) = 0.2716$
(e) Yes; it would be unusual to observe an individual who consumes at least eight drinks. $P(X \geq 8) = 0.0082$.
(f) The $\bar{x}$-distribution is normal. Since the sample size $n = 243$ is large, the Central Limit Theorem applies.
(g) Lower bound: 1.8 [Tech: 1.9], upper bound: 2.2; we are 95% confident that the mean number of drinks consumed, when people drink, is between 1.8 and 2.2 drinks.

55. The t-distribution has less spread as the degrees of freedom increase because as n increases s becomes closer to σ by the Law of Large Numbers.

56. Robust means that the procedure is still accurate when there are moderate departures from the requirements, such as normality in the distribution of the population.

57. The degrees of freedom are the number of data values that are free to vary.

58. The researcher used the entire population as the sample.

59. We expect that the margin of error for population A will be smaller since there should be less variation in the ages of college students than in the ages of the residents of a town, resulting in a smaller standard deviation for population A.

60. To estimate μ with the same margin of error, the sample size from population B must be 4 times that from population A, since $\frac{10}{\sqrt{4n}} = \frac{10}{2\sqrt{n}} = \frac{5}{\sqrt{n}}$.

9.3 Assess Your Understanding (page 421)

1. Lower bound: 0.069, upper bound: 0.165 [Tech: 0.164]
2. Lower bound: 0.317, upper bound: 0.383 [Tech: 0.384]
3. Lower bound: 37.74, upper bound: 52.26
4. Lower bound: 2.65, upper bound: 3.85
5. Lower bound: 114.98, upper bound: 126.02
6. Lower bound: 19.73 [Tech: 19.74], upper bound: 20.47 [Tech: 20.46]
7. Lower bound: 51.4, upper bound: 56.6; we can be 95% confident that felons convicted of aggravated assault serve a mean sentence between 51.4 and 56.6 months.

8. Lower bound: 0.829, upper bound: 0.873; the Centers for Disease Control can be 95% confident that the proportion of adults who always wear seat belts is between 0.829 and 0.873.

9. Lower bound: 2992.2, upper bound: 3849.9; the Internal Revenue Service can be 90% confident that the mean additional tax owed is between $2992.2 and $3849.9.

10. Lower bound: 861.98, upper bound: 864.02; we can be 99% confident that the mean muzzle velocity of the projectile is between 861.98 and 864.02 meters per second.

11. Lower bound: 0.496, upper bound: 0.548; the Gallup organization can be 90% confident that the proportion of adult Americans who are worried about having enough money for retirement is between 0.496 and 0.548.

12. Lower bound: 87.007 [Tech: 87.008], upper bound: 99.853 [Tech: 99.852]; we can be 99% confident that the mean amount spent per person in one day at the theme park is between $87.007 and $99.853.

13. The distribution is normal and there are no outliers, so we can use a t-interval. Lower bound: 262.4, upper bound: 273.1; we are 95% confident that the mean gestation period of humans is between 262.4 and 273.1 days.

14. The distribution is normal and there are no outliers, so we can use a t-interval. Lower bound: 0.851, upper bound: 0.894; we are 95% confident that the mean weight of plain M&Ms is between 0.851 and 0.894 gram.

15. We cannot construct a t-interval; there is an outlier in the data set.

16. We cannot construct a t-interval; the data are not normally distributed and the sample size is small.

Chapter 9 Review Exercises (page 424)

1. (a) $t_{0.005} = 2.898$
(b) $t_{0.05} = 1.706$

2. We would expect 95 of the 100 intervals to include the mean 100. Random chance in sampling causes a particular interval to not include the mean 100. Any sample statistic in the tails of the distribution will result in a confidence interval that does not include the parameter.

3. In a 95% confidence interval, the 95% represents the proportion of intervals that would contain the parameter (e.g., the population mean or population proportion) if a large number of different samples is obtained.

4. If a large number of different samples is obtained, a 90% confidence interval for a population mean will not capture the true population mean 10% of the time.

5. Area to the left of $t = -1.56$ is 0.0681 because the t-distribution is symmetric about zero.

6. There is more area under the t-distribution to the right of $t = 2.32$ than under the standard normal distribution to the right of $z = 2.32$, because the t-distribution uses s to approximate σ, making it more dispersed than the z-distribution.

7. The properties of Student's t-distribution:

1. It is symmetric around $t = 0$.

2. It is different for different sample sizes.

3. The area under the curve is 1; half the area is to the right of 0 and half the area is to the left of 0.

4. As t gets extremely large, the graph approaches, but never equals, zero. Similarly, as t gets extremely small (negative), the graph approaches, but never equals, zero.

5. The area in the tails of the t-distribution is greater than the area in the tails of the standard normal distribution.

6. As the sample size n increases, the distribution (and the density curve) of the t-distribution becomes more like the standard normal distribution.

8. (a) Lower bound: 51.54, upper bound: 58.06
(b) Lower bound: 52.34, upper bound: 57.26; increasing the sample size decreases the width of the interval.
(c) Lower bound: 49.52, upper bound: 60.08; increasing the level of confidence increases the width of the interval.

9. (a) Lower bound: 97.07, upper bound: 111.53
(b) Lower bound: 98.86, upper bound: 109.74; increasing the sample size decreases the width of the interval.
(c) Lower bound: 95.49, upper bound: 113.11; increasing the level of confidence increases the width of the interval.

10. (a) Because the distribution is likely skewed left, a large sample size is needed to invoke the Central Limit Theorem.
(b) Lower bound: 82.58, upper bound: 93.22; we are 95% confident that the mean age adult Americans would like to live is between 82.58 and 93.22 years.
(c) A sample size of $n = 231$ is required to estimate the mean age adult Americans would like to live within 2 years with 95% confidence.

11. (a) The distribution is skewed right.
(b) Lower bound: 8.86, upper bound: 11.94; we are 90% confident that the population mean number of e-mails sent per day is between 8.86 and 11.94 e-mails.

12. (a) The sample is probably small because of the difficulty and expense of gathering data.
(b) Lower bound: 201.5, upper bound: 234.5; the researchers can be 95% confident that the population "mean total work performed" for the sports-drink treatment is between 201.5 and 234.5 kilojoules.
(c) Yes; it is possible that the population "mean total work performed" for the sports-drink treatment is less than 198 kilojoules, since it is possible that the true mean is not captured in the confidence interval. It is not likely.
(d) Lower bound: 161.5, upper bound: 194.5; the researchers can be 95% confident that the population "mean total work performed" for the placebo treatment is between 161.5 and 194.5 kilojoules.
(e) Yes; it is possible that the population "mean total work performed" for the placebo treatment is more than 198 kilojoules, since it is possible that the true mean is not captured in the confidence interval. It is not likely.
(f) Yes; our findings support the researchers' conclusion. The confidence intervals do not overlap, so we are confident that the mean for the sports-drink treatment is greater than the mean for the placebo treatment.

13. (a) From the Central Limit Theorem, when the sample is large, $\bar{x}$ is approximately normally distributed.
(b) Lower bound: 1.95, upper bound: 2.59 [Tech: 2.58]; we can be 95% confident that couples who have been married for 7 years have a mean number of children between 1.95 and 2.59.
(c) Lower bound: 1.85, upper bound: 2.69; we can be 99% confident that couples who have been married for 7 years have a mean number of children between 1.85 and 2.69.

14. (a) $\bar{x} = 147.3$ cm, $s = 28.8$ cm
(b) The conditions are met. The data are approximately normal, and there are no outliers.
(c) Lower bound: 129.0, upper bound: 165.6; we are 95% confident that the population mean diameter of a Douglas fir tree in the western Washington Cascades is between 129.0 and 165.6 cm.

15. (a) $\hat{p} = 0.086$
(b) Lower bound: 0.065, upper bound: 0.107 [Tech: (0.064, 0.107)]; the Centers for Disease Control is 95% confident that the proportion of adult males 20 to 34 years old who have hypertension is between 0.065 and 0.107.
(c) 336 subjects would be needed if we use the point estimate of the proportion found in part (a).
(d) 1068 subjects would be needed if no prior estimate is available.

Chapter 9 Test (page 425)

1. The properties of the Student's t-distribution:
1. It is symmetric around $t = 0$.
2. It is different for different sample sizes.
3. The area under the curve is 1; half the area is to the right of 0 and half the area is to the left of 0.
4. As t gets extremely large, the graph approaches, but never equals, zero. Similarly, as t gets extremely small (negative), the graph approaches, but never equals, zero.
5. The area in the tails of the t-distribution is greater than the area in the tails of the standard normal distribution.
6. As the sample size n increases, the distribution (and the density curve) of the t-distribution becomes more like the standard normal distribution.

2. (a) $t_{0.02} = 2.167$
(b) $t_{0.01} = 2.567$

3. $\bar{x} = 139.2$, $E = 13.4$

4. (a) The distribution is skewed right.
(b) Lower bound: 1.151, upper bound: 1.289 [Tech: (1.152, 1.288)]; we are 99% confident that the population "mean number of family members in jail" is between 1.151 and 1.289 members.

5. (a) Lower bound: 4.319, upper bound: 4.841; we are 90% confident that the population "mean time to graduate" is between 4.319 and 4.841 years.
(b) Yes; our result from part (a) indicates that the mean time to graduate is more than 4 years. The entire interval is above 4.

6. (a) $\bar{x} = 57.8$ inches; $s = 15.4$ inches
(b) Yes; the conditions are met. The distribution is approximately normal, and there are no outliers.
(c) Lower bound: 48.0 [Tech: 47.9], upper bound: 67.6; the student is 95% confident that the mean depth of visibility of the Secchi disk is between 48.0 and 67.6 inches.
(d) Lower bound: 44.0 [Tech: 43.9], upper bound: 71.6; the student is 99% confident that the mean depth of visibility of the Secchi disk is between 44.0 and 71.6 inches.

7. (a) $\hat{p} = 0.948$
(b) Lower bound: 0.932, upper bound: 0.964 [Tech: 0.965]; the EPA is 99% confident that the proportion of Americans who live in neighborhoods with acceptable levels of carbon monoxide is between 0.932 and 0.964.
(c) 593 Americans must be sampled if the prior estimate of p is used.
(d) 3007 Americans must be sampled for the estimate to be within 1.5 percentage points with 90% confidence if no prior estimate is available.

8. (a) $\bar{x} = 133.4$ minutes
(b) Since the distribution of the lengths of matches is not normally distributed, the sample must be large so that the distribution of the sample mean will be approximately normal.
(c) Lower bound: 114.9, upper bound: 151.9; the tennis enthusiast is 99% confident that the population "mean length of matches at Wimbledon" is between 114.9 and 151.9 minutes.
(d) Lower bound: 119.6, upper bound: 147.2; the tennis enthusiast is 95% confident that the population "mean length of matches at Wimbledon" is between 119.6 and 147.2 minutes.
(e) Increasing the level of confidence increases the width of the interval.
(f) No; because the tennis enthusiast only sampled matches at Wimbledon, the results cannot be generalized to include other professional tennis tournaments.

CHAPTER 10 Hypothesis Tests Regarding a Parameter

10.1 Assess Your Understanding (page 434)

1. hypothesis	**2.** Hypothesis testing	**3.** null hypothesis
4. alternative hypothesis	**5.** I	**6.** II
7. level of significance	**8.** False	**9.** Right-tailed, μ
10. Left-tailed, p	**11.** Two-tailed, σ	**12.** Right-tailed, p
13. Left-tailed, μ	**14.** Two-tailed, σ	

15. (a) H_0: $p = 0.105$; H_1: $p > 0.105$
(b) The sample evidence led the researcher to believe that the proportion of births to teenage mothers increased, when in fact the proportion had not increased.
(c) The sample evidence did not lead the researcher to believe that the proportion of births to teenage mothers increased, when in fact the proportion did increase.

16. (a) H_0: $\mu = \$17{,}072$, H_1: $\mu \neq \$17{,}072$
(b) The researcher rejects the hypothesis that the mean charitable contribution per household is \$17,072, when in fact it is \$17,072.
(c) The researcher fails to reject the hypothesis that the mean charitable contribution per household is \$17,072, when in fact it is different from \$17,072.

17. (a) H_0: $\mu = \$218{,}600$; H_1: $\mu < \$218{,}600$
(b) The sample evidence led the real estate broker to conclude that the mean price of an existing single-family home has decreased, when in fact the mean price had not decreased.
(c) The sample evidence did not lead the real estate broker to conclude that the mean price of an existing single-family home decreased, when in fact the mean price did decrease.

18. (a) H_0: $\mu = 32$ ounces, H_1: $\mu < 32$ ounces
(b) The consumer advocate rejects the hypothesis that the mean net weight of the peanut butter is 32 ounces, when in fact the true mean weight of the peanut butter is 32 ounces.
(c) The consumer advocate fails to reject the hypothesis that the mean net weight of the peanut butter is 32 ounces, when in fact the mean weight of the peanut butter is less than 32 ounces.

19. (a) H_0: $\sigma = 0.7$ psi, H_1: $\sigma < 0.7$ psi
(b) The quality control manager rejects the hypothesis that the variability in the pressure required is 0.7 psi, when the true variability is 0.7 psi.

(c) The quality control manager fails to reject that the variability in the pressure required is 0.7 psi, when the variability is less than 0.7 psi.

20. (a) H_0: $p = 0.196$, H_1: $p > 0.196$
(b) The school nurse rejects that the proportion of children who are overweight is 0.196, when in fact the true proportion of overweight children in her school district is 0.196.
(c) The school nurse fails to reject that the proportion of children who are overweight is 0.196, when the true proportion of overweight children in her school district is more than 0.196.

21. (a) H_0: $\mu = \$47.47$, H_1: $\mu \neq \$47.47$
(b) The sample evidence led the researcher to believe the mean monthly cell phone bill is different from $47.47, when in fact the mean bill is $47.47.
(c) The sample evidence did not lead the researcher to believe the mean monthly cell phone bill is different from $47.47, when in fact the mean bill is different from $47.47.

22. (a) H_0: $\sigma = 112$, H_1: $\sigma < 112$
(b) The sample evidence implies that the standard deviation test score is less than 112, when in fact the standard deviation test score is 112.
(c) The sample evidence did not imply that the standard deviation test score is less than 112, when in fact the standard deviation test score is less than 112.

23. There is sufficient evidence to conclude that the proportion of births to teenage mothers has increased above its 2007 proportion of 0.105.

24. There is not sufficient evidence to conclude that the mean charitable contribution per household has changed from its 2005 level of $17,072.

25. There is not sufficient evidence to conclude that the mean price of an existing single-family home has decreased from its 2009 level of $218,600.

26. There is sufficient evidence to conclude that the mean content in a jar of peanut butter is less than 32 ounces.

27. There is not sufficient evidence to conclude that the variability in pressure has been reduced.

28. There is not sufficient evidence to conclude that the proportion of 6- to 11-year-olds who are overweight is greater than 0.196.

29. There is sufficient evidence to conclude that the mean monthly cell phone bill is different from its 2010 level of $47.47.

30. There is not sufficient evidence to conclude that the standard deviation SAT Critical Reading Test score has decreased from its 2010 value of 112.

31. There is not sufficient evidence to conclude that the proportion of births to teenage mothers has increased from its 2007 level of 0.105.

32. There is sufficient evidence to conclude that the mean charitable contribution has changed from its 2005 level of $17,072.

33. There is sufficient evidence to conclude that the mean price of an existing single-family home has decreased from its 2009 level of $218,600.

34. There is not sufficient evidence to conclude that the mean content in a jar of peanut butter is less than 32 ounces.

35. (a) H_0: $\mu = 54$ quarts, H_1: $\mu > 54$ quarts
(b) Congratulations to the marketing department at popcorn.org. After a marketing campaign encouraging people to consume more popcorn, our researchers have determined that the mean annual consumption of popcorn is now greater than 54 quarts, the mean consumption prior to the campaign.
(c) A Type I error was made. The probability of making a Type I error is 0.05.

36. (a) H_0: $\mu = 516$, H_1: $\mu > 516$
(b) There is not sufficient evidence to conclude that the mean score on the SAT Math Reasoning exam of students who take the company's course is higher than 516.
(c) A Type II error was committed because the researcher failed to reject a false null hypothesis. When $\alpha = 0.01$, the probability of committing a Type I error is 0.01.
(d) To decrease the probability of making a Type II error, we need to increase the level of significance.

37. (a) H_0: $\mu = 0.067$, H_1: $p < 0.067$
(b) There is not sufficient evidence to conclude that the changes at DARE have resulted in a decrease in the proportion of 12- to 17-year-olds who have used marijuana in the past 6 months.
(c) A Type II error was committed.

38. (a) H_0: $p = 0.152$, H_1: $p < 0.152$
(b) We are proud to announce a new massage therapy program that is clinically proven to reduce the proportion of individuals who experience migraine headaches.
(c) A Type I error was committed.

39. H_0: $\mu = 0$, H_1: $\mu > 0$, where μ is the mean increase in gas mileage when using the device.

40. (a) H_0: $\mu = 4$ hours, H_1: $\mu < 4$ hours
(b) *Consumer Reports* might reject the null hypothesis and conclude that a car with Prolong will not run 4 hours without oil.

41. If you are going to accuse a company of wrongdoing, you should have fairly convincing evidence. In addition, you likely do not want to find out down the road that your accusations were unfounded. Therefore, it is likely more serious to make a Type I error. For this reason, we should probably make the level of significance $\alpha = 0.01$.

42. $\alpha = 0.01$; choose a small α to make it difficult to reject H_0.

43. As the level of significance, α, decreases, the probability of making a Type II error, β, increases. As we decrease the probability of rejecting a true null hypothesis, we increase the probability of not rejecting the null hypothesis when the alternative hypothesis is true.

44. Answers will vary.

45. Answers will vary.

10.2 Assess Your Understanding (page 445)

1. statistically significant

2. True **3.** False **4.** 2.33

5. −1.28 **6.** ±1.96

7. $np_0(1 - p_0) = 42 > 10$
(a) Classical approach: $z_0 = 2.31 > z_{0.05} = 1.645$; reject the null hypothesis.
(b) *P*-value approach: *P*-value = 0.0104 [Tech: 0.0103] $< \alpha = 0.05$; reject the null hypothesis. There is sufficient evidence at the $\alpha = 0.05$ level of significance to reject the null hypothesis.

8. $np_0(1 - p_0) = 60 > 10$
(a) Classical approach: $z_0 = -3.36 < -z_{0.01} = -2.33$; reject the null hypothesis.
(b) *P*-value approach: *P*-value = $0.0004 < \alpha = 0.01$; reject the null hypothesis. There is sufficient evidence at the $\alpha = 0.01$ level of significance to reject the null hypothesis.

9. $np_0(1 - p_0) = 37.1 > 10$
(a) Classical approach: $z_0 = -0.74 > -z_{0.10} = -1.28$; do not reject the null hypothesis.
(b) *P*-value approach: *P*-value = 0.2296 [Tech: 0.2301] $> \alpha = 0.10$; do not reject the null hypothesis. There is not sufficient evidence at the $\alpha = 0.10$ level of significance to reject the null hypothesis.

10. $np_0(1 - p_0) = 75 > 10$
(a) Classical approach: $z_0 = -0.46 > -z_{0.10} = -1.28$; do not reject the null hypothesis.
(b) *P*-value approach: *P*-value = 0.3228 [Tech: 0.3221] > $\alpha = 0.10$; do not reject the null hypothesis. There is not sufficient evidence at the $\alpha = 0.10$ level of significance to reject the null hypothesis.

11. $np_0(1 - p_0) = 45 > 10$
(a) Classical approach: $z_0 = -1.49$ is between $-z_{0.025} = -1.96$ and $z_{0.025} = 1.96$; do not reject the null hypothesis.
(b) *P*-value approach: *P*-value = 0.1362 [Tech: 0.1360] $> \alpha = 0.05$; do not reject the null hypothesis. There is not sufficient evidence at the $\alpha = 0.05$ level of significance to reject the null hypothesis.

12. $np_0(1 - p_0) = 240 > 10$
(a) Classical approach: $z_0 = 1.29$ is between $-z_{0.005} = -2.575$ and $z_{0.005} = 2.575$; do not reject the null hypothesis.
(b) *P*-value approach: *P*-value = 0.1970 [Tech: 0.1967] $> \alpha = 0.01$; do not reject the null hypothesis. There is not sufficient evidence at the $\alpha = 0.01$ level of significance to reject the null hypothesis.

13. About 27 in 100 samples will give a sample proportion as high or higher than the one obtained if the population proportion really is 0.5. Because this probability is not small, we do not reject the null hypothesis. There is not sufficient evidence to conclude that the dart-picking strategy resulted in a majority of winners.

14. (a) H_0: $p = \frac{1}{12}$, H_1: $p > \frac{1}{12}$
(b) About 17 in 100 samples will give a sample proportion as high or higher than the one obtained if the population proportion really is $\frac{1}{12}$. Because this probability is not small, we do not reject the null hypothesis. There is not sufficient evidence to conclude that the individual has the ability to determine birth month.

15. $np_0(1 - p_0) = 16.1 > 10$ and $n \le 0.05N$. Hypotheses: $H_0: p = 0.019$, $H_1: p > 0.019$

(a) Classical approach: $z_0 = 0.65 < z_{0.01} = 2.33$; do not reject the null hypothesis.

(b) *P*-value approach: *P*-value $= 0.2578$ [Tech: 0.2582] $> \alpha = 0.01$; do not reject the null hypothesis. There is not sufficient evidence at the $\alpha = 0.01$ level of significance to conclude that more than 1.9% of Lipitor users experience flulike symptoms as a side effect.

16. $np_0(1 - p_0) = 12.6 > 10$ and $n \le 0.05N$. Hypotheses: $H_0: p = 0.94$, $H_1: p > 0.94$

(a) Classical approach: $z_0 = 0.69 < z_{0.01} = 2.33$; do not reject the null hypothesis.

(b) *P*-value approach: *P*-value $= 0.2451$ [Tech: 0.2462] $> \alpha = 0.01$; do not reject the null hypothesis. There is not sufficient evidence at the $\alpha = 0.01$ level of significance to support the manufacturer's claim that more than 94% of patients taking Nexium are healed within 8 weeks.

17. $H_0: p = 0.5, H_1: p > 0.5$; $np_0(1 - p_0) = 169 > 10$ and $n \le 0.05N$. Classical approach: $z_0 = 1.09 < z_{0.05} = 1.645$; do not reject the null hypothesis. *P*-value approach: *P*-value $= 0.1379$ [Tech: 0.1408] $> \alpha = 0.05$; do not reject the null hypothesis. There is not sufficient evidence to conclude that a majority of adults in the United States believe they will not have enough money in retirement.

18. $H_0: p = 0.5, H_1: p > 0.5$; $np_0(1 - p_0) = 125 > 10$ and $n \le 0.05N$. Classical approach: $z_0 = 1.70 > z_{0.05} = 1.645$; reject the null hypothesis. *P*-value approach: *P*-value $= 0.0446 < \alpha = 0.05$; reject the null hypothesis. There is sufficient evidence to conclude that a majority of students in the state of Illinois are prepared for social science in college upon graduation.

19. $np_0(1 - p_0) = 118.272 > 10$ and $n \le 0.05N$.Hypotheses: $H_0: p = 0.56$, $H_1: p > 0.56$. Classical approach: $z_0 = 2.60 > z_{0.05} = 1.645$; reject the null hypothesis. *P*-value approach: *P*-value $= 0.0047 < \alpha = 0.05$; reject the null hypothesis. There is sufficient evidence at the $\alpha = 0.05$ level of significance to support the claim that the proportion of employed adults who feel basic mathematical skills are critical or very important to their job is greater than 0.56.

20. $H_0: p = 0.38, H_1: p < 0.38$; $np_0(1 - p_0) = 264.3432 > 10$ and $n \le 0.05N$. Classical approach: $z_0 = -1.45 > -z_{0.05} = -1.645$; do not reject the null hypothesis. *P*-value approach: *P*-value $= 0.0735$ [Tech: 0.0754] $> \alpha = 0.05$; do not reject the null hypothesis. There is not sufficient evidence to conclude that the proportion of families with children under the age of 18 years of age who eat dinner together 7 nights a week has decreased since December 2001.

21. $H_0: p = 0.52, H_1: p \neq 0.52$; $np_0(1 - p_0) = 199.68 > 10$ and $n \le 0.05N$. Classical approach: $z_0 = -11.32 < -z_{0.05/2} = -1.96$; reject the null hypothesis. *P*-value approach: *P*-value $< 0.0001 < \alpha = 0.05$; reject the null hypothesis. There is sufficient evidence to conclude that the proportion of parents with children in high school who feel it was a serious problem that high school students were not being taught enough math and science has changed since 1994.

22. $np_0(1 - p_0) = 121.8 > 10$ and $n \le 0.05N$. Hypotheses: $H_0: p = 0.58$, $H_1: p \neq 0.58$. Classical approach: $z_0 = -0.45$ is between $-z_{0.05} = -1.645$ and $z_{0.05} = 1.645$; do not reject the null hypothesis. *P*-value approach: *P*-value $= 0.6528$ [Tech: 0.6505] $> \alpha = 0.10$; do not reject the null hypothesis. There is not sufficient evidence at the $\alpha = 0.10$ level of significance to support the claim that the percentage of females aged 15 years or older who live alone has changed.

23. $H_0: p = 0.47, H_1: p \neq 0.47$; $\hat{p} = 0.431$; $n\hat{p}(1 - \hat{p}) = 248.427 > 10$ and $n \le 0.05N$. Lower bound: 0.401, upper bound: 0.461 [Tech: 0.462]. Since 0.47 is not contained in the interval, we reject the null hypothesis. There is sufficient evidence to conclude that parents' attitude toward the quality of education in the United States has changed since August 2002.

24. (a) Answers will vary. The survey would need to be clearly anonymous and untraceable. In addition, the questions need to be phrased so as to not sound judgmental.

(b) $H_0: p = 0.22$, $H_1: p \neq 0.22$; $\hat{p} = 0.244$; $n\hat{p}(1 - \hat{p}) = 92.232 > 10$ and $n \le 0.05N$. Lower bound: 0.206, upper bound: 0.282. Since 0.22 is contained in the interval, we do not reject the null hypothesis. There is not sufficient evidence to conclude that the proportion of males who have strayed at least once during their married life is different from 0.22.

25. $np_0(1 - p_0) = 35 > 10$ and $n \le 0.05N$. Hypotheses: $H_0: p = 0.37$, $H_1: p < 0.37$. Classical approach: $z_0 = -0.25 > -z_{0.05} = -1.645$; do not reject the null hypothesis. *P*-value approach: *P*-value $= 0.4013$ [Tech: 0.3999] $> \alpha = 0.05$; do not reject the null hypothesis. No; there is not sufficient evidence at the $\alpha = 0.05$ level of significance to conclude that less than 37% of pet owners speak to their pets on the answering machine or telephone. The sample data do not contradict the results of the Animal Hospital Association.

26. $np_0(1 - p_0) = 25.5 > 10$ and $n \le 0.05N$. Hypotheses: $H_0: p = 0.85$, $H_1: p > 0.85$

(a) Classical approach: $z_0 = 0.20 < z_{0.10} = 1.28$; do not reject the null hypothesis.

(b) *P*-value approach: *P*-value $= 0.4207$ [Tech: 0.4215] $> \alpha = 0.10$; do not reject the null hypothesis. There is not sufficient evidence at the $\alpha = 0.10$ level of significance to conclude that more than 85% of the adult population eats salad at least once a week.

27. Hypotheses: $H_0: p = 0.5$, $H_1: p > 0.5$. $np_0(1 - p_0) = 4 < 10$. *P*-value $= 0.1051 > \alpha = 0.05$; do not reject the null hypothesis. There is not sufficient evidence at the $\alpha = 0.05$ level of significance to support the conclusion that the experimental course was effective.

28. Hypotheses: $H_0: p = 0.04$, $H_1: p < 0.04$. $np_0(1 - p_0) = 4.6 < 10$. *P*-value $= 0.2887 > \alpha = 0.05$; do not reject the null hypothesis. There is not sufficient evidence at the $\alpha = 0.05$ level of significance to support the obstetrician's belief that less than 4% of mothers smoke 21 or more cigarettes during pregnancy.

29. Hypotheses: $H_0: p = 0.021$, $H_1: p > 0.021$. $np_0(1 - p_0) = 3.1 < 10$. *P*-value $= 0.0976 > \alpha = 0.05$; do not reject the null hypothesis. There is not sufficient evidence at the $\alpha = 0.05$ level of significance to conclude that more than 2.1% of Americans work at home.

30. Hypotheses: $H_0: p = 0.078$, $H_1: p > 0.078$. $np_0(1 - p_0) = 5.8 < 10$. *P*-value $= 0.0461 < \alpha = 0.10$; reject the null hypothesis. There is sufficient evidence at the $\alpha = 0.10$ level of significance to support the urban economist's belief that the percentage of Americans who spend more than 60 minutes traveling to work has increased since 2009.

31. (a) The proportion could be changing due to sampling error—different people are in the sample. The proportion could also be changing because people's attitudes are changing.

(b) No; the probability of obtaining a sample proportion of $\hat{p} = 0.498$ if $p = 0.48$ is 0.0808 [Tech: 0.0814]. That is, about 8 samples out of 100 samples will result in a sample proportion of 0.498 or greater, if the population proportion is 0.48.

32. $H_0: p = 0.65, H_1: p < 0.65$; *P*-value $= 0.1922$ [Tech: 0.1928]. There is a 0.19 probability of obtaining the results we obtained if the null hypothesis is true. That is, about 19 samples in 100 will yield results similar to those found, if the null hypothesis is true. The headline is inaccurate.

33. Hypotheses: $H_0: p = 0.21$, $H_1: p > 0.21$. $np_0(1 - p_0) = 33.01 > 10$ and $n \le 0.05N$. *P*-value $= 0.0255 < \alpha = 0.1$; reject the null hypothesis. There is sufficient evidence at the $\alpha = 0.1$ level of significance that more than 21% of Americans consider themselves to be liberal.

34. Hypotheses: $H_0: p = 0.21$, $H_1: p < 0.21$. $np_0(1 - p_0) = 33.01 > 10$ and $n \le 0.05N$. *P*-value $= 0.0017$; reject the null hypothesis. Yes, the survey results suggest that the proportion of adult Americans who are current smokers has declined.

35. Hypotheses: $H_0: p = 0.5$, $H_1: p \neq 0.5$. $np_0(1 - p_0) = 11.25 > 10$ and $n \le 0.05N$. *P*-value $= 0.2984$ [Tech: 0.297]; do not reject the null hypothesis. Yes, the data suggest that the spreads are accurate.

36. (a) The researcher would be testing whether more than 40% of registered voters are Republican. $np_0(1 - p_0) = 76.8 > 10$ and $n \le 0.05N$. *P*-value $= 0.0537$ [Tech: 0.0551] $> \alpha = 0.05$; do not reject the null hypothesis. There is not sufficient evidence at the $\alpha = 0.05$ level of significance that more than 40% of registered voters are Republican.

(b) The researcher would be testing whether more than 41% of registered voters are Republican. $np_0(1 - p_0) = 77.4 > 10$ and $n \le 0.05N$. *P*-value $= 0.1075$ [Tech: 0.1098] $> \alpha = 0.05$; do not reject the null hypothesis. There is not sufficient evidence at the $\alpha = 0.05$ level of significance that more than 41% of registered voters are Republican.

(c) The researcher would be testing whether more than 42% of registered voters are Republican. $np_0(1 - p_0) = 78.0 > 10$ and $n \le 0.05N$. *P*-value $= 0.1922$ [Tech: 0.1947] $> \alpha = 0.05$; do not reject the null hypothesis. There is not sufficient evidence at the $\alpha = 0.05$ level of significance that more than 42% of registered voters are Republican.

(d) If we "accept" rather than "not reject" the null hypothesis, then we are saying that the population proportion is a specific value such as 0.41 in part (b) or 0.42 in part (c), and so we have used the same data to conclude that the population proportion is two different values. However, if we do not reject the null hypothesis, then we are saying that the population proportion could be 0.41 or 0.42 or even some other value; we are simply not ruling them out as the value of the population proportion. "Accepting" the null hypothesis can lead to contradictory conclusions, whereas "not rejecting" does not.

37. (a) We do not reject the null hypothesis for values of p_0 between 0.44 and 0.62, inclusive. Each of these values of p_0 represents a possible value of the population proportion at the $\alpha = 0.05$ level of significance.
(b) Lower bound: 0.432, upper bound: 0.628
(c) At $\alpha = 0.01$, we do not reject the null hypothesis for any of the values of p_0 given in part (a), so that the range of values of p_0 for which we do not reject the null hypothesis increases. The lower value of α means we need more convincing evidence to reject the null hypothesis, so we would expect a larger range of possible values for the population proportion.

38. (a) Answers will vary.
(b) At the $\alpha = 0.1$ level of significance, we expect 10 of the 100 samples to result in a Type I error.
(c) Answers will vary.
(d) We know the population proportion.

39. (a) Answers will vary.
(b) At the $\alpha = 0.1$ level of significance, we expect 10 of the 100 samples to result in a Type I error.
(c) Answers will vary. The sample size is small.
(d) We know the population proportion.

40. (a) The researchers simply looked at records. There was no treatment imposed on the individuals in the study.
(b) Retrospective
(c) 102 females
(d)

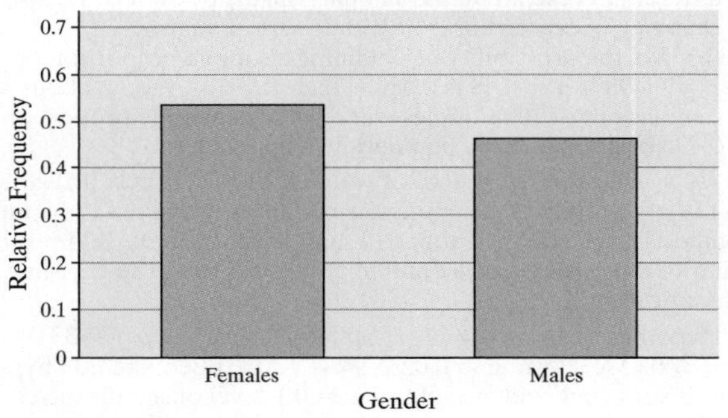

(e) $\hat{p} = \frac{92}{194} = 0.474$
(f) $H_0: p = 0.51, H_1: p < 0.51$. Classical approach: $z_0 = -1.00 > -z_{0.05} = -1.645$; do not reject the null hypothesis. *P*-value approach: *P*-value $= 0.1587$ [Tech: 0.1594]; do not reject the null hypothesis. The sample evidence does not indicate that the proportion of males in families where a sibling has lupus is less than 0.51, the accepted proportion of males in the general population at birth.
(g) Lower bound: 0.404, upper bound: 0.544. We are 95% confident that the proportion of males in a family where a sibling has lupus is between 0.404 and 0.544.

41. (a) The randomness in the order in which the baby is exposed to the toys is important to avoid bias.
(b) $H_0: p = 0.5$, $H_1: p > 0.5$
(c) *P*-value $= 0.0021$; there is sufficient evidence to suggest the proportion of babies who choose the "helper" toy is greater than 0.5.
(d) If the population proportion of babies who choose the helper toy is 0.5, a sample where all 12 babies choose the helper toy will occur in about 2 out of 10,000 samples of 12 babies.

42. A *P*-value is the probability of getting a result at least as extreme as the one obtained in a sample assuming the null hypothesis to be true. If the *P*-value is less than a predetermined level of significance α, we reject the null hypothesis.

43. If the *P*-value for a particular test statistic is 0.23, we expect results at least as extreme as the test statistic in about 23 of 100 samples if the null hypothesis is true. Since this event is not unusual, we do not reject the null hypothesis.

44. If the *P*-value for a particular test statistic is 0.02, we expect results at least as extreme as the test statistic in about 2 of 100 samples if the null hypothesis is true. This result is significant at the $\alpha = 0.01$ level of significance, but not at the $\alpha = 0.05$ level of significance. We need to consider the consequences of making a Type I error before deciding whether to reject the null hypothesis.

45. For the Classical Approach, the calculation of the test statistic is simple, but you need to be very careful when determining the rejection region to interpret the result. For the *P*-value method, the *P*-value is harder to calculate than the test statistic but the decision to reject or not is the same, regardless of the test. Plus, evidence as to the strength of evidence against the null hypothesis is reported. Most software will calculate both the test statistic and the *P*-value, which eliminates the disadvantages of the *P*-value method. Since the *P*-value is easier to interpret, the *P*-value method is easier to use with technology.

46. If we construct a confidence interval using the margin of error, we obtain *lower bound*: 52% and *upper bound*: 58%. Because a majority would be any percentage greater than 50%, the headline is accurate.

47. Statistical significance means that the result observed in a sample is unusual when the null hypothesis is assumed to be true.

10.3 Assess Your Understanding (page 454)

1. (a) $t_{0.01} = 2.602$
(b) $-t_{0.05} = -1.729$
(c) $\pm t_{0.025} = \pm 2.179$

2. (a) $t_{0.1} = 1.321$
(b) $-t_{0.01} = -2.426$
(c) $\pm t_{0.005} = \pm 2.738$

3. (a) $t_0 = -1.379$ **(b)** $-t_{0.05} = -1.714$
(c)

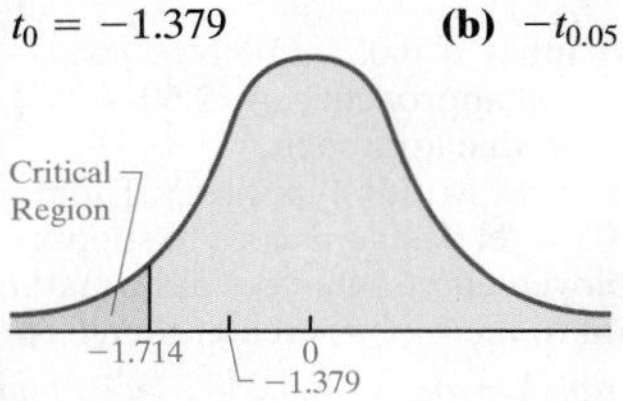

(d) There is not enough evidence for the researcher to reject the null hypothesis because it is a left-tailed test and the test statistic is greater than the critical value ($-1.379 > -1.714$).

4. (a) $t_0 = 2.674$ **(b)** $t_{0.1} = 1.318$
(c)

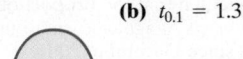

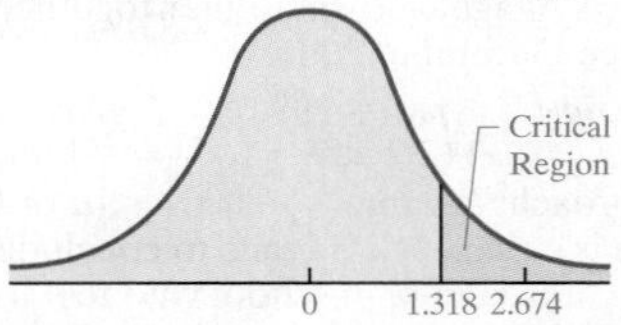

(d) The researcher will reject the null hypothesis because it is a right-tailed test and the test statistic is greater than the critical value ($2.674 > 1.318$).

5. (a) $t_0 = 2.502$ **(b)** $-t_{0.005} = -2.819$; $t_{0.005} = 2.819$
(c)

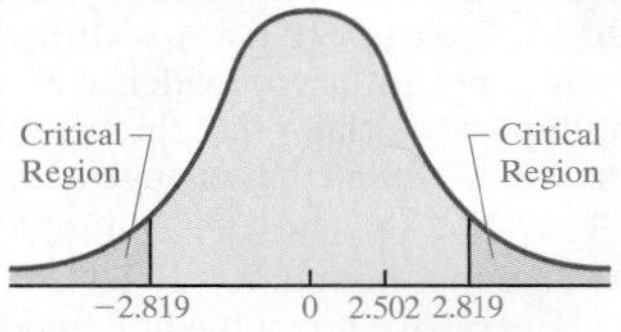

(d) There is not sufficient evidence for the researcher to reject the null hypothesis, since the test statistic is between the critical values ($-2.819 < 2.502 < 2.819$).
(e) Lower bound: 99.39, upper bound: 110.21. Because the 99% confidence interval includes 100, we do not reject the statement in the null hypothesis.

6. (a) $t_0 = -1.711$ **(b)** $-t_{0.02} = -2.189$
(c)

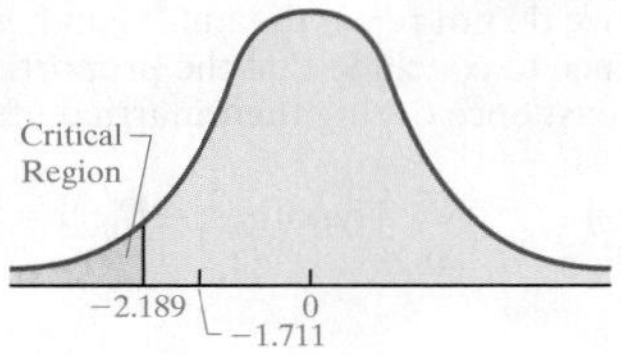

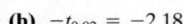

(d) The researcher will not reject the null hypothesis because it is a left-tailed test and the test statistic is greater than the critical value $(-1.711 > -2.189)$.

7. (a) $t_0 = -1.677$
(b)

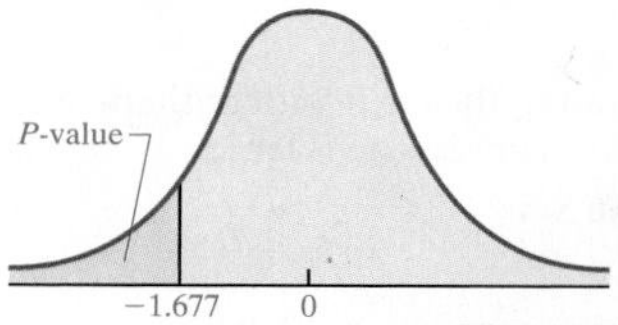

(c) $0.05 < P\text{-value} < 0.10$ [Tech: $P = 0.0559$]. If we take 100 random samples of size 18, we would expect about 6 of the samples to result in a sample mean of 18.3 or less if $\mu = 20$.
(d) The researcher will not reject the null hypothesis at the $\alpha = 0.05$ level of significance because the *P*-value is greater than the level of significance.

8. (a) $t_0 = 1.109$
(b)

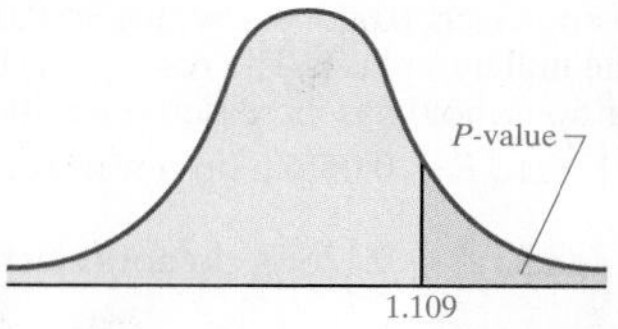

(c) $0.10 < P\text{-value} < 0.15$ [Tech: $P = 0.1445$]. If we obtain 100 random samples of size $n = 13$, we would expect about 14 of the samples to result in a sample mean of 4.9 or higher if $\mu = 4.5$.
(d) The researcher will not reject the null hypothesis at the $\alpha = 0.10$ level of significance because the *P*-value is greater than the level of significance.

9. (a) No; $n \geq 30$ **(b)** $t_0 = -3.108$
(c)

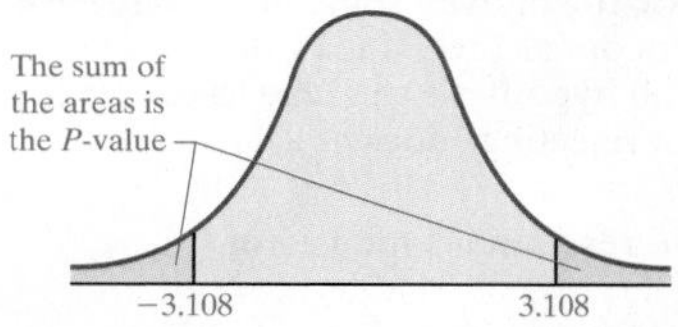

(d) $0.002 < P\text{-value} < 0.005$ [Tech: *P*-value $= 0.0038$]. If we obtain 1000 random samples of size $n = 35$, we would expect about 4 samples to result in a mean as extreme or more extreme than the one observed if $\mu = 105$.
(e) The researcher will reject the null hypothesis at the $\alpha = 0.01$ level of significance because the *P*-value is less than the level of significance $(0.0038 < 0.01)$.

10. (a) No; $n \geq 30$ **(b)** $t_0 = 2.455$
(c)

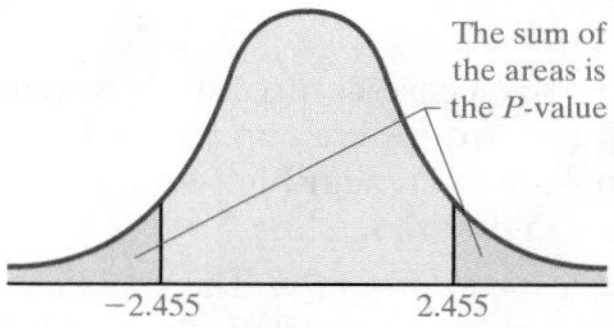

(d) $0.01 < P\text{-value} < 0.02$ [Tech: *P*-value $= 0.0186$]; If we obtain 100 random samples of size $n = 40$, we'd expect about 2 samples to result in a mean as extreme or more extreme than the one observed if $\mu = 45$.
(e) The researcher will not reject the null hypothesis at the $\alpha = 0.01$ level of significance because the *P*-value is greater than the level of significance $(0.0186 > 0.01)$.
(f) Lower bound: 44.66, upper bound: 51.94. Because the confidence interval includes 45, we do not reject the null hypothesis.

11. (a) H_0: $\mu = \$67$, H_1: $\mu > \$67$
(b) There is a 0.02 probability of obtaining a sample mean of $73 or higher from a population whose mean is $67. So, if we obtained 100 simple random samples of size $n = 40$ from a population whose mean is $67, we would expect about 2 of these samples to result in sample means of $73 or higher.
(c) Because the *P*-value is low ($P\text{-value} = 0.02 < \alpha = 0.05$), we reject the statement in the null hypothesis. There is sufficient evidence to conclude that the mean dollar amount withdrawn from a PayEase ATM is more than the mean amount from a standard ATM (that is, more than $67).

12. (a) H_0: $\mu = 63.7$ inches, H_1: $\mu > 63.7$ inches
(b) There is a 0.35 probability of obtaining a sample mean of 63.9 inches or greater from a population whose mean is 63.7 inches. So, if we obtained 100 simple random samples of size $n = 45$ from a population whose mean is 63.7 inches, we would expect about 35 of these samples to result in a sample mean of 63.9 inches or higher.
(c) Because the *P*-value is large ($P\text{-value} = 0.35 > \alpha = 0.10$), we do not reject the statement in the null hypothesis. There is not sufficient evidence to conclude that the mean height of women 20 years of age or older is greater than it was in 1990.

13. (a) H_0: $\mu = 22$; H_1: $\mu > 22$
(b) The sample is random. The sample size is large, $n = 200 \geq 30$. We can reasonably assume that the sample is small relative to the population, so the scores are independent.
(c) Classical approach: $t_0 = 2.176 > t_{0.05} = 1.660$; reject the null hypothesis. *P*-value approach: $0.01 < P\text{-value} < 0.02$ [Tech: $P = 0.0154$]; reject the null hypothesis.
(d) There is sufficient evidence to conclude that students who complete the core curriculum are scoring above 22 on the math portion of the ACT.

14. (a) H_0: $\mu = 501$; H_1: $\mu < 501$
(b) The sample is random. The sample size is large, $n = 100 \geq 30$. We can reasonably assume that the sample is small relative to the population, so the scores are independent.
(c) Classical approach: $t_0 = -1.379 < -t_{0.1} = -1.290$; reject the null hypothesis. *P*-value approach: $0.05 < P\text{-value} < 0.10$ [Tech: $P = 0.0855$]; reject the null hypothesis.
(d) There is sufficient evidence to conclude that students who learn English as well as another language simultaneously score worse on the SAT Critical Reading Exam.

15. Hypotheses: H_0: $\mu = 9.02$, H_1: $\mu < 9.02$. Classical approach: $t_0 = -4.553 < -t_{0.01} = -2.718$; reject the null hypothesis. *P*-value approach: $P\text{-value} < 0.0005$ [Tech: *P*-value $= 0.0004$] $< \alpha = 0.01$; reject the null hypothesis. There is sufficient evidence to conclude that the mean hippocampal volume in alcoholic adolescents is less than the normal mean volume of 9.02 cm^3.

16. Assuming that the population of kidney weights is normally distributed, with no outliers: Hypotheses: H_0: $\mu = 355.7$, H_1: $\mu > 355.7$. Classical approach: $t_0 = 3.144 > t_{0.05} = 1.796$; reject the null hypothesis. *P*-value approach: $0.0025 < P\text{-value} < 0.005$ [Tech: *P*-value $= 0.0047$] $< \alpha = 0.05$; reject the null hypothesis. There is sufficient evidence to conclude that the mean weight of kidneys of first-generation mice whose both parents were exposed to para-nonylphenol is greater than the mean weight of the kidneys of nonexposed mice.

17. H_0: $\mu = 703.5$, H_1: $\mu > 703.5$. Classical approach: $t_0 = 0.813 < t_{0.05} = 1.685$ (39 degrees of freedom); do not reject the null hypothesis. *P*-value approach: $0.25 > P\text{-value} > 0.20$ [Tech: *P*-value $= 0.2105$] $> \alpha = 0.05$; do not reject the null hypothesis. There is not sufficient evidence to conclude that the mean FICO score of high-income individuals is greater than that of the general population. In other words, it is not unlikely to obtain a mean credit score of 714.2 or higher even though the true population mean credit score is 703.5.

18. H_0: $\mu = 154.8$ minutes, H_1: $\mu < 154.8$ minutes. Classical approach: $t_0 = -3.969 < -t_{0.05} = -1.676$ (using 50 degrees of freedom); reject the null hypothesis. *P*-value approach: $P\text{-value} < 0.0005$ [Tech: *P*-value $= 0.0001$] $< \alpha = 0.05$; reject the null hypothesis. There is sufficient evidence to conclude that Internet users watch less television per day.

19. H_0: $\mu = 40.7$ years, H_1: $\mu \neq 40.7$ years; 95% confidence interval: Lower bound: 35.44 years, upper bound: 42.36 years. Because the interval includes 40.7 years, there is not significant evidence to conclude that the mean age of a death-row inmate has changed since 2002.

20. H_0: $\mu = \$1493$, H_1: $\mu \neq \$1493$; 95% confidence interval: Lower bound: $1507.7, upper bound: $1728.3. Because the interval does not include $1493, there is significant evidence to conclude that the mean energy expenditure (adjusted for inflation) has changed since 2001.

21. (a) Yes; the conditions are satisfied. The data appear to be normally distributed, and there are no outliers.
(b) Hypotheses: H_0: $\mu = 84.3$ seconds, H_1: $\mu < 84.3$ seconds. Classical approach: $t_0 = -1.310 > -t_{0.10} = -1.383$ with 9 degrees of freedom; do not reject the null hypothesis. *P*-value approach: $0.15 > P\text{-value} > 0.10$ [Tech: *P*-value $= 0.1113$] $> \alpha = 0.10$; do not reject the null hypothesis. There is not sufficient evidence to conclude that the new system is effective.

22. (a) Yes; the normal probability plot suggests that the data could come from a population that is normally distributed, and the boxplot does not show any outliers.
(b) H_0: $\mu = 198$, H_1: $\mu > 198$; $t_0 = 3.499$ and $t_{0.10} = 1.383$ with 9 degrees of freedom; reject the null hypothesis. $0.0025 < P$-value < 0.005 [Tech: P-value $= 0.0033$] $< \alpha = 0.10$; reject the null hypothesis. Conclusion: There is sufficient evidence to conclude that the class was effective.

23. (a) Yes; all the data lie within the confidence bands of the normal probability plot, and the boxplot does not show any outliers.
(b) H_0: $\mu = 0.11$ mg/L, H_1: $\mu \neq 0.11$ mg/L. Classical approach: $t_0 = 1.707$ is between $-t_{0.025} = -2.262$ and $t_{0.025} = 2.262$; do not reject the null hypothesis. P-value approach: $0.1 < P$-value < 0.2 [Tech: $P = 0.122$]; do not reject the null hypothesis. Conclusion: There is not sufficient evidence to indicate that the calcium concentration in rainwater in Chautauqua, New York, has changed since 1990.

24. (a) Yes; all the data lie within the confidence bands of the normal probability plot, and the boxplot does not show any outliers.
(b) H_0: $\mu = 64.05$ oz, H_1: $\mu \neq 64.05$ oz. Classical approach: $t_0 = -4.482$ is less than $-t_{0.005} = -2.831$; reject the null hypothesis. P-value approach: P-value < 0.001 [Tech: $P = 0.0002$]; reject the null hypothesis. Yes; the machine should be recalibrated.
(c) Remember, α is the probability of making a Type I error. With $\alpha = 0.01$, there is a 1% probability of rejecting the null when the null is true; with $\alpha = 0.1$, there is a 10% probability of rejecting the null when the null is true. Making a Type I error means shutting down the machine and recalibrating when the procedure is unnecessary. Quite a bit of revenue would be lost for no reason.

25. (a) The data are skewed to the right with outliers.
(b) H_0: $\mu = 35.1$, H_1: $\mu \neq 35.1$. Classical approach: $t_0 = -6.216$ is less than $-t_{0.025} = -2.023$; reject the null hypothesis. P-value approach: P-value < 0.001 [Tech: $P < 0.0001$]; reject the null hypothesis. Yes; the evidence suggests that the volume of Apple stock has changed since 2007.

26. (a) The data are skewed to the right with outliers.
(b) H_0: $\mu = 5.44$, H_1: $\mu \neq 5.44$. Classical approach: $t_0 = -7.606$ is less than $-t_{0.025} = -2.032$; reject the null hypothesis. P-value approach: P-value < 0.001 [Tech: $P < 0.0001$]; reject the null hypothesis. Yes; the evidence suggests that the volume of Google stock has changed since 2007.

27. H_0: $\mu = 0.11$ mg/L, H_1: $\mu \neq 0.11$ mg/L. Lower bound: 0.0677, upper bound: 0.2459. Because 0.11 is in the 99% confidence interval, we do not reject the statement in the null hypothesis. There is not sufficient evidence to indicate that the calcium concentration in rainwater in Chautauqua, New York, has changed since 1990.

28. H_0: $\mu = 64.05$ oz, H_1: $\mu \neq 64.05$ *oz*. Lower bound: 63.987, upper bound: 64.027. Because 64.05 is not in the 95% confidence interval, we reject the statement in the null hypothesis. The machine should be recalibrated.

29. H_0: $\mu = 35.1$, H_1: $\mu \neq 35.1$. Lower bound: 19.858, upper bound: 27.342. Because 35.1 is not in the 95% confidence interval, we reject the statement in the null hypothesis. The evidence suggests that the volume of Apple stock has changed since 2007.

30. H_0: $\mu = 5.44$, H_1: $\mu \neq 5.44$. Lower bound: 2.703, upper bound: 3.857. Because 5.44 is not in the 95% confidence interval, we reject the statement in the null hypothesis. The evidence suggests that the volume of Google stock has changed since 2007.

31. (a) H_0: $\mu = 515$, H_1: $\mu > 515$
(b) Classical approach: $t_0 = 1.49 > t_{0.10} \approx 1.282$; reject the null hypothesis. P-value approach: $0.10 < P$-value < 0.05 [Tech: 0.0632] $< \alpha = 0.10$; reject the null hypothesis.
(c) Answers will vary.
(d) With $n = 400$ students: Classical approach: $t_0 = 0.70 < t_{0.10} \approx 1.29$; do not reject the null hypothesis. P-value approach: $0.20 < P$-value < 0.25 [Tech: 0.2358] $> \alpha = 0.10$; do not reject the null hypothesis.

32. (a) H_0: $\mu = 0$, H_1: $\mu > 0$
(b) Classical approach: $t_0 = 3.85 > t_{0.10} \approx 1.282$; reject the null hypothesis. P-value approach: P-value $= 0.0005 < \alpha = 0.10$; reject the null hypothesis.
(c) Answers will vary.
(d) With $n = 40$ subjects: Classical approach: $t_0 = 0.79 < t_{0.10} \approx 1.304$; do not reject the null hypothesis. P-value approach: $0.20 < P$-value < 0.25 [Tech: 0.2170] $> \alpha = 0.10$; do not reject the null hypothesis.

33. H_0: $\mu = \$4951$, H_1: $\mu < \$4951$. Classical approach: $t_0 = -4.479$ is less than $-t_{0.05} = -1.66$ for 100 degrees of freedom; reject the null hypothesis. P-value approach: P-value< 0.001 [Tech: $P < 0.0001$]; reject the null hypothesis. The results suggest that the mean credit-card debt is less than \$4951.

34. (a) $\bar{x} = 3.2$; $s = 1.7$
(b) The distribution is skewed to the right with outliers. We can use the normal model because the sample size is large.

Television Sets

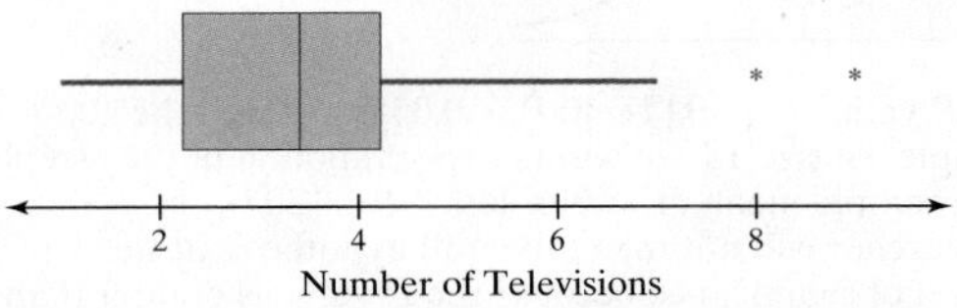

(c) H_0: $\mu = 2.9$, H_1: $\mu > 2.9$. Classical approach: $t_0 = 2.518$ is greater than $t_{0.05} = 1.66$ for 100 degrees of freedom; reject the null hypothesis. P-value approach: $0.005 < P$-value < 0.01 [Tech: $P < 0.0063$]; reject the null hypothesis. The results suggest that the number of televisions per household has increased since 2009.

35. (a) $0.05 < P$-value < 0.10 [Tech: $P = 0.0557$]; do not reject the null hypothesis.
(b) $0.10 < P$-value < 0.15 [Tech: $P = 0.1286$); do not reject the null hypothesis.
(c) P-value > 0.25 [Tech: $P = 0.2532$]; do not reject the null hypothesis.
(d) If we "accept" rather than "not reject" the null hypothesis, we are saying that the population mean is a specific value, such as 100, 101, or 102, and so we have used the same data to conclude that the population mean is three different values. However, if we do not reject the null hypothesis, we are saying that the population mean could be 100, 101, or 102 or even some other value; we are simply not ruling them out as the value of the population mean. "Accepting" the null hypothesis can lead to contradictory conclusions, whereas "not rejecting" does not.

36. (a) Answers will vary.
(b) We would expect 5 to result in a Type I error.
(c) Answers will vary.
(d) We know the population mean.

37. (a) Answers will vary.
(b) Answers will vary.
(c) We would expect 5 to result in a Type I error.
(d) Answers will vary. The distribution is skewed right and the sample size is small.

38. (a) *Step 1: Research objective.* To determine whether there is an association between distance of home address at birth from high-voltage power lines and the incidence of leukemia and other cancers in children in England and Wales.

Step 2: Collect information. This is a case-control study, which is an observational study in which two groups are compared. Here the two groups are children who were born near high-voltage lines and those who were not born near high-voltage lines.

Step 3: Organize and summarize the information. The statistics based on the sample are based on relative risk. The relative risk of leukemia for children born within 200 meters (m) of high-voltage power lines was 1.69 (these children were 1.69 times more likely to contract cancer than those who lived more than 600 m from the power lines). The relative risk of leukemia of children who lived between 200 and 600 m from high-voltage lines was 1.23 when compared with children who lived more than 600 m from the power line.

Step 4: Draw conclusions. The 95% confidence interval for relative risk of children who lived within 200 m of the high-voltage power lines compared to those who lived more than 600 m from the power lines was lower bound: 1.13, upper bound: 2.53. The researchers are 95% confident that the relative risk is between 1.13 and 2.53. Because a relative risk of 1 would imply no association, and this interval does not contain 1, we would reject the null hypothesis of no association. The 95% confidence interval for relative risk for children who lived between 200 and 600 m of high-voltage power lines compared to those who lived more than 600 m from the power lines was lower bound: 1.02, upper bound: 1.49. The researchers are 95% confident that the relative risk is between 1.02 and 1.49. Because a relative risk of 1 would imply no association, and this interval does not contain 1, we would reject the null hypothesis of no association. There is a relation between the distance one is from the power lines and the relative risk of contracting leukemia with a P-value < 0.01. The likelihood of observing the relation observed when there is no relation between proximity to the power lines and leukemia is 0.01. There is an association between childhood leukemia and proximity of home address at birth to high-voltage power lines.

(b) It would be highly unethical to conduct this experiment on human subjects. A researcher could try to replicate the results of this experiment with lab rats. We need a case-control to help diminish the likelihood of lurking variables. We must assume that the subjects are similar in all other traits that might affect the likelihood of contracting leukemia.

39. Yes; because the head of institutional research has access to the entire population, inference is unnecessary. He can say with 100% confidence that the mean age decreased because the mean age in the current semester is less than the mean age in 1995.

40. This means that minor departures from normality will not adversely affect the results of the test.

41. Statistical significance means that the sample statistic likely does not come from the population whose parameter is stated in the null hypothesis. Practical significance refers to whether the difference between the sample statistic and the parameter stated in the null hypothesis is large enough to be considered important in an application. A statistically significant result may be of no practical significance.

42. Answers will vary.

10.4 Assess Your Understanding (page 461)

1. Hypotheses: H_0: $\mu = 1$, H_1: $\mu < 1$. Classical approach: $t_0 = -2.179 > -t_{0.01} = -2.552$ with 18 degrees of freedom; do not reject the null hypothesis. P-value approach: $0.025 > P\text{-value} > 0.02$ [Tech: P-value $= 0.0214$] $> \alpha = 0.01$; do not reject the null hypothesis. There is not sufficient evidence at the $\alpha = 0.01$ level of significance to conclude that the mean is less than 1.

2. Hypotheses: H_0: $p = 0.5$, H_1: $p > 0.5$; $np_0(1 - p_0) = 50 > 10$ and $n \le 0.05N$. Classical approach: $z_0 = 2.12 > z_{0.05} = 1.645$; reject the null hypothesis. P-value approach: P-value $= 0.0170$ [Tech: 0.0169] $< \alpha = 0.05$; reject the null hypothesis. There is sufficient evidence at the $\alpha = 0.05$ level of significance to conclude that more than half of the individuals with valid driver's licenses drive an American-made automobile.

3. Hypotheses: H_0: $\mu = 25$, H_1: $\mu \ne 25$. Classical approach: $t_0 = -0.738$ is between $-t_{0.005} = -2.977$ and $t_{0.005} = 2.977$ with 14 degrees of freedom; do not reject the null hypothesis. P-value approach: P-value > 0.25 [Tech: P-value $= 0.4729$] $> \alpha = 0.01$; do not reject the null hypothesis. There is not sufficient evidence at the $\alpha = 0.01$ level of significance to conclude that the population mean is different from 25.

4. Hypotheses: H_0: $\mu = 600$, H_1: $\mu \ne 600$. Classical approach: $t_0 = -1.186$ is between $-t_{0.05} = -1.671$ and $t_{0.05} = 1.671$ with 60 degrees of freedom; do not reject the null hypothesis. P-value approach: $0.30 > P\text{-value} > 0.20$ [Tech: P-value $= 0.2401$] $> \alpha = 0.10$; do not reject the null hypothesis. There is not sufficient evidence at the $\alpha = 0.10$ level of significance to conclude that the population mean is different from 600.

5. Hypotheses: H_0: $\mu = 100$, H_1: $\mu > 100$. Classical approach: $t_0 = 3.003 > t_{0.05} = 1.685$; reject the null hypothesis. P-value approach: $0.001 < P\text{-value} < 0.0025$ [Tech: P-value $= 0.0023$] $< \alpha = 0.05$; reject the null hypothesis. There is sufficient evidence at the $\alpha = 0.05$ level of significance to conclude that the population mean is greater than 100.

6. Hypotheses: H_0: $p = 0.25$, H_1: $p < 0.25$; $np_0(1 - p_0) = 60 > 10$ and $n \le 0.05N$. Classical approach: $z_0 = -2.84 < -z_{0.01} = -2.33$; reject the null hypothesis. P-value approach: P-value $= 0.0023 < \alpha = 0.01$; reject the null hypothesis. There is sufficient evidence at the $\alpha = 0.01$ level of significance to conclude that less than 25% of adults prefers mint chocolate chip ice cream.

7. H_0: $\mu = 100$, H_1: $\mu > 100$. Classical approach: $t_0 = 1.28 < t_{0.05} = 1.729$; do not reject the null hypothesis. P-value approach: $0.10 < P\text{-value} < 0.15$ [Tech: 0.1084] $> \alpha = 0.05$; do not reject the null hypothesis. There is not sufficient evidence to conclude that mothers who listen to Mozart have children with higher IQs.

8. H_0: $p = 0.5$, H_1: $p > 0.5$. Classical approach: $z_0 = 2.31 > z_{0.05} = 1.645$; reject the null hypothesis. P-value approach: P-value $= 0.0104$ [Tech: 0.0105] $< \alpha = 0.05$; reject the null hypothesis. There is sufficient evidence to conclude that a majority of Americans in 1945 believed that the United States could develop a way to protect itself from atomic bombs.

9. Hypotheses: H_0: $p = 0.23$, H_1: $p \ne 0.23$; $np_0(1 - p_0) = 181.7 > 10$ and $n \le 0.05N$. Classical approach: $z_0 = 1.37$, which is between $-z_{0.05} = -1.645$ and $z_{0.05} = 1.645$; do not reject the null hypothesis. P-value approach: P-value $= 0.1706 > \alpha = 0.10$; do not reject the null hypothesis. There is not sufficient evidence at the $\alpha = 0.10$ level of significance to conclude that the percentage of university undergraduate students who have at least one tattoo has changed since 2001.

10. Hypotheses: H_0: $\mu = 3.5$, H_1: $\mu < 3.5$; Classical approach: $t_0 = -1.0999 > -t_{0.05} = -1.660$ with 100 degrees of freedom; do not reject the null hypothesis. P-value approach: $0.10 < P\text{-value} < 0.15$ [Tech: P-value $= 0.1365$]; do not reject the null hypothesis. There is not sufficient evidence at the $\alpha = 0.05$ level of significance to conclude that the mean number of credit cards per individual is less than 3.5.

11. (a) Yes; the conditions are satisfied. The data appear to be normally distributed, and there are no outliers.

(b) Hypotheses: H_0: $\mu = 10{,}000$, H_1: $\mu < 10{,}000$. Classical approach: $t_0 = -1.343 > -t_{0.05} = -1.771$; do not reject the null hypothesis. P-value approach: $0.15 > P\text{-value} > 0.10$ [Tech: P-value $= 0.1012$] $> \alpha = 0.05$; do not reject the null hypothesis. There is not sufficient evidence at the $\alpha = 0.05$ level of significance to conclude that the toner cartridges have a mean of less than 10,000 copies. The consumer advocate's concerns do not appear to be founded.

12. Hypotheses: H_0: $\mu = 8$, H_1: $\mu < 8$. Classical approach: $t_0 = -1.444$, $t_{0.01} = -2.403$; do not reject the null hypothesis. P-value approach: $0.10 > P\text{-value} > 0.05$ [Tech: 0.0777] $> \alpha = 0.01$; do not reject the null hypothesis. There is not sufficient evidence at the $\alpha = 0.01$ level of significance to conclude that the mean wait time is less than 8 minutes. The evidence supports the resident's skepticism.

13. (a) Yes; the conditions are satisfied. The data appear to be normally distributed, and there are no outliers.

(b) Hypotheses: H_0: $\mu = 3.2$, H_1: $\mu > 3.2$. Classical approach: $t_0 = 1.989 > t_{0.05} = 1.796$; reject the null hypothesis. P-value approach: $0.025 < P\text{-value} < 0.05$ [Tech: P-value $= 0.0361$] $< \alpha = 0.05$; reject the null hypothesis. There is sufficient evidence at the $\alpha = 0.05$ level of significance to conclude that the new contractor is not getting the streetlights replaced as quickly.

14. Hypotheses: H_0: $p = 0.26$, H_1: $p \ne 0.26$; $np_0(1 - p_0) = 11.544 > 10$ and $n \le 0.05N$. Classical approach: $z_0 = 1.589$ is between $-z_{0.025} = -1.96$ and $z_{0.025} = 1.96$; do not reject the null hypothesis. P-value approach: P-value $= 0.1118$ [Tech: 0.112] $> \alpha = 0.05$; do not reject the null hypothesis. There is not sufficient evidence at the $\alpha = 0.05$ level of significance to conclude that the proportion of individuals who text while driving is different from 0.26. The data do not contradict the results from Toluna.

15. Assuming the congresswoman wants to avoid voting for the tax increase unless she is confident that the majority of her constituents are in favor of it, the value of α should be small, such as $\alpha = 0.01$ or $\alpha = 0.05$, to avoid a Type I error. Let p be the population proportion in favor of the tax increase. Hypotheses: H_0: $p = 0.5$, H_1: $p > 0.5$; $np_0(1 - p_0) = 2062.5 > 10$ and $n \le 0.05\,N$. P-value $= 0.0392$ [Tech: 0.0391]. The P-value is greater than $\alpha = 0.01$ but less than $\alpha = 0.05$, so the conclusion depends on the value of α. Recommendations will vary.

16. Hypotheses: H_0: $\mu = 43$, H_1: $\mu < 43$; Classical approach: $t_0 = -2.635 < -t_{0.05}, = -1.660$ with 100 degrees of freedom; reject the null hypothesis. P-value approach: $0.0025 < P\text{-value} < 0.005$ [Tech: P-value $= 0.0045$]; reject the null hypothesis. There is evidence at the $\alpha = 0.05$ level of significance to conclude that the mean wait time is less than 43 seconds, so the policies seem to have been effective. However, there is no practical significance because reducing the wait time by a fraction of a second is not going to be noticeable to the customers.

17. (a)

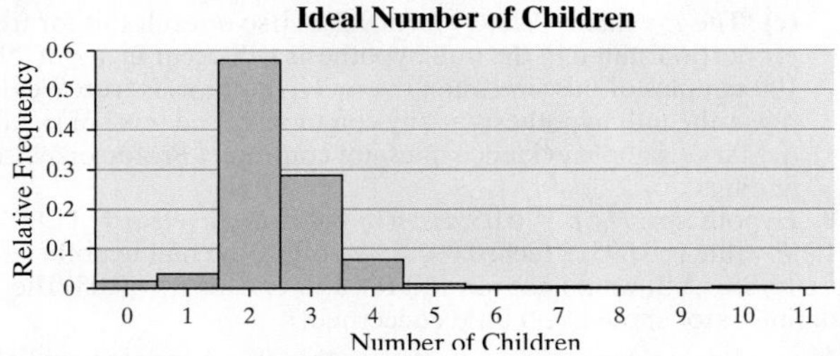

The distribution is skewed right.

(b) 2
(c) $\bar{x} = 2.47$, $s = 1.02$
(d) The data are clearly skewed to the right, so we need a large sample size to use the Central Limit Theorem.
(e) H_0: $\mu = 2.64$, H_1: $\mu \neq 2.64$; $t_0 = -5.041 < -t_{0.05/2} = -1.962$; reject the null hypothesis. *P*-value < 0.0001; reject the null hypothesis. The results of the poll indicate that people's beliefs as to the ideal number of children have changed.

Chapter 10 Review Exercises (page 463)

1. (a) H_0: $\mu = 3173$; H_1: $\mu < 3173$
(b) If we reject the null hypothesis and the mean credit card debt of college undergraduates has not decreased, then we make a Type I error.
(c) If we do not reject the null hypothesis and the mean credit card debt of college undergraduates has decreased, then we make a Type II error.
(d) There is not sufficient evidence at the α level to support the researcher's belief that the mean credit card debt of college undergraduates has decreased.
(e) There is sufficient evidence at the α level to support the researcher's belief that the mean credit card debt of college undergraduates has decreased.

2. (a) H_0: $\mu = 0.13$; H_1: $\mu \neq 0.13$
(b) If we reject the null hypothesis and the proportion of cards that result in default is not different today, we make a Type I error.
(c) If we do not reject the null hypothesis and the proportion of cards that result in default is different today, we make a Type II error.
(d) There is not sufficient evidence at the α level to support the credit analyst's belief that the proportion of cards that result in default is different today.
(e) There is sufficient evidence at the α level to support the credit analyst's belief that the proportion of cards that result in default is different today.

3. The probability of a Type I error is 0.05.

4. The probability of a Type II error is 0.113. The power of the test is $1 - \beta = 0.887$. The power of the test is the probability of correctly rejecting the null hypothesis.

5. (a) The sample size must be large to use the Central Limit Theorem because the distribution of the population may not be normal.
(b) Classical approach: $t_0 = 2.0515 > t_{0.05} = 1.691$ for 34 degrees of freedom; reject the null hypothesis. *P*-value approach: $0.02 <$ *P*-value < 0.025 [Tech: $P = 0.0240$]; reject the null hypothesis.

6. (a) The distribution must be normal because the sample size is small.
(b) Classical approach: $t_0 = -1.795$ is between $-t_{0.025} = -2.145$ and $t_{0.025} = 2.145$ for 14 degrees of freedom; do not reject the null hypothesis. *P*-value approach: $0.05 <$ *P*-value < 0.10 [Tech: $P = 0.0943$]; do not reject the null hypothesis.

7. Hypotheses: H_0: $p = 0.6$, H_1: $p > 0.6$; $np_0(1 - p_0) = 60 > 10$ and $n \le 0.05N$. Classical approach: $z_0 = 1.94 > z_{0.05} = 1.645$; reject the null hypothesis. *P*-value approach: *P*-value $= 0.0262$ [Tech: 0.0264] $< \alpha = 0.05$; reject the null hypothesis. There is sufficient evidence at the $\alpha = 0.05$ level of significance to conclude that $p > 0.6$.

8. Hypotheses: H_0: $p = 0.35$, H_1: $p \neq 0.35$; $np_0(1 - p_0) = 95.6 > 10$ and $n \le 0.05N$. Classical approach: $z_0 = -0.92$ is between $-z_{0.025} = -1.96$ and $z_{0.025} = 1.96$; do not reject the null hypothesis. *P*-value approach: *P*-value $= 0.3576$ [Tech: 0.3572] $> \alpha = 0.05$; do not reject the null hypothesis. There is not sufficient evidence at the $\alpha = 0.05$ level of significance to conclude that $p \neq 0.35$.

9. (a) H_0: $p = 0.733$, H_1: $p \neq 0.733$.
(b) The sample is random. $np_0(1 - p_0) = 19.57 \ge 10$. We can reasonably assume that the sample is less than 5% of the population.
(c) The *P*-value is 0.2892 [Tech: 0.2881], so a result this far from the proportion stated in the null hypothesis will occur in about 29 of 100 samples of this size when the null hypothesis is true. We do not reject the null hypothesis at any commonly used level of significance α. Mary's sample evidence does not contradict Professor Wilson's findings.

10. Hypotheses: H_0: $p = 0.05$, H_1: $p > 0.05$. $np_0(1 - p_0) = 11.875 \ge 10$. The *P*-value is 0.0951 [Tech: 0.0958]. We reject the null hypothesis at $\alpha = 0.10$, but we do not reject it for $\alpha = 0.01$ or $\alpha = 0.05$. The administrator should be a little concerned.

11. (a) Yes, we can reasonably assume that the distances between retaining rings is normally distributed. In addition, the sample size is large.
(b) H_0: $\mu = 0.875$, H_1: $\mu > 0.875$
(c) Recalibrating the machine could be very costly, so he wants to avoid the consequences of making a Type I error.
(d) Classical approach: $t_0 = 1.2 < t_{0.01} = 2.438$; do not reject the null hypothesis. *P*-value approach: $0.10 <$ *P*-value < 0.15 [Tech: *P*-value $= 0.1191$]; do not reject the null hypothesis. No, the evidence does not suggest that the machine be recalibrated.
(e) The quality-control engineer would make a Type I error if he recalibrated the machine when it did not need to be recalibrated. He would make a Type II error if he did not recalibrate the machine when it actually did need to be recalibrated.

12. Hypotheses: H_0: $\mu = 98.6$, H_1: $\mu < 98.6$. Classical approach: $t_0 = -15.119 < -t_{0.01} = -2.364$, using 100 degrees of freedom; reject the null hypothesis. *P*-value approach: *P*-value < 0.0005 [Tech: *P*-value < 0.0001]; reject the null hypothesis. The evidence suggests that the mean temperature of humans is less than 98.6°F.

13. (a) Yes, all the data lie within the confidence bands of the normal probability plot and the boxplot does not show any outliers.
(b) Hypotheses: H_0: $\mu = 1.68$, H_1: $\mu \neq 1.68$. Lower bound: 1.6781 [Tech: 1.6782], upper bound: 1.6839 [Tech: 1.6838]. The mean stated in the null hypothesis is included in the 95% confidence interval, so do not reject the null hypothesis. Conclusion: There is not sufficient evidence to conclude that the golf balls do not conform to USGA standards.

14. Hypotheses: H_0: $\mu = 480$, H_1: $\mu < 480$. Classical approach: $t_0 = -1.577 > -t_{0.05} = -1.812$; do not reject the null hypothesis. *P*-value approach: $0.05 <$ *P*-value < 0.10 [Tech: *P*-value < 0.0730]; do not reject the null hypothesis. There is not sufficient evidence to suggest that the students are studying less than 480 minutes per week.

15. H_0: $p = 0.5$, H_1: $p > 0.5$; $np_0(1 - p_0) = 150(0.5)(1 - 0.5) = 37.5 > 10$ and $n \le 0.05N$. Classical approach: $z_0 = 0.98 < z_{0.05} = 1.645$; do not reject the null hypothesis; *P*-value approach: *P*-value $= 0.1635$ [Tech: 0.1636] $> \alpha = 0.05$; do not reject the null hypothesis. There is not sufficient evidence to suggest that a majority of pregnant women nap at least twice each week.

16. Hypotheses: H_0: $p = 0.52$, H_1: $p > 0.52$. The *P*-value is 0.0793 [Tech: 0.0788]. Reject the null hypothesis at the $\alpha = 0.10$ level of significance. The results are statistically significant. The new retention rate was about 53.3%, not a great increase over 52%, so the results might not be considered practically significant. The cost of the new policies would have to be weighed against such a small increase in the retention rate when considering whether other community colleges should implement the policies.

17. Hypotheses: H_0: $p = 0.4$, H_1: $p > 0.4$; $np_0(1 - p_0) = 9.6 < 10$. *P*-value $= 0.3115 > \alpha = 0.05$; do not reject the null hypothesis. There is not sufficient evidence at the $\alpha = 0.05$ level of significance to support the researcher's notion that the proportion of adolescents who prays daily has increased.

18. Hypotheses: H_0: $\mu = 73.2$, H_1: $\mu < 73.2$. Classical approach: $t_0 = -2.018 < -t_{0.05} = -1.645$; reject the null hypothesis. *P*-value approach: *P*-value $= 0.0218 < \alpha = 0.05$; reject the null hypothesis. There is sufficient evidence at the $\alpha = 0.05$ level of significance to support the coordinator's concern that the mean test scores decreased. The results do not illustrate any practical significance. The average score only declined 0.4 point.

19. If we accept the null hypothesis, we are saying it is true. If we do not reject the null hypothesis, we are saying that we do not have enough evidence to conclude that it is not true. It is the difference between saying H_0 is true and saying we are not convinced that it is false.

20. H_0: $\mu = 1.22$, H_1: $\mu < 1.22$. The *P*-value indicates that if the population mean is 1.22 hours as stated in the null hypothesis then results as low as or lower than those obtained by the researcher would occur in about 3 of 100 similar samples.

21. In the Classical Approach, a test statistic is calculated and a rejection region based on the level of significance α is determined within the appropriate distribution for the population parameter stated in the null hypothesis. The null hypothesis is rejected if the test statistic is in the rejection region.

22. In the *P*-value approach, the probability of getting a result as extreme as the one obtained in the sample is calculated assuming the null hypothesis to be true. If the *P*-value is less than a predetermined level of significance α, we reject the null hypothesis.

Chapter 10 Test (page 465)

1. (a) H_0: $\mu = 42.6$ minutes, H_1: $\mu > 42.6$ minutes
(b) There is sufficient evidence to conclude that the mean amount

of daily time spent on phone calls and answering or writing emails has increased since 2006.
(c) We would reject the null hypothesis that the mean is 42.6 minutes, when, in fact, the mean amount of daily time spent on phone calls and answering or writing emails is 42.6 minutes.
(d) We would not reject the null hypothesis that the mean is 42.6 minutes, when, in fact, the mean amount of time spent on phone calls and answering or writing emails is greater than 42.6 minutes.

2. (a) H_0: $\mu = 167.1$ seconds, H_1: $\mu < 167.1$ seconds
(b) By choosing a level of significance of 0.01, the probability of rejecting the null hypothesis that the mean is 167.1 seconds in favor of the alternative hypothesis that the mean is less than 167.1 seconds, when, in fact, the mean is 167.1 seconds, is small.
(c) Classical approach: $t_0 = -1.75 > -t_{0.01} = -2.381$ (using 70 df); do not reject the null hypothesis. *P*-value approach: $0.025 < P\text{-value} < 0.05$ [Tech: *P*-value = 0.0423] is greater than $\alpha = 0.01$; do not reject the null hypothesis. There is not sufficient evidence to conclude that the drive-through service time has decreased.

3. H_0: $\mu = 8$, H_1: $\mu < 8$. Classical approach: $t_0 = -1.755 < -t_{0.05} = -1.660$ (using 100 df); reject the null hypothesis; *P*-value approach: $0.025 < P\text{-value} < 0.05$ [Tech: *P*-value = 0.0406] $< \alpha = 0.05$; reject the null hypothesis. There is sufficient evidence to conclude that postpartum women get less than 8 hours of sleep each night.

4. H_0: $\mu = 1.3825$ inches, H_1: $\mu \neq 1.3825$ inches. Lower bound: 1.3824 inches; upper bound: 1.3828 inches. Because the interval includes the mean stated in the null hypothesis, we do not reject the null hypothesis. There is not sufficient evidence to conclude that the mean is different from 1.3825 inches. Therefore, we presume that the part has been manufactured to specifications.

5. H_0: $p = 0.6$, H_1: $p > 0.6$; $np_0(1 - p_0) = 1.561(0.6)(0.4) = 374.64 > 10$ and $n \leq 0.05N$. We will use an $\alpha = 0.05$ level of significance. Classical approach: $z_0 = 0.89 < z_{0.05} = 1.645$; do not reject the null hypothesis. *P*-value approach: *P*-value = 0.1867 [Tech: 0.1843] $> \alpha = 0.05$; do not reject the null hypothesis. There is not sufficient evidence to conclude that a supermajority of Americans did not feel that the United States would need to fight Japan in their lifetimes. It is interesting, however, that significantly fewer than half of all Americans felt the United States would not have to fight Japan in their lifetimes. About 2.5 years after this survey, the Japanese attack on Pearl Harbor thrust the United States into World War II.

6. H_0: $\mu = 0$, H_1: $\mu > 0$. Classical approach: $t_0 = 2.634 > t_{0.05} = 1.664$ (using 80 df); reject the null hypothesis. *P*-value approach: $0.0025 < P\text{-value} < 0.005$ [Tech: *P*-value = 0.0051] $< \alpha = 0.05$; reject the null hypothesis. There is sufficient evidence to suggest that the diet is effective. However, losing 1.6 kg of weight over the course of a year does not seem to have much practical significance.

7. H_0: $p = 0.37$, H_1: $p > 0.37$, $np_0(1 - p_0) = 6.993 < 10$. *P*-value = $P(\hat{p} \geq 0.37) = P(X \geq 16) = 0.0501 < \alpha = 0.10$; reject the null hypothesis. There is sufficient evidence to conclude that the proportion of 20- to 24-year-olds who live on their own and do not have a land line is greater than 0.37.

CHAPTER 11 Inferences on Two Samples

11.1 Assess Your Understanding (page 479)

1. Independent
2. Dependent
3. Dependent; quantitative
4. Independent; quantitative
5. Independent; qualitative
6. Dependent; qualitative
7. Independent; quantitative
8. Dependent; quantitative

9. (a) H_0: $p_1 = p_2$ versus H_1: $p_1 > p_2$
(b) $z_0 = 3.08$
(c) $z_{0.05} = 1.645$
(d) *P*-value = 0.0010. Because $z_0 > z_{0.05}$ (or *P*-value $< \alpha$), we reject the null hypothesis. There is sufficient evidence to support the claim that $p_1 > p_2$.

10. (a) H_0: $p_1 = p_2$ versus H_1: $p_1 < p_2$
(b) $z_0 = -0.35$
(c) $-z_{0.05} = -1.645$
(d) *P*-value = 0.3649. Because $z_0 > -z_{0.05}$ (or *P*-value $> \alpha$), we do not reject the null hypothesis. There is not sufficient evidence to support the claim that $p_1 < p_2$.

11. (a) H_0: $p_1 = p_2$ versus H_1: $p_1 \neq p_2$
(b) $z_0 = -0.34$
(c) $-z_{0.025} = -1.96$; $z_{0.025} = 1.96$
(d) *P*-value = 0.7307. Because $-z_{0.025} < z_0 < z_{0.025}$ (or *P*-value $> \alpha$), we do not reject the null hypothesis. There is not sufficient evidence to support the claim that $p_1 \neq p_2$.

12. (a) H_0: $p_1 = p_2$ versus H_1: $p_1 \neq p_2$
(b) $z_0 = -2.19$
(c) $-z_{0.025} = -1.96$; $z_{0.025} = 1.96$
(d) *P*-value = 0.0286. Because $z_0 < -z_{0.025}$ (or *P*-value $< \alpha$), we reject the null hypothesis. There is sufficient evidence to support the claim that $p_1 \neq p_2$.

13. Lower bound: −0.075, upper bound: 0.015
14. Lower bound: −0.090, upper bound: 0.068
15. Lower bound: −0.063, upper bound: 0.043
16. Lower bound: −0.039, upper bound: 0.009

17. (a) H_0: $p_A = p_B$ vs. H_1: $p_A \neq p_B$
(b) $z_0 = 0.70$
(c) $z_{0.025} = 1.96$; do not reject the null hypothesis
(d) *P*-value = 0.4840

18. (a) H_0: $p_A = p_B$ vs. H_1: $p_A \neq p_B$
(b) $z_0 = 1.59$
(c) $z_{0.025} = 1.96$; do not reject the null hypothesis
(d) *P*-value = 0.1118

19. Each sample is the result of a randomized experiment; $n_1\hat{p}_1(1 - \hat{p}_1) = 91 \geq 10$ and $n_2\hat{p}_2(1 - \hat{p}_2) = 60 \geq 10$; and each sample is less than 5% of the population size. H_0: $p_1 = p_2$: H_1: $p_1 > p_2$. Classical approach: $z_0 = 2.20 > z_{0.05} = 1.645$; reject H_0. *P*-value approach: *P*-value $= 0.0139 < \alpha = 0.05$; reject H_0. There is sufficient evidence at the $\alpha = 0.05$ level of significance to conclude that a higher proportion of subjects in the treatment group (taking Prevnar) experienced fever as a side effect than in the control (placebo) group.

20. Each sample is the result of a randomized experiment; $n_1\hat{p}_1(1 - \hat{p}_1) = 95 \geq 10$ and $n_2\hat{p}_2(1 - \hat{p}_2) = 21 \geq 10$; and each sample is less than 5% of the population size. H_0: $p_1 = p_2$, H_1: $p_1 < p_2$. Classical approach: $z_0 = -0.20$ is greater than $-z_{0.05} = -1.645$; do not reject H_0. *P*-value approach: *P*-value =0.4207 [Tech: 0.4221] $> \alpha = 0.05$; do not reject H_0. There is not sufficient evidence at the $\alpha = 0.05$ level of significance to conclude that a lower proportion of subjects taking Prevnar experienced drowsiness as a side effect than in the control (placebo) group.

21. $\hat{p}_{1947} = 0.37$, $\hat{p}_{2010} = 0.30$. Each sample is a simple random sample; $n_{1947}\hat{p}_{1947}(1 - \hat{p}_{1947}) \geq 10$ and $n_{2010}\hat{p}_{2010}(1 - \hat{p}_{2010}) \geq 10$. The sample size is less than 5% of the population for each sample. H_0: $p_{1947} = p_{2010}$ vs. H_1: $p_{1947} \neq p_{2010}$. Classical approach: $z_0 = 3.33$ is greater than $z_{0.025} = 1.96$; reject H_0. *P*-value approach: *P*-value $= 0.0008 < \alpha = 0.05$; reject H_0. There is sufficient evidence at the $\alpha = 0.05$ level of significance to conclude that the proportion of adult Americans who were abstainers in 1947 is different from the proportion of abstainers in 2010.

22. $\hat{p}_C = 0.310$; $\hat{p}_S = 0.397$. Each sample is a simple random sample; $n_C\hat{p}_C(1 - \hat{p}_C) \geq 10$ and $n_S\hat{p}_S(1 - \hat{p}_S) \geq 10$. The sample size is less than 5% of the population for each sample. H_0: $p_C = p_S$ vs. H_1: $p_C \neq p_S$. Classical approach: $z_0 = -3.12 < -z_{0.005}$; reject H_0. *P*-value approach: *P*-value = 0.0018 [Tech: 0.0019] $< \alpha = 0.01$; reject H_0. There is sufficient evidence at the $\alpha = 0.01$ level of significance to conclude that the proportion of Catholics who favor capital punishment for persons under the age of 18 is different from the proportion of seculars who favor capital punishment for persons under the age of 18.

23. H_0: $p_m = p_f$ vs. H_1: $p_m \neq p_f$. Lower bound: −0.008 [Tech: −0.009], upper bound: 0.048. We are 95% confident that the difference in the proportion of males and females that have at least one tattoo is between −0.008 and 0.048. Because the interval includes zero, we do not reject the null hypothesis. There is no significant difference in the proportion of males and females that have tattoos.

24. H_0: $p_m = p_f$ vs. H_1: $p_m \neq p_f$. Lower bound: −0.128 [Tech: −0.129], upper bound: −0.050. We are 90% confident that the difference in the proportion of males and females that are normal weight is between −0.128 and −0.05. Because the interval does not include zero, we have evidence to conclude that there is a difference in the proportion of males and females that are normal weight. It would appear a higher proportion of males are not normal weight.

25. (a) Each sample is the result of a randomized experiment, $n_1\hat{p}_1(1 - \hat{p}_1) = 48 \geq 10$ and $n_2\hat{p}_2(1 - \hat{p}_2) = 30 \geq 10$, and each sample is less than 5% of the population size. H_0: $p_1 = p_2$, H_1: $p_1 > p_2$. Classical approach: $z_0 = 2.13 > z_{0.05} = 1.645$; reject H_0. *P*-value =0.0166 $< \alpha = 0.05$; reject H_0. There is sufficient evidence

at the $\alpha = 0.05$ level of significance to conclude that the proportion of individuals taking Clarinex and experiencing dry mouth is greater than that of those taking a placebo.
(b) No

26. (a) Each sample is the result of a randomized experiment, $n_1\hat{p}_1(1 - \hat{p}_1) = 446 \geq 10$ and $n_2\hat{p}_2(1 - \hat{p}_2) = 468 \geq 10$, and each sample is less than 5% of the population size. H_0: $p_1 = p_2$, H_1: $p_1 < p_2$. Classical approach: $z_0 = -1.71 < -z_{0.05} = -1.645$; reject H_0. P-value $= 0.0432 < \alpha = 0.05$; reject H_0. There is sufficient evidence at the $\alpha = 0.05$ level of significance to conclude that a higher percentage of patients are cured with the new proposed treatment than with the current standard treatment.
(b) Answers will vary.

27. (a) To remove any potential nonsampling error due to the respondent hearing the word "right" or "wrong" first.
(b) Lower bound: 0.282, upper bound: 0.338 [Tech: 0.339]. We are 90% confident that the difference in the proportion of adult Americans who believe the United States made the right decision to use military force in Iraq from 2003 to 2010 is between 0.282 and 0.338. The attitude regarding the decision to go to war changed substantially.

28. (a) The response variable is whether the student passed or not. The explanatory variable is the delivery method: traditional lecture or student-centered.
(b) H_0: $p_{\text{lecture}} = p_{\text{student-centered}}$ vs. H_1: $p_{\text{lecture}} < p_{\text{student-centered}}$. Classical approach: $z_0 = -3.59$ [Tech: -3.63] is less than $-z_{0.05} = -1.645$; reject H_0. P-value approach: P-value < 0.0002 [Tech: P-value $= 0.0001$] $< \alpha = 0.05$; reject H_0. There is sufficient evidence at the $\alpha = 0.05$ level of significance to conclude that the student-centered model results in a higher pass rate than the traditional lecture model.

29. (a) $\hat{p}_{\text{male}} = 0.317$, $\hat{p}_{\text{female}} = 0.216$
(b) H_0: $p_{\text{male}} = p_{\text{female}}$ vs. H_1: $p_{\text{male}} \neq p_{\text{female}}$. Classical approach: $z_0 = 1.61$ is between $-z_{0.025} = -1.96$ and $z_{0.025} = 1.96$; do not reject H_0. P-value approach: P-value $= 0.1075 > \alpha = 0.05$; do not reject H_0. There is not sufficient evidence at the $\alpha = 0.05$ level of significance to conclude that the proportion of males and females willing to pay higher taxes to reduce the deficit differs.

30. (a) $\hat{p}_{\text{male}} = 0.695$, $\hat{p}_{\text{female}} = 0.845$
(b) H_0: $p_{\text{male}} = p_{\text{female}}$ vs. H_1: $p_{\text{male}} < p_{\text{female}}$. Classical approach: $z_0 = -2.52$ is less than $-z_{0.05} = -1.645$; reject H_0. P-value approach: P-value $= 0.0059 < \alpha = 0.05$; reject H_0. There is sufficient evidence at the $\alpha = 0.05$ level of significance to conclude that a higher proportion of females than males have a Facebook account.

31. (a) In sentence A, the verbs are "was having" and "was taking." In sentence B, the verbs are "had" and "took."
(b) H_0: $p_A = p_B$ vs. H_1: $p_A \neq p_B$, P-value $= 0.0013$. A level of significance is not specified, but since the P-value is very small we reject H_0. There is sufficient evidence to conclude that the sentence structure makes a difference.
(c) Answers will vary. The wording in sentence A suggests that the actions were taking place over a period of time and habitual behavior may be continuing in the present or might be expected to continue at some time in the future. The wording in sentence B suggests events that are concluded and were possibly brief in duration or one-time occurrences.

32. (a) The response variable is whether John secures a sale or not. The explanatory variable is the web page design.
(b) H_0: $p_{\text{I}} = p_{\text{II}}$ vs. H_1: $p_{\text{I}} \neq p_{\text{II}}$, P-value $= 0.3576$ [Tech: P-value $= 0.3629$]. A level of significance is not specified, but since the P-value is quite large we do not reject H_0. There is not sufficient evidence to conclude that the Web page design makes a difference in securing a sale.

33. (a) The same person answered both questions.
(b) H_0: $p_{\text{seat belt}} = p_{\text{smoke}}$ vs. H_1: $p_{\text{seat belt}} \neq p_{\text{smoke}}$. Classical: $z_0 = 4.31 > z_{0.025} = 1.96$; reject the null hypothesis. P-value < 0.0001; reject the null hypothesis. There is sufficient evidence at the $\alpha = 0.05$ level of significance to conclude that there is a difference in the proportion who do not use a seat belt and the proportion who smoke. The sample proportion of smokers is 0.17, while the sample proportion of those who do not wear a seatbelt is 0.13. Smoking appears to be the more popular hazardous activity.

34. H_0: $p_{\text{low}} = p_{\text{high}}$ vs. H_1: $p_{\text{low}} \neq p_{\text{high}}$. Classical: $z_0 = 6.20 > z_{0.025} = 1.96$; reject the null hypothesis. P-value < 0.0001; reject the null hypothesis. There is sufficient evidence at the $\alpha = 0.05$ level of significance to conclude that there is a difference in the proportion who believe low-income and high-income people pay their fair share in taxes.

35. H_0: $p_{\text{NN}} = p_{\text{RN}}$ vs. H_1: $p_{\text{NN}} \neq p_{\text{RN}}$. Classical: $z_0 = 2.41 > z_{0.025} = 1.96$; reject the null hypothesis. P-value $= 0.016$; reject the null hypothesis. There is sufficient evidence at the $\alpha = 0.05$ level of significance to conclude that there is a difference in the proportion of words not recognized by the two systems.

36. H_0: $p_A = p_B$ vs. H_1: $p_A \neq p_B$. Classical: $z_0 = 1.28 < z_{0.025} = 1.96$; do not reject the null hypothesis. P-value $= 0.2006$; do not reject the null hypothesis. There is not sufficient evidence at the $\alpha = 0.05$ level of significance to conclude that there is a difference in the proportion who have their poison ivy healed using ointment A versus ointment B.

37. No. The difference between the two sample proportions is not significant.

38. We are testing H_0: $p_1 = p_2$ versus H_1: $p_1 > p_2$. The P-value is 0.072, which is moderately low, suggesting the Accupril has more dizziness than the placebo.

39. (a) $n = n_1 = n_2 = 1406$
(b) $n = n_1 = n_2 = 2135$

40. (a) $n = n_1 = n_2 = 2551$
(b) $n = n_1 = n_2 = 3383$

41. (a) Completely randomized design
(b) Whether the subject contracted polio or not
(c) The vaccine or placebo
(d) A placebo is an innocuous medication that looks, tastes, and smells like the experimental treatment.
(e) Because the incidence rate of polio is low, a large number of subjects is needed so that we are guaranteed a sufficient number of successes.
(f) H_0: $p_1 = p_2$, H_1: $p_1 < p_2$. Classical approach: $z_0 = -6.74 < -z_{0.01} = -2.33$; reject H_0. P-value approach: P-value $<0.0001 < \alpha = 0.01$; reject H_0. There is sufficient evidence at the $\alpha = 0.01$ level of significance to conclude that the proportion of children in the experimental group who contracted polio is less than the proportion of children in the control group who contracted polio.

42. A pooled estimate of p is the best point estimate of the common population proportion p. However, when finding a confidence interval, the sample proportions are not pooled because no assumption about their equality is made.

43. In an independent sample, the individuals in sample A are in no way related to the individuals in sample B; in a dependent sample, the individuals in each sample are somehow related.

11.2 Assess Your Understanding (page 488)

1. $<$ **2.** $>$

3. (a)

Observation	1	2	3	4	5	6	7
d_i	-0.5	1	-3.3	-3.7	0.5	-2.4	-2.9

(b) $\bar{d} = -1.614$; $s_d = 1.915$
(c) Classical approach: $t_0 = -2.230 < -t_{0.05} = -1.943$; reject the null hypothesis. P-value approach: $0.025 < P$-value < 0.05 [Tech: P-value $= 0.0336$] $< \alpha = 0.05$; reject the null hypothesis. There is sufficient evidence at the $\alpha = 0.05$ level of significance to reject the null hypothesis that $\mu_d = 0$.
(d) We can be 95% confident that the mean difference is between -3.39 and 0.16.

4. (a)

Observation	1	2	3	4	5	6	7	8
d_i	-0.4	1.5	1	-1.3	-2.3	-6.9	5.1	-5.3

(b) $\bar{d} = -1.075$; $s_d = 3.833$
(c) Classical approach: $t_0 = -0.793$; do not reject the null hypothesis since $-t_{0.005} = -3.499 < -0.793 < t_{0.005} = 3.499$. P-value approach: $0.50 > P$-value > 0.40 [Tech: P-value $= 0.4537$] $> \alpha = 0.01$; do not reject the null hypothesis. There is not sufficient evidence at the $\alpha = 0.01$ level of significance to support the claim that $\mu_d \neq 0$.
(d) We can be 99% confident that the mean difference is between -5.82 and 3.67.

5. (a) H_0: $\mu_d = 0$ vs. H_1: $\mu_d > 0$

(b) Classical approach: $t_0 = 2.606 > t_{0.05} = 1.753$; reject the null hypothesis. *P*-value approach: $0.005 < P\text{-value} < 0.01$ [Tech: $P\text{-value} = 0.0099$] $< \alpha = 0.05$; reject the null hypothesis. There is sufficient evidence at the $\alpha = 0.05$ level of significance that a baby will watch the climber approach the hinderer toy for a longer time than the baby will watch the climber approach the helper toy.
(c) Answers will vary. The fact that the babies watch the surprising behavior for a longer period of time suggests that they are curious about it.

6. (a) H_0: $\mu_d = 0$ vs. H_1: $\mu_d > 0$
(b) Classical approach: $t_0 = 2.996 > t_{0.05} = 1.833$; reject the null hypothesis. *P*-value approach: $0.005 < P\text{-value} < 0.01$ [Tech: $P\text{-value} = 0.0075$] $< \alpha = 0.05$; reject the null hypothesis. There is sufficient evidence at the $\alpha = 0.05$ level of significance that caffeine increases energy expenditure.

7. (a) This is matched-pairs data because two measurements (A and B) are taken on the same round.
(b) Hypotheses: H_0: $\mu_d = 0$, H_1: $\mu_d \neq 0$; $d_i = A_i - B_i$. Classical approach: $t_0 = 0.852$; do not reject the null hypothesis since $-t_{0.005} = -3.106 < 0.852 < t_{0.005} = 3.106$. *P*-value approach: $0.50 > P\text{-value} > 0.40$ [Tech: $P\text{-value} = 0.4125$] $> \alpha = 0.01$; do not reject the null hypothesis. There is not sufficient evidence at the $\alpha = 0.01$ level of significance to conclude that there is a difference in the measurements of velocity between device A and device B.
(c) Lower bound: -0.309, upper bound: 0.543. We are 99% confident that the mean difference in measurement is between -0.31 and 0.54 feet per second.
(d)

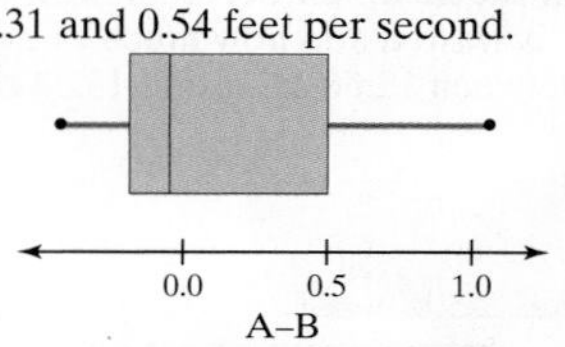

Yes, the boxplot supports that there is no difference in measurements.

8. (a) These are matched-pairs data because the same person is being timed for both the red and blue stimuli.
(b) To control for any "learning" that may take place in reaction time.
(c) Hypotheses: H_0: $\mu_d = 0$, H_1: $\mu_d \neq 0$; $d_i = \text{red}_i - \text{blue}_i$. Classical approach: $t_0 = -1.312$; do not reject the null hypothesis since $-t_{0.005} = -4.032 < -1.312 < t_{0.005} = 4.032$. *P*-value approach: $0.30 > P\text{-value} > 0.25$ [Tech: $P\text{-value} = 0.2466$] $> \alpha = 0.01$; do not reject the null hypothesis. There is not sufficient evidence at the $\alpha = 0.01$ level of significance to conclude that there is a difference in the reaction time to the blue and red stimuli.
(d) We can be 99% confident that the mean difference in reaction time between blue and red stimuli is between -0.3789 second and 0.1929 second.
(e)

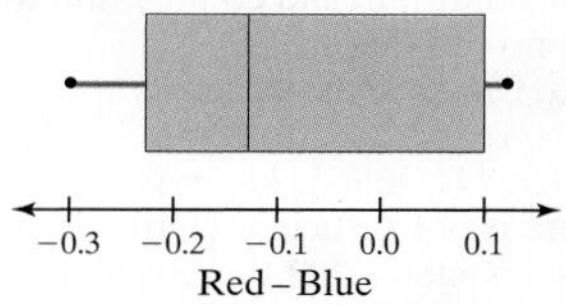

Yes, the boxplot supports that there is no difference in reaction times.

9. (a) These are matched pairs because the car and the SUV were involved in the same collision.
(b)

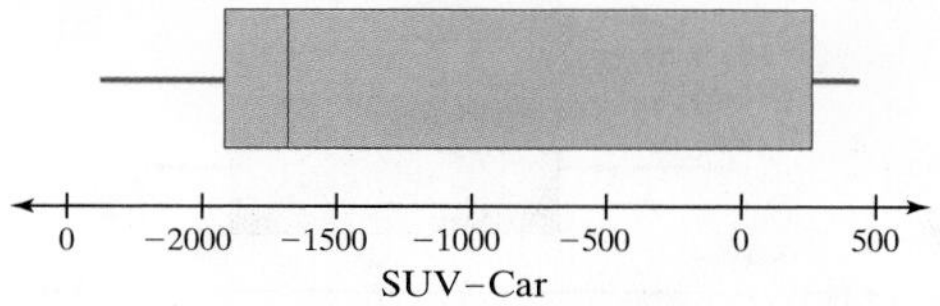

The median of the differences is well to the left of 0 suggesting that SUVs do have a lower repair cost.
(c) H_0: $\mu_d = 0$ vs. H_1: $\mu_d < 0$. Classical approach: $t_0 = -2.685 < -t_{0.05} = -1.943$; reject the null hypothesis. *P*-value approach: $0.01 < P\text{-value} < 0.02$ [Tech: $P\text{-value} = 0.0181$] $< \alpha = 0.05$; reject the null hypothesis. There is sufficient evidence at the $\alpha = 0.05$ level of significance to suggest that the repair cost for the car is higher.

10. (a) To control for any role that season might have on lake clarity.
(b) Hypotheses: H_0: $\mu_d = 0$, H_1: $\mu_d > 0$; $d_i = Y_i - X_i$. Classical approach: $t_0 = 2.384 > t_{0.05} = 1.895$; reject the null hypothesis. *P*-value approach: $0.02 < P\text{-value} < 0.025$ [Tech: $P\text{-value} = 0.0243$] $< \alpha = 0.05$; reject the null hypothesis. Yes; there is sufficient evidence at the $\alpha = 0.05$ level of significance to conclude that there has been an improvement in the clarity of the water in the 5-year period.
(c)

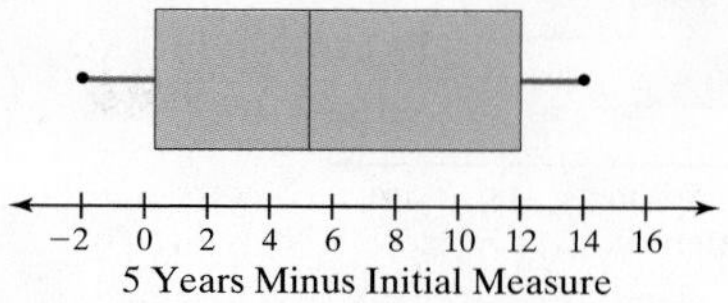

Yes, the boxplot supports that the lake is becoming more clear, since most differences are positive.

11. Hypotheses: H_0: $\mu_d = 0$, H_1: $\mu_d > 0$; $d_i = Y_i - X_i$. Classical approach: $t_0 = 0.398 < t_{0.10} = 1.356$; do not reject the null hypothesis. *P*-value approach: $P\text{-value} > 0.25$ [Tech: $P\text{-value} = 0.3508$] $> \alpha = 0.10$; do not reject the null hypothesis. No; there is not sufficient evidence at the $\alpha = 0.10$ level of significance to conclude that sons are taller than their fathers.

12. Hypotheses: H_0: $\mu_d = 0$, H_1: $\mu_d < 0$; $d_i = Y_i - X_i$. Classical approach: $t_0 = -1.220 > -t_{0.05} = -1.860$; do not reject the null hypothesis. *P*-value approach: $0.15 > P\text{-value} > 0.10$ [Tech: $P\text{-value} = 0.1286$] $> \alpha = 0.05$; do not reject the null hypothesis. No; there is not sufficient evidence at the $\alpha = 0.05$ level of significance to conclude that the new loading procedure reduces wait time.

13. H_0: $\mu_d = 0$; H_1: $\mu_d \neq 0$; $d_i = \text{diamond} - \text{steel}$, $\bar{d} = 1.3$; $s_d = 1.5$, $t_{0.025} = 2.306$. Lower bound: 0.1 [Tech: 0.2]; upper bound: 2.5. We are 95% confident that the difference in hardness reading is between 0.1 and 2.5. Because the interval does not include 0, we reject the null hypothesis. There is sufficient evidence to conclude that the two indenters produce different hardness readings.

14. Hypotheses: H_0: $\mu_d = 0$, H_1: $\mu_d < 0$; $d_i = T_i - H_i$. Classical approach: $t_0 = 0.089 > -t_{0.10} = -1.383$; do not reject the null hypothesis. *P*-value approach: $P\text{-value} > 0.25$ [Tech: $P\text{-value} = 0.5345$] $> \alpha = 0.10$; do not reject the null hypothesis. There is not sufficient evidence at the $\alpha = 0.10$ level of significance to conclude that Thrifty is less expensive than Hertz.

15. (a) To control for any "learning" that may occur in using the simulator.
(b) Hypotheses: H_0: $\mu_d = 0$, H_1: $\mu_d \neq 0$. Lower bound: 0.688, upper bound: 1.238. $d_i = Y_i - X_i$. We can be 95% confident that the mean difference in reaction time when teenagers are driving impaired from when driving normally is between 0.688 second and 1.238 seconds. Because the interval does not contain zero, we reject the null hypothesis. There is sufficient evidence to conclude there is a difference in braking time with impaired vision and normal vision.

16. Lower bound: 29.55, upper bound: 35.85. We can be 95% confident that the mean difference in braking distance on a wet road from a dry road is between 29.55 and 35.85 feet when driving at 40 miles per hour.

17. (a) Drivers and cars behave differently, so this reduces variability in mpg attributable to the driver's driving style.
(b) Driving conditions also affect mpg. By conducting the experiment on a closed track, driving conditions are constant.
(c) Neither variable is normally distributed.
(d) The difference in mileage appears to be approximately normal.
(e) H_0: $\mu_d = 0$; H_1: $\mu_d > 0$; $d_i = 92\ \text{Oct}_i - 87\ \text{Oct}_i$. *P*-value = 0.141. We would expect to get the results we obtained in about 14 samples out of 100 samples if the statement in the null hypothesis were true. Our results are not unusual; therefore, do not reject H_0.

18. (a) It is matched-pairs data because the flying conditions are similar for each windmilling/stopped-propeller matching.
(b) The decision to windmill or stop the propeller first was determined randomly to control for any "learning" that may take place while flying without the aid of an engine.
(c) The pilot can see whether the propeller is spinning or not.
(d) Response: time to descend 800 feet; treatments: windmilling or stopped propeller.
(e)

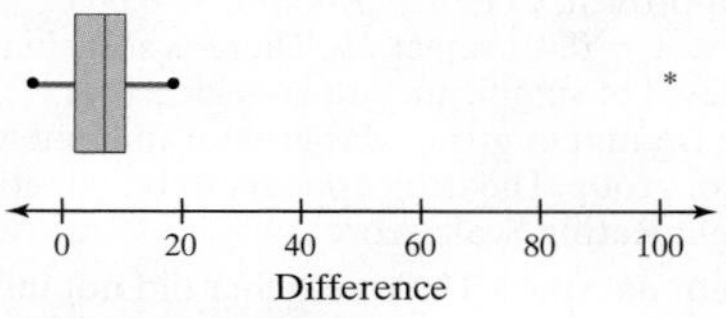

An outlier is present.

(f) The conditions of windmilling and stopped propeller were not the same, so the data are not matched by weather conditions.

(g)

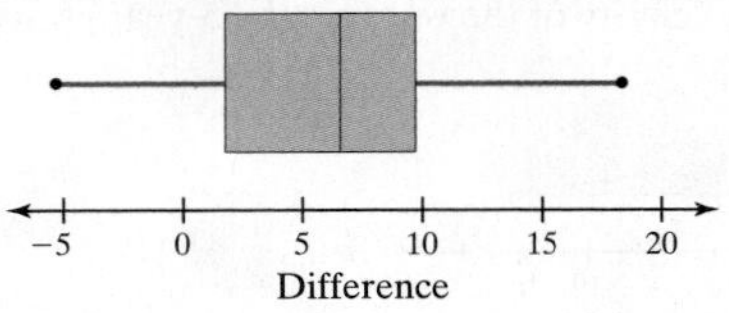

Yes

(h) H_0: $\mu_d = 0$ vs. H_1: $\mu_d > 0$

(i) Classical: $t_0 = 5.49 > t_{0.05} = 1.708$, reject the null hypothesis; *P*-value < 0.0005 [Tech: < 0.0001], reject the null hypothesis. There is sufficient evidence to conclude that stopping the propeller increases the time to fall 800 feet (thereby increasing the horizontal distance that the plane will travel).

(j) If you experience engine failure, you should stop the propeller from windmilling to increase the distance that the plane will glide.

11.3 Assess Your Understanding (page 500)

1. (a) H_0: $\mu_1 = \mu_2$, H_1: $\mu_1 \neq \mu_2$. Classical approach: $t_0 = 0.898$ is between $-t_{0.025} = -2.145$ and $t_{0.025} = 2.145$; do not reject H_0. *P*-value approach: $0.40 > P\text{-value} > 0.30$ [Tech: *P*-value $= 0.3767$] $> \alpha = 0.05$; do not reject H_0. There is not sufficient evidence at the $\alpha = 0.05$ level of significance to conclude that the population means are different.
(b) Lower bound: -1.53 [Tech: -1.41], upper bound: 3.73 [Tech: 3.61]

2. (a) H_0: $\mu_1 = \mu_2$, H_0: $\mu_1 \neq \mu_2$. Classical approach: $t_0 = 2.486 > t_{0.025} = 2.093$; reject H_0. *P*-value approach: $0.02 < P\text{-value} < 0.04$ [Tech: *P*-value $= 0.0175$] $< \alpha = 0.05$; reject H_0. There is sufficient evidence at the $\alpha = 0.05$ level of significance to conclude that the population means are different.
(b) Lower bound: 1.11 [Tech: 1.30], upper bound: 12.89 [Tech: 12.70]

3. (a) H_0: $\mu_1 = \mu_2$, H_1: $\mu_1 > \mu_2$. Classical approach: $t_0 = 3.081 > t_{0.10} = 1.333$; reject H_0. *P*-value approach: $0.0025 < P\text{-value} < 0.005$ [Tech: *P*-value $= 0.0024$] $< \alpha = 0.10$; reject H_0. There is sufficient evidence at the $\alpha = 0.10$ level of significance to conclude that $\mu_1 > \mu_2$.
(b) Lower bound: 3.57 [Tech: 3.67], upper bound: 12.83 [Tech: 12.73]

4. (a) H_0: $\mu_1 = \mu_2$, H_1: $\mu_1 < \mu_2$. Classical approach: $t_0 = -4.393 < -t_{0.05} = -1.696$; reject H_0. *P*-value approach: *P*-value < 0.0005 [Tech: *P*-value < 0.0001] $< \alpha = 0.05$; reject H_0. There is sufficient evidence at the level of significance to conclude that $\mu_1 < \mu_2$.
(b) Lower bound: -30.75 [Tech: -30.59], upper bound: -11.25 [Tech: -11.41].

5. H_0: $\mu_1 = \mu_2$: H_1: $\mu_1 < \mu_2$. Classical approach: $t_0 = -3.158 < -t_{0.02} = -2.172$; reject H_0. *P*-value approach: $0.001 < P\text{-value} < 0.0025$ [Tech: *P*-value $= 0.0013$] $< \alpha = 0.02$; reject H_0. There is sufficient evidence at the $\alpha = 0.02$ level of significance to conclude that $\mu_1 < \mu_2$.

6. H_0: $\mu_1 = \mu_2$, H_1: $\mu_1 > \mu_2$. Classical approach: $t_0 = 1.237 < t_{0.05} = 1.782$; do not reject H_0. *P*-value approach: $0.15 > P\text{-value} > 0.10$ [Tech: *P*-value $= 0.1144$] $> \alpha = 0.05$; do not reject H_0. There is not sufficient evidence at the $\alpha = 0.05$ level of significance to conclude that $\mu_1 > \mu_2$.

7. (a) H_0: $\mu_{CC} = \mu_{NT}$ vs. H_1: $\mu_{CC} > \mu_{NT}$. Classical approach: $t_0 = 12.977 > t_{0.01} \approx 2.364$ (using 100 df); reject H_0. *P*-value approach: *P*-value < 0.0005 [Tech: *P*-value < 0.0001]; reject H_0. The evidence suggests that the mean time to graduate for students who first start in community college is longer than the mean time to graduate for those who do not transfer.
(b) Lower bound: 0.818 [Tech: 0.848], upper bound: 1.182 [Tech: 1.152]. We are 95% confident that the mean additional time to graduate for students who start in community college is between 0.818 year and 1.182 years.
(c) No; this is observational data. Community college students may be working more hours, which does not allow them to take additional classes.

8. H_0: $\mu_1 = \mu_2$, H_1: $\mu_1 > \mu_2$. Classical approach: $t_0 = 2.849 > t_{0.01} = 2.403$; reject H_0. *P*-value approach: $0.0025 < P\text{-value} < 0.005$ [Tech: *P*-value $= 0.0026$] $< \alpha = 0.01$; reject H_0. There is sufficient evidence at the $\alpha = 0.01$ level of significance to conclude that mean improvement in the treatment group was greater than mean improvement in the control group. The drug appears to be effective in improving the Young Mania Rating Scale score.

9. (a) This is an observational study. The researcher did not influence the data.
(b) Large, independent samples
(c) H_0: $\mu_A = \mu_D$, H_1: $\mu_A \neq \mu_D$. Classical approach: $t_0 = 0.846$ is between $-t_{0.025} = -2.032$ and $t_{0.025} = 2.032$; do not reject H_0. *P*-value approach: $0.50 > P\text{-value} > 0.40$ [Tech: *P*-value $= 0.4013$] $> \alpha = 0.05$; do not reject H_0. There is not sufficient evidence at the $\alpha = 0.05$ level of significance to say that travelers walk at different speeds depending on whether they are arriving or departing an airport.

10. (a) This is an observational study. The researcher did not influence the data.
(b) Since the samples are small, the populations must be normally distributed, with no outliers.
(c) H_0: $\mu_B = \mu_L$, H_1: $\mu_B \neq \mu_L$. Classical approach: $t_0 = 0.772$ is between $-t_{0.025} = -2.093$ and $t_{0.025} = 2.093$; do not reject H_0. *P*-value approach: $0.50 > P\text{-value} > 0.40$ [Tech: *P*-value $= 0.4448$] $> \alpha = 0.05$; do not reject H_0. There is not sufficient evidence at the $\alpha = 0.05$ level of significance to say that business travelers walk at different speeds than leisure travelers when walking in an airport.

11. (a) Lower bound: 4.71, upper bound: 6.29, using 100 degrees of freedom. We are 95% confident that the mean difference in scores between students who think about being a professor and students who think about soccer hooligans is between 4.71 and 6.29.
(b) Since the 95% confidence interval does not contain 0, the results suggest that priming does have an effect on scores.

12. Lower bound: 12.66, upper bound: 13.34, using 100 degrees of freedom. We are 95% confident that the mean difference in how much of every tax dollar Republicans say is wasted and how much of every tax dollar Democrats say is wasted is between 12.66 cents and 13.34 cents.

13. (a)

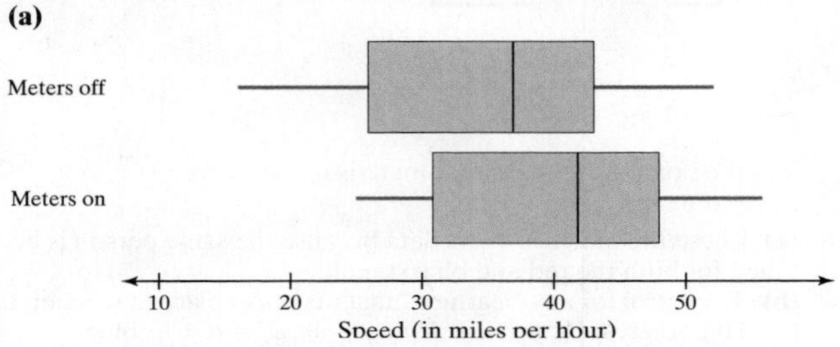

(b) H_0: $\mu_{on} = \mu_{off}$, H_1: $\mu_{on} > \mu_{off}$. Classical approach: $t_0 = 1.713 > t_{0.10} = 1.345$; reject the null hypothesis. *P*-value approach: $0.05 < P\text{-value} < 0.10$ [Tech: *P*-value $= 0.0489$]; reject the null hypothesis. There is sufficient evidence at the $\alpha = 0.10$ level of significance that the ramp meters are effective in maintaining higher speed on the freeway.

14. (a) Yes; each sample is the result of a randomized experiment. The samples were obtained independently. We are told that a normal probability plot indicates that the data could come from a population that is normal, with no outliers.
(b) H_0: $\mu_F = \mu_M$, H_1: $\mu_F \neq \mu_M$. Classical approach: $t_0 = 0.619$ is between $-t_{0.025} = -2.145$ and $t_{0.025} = 2.145$; do not reject H_0. *P*-value approach: *P*-value > 0.50 [Tech: *P*-value $= 0.5403$] $> \alpha = 0.05$; do not reject H_0. There is not sufficient evidence at the $\alpha = 0.05$ level of significance to conclude that there is a difference in reaction time between females and males.
(c)

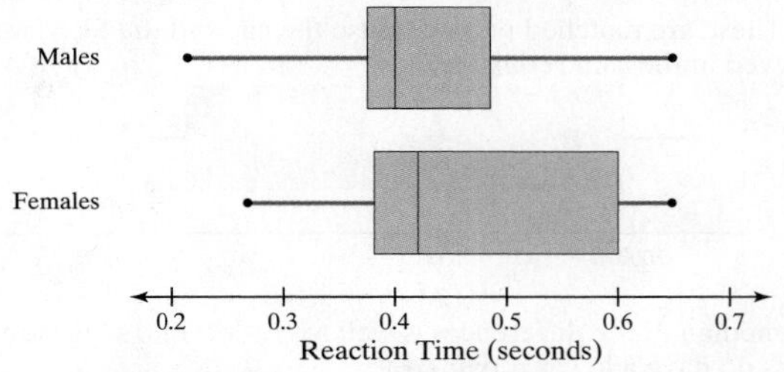

Yes, the boxplots support that there is no difference in reaction times.

15. H_0: $\mu_{carpet} = \mu_{no\ carpet}$, H_1: $\mu_{carpet} > \mu_{no\ carpet}$. Classical approach: $t_0 = 0.956 < t_{0.05} = 1.895$; do not reject H_0. *P*-value approach: $0.20 > P\text{-value} > 0.15$ [Tech: *P*-value $= 0.1780$] $> \alpha = 0.05$; do not reject H_0. There is not sufficient evidence at the $\alpha = 0.05$ level of significance to conclude that carpeted rooms have more bacteria than uncarpeted rooms.

16. (a) This is an experiment using a completely randomized design.
(b) The treatments are multimodal teaching style and unimodal teaching style.

(c) H_0: $\mu_{\text{visual}} = \mu_{\text{textual}}$, H_1: $\mu_{\text{visual}} \neq \mu_{\text{textual}}$. Classical approach: $t_0 = 2.378 > t_{0.025} = 2.110$; reject H_0. *P*-value approach: $0.02 <$ *P*-value < 0.04 [Tech: *P*-value $= 0.0236$] $< \alpha = 0.05$; reject H_0. There is sufficient evidence at the $\alpha = 0.05$ level of significance to conclude that there is a difference in the test scores of people who use the visual manual and those who use the textual manual.

17. H_0: $\mu_{\text{AL}} = \mu_{\text{NL}}$, H_1: $\mu_{\text{AL}} > \mu_{\text{NL}}$. Classical approach: $t_0 = 2.136 > t_{0.05} = 1.699$; reject H_0. *P*-value approach: $0.02 <$ *P*-value < 0.025 [Tech: *P*-value $= 0.0187$] $< \alpha = 0.05$; reject H_0. There is sufficient evidence at the $\alpha = 0.05$ level of significance to conclude that games played with a designated hitter result in more runs.

18. H_0: $\mu_{\text{RB}} = \mu_{\text{ALT}}$, H_1: $\mu_{\text{RB}} \neq \mu_{\text{ALT}}$. Classical approach: $t_0 = 0.610$ is between $-t_{0.05} = -1.699$ and $t_{0.05} = 1.699$; do not reject H_0. *P*-value approach: *P*-value > 0.50 [Tech: *P*-value $= 0.5440$] $> \alpha = 0.10$; do not reject H_0. There is not sufficient evidence at the $\alpha = 0.10$ level of significance to conclude that the lengths of rhythm & blues songs differ from the length of alternative songs.

19. H_0: $\mu_{\text{Male}} = \mu_{\text{Female}}$, H_1: $\mu_{\text{Male}} \neq \mu_{\text{Female}}$. Classical approach: $t_0 = -2.756 < -t_{0.025} = -1.990$; reject the null hypothesis. *P*-value approach: *P*-value $= 0.0064 < \alpha = 0.05$; reject the null hypothesis. There is sufficient evidence at the $\alpha = 0.05$ level of significance that there is a difference between males and females regarding the ideal number of children.

20. H_0: $\mu_{\text{male}} = \mu_{\text{female}}$, H_1: $\mu_{\text{male}} > \mu_{\text{female}}$. Classical approach: $t_0 = 2.362 > t_{0.05} = 1.664$; reject the null hypothesis. *P*-value approach: *P*-value $= 0.0096 < \alpha = 0.05$; reject the null hypothesis. There is sufficient evidence at the $\alpha = 0.05$ level of significance that males watch more television each week than females.

21. Lower bound: 0.71 [Tech: 0.72], upper bound: 2.33 [Tech: 2.32]. We can be 90% confident that the mean difference in daily leisure time between adults without children and those with children is between 0.71 and 2.33 hours. Since the confidence interval does not include zero, we can conclude that there is a significant difference in the leisure time of adults without children and those with children.

22. Lower bound: 38.08 [Tech: 38.13], upper bound: 44.72 [Tech: 44.67]. We can be 90% confident that the mean difference in cooling time between filled clear glass bottles and filled aluminum bottles is between 38.08 and 44.72 minutes. Since the confidence interval does not include zero, we can conclude that there is a significant difference in the cooling times of glass bottles and aluminum bottles.

23. (a) H_0: $\mu_{\text{men}} = \mu_{\text{women}}$ versus H_1: $\mu_{\text{men}} < \mu_{\text{women}}$
(b) *P*-value $= 0.0051$. Because *P*-value $< \alpha$, we reject the null hypothesis. There is sufficient evidence at the $\alpha = 0.01$ level of significance to conclude that the mean step pulse of men is lower than the mean step pulse of women.
(c) Lower bound: -10.7, upper bound: -1.5. We are 95% confident that the mean step pulse of men is between 1.5 and 10.7 beats per minute lower than the mean step pulse of women.

24. (a) H_0: $\mu_{\text{men}} = \mu_{\text{women}}$ versus H_1: $\mu_{\text{men}} < \mu_{\text{women}}$
(b) *P*-value $= 0.0001$. Because *P*-value $< \alpha$, we reject the null hypothesis. There is sufficient evidence at the $\alpha = 0.01$ level of significance to conclude that the women are more flexible than the men.
(c) Lower bound: -3.58, upper bound: -1.12. We are 95% confident that the mean flexibility of women is between 1.12 and 3.58 inches higher than the mean flexibility of men.

25. (a) Completely randomized design
(b) Final exam; online versus traditional homework
(c) Teacher; location; time; text; syllabus; tests
(d) The assumption is that the students "randomly" enrolled in the course.
(e) H_0: $\mu_F = \mu_S$; H_1: $\mu_F > \mu_S$. Classical: $t_0 = 1.795 > t_{0.05} = 1.711$; reject H_0. $0.025 <$ *P*-value < 0.05 [Tech: *P*-value $= 0.039$] $< \alpha = 0.05$; reject H_0. There is sufficient evidence at the $\alpha = 0.05$ level of significance to conclude that the final exams in the fall semester were higher than the final exams in the spring semester. It would appear to be the case that the online homework system helps in raising final exam scores.
(f) One factor is the fact that the weather is pretty lousy at the end of the fall semester, but pretty nice at the end of the spring semester. If "spring fever" kicked in for the spring semester students, then they probably studied less for the final exam.

26. The degrees of freedom obtained from Formula (2) are larger than the smaller of $n_1 - 1$ or $n_2 - 1$, and t_α decreases as the degrees of freedom increase. The larger the critical value is, the harder it is to reject the null hypothesis.

11.4 Assess Your Understanding (page 507)

1. H_0: $p_A = p_B$ vs. H_1: $p_A \neq p_B$. Classical: $z_0 = 0.64 < z_{0.025} = 1.96$; do not reject the null hypothesis. *P*-value $= 0.5222 > \alpha = 0.05$; do not reject the null hypothesis. There is not sufficient evidence at the $\alpha = 0.05$ level of significance to conclude that there is a difference in the proportions.

2. H_0: $p_1 = p_2$ vs. H_1: $p_1 \neq p_2$. All requirements to conduct the test are satisfied. Classical: $z_0 = -1.18$ is between $-z_{0.005} = -2.575$ and $z_{0.005} = 2.575$; do not reject the null hypothesis. *P*-value $= 0.238$ [Tech: 0.242] $> \alpha = 0.01$; do not reject the null hypothesis. There is not sufficient evidence at the $\alpha = 0.05$ level of significance to conclude that there is a difference in the proportions.

3. H_0: $\mu_1 = \mu_2$ vs. H_1: $\mu_1 \neq \mu_2$. All requirements to conduct the test are satisfied. Classical: $t_0 = -1.39$ is between $-t_{0.025} = -2.179$ and $t_{0.025} = 2.179$; do not reject the null hypothesis. $0.20 >$ *P*-value > 0.10 [Tech: *P*-value $= 0.1745$] $> \alpha = 0.05$; do not reject the null hypothesis. There is not sufficient evidence at the $\alpha = 0.05$ level of significance to conclude that there is a difference in the means.

4. H_0: $p_1 = p_2$ vs. H_1: $p_1 < p_2$. All requirements to conduct the test are satisfied. Classical: $z_0 = -1.84 < -z_{0.05} = -1.645$; reject the null hypothesis. *P*-value $= 0.0329$ [Tech: 0.0335] $< \alpha = 0.05$; reject the null hypothesis. There is sufficient evidence at the $\alpha = 0.05$ level of significance to conclude that proportion 1 is less than proportion 2.

5. H_0: $\mu_1 = \mu_2$ vs. H_1: $\mu_1 \neq \mu_2$. All requirements to conduct the test are satisfied. Classical: $t_0 = -3.271 < -t_{0.005} = -2.704$; reject the null hypothesis. $0.002 <$ *P*-value < 0.005 [Tech: *P*-value $= 0.0016$] $< \alpha = 0.01$; reject the null hypothesis. There is sufficient evidence at the $\alpha = 0.05$ level of significance to conclude that there is a difference in the means.

6. H_0: $\mu_d = 0$ vs. H_1: $\mu_d > 0$; $d_i = Y_i - X_i$. Classical: $t_0 = 1.324 < t_{0.05} = 2.132$; do not reject the null hypothesis. $0.15 >$ *P*-value > 0.10 [Tech: *P*-value $= 0.128$] $> \alpha = 0.05$; do not reject the null hypothesis. There is not sufficient evidence at the $\alpha = 0.05$ level of significance to conclude that the treatment is effective.

7. H_0: $\mu_d = 0$ vs. H_1: $\mu_d < 0$; $d_i = Y_i - X_i$. Classical: $t_0 = -1.754 < -t_{0.1} = -1.533$; reject the null hypothesis. $0.05 <$ *P*-value < 0.10 [Tech: *P*-value $= 0.0771$] $< \alpha = 0.1$; reject the null hypothesis. There is sufficient evidence at the $\alpha = 0.1$ level of significance to conclude that the treatment is effective.

8. H_0: $p_A = p_B$ vs. H_1: $p_A \neq p_B$. Classical: $z_0 = 1.18 < z_{0.025} = 1.96$; do not reject the null hypothesis. *P*-value $= 0.238 > \alpha = 0.05$; do not reject the null hypothesis. There is not sufficient evidence at the $\alpha = 0.05$ level of significance to conclude that there is a difference in the proportions.

9. (a) There are a few very large collision claims relative to the majority of claims.
(b) H_0: $\mu_{30-59} = \mu_{20-24}$ vs. H_1: $\mu_{30-59} < \mu_{20-24}$. All requirements to conduct the test are satisfied; use $\alpha = 0.05$. Classical: $t_0 = -1.890 < -t_{0.05} = -1.685$; reject the null hypothesis. $0.025 <$ *P*-value < 0.05 [Tech: *P*-value $= 0.0313$] $< \alpha = 0.05$; reject the null hypothesis. There is sufficient evidence at the $\alpha = 0.05$ level of significance to conclude that the mean collision claim of a 30- to 59-year-old is less than the mean claim of a 20- to 24-year-old. Given that 20- to 24-year-olds tend to claim more for each accident, it makes sense to charge them more for coverage.

10. H_0: $p_{\text{nk}} = p_{\text{k}}$ vs. H_1: $p_{\text{nk}} < p_{\text{k}}$. Independent samples; all requirements to conduct the test are satisfied; use $\alpha = 0.05$. Classical: $z_0 = -4.63 < -z_{0.05} = -1.645$; reject the null hypothesis. *P*-value $< 0.0001 < \alpha = 0.05$; reject the null hypothesis. There is sufficient evidence at the $\alpha = 0.05$ level of significance to conclude that the proportion of non-Kumon students who answered the question correctly is less than the proportion of Kumon students who answered the question correctly. The Kumon students performed better on the exam question. A confounding factor is that it may be the case that stronger students enroll in Kumon (since it is an after-school program). So, it is not clear what role Kumon plays in the performance of the students compared to their ability.

11. H_0: $p_{\text{HE}} = p_{\text{HA}}$ vs. H_1: $p_{\text{HE}} \neq p_{\text{HA}}$. Classical: $z_0 = 3.74 > z_{0.025} = 1.96$; reject the null hypothesis. *P*-value $= 0.0002 < \alpha = 0.05$; reject the null hypothesis. There is sufficient evidence at the $\alpha = 0.05$ level of significance to conclude that there is a difference in the proportions. It seems that the proportion who are healthy differs from the proportion who are happy. The data imply that more people are happy even though they are unhealthy.

12. (a)

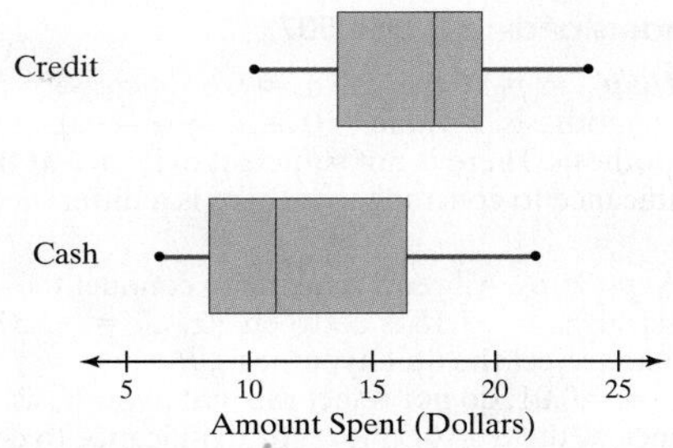

The boxplots indicate that people do spend more on fast food when they use a credit card.
(b) H_0: $\mu_{cr} = \mu_{ca}$ vs. H_1: $\mu_{cr} > \mu_{ca}$. All requirements to conduct the test are satisfied. Classical: $t_0 = 2.247 < t_{0.01} = 2.821$; do not reject the null hypothesis. $0.05 > P$-value > 0.025 [Tech: P-value $= 0.0191$] $> \alpha = 0.01$; do not reject the null hypothesis. There is not sufficient evidence at the $\alpha = 0.01$ level of significance to conclude that the mean amount spent with credit cards is more than the mean amount spent with cash.
(c) With $\alpha = 0.05$ level of significance, we would reject the null hypothesis. However, once the level of significance is decided on, you should not change it. With that said, the P-value does suggest that the mean amount on credit-card sales is more than the mean amount on cash sales. It would be legitimate to suggest to your manager that further investigation is warranted (such as looking at larger samples).

13. H_0: $\mu_d = 0$ vs. H_1: $\mu_d \neq 0$; $d_i = W_i - T_i$. Classical: $t_0 = -1.244$ is between $-t_{0.025} = -2.262$ and $t_{0.025} = 2.262$; do not reject the null hypothesis. $0.30 > P$-value > 0.20 [Tech: P-value $= 0.2451$] $> \alpha = 0.05$; do not reject the null hypothesis. There is not sufficient evidence at the $\alpha = 0.05$ level of significance to conclude that there is a difference in the pricing of health and beauty products at Walmart and Target.

14. H_0: $p = 0.5$ vs. H_1: $p > 0.5$. All requirements to conduct the test are satisfied. Classical approach: $z_0 = 9.217 > z_{0.05} = 1.645$; reject the null hypothesis. P-value approach: P-value < 0.0002 [Tech: P-value < 0.0001] $< \alpha = 0.05$; reject the null hypothesis. There is sufficient evidence at the $\alpha = 0.05$ level of significance to suggest that a quick 1-second view of a black and white photo represents enough information to judge the winner of an election.

15. H_0: $\mu = 3.101$ vs. H_1: $\mu > 3.101$. All requirements to conduct the test are satisfied. $t_0 = 4.064$ and P-value < 0.0005 [Tech: P-value $= 0.0003$]; no level of significance is stated but given that the P-value is so small we reject the null hypothesis. There is sufficient evidence to conclude that gas in Chicago is more expensive than the national average.

16. H_0: $\mu_c = \mu_{nc}$ vs. H_1: $\mu_c > \mu_{nc}$. All requirements to conduct the test are satisfied. Classical: $t_0 = 1.875 > t_{0.1} = 1.299$; reject the null hypothesis. $0.025 < P$-value < 0.05 [Tech: P-value $= 0.0319$] $< \alpha = 0.1$; reject the null hypothesis. There is sufficient evidence at the $\alpha = 0.1$ level of significance to conclude that the teacher evaluations were better for the chocolate group than for the nonchocolate group.

17. H_0: $p_{>100K} = p_{<100K}$ vs. H_1: $p_{>100K} \neq p_{<100K}$. Lower bound: 0.019 [Tech: 0.020], upper bound: 0.097. Because the confidence interval does not include 0, there is sufficient evidence at the $\alpha = 0.05$ level of significance to conclude that there is a difference in the proportions. It seems that a higher proportion of individuals who earn over \$100,000 per year feel it is morally wrong for unwed women to have children.

18. (a) Since the sample size is small, the distribution of differences must be normal with no outliers.
(b) H_0: $\mu_d = 0$ vs. H_1: $\mu_d > 0$; $d_i = GE_i - P_i$. Classical: $t_0 = 2.974 > t_{0.05} = 1.782$; reject the null hypothesis. $0.005 < P$-value < 0.01 [Tech: P-value $=0.0058$] $< \alpha = 0.05$; reject the null hypothesis. There is sufficient evidence at the $\alpha = 0.05$ level of significance to conclude that the daily volume of General Electric stock is greater than that of Pfizer stock.

19. (a) Yes
(b)

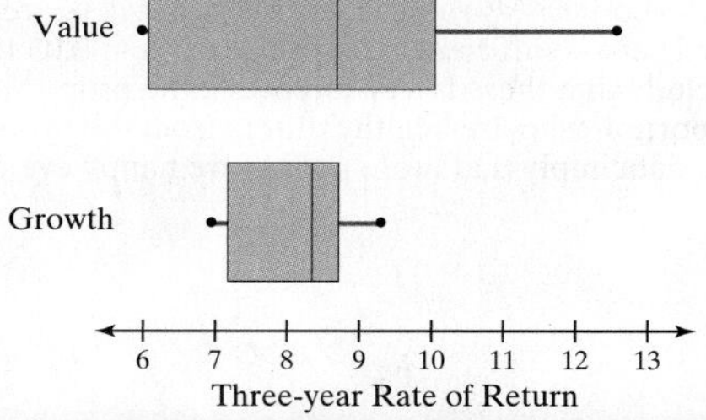

There are no outliers in either data set.
(c) H_0: $\mu_v = \mu_g$ vs. H_1: $\mu_v \neq \mu_g$. Classical: $t_0 = 0.587$ is between $-t_{0.025} = -2.262$ and $t_{0.025} = 2.262$; do not reject the null hypothesis. P-value > 0.50 [Tech: P-value $= 0.5691$] $> \alpha = 0.05$; do not reject the null hypothesis. There is not sufficient evidence at the $\alpha = 0.05$ level of significance to conclude that the rate of return of value funds is different from the rate of return of growth funds.

20. Use matched-pairs design to eliminate variability due to overall market fluctuations.
21. Hypothesis test for a single mean
22. Hypothesis test for two proportions, independent sample
23. Matched pairs t-test on difference of means
24. Confidence interval for a single mean
25. Confidence interval for a single proportion
26. Two sample t-test of independent means

Chapter 11 Review Exercises (page 511)

1. Dependent; quantitative **2.** Independent; quantitative
3. (a)

Observation	1	2	3	4	5	6
$d_i = X_i - Y_i$	-0.7	0.6	0	-0.1	-0.4	-0.4

(b) $\bar{d} = -0.167$; $s_d = 0.450$
(c) Hypotheses: H_0: $\mu_d = 0$, H_1: $\mu_d < 0$. Classical approach: $t_0 = -0.907 > -t_{0.05} = -2.015$; do not reject the null hypothesis. P-value approach: $0.25 > P$-value > 0.20 [Tech: P-value $= 0.2030$] $> \alpha = 0.05$; do not reject the null hypothesis. There is not sufficient evidence to conclude that the mean difference is less than zero.
(d) Lower bound: -0.79, upper bound: 0.45

4. (a) Hypotheses: H_0: $\mu_1 = \mu_2$, H_1: $\mu_1 \neq \mu_2$. Classical approach: $t_0 = 2.290 > t_{0.05} = 1.895$; reject the null hypothesis. P-value approach: $0.05 < P$-value < 0.10 [Tech: P-value $= 0.0351$] $< \alpha = 0.10$; reject the null hypothesis. There is sufficient evidence at the $\alpha = 0.1$ level of significance to conclude that $\mu_1 \neq \mu_2$.
(b) Lower bound: 0.73 [Tech: 1.01], upper bound: 7.67 [Tech: 7.39]

5. Hypotheses: H_0: $\mu_1 = \mu_2$, H_1: $\mu_1 > \mu_2$. Classical approach: $t_0 = 1.472 < t_{0.01} = 2.423$; do not reject the null hypothesis. P-value approach: $0.10 > P$-value > 0.05 [Tech: P-value $= 0.0726$] $> \alpha = 0.01$; do not reject the null hypothesis. There is not sufficient evidence at the $\alpha = 0.01$ level of significance to conclude that the mean of population 1 is larger than the mean of population 2.

6. H_0: $p_1 = p_2$, H_1: $p_1 \neq p_2$. Classical: $z_0 = -1.70$ is between $-z_{0.025} = -1.96$ and $z_{0.025} = 1.96$; do not reject the null hypothesis. P-value $= 0.093$ [Tech: 0.0895] $> \alpha = 0.05$; do not reject the null hypothesis. There is not sufficient evidence at the $\alpha = 0.05$ level of significance to conclude that the proportion in population 1 is different from the proportion in population 2.

7. (a) The sampling method is dependent because the same individual is used for both measurements.
(b) Hypotheses: H_0: $\mu_d = 0$, H_1: $\mu_d \neq 0$. Classical approach: $t_0 = 0.512$ is between $-t_{0.025} = -2.262$ and $t_{0.025} = 2.262$; do not reject the null hypothesis. P-value approach: P-value > 0.50 [Tech: P-value $= 0.6209$] $> \alpha = 0.05$; do not reject the null hypothesis. There is not sufficient evidence at the $\alpha = 0.05$ level of significance to conclude that arm span is different from height. The sample evidence does not contradict the belief that arm span and height are the same.

8. (a) The testing method is independent since the cars selected for the McDonald's sample had no bearing on the cars chosen for the Wendy's sample.
(b) Hypotheses: H_0: $\mu_{McD} = \mu_W$, H_1: $\mu_{McD} \neq \mu_W$. Classical approach: $t_0 = -4.059 < -t_{0.05} = -1.706$; reject the null hypothesis. P-value approach: P-value < 0.0005 [Tech: P-value $= 0.0003$] $< \alpha = 0.10$; reject the null hypothesis. There is sufficient evidence at the $\alpha = 0.10$ level of significance to conclude that the wait times in the drive-throughs of the two restaurants differ.

(c)

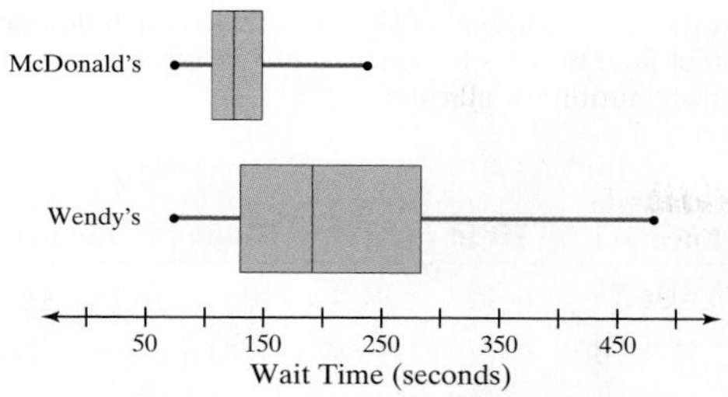

Based on the boxplots, it would appear to be the case that the wait time at McDonalds is less than the wait time at Wendy's.

9. **(a)** Each sample is the result of a randomized experiment; $n_1\hat{p}_1(1-\hat{p}_1)=26 \geq 10$ and $n_2\hat{p}_2(1-\hat{p}_2)=45 \geq 10$; and each sample is less than 5% of the population size. Hypotheses: H_0: $p_{\text{exp}} = p_{\text{control}}$, H_1: $p_{\text{exp}} < p_{\text{control}}$. Classical approach: $z_0 = -2.71 < -z_{0.01} = -2.33$; reject the null hypothesis. *P*-value approach: *P*-value $=0.0033 < \alpha = 0.01$; reject the null hypothesis. There is sufficient evidence at the $\alpha = 0.01$ level of significance to conclude that a lower proportion of women in the experimental group experienced a bone fracture than in the control group.
(b) Lower bound: -0.06, upper bound: -0.01. We are 95% confident that the difference in the proportion of women who experienced a bone fracture between the experimental and control group is between -0.06 and -0.01.
(c) This is a completely randomized design with two treatments: placebo and 5 mg of Actonel.
(d) A double-blind experiment is one in which neither the subject nor the individual administering the treatment knows which group (experimental or control) the subject is in.

10. H_0: $p_J = p_V$, H_1: $p_J \neq p_V$. Classical: $z_0 = 1.81 < z_{0.025} = 1.96$; do not reject the null hypothesis. *P*-value $= 0.0702 > \alpha = 0.05$; do not reject the null hypothesis. There is not sufficient evidence at the $\alpha = 0.05$ level of significance to conclude that there is a difference in the proportions. It seems that the proportion who feel serving on a jury is a civic duty is the same as the proportion who feel voting is a civic duty.

11. **(a)** $n = n_1 = n_2 = 2136$ **(b)** $n = n_1 = n_2 = 3383$

12. Lower bound: -1.37, upper bound: 2.17. Since the interval includes zero, we conclude that there is not sufficient evidence at the $\alpha = 0.05$ level of significance to reject the claim that arm span and height are equal.

13. Lower bound: -128.868 [Tech: -128.4]; upper bound: -42.218 [Tech: -42.67]. A marketing campaign could be initiated by McDonald's touting the fact that wait times are up to 2 minutes less at McDonald's.

Chapter 11 Test (page 513)

1. Independent

2. Dependent

3. **(a)**

Observation	1	2	3	4	5	6	7
$d_i = X_i - Y_i$	0.2	-0.5	0.2	0.6	-0.6	-0.5	-0.8

(b) $\bar{d} = -0.2$; $s_d = 0.526$
(c) Hypotheses: H_0: $\mu_d = 0$, H_1: $\mu_d \neq 0$. Classical approach: $t_0 = -1.006$ is between $-t_{0.005} = -3.707$ and $t_{0.005} = 3.707$; do not reject the null hypothesis. $0.40 >$ *P*-value > 0.30 [Tech: *P*-value $= 0.3532$] $> \alpha = 0.01$; do not reject the null hypothesis. There is not sufficient evidence to conclude that the mean difference is different from zero.
(d) Lower bound: -0.69, upper bound: 0.29

4. **(a)** Hypotheses: H_0: $\mu_1 = \mu_2$, H_1: $\mu_1 \neq \mu_2$. Classical approach: $t_0 = -2.054 < -t_{0.05} = -1.714$. Reject the null hypothesis. $0.05 <$ *P*-value < 0.10 [Tech: *P*-value $= 0.0464$] $< \alpha = 0.1$; reject the null hypothesis. There is sufficient evidence at the $\alpha = 0.1$ level of significance to conclude that the means are different.
(b) Lower bound: -12.44 [Tech: -12.3], upper bound: 0.04 [Tech: -0.10]

5. Hypotheses: H_0: $\mu_1 = \mu_2$, H_1: $\mu_1 < \mu_2$. Classical approach: $t_0 = -1.357 > -t_{0.05} = -1.895$; do not reject the null hypothesis. $0.15 >$ *P*-value > 0.10 [Tech: *P*-value $= 0.0959$] $> \alpha = 0.05$; do not reject the null hypothesis. There is not sufficient evidence at the $\alpha = 0.05$ level of significance to conclude that the mean of population 1 is less than the mean of population 2.

6. H_0: $p_1 = p_2$ vs. H_1: $p_1 < p_2$ Classical: $z_0 = -0.80 > -z_{0.05} = -1.645$; do not reject the null hypothesis. *P*-value $= 0.2119$ [Tech:0.2124] $> \alpha = 0.05$; do not reject the null hypothesis. There is not sufficient evidence at the $\alpha = 0.05$ level of significance to conclude that the proportion in population 1 is less than the proportion in population 2.

7. **(a)** The testing method is independent since the dates selected for the Texas sample have no bearing on the dates chosen for the Illinois sample.
(b) Both samples must come from populations that are normally distributed.
(c)

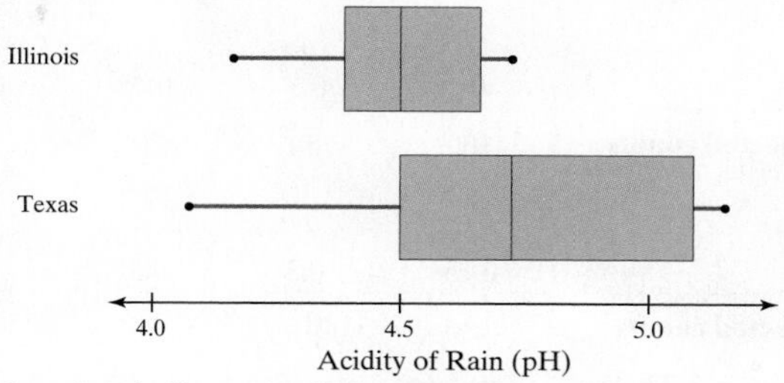

The boxplots indicate the Chicago rain has a lower pH than Houston rain.
(d) Hypotheses: H_0: $\mu_{\text{Texas}} = \mu_{\text{Illinois}}$, H_1: $\mu_{\text{Texas}} \neq \mu_{\text{Illinois}}$. Classical approach: $t_0 = 2.276 > t_{0.025} = 2.201$; reject the null hypothesis. $0.04 <$ *P*-value < 0.05 [Tech: *P*-value $= 0.0387$] $< \alpha = 0.05$; reject the null hypothesis. There is sufficient evidence at the $\alpha = 0.05$ level of significance to conclude that the acidity of the rain near Houston is different from its acidity near Chicago.

8. **(a)** The response variable is the student's GPA. The explanatory variable is whether the student has a sleep disorder or not.
(b) Hypotheses: H_0: $\mu_{\text{sleep disorder}} = \mu_{\text{no sleep disorder}}$, H_1: $\mu_{\text{sleep dlsorder}} < \mu_{\text{no sleep disorder}}$. Classical approach: $t_0 = -3.784$ [Tech: -3.866] is less than $-t_{0.05} = -1.660$; reject H_0. *P*-value approach: *P*-value < 0.0005 [Tech: *P*-value < 0.0001] $< \alpha = 0.05$; reject H_0. There is sufficient evidence at the $\alpha = 0.05$ level of significance to suggest that sleep disorders adversely affect a student's GPA.

9. Hypotheses: H_0: $\mu_d = 0$ vs. H_1: $\mu_d < 0$; Classical approach: $t_0 = -1.927 < -t_{0.10} = -1.440$; reject the null hypothesis. *P*-value approach: $0.05 <$ *P*-value < 0.10 [Tech: *P*-value $= 0.0511$] $< \alpha = 0.1$; reject the null hypothesis. There is sufficient evidence at the $\alpha = 0.1$ level of significance to suggest that the repair cost for the car is higher.

10. **(a)** Completely randomized design.
(b) Whether the subject gets dry mouth or not.
(c) Each sample is the result of a randomized experiment. $n_1\hat{p}_1(1-\hat{p}_1) = 66 \geq 10$ and $n_2\hat{p}_2(1-\hat{p}_2) = 31 \geq 10$; and each sample is less than 5% of the population size. Hypotheses: H_0: $p_{\text{exp}} = p_{\text{control}}$ H_1: $p_{\text{exp}} > p_{\text{control}}$. Classical approach: $z_0 = 2.21 > z_{0.05} = 1.645$; reject the null hypothesis. *P*-value $= 0.0136 < \alpha = 0.05$; reject the null hypothesis. There is sufficient evidence at the $\alpha = 0.05$ level of significance to conclude that a higher proportion of subjects in the experimental group experienced a dry mouth than in the control group.

11. H_0: $p_M = p_F$, H_1: $p_M \neq p_F$. Lower bound: 0.051, upper bound: 0.089. Because the confidence interval does not include 0, we reject the null hypothesis. There is sufficient evidence at the $\alpha = 0.1$ level of significance to conclude that the proportion of males and females for which hypnotism led to quitting smoking is different.

12. H_0: $p_A = p_{CP}$, H_1: $p_A \neq p_{CP}$. Classical: $z_0 = 76.6 > z_{0.025} = 1.96$; reject the null hypothesis. *P*-value $< 0.0001 < \alpha = 0.05$; reject the null hypothesis. There is sufficient evidence at the $\alpha = 0.05$ level of significance to conclude that the proportion of individuals who favor the death penalty is different from the proportion who favor abortion.

13. **(a)** $n = n_1 = n_2 = 762$
(b) $n = n_1 = n_2 = 1201$

14. H_0: $\mu_p = \mu_n$; H_1: $\mu_p \neq \mu_n$. Lower bound: 1.03 pounds, upper bound: 1.17 pounds. Because the confidence interval does not contain 0, we reject the null hypothesis. There is sufficient evidence to conclude that Naltrexone is effective in preventing weight gain among individuals who quit smoking. Answers will vary regarding practical significance, but one must ask, "Do I want to take a drug so that I can keep about 1 pound off?" Probably not.

CHAPTER 12 Additional Inferential Procedures

12.1 Assess Your Understanding (page 522)

1. True
2. goodness-of-fit
3. expected counts; np_i
4. To perform a goodness-of-fit test, all expected frequencies must be greater than or equal to 1, and at least 80% of the expected frequencies must be greater than or equal to 5.
5.

p_i	0.2	0.1	0.45	0.25
Expected counts	100	50	225	125

6.

p_i	0.15	0.3	0.35	0.20
Expected counts	105	210	245	140

7. (a) $\chi_0^2 = 2.72$
(b) df = 3
(c) $\chi_{0.05}^2 = 7.815$
(d) Do not reject H_0, since $\chi_0^2 < \chi_{0.05}^2$. There is not sufficient evidence at the $\alpha = 0.05$ level of significance to conclude that any one of the proportions is different from the others.
8. (a) $\chi_0^2 = 2.2$
(b) df = 4
(c) $\chi_{0.05}^2 = 9.488$
(d) Do not reject H_0, since $\chi_0^2 < \chi_{0.05}^2$. There is not sufficient evidence at the $\alpha = 0.05$ level of significance to conclude that any one of the proportions is different from the others.
9. (a) $\chi_0^2 = 12.56$
(b) df = 4
(c) $\chi_{0.05}^2 = 9.488$
(d) Reject H_0, since $\chi_0^2 > \chi_{0.05}^2$. There is sufficient evidence at the $\alpha = 0.05$ level of significance to conclude that X is not binomial with $n = 4, p = 0.8$.
10. (a) $\chi_0^2 = 11.987$
(b) df = 4
(c) $\chi_{0.05}^2 = 9.488$
(d) Reject H_0, since $\chi_0^2 > \chi_{0.05}^2$. There is sufficient evidence at the $\alpha = 0.05$ level of significance to conclude that X is not binomial with $n = 4, p = 0.3$.
11. H_0: the distribution of colors is as stated by M&M; H_1: The distribution is different from that stated by M&M. Classical approach: $\chi_0^2 = 18.738 > \chi_{0.05}^2 = 11.071$; reject the null hypothesis. *P*-value approach: *P*-value $< 0.005 < \alpha = 0.05$ [Tech: *P*-value $= 0.002$]; reject the null hypothesis. There is sufficient evidence at the $\alpha = 0.05$ level of significance to conclude that the distribution of candies in a bag of M&Ms is not 13% brown, 14% yellow, 13% red, 20% orange, 24% blue, and 16% green.
12. Classical approach: $\chi_0^2 = 3.569 < \chi_{0.05}^2 = 11.071$; do not reject the null hypothesis. *P*-value approach: *P*-value $> 0.10 > \alpha = 0.05$ [Tech: *P*-value $= 0.613$]; do not reject the null hypothesis. There is not sufficient evidence at the $\alpha = 0.05$ level of significance to reject M&M/Mars' stated distribution of 12% brown, 15% yellow, 12% red, 23% orange, 23% blue, and 15% green candies in a bag of peanut M&Ms.
13. (a) Answers will vary depending on the desired probability of making a Type I error. One possible choice: $\alpha = 0.01$.
(b) H_0: The digits follow Benford's Law; H_1: The digits do not follow Benford's Law. Classical approach: $\chi_0^2 = 21.693$; compare χ_0^2 to your chosen χ_α^2. *P*-value approach: *P*-value is between 0.01 and 0.005 [Tech: *P*-value $= 0.006$].
(c) Answers will vary. One possible answer: Since *P*-value < 0.01, there is sufficient evidence to conclude that Benford's Law is not followed and the employee is guilty of embezzlement.
14. Classical approach: $\chi_0^2 = 5.092 < \chi_{0.05}^2 = 15.507$; do not reject the null hypothesis. *P*-value approach: *P*-value $> 0.10 > \alpha = 0.05$ [Tech: *P*-value $= 0.748$]; do not reject the null hypothesis. At the $\alpha = 0.05$ level of significance, the evidence supports the belief that the distribution of the surface area of rivers follows Benford's Law.
15. (a) Classical approach: $\chi_0^2 = 121.367 > \chi_{0.05}^2 = 9.488$; reject the null hypothesis. *P*-value approach: *P*-value $< 0.005 < \alpha = 0.05$ [Tech: *P*-value < 0.0001]; reject the null hypothesis. There is sufficient evidence at the $\alpha = 0.05$ level of significance to conclude that the distribution of fatal injuries for riders not wearing a helmet does not follow the distribution for all riders.
(b)

Location of Injury	Multiple Locations	Head	Neck	Thorax	Abdomen/ Lumbar/Spine
Observed	1036	864	38	83	47
Expected	1178.76	641.08	62.04	124.08	62.04

We notice that the observed count for head injuries is much higher than expected, while the observed counts for all the other categories are lower. We might conclude that motorcycle fatalities from head injuries occur more frequently for riders not wearing a helmet.
16. (a) Classical approach: $\chi_0^2 = 511.475 > \chi_{0.05}^2 = 7.815$; reject the null hypothesis. *P*-value approach: *P*-value $< 0.005 < \alpha = 0.05$ [Tech: *P*-value < 0.0001]; reject the null hypothesis. There is sufficient evidence at the $\alpha = 0.05$ level of significance to conclude that the distribution of weapons used in robberies on school property does not follow the national distribution of weapons used in robberies generally.
(b)

Weapon	Gun	Knife	Strong-Arm	Other
Observed	329	122	857	344
Expected	693.84	148.68	660.8	148.68

We notice that the observed counts for gun and knife are lower than expected, while the observed counts for strong-arm and other are higher. We might conclude that guns and knives are used less frequently in robberies on school property than they are used in robberies generally.
17. (a) Group 1: 84; Group 2: 84; Group 3: 84; Group 4: 81. Classical approach: $\chi_0^2 = 0.084$ [Tech: 0.081] $< \chi_{0.05}^2 = 7.815$; do not reject the null hypothesis. *P*-value approach: *P*-value $> 0.99 > \alpha = 0.05$ [Tech: *P*-value $= 0.994$]; do not reject the null hypothesis. There is not sufficient evidence at the $\alpha = 0.05$ level of significance to conclude that there are differences among the groups in attendance patterns.
(b) Group 1: 84; Group 2: 81; Group 3: 78; Group 4: 76. Classical approach: $\chi_0^2 = 0.463$ [Tech: 0.461] $< \chi_{0.05}^2 = 7.815$; do not reject the null hypothesis. *P*-value approach: *P*-value $> 0.90 > \alpha = 0.05$ [Tech: *P*-value $= 0.927$]; do not reject the null hypothesis. There is not sufficient evidence at the $\alpha = 0.05$ level of significance to conclude that there are differences among the groups in attendance patterns. It is curious that the farther a group's original position is located from the front of the room, the more the attendance rate for the group decreases.
(c) Group 1: 20; Group 2: 20; Group 3: 20; Group 4: 20. Classical approach: $\chi_0^2 = 2.55$ [Tech: 2.57] $< \chi_{0.05}^2 = 7.815$; do not reject the null hypothesis. *P*-value approach: *P*-value $> 0.10 > \alpha = 0.05$ [Tech: *P*-value $= 0.463$]; do not reject the null hypothesis. There is not sufficient evidence at the $\alpha = 0.05$ level of significance to conclude that there is a significant difference in the number of students in the top 20% of the class by group.
(d) Though not statistically significant, the group located in the front had both better attendance and a larger number of students in the top 20%. Choose the front.
18. (a) Classical approach: $\chi_0^2 = 3.257 < \chi_{0.05}^2 = 7.815$; do not reject the null hypothesis. *P*-value approach: *P*-value $> 0.10 > \alpha = 0.05$ [Tech: *P*-value $= 0.354$]; do not reject the null hypothesis. There is not sufficient evidence at the $\alpha = 0.05$ level of significance to conclude that the distribution of races in traffic stops is different from the distribution of drivers in Mundelein. That is, there is not sufficient evidence of racial profiling in Mundelein.
(b)

Race	White	African American	Hispanic	Asian
Observed	7079	273	2025	491
Expected	7095.092	276.304	2042.676	453.928

We notice that the observed counts for the races are close to the expected counts. Only the Asian traffic stops are higher than expected.
19. Classical approach: $\chi_0^2 = 18.8895 > \chi_{0.01}^2 = 11.345$; reject the null hypothesis. *P*-value approach: *P*-value < 0.005 [Tech: *P*-value $= 0.0003$];

reject the null hypothesis. No level of significance is given, but the result is significant for $\alpha = 0.1$, $\alpha = 0.05$, and $\alpha = 0.01$. There is sufficient evidence to suggest that hockey players' birthdates are not evenly distributed throughout the year.

20. Classical approach: $\chi_0^2 = 19.03 > \chi_{0.05}^2 = 12.592$; reject the null hypothesis. *P*-value approach: *P*-value $< 0.005 < \alpha = 0.05$ [Tech: *P*-value $= 0.004$]; reject the null hypothesis. There is sufficient evidence at the $\alpha = 0.05$ level of significance to reject the belief that bicycle fatalities occur with equal frequency over the days of the week. We might conclude that fewer bicycle fatalities occur on Sundays and Tuesdays.

21. Classical approach: $\chi_0^2 = 13.227 > \chi_{0.05}^2 = 12.592$; reject the null hypothesis. *P*-value approach: *P*-value $< 0.05 = \alpha$ [Tech: *P*-value $= 0.040$]; reject the null hypothesis. There is sufficient evidence at the $\alpha = 0.05$ level of significance to reject the belief that pedestrian deaths occur with equal frequency over the days of the week. We might conclude that fewer pedestrian deaths occur on Tuesdays and more occur on Saturdays.

22. (a) Classical approach: $\chi_0^2 = 4.67 < \chi_{0.01}^2 = 15.086$; do not reject the null hypothesis. *P*-value approach: *P*-value $> 0.10 > \alpha = 0.01$ [Tech: *P*-value $= 0.457$]; do not reject the null hypothesis. There is not sufficient evidence at the $\alpha = 0.01$ level of significance to conclude that the die is loaded.
(b) The player does not want to incorrectly conclude that the die is loaded. That is, the player does not want to make a Type I error.

23. (a)

Grade	Relative Frequency	Observed Frequency	Expected Frequency
K–3	0.329	15	8.225
4–8	0.393	7	9.825
9–12	0.278	3	6.95

(b) Classical approach: $\chi_0^2 = 8.638 > \chi_{0.05}^2 = 5.991$; reject the null hypothesis. *P*-value approach: *P*-value $< 0.025 < \alpha = 0.05$ [Tech: *P*-value $= 0.013$]; reject the null hypothesis. There is sufficient evidence at the $\alpha = 0.05$ level of significance to conclude that the grade distribution of home-schooled children in her district is different from the national proportions. We might conclude that a greater proportion of students in grades K–3 are home-schooled in this district than nationally.

24. Classical approach: $\chi_0^2 = 1.201 < \chi_{0.05}^2 = 15.507$; do not reject the null hypothesis. *P*-value approach: *P*-value $> 0.995 > \alpha = 0.05$ [Tech: *P*-value $= 0.997$]; do not reject the null hypothesis. There is not sufficient evidence at the $\alpha = 0.05$ level of significance to reject the belief that the first digit in Fibonacci numbers follows Benford's Law.

25. (a) Northeast: 950; Midwest: 1145; South: 1780; West: 1125
(b) Northeast: 0.18; Midwest: 0.218; South: 0.369; West: 0.233. The proportions are the same.
(c) Classical approach: $\chi_0^2 = 9.240 > \chi_{0.05}^2 = 7.815$; reject the null hypothesis. *P*-value approach: $0.025 <$ *P*-value < 0.05 [Tech: *P*-value $= 0.0263$] $< \alpha = 0.05$; reject the null hypothesis. Assuming the level of significance is $\alpha = 0.05$ as in Example 2, there is sufficient evidence to suggest that the distribution of residents in the United States has changed since 2000.
(d) Higher sample sizes require less significant evidence.

26. (a) Answers will vary.
(b) Expect 0.3277 of the numbers to be 0, 0.4096 of the numbers to be 1, 0.2048 to be 2, 0.0512 to be 3, 0.0064 to be 4, and 0.0003 to be 5.
(c) Answers will vary.

27. (a) Expected number with low birth weight: 17.04; expected number without low birth weight: 222.96.
(b) H_0: $p = 0.071$ vs. H_1: $p > 0.071$. Classical approach: $\chi_0^2 = 1.554 < \chi_{0.05}^2 = 3.841$; do not reject the null hypothesis. *P*-value approach: *P*-value $> 0.10 > \alpha = 0.05$ Tech: *P*-value $= 0.213$]; do not reject the null hypothesis. There is not sufficient evidence at the $\alpha = 0.05$ level of significance to conclude that mothers between the ages of 35 and 39 have a higher percentage of low-birth-weight babies.
(c) H_0: $p = 0.71$ vs. H_1: $p > 0.71$; $np_0(1 - p_0) = 15.83 > 10$. Classical approach: $z_0 = 1.25 < z_{0.05} = 1.645$; do not reject the null hypothesis. *P*-value approach: *P*-value $= 0.1056 > \alpha = 0.05$ [Tech: *P*-value $= 0.1063$]; do not reject the null hypothesis. There is not sufficient evidence at the $\alpha = 0.05$ level of significance to conclude that mothers between the ages of 35 and 39 have a higher percentage of low-birth-weight babies.

28. (a) We would expect 103.2 of the 400 individuals sampled to live alone and 296.8 to not live alone.
(b) H_0: $p = 0.258$ vs. H_1: $p > 0.258$. Classical approach: $\chi_0^2 = 48.275 > \chi_{0.05}^2 = 3.841$; reject the null hypothesis. *P*-value approach: *P*-value $< 0.001 < \alpha = 0.05$; reject the null hypothesis. There is sufficient evidence at the $\alpha = 0.05$ level of significance to conclude that the percentage of Americans living alone is more than 25.8%.
(c) H_0: $p = 0.258$ vs. H_1: $p > 0.258$; $np_0(1 - p_0) = 76.5744 > 10$. Classical approach: $z_0 = 6.948 > z_{0.05} = 1.645$; reject the null hypothesis. *P*-value approach: *P*-value $< 0.0001 < \alpha = 0.05$; reject the null hypothesis. There is sufficient evidence at the $\alpha = 0.05$ level of significance to conclude that the percentage of Americans living alone is more than 25.8%.

29. (a) $\mu = 0.9323$ hits
(b) All expected frequencies will not be greater than or equal to 1. Also, more than 20% (37.5%) of the expected frequencies are less than 5.
(c), (d)

x	$P(x)$	Expected Number of Regions
0	0.3936	226.741
1	0.3670	211.390
2	0.1711	98.540
3	0.0532	30.623
4 or more	0.0151	8.698

(e) Classical approach: $\chi_0^2 = 1.0116 < \chi_{0.05}^2 = 9.488$; do not reject the null hypothesis. *P*-value approach: *P*-value $> 0.90 > \alpha = 0.05$ [Tech: *P*-value $= 0.907$]; do not reject the null hypothesis. There is not sufficient evidence at the $\alpha = 0.05$ level of significance to conclude that the distribution of rocket hits is different from the Poisson distribution. That is, the rocket hits do appear to be modeled by a Poisson random variable.

30. (a) The probability of rolling a 5 or a 6 is $\frac{1}{3}$.
(b), (c)

Number of Successes	Probability	Expected Frequency
0	0.0077	202.75
1	0.0462	1216.50
2	0.1272	3345.37
3	0.2120	5575.61
4	0.2384	6272.56
5	0.1908	5018.05
6	0.1113	2927.20
7	0.0477	1254.51
8	0.0149	392.04
9	0.0033	87.12
10	0.0005	13.07
11	0.00005	1.19
12	0.000002	0.05

(d) Classical approach: $\chi_0^2 = 34.640 > \chi_{0.01}^2 = 23.209$, using 10 degrees of freedom; reject the null hypothesis. *P*-value approach: *P*-value < 0.005 [Tech: *P*-value < 0.0001]; reject the null hypothesis. No level of significance is given, but the result is significant for $\alpha = 0.1$, $\alpha = 0.05$, and $\alpha = 0.01$. There is sufficient evidence to suggest that the number of successes does not follow a binomial distribution.

31. Answers will vary. One possible answer: *Goodness of fit* is appropriate because we are testing to see if the frequency of outcomes from a sample fits the theoretical distribution.

32. The χ^2 goodness-of-fit tests are always right tailed because the numerator in the test statistic is squared, making every test statistic other than a perfect fit positive. So we are measuring if $\chi_0^2 > \chi_\alpha^2$.

33. If the expected count of a category is less than 1, two (or more) of the categories can be combined so that a goodness-of-fit test can be used. Alternatively, the sample size can be increased.

12.2 Assess Your Understanding (page 537)

1. True

2. homogeneity

3. (a) $\chi_0^2 = 1.701$
(b) Classical approach: $\chi_0^2 = 1.701 < \chi_{0.05}^2 = 5.991$; do not reject the null hypothesis. *P*-value approach: *P*-value $> 0.10 > \alpha = 0.05$ [Tech: *P*-value $= 0.427$]; do not reject the null hypothesis. There is evidence at the $\alpha = 0.05$ level of significance to conclude that *X* and *Y* are independent. We conclude that *X* and *Y* are not related.

4. (a) $\chi_0^2 = 13.053$
(b) Classical approach: $\chi_0^2 = 13.053 > \chi_{0.05}^2 = 5.991$; reject the null hypothesis. *P*-value approach: *P*-value $< 0.005 < \alpha = 0.05$ Tech: *P*-value $= 0.001$]; reject the null hypothesis. There is sufficient evidence at the $\alpha = 0.05$ level of significance to conclude that *X* and *Y* are dependent. We conclude that *X* and *Y* are related to each other.

5. Classical approach: $\chi_0^2 = 1.989 < \chi_{0.01}^2 = 9.210$; do not reject the null hypothesis. *P*-value approach: *P*-value $> 0.10 > \alpha = 0.01$ [Tech: *P*-value $= 0.370$]; do not reject the null hypothesis. There is not sufficient evidence at the $\alpha = 0.01$ level of significance to conclude that at least one of the proportions is different from the others.

6. Classical approach: $\chi_0^2 = 3.533 < \chi_{0.01}^2 = 9.210$; do not reject the null hypothesis. *P*-value approach: *P*-value $> 0.10 > \alpha = 0.01$ [Tech: *P*-value $= 0.171$]; do not reject the null hypothesis. There is not sufficient evidence at the $\alpha = 0.01$ level of significance to conclude that at least one of the proportions is different from the others.

7. (a)

Had Sexual Intercourse?	Both Biological/ Adoptive Parents	Single Parent	Parent and Stepparent	Nonparental Guardian
Yes	78.553	52.368	41.895	26.184
No	71.447	47.632	38.105	23.816

(b) (1) All expected frequencies are greater than or equal to 1, and (2) no more than 20% of the expected frequencies are less than 5.
(c) $\chi_0^2 = 10.357$
(d) H_0: Family structure and sexual activity are independent; H_1: Family structure and sexual activity are not independent. Classical approach: $\chi_0^2 = 10.357 > \chi_{0.05}^2 = 7.815$; reject the null hypothesis. *P*-value approach: *P*-value $< 0.025 < \alpha = 0.05$ Tech: *P*-value $= 0.016$;] reject the null hypothesis. There is sufficient evidence at the $\alpha = 0.05$ level of significance to conclude that sexual activity and family structure are associated.
(e) The biggest difference between observed and expected occurs under the family structure in which both parents are present. Fewer females were sexually active than was expected when both parents were present. This means that having both parents present seems to have an effect on whether the child is sexually active.
(f)

Had Sexual Intercourse?	Both Biological/ Adoptive Parents	Single Parent	Parent and Stepparent	Nonparental Guardian
Yes	0.427	0.59	0.55	0.64
No	0.573	0.41	0.45	0.36

Family Structure and Sexual Activity

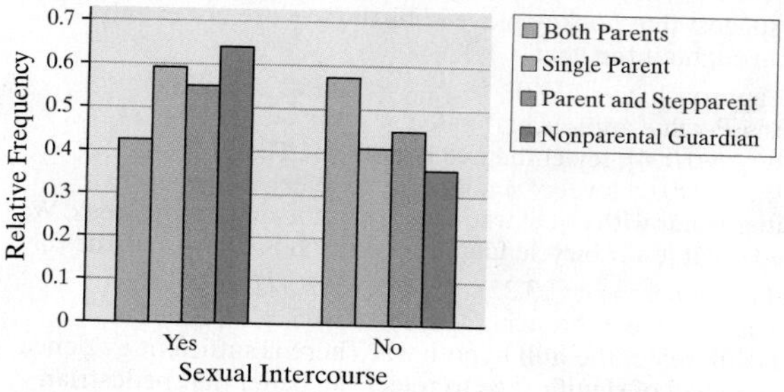

8. (a)

	Less Than 3 Months	3–5 Months	More Than 5 Months (or Never)
Intended	573.54	36.80	41.66
Unintended	73.01	4.68	5.3
Mistimed	179.45	11.51	13.04

(b) (1) All expected frequencies are greater than or equal to 1, and (2) no more than 20% of the expected frequencies are less than 5.
(c) $\chi_0^2 = 21.357$
(d) Classical approach: $\chi_0^2 = 21.357 > \chi_{0.05}^2 = 9.488$; reject the null hypothesis. *P*-value approach: *P*-value $< 0.005 < \alpha = 0.05$ [Tech: *P*-value < 0.0001]; reject the null hypothesis. There is sufficient evidence at the $\alpha = 0.05$ level of significance to conclude that wantedness of pregnancy and months pregnant before prenatal care are associated.
(e) The biggest difference between observed and expected occurs between intended and less than 3 months. The observed is greater than the expected, which implies that intended pregnancies are likely to have early prenatal care.
(f)

	Less Than 3 Months	3–5 Months	More Than 5 Months (or Never)
Intended	0.910	0.040	0.051
Unintended	0.771	0.096	0.133
Mistimed	0.828	0.093	0.078

Prenatal Care by Wantedness of the Pregnancy

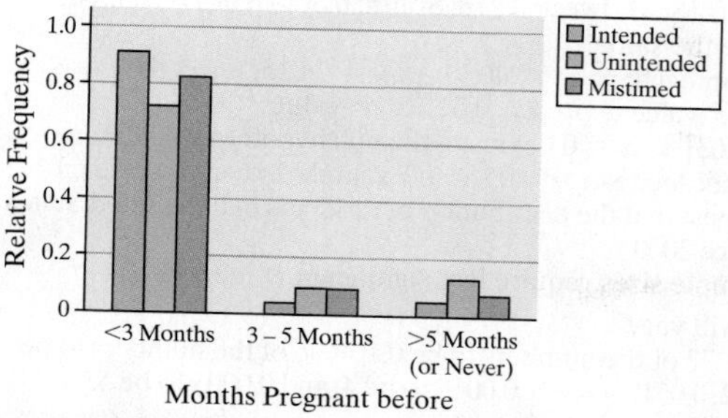

9. (a) H_0: Health and happiness are independent; H_1: Health and happiness are not independent. Classical approach: $\chi_0^2 = 182.174 > \chi_{0.05}^2 = 12.592$; reject the null hypothesis. *P*-value approach: *P*-value $< 0.005 < \alpha = 0.05$ [Tech: *P*-value < 0.0001]; reject the null hypothesis. There is sufficient evidence at the $\alpha = 0.05$ level of significance to conclude that happiness and health are dependent. That is, happiness and health are related to each other.

(b)

	Health			
Happiness	**Excellent**	**Good**	**Fair**	**Poor**
Very Happy	0.492	0.280	0.202	0.183
Pretty Happy	0.448	0.609	0.570	0.486
Not Too Happy	0.060	0.111	0.227	0.330

Health and Happiness

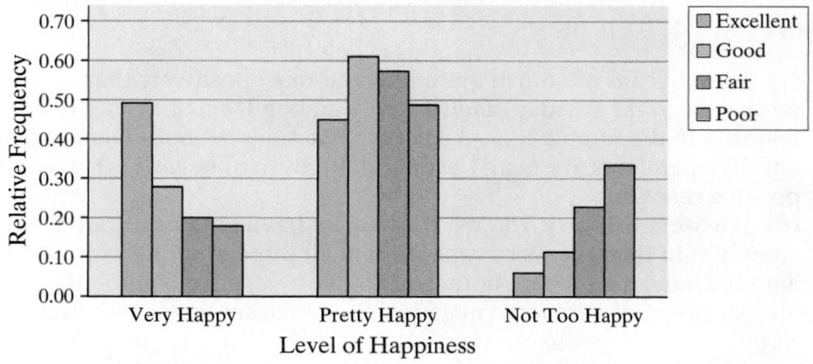

(c) The proportion of individuals who are "very happy" is much higher for individuals in "excellent" health than any other health category. Further, the proportion of individuals who are "not too happy" is much lower for individuals in "excellent" health compared to the other health categories. Put simply, the level of happiness seems to decline as health status declines.

10. (a) Classical approach: $\chi_0^2 = 285.061 > \chi_{0.05}^2 = 21.026$; reject the null hypothesis. P-value approach: P-value $< 0.005 < \alpha = 0.05$ [Tech: P-value $= 0.000$]; reject the null hypothesis. There is sufficient evidence at the $\alpha = 0.05$ level of significance to conclude that happiness and education are dependent. That is, happiness and education are related to each other.

(b)

	Health			
Education	**Excellent**	**Good**	**Fair**	**Poor**
Less than High School	0.135	0.378	0.372	0.116
High School	0.257	0.485	0.198	0.060
Junior College	0.288	0.496	0.176	0.040
Bachelor	0.394	0.475	0.110	0.021
Graduate	0.418	0.473	0.103	0.006

Health and Education

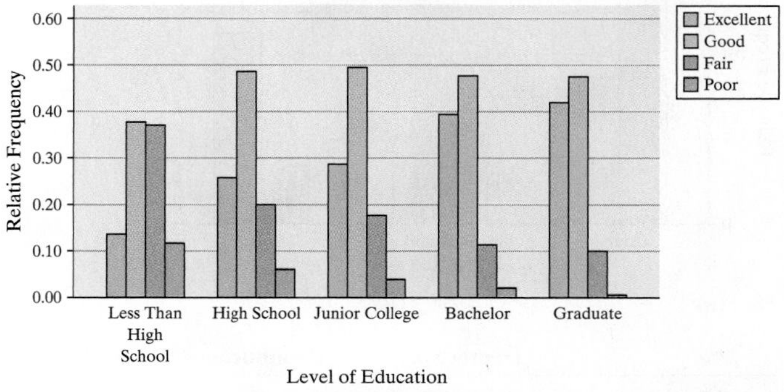

(c) The proportion of individuals with a "less than high school" education is less than the proportions for the other education levels in both the "excellent" and "good" health categories. Further, the proportion of individuals with "less than high school" is greater than the proportions of the other education levels in both the "fair" and "poor" health categories. Similarly, the proportion of individuals with a "graduate" education is higher than the proportions for the other education levels in the "excellent" health category. Likewise, the proportion of individuals with a "graduate" education is lower than the others proportions in the "poor" health category. Generally, a better health category seems to indicate a higher level of education, and a worse health category seems to indicate a lower level of education. Answers for lurking variables will vary. One possible lurking variable is age, since younger individuals are less likely to not have a high school diploma.

11. (a) Classical approach: $\chi_0^2 = 7.803 < \chi_{0.05}^2 = 12.592$; do not reject the null hypothesis. P-value approach: P-value $> 0.10 > \alpha = 0.05$ [Tech: P-value $= 0.253$]; do not reject the null hypothesis. There is not sufficient evidence at the $\alpha = 0.05$ level of significance to conclude that smoking status and number of years of education are associated. It does not appear to be the case that number of years of education plays a role in determining smoking status.

(b)

Years of Education	Current	Former	Never	Total
<12	0.376	0.186	0.439	1
12	0.393	0.198	0.410	1
13–15	0.389	0.221	0.389	1
≥16	0.288	0.280	0.432	1

Smoking Status vs. Level of Education

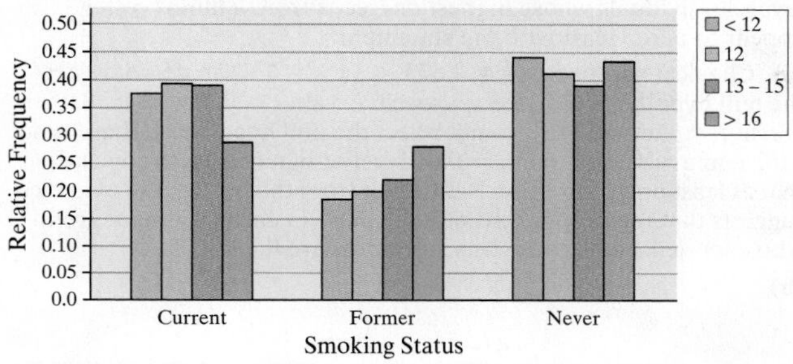

12. (a) Classical approach: $\chi_0^2 = 0.036 < \chi_{0.10}^2 = 2.706$; do not reject the null hypothesis. P-value approach: P-value $> 0.10 = \alpha$ [Tech: P-value $= 0.849$]; do not reject the null hypothesis. There is not sufficient evidence at the $\alpha = 0.10$ level of significance to conclude that gender and opinion are associated. It appears to be the case that gender is not associated with one's opinion regarding choice.

(b)

Gender	Pro-Life	Pro-Choice	Total
Men	0.496	0.504	1
Women	0.490	0.510	1

Opinion on Abortion

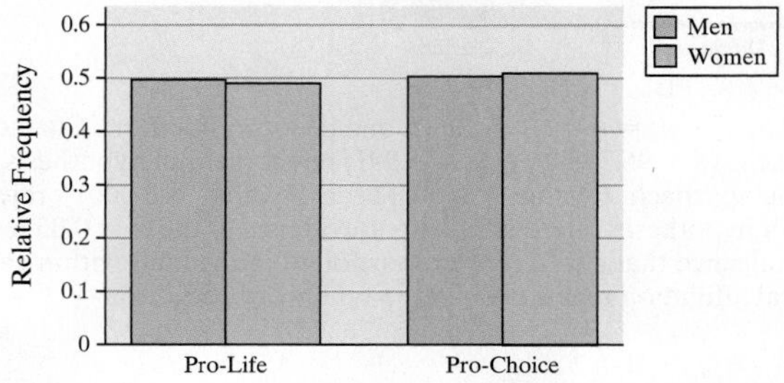

13. (a) H_0: $p_{<HS} = p_{HS} = p_{JC} = p_B = p_G$; H_1: At least one proportion differs. Classical approach: $\chi_0^2 = 37.198 > \chi_{0.05}^2 = 9.488$; reject the null hypothesis. P-value approach: P-value $< 0.005 < \alpha = 0.05$ [Tech: P-value < 0.0001]; reject the null hypothesis. There is sufficient evidence at the $\alpha = 0.05$ level of significance to conclude that at least one of the proportions is different from the others. That is, the evidence suggests that the proportion of individuals who feel everyone has an equal opportunity to obtain a quality education in the United States is different for at least one level of education.

(b)

	Less Than High School	High School	Junior College	Bachelor	Graduate
Yes	0.784	0.734	0.547	0.585	0.597
No	0.216	0.266	0.453	0.415	0.403

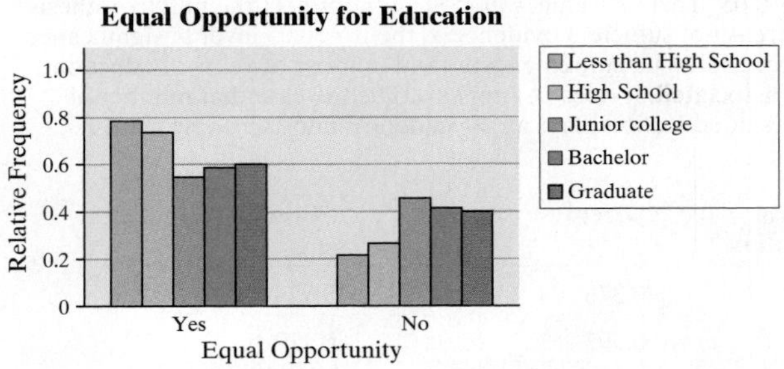

Higher proportions of individuals with either a "high school" education or "less than a high school" education seem to agree with the statement that everyone has an equal opportunity to obtain a quality education than individuals in the other three education levels. Individuals whose highest degree is from a junior college appear to agree least with the statement.

14. **(a)** Classical approach: $\chi_0^2 = 4.673 < \chi_{0.01}^2 = 13.277$; do not reject the null hypothesis. *P*-value approach: *P*-value $> 0.10 > \alpha = 0.01$ [Tech: *P*-value $= 0.323$]; do not reject the null hypothesis. There is not sufficient evidence at the $\alpha = 0.01$ level of significance to conclude that at least one proportion is different from the others. The evidence suggests that the proportions of individuals in each treatment group who experienced dizziness as a side effect are the same.

(b)

	Drug				
Side Effect	**Celebrex**	**Placebo**	**Naproxen**	**Diclofenac**	**Ibuprofen**
Dizziness	0.020	0.017	0.026	0.013	0.023
No Dizziness	0.980	0.983	0.974	0.987	0.977
Total	1	1	1	1	1

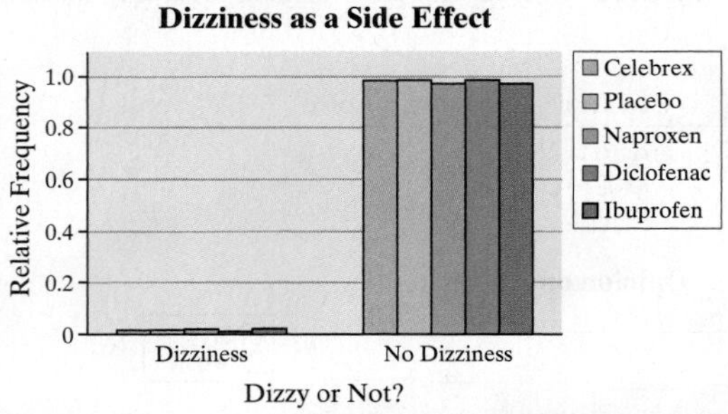

15. **(a)** $H_0: p_D = p_I = p_R$; H_1: At least one proportion differs. Classical approach: $\chi_0^2 = 96.728 > \chi_{0.05}^2 = 5.991$; reject the null hypothesis. *P*-value approach: *P*-value < 0.005[Tech: *P*-value < 0.0001]; reject the null hypothesis. There is sufficient evidence at the $\alpha = 0.05$ level of significance that a different proportion of individuals within each political affiliation reacts positively to the word socialism.

(b)

	Democrat	Independent	Republican
Positive	0.4409	0.2599	0.1501
Negative	0.5591	0.7401	0.8499
Total	1	1	1

(c) Independents and Republicans are far more likely to react negatively to the word *socialism* than Democrats are. However, it is important to note that a majority of Democrats in the sample did have a negative reaction, so the word *socialism* has a negative connotation among all groups.

16. **(a)** Classical approach: $\chi_0^2 = 20.591 > \chi_{0.05}^2 = 5.991$; reject the null hypothesis. *P*-value approach: *P*-value < 0.005 [Tech: *P*-value < 0.0001]; reject the null hypothesis. There is sufficient evidence at the $\alpha = 0.05$ level of significance that a different proportion of individuals within each political affiliation reacts positively to the word *capitalism*.

(b)

	Democrat	Independent	Republican
Positive	0.4709	0.5199	0.6199
Negative	0.5291	0.4801	0.3801
Total	1	1	1

(c) Republicans are much more likely to react positively than negatively to the word *capitalism*. Only among Democrats did the majority in the sample have a negative reaction, but both Democrats and Independents are nearly evenly split between negative and positive reactions.

(d) Answers will vary. The word *socialism* has a greater negative connotation than the word *capitalism* in all three groups. Even among Democrats where both words have a negative connotation, a greater proportion reacted negatively to socialism than capitalism.

17. **(a)**

	Course	Personal	Work
Female	13	5	3
Male	10	6	13

(b) Classical approach: $\chi_0^2 = 5.595 > \chi_{0.10}^2 = 4.605$; reject the null hypothesis. *P*-value approach: *P*-value $< 0.10 = \alpha$ [Tech: *P*-value $= 0.061$]; reject the null hypothesis. The evidence suggests a relation between gender and drop reason. Females are more likely to drop because of the course, while males are more likely to drop because of work.

(c)

	Reason		
	Course	**Personal**	**Work**
Female	0.619	0.238	0.143
Male	0.345	0.207	0.448
Total	1	1	1

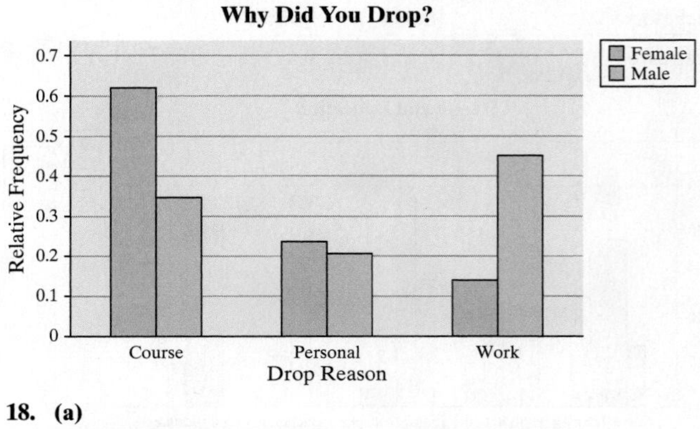

18. **(a)**

	Democrat	Republican
Grade school	7	2
High school	10	6
College	9	12

(b) Classical approach: $\chi_0^2 = 3.483 < \chi_{0.10}^2 = 4.605$; do not reject the null hypothesis. *P*-value approach: *P*-value $> 0.10 = \alpha$ [Tech: *P*-value $= 0.175$]; do not reject the null hypothesis. The evidence suggests that there is no association between level of education and political affiliation.

(c)

	Democrat	Republican	Total
Grade school	0.778	0.222	1
High school	0.625	0.375	1
College	0.429	0.571	1

Political Affiliation by Education

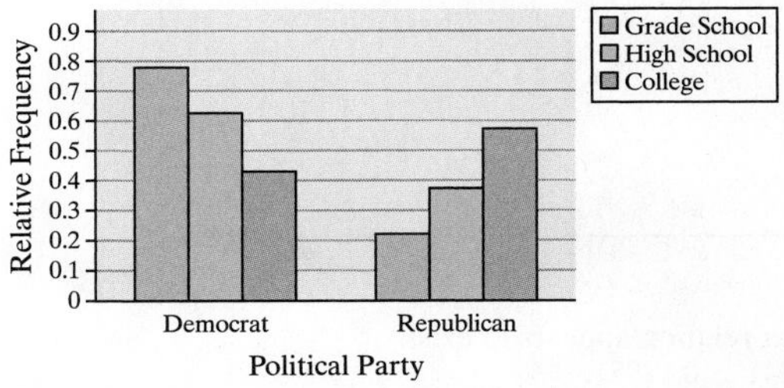

19. Classical approach: $\chi_0^2 = 2.769 < \chi_{0.05}^2 = 5.991$; do not reject the null hypothesis. *P*-value approach: *P*-value = 0.2504; do not reject the null hypothesis. There is not sufficient evidence at the $\alpha = 0.05$ level of significance to suggest that there is an association between political affiliation and willingness to pay higher taxes to reduce the federal debt.

20. Classical approach: $\chi_0^2 = 0.983 < \chi_{0.05}^2 = 5.991$; do not reject the null hypothesis. *P*-value approach: *P*-value = 0.6117; do not reject the null hypothesis. There is not sufficient evidence at the $\alpha = 0.05$ level of significance to suggest that there is an association between political philosophy and whether a language other than English is primarily spoken at home.

21. (a) All healthy women 45 years of age or older
(b) Whether or not a cardiovascular event (such as heart attack or stroke) occurs: qualitative
(c) 100 mg aspirin, placebo
(d) Completely randomized
(e) The women were randomly assigned into two groups (aspirin versus placebo). This randomization controls for any other explanatory variables, since individuals affected by these lurking variables should be equally dispersed between the two groups.
(f) Classical approach: $z_0 = -1.44 > z_{0.025} = -1.96$; do not reject the null hypothesis. *P*-value approach: *P*-value = 0.1498 [Tech: 0.1511]; do not reject the null hypothesis. There is not sufficient evidence to conclude that a difference exists between the proportions of cardiovascular events in the aspirin group versus the placebo group. The test statistic, rounded to three places, is $z_0 = -1.435$.
(g) Classical approach: $\chi_0^2 = 2.061 < \chi_{0.05}^2 = 3.841$; do not reject the null hypothesis. *P*-value approach: *P*-value > 0.10 > $\alpha = 0.05$ [Tech: *P*-value = 0.151]; do not reject the null hypothesis. There is not sufficient evidence to conclude that a difference exists between the proportions of cardiovascular events in the aspirin group versus the placebo group.
(h) $(z_0)^2 = (-1.435)^2 = 2.059 \approx \chi_0^2 = 2.061$. Conclusion: $(z_0)^2 = \chi_0^2$.

22. Answers may vary, but differences should include chi-square test for independence compares two characteristics from a single population, whereas the chi-square test for homogeneity compares a single characteristic from two (or more) populations. Similarities should include the procedures of the two tests and the assumptions of the two tests are the same.

23. Answers may vary.

12.3 Assess Your Understanding (page 552)

1. 82.7 **2.** True **3.** 0; σ

4. If the null hypothesis, H_0: $\beta_1 = 0$, is not rejected, the best guess for the value of the response variable for any value of the explanatory variable is the sample mean of y, $\bar{y}$.

5. (a) $\beta_0 \approx b_0 = -2.3256$, $\beta_1 \approx b_1 = 2.0233$
(b) $s_e = 0.5134$ is the point estimate for σ.
(c) $s_{b_1} = 0.1238$
(d) Because the *P*-value < 0.001 < $\alpha = 0.05$ (or $t_0 = 16.343$[Tech: 16.344] > $t_{0.025} = 3.182$), we reject the null hypothesis and conclude that a linear relation exists between x and y.

6. (a) $\beta_0 \approx b_0 = -3.700$, $\beta_1 \approx b_1 = 1.100$
(b) $s_e = 0.7303$ is the point estimate for σ.
(c) $s_{b_1} = 0.1155$
(d) Because the *P*-value = 0.002 < $\alpha = 0.05$ (or $t_0 = 9.524$ [Tech: 9.526] > $t_{0.025} = 3.182$), we reject the null hypothesis and conclude that a linear relation exists between x and y.

7. (a) $\beta_0 \approx b_0 = 1.200$, $\beta_1 \approx b_1 = 2.200$
(b) $s_e = 0.8944$ is the point estimate for σ.
(c) $s_{b_1} = 0.2828$
(d) Because the *P*-value = 0.004 < $\alpha = 0.05$ (or $t_0 = 7.778$ [Tech: 7.779] > $t_{0.025} = 3.182$), we reject the null hypothesis and conclude that a linear relation exists between x and y.

8. (a) $\beta_0 \approx b_0 = 3.600$, $\beta_1 \approx b_1 = -1.800$
(b) $s_e = 0.5164$ is the point estimate for σ.
(c) $s_{b_1} = 0.1633$
(d) Because the *P*-value = 0.002 < $\alpha = 0.05$ (or $t_0 = -11.023 < -t_{0.025} = -3.182$), we reject the null hypothesis and conclude that a linear relation exists between x and y.

9. (a) $\beta_0 \approx b_0 = 116.600$, $\beta_1 \approx b_1 = -0.7200$
(b) $s_e = 3.2863$ is the point estimate for σ.
(c) $s_{b_1} = 0.1039$
(d) Because the *P*-value = 0.006 < $\alpha = 0.05$ (or $t_0 = -6.929$ [Tech: -6.928] < $-t_{0.025} = -3.182$), we reject the null hypothesis and conclude that a linear relation exists between x and y.

10. (a) $\beta_0 \approx b_0 = -3.30$, $\beta_1 \approx b_1 = 0.78$
(b) $s_e = 1.7416$ is the point estimate for σ.
(c) $s_{b_1} = 0.1102$
(d) Because the *P*-value = 0.006 < $\alpha = 0.05$ (or $t_0 = 7.078$ [Tech: 7.081] > $t_{0.025} = 3.182$), we reject the null hypothesis and conclude that a linear relation exists between x and y.

11. (a) $\beta_0 \approx b_0 = 69.0296$; $\beta_1 \approx b_1 = -0.0479$
(b) $s_e = 0.3680$
(c) $s_{b_1} = 0.0043$
(d) Because the *P*-value < 0.001 [Tech: *P*-value = 0.0001] < $\alpha = 0.05$ (or $t_0 = -11.140$ [Tech: -11.157] < $-t_{0.025} = -2.571$), we reject the null hypothesis and conclude that a linear relation exists between commute time and score on a well-being survey.
(e) 95% confidence interval: lower bound: -0.0589, upper bound: -0.0369

12. (a) $\beta_0 \approx b_0 \approx 61.3687$; $\beta_1 \approx b_1 = -0.0764$
(b) $s_e = 1.4241$
(c) $s_{b_1} = 0.0085$
(d) Because the *P*-value < 0.001 [Tech: *P*-value = 0.0009 < $\alpha = 0.05$ (or $t_0 = -8.938$ [Tech: -8.939] < $-t_{0.025} = -2.776$), we reject the null hypothesis and conclude that a linear relation exists between credit score and interest rate.
(e) 95% confidence interval: lower bound: -0.1001, upper bound: -0.0527

13. (a) $\beta_0 \approx b_0 = 12.4932$, $\beta_1 \approx b_1 = 0.1827$
(b) $s_e = 0.0954$
(c) A normal probability plot of the residuals shows that they are approximately normally distributed.
(d) $s_{b_1} = 0.0276$
(e) Because the *P*-value < 0.001 < $\alpha = 0.01$ (or $t_0 = 6.62$ [Tech: 6.63] > $t_{0.005} = 3.250$), we reject the null hypothesis and conclude that a linear relation exists between a child's height and head circumference.
(f) 95% confidence interval: lower bound: 0.1204; upper bound: 0.2451
(g) A good estimate of the child's head circumference would be 17.34 inches.

14. (a) $\beta_0 \approx b_0 = 1.1140$, $\beta_1 \approx b_1 = 1.3902$
(b) $s_e = 0.4944$
(c) A normal probability plot of the residuals shows that they are approximately normally distributed.
(d) $s_{b_1} = 0.1501$
(e) Because the *P*-value < 0.001 < $\alpha = 0.01$ (or $t_0 = 9.262$ [Tech: 9.260] > $t_{0.005} = 3.250$), we reject the null hypothesis and conclude that a linear relation exists between the right humerus and the right tibia of rats sent to space.
(f) 99% confidence interval: lower bound: 0.9024; upper bound: 1.8780
(g) The mean length of the right tibia on a rat whose right humerus is 25.93 mm is 37.162 mm.

15. (a) $\beta_0 \approx b_0 = 2675.6$, $\beta_1 \approx b_1 = 0.6764$
(b) $s_e = 271.04$

(c) A normal probability plot of the residuals shows that they are approximately normally distributed.
(d) $s_{b_1} = 0.2055$
(e) Because the P-value $= 0.011 < \alpha = 0.05$ (or $t_0 = 3.291 > t_{0.025} = 2.306$), we reject the null hypothesis and conclude that a linear relation exists between the 7-day and 28-day strength of this type of concrete.
(f) 95% confidence interval: lower bound: 0.2025; upper bound: 1.1503
(g) The mean 28-day strength of this concrete if the 7-day strength is 3000 psi is 4704.8 psi.

16. (a) $\beta_0 \approx b_0 = 0.2088, \beta_1 \approx b_1 = 0.0575$
(b) $s_e = 0.1121$
(c) A normal probability plot of the residuals shows that they are approximately normally distributed.
(d) $s_{b_1} = 0.0046$
(e) Because the P-value $< 0.001 < \alpha = 0.10$ (or $t_0 = 12.500$ [Tech: 12.502] $> t_{0.05} = 1.796$), we reject the null hypothesis and conclude that a linear relation exists between the tar and nicotine levels in cigarettes.
(f) 90% confidence interval: lower bound: 0.0492; upper bound: 0.0658
(g) The mean amount of nicotine in a cigarette that has 12 mg of tar is 0.90 mg.

17. (a) $\beta_0 \approx b_0 = 0.1200, \beta_1 \approx b_1 = 1.0997$
(b) Because the P-value $< 0.001 < \alpha = 0.10$ (or $t_0 = 11.168 > t_{0.05} = 1.833$), we reject the null hypothesis and conclude that a linear relation exists between the rate of return of the S&P 500 index and the rate of return of UTX.
(c) 90% confidence interval: lower bound: 0.9192; upper bound: 1.2802
(d) When the mean rate of return of the S&P 500 index is 3.25%, the mean rate of return for United Technologies is 3.694%.

18. (a) $\beta_0 \approx b_0 = -142.4700, \beta_1 \approx b_1 = 1.6942$
(b) Because the P-value $= 0.011 < \alpha = 0.05$ (or $t_0 = 3.134 > t_{0.025} = 2.228$), we reject the null hypothesis. We conclude that a linear relation exists between the total length and weight of American black bears.
(c) 95% confidence interval: lower bound: 0.4897; upper bound: 2.8989
(d) American black bears with a total length of 146.0 cm have a mean weight of 104.8 [Tech: 104.9] kg.

19. (a) $\beta_0 \approx b_0 = 33.2350; \beta_1 \approx b_1 = -0.9428$
(b) Because the P-value > 0.5 [Tech: P-value $= 0.5678$] $> \alpha = 0.05$ (or $t_0 = -0.596 > -t_{0.025} = -2.306$), we do not reject the null hypothesis. There is not sufficient evidence to conclude that a linear relation exists between compensation and stock return.
(c) 95% confidence interval: lower bound: −4.5924, upper bound: 2.7068 [Tech: 2.7067]
(d) No, the results do not indicate that a linear relation exists. We could use $\bar{y} = 17.317\%$ as an estimate of the stock return.

20. (a)

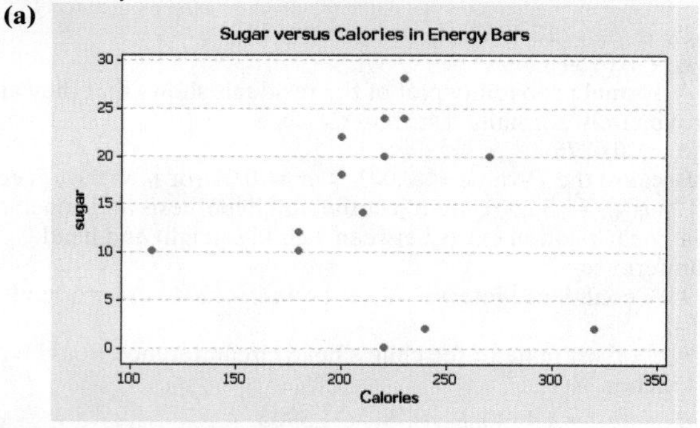

No linear relation appears to exist.
(b) $\hat{y} = 17.8675 - 0.0146x$
(c) $s_e = 9.3749$
(d) A normal probability plot of the residuals shows that they are approximately normally distributed.
(e) $s_{b_1} = 0.0549$
(f) Because the P-value $= 0.795 > \alpha = 0.01$ (or $t_0 = -0.266$ [Tech: −0.265] $> -t_{0.005} = -3.055$), we do not reject the null hypothesis. We conclude that a linear relation does not exist between the number of calories per serving and the number of grams per serving in high-protein and moderate-protein energy bars.
(g) 95% confidence interval: lower bound: −0.1342 [Tech: −0.1343]; upper bound: 0.1050 [Tech: 0.1051]
(h) Do not recommend using the least-squares regression line to predict the sugar content of the energy bars because we did not reject the null hypothesis. A good estimate for the sugar content is $\bar{y} = 14.7$ grams.

21. (a)

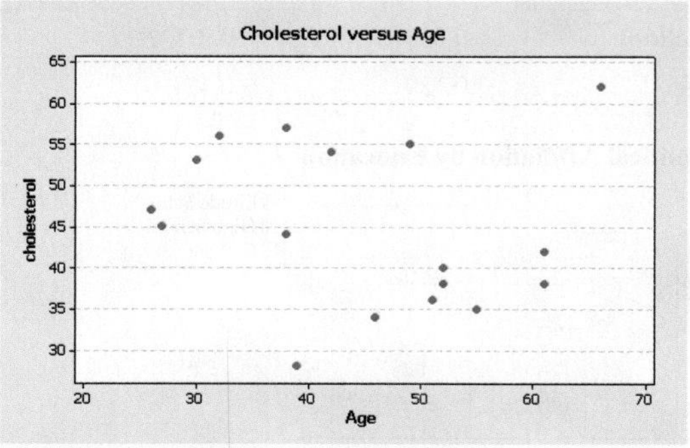

No linear relation appears to exist.
(b) $\hat{y} = 50.7841 - 0.1298x$
(c) Because the P-value $= 0.530 > \alpha = 0.01$ (or $t_0 = -0.642$ [Tech: −0.643] $> -t_{0.005} = -2.947$), we do not reject the null hypothesis and conclude that a linear relation does not exist between the age and HDL levels.
(d) 95% confidence interval: lower bound: −0.5605; upper bound: 0.3009 [Tech: 0.3008]
(e) Do not recommend using the least-squares regression line to predict the HDL cholesterol levels since we did not reject the null hypothesis. A good estimate for the HDL cholesterol level would be $\bar{y} = 44.9$.

22. (a) $\hat{y} = 26.36$ when $x = 10$.
(b) $\mu_{y|10} = 26.36$
(c) An estimate of the standard deviation of y when $x = 10$ is $s = 2.167$.
(d) If the requirements for the least-squares regression model are satisfied, y will be normally distributed with $\mu_{y|10} = 26.36$ and $\sigma = 2.167$.

23. (a)

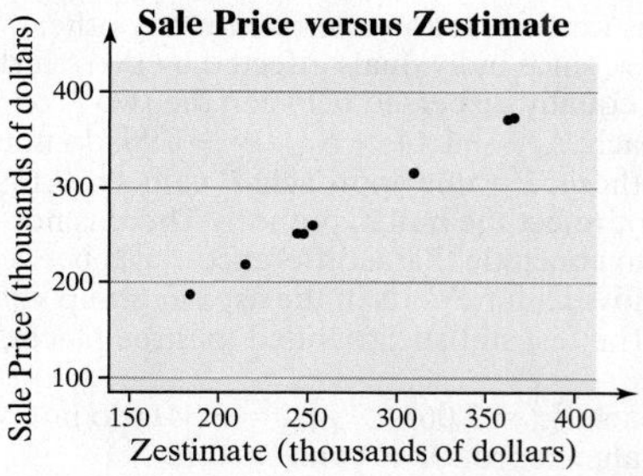

(b) $\hat{y} = 1.0228x - 0.7590$; because the P-value $< 0.001 < \alpha = 0.05$ (or $t_0 = 105.426 > t_{0.025} = 2.447$), we reject the null hypothesis and conclude that there is a linear relation between the Zestimate and the sale price.
(c) $\hat{y} = 0.5220x + 115.8094$; because $0.20 > P$-value > 0.10 [Tech: P-value $= 0.1927$] $> \alpha = 0.05$ (or $t_0 = 1.441 < t_{0.025} = 2.365$), we do not reject the null hypothesis. There is not sufficient evidence to conclude that a linear relation exists between the Zestimate and the sale price. Yes, this observation is influential.

24. It is important to perform both graphical and analytical analyses when analyzing relations between two quantitative variables because the graph describes the type of relation that exists and the analytical description allows for statistical inference to be conducted.

25. The y-coordinates on the least-squares regression line represent the mean value of the response variable for any given value of the explanatory variable.

26. It is desirable to have the explanatory variables be widely dispersed so that the standard deviation of b_1 is smaller.

27. We do not conduct inference on the linear correlation coefficient because a hypothesis test on the slope and a hypothesis test on the linear correlation coefficient yield the same conclusion. Moreover, the requirements for conducting inference on the linear correlation coefficient are very hard to verify.

12.4 Assess Your Understanding (page 561)

1. confidence; mean

2. prediction; individual

3. **(a)** $\hat{y} = 11.8$
(b) Lower bound: 10.8 [Tech: 10.9]; upper bound: 12.8
(c) $\hat{y} = 11.8$
(d) Lower bound: 9.9; upper bound: 13.7
(e) The confidence interval is an interval estimate for the mean value of y at $x = 7$, whereas the prediction interval is an interval estimate for a single value of y at $x = 7$.

4. **(a)** $\hat{y} = 5.1$
(b) Lower bound: 4.0; upper bound: 6.2
(c) $\hat{y} = 5.1$
(d) Lower bound: 2.5; upper bound: 7.7
(e) The confidence interval is an interval estimate for the mean value of y at $x = 8$, whereas the prediction interval is an interval estimate for a single value of y at $x = 8$.

5. **(a)** $\hat{y} = 4.3$
(b) Lower bound: 2.5; upper bound: 6.1
(c) $\hat{y} = 4.3$
(d) Lower bound: 0.9; upper bound: 7.7

6. **(a)** $\hat{y} = 0.4$
(b) Lower bound: −0.8; upper bound: 1.6
(c) $\hat{y} = 0.4$
(d) Lower bound: −1.6 [Tech: −1.7]; upper bound: 2.4

7. **(a)** $\hat{y} = 68.07$
(b) Lower bound: 67.723; upper bound: 68.420
(c) $\hat{y} = 68.07$
(d) Lower bound: 67.252; upper bound: 68.891
(e) The prediction made in part (a) is an estimate of the mean well-being index composite score for all individuals whose commute time is 20 minutes. The prediction made in part (c) is an estimate of the well-being index composite score of one individual, Jane, whose commute time is 20 minutes.

8. **(a)** $\hat{y} = 5.619\%$
(b) Lower bound: 3.729%; upper bound: 7.509%
(c) $\hat{y} = 5.619\%$
(d) Lower bound: 2.043%; upper bound: 9.196% [Tech: 9.195%]
(e) The prediction made in part (a) is an estimate of the mean interest rate for all individuals whose credit score is 730. The prediction made in part (c) is an estimate of the interest rate of one individual, Kaleigh, whose credit score is 730.

9. **(a)** $\hat{y} = 17.20$ inches
(b) 95% confidence interval: lower bound: 17.12 inches; upper bound: 17.28 inches
(c) $\hat{y} = 17.20$ inches
(d) 95% prediction interval: lower bound: 16.97 inches; upper bound: 17.43 inches
(e) The confidence interval is an interval estimate for the mean head circumference of all children who are 25.75 inches tall. The prediction interval is an interval estimate for the head circumference of a single child who is 25.75 inches tall.

10. **(a)** $\hat{y} = 37.023$ [Tech: 37.022] mm
(b) 95% confidence interval: lower bound: 36.647 [Tech: 36.646] mm; upper bound: 37.399 [Tech: 37.398] mm
(c) $\hat{y} = 37.023$ [Tech: 37.022] mm
(d) 95% prediction interval: lower bound: 35.843 [Tech: 35.842] mm; upper bound: 38.203 [Tech: 38.202] mm
(e) Although the predicted lengths of the right tibia in parts (a) and (c) are the same, the intervals are different because the distribution of the means, part (a), has less variability than the distribution of the individuals, part (c).

11. **(a)** $\hat{y} = 4400.4$ psi
(b) 95% confidence interval: lower bound: 4147.8 psi; upper bound: 4653.1 psi
(c) $\hat{y} = 4400.4$ psi
(d) 95% prediction interval: lower bound: 3726.3 psi; upper bound: 5074.6 psi
(e) The confidence interval is an interval estimate for the mean 28-day strength of all concrete cylinders that have a 7-day strength of 2550 psi. The prediction interval is an interval estimate for the 28-day strength of a single cylinder whose 7-day strength is 2550 psi.

12. **(a)** $\hat{y} = 0.90$ mg
(b) 95% confidence interval: lower bound: 0.83 mg; upper bound: 0.97 mg
(c) $\hat{y} = 0.90$ mg
(d) 95% prediction interval: lower bound: 0.64 mg; upper bound: 1.16 mg
(e) Although the predicted nicotine contents in parts (a) and (c) are the same, the intervals are different because the distribution of the mean nicotine level, part (a), has less variability than the distribution of the individual nicotine levels for a particular tar level, part (c).

13. **(a)** $\hat{y} = 4.739\%$
(b) 90% confidence interval: lower bound: 3.662%; upper bound: 5.815%
(c) $\hat{y} = 4.739\%$
(d) 90% prediction interval: lower bound: 1.441%; upper bound: 8.036% [Tech: 8.037%]
(e) Although the predicted rates of return in parts (a) and (c) are the same, the intervals are different because the distribution of the mean rate of return, part (a), has less variability than the distribution of the individual rate of return of a particular S&P 500 rate of return, part (c).

14. **(a)** $\hat{y} = 119.2$ [Tech: 119.3] kg
(b) 95% confidence interval: lower bound: 99.8 [Tech: 99.9] kg; upper bound: 138.6 [Tech: 138.7] kg
(c) $\hat{y} = 119.2$ [Tech: 119.3] kg
(d) 95% confidence interval: lower bound: 68.9 kg; upper bound: 169.6 kg
(e) Although the predicted weights in parts (a) and (c) are the same, the intervals are different because the distribution of the mean weights, part (a), has less variability than the distribution of individual weights, part (c).

15. **(a)** It does not make sense to construct either a confidence interval or prediction interval based on the least-squares regression equation because the evidence indicated that there is no linear relation between CEO compensation and stock return.
(b) Since there is no linear relation between x and y, we use the techniques of Section 9.2 on the y-data to construct the confidence interval. 95% confidence interval for the mean stock return: lower bound: −0.679% [Tech: −0.681%], upper bound: 35.313% [Tech: 35.315%].

16. **(a)** It does not make sense to construct either a confidence interval or prediction interval based on the least-squares regression equation because the evidence indicated that there is no linear relation between calories and sugar.
(b) Since there is no linear relation between x and y, we use the techniques of Section 9.2 on the y-data to construct the confidence interval. 95% confidence interval for the mean sugar content: lower bound: 9.5 grams; upper bound: 19.9 grams.

17. **(a)**

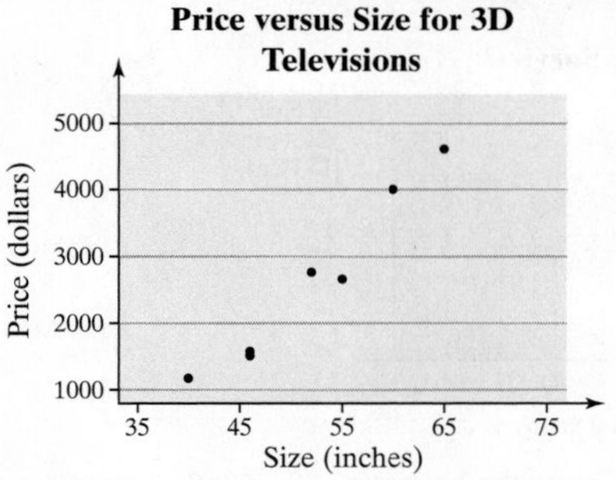

(b) $r = 0.979$
(c) Yes, because $0.979 > 0.666$ (Table II)
(d) $\hat{y} = -4599.217 + 137.6711x$
(e) For each inch added to the size of the 3D television, the price will increase by $137.67, on average.
(f) It is not reasonable to interpret the intercept. It would indicate the price of a 0-inch 3D television, which makes no sense.
(g) About 95.7% of variability in price is explained by the variability in size (or the least-squares regression).
(h) $\beta_0 \approx b_0 = -4599.2$; $\beta_1 \approx b_1 = 137.67$
(i) $s_e = 269.0488$
(j) A normal probability plot of the residuals shows that they are approximately normally distributed.
(k) $s_{b_1} = 10.9656$
(l) Because the P-value $< 0.0001 < \alpha = 0.05$ (or $t_0 = 12.555 > t_{0.025} = 2.365$), we reject the null hypothesis. We conclude that a linear relation exists between the size and price of 3D televisions.
(m) 95% confidence interval: lower bound: 111.7416; upper bound: 163.6007
(n) $2560

(o) 95% confidence interval: lower bound: \$2341.4; upper bound: \$2778.0
(p) The price of the 52-inch Sharp 3D television is neither below nor above the mean price for 52-inch 3D televisions. Its price, \$2700, is within the bounds of the confidence interval found in part (o).
(q) \$2560
(r) 95% confidence interval: lower bound: \$1887.0; upper bound: \$3232.3.
(s) Answers will vary. Possible lurking variables: brand name, picture quality, and audio quality.

Chapter 12 Review Exercises (page 565)

1. H_0: The wheel is in balance; H_1: The wheel is out of balance. Classical approach: $\chi_0^2 = 0.578 < \chi_{0.05}^2 = 5.991$; do not reject the null hypothesis. *P*-value approach: *P*-value $> 0.10 > \alpha = 0.05$ [Tech: *P*-value $= 0.749$]; do not reject the null hypothesis. There is not sufficient evidence at the $\alpha = 0.05$ level of significance to conclude that the wheel is out of balance. That is, the evidence suggests that the wheel is in balance.

2. H_0: The teams are evenly matched; H_1: The teams are not evenly matched. Classical approach: $\chi_0^2 = 5.91 < \chi_{0.05}^2 = 7.815$; do not reject the null hypothesis. *P*-value approach: *P*-value $> 0.10 > 0.05 = \alpha$ [Tech: *P*-value $= 0.1161$]; do not reject the null hypothesis. There is not sufficient evidence at the $\alpha = 0.05$ level of significance to conclude that the teams playing in the World Series have not been evenly matched. That is, the evidence suggests that the teams have been evenly matched. On the other hand, the *P*-value is suggestive of an issue. In particular, there are fewer six-game series than we would expect. Perhaps the team that is down "goes all out" in game 6, trying to force game 7.

3. (a) H_0: Class is independent of survival status; H_1: Class is associated with survival status. Classical approach: $\chi_0^2 = 133.052 > \chi_{0.05}^2 = 5.991$; reject the null hypothesis. *P*-value approach: *P*-value $< 0.005 < \alpha = 0.05$ [Tech: *P*-value $= 0.000$]; reject the null hypothesis. There is sufficient evidence at the $\alpha = 0.05$ level of significance to conclude that the class of service and survival rates are dependent.
(b)

	Class		
Titanic	**First**	**Second**	**Third**
Survived	0.625	0.414	0.252
Did Not Survive	0.375	0.586	0.748

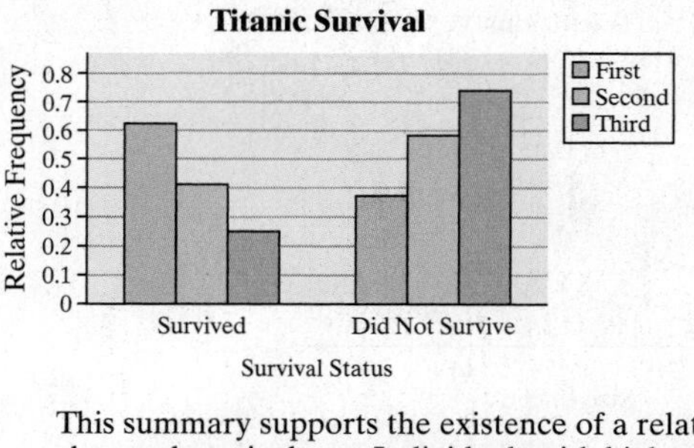

This summary supports the existence of a relationship between class and survival rate. Individuals with higher-class tickets survived in greater proportions with lower-class tickets.

4. H_0: Gestational period is independent of degree; H_1: Gestational period is not independent of degree. Classical approach: $\chi_0^2 = 10.239 > \chi_{0.05}^2 = 9.488$; reject the null hypothesis. *P*-value approach: *P*-value < 0.05 [Tech: *P*-value $= 0.037$]; reject the null hypothesis. There is sufficient evidence at the $\alpha = 0.05$ level of significance to conclude that length of the gestational period and completion of a high school diploma are dependent.

5. (a) Classical approach: $\chi_0^2 = 37.537 > \chi_{0.05}^2 = 7.815$; reject the null hypothesis. *P*-value approach: *P*-value < 0.005[Tech: *P*-value < 0.0001]; reject the null hypothesis. There is sufficient evidence at the $\alpha = 0.05$ level of significance that the level of funding received by the counties is associated with the candidate.

(b)

	High-Funded	Medium-Funded	Low-Funded	No Funding
Roosevelt	0.5994	0.5698	0.5400	0.4692
Landon	0.4006	0.4302	0.4600	0.5308
Total	1	1	1	1

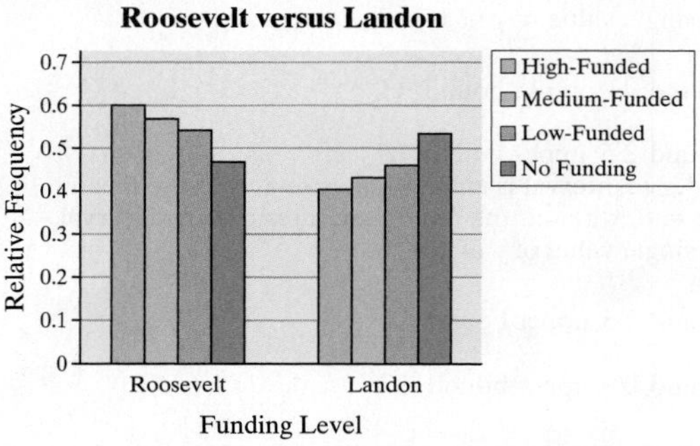

6. The least-squares regression model is $y_i = \beta_0 + \beta_1 x_i + \varepsilon_i$. The requirements to perform inference on the least-squares regression line are (1) for any particular values of the explanatory variable *x*, the mean of the corresponding responses in the population depends linearly on *x*, and (2) the response variables, y_i, are normally distributed with mean $\mu_{y|x} = \beta_0 + \beta_1 x$ and standard deviation σ. We verify these requirements by checking to see that the residuals are normally distributed, with mean 0 and constant variance σ^2 and that the residuals are independent.

7. (a) $\beta_0 \approx b_0 = 3.8589$; $\beta_1 \approx b_1 = -0.1049$; $\hat{y} = 3.334$
(b) $s_e = 0.5102$
(c)

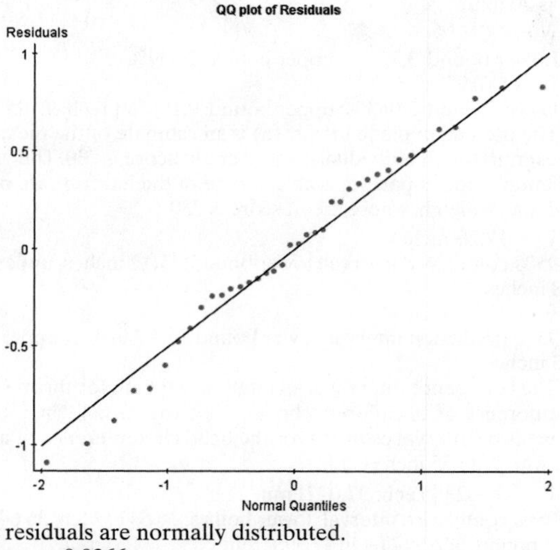

The residuals are normally distributed.
(d) $s_{b_1} = 0.0366$
(e) Because the *P*-value $= 0.007 < \alpha = 0.05$ (or $t_0 = -2.866$ [Tech: -2.868] $< t_{0.025} = -2.028$), we reject the null hypothesis and conclude that a linear relation exists between the row chosen by students on the first day of class and their cumulative GPAs.
(f) 95% confidence interval: lower bound: -0.1791; upper bound: -0.0307
(g) 95% confidence interval: lower bound: 3.159; upper bound: 3.509
(h) $\hat{y} = 3.334$
(i) 95% prediction interval: lower bound: 2.285; upper bound: 4.383 [Tech: 4.384]
(j) Although the predicted GPAs in parts (a) and (h) are the same, the intervals are different because the distribution of the mean GPAs, part (a), has less variability than the distribution of individual GPAs, part (h).

8. (a) $\beta_0 \approx b_0 = -399.2$; $\beta_1 \approx b_1 = 2.5315$; $\hat{y} = 1879.15$, so the mean rent of a 900-square-foot apartment in Queens is \$1879.15.
(b) $s_e = 229.547$

(c)

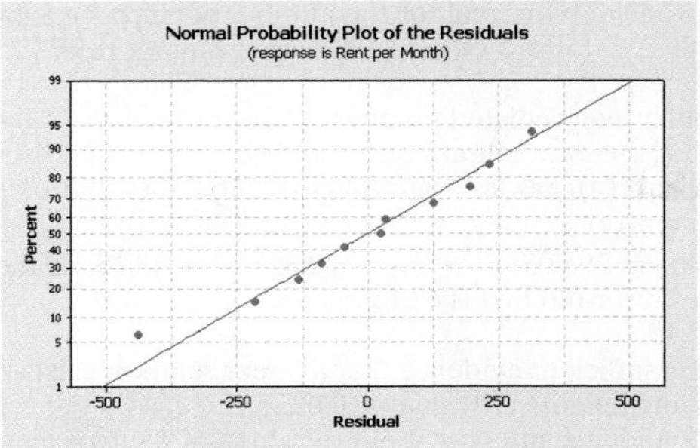

The residuals are normally distributed.

(d) $s_{b_1} = 0.2166$

(e) There is evidence that a linear relation exists between the square footage of an apartment in Queens, New York, and the monthly rent.

(f) 95% confidence interval about the slope of the true least-squares regression line: lower bound: 2.0416, upper bound: 3.0214.

(g) 90% confidence interval about the mean rent of 900-square-foot apartments: lower bound: \$1752.20; upper bound: \$2006.00.

(h) When an apartment has 900 square feet, $\hat{y} = \$1879.15$ [Tech: 1879.1].

(i) 90% prediction interval for the rent of a particular 900-square-foot apartment: lower bound: \$1439.60; upper bound: \$2318.60.

(j) Although the predicted rents in parts (a) and (h) are the same, the intervals are different because the distribution of the means, part (a), has less variability than the distribution of the individuals, part (h).

Chapter 12 Test (page 567)

1. H_0: The dice are fair; H_1: The dice are not fair. Classical approach: $\chi_0^2 = 4.940 < \chi_{0.01}^2 = 23.209$; do not reject the null hypothesis. P-value approach: P-value $> 0.10 > \alpha = 0.01$ [Tech: P-value $= 0.895$]; do not reject the null hypothesis. There is not sufficient evidence at the $\alpha = 0.01$ level of significance to conclude that the dice are loaded. That is, the evidence suggests that the dice are fair.

2. H_0: Educational attainment is the same today as 2000; H_1: Educational attainment has changed since 2000. Classical approach: $\chi_0^2 = 2.661 < \chi_{0.10}^2 = 9.236$; do not reject the null hypothesis. P-value approach: P-value $> 0.10 = \alpha$ [Tech: P-value $= 0.752$]; do not reject the null hypothesis. There is not sufficient evidence at the $\alpha = 0.10$ level of significance to conclude that the distribution of educational attainment of Americans today is different from the distribution of education attainment in 2000. That is, the evidence suggests that educational attainment has not changed.

3. (a) $H_0: p_R = p_I = p_D$; H_1: At least one proportion differs. Classical approach: $\chi_0^2 = 41.767 > \chi_{0.05}^2 = 5.991$; reject the null hypothesis. P-value approach: P-value $< 0.005 < \alpha = 0.05$ [Tech: P-value < 0.001]; reject the null hypothesis. There is sufficient evidence at the $\alpha = 0.05$ level of significance to conclude that at least one proportion is different from the others. That is, the evidence suggests that the proportion of adults who feel morality is important when deciding how to vote is different for at least one political affiliation.

(b)

	Republican	Independent	Democrat
Important	0.920	0.810	0.820
Not Important	0.080	0.190	0.180

Importance of Morality

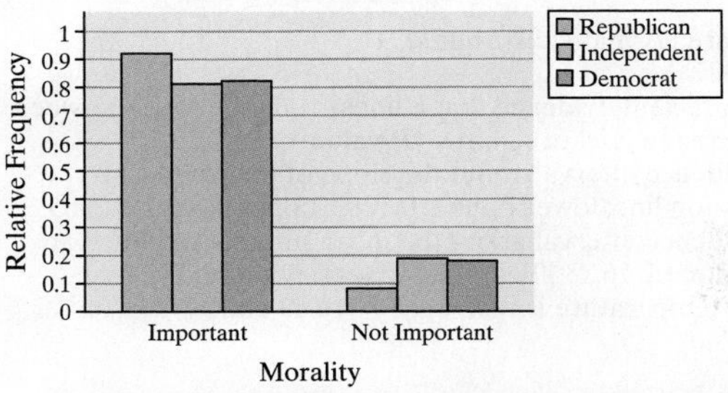

A higher proportion of Republicans appears to feel that morality is important when deciding how to vote than do Democrats or Independents.

4. Classical approach: $\chi_0^2 = 4155.285 > \chi_{0.05}^2 = 7.815$; reject the null hypothesis. P-value approach: P-value < 0.005 [Tech: P-value < 0.0001]; reject the null hypothesis. There is sufficient evidence at the $\alpha = 0.05$ level of significance that different proportions of 18- to 29-year-olds have been affiliated with religion in the past four decades.

5. Classical approach: $\chi_0^2 = 330.803 > \chi_{0.05}^2 = 12.592$; reject the null hypothesis. P-value approach: P-value $< 0.005 < \alpha = 0.05$ [Tech: P-value < 0.0001]; reject the null hypothesis. There is sufficient evidence at the $\alpha = 0.05$ level of significance to conclude that the proportions for the time categories spent in bars differ between smokers and nonsmokers. From the conditional distribution and bar graph, it appears that a higher proportion of smokers spends more time in bars than nonsmokers.

	Almost Daily	Several Times a Week	Several Times a Month	Once a Month	Several Times a Year	Once a Year	Never
Smoker	0.584	0.539	0.437	0.435	0.430	0.372	0.277
Nonsmoker	0.416	0.461	0.563	0.565	0.570	0.628	0.723

Smoking and Bars

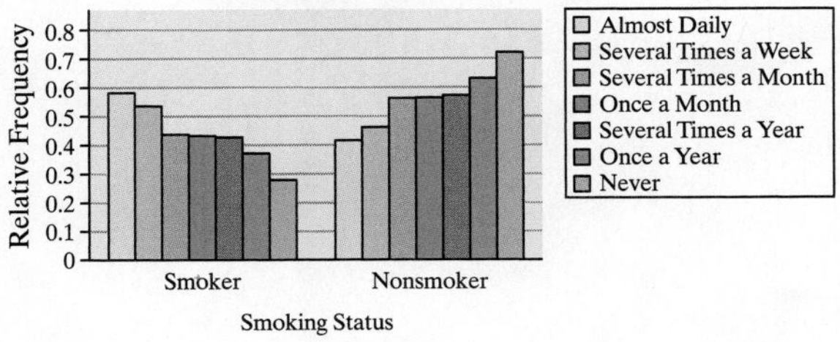

6. (1) For any particular values of the explanatory variable x, the mean of the corresponding responses in the population depends linearly on x.
(2) The response variable, y_i, is normally distributed with mean $\mu_{y|x_i} = \beta_0 + \beta_1 x$ and standard deviation σ.

7. (a) $\beta_0 \approx b_0 = -0.309$; $\beta_1 \approx b_1 = 0.2119$; $\hat{y} = 16.685$ [Tech: 16.687]; so the mean number of chirps when the temperature is 80.2°F is 16.69.
(b) $s_e = 0.9715$
(c)

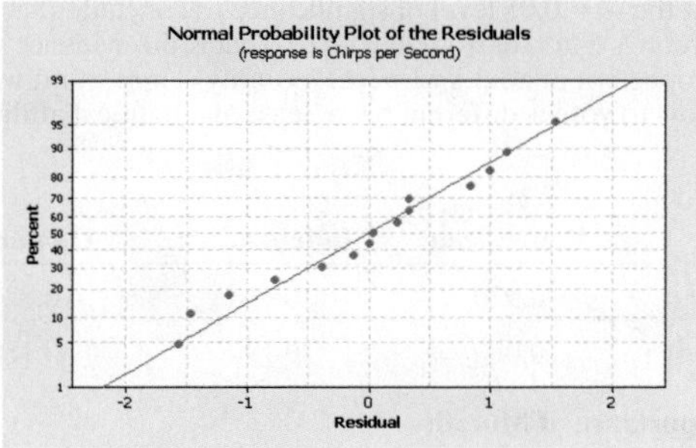

The residuals are normally distributed.
(d) $s_{b_1} = 0.0387$
(e) There is sufficient evidence that a linear relation exists between temperature and the cricket's chirps (P-value < 0.001).
(f) 95% confidence interval about the slope of the true least-squares regression line: lower bound: 0.1283; upper bound: 0.2955.
(g) 90% confidence interval about the mean number of chirps at 80.2°F: lower bound: 16.25 [Tech: 16.24]; upper bound: 17.13.
(h) When the temperature is 80.2°F, $\hat{y} = 16.69$ chirps.
(i) 90% prediction interval for the number of chirps of a particular cricket at 80.2°F: lower bound: 14.91; upper bound: 18.47 [Tech: 18.46].
(j) Although the predicted numbers of chirps in parts (a) and (h) are the same, the intervals are different because the distribution of the means, part (a), has less variability than the distribution of the individuals, part (h).

8. (a) $\beta_0 \approx b_0 = 29.705$; $\beta_1 \approx b_1 = 2.6351$; $\hat{y} = 48.15$; so the mean height of a 7-year-old boy is 48.15 inches.
(b) $s_e = 2.45$
(c) There is sufficient evidence that a linear relation exists between boys' ages and heights (P-value < 0.001).
(d) 95% confidence interval about the slope of the true least-squares regression line: lower bound: 2.2008; upper bound: 3.0694.
(e) 90% confidence interval about the mean height of 7-year-old boys: lower bound: 47.11 [Tech: 47.12]; upper bound: 49.19 inches.
(f) The predicted height of a randomly chosen 7-year-old boy is 48.15 inches, $\hat{y} = 48.15$.
(g) 90% prediction interval for the height of a particular 7-year-old boy: lower bound: 43.78; upper bound: 52.52 inches.
(h) Although the predicted heights in parts (a) and (f) are the same, the intervals are different because the distribution of the means, part (a), has less variability than the distribution of the individuals, part (f).

9. (a) $\beta_0 \approx b_0 = 67.388$; $\beta_1 \approx b_1 = -0.2632$
(b) There is not sufficient evidence at the $\alpha = 0.05$ level of significance to support that a linear relation exists between a woman's age and grip strength (P-value $= 0.138$).
(c) Based on the answer to (b), a good estimate of the grip strength of a 42-year-old female would be the mean strength of the population, 57 psi.

Index

D

N

O

P

Q

T

U

V

W

Y

Z

Photo Credits

Preface Page xv, Michael Sullivan

Chapter 1 Pages vii, 2, 60, Discpicture/Shutterstock; Page 8, Felicia Martinez/PhotoEdit, Inc.; Page 39, Johnkwan/Dreamstime; Page 45, A. Barrington Brown/Photo Researchers, Inc.; Page 49, Pete Saloutos/Shutterstock; Page 52, Matka Wariatka /Shutterstock.

Chapter 2 Pages vii, 62, 114, Tony Freeman/PhotoEdit, Inc.; Page 81, Library of Congress Prints and Photographs Division [LC-USZ62-5877].

Chapter 3 Pages vii, 116, 176, Ryan McVay/Photodisc/Getty Images; Page 139, Ria Novosti/Alamy; Page 163, Alfred Eisenstaedt/Time Life Pictures/Getty Images.

Chapter 4 Pages viii, 177, 230, Goddard Space Flight Center/NASA; Page 183, SPL/Photo Researchers, Inc.; Page 197, Sheila Terry/Photo Researchers, Inc.; Page 199, Mary Evans Picture Library/Alamy.

Chapter 5 Pages viii, 232, 296, Kasia/Shutterstock; Page 238, Mary Evans Picture Library/The Image Works; Page 240, SPL/Photo Researchers, Inc.; Page 241, SPL/Photo Researchers, Inc.; Page 244, Victor de Schwanberg/Alamy; Page 269, RIA Novosti/Alamy; Page 278, Churchill Downs/AP Images; Page 282, Andy Marlin/Reuters.

Chapter 6 Pages viii, 297, 327, Dorling Kindersley, Inc.; Page 304, SPL/Photo Researchers, Inc.; Page 310, North Wind Picture Archives/Alamy; Page 311, Gary Conner/PhotoEdit, Inc.

Chapter 7 Pages ix, 328, 364, Marema/Shutterstock; Page 332 top, SPL/Photo Researchers, Inc.; Page 332 bottom, North Wind Picture Archives; Page 334, Interfoto/Personalities/Alamy; Page 356, North Wind Picture Archives.

Chapter 8 Pages ix, 366, 389, Juan David Ferrando Subero/Shutterstock; Page 373, Prisma/Newscom; Page 379, Victor de Schwanberg/Alamy.

Chapter 9 Pages ix, 390, 427, Somatuscan/Shutterstock.

Chapter 10 Pages ix, 428, 466, Almagami/Shutterstock; Page 432, FogStock, LLC./PhotoLibrary New York.

Chapter 11 Pages x, 467, 514, Galyna Andrushko / Shutterstock.

Chapter 12 Pages x, 515, 569, Kimberly Butler/Time & Life Pictures/Getty Images; Page 516, Carolyn Jenkins/Alamy; Page 521, SPL/Photo Researchers, Inc.

Case Studies (CD) Chapter 1, Marie C. Fields/Shutterstock; Chapter 2, Gregor Kervina/Shutterstock; Chapter 3, The Pierpont Morgan Library/Art Resource, New York; Chapter 4, Mark Liebowitz/Masterfile; Chapter 5, Peter Gatherole/Dorling Kiindersley, Inc.; Chapter 6, North Wind Picture Archives; Chapter 7, Science Photo Library/Custom Medical Stock; Chapter 8, 6493866629/Shutterstock; Chapter 9, Valvee/Shutterstock; Chapter 10, George Bailey/Shutterstock; Chapter 11, Kurhan/Shutterstock; Chapter 12, Photo Library New York.